COMPOSING INQUIRY

METHODS AND READINGS FOR INVESTIGATION AND WRITING

Margaret J. Marshall Ph.D.

CONTRIBUTORS

Isis Artze-Vega
James Britton
Deirdre Fagan
Judy Hood
Joanna Johnson
April Mann
Gina Maranto
Adina Sanchez-Garcia
Andrew Strycharski
John Wafer

PEARSON

Prentice
Hall

Upper Saddle River, New Jersey 07458

Editorial Director: Leah Jewell
Senior Acquisitions Editor: Brad Potthoff
Editorial Assistant: Tracy Clough
Production Liaison: Joanne Hakim
Senior Marketing Manager: Windley Morley
Marketing Assistant: Heather Halpern
Senior Operations Supervisor: Sherry Lewis
Creative Director: Jayne Conte
Cover Design: Bruce Kenselaar
Permissions Specialist: Kathleen Karcher
Director, Image Resource Center: Melinda Patelli
Manager, Rights and Permissions: Zina Arabia
Manager, Visual Research: Beth Brenzel
Photo Coordinator: Angelique Sharps
Photo Researcher: Kathy Ringrose
Full-Service Project Management: Patty Donovan/Pine Tree Composition
Composition: Laserwords Private Limited
Printer/Binder: RR Donnelley & Sons Company
Cover Printer: RR Donnelley & Sons Company

Credits and acknowledgments borrowed from other sources and reproduced, with permission, in this textbook appear on appropriate page within text (or on page 625).

Pearson Education LTD., London
Pearson Education Singapore, Pte. Ltd
Pearson Education, Canada, Ltd
Pearson Education–Japan
Pearson Education Australia PTY, Limited

Pearson Education North Asia Ltd
Pearson Educación de Mexico, S.A. de C.V.
Pearson Education Malaysia, Pte. Ltd
Pearson Education, Upper Saddle River, New Jersey

10 9 8 7 6 5 4 3 2 1

CONTENTS

Readings

PREFACE

Composing Inquiry is a reader/rhetoric for first-year composition courses that takes seriously the call to engage undergraduates in intellectual work. All the readings included here serve to illustrate methods of research and investigation used in various academic disciplines, and all inspire similar projects that can be done by undergraduate students as they learn to work on their writing. Unlike traditional readers, *Composing Inquiry* also includes chapters meant to help students understand methods of inquiry commonly used by scholars to collect data or test theories. These method chapters can be used in conjunction with the readings or independently, depending on the program/course goals or the preferences of individual teachers. The methods chapters are structured in similar ways to include:

- A general explanation of the method, including how it is used in the academic world and how to use the method to further an inquiry
- Examples of special cases, that is, modifications of the method or specific kinds of materials that researchers work with using a version of the primary method
- A discussion of ethical considerations connected to the method
- Practice activities that can be done independently or with classmates
- Highlights of rhetorical issues that often appear as students work to present their research in writing
- Samples of student writing featuring that method
- A list of Internet Resources relevant to the featured method and special cases
- Links to the readings and assignments that appear later in the book

Methods covered include:

- **Observing**, including working with visual materials and artifacts
- **Interviewing**, including conducting focus group interviews and collecting oral histories
- **Working with numbers**, including analyzing statistics and conducting surveys
- **Working with texts**, including analyzing public speech and music, and working with formal and informal archives

The second section of the book presents four **model projects** that invite students to engage with real questions, conduct real research, and produce real documents that contribute to knowledge-making. Each project can sustain an entire term's worth of writing or be combined with methods or readings as the instructor chooses. In some programs these projects might serve to structure a writing course with a more focused topic; in other programs the model projects, or portions of the projects, might be interspersed with the assignment sequences. The four projects are also structured in slightly different ways to illustrate variations in project-based courses that might be adapted by teachers or programs to other topics or themes in conjunction with the research that is happening in their own institutions.

- **The Water Project** features a documentary film on the problems of sustainable water, invites students to contribute to the companion Web site, and suggests a series of writing and investigation activities which can be completed in other locales. The project is meant to also serve as an example of linking first-year writing courses to the research or scholarly productions of faculty in local institutions.

- **The Local History Project** suggests ways that students can inquire and write about their own area's history. Using a variety of methods and linking to institutional or community interests, the project also allows students to work individually or to combine in collaborative teams to produce a more comprehensive history of a particular institution or area. While links to ongoing scholarly work are provided as examples, this project, unlike The Water Project, does not invite students to contribute directly to these existing Web sites, though it is certainly possible that regional sites will welcome student submissions.

- The third project, **Public Spaces**, again features the ongoing work of a university professor and his existing Web site, and also models ways for students to do similar work in their own areas or for their own purposes. Combining oral history, land use, public policy, community planning, and governmental decision-making, Public Spaces allows students to take research into the areas of community service and public action.

- The final project, **Organizational Needs Assessment**, demonstrates how a single investigation, this time of a local organization or business, can draw upon multiple methods of research and lead to both oral presentations and written documents. This project moves students even further into the local community by asking that they produce documents meant to be useful in a real-world setting. Though neither service learning nor technical writing, the Organizational Needs Assignment project could be used in either type of course as the primary writing assignment of the term or be adjusted to serve as one project among many.

Assignment sequences, the third section of the book, demonstrate how readings can be used together to investigate a particular theme or topic, expose students to a number of different methods in a single term, work between readings and methods, or sustain and complicate the work with a single method. Our intention is again to offer sequences as models for how individual teachers might sequence writing and inquiry over a term while also giving students and teachers several already developed plans of action. None of the assignments ask students to write directly about the readings, so teachers can be sure that the work produced will be varied even as students work on particular strategies. Such unity of purpose means class activities will be coherent, and peer groups can be useful to individuals even though topics might be quite varied. Several of the sequences are designed without readings for those who find that kind of work fits their program or individual course better. Most sequences offer five or six assignments, though some without readings have slightly more, giving teachers (or students) the opportunity to select the ones that seem most appropriate to their work. Most of the sequences include assignments that invite students to experiment with different kinds of revision, a key component of learning to write well. We know that experienced teachers will write their own assignments or rearrange existing assignments to reflect the goals of their own programs. However, teachers (and program directors) can be assured that following the sequences as they are written will generate writing appropriate to undergraduate courses without being formulaic because we've taken care to write assignments that pose challenges from the beginning assignment, as well as to avoid asking students to do the same work in multiple assignments. Every sequence also includes suggestions for how students can reflect on their own writing and writing processes after each assignment, and every sequence ends with an invitation to synthesize what has been learned about both the topic and about writing, an assignment that works especially well with portfolio grading.

Reading selections are the final section of the book. All the readings have been chosen because they connect to one another around themes or areas of investigation that are still being actively pursued by researchers, policy makers, and educated citizens. In other words, the readings lend themselves to assignments that invite students to join in this ongoing intellectual work. The readings also demonstrate the use of the methods discussed earlier. The articles are all examples of scholarly writing, represent a wide range of disciplines and writing styles, and have not already been widely anthologized. All the articles are presented in their entirety as they first appeared in scholarly journals, or as book chapters. Suggestions for adding literary texts and movies are included in the teachers' resource guide since literary texts are not represented in the readings collected here. The teachers' resource guide also includes strategies for helping students who might find the readings difficult.

We expect that any course that uses an inquiry approach makes student writing and their real dilemmas of investigation and communication a centerpiece of the course. At the suggestion of reviewers, we have added an additional introductory chapter discussing rhetorical choices that often arise as students present their inquiries in written form; in each method chapter, we've highlighted two or three of the most common difficulties of presenting research that arises from that method. Sample student writing is included in each method chapter for illustration and discussion. In addition the individual method chapters and the sample projects highlight ethical issues of research and writing, and the practice activities guide students through specific skills necessary to the particular method. Written by a team of composition teachers at the University of Miami under the direction of Dr. Margaret J. Marshall, *Composing Inquiry* enacts a vision of collaborative program development that values the intellectual work of classroom teachers regardless of their rank or degree level. We hope that other instructors who use our book will make suggestions, contribute new material, and join in expanding the projects for subsequent editions. We also invite students to submit their writing or their suggestions for revisions for subsequent editions to mmarshall@miami.edu.

ACKNOWLEDGMENTS

We would like to take this opportunity to thank our students for their patience as we worked through early drafts of this material and for their many suggestions for making the book better; our friends and family for bearing with us, especially in moments when deadlines loomed; and our colleagues both near and far for their good ideas, encouragement, and suggestions that have made the book stronger. We particularly want to thank the reviewers who examined earlier drafts of this text, including G. Douglas Atkins, University of Kansas; David Beach, George Mason University; Lisa Beckelhimer, University of Cincinnati; Glenn Blalock, Texas A&M; Beth Buyserie, Washington State University; MaryAnn Crawford, Melinda Kreth, Central Michigan University; Jason DePolo, North Carolina A&T State University; Terrence Doody, Rice University; Heidi Emmerling, University of Nevada; Joan Graham, University of Washington; Rebecca Jackson, Texas State University; Linda Kornasky, Angelo State University; Christine Ross, Quinnipiac University; Lisa Ruch, Bay Path College; Jason Saphara, California State University; Virginia Skinner-Linnenberg, Nazareth College; Trixie Smith, Middle Tennessee State University; and Derek Soles, Drexel University.

We want to publicly thank the many students who submitted writing for us to consider and especially those who agreed to let their writing be published here: Hattie Wellington, Christopher Perin, Bryan McLucas, Samantha Sanderson, Kenny Rosina, and Stephen Fuller. We also want to thank the sisters who agreed to have their experiences at Columbine appear in Samantha Sanderson's essays.

Many teachers contributed to this project by testing out assignments, suggesting articles to be included as readings and reviewing the suggestions made by others, considering student writing that might serve as examples, and drafting assignments. We are most grateful for those contributions and the collegial conversations they fostered that made us better teachers, and improved the quality of this text. We want to especially acknowledge the work of Lara Cahill, Darrel Elmore, Zisca Burton, Kileen Marshall, Andrew Strycharski, John Wafer, and April Mann who helped with copyediting earlier drafts; Joanna Johnson, Isis Artze-Vega, and Adina Sanchez-Garcia, who found many of the reading selections; and Judy Hood, who found the piece of student art work included in Chapter 3 and did the work necessary to get permission for its use.

To the many people at Pearson Education, especially Emma Christensen, who helped us produce custom editions to test with our students at Miami, we offer heartfelt thanks. We were especially blessed that Leah Jewell had enough faith in our vision to help us figure out how to undertake such a massive project despite heavy teaching loads that seemed to make such a long-term commitment unimaginable. Finally, to our editor at Prentice-Hall, Brad Potthoff, who pushed us to do more when we thought we had done all we could: thanks for your patience, your sound advice, and your faith that we could indeed make a better book for students and teachers working, writing, and inquiring together.

CHAPTER 1

INTRODUCTION

WHAT'S INQUIRY?

This is a book that invites students and teachers to engage in *inquiry*. Inquiry might seem to be just another word for *research*, and many students associate research with hunting for information in the library and summarizing what they find there. But, if you look up inquiry in the *Oxford English Dictionary*, you'll find that it is "the action of seeking, especially (and now always) for truth, knowledge, or information concerning something; search, research, investigation, examination. Or, the action of asking or questioning, interrogation." We think two things are especially interesting in this definition. First, inquiry already has embedded *action*. Second, the action—seeking or asking—implies a purpose or goal: "for truth, knowledge, or information concerning something." For our purposes, then, inquiry is distinct from asking questions where the answers are already known, just as it is different from answering questions to prove that you have learned someone else's answers. To engage in inquiry means that real people are considering something carefully and deliberately enough that they aren't going to settle for a sound-bite answer or a trivia quiz response. All kinds of people value such careful and deliberate thinking and the writing that accompanies it, and the academic world in particular is built around these efforts to investigate, think through, reconsider, and generate new knowledge. Because such thinking and investigation is complicated and almost always requires working with an array of material over time, writing is integral to the process. Writing helps researchers sort things out, put the parts together, and figure out the importance, the implications, and the consequences of whatever is being explored.

Inquiry doesn't happen in a vacuum, nor does it always follow predictable paths or a set process. Instead, inquiry relies on the investigator's interests and previous experiences, and it draws on work that others have done earlier. Thus, reading and utilizing secondary sources is an important part of inquiry, but the basic methods of investigation—observing, interviewing, working with numbers, and working with texts—involve primary research and questions that cannot be looked up or answered by summarizing what is already known. Likewise, as researchers interpret data, juxtapose previously existing information in new ways, or apply a theory to a new set of examples, they form arguments and work to convince others that their insights are accurate, reliable, and significant. Arguments that arrive from inquiry aren't the same as arguments that happen when people take a stance in a controversy or try to persuade others to accept a particular point of view. In those kinds of arguments, the desire to prove the point, win the debate, or get the last word almost always works against the careful consideration and suspension of judgment valued in inquiry. Inquiry arguments almost always try to show the reader or listener *how* the conclusion was reached not just what the conclusion is. Inquiry-based arguments value deliberation, consideration of alternative points of view or contrary interpretations, logical reasoning over emotion, and an awareness of one's own biases and the limitations of method, evidence, and conclusions. We don't know anyone who can produce sound arguments or careful deliberations of complex issues without writing and rewriting, and we don't know very many people who are willing to work on writing that they don't really care about. So, a writing course is a particularly good place for introducing the methods, writing processes, and habits of mind essential to inquiry.

Figure 1.1 details the qualities we mean when we say "habits of mind."

FIGURE 1.1 Habits of mind

- **Curiosity:** wondering why and what if; using interests and prior knowledge to develop new angles or consider different perspectives; knowing how to formulate questions for investigation and consideration

- **Flexibility**: being able to classify and distinguish related items or terms; knowing different ways to find answers to questions; trying different strategies to complete a project; being able to write for different audiences, purposes, and in different styles; recognizing what's gained or lost by using different techniques; understanding how to revise an inquiry or a written product; taking reasonable risks to consider divergent ideas or approaches; being able to revise a position in light of new evidence

- **Tolerance**: being comfortable with multiple perspectives and the lack of simplistic answers; looking at an issue or topic from different perspectives even if those perspectives aren't the ones you would usually take; understanding bias or the cultural, historical, and socioeconomic factors that constitute a particular perspective; recognizing what's been left out and considering why

- **Precision**: striving for accuracy; understanding consequences of choices; considering ethical implications of methods of investigation and representation; recognizing differences in word choice and definitions of key terms and how those differences might alter meaning

- **Deliberation**: considering implications or consequences; evaluating evidence and conclusions systematically and without a rush to judgment; proposing ways to mitigate negative consequences to proposed solutions; weighing different problems against one another and against various kinds of principles or standards; appreciating complexity rather than simplistic or reductive answers; recognizing sound logic

- **Self-Reflection**: being able to consider (and reconsider) one's own point of view and assess one's own work; imagining alternatives and limitations

Because these "habits of mind" are so varied and numerous, we think it is clear that no single course can ensure that all these abilities will be mastered and then used successfully from that point on. In fact most people use such careful and intentional thinking only some of the time, for some problems or issues, because to be so deliberate all the time about every action or question that presents itself would be debilitating. Thus a crucial part of using such thinking is distinguishing when it is appropriate and when it is not. We, and others, call these *habits* to emphasize the action—that is, to focus on the **ability** to think rather than the **content** of that thinking. Habits also suggests that abilities have become commonplace enough that they are no longer a part of the conscious decision-making process but have become implicit in the thinker's predilections and routine practices. Habits begin with conscious practice and even old habits can be scrutinized, reconsidered, revised, or rejected. An inquiry approach that aims to foster these habits of mind is both instructive and contemplative, both rigorous and experimental.

WHY INQUIRY? WHY COMPOSING?

Over the years many of our students have asked us why they have to take yet another English course to learn to write. After all, our students often say, we wouldn't be in college if we didn't already know how to write. Most of our students have indeed taken high school classes that focused on writing. Many have taken Advanced Placement classes and performed well on standardized tests and in courses where they were required to write both in and out of class. Our students seem to know that a college-level writing course doesn't need to treat them as if they know nothing, and we agree. Interestingly the research of Harvard Professor Richard Light found that when college students are asked what skills they want to improve, they list writing three times more often than anything else.[1] Harvard students have clearly also had these prior experiences, yet apparently they don't feel confident that their writing abilities are as good as they need to be. Most of our students, even those who have decided that writing isn't one of their strengths, agree that it's important to be able to communicate well on paper, but they aren't quite sure what more there is to know about writing and they assume that the college composition course will be nothing new. That doesn't have to be the case; college courses can help students develop as writers, and they can do so without just repeating the same routines students have already experienced.

We know our students can read and write, often very well. We also know that the level of literacy expected from educated citizens is always shifting. Because we believe that college composition courses represent the newest expectations for critical literacy—both reading and writing—we've built this book around those expectations. Knowing a bit more about the scholarship of literacy has helped our students to understand why they might *want* to take yet another course to learn to write, and so we turn now to a brief explanation of that scholarship.

LITERACY

Although "literacy" is a term commonly used to mean the decoding skills necessary to read a written text, literacy researchers such as Lawrence Stedman and Carl Kaestle[2]

---

[1] Richard Light, *Making the Most of College: Students Speak Their Minds* (Cambridge: Harvard UP, 2001).
[2] Lawrence Stedman and Carl Kaestle, "Literacy and Reading Performance in the United States, from 1880 to the Present," *Reading Research Quarterly* 22.1 (1987): 8–46.

point out that "literacy is not a single skill, but a set of skills that people have to varying degrees" (10). If you've ever had to figure out how to choose a new car, for example, or operate a new technology, you know what Stedman and Kaestle mean: you weren't suddenly "illiterate" just because you never knew what "dealer's preparation" meant to the sticker price. Or think about some of the very different kinds of texts that *some* people know how to read but most of us find strange and indecipherable at least the first time we encounter them. Architectural blueprints, corporate financial records, court orders, historical ledgers, legislative acts, statistical data, even computer manuals can leave readers feeling illiterate until they learn key vocabulary, figure out how to attend to the various symbols on the page, and become used to the form, or genre, of the presentation. Likewise, though reading is often portrayed as an activity we do alone, literacy often depends on interactions with others. You could certainly read the instructions that came with your new iPod or digital camera even if the first few times you tried to follow those instructions, the results were not as you expected. Most of us turn to a friend to help in such situations, to show us the tricks and explain the references that seem so obscure in the written instructions. Learning from those around us is substantiated in research as well, and educational psychologists regularly note the difference between what we can learn on our own and what we can do with the help of others.[3] So all of us operate on a scale of literacy, and new kinds of texts, new technologies, even new expectations are added regularly into our repertoire of literate practice.

Literacy expectations also change over time and because literacy is connected to status, schooling, and conceptions of success, what counts as evidence of being literate also changes over time. Historical scholarship tracking the evolution of literacy and its connections to schooling demonstrates that each time the general population achieves an expected level of literacy, the definition of literacy shifts.[4] Thus the number of people considered literate grows until the majority of the population achieves that level of literacy, and then the expected level of literacy rises and the process begins again. Today being literate requires much more than the simple decoding of texts, the ability to sign one's own name on formal documents, or even the written fluency necessary to produce the answer to an essay test question, although these abilities have served as signs of being literate in the past. Rather, educated (i.e., literate) citizens are now expected to read complex texts critically, to synthesize information from a variety of sources, to evaluate those sources not only for their believability and accuracy but also for their motives, biases, and assumptions. Literate people are also expected to be able to compose critical arguments, manipulate prose for different audiences and purposes, talk with others about the production or revision of these written documents, and know how to use a range of rhetorical strategies for any given writing task. In addition, being able to understand and use visual texts is increasingly important.[5]

---

[3]Lev Vygotsky's work is among the most famous for detailing this difference in relation to language and literacy. See, for example, *Thought and Language* (Cambridge: MIT Press, 1986) or *Mind in Society: The Development of Higher Psychological Processes*, ed. Michael Cole (Cambridge: Harvard UP, 1978).

[4]See Geraldine Joncich Clifford, "Buch und Lesen: Historical Perspectives on Literacy and Schooling," *Review of Educational Research* 54.4 (1984): 472–500.

[5]For a fuller explanation and additional details of this argument connecting literacy, schooling, and public criticism of higher education, see Margaret J. Marshall, *Response to Reform: Composition and the Professionalization of Teaching* (Carbondale: Southern Illinois UP, 2004), especially pages 4–9.

In 1998 when the Boyer Commission[6] first released its report on improving education for undergraduates at research universities, this expectation for higher levels of literacy and the role of universities in ensuring that undergraduates were educated as literate citizens was publicly connected to a call for engaging students in *inquiry*. The Boyer Commission argued that research universities have a particular responsibility to alter the methods of education so as to expose undergraduates to real research projects and actively engage them in the production of knowledge. Although we don't agree that this pedagogy should be limited to research universities, we do believe that active learning and intellectual engagement are central to the level of literacy expected of college-educated students. Indeed, theories of teaching based on the active engagement of students rather than on the transference of static knowledge have a long history, dating in this country to at least the work of John Dewey[7] at the beginning of the twentieth century, but also to international figures in education such as Paulo Freire.[8] Many universities now have taken up the challenge to provide students with significant learning experiences by helping faculty members to rethink their courses in light of current research into learning and teaching.[9] Experience tells most of us the same thing: we learn more when we actually *do* something than when we just read or hear about it.

Writing courses are often considered more interactive by nature; we learn to write by writing—not by listening to others talk about writing. Of course it's possible to have a writing course where hands are busy but minds are not. When some of us were in elementary school, we had writing lessons where the teacher read out sentences, and we wrote them down. We were graded on how well we shaped the letters, and whether we remembered to skip lines, used capital letters correctly, and ended with a period. Later we wrote as we entered that week's spelling words into blanks left in sentences the teacher provided. We were *writing*, but certainly not *composing*. Eventually we learned to write what is known as the five-paragraph essay, a form that works well to answer an essay question exam, but that is hard to utilize to convey complex arguments or original research. College writing courses are, of course, not lessons in penmanship, spelling, or exam writing, and inquiry can help such courses stay focused on composing meaning rather than on learning forms.

Indeed, the inquiry projects of undergraduate students are getting considerable attention. Several institutions sponsor publications for undergraduate research that parallel publications of creative writing. For a short list of such publications available online, see Internet Resources at the end of this chapter.[10] Many institutions also fund students to work on research projects in collaboration with faculty members, especially in special summer internships, and events that showcase undergraduate research and publications

[6]The Boyer Commission on Educating Undergraduates in the Research University. *Reinventing Undergraduate Education: A Blueprint for America's Research Universities*. Shirley Strum Kenny-State University of New York at Stony Brook 1998. Also available online now at http://www.reinventioncenter.miami.edu/The BoyerReport.html.
[7]See, especially, John Dewey, *Experience and Education* (New York: Macmillan, 1938).
[8]See, especially, Paolo Freire, *Pedagogy of the Oppressed* (New York: Continuum Publishing, 1970).
[9]See Dee L. Fink, *Creating Significant Learning Experiences: An Integrated Approach to College Courses* (San Francisco: J Wiley, 2003) for an overview of the research supporting these efforts. Professor Light's research cited in footnote 1 of this chapter also confirms the importance of writing in relation to the level of student engagement in the course.
[10]A special edition of *New Directions for Teaching and Learning* in spring 2003 focused on "Valuing and Supporting Undergraduate Research," and academic journals from nearly every discipline have included reports of, or arguments for encouraging, primary research conducted by undergraduates.

have become a common occurrence. So, "why inquiry" and "why composing"? The short answer, one that we hope is clearer because of what we've said about literacy, is this: *Inquiry* and *composing* represent the most recent demands for the advanced literacy required of college-educated citizens. Both inquiry and composing emphasize writing as an activity of making meaning, an activity that involves all those habits of mind we talked about earlier—curiosity, flexibility, tolerance, precision, deliberation, and self-reflection.

READING AND WRITING TOGETHER

As we pointed out earlier, inquiry doesn't happen in a vacuum. Reading what others have done and incorporating these other sources into our own projects are essential steps of any inquiry project. But reading for these academic purposes is not the same as reading for fun or as straightforward as reading to get information. Our students often tell us that the reading we ask them to do to learn inquiry methods is hard stuff—boring, unfamiliar, difficult to decipher. Rarely are the pieces written for a student audience, so we know that our students have reason to complain, but we also ask them to think more carefully about the assumptions they bring to this reading. Why should reading always be easy? Do we really learn most when we exert the least effort? Does easy or familiar necessarily equate to fun or are there times when something difficult also ends up providing pleasure? Intellectual work *can* be fun, but it almost always is difficult as well. We think most students come to college expecting such challenges, and are more satisfied with the college experience when they encounter such work earlier rather than later.[11] The readings we've selected for this book are meant to be challenging enough that they help readers learn to work with unusual material, stretch the range of literacy abilities most college students already possess, and provide examples of different kinds of inquiry methods and final written forms for presenting such inquiries. Reading, especially hard reading, is naturally active: it generates opportunities to interact with others as we talk about what the text means and how it matters in our lives.

STRATEGIES FOR ACTIVE READING

We've all had the experience of reading something, but discovering part way through that our mind has wandered and that we really have no idea what we've supposedly just read. To combat such drifts of attention, we find it helpful to read with a pen in hand, to mark the things that seem intriguing with checks in the margin so we can return to them once we've read the whole piece. Actually we find that most of the things we really want to learn from need to be read more than once, and that we need to read when our energy level is high enough that we can actually pay attention. Oh sure, we have the bedside reading that puts us to sleep, and the airplane or beach reading that we expect to go fast and not be remembered for long, but for things we know we'll need to think about carefully, we try not to read when we're tired or where there are lots of distractions.

Especially when we are reading material that is in a form we are not used to reading, we find it helpful to use a modified version of the SQ3R approach. SQ3R stands for Survey, Question, Read, Recite, Review and is a fairly well-known approach to reading

---

[11]Indeed, Professor Light's studies that we referenced in footnote 1 indicate that students are more satisfied with courses that present them with a challenge than with courses that are perceived as too easy.

texts that need to be remembered. Reading as a basis for writing, though, doesn't necessarily require that we *remember* everything as we might if we were going to be tested
on the content. Still, being an active reader is useful to writers in part because it provides
a structure that harnesses curiosity. Every time we approach a reading assignment, we
bring our prior experiences and personal interests with us, and we can use what we
already know to make the new reading more understandable and meaningful with a
strategy of SQRMR—Survey, Question, Read, Mark, Respond.

First, we look over, or **Survey**, the organization of a text before we actually begin to
read. In surveying we note headings, read captions under illustrations and graphic material, and notice other features (e.g., italicized words, quoted passages, footnotes, definitions, questions, etc.) that seem distinctive. In effect surveying provides a mental outline
for the reading that is about to begin and that mental framework helps us to connect new
information to something that we already know.[12] When we survey a text from the point
of view of a writer, we pay attention to *how* the author has put the text together, that is,
to the *rhetorical* choices the author has made. We look carefully at the beginning and ending of the piece in order to see how the specific issue has been framed; we notice where
and how visual material has entered the text; we watch for other signs that the author
is working within the expectations of a particular genre or following the conventions of
a particular discipline. We'll have more to say about these rhetorical issues in the next
chapter, but for now it's important to note that all texts have authors who make decisions about how they should be written. Even texts that don't seem to have an author—
phone books, for example, or university Web sites—are actually constructed by someone.

Depending on the difficulty of the text, we may write down the headings or other
organizational features of the text and pose a few **Questions** that we expect the reading
will answer. The questioning step in this process gives us a chance to consider the text
in terms of our own purposes and to anticipate what might be learned from this particular piece of writing. Once we begin to **Read** the text, we **Mark** the passages that we think
are important or confusing so that we can return to them later and consider them more
carefully. It's useful to develop several ways to mark the text and not rely only on highlighting. A simple check mark in the margin, for example, helps a reader to locate places
to refer to later. Penciled notes in the margin can be used to identify the function of the
paragraph, raise a question, or put the main idea into a few words. Some readers like to
read through the entire text without marking in order to get a general idea of the content and style, and then to read through more slowly and carefully, marking the text for
further study. Most of us, however, rarely have the time to read without simultaneously
marking the text. Whether we read the text once, twice, or thirty times, each time we
return to a passage we will notice things that we hadn't noticed before, and thus the
meaning of the text changes as we work with it. The marks we've made on the page not
only help us to make sense of the material, but also gives us a set of personalized notations that remind us of the important points when we review the material later.

Sometimes we find it helpful to write in **Response** to a reading. Marginal notations
are like shorthand, but it can be useful to keep a reading log that helps us move from
reading to writing. When we finish a reading assignment, for example, we sometimes
make an entry in a reading log about our reactions, the key points, and what we think

---

[12]There is a good deal of research about how readers are able to process new information. See, in particular,
Frank Smith, *Understanding Reading: A Psycholinguistic Analysis of Reading and Learning to Read* (Hillsdale,
NJ: L. Erlbaum, 1988).

> ╭─────────────────────╮
> │ **PRACTICE ACTIVITY 1-1** │
> ╰─────────────────────╯
>
> ## Marking a Text
>
> Compare the way you've marked a reading assignment in one of your courses with class-mates taking the same course. If possible, compare your markings to someone who took the course previously and did well. You may also want to visit the professor of the course during office hours to ask about strategies for reading the material of the course more successfully.
>
> **Consider:** Are you and your classmates marking the same information? In the same ways? How do your techniques compare with those of students who did well in the course?

of those ideas. Sometimes we copy sentences or short passages that we find difficult and then spend some time writing about what we understand, or why we find this passage challenging.[13] We find that we often understand smaller sections of the prose even when we don't understand everything in the text. Breaking apart complex sentences helps us to figure out what's being said. When we've participated in scholarly reading groups and read highly theoretical or obscure texts, we've found that our colleagues use these same strategies; working with others to unpack a complicated text, to test interpretations against what others understand is a common literate practice. Obviously using a dictionary can help us understand unknown vocabulary, but often writers explain unusual terms or an uncommon use of a term in the passage itself. Since such definitions are not always offered directly or simplistically, we've learned to look for repetitions or key words that can signal such definitions. Writers also use words that signal relationships between ideas and finding those words can help a complicated passage suddenly seem clearer. Summarizing the reading, or parts of the reading, can help crystallize the meaning and gives us a way of comparing our sense of the text with other readers' understandings.

Some readers use a notebook with legal margins (also called Cornell margins) as a reading log. Legal margins are wider than standard margins and we find it useful to copy passages from the text on the left and use the right hand side for our own notes. Sometimes we put our thoughts on one side, and use the other for points that arise in class discussions; or we make an initial entry on one side, and leave the other side for questions or comments that occur to us when we return to read our entry later. Others use a computer even for informal reading logs, saving each entry as a separate file or using different fonts to separate initial reactions from later ones. You should experiment with these suggestions, and talk with your classmates and teachers about techniques that they have developed to be good readers or to move from reading to writing. No one method works for everyone, and different techniques work for different kinds of reading or at different stages of a project, so most of us find it useful to know a range of strategies, choosing the most appropriate—or the most comfortable—for the task at hand. Writers who

---

[13]The Double-Entry Reading Log is a method explained by Anne Berthoff in her book *Forming/Thinking/Writing*, 2nd ed. with James Stephens (Portsmouth, NH: Boynton/Cook, 1988).

use reading logs of any kind usually find it useful to date each entry so when they return to the log they can track the progression of their own thinking.

Reading logs can also be useful when we want to speak back to the writer, argue against her ideas or provide our own examples to illustrate the meaning. Even when a reading is not difficult to understand, the issues it raises and the evidence it uses to support its point of view can be worth closer scrutiny, and we find writing can help us sort out which parts are worth more careful consideration. Some writers, and teachers of writing, talk about "joining the conversation" that the reading represents, and that conversation may have multiple parts that are not all well developed in any single piece of writing. Sometimes writers help us figure out those larger conversations, but often the only evidence of that larger debate is hiding in the footnotes or citations. Likewise some writers and teachers of writing talk about "reading with and against the grain." When we read "with the grain," we're trying to accept as much of the author's project as we possibly can, to think with her about the implications of the work and to imagine other cases that would support this point of view. But when we read "against the grain," we're trying to see what the author has left out, what his assumptions have kept him from noticing. We're also considering other examples that would contradict or raise questions about his work. To read both with and against the grain, then, requires that we balance these two impulses to see both the possibilities and the limitations in alteration and simultaneously.

We see this shift in attention and imagination as analogous to the famous illustrations of perception such as that of the old hag or the beautiful lady. When viewers first

FIGURE 1.2 Old or young woman?

see this image, they usually see either an old hag or a beautiful lady, but rarely both. Once you can shift your perception to see the alternative, psychologists say that your perception will alternate first to one, then to the other. This fluctuation of vision can happen so quickly that it can seem as if we are seeing both images simultaneously. When we read both with and against the grain, we have to practice seeing the possibilities and the limitations, and while we might take each one in turn, both can be valuable strategies for developing our own take on the conversation.

We also sometimes read, or reread, to pay specific attention to *how* the writer has constructed the piece. In such cases, we're letting the content fade to the background a bit in order to bring the rhetorical strategies and choices of the author more to the center of attention. We'll have more to say about rhetorical choices in the next chapter and Chapter 6 also considers how to attend to the features of a written text, but we think it's important for students to recognize from the beginning that reading as a writer is a bit different from reading as a scholar or student. When we read as a writer, the notes we make in the margins and the features we talk about with others are less about content and more about structure, style, or technique. As writers, we may copy into our reading logs those sentences that we find artfully crafted rather than the ones that hold the central point of the reading. And, in response, we may try to imitate the structure of that sentence, substituting new content and new words rather than responding to the meaning of that sentence. Some writers have a page in their reading logs for unusual words, figures of speech, or clever turns of phrase. Many writers create a page of their own common errors or a checklist of writing issues they use as they proofread, and they may include examples from their own writing as well as from what they read.

Our students sometimes complain that they've heard some of these suggestions before and that taking notes, stopping to ask questions and anticipate what they will read, or keeping a reading log or writer's notebook just takes too much time and isn't practical in the busy world of most college students. We certainly understand that these steps can take time to learn, but once you've learned to use them, they can help you to be more efficient and needn't take any more effort than sorting through your mail to decide what to read first. We also agree, as we said before, that not everything we need to read—whether in courses or in life—is worth this kind of careful attention. However, it's useful to develop strategies for learning from material that we find initially inaccessible or uninviting. Writing is one way to work on difficult material. When we write about what we've read, we often come to understand it better, and in understanding, find ways to connect the reading to our own interests and experiences. Talking with others about what we've read is also useful. Being an active reader—posing questions, paying attention to what has motivated the writer to produce the piece, noticing how pieces are put together—can help even the most difficult pieces of writing seem more interesting to us. Knowing how to work on a reading assignment—or better still how to use it for our own purposes—and being able to move between the active reading of a scholar and the active reading of a writer are marks of an educated, that is, literate, adult. Practice these skills in the writing course, and then use them, or not, as the situation requires. Practicing these strategies intentionally enough that you don't have to consciously think about them will transform them into habits that will serve you well long after your college courses are completed.

POSING QUESTIONS

Some writing is meant to reproduce the ideas, observations, and arguments of others, and those others are often experts of some sort. Encyclopedias or almanacs, for example, summarize information and present what is known in a compact and direct way. Writers of encyclopedias are not trying to make *new* knowledge; they aim to tell their readers what is already known. Likewise most newspaper articles provide an account or summary of some event or situation rather than make an argument; the arguments about news events appear in the editorials or feature columns. So, although lots of writing includes reporting on what is already known and may require synthesizing different sources of information together into a single account, repeating information is seldom — if ever — the most important part of college-level writing. Instead, making claims about what that information means, or how it might be used, or even why it is significant is at the heart of most academic writing because academics are writing, most often, to share their inquiry work with others. In the kind of writing that is at the center of this book — writing organized around and defined by the process of inquiry — the goal is decidedly not simply to replicate or rearrange what other writers have already told the world. Instead your writing will be an act of creation — a composing of meaning — and one of the primary ways such meaning making happens is through what Paulo Freire calls "problem-posing." Unlike problem solving where the task is to arrive at an answer or solve a problem, the work of problem-posing is to generate questions that enable us to investigate, reexamine, rethink, and even reimagine the worlds we inhabit. Posing problems, or problematizing, requires active engagement of a mind at work.

If questioning is at the heart of inquiry, what kinds of questions are most useful and how do you learn what to ask? Often writers use factual questions such as "who, what, where, when, and how" to investigate and shape their writing. Such questions are very common in journalistic writing, but they can be useful at various stages of an inquiry project as well. But again, if the factual question can be easily looked up or has a simple, straightforward answer, it probably will not produce a very interesting or engaging inquiry. For example, if you were to ask who owns a particular building in your neighborhood, the answer is usually relatively easy to discover, and your inquiry comes to a halt. However, if you ask a more complicated who question — who *uses* this building, or who *has used* this building — you might end up with a rich descriptive essay or uncover an interesting history or stories of individuals that are worth writing and reading. If you ask an even more complicated question — *why* is this building designed in this way, or *how* has this building changed over time in relation to how it was used — you could end up with an even richer piece that considers a particular place in relation to social and cultural values.

Of course factual or journalistic questions are not the only kind of questions researchers use. More often researchers are interested in the significance of the information they collect, so they ask a version of "so what?" or "who cares?" throughout the inquiry and writing process. We don't mean "so what?" here to be the cynical or sarcastic "so what?" that suggests in the very asking that *nobody* cares or at least that no one is interested. Rather the "so what?" of academic work relies on a deeply ingrained belief that of course people care, and of course they want to know why. In this context, "so what?" is a prompt to curiosity and an invitation to speculate rather than an accusation that nothing matters or that to be interested is somehow silly. Finding what you care about, what interests you, what primes the pump of your mind is the key to making your questions ones you'll want to pursue.

Researchers don't stop with just one question. Instead questions lead to other questions, and that's how inquiry progresses. If you were reading Leo Chavez's essay on immigration, you might get curious about where particular immigrant groups have settled in the United States, and you might turn to the MLA language map based on census data at http://www.mla.org to get a quick answer to that question. But once you saw the map, you would probably start asking other questions, and those additional questions could lead to an inquiry. Asking "how does the distribution of the Hmong immigrants compare with that of other immigrants from Southeast Asia?" would let you use the comparison feature on this same Web site to find a satisfactory answer. But asking "why did the Hmong cluster in these areas?" is a more complicated question that would require you to locate other sources of information. Asking "what problems have the Hmong (or other immigrants) encountered?" might require you to use not only secondary sources such as newspaper accounts, government reports, or ethnographic accounts,[14] but also to interview people in your own area.

Of course sometimes the questions you start with lead in very different, seemingly unrelated, directions. Let's take that same example of wondering where immigrant groups have settled in the United States and finding the language map. If, at that point, you took a step back to consider a broader issue such as language diversity, or the map itself, your investigation would lead in a totally new direction than if you began to follow questions about specific immigrant groups or patterns of settlement. Again, some of the questions you might ask—who created this language map? how is the information generated? what do the creators hope to achieve?—can be answered by carefully reading information on the site itself. But if you asked "how has this language map been used so far?" you would have to develop a different strategy for investigation. Perhaps that strategy would include using a citation index to see which scholars have referenced the map in their work, and you would need to learn how to use a citation index[15] in order to continue your investigation. Of course you might not ask any of these questions because you aren't interested in language differences, immigration, or the role of professional organizations in language study or policy questions. Curiosity and interest are central to good inquiry, and if you aren't interested, it's doubtful that you can ask questions that are complex enough to sustain a real inquiry.

Researchers are always working out of their own experiences, bringing their own interests to bear on what they encounter. If you read carefully, or investigate the body of work of any particular scholar, you'll probably uncover the signs of personal experience, interest, and of who or what is influencing the direction of a scholar's research. Most academics follow a trajectory—what is sometimes called a "research agenda"—as they work with similar questions across a number of different situations, or try to answer big questions by thinking very specifically about smaller ones. Our students rarely have decided on big issues that they want to spend their lives investigating, but they all have the ability to make connections to what they already know or are interested in, and they all have the capacity to step back from those specific interests to consider why such issues matter, who should care, or what their work might mean.

---

[14]See, for example, Anne Fadiman, *The Spirit Catches You and You Fall Down: A Hmong Child, Her American Doctors, and the Collision of Two Cultures* (New York: Farrar, 1997).
[15]Citation indexes are now included in most libraries' electronic databases and separated into Arts and Humanities Citation Index, Science Citation Index, and Social Science Citation Index. The research staff at most libraries will help you learn to use this resource free of charge.

Generating Questions

Spend some time exploring the MLA language map. (http://www.mla.org), and use it to generate several questions that you might investigate about specific language groups, the patterns of language use in the United States, or the uses of the map itself. Use your own experiences and interests to find connections that you could explore.

Consider: How would you go about answering any of the questions you've generated? What resources would you turn to or what methods of investigation do you think you would have to use? What would make such work interesting to you?

While curiosity, experience, and intuition are important to good inquiry, there are some standard strategies for learning to ask good questions. In fact asking questions is so common in investigation and inquiry that there are questions—usually called heuristics— that are frequently listed in writing texts as "invention" strategies. Used as an invention strategy, the questions are meant to help writers figure out what can be said about any given topic X. In the chart we've included as Figure 1.3, notice that these questions are followed by a type (or mode) of writing. In a more traditional writing curriculum, students are often assigned to write in a particular mode, say definition, and the corresponding question can be used to generate content that is likely to fit the required mode. Researchers use heuristics not to fill in a mode, however, but to consider the range of information that is known and unknown about their topic of investigation.

Another useful way of organizing questions is via Bloom's taxonomy. Originally developed by Benjamin Bloom in 1956, Bloom's taxonomy was revised in 2001 to reflect further research in cognition and learning. Both versions identify six different levels of critical thought and the types of questions that lead to these levels of cognition. See Figure 1.4.[16] The most common use of Bloom's taxonomy is by teachers in crafting assignments or test questions. Teachers often try to begin with knowledge/factual questions in discussions in order to determine that everyone has the same basic understanding of the material. More advanced assignments usually ask students to analyze, synthesize, or apply information. In terms of inquiry projects, Bloom's taxonomy can allow you to think more deeply about your project and shape more difficult questions for yourself.

The movement from knowledge to evaluation reflects increasingly complex and sophisticated ways of thinking about your work, but this is less a simple linear progression than it might seem. In fact these different levels of questions tend to overlap and

---

[16]There are some interesting changes in the two versions, including shifting from nouns to verbs, adding a second element to reflect a knowledge dimension in addition to a cognitive process dimension, and reversing the order of the final two stages. These shifts, however, are not so important to our purpose here—demonstrating ways of conceptualizing and using questions in inquiry projects. For further explanation of the differences in the original and the revised versions of Bloom's taxonomy, see Jackie Acree Walsh and Beth Dankert Sattes, *Quality Questioning: Research-Based Practice to Engage Every Learner* (Thousand Oaks, CA: Corwin Press; [Charleston, WV]: AEL, 2005).

FIGURE 1.3 Heuristic questions

Heuristic Questions	Modes of Writing
What is X?	Definition
How can X be described?	Description
What are the component parts of X?	Simple Analysis
How is X made or done?	Process Analysis
How should X be made or done?	Directional Analysis
What is the essential function of X?	Functional Analysis
What are the causes of X?	Causal Analysis
What are the consequences of X?	Causal Analysis
What are the types of X?	Classification
How does X compare with Y?	Comparison
What is the present status of X?	Comparison
How can X be interpreted?	Interpretation
What are the facts about X?	Reportage
How did X happen?	Narration
What kind of person is X?	Characterization
What is my personal response to X?	Reflection
What is my memory of X?	Reminiscence
What is the value of X?	Evaluation
How can X be summarized?	Summary
What case can be made for/against X?	Argumentation

Adapted from Berke, Jacqueline. *Twenty Questions for the Writer: A Rhetoric with Readings.* 2nd ed. New York: Harcourt, 1976.

be used in a more recursive way by researchers. If you use Bloom's taxonomy as a guide to inquiry, some of the kinds of thinking you do in the early stages can also be useful at later stages. For example, you might begin with the question about how the Hmong compare with other immigrant groups—a comprehension level question in Bloom's taxonomy—but as you do your investigation, you would probably have to analyze a number of different features of the immigrant experience and analysis is clearly a "higher" stage of Bloom's taxonomy. When you start compiling your data into a written form to share with others, though, the questions of comparison, or even factual information, will still be important.

When you were deciding on which colleges to attend, you probably went through an inquiry process, even though it may not have seemed very much like formal research. You might have browsed Web sites, talked to friends or family members, collected data about costs and student profiles. You might not have done any formal writing during this process, but you probably did keep lists, send letters or e-mail to

FIGURE 1.4   Bloom's original taxonomy

- **Knowledge**: factual answers (who, what, where, when, how), describe, recall and recognition, define, list
- **Comprehension**: interpreting and extrapolating, understanding of facts, translating, compare and contrast, classify, represent, tell or narrate
- **Application**: applying to new situations, taking a new slant, solving problems by applying acquired knowledge, fact, or rules in a new way, predict, apply
- **Analysis**: breaking down into parts, forms by identifying motives or causes
- **Synthesis**: combining elements into a new pattern, something not there before
- **Evaluation**: employing some set of criteria, explaining the criteria, explaining why

request information, and compose, at least orally, descriptions for friends and arguments for your family about why one choice was better than another. As you worked your way through this decision-making process, then, you probably asked different questions at different times, and returned to the same questions more than once in the process.

Researchers also have to recognize when they are asking questions that just can't be answered, or at least not answered very convincingly with the resources and time they have available. If, when you were investigating which college to attend, you posed the question "where will I meet my true love?" you would have recognized that no amount of research could answer that question with much certainty. Likewise, if you are interested in investigating how a particular building on your campus reflects the values of the time in which it was built, you wouldn't try to do a survey to answer that question. And if you wanted to understand the reasons behind the language patterns visible on the MLA language map, you wouldn't expect to conduct oral histories in multiple states in only a couple of weeks. So, choosing an appropriate method for your inquiry and recognizing the limits of what can reasonably be done can help you refine your inquiry before you ever get started.

Because figuring out which questions to ask and how you might begin an inquiry can require more time than is available in the standard college term, we've designed assignments that jump-start this process by suggesting a beginning question and method of inquiry. We understand that it's difficult for students at the beginning of their academic careers to have the depth of knowledge to carry out complicated inquiry projects, so we've structured the assignment sequences to build on one another, indicated where collaborative efforts might be useful, and provided more assignments than most classes will use so that teachers and/or students can make choices without losing the unity of the inquiry. The best work, however, will come when your own curiosity and interests take over and you become invested enough in the work you are doing that you go off in directions that we simply can't anticipate, but which your teacher and classmates can help you pursue.

PRACTICE ACTIVITY 1-3

Posing Questions to Continue an Inquiry

The various articles and videos collected on the Modern Media Initiatives for a Sustainable Future at http://www.onewater.org/index.htm are, in many ways, "finished" products, but they also represent an ongoing inquiry. Examine any of the articles or videos at this site, and consider what additional questions you would pose for yourself if you were going to carry this work further? What questions do you think these contributors have begun to ask, but not quite answered in their presentations?

Consider: When have you used questions to guide you in some real-life process? How did that inquiry process work for you? Thinking back, what additional questions could you have asked to push your inquiry further?

USING THIS BOOK

The material we've collected into this book is meant to be used in a variety of ways, depending on the goals of the particular course, the judgments of individual teachers, and the needs of specific students or classes. Unlike most textbooks our students are accustomed to using, this book is unlikely to be read from front to back in the order material appears, and some parts of the book—like the next chapter on presenting inquiries in writing—are often turned to several times over the course of the term.

The assignment sequences are designed for the most part to take you through a variety of methods as you work to investigate a particular topic. A few of the sequences have been designed to center on a single method for the entire course, experimenting with different ways to use that method to generate inquiry projects that can then be revised or adapted for different purposes. Most sequences are built around readings and so invite you to think about your own inquiry projects in relation to the work of other scholars. These readings also serve, then, to exemplify methods or combinations of methods as well as the ways that scholars have presented their work in a final piece of writing. Because the readings have been chosen to reflect a wide array of disciplinary perspectives, there are significant differences in how these writers present their work as well as in the kinds of questions they choose to address, and we think those differences are well worth your attention. The sequences that are focused on a single method, however, have been designed to work without the readings, though it is certainly possible to turn to the readings to see examples of that method in practice. We've also provided sample projects that can serve as an alternative to the sequences. In classes that choose to work with the projects, readings and the methods chapters may still be used, but the work that is generated by the class itself will dictate which methods and which readings may prove useful.

Like the sample projects, the assignment sequences invite you to construct your own inquiry projects, most often by testing the ideas or conclusions of the readings in a new situation or with new material or by trying the same method in a different context. The methods chapters are meant to explain in more detail how you might go about doing this work. Because they work together, then, most teachers move back and forth between the readings and the methods chapters. We've also included some samples of student writing so you can see how other students worked with these methods or pursued the questions raised in the sequence of assignments. We don't want to suggest that these examples of inquiry—neither the student inquiries nor those of more experienced scholars—are without problems. Rather we think most readers will see both possibilities and limitations of this work, and sometimes it will be the gaps that will inspire you or get you thinking in new ways. This is how writing functions in the academic world, and in lots of other contexts as well: what seems most problematic generates new ideas and new investigations.

We've included in the assignment sequences two aspects that we believe are critical to developing those habits of mind we discussed earlier. First, after each assignment we invite you to take a few minutes to record your reflections about your own learning, and at the end of the sequence, we invite you to look back over your work, including those notes of reflection, and take stock of what you've done and learned. We've found that many students see these reflections as an opportunity to praise (or find fault with) themselves, the course, or the teacher, but we want to encourage you to move past such simple reactions and instead think more deeply about your own work. This ability to analyze your own work—to see its limits and possibilities, to consider what else might be done and why you didn't do those things already, to identify what else you need to learn and how you might go about doing so—will serve you well as you move through your other college courses and into your life beyond college. As you've probably noticed, these reflective opportunities are specifically tied to the quality of self-reflection that we identified as an important habit of mind essential to inquiry.

The second feature we've included in every sequence is an emphasis on different kinds of revision. One of us has a son who learned to do revisions in elementary school, but his strategy was to compose his essay at the computer, print it out, and then run the spell checker. As the computer identified each misspelled word, he would circle it on the printed copy and accept the correction on the screen. By printing a new copy of the corrected essay, he could present the "first draft" and "final copy" to his teacher. Revising done. We know that our college-level students do more than run the spell checker when we ask for revisions, but many of our students have come to equate revising with "fixing mistakes" or "adding what the teacher wants" and neither of these is what most writing teachers mean when they ask students to revise. So, the assignment sequences frequently suggest revising previous work by adding another method, incorporating the work of other scholars, or representing the work in a different form for a different audience. In the next chapter we have more to say about different kinds of revision because even when the assignments don't specify a particular kind of revision, we think it's useful to be thinking about how the inquiry might be furthered through revision and how the presentation of the inquiry in writing might be altered. We know very few strong writers who aren't also adept at revision, and revising helps foster the habit of mind of flexibility.

As you use this book, we hope that you'll find something that sparks your interest and that you'll discover the pleasure of deliberation, figuring out what to ask and how to find possible answers. If you stay flexible in your thinking, taking time to think through options and to consider your work from different angles, the risks you take can pay off in interesting writing that may very well have a life outside the class assignment. If you learn to see what isn't already done, to be precise in making distinctions and to be reflective as you weigh possible meanings, you will be engaged in using and developing the habits of mind that will last far beyond a single course—habits of mind that will mark you as a literate citizen.

INQUIRY AND THE INTERNET

Throughout this text you'll find references to Web sites and other Internet resources. We know that most of our students are accustomed to using the Internet to locate information and that they are often comfortable writing for Internet audiences as well. Handbooks and research guides, particularly those that are regularly updated by your own institution's library, will provide an overview of the strategies for searching the web, as well as the dangers inherent in using such resources. Your instructor may have particular guidelines for you to follow because courses that use this text may also have a responsibility to ensure that you are comfortable using more traditional print sources and understanding the resources of your own institution's library. We'll offer just two quick cautions and hope that these spark a discussion among you and your classmates about using the Internet effectively.

First, remember that information you find on the Internet may not be reliable or even accurate, and that like print sources, Web sites are written by people who have a particular point of view and their own purposes. Pay attention to who sponsors (or creates) the Web sites you consult and to how recently the information was updated. A study by Graham and Metaxas reported in *Communications of the ACM* (May 2003) indicated that while undergraduate students regularly use the Internet for research, they tend to rely on a single search engine even though none of the engines available cover more than an estimated sixteen percent of the material available. Graham and Metaxas also found that students rarely check the accuracy of the information and are usually more confident than they should be about the reliability of the data they find. The study also suggests that students are particularly susceptible to advertisements and government misinformation, and are not more critical consumers of Internet information as their skills increase.

Second, the ability to cut and paste information from the Internet can make it very easy to unintentionally plagiarize material. Remember that any material you use in your own writing should be acknowledged by properly citing the original source. Even if you are borrowing ideas and not using the exact words of the original, you should still provide a citation. To avoid unintentional wholesale copying, take notes from Internet sources as you would from print material—paraphrasing or summarizing rather than merely pasting in the information. Handbooks will provide you with examples of citation forms, but the general principle of helping your reader to locate the information applies to material from the Internet just as it does to print documents.

At the end of each chapter, we provide you with a list of Internet Resources relevant to the chapter. We also repeat any Web sites that are referenced in the chapter so they will be easier to locate.

Internet Resources

A list of undergraduate research journals is available through the Council on Undergraduate Research at http://www.cur.org/ugjournal .html which also sponsors conferences and solicits donations to help fund undergraduate projects.

The Boyer Report is available online at http://www .reinventioncenter.miami.edu/TheBoyerReport .html. Other education-related work undertaken by the Carnegie Corporation is described and regularly updated at http://www. carnegie.org/sub/ program/education.html.

Several national foundations and grant agencies sponsor or coordinate undergraduate research opportunities. See, for example, the grants available from The National Science Foundation at http://www.nsf.gov/funding/pgm_summ.jsp?pims_id=5517&from=fund and the summer programs offered by The National Institute of Environmental Health Sciences at http://www.niehs.nih.gov/summers/ and by NASA at http://research.nianet.org/larss/index.html. You can find others by using search terms like "undergraduate research," "summer research," or "research funding for students." Many states also provide programs and funding for undergraduates. Consult your own institution's office of undergraduate research or career planning program for additional resources.

The materials at http://www.socialresearchmethods.net/ are particularly useful for those doing social science research and needing to formulate appropriate research questions either alone or in collaboration with others. The "project gallery" on this site is particularly interesting for its collection of student research projects from a number of different disciplinary areas.

Web Sites Referenced in This Chapter

The MLA language map
   http://www.mla.org

The Modern Media Initiatives for a Sustainable Future
   http://www.onewater.org/index.htm

CHAPTER 2

PRESENTING INQUIRY: RHETORICAL CHOICES AND WRITING ISSUES

As we discussed in Chapter 1, researchers don't really do their research and then "write it up." Instead, researchers write throughout the process of their inquiries, in both formal and informal forms. Nevertheless there comes a moment when researchers are ready to share their work with others, and most of the time that sharing requires a written document. In this chapter we want to consider some of the choices that researchers make as they shape written products to share their work, choices that depend on who they want to speak to (the audience) and what goals they have for that particular piece of writing (the purpose). We also want to consider some of the common issues that arise as researchers present their inquiry projects in writing. While it may be helpful to read through this chapter as you begin to shape the presentation of your inquiry, we think it will probably be most helpful to turn to the various sections as you write or rewrite to work on these particular issues. Though we present these issues separately, it's important to remember that these rhetorical choices are actually interconnected.

WHAT DOES AUDIENCE HAVE TO DO WITH IT?

As writers we commonly think of our audience as someone who will read or might read our work, and in a class setting it is easy to think that the only reader who matters is the teacher. To engage in the active learning required of inquiry projects, however, requires that you think beyond the immediate audience of your teacher, or even the few classmates who may read your writing, and instead consider as rhetorical scholars Lisa Ede and Andrea Lunsford have suggested that your work is directed "not just to the intended, actual, or eventual readers of a discourse [the audience addressed], but to all those whose image, ideas, or actions influence a writer during the process of composition [the audience invoked]."[1] For Ede and Lunsford, this invoked audience requires us to think about the various interested parties or stakeholders—people who have informed our project and those who might be interested in what we've done.

Interested parties and stakeholders are terms that allow us to think about different kinds of audiences even as we conduct our inquiry. Those who are interested may be interested for a variety of personal or professional reasons. The various photo essays, articles, and videos of the University of Miami's Modern Media Initiatives for a Sustainable Future[2] mentioned in Practice Activity 3 of Chapter 1 are good examples of how researchers deal with these complex audiences. For example we're sure that those *interested* in the various student-produced essays on this site include friends and family, residents of Miami, ecologists, and perhaps government officials. We're also certain that these essays have been informed by a number of different people, and different primary and secondary sources. Because wrong or misrepresented information could have serious consequences, each of these contributors had to be sure to get permission for the photographs they took, and they had to tell people they interviewed what they were doing. As these writers composed and revised their work, they were thinking about all the different individuals who would see the finished product, about how to accurately represent what they had found, and about how to inform some members of their audience, challenge some, and motivate still others. If all these authors wanted to do was to create an interesting collection of photographs, they might be able to ignore the concerns of those who didn't support or like their work. Inquiry projects, however, like these documentary photo essays, are more interested in thinking through complicated issues than in coming up with simple pro/con stances or tidy solutions. Thus inquiry projects force writers to consider how to speak to the full spectrum of possible audiences rather than only to those who already share a particular point of view or those who are easily positioned as the opposing side in need of persuasion or enlightenment.

Likewise the Organizational Needs Assessment Project described in the Sample Projects section later in this book invites students to investigate and then make recommendations for improving some aspect of an organization, group, or business. When students have chosen to focus on a particular feature of the campus, say the dining services, their work becomes more interesting, complex, and responsible when they recognize that those who work in the dining hall are as much a part of their invoked audience as are their friends who eat there. When we consider audience in relation to our writing, we are working to determine not only what form our final work should take, but also what values and assumptions our potential readers will share with each other and with us. Even when the immediate reader is an individual or group that is very specific, other readers are still possible and ought not to be forgotten. When we think about these different audiences, even if we can convince ourselves that they will never actually see our writing, we are also forced to think about how our writing will represent them and us; the way we write can make us seem silly or thoughtful, scrupulous or prejudicial, trustworthy or flippant. The decisions we make are not simply a matter of ethical behavior or effective persuasion; they demonstrate tolerance for diverse perspectives which is one of the habits of mind that inquiry work values and seeks to develop.

---

[1] Lisa Ede and Angela Lunsford. "Audience Addressed Audience Invoked: The Role of Audience in Composition Theory and Pedagogy," *College Composition and Communication* 35.2 (1984): 155–71.
[2] http://www.onewater.org/.

DISCOURSE COMMUNITIES AND GENRE EXPECTATIONS

One way to think about how audience can alter our writing is to consider discourse communities. Discourse communities are groups of people who share a common language, common interests, and sometimes common goals even if they are not physically located in the same place. In fact many discourse communities meet only through the writing they share. When scholars think about writing a piece directed to others in the same field of study, they are writing to a particular discourse community. In such cases some of the decisions about how to shape the writing may be made by simply following the standards expected in their field. When you look at the readings in this book, you'll notice several very different styles of writing, even different ways of documenting sources. Such differences are usually because the writers were originally following expectations of their discipline or conforming to the stylistic choices of a particular journal. You may have encountered a form commonly used in the sciences and social sciences that begins with an abstract summarizing the study, introduces the reasons for the study or its central questions by outlining the relevant prior research, and then includes separate sections for explaining methods, data analysis, results, and discussion or conclusions. Though such an overt form is not used in the humanities, many researchers still make these gestures someplace in their formal presentation. That is, they will refer to relevant prior research, often using such prior work to introduce their own investigation or establish its distinctive features, key terms, and place within a larger discussion. Likewise most researchers reveal relevant aspects of their method of investigation, in part to establish that their conclusions are trustworthy and that readers can believe the evidence because it has been collected in a systematic way, but also in part because revealing the method identifies the work as fitting the expectations of the discourse community. Researchers who use the method of direct observation are probably in a different discourse community than researchers who do surveys, and those who analyze archival materials are usually working from a different disciplinary training than those who conduct focus group interviews. These different methods, however, cannot be said to belong to only one discipline or one discourse community. Similarly different discourse communities rely on different forms for providing evidence or referencing the work of others, but all research communities expect to find citations that will lead readers back to the original sources and to the work of others that has been referenced or summarized. Although there are some studies whose primary purpose is to summarize what has already happened, or to pull together different studies on a similar topic, even these summary-based research reports analyze data and draw conclusions. In other words all researchers, no matter what form of presentation they use to share their work with others, are moving beyond the direct reporting common to encyclopedias and engaging in analysis and deliberation.

Because discourse communities can be counted on to have some knowledge in common, specialized terms can be used without elaborate explanation, theories or common procedures can be assumed, and the value of the work can be treated as a given rather than justified through argument. A discourse community, though, will also expect the writer/researcher to adhere to common good practice and will question the work with a more informed eye than will a reader from outside the community. Members of a discourse community are not just looking for others to agree with them. After all, who wants to read (or write) something that everyone already knows or finds obvious? In the academic world, researchers routinely send their writing out for "peer review" and revise their presentation, or even redesign their research, to address concerns raised by these knowledgeable peers.

PRACTICE ACTIVITY 2-1

Language and Discourse Communities

Make a list of the various groups and organizations that you belong to or have belonged to in the past. Remember to think of groups that aren't official—skateboarders, babysitters, stepchildren—as well as the more formally organized ones—scouting groups, high school bands, church choirs. Choose one or more of these groups and make another list of the specific language or language practices that this group uses that might be considered unusual or specialized or that outsiders would not immediately understand in the same way as members of the group. Make a third list of the ways new members to the group learn (or are taught) the language and language practices.

Consider: Compare your lists with those of your classmates. What commonalities can you find across different kinds of groups? How would you describe the categories of language, language practices, and language learning that you've uncovered in this brief practice? How might you go about investigating the language-related practices of a group to which you did not already belong?

While it's common to think of discourse communities as primarily represented by different disciplines and to imagine these different disciplines have particular genres they expect writers to use when they present their research, neither discourse communities nor forms for writing are this simple. Because scientists understand their role to be investigators of the natural world testing hypotheses and looking for consequences, they present their research primarily as a report of what they've done and what happened. They often frame their individual study with a review of the literature, that is, the prior research that is related to the question they are investigating or the precise procedure they are trying to replicate. Since there are often a number of different ways to position a study in relation to prior work, scientists make choices about which studies to cite and which features of their work they want to emphasize for a particular audience. These reports are usually presented using language that is as neutral as possible, and the sentence structure is commonly passive voice because the emphasis is on what happened—not on who did what. Researchers in the humanities, however, see their role as interpreters of textual evidence looking for meanings in human cultures and artifacts. Research in the humanities often works to examine singular examples in careful detail, or compares a small number of carefully chosen exemplars meant to reflect a pattern or generalization of some kind. Often these researchers are working within a particular theoretical perspective to read the particular text as fitting within or challenging that theory. Social scientists understand their role to be theorizers working to understand human behavior and the social systems humans create. Social scientists can do work that draws on scientific traditions and so employ hypotheses and fixed procedures, or they may draw on a more humanistic tradition and interpret data of various kinds as if they were reading a set of texts.

While these broad distinctions among the three primary divisions of academic work—sciences, humanities, and social sciences—may still be generally true, more and more research reflects a crossing of disciplinary boundaries as researchers ask questions or work with materials that cannot be confined to traditional disciplines. Such interdisciplinary work speaks to an audience with members from different discourse communities and different disciplinary expectations so it may combine features from sciences, humanities, and social sciences in unusual ways. In fact many researchers in the social sciences in particular have called into question the reliance on forms that originated in the sciences, forms that tend to hide the actions of the researcher. Especially in such fields as anthropology, researchers openly have argued about how to present their research and have often turned to narrative formats that make their own perspectives and biases a more explicit part of the presentation.

One of the difficulties for students who are just beginning their college studies is that they aren't yet fully members of any disciplinary community; they don't have the background knowledge that members of the discipline have, they aren't aware of the ongoing debates in that field, and they may not recognize the differences in the usual forms for presenting research that are treated as commonplaces in various disciplines or the way these forms have been challenged. In addition, academic disciplines aren't the only place where the work of inquiry projects matters, so there are many more genres available for presenting research than are represented by the usual forms in these three broad disciplinary divisions. Think, for example, of the forms that might be used to present research in a business setting, or how those in various governmental bodies charged with making decisions might consider the implications of an inquiry. Furthermore, even when academics present their research outside of academic journals or scholarly books, they are unlikely to follow the standard academic forms, though many of the same rhetorical moves may still be required. For example, when academics apply for funding to continue their research, they almost always have to present their work to an audience that includes scholars from other disciplines. They may still provide a summary of prior research, lay out their methods, argue for the importance of the particular example they are concerned with exploring, and give credit to others through citations, but these moves will not appear in the same form that they would take if the research was being written for a scholarly publication.

So, as we said before, it would be easier if the forms for presenting research matched up neatly to the methods of investigation or to the questions asked, but such is not the case. When you think about presenting your research, you have to think about different genres and the possibilities and limits of each. It may be useful to think of music as an example. We might say that in general country music tells a story of lost love or heartbreak, but we recognize a song as "country" long before we've heard the story told in the lyrics. There are particular rhythms and even different instruments that separate country from jazz, classical from new age, or gospel from rap. When a song sounds like country but violates one or more of the expected conventions, it will either be touted as a new innovation or dismissed as failing to fit. As another example, think of the various genres for oral speech. Telling a joke is different from delivering a sermon, and those differences aren't just a matter of length or subject matter. While those hearing a sermon might appreciate the interjection of a joke, such a blending of genres needs to be done with careful attention to the audience's expectations or the attempt at humor will be seen as inappropriate, perhaps even sacrilegious. Many people have preferences for particular genres when they read for pleasure; some prefer mysteries, poetry, romance, or spy thrillers. Likewise most of us have our favorite type of movies—documentaries, comedies, historical dramas, suspense—but enjoy different genres at different times depending on our mood or the subject being depicted. Again, we recognize these types by their subject matter *and* by the way they make use of particular stylistic features. While it is possible for books and movies, like talk and music, to employ features of more than one genre, such combinations must be done with skill to create a hybrid that is innovative rather than a confusing failure. Those decisions are not made without considering both the intended audience and the intended purpose.

We don't believe an introductory writing course can teach you all these variations for presenting your inquiry because each inquiry can be presented in so many different forms and to so many different audiences with a number of different purposes in mind. Nor do we think it is useful to try to force inquiries into formulaic versions of standard disciplinary genres. You'll learn the various forms for presenting your research to academic audiences as you move through different classes, and the forms used most often in your major area of study will eventually seem obvious to you. Instead of concentrating on learning the features of traditional formats, then, we want to encourage you to be aware of genre differences, to choose a form that matches your audience and purpose, to experiment with different ways of presenting your research, and to pay attention to what happens to your research and your writing as you move from one form to another or work to combine usual forms into something new. Meanwhile your classmates comprise an immediate discourse community that can hold you accountable for what you say and how you say it. Your peer readers can help you consider what format you should use to present your research, and they can help you see if you are following the style of a particular genre effectively and correctly. Being a peer reviewer in an inquiry class, then, requires your serious attention and your honest assessment of the work and the writing. Figure 2.1 provides examples of questions that peer reviewers can consider as they respond to work done by their classmates.

FRAMING YOUR WORK

In written work something has to come first, and this introductory move is an important place to establish the authority to speak, set the tone, and capture the readers' interest. We think it's useful to think not just about the specific paragraph(s) of introduction, but of how you want to frame the presentation of your inquiry. Like framing a photograph or piece of artwork, the frame for the written presentation of your inquiry depends on a number of issues. Frames are partly a matter of taste (do you like the elaborate carving of an antique wood frame or sleek black metal?), partly determined by the content (you probably wouldn't use the same frame for a candid snapshot of friends as you would for a formal wedding portrait of your grandparents), and partly dependent on where you intend to display the final result (the photos on your desk would probably be framed differently if they were to appear as part of an art exhibit). So, when you think about how to frame your work, you will find yourself once again considering those questions of audience, purpose, and genre that we've already discussed, but you will also have to consider even more closely the question of authority: How do you want to present yourself, and how do you establish for your reader that you know what you're talking about?

There are several common strategies for developing introductions, including: the inverted triangle (start broad, narrow to the specific topic), the interesting anecdote, the startling statistic, the interesting example, the provocative question, and the dictionary definition. Many students think they need to retell the story of their inquiry when they present their work, in writing. Such a narrative *might* be an appropriate

FIGURE 2.1 Questions for peer review

- Is the overarching question or point of the inquiry clear? If not, what should the writer do to clarify the project? Look at the introduction or frame as well as the conclusion. Consider the relationship of the parts to the whole. Are any promises made in the beginning kept? Are issues raised in the conclusion connected to what has come before but without being redundant? Try summarizing the project and the main points, and see if other readers and the author agree.

- Is the method of investigation either clear or can be assumed as obvious? Is it clear how the evidence was obtained, and does that method seem reliable, consistent, and ethical? Have shortcuts been taken with the method of investigation that make the conclusions suspicious? Is the method appropriate for the questions being considered? What other methods might be useful to advance the inquiry?

- Is the evidence appropriate to support the conclusions drawn? Are the claims logical given the evidence? If data are presented in tables, charts, or other graphics, are those insertions appropriate and correct? What shortcomings might be overcome by additional work? Which evidence or conclusions are difficult to accept and why?

- What questions arise upon reading through the piece? Should those questions be answered in this work or do they suggest additional inquiry possibilities? Are there places that are confusing? What could the writer do to help readers follow the presentation better or to answer the questions that arise?

- What stakeholders or interested parties are apparent in this work? How are those potential audiences constructed in this piece of writing? Is that construction fair and ethical?

- How has the writer established the authority to write on the topic? Does the writer seem believable and trustworthy? What could be done to correct any problems with the authorial construction?

- Is the form for presenting the work appropriate? Does the writer follow the usual conventions of the genre being used? What changes would make the presentation fit more effectively into the expectations readers are likely to have when they see this research presented in this form?

frame, but usually readers are not interested in all the details of your search and would rather know what you found, why it matters, how you did your work and what it all means. Telling the story of your research will lead you to present your work in chronological order, but such an arrangement rarely helps readers understand what is most important and part of the researcher's task is to present the inquiry in a way that shows the patterns of analysis, demonstrates the connections between different sources of information, and confirms the appropriateness of the interpretations or conclusions. Some genres for presenting research—such as the usual social-science form that we described earlier—may seem to settle the problem of framing by insisting that particular sections be included, but even in these forms, the opening gesture that positions the research being reported in relation to prior research or current concerns requires that the writer make choices.

Very few research studies have an introduction that is only a single paragraph in length, yet students are usually taught to write introductory paragraphs that end with a single sentence that states the point they intend to prove or the conclusion they have reached through their analysis (what is sometimes called the "thesis statement"). A single sentence that functions as a thesis is as rare as single paragraphs of introduction. Indeed, if you look carefully at the readings included here, you will see that these authors almost always have several paragraphs of introduction before they identify the specific question or issue that is at the heart of the research they are presenting. While there is probably a point that these researchers want to convey, it may have several interconnected parts, need to move from one point to another with supporting evidence for each part, or require a preliminary discussion to contextualize the research they conducted. Thus, those beginning paragraphs usually do a number of different moves, including:

- Position the work in relation to prior research or a current concern.
- Provide definitions that establish the perspective or underlying theory informing the research.
- Explain the method used for the investigation.
- Clarify what is and isn't addressed (i.e, narrow the focus to a doable project).

Clearly this is a lot to do while also getting the reader's interest and establishing the authority to speak, so it's really no wonder that research is rarely introduced with a single paragraph. On the other hand, the introductory frame has to get to the point efficiently without wandering off on irrelevant tangents or providing details that more properly belong later. As you work on framing your research, you'll want to take time to establish what you are doing and why it matters and you'll probably need to revise your prose to be as concise as possible. Some writers think of this framing move as similar to introducing people you really like and respect to one another. If you've ever tried to do such an introduction, or watched others who make such introductions well, you know that you need to give these people some key information about each other. In effect you're establishing some common ground so these guests can continue to talk together. Some writers think of the frame as the opening bid in a card game. You want your readers to have a sense about what you have in your hand, but you probably don't want to give away everything or overbid by making claims that are grander than you can really establish with the research you've done. Some writers think of the frame as providing an outline, especially if the research is complicated or has multiple parts. Some writers speak of the frame as if they are entering a conversation that has been going on for some time; they want to show that they have been listening well enough to know what the key issues are, and then they offer the new idea, or new research, that contributes to that conversation.

Of course introducing your inquiry is not the same as introducing people to one another or playing a card game or sketching an outline or joining a conversation, but these analogies each suggest something important about the task of framing your work: you want your readers to be curious about the issues you're raising, to think well of you, to have some sense of what to expect, and to trust that you've paid attention to related work. Making these moves with confidence usually requires considerable practice and lots of rewriting. Probably the best way to learn to write the introductory frame is to spend some time carefully examining the frames of a number of different research presentations. The readings in this book give you easy access to a wide array of frames, and you can watch for other examples as you read scholarship in other courses or turn to library resources to support your own inquiry projects.

Some writers use a quotation from another source to begin their presentation, and they may or may not make explicit reference to this quotation. Likewise most academic writers use the title to help frame the presentation, but different conventions exist for how explicit or "catchy" the title should be. Sometimes a formal abstract precedes the beginning frame, especially in the sciences and social sciences. Headings and subheadings within a piece can help reinforce the frame by echoing key words or employing parallel construction as they signal divisions and connections. When researchers are presenting their work as a book-length project, they typically write an introduction to the whole book that includes a summary of the various chapters or sections in addition to establishing the overarching questions the work is addressing. Then each chapter must establish how the work in that particular chapter relates to what has come before; this move is often made through summary and repetition. Frames help readers to determine whether the study is relevant to their interests, or to locate the particular sections within a longer study that are of most interest to their own purposes. The framing move, then, is dependent on genre, length, audience, publication requirements, and the specific material being presented. In almost every case, the writer is implicitly answering the questions: Why should anyone be interested in reading this research and what questions does it attempt to answer?

PRACTICE ACTIVITY 2-2

Identifying the Frame

Look through the opening paragraphs of several of the readings to identify how these writers have framed their projects. What strategies do you see them using? How exactly do they signal the purpose of their own work? How do these frames help the writer establish a relationship with the reader? Where do you see the writer using common features of a particular genre and thereby signaling a discourse community or expected audience? Compare these frames to those you find in nonacademic publications. How are the frames for newspaper stories, feature articles in different kinds of magazines, government reports, or business documents different from those used in academic work? With your classmates make a list of the strategies you've identified. Which of these techniques might be appropriate for the presentation of your inquiry? If you've already written an introduction to your inquiry, try revising it to employ a different strategy.

Consider: Does thinking about the beginning of your writing as a "frame" for your inquiry differ from thinking about the beginning as an "introduction"? When you change the frame, what other parts of the presentation need to change as well?

DEVELOPING AN ARGUMENT THROUGH ANALYSIS

As we discussed earlier, the presentation of research is not simply a narrative account of what you did and how you did it. Writing research is also not a matter of creating an encyclopedic-type summary of what is already known and whatever new information your inquiry has uncovered. Research may include these moves of narrative, summary, or explanation, but it also includes moves of analysis where the researcher demonstrates what patterns have been discerned either by breaking the issue into smaller parts or by combining separate pieces of evidence together. Moving from summary or narrative to answer the so what question, having a point, is among the most difficult and important work researchers do.

Most of us have had the experience of taking a stance about some issue in a pro/con type debate. Political debates, in particular, lend themselves to this kind of for-or-against positioning. Likewise most of us have had the experience of having to offer up evidence to support an opinion or justify a decision. Why should I buy this car over that one? Which extracurricular activities should I join? What reasons can I give my parents to convince them to let me spend spring break in Mexico? Some of what we already know how to do in taking a stand or using evidence to support a conclusion is useful in sharing the results of inquiry projects, but because researchers are interested in thinking things through, considering multiple points of view, and avoiding the simplistic rush to judgment, they almost never write the pro/con argument. Instead researchers develop a stance that demonstrates their mind at work with the evidence they have collected, and their arguments are almost always attempts to help readers follow their analysis. In this kind of written research, the writer is taking the stance of a guide who demonstrates connections, showcases the most important information, and points out which evidence needs to be accepted and which might be treated more skeptically. Of course researchers sometimes do argue for a particular point of view or specific conclusion, or they might use their research to make such an argument, and if they do, they are taking a stance much like a defense attorney who argues for a particular verdict by pointing to the evidence that supports the desired conclusion while acknowledging the existence of counterevidence.

Many writing courses ask students to develop a position—form an argument—and support that argument as convincingly as they can with the evidence at their disposal. It is also possible, however, to make tentative arguments, based on a limited amount of evidence, and to suggest what other kinds of work would have to be done in order to confirm this tentative position. Sometimes researchers start with a tentative argument—a hypothesis—based on their best guess or on their understanding of prior research. Often, however, researchers start out with an interesting case, a set of material they want to understand better, or with an idea that they might answer a particular kind of question by looking at a collection of evidence in a particular way. Researchers want to know something about the experience of first-generation students, for example, so they collect oral histories of students who fit this profile. They may want to understand American attitudes toward immigration, so they collect examples of how this issue has been portrayed in the popular press. However the research begins, whatever methods researchers use, they eventually have to analyze the evidence and try to determine what that evidence means. It is the analysis that forms the base for any arguments they may be able to make.

FIGURE 2.2   Elements of analysis

- **Attend to details:** break into parts
- **Identify patterns:** look for repetitions
- **Label similarities and distinctions:** define key terms; group patterns into meaningful units, that is, regroup the details
- **Consider context:** what are these particular data a part of; what social, political, historical, economic conditions produced these data and these patterns?
- **Watch for oddities:** what's missing; what doesn't seem to fit; what contradicts the patterns?
- **Make an interpretive leap:** what do these details, patterns, context and groupings mean?
- **Consider alternatives:** what other possible interpretations are there; what if the apparent oddity is more important than what seems to fit; what if the key terms are changed; what if the details were broken apart in a different way?
- **Acknowledge limits:** what constraints might have altered or influenced the data; how reproducible are these results; where might mistakes have been introduced; what assumptions have been made in order to interpret the data a particular way?

How do researchers analyze the data they've collected? Each of the method chapters has more specific suggestions for analyzing evidence collected by that method or for working with special types of data, but whether the data are numerical, textual, or visual or whether the data were amassed from a survey, direct observation, or interviews, analyzing data involves the elements identified in Figure 2.2.

PRACTICE ACTIVITY 2-3

Separating the Argument from the Evidence

Turn to the readings and locate places where the evidence, or a portion of the evidence, is presented in a graphic either through an illustration, chart, or graph of some kind. Using the elements of analysis given in Figure 2.2, see if you can make any tentative interpretations of this evidence. What more do you need to know in order to make sense of the data? Can you tell from the visual material how the author has interpreted the material or do you need to read the text in order to find the argument? Try reading the editorials in a local newspaper or following the evidence and conclusions in a popular magazine account of some issue. Can you identify the evidence that these writers are using to support their conclusions?

Consider: Compare your interpretations of graphic data with your classmates. Did you research similar tentative interpretations? What differences do you find in the use of evidence in nonacademic writing?

INCLUDING THE WORK OF OTHERS: PARAPHRASES, QUOTATIONS, CITATIONS

In addition to summarizing prior research as a frame for one's own work, researchers regularly use the work of others alongside their own original research. These secondary sources can provide background information, establish the key terms or primary questions that guide the research, serve as a theoretical lens for interpreting the data, or position the research as fitting with a particular stance or tradition. When secondary sources enter the research, they may be summarized or quoted, but in either case the reference will be cited so that readers could, if they wished, track down the original to verify the researcher's appropriation of this material. Thus the citation isn't just a matter of helping readers see what has influenced the researcher's thinking. Nor are citations only a matter of academic honesty or politeness as researchers acknowledge each other's work. Rather citations are part of the rhetorical move that researchers make to establish that they know what they are talking about, have studied the work of others, and so have the authority to be trusted. Failure to cite work that has informed your own is, of course, a serious breach of academic ethics, but it is also rhetorically foolish since it denies you the opportunity to position yourself as a serious scholar and undercuts your authority.

Any handbook will provide you with examples of different ways to incorporate a direct quotation and cite the source following standard conventions. The general principles, however, are fairly straightforward no matter which citation form you use. Those principles include the information that will allow a reader to locate the original, including:

- Name of author
- Name of specific article or chapter
- Name of publication—journal, book, Web site, album, archival collection, etc.
- Date of source (or date you accessed the Web site)
- Page numbers if you didn't use the entire source

Learning to summarize secondary sources, what is often called the "review of prior research" in the sciences or social sciences, takes time and practice. In general, however, these summaries aim to present the key elements of earlier work in relation to what the current research is contributing, so identifying which sources should be included, arranging them in an order that fits your own purposes, synthesizing the relevant portions, and recognizing the controversy or unanswered questions are important steps in presenting the literature review. Whether your study is following the traditions of the sciences, social sciences, humanities, or blending two or more of these in an interdisciplinary approach, you will probably at some stage look for relevant prior research, and whether you do this search for prior research in order to identify a workable focus or only after you've done some initial investigation of your own, you'll need to keep careful records of the source information and prepare your own annotation of each of the sources you locate. Such annotations will be useful as you arrange and synthesize this work, but writing brief summaries as you read will help you avoid unintentionally misrepresenting others' work as your own. As you search for relevant prior research, you'll also need to keep in mind what kind of research you are seeking. For example, are you looking for studies that use the same theory or the same method of investigation? Are you interested in establishing a trend over a specific period of time or mapping the scope of prior work? Would quantitative research be most relevant to the questions you are considering, or should you be looking for qualitative studies? Does it matter if this research was related to the same group (e.g., age, race, gender) or used the same type of material that you are working with? In short, because you can't possibly read everything, you need to make some logical selections by considering your purpose and reading with a critical eye to select the best — most relevant, most well-regarded, most important — prior work. Chapter 6 has additional suggestions for locating and then working with secondary sources and for summarizing or paraphrasing both primary and secondary sources. Figure 2.3 provides some questions you might consider as you conduct a review of prior research and incorporate prior research into your inquiry presentation.

As we said before, sometimes researchers find it appropriate to insert a quotation rather than rely only on summary, and sometimes quoted material is treated as the direct evidence to support the researcher's conclusions, illustrate the analysis, or demonstrate how the researcher is working with the textual material that is the evidence in the study. When researchers incorporate quotations, then, they do so for a number of different reasons and so the way they introduce those quotations, how much space they take up, or what they have to say about the quoted passage after they've presented it is infinitely variable. We have more to say about working with specific kinds of quoted materials in the chapters on interviewing and working with texts. Still, as Figure 2.4 shows, there are several common principles that can make the use of quotations more effective.

FIGURE 2.3 Questions for reviewing prior research

- What is already known about this topic or issue?
- Why study this issue any further? That is, what *isn't* known?
- What are the key concepts or main variables in the efforts to study this issue?
- What are the relationships between these concepts or variables?
- What are the existing theories that have informed research on this topic?
- What research designs or methods have been used, and which of those seem unsatisfactory?
- Where are there inconsistencies or gaps in the previous work on this topic?
- What prior findings need to be further explored, tested, or verified?
- What kinds of evidence have been omitted or overlooked in prior studies?
- What contribution can a new study be expected to make?

FIGURE 2.4   Principles for effective use of quotations

- Quoted material must be introduced, usually by providing the source information or some context that links the quotation to the author's own prose.

- Vary the way you introduce quoted material by using appropriate synonyms for "said" (claimed, argued, found, believed, asserted, thought), inserting a short quotation in the middle of your own sentence, or by extracting only the most relevant portion (see specific examples in Chapter 6's Working on Writing with Texts).

- The amount of quoted material should never outweigh the amount of original material written by the author (try using a highlighter to identify where you are quoting or paraphrasing so you can clearly see how much of the writing is your own work and how much is coming from others).

- Readers will not read the quotation or understand it in exactly the same way as the writer, so quotations should never just be dropped in without comment or analysis by the author.

- If the quotation is the evidence that is being interpreted, the author must demonstrate through analysis exactly how the quoted passage is being interpreted— which details are important and how those details combine with other portions of the author's analysis to support the conclusions (see Chapter 6 for more detail about how to do textual analysis).

ARRANGEMENT

If researchers aren't just telling the story of what they did in the order they did it and if they aren't following a set form for presenting their research, how do they arrange the material they want to present? What strategies do researchers use to organize the material, help guide readers through various parts, and show the connections or distinctions between different kinds of evidence or different interpretations? Obviously, such decisions depend, once again, on purpose and intended audience, but three strategies are particularly useful for keeping complex material organized and helping readers follow your work: foregrounding, headings and transitions.

FOREGROUNDING

Like framing, foregrounding helps readers anticipate what is coming and so helps writers lay out the scope of their work—what they will and won't be talking about. When writers make statements like, "This article addresses the gendered assumptions about men and women's roles within the University" (Bachin) or "Our argument proceeds in three stages" (Edwards and Winkler), they are setting out the scope of the work to come. These sorts of explicit statements are often a part of the frame that introduces the research presentation. Sometimes such foregrounding moves require more than a single sentence as researchers lay out the theories that inform their work or the assumptions they made as they undertook their projects. In the study by Len-Ríos and her colleagues (p. 451) comparing the representation of women in newspapers to the perceptions of that representation, for example, a section headed "Theoretical Framework" comes before the review of prior research. In this section the researchers summarize their understanding of a key term, "hegemony," and the various feminist perspectives that lead them to do this study in this particular way. This kind of foregrounding does more than frame the particular research they conducted because it provides an explanation that establishes a common ground which they expect readers to accept. Of course it's possible to disagree with their perspective, to argue against their view of how power works within a culture, but if we were to disagree with those fundamentals, the details of their particular study would hardly matter; we simply wouldn't read any further, or we would reject the study as a whole rather than worry about the small details. To read *with* a writer's project, we have to accept the grounds and scope of that project. To read *against* a writer's project, we have to show how the details that follow contradict the grounds or scope that has been established. In the end we may decide that the grounds or scope that the researcher has laid out is inadequate, flawed, or otherwise unacceptable; but we can't really evaluate the project itself if we don't, at least temporarily, accept the premises that the writer lays out for her work.

Foregrounding can also take the form of dismissing some aspects of the topic or issue that this particular piece of writing is just not going to consider. Again, such a gesture is a way of establishing the scope of what is about to be read—a way of clearing the terrain so that the path ahead is more visible. Notice, for example, how Len-Ríos and her colleagues dismiss demographics as a basis for comparison in their introductory frame, explaining as they do so why these kind of data will not be found in their study. Here's the relevant section:

> We compare content to perceptions rather than actual demographics because occupational statistics (e.g., the number of females in elite societal positions) tend to represent the outcomes of a patriarchal system. Rather, by examining both male and female perceptions, we get a better sense of attitudes toward the system and determine how well content matches perceptions. This is not to say actual demographics do not matter; they do. However, for our analysis, perceptions reflect fewer institutional biases than occupational statistics. (p. 452)

Again, we might decide that eliminating demographics was a mistake and undertake a replication of this study that would include demographics, but these researchers have been very clear to foreground this absence and explain their decision to eliminate this aspect from their study so we cannot be surprised later. Foregrounding in qualitative studies often takes the form of providing a description of the setting or the participants (see, e.g., Benmayor, p. 324 and Frisch, p. 383), and foregrounding regularly includes setting out the kinds of questions the researcher is interested in considering (see Dilworth, p. 353 and Lewis, p. 464, for examples of this foregrounding with questions).

HEADINGS

Statements that indicate what is to come next often appear later in the text as well, especially if the study is long or takes the form of a book with multiple chapters. "In the next section, I will turn to . . . ," or "I'll return to this issue later, but first . . . ," are common examples of statements that foreshadow not the entire study but only some small piece of what is to come. In the study by Lutz and Collins, a general paragraph sets up, or foreshadows, the seven kinds of gaze they identified. Let's look carefully at this paragraph to see how it functions to tell readers what's coming next.

Many gazes can be found in every photograph in the *National Geographic*. This is true whether the picture shows an empty landscape; a single person looking straight at the camera; a large group of people, each looking in a different direction but none at the camera; or a person in the distance whose eyes are tiny or out of focus. In other words, the gaze is not simply the look given by or to a photographed subject. It includes seven kinds of gaze. (p. 495)

Notice how this paragraph moves from a very general statement—"Many gazes can be found"—to the specific claim "gaze is not simply the look given by or to a photographed subject. It includes seven kinds of gaze." What these researchers are doing is redirecting our attention away from the kind of picture (landscape, single person, etc.) to "gaze" as a key term that they intend to describe in more detail or with more precision by mapping out seven different types. They don't explicitly name these seven kinds in this paragraph (though they did name them in the opening abstract), but they've set their readers up to expect that seven kinds will be named, and indeed the headings that follow name seven kinds of gaze. In effect the authors have moved from what anyone might notice (there are lots of gazes and these occur in every photograph) to what their research has helped them articulate (there are seven different kinds of gaze). An attentive reader might well be a bit surprised at the suggestion that even pictures of an empty landscape include a gaze, but their attention is directed not toward this rather easily explained example but to the larger point of the study which is to define these different kinds of gaze and, as we've learned from the earlier frame, to consider how these photographs have influenced the Western worldview of those depicted. This kind of foreshadowing is thus a way of keeping the reader heading in the same direction as the writing that is coming next. Notice again how these researchers have used both a foreshadowing sentence and the graphic device of headings.

Headings can also serve to keep the reader on track by visually separating the parts and providing a title that glosses the small section that follows. Headings are often cast in parallel construction, especially if the piece contains both headings and subheadings. In Peirce Lewis's explanation of reading landscapes (p. 464) as historical evidence, for example, the following headings appear:

Learning by Doing: Reading the Landscape of a Small Town

Putting Things in Context: Three Levels of Magnification

Two Views from a Distance

Maximum Magnification: The View from High Street

Lessons from the Landscape

Even without the differences in font size that Lewis includes, we can tell by the structure of these headings that the first and second are of equal importance and that the third and fourth identify the "levels of magnification" referred to in the second heading. These headings also serve as a kind of outline of the entire piece, helping readers to anticipate the information that is included. It is because headings work this way that the suggestions for active reading in Chapter 1 include surveying the headings and forming questions from them that you think the reading will answer.

TRANSITIONS

Another device writers use to help organize their material and provide signposts that keep readers with them is transitions. Sometimes transitions take the form of *single words*. First, second, third, next, then, thus, moreover, furthermore, nevertheless, and however are common transition words, and most handbooks will provide you with other examples. But transitions can also come in the form of *phrases*:

- As a means of illustrating
- In summary
- I shall begin with . . .
- As we have seen
- Based on this work, we can conclude that . . .

Although transitions often appear at the beginnings of paragraphs as writers move from one point to another and need to signal to the reader that they are moving on to something new or to a related issue or additional example, transitions also help paragraphs hold together. Without transitions, sentences would seem disconnected, and the reader would have to do all the work of blending ideas and examples together. So, a third kind of transition, what is often referred to as *paragraph coherence*, happens when writers repeat key words or phrases to tie the ideas within sentences together or use subordinate conjunctions to show the relationships between ideas and/or details. Writers can't just sprinkle transition words and phrases randomly, so the common advice to "use transitions" ought properly to be understood as *"build connections between ideas and show relations both within a paragraph and from section to section."* Let's look at how one writer does this work of connecting ideas and showing relationships with various kinds of transitions. This paragraph is from James Boyd White's comparison of Greek tragic plays with Supreme Court opinions, particularly the opinion of Justice Harlan at the height of the Vietnam War. The case involved a citizen arrested for wearing a jacket with the phrase "Fuck the War." In this section White summarizes the "argumentative structure" of Harlan's opinion.

> He begins a bit like a modernist painter sculpting out negative space by telling what, in his words, this case "does *not* present" (emphasis in original). First, he says this is a case in which the state seeks to punish, not conduct that is associated with speech, but speech itself. Likewise, it does not involve a statute directed at the special need for decorous speech and conduct in the court house or its precincts, but one of general applicability. This means that no special deference is due any judgment of the legislature as to the proper control of speech in the halls of a courthouse, for no such judgment has been made. And, despite the sexual vulgarity of the central term employed, this is not an obscenity case, for the expression is in no way erotic. Furthermore, the phrase in question does not qualify as the sort of expression the Court has termed *"fighting* words," unprotected by the First Amendment for it was not a direct personal insult. Nor is a prohibition of this phrase justified by the fact that it was forced upon "unwilling or unsuspecting viewers," as a "captive audience"; to justify suppression on such grounds, the government must show that "substantial privacy interests are being invaded in an essentially intolerable manner," which is not the case here. (pp. 605–606)

There are clearly a number of single transition words that White uses to keep his summary moving forward, including first, likewise, and, nor, and furthermore. Notice that these transition words mark both order (first), comparison (likewise), and addition (and, furthermore). The use of nor also signals a kind of addition since in this paragraph it echoes other examples of what the case is not. White also uses the construction "this means" to signal a recasting of what has come before in terms of its significance. In addition throughout this paragraph are sentences constructed to show negation. Sometimes that negation works to balance two parts of the sentence against one another through the use of a conjunction. Think of the conjunction as the pivot point in a seesaw. Thus,

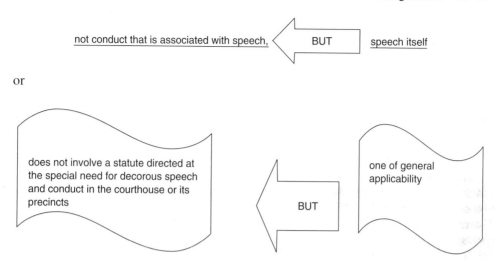

not conduct that is associated with speech, ⟵ BUT | speech itself

or

does not involve a statute directed at the special need for decorous speech and conduct in the courthouse or its precincts ⟵ BUT | one of general applicability

Sometimes the negation works by balancing one clause against a subordinate, or lesser, clause as in

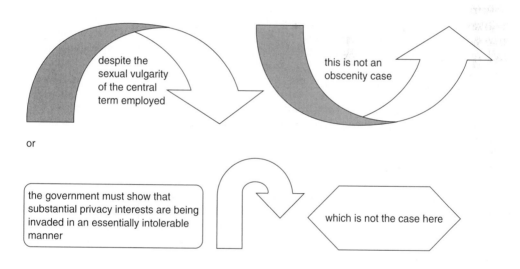

despite the sexual vulgarity of the central term employed | this is not an obscenity case

or

the government must show that substantial privacy interests are being invaded in an essentially intolerable manner | which is not the case here

So, White has not only summarized Harlan's points, but shown how those points are related to one another. In the process he has demonstrated what he has said at the beginning of the paragraph is significant about how Harlan begins his argument: that he begins by sculpting out the negative, by examining what the case is not. Perhaps it will be easier to see these efforts to stitch the paragraph together if we repeat it with all the connective tissue highlighted.

He **begins** a bit like a modernist painter sculpting out negative space by telling what, in his words, this case "does *not* present" (emphasis in original). **First**, he says this is a case in which the state seeks to punish, <u>not conduct</u> that is associated with speech, <u>but speech</u> itself. **Likewise**, it does <u>not</u> involve a statute directed at the special need for decorous speech and conduct in the court house or its precincts, <u>but</u> one of general

> ## PRACTICE ACTIVITY 2-4
>
> ### Identifying Arrangement Strategies
>
> Turn to any one of the readings and examine it for the arrangement strategies it uses. Select one paragraph in the readings that seems to you to make use of a variety of transition devices. Circle, underline, or otherwise mark those devices and be ready to explain how they work. Have a classmate work with the same paragraph and see if you both marked the same features and understand them in the same way. Turn to one of your own paragraphs and mark the transitions you've used. Can you strengthen your paragraph by using a kind of transition you haven't already used or by adding more "stitching"?
>
> **Consider:** With your classmates make a list of the arrangement strategies used in the different readings you examined. Which of these do you regularly use in your own writing and which ones are new to you? What happened as you tried to rework your paragraph to include different kinds of transitions? Which version do you like best and why?

applicability. **This means** that no special deference is due any judgment of the legislature as to the proper control of speech in the halls of a courthouse, for no such judgment has been made. **And,** despite the sexual vulgarity of the central term employed, this is not an obscenity case, for the expression is in no way erotic. **Furthermore,** the phrase in question does not qualify as the sort of expression the Court has termed "*fighting* words," unprotected by the First Amendment for it was not a direct personal insult. **Nor** is a prohibition of this phrase justified by the fact that it was forced upon "unwilling or unsuspecting viewers," as a "captive audience"; to justify suppression on such grounds, the government must show that "substantial privacy interests are being invaded in an essentially intolerable manner," which is not the case here.

CLARITY AND STYLE

As we saw in the discussion of arrangement, the choices a writer makes involve both big moves that provide structure to the whole piece, and small moves that alter the way sentences are put together to convey meaning. Some of these moves are simply a matter of style—either following your own ear for the language or adhering to standard conventions laid out in style manuals or in the directions to authors section of journals. But matters of style can also alter the meaning, shift the tone, and thereby convey a different sense of authorship; there simply isn't one right way to say whatever needs to be said, even in the most formal presentations of research. It is true that many researchers try to present their work using objective language, avoid using personal pronouns, and work to eliminate language that is emotionally charged or sexist. It is also true that all research involves human actors who necessarily have a point of view just as they have a personal interest in the work at hand. Balancing these apparently contradictory forces depends on the audience, purpose, type of publication, genre for presentation, and personality. We think students, especially students in composition courses, should try to avoid the one-type-fits-all writing and instead actively experiment with shifting the style of presentation, learning in the process to read critically the results and revise accordingly. Two specific issues, however, are worth discussing: sentence length and word choice.

PRACTICE ACTIVITY 2-5

Building Paragraph Coherence

Here is a paragraph written by a student that has very little of the connective tissue provided by transitions, conjunctions, and subordination. Rewrite the paragraph using whichever of these strategies you think appropriate.

India became a free country in 1947, at the beginning of the nuclear age. The leaders of nations have chosen to opt for self-reliance, and freedom of thought and action. India had rejected the Cold War example by the United States and Russia, and had chosen the harder path of nonalignment. National strength was built through India's own resources; the skills and creativity of the people. One of the first initiatives by Prime Minister Nehru was the development of science and scientific spirit. Disarmament was a major part in India's foreign policy.

Consider: Compare your revision of this paragraph to those produced by your classmates. What happened as you tried to rework this paragraph to build connections? Are the differences matters of personal style or a different understanding of the meaning? Which version(s) do you like best and why?

SENTENCE LENGTH

In considering how to build connections, you may have discovered that long sentences can help you hold several ideas together at once. Compound or complex sentences—those with multiple phrases or clauses—can often get tangled and lead to errors in grammar that would not otherwise occur. Most students at the college level know, for example, that subjects have to agree with verbs and that some adjectives cannot be used with singular nouns. They would never say "My book are missing," or "Children does require many attention." But, even the most talented of writers, or the most advanced researchers, have produced sentences that are so complicated that they make such mistakes. Is the answer then to write only short, simple sentences? Obviously not, since short sentences can't build the kind of relationships or signal connections that make meaning.

Whether you write short or long sentences, you need to learn to proofread carefully to see what you've actually written and not what you thought you wrote. When we compose at the computer, it is especially easy to introduce errors as we erase portions of sentences and start again, altering the structure without getting all the parts to mesh together properly. We have more to say about proofreading in the next section on different kinds of revision, but four strategies that we find especially helpful are summarized in Figure 2.5.

WORD CHOICE

Choosing appropriate words involves making decisions about tone, meaning, and audience. Can we use technical vocabulary without definition and assume that our readers will understand or do we need to use a more general vocabulary? Should we eliminate value-laden terms and try to present the material as objectively or neutrally

FIGURE 2.5   Suggestions for proofreading

- Print out and read a hard copy with a pen in hand, reading both from the beginning to the end for overall structure and logic and from the end to the beginning to catch sentence-level gaffs.

- Let the draft sit for a while before returning to it. Having time to let a draft sit depends on starting early and planning well, but even a simple e-mail can profit by sitting for a few minutes and then being reread for correctness before hitting the send button.

- Solicit feedback from peer readers. When we ask for feedback from peers, we try to identify what kind of feedback we need as precisely as possible, and we never relinquish the responsibility or the right to make decisions as the author. In other words, others can tell us what problems they have as readers of our work, but what to do about those problems is up to the author.

- Don't blindly accept the corrections of your computer's grammar or spell checkers. Grammar checkers look for general patterns based on common word lists and don't represent an intelligent reader attending to meaning. Especially in long sentences, these grammar checkers may not really be able to tell which word is the subject and so can introduce an error by matching the verb to a word that is close by rather than to the real subject of the sentence. Likewise spell checkers cannot recognize the misuse of a correctly typed word (like typing "on" when you meant "no"). Furthermore, if you ever accept a word as correct, it might be added to your computer's dictionary and never again be identified as wrong.

as possible? Will a more precise word help convey the meaning better or serve only to make our writing sound as if we've opened the thesaurus and made substitutions for common words without considering the impact these words have on the overall tone? While it may be generally true that precision is better than vagueness and that defining unusual terms is essential, we can think of plenty of examples where people argue about which term is more precise in a given situation. Defining terms that the audience already knows and thinks are commonplace creates the impression that the writer doesn't know the discourse community, or the subject, very well. Likewise, how you name something matters. Think, for example, about how the abortion debates circle around how to name this practice—prochoice versus prolife doesn't just represent different sides; they are significantly different ways of naming. You can probably think of other examples where a controversy wasn't just about the event but about how to name it.

Good writers pay attention to individual words, despite these potential difficulties. They watch for repetition and determine whether it was the necessary repetition of key words that built coherence or the unintentional redundancy caused by a failure to be precise. One strategy that helps in both word choice and sentence structure is to look at the first word of each sentence. If the same word starts every sentence in the paragraph, or nearly every sentence, consider revising to combine sentences together, alter the structure, or provide a synonym.

Good writers also look for places where extra words have crept into the prose, making the passage longer but not necessarily clearer. Five common ways to eliminate unnecessary words are highlighted in Figure 2.6.

Paying attention to these issues of arrangement, clarity, and style often requires that you write a draft and then revise it rather than trying to get everything exactly right as you compose. Good writers—like good researchers—revise in a number of different ways, often more than once, so we want to end this chapter with a closer consideration of revision.

FIGURE 2.6　Strategies for eliminating unnecessary words

- Look for forms of the verb "to be" (is, am, are, was, were, be, being, been). These be verbs create wordiness because they are often found in structures that require other words to be complete. Thus, *The importance of this issue is not to be taken lightly* could be recast as *This issue is important* or, *There are hundreds of people who frequent the park every day* can become *Hundreds of people frequent the park every day* with no loss of meaning. In fact the "there are" or "there is" construction is almost always ripe for recasting.

- Constructions that utilize prepositional phrases often can be pruned to do the same work with fewer words. Thus,

During the course of the study	becomes	*During the study*
We came to the realization that	becomes	*We realized that*
In the event that	becomes	*If*
Due to the fact that	becomes	*Because*
Realizing the fact that	becomes	*Knowing*
The population that participated in the study was	becomes	*The participants were*

- Nouns that are formed from verbs—those ending in *ion, ment,* or *ence*—often signal a sentence that can be improved by recasting. For example, *Validation of the participants' views could not be obtained* becomes *The participants' views could not be validated.* Or, *Our study made an assessment of student responses to four questions* becomes *Our study assessed student responses to four questions.*

- Eliminate modifiers if the meaning is better conveyed by a different word altogether. Thus, if you say *rather angry* do you really mean *annoyed*? If the storm was *very destructive*, wasn't it really *devastating*? If the area was *rectangular in shape*, couldn't you just call it *rectangular* and be done?

- Try underlining the new information that each sentence in a paragraph contributes. Once you can clearly see which words in the sentence are doing the work and which are filler, see if you can combine any of those sentences to eliminate as much filler as possible.

PRACTICE ACTIVITY 2-6

Pruning Prose

Turn to any piece of your own writing and examine it for wordiness. Try revising the piece to reduce the word count by 25 percent. In other words, if your original version was 1,000 words, see if you can create a version with no more than 750 words. You might also try this exercise using a classmate's writing rather than your own.

Consider: Does the revised, and shorter, piece of prose seem to you to be clearer? Which strategies for pruning the prose did you use most often? If you did the reduction on a classmate's paper, does the original author think that the cut version alters the meaning in any important ways? Which version do you like best and why?

AN EYE TOWARD REVISION

One of the most important things to know about writing, especially writing that comes from inquiry, is that it is rarely done without considerable work. Not only do writers spend time collecting information, analyzing their "data," and considering their arguments, but they also spend time putting words on the page, reading what they've written, and reworking their prose. Sometimes our students are surprised to learn how much time researchers spend at their computers writing and rewriting before presenting their work to others. From our point of view, one of the functions of a first-year writing course is to help students develop strategies for working on the writing once it appears on the page. Posing questions, shaping the prose to fit audience expectations, and clarifying the purpose are important elements of working on writing; but almost none of that work happens without considerable time spent on revision. The good news in all this time and effort is, as we mentioned in the first chapter, that college graduates say they learned more in courses where they spent more time than in courses that required little effort.[3] We believe that learning to do revisions helps students continue to learn and develop as writers even beyond the first-year writing course. We also believe that it can be useful to recognize different kinds of revisions rather than assuming that every piece of writing needs to go through the same revision process. We've identified six different kinds of revision, and many of the assignment sequences include one or more opportunities to revise, though most of us encourage students to revise the writing they find most engaging and to choose the kind of revision that makes the most sense for the work at hand.

Revisions that rethink the project and thus require massive changes are sometimes called "global revisions." Students, we find, think of these as "starting over," but even if what you produce seems to be an entirely different paper, you're probably drawing upon the experience of the first writing. You may have misunderstood the assignment, or chosen a topic that didn't let you do your best work. You may also need a massive revision, even if you keep the same kernel of an idea, when you find that your

---

[3]Richard Light, *Making the Most of College: Students Speak Their Minds* (Cambridge: Harvard UP, 2001).

thoughts on the topic have changed substantially or when you want to try for a different overall tone or effect. Scholars also do global revisions like these if they realize that their original question was not appropriate, that the data they thought they would be able to find are not available, or that their own thinking has changed in radical ways as they work on an issue over time.

Revisions that expand, rearrange, or reconsider aspects of your original paper allow you to keep something of the original writing, though you may have to create a different frame. Sometimes it is possible to blend together two or more assignments into a single effective paper, but such a revision of blending will require careful thinking about organization, transitions, and framing to make the finished product smooth, coherent, and effective. Some of the assignment sequences in this book invite you to extract from earlier work, to blend different assignments together for a later paper, or to build on what you have already done and extend the project by adding another method. If you look closely at the body of work of most scholars, you will find evidence of expansion, rearrangement, or reconsideration. Scholars often excerpt book-length projects into shorter article-length versions. Likewise some scholars who have written several articles on the same topic compile that work into a book-length analysis or argument.

Perhaps the most common revision for required writing is *revising to eliminate the marks of the assignment*. If, for example, you have referred to the requirements of the assignment, your paper will be more effective if you imagine transforming it to stand alone outside the class. References to readings or to class discussions also mark the paper as "class work," but the most effective essays make these references understandable to readers who have not been members of the class. Making the transition from class assignment to independent essay will require you to think about why you would want an audience to know about the things you write about, and who exactly that audience is. As discussed earlier, if you have a purpose and an audience in mind, your writing will probably be more coherent and effective, but often who that audience is just really can't be clear until after you've done some writing. This may seem to be a kind of revision that scholars would never have to do, but actually many pieces of scholarship start out as a direct response to a conversation, even if that conversation is happening in printed discourse rather than in oral exchanges. Scholars want their writing to join the conversation on the critical issue, and as we said earlier, the frame of "reviewing the literature" helps scholars to signal which conversations they are trying to join. In responding to others, though, scholars don't usually want to sound as if they are responding to a single point or taking on a particular person. There are, of course, some pieces of scholarship that do take on a particularly famous person (theory, or study) directly, or that frame the piece as a direct response to someone else, but even these direct responses are usually not constituted as an attack or rebuttal, but rather as a reconsideration of key ideas or claims. Take a look at Frisch's essay, for example (p. 383). He makes clear that he is writing, at least in part, in response to the claims made by a number of critics of education in the mid-1980s, and his use of terms such as "improbable best sellers" and "recent sensation" make his opposition pretty transparent, though not directly confrontational.

Probably the most frequent revision we ask students to do is to *continue* from where they left off. Many essays may be good enough to seem complete as far as they go, but leave unanswered a more interesting or pressing question/issue that hasn't been considered. Revising to consider this previously unacknowledged issue may be a matter of simply adding on to what you already have, but frequently the addition requires a slightly different frame as well. In some cases the "larger" question allows you to reposition prior writing as an illustration or example and requires that you add additional examples to fully support the larger analysis. This kind of revision makes us think harder about what we've already said, complicate our understanding of the issue, and ask additional questions. Whenever we find ourselves writing endings that tie everything up into a neat package, we get suspicious that we haven't yet asked the most interesting or useful questions. As we discussed in the Posing Questions section, stepping back from what we've already said to imagine a counterargument can help us carry on.

The last kind of revision we ask students to do is actually what we've found most students think of when asked to revise: *editing and fine-tuning* to produce correct, standard written English. Most college level writing courses expect students to be able to produce "reasonably correct prose," and so we encourage students to learn to proofread for slips of the pen, punctuation, and spelling errors; grammatical mistakes; redundancy in word choice or sentence structure; and poor word choice as we discussed earlier. Sometimes errors in sentences are a signal that something more serious is wrong. If you can't get a series of items into parallel structure, for example, maybe it's because the items you've tried to make parallel are really not similar, and so more than your sentence structure needs to be clarified. Likewise, if your sentences have no connections and seem "choppy," perhaps you aren't explaining the relationships between your assertions and your evidence. A complex sentence that gets tangled up grammatically is often an opportunity to rethink how the parts of that sentence relate to one another and why it is important for all of the parts to be in the same sentence. Clarifying vague pronouns—the pronoun "this" standing alone at the beginning of a sentence is almost always vague—makes us rethink what we were trying to say. Sorting out grammatical issues, then, can be a way to attend more carefully to the nuances of the meaning you are creating, and these kinds of sentence problems need to be separated from the sloppy mistakes writers make when they are typing and thinking at the same time.

A more difficult level of such fine-tuning is considering tone and the ways that your writing has represented you and your topic. Depending on your audience, purpose, and style, you may have to undertake massive changes in content as well as sentence form and word choice in order to create a consistent rhetorical style. If, for example, you are trying to write parody, you must be consistent, and you must consider carefully how you will signal that parody to your readers (e.g., through overstatement, or through a consistent play on a well-known form). Readers can help you determine how you are coming off to others if you let them know that you want this kind of information. It isn't the case that you never want to offend your readers, insult them, or appear to be self-righteous or egotistical, but you do want to intend these results for a reason and consider carefully why you would want these reactions. You may find it helpful to think about what you gain and/or lose by speaking of your topic, or to your readers, in particular ways. Some writing is clearly meant to incite rather than persuade, but very little academic writing takes this stance since academic writing values analysis and deliberation over either strident persuasion or entertainment.

The most successful revisions (at least for composition courses) are ones where you use the opportunity to write again as a way of *thinking further* about the topic or issue you have chosen. If you aren't really interested in the topic, if you can't make yourself care about the issues involved, your writing is not likely to demonstrate the kind of engaged mind thinking through and responding to the intellectual conversations that inquiry projects are meant to engender. It is perfectly reasonable in doing inquiry projects to be able to articulate the problems without knowing the solutions, or to see more than two sides of an issue. You need not have neat solutions, and your papers don't have to arrive at a tidy conclusion in order to be effective. Academic writing frequently ends by pointing to the issues that remain unresolved, or to the way that commonplace renditions of the issues are unsatisfying once the complexity of the situation is acknowledged. Your papers can also end in this state of "uncertainty" in which you can describe the problem but don't have the solution. This stance is often called "problematizing" as opposed to "problem solving" as we explained earlier. Although sometimes writers revise to put where they ended up at the beginning of their writing in a clearly articulated thesis, it is just as likely that they will begin with one set of questions or curiosities and end with others which they hope to pick up in subsequent research. Remember, then, that the best academic papers are often those where it is clear that the scholar has done some careful and detailed thinking, and can no longer be satisfied with the easiest answers. Whatever conclusions are advanced are offered with careful qualifications that limit the scope and acknowledge alternative perspectives.

Most of the assignment sequences give students the chance to try out different methods and to work from different perspectives. Inevitably some of that work will be worth revising, and some won't. We think that's okay; not every project we've started has led to a publication either, but we still learned something from doing the research and our writing abilities were stretched as we tried to present the inquiry. Sometimes what seemed like a false start turned out later to be salvageable as new resources became available or we learned more. Sometimes we've revised a piece by adding more, reframing the work, or trying to shift to a different audience and discovered that our first effort was actually more successful. So, while we encourage our students to learn to revise, we would never require our students to revise everything they write or to assume that revisions will always make a piece of writing better. Learning to choose, experimenting, and then evaluating the results are key components of being a good writer with strong habits of mind.

We hope it is clear to readers who have worked through both of these introductory chapters that the habits of mind that form the basis of inquiry work—curiosity, flexibility, tolerance, precision, deliberation, and self-reflection—are also involved in the rhetorical choices that writers make as they present their inquiries in a written form. The reverse is also true. Rhetorical choices—like how to frame your work, how to arrange your data and analyze the evidence to reach conclusions, which words to choose and how best to say what you mean—are clearly at work from the earliest moments of any inquiry project.

Internet Resources

Some Web sites are organized to group information together for different potential audiences. See, for example, the Department of Labor audience index at http://www.dol.gov/dol/audience/index.htm. See if you can find similarly organized sites, compare the categories of "audience" such sites create and the kinds of documents that are sorted into each audience type. Compare your findings with those found by your classmates. What does your data suggest about how these Internet sites understand "audience."

Quotations used as epigraphs to frame a piece of writing need to be chosen carefully in order to have the intended impact. Usually these will emerge from the material you are working with, but sometimes it is useful to consult published books of quotations. Several of these appear online, including one by John Bartlett at http://www.bartleby.com/100, which allows you to search by subject, author, or genre.

Several classic books of English usage and style, including William Strunk's *Elements of Style*, are now available in a searchable form at http:/ /www.bartleby.com/usage/.

Web Sites Referenced in This Chapter

The Modern Media Initiatives for a Sustainable Future

http://www.onewater.org/index.htm

CHAPTER 3

OBSERVING

You've been learning through observations from the moment you were born. In fact babies take in so much new information through their senses that one of the first things they learn to do is to screen out much of this stimulus so they can focus on individual sensory data. Newborns learn to focus on faces and to distinguish between background noise and sounds directed at them as a natural biological and psychological process. In the normal process of growing up, we learn how to pay attention to the world around us and how to draw inferences from the data we take in. We learn to recognize the subtle signals of our parents being too tired to agree to an allowance increase, for example, or to the clues that a new classmate may be interested in establishing a closer friendship. Often, of course, we misread these signals, or we encounter "mixed" signals in these human relationships.

We read the physical environment around us as well, knowing when it "looks like snow" or that "spring is coming." If we commute over the same roads each day, we learn to recognize the key spots where a slowdown indicates a real problem up ahead, or how to time our travels to miss the worse of the traffic jams. We "read" the parking lots and make educated guesses about how good a restaurant is likely to be even if we've never eaten there, and we know if the grocery store or mall is going to be crowded before we ever get out of our cars. Much of these data are unconsciously processed and may seem trivial or unimportant, but paying attention to what we notice and to how we make inferences or conclusions based on such information can actually teach us quite a bit and lead us to new insights.

Many scholars make knowledge through a similar but more consciously focused process of close and careful observation. Scientists in lab settings are one such example, but many other scholars from anthropologists to sociologists, from art historians to cultural critics begin their investigations with what they observe. Scholars also teach themselves to pay attention to things that ordinarily would be ignored. You've certainly experienced this phenomenon when learning to drive or navigating a new city. In these situations you've undoubtedly had to direct your observations to the signals of street

---

PRACTICE ACTIVITY 3-1

Identifying Signals

Brainstorm a list of the signals for the situations used as examples in the earlier paragraphs or for other situations that you think are "read" by visual clues of some kind.

Consider: How did you learn which signals mean what? Can you remember a particular incident where you misread the signals? What caused that misreading?

---

signs, traffic lights, and other vehicles on the road. You also had to learn to ignore the signals that passengers are more likely to notice such as flowers in bloom, scantily clad joggers, or which stores are in the malls you pass. What you paid attention to shifted because your needs are different as a driver than they are as a passenger; those needs are also different when you know the terrain and when you don't.

You've probably seen that when people are presented with a list of items or a collection of objects, different people remember different items and some people remember items that others never notice at all. Those items didn't disappear, so of course everyone must have seen them in a physical sense, but those viewers who failed to focus on a particular item had no recognition of having seen it. Perhaps you've had the same experience in the process of recounting memories from your childhood with your parents or siblings. It is not at all uncommon for different participants to remember different details because of their own interests, degree of attention, or how they connected new information or experiences to what they already knew or believed.

Psychologists have studied what people notice or fail to notice under various conditions. A Web site of such experiments conducted by Professor Daniel J. Simons and the researchers at the Visual Cognition Lab at the University of Illinois includes videos of various experiments that demonstrate what researchers call "change blindness" or "inattentional blindness." See http://viscog.beckman.uiuc.edu/djs_lab/demos.html Change blindness experiments demonstrate how often people miss changes in a scene or situation while they are participating in the event. Inattentional blindness is the ability to "not see" an interruption or unexpected event while attending to some kind of action or performing an activity.[1] The Web site demos allow you to test your own powers of observation, as well as learn more about how researchers study visual awareness.

Throughout the eighteenth and nineteenth centuries, people who made careful observations of the natural world and supplemented those observations with drawings or sketches helped add to the knowledge of the natural sciences. Charles Darwin, Sir Hans Sloane, and an expedition led by Captain James Cook are some famous

---

[1] Lester Hussie, Jr., a student who read an early version of this chapter, pointed out that actors are trained to ignore interruptions like flash photography, cell phones, or crying babies. Hussie also suggested that students regularly use inattentional blindness to block out distractions when they study in such public settings as libraries or computer labs. We agree. Knowing what to ignore and what to pay attention to and how to shift between noticing and intentional blindness are important skills that most of us use unconsciously. It seems to us, however, that students can consciously work on attending and learn to evaluate whether their blindness (intentional or unintentional) is necessary or detrimental to their purposes.

PRACTICE ACTIVITY 3-2

Change Blindness and Inattentional Blindness

Watch any of the videos at the Visual Cognition Lab Web site (http://viscog.beckman.uiuc.edu/djs_lab/demos.html). How many changes did you notice in the change blindness experiments? How did you do on the inattentional blindness experiments? Do you think your results would be different in the second set of experiments if you were actually a part of the experiment rather than watching others doing the experiment? Why or why not?

Consider: How do your results compare with those of your classmates? What might you do as a researcher relying on observation to counter the difficulties of change blindness and inattentional blindness?

---

examples of British explorations that contributed to scientific knowledge. Lewis and Clark and other explorers of the North American continent also collected specimens, recorded observations, and made drawings and maps as a part of their work. Similar explorations of the ocean or of outer space have relied on close observation of the natural environment, including the flora and fauna of new locations. All these naturalists had to learn to record what they observed and to notice small details and actions, as well as patterns and anomalies. In the process they developed procedures for recording and observing which were systematic enough that others could repeat the observation and check the results. These early researchers recognized that they could not draw reliable conclusions or make meaningful interpretations based on their observations unless they could be reasonably certain that their observations were typical rather than idiosyncratic.

One problem that observers often face in watching an event or interaction carefully and simultaneously recording those observations is that subjects are active and so the details change before the observer can get them down on paper. Taking field notes on a scene involving multiple subjects or interactions is even more complicated and can take years of practice to perfect. Our goal is not to make you expert ethnographers or naturalists, but you can adapt some common techniques used by these researchers to

---

PRACTICE ACTIVITY 3-3

Historical Observation Records

Visit any of the Web sites listed at the end of this chapter in Internet Resources as "Historical Observation Sites" just to see what catches your interest. Practice generating questions for further investigation using these materials. What other historical sites that preserve the earlier work of naturalists, explorers, or expositions can you find?

Consider: What ideas for inquiry projects built on historical observation records occur to you as you visit these sites, and how might you pursue those projects?

make observing and recording more manageable and more intentional. See Figure 3.1 for some suggested techniques.

Learning to notice rather than be blind in your observations is not only a matter of learning to pay attention and get enough details recorded, but also an intellectual activity that anthropologist Clifford Geertz calls establishing the authority of "being there." For Geertz, collecting enough details to be believable is not the issue; rather, the

FIGURE 3.1 Strategies for focusing observations and taking notes

- To prevent interference from your own prior assumptions, choose a place or event that you are not directly involved in or do not know much about.

- You can participate casually in the place, event, or group, but should not be a complete participant. Example: You observe an athletic event, but you are *not* a member of the team.

- Do not talk to people or interview people during your observation.

- Note the time and date, as well as the exact location of where you make your observations. Describe the setting and the mood and use your senses (what do you hear or smell?), but most of your data should come from what you see.

- Note concrete details, not general impressions. Avoid making judgments or evaluations while you are observing. Instead take as many notes as you can so you have lots of data to consider when you start analyzing. Remember, sometimes what seems to be minor can be central to the meaning you want to claim for your observation.

- Concentrate on taking notes (jotting) rather than recording the scene in full sentences in order to avoid missing important details. If there is a lot of activity and you find you can't keep up, try wearing a watch or setting a timer to record what is happening only at a set interval, say every five minutes, or record the action at the same time of day over several days. If you were interested in animal behavior, for example, you might record only the behavior just before or after the animal is fed.

- Choose just one thing to observe. Ignore everything but that selected feature. If you're observing the food court at a local mall, for example, you might focus only on what happens at a particular table, ignoring the traffic at the various vendors. This focusing strategy is especially useful for follow-up observations when you think you've identified a pattern and want to confirm your interpretation.

- Record the plot line. What happens first, second, third, and so on? To observe the plot line, you have to be present at the beginning and stay attentive until the end. Thus this method works for events but is more difficult for observations of places. Observations of rituals (football games, class sessions) or time-limited events (like an elevator ride from the bottom to top floor of a building) can be "plotted" in this way.

- Use a geographic frame—left to right, top to bottom or panoramic sequence— ignoring things that change once you've passed by that specific spot. Static scenes such as a piece of art or a landscape with little action work well with a geographic focus, but most observers find it is difficult to capture everything without circling back to the starting point and starting again.

difficulty is in engaging with the details that have been collected in order to make meaning. Here's how he makes this point in his essay "Being There"[2]:

> The ability of anthropologists to get us to take what they say seriously has less to do with either a factual look or an air of conceptual elegance than it has with their capacity to convince us that what they say is a result of their having actually penetrated (or, if you prefer, been penetrated by) another form of life, of having, one way or another, truly "been there." And that, persuading us that this offstage miracle has occurred, is where the writing comes in. (4–5)

For scholars, observation is rarely a method used in isolation. When an anthropologist goes into a different culture to observe, he doesn't do so without other sources of information as well. He asks questions, reads about the culture in advance, studies what others have done before him, and tries to connect those direct observations he can make to these other sources of information. He speculates on what he observes, asking questions of himself and others about why things are done the way he sees them being done, what significance certain activities have, and whether a particular observation is typical of the culture or is an idiosyncrasy of the individual(s) he is observing. Likewise, when you use observation as a method of inquiry, you will be doing so with some purpose in mind. You will have chosen the site, and even the time, of your observation intentionally so as to match the interests you have or the questions you want answered.

Likewise, when a chemist in the lab observes a particular reaction, she has to determine whether that event is typical or unique, mundane or significant. One way that the chemist would determine the significance of her experiment would be to refer to the publications of other scientists in her field who had done similar or related experiments. Such experiments require a replication of results in order to be considered reliable, so describing exactly what was done and what happened or did not happen is a key part of the way scientists share their findings and make their conclusions available to others to validate. Contrary to the commonplace notion that first you do the experiment and then you "write it up," writing is an integral part of the process from the very moment you begin to be serious about observing—not just at the end of the process. It just isn't possible to observe carefully enough to make sense of what you're seeing without making notes of some kind. Likewise it is impossible not to think as you capture details in language, even the language of notations. When you write down speculations about significance or reread your notes and arrange them in an order that lets others follow your sense of what's important, you are composing meaning. Writing and rewriting is how researchers make experiences like observing into knowledge.

Noticing what we notice and reflecting on what it is about our own background, experience, and interests that allows us to see what we see is a good way to begin to see what else is there and to experience that miracle of penetrating (or being penetrated by) our experiences. Did you notice, for example, the pronouns used in the preceding paragraphs? Most readers still tend to notice feminine pronouns but read past the male pronouns. This ability to "miss" the male indicators is especially common when talking about groups that are commonly assumed to be male or a mixture of males and females. Using the female pronoun for groups of mixed gender is still unusual enough in English that these feminine pronouns create dissonance for readers; their expectations are not

---

[2]Clifford Geertz, "Being There: Anthropology and the Sense of Writing," *Works and Lives: The Anthropologist as Author* (Stanford, CA: Stanford UP, 1988).

matched by what is on the page. In an earlier draft of this chapter, the pronouns used to describe archaeologists and chemists were switched. When the female pronouns came first, several readers began to question the pronouns of all the paragraphs because the dissonance that was created caused them to begin to notice *all* the pronouns. Perhaps this was not the case for you and your classmates. Are you accustomed to seeing a variety of pronouns in textbooks or other reading material? Discuss this phenomenon with your classmates. If there are differences among you in noticing or not noticing the pronouns, what could account for those differences? Why might those differences be significant?

But, as we've already noted, observation is rarely used in isolation in any serious inquiry though observing, or noticing, is often the beginning point. If you observed that readers' reactions to pronoun usage varied, observing alone wouldn't enable you to say how often readers notice pronouns, under what conditions they notice or ignore pronouns, or even how many readers are noticing or not noticing pronouns in any given passage. To investigate this phenomenon, then, you would have to decide which question(s) you wanted to explore, and select a method of investigation that would help you answer the question(s). If, for example, you wondered whether feminine pronouns were noticed more often than masculine pronouns, you might create a passage where everything was the same except the pronouns, give that passage to a number of different readers, and then ask the readers questions about what they remember, including questions that ask them about the pronouns of the passage. If you wanted to know if men or women notice feminine pronouns more often, you would have to design your study to include a balance of men and women readers.[3]

Another way to test gendered pronoun use would be to survey printed texts to determine common practice. The articles by Leo Chavez, Julia Koza, and María Len-Ríos included in the Readings section are examples of researchers surveying textual and visual features of popular magazines and drawing conclusions about meaning from what they observe in a more systematic way. If you were going to investigate pronoun use by surveying written texts, you would have to begin by figuring out, as these researchers did, how to make the investigation manageable. You would need to narrow your survey in similar ways—by selecting a particular kind of text (perhaps newspapers, textbooks, or magazine articles) or considering only publications geared for a particular audience. You might be interested in shifts in pronoun use over time, and if so, you would need to include multiple years in your survey. You might decide, as some of our students have in similar work, to look at the same newspaper on the same date every year. In any case, you would need to acknowledge the limits of your survey and be careful not to make claims that are larger than your data can really support.[4]

Observations of the physical world also require additional strategies of inquiry to move from reporting the phenomena to making an interpretation, argument, or claim of significance. Let's say, for example, that you notice that a particular neighborhood has a similar architectural style, a structure of buildings that is very different from another neighborhood nearby. In order to say something about why or how these differences in style emerged, you would need to do some library research that would help you characterize

---

[3]Chapter 4, Interviewing, and the second section of Chapter 5, Conducting Surveys, provide additional ideas about how to structure an inquiry using these additional methods.
[4]Chapter 6, Working with Texts, provides additional suggestions for analyzing textual features like pronouns and for using textual evidence in support of other kinds of inquiry. To the extent that tracking features of publications produces numerical data, Chapter 5, Working with Numbers, may prove helpful in this kind of inquiry.

the styles you've observed, identifying in the process the time period when those styles emerged or were popular. You might use the archives of the local historical museum to track the development of these different neighborhoods and consult historical maps to pinpoint the dates of construction. City or county offices often have an archives department that preserves the records associated with the development of the locale area, including the meetings of zoning commissions that authorize what kind of development can occur in a particular location. If you could identify the architect who designed key buildings, you would be able to research that architect's training or career profile to see what traditions influenced her designs. You might interview people who have lived in the neighborhood for a long time to see what they remember about the construction of various structures. This additional information would allow you to contextualize your own direct observations, pinpointing the features that are common to the style and those that might have emerged for other reasons.

Researchers who are interested in architecture might expect such an investigation to say something interesting or new about how architectural styles respond to local conditions or how individual architects create a new style by combining features of old ones. Historians, on the other hand, would probably be more interested in the way physical structures reflect the values or conditions of their period of construction. Economists and sociologists would probably pursue how the economic class of the people for whom buildings are intended influences the way such structures are constructed. And if a city commission had to determine where to construct a new roadway through these neighborhoods, they might be interested in both the historical value of the buildings, their status as architectural specimens, and their impact on the local ecology. Thus, what kind of meaning is made, like what kinds of questions to ask and what kinds of additional sources of information to turn to are variable, often a product of the researcher's interests, training, methods, and habits of mind, and clearly shaped by the purpose for the inquiry and the audience who will read the researcher's final work.

SPECIAL MATERIALS: VISUALS

Scholars who work with visual materials rely heavily on observation as a method of inquiry and investigation, and their work can teach us about methods of observing and ways of writing about what is observed.[5] Art historians and art critics, for example, often begin with descriptions that help less experienced viewers see the work of art as they do, and they often take a big-picture view to position the piece in a larger historical or cultural context as they answer such questions as:

- When and where was the work made? By whom and for whom?
- What did the work originally look like, and what accounts for the changes visible in its current condition?

---

[5]While many scholars of visual materials eventually compile their own extensive collections, published collections are a good place to begin your studies, and most libraries will have several such publications featuring individual artists, artistic periods, themed topics, or genres. Some common collections of photographs, for example, include Gordon Parks's *Half-Past Autumn*, Walker Evans and James Agee's *Let Us Now Praise Famous Men*, Jean Mohr and Edward Said's *After the Last Sky*, Jacob Riis's *How the Other Half Lives*, Dorothea Lange's *American Photographs*, or Michael Carlebach's *Working Stiffs* or his *Origins of Photojournalism*. Use these titles to help you generate key terms and categories to locate similar books in your own library.

- Where would the work originally have been seen? By whom?
- What purpose did the piece originally serve?
- How does the piece reflect its culture or historical origin, the materials available to the artist, or the common practices of the era of its creation? How and where did the artist break from tradition or common practice to do something new or different?
- How has the piece been seen over time? How has its reception changed over time, and why did these changes occur?

PRACTICE ACTIVITY 3-4

Applying "Big-Picture" Questions

Although the pictures presented in Figures 3.2 and 3.3 are not examples of famous artwork, see if you can apply any of the big-picture questions to these photographs. Do you recognize the images immediately? If you don't, what clues exist in the picture itself that help you figure out something of its historical and social context?

Consider: What makes some images immediately recognizable? What images resonate for you as emblematic of particular events, cultures, or generations?

FIGURE 3.2

FIGURE 3.3

   Scholars also concern themselves with the inner working of the piece—the close-up view, if you will. They use specialized vocabulary and an understanding of techniques and stylistic features to consider such features as:

- What does the form of the piece contribute to the overall effect? How do the materials used, the size, or techniques of construction contribute to the piece?

- What is the subject or content of the work? What is the source of this image? That is, myth, religion, natural world, and so on?

- What is the relationship of the objects represented in the piece? What relationship do the figures, for example, have to one another or to the viewer? How does the staging of the piece—even if it appears to be a naturally occurring scene—convey meaning or significance?

- How does color (hue, density, shadow) contribute to the piece?

- If there is text accompanying the piece, how does that text interact with or illuminate the piece. If there is a title, for example, how does it affect our understanding of the piece? If there is no title, what does its absence mean?

PRACTICE ACTIVITY 3-5

Applying "Close-up" Questions

See if you can apply any of the close-up questions to either of the pictures presented in Figures 3.4 or 3.5. Practice writing a description of either of these images.

Consider: Compare your written description with those produced by your classmates. Which elements were consistent across the different descriptions? How are the differences in your description reflective of your own tastes, personality, or interests?

FIGURE 3.4 "Zulus" photograph by Ed Kashi, September 1, 1998.

FIGURE 3.5 "Boy Holding Machete during Yard Work." Orphans of Peru series photograph by Cecilia Larrabure, September 23, 2003.

As scholars work to answer big-picture and close-up view questions, they draw upon historical studies as well as a body of knowledge related to *iconography*, or the symbolic meanings of images. Most of us would recognize, for example, that a crucifix is a symbol of Christianity and that a star and crescent moon are images that represent Islam. Likewise certain items are so regularly associated with particular historical, mythological, religious, or legendary figures that they become known as *attributes* that serve to identify the figure. Just as every American child knows to associate four leaf clovers with good luck and Saint Patrick's Day or black cats and skeletons with Halloween, scholars who analyze visual materials learn to recognize the symbolic meaning of animals, plants, and other objects in the works they study. Of course many of these interpretations are subject to debate, so scholars write out their arguments for understanding a piece of art in a particular way, pointing to specific details in the work and combining those details with secondary sources that allow them to make the case for their interpretation. Colors as well as shapes or objects can have symbolic meaning, though these meanings vary by culture and context. White, for example, is the symbol of purity and virginity in western European cultures, but in Oriental cultures, as in ancient Greece and Rome, white was the color of mourning.[6]

Scholars are also interested in *iconology*, or the study of images for what they reveal about cultural beliefs and values. The studies of images used in advertising or those on the covers of magazines mentioned earlier are examples of the scholarship of iconology. These researchers are more interested in what the images they are examining say about the culture they represent than they are in how the images construct the artistic world or reflect artistic development. Editorial cartoons almost always make use

---

PRACTICE ACTIVITY 3-6

Common Symbols and Their Meanings

Make a list of common symbols and the meaning usually associated with that symbol. For example: four leaf clover = good luck; black cats = bad luck. Compare your list with those generated by classmates.

Consider: What accounts for any differences in the associations on your lists? Can you find the origin of the association for one of the symbols on your list using one of the resources suggested in footnote 6?

---

[6]There are encyclopedias and dictionaries that can help you interpret and analyze symbols. See, for example, *An Illustrated Encyclopaedia of Traditional Symbols* by J. C. Cooper (Thames and Hudson, 1978); *Encyclopedia of Comparative Iconography: Themes Depicted in Works of Art* Helene E. Roberts, editor (Fitzroy Dearborn, 1998); or *The Dictionary of Subjects and Symbols in Art* by James Hall (Harper and Row, 1979). Likewise many university libraries subscribe to electronic databases that allow scholars to search online for both images and articles about art. See the list of Internet Resources at the end of this chapter for additional suggestions.

of symbolic imagery and icons in order to convey meaning succinctly and visually. Edwards and Winkler's study of the appropriation of the photographic image of the Iwo Jima flag raising into editorial cartoons is concerned with the distinction between iconographs and ideographs, a term that has previously been limited to texts rather than images. In either iconography or iconology using secondary resources is essential to

---

PRACTICE ACTIVITY 3-7

Recognizing and Interpreting Symbols

The historical images presented in Figures 3.6 and 3.7 make use of various kinds of symbolic imagery. Make a list of the symbols you recognize in these illustrations. Next to each symbol you've listed, indicate what you think the symbol is conveying in the context of this illustration.

Consider: Compare your lists and the meanings you've identified with the lists generated by your classmates. If you were going to further investigate these historical images and their original contexts, how would you go about doing so and who might be interested in the results of your work? In other words, what research questions would you be trying to answer by such an investigation?

FIGURE 3.6 *Welcome to the Land of Freedom Illustration.* **Frank Leslie's Illustrated Newspaper, July 2, 1887**

FIGURE 3.7   Union Labor Party Presidential Election Poster, Kurz and Allison, 1888.

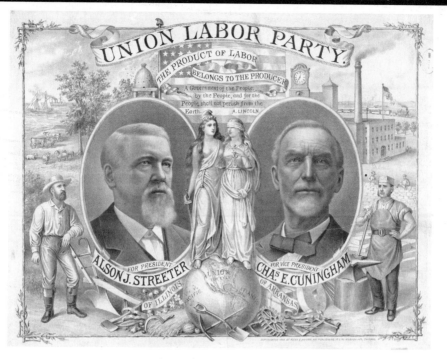

transform simple reporting or description to analysis, argument, or interpretation, but observation is always also necessary. Figure 3.8 is a checklist for analyzing editorial cartoons developed by Jonathan Burack of highsmith.com, which our students have found very helpful.

Another avenue of inquiry into images involves the implications inherent in using images. In a world saturated with images, do we choose to look and consciously interpret, or does the image capture our gaze and manipulate our reaction? Do we have the power, or does the image have power over us? Is "effective rhetoric," as W. J. T. Mitchell declares, "a two-pronged strategy of verbal and visual persuasion?"[7] Since many images are derivative of earlier works, what is the relationship between originality and mimicry? Are reproductions or imitations a form of plagiarism? Figure 3.11 is an example of a student artist's painting "copied" or "inspired" by Cézanne's *Card Players* and incorporated into a different piece of art. Malcolm Gladwell's November 22, 2004, *New Yorker* essay "Something Borrowed" considered this very issue of imitation or appropriation in the context of the controversy surrounding the dramatic production *Frozen*. Parody, satire, imitation, appropriation, and fraudulent copying envelop the visual art world as well. Indeed, *intertextuality*—subtle or overt references to earlier works—is such an important component of the artistic world that scholars spend considerable time arguing about how to

---

[7]W. J. T. Mitchell, "The Photographic Essay: Four Case Studies," *Picture Theory: Essays on Verbal and Visual Representation* (Chicago: U of Chicago Press, 1994).

FIGURE 3.8 A mindsparks editorial cartoon checklist, courtesy of Jonathan Burak

- **The Issue:** Editorial cartoons are NOT just like other comics. They may be funny. But their main purpose is to offer an opinion or point of view about some issue or problem in the news. First try to decide what the issue or problem is in the cartoon you are studying.

- **Symbols:** A symbol is any object or design that stands for some other thing, person, or idea. For example, a huge thug may stand for the problem of crime. Describe objects in the cartoon that are symbols.

- **Exaggeration and Distortion:** Which features in the cartoon are exaggerated? That is, which appear much larger or smaller than they actually are? Changes in size or shape of this sort often add to the cartoon's point. Distorting an object means changing it in some way to make it look funny, ugly, etc. What symbols or other objects in the cartoon are distorted, and how does this add to the cartoon's point?

- **Stereotypes:** A stereotype is a simplistic view of some group. It is often insulting. But it can also help the cartoon make its point quickly. What stereotypes are used in the cartoon? Are they used unfairly, or are they used just to help the cartoon make its point?

- **Caricature:** Caricature is a portrayal of an individual's features in an exaggerated or distorted way. Is caricature used in the cartoon? If so, does it help to make an important point about the person portrayed?

- **Humor and Irony:** Humor is important in many editorial cartoons. Irony is one kind of humor. In it, a viewpoint is expressed in such an odd way as to make that view actually seem ridiculous. Is the cartoon you are studying funny or ironic? Does the humor add to the cartoon's point? Does the humor present an unfair or highly exaggerated idea of the other side's point of view?

- **Background Knowledge:** A reader usually must know certain things about an issue in order to understand an editorial cartoon on that issue. What kinds of background knowledge do you need to make sense of the cartoon you are studying? Where might you get that knowledge if you do not already have it?

- **The Argument:** Slogans tell us what to do or think. "Smoking Kills," or "Give a Hoot, Don't Pollute" are slogans. A good editorial cartoon is NOT just a slogan. It gives reasons for its opinion. In other words, it is an argument. What point of view does your cartoon present, and what argument does it offer? How do its symbols, distorted features, stereotypes, caricature or other features help it to make a good argument for its point of view?

interpret such recycled images and what affect they have on the viewer's experience of new work.

Finally, scholars working with images also investigate the effects of technology on the production or use of visuals. For example, Michael Carlebach, an historian of photojournalism, argues that the technology that made tintypes easily available and relatively inexpensive led workers to pose for personal photographs when previously such portraits would have been reserved for wealthier patrons with a

PRACTICE ACTIVITY 3-8

Interpreting Editorial Cartoons

Choose one of the editorial cartoons presented in Figures 3.9 or 3.10 or find another example to work with. The Internet Resources at the end of this chapter provide some suggestions for searching for editorial cartoons online. Use Burak's checklist to compile a list of the features the cartoonist has used to make the point. Then write a short explanation of the cartoon for someone who might not understand it or its message.

Consider: Compare your list of features with those compiled by your classmates. Are editorial cartoons only funny if we already understand the issue? Recognize the symbols? Agree with the position being advocated? Why do such images create such heated controversy, at least on occasion?

FIGURE 3.9 **"Liberty has been Secured," Lalo Alcaraz, 2002.**

different sense of artistic composition.[8] Leah Dilworth's essay included in the Readings is another example of a scholar who reads images and considers their participation in the economic, social, and legal dimensions of our world even as she asks which images count as "art" and which ones don't. Obviously, then, the investigation of visual materials has many possible directions and draws upon a wide array of scholarly perspectives.

[8]See *Working Stiffs: Occupational Portraits in the Age of Tintypes* (Washington, D.C.: Smithsonian Institution Press, 2002).

FIGURE 3.10 "Democratic Plan," Bob Gorrell, September 12, 2006.

FIGURE 3.11 *Untitled*, Izlia Fernandez. Savannah College of Art and Design, 2003. Courtesy of owner, Don C. Shipp, Miami, Florida, 2004.

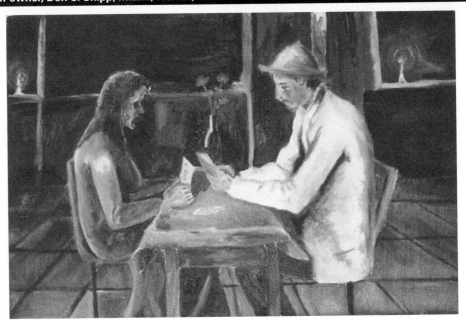

> **PRACTICE ACTIVITY 3-9**
>
> ## Imitation, Appropriation, Parody
>
> Locate a copy of Cézanne's *Card Players*, and compare it to the student work in Figure 3.11. See if you can locate other imitations or parodies based on this work as well. Then see if you can find imitations or parodies of other famous pieces of art. You might try, for example, looking for imitations and parodies of Grant Wood's *American Gothic* or of Edvard Munch's *The Scream*.
>
> **Consider:** What makes these imitations, appropriations, and parodies recognizable? Are there features that remain the same in the examples you've found that are based on the same original artwork? For example, do all of the pieces that play off Cézanne's *Card Players* include two people, one with a hat, and a table? Is the flower always present? What's the difference between an imitation, appropriation, parody, and plagiarism?

SPECIAL MATERIALS: ARTIFACTS

As already noted many different kinds of scholars use observation as a means of inquiry, and among them are researchers who work with objects—such as archaeologists, art critics, cultural anthropologists, and architects. Because man-made objects have regularly been designed to carry symbolic meaning even as they function to accomplish practical tasks, scholars who work with objects are able to connect their observations of a single object to the patterns that have been established by prior scholarship. Working with artifacts, then, like working with works of visual art, requires contextualizing the *symbolic* meanings embedded in objects. In order to contextualize when you don't already have the depth of knowledge of someone who has been working in a particular discipline for a long time, you will have to combine secondary sources such as those you are most likely to find in the library with what you can discern from your own direct examination. Learning to observe and interpret objects, however, is a fascinating practice, and one we've found beginning students can use to enhance the habits of mind of curiosity and precision essential to much academic inquiry.

Archeology developed as a way to discover elements of human civilizations that systems of recording and storing language did not preserve, even when the civilization had such systems. The restraints naturally placed on the information early archeologists could gather led them (and continues to lead them) to develop methods of inquiry into artifacts, those objects that people use to communicate and shape their social worlds. Researchers now accept, thanks in large part to pioneering work in archeology, that we communicate with artifacts and that even ordinary objects reflect the cultural values of those who create them. Thus, when we build houses, for example, we communicate a complex set of beliefs about family relationships, gender roles, and public and private life. When we create new tools or adapt old ones for a new use, we are at the same time reflecting the economic and social features of our culture at that moment in time. Because objects are often embellished with details to make them more aesthetically appealing, scholars can recognize patterns or styles that position the object within a particular culture, historical moment, or decorative tradition. Sometimes these embellishments carry religious symbolism; sometimes they reflect local raw materials or signal trade relationships with neighboring communities. Almost always the ways that the material is shaped into the object reflects learned knowledge, individual skill, and technological innovation. So, although the study of artifacts is often identified with the work of archaeologists trying to understand a mysterious object from an ancient culture, scholars interested in understanding culture, even current culture, regularly turn to material artifacts.

Figure 3.12 presents a rough heuristic to guide you as you investigate artifacts and consider the relationship between their physical composition and their social, communicative,

---

FIGURE 3.12 Ways of understanding artifacts

- **Substance:** Any object can be experienced by the senses. Look at it carefully, and see it from different points of view. Touch it and feel its textures. Hold it and feel its weight and balance. Taste it, if possible (and safe!). Smell it carefully. Listen to the object. If possible, and if it will not damage the object, strike it gently against or with other objects. Are there features of the object that are embellishments or decorative elements added onto the basic object? If so, how are these features different from or integrated into the primary object?

- **Materiality:** From what materials is the object constructed? What do you know about the properties, sensory and otherwise, of these materials? Does it have parts? Are those parts interchangeable with other objects of its kind? Measure the artifact and/or its parts. Does the relative size or proportion suggest importance or priority?

- **Function:** What is it for? How is it used? How do elements of its thingy-ness and materiality help it to perform its function? Does it have multiple functions? Does it lend itself to other uses? Is there evidence of *wear*, and does this tell you anything about patterns of use? Are there other objects that perform the same or a similar function? In what ways are they like and unlike this one?

- **Transformations:** How were the materials shaped to form this object? What processes did those materials undergo? Do you see evidence of hand-crafting, machine-crafting, mass production? Has this object (or others like it) changed form several times? Have these transformations been related to its function or functions or were they merely aesthetic? Are there other versions of this object that show stages of transformation?

- **Maintenance:** In what ways can the object break or become unusable? How much special knowledge does it take to make it usable again, or to adapt it for different circumstances? What kind of standard maintenance does it require and who performs that maintenance? Is there evidence of maintenance or repairs on this particular object?

- **Place:** See the object as it exists or existed in its environment. Where does it reside? Why? How are other objects arranged around it? How does its location make it part of the social world? Can you sketch its place?

- **Communication:** What kinds of material meanings does it communicate in the way it is or was used? What messages does it send, purely by virtue of its function? By virtue of its place or location? Are there ways it communicates "symbolically," as well as functionally? How does its substance contribute to its symbolic communication? To its aesthetic communication?

╔══╗
║ **PRACTICE ACTIVITY 3-10** ║
╚══╝

Practice with Artifacts

Choose any man-made object that you can examine directly. Use the suggestions in Figure 3.12 to guide you in making a list of the object's characteristics. Share your descriptive list with your classmates without revealing the object or its usual name. Can your classmates identify the object by its characteristics alone?

Consider: What questions can you generate about your object from this preliminary examination? What does the collection of objects you and your classmates have chosen say about modern culture?

and cultural uses. Some of these suggestions will be more apropos of certain objects than others, but all are useful to consider. When you have answered the kinds of questions presented in Figure 3.12, you will have developed a greater familiarity with the object, and you will begin to notice things about it that had escaped your attention. Although it may seem a laborious process, actually writing out answers will spur you to think about the object more deeply and with greater attention to detail than only answering them in your head.

Any one of the features of an artifact might also become an area for secondary investigation. If the object is made of iron, for example, knowing more about the properties of iron, when human beings began using iron, what procedures are necessary to shape iron, what dangers exist in its use—any of this secondary information may help you make more sense of the object you are examining. Scholars do not operate in a vacuum, but rather stand on the shoulders of those who have come before. Being able to identify patterns; positioning a particular object within a category, type, or style of similar objects; and knowing background information about those categories, types, and styles are indispensable to the investigation of artifacts.

As we continue to see new ways that artifacts carry meaning, we often simultaneously place distance between those artifacts and ourselves. In museums, we are encouraged to observe the artifacts archeologists study, but are rarely allowed to touch or hold them. Similar things happen when old monuments (which we often call sculpture), murals, paintings, or photographs are placed in galleries and museums. There are, of course, good reasons for such practices and prohibitions, not the least of which is that too much human contact can destroy the artifact. But the distance established by museums or galleries and the special efforts they take to preserve artifacts can lead us to feel that we do not need to encounter an artifact fully in order to understand it or that only those objects that have obtained museum status are worthy of our careful investigation and attention.

Consider some uses of photographs or reproductions, for instance. Photographs are themselves artifacts, but a photograph or image of something is not as useful in apprehending its meaning as the real object. Artifacts have mass, proportion, density, weight, three dimensions. We "know" things about a hammer by holding it—feeling its center of gravity, for instance—in a way that a picture cannot reveal and words never fully describe. There are many artifacts, ones stored or on display in museums, that you cannot hold. But there are many in the world around you that you know because you do hold them. Hold

---

PRACTICE ACTIVITY 3-11

Artifacts across Time

Can you figure out what the object in Figure 3.13 is? What features give you a clue about its use or age? What features are the same as more modern versions of the same object? See if you can find other pictures of this object that demonstrate how it has changed over time, or collect several versions of any man-made object—phones, clocks, or radios might be good choices.

Consider: What features remain the same across several versions of the same object? How do your objects reflect considerations of style or aesthetics? What do any of these objects suggest about the culture that produced or used them? What limitations did you encounter working with photographs of these objects rather than with the objects themselves?

---

a contemporary cellular phone and compare it with the ones people used five years ago, and you will notice a pronounced difference. People use these objects differently because their dimensionality is different, and the phones developed a different dimensionality to suit the way people wanted to use them. A house feels different when you stand on its porch or in its kitchen, even if you occupy the space of its ruins, than if you observe a picture of it. This difference in how we can know a place or an object by experiencing it directly—physically—accounts for why people visit the Grand Canyon or the Statue of Liberty instead of just looking at pictures.

That's not to disparage photographs. In fact, because they are themselves artifacts, objects people use to communicate, photographs can be investigated in much the same way as other

FIGURE 3.13

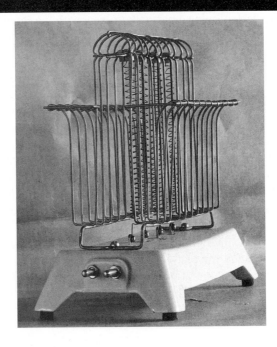

artifacts. Think, for instance, about typical family photos. They are usually a certain size, and are printed on a certain kind of paper. Think also about the ways current technologies change our relationships with photos—changing their dimensions, pushing them between digital and analog worlds, increasing the ease of capturing images, and, perhaps, decreasing their permanence at the same time—just as e-mail has transformed letter writing.[9]

To say that technologies transform the nature of artifacts and the way we interact with them is only to say something that has always been true of human societies. Although the pace of change in our time may have quickened, we do not (impressions to the contrary notwithstanding) live in a uniquely technological age. Humans surrounded themselves with technologies—things they made to help them shape their world—long before their gadgets depended on electricity. Because using a plethora of artifacts is one thing that ties all human beings together, investigating them can often be a window on our societies and ourselves.

ETHICAL CONSIDERATIONS IN OBSERVING

Researchers who use observation know that their very presence may well change what they are observing. When scientists tried to observe the nesting behaviors of birds, for example, they had to figure out how not to disrupt the process. Setting up nesting stations with Plexiglas backs that allowed researchers to peek inside without disturbing the nest itself was an important innovation in their research. We don't expect our students to invent elaborate controls on their observation for the sake of the work we are interested in accomplishing in a writing course, but we do expect them to be aware of how their presence can alter the subjects they are trying to observe.

Observing human beings is even more complicated. Imagine, for example, if a researcher came with you to observe as you went about your daily activities. Would the presence of the researcher alter the way you get to campus, take notes in class, or buy books at the bookstore? How about the way you wash your face, eat lunch, or party with friends? Would you be offended if someone reported on your behavior without your knowledge? What if they reported on your behavior but kept your identity a secret? Would you expect the researcher to tell you in advance what he was looking for or how he would be reporting the information he collected? How would you react if a researcher who clearly did not share your beliefs showed up at a religious service, a wedding, or a funeral? Would you be less concerned about the presence of such a researcher if you knew she had asked someone in authority for permission to attend and take notes on what she was observing?

Of course, the problem with telling participants what the research is about or even that the observer is present is that such knowledge can alter the very behavior the researcher is interested in understanding. Two-way mirrors in psychology studies only partially solve this problem because participants are usually aware that behind the mirror is a researcher. When researchers become "participant observers," they hope that their continued presence will help make their subjects comfortable enough that they act as they normally do and at least momentarily forget that the researcher is there for other purposes. Researchers typically use triangulation—three or more methods of investigation, observers, ways of gathering data, or better still a combination of all—to

---

[9]For more on photographs, see the earlier section in this chapter Special Materials: Visuals.

provide a check on the information they get through direct observation and increase the validity of the research.[10]

Since the likelihood of influencing the observation by the presence of a researcher is difficult to overcome in studies involving human subjects, many researchers take the stance that they need to make their presence visible in the written record, to be as clear as possible about how they conducted the observation, and to speculate on the impact they had on the information they collected. This kind of reflective practice has to be balanced, however, so that the subject doesn't become the researcher rather than the subject being researched. No matter how much someone tells you *about* such balance, though, you'll learn it in practice as you write, have others read and respond to your writing, and write again. Even practiced researchers write and rewrite before they publish their work. Because ethnographers typically use one or more local informants who are a part of the group being observed to provide additional information about the significance or "normal-ness" of the things the researcher has observed, many researchers treat their informants as coresearchers. The researcher may ask the informant to read and comment on the analysis in a draft form, and then write into the final version any differences of interpretation that the informants point out. Often informants have their own interpretation of what's important and what's not about both their own culture and the researcher's culture. David Thelen's essay interviewing Alexander Butterfield about his memory of the revelation of the Watergate tapes is a good example of a researcher working with his informant to both interpret and present the research.

If a researcher goes into an observation/data collection phase with a theory or interpretation already in mind, the observation is certainly influenced by those expectations. Researchers who work from observations have to check their tendencies to see what they expected and be open to alternatives. Sometimes, in fact, researchers do observations focusing on specific details in order to see if their speculation is accurate. Researchers are frequently working to prove (or disprove) a hypothesis, to replicate the results of prior research or to test a theory in a new situation. But researchers are also regularly involved in serendipity; that is, they start out to examine one thing and discover something much more compelling or intriguing along the way that is worth their attention and systematic investigation.

Almost all institutions have human subject research review boards charged with reviewing research involving human subjects with an eye to protecting participants. Such boards might approve a study where subjects are not told that they are being observed as long as the researcher took precautions to protect the identity of individuals, did not encourage or promote illegal or dangerous behavior, and acted in ways that minimized the harm to those who became the subject of this research. Most of these institutional research review boards (often referred to as IRBs) will not expect students who are just learning to use research methods to submit their planned research for review, but they will expect that your instructor is helping you to consider how to do your work in an ethical way and how to minimize any negative impact on your subjects. Observing in public places, protecting the identity of those you observe, being forthcoming about your purpose to anyone who questions your presence, and thinking through your plan of observation from the perspective of those who will be observed or represented in writing are some of the ways you can ensure that your research, however informal, is in keeping with sound ethical practices.

---

[10]See "triangulation," Dictionary of the Social Sciences. Craig Calhoun, ed. Oxford University Press, 2002. Oxford Reference Online, Oxford University Press <http://www.oxfordreference.com/views/ENTRY .html?subview=Main&entry=t104.e1711>.

PRACTICE ACTIVITY 3-12

Ethics and Surveillance

The increased use of video surveillance has generated considerable controversy and concerns about privacy. Sometimes surveillance cameras are easily discernable, other times their presence is not so obvious. The Web site http://www.observingsurveillance.org/ is an example of one group's efforts to bring attention to such surveillance. Surveillance cameras are often used as security devices, but they can also be used for advertising or promotional purposes. Many college campuses have webcams so prospective students can see the campus from afar. You can see the live video of the University of Miami campus, for example, by visiting http://www.miami.edu/webcams/. Does your campus have a similar system? If so, are students (and faculty) aware of the various locations of such cameras?

Consider: Are such uses of surveillance cameras ethical? What if the surveillance is combined with face recognition technology? How is surveillance different from or similar to the observing done by researchers?

WORKING ON WRITING OBSERVATIONS

When researchers work with observation data, they aren't just trying to re-create a scene or describe what they have observed. Rather these researchers are using their observations as data that lead them to specific conclusions, interpretations, or arguments. Thus, in representing their observations in writing, these researchers have to be certain they are analyzing the data and arranging the details they present in such a way that readers can follow the analysis to the conclusion or generalization. As we said in Chapter 2, analysis involves:

- Attending to details by breaking into parts
- Identifying patterns by looking for repetitions
- Regrouping the details into meaningful units by labeling similarities and distinctions, and defining key terms
- Considering the context for the data by noting what social, political, historical, economic conditions produced these data and these patterns
- Watching for oddities by considering what's missing or what doesn't seem to fit, and where there are contradictions to the patterns you've observed
- Making an interpretive leap by articulating what the details, patterns, context, and groupings mean or how they should be understood as significant
- Considering alternative interpretations by imagining the apparent oddity as more important than those elements that seem to fit, by changing the key terms, or by breaking the details into different kinds of groups
- Acknowledging the limits of your interpretation by noting what constraints might have altered or influenced the data, how reliable are the results, where mistakes might have been introduced, and what assumptions have been made in order to interpret the data in this particular way

Although all these elements are important when researchers analyze observation data, two issues are particularly visible in writing from observations: moving from summary descriptions to generalizations of meaning, and vivid versus "objective" word choice.

SUMMARY DESCRIPTIONS TO GENERALIZATIONS

For observations to serve as data, they first have to be transferred onto the page. That is, the details of what we've seen can't remain in our heads or as rough notes if they are to be the source of meaning for readers, especially readers who have not seen the event, object, structure, or scene. Even in cases where the observed data might be commonplace, authors have to render the features that they find most relevant to their purposes onto the page so that readers are directed to attend to specific details rather than a general memory. Look, for example, at how Jules David Prown directs his readers to attend to the details of a teapot, even though his audience has surely seen teapots before and his essay includes an illustration of the teapot he is describing.

> As an example, I will analyze a single artifact. This object is $6\frac{3}{8}$ inches high, $4\frac{3}{4}$ inches wide at the widest part of the body, and $7\frac{7}{8}$ inches wide from spout tip to handle. It is wider than it is high and could be inscribed within a rectangle. The primary material is pewter, although the handle and lower ring of the finial are of wood. There is a small hole in the top of the lid, and inside the vessel there is a circular arrangement of small holes where the spout joins the body. (p. 524)

This description actually continues for several more paragraphs before Prown introduces the concept of metaphor, how metaphors help anthropologists decode culture and how this concept can help us understand "how artifacts function as metaphorical expressions of culture." At this point, Prown offers another description of the teapot, one that makes use of the physical details he has presented earlier in order to make claims about how that teapot can be read metaphorically.

> The object, which we can now refer to as a teapot since our analysis of it is complete, invokes multiple textual metaphors—cheerful, comfortable, reliable, grandmotherly, and so forth—metaphors based on the feelings of experience. It also embodies structural metaphors based on the shape of experience. The lid and finial, for example, can be read as a bell metaphor. And the bell shape suggests calling—whether by a dinner bell or ringing from a sick bed—calling for and receiving help or comfort or sustenance. Another structural metaphor, equally obvious, is less easily retrieved, however, perhaps because repressed. If you ask the respondent (or the analyst asks him- or herself) to identify the Ur-experience, the earliest human experience of ingesting warm liquids, the immediate response is a baby feeding from a mother's breast. Structural analogies between the shape of the lower section of the body of the vessel and the female breast now become evident. And when the object is viewed from above, with the finial at the center like a nipple, the object is even more breastlike. The teapot is revealed, unexpectedly, as a structural metaphor for the female breast. (p. 526)

Although these two paragraphs both include descriptive details of the teapot, the second one also has sentences, or parts of sentences, that make claims about how the teapot ought to be understood. These claims for meaning are all related to the opening "as an example" which links this specific case to a larger point Prown is making about how examining artifacts can help us understand cultural beliefs. Prown returns to this larger point at the end of this specific example and before he moves on to the second example of card tables when he writes:

> If artifacts express culture metaphorically, what kinds of insight can they afford us? What for example, does the teapot tell us about belief? The object has given us a clue that the drinking of tea, and perhaps the entire ceremony of tea drinking, may be related metaphorically to the fundamental human act of giving and receiving and has the potential of being a symbol of generosity or charity, of *caritas*. The humanness as well as the humaneness of the act is suggested in this teapot by the fact that the liquid is encased in an organic, breastlike form. (pp. 526–527)

Sometimes the observed details are not the central evidence for the researchers' claims, but simply one kind of evidence among many. In Robin Bachin's historical examination of the creation of the women's gymnasium at the University of Chicago, for example, the physical description of the building adds to the point she is developing from the textual evidence of correspondence and archival records. Notice how Bachin uses those descriptive details to support her point that the women's gymnasium, though recognizing nontraditional views of women, had to conform to expectations for proper female activity.

> Indeed, unlike Bartlett Gymnasium's [the men's gym] focus on virility and competition, the new women's gym would be structured around patterns of appropriate female physical activity and sociability. Marion Talbot and Gertrude Dudley, along with several female faculty and students, contributed ideas for the design of the building to the architects Shepley, Rutan and Coolidge (RCBG 24:12; see also Block 1983:123). Ida Noyes Hall was built to resemble a Tudor manor house, with elegant interior details that symbolized women's domestic arts. The Hall contained a large Common Room, as well as a library, social rooms for serving refreshments, offices for women's clubs and a sun parlour. It also included a personal service department, with provisions for shining shoes and giving manicures. The Hall featured a swimming pool, a game room, two bowling alleys and a large room for "corrective gymnasium work" (Goodspeed 1916: 441–2). The latter room was finished off with a large mural depicting the *Masque of Youth*, led by the Spirit of Gothic Architecture, illustrating, according to University Professor Edith Flint Foster, that "beauty ought to be educative" (see Block 1983: 123). (pp. 318–319)

Most of us learn that we can arrange information to move from specifics to the general or we can start with the general and then offer the specifics to substantiate our claim. As these examples illustrate, the movement between generalization and specific details can be either or both; often in complicated research, the observed details lead to a claim which in turn becomes a specific example in support of some larger claim. But when our students do an observation and come to class with notes, what claims they can make from the data they've collected is often just not clear. We think most researchers have similar moments; they've investigated some object or scene or text, taken detailed notes, but what it all means just isn't yet clear. At that moment they don't have to produce a "finished" paper, but they probably do start writing and organizing the details, asking themselves questions like "so what?" "why is this interesting?" or "what could account for what I've observed?"

If you began your observation with a particular research question in mind—how do people use this park?—then that question will guide your presentation of the details you observed. If, however, you begin as many of the assignments suggest—find a place to observe, record what happens, and then think about what those details tell you about the culture, community, and so on—you'll have to look for patterns in your details that lead you to a generalization, and you'll probably need to think about what the larger issue is that your observation speaks to. In the essay we've included at the end of this chapter, Hattie Wellington works from her detailed observations of the intramural fields to make an argument about the importance of this physical space in the culture of undergraduates. Notice how she arranges the details to work toward this point. Notice, too, that she includes a short interview with a particular student as a supplement to what she could observe directly. We're not suggesting that Wellington's essay is perfect, but we do believe she demonstrates careful observation and that she has successfully analyzed the details she observed to move from a simple description or summary to generalize a point of what those details say about the space she observed in the culture of the university.

VIVID DETAILS *VERSUS* "OBJECTIVE" LANGUAGE

Many of our students have written direct observation in the context of science labs and in that context they were encouraged to present the facts as objectively as possible. Some of our students have written creative fiction where they were encouraged to create vivid descriptions by using their senses, substituting active verbs for to-be verbs' and choosing appropriate metaphors. Our students have also learned that some words carry connotations that skew the prose and reveal the point of view and that such language is usually discouraged in academic writing but commonplace in politics and advertising. Such apparently contradictory standards for how to present descriptions often surface as our students work with observing. Though we've said it before, we want to remind

FIGURE 3.14 Suggestions for writing from observations

- Don't feel as if you have to mention everything you observed. Instead, choose excerpts from your notes that serve as examples of a theme or pattern that you find significant for some reason.

- Don't expect the reader to interpret your description or excerpt. Provide analytical commentary that explains your claims or theories.

- Make sure to provide sufficient evidence (in the form of observational details) for your claims.

- Comparing your findings with your assumptions or expectations might help you analyze your data or explain why your findings are significant.

- Your generalization does not have to be earth shattering. What you can responsibly claim based on your observations may seem pretty straightforward and unexciting.

- Resist the urge to draw one conclusion about what you observed. Instead, entertain multiple explanations for why you saw what you saw, even if these interpretations contradict each other. Then, if you can, help your readers understand why one of these interpretations is more probable, interesting, or significant.

you that word choice, like many of the rhetorical choices you have to make, is a matter of audience and purpose. There simply isn't one right way to do description, and even if you want to be totally objective, your point of view is likely to creep into the presentation. You should, however, aim for consistency. If you're presenting the facts, and nothing but the facts, neutral language is going to seem more appropriate than vivid embellishments.

As you can see in the passage we quoted earlier by Robin Bachin, even mostly factual descriptions can choose words intentionally. Take this sentence, for example: "Ida Noyes Hall was built to resemble a Tudor manor house, with elegant interior details that symbolized women's domestic arts." The word "elegant" provides an important descriptive detail, but it also conjures up a scene of luxury that is echoed in the list of amenities that follow—a large Common Room, library, sun parlour, swimming pool, game room, bowling alleys, decorative murals, and a department for personal services such as shoe shining and manicures. This bountiful list of rooms and features is as much an echo of the Victorian era as the use of the British spelling of "parlour." Further, the closing quotation that "beauty ought to be educative" serves to underscore the characterization that elegance is being intentionally linked to "women's domestic arts." It's hard, then, to say that Bachin is *only* presenting the facts.

Look again at Prown's choice of words in describing and then interpreting the teapot. The initial description is more straightforward, to be sure, but doesn't that style help create the contrast between recording objects and interpreting objects that is at the heart of his essay? In other words Prown is actually enacting the very difference that he is trying to discuss. Both Bachin and Prown are choosing words, deciding on styles of presenting description, and arranging details to intentionally create both meaning and effect. Further, Geertz's advice that writers must convey the sense of "being there" would seem to require the use of vivid details, precise vocabulary, and narrative-type re-creations of the event. So we think that the usual advice to present your research "objectively" is not only misleading, but also actually not followed by more experienced researchers/writers. How, though, do you make your observations vivid?

One strategy many writers use is to convey the scene using specific details rather than glossing over the scene with an impression. If the location you observed seemed to you chaotic, don't just give that generalization. Instead look carefully at your notes for the details that gave you that impression—people rushing past, phones ringing, doors opening and closing, computers humming, conversations starting and stopping or being interrupted, a loudspeaker giving announcements to which no one seemed to be listening, radios on different stations, several televisions broadcasting different stations simultaneously, and two vendors competing for customers by calling out the specialties featured at their stands. This list of details could be enhanced by re-creating the scene with sensory details—sight, sound, smell, taste, touch. Here's an example of sensory-based description:

> Grand Central Station is never calm, but in the heat of summer vacation, travelers and businessmen converge to make the cavernous station echo with chaos. Businessmen in their dark suits and power ties rush past toting leather cases, their pockets bulging with cell phones or BlackBerries. Students on summer holiday elbow through the crowd, iPods blocking the exterior noise for them but creating fleeting moments of song or rhythm for those they pass. The aroma of fresh-popped corn vies with the steamy odor of greasy water that has cooked too many hot dogs for too many days, and if you get too close, the acrid smell of sauerkraut, pickles, and chopped onions momentarily overwhelms the odors of train oil, sweat, and wet newspapers that cling

PRACTICE ACTIVITY 3-13

Vivid or Objective Descriptions

Turn to either of the student essays at the end of this chapter and try to identify where these writers have chosen words that echo their points. Try rewriting one of the paragraphs of description, making it either more vivid or more objective. Try the same experiment with a piece of your own writing.

Consider: Compare your results with revisions done by your classmates. Which versions do you like best and why? What else would have to change in the rest of the essay in order to make these new paragraphs fit it?

to the walls and seep into your pores. Red, yellow, hot pink, lavender, green. All the colors of the rainbow congregate in the shops that line the periphery, but there is no order to this array, no orderly blending from one to the next in an arch that leads to these pots of gold. A lone trumpet player stands against the wall, the threads of old show tunes wafting in and out of the crowd. If you stay long enough, you'll hear the whole repartee repeat in endless, unsolicited encores, but for those who pass by and drop leftover quarters and the occasional dollar bill into the open case with frayed, red velvet lining, the melodies are a break from the drone of an intercom system announcing the next train in a voice that isn't quite clear nor quite human.

If you reread the previous paragraph and pay close attention to how it is constructed, we think you'll see pretty quickly that the writer takes us through the details via various senses. Notice, too, that adjectives and verbs help make the scene more specific. The station is *cavernous*—not just large. The music *wafts*, and replaces the *drone* of the intercom. The corn is *fresh-popped*, and *vies* with other odors; the trumpet case has a *frayed, red velvet* lining; colors *congregate*. The writer also uses repetition and metaphor to re-create the scene, and there is some attempt to point to what is missing— order, pattern, human interactions—so as to underscore the conclusion that this is a scene of chaos. Senses, specific words rather than general ones, figurative language, and pointing to what isn't there can make the re-creation of an observed scene more vivid and believable.

STUDENT ESSAY: OBSERVATION OF A PLACE

A Health Sciences major at the University of Miami, Hattie Wellington was a first-year student when she wrote her essay. Hattie remembers having to step outside of the five-paragraph form she had learned so well in high school in order to combine interviews, observations, and narration into one essay. Hattie says, "The IM fields are nothing spectacular, but writing a good observation essay is about observing the depth of things and making connections as to why it is that way, who cares about it, and where the observations fit into the story."

The Fields of Dreams

Hattie Wellington

Imagine going to college where thousands of people go on vacation. My school feels more like a summer camp than a university. I lay out in between my classes. People play sports all the time and anytime between the hours of 10 AM and 10 PM. Some afternoons I can hear the band practicing right outside my window. Every morning on my way to class, I see people with their books open and laptops on, in their bathing suits. Every evening on my way to dinner, I witness games of soccer, frisbee, football, baseball, or lacrosse being played by people from every walk of life. Every night when I return to my dorm room, I notice a couple of tables and chairs pulled out onto the fields with twenty kids gathered around each of them. Welcome to the University of Miami: life on the intramural fields.

Around here, we call them the "IM fields," and everyone will know what you're talking about when you say that. They are the intramural fields: home to everything from band practice to tanning and from sports to smoking. Sororities and fraternities brag about their intramural successes. Posters from club sports line the bulletin boards posted in dorms, dining halls, classrooms, and the wellness center. Intramural sports, here at the University of Miami, are no joke. They are something people take very seriously; something that is a source of both pride and enjoyment to many students. The intramural fields are, in many ways, an epicenter for social life.

There's Something For Everybody

Friday afternoons are an enjoyable place wherever you go. It's the beginning of a new era, turning over a new leaf: the weekend. Last Friday afternoon after I finished class and running a few errands, I walked back to my dorm and passed by the intramural fields. It was nearing four o'clock. I was amazed at the variety of activities that occur spontaneously on these fields. They're not just for sports; there's something for everybody.

The band practiced loud and proud on the edge of one of the fields, facing away from everybody else. The band was large and took up a lot of space. They were practicing a song, often starting, stopping, and repeating portions they had already played. About 40 feet from the edge of the band there was a group of 20 girls dressed in sweats, shorts, and tank tops who kept their eyes on a guy who led them dressed in a camouflaged T-shirt and black pants. The guy looked pretty muscular and masculine, while all the girls looked rather slim and petite. The girls, nonetheless, paid close attention to this man who I assumed to be their instructor. They mostly danced along with the band's rhythm, but they kept going when the band stopped. They, too, started and stopped several times, taking time to repeat and work on the moves they missed.

There were only about 40 feet separating the dancers from the band, but somehow within that space two girls on towels found their niche to sunbathe in. I found it odd that they chose to lay so close to the band in the midst of a loud practice, but maybe they were already there when the band started playing; maybe they didn't want to make the effort to move. I wondered if maybe the band or dancers found them obtrusive, maybe they *should* move. They weren't the only sunbathers either though. In the middle of the fields there were four girls on towels sunbathing, and next to them there was a girl with a pile of books and her laptop open. She looked like she was in the middle of a good study session, but I had trouble believing that since she was wearing a bikini. I don't know why, but I can't put bikini and studying together like that.

The sun was beating down on my shoulders as if someone was pressing a warm iron to my skin. Sweat was beading on my upper lip and trickling down the small of my back. It was hot. I took a drink of water, but it only cooled me for the instant the coolness touched my lips, then I was hot again. Shade was scarce. Either cower in the shadiness of the Stanford patio or bake in the sun burning down on the intramural fields. Trees lined the perimeter of the fields, but as for me, the person in the middle of a large, open field, I was scorched by the unmitigated rays of the sun while another person's eyes squinted to read the words on the page of her textbook. These fields are filled with distractions, not to mention the sun.

Furthermore, there was a group of soccer players congregated on the far field. Each of these boys wore something different, but all of them dressed in the same general form: dark athletic shorts and a white T-shirt. Some went shirtless, but not many. I wondered how they knew which players were on their team since I didn't see any sort of distinguishing marks. They played in between two small goals that they had set up, constantly hustling, constantly running. They didn't stop the game for more than 30 seconds the whole time I watched. They talked to each other, and sometimes they yelled commands to their teammates on the other end of the field. I was sweating under that hot sun, but they kept the ball in motion, seemingly un-phased by the burning rays.

So, simultaneously, all of this occurred on the intramural fields. Within feet of each other, everyone kept their own activity to themselves. It seemed everyone followed the implicit rules of the fields: 1) do whatever you want, 2) don't bother anybody else, and 3) don't let anybody else bother you. Although these fields may not have all the liberation of South Beach, they do have an element of freedom that makes most people feel as though they can do what they choose, whether that be sports, sunbathing, or something else, that is, with their bathing suit tops on and without the alcohol. Certain explicit rules do still apply seeing as these fields *are* on campus. The intramural fields: a place to practice, to play, to tan, to study, to hang out. There's something for everybody.

The Fields Don't Sleep

It was a Sunday morning, normally a pretty quiet morning after students have spent their Saturday nights out and about in the lively Miami area. I, however, woke up at 9 o'clock this morning, a decent but almost unheard of hour for a college student to wake up on a weekend. Walking out of my dorm on the way to the dining hall, I noticed something, something that struck my fancy on an otherwise lonely Sunday morning. What I noticed first were six chairs and a table sitting out in the middle of the intramural fields, but no one was there. No one sat in those chairs or used that table yet this morning, but I could only imagine who did what there last night. Why were they in the middle of the field? Who brought them there? What did they do there?

To the left of the chairs a group of four boys passed a football in a square formation. They appeared to be fairly laid back, simply working on their passing techniques and chatting amongst themselves. They wore athletic shorts, tennis shoes, and T-shirts. They weren't really sweating or hustling to get anywhere; they were just passing a football around their square.

However, my attention was shifted to the location of a whistle on the field furthest from me. Evidently, a group had already begun playing a game of football this morning. This game was obviously more serious, more competitive. Five cones lined each side of the field and there were two cones placed on the sides of what I assumed to be the end zones. They wore either red or blue mesh jerseys with their athletic shorts and tennis shoes, giving them the more uniform look. These were teams; they weren't just a couple of guys tossing a ball around. On the sidelines there stood a messy line of players chugging on their water bottles and yelling at the players on the field. I watched these players line up and execute several plays until a flag was pulled, a whistle was blown, and they walked back into their formation. Occasionally, somewhere close to every other play, they would have a brief meeting and break on what sounded like an "uhhh" sound. They had hustle in their step and competition in their game.

Keep in mind it was only nearing 10 o'clock on a weekend morning. Not a lot of people were out, but these players had already engaged themselves in an intense game of flag football on the intramural fields. The games had already begun for the day, and I didn't expect them to end any time soon. These intramural sports maintained a sense of competition, while still adding to the harmony of the fields. The noise from the variety of activities meshed into one harmonious sound coming from the fields. Even though there were many different activities occurring simultaneously, the fields became a melting pot of amusement, competition, and relaxation.

Later, on the same Sunday night when I was returning to my dorm for the night I walked the usual path along the IM fields. The time was 10 o'clock at night, but the fields were still going strong. The table and chairs from the middle of the field has long since been moved to their standard location on the patio adjacent to the fields. The chairs, though, were no longer empty; the table was no longer abandoned. Now, the night blessed these table and chairs with two girls and a boy. Both of the girls slouched in the chair, looking very comfortable in their pink sweatpants and tank tops. Each of them puffed on their cigarettes, talking to each other and the boy between puffs. He propped his feet up on the table and flaunted his tan suede slippers that he paired with jeans and a T-shirt. So there they were, chatting and smoking right next to their beloved fields. What had been a source of healthy games and (unhealthy) sun bathing during the day was home to a social gathering at night. They weren't the only ones out there; people are there at the tables by the IM fields every night. Gathering there to kick back, relax, and maybe play on the fields. Over 12 hours of play. These fields never seemed to grow tired of social activity. They flourish with social life, of all sorts, night and day. The fields don't sleep.

Home Is Where the Fields Are

The IM fields can also serve as the food for those who didn't want to leave their appetite for sports back at home. This is the University of Miami, so maybe playing for an athletic team was a bit out of your league. Then again, the fields are home to so many club and intramural sports that you don't have to totally leave that sport behind. I interviewed a girl on my floor, Jess, who comes all the way from Chicago. Chicago and Miami certainly lack many similarities. That is, except the fact that the girl can maintain her love for soccer a good 1500 miles from home. Jess started playing club soccer two weeks ago. They practice every Monday and Tuesday from 5:30 to 6:30, but it's not as strict as playing for a real team; you just come when you can. Jess just came out for the first club soccer practice because she loved and loves to play soccer. In fact, she is getting her mom to mail her a soccer ball very soon. Obviously, Jess has proven her dedication to the game because on the first day of club soccer, the UM Women's soccer coach approached Jess and asked her to try out for the team in the spring. Jess says she is definitely considering doing it, but is sort of afraid of the time commitment of joining an official team.

I asked Jess what she thought about the IM fields and if she does anything else besides play club soccer on them. Sure enough, Jess is one of the girls that tans on the IM fields. She complained about the intense heat though, saying she really prefers to lay out by the pool, but it's just so convenient to have the fields right outside the entrance to our dorm. Also, Jess told me that she wants to run on the IM fields, that is, once it's not so hot in a couple of months. I think a lot of people probably have this idea too, but it sounds good to me. The IM fields are soft, luscious grass, it seems like it would be so peaceful and easy on the knees to take a jog around them. Plus, you'd always have something to look at.

In addition, Jess is going to play flag football with her sorority on Sunday evening. Many sororities and fraternities play flag football throughout the week, sometimes turning a peaceful game into a bitter rivalry. IM fields are good for that too though. What makes the games even more intense is that there are actual flag football officials, which basically means the competition is real. Jess admitted that she didn't even think she was very good at flag football, but that it would be fun anyways. That's the beauty of the fields: they don't judge you on how good you are at sports.

Jess and I talked about how it's hard to get homesick when there's always something to do. She said she had no trouble keeping busy between class, working out, going out, her sorority, and soccer. When I reminded her that she was lucky to not have to drop soccer, she enthusiastically agreed, believing that losing soccer would make her much more homesick. "At least I can still play it [soccer] here; it makes it more like home," Jess confirmed my belief that keeping busy and that wholesome fun is made more possible by the IM fields. Furthermore, she made me notice just how intense an appetite for sports can grow and the need for a non-judgmental place at a university. On these fields, Jess flourishes in the excitement of sports, fueling her desire to play soccer that she had thought she might have to leave behind. Coming to college is a big step, but these fields, in protecting health and fitness values provide a safe-haven for some students like Jess. She may not be ready to play soccer for the University, and other students may not even have the ability to do so, but one thing is for sure: the intramural fields won't deny her access to a good game. In addition, these fields, in all of their freedom, don't judge someone on their activity. These fields cannot be limited to simply intramural sports; in fact, they are a social gathering place and a realm of relaxation. While Jess spends the majority of her days being graded in classes, the intramural fields aren't just about keeping score. The real idea of her playing club soccer is not based on winning or losing, but on finding friends and doing what she enjoys. Find your home on the IM fields, whether it is tanning, playing any sport, smoking, jogging, or just socializing. The key to not getting homesick, I believe, is keeping busy.

Discussion

At first, you may think the IM fields are what they appear to be: fields. But they are so much more. Jocks run alongside the band. Tanning-fiends and smokers can both feed their unhealthy habits. No one is judging you for what you're doing or how good you are at intramural sports. It's harmony. These fields are a melting pot of all social backgrounds, and to top it off they're open 24 hours a day. More so than the uniqueness of South Beach or the diversity on the Metro, these fields have shown me that everyone can have fun. Everyone can have fun together in the same place. The same place to one person may be fun for different reasons to another, but fun nonetheless. Respect others and enjoy yourself: golden rules for living and golden rules for the IM fields.

STUDENT ESSAY: VISUAL ANALYSIS

Christopher Perin, a native of New York City, wrote his essay for a composition course for transfer students at the University of Miami. Christopher is an accounting major who feels that "writing is as important to business and accounting as math and numbers are." He hopes to work in an upper-management position for a large firm after graduate school. This essay was started as a response to an assignment modeled on Leo Chavez's work with magazine covers and then revised to include textual analysis, as well as the analysis of visual materials.

Web Pages in the Automobile Industry

Christopher Perin

The Internet is one of the most useful tools for companies to communicate with their customers. Internet Web sites allow their audiences to interact and learn about a company's products through text pictures available to them twenty-four hours a day. They are possibly the most efficient advertisements for companies as they are cheap to maintain and can reach to everyone across the world at the same time. In the auto industry, the Web site can be thought of as the interactive, electronic brochure. Each product in the brochure is displayed in a different way to highlight its attributes and strong qualities, and downplay its weak ones. Speaking strictly of the automobile industry, different car manufacturers advertise their products through pictures and text using different photographic and literate techniques.

Hummer is a car that many believe stands for America. Its massive size, wasteful gas mileage and rugged appearance all contribute to this image. Furthermore, it is used by the U.S. Military as a transport vehicle. However, recently the Hummer has become an extremely popular vehicle to the public. Hummer has used pictures and displayed their product in a specific way to target certain audiences and display what this truck is all about. The picture (opposite) is of the first adaptation of the H1 Hummer, the truck used by the U.S. Military. This truck was and still is wildly popular in spite of its wide stance and dismal gas mileage.

This picture was taken from Hummer's official Web site and shows the H2 in a forest. Notice the angle of the camera and the position of the truck at the edge of a cliff. The picture is comparable to the classic image of a man who has reached the peak of a mountain and essentially "conquered" the mountain. Here, this picture seems to say that the Hummer H2 has conquered the wilderness. Furthermore, the truck is not displayed as sparkling clean, as there is definite dirt shown on the left side of the truck as well as on the tires. On top of this, the angle the picture is taken from makes the truck seem enormous and intimidating; possibly stating that this is how one would feel while driving the H2.

The Hummer H2 from www.hummer.com

Therefore, it can be inferred that Hummer is trying to appeal to the more outdoorsy crowd with this photo, showing them that this is not a tame, domesticated SUV, rather, it is the strong, wild, king of the jungle.

In its introduction of the H2, the text reads:

> In a world where SUV's have begun to look like their owners, complete with love handles and mushy seats the H2 proves that there is still one out there that can drop and give you 20 (H2 "Highlights: Introduction" www.hummer.com).

This is a very interesting sentence which attacks the general population of SUV's and their owners. The general tone of the sentence enforces Hummer's tactic to convey an aggressive image of the car. It conveys a sense of power and confidence which they believe will be translated to the driver of this car. It also seems to state that this car will not pamper its driver, but will do what an SUV is meant to do better than any of its competitors. It states that the driver can push the H2 to do more and it will not hesitate. These few words convey a lot about the Hummer's confidence, strength and hard-working attitude. It gives the car the feel of a soldier who is at your command, alluding to its original uses in the US Army and implying that even though the exterior has been revamped, it is still true to its roots.

Not all car manufacturers want or are even able to appeal to the outdoorsman or woman and, therefore, must take a different approach in displaying their automobiles. For example, Porsche prides itself on being a finely crafted, German sports car, meant for the driving enthusiast. The next picture is taken from the Porsche USA homepage. It shows the new 911 Targa 4, a variation on their flagship car, the 911 Carrera. This car's selling point is its all glass top and all wheel drive.

This is a very interesting picture, because like Hummer, Porsche has displayed its product in the wilderness, looking over a cliff. The difference in this picture is the focus of it. Notice that the sky takes up a very large amount of space in the picture. The implications of this are that you can take in the view in this car. The interesting thing about this picture is that this is a sports car;

The Porsche 911 Targa 4 http://www.porsche.com/usa/models/911/911-targa-4/gallery/

however, it is shown off the road in the wilderness somewhere. Porsche is showing us that, although so many cars have sunroofs, none have a sunroof like the Targa 4, and more importantly, the Targa 4 can get you to a place where you can put that sunroof to good use with its all-wheel drive. Compared to the picture of the Hummer, this picture is also taken from a different angle which rather than enlarging the car, diminishes it allowing it to look sporty and small. Furthermore, the car is shown in a pristine form, no blemishes, dirt or anything on the car, because after all, it is not a rally car. It is still a high end sports car intended for a wealthier consumer. Therefore, Porsche intends to imply this by showing that the car still has class, even in the wilderness, and isn't meant for getting down and dirty.

An interesting aspect of the display of the 911 Targa 4 on Porsche's Web site was the text below the picture. It reads:

> Conventions shaken. Senses stirred. A sweeping glass roof reveals the wide-open sky. Discover the new views—take a look up! See the world in a new light and experience the fascination of the new 911 Targa 4 models. (http://www.porsche.com/usa/"Home page")

Although only a short excerpt of text, these few sentences convey a lot about the car and its strengths. The text is written in a poetic form with two stanzas and incomplete sentences, possibly inferring that the car is poetic itself or at least a honed form of art. As stated before, the car's selling point is its all glass roof, and the first line seems to allude to that. The conventions of a regular square sunroof have been challenged by this new glass top and the views bring the senses to life. It is possible that Porsche means to refer to the feeling of the drive as well in the second portion of the line, postulating that this car can make you feel things other sports cars can not. The second sentence is especially interesting as the glass top is described as "sweeping" and the sky as "wide-open." Sweeping is an interesting word to describe a roof and would seem more appropriate to describe the sky and wide-open would seem to describe a glass top well. What Porsche may be trying to say here is that the Targa 4 makes the sky and the roof one in the same. In other words, they are saying the sky is your roof in the Targa 4. Finally, the last sentence challenges the reader to take a look up and

BMW 760 Li http://www.bmwusa.com/vehicles/7/760liSedan/gallery.htm

experience views they've never seen before in this car. Although less interesting, the second stanza reemphasizes the points of the first stanza but refers to a "new light" drawing a parallel between the new light shining through the roof and the new light shining on the reader's outlook on the world.

The last picture shown is of the new BMW 760Li Sedan. This is BMW's flagship car which showcases their best technology, and luxury. This car has a starting MSRP of $121,400; a price tag not meant for the average American. The picture is taken from BMW USA's Web site and is a common format for high-end luxury vehicles in this price range.

To begin with the setting of this picture is indicative of the car's intended audience. It appears that the car is set in front of a building, implying that the owner of this car might work in this posh office building. BMW may be trying to tell corporate America that this is the car that they belong in. The colors in this photo are also interesting. The picture is full of gunmetal grays and steel blues and silver. These colors create a very modern appearance of the car and suggest that this car is also very modern, alluding to its extensive list of technological features. Finally, the angle of the photograph is from straight ahead, neither enlarging nor diminishing the car. This angle makes the viewer take the car as it is, and does not attempt to deceive them at all. Therefore, it is possible, that BMW believes that they don't need to get tricky with the photography to make this car appealing; its appearance alone sells the car. What this angle does do however, is highlight the many different body lines on the car creating an elegant appearance which again may highlight the class that BMW believes this car stands for.

In another very interesting move BMW begins to summarize their 760Li like this:

> The Flagship of all BMW Sedans, the 760Li is the most luxurious, refined, and gifted of all production luxury sedans in the world. The longer wheelbase provides more room to share the joy of the 760Li experience with others. (http://www.bmwusa.com/vehicles/7/ 760lisedan/default "760 Li Sedan Overview")

It goes on solely to describe different features of the car, such as its unique wood trim and its premium leather interior and something called a "cool box," essentially a cooler in the car, rear climate control and finally the "breathtaking performance of its V-12 engine." Somewhat similar to the picture above of the BMW, the introduction of the 760Li does not seem to be analyzable. Again, BMW implies their belief that they do not need to use tricks to sell this car. Its impressive feature set, luxury and performance sell the car by themselves. Though the least interesting of the three introductions, BMW's text subtly conveys a feeling of confidence, boasting outright about its features and performance without trying to woo the viewer at all.

Comparing these three pictures, there is a definite difference in the way that different types of cars are conveyed to their audience through pictures. To begin with, SUVs tend to be portrayed as rugged, large and strong as shown in the picture of the Hummer H2. Sports cars are generally shown in motion on the road; however, Porsche chooses to highlight their all-wheel drive and all glass roof by showing the car off road in front of an expansive view. Finally, BMW shows their flagship, 760Li in front of a corporate building intending to appeal to high class clients. These three pictures together show that car manufacturers put a lot of thought into their cars, their target audience and each car's selling point before they take pictures of them to present to the public. These different things can not only be presented through just the car, but also through its setting and the angle of the photograph. Furthermore, a few well chosen words about a particular product can take a great photograph and make it incredible. Hummer made a connection between a soldier and the car to insinuate its hardworking, driven nature. Porsche chose a poetic formula of text to reinforce and subtly tell the reader/viewer of the advertisement that the Targa 4 is a work of art they have never experienced and BMW chooses a similar strategy to their picture by creating a straightforward passage which solely boasts about the performance, luxury and overall feature set of the car, stating with confidence that the car can speak for itself and does not need to be photographed or portrayed in a certain light to be desirable. All of this together shows some of the interesting techniques that auto manufacturers use to describe and highlight their products in the best light possible.

WORKS CITED

BMW of North America, LLC. 1/19/2007. "Home page" BMWUSA. 30 October, 2006.
    http://www.bmwusa.com/default.
BMW of North America, LLC. 1/19/2007. "BMW 760 Li Gallery" BMWUSA 30 October, 2006.
    http://www.bmwusa.com/vehicles/7/760liSedan/gallery.htm.
General Motors Corporation. 2004 "H2 Highlights: Introduction" Hummer 30 October 2006.
    www.hummer.com.
General Motors Corporation. 2004 "H2 Gallery: Off-Road" Hummer 30 October 2006.
    www.hummer.com.
Porsche Cars North America. 2007. "911 Targa 4: Gallery" Porsche 30 October 2006.
    http://www.porsche.com/usa/models/911/911-targa-4/gallery/.
Porsche Cars North America. 2007. "Home page" Porsche 30 October 2006.
    http://www.porsche.com/usa/.

Internet Resources

General Observation Sites

Use resources like the United States Geographical Survey maps at http://www.usgs.gov/ to help you map the physical spaces in your area. Locating public art to observe and investigate is made easier by Web sites like Connecticut's Art in Public Places initiative at http://www.ct.gov/cct/cwp/view.asp?a=2214&q=293756. A similar project by Miami Dade County can be found at http://www.co.miami-dade.fl.us/publicart/. Search for similar sites in your own community using key terms like "public art" or "community art." The Association of Zoos and Aquariums provides links to online zoo cams from around the world featuring a number of different kinds of animals. Find these zoo cams at http://www.zoos-worldwide.de/zoocams.html.

Historical Observation Sites

Many historical exposition journals and drawings have been preserved in libraries and archives and a number are now available online. See, for example, the journals of Lewis and Clark at http://libtextcenter.unl.edu/lewisandclark/index.html and their collection of naturalist

drawings at the Smithsonian at http://web4.si
.edu/lewisandclark/index.html?loc=/lewis
andclark/home.html; an online transcription of
the Charles Darwin's *Voyage of the Beagle* can
be found at http://www.literature.org/authors/
darwin-charles/the-voyage-of-the-beagle/; a
summary of several British voyages of discovery, including those by Cook, Sloane, and Darwin can be found at http://www.nhm.ac.uk/
nature-online/science-of-natural-history/
expeditions-collecting/voyages-discovery/. Sir
Hans Sloan's Jamaican Botanical Collection is
available at the British Museum of Natural
History along with other historical collections
which can be searched or browsed online at
http://www.nhm.ac.uk/research-curation/
projects/sloane-herbarium/hanssloane.htm; the
Australian Research Council and the Australian National University sponsor the
Endeavour Project which includes journals,
maps, and images from Captain James Cook's
South Pacific travels at http://coombs.anu.edu
.au/~cookproj/home.html. National Archives
and Museum sites are good starting places for
such collections. The pictures for the original
Audubon collection were produced in combination with careful observations of the birds,
insects, and wildlife in their natural habitat.
You can see some of Audubon's work at
http://piclib.nhm.ac.uk/piclib/www//search.php?
search=audubon. Another of the naturalists
who contributed to Audubon's collection was
William MacGillivray. His collection is also on
view at the British Natural History Museum at
http://internt.nhm.ac.uk/jdsml/nature-online/
macgillivray/.

Sites Useful for Visual Analysis

An online dictionary of artistic terms is available
at http://www.artlex.com/. Many sites provide
images of art as well as historical information
and biographies of the artists. See for example, www.groveart.com. Included in this Web
site is the thirty-four volume work, *The Dictionary of Art* edited by Jane Turner (Grove's
Dictionaries, 1996) which has articles on
artists, architects, painters, and photographers
as well as materials, theories, and movements.
Both Artstor (http://www.artstor.org/info/)
and the Associated Press photo archive
(http://ap.accuweather.com/) will allow you to

search for specific kinds of images—historical
or current.

Art Abstracts and Art Retrospective are two
online databases for scholarly publications
about art that are a part of Wilson Web system
available through many libraries. Online government sources such as the National Park
Service also offer photographic records of the
environment, while other Web sites such as
http://tenbyten.org/info.html and http://news
.bbc.co.uk/offer current news photographs.
Some of these resources require licensing
agreements with institutions that limit their
use to current students and faculty, so begin
your search by accessing your library's database collections. Online photo collections
make a wide range of options available to view
and to download. Try, for example, the Institute for Public History's *Public Spaces* project
at http://www.education.miami.edu/iph/ or
http://www.eyewitnesstohistory.com/, or
http://www.worldpressphoto.org/or http://bop
.nppa.org/archive.html for award-winning photojournalism. Visit the Bettmann Archives at
http://pro.corbis.com/ or the American Memory project at the Library of Congress:
http://memory.loc.gov/ammem/index.html.
Newspapers such as the *New York Times*,
Seattle Times, *Washington Post*, and search
engines such as Google.com also offer photo
archives. The Association of American Editorial Cartoonists maintains a searchable site at
http://editorialcartoonists.com/cartoon/browse
.cfm/. You can also search for political cartoons
by topic at http://politicalcartoons.com/. There
are regular exhibits of editorial cartoons, usually featuring a single cartoonist. One that's
available online is the Library of Congress's
exhibit of Herbert Block's cartoons at
http://www.loc.gov/rr/print/swann/herblock/,
which also includes historical information and
essays. Finally many cartoonists maintain their
own sites, so try a search using the name of
cartoonists whose work you are interested in
examining.

Sites for Artifacts

Many museums include photographs and
descriptions of artifacts in their possession. A
good place to begin is at the Smithsonian's
Web site http://www.si.edu/museums/. Also

useful is the Virtual Library Museum pages at
http://icom.museum/vlmp/. This site lets users
search by country or topic and is maintained
by Professor Jonathan Bowen, but be aware
that not every link (or even every museum)
will take you to photographs or descriptions
of artifacts.

Individuals have also constructed sites featuring
artifacts, often winning awards for their work.

See, for example, Anthony Stein's *Mississippian
Moundbuilders and Their Artifacts* at
http://www.mississippian-artifacts.com/.
Searching for the particular kind of artifact
you are interested in will take you to more
specific sites.

Web Sites Referenced in This Chapter

Visual Cognition Lab
http://viscog.beckman.uiuc.edu/djs_lab/
demos.html

Dictionary of the Social Sciences. Oxford Reference Online.
http://www.oxfordreference.com/views/
ENTRY.html?subview=Main&entry=t104.e1711

Observing Surveillance Project
http://www.observingsurveillance.org/

University of Miami campus live webcam
http://www.miami.edu/webcams/

Links to the Readings

Many of the assignments in the assignment
sequences tied to the readings require observation
either alone or in combination with other
methods. Each of these readings also includes passages
where the authors present their observations,
discuss the limits of their observations, or
demonstrate how to combine information gathered
from observation with other kinds of data.
Several of these readings (marked with an asterisk)
demonstrate careful investigation of artifacts.
Those marked with a plus sign are concerned with
examining visual materials.

*+Bachin, Robin. "Courage, Endurance and
Quickness of Decision: Gender and Athletics
at the University of Chicago, 1890–1920"

+Chavez, Leo R. "Developing a Visual Discourse
on Immigration"

*+Dilworth, Leah. "'Handmade by an American
Indian': Souvenirs and the Cultural Economy
of Southwestern Tourism"

+Edwards, Janis L. and Carol K. Winkler. "Representative
Form and the Visual Ideograph:
The Iwo Jima Image in Editorial Cartoons"

+Len-Ríos, María et al. "Representation of
Women in News and Photos: Comparing Content
to Perceptions"

*+Lewis, Peirce. "Common Landscapes as Historic
Documents"

+Lowe, Melanie. "Colliding Feminisms: Britney
Spears, 'Tweens,' and the Politics of Reception"

+Lutz, Catherine A. and Jane L. Collins. "The
Photograph as an Intersection of Gazes"

*Prown, Jules David. "The Truth of Material
Culture: History or Fiction?"

*Shackel, Paul A. "Public Memory and the
Search for Power in American Historical
Archaeology"

+Spence, Steve. "Van Gogh in Alabama, 1936"

Assignments Using Observing

Collective Memory Assignment 6 (Lewis)
Considering "Public" Assignment 1; Assignment 4
Constructing Public Spaces Assignment 1

(Lewis); Assignment 2 (add interviews or
survey data); Assignment 4; Assignment 5
(Bachin)

Cultural Politics and Public Discourse
 Assignment 1
Direct Observation
Ethnicity in America II: Defining America
 Assignment 2 (with interviews or history)
Reclaiming the Past Assignment 3 (Lewis)

Representing Community Assignment 1
 (Bachin); Assignment 2 (add interview);
 Assignment 3 (add interview and texts)

Assignments Working with Visual Materials

Between Writing and Knowing Assignment 3
Collective Memory Assignment 2 (Spence);
 Assignment 5 (Frisch)
Cultural Politics and Public Discourse Assign-
 ment 3 (Lowe) with focus group
*Cultural Politics and Public Discourse II: Shaping
 Values* Assignment 5 (Edwards & Winkler)
Ethnicity in America: Identity Assignment 2
 (Chavez)
Ethnicity in America II: Defining America
 Assignment 4
Examining Visuals

Eye on Campus Assignment 4; option in
 Assignment 6
Gender Investigations Assignment 3 (Edwards &
 Winkler)
Humanizing Numbers Assignment 4
Material Culture Assignment 5 (Lutz & Collins)
Reading Media Assignment 3 (Chavez); Assign-
 ment 5 (Edwards & Winkler)
Reclaiming the Past Assignment 2 (Edwards &
 Winkler)
Visual Rhetoric: Photographs
Working with Texts Assignment 3; Assignment 4

Assignments Working with Artifacts

Between Writing and Knowing Assignment 5
Collective Memory Assignment 4 (Shackel)
Considering "Public" Assignment 2 (Shackel)
Ethnicity in America: Identity Assignment 1
 (Dilworth)
Eye on Campus Assignment 1 (Bachin)
Gender Investigations Assignment 5 (Bachin)
Histories: Official and Unofficial Assignment 1;
 Assignment 2 (Shackel, plus interview)

Investigating Artifacts
Material Culture Assignment 1 (Prown); Assign-
 ment 2 (Bachin, add history)
Reclaiming the Past Assignment 4 (Prown)
Representing Community Assignment 4
 (Shackel)

CHAPTER 4

INTERVIEWING

An interview is, basically, a conversation with a purpose, and conversations are an ancient form of acquiring knowledge. Long before people turned to the Internet, television, or public libraries to find answers to their questions, they relied on spoken inquiries.

Today interviews take a variety of forms—from the type conducted by journalists and popularized by talk shows and late-night television to the diverse kinds of academic interviews explored in this chapter. Among the wide range of scholars who regularly conduct interviews in their field are anthropologists, sociologists, political scientists, and educators. Chemists testing a new drug or treatment, for instance, question subjects about changes in their health or side effects, just as historians strive to depict events from multiple perspectives by interviewing diverse participants. We hope to demonstrate that, with preparation and practice, interviews can be extremely useful to you in your own academic pursuits, whether you've had no prior experience with this method or have done numerous interviews while working for a school newspaper.

Many might argue that interviews are an outdated or impractical means of finding answers, especially when compared with the lightning speed of the World Wide Web in which data are only a few clicks away. In fact the kinds of interview-based studies addressed in this chapter are precisely those for which there are no definitive answers, and so personal experience, impressions, or expertise are essential to making meaning or developing a position. In other words, you'll be discovering new information through your interview, just as professional researchers do.

Take, for instance, former University of Georgia student Bryan McLucas, who was enrolled in the course Language Use in the African American Community in the fall of 1996. He was assigned to conduct a sociolinguistic interview—one that examined an African American individual's language use and views on the language issues covered in the class. Bryan chose one of his classmates, Irving (a pseudonym), and Bryan's essay is an example of original scholarship. That is, no one else had ever taken the time to record and examine Irving's sociolinguistic experiences, and, as a result, Bryan—an undergraduate student—contributed to the field of sociolinguistics. You'll find Bryan's essay at the end of this chapter along with his transcript of the interview. This kind of interview is usually called a *case study* and is meant to add the nuance and depth to more generalized information frequently collected from surveys. Sometimes researchers follow several "cases" in a single study, selecting their informants to reflect different aspects of the population they are interested in or randomly selecting informants who are meant to be generally representative. Case studies are often used in such fields as education and sociology, especially in combination with other methods.

In some cases, however, interviewers are interested in the experiences or impressions of experts rather than the responses of random subjects. Interviews with experts are common in journalism, but are also valuable for researchers who need the latest information or perspective from those with firsthand knowledge. For example, if your project involves a current environmental concern, you would want to interview an expert in the field of environmental studies, preferably someone who works with the specific topic of your investigation. Unlike a book that was written two years ago, or a newspaper article written six months ago, an individual with extensive expertise could provide you with up-to-the-minute information. Interviewing authorities is also useful when you can't find answers to your specific questions in written sources, when the texts you've read have raised new questions for you, or when the viewpoint you seek is one not usually included. A communication student we know was investigating the architecture of a particular building and how its appearance seemed to isolate its residents from the neighboring community. She was able to locate and interview the original architect, adding information about his intentions for the design that she could not have learned elsewhere.

How can you locate an expert? Authors of books or articles on your subject are potential interview subjects, as are people quoted or cited within them. A quick online search using key words related to your topic—such as "environment expert"—could lead you to two additional kinds of experts: (1) professors, whose college Web sites usually indicate in what topics they're considered authorities, and (2) leaders/members of organizations, such as the Ecologic-Institute for International and European Environmental Policy. The student who interviewed the architect of the building she was investigating found his name while looking at archival records at the city zoning office. Keeping your eyes open for such unexpected sources of information and other directions for your study are important features of good research. If you're intimidated by the idea of interviewing an expert, just remember that most people love discussing their specialty, and most will also be flattered that you consider their viewpoint worth documenting.

Despite the many applications of interviewing we've described, we're not suggesting that interviewing is always the most effective mode of inquiry. When a researcher is interested in a group's natural behavior, observations may be more suitable than an interview. Likewise, if you want to know what the majority of people think or do, surveying is more appropriate than interviewing. When should you opt for an interview, as opposed to an observation or survey? When your interest is not in how a group behaves or thinks, but rather in what individual people know, think, or perceive; when your topic is too narrow, obscure, private, or distant to be readily observed; or, as pointed out in the chapters on observing and working with numbers, when you need an informant to help you understand what you've observed or to provide more specific details to the generalities of numbers. Clearly, then, interviews can be used alone, as an isolated method of inquiry, or in conjunction with other methods. Anthropologists, for instance, often use interviews to help interpret or expand upon their observations, and market researchers often use this method to help generate survey questions and the most effective wording for their studies.

ETHICAL CONSIDERATIONS AND THE 4 Cs OF RESPONSIBLE INTERVIEWING

Because interviewing necessarily involves human subjects, as opposed to texts, artifacts, statistical data, or images, student and professional interviewers alike must take a number of precautions to ensure the integrity of their work. Before asking any questions, we encourage you to reflect on what we'll call the four Cs of responsible interviewing: consent, confidentiality, consequences, and culture.

1. Informed **CONSENT** means it is your obligation as an interviewer to explain to your subjects why you are questioning them; to provide them with information about if, where, when, and how your findings might be shared with others (e.g., your instructor and classmates); and to give them the opportunity to refuse to participate once they have this information. Using a hidden tape recorder while having a supposedly private conversation would clearly violate this rule and render your interview disreputable.

2. The second "c" stands for **CONSEQUENCES**, meaning that you should contemplate any potentially harmful effects both for your subject and for yourself that could result from the interview. The consequences can range from legal repercussions to emotional ones. If you question illegal immigrants, for example, revealing their full names and whereabouts could lead to their deportation or imprisonment. Individuals who speak negatively about their company's inner workings or employers could lose their jobs. Also take into account your relationship to your interviewee and the potential emotional effects of your interview. When questioning a relative or friend, think about whether the interaction and/or topic could negatively impact your relationship. Likewise, if you ask someone to disclose information about a sensitive topic such as an illness or painful memory, you should be prepared to give them time to regroup if they become distraught and be sensitive to their needs. Generally speaking, if there are potentially harmful consequences, your study should probably be reviewed in advance by your institutional research board. All universities have guidelines about doing research with human subjects and a review committee to ensure that the human subjects are protected. We have tried to design assignments that will involve no harmful consequences and thus not require review by such a committee, but your instructor can help you determine if your research plan warrants a review.

3. Because of potential consequences such as these, the third factor to consider is **CONFIDENTIALITY**. If subjects feel uncomfortable disclosing their real names or that of their organizations, you must respect their wishes. Think carefully about why the individuals might prefer to remain anonymous. Perhaps they envision more serious consequences resulting from your interview than you are aware of. Researchers often err on the side of protecting their informants and so provide pseudonyms, which may be appropriate for your own essays as well. The choice,

and the consequences for your research, will depend in large part on the particulars of your study and what you hope to do with it. Keep in mind, however, that in some cases anonymity could cast doubt on the credibility of your interview.

4. **CULTURE**, the final "c," is meant to remind us that human beings are complex and heterogeneous, differing in class, gender, age, generation, ideology, and many other factors. Complete objectivity is unattainable, we know, but respecting differences is essential when using interviews to make knowledge. Several of the readings in this text illustrate the difficulties of interviewing across cultural divides, but such differences are often at the heart of the questions researchers are interested in exploring. Judy Yung's "'A Bowlful of Tears' Revisited: The Full Story of Lee Puey You's Immigration Experience at Angel Island," which you'll find in the Readings, is a particularly good example of how a researcher learned to balance respect for her subject with the need to press for additional information, as well as how self-reflection enabled this researcher to reconsider her own earlier work in a new way.

These ethical questions can be difficult to work through, but it's essential that you contemplate all of them before, during, and after each interview you conduct. Don't take any chances along the way; when in doubt, consult with your instructor.

One way to ensure a responsible interviewing process is to draft an ethical protocol along with your interview design plan. Steinar Kvale, whose seven interviewing stages are explained in the next section, suggests the following process to ensure attention to ethical concerns (112)[1]. First, draw a vertical line through the middle of a sheet of paper, dividing the paper into two. On the left side of the line write out a brief description of your plans for each of the seven interviewing stages. For each step, think about what ethical concerns might arise and how to resolve or ameliorate them. During Stage 3, for example, the interviewing day itself, you could remind yourself to clearly explain to your subject the purpose of your interview and how the information will be used, and to ask for your subject's consent. If an individual has asked you to conceal his/her identity, you might write yourself a reminder during Stage 7, Reporting, not to disclose their identity.

PRACTICE ACTIVITY 4-1

Interviewer Impact

Go to the History Matters, "Making Sense of Oral Histories" Web site at http://history matters.gmu.edu/mse/oral/question2.html, and read the two transcripts of the interviews given by the same woman to two different interviewers. As Linda Shopes indicates, this exercise "present[s] a stark example of the way the narrator's response to the social identity of the interviewer shapes the interview."[2]

Consider: Can you tell which of the interviewers is white and which is African American? How? And how might this activity inform your own interviewing practices?

---

[1] Steinar Kvale, *InterViews: An Introduction to Qualitative Research Interviewing* (Thousand Oaks, CA: Sage, 1996).

[2] Linda Shopes, "Making Sense of Oral History," *History Matters: The U.S. Survey Course on the Web*, http://historymatters.gmu.edu/mse/oral, February 2002.

PRACTICE ACTIVITY 4-2

Ban Your Biases

First, make a list of your gender, age, ethnic or racial group, religion or philosophy, political party, and socioeconomic group. Next, list a few additional words or phrases that describe you. Think about how each of these categories and terms might bias your interviewing efforts and write down each potential bias next to the appropriate term. For each potential bias you identify, think about a way in which you might counteract it, and write a brief description of each resolution next to its corresponding bias. Keep this bias worksheet handy, and review it before conducting each of your interviews.[3]

Consider: Which of your biases do you think would be the most difficult one for you to "ban" in an interview situation and why?

STAGING THE INTERVIEW

Ethical concerns and identifying one's biases may be difficult, but you'll be relieved to learn that your two main tasks as an interviewer could not be more straightforward. You'll have to ask questions and listen. The main difference between a scholarly interview and a conversation with your best friend or sibling, then, is not *what* you'll be doing, but *why*—that is, your objective. An interview should be focused on a particular subject matter and have a specific set of goals, and it thus requires considerable preparation.

In his text *InterViews: An Introduction to Qualitative Research Interviewing*, Steinar Kvale outlines the seven stages of an interview investigation: (1) thematizing, (2) designing, (3) interviewing, (4) transcribing, (5) analyzing, (6) verifying, and (7) reporting. The activities and assignments in this unit will explain what each phase entails and will provide you with opportunities to practice and execute them.

Whether your interview is part of a larger project or an exercise of its own, the challenge is to formulate thoughtful and informed queries, pay close attention to your subject's words, critically examine your data, and then communicate to readers the value of your inquiry.

STAGE ONE *THEMATIZING: CRAFTING TWO KINDS OF QUESTIONS*

As mentioned earlier, an interview differs from a regular conversation in that it has a purpose, and so the first interviewing stage, which Kvale calls "thematizing," begins with exploring your objectives, identifying main concepts, and recognizing themes.

Suppose the general topic of your analysis is the relationship between your college or university and your campus city or town. You might consider whether the two units complement each other and interact smoothly and interdependently, or whether there is any conflict or animosity between them. You might consider questions such as: How

---

[3]Activity source: C. George Boeree, Shippensburg University, "Qualitative Methods: Part 4," http://www .ship.edu/~cgboeree/qualmethfour.html.

have they impacted each other? How has each changed since the beginning of their interaction?

When University of Georgia student Bryan McLucas was assigned to conduct an interview for his sociolinguistics class, the main theoretical question posed by his instructor was: What is the relationship between the interviewee's "attitudes toward specific linguistic issues relevant to language use in the African American community" and "the participant's prior experiences and current behavior"?

When developing theoretical questions, conducting a bit of background library research on the topic will help you formulate thoughtful areas of investigation. You'll want to be aware of your assumptions and consider multiple hypotheses as you formulate your theoretical questions. The next step is to transform these theoretical questions into questions you would actually pose to a subject. Theoretical questions and theories are usually far too abstract, broad, and formal to be useful for the actual interview, so you'll want to break them down into conversational and straightforward questions.

For the most part, avoid writing questions that can be answered with a simple yes or no, and instead use open-ended formulations such as "Tell me about . . ." and "Can you describe . . ." This strategy is particularly useful toward the beginning of the interview because direct, detailed, or compound questions often intimidate interviewees. Later, in the section on Stage 3, however, you'll learn how to create impromptu questions during the interview in order to steer the conversation in various directions.

It may be helpful to compare the theoretical questions Bryan used to three of his actual interview questions:

Bryan's Theoretical Question   What is the relationship between people's "attitudes toward specific linguistic issues relevant to language use in the African American community" and their "prior experiences and current behavior"?

Bryan's Interview Questions

- "How did you learn AAE [African American English]?"
- "Have you had any difficulties or confrontations because of language?"
- "What dialect did you speak at home with your family? With guests or other relatives?"

PRACTICE ACTIVITY 4-3

Theoretical Questions

Brainstorm a set of theoretical questions on any topic you're interested in (or perhaps on a subject that was assigned to you). Remember to consider more than the easiest who, what, when, where, why, and how of reporting. Instead try questions like: What is the relationship of x to y? What is x a part of? What are the parts of x? Who benefits by z? Who is left out of z? How does x impact y? Review the other heuristic questions in Figure 1.3 for additional ideas. Next identify whether you could explore your questions through an interview; and if so, with whom?

Consider: What makes a question accessible via an interview?

FIGURE 4.1   Question categories (adapted from Kvale 133)

- **Opening Questions**

  "Could you please describe . . . ?"

  "Can you tell me about . . . ?"

  "Please discuss . . ."

  "I'm interested in _____. What can you tell me about the subject?"

- **Follow-up Questions**

  "Really?" (Pronounced so that it conveys interest, not doubt, encouraging the subject to continue discussing x)

  "How so?"

- **Probing Questions**

  *Especially when your subject provides short or yes/no answers

  "Can you tell me more about . . . ?"

  "Could you please give me an example of . . . ?"

Notice how straightforward and conversational Bryan's interview questions are compared with the abstract and complex theoretical question he sought to explore.

When formulating conversational questions, consider the type of information you're seeking and tailor your inquiries accordingly, but be careful not to phrase questions in a leading way. In other words, you don't want to ask questions that will influence your subjects' answers. Framing nonleading questions is especially important in situations where you intend to interview several people and compile the results. In such cases you'll want to pose questions that will elicit varied and even contradictory responses. Work with others to revise your questions, rewriting to clarify any confusing points, as well as to eliminate leading questions, those that reveal your own biases, or any that are culturally insensitive.

After developing a list of interview questions, you'll also need to arrange them such that you start with easy, "warm-up" questions that won't intimidate your subject. Organize them logically, thinking about which responses might lead smoothly into another of your questions. Leave the difficult or controversial questions for late in the conversation, when your subject will probably be more open and feel more comfortable responding.

STAGE TWO DESIGNING: PRACTICAL MATTERS

The Setup   After crafting some theoretical and interview questions, you'll have to figure out who to interview and set up the meeting. There's no foolproof way to select an ideal subject, and there's no guarantee that the person you choose will speak openly or eloquently on the topic. However, the more educated and informed your selection

| PRACTICE ACTIVITY 4-4 |

Conversational Questions

Go back to the theoretical questions you generated in Practice Activity 4.3 and turn them into conversational questions you would actually ask someone you will interview.

Consider: What is required to make the transformation from theoretical to conversational questions?

process—through, for example, research, observation, and word-of-mouth—the better your chances of conducting a fruitful interview.

How many people you should interview, how many times, and for how long depends completely on the project at hand and your objectives. As with every other mode of inquiry, the more you practice it, the better sense you'll have of these logistics. Obviously a project that seeks out an interview to provide expert opinion is different from a project such as that of Portland State University student Wynde Dyer[4] who interviewed multiple subjects who had used the Internet to locate dates. Dyer's study is interested not in one expert's opinion, but in how the experiences of her subjects suggest general (or common) perceptions. Sometimes scholars find it convenient and appropriate to interview groups of people at a time instead of individuals. We have more to say about such *focus-group interviewing*, as the process is called, in the special section later in this chapter. You should think carefully about the kind of interviewing that best fits your investigation in advance so you can plan appropriately.

Once you've identified a potential interviewee, get in touch with them via phone or e-mail. Begin by introducing yourself and your project, and explain why you are contacting them. If you've already had an encounter with the person you want to interview, you can mention that, especially if you're afraid they won't remember you. If you haven't met the person before, you should explain how you determined that they would be a good person for your study. In either case, you might mention why you think their input would be useful to you. If you're sending an introductory query in order to invite participants to opt into your study, you will want to inform these potential subjects how the interview materials will be used and who will see them. Be sure to mention your time frame, that is, how soon you would need to meet with them, where you would like to conduct the interview, and how long you think the interviewing will last. Finally, since many e-mail users screen out e-mail from those they don't know, announcing the purpose in the subject line is a good idea. Remember: On the day before your interview is scheduled, call or e-mail your subject to confirm the location and time.

When a face-to-face discussion is not feasible, a telephone interview may work, but you should still arrange the interview in advance, not expect your interviewee to stop what she is doing to talk with you. Computer-assisted interviews, as with an instant messaging system or via e-mail, are not recommended because you won't be able to perceive any nonverbal signals such as intonations or body language. You'll also miss out

---

[4]Dyer's study, "Desperate, Lonely and Socially Inept," can be found at http://www.inq.pdx.edu/journal/article6.html.

on the impromptu quality of your subjects' responses, since they'll have the time to carefully select their words and craft their answers. If you do conduct an interview via phone or the Internet, be sure to disclose this information to your readers and to factor in the potential influence of the medium used in your analysis.

Getting It Down   Your goal in any interview situation is to secure your subject's words verbatim. Yet even if you arrive at your first interview on time, confident, and with a great list of questions, chances are that as you begin, you'll hear an interesting quote, scramble to write it down, and notice immediately that this person speaks much more quickly than you can write. The solution? Simple, you say: Use a tape recorder, and if one is available to you, by all means, use it. Among the benefits of recording an interview is that you don't have to rely on the accuracy of your notes or memory; you can simply replay the tape and transcribe, or write out the content, at your own pace. If you do use a recorder, remember to get the interviewee's permission before you start recording.

Many reporters, however, warn never to use *only* a recording device. They recommend documenting the conversation on a piece of paper as well. Otherwise you run the risk of having nothing to show for your time but a blank or inaudible tape, and a repeat interview is often unattainable. Writing also gives you something to do during your interview while your subject is speaking, so that you're not left staring back at him, which would probably make you both uncomfortable. Pen/pencil and paper are also more readily available than a recorder.

Whether you use a recording device or not, the key to successfully chronicling an interview by hand is to create a personalized shorthand and to listen astutely. Using abbreviations and symbols such as those included in Figure 4.2 will save you a great

---

FIGURE 4.2   Common symbols and abbreviations

vs.	against	&	and
@	at	b/c	because
b/w	between	↓	decrease
=	equal	esp.	especially
etc.	etcetera	1st	first
4	for	>	greater than
↑	increase	info.	information
<	less than	max.	maximum
min.	minimum	no or #	number
+	plus	prob	probable/probably
2nd	second	?	therefore
3rd	third	2	to
w/	with	w/o	without

deal of time when conducting an interview, but don't limit yourself to these common symbols. When creating your own individual shorthand, use symbols you've learned in math or science courses such as —> for "resulting in" or perhaps symbols you use online when writing e-mails or instant messaging. Another approach is to write only enough of a word to recognize it, as in "asso" for associated or association. Leaving out unimportant words and articles such as "is," "was," "were," "a," "an," and "the" will also save you time, as will omitting vowels ("mvmt" for "movement"). Comparing symbols you use in taking notes in class with your classmates will probably introduce you to a few new shortcuts that you can utilize while interviewing.

Listening carefully might seem like obvious advice when conducting an interview, but it's essential to effective transcription. You might otherwise find yourself trying to write down your subject's every word. With practice, you'll be able to distinguish between sentences or phrases that you'll want to quote fully and those whose general idea will do. For the most part, however, the experience of transcription will follow a pattern along the following lines: You begin writing down one seemingly valuable sentence, the following one, and then hear a third sentence that is poorly phrased, unclear, or irrelevant to your topic. Perfect. That gives you the opportunity to turn back to your notes and complete the first two sentences (before you forget them). If you find yourself unable to catch up quickly enough or hear an extraordinary idea you don't want to miss, it is perfectly acceptable to kindly ask your subject to pause for a moment.

STAGE THREE *INTERVIEWING: SEMISTRUCTURED CONVERSATION*

When you begin your interview, don't start asking questions immediately. The success of this method depends largely on your subject's level of comfort and willingness to open up to you, a stranger, so spend the first few minutes breaking the ice. Just as you did when setting up the meeting, briefly discuss the topic of your study, your goals, and what you will do with the information or narrative you collect.

In the previous stage, we stressed that listening carefully will help you in note taking and transcription, but listening is also essential in guiding the interview. For instance, if your subject phrases a statement too abstractly for you to comprehend, you could interrupt and ask them to rephrase or explain what they said. One technique is to rephrase their vague statement as a question, subtly indicating to them that you want more details. If someone says, "that was an important moment," for example, you could ask: "So that moment had a great impact on you?" If you detect a long digression, one way to steer the interviewee back to the matter at hand is to ask them a question that relates their current topic of conversation to the interests of your study. For instance, "_____ (their current topic) is very interesting. How do you see that relating to _____ (your topic of interest)?"

Use the questions you developed in Stage 1 as a guide and to help keep you on track, but don't let them stifle or disrupt the discussion, which could take a completely different (and more fruitful) direction than you had planned, and which should remain conversational and informal. Your subject's responses will probably lead you to develop new questions during the actual interview.

Keep in mind that your interviewee should be doing most of the talking—not you! You're interested in what *they* have to say, and your own statements and opinions could affect your subject's responses. If you look at Bryan's sociolinguistic transcript at the end of this chapter, you'll see that he did a great deal of talking during the conversation and often mentions his own take on things, which may have limited and/or altered some of Irving's answers. As you prepare for your interview, it may be useful to anticipate some common difficulties. See Figure 4.3 for examples of difficult interview scenarios, and think about how you would attempt to resolve them.

When the interview is coming to an end, review your list of questions to make sure you haven't forgotten any important ones. You could then ask, "Is there anything else you'd like to say?" or "Is there any question you would have liked for me to ask?"

Before you go, thank your subject for his time and input; ask him for the spelling of any unfamiliar words (such as people's names), and double check dates or figures. Review your notes as soon after the meeting as possible to fill in any blanks or complete any sentences, as well as to jot down your impressions and nonverbal signals you perceived. Did your subject seem reluctant to answer any of your questions? Did her words become forceful or loud at any point? All these notes will help you in the analysis stage, and you run the risk of forgetting them if you don't record them when the conversation is still fresh in your mind.

STAGE FOUR *TRANSCRIBING: FROM ORAL TO WRITTEN FORM*

We explained in Stage 2 that "transcribe" means to write out what is spoken during an interview, but we must return to this process here because (1) many scholars use recording devices and transcribe after interviewing, and (2) even those who take notes during the interview should type them out before the analyzing and reporting processes. Transcription is also an important interviewing step because many final products are in text form—as in a scholarly article, text, or Web site content—as opposed to audio or visual formats. One reason for the continued prevalence of text is that it is more easily disseminated and reviewed than audio recordings. The written form facilitates sharing, and it is easier for researchers to scan through textual data.

Although it might seem straightforward and even mechanical, transcribing requires careful attention. If your study involves more than one subject interviewed about the same issue, or if you are using focus groups where more than one person may be talking at the same time, you'll need to be consistent in transcribing interruptions, places where

---

FIGURE 4.3 What would you do if?

- . . . your subject responds with one-word answers?
- . . . your interviewee strays completely from the topic?
- . . . you are late for a scheduled interview?
- . . . your tape recorder battery dies during an interview?
- . . . your subject has a strong accent which you cannot understand?
- . . . your interviewee speaks too softly for you to hear?

there are talkovers, and any pauses. As we mention in the special section about oral speech in Chapter 6, Working with Texts, researchers have developed special marks for coding these oral features. Even if you are doing only a single interview, transcribing consistently will be essential to your ability to analyze the information you've been given. It often happens that two scholars given the same tape to transcribe come up with different versions of an interview. Why? One reason is that subjects do not always enunciate, or pronounce every sound, which leads to trouble with homonyms and words that sound similar. If you're working with a recording, take the time to replay any unclear moments. Also use your common sense. Make sure that what you write down seems logical and coherent. Scholars and students alike are often unsure what to do about accents, expressions, colloquialisms, slang, grammatical errors, and other nonstandard features of English. You should know that such "errors" frequently occur even with well-educated interviewees who speak English fluently. Since oral and written languages vary significantly, what makes perfect sense in a conversation between two people often seems incoherent on paper.

So, should one aim for a transcription that's as close to the spoken words as possible, or is it a scholar's responsibility to produce a grammatically correct text in standard written English? Truth is, there's no simple solution; the answer will depend on each individual study and its objectives. On the other hand, most academics agree that, whenever possible, it's important not to portray a subject as ignorant or incoherent, so that minor grammatical corrections and editing are standard practice.

In Rina Benmayor's article included in the Readings, "Narrating Cultural Citizenship: Oral Histories of First-Generation College Students of Mexican Origin," it seems she chose to present the students' responses as closely to how they were spoken as possible. She did not correct sentences with minor grammatical mistakes such as "I think she treated me bad"; this choice reflects her determination to allow these students to speak for themselves and to accurately represent their voices.[5]

PRACTICE ACTIVITY 4-5

Representing Your Subject

Scan the essay Bryan wrote after interviewing Irving—available at the end of this chapter—looking at the exact quotations he selected. How did he represent Irving's voice? How do you account for the changes/revisions he made? What is your impression of Irving based on the quotes Bryan has used?

Consider: What can you do as an interviewer to ensure that you represent your subject in an honest, objective way?

---

[5]Although transcription and determining how to treat issues of voice and dialect are indispensable to all scholars who conduct interviews, the process of transcription is of particular significance to oral historians, whose final product is often an edited transcript. See the section about collecting Oral Histories for additional suggestions.

STAGE FIVE *ANALYZING: PAYING CRITICAL ATTENTION*

After examining your topic, conducting an interview, and transcribing it, what do you do with the pages of quoted material? The short answer is in the title and subtitle of this section. You analyze them; pay critical attention to them. You should know that this is one of the main stages of interviewing. The critical attention scholars dedicate to an oral exchange is in large part what distinguishes interviews from everyday conversations.

Read your transcript closely, looking for passages, words, and phrases that stand out to you somehow—whether because they were spoken eloquently or in an unconventional or vivid way (perhaps using a simile or metaphor), or because they were repeated several times. Think about why these quotes stand out to you and what they suggest about the significance of your interview. Consult Chapter 6 Working with Texts, especially the section on public speech, for more suggestions on analyzing the transcription of your interview. Analyzing the interview requires you to think about these "data" in relation to your theoretical question—what were you trying to find out—and that you move from summary to some point of significance. As we pointed out in Chapters 2 and 3, analysis requires that you think about the parts in relation to the whole, that you look for patterns and abnormalities, that you consider context, allow for multiple interpretations, and acknowledge your limits.

STAGE SIX *VERIFYING: EVALUATING YOUR FINDINGS*

During this stage, think about the generalizability, reliability, and validity of your interview findings.

- What generalizations can you make based on your findings? Do you have sufficient data to make generalizations, or might your analysis suggest that you have a unique case?
- How reliable are your findings? Do you have reason to doubt the reliability of your subject? Has your own view interfered with your interview data in some way, thereby tainting the reliability?
- An interview is considered "valid" if it examined what it intended to examine. Is your interview "valid"?

PRACTICE ACTIVITY 4-6

Examining Words

Go to http://historymatters.gmu.edu/mse/oral/question3.html, listen to (or read) the excerpt, and respond to the questions on the Web site about the significance of this portion of interview material. Then, compare your interpretations with those of your classmates. How might you account for the similarities and differences between the varying analyses? Be sure to refer to concrete examples from the interview during your discussion.

Consider: What makes one interpretation of interview material more convincing than another? How can you convince others that your reading is a valid one?

Usually interviews, especially case study interviews of single subjects, are combined with secondary sources—published research studies, theoretical perspectives from scholars in the field, or statistical data, for example. To make his analysis even more authoritative and to determine the validity of his claims, Bryan could have conducted research on African American sociolinguistics or brought in some of the texts used in his class. Again, the chapter on working with textual materials suggests some strategies for finding appropriate secondary sources relevant to your project.

STAGE SEVEN *REPORTING: SHAPING FOR AUDIENCES*

Although there's no template for a written work based on an interview, your final product should include:

- Introductory information about your general topic.
- A description of your process, that is, who you interviewed and why.
- An awareness of your involvement in the project (such as potential bias).
- Carefully selected interview data, usually both quoted and paraphrased.
- Your analysis of the data.
- The "so what?" factor: How does your analysis respond to/complicate/impact your initial theoretical questions? Will your readers recognize the significance of your interview data and essay, or will they be left wondering, "So what?"?

We'll have more to say in the section on Working on Writing Interviews about different genres of interview presentation.

SPECIAL CASE: FOCUS GROUPS

Although originally a strategy developed by market researchers, focus groups (or group interviews) are now a widely accepted method for academic research. It's easy to understand the appeal of focus groups: They usually take less time than multiple, individual interviews, yet provide multiple perspectives that wouldn't be available from a single, case-study approach. Focus groups can provide detailed experiences to flesh out statistical data and can help researchers get a sense of the usual thinking of the target population in a way that open-ended surveys cannot. However, such advantages do not

---

PRACTICE ACTIVITY 4-7

Moving from Transcript to Essay

Reread Bryan's paper "A Sociolinguistic Interview," and consider the criteria presented in stage seven. How does Bryan introduce Irving and does he do so effectively? How well has he chosen his interview data? How has Bryan analyzed Irving's words? Do you agree with his analysis? What is the significance of this essay?

Consider: What could Bryan have done that would have improved the quality of his final paper? What other choices could Bryan have made in presenting the data from his interview?

mean that focus groups are always the most fitting research method. Like observations, the focus group process involves group interaction, but, unlike a natural setting, the focus group scenario is contrived and controlled. Since observing the natural setting is not always an option, a focus group may be a researcher's only alternative if the project is concerned with human interactions around a particular topic, but it will never be a replacement for naturalistic observation. Choosing to use a focus group interview, then, is as dependent on the inquiry's questions and purpose as any other research method choice would be.

Focus groups are especially effective when the researcher is not interested in individual people's thoughts or insight, but rather in less detailed data from a greater sample of individuals or in the interactions of responses generated by participants. In "Colliding Feminisms: Britney Spears, 'Tweens,' and the Politics of Reception," one of the readings in this text, author Melanie Lowe explains that one of the reasons she worked with focus groups was that this method resembles "the local, social organization of talk," that is to say, they're similar to everyday life. For Lowe's study, such interaction was an important part of her study of how preteens understood Spears and her shifting images.

The typical focus group session is comprised of six to ten subjects and lasts one to two hours, and the average study uses three to five different groups. Specialists also suggest that the most effective focus groups consist of homogeneous strangers, which means that the group members are similar, particularly in such features as sex, age, and race, and that they are unfamiliar to the interviewer and to each other (*Focus Groups as Qualitative Research*).[6] This standard of best practice means that you can't just have a chat with friends, roommates, or relatives and call that discussion a focus group. Identifying so many participants who can meet together at the same time for a couple of hours is one of the difficulties many students encounter in trying to use focus group methods. Work with your instructor to determine the minimum number of subjects you should include for your study.

During the session, the interviewer plays the role of a moderator, which means that there will be much less dialogue between researcher and subjects than during a standard interview. Focus group interviews are often less structured than their one-on-one counterparts, but the loose structure does not mean that you don't need to prepare questions. On the contrary, since you don't know where the conversation will lead, you should plan for a variety of possibilities and have key questions ready if the conversation falters after you introduce the initial topic. Notice, for example, in Lowe's study that she came to the focus group sessions with different photographs of Spears ready for her participants to consider if they ran out of things to say. She also had recordings of Spears's music, copies of lyrics, and articles from popular magazines to spur the conversation she was interested in generating for her study.

In the actual session, it's a good idea to write down participants' names and keep track of who said what, in case you want to refer to them later. If you see that the discussion is getting off track, or that the participants are not reacting to each other's points, you will need to intervene to redirect the conversation without taking over. You could, for example, say something along the lines of, "Enrique, you said earlier that . . . ; how do you feel about the point Megan raised that . . . ?"

---

[6]David L. Morgan, *Focus Groups as Qualitative Research* (Thousand Oaks, CA: Sage, 1997).

One important factor to consider before the meeting, during the session, and when analyzing the data is the potential influence of the group members on individual responses. For instance, does it seem that one person agreed with the others simply to avoid setting him/herself apart from the group? Is there one person who is dominating the group? Pay attention as well to the gender dynamics and to indications of cultural or personality differences that may affect who speaks or what gets said. Keeping track of such interactions can be difficult even for an experienced researcher, so consider working with a partner and dividing up responsibilities in advance.

SPECIAL CASE: ORAL HISTORIES

Oral history is essentially the practice of interviewing to collect data about an individual's life and times, and the scholars and students participating in the hundreds of existing international oral history projects worldwide are creating historical records from far more perspectives and with much more detail than ever before. Like any other field, oral history includes its own practices and protocols, but at its core is the organized and ethical scholarly interview described in this chapter.

One significant distinction between journalistic and even general academic interviewing and the oral history interview is that the latter must be recorded on tape or, even better, on an audiovisual device since, as the name suggests, the interview itself is the "oral history." Producing a clear recording is essential because the subject's words must be carefully transcribed, often including such details as regional accents, slang, or grammatical errors that other researchers and reports often disregard or simply adapt to standard written English. The precise written record is crucial because texts are much easier to examine and disseminate than audio- or videotapes, but in oral histories, the recordings themselves are often archived so as to preserve the individual's original voice and mannerisms. Obviously, then, researchers have developed tips for producing the clearest recordings, and several of these are available on the Web sites listed in the Internet Resources section at the end of this chapter.

Another distinguishing feature of the oral history interview is the role of the interviewer. Even more than in focus-group interviewing, the interviewer must refrain from engaging in a dialogue with the subject. Instead, oral history subjects, often called the "narrators," should be allowed to tell their story, at their own pace, and with little interruption (except, perhaps, for clarification of a point, or to ask for more details). Again, suggestions for interviewing strategies that are specific to collecting an official oral history are available at the sites included in the Internet Resources.

Finally, archiving an oral history is essential to preserving it for future scholars, and if you're participating in an official oral history project, or wish to start one, you should consult with your local historical society or university library about the technical and legal aspects of this work. Obtaining a signed permission form is standard, and examples of such forms are available at several Web sites as indicated in the Internet Resources section. Unless you are participating in a more formal oral history initiative, the sample permission form included as Figure 4.4 should be sufficient.

Though important and often complicated, collecting the oral history is really just the first step. The more important work is to analyze that oral history and decide what it means. Indeed so many oral histories have been collected and preserved that scholars can use existing oral histories for many interesting inquiry projects. Many of these

FIGURE 4.4   Sample permission form

I, (name of interview subject), give my permission for (name of interviewer) to use the transcript or recording of the interview/oral history conducted on (date) for purpose of writing assignments associated with (course at institution).

I understand that this work will be read by the instructor and students in the class and that the writing might lead to subsequent publications or presentations beyond the initial classroom setting. Giving my permission for such use does not prohibit me from using the information contained in this interview for my own purposes now or in the future, or from granting similar permission to others for subsequent interviews.

(signature of the interview subject)   (date)

collections are available online, and the Internet Resources will get you started on locating these existing collections. So whether you collect your own oral history or use an existing transcript or tape, it's important to remember that, as Linda Shopes puts it in "Making Sense of Oral History," one person's story does not necessarily represent the "truth." "The first step in assessing an interview," she advises, "is to consider the reliability of the narrator and the verifiability of the account" (6).

WORKING ON WRITING INTERVIEWS

As we've indicated in the stages of interviewing, there are two issues that always arise for researchers working from interviews: what form to use to present the interview and what to do about quotations. We'll take each in turn.

FORM OF PRESENTATION

Interviews can be presented in a form that looks more like a transcript with Q/A or the initials of the interviewer/subject serving as markers of the dialogue turns. This format is common in news magazines and in cases where the questions are as important as the answers. It is a form that allows for minimum alteration of the subjects' words, but

---

PRACTICE ACTIVITY 4-8

Family History

Go to the History Matters, "Making Sense of Oral Histories" Web site http://historymatters.gmu.edu/mse/oral/question1.html, and listen to (or read) the three interviews with members of the same family.

Consider: As the site suggests, consider how gender and generational differences shape the stories.

requires that the questions be clear and direct. Though this format may seem very close to a transcript presentation, it often requires that the interviewer omit questions that did not generate interesting answers, so some editing may be necessary to make the conversation easier to follow. Interviews can also be presented as extracts so that key moments of the interview become supporting evidence in an essay-type argument. Sometimes researchers want the subject's voice and personality to come through so that their story takes center stage, and then the interview may seem like a first-person narrative rather than the work of an interviewer. Though we fear sounding like a broken record to those who have read earlier chapters, decisions about format are influenced by audience and purpose.

When David Thelen interviews three key participants in the revelation of the Watergate tapes, for example, he does so because he's interested in historical memory and how individuals reshape the stories of their lived experiences over time rather than in the usual historical question of "what happened?" In fact Thelen is making an argument about history and historical memory based on the evidence of this specific historical case with these three accounts as the data. He says, "What is interesting for a conception of history that places memory close to its center is not that there are errors and discrepancies in accounts published fifteen years after an event, but how each of the participants has created a different narrative from the same original event in the years since 1973. Rather than our customary concern with what actually happened in room G-334, we can focus on which parts of the story each participant 'forgot,' 'remembered,' and reshaped, when and why" (p. 574). Thelen's purpose makes it important that each of the three participants gets to tell his own story in his own way, so that his readers can see that they forget, remember and reshape differently. That doesn't mean that Thelen isn't doing any analysis, but it does mean that his analysis happens almost completely in the frame he establishes to introduce these three stories and in the comments he makes about the process of agreeing on the transcript presentation with one of those participants. As you can easily see if you turn to this reading, two of those participants write their own firsthand accounts (though they are surely doing so at Thelen's prompting, answering his questions). In the third account, Thelen works with the informer and presents most of his story in the Q/A format with the questions and answers identified by initials. The differences in the form seem to echo Thelen's point about differences in memory, and the introductory frame allows Thelen to make his argument about how these accounts should be considered.

In contrast to this full-story approach, Benmayor's presentation and analysis of the oral histories of first-generation students uses only isolated moments from these interviews, arranged to illustrate her interpretation of these stories. Likewise, Lowe's analysis of the focus group interviews is presenting only those pieces of the interviews that she finds most illustrative of her conclusions, but all these researchers had to work with the full transcripts to decide what significance they could make from what their subjects were telling them. In each case these researchers turned to interviews for specific purposes and then presented their findings with those purposes in mind.

QUOTATIONS

Deciding which passages of the transcription to quote directly and which to paraphrase or summarize depends in large part on your project and how the interview fits with the other data you're including. If the person you interviewed is an authority, if their voice is distinctive or having their personality appear on the page is essential to your project, or if you can't summarize what they've said in other words, you'll probably choose to include a direct quotation. Usually direct quotations should be treated like salt in a well-prepared meal: used only as absolutely necessary. As you work with your interview material, you'll also make decisions about what to include and what to leave out based on your intended audience and the form you've decided to use for your final written product. Researchers begin to make these decisions by reading through the transcript, looking for those portions that are especially compelling, meaningful, or interesting. Toward the end of his interview, for example, Bryan asks Irving whether he feels that African American Vernacular English (AAVE) promotes exclusion between African Americans and Caucasians, and he includes Irving's response in his essay as a block quotation:

> I think probably no, because the exclusion is really from the other side of it because the Asian community, Hispanic, AAVE—what have you—all have a clear understanding of what SE [Standard English] is but the SE environment doesn't have a clear and total understanding of all of these other environments, so therefore it's sort of like, well, we're not being invited in the door so we're gonna create our own little tiny door and it is a . . . progressional type thing . . . building on AAVE, but at the same time it does exclude, but I feel like the people who are speaking AAVE . . . are not accepted socially or linguistically so therefore we have to create our own thing and then from that microcosm and the SE microcosm, that's where the problems come from. (p. 108)

We've found that when students read the transcript of this interview, they, too, are drawn to this passage. Not only does it appear toward the end of the meeting, when some of the toughest questions often come up, and is clearly an important point Irving feels strongly about, but also this passage stands out because "tiny little door" is a memorable visual metaphor.

But Bryan doesn't expect these words from the interview to stand alone and mean the same thing to his readers that he thinks they mean. Instead Bryan provides his own analysis of Irving's words when he says:

> I believe that this idea illustrates the rift that exists between black culture and white America. Each side believes that the other is excluding it. From a linguistic standpoint, whites are excluded—for the most part—from AAVE. This is good for African-Americans because it creates a culture for them with which they can identify. African-Americans also want for their culture to be accepted by mainstream society, but unfortunately, whites don't usually get a chance to immerse themselves in that culture to study it in the same way that Irving studied the German culture. Without first-hand exposure, whites, to some degree, are going to be uncomfortable around this culture and be less willing to accept it. (p. 108)

In the first sentence of this passage, Bryan indicates that he finds Irving's statement representative of many African Americans' view. In other words he takes one interview subject's response and relates it to a larger group. Although Irving did not say so explicitly,

Bryan also intelligently deduces that Irving believes having an unique linguistic code benefits AAVE speakers because it "creates a culture for them with which they can identify." And, as all scholars should, Bryan adds his own spin on things. While Irving suggests African Americans have no choice but to create their own language and seems to blame Caucasians, Bryan provides an alternative explanation, attributing some of this exclusion to the fact that whites "don't usually get a chance to immerse themselves in that [black] culture to study it."

Since we're not sociolinguistic experts, we're not suggesting that either student's perspective is the "right" one. What we can learn from Bryan's analysis, however, is how to examine words and make meaning from them. Further we think Bryan is doing precisely what researchers are expected to do when they include quoted material: he explains why he thinks that material is relevant to his own purposes. When you decide to include a quoted passage from your transcripts, be certain that you don't expect those words to stand by themselves and convey to your readers precisely what you think they mean without doing the work to explain your interpretation or analysis.

Researchers don't always present the entire passage; they can lift key words or phrases and insert those relevant portions into their own sentences. Notice, for example, that Wynde Dyer frames the words of her subjects with her own analysis and that she selects when to incorporate short phrases or key words (from either her subjects or the secondary sources she is consulting) and when to provide her readers with a longer quotation from those she interviewed. Here's an example from one place in her essay where she is making such decisions:

> Because most of our subjects—the major exception being one of the deviant cases—had positive first experiences with internet dating, the primacy effect, or "the tendency for first impressions to be lasting ones" (Trenholm & Jensen, 2004, p. 157), becomes apparent. Sam said because "his first few experiences went really well" he "kept on doing it," and David also continued with his internet dating practices because "the first girl [he] met was really cute and cool." Both Matt and Maria maintained that if they ever broke up, they would both go back to the Internet in search of love. Jennifer's testimonial to the importance of first impressions is the most powerful example of the primacy effect in action:
>
> > *I'd say the first person I went on a date with was the one I felt like I had the most chemistry with so it kind of hooked me. I still kind of long for that person, it's kind of odd. The first person I met was just kind of the kick start to get the ball rolling. So maybe what also got me hooked was, "Well, can everyone be this great?" (8)*

What we particularly admire about this paragraph is that Dyer blends the shorter excerpts from both her own interviews and her secondary sources into her own sentences in a clear and effective way, and reserves the longer block quotation to underscore the point she's making. She doesn't analyze this quotation, but the work she's done earlier in the paragraph and the characterization she uses to introduce this passage—"the most powerful example of the primacy effect"—makes it clear to her readers how this passage is to be understood.

> **PRACTICE ACTIVITY 4-9**
>
> ## Working with Quotations
>
> Turn to any of the readings that utilize interviews, or to one of your own papers that has incorporated interview material, and find a section that includes a block quotation. Try rewriting this section to eliminate the block quotation by first paraphrasing or summarizing. Then, rewrite again extracting key phrases as quotations blended with your own sentences. Compare your versions with those done by classmates working on the same sections.
>
> **Consider:** Which versions of the passage do you like best and why? What is difficult about rewriting to eliminate full quotations?

STUDENT ESSAY: CASE STUDY INTERVIEW

Bryan McLucas was a student of Dr. Sonja Lanehart at the University of Georgia when he wrote the following essay for a course on African American Vernacular English. Bryan has since graduated with an undergraduate major in Linguistics and a minor in English. He stayed at UGA and obtained an MEd in Instructional Technology. Currently Bryan works for the Hugh Hodgson School of Music at UGA as an Information Technology Professional.

A Sociolinguistic Interview

Bryan McLucas

Irving and I sit across from each other at a vintage 60's Formica table, my trusty Panasonic RN-111 micro-cassette recorder in hand. He is a black male in his mid 20's who grew up in a region of Atlanta called the "SWAts" (South West Atlanta), for the most part, except for the five years that he spent in a little Georgia town called Hogansville with his grandmother. After high-school, he joined the Army and then went on to college. This is where we are now. Irving and I are both in the same AAVE class, and we discussed some of the topics that have been brought up in that class over a banana and a bowl of cereal.

After Irving explained his background to me, which situations in his life he felt had the strongest influence on his idiolect. He had learned his speech style, in part, from his parents (who are both college graduates) from his teachers and from television. The biggest influence, however, was his grandmother. "She was a huge influence," he replied. He went on to say that both she and his grandfather were schoolteachers. This had an enormous impact on the way that he spoke because he was always being corrected by his grandmother for using improper grammar. Although at the time she was retired, Irving's grandmother had been a kindergarten teacher—so she was accustomed to teaching children Irving's age how to speak. I asked if the types of things that she corrected were AAVE-isms or normal, everyday kid-learning-how-to-speak-isms. "She didn't care what wordage I used." He went on to say that his grandmother used AAVE so she was not trying to dissuade him from speaking it. She wanted for him to know how to speak correctly so that he could code-shift when necessary. There was even code-shifting within his family. There were some situations where his family would use AAVE, and some situations where they would use SE, even among themselves. Everyone, he explained, knew what each language was and utilized it. "It's [SE's] a weapon that you use wherever you need to go if you're black."

After his grandmother taught him "correct" speech at such an early age, I was certain that when he returned to Atlanta there had to be a pretty significant difference in his speech vs. the urban kid's speech. He went on to explain the term "proper" to me. According to Irving, "proper" is the term that most African-Americans use to describe a fellow African-American who speaks Standard English, or they at least speak a more standard dialect than the accuser. This is how people described Irving in his childhood. "I did use to get in trouble for speaking proper," he admitted. Irving was quick to point out that he didn't feel that he was not a speaker of AAVE, but rather that the people he surrounded himself with spoke it more heavily than he did. This leads way to Irving's spectrum theory.

The spectrum theory is that everyone's pattern of speech falls somewhere on a continuum. There is no true speaker of AAVE nor a true speaker of Standard English. To illustrate further, let's put the clear speakers of Standard English on the left of this spectrum, and the clear speakers of AAVE on the right. It would depend on if someone fell to the right or left of your own position on that scale whether you considered them an AAVE or an SE speaker. Also, their distance from your position would indicate how severe you considered their dialect. Irving wasn't sure where he fit on this scale, but from my observation he would be in the SE half, at the very least. Keep in mind that this scale assumes that someone speaks the same way to everybody and ignores code-shifting, which he feels applies to him "all day long."

On the subject of code-shifting, I asked Irving which situations he would apply to SE and in which situations AAVE would be more preferable. He was quick to point out that SE, the Language of Wider Communication, is the only language that is acceptable in a corporate environment. In other words, that language has a certain utility for him, and "otherwise [he] wouldn't care necessarily to speak Standard English" He would, however make sure that his children understand the mechanics of how to use SE because he feels that it is an integral part of functioning in a formal setting and this is how the language was presented to him by his grandmother.

When asked about the benefits of AAVE, I received two answers—the descriptive nature of the language has more utility and secondly, one would receive more social acceptance. The latter ties into the social theory of group acceptance. To quote directly, "social acceptance is probably the number one functional reason [for speaking AAVE]." "Fitting in" seems to be a reoccurring motif, and I wondered if maybe this idea of group cohesion includes a degree of exclusion. Irving feels that exclusion definitely goes on, but that it is a by-product of AAVE, rather than a goal. I asked how he viewed white people that used AAVE and he expressed a little dissention about the matter.

Originally, Irving could not accept a white person using an African-American dialect. Eventually, however, he realized that some whites have grown up in the same environment that he did, and that it is just as true a language to them as it is to him. As long as it isn't someone trying to come into something that they don't understand. Irving views this as patronizing. He then drew a puzzling analogy to the time he spent in Germany. He did not speak German before he got there, but as he learned more of the language he decided to throw himself into it and use the language around native Germans. He claimed to feel totally out of place, originally, but that it helped him to understand what the Germans were all about. I wondered why this couldn't apply to AAVE also, and why whites would not be allowed to engage in a similar practice to try and understand black culture. It became clearer to me when Irving added that it was all about respect. Germany has an established language and culture, and that was respected by most people. Black Americans are people without a culture, or rather, they are people who have been robbed of their culture. Because of this, African-Americans are trying to create their own culture—something that they can identify with—and the continuation of AAVE is a large part of this. Irving doesn't think that AAVE, at this point, could be approached in a respectful manner by someone who isn't black.

The picture that he has painted for me is that language is a very tender matter for African-Americans. He relates that in the Army, which is disproportionately black, you would never use AAVE when talking to your superior. I asked, "if the majority of people in the army are black speakers of

AAVE, then is this a case of the minority trying to control the majority?" "Yes, totally," he replied. He explains that the best way to subjugate people is to take away their language. Without language you don't have identity, you belong to no group, and you are thereby easier to control. I added that maybe African-Americans were trying to resist this control by holding on to this language. He explained that "it's like trying to make a linguistic culture out of nothing." Irving then digresses slightly in saying that he thinks that it won't last, that the language is in a constant state of decreolization and will eventually phase out. I mistakenly added that because of the number of blacks and white were about the same, that the two languages would eventually fall together. This opened up a new topic over a common misconception about the black population.

Irving insists that out of 300 million people in this country, 10% are black, 7% are Hispanic, 4% are Asian and the rest are miscellaneous. He admits that even to him the numbers of blacks seem much higher, but they really only make up a relatively small percentage. It has to be the case in so many places, he goes on to say, that there are white people who have never seen a black person before. I related that in many places this was the case, especially among the affluent. When the children of these families meet a black person for the first time, they are very uncomfortable—simply because it is unfamiliar. This doesn't make them racist, necessarily; it just means that they will be uncomfortable until they get some exposure. "That's all it is, man, totally," Irving replied, ". . . exposure." I then inquired, "would you say that the key to racial harmony is . . ."

"Exposure. Yep," he concluded.

Returning to my previous hypothesis about exclusionary practices, I asked if exposure is the key to people understanding each other and getting along, then was AAVE a vehicle by which exclusion and separation continues to occur. His reply, which concluded our interview, was as follows:

> I think probably no, because the exclusion is really from the other side of it because the Asian community, Hispanic, AAVE—what have you—all have a clear understanding of what SE is but the SE environment doesn't have a clear and total understanding of all of these other environments, so therefore it's sort of like, well, we're not being invited in the door so we're gonna create our own little tiny door and it is a progressional type thing building on AAVE, but at the same time it does exclude, but I feel like the people who are speaking AAVE are not accepted socially or linguistically so therefore we have to create our own thing and then from that microcosm and the SE microcosm, that's where the problems come from.

I believe that this idea illustrates the rift that exists between black culture and white America. Each side believes that the other is excluding it. From a linguistic standpoint, whites are excluded—for the most part—from AAVE. This is good for African-Americans because it creates a culture for them with which they can identify. African-Americans also want for their culture to be accepted by mainstream society, but unfortunately, whites don't usually get a chance to immerse themselves in that culture to study it in the same way that Irving studied the German culture. Without first-hand exposure, whites, to some degree, are going to be uncomfortable around this culture and be less willing to accept it. There is a continual push-pull among African-Americans who want to belong to both the smaller group and at the same time be accepted in the larger. This idea not exclusively a group goal, but is even expressed on the individual level as shown in this interview. The language that the individual associates him or herself with seems to play a key role as to which group the individual wishes to belong. Speakers of SE identify with mainstream America, speakers of AAVE with the black culture created in opposition of the mainstream culture. Bi-dialectal people, like Irving, identify with the black culture almost exclusively, but seem to use SE as a tool or "weapon" within the mainstream society. Irving doesn't seem to accept Standard English as anything other than a necessity. He doesn't believe that SE is an integral part of himself, but rather an extension of his ability to communicate with others. Standard English really is a weapon to Irving, and a weapon that he wields proficiently.

Sociolinguistic Interview Transcript

B: Okay, so give me some history about you, like, where you grew up, where you went to school.

I: Okay, where I went to school, uh . . . well I'm originally from Atlanta, I was there until like seventh grade and then my parents got divorced and then I lived with my Grandmother in the country and I lived there until I was like ten or twelve and then I moved back to Atlanta. So I guess I had a mixture of like urban/rural upbringing.

B: So all of your starting social whatever was in Atlanta when you were young, then you went to live with your Grandmother. Did she live in the country all of her life?

I: Yeah.

B: So she was "southern belle."

I: You could possibly describe her as that, not quite that . . . that's almost on, yeah.

B: Whenever I listen to tapes of me when I was that age it sounds so southern. . . . I sound like country bumpkin and like it wasn't until like sixth, seventh eighth grade before I started cuttin' out all this /pai/ and stuff like that . . . did you have a similar, like if you listened to yourself when you were that age livin' with her was it . . .

I: Nope, not really.

B: It wasn't?

I: Well my immediate family, my father, mother, . . . we didn't really have southernisms in our speech so that wasn't really a big deal. I did use to get in trouble because I talked real "proper." That's what it's called.

B: That was gonna be my next question. Where does the proper speech fit in to all of this? In other words did you learn proper speech from your parents?

I: Umm, I wouldn't say that I learned it from them, per se, I would say that I learned it more from school, and television and like. . . . Walter Cronkite and shit like that.

B: So you went to school in the city of Atlanta for the first few years and, I don't know because I didn't go to school in Atlanta, but, I would suspect that there would be a higher incidence of AAVE in Atlanta schools.

I: I would definitely say that, especially in an any urban environment.

B: So it was only because you went to school for a couple of years in that environment that it didn't affect you that much?

I: Ummm . . . I dunno, that's hard to say, that's definitely hard to say. I think that what happens is AAVE has to be put on a continuum, ya know, like a spectrum and I would say that I'm definitely somewhere in the middle of that spectrum, but probably the people that I knew . . . the majority of the people that I knew were somewhere to the left or right of that but they were definitely somewhere in a different place than I was and probably because of that fact that's why they considered me to speak "proper" or whatever, ya know? These are like little school kids or whatever.

B: So it's relative, someone that's a very standard speaker would see how you speak as very "dialectal" but someone who was a very heavy dialectal speaker would say that he speaks very "proper" so it all depends on your perspective.

I: It's all really relative, but let me say that as a matter of fact that there are definitely black people who aren't even on the spectrum at all, so you know . . . there's a difference there also.

B: Right, okay, so uh, where you went to school for the majority of your life, in the country setting . . .

I: That wouldn't be the majority of the time, the majority of the time would be, like, Atlanta. It was only there for like four or five years. From like one to eight I was in Atlanta, then maybe like nine to twelve I was there and then maybe the rest of the time I was back in Atlanta, that was just like a small portion.

B: Okay, so in those five years that you were in the more "country" setting, what percentage of your school was black . . .

I: Yeah, yeah, uhhh . . . it was like 50/50.

B: even at that time the people of that school noticed that you were more "proper" speaking?

I: Yeah, these were like the black students though . . .

B: The white students weren't like "Man . . ."

I: No.

B: So those would be some of the difficulties that you had with language at the time? Fitting in, maybe?

I: Yeah, I would say that definitely. That's part of that thing that if you don't speak AAVE, you are perceived to speak proper or whatever, um, and you're gonna get some degree of ostracism, ya know what I'm sayin'? placed on you.

B: That holds true for anything though, like, I would say that for the most part anything thats different is seen as the outside.

I: True, true, as far as the deviance.

B: In your life have you ever been bi-dialectal where you speak different around black people than you do white people or even black people that speak Standard English.

I: Yeah, I mean that code shifting thing applies to me all day long. It's so cool now because it's like I don't even have to think about it. I think maybe when I was younger it was definitely something that I had to think about, but now it's like, strictly involuntary.

B: I can relate to that too because . . . especially when you're younger there's a huge difference between the way you talk around your friends and how you talk when you come home and talk to your parents, so, that's another big example of code-shifting.

I: Yeah, it then applies across the board, I think.

B: yeah, and, uh, what do you see as the benefits of speaking a Standard English as opposed to AAVE?

I: Um, Standard English is like, of course, the language of wider communication and it's just like, it's the language that is the language of, ya know, where we are, right now. So, as opposed, say like I wouldn't necessarily have free reign to speak AAVE in some corporate environment, ya know, therefore speaking in a standard dialect would benefit me there. So that's the purpose, that's the utility for having it, otherwise I wouldn't care necessarily to speak Standard English.

B: All right, here's a perhaps more fun question. What benefits do you see of speaking African American Vernacular as opposed to standard?

I: Umm, well, social . . . social acceptance is probably the number one as far as like a functional reason and then secondly, and more importantly than the other, I just think that it has more like, vigor to it, ya know what I'm sayin'? It's almost musical to me.

B: There's more soul.

I: Yeah, to use a cliché, it definitely has more soul. It's colorful as shit.

B: More descriptive.

I: Yeah and to me that's just beautiful and to me that just ties into music to me because I'm like this crazy hip-hop fan and that's just like basically a language, it's like poetry.

B: Um, well, how do you view, we were talking about this in class discussion once, about white people who speak an African American Vernacular?

I: Whew, uh, I have a love hate relationship with that. Umm, you see, I used to just totally disrespect people across the board who did that but then I finally had to realize that there were some people who grew up in that same environment that you grew up in without necessarily having to patronize you, so therefore, it's cool but if it's something that's goin' on that you don't really understand. I mean, it's like sayin' somethin', like, repeating something that someone else said to you but you don't know exactly what it is and to me that doesn't really make sense and that would be the same thing to me.

B: Would you compare it more to like, if you think of AAVE as a language within itself, does it seem more to you like it's, I dunno, exclusively a social thing, people in your same social setting would use it or do you see it more as like a language and if a white person were to speak it it would be just as silly as like a white person walking into a circle of a bunch of Japanese people and speaking Japanese slang or throwing Japanese words around even though their culture didn't belong.

I: Well, no, not necessarily because it's all about understanding because I used to, um, I've been in the same sort of situation because I used to live in Germany for a couple of years and I didn't like get fluent in German but all the Germans would be like, damn, you speak pretty good German so like after a while I was like, okay, I'm gonna do this, and um, so I felt totally out of place, like a fish out of water, but, it was cool, but, at the same time it was like, I understood the mind set of Germans and Germany or whatever and there-fore I had respect for it and I could approach it in like that manner but I think that a lot of people don't have respect for AAVE. They approach it in a manner where they don't have a lot of respect and therefore they don't really, ya know, to me, ya know, that's the one that doesn't belong so get out, ya know, whatever.

B: To shift gears a little, if you have children would you make a conscious effort to teach them Standard English or would you just let them pick up, ya know, what they will?

I: Um, I'd definitely make sure that they under-stood all of the mechanics behind Standard English, ya know, to be viable in the society and I think that that's something that's a necessity, so I'm gonna be the mother of that invention. No, doubt.

B: Umm, what about, let me put you in a situa-tion: Let's say that your living in an urban area and the kids that your kids want to fit in with are heavy speakers of African American Ver-nacular, and except for the small amount of time that they are around their teachers or you or whatever, that's the only standard that they, uh, receive. Would you make a conscious effort to adjust their idiolect?

I: Well, not necessarily adjust but once again make sure that they have, like. . . . See all, the only difference between like people who speak AAVE only and people who are bi-dialectal, in my mind anyway, is that the people that aren't bi-dialectal didn't get exposure, or exposure enough to um, SE. See that's the only difference. If you're exposed to it, you will pick it up, period. Even if you don't use it. So, you know, pseudo naturally.

B: So, just being in the home setting you think that would be enough exposure.

I: Well, not necessarily even me because I speak more of a vernacular. I dunno, I don't know how you would describe my vernacular.

B: I dunno, personally listening to you, coming from the white side of it you don't seem to speak vernacular very heavily if that's the adverb I'm looking for.

I: It's weird, because it's like a huge mixture. It's like my own personal . . .

B: Idiolect.

I: It is like an idiolect with heavy vernacular, I call it like, intellectual vernacular so I dunno, it's like strange.

B: That works, that works.

I: Not that I'm sayin' I'm a smart guy or any-thing.

B: Like what we were saying before . . . it's all on a continuum and in my experience as far as people who consider themselves to be AAVE speakers. Um examples on this continuum would be Bryant Gumbel, the other end being those guys on *Airplane*! The movie, and I dunno, if you want to cut it in quarters I would see how you speak on the three-quarter mark going one way and maybe how [this guy in our class, who we shall call Englebert] talks as the three-quarter mark going the other way.

I: That could be it, possibly, and the whole deal is like that I'll swing between the three.

B: Yeah, it's a shifting scale and it's all relative. Umm.

I: Just being in this class I notice it so much more, whereas, I knew it before but it was never anything that I thought of.

B: In this class, for the most part, It makes you very conscious of the way that you talk. Even I, I sit there and I'm like, "man, I'm so white."

I: It's funny, but its like there . . . it's definitely a reality.

B: And I like what [Englebert] said, "I dunno about this bi-dialectal thing, this is the way I am . . . what you see is what you get" so there are definitely a lot of prejudices on one side or the other. When you stereotype somebody you assume things about them, we talked about this in class about if you have a really coarse south-ern dialect then automatically you're stupid because you "sound" stupid and people tend to do the same thing when it comes to AAVE, and [Englebert] for instance is a very bright guy and it seems like, what I'm gettin' at is that [Englebert] could have an I.Q. of like 180 and talk the way he does and sit next to Bryant Gumbel who could have an I.Q. of like 85 and just from the way they speak people are gonna assume different things about them.

I: Just the opposite, but also on the topic of [Englebert], he feels very uninhibited in our class, but I guarantee you, that if you were to see him in some other class, or in some other important, standard situation in which AAVE wouldn't be quite so open armed, he would speak a whole lot differently, I guarantee you.

B: I agree totally, people tend to have ideals about themselves and even though, I'm sure that he would like to live up to those ideals.

I: I'm sure that's the way that he feels most comfortable speaking, but it would be lovely to see him in a different environment.

B: So what do you think about this issue of teachers taking classes on AAVE. Good idea?

I: Excellent. Especially, ya know, since I'm in the English Ed department, I wouldn't ever need to take any of those classes, because I am those classes. But, I know that especially in the city, the people that are teaching it need to be very enculturated as to the people that they are teaching. I think that that may be the missing link in the communication line between a lot of students. So let's do it.

B: The title of these courses would lend you to believe that you're supposed to go in and learn it as if it is a different language and be able to communicate in it. Do you think that that's actually the goal, or that it's to prove to the people that take the class that it's a perfectly viable language?

I: No, I don't think it's important to prove to the people that it's viable. I think that it's important to prove to people that this is something that you're going to have to deal with, this is something, literally, that you're gonna have to face. All those people that go to Japan and Taiwan to teach English, they don't ever learn the language, but they can still teach English, and those people who learn English from people who don't know their language learn so much better . . . and it would be that same principle. Those people don't have to learn AAVE, they just have to learn, ya know, what pitfalls of AAVE would not

allow students to learn SE effectively. See I look at it more as a grammatical issue, ya know, and when you really break it down that's what it comes down to because I don't care where you are, where you live, I mean, you can pretty much understand everybody as long as they are speaking some form of English, if you like, stop and slow down enough . . . that could be the biggest thing that you have to do to understand that person. So, I know those people understand what they're saying, it's just like, once again, getting them to be able to, in part, knowledge of SE onto their students is what is the focus and is what is being missed.

B: Okay, here's a tougher question, how do you feel about people who are exclusive speakers of AAVE and through growing up their parents speak it, their friends speak it, and they don't learn any version of SE. How do you feel about their ability to communicate with others?

I: There again you're getting into that little funny area because anyone who speaks AAVE automatically, I mean they may not speak it, like, literally but they understand it because there's no way that you could be like totally isolated in the world only with AAVE simply because we live in America and you might have a nice homogenous environment where you get a heavy dose of AAVE, and you may . . . I think that after so long of not having to, being forced to speak SE, you're just like, fuck it, even when you do go into that environment. . . .

B: I think I was talking specifically more, what about them trying to get across what they have to say to someone that speaks SE because I hear what you're saying about, ya know, they're gonna be able to understand anybody that speaks SE, no problem, because, ya know, television . . . you hear it everywhere, but there are a lot of standard English speakers that will listen to an AAVE speaker and not know what the *hell* they're talking about.

I: Well, see that's what I'm sayin', like, I think that's constant because AAVE speakers can communicate in SE if they choose.

B: Ahhh, so you're saying that these people. . . . If it is the case that a white person listens to an AAVE speaker and can't understand them, there's a reason why they can't understand them. If they wanted to get across what they had to say they could do it.

I: Crystal. Every single time. There's not one exception if you ask me. I'll give you an example: When I was in the Army, basically you can't speak AAVE to your superiors, if you go see the first sergeant, you're gonna be speakin' some real straight up, G.I. Joe English which is, to me, basically Standard English with a double caffeine shot of military jargon.

B: You bring up being in the Army. What other little anecdotes do you have specifically dealing with your stint in the service?

I: Not necessarily. I think that was one of the biggest parts of my exposure in life to different varieties of language. It didn't really start there, though, like when I was in high school I went to a real melting pot sort of school so I got exposure to a lot of things in there, and then when I went into the army I went to New Jersey first and got the New Jersey version for a little while and then I moved to Boston and I used to hang out in Rhode Island so I did that whole thing with "park the car" and all that other crap, and then I went to Germany after that. And you wanna know what the funny thing is? A lot of Germans learn English from Black G.I.'s and to me there's AAVE goin' on all over Germany because that's the only place where they learn their English from and it's like an AAVE version of English and it's weird as hell to see all of these German people speaking it and it's like totally out of place.

B: Why do you think that is, I mean, like what specifically puts more African American people in the position of teaching English?

I: Well, first of all, there's a disproportionate amount of black people in the Army as opposed to like the rest of society. Sort of like that same thing with the prison thing, jail thing, army, what else. . . . So you're gonna get like major instances of AAVE speaking and speech patterns so therefore I would say that that would probably be the reason.

B: That brings to mind a question: If there's a disproportionate amount of black people in the armed services and you were saying before that AAVE is just right out, is this another case of the minority controlling the majority? Like the minority of people in the army are imposing SE on the majority of speakers of AAVE?

I: Yes, totally, if you know anything about imperialization, that's the reason why we still have this predicament now. All this other race issue and all that bullshit is totally gotten out of language. If you want to subjugate someone, you take away their language. That's what happened and that's why black people are still fucked, basically, because they don't have a language. Go look at the Asian community, that's why they're so economically viable, they have their own language.

B: One thing that I've learned about war is that if you want to subjugate people, you go in and destroy their art museums, their theaters and take away their culture and without culture there is no group cohesion, which is a sociological issue, and language is a huge part of culture. Which brings to mind another question: Do you think that AAVE has persisted for so long is to create group cohesion and make a culture?

I: There we go. I would definitely say that, and it's like trying to make a linguistic culture, if you will, out of nothing, out of that pidgin/creole and we're totally in that like, decreolization point right now, umm . . . but I think that it would only decreolize to a certain extent because you can't like totally wipe it out, because I like to watch those futuristic type movies where they all talk the same and I think that it will happen like that.

B: I think the same thing because if you look at the way black people spoke before school integration and where we are now it's like, worlds different and I think that it's gonna be the same on both sides with like, AAVE being incorporated into white speech and . . .

I: Like a share thing.

B: Yeah, it's not like the Mexican community which, in Georgia is not as large as it would be in like Texas, so it wouldn't be as heavy an influence, I don't know the exact statistics but blacks and whites are about 50/50 most places.

I: See that's the common misconception . . . that's what I wanted to say. . . . See that is the key to this whole class, to this whole everything. Everything that we've ever talked about in class but nobody has said anything about it and sometimes, ya know, I want to bring in like other issues and they're not like totally relevant like linguistics so it's not totally relevant but it is at the same time. What people don't realize is that there are only like 300 million people in this country, okay, and 10% of them are black 7% of them are Hispanic 4% are Asian and the rest are etc. I hate to group the rest of whoever ya'll are as etc. umm, so there's only like a 10% black population in this whole country and that's only like 1 out of 10 people and it doesn't look like that even to me, but it is and it's so weird. I always say, "where the fuck are all of these white people" but they're out there and I know it and it's like the other day when Dr. Lanehart said that there's some white person who had never seen a black person before and that has to be the case in like so many places.

B: It's like preppy little white girl that goes to private school her entire life and then goes to a state college and suddenly there's black people, ya know? That girl is gonna be uncomfortable because she's never seen a black person before . . . . It doesn't make her racist or anything else, it just means that she's uncomfortable until she gets some exposure.

I: That's all it is man, totally.

B: So, would you say that the key to racial harmony is . . .

I: Exposure? Yep. It's just like I said. The people that speak AAVE, in order for them to speak AAVE as well as you or I or anyone else they just need to be exposed.

B: That brings to mind a question: We've already established that AAVE is a way of bringing culture to people with no culture in relation to the way that Asians and Hispanics do when they create their little communities and exclude other people. Do you see that the same kind of thing with AAVE and people who adamantly speak AAVE are trying to exclude . . .

I: Well, I think that the exclusionary practice part of it is like a by-product as opposed to a goal, but I think that it definitely happens, yeah.

B: If exposure is a key to people getting along, going on that model, do you think that AAVE in some way is a vehicle by which exclusion continues to happen and there's not as much exposure between cultures?

I: Um, I think that probably no, because the exclusion is really like from the other side of it because the Asian community, Hispanic, AAVE what have you, all have a clear understanding of what SE is but the SE environment doesn't have a clear and total understanding of all these other environments, so therefore it's sort of like, well, we're not being invited in the door so we're gonna create our own little tiny door and it is a, like, progressional type thing as far as, like building on AAVE, but at the same time it does exclude, but I feel like the people who are speaking AAVE are feeling like, hey, we're not accepted socially or linguistically so therefore we have to create our own thing and then from that microcosm and the SE microcosm, that's where the problems come from.

B: Any assorted comments before we wrap up?

I: I think that we just about covered it. I just wanted to make it really clear that all AAVE speakers have a total grasp of SE, um, at least from a speaking standpoint, maybe not writing and that sort of thing.

B: Well, okay. Ta da.

STUDENT ESSAY: ORAL HISTORY INTERVIEW

Samantha Sanderson is a native of Ohio who transferred to the University of Miami in 2006. A Biochemistry major, Samantha also plays on the university's soccer team. Although Samantha began the composition class where she wrote this essay saying that she was not a very good writer, she discovered that writing was mostly about revising. This essay was written in response to an assignment to conduct interviews, but as you'll see if you turn to Chapter 6, it was also revised to focus more on analyzing specific language.

Columbine: A Day to Remember

Samantha Sanderson

One of the worst school shootings in history occurred on April 20, 1999, in Jefferson County, Colorado, at Columbine High School. Eric Harris and Dylan Klebold, two Columbine students, went on a rampage against fellow classmates with numerous weapons, including guns, homemade bombs and knives. Killing twelve students and one teacher before committing suicide, these two boys changed the lives of everyone there and their families, who were forced to look on, wait and wonder.

Many victims' families got to speak out in the aftermath of this tragedy, but what about the survivors and their family members? A few survivors got interviewed, however, the main stories one remembers from this attack are those about the victims, not families of survivors or survivors themselves. In light of this fact, there are two oral histories that need to be shared in order for one to see the difference that an event such as Columbine can have on the survivor's family versus the survivors. The first is from the younger sister of a survivor from the Columbine massacre, who I've called Linda. She will share how her day went, being reunited with her sister and all that she remembers of the next few days, including her neighbor's funeral. The second is the perspective of a survivor, who I've called Jenny, who will walk through the event, being reunited with her mother and family, the funeral of her neighbor and the decision she made from all she has witnessed.

WAITING AND WATCHING IN WONDER: LINDA'S STORY

I was in the fifth grade and we were having class in one of the outside tent classrooms. Around eleven it was time for lunch and we usually just filed into the main building and got our food, but something was different that day. At first we weren't allowed to go into the building to get our food. Then the teachers told us to run as quickly as we could from the tent to the lunchroom. We all knew something was wrong but nobody knew what. After we ate, we didn't return to class; instead we went into a room and watched a movie. The principal came on over the loud speaker and told us that if our parents came, we could leave but could only leave with our parents. My neighbor showed up to get me; I kept saying I couldn't go because my mom was to come. After she convinced me that she had it approved by the school, I finally left with her. On our way home my neighbor asked me if I knew where my sister was and I simply replied, "School." That is when she informed me that there was a shooting at my sister's school.

As soon as I walked in the house I saw my aunt with the phone in her hand staring at the television. She told me to watch the news with her; people were running from the building with their hands over their heads. I was very confused; where were my mom and sister? What was going on? My aunt informed me that my mother was at the library waiting to hear news from Jenny. The students were being taken to either the local library or Leigh Wood Elementary. The whereabouts of the students were being posted at both locations, so my mother was waiting at the library. My dad kept calling my aunt to see if there was any word on Jenny; he was out of town for business and had to drive home three hours to get back. All he knew was what he heard on the radio and they had said 200 people were dead, plus he knew they couldn't find my sister.

Around four o'clock, five hours after we had first heard news of what was going on, my aunt got a call from my mom and she had found Jenny. When my mom pulled up, I ran to the car as fast as I could and embraced Jenny with the tightest hug possible. I remember telling her I never thought that I would see her again.

All night I watched the news; we were looking for our neighbor's son, Danny, who we still had no word on. Plus, there was nothing else to do. Jenny had left with some friends to go to a candlelight vigil at a church, so I just sat and watched the news all night.

I relive that day a lot. I relive the next few days a lot. My neighbor, Danny, his body turned up on the front page news the next day, sprawled out on the cement. That is how his parents found out he was dead. I remember his funeral, lines of people out the doors of the church. We thought we weren't going to get to say good-bye to him because we couldn't even get in, but family members recognized my parents from the small open casket showing the night before so they led us into the church to say good-bye. They played "In the Arms of an Angel" by Sarah McGlocklin as they brought his casket down the aisle. All I remember is his grandfather speaking and his youngest stepbrother speaking; they were really close.

Danny's mom took the cement that Danny had died on and put it in her backyard and built a swing above it. Danny was her only child; she had children through marriage but that was all. I remember seeing her slowly swing back and forth over that cement every morning. It was so sad. They finally moved into the mountains to get away from the news reporters who bothered them endlessly and to take a break from it all.

STUCK INSIDE: JENNY'S STORY

I apologize if things seem out of order; I don't think about this day a lot. In fact, sometimes I forget the anniversary of that day. I remember that it was freshman year and I was in Earth Science class. The fire alarm sounded and so we began to file out into the hallway, but it was just a mob of students; nobody was going anywhere. I can't remember specifically but I am pretty sure that someone yelled get back into the classroom. So we all turned to get back into our rooms but another girl and I got separated into a science office. At first there were eleven students and a teacher in there, but there was another teacher that came in later. I remember this because there were thirteen people in our room and that was the number of fatalities. The teacher that came later had blood on his shirt, which we later found out was from Dave Sanders, the teacher who was killed. When this teacher had left Dave Sanders he came to our office and locked the door. We heard a lot of popping sounds, but I couldn't tell you if they were bombs or gun shots because after a while they all sound the same.

I was holding this girl's hand the whole time we were in the room; she was looking to me to be her rock. At one point we heard the gunmen in our hall. They shot into the room next door and we heard it hit the wall and someone screamed. I remember thinking selfishly that this stupid girl was going to get us killed because we were hiding behind a bookshelf so nobody could see us, but now they would know we were there.

I have no idea why I did this, but I rolled onto my left side and tucked my head down. All I wanted was to make sure that if they shot through our window my heart would be protected. One teacher was next to the door, an Exacto knife in hand. I have never seen anyone hold a knife with intent to kill until that moment and I haven't since. The other teacher, the one who had been with Mr. Sanders, was sprawled out over us to protect us. A gunman came to our door and rattled the doorknob. The teacher with the knife was standing out of sight but right by the door as the gunman looked in. He tried a few times to get in, but then the other gunman started yelling something; I honestly couldn't tell you what he said, but the other gunman gave up and they left. After that, it was just waiting.

There was a radio in the room but we dared not use it because we didn't know who was behind everything that was going on. A girl in the room had a father who was a sergeant of police and she also had a cell phone on her. He had been trying to get a hold of her all day but we were all scared of making noise so she didn't answer. She finally called him and told him that she was in the room, safe but with twelve others. Her dad told her to let everyone make one call so I called home and talked to my aunt to let her know I was ok. My aunt was crying; she just lost it and we both were kind of speechless. She asked me if I knew where I would be going, but I didn't. I still think that this girl's dad was the one who got the ball rolling on getting us out of there.

Eventually the SWAT team arrived and they had to bust down our door because nobody wanted to answer it. They were serious and pointing guns at our heads because they didn't know if the shooters were hiding in there with us or what was going on. We were pushed into the hallway and patted down. I was really nervous so I started giggling, which was obviously the wrong thing to do because a SWAT member nudged me with a gun and told me to stop laughing. Once the door opened to the outside we all wanted to run, but we couldn't; we had to go single file through a hole someone cut in the fence and onto a bus. There were two exit pathways from the building; one was the way I went and the other went by two slain bodies, including the body of my neighbor so I am glad I was spared that sight. All I saw were shoes and book bags, things people didn't come back for.

I was taken to the elementary school and I waited for about an hour before my mom got there, due to the traffic. They had counselors there and I talked to about six of them. Nobody could believe how talkative I was being, but I talk when I'm nervous. A lot of people got interviewed by CSI personnel as we got off the bus, but I got skipped over pretty easy because they wanted to talk to the kids who walked by bodies or saw more things than I did.

My friend was the one who informed me that my mom was there and I walked up to her, my brother and my cousin, who were with her. For some reason as I came up behind her I tapped her on the shoulder; everyone else was running to their parents but I calmly got her attention. She spun around and everyone began to cry and hug me. It was very emotional. I asked where my dad was and my mom said he was driving back as quickly as he could. I spoke with him later and he told me he was driving 100 miles an hour and would not have stopped for anything. After seeing the way it affected my parents, I felt like I was the lucky one because I didn't have to worry the way they did.

I saw my neighbors; they were looking for Danny, but we couldn't find him and they said it would be ok if we left. Stories began to come out about different occurrences; people who had missed school for doctor's appointments, a cop exchanging gunfire with the gunmen, my friends who were in the cafeteria and saw the duffle bags with bombs in them but thought nothing about it; they were so lucky that the bombs malfunctioned.

I went to a church that night and the atmosphere was so sad and horrible, I was just happy to be alive. I didn't really have survivor's guilt. I obviously wondered why me? Why did I live? But I never really felt like I should have died instead of others. There were reports of dead students but no names or numbers. We were still looking for Danny.

When we saw the newspaper the next morning and realized that Danny was gone, I had to do the hardest thing I have ever done. I walked over to my neighbors' house to give my condolences. I said, "I'm sorry they took him." His mom just hugged me and said how glad she was that they hadn't taken me too.

I tried to take the positive out of this situation. Seeing all the people and the efforts they made helped me realize that I wanted to give back just as they had. I have stuck with that and I am graduating with a degree in nursing. I want to be a missionary nurse and give back to those in trouble.

COMPARISON

When I was interviewing these sisters it was amazing to see the difference between the two; there seemed to be a lot of emotion coming from the younger sister versus the older one. Linda, the younger sister, could recall moments and songs that she heard and experiences that still affect her today. She spoke nonstop for almost an hour and when she spoke about seeing Danny's body in the paper she choked up for a minute. Jenny, the older sister, barely thinks about the day and her memories came back in pieces all out of order. She would begin talking about something and remember a detail she had forgotten and would go back to it; she jumped around a lot. Both mentioned their mother having them go to counseling to make sure that everything was ok and they were dealing with it all in an appropriate manner.

Although it was a hard time for both of them, Linda says that when she attended Columbine three years later that it just seemed like a normal high school. She never felt unsafe and things just seemed right. Jenny didn't talk much about what happened afterward, but she did seem to move on. Also, I thanked them for speaking with me about such a sensitive subject but both assured me they did not mind. They said they would rather talk about it and get a real story out there than people just assuming that the crazy news stories are all true.

Internet Resources

The Oral History Society of the United Kingdom provides useful information about identifying subjects for oral histories, preparing interview questions and the logistics of recording the interview at http://www.ohs.org.uk/advice/. Additional suggestions, including examples of legal releases that must be obtained for any oral history that is going to be preserved and diagrams of the most effective setup for producing clear audiovideo tapes, can be found at the UCLA Oral History Program at http://www.library.ucla.edu/libraries/special/ohp/ohpdocs.htm. Another example of signed releases is available through the T. Harry Williams Center for Oral History at Louisiana State University. You can access this site at http://www.lib.lsu.edu/special/williams/index.html.

Both the UCLA site and the University of Miami's Oral History Project site at http://www.library.miami.edu/archives/ohp/mission.html are examples of archived oral histories of local regions. Both sites contain links to some of the many other oral history projects, as well as bibliographies and indexes of the archived recordings already in their collections. Another annotated list of online sites that have archived transcripts is available at the History Matters site mentioned in the Practice Activities in this chapter (http://historymatters.gmu.edu/mse/oral/online.html#exemp).

Web Sites Referenced in this Chapter

History Matters, "Making Sense of Oral Histories" http://historymatters.gmu.edu/mse/oral

Boeree, C. George, Shippensburg University, "Qualitative Methods: Part 4" http://www.ship.edu/~cgboeree/qualmethfour.html

Dyer, Wynde, "Desperate, Lonely and Socially Inept" http://www.inq.pdx.edu/journal/article6.html

Links to the Readings

In each of the following readings, the authors conducted interviews as their primary method of investigation.

Benmayor, Rina. "Narrating Cultural Citizenship: Oral Histories of First-Generation College Students of Mexican Origin"

Lowe, Melanie. "Colliding Feminisms: Britney Spears, 'Tweens,' and the Politics of Reception"

Thelen, David. "Remembering the Discovery of the Watergate Tapes"

Yung, Judy. "'A Bowlful of Tears Revisited': The Full Story of Lee Puey You's Immigration Experience at Angel Island"

Assignments Using Interviewing

Collective Memory option in Assignment 2 (Spence); Assignment 3 (Thelen)
Considering "Public" option in Assignment 4
Constructing Public Spaces option in Assignment 2, 4, 5; Assignment 3 (with history)
Cultural Politics and Public Discourse II: Shaping Values Assignment 2 (Thelen)
Direct Observation option in Assignment 3 and 4

Ethnicity in America: Identity Assignment 3 (Yung)
Ethnicity in America II: Defining America option in Assignment 2; Assignment 3
Expanding a Trends Report Assignment 4; option in Assignment 5
Eye on Campus Assignment 2 (Benmayor); option in Assignment 5 and 6

Histories: Official and Unofficial Assignment 3 (Thelen); option in Assignment 4
Humanizing Numbers Assignment 3
Investigating Artifacts option in Assignment 3 (with history)

Representing Community Assignment 2; option in Assignment 3
Trying Out Interviews

Assignments Working with Focus Groups

Between Writing and Knowing Assignment 4
Cultural Politics and Public Discourse Assignment 3 (Lowe)

Gender Investigations Assignment 4 (Lowe)
Reading Media Assignment 6 (Lowe)

Assignments Using Oral Histories

Ethnicity in America: Identity option in Assignment 4
Ethnicity in America II: Defining America Assignment 1

Gender Investigations Assignment 6 (Yung)
Reclaiming the Past Assignment 1 (Yung)

CHAPTER 5

WORKING WITH NUMBERS

Researchers work with numbers, as they work with texts, in two primary ways: They investigate numbers directly, and they use numbers as evidence along with other kinds of data to support a broader inquiry project. In the first case, researchers work to interpret numerical data accurately and make claims (or arguments) about how such data ought to be understood. Research that argues about the correct interpretation of government-sponsored economic data is a good example of this first kind of inquiry. In this case, the numbers come first; the economic data have been released by the government, and the research is attempting to understand and interpret the data. In the second case, some other kind of project comes first, and the researchers turn to numbers as one part of their analysis, positioning relevant figures alongside other kinds of information. A researcher interested in the impact of a particular presidency, for example, might analyze the president's success in shepherding legislation through congress, his appointment of key judicial leaders, and his handling of foreign and domestic issues—evidence that is primarily non-numerical—alongside data about the economy. In this second case, the economic numbers would still require careful interpretation (by the author and then by readers) even though they would not be the central or only focus of the study.

In either case, researchers can use numbers collected by others or they might design research to collect their own numbers. If you questioned the National Endowment for the Arts (NEA) report on declining literary reading you might conduct a careful analysis of the numbers presented in this report. How were the numbers collected? How might responders' interpretation of key terms have influenced the numbers? Are the percentages misleading in some way? Doing so would have you working primarily with the numbers already collected. Alternatively you might decide to conduct your own survey to see whether students on your campus fit this general profile or if you could uncover what college-age students *are* reading if they aren't reading literature. Either way, you would generate numbers that you would then need to analyze. In the first part of this chapter, we provide guidance in working with numbers—both those provided by others or the ones you collect on your own. In the second part of the chapter, we outline the basic steps in designing and conducting a survey, the most common method of research involving numerical data.

We often think of numbers as hard data, the substantive and the real, what helps to "prove" an idea is true. But numbers are creative entities as well. Looking at numbers is often a way to generate ideas, a way to find interesting arguments, perspectives, or information, and thus a place for inquiry. Even those college students who hate or fear math (and some of their instructors who feel the same!) usually have enough experience, knowledge, and creativity to use statistical data in investigating topics of interest.

We are going to ask that you begin looking at numbers in a way that will probably be a little different than how you have approached them before. We will keep the formulas and equations to a minimum, and instead ask that you use numbers as you would use an interview or observation: as data that must be interpreted to become meaningful. Whether you are working with numbers collected by others or conducting surveys that produce numerical data, whether you are investigating numbers as the focus of your research or turning to numbers as additional support for an inquiry into some other topic, the new levels of literacy we discussed in the introduction increasingly demand that college students have "numeracy" as well. Learning not only to manipulate numbers in increasingly complex ways—as you surely will in college-level math classes—but also to write about them clearly and coherently is knowledge that benefits all educated citizens.

PART I: INTERPRETING NUMBERS: SOME BASICS

The following section describes different kinds of numbers. You may think you already know the difference between, say, raw numbers and rates. Alternatively you may be one of those people whose eyes glaze over any time they are faced with a set of numbers or (gasp!) a variable. In either case you should pay attention to what comes next because it has less to do with defining these various numbers than with explaining how to work with them.

TYPES OF NUMBERS: RAW NUMBERS, PERCENTAGES, MEASURES OF CENTRAL TENDENCY (MEAN, MEDIAN, AND MODE), RATES

All numbers are not equal. Different types have their uses and abuses, which you should consider when conducting and presenting your inquiries. Raw numbers are most useful for presenting actual data, but their significance is not always obvious. When literacy researchers Helen Damon-Moore and Carl Kaestle[1] tell us that *The Ladies' Home Journal's* "circulation was 25,000 at the end of its first year (1884), double that in six more months, and by 1886 had reached the impressive figure of 400,000" (250), they are giving us raw numbers, but they are doing so in a way that helps make the significance of these numbers clearer. Without additional information, however, we really don't know what to make of those numbers. What was the population of readers in 1884 and 1886? Surely a number of magazines were purchased by libraries (or families) where more than one reader saw the publication, so circulation can't be easily equated with readership. The simple difference between 25,000 and 400,000 in two years does seem to justify characterizing the circulation as "impressive," and in the

---

[1]See Helen Damon-Moore and Carl F. Kaestle, "Gender, Advertising, and Mass-Circulation Magazines," *Literacy in the United States: Readers and Reading since 1880* (New Haven, CT: Yale University Press, 1991).

paragraph where these numbers appear, that characterization is the authors' point—the numbers are being used as data to support the authors' argument that "the time was ripe for a practical magazine geared to a new broad group of women readers" and that advertisers were looking for such a venue.

Often it is not the raw numbers that are presented but a percentage. Imagine, for example, if a survey comparing the experiences of students attending large and small colleges found that sixty-nine of the ninety-one students attending small colleges were satisfied with their schools, while fifty-two of the ninety-five people who attended large universities were satisfied. Instead of giving the reader these raw numbers, it would probably be more effective to calculate the percentage and say that seventy-five percent of the small college graduates were satisfied, while only about fifty percent of those who attended large universities were. Researchers usually still present the raw numbers, perhaps in a table, so that readers can check the work, but in this case percentages communicate the significant information more clearly.

Additionally, calculating a percentage change can reveal vital information that might otherwise go unnoticed. Growth rates, in populations or stocks, are one form of percentage change. Consider the data on college enrollment in Table 5.1.

The college enrollment for both white and black individuals increased from 1985 to 2000. If you look at the raw numbers, you can see that white enrollment increased considerably more than black enrollment. Indeed, 1,218,000 (notice that the label indicates these numbers are in thousands) more white students attended college in 2000 than in 1985. By contrast, 901,000 more black students attended college. That means that white enrollment increased by 317,000 more individuals than black enrollment—a considerable number. But these raw numbers do not tell the whole story. Percentage changes, which are a way to figure out the rate of change that takes the relative sizes of the populations into account, might be better here. When you calculate the rate of change,[2] you discover that white attendance increased by about eleven percent, while black attendance increased by about seventy-one percent. That means that black attendance increased sixty percent more than white attendance.

Percentage changes are one form of rate or proportion. Like percentages, rates and proportions are a kind of fraction that will help to clarify information, and perhaps even correct mistakes, when used properly. Rates are often expressed as "per something," the something often being a measure of time (per second, per diem) or some other object (per capita). To understand the significance of rates, imagine that we want to know what percentage of white or black people are enrolled in college. We can easily supplement the data in Table 5.1 on educational enrollment with data on population totals.

Now, to determine the rates of college attendance, we simply express the numbers who attend college (Table 5.1) in comparison to the total population (Table 5.2). We

TABLE 5.1 U.S. College Enrollment by Race, in Thousands. U.S. Census Bureau, 2003		
Race/Ethnicity	*1985*	*2000*
White	10,781	11,999
Black	1,263	2,164

---

[2]Calculating a percentage change is easy. Take the earlier number and subtract it from the later one. Then divide that difference by the earlier number. This works whether you are calculating an increase or a decrease. To practice, try it on the numbers in Table 5.1, and see if you come up with the same results as you see here.

TABLE 5.2	Total U.S. Resident Population by Race, in Thousands. U.S. Census Bureau, 2001	
Race/Ethnicity	*1985*	*2000*
White	202,031	226,232
Black	28,569	35,307

can use different types of fractions to portray this relationship. For the sake of convenience, let's use percentages (Table 5.3) and see what comes up.

Now we can see that, compared with each group's total population, the rate of college enrollment remained steady for whites and grew substantially for blacks. If these numbers are correct, the per capita rate of college attendance in 2000 was higher for blacks than for whites. However, the rate of increase does not seem as dramatic as the seventy-one percent growth rate in total college attendance the numbers at first seemed to indicate. Per capita data are not always expressed as percentages; the data are commonly presented in a number per 100,000. Death rates and crime rates are often reported in this way, and you should be aware that when you encounter a per capita number without further explanation, oftentimes it means "per 100,000 people."

Averages are another kind of useful number, though the term can mean different things, so the phrase *measures of central tendency* is sometimes clearer, if more wordy. Averages, for instance, are often useful when you wish to depict a middle-of-the-road case, but there are different kinds of averages and you should be sure to use the kind of average that best suits your needs. In particular it pays to distinguish between the mean, the median, and the mode. Measures of central tendency all look for some kind of center point to the data. The *median* simply refers to the middle value in a set of values. The *mean* refers to the mathematical average of all the values and is what people usually mean when they say "the average." The *mode* is the value that occurs most often.

Other useful information can be provided by measures of spread, different ways of indicating how much the data are either spread out or how tightly the data cluster around the center. The *range*, the most basic measure of spread, is the difference between the lowest and the highest values. Among other measures of spread, the most robust, most useful, and most complicated is the *standard deviation*, which averages how far all data tend to be spread out from the mean.[3]

TABLE 5.3	Per Capita College Enrollment by Race, Expressed as Percentage. Based on data from 2001 and 2003 Statistical Abstract (see Figures 5.2 and 5.3)	
Race/Ethnicity	*1985*	*2000*
White	5.34	5.30
Black	4.42	6.13

---

[3]For further explanation of standard deviations, including how to calculate them by hand or (much more easily) using Excel, see "Standard Deviation" on Robert Niles's excellent *Statistics Every Writer Should Know* site (http://www.robertniles.com/stats/stdev.shtml). Niles provides a vibrant introduction to statistical concepts aimed at practicing journalists. If you want a humorous and energetic introduction to statistics that provides more depth than Niles, see Fred Pyrczak's *Success at Statistics: A Worktext with Humor*, 3rd ed. (Los Angeles, CA: Pyrczak, 2003). Links to online statistics information, including interactive programs, hypertextbooks (for different levels), free software, interactive tutorials, and related resources, are available at John C. Pezzullo's multiaward winning *Interactive Statistics Pages* (http://www.statpages.net).

TABLE 5.4	Annual Income Distribution of Imaginary Group, in Dollars 2006
	Annual Income
Family 1	30,252
Family 2	194,500
Family 3	28,766
Family 4	14,128
Family 5	45,676
Total	313,322

To find the mean, simply add all the data together and then divide by the total number of cases. For instance, let's say you have five families with incomes as represented in Table 5.4. To find the mean, you would add these and get the total of $313,322. You would then divide by five (since there are five families) and your mean (average) income would be $62,664. Let's say, however, that you want to understand how the average family in the sample paid expenses. Because one of the families has a high income compared with the rest, the mean is misleading. In this case it might be better to use the median.

To find the median, arrange all your cases in descending order, and then find the one in the middle. In this example, Family 1 with an annual income of $30,252 is the median. If you look over the information in the chart, you will see that this is a better representation of the average family income for your particular purposes. Usually, when you want to depict the "Average Joe" from within a sample, use the median.

READING SURVEY REPORTS

As you read survey reports, use the same skills that you use when reading other kinds of material. You will likely encounter confusing numbers, or you may see charts that at first seem to make more sense than the surrounding text but that also include a lot of unfamiliar numbers or symbols. Skim over what you do not understand, and focus on what makes sense. You can go back to the confusing parts later, remembering that some of the data will only be of real interest to those who know the math side of statistics.

As you look over the data, keep in mind the difference between descriptive statistics and inferential statistics. Some of the data, for instance the mean or the odds ratio, *describe* patterns in the data and are the "juicy" part of the analysis—they are the claims about what these data reveal. Numbers and figures related to statistical *inference*, such as chi-square, ANOVA results, or p-values, deal with the question of whether the descriptions of the sample data (the "juicy" part of the analysis) can be generalized to the broader population. They are useful to understand, if only so you don't end up being misled, but they will not reveal much about the relationship between variables. In other words descriptive statistics might tell you that people in a survey who attended small colleges were more satisfied with their experience than were people who attended large colleges. Inferential statistics would tell you whether that interesting insight is generally true, or if it's just a fluke of the particular group who took the survey.

FIGURE 5.1 Glossary of terms

- **ANOVA:** ANOVA stands for ANalysis Of VAriance and is a common way to test for statistical significance.[4] Results of ANOVA tests will commonly appear as follows: $F(2,26) = 7.519$, $p = .003$. You can safely ignore everything before the p-value, noting that if p is less than .05, the effect is statistically significant. ANOVA tests whether the differences found between two or more groups of data are significant.

- **Chi-square (X^2):** If you see X^2 in a piece of statistical reporting, it probably refers to results of the chi-square test (the Greek letter chi looks like the roman letter X). The chi-square test seeks to determine the likelihood that a particular correlation or other result is statistically significant. The actual numbers here are unimportant for our purposes (they matter to statisticians). Chi-square should be reported along with the "degrees of freedom" (df), which you can also ignore. Instead, look for the p-value associated with a reported X^2 value (sometimes it will only be footnoted—researchers will often only report correlations when the chi-square test demonstrates statistical significance). If this value is .05 or less, then the proportion that is being tested is statistically significant.

- **Confidence Interval (CI):** Reports will sometimes reveal confidence intervals (CI), usually the ninety-five percent confidence interval, but sometimes the ninety-nine percent one. A confidence interval is a measure of statistical inference. When using a confidence interval, the author is saying that the real score lies somewhere between the two numbers presented (or, with a ninety-five percent confidence interval, that the score will be in the stated range ninety-five percent of the time). For example, if I am dealing with odds ratios (see below), and I report that the ninety-five percent confidence interval for the odds ratio (OR) of a female student feeling upset after the September 11 attacks is 1.3–1.7, I am saying that it's pretty certain (ninety-five percent likely) that the real OR lies somewhere between these numbers. Researchers will provide confidence intervals for all sorts of data, not just odds ratios. A report may make the following claim: "Female college students were more likely than male students to feel emotionally upset after the September 11 attacks (OR, 1.5, 95% CI, 1.3–1.7)." This means that within the sample, the odds ratio was exactly 1.5 and that in performing statistical tests the researchers know that in the broader population of female college students, the real odds ratio is likely to be between 1.3 and 1.7. The larger the confidence interval, the harder it is to make substantive claims about the data. Furthermore, if the CI spans the reference number, then we cannot make even basic claims with any confidence. For instance, if the confidence interval for an odds ratio is 0.8–1.4, we do not even know if the thing we are measuring is more or less likely to happen, which is the whole point (usually) of having an odds ratio. CIs are part of inferential statistics, but they are probably the most interesting and useful part of inferential statistics for casual readers. For an example of why, see *Margin of Error*.

- **Correlation (p, r, or rho):** The indication of degree of correlation, this number may also be called Pearson's rho, the correlation coefficient or the regression coefficient. The value of r or rho will always be a number between −1 and 1. The number "0" means absolutely no correlation. The number "1" means a perfect positive correlation and the

---

[4]Ninety-five percent is the classic cutoff for statistical significance. This number is not magical, however, and a number of people have argued that the cutoff number ought to be different depending on the context of the test. For instance clinical significance might be something very different from statistical significance, so in certain contexts a clinical researcher may be willing to report a correlation that does not "pass" the test of statistical significance.

FIGURE 5.1 (Continued)

number "–1" means a perfect negative correlation. A negative correlation means that as the first number decreases, the second number increases in equal measure. If people who had higher levels of education, from high school through college to graduate school, were also less likely to watch daytime television, there would be a negative correlation between level of education and daytime television watching. A correlation of 0 means that there is absolutely no relationship between the two measures. In the real world, you will never see any of these perfect numbers. However, very weak correlation, numbers around zero, can be treated as zero, while numbers that approach one or negative one suggest a strong correlation. The correlation coefficient is the odds ratio (see below) in a different form. Sometimes surveys will report one, sometimes the other, sometimes both.

- **Margin of Error:** The margin of error is often reported in opinion polls. Margin of error is just a specialized case of the confidence interval, so if you are still confused by that concept maybe thinking about the margin of error will help. The margin of error means that the researchers are fairly confident (unless otherwise specified assume a ninety-five percent CI in an opinion poll) that the actual opinion people hold is within the margin of error of the reported figure. So if, in a poll with a four percent margin of error, Candidate X is predicted to receive forty-three percent of the vote one month, and the next month he is expected to receive forty-six percent of the vote, his number has not changed. Take that margin of error seriously. (If, however, on the following month his number drops to forty percent, this represents a real change from the second month, even though it is still within the four percent margin of error from the first month.) What does the ninety-five percent mean? It means that ninety-five percent of the time (or 19 out of 20 times) the responses of people to the questions in the poll would fall within the stated margin of error. Note that this means that 1 in 20 times the response would be outside this margin of error.

- **Mean (M, m, μ):** This is the mean, usually the arithmetic mean, but sometimes the geometric mean. (Geometric means are used to find numbers like average growth rates. When conducting your own analysis, figure out growth rates or percentage changes using two discrete points, but do not try to figure out a mean growth rate until you know how to find a geometric mean.)

- **Odds Ratio (OR):** A very important statistic for demonstrating degree of correlation. An OR above one is a positive correlation, and below one is a negative correlation. Although ORs are often given as a single number, this number is always in ratio to 1. Thus an odds ratio of 1.5 is really 1.5:1. Let's say researchers note that the OR for female students feeling emotionally upset after the September 11 attacks is 1.5. This means that for every one student in the reference group (probably male students) who feels upset, there are 1.5 female students who feel upset. So if there were a group of 60 students, 30 male and 30 female, and 10 of the male students felt upset, then 15 women would feel upset. Likewise, a number below 1 represents a negative correlation compared to the reference group.

- **p-value (p):** This is one of the most important figures in inferential statistics. The smaller the p-value, the more "significant" the finding, and the larger the p-value, the greater the chance that these particular results could be obtained merely by chance (and therefore do not represent a real difference). P-values are similar, then, to CIs. The traditional cut-off for statistical significance is .05, which equals five percent (which is the inverse of the ninety five percent CI). A p-value of .05 or smaller is good, the smaller the better. This number only means "there is a strong likelihood that the correlation is real." So even if the correlation seems small, say, an OR of 1.13, a high p-value means that this weak

FIGURE 5.1 (Continued)

correlation is real. On the other hand, a strong correlation, say an OR of 2.3, will be ignored by many researchers if the p-value is above .05, because there is too great a chance that this correlation is just a chance occurrence in the sample and does not represent a true correlation in the larger population.

- **Total number (N):** Responsible researchers always report the total number of respondents to the survey they include in their analysis, and use the variable N to signal this number. If you see $N = 224$, that means 224 people are included in the analysis. Many researchers will also indicate how many people they sent surveys to, how many responded and the response rate, and the number of surveys they had to discount (because, for instance, the returned surveys were incomplete or illegible).

PRACTICE ACTIVITY 5-1

Interpreting Numbers

The following exercises use the complete data tables from the 2001 and 2003 Statistical Abstract upon which Tables 5.1, 5.2, and 5.3 from this chapter are based. Questions appear first, and the complete data sets follow in Figures 5.2 and 5.3.

1. Compare the original data in these tables with Tables 5.1, 5.2, and 5.3 in the text. Where has the text presented the data exactly as it appears here? Where has it modified that data by performing certain operations on it? Are those operations clearly explained in the text? Are they appropriate for the kind of information sought? What kinds of information do the tables in the text leave out that appear in these data tables? How does leaving this information out affect the presentation?

2. The tables in the text take measurements at discrete points in time—the years 1985 and 2000. The original data tables present a more complete picture, though. What are the advantages of using only two points in time? What are the disadvantages? Do you think choosing only 1985 and 2000 is a legitimate way to parse this data? (Why or why not?)

3. Figure out the percentage change (the growth rate) in the total white and black U.S. populations between 1985 and 2000. Compare these numbers with the percentage change in college enrollment by race that was calculated from Table 5.1. Then compare the growth rate to the percentage enrollment by race that appears in Table 5.3. What do you see? Do these numbers suggest anything to you? Think about how growth rate in a population affects the age distribution. How do such considerations affect the significance of the "per capita college enrollment by race," as presented in Table 5.3?

4. Working with statistics is not only about crunching numbers, but should also engage your imagination and creativity. Although these census data provide numbers that reflect certain demographic trends, the trends themselves do not explain why certain changes have been occurring or the significance of those changes. Think about the reasons why the changes in college enrollment and graduation reflected here may have occurred, and come up with a few alternate explanations. This is not about what you know, it is about plausible explanations (some of which you could subsequently test, if you wanted). What reasons are there to be optimistic about social improvements for African Americans? What are some explanations that would mitigate this optimism?

FIGURE 5.2 Statistical Abstract Population Chart for Practice Activity 5.1.

No. 14. Resident Population by Race, 1980 to 2000, and Projections, 2005 to 2050

[In thousands, except as indicated (226,546 represents 226,546,000). As of July, except as indicated. These data are consistent with the 1980 and 1990 decennial enumerations and have been modified from the official census counts; see text of this section for explanation.]

Year	Total	White	Black	American Indian, Eskimo, Aleut	Asian, Pacific Islander
1980 (April)[1]	226,546	194,713	26,683	1,420	3,729
1981	229,466	196,635	27,133	1,483	4,214
1982	231,664	198,037	27,508	1,537	4,581
1983	233,792	199,420	27,867	1,596	4,909
1984	235,825	200,708	28,212	1,656	5,249
1985	237,924	202,031	28,569	1,718	5,606
1986	240,133	203,430	28,942	1,783	5,978
1987	242,289	204,770	29,325	1,851	6,343
1988	244,499	206,129	29,723	1,923	6,724
1989	246,819	207,540	30,143	2,001	7,134
1990 (April)[2]	248,791	208,741	30,517	2,067	7,467
1991	252,153	210,975	31,137	2,112	7,929
1992	255,030	212,874	31,683	2,149	8,324
1993	257,783	214,691	32,195	2,187	8,710
1994	260,327	216,379	32,672	2,222	9,054
1995	262,803	218,023	33,116	2,256	9,408
1996	265,229	219,636	33,537	2,290	9,765
1997	267,784	221,333	33,989	2,326	10,135
1998	270,248	222,980	34,427	2,361	10,479
1999	272,691	224,611	34,862	2,397	10,820
2000[3]	275,130	226,232	35,307	2,434	11,157
Projections[4]					
2005	287,716	234,221	37,619	2,625	13,251
2010	299,862	241,770	39,982	2,821	15,289
2015	312,268	249,468	42,385	3,016	17,399
2020	324,927	257,394	44,736	3,207	19,589
2025	337,815	265,306	47,089	3,399	22,020
2030	351,070	273,079	49,535	3,599	24,858
2040	377,350	287,787	54,462	4,006	31,095
2050	403,687	302,453	59,239	4,405	37,589

FIGURE 5.2   (Continued)

Percent distribution:					
2005........................	100.0	81.4	13.1	0.9	4.6
2010........................	100.0	80.6	13.3	0.9	5.1
2015........................	100.0	79.9	13.6	1.0	5.6
2020........................	100.0	79.2	13.8	1.0	6.0
2025........................	100.0	78.5	13.9	1.0	6.5
2030........................	100.0	77.8	14.1	1.0	7.1
2040........................	100.0	76.3	14.4	1.1	8.2
2050........................	100.0	74.9	14.7	1.1	9.3
Percent change:					
2010–2020..............		8.5	6.5	12.7	14.9	31.3
2020–2030..............		8.4	6.5	11.9	13.7	28.1
2030–2040..............		8.2	6.3	11.1	12.7	26.6
2040–2050..............		8.0	6.1	10.7	12.2	26.9

[1]See footnote 4, Table 1. [2]The April 1, 1990, estimates base (248,790,925) includes count resolution corrections processed through August 1997. It generally does not include adjustments for census coverage errors. However, it includes adjustments estimated for the 1995 Test Census in various localities in California, New Jersey, and Louisiana; and the 1999 census dress rehearsals in localities in California and Wisconsin. These adjustments amounted to a total of 81,052 persons. [3]These 2000 figures do not reflect the results of the 2000 census. [4]Based on middle series of assumptions. See footnote 1, Table 3.
Source: U.S. Census, Statistical Abstract Section 1: Population (2001), 17.

FIGURE 5.3   Statistical Abstract College Enrollment Chart for Practice Activity 5.1.

No. 280. College Enrollment by Sex, Age, Race, and Hispanic Origin: 1980 to 2001

[In thousands (11,387 represents 11,387,000). As of October for the civilian noninstitutional population, 14 years old and over. Based on the Current Population Survey; see text, Section 1, and Appendix III.]

Characteristic	1980	1985	1990[1]	1994	1995	1996	1997	1998	1999	2000	2001
Total[2].................	11,387	12,524	13,621	15,022	14,715	15,226	15,436	15,546	15,203	15,314	15,873
Male[3].................	5,430	5,906	6,192	6,764	6,703	6,820	6,843	6,905	6,956	6,682	6,875
18 to 24 years	3,604	3,749	3,922	4,152	4,089	4,187	4,374	4,403	4,397	4,342	4,437
25 to 34 years	1,325	1,464	1,412	1,589	1,561	1,523	1,509	1,500	1,458	1,361	1,476
35 and over	405	561	772	958	985	1,013	899	953	1,024	918	908
Female[3].............	5,957	6,618	7,429	8,258	8,013	8,406	8,593	8,641	8,247	8,631	8,998
18 to 24 years	3,625	3,788	4,042	4,576	4,452	4,582	4,829	4,919	4,863	5,109	5,192
25 to 34 years	1,378	1,599	1,749	1,830	1,788	1,920	1,760	1,915	1,637	1,846	1,946
35 and over	802	1,100	1,546	1,766	1,684	1,765	1,892	1,732	1,675	1,589	1,776

FIGURE 5.3 (Continued)

White[3]	9,925	10,781	11,488	12,222	12,021	12,189	12,442	12,401	12,053	11,999	12,208
18 to 24 years	6,334	6,500	6,635	7,118	7,011	7,123	7,495	7,541	7,446	7,566	7,548
25 to 34 years	2,328	2,604	2,698	2,735	2,686	2,644	2,522	2,568	2,345	2,339	2,469
35 and over	1,051	1,448	2,023	2,267	2,208	2,254	2,297	2,199	2,174	1,978	2,103
Male	4,804	5,103	5,235	5,524	5,535	5,453	5,552	5,602	5,562	5,311	5,383
Female	5,121	5,679	6,253	6,698	6,486	6,735	6,890	6,799	6,491	6,689	6,826
Black[3]	1,163	1,263	1,393	1,800	1,772	1,901	1,903	2,016	1,998	2,164	2,230
18 to 24 years	688	734	894	1,001	988	983	1,085	1,115	1,146	1,216	1,206
25 to 34 years	289	295	258	440	426	519	423	539	453	567	562
35 and over	156	213	207	323	334	354	372	340	354	361	429
Male	476	552	587	745	710	764	723	770	833	815	781
Female	686	712	807	1,054	1,062	1,136	1,180	1,247	1,164	1,349	1,449
Hispanic origin[3,4]	443	580	748	1,187	1,207	1,223	1,260	1,363	1,307	1,426	1,700
18 to 24 years	315	375	435	662	745	706	806	820	740	899	1,035
25 to 34 years	118	189	168	312	250	310	254	336	334	309	392
35 and over	(NA)	(NA)	130	205	193	184	151	198	226	195	260
Male	222	279	364	529	568	529	555	550	568	619	731
Female	221	299	384	659	639	693	704	814	739	807	969

NA Not available. [1]Beginning 1990, based on a revised edit and tabulation package. [2]Includes other races not shown separately. [3]Includes persons 14 to 17 years old, not shown separately. [4]Persons of Hispanic origin may be of any race.

Source: U.S. Census Bureau, Statistical Abstract, Section 4: Education, (2003), 39.

DATA ANALYSIS

If you understand different kinds of numbers, you have already taken the first step in data analysis. The mathematical science of data analysis is statistics, and good statisticians can use their skills in data analysis for everything from playing poker to determining how many fish live in the sea. But the statistician's precise formulae are ultimately based on a commonsensical understanding of how numbers work—basic analysis that even non-specialists can perform. Analyzing numbers is similar to analyzing other forms of data. You're still attending to details, looking for patterns, considering the context, making an interpretative leap, considering alternative explanations, and acknowledging the limits, but there are also some specific strategies you can use when analyzing numerical data. What follows are a few suggestions for how to analyze numerical data, and then an example that illustrates some of these ideas.

- *Plot the data.* Visual representations give you a better "feel" for relationships than just looking at numbers. They are good for you as a researcher as well as for your readers, so plot your data early in the writing process as a way to discover ideas about it. Bar graphs are often useful, and you can supplement them with line graphs if you are charting the "spread" of a single variable. You can build these effortlessly if you have recorded your data in a spreadsheet program such as Excel, though not all spreadsheet programs include chart wizards.[5] Note that at this stage you are just sensing the texture for your data, so look at a variety of charts or graphs just to see what it looks like and to see if you notice anything interesting. This is a good chance to experiment with the chart wizard because you will learn more about how to make charts and you will get to see your data from a few different perspectives.

- *Figure out central tendencies.*   This includes figuring out the mean, the median, and the mode. Knowing the center point of your data (or its central points) can give you a focus. When you compare different sets of data, it is especially useful to compare their central tendencies. Often the *differences* among these measures are themselves instructive. If the mean and the mode are significantly different, for instance, ask yourself why.

- *Look for changes over time.*   If you are dealing with data sets that measure something at different points in time, changes in these data can often suggest trends. Figure out growth or decline in certain raw numbers, and use these as the basis for determining percentage changes. Look for changes in similar factors or, especially, in the *underlying* data set. A growing number of college attendees is only meaningful when compared with the growth in the overall population, for instance. In the National Endowment for the Arts "Trends in Literature Participation" what at first looks like a *growth* in the number of literary readers in fact is revealed as a *decline* in the percentage of literary readers when compared with the growth in the overall population. Make sure that you compare apples to apples when looking for changes over time. For instance it is only useful to compare an opinion survey from 1990 with one in 2000 if the exact same questions were used and the researchers were consistent in selecting their data sample.

- *Compare individual factors.*   Sometimes you can supplement generalizations about data by comparing individual factors. Sometimes, you need to compare these individual factors before making any useful generalizations. Always, paying careful attention to a variety of unique factors will help you to develop a better grasp of complexities. Imagine, for instance, that you are comparing "educational achievement" for different ethnic groups in the United States between 1985 and 2005. There are many different individual factors that help to reveal educational achievement: high school graduation, college attendance, college attendance by institution type, degrees conferred, average time for completion of degree, literacy rates, field of study, and others. To build a complete picture, compare each of these individual factors. Keep your eye open for any striking, unusual, or "counterintuitive" data you come across. Counterintuitive data are observations that go against common assumptions, and these are always interesting to note and consider.

- *Group factors.*   Sometimes, in addition to comparing individual factors, you can group these factors together and compare the groups. For instance, you may have

---

[5]Statisticians use other kinds of graphics to help them see characteristics of or relationships between data sets. Stem and leaf diagrams and box plots are good for getting a visual overview of particular data sets, and scatter plots are good for "seeing" correlations between variables. For directions on stem and leaf plots, dot plots, box and whisker plots, and histograms (as well as an introduction, not included here, to data types), see the "Data Display and Summary Chapter" in *Statistics at Square One* (http://bmj.bmjjournals.com/collections/statsbk/1.shtml).

figures for earned degrees in a variety of specific fields (biology, engineering, history, chemistry, philosophy, etc.) and want to group them by field—sciences and liberal arts—for the purpose of comparison. Use your imagination and your common sense when grouping factors.

- **Look for correlations.** Researchers who conduct surveys or experiments are looking for some kind of correlation between variables. Statisticians have some pretty nifty tests that allow them to measure correlations quite precisely. As a beginning researcher, though, you can rely on "eyeballing" the data to find some kinds of correlations. Correlations, broadly, establish links between certain data. If, as the number of earned college degrees rises, income in a group also rises, there is a correlation between the two factors. *Correlation does not itself demonstrate cause.* Perhaps increased college attendance is a result of higher income, rather than the other way around. Or there may be a third factor (or set of factors) that is the cause of both income and college degrees rising. Correlations do establish a link, but researchers understand that establishing a link is only the first step in explaining why. So, finding correlations is an occasion for further research. If you see something interesting as you analyze your data, ask what might explain what you've noticed and search for correlations. If, for instance, you notice that violent crime declined in a particular city throughout the 1990s and then rose again starting in 2000, you might reasonably ask what factors might have played into the decline and rise. Were there economic changes? Were new handgun laws passed? Did the police initiate new policies? Was there a different federal response to crime? Each of these guesses will require you to turn to other records for data that lets you confirm or reject your imagined correlation. Try not to settle on one factor, even once you believe you have found a correlation; instead compare a variety of possibilities, and always remain open to discovering that your assumptions need to be modified.

DATA ANALYSIS EXAMPLE: A SURVEY OF STUDENTS ATTENDING LARGE AND SMALL SCHOOLS

Imagine the data presented in Tables 5.5 and 5.6 represent summaries from a survey a student, Juana, constructed measuring satisfaction of students attending schools of different sizes. Juana had respondents rank their level of satisfaction for each item (library, cafeteria, etc.) on a Likert scale, with responses from 1–5 indicating low to high levels of satisfaction.[6] Let's look at how Juana could use some of the data analysis strategies we've been discussing to examine these scores.

Figure out Central Tendencies. Using the scaled data (from the Likert scale), Juana finds the mean adjusted score by multiplying the total number of responses within each category by the value of that category (1 for "very unsatisfied" and up to 5 for "very satisfied"), adding those numbers, and then dividing by the total number of responses. This is presented in the chart as the "Satisfaction Index." The Adjusted Response Score in the chart finds the mean for each category (question). These scores are useful for thinking about ranking the data and also for comparing categories. The median score in each example is the score in the middle. In the first table, there are a

---

[6]Note that the survey and the data are fictitious and have been presented only to illustrate the ideas that follow.

TABLE 5.5 Frequency of Responses from Large University Attendees to Questions about Satisfaction with College Experience, Imaginary Data

(*N = 20*)

Likert Scale Ranking Likert Scale Value	Very Unsatisfied 1	Unsatisfied 2	Neutral 3	Satisfied 4	Very Satisfied 5	# Response	Adjusted Response Score
Library	2	4	8	2	4	20	3.1
Cafeteria	8	6	4	1	1	20	2.05
Professors' knowledge	0	3	4	9	4	20	3.7
Entertainment options	1	1	4	8	6	20	3.85
Amount you learned	0	1	5	6	8	20	4.05
Contact w/ professors	0	6	6	2	6	20	3.4
Clubs/organizations	0	2	6	7	5	20	3.75
Classrooms	0	2	12	4	2	20	3.3
Campus environment	1	3	6	5	5	20	3.5
Classmates	2	3	4	4	7	20	3.55
Total	**14**	**31**	**59**	**48**	**48**	**200**	
Percentage	0.07	0.155	0.295	0.24	0.24		
Average							**3.425**

Satisfaction Index	**3.425**
(mean adjusted response score)	
Median	3
Mode	3

total of two hundred scores, so there is no score exactly in the middle. In such cases, the median is the mean of the two middlemost scores. In this chart, both of these scores (the 100th and the 101st) are 3, so their average is also 3. The mode is the number that appears most frequently. In Table 5.5, the mode is 3 because people responded with the score of 3 more often than with any other score. When you figure out central tendencies, you can compare the two groups (noting, for instance, that the satisfaction index is higher for small school attendees than for large school attendees). You can also consider what this information might tell you about each group.

Compare Individual Factors.   Based on an analysis of central tendencies, Juana may be able to conclude that small school attendees score higher on her satisfaction index than large school attendees. But do the data reveal anything more? Can she observe reasons why this may be true, or discover any other interesting information?

She can rank her factors. Which area scored highest within each of the groups? How do the individual scores differ for each of these? In what areas are small schools strongest? What about large schools? Where is each weakest? What area or areas account for the biggest differences between them?

TABLE 5.6 Frequency of Responses from Small College Attendees to Questions About Satisfaction with College Experience, Imaginary Data

(N = 25)

Likert Scale Ranking Likert Scale Values	Very Unsatisfied *1*	Unsatisfied *2*	Neutral *3*	Satisfied *4*	Very Satisfied *5*	# Response	Adjusted Response Score
Library	2	2	8	6	7	25	3.56
Cafeteria	8	7	3	2	5	25	2.56
Professors' knowledge	0	3	4	8	10	25	4
Entertainment options	1	2	5	8	9	25	3.88
Amount you learned	0	2	5	8	10	25	4.04
Contact w/ professors	0	4	5	4	12	25	3.96
Clubs/organizations	2	4	7	7	5	25	3.36
Classrooms	0	2	15	6	2	25	3.32
Campus environment	3	3	6	6	7	25	3.44
Classmates	3	2	5	6	9	25	3.64
Total	**19**	**31**	**63**	**61**	**76**	250	
Percentage	0.076	0.124	0.252	0.244	0.304		
Average							**3.576**

Satisfaction Index (mean adjusted response score)	**3.576**
Median	4
Mode	5

In general, although she has set out to make a particular set of observations, Juana should remain open to the possibility that she will discover something interesting she had not been looking for. In this data set, for instance, the most highly ranked item for each group is the amount they learned, and these scores are nearly identical for both the small school and large school groups. So, if this survey reflects reality, individuals who are most interested in learning will likely find equal satisfaction in both small and large schools, and that level of satisfaction is likely to be high.

Group Factors. Juana has broken her broad categories down into more specific questions. For example, instead of just asking about facilities, she asked questions about the cafeteria, the library, and classrooms. She knows that in doing so she has weighted the survey so the broad category of "facilities" influences the satisfaction index more than the broad category "professors," since there are two questions that are directly about professors. If Juana wanted to, she could double the value of the two questions about professors in order to increase its rating in her index, or she could combine the facilities scores into one average in order to minimize the effects of this category. Since it is usually easier to decide on weightings for various categories and plan the appropriate number of questions than to calculate weighting formulas after the questions have been asked, it's important to consider such issues as you design your survey.

In addition to working with these weightings, Juana can simply group these broad categories together and see if anything interesting appears. For instance, she might ask if they are consistently rated high or low in one or the other group. Or she might ask if one particular item within that group had a greater impact on the overall group score than another.

Juana can also regroup items. Under one set of groupings, she might have "facilities," "professors," and "students" as three exclusive groups. In this case, libraries, cafeteria, and classrooms would all go under "facilities." But she might also have another set of groupings that includes "academics" and "extracurriculars." In this case, libraries and classrooms would be part of "academics," while cafeteria would be in the "extracurricular" category. When she writes her report, Juana may want to present comparative scores for these groupings.

Look for Correlation. In the broadest sense, Juana wants to know if attending one type of school correlates with a higher level of satisfaction. Her different satisfaction index scores seem to indicate a correlation between attending small schools and being satisfied with the college experience.[7]

Juana can look for correlations in her other data as well—places where certain factors seem to be grouped or go together, where increases in one score are mirrored by increases in another. If she is attuned to relationships among factors, Juana may be able to "eyeball" some of the important correlations.

PRACTICE ACTIVITY 5-2

Data Analysis

Using the data in the Tables 5.5 and 5.6, answer the following questions. (Remember that the data are "invented" and do not represent real answers to a real survey.)

1. Look at the satisfaction index (mean), median, and mode for each group. What do you notice about these numbers? What do these numbers suggest about the responses?

2. Rank the responses in each group from highest adjusted response score to lowest and compare them. What are the highest three factors in each? What are the lowest? What can you conclude from these rankings?

3. Looking over all the adjusted response scores, what factors most account for differences between the groups? If you were giving advice to someone who was trying to decide between a large and a small school, what would you tell them based on this information?

---

[7]Many researchers would be more careful about this claim. They would say that there is a correlation between attending a small school and scoring high on the satisfaction index. Although they hope that the satisfaction index measures something real called "satisfaction," they realize that the relationship between measures and the reality to which they refer is not always incontrovertible. Who is to say, for instance, that students' opinion of their professors' knowledge has any real impact on their sense of satisfaction? And more broadly, different people will be satisfied by different things, so Juana's measure may not end up measuring real satisfaction at all, but only certain factors that she has decided are important.

PART II: COLLECTING YOUR OWN NUMBERS: SURVEYS

In the previous section we introduced you to Juana, a fictional undergraduate student who is interested in whether the size of the school changes how satisfied students are with their college experience. In that section we provided the summarized results of her survey and suggested ways she might analyze the responses she had collected. But the process of arriving at those numbers is an extensive and fascinating inquiry method itself: constructing and conducting surveys. You may use an informal survey as part of a broader project, or you may construct a more formal survey, along the lines of what Juana has completed, as the focal point of your research. Below you will find recommended steps for conducting a survey. But before you conduct a survey, you should have some idea of what kinds of questions surveys can and cannot answer.

Because surveys attempt to discover reliable statistical data about a particular group rather than detailed information about individuals, surveys are useful when the inquiry question is about human attitudes, thoughts, or behavior or when the issue is whether there is a relationship between two factors (e.g., reading behavior and level of education). Surveys cannot, however, establish a causal relationship between the factors or provide detailed illustrations of individual experiences.[8] A survey will not answer the question "Was the second Iraq war a good idea?" But good survey research can examine attitudes among students about the war and might answer a research question like: "What do students at my college think about the war in Iraq?"

If we sought to know if female plumbers tended to earn less than male plumbers, a survey probably would be the best way to answer the question. If we discovered (perhaps as a result of our survey) that female plumbers tended to earn more than male plumbers, we might want to know why, but we would then need to turn to case studies to provide the kinds of in-depth information about multiple causes and effects because no survey could provide us with such insight. Methods of investigation can be combined of course, so long as there are enough time and resources to do so; surveys are often combined with focused interviews of individuals to provide more detailed information. When reading social scientific arguments, it is important to ask if the researchers' methods are appropriate for the kinds of conclusions they draw.

Like experiments that involve people or other phenomena, surveys test the effect of an independent variable on a dependent variable. However, in experiments, the researcher manipulates this independent variable directly. For instance, in a psychological experiment, the psychologist might change the color of a room (independent variable) to test the effect of this change on people's moods (dependent variable). Surveys define variables, for instance, sex or income level, but the investigator does not control these. When conducting surveys, researchers do not perform a sex change on their subjects to see how this affects their income, nor do they control the amount of money their subjects receive. Such limitations mean that researchers must take care in selecting the

---

[8]In contrast to surveys, case studies provide an in-depth perspective on a member or a few members of a group rather than on the group more generally. In the social sciences, an individual member of a particular group is often referred to as a "case." A case can be a person, if people are the basic unit of measure, but it can also be a family, group, or organization. In a study that compares the income of men to women, each person is a case. In a study that compares household income in rural to urban areas, each household is a case. In this second example, case studies would provide an in-depth exploration of particular households, listing their members, how much each member earns, their jobs, and so forth. A survey, or "case-classificatory" research, on the other hand, would probably seek to determine if there are general differences between the household income of city folk and country folk.

group to survey—the sample—in order to be certain that a fair distribution of cases (or individuals) across variables (or categories) is included. If you want to investigate sex differences in income, for example, you would have to be sure that your sample included both men and women to survey.[9] In our earlier example, because Juana wanted to know whether people who attend large schools or small schools have more satisfactory experiences, she had to interview people who attended different kinds of schools to get a distribution of cases (people who attended college) across her categories (type of college attended).

Even if Juana were only interested in people who attended large schools, she would do better to compare their degree of satisfaction to some other group. Why? For one, people's responses to questions on attitude or opinion surveys can vary by twenty percent with small changes in wording. Furthermore, single variables often only reflect arbitrary cutoff points. Imagine Juana distributes a "degree of satisfaction" questionnaire only to people who attended large schools and establishes a 100-point scale. She sorts her responses into "high" (85–100), "medium" (16–84), and "low" (0–15), and discovers that seventy-five percent of respondents were "highly satisfied." The results would not tell us how highly satisfied people really were because Juana could just as easily have established 75 or 90 as her cutoff, and come up with very different results.

Be especially wary of single variable findings that imply a comparison. If you read that American students today are ignorant of geography since only ten percent can find their state capital on the map, ask what percentage of Americans fifty years ago could. If there is no measure, then the ten percent number is basically meaningless as a comparison, and no conclusions should be trusted. This is not to say that this ten percent number might not be meaningful itself—perhaps it would be good if more than ten percent of our citizens could find their state capital. It is to say that this number tells us nothing about education today as compared with some other time; nor does it tell us anything about Americans' geographic knowledge compared with that of citizens of other countries.

Do not investigate a question whose answer you can find through other means. You do not need a survey to find out "What electronic resources are available in the library to help students complete research?" But a survey might be useful in determining "What electronic resources do communication majors at my university tend to use most when completing research projects?" or "In what ways do first–year students use the library?" Good questions seek either to discover something or to test a hypothesis, not prove a predetermined point. You may go into your research project wanting to show that students who smoke just don't understand how bad it is for them. However, you should formulate your project to test that hypothesis objectively, and here is where the value of comparisons comes into play. You might ask, "How knowledgeable are smokers compared to nonsmokers about various physical consequences of smoking?"

When conducting surveys, you may end up collecting your data through interviews or through questionnaires. If you have read the chapter on interviews in this book, you should be aware that the survey interview is a different kind of creature from the journalistic or ethnographic interview. In these latter cases, you use the interview as an opportunity to explore a number of different issues, to gain understanding, to engage your subject in conversation. As an interviewer, flexibility is one of your goals. When you conduct interviews as part of a survey, however, you do not want to modify the responses you receive by

---

[9]Selecting a sample can be a complex undertaking, and entire, indeed quite fat, books have been written about techniques for selecting samples effectively. We discuss some of the issues involved later, but understand that sample selection is perhaps the least-well addressed topic in this chapter.

changing the questions you ask or the kind of feedback you give. Develop a script and stick to it, asking the same sets of questions in the same order, using the same wording.

STEPS FOR CONDUCTING A SURVEY

There are considerations at each stage of surveying. We can cover some of them, remembering that any one of these stages of survey research has spawned books and even lifetimes of study. The fundamental issue for researchers who design and conduct their own surveys is making certain the questions asked lead to consistent, reliable, and valid data.

Determine the Research Questions   The first step in developing a survey is determining what you want to find out. As we pointed out earlier, not all research questions lend themselves to surveys, but the assignments we provide in this book that ask you to conduct a survey jump-start the process by presupposing an area of investigation that is susceptible to survey methodology. Still, developing more specific research questions involves some background reading or research. At the very least, a preliminary search of already published research—what researchers often call a "review of the literature"—will help you to determine whether researchers have previously attempted to answer a similar question, or conducted a survey that might serve as a model for your own confirming (or disputing) study. To find such previous studies, consult your library's databases and search using relevant key terms. Once you find a study that seems relevant to your work, look at the descriptors that are attached to that study so you can consider refining your search. Use the abstracts to get an overview of the study so that you can select the most relevant studies to read more carefully. Finally look up any reference that seems pertinent to your work, especially if a particular researcher or a particular study is sited repeatedly.

For example Juana's proposed study of satisfaction among students who attend schools of different size begins with a search of a database such as Academic Search Elite. Using the key term "college satisfaction," Juana finds five articles, two of which seem related to her interest: "An Investigation of Broad and Narrow Personality Traits in Relation to General and Domain-Specific Life Satisfaction of College Students" by Lounsbury et al. and "Achievement motivation and college satisfaction in traditional and nontraditional students" by Donahue et al. The list of subject terms for these two articles lead Juana to refine her search to "satisfaction and college students" as subject terms rather than general terms, and this search produces thirty-nine articles. Even without reading all these studies, Juana can discern from the titles and abstracts that other factors—including students' classification as traditional or nontraditional, parental attitudes, sleep length, and emotional awareness—might influence student satisfaction. Juana might then decide to modify her survey to include a question about age when attending college in order to sort out those who researchers would categorize as traditional (ages seventeen to twenty-four) from nontraditional (twenty-five and older).

Define Variables   Defining variables is an important and easily overlooked part of the survey process. It involves something researchers sometimes call "operationalizing" their ideas. That's a fancy way of saying that a researcher might have a pretty clear research question, but still must develop measures that will be highly reliable, with clear objective definitions.

Let's take Juana's seemingly simple question: Were people who attended small colleges or large universities more satisfied with their experiences? There are two parts of the first variable here: the people who attended school and the type of school they attended. (The second variable is level of satisfaction.)

Juana should first think about that first variable: People who attended school. "People" is easy enough, especially once she's learned that previous researchers have already determined that the age of college attendance makes a difference in satisfaction. What does it mean, though, to "attend" a school? Would spending a single semester, or even part of a single semester count? Does she want to limit her study to people who graduated from a particular kind of school? What will she do with people who attended one type of school first and then another? What about people who ended up at one kind of school even though their first choice was another, or who decided to go to one type of school for a couple of years, such as a junior college, with the intention of transferring to a different kind? Should she treat all these different kinds of attendance differently? At the same time, Juana does not want to make her system so complicated that completing the survey becomes impossible, and "operationalizing" the second part of the variable—school—promises to add more complexity.

There are some obvious problems with defining "type of school" in terms of size. What counts as a small school and what counts as a large one? It's possible that Juana is using "size" when she really is interested in local schools (such as community colleges) versus ones that are farther away. Or she may be substituting size for the difference between a liberal arts college with a primary interest in teaching undergraduates and a research university where graduate programs and professorial research can take precedence over undergraduate instruction. Even if size really is the issue Juana is concerned about, would it be legitimate to define the cutoff in terms of student body size (five thousand students, ten thousand students), or should she measure size by the number of departments or majors offered? Whichever measure she decides on, should she predetermine the cutoffs (so that up to five thousand students is small, but more than ten thousand is large) or should she let respondents say whether the school they attended was large or small without defining this term? How would she deal (or expect her responders to deal) with the small branch campus of a large state university?

In other words Juana has considerable work to do defining her variables. She wants to develop variables that will be reliable, and she wants to think about their validity—that is, whether they will measure the things she wants to measure—as she develops these reliable definitions.

Define Sample (Population)   Surveys (such as a census) can involve an entire population. Unless the population of interest is small, it usually is not possible to survey everyone. Juana, for example, cannot possibly ask all the people who ever attended any institution of higher learning about their experiences, but a researcher interested in which campus events students on a particular floor of a dorm are attending might be able to survey the entire targeted population. Because most research involves larger populations, however, researchers have developed strategies for surveying a sample and extrapolating the data to the whole population. The political polls you see tracking candidates or officeholders always involve a relatively small sample of the population, making claims about what Americans think about the presidential candidates based on the opinions of relatively few people. Likewise the famous Nielsen Rating of television viewing is based on a sample of viewers rather than a direct count of everyone.

You probably do not have the background or resources to generate a sample in the same way experienced social scientists do, but you should try to take a few precautions that will increase the reliability of your data. First, try to make sure your sample is chosen at random. Juana will not have a random sample if she surveys only members of her family, and if she distributes her survey outside a local grocery store she'll probably have a more reliable survey than if she distributes her survey at a café popular with students from the local community college.

Second, to the extent possible, know the nonrandom limits that are naturally placed on your sample, and restrict your research question, and your claims, accordingly. For instance Juana will be interviewing people in her local area, an ethnically and racially diverse small town in the middle of an agricultural area. She recognizes that her claims may be valid for "people who come from small towns," but may not be applicable to the broader population, to city folk, or to children of farmers. When she reports her results, she will be careful to provide the information about who she surveyed just as Kenneth Rosina does in his essay "Satisfaction among First–Year University of Miami Students" which we've included at the end of this chapter. Sometimes small scale surveys can still be interesting and instructive. Rosina's study, for example, included only "35 students, 21 male and 14 female" and all were first-year students at the University of Miami. The problem occurs when researchers overreach, making claims that are larger than their sample can support. A student who conducts a survey of students in one dorm and gets only a few responses will probably recognize that the results can't be generalized to college students in the United States, but it may be easy to miss that the sample also doesn't allow claims about all students on the particular campus (because not all students live in the dorms), or even about all of the residential housing system (because not all buildings were included in the sample). We think this problem of overreaching, allowing for alternative interpretations of the data, and acknowledging the limits of your work is a central feature of making meaning from survey data, and so we'll have more to say about this later in the chapter in the section on Writing from Numbers.

As you develop your own surveys, you should be conscientious in these ways, as well. Often the people you will have immediate access to are other college students—a group that is usually close to the same age and income level. Make sure you are aware of the characteristics of your sample as you develop your research. At this stage try to be as specific as you can about the people you will survey and write out a plan for defining and gathering information (e.g., "Will request interviews from every woman who enters or leaves library until I have forty interviews," or "Will distribute questionnaires to all residents of my floor and the floors above and below"). Letting others critique your plan in advance is a way of checking on what you might be overlooking and gives you the chance to refine your plan before you spend time surveying irresponsibly.

Develop Questions for Polling (Interview Protocol) or Questionnaire   How researchers question people is another area where reliability comes into play. First, recognize that there is a difference between polls (survey interviews) and questionnaires, which are forms you would distribute and then ask people to fill out and return. Longer sets of questions are better handled in questionnaires, but if you distribute questionnaires, many of them will never be returned. Polls are more time intensive but usually get a better return rate. If you conduct a survey, you will have to think through which of these methods is right for you. If you decide on a questionnaire, try to make it as easy as possible for people both to fill out the questionnaire and return it. **DO NOT** simply spam a bunch of people with an unsolicited e-mail survey. If you want to try to conduct a survey over e-mail, make contact first through other means and have people "opt in" by giving you their e-mail addresses.

Figure 5.4 provides some general guidelines to follow when developing questions.

FIGURE 5.4 General Guidelines for Developing Survey Questions

- ***Collect information important to your variable (comparison) first***. In doing so, be sure to define the options clearly for your interviewees. Juana does not want to have collected lots of rich data about how satisfied respondents were with their college experience and then discover that she forgot to find out what kind of school they attended.

- ***Make sure the wording is clear and simple***. Test your questions on a few people and ask them how they interpret the questions and if any of the questions are confusing. Part of making the wording clear and simple is being sure your questions only ask one thing at a time. Thus, you can't ask such questions as: "the teachers at the school I attended were well prepared and available to help me" or "I took advantage of the numerous opportunities to get involved in nonacademic activities." In the first question, there clearly are two different issues about teachers that need to be separated into two questions. In the second question, the respondents are being asked simultaneously about their involvement in nonacademic activities and whether there were a number of such activities.

- ***Ask the same questions at different points, in both a positive and negative form***. There is a tendency for people to answer yes aimlessly or to fill in "highly satisfied" or make similar moves when filling out questionnaires or responding to polls. Try to correct for this tendency by asking for the same information twice, once in an affirmative and once in a negative form. For example, Juana might ask at one point, "Did you find your experience at the college you attended satisfactory?" and then at another, "Were you dissatisfied with the experience at the college you attended?" When she analyzes her data, she will be able to check for a correlation in similar questions as a measure of overall reliability of the responses.

- ***Avoid the overlong poll or questionnaire***. Define a few variables clearly and try to be efficient in your questionnaire. This advice may seem to contradict some of the other suggestions (such as asking for the same information more than once and being sure to spread it out), but you want to aim for appropriate balance.

- ***Consider how to ask questions and record responses in relation to the kind of analysis you will perform***. You might ask open-ended questions. If you do this, you will get complex responses that often reveal subtleties in people's attitudes, but will have a hard time "operationalizing" the responses with reference to your variables. If Juana asks, "How would you describe your level of satisfaction with the school you attended?" she is likely to get a wide variety of interesting responses, but she will have a difficult time sorting reliably. Many researchers prefer some sort of closed response or prefer to mix response types. If Juana asks a yes or no question, such as, "Were you satisfied with your college experience?" she is more likely to get responses she can sort effectively. Even here, though, she will likely get some vague responses that she will need to edit (see comments about the editing step below). She might instead include check boxes with "Yes" and "No" columns. This will minimize the amount of editing she has to do, but for certain kinds of questions it will decrease the reliability of the survey. People who have no opinion on a particular issue will either have to check a box they do not fully agree with, leave the question blank, or pencil in an alternative in the margins, and any of these options can cause problems when Juana begins to analyze the data. To avoid such confusion when measuring attitudes many researchers prefer to use the Likert Scale, which asks respondents to rank attitudes from strongly agree to strongly disagree on a five-point scale. Thus Juana might ask for responses to the statement, "I was satisfied with the education I received in my first year of college" and have people respond between 1 and 5.

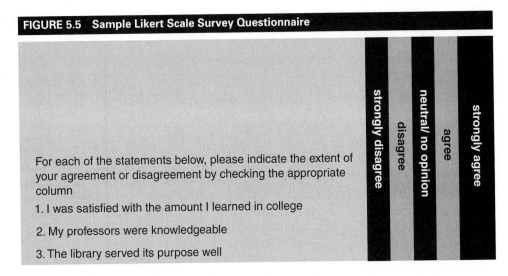

FIGURE 5.5 Sample Likert Scale Survey Questionnaire

For each of the statements below, please indicate the extent of your agreement or disagreement by checking the appropriate column

	strongly disagree	disagree	neutral/ no opinion	agree	strongly agree
1. I was satisfied with the amount I learned in college					
2. My professors were knowledgeable					
3. The library served its purpose well					

If you use a Likert Scale, make sure to be clear about which number corresponds to strongly agree and which to strongly disagree. It is usually best if you can provide check boxes in columns, as in Figure 5.5. Also, when using the Likert scale, you will usually, instead of asking questions, make statements and request that respondents mark their level of agreement, or something similar (e.g., "rate your level of satisfaction with the library"). You have many options: determine the kinds of questions to ask based on the kind of information you seek and the kind of analysis you plan to perform. Sometimes you will collect factual information, sometimes you will seek yes or no answers, and sometimes you will be measuring attitudes or opinions.

Pilot the Survey   Researchers usually like to pilot a survey with a small group in order to flush out unforeseen problems. Having invested a great deal of time, effort, and often money into the survey, they do not want to discover, once they are out of funds, that respondents did not understand a crucial question or discover that they had not defined an important variable clearly enough. Piloting the survey gives researchers the opportunity to work out the kinks and clarify their research operations.

You may or may not have the chance to pilot your survey with a small group, but if you conduct a survey, you should develop some method for testing it, including testing your interview protocol or questionnaire, at least by showing it to group members or a classmate or roommate.

Adjust   Obviously the point of piloting the survey is to adjust it to correct problems. If you run a small pilot, think carefully about the implications of problems you may have encountered. You may not need any changes, or you may need to make some adjustments to the wording of questions or the way you approach subjects. Furthermore it is not too late, at this point, to revise your research question so it better accords with the information you believe you will be able to obtain.

Conduct Survey   This step may seem obvious, and much of it is. By the time researchers conduct their survey, they have their questionnaire or interview protocol prepared, know their sample and how to reach them, and have thought through their variables and their research question from several angles. One thing researchers want to do at this point is make sure they have a mechanism for keeping track of the preparation, distribution, and return of questionnaires, for the kinds of external records they will keep on respondents. Once the survey has been distributed, it is not appropriate to expand to include a larger sample if the return rate is low. Because return rates are greatly increased when researchers follow up with respondents and because researchers often work in teams when conducting surveys, they need to have a procedure that each of the researchers will use for following up with people who have received questionnaires but haven't responded. Even if a researcher is working independently, she needs a system for keeping records of these follow-ups. Clear records are also important when the time comes to analyze the data. Perhaps you will distribute your surveys in envelopes. You can number the envelopes (instead of putting names on them) and keep separate sheets (of paper or in a spreadsheet program) where you record and check off who you have distributed surveys to (e.g., by matching names with the number on the envelope), who has returned them, who you have followed up with, and who has responded to your follow-up. If you cannot afford envelopes, instructing respondents to staple questionnaires and return them (perhaps by sliding them under a dorm door) can be effective. Know that the more effort you ask of respondents, even seemingly simple effort, the lower the response rate will be. Plan carefully to make the process easy for your respondents and efficient for you.

It is also important to let your respondents know that you will not share personal information with anyone. (See the Ethical Considerations section for more details.) You should include a statement about respondents' anonymity prominently on the questionnaire, or include it early in the interview protocol you write up. Remember, if you guarantee anonymity, you are legally bound to preserve it.

Analyze Results   The last step in the survey involves analysis of survey data. Review Part I of this chapter for suggestions on Data Analysis. When you conduct your own survey, a couple of steps, which you may conduct simultaneously, will intervene before you can begin this actual analysis.

For one, you will have to record the data. You will probably have a stack of questionnaires or interview records, and will need to tabulate all the data on another sheet of paper or in spreadsheets. As you engage in this process, you will probably also notice the need to edit your data. Some surveys will be incomplete; some of the answers people provided will be nonsensical or illegible. There will likely be a certain number of surveys that you simply cannot use. When researchers use open-ended questions, they discover that they have many judgment calls to make and must develop strategies to make sure that they are consistent when recording results. For instance, if Juana is recording experiences as either satisfactory or unsatisfactory, and she asks the question "Were you satisfied with your college experience?" what is she to do when she receives this response, "Well, I enjoyed the time I spent in school but believe the education I received could have been better"? Juana will need to develop a clear operational definition of "satisfied" to mean, perhaps, "indicated appreciation or enjoyment of at least one major aspect of college experience, including social life, quality of instruction, or quality of learning." Under this definition, the ambiguous response given earlier above would count as "satisfied." She can continue to develop this definition as she sorts through her results, but she wants to be sure to apply it consistently and use it as a guide for sorting ambiguous responses.

Juana could just as easily develop an operational definition that ranked the ambiguous response as "not satisfied." Ultimately, though, if she has constructed her survey and her analytical measures well, which group the response was sorted into would not matter so much as the fact that she had a clear definition that reliably, that is consistently, sorted similar responses. This is another important reason why, as was mentioned at the beginning of the chapter, studies should use more than one variable and compare them. Significance comes from comparing the responses, not (in many cases, at least) in raw measures of a particular response. However the cases are sorted, so long as they are done so reliably, Juana will still be able to gauge which group experienced a greater degree of satisfaction with the college experience.

A second step inherent in analyzing your data is deciding how to present it. As we pointed out earlier, raw numbers are rarely the most useful or meaningful way to present the numbers. As you work with the data you've collected, you may well find that its significance becomes clearer to you as you represent it differently.

ETHICAL CONSIDERATIONS

Researchers have different kinds of ethical responsibilities depending on the kinds of research they conduct. If you are dealing with data that others have collected, you will have to consider carefully what these numbers do and do not represent, what they can and cannot portray. Should you conduct your own survey, you have added responsibilities in protecting your respondents' identities and respecting them as people.

When you make claims about survey data in your writing, you should remain aware that an opinion or attitude survey is never a direct reflection of reality, but rather that it measures something you hope approximates a reality. Consider the example of Juana, who after conducting a survey about what former students from large and small colleges thought about their experiences, developed a "satisfaction index" averaging the tallies from a five-point scale for different factors. There may be a real difference between how people from large and small schools score on her measure, and so the measure measures something, but exactly what it measures is not entirely clear. (The measure is reliable— that is, consistent, but the question of validity always remains, to some degree, open.) So in reporting her data, Juana will probably want to qualify her claims about what kind of college a person should attend. She might say something like, "The survey seems to indicate that people who value academics and relationships with their professors are likely to have a better experience at a small school." You can also be open about potential problems with your measure. Researchers often do this in the hope that future research will fill in the gaps, because no piece of social science is ever finally and fully conclusive.

In introducing the use of statistical data and surveying, we have not been able to do more than mention *statistical inference,* but it's important to know that statistical inference influences the claims that researchers can responsibly make from the data they've collected. As we mentioned in the discussion of defining a sample, a census is one of the few instances when surveyors gather information about an entire population. In most cases, researchers must choose a small sample and extrapolate their responses to the larger population. Statistical inference helps to measure whether such extrapolations are legitimate. In completing informal research, you'll want to try to select representative samples and to select a large enough sample that the chances of getting a response biased by outliers are minimized. As you move forward to complete more advanced social scientific research, you will learn how to measure whether the data you gather from a sample are likely to represent the broader population.

As a developing researcher, your ethical responsibility to the data you collect and the claims you make about it are important, but your ethical responsibilities to survey respondents is paramount. It is very important that you protect the identity of your respondents, even if you feel that the questions you ask are not particularly revealing. This means that no one—not your roommate, not your professor, no one, no matter how much your best friend begs—should know who responded in what manner, or even, to the extent possible, who the respondents to your survey are. You cannot share this information. Because we all have biases that might lead us to consciously or unconsciously weight some responses as more significant than others if we knew who responded in particular ways, *try to hide information about respondents' identity even from yourself.* Hiding responder identity from yourself is even more important when you are surveying people you may encounter again, as is often the case in the kind of informal surveys beginning students conduct. Thus, while you may want to keep track of who has or has not responded to a questionnaire, organize your paperwork so no personally identifying information appears on the questionnaire form itself, and sort these separately before recording your data. It's fine, however, to request personal information related to your variables on the questionnaire form, but such information should not allow you to identify the particular individual who is responding. If you are measuring differences between the responses of males and females to questions about study habits, be sure that concerns about protecting confidentiality do not lead you to forget to have respondents identify their gender. On the other hand, if you ask for the gender of your responders and then do not ensure that you have multiple responders of both genders in your sample, you could unwittingly make the responses of the sole male responder identifiable.

Standard protocol is to let survey respondents know that their responses will remain completely anonymous. In part this will help prevent the problem of people providing what they perceive to be socially acceptable responses. Remember that if you guarantee anonymity, you are legally bound to preserve it.

Finally think carefully about the potential emotional impact of your survey questions. We recommend that, as you hone your survey skills, you avoid topics that may force people to confront painful memories or confess illegal activity. As you gain more experience and training in conducting surveys, you can work with your professors and your school's human research review board if you wish to conduct research exploring sensitive areas.

WORKING ON WRITING FROM NUMBERS

Much of the research that is centered around numbers happens in the social sciences, so often this research is presented in the standard social science format with an introduction that provides the context and background, a review of relevant prior literature, a discussion of the methods used, followed by the results, discussion or analysis of the data, and a conclusion that usually suggests the areas for future study. There are variations of this form, of course, even within the social sciences. María Len-Ríos's study that we've included in the Readings is a good example of a version of this form for presenting survey research. But the essay by Frisch, which also includes a survey, doesn't follow this format. Likewise, Leo Chavez's study of magazine covers and immigration, Julia Koza's examination of the treatment of rap music in popular media, and the NEA report on reading literature all require the analysis and presentation of numbers and none of these pieces follow the standard social science format. As we explained in Chapter 2, we believe that it is more useful for students early in their undergraduate career to consider audience, purpose, and responsible presentation rather than concentrating on following a precise format. Thus we want to highlight two issues that we think research from numbers regularly generates for writers: acknowledging limits and including graphic representations of data.

ACKNOWLEDGING LIMITS

When researchers give the specifics of their method, they are setting up the grounds for later limits. When researchers explain alternative interpretations of the data, they are inviting consideration of the limits of whatever claims they want to advance as the most convincing interpretation. When researchers offer insight into the assumptions or hypotheses they bring with them into their investigations, they are acknowledging that there may well be factors that make them inclined to interpret the evidence in a particular way, ignore contrary cases, or create particular kinds of patterns from the data at hand. Why would anyone who expects to be persuasive make gestures like these that would seem to invite readers to doubt their conclusions? In part researchers acknowledge limits, admit biases, and entertain alternatives because they are members of a discourse community that values deliberation and rigorous thinking over pure persuasion. Following these practices demonstrates not only their reliability as good researchers, but also their commitment to values that go beyond their own immediate interests. In other words they strengthen their authority—and thereby their ability to persuade—by behaving in these expected ways.

We're not suggesting that researchers' gestures to acknowledge their limits, or the limits of their research, should be seen cynically—just a gesture to *appear* more credible. Rather, what we mean to suggest is that these values are more important to researchers than the particular point they may want to advance in any single article or research study. For our students, the shift we are suggesting—valuing responsible research over the point you want to make—often seems new and startling, certainly contrary to much of the writing that we are all exposed to on a daily basis. Imagine if advertisers said, "Dentists recommend any toothpaste that has fluoride and ours does," rather than "Our toothpaste carries the approval of the American Dentistry Association." Or, what if politicians said, "I don't really know how we can solve this problem. We could do x, or y, or z and each of these has advantages and disadvantages." Some of us would appreciate such honesty, but many voters would find such comments unpersuasive.

Even when writers are convinced that acknowledging limits is appropriate, how exactly they should do so remains a problem that has to be solved in writing. Kenneth Rosina acknowledges the limits of his work throughout his essay. He gives his starting hypothesis in the opening paragraph when he writes:

> I thought that those who reached for their college and had it listed as their "first choice school" would appreciate everything more and be more satisfied with the college they attend. It only makes sense to think that if you really strive for something and want it most, when you get it, you'll enjoy it to its fullest capacity and be bursting with delight. I created a study to test just this logical thought process, and show exactly who is more satisfied with their school choice: those who listed University of Miami as their first choice school, or those who did not. (p. 152)

Later, however, he admits that his hypothesis was not supported by the data he collected.

> Upon beginning this survey, the expected outcome was that those students who had the University of Miami as their first choice school would be more satisfied with their school choice, but the data seem to point otherwise. (p. 152)

Rosina then does additional research—by interviewing admissions officers—to try to account for this unexpected result. And he develops several alternative explanations, including, "It could have been the Advanced Placement program that put these students on an early track to college life that enables them to find college more pleasurable, or it could be more centralized around the financial aspect." Rosina then develops the rationale behind each of these alternatives with specific examples, though he cannot use his survey data to support or refute either of them since he didn't ask questions that would allow him to do so. Later in the essay, Rosina considers another aspect of the data he did collect—about social activities—and again offers different possible interpretations:

> The data collected on clubs and sports were too similar from group to group to be conclusive. Is it that alcohol leads to a higher satisfaction among first–year freshmen? Or could it be that those who enjoy their school the most are those who can appreciate not only the academics of the school, but also its fun side? It seems to be a matter of what causes what, and which came first, the chicken or the egg, and unfortunately my study isn't able to conclude that order, but it does make the correlation between the two known, and that correlation is something to be left for another further survey. (p. 154)

After wondering if the University of Miami's increasing academic rigor might explain the correlation he has noted between social life and satisfaction, Rosina accepts an interpretation from a colleague: "People have very high expectations of their first choice schools, and they might not be met," so those who have lower expectations may actually turn out to be more satisfied. In his conclusion, Rosina summarizes all these possible alternative interpretations, notes that his expectations were not confirmed by the data he collected, points to additional work that would have to be done to determine which of these possibilities is more likely, and couches all of this in the tentative language of "seems" or "suggests."

> My study seems to show that out of first-year University of Miami students, those who didn't list UM as their first choice school are more satisfied than those who did list UM as their first choice school. This seems to be due to the dramatic difference between scholarships given to the two groups, and reasons for attending the University of Miami in comparison to the University's rapidly changing academic reputation. My survey, however, doesn't ask about Advanced Placement programs in high school, which could be a vital piece of information in determining which factor is the leading reason for large or little satisfaction between groups, and a further study should include such questions. Ward's testimony, along with colleague Jessica Vogel's statement on first choice expectations also indicates the method of ranking schools and the accuracy of student's expectations of the school may not always be the most accurate or beneficial. My study and discussion with Matthew G. Ward seemed to clear up some of the confusion about who is more satisfied as a first–year freshman on the University of Miami campus and brought up other factors that I had not thought of and my survey didn't include either. Ward also points to expectations and scholarships as two main focuses, but more research would need to be done in order to pinpoint the most important aspect of first-year freshmen's experiences here at UM, and why exactly one group is more satisfied than the other, and how to satisfy them both. (p. 156)

Throughout his essay, then, Rosina entertains alternative possibilities for interpreting the data he has collected, acknowledges what his data can't prove, and tries to investigate further to explain the results. With more time Rosina might have developed a second survey or interviewed a broader range of students. To make generalizations about students and their satisfaction with their first choice schools, Rosina would have to devise a way to survey students at several institutions and determine whether the same factors of advanced placement, scholarships, and social life played a part in the level of satisfaction on other campuses. He might also want to consider whether first-year students' level of satisfaction changes as they progress to sophomore, junior, or senior status, but he would have to figure out how to include those students who are so dissatisfied that they transfer out of the institution. Still we think Rosina has made appropriate gestures to acknowledge the limits of his research and present his work responsibly.

Look at how Michael Frisch acknowledges the limits of his interpretations of the results of asking students to list the first ten associations they think of for American History:

> It is hard to know how much we can generalize from the uniformity of these lists, or how much interpretive weight they can bear. Perhaps all this is merely an artifact of my western New York sample, or the curriculum of New York State's primary and secondary schools; I would be the first to concede that a similar survey in Waco, Texas, for example, would produce a somewhat different list. But I believe regional variation would be far less than might be expected, and that the consistency of the lists—arguably closer to the heart of their significance than the precise content—might well be as striking. (p. 393)

Frisch goes on to offer evidence from a colleague in another state, thus showing the same impetus to further research that Rosina exhibited. He also uses the same tentative language in summarizing his findings and argument that Rosina used:

> As I have argued, however, the surveys are more interesting when taken as evidence of what students do know, rather than what they don't. If the results say little one way or the other about how much history the students surveyed may actually know, they are evidence that cultural imagery seems to be reproduced in our young people with startling consistency and regularity. And this conclusion casts something of a shadow over the current jeremiads, whose core concerns, I would argue, are at bottom more fundamentally cultural and political than educational. This point is worth at least brief examination by way of conclusion. (p. 399)

Notice, in particular, that Frisch's paragraph is both summarizing and setting up a further point. He asserts (claiming that the survey results provide evidence about cultural imagery being reproduced), but qualifies these assertions with "seems to be." Further, he reminds us repeatedly that he is arguing—"as I have argued" and "I would argue"—suggesting in the process that these are not ironclad facts but assertions made from the analysis of the data at hand and subject to debate. Such gestures are another form of acknowledging limits.

As another example, take a close look at the way Len-Ríos acknowledges the limits of her study at the end of her paper.

> Our study has its limitations. The two Midwestern U.S. newspapers we studied may not be representative of others. Our survey measures were single-item measures. Future studies should use multiple-item constructs. In addition, our data were staggered. We first examined news content, then newsroom perceptions, and finally news reader perceptions. It could be that there were changes in content and perceptions between study times that affected the results. It is also possible that the newspapers changed substantially over the past 5 years. However, with stable newsroom demographics, with research spanning several decades indicating similar results, and with little culture shift in the United

States, we believe masculine cultural hegemony would still be supported today. If news readers and staff are continually socialized to see certain types of news as gendered, then there is little expectation for change. Consistent with feminist theory, future research should use qualitative techniques to track cross-cultural training and newsroom socialization to determine how they actually influence newsroom decisions. (p. 461)

While these authors are certainly acknowledging other possibilities and pointing to the limits of their study, they don't spend nearly as much time developing what those alternatives would mean as Rosina does. Their confidence could be because their study is complete and persuasive; after all these researchers worked in a team, conducted their research over a long period of time, and all were experienced researchers/scholars. On the other hand, offering up possible limitations and sweeping them away all in the same paragraph strikes us as the kind of minimal gesture that will rarely work, especially for student writers with more limited surveys.

INCORPORATING GRAPHICS

It is often more effective to present numerical information graphically than by listing numbers in the text. Consider, for instance, how much easier it is to understand the family incomes in the earlier section of this chapter when they are presented in a table (Table 5.4) than they would have been if listed in the text. Tables are the most basic and perhaps handiest form of graphic. Before using other types of graphics, first put your data

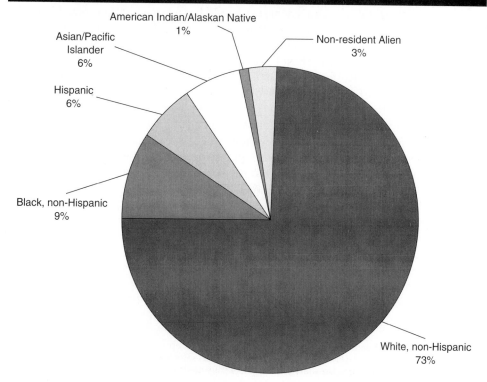

FIGURE 5.6   Sample Pie Chart Based on Table 5.7: Bachelor's Degree Conferrals, by Race/Ethnicity, 2000. U.S. Census Bureau, 2004.

TABLE 5.7	Bachelor's Degree Conferrals, by Race, in Thousands. U.S. Census Bureau, 2003
Race	*Bachelor's Degrees Conferred*
White, non-Hispanic	929,106
Black, non-Hispanic	108,013
Hispanic	75,059
Asian or Pacific Islander	77,912
American Indian/Alaskan Native	8,719
Nonresident alien	39,066
Total	1,237,875

in a table (even just for your own use) and then build your other graphics[10] from the data table. Many researchers present the raw data in a table, along with other graphics intended to enhance visual understanding.

The kind of graphics you use depends on the kind of information you want to convey. Use a pie chart to depict the relationship of parts to a whole. A bar graph is useful for comparing one element with another or others. Line graphs are most useful for demonstrating change over time or comparing change over time between multiple elements.

Here's an example. Imagine you want to show the percentage of people receiving bachelor's degrees, broken down by race/ethnicity. The most effective way to present these data, which show relationships of parts (racial/ethnic groups) to a whole (total bachelor's degrees), would be to use a pie chart (see Figure 5.6). But let's say instead you wanted to display the growth in bachelor's degree conferrals for African Americans over the fifteen years from 1985 to 2000. In this case, a line graph would be your best bet (see Figure 5.7).

Turn to Rosina's paper at the end of this chapter, and notice how he has incorporated different kinds of graphics to illustrate his findings. Turn also to the essays in the Readings by Chavez, Frisch, Koza, Len-Ríos, and the NEA. Notice how these writers have used various kinds of charts and graphs to illustrate key points of their research, but also how they present these data in prose. Sometimes a graph can substitute for a narrative explanation, but often it only illustrates that information visually, reinforcing but not substituting for the discursive version.

Whenever you present data in tables or graphs, be sure to label these visuals. Number tables or figures consecutively throughout a paper, section, or chapter, with separate numbering for tables and for figures. If the data come from a separate source, even if you have designed the graphic yourself, tell your readers in the label where the data come from. This will help them to understand your presentation. If you collected the data yourself, the text of your essay or report should make that clear. Be sure you have an informative title for your graphic. Do not try to be clever with the titles; just communicate what the graphic presents as clearly and completely as you can so anyone looking at it would know what it represents.

---

[10]You can easily create tables and graphics with a spreadsheet program and paste them into your document using your word processor. Do not be intimidated by this software if it is unfamiliar to you. A spreadsheet is really just a fancy name for a table. Spreadsheet software is useful for creating and manipulating tables.

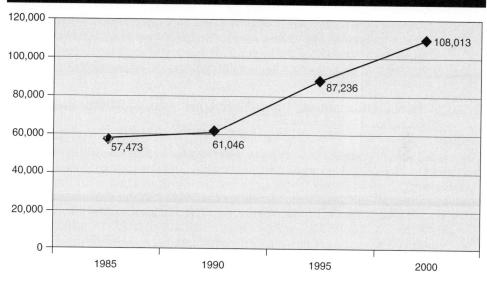

FIGURE 5.7   Sample Line Graph Based on Table 5.8: Bachelor's Degrees Earned by Black, Non-Hispanics, 1985–2000. U.S. Census Bureau, 2003

TABLE 5.8   Bachelor's Degrees Earned by Black, Non-Hispanics, 1985–2000. U.S. Census Bureau, 2003

Year	Number
1985	57,473
1990	61,046
1995	87,236
2000	108,013

PRACTICE ACTIVITY 5-3

Creating Graphics

Using any source of numerical data you wish—examples from this chapter, sections of the readings, or information from a newspaper or magazine—create a graphic representation of the numbers. Then write the information in discursive form. Give the discursive form to one classmate and the graphic representation to another and have them translate the information into the alternative form (text becomes graphic, graphic becomes text). Compare the results.

Consider: What gets lost as information is translated from graphic form to text and back? What problems did you encounter doing this activity, and how could you keep those problems from occurring as you represent your research data?

Kenny Rosina is originally from Long Island. He plans to pursue a doctoral degree in chemistry and forensic science after graduating from the University of Miami. Kenny started this investigation as a first-year student because he was thinking about transferring and wanted to find out what contributed to students' satisfaction with their university experience.

Satisfaction among First–Year University of Miami Students

Kenny Rosina

When going into college, I had many thoughts about who felt as I did, who was having fun as I was, and who was disappointed as I was. I thought that those who reached for their college and had it listed as their "first choice school" would appreciate everything more and be more satisfied with the college they attend. It only makes sense to think that if you really strive for something and want it most, when you get it, you'll enjoy it to its fullest capacity and be bursting with delight. I created a study to test just this logical thought process, and show exactly who is more satisfied with their school choice: those who listed University of Miami as their first choice school, or those who did not.

The Survey

The populations that received and participated in the study were all first-year University of Miami students, and all consented to filling out a survey and allowing their results to be used for data and published anonymously. The population consisted of 35 students, 21 male and 14 female.

This study was aimed to determine which group of first–year students was most satisfied with their decision to attend the University of Miami, mainly those who had UM as their first choice school, and those who didn't. The study consisted of a survey with baseline questions, to distinguish different types of students, and Likert ranking questions, to assign numerical values to positive and negative experiences at UM. Such Likert rankings consisted of statements such as "I am happy with the academic program I'm in at UM," or "I am thinking about transferring to another school," and asked them to quantify their agreement to these questions on a 0–10 scale. The positive questions that aimed at how much the students *liked* something were given the positive value the students circled (a 7 correlates to a +7), where the negative statements, such as the one regarding transferring, were given the corresponding negative number to the one they circled (a 7 correlates to a –7). These values were then added together to make the Likert average of the student, with the highest and most pleased value being 50 and lowest and most displeased value –20. To then attain a better picture of which groups of students answered which way, five numerical fill-in questions pertaining to things such as amount of sports played, clubs participated in, and times a week they go out and drink alcohol were answered at the end of the survey.

In grouping the data, the results of the survey were compiled into four distinct subsets: males whose first choice for college was the University of Miami, males whose first choice for college was *not* the University of Miami, females whose first choice for college was the University of Miami, and females whose first choice for college was *not* the University of Miami. The average Likert number for each question was taken from each of these subsets, and the average compounded Likert number was taken from each subset as well. These are then compared to the average Likert number for each individual question and the compounded Likert number of all participants. (See survey and data table on last page.)

Data Analysis

Upon beginning this survey, the expected outcome was that those students who had the University of Miami as their first choice school would be more satisfied with their school choice, but the data seem to point otherwise. The compounded Likert numbers, which are the numerical value for how much a student is satisfied with the University of Miami, are higher for males and females who didn't have

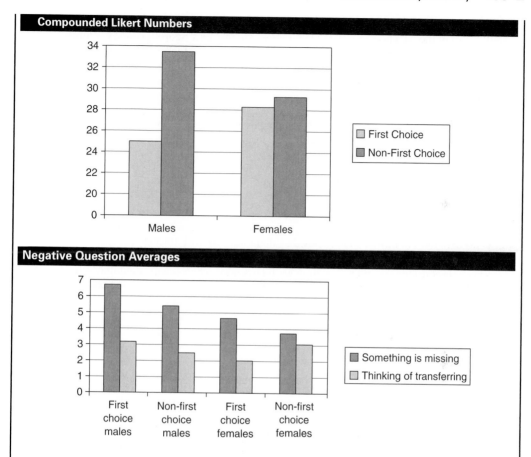

Compounded Likert Numbers

Negative Question Averages

UM as their first choice school. Those who listed University of Miami as a non-first choice school are more satisfied at UM than those who listed it as their first choice school. The compounded Likert number was 24.9 for first choice males, 33.4 for non-first choice males, 28.1 for first choice females, and 29.0 for non-first choice females. The two negative questions, regarding if something seems missing in their college experience and transferring, are also good portrayers like the Likert numbers. These negative averages are, on a 1–10 scale, 6.6 and 3.1, and 4.6 and 1.9 for first choice males and females respectively, and 5.3 and 2.4, and 3.7 and 3.0 for non-first choice males and females respectively.

First choice males have higher dissatisfaction numbers than non-first choice males, and first choice females have a higher dissatisfaction number than non-first choice females. This seems counterintuitive, since those who reached for UM as a school and wanted to attend this school the most are taking a backseat in enjoying it.

Looking Further

Why are the students that didn't have University of Miami as their first choice more satisfied with their college experience at UM than those who strived to get here? This was a question I deemed fit for Matthew G. Ward, the Senior Associate Director of Admissions. I informed Ward about the survey I conducted and of the unexpected results, and asked him to try to explain why he thought I received the results I did. When looking at the two groups, first choice students and non-first choice students, the biggest difference is scholarship money. Most of the non-first choice students received scholarships, with most being 50% tuition or more, and first choice students received significantly less scholarship money. With scholarship money comes advanced programs, harder and more interesting classes, and to receive scholarships, it's almost necessary to be in the Advanced Placement programs in high school. "Most of the AP classes taught in high school are the most rigorous courses, offering the best preparation for college," says Ward. These kinds of students might feel as if they were already in college, since most AP courses give college credit, and Ward explains that most of the friends an AP student has go onto 4 year institutions, so the student lives with college choices and college in their academic sights for years before they actually reach college. Perhaps it's this pre-college experience that allows them to be more satisfied with what college actually is than those who had UM as their first choice school and didn't receive much scholarship money.

It could have been the Advanced Placement program that put these students on an early track to college life that enables them to find college more pleasurable, or it could be more centralized around the financial aspect. My survey was unable to determine which was the main reason, but Ward explains, "Scholarships certainly provide a comfort level, and students also like the fact that they're being recognized for their achievements." Scholarship money eases the pressure of paying for college, and many students that receive scholarships either pay the rest themselves by taking out college loans and paying them off after college, or have parents pay the resulting tuition costs, since it's significantly less than normal tuition. This means they don't have to work through college, and can choose when they want a job for spending money, if they ever want a job. The control of employment, ease of financial responsibilities, and recognition for high school achievements definitely puts the scholarship winner more at ease than those who didn't receive any scholarships, and could make them more satisfied even if the University of Miami wasn't their first choice school.

Another possibility is that those students that received scholarships and didn't list the University of Miami as their first choice are in more interesting and more challenging classes. When a student takes an AP test and scores high enough, they receive college credit from UM, allowing them to bypass a lower level course and go straight to a more challenging and demanding course. One factor for deciding if a student likes a school is their class size, performance in that class, and how interesting their classes are. Why like a school if the classes offered are great, but the ones you can take are boring and not as educational as you would like? From discussing classes with my friends from high school, who were all AP students, and students here at UM, both AP and non-AP students, it becomes clear that second choice students, thanks to AP exams, are more often in higher level courses from the beginning of college that challenge them, keep them interested, and often involve heated debates or discussions. Many introductory and low level courses are skipped from Advanced Placement credit, and the more likely to be intellectually stimulating and gripping courses are taken right away. However, this is only available for those students that received scholarship money and passes intro-level courses. Many first choice students aren't in this position to take these riveting courses right away, and therefore are drilled with lethargic and brain numbing classes. Classes are a huge part of college life and satisfaction with your school, so it's obvious to see how such a large difference in classes between first choice and non-first choice students could create a difference in satisfaction with the University of Miami.

Survey's Background Info Takes Center Stage

As for the later questions regarding social behavior, slight trends were noticed. Non-first choice students drank alcohol, on average, one more time per week than first choice students. The data collected on clubs and sports were too similar from group to group to be conclusive. Is it that alcohol leads to a higher satisfaction among first–year freshmen? Or could it be that those who enjoy their school the most are those who can appreciate not only the academics of the school, but also its fun side? It seems to be a matter of what causes what, and which came first, the chicken or the egg, and unfortunately my study isn't able to conclude that order, but it does make the correlation between the two known, and that correlation is something to be left for another further survey.

With regard to the questions about why they came to the University of Miami, non-first choice students listed "academics" or "scholarship" as the reason for attending, whereas first choice students listed "weather," "social atmosphere," "location," and "academics" all evenly. (Note: Black areas in the following graph represent empty data fields.)

Reasons for Attending UM

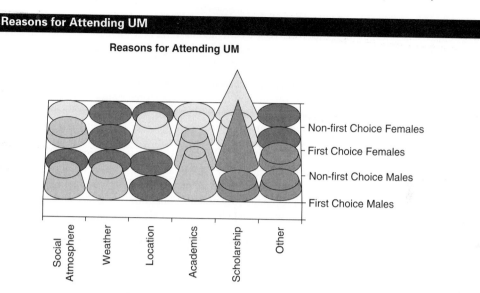

Reasons for Attending UM

- Non-first Choice Females
- First Choice Females
- Non-first Choice Males
- First Choice Males

Social Atmosphere · Weather · Location · Academics · Scholarship · Other

Explaining the Differences

There is a large discrepancy to why students applied to the University of Miami, with most non-first choicers aiming for academics and scholarships and first choicers aiming for location and social atmosphere. One reason those who applied for academics might be more satisfied than those who applied for the social atmosphere could be because the University of Miami is dramatically changing what defines the University, and is in a revolutionary time bent on academic prosperity and gaining a dominant academic reputation.

President Donna E. Shalala recently turned down offers from what Ward describes as the "traditional elites of the United States," because she "wanted to go to a school that wanted to get better, not one that thought it already was great." It's exactly this attitude and determination that is changing the University of Miami from "Suntan U." to an academically rich and challenging environment. The Momentum Campaign is doing exactly this, and it's this momentum of change that those students that came here for academics and scholarships approve of and are attracted by, and in the process of changing, we're weeding out the weaker students that wouldn't be able to hold their own in a "traditional elite." Unfortunately, it's these students that are the first choice students and have higher populations in the lower percentages of the academic student body that feel negative effects of growing academic and work ethics.

The more than likely desired "Suntan U." is becoming a thing of the past, and as Ward describes, the University of Miami is taking advantage of the influx and the wave of children from the baby-boom era, and using the increase of students to make UM more selective and nurture its academic reputation and performance for future generations. First choice students can feel it more than others who are bent on excellent academic performance. A colleague, Jessica Vogel, stated, "People have very high expectations of their first choice schools, and they might not be met," and this is just the case with first choice students and the changing scope of the former "Suntan U."

As far as expectation of the school are concerned, there are many aids to help high school students choose the right college: high school counselors, college counselors, and Princeton Review, College Board, and Barron's books with synopses of each college. When I asked Matthew about these aids, he clarified my misguided notions of strict admissions office facts by noting:

> Princeton's method gives surveys to kids on campus and gets true survey data, but sample population can vary depending on day or location. But depending on who they talk to, they're not going to hit every one of our students, and you know as well as I do that this

place is very diverse, and has a lot of different kinds of students that have a lot of different opinions on whether their expectations are being met. I think that some of the bigger items that come out tend to be on point. It's the minutia of things that students say that you're like, well, that may be true for one person but not another.

So as far as college books are concerned, admissions facts, SAT scores and the like are accurate, as well as the general idea of UM, but for student quotes and personal opinions, it seems like none can be really trusted and portray a fair perspective of the University of Miami. For a true student perspective of the school, you really have to know or find someone like yourself here, and ask them directly what they think of it, because that's as close as you can come to getting a student opinion that means something to you. When speaking of college counselors, Ward also stated, "A high school junior sitting down with their college counselor in the spring putting together their list of colleges is usually ordering their list by competitiveness of admission and not necessarily fit." This common trend, which most of my colleagues and I can all say is commonly practiced and how we made our first list of colleges, can also attribute to reasons that many first choice students are more disappointed than non-first choices. With seven or eight schools on a list ranked by difficulty of admissions, it's unlikely that most students' best fit will be their first choice school.

My study seems to show that out of first-year University of Miami students, those who didn't list UM as their first choice school are more satisfied than those who did list UM as their first choice school. This seems to be due to the dramatic difference between scholarships given to the two groups, and reasons for attending the University of Miami in comparison to the University's rapidly changing academic reputation. My survey, however, doesn't ask about Advanced Placement programs in high school, which could be a vital piece of information in determining which factor is the leading reason for large or little satisfaction between groups, and a further study should include such questions. Ward's testimony, along with colleague Jessica Vogel's statement on first choice expectations, also indicates the method of ranking schools and the accuracy of student's expectations of the school may not always be the most accurate or beneficial. My study and discussion with Matthew G. Ward seemed to clear up some of the confusion about who is more satisfied as a first–year freshman on the University of Miami campus and brought up other factors that I had not thought of and my survey didn't include either. Ward also points to expectations and scholarships as two main focuses, but more research would need to be done in order to pinpoint the most important aspect of first-year freshmen's experiences here at UM, and why exactly one group is more satisfied than the other, and how to satisfy them both.

WORKS CITED

Vogel, Jessica. Personal Interview. 10 November 2004
Ward, Matthew G. Personal Interview. 10 November 2004

ROSINA'S SURVEY

Please be aware that in completing this survey, you're allowing the use of this data for statistical publications and your identity is kept completely confidential. Professors, reviewers of data, and all UM personnel are forbidden to know the identities of any survey participants, and by completing this survey, I'm legally bound to keep your identity private. Thank you.

Gender: *Male*   *Female*

Are you a first–year University of Miami Student?   Y   N

Was the University of Miami your first choice school?   Y   N

Why did you come to University of Miami? (Please circle one or fill in other)

Scholarship   Social Atmosphere   Academic Program   Athletics   Other:

Are you attending University of Miami on a scholarship?   Y   N

If yes, please circle the type (academic or athletic) of scholarship and specify amount

$_____ or _____% tuition.

Please indicate your satisfaction level regarding the following statements (0 completely disagree - 10 completely agree)

I am happy with the academic program I'm in at UM.

   0   1   2   3   4   5   6   7   8   9   10

I am happy with the friends I've found so far at UM.

   0   1   2   3   4   5   6   7   8   9   10

I am satisfied with the student body's academic performance here at UM.

   0   1   2   3   4   5   6   7   8   9   10

I am happy with campus life and on–campus activities here at UM.

   0   1   2   3   4   5   6   7   8   9   10

My experience at UM has been exactly what I thought it would be.

   0   1   2   3   4   5   6   7   8   9   10

Something feels missing in my college experience here at UM.

   0   1   2   3   4   5   6   7   8   9   10

I am thinking about transferring to another school.

   0   1   2   3   4   5   6   7   8   9   10

Please fill in the appropriate amount:

I participate in _____ on-campus clubs or organizations (not counting intramural sports).

I participate in _____ intramural sports.

I participate in _____ team sports.

I go out to Coconut Grove, South Beach Strip, or any bar or club _____times a week.

I drink alcohol _____ times a week.

Thank you for completing this survey, please fold in half and return to Kenny Rosina personally, or place inside envelope outside Hecht-McDonald Tower room 407.

Rosina's Data Table

Gender	Choice	Why come here	Scholarship	Academics	Friends	Stud. Perf.	Cmps Lfe	Expectations	Missing?	Transfer	Compounded Likart	Clubs	IM Sports	Team Sport	Clubs/week	Alch/week
Male	1st choice	Social Atmosphere	Yes - $???	6	8	6	10	9	4	0	35	0	0	0	2	4
		Weather	100%	7	7	6	7	8	6	0	29	2	1	6	1	0
		Scholarship	75%	8	10	7	9	9	2	2	39	0	0	0	1	1
		Academics	"12,000"	9	10	9	9	6	9	9	25	5	1	0	1	0
		Academics	No	8	8	8	9	9	1	0	41	2	4	0	7	7
		Social Atmosphere	No	5	10	10	4	0	10	5	14	0	2	1	1	1
		Music (academics)	No	6	7	6	6	4	6	2	21	0	0	0	1	0
		Weather	No	8	7	7	8	6	9	0	27	0	0	0	0	0
		Academics	No	6	8	7	9	7	9	5	23	0	1	0	2	3
		Girls	No	1	4	5	8	3	10	8	3	1	1	1	3	0
		Avg:		5.6	7.9	7.1	7.9	6.1	6.6	3.1	24.9	1	1	0.8	1.8	1.5
Male	X > 1 choice	Scholarship	25%	8	9	10	8	9	7	0	37	1	1	0	3	3
		Scholarship	75%	7	8	7	7	6	4	5	26	2	1	0	1	1
		Scholarship	"18,000"	5	9	3	5	2	8	7	9	1	3	0	3	6
		Academics	No	10	10	10	8	5	0	1	42					2
		Academics	25%	8	10	9	9	9	2	0	43	0	0	0	1	1
		Academics	"8,000"	4	6	4	2	3	10	6	3	3	1	0	1	
		Scholarship	"15,000"	10	10	5	8	5	5	0	33	0	1	1	1	0
		Scholarship	75%	8	10	7	3	5	10	0	23	2	1	0	0.5	0
		Scholarship	75%	8	9	6	9	8	1	0	39	1	0	0	1	7
		Family Faculty	100%	8	7	9	3	4	9	7	15	0	0	0	0	1
		Scholarship	50%	7	10	9	10	7	2	0	41	0	0	0	1	1
		Avg:		7.5	8.9	7.2	6.5	5.7	5.3	2.4	33.4	1	0.8	0.1	1.25	2.2
Female	1st choice	Scholarship	50%	7	8	5	7	8	5	0	30	0	0	0	0	0
		Social Atmosphere	No	10	10	10	10	10	0	0	50	0	0	0	3	3
		All	No	10	10	10	10	10	0	0	50	1	0	0	2	2
		Location	50%	10	6	8	4	3	7	0	24	0	0	0	2	0
		Academics	No	7	8	8	8	8	3	0	36	2	0	0	2	0
		Parents (Scholarship)	"10,000"	8	6	7	7	5	7	5	21	1	1	1	1	1
		Avg:		8.7	8	8	7.7	7.3	3.7	0.8	35.2	0.666	0.167	0.167	1.33	1
Female	X > 1 choice	Scholarship	Yes - $???	8	10	8	8	5	2	0	37	0	0	0	4	5
		Social Atmosphere	No	5	5	4	8	3	5	5	15	1	1	0	1	3
		Academics	"8,000"	9	7	6	8	8	8	6	24	2	0	0	1	1
												1	0	1	1	0

Internet Resources

Most governments make census data freely available on the web, and such data can be the subject of inquiry or used to support other kinds of inquiry methods. The U.S. Census Bureau's *Statistical Abstract of the United States* is updated each year and available at http://www.census.gov/compendia/statab/. Canadian Census Data is available online through the Statistics Canada Web site: http://www12.statcan.ca/. The Mexican Census Bureau also makes its information available via the Web http://www.inegi.gob.mx/est/default.asp (in Spanish, of course), and UCLA publishes a yearly Statistical Abstract of Latin America, which is not available online but which is available in the reference section of many university libraries. The United Kingdom's Census Bureau can be located at: http://www.statistics.gov.uk/, and Australia's Bureau of Statistics at: http://www.abs.gov.au/. You can find most countries' Census Bureaus simply by typing that country's name and "census" into any search engine.

Governments also provide other kinds of statistical data and reports. A good place to start when you want to locate such information from the U.S. government is at the FedStats Web site http://www.fedstats.gov/), which provides links to statistical data from over one hundred federal agencies. Reports, both regular and occasional, from many of these agencies will also be available in many libraries.

Web sites Referenced in this Chapter

Niles, Robert. *Statistics Every Writer Should Know*
  http://www.robertniles.com/stats/stdev.shtml

Pezzullo, John C. *Interactive Statistics Pages*
  http://www.statpages.net

Statistics at Square One
  http://bmj.bmjjournals.com/collections/statsbk/1.shtml

Links to the Readings

While only a few of the readings included in this text use work with numbers as a primary method of investigation, numerical data often underlie or support other kinds of analysis. An asterisk in the list below indicates that the primary research method of the piece is a survey or other numerical analysis. Assignment sequences, however, often invite students to conduct a survey or turn to numerical data, often as an option for developing an investigation.

Benmayor, Rina. "Narrating Cultural Citizenship: Oral Histories of First-Generation College Students of Mexican Origin"

Chavez, Leo R. "Developing a Visual Discourse on Immigration"

*Frisch, Michael. "American History and the Structures of Collective Memory: A Modest Exercise in Empirical Iconography"

Koza, Julia Eklund. "Rap Music: The Cultural Politics of Official Representation"

*National Endowment for the Arts. "Trends in Literature Participation, 1982–2002."

*Len-Ríos, María E. et al. "Representation of Women in News and Photos: Comparing Content to Perceptions"

Assignments Working with Numbers

Between Writing and Knowing Assignment 1
Cultural Politics and Public Discourse Assignment 5 (Len-Ríos et al.)
Direct Observation option in Assignment 3 and 4
Expanding a Trends Report

Gendered Investigations Assignment 1 (Len-Ríos et al.)
Humanizing Numbers
Working with Texts Assignment 1 and 2

Assignments Working with Surveys

Between Writing and Knowing Assignment 2

Collective Memory Assignment 1 (Frisch); option in Assignment 2

Considering "Public" option in Assignment 5 (NEA)

Constructing Public Spaces option in Assignment 2 and 4

Cultural Politics and Public Discourse II: Shaping Values Assignment 1 (Frisch)

Expanding a Trends Report Assignment 2 and 5

Eye on Campus Assignment 3 (Frisch); option in Assignment 5 and 6

Gendered Investigations Assignment 2 (Len-Ríos et al.)

Histories: Official and Unofficial option in Assignment 4

Reading Media Assignment 4 (Len-Ríos et al.)

Reclaiming the Past Assignment 5 (Frisch)

Representing Community option in Assignment 3

CHAPTER

WORKING WITH TEXTS

All kinds of researchers work with texts of many different kinds to make new knowledge. Like other kinds of data, textual evidence is used both in isolation and in combination with other methods. When historians analyze archival records, for example, they often extract only the most relevant passages from letters, memos, or other records and then synthesize these textual moments, sometimes adding other forms of data such as interviews or photographs in order to make an argument about how this history ought to be read or why it is significant. Religious studies scholars regularly work to trace variations in translations of single words, or compare the use of key phrases in different passages of sacred texts. Literary and legal scholars, however, often work with whole texts—short stories, poems, novels, or judicial opinions—in order to understand those texts or their impact on readers. Often this kind of textual analysis operates from an assumption that the texts themselves can teach us something about human culture—about our values and conceptions—and that language (most easily analyzed in written texts) both reflects and constitutes that human world. Like the explication of other art forms, some writing about texts aims to teach us how to see what's really there, what a casual or less experienced reader might miss, and such writing can either focus exclusively on the text itself—the interplay of form and meaning—or might include historical, social, political, or economic contexts.

Like other researchers, scholars who turn to texts for their data do not usually begin their work with a firm thesis and then set to work to find "evidence" to support their argument. Instead these scholars begin with a question or an observation that makes them curious. They turn to particular texts just as other researchers might turn to observation or interviews or statistics, because they suspect that doing so will help them answer that question or work out the significance of what they've noticed. This is not to say that those who work with texts don't sometimes have hunches, or that they don't develop hunches as they work with texts. Just as scientists in the lab have hunches and set up experiments to prove or disprove a hypothesis, researchers who work with texts take care not to let their hunches lead them to ignore counterevidence or alternative interpretations.

In working with textual material in a spirit of inquiry, you'll need to draw upon skills you've certainly used before in writing about texts, but you'll also need to consider when to turn to texts and what kinds of questions you might ask to investigate texts. To help you with this work, we've divided this chapter into two parts. In the first section, we outline some ways for inquiring into texts—posing questions and imagining projects that can reasonably be answered by selecting appropriate textual cases and reading them as "data." In the second section, we lay out common strategies for close reading, strategies that can be used alone or in combination, with small passages or whole texts—work that might be a review of strategies you learned in prior English courses but that may well make those strategies more explicit.

PART I: INQUIRY INTO TEXTS

In this section we want to talk about several different kinds of inquiry involving textual materials, and we'll make some distinctions that, while common, are actually the subject of intense debates between scholars who specialize in textual studies. We want to emphasize up front that we're not trying to provide a complete, or even introductory, overview of literary criticism, theory, or history nor are we attempting to provide specifics about hermeneutics, philosophy, legal analysis, or semiotics though all of these rely at least in part on work with texts. Instead we want to provide just enough of a sense of the underlying issues so you can begin to experiment with what it means to engage in textual inquiry, just as in other chapters we've tried to give just enough information about other methods of inquiry so that you could enter into the work of academics without already having to be a specialist.

One distinction that we've made in organizing this book is between written texts and visual ones. In fact, many of us believe that nearly *everything* can be thought of as a text. Thus, films, photographs, even lived experience can be thought of as having features that are like a written text. Events and certainly visual texts often have characters, for example, as well as scenes and even plot lines; these texts often unfold in linear time but contain recursive elements that foreshadow events to come or make reference to the past. There can be elements of symbolism, references to other texts, or metaphors. So, while we're foregrounding written texts in this chapter and have tried to limit our examples to written discourse, much of what we have to say here can be applied to visual or aural materials as well. Indeed we include music and public speech—both examples of aural materials—as special cases in this chapter, but we put our discussion of working with visual materials in the chapter on observing. We actually argued back and forth among ourselves about this organization and chose the final placement less because the categories are absolutely distinct than because chapters of similar length provide a pleasing symmetry.

Likewise it is common to separate *literary* texts from other written work. Like other art forms, literature has a long history of being treated as different from everything that is not art. In this tradition literature is more highly valued as a reflection of aesthetic value and conscious creation, and it is assumed to be more layered with meanings that may not be apparent in an initial reading. But this distinction, too, has been challenged in scholarly debates, and techniques that had been restricted to literature have been used to read advertisements, legal documents, and other writing from the nonliterary world. While most of us writing this text have a background in literature and literary analysis that makes us think first of examples from the literary world, the collapse of the distinction between literary/nonliterary certainly informs our discussion of how to work with texts. Even the decision to use "texts" rather than "literature" throughout this chapter underscores that collapsed distinction.

Let's begin, then, with the broadest kind of inquiry into texts: questions about the nature of texts. The debate over what literature should be taught in school is fueled by these kinds of broad questions as well as by the answers that different people offer to such questions as: What counts as "good" literature? What role does literature play in shaping cultural values? What can we learn about other cultures by reading literature in translation? Why should students read/study imaginative literature? Likewise questions about which writing deserves the recognition of special prizes, or what makes some writing endure "the test of time," or how sacred (or foundational) texts should be read are fundamentally questions about the nature of texts and our practices in reading them.

Some of the discussion about books that gain wide popularity—such as *Harry Potter* or *The Da Vinci Code* in recent years—involve similar broad questions about the qualities that make literature great (or enduring) and the effect of stories (whether great literature or not) on readers. When parents or others object to children reading a particular book or argue that a particular kind of writing ought to be banned (or burned), they are arguing from a set of assumptions about how texts work to shape our culture and the individuals in it, and these assumptions—as well as the particular solution being advanced—are usually countered by others who read the same texts and the role of texts very differently.

One way that scholars inquire into texts, then, is when they have a question that might be reasonably answered by turning to whole texts, reading those texts carefully, and contrasting the features of some texts to others. In the second part of the chapter, we consider some of the strategies researchers use for this careful (close or critical) reading of text, but let's consider first how researchers choose the texts with which they will work once they've determined that texts are the appropriate material to use to try to answer their questions. Clearly some questions start with a text: Are the *Harry Potter* books enduring literature? Is *The Da Vinci Code* misrepresenting Catholicism? But what do researchers do when they have a question that doesn't presuppose a particular work? Just like other researchers, those who work with textual material often start with what they already know and then seek connections to what other researchers have already done.

PRACTICE ACTIVITY 6-1

Textual Controversy

Make a list of texts that have generated controversy. Were there books you (or your friends) weren't allowed to read as you were growing up? What movies are considered controversial? While you may be most aware of current controversies, try to think of texts that were controversial in previous times as well.

Consider: What makes the texts on your list controversial? What are the underlying issues in these controversies? Is there a pattern to such debates? How might you investigate any of these controversies?

Let's say, for example, that you are asked to recommend a novel that all beginning students entering your institution next year should be asked to read. Of course such a requirement is based on a belief that students should have a "general" or "liberal arts" education as well as the professional or career-preparing education many students seek in coming to college. The requirement also assumes that there is a positive value to having students at the same institution read the same text (perhaps to build community among students of diverse backgrounds and experiences), and that the experience of reading "good" writing teaches more than just information about the topic. You might, of course, question any of these assumptions, trace their foundation in prior research/writing, or try to test whether the assumptions are accurate through surveys or empirical evidence. But even if you accept the assumptions, there are a number of questions that must be investigated before you can make your recommendation if you are not just to recommend your own favorite book.

You might begin, for example, by investigating what criteria has been used in selecting books in previous years, or you might try to determine a set of criteria by analyzing these prior selections directly. The criteria used to select a book for first-year college students is certainly different than the criteria used to select books for other lists or prizes, say the Oprah Winfrey Book Club, the Nobel Peace Price for Literature, or the Newberry Award for Children's Literature. Once you knew the criteria, you would have to identify possible selections that fit this standard and then weigh all of the possible selections against one another to arrive at your recommendation. If your school used "widely read" as one of the criterion, you might begin by generating a list of best sellers. Using the term "best books" (a Library of Congress subject term) will lead you to a number of reference books and journals that compile such lists. Some of these compilations are limited by genre, subject matter, or age of reader. Some include reviews or abstracts of the work. Many are interested in nonimaginative works. "Best books" is a term that will also lead you to other terms that might be useful for narrowing your search.[1] Once you find a source that seems to be what you are looking for, be sure to check which subject terms have been used to classify that source and consider using these descriptor terms to expand your search.

PRACTICE ACTIVITY 6-2

Library of Congress Subject Terms

Use the ERIC database to explore Library of Congress Subject terms. If your library does not have the ERIC database online, you can find it at www.eric.ed.gov.[1] Use the thesaurus feature to gain access to the list of key terms. Browse or search for specific terms, paying careful attention to the narrower, broader, and related terms. Since ERIC is a database related to education, it will not contain all topics of interest, but it is a convenient site for seeing how Library of Congress key terms are structured.

Consider: How would you explain the difference between key terms and subject terms? How might features like "scope note," "used for," and "add date" be important to researchers?

---

[1]Researchers use the *Library of Congress Subject Headings* to determine the many possible terms related to their project. Often researchers have to try several different key terms, or combinations of terms, before they find the kind of material they are seeking. If you don't know how to use the *Library of Congress Subject Headings* or how to combine key terms in what is called a Boolean search, ask the reference librarian for help.

Likewise, several databases, including *Books in Print* and *WorldCat*, would be useful in your attempt to generate a list of books that would satisfy the criterion of "widely read." *Books in Print*, for example, has a search feature that generates best sellers by year, or by name of list (e.g., *New York Times* or Amazon). You can also search for books that have won awards, narrowing by year or name of award (e.g., Pulitzer Prize or the Dartmouth Book Award). These databases will allow you to then cross-search the author or the publisher. The database also provides basic information about cost and availability and gives a short synopsis for most entries.

Two principles of locating texts, then, are to use library databases appropriate to your purposes and Library of Congress subject terms to narrow your search and identify appropriate resources. These same two principles work in situations where you are not looking for literary materials but need to identify appropriate book-length works. Since so many new library resources become available every year, even experienced scholars often turn to research librarians for help with such searches, and many university libraries have special research staff to help scholars and students locate the most useful databases and identify the best key terms for specific investigations.

A slightly different process is used when the inquiry question requires the researcher to collect numerous examples from a number of different texts. If, for example, you were trying to do a project similar to Leo Chavez's investigation of public perceptions of immigration, you would want not a single text to analyze but a whole collection of texts, or at least portions of texts. Your first step would be to amass numerous possible snippets, and to do so you would probably still begin in the library with Library of Congress subject headings, key words, and appropriate databases. *ProQuest*, for example, will let you search both major current newspapers and historical newspapers such as the *New York Times* or *The Wall Street Journal*, using key terms with or without limiting the dates. If you're looking for general patterns rather than the discussions of a specific topic, you would begin with a systematic survey of a body of texts you were interested in. For example suppose you wanted to know what other topics regularly appeared on the covers of the magazines Chavez studied. The only way to determine the answer to such a question is to examine the magazines themselves, determining how to classify or group the covers as you examine them.

PRACTICE ACTIVITY 6-3

Searching with Databases

Spend at least half an hour exploring one of the databases available at your library. What kind of information is available on the database? Try searching for various topics using both key words and subject terms. Experiment with the ways you can limit the search. If you do this exercise with classmates, consider dividing up the possible databases and reporting your findings. You might also want to try searching for the same topic in two or three different databases.

Consider: What did you learn about the databases at your library? How would you explain to someone who has never used a database how to use it effectively? As you work with the database, what questions for inquiring into databases occur to you?

Knowing where to turn for the data you seek is a complicated process and depends, of course, on the topic or focus of your investigation. Thus it's difficult for a book like this one to give you all the possibilities. Instead we suggest you work with your teacher, your classmates (colleagues), and research librarians, just as any researcher would, narrowing your search, trying out possibilities, and learning about new databases and other research tools as you need them.

PART II: CLOSE (OR CRITICAL) READING

Close reading is a term that often substitutes for *analysis* for those who work with textual material. By breaking the larger text into parts, readers are able to notice features they might otherwise have missed and in the process come to understand the whole text in a new way. Such reading is not, of course, limited to written texts since images and lived events can also be examined as "texts." When football players spend hours viewing film, for example, they're not looking for highlights to make them feel good about previous games. They're combing through specific plays, training themselves to recognize patterns in small movements that might seem random to a casual fan. These patterns can reveal a great deal: their own team's or the opposing team's strengths and weaknesses or their own personal strengths and weaknesses, opportunities they might exploit against an opponent in an upcoming game. Commentators often point out the extended hours certain players spend viewing film; the commentators' implied or sometimes explicit message is that the extra effort these players put into their "reading" helps them better understand the game and gives them the edge over players who don't "read" as well or as often. In any type of analysis, a careful and sustained reading teaches you how to see and how to interpret and understand what you're seeing. This type of reading is hard work because you're not just reading the text; you are using the act of reading to teach yourself how to better understand what you read.

Scientists go through the same process of learning to analyze and read carefully. When novices first look into a microscope, it's hard for them to make out anything. It takes careful training and effort to see what they're supposed to see on the slide. Similarly, when most of us look at the night sky, we don't see what an astronomer sees. Partly the difference is that we don't even use the same reading "equipment" as the astronomer. We might, depending on our previous experience, see some constellations and not others. Those who have had a long-standing interest in the stars, those who have spent night after night watching, or those who have taken special trips to remote locations so that city or residential lights don't interfere with night vision can probably see a great deal in the night sky. Such sky-readers can identify which lights are stars and which are the planets in our solar system visible to the naked eye. They know where to point the telescope to find more distant objects. Professional astronomers use specialized reading tools to judge distances between celestial bodies, deduce the ages of the objects they're observing, and determine the physical composition of those bodies. However, for those of us who have never spent any time looking through a telescope, our vision is limited. We don't really know how to see what's out there waiting to be seen.

When scholars read texts, they do so with their own arsenals of specialized tools and precise terminology. Like the astronomer and the football player, those who engage in serious study of written texts learn to recognize meanings and patterns not readily visible to the untrained eye. Like the astronomer and football player, those who practice "close reading" on some texts develop habits that enable them to see more even on a first reading than inexperienced readers do. In other words, practice improves ability.

This more systematic and analytical type of reading is also called a *critical reading*. When you do a critical reading, you're not being asked to be "critical" in the pejorative sense or to provide a list of why you liked or disliked a text the way a movie or book critic might. What a critical reading asks you to do is connect the way the text was written with the meaning(s) you think the text is trying to convey or you think the text is conveying unintentionally. You're being asked to view the text as a collection of component parts, which you are able to identify and discuss in relation to the whole.

There are, of course, several variations of textual analysis and different theoretical perspectives that shape how academics interpret textual features and the patterns they discern. In *content analysis*, a form of textual analysis sometimes called *discourse analysis*, readers look carefully at the language of a text or texts, counting repetitions of words and phrases and determining connections between those words and phrases, all in an attempt to "[uncover] some underlying thematic or rhetorical pattern" (Huckin 14). In his essay "Content Analysis: What Texts Talk About," Thomas Huckin[2] describes the often-painstaking work of examining this type of textual data and the benefits and values of this type of thorough textual research. This work uncovers patterns that casual readers would find difficult to notice. These patterns, in turn, can suggest meaning where there had been only random examples. Included in the readings at the end of this book are a number of texts which use content analysis, a method that can be especially helpful in uncovering patterns of biases—deliberate or incidental—in texts or a series of related texts.[3] Sometimes content analysis is interested in small details like the shift of terms or repeated use of particular words. Leo Chavez, for example, in a part of his study of magazine covers devoted to the issue of immigration that we do not include in this volume, looks at how frequently these covers use terminology such as "invasion," "crisis," and "time bomb." Likewise, in her examination of the way media portrayed the emergence of rap music in the 1980s, Julia Koza notes the surprising frequency of words such as "underclass," and she notes how such semantic formulations have the power to move the media coverage of rap music from the "Music and Arts" section of a magazine to its "Social Issues" section (pp. 00). But content analysis can also be concerned with larger trends visible through counting how often the topic is considered. The study by Len-Ríos and her colleagues following the representation of women in two major newspapers is an example of content analysis that considers the big picture rather than individual words.

In *rhetorical analysis*, a form closely related to content analysis, the focus is on the persuasive intent of the text. Based on the belief that all texts exist, at least in part, as an argument, rhetorical analysis, as Jack Selzer[4] explains, "can be understood as an effort

---

[2]Thomas Huckin, "Content Analysis: What Texts Talk About," *What Writing Does and How It Does It: An Introduction to Analyzing Texts and Textual Practices*, ed. Charles Bazerman (Mahwah, NJ: Lawrence Erlbaum, 2003), 12–32.

[3]For a discussion of the way content analysis can itself be broken down into different approaches, see S. Titscher, M. Meyer, R. Wodak, and E. Vetter's *Methods of Text and Discourse Analysis* (Newbury Park, CA: Sage, 2000).

[4]Jack Selzer "Rhetorical Analysis: Understanding How Texts Persuade Readers" *What Writing Does and How It Does It: An Introduction to Analyzing Texts and Textual Practices*, ed. Charles Bazerman (Mahwah, NJ: Lawrence Erldaum, 2003), 279–307.

to understand how people within specific social situations attempt to influence others through language" (281). American society in the twenty-first century is deeply committed to the idea that language and the way it is used, that is, *rhetoric*, is persuasive. Consider the billions of dollars that advertisers spend to convince us to buy their products.[5] Similarly the uproar that often arises over foul language on television or radio attests to our beliefs that language is profoundly persuasive, even dangerous. Rhetoricians read to reveal the strategies that writers use to manipulate their readers, the ways in which writers exert the power of their language. Although manipulation often has a negative connotation, rhetorical analysis looks at the manipulation inherent in all textual acts, from politicians looking for votes to dentists encouraging better oral hygiene. Like those who are interested in content analysis, rhetoricians frequently examine the connections or disjunctions between the form of presentation and the surface content. Those who analyze political speech, for example, are often attending to the gaps between the overt message and the forms (or context) for its presentation. Janis Edwards and Carol Winkler's examination of the appropriation and reconfiguration of the Iwo Jima image in editorial cartoons is an excellent example of this kind of rhetorical analysis, though of course they are also arguing against scholars who have claimed that only discursive texts can function as ideographs.

Some rhetoricians are interested not just in overtly persuasive texts such as advertisements or political speech but rather in the way all discourse serves to create a world with relationships between the writer, the reader, and the topic. These rhetoricians are interested in how writers (or speakers) create these relationships in the decisions they make about how to write or what to say. James Boyd White's essay comparing Greek theater to judicial opinions is an example of a scholar working in the *constitutive rhetoric* tradition. For White and other scholars who use this approach, unpacking the language of such documents can help us understand the complex dynamics of relationships and the significance of key terms that reflect cultural values, values that often go unexamined and unchallenged.

In *literary analysis*, the form of textual analysis with which most college students are at least somewhat familiar, readers have traditionally looked at specific features of the prose to help decipher or complicate the surface meaning of a poem, story, play, or novel. These standard literary devices—including metaphor, metonymy, synecdoche, simile, setting, plot, and characterization—provide a richer, more suggestive reading experience, and the study of these literary devices allows readers access to multiple levels of textual meaning. In literature classrooms today, literary analysis and rhetorical analysis often go hand in hand. Scholars influenced by incarnations of literary criticism from postcolonialism to feminist theory read literary texts as implicit arguments for (or against) social change or as arguments asserting or limiting the power and agency of the individual in the world.[6] In this context literary features are noted alongside other rhetorical strategies. This type of reading has moved outward from literature classrooms, so that rhetoricians are also looking at the literary features of nonliterary texts, trying

---

[5]Commercials combine text with persuasive use of visual and aural appeals, all designed to manipulate consumers into purchasing a given product.

[6]For an examination of the different branches of literary criticism, take a look at John Anthony Cuddon's *A Dictionary of Literary Terms and Literary Theory* or Terry Eagleton's *Literary Theory: An Introduction*, or one of the many other similar works at your institution's library. Literary theory resources are also available on the web, and we provide a few such links in the Internet Resources at the end of this chapter.

to determine the way writers and speakers use features of narrative and metaphor to tell "stories" about ourselves. Some scholars argue that everything that we think we know, from history to religion to science, has its basis in the stories that we tell ourselves about the world; thus, for these scholars understanding the features of our storytelling patterns is crucial to understanding our knowledge of the world around us.

FACETS OF A CRITICAL READING

Consider the various facets of careful close reading to be a means of gathering information and developing ideas. Instead of researching in the library or surfing the Internet or peering through a telescope at the night sky, you do a close or critical reading by searching through a text. The act of writing about the text also helps you to think about the text more carefully, so we can't really say that first you read, and then you write; rather, critical/close reading is an activity of reading and writing simultaneously. It might be helpful, then, to review the strategies outlined in the introduction in the section headed "Active Reading." As researchers work with texts they consider such big issues as:

- *Purpose:* What's the author's intent or message? Where is that message made clear, and where is it implied? Try saying this message in your own words. Chances are high that the message is not new but rather a restatement of a point others have made in other ways. So what makes this writer's message different from those other versions? What's the *spin* here? How is the topic written about? Is the message (or primary topic) presented positively or negatively?

- *Audience:* Who is the author writing to and why? How can you tell who the intended audience is meant to be? Is there another audience (an implied audience) hiding behind this direct audience? Consider, for example, the syllabi that you receive from your professors. Most such documents are written to students in the class — the direct audience. But because professors know that these documents will be read by others — department chairs, university officials, colleagues — they often have features that are meant for these other readers more than they are for the students taking the course. Speeches by politicians have a similar double audience — the audience who hears the speech at the time it is given and the many

---

PRACTICE ACTIVITY 6-4

Close Reading of Course Syllabi

Using the syllabi for the courses you are taking this term, do a close reading that employs content analysis (what features are similar across all courses), rhetorical analysis (what strategies are the authors using and how do these documents construct you, the course, and the teacher), and literary analysis (what metaphors or other literary devices are present). You may want to pay particular attention to the pronouns (see the discussion of pronoun use in Chapter 3 in the section after Figure 3.1).

Consider: What claims would you make about the genre of course syllabi given your analysis? What could you say about the culture of college courses based on these documents?

others who will read (or hear about) the speech later. Likewise business letters often have an immediate audience, but are consciously written for the potential audience that might emerge in a lawsuit. How are these various audiences/readers spoken to (or about)? How does that way of talking fit with or contradict the message? What specific features of the words on the page clue you into these issues of audience?

- *Context:*   When did this text appear and what prompted its creation? Whether the text is imaginary literature (a short story, novel, play, or poem) or a piece of transactional writing (a memo or letter, for example), it was created at a particular moment in time and in a particular culture and that context is not the same as the one in which it has continued to exist (or in which it has reemerged if the document is one that was "lost" and then "rediscovered" and republished). Some of the features of the text will inevitably be a result of the context of its creation, but other features will reflect the author's interpretations of this context. Think, for example, of what features let you recognize a poem when you see it or how you can classify a play as tragedy or comedy. Business letters have different features than love letters. What can be written in an e-mail today is different from what would have been written in an eighteenth-century letter, and either of these is different from an entry in a diary. Context matters. Where can you *see* that context in the writing?

- *Author:*   Who the writer actually is as a human being is different from the author who is constructed through the writing. In imaginative texts this issue is often discussed in terms of the point of view or narrative voice. Is the story told through a main character or by an omniscient presence? In nonliterary texts, point of view, and the construction of the authorial voice is also an issue, though one that is regularly ignored. Take, for example, documents such as travel brochures, government regulations, or institutional mission statements. Some individual (or group of individuals) writes these documents, but they are often constructed to appear author-less. Why would this stance be useful, even desirable? What features contribute to such a stance? Are there contradictions in the authorial voice, shifts in tone, for example, or places in the text where the message is at odds with the authorial construction?

Close/critical reading also involves attention to small features, to individual words and matters of style because the larger features are constructed through such small details. Close reading of texts means considering such items as:

- *Word Choice:*   What are the key words that are repeated throughout the text and how are those terms defined in the writing? Sometimes, for example, a key term is explicitly defined. More often it is defined through example or illustration, through juxtaposition with other terms, by being repeated in different situations with different nuances. Don't forget that words have connotations as well as denotations. Note metaphors and other figures of speech which create both literal and symbolic meaning. Look for repetitions of sounds even when the words are different. Consider the way that words reflect the intended audience, convey information about characters, or signal the bias of the author. Note, too, any foreign words or phrases and consider why these words are not translated. Jargon or specialized terms, like words rendered in dialect, are worth your attention.

- *Organization:* How is the material organized? Common organizational strategies are cause/effect, comparison/contrast, chronological (or narration), process, and classification and division. But these organizational strategies are not always clear-cut and longer pieces of writing often use more than one strategy or a variation of one of these. Try outlining the text you are working with using either a formal outline or a flowchart. Look for transition words and phrases that often signal the organization. Headings and subheadings usually signal different points, but the type or format of these headings indicates material that is of the same level of importance (or generality). In literary texts, chapter (or scene) breaks are important indicators of organization and often are used when the point of view shifts or to jump forward or backward in time. Some features of organization might seem to be only the result of the genre. For example, the salutation is a standard feature of a business letter. But sometimes important distinctions are lurking in these common places. When Jane Austen includes letters in her novels, for example, it's worth thinking about why she does so (and when) since she has other choices for presenting the information revealed in these epistolary moments of her texts. Likewise, when narrative moments enter into nonliterary texts, their use should be examined carefully. Presidential speeches often make use of such narrative moments, and these are rarely simple insertions of personal accounts that illustrate the overall message.

- *Evidence:* What details, examples, illustrations, or data are presented to support the points being made? Are the evidence and conclusions presented inductively or deductively? Is this evidence believable, logical, and sound (i.e., can you trust it or are there indications that it is meant to be taken as satire, irony, parody, or that it is unreliable, biased, or fallacious)? Try sorting out the primary claims (or conclusions) from the text that supports, illustrates, or explains those claims. Not every claim will be supported with evidence, let alone the same kind of evidence, so notice what gets treated as an assumption and what gets support. Often writers will consider counterarguments, or how the evidence can make a different argument from the one they are advancing. Try to track these moves and consider whether the author is giving all sides the same level of consideration. Evidence often appears as quotations or paraphrases of other people's words. In academic writing, it is common to separate the primary text (or evidence) from the secondary texts (or sources). Textual analysis often considers not only who gets quoted and how reliable that source is, but also how the quoted material works within the primary text. It's usually worth the trouble to look up the quoted material to see how the writer has made the extraction. Is the passage quoted in total or extracted in a way that shifts its meaning or emphasis? What gets quoted and what gets left out (or summarized) is worth considering. Does the quoted passage get explained or explicated or does it simply appear, as if *how* it supports the primary author's argument is obvious? Legal analysis often hinges on such tracing of cited texts (prior legal cases) because the interpretation of those cases is the essence of establishing (or countering) legal precedence. Even in imaginative literature, attention should be paid to various kinds of evidence that make up the plot, characters, and thematic issues. Since few stories are told completely in dialogue, paying attention to when dialogue enters the story, who speaks, what they say, and how they say it is a useful and common strategy of analysis. Likewise many scholars are interested in the interaction between text and visual materials—charts, graphs, tables, or illustrations—and whether visual or textual material takes precedence in readers' experience of the text.

- *Character:* Who are the actors in the piece and how are they constructed? How do we learn about these characters—from their own words, those of other characters, or those of the author? Are these different sources of information equally reliable? What role do the characters play in developing the message? Do any of the characters function as symbols? Character may seem to be a feature that applies only to imaginative texts, but nonimaginative texts often have characters as well. A business letter, for example, may complain about or praise a store clerk, judicial opinions construct the characters involved in the suit when they repeat the facts of the case or summarize the rulings of a lower court, and travel brochures feature characters in the form of local merchants or visiting tourists. And characters can fall into common types (see Symbolism) so pay attention to the details that make the characters complex human beings or symbolic figures.

- *Symbolism:* Like visual works, textual material makes use of a wide array of symbols to convey additional meaning. Metaphors and other figurative language are clearly symbolic, but other features of the text can carry symbolic meaning as well. Characters, for example, might replicate behavior or characteristics that are similar to other cultural figures (the Christ figure, the Cinderella figure, the wicked stepmother, the tragic hero, the long-suffering saint are among the common character types). Any story can follow familiar lines, and some of these are employed even in nonliterary writings (the rags to riches tale, the American success story, the cautionary tale are all familiar tropes). Symbolic meaning also emerges when researchers read the parallels and disjunctions between form and meaning.

- *Style:* Visual features, layout, tone, sentence length, even punctuation are reflections of authorial choices (and contextual conditions) that enhance meaning either by reinforcing the message or contradicting it. Authors, especially literary authors, regularly make such choices consciously for their intended impact, but all writers produce words on the page that are consistent with expectations of their time and the genre they are working within. Presenting information as a bulleted list, for example, has a different effect than presenting the same information as a series of short sentences. Either of those choices produces a different impact on readers than if the information is presented in a long, complex sentence. Some of these stylistic differences are simply idiosyncratic—up to the author alone—but many are choices made unconsciously or because they seem right, and they seem right because they are consistent with the writers' background, training, or understanding of what is expected of them. As you can see by flipping through the readings collected in this text, historians follow different expectations for their scholarship than sociologists, general readership publications look and sound different from scholarly journals, and British writers use a different style from that of American authors. One place to see such stylistic differences is in the references section of scholarly publications. All researchers are careful to provide information about their sources, but how that information is arranged follows conventions that vary from discipline to discipline. Experienced readers of texts can classify a piece of writing as belonging to one discipline or another based simply on looking at the style of presentation of the references. But authors, especially authors of imaginative literature, also regularly challenge the expected features of genres. One common way of reading literary works is for these challenges to the conventions of the time or the expectations of the genre for it is through such a process that new forms are produced and old ones are revised. You might remember, for example, the moment when reality television shows began to be popular and how those shows altered the usual genres of sitcoms, dramas, game shows, or televised news. If you've watched any of these shows over time, you're probably aware of the many variations in structure that are not easily reduced to new characters, new situation. So, as you analyze textual material, pay attention to the many stylistic devices that authors employ—consciously or not—and read them for their consistency or disjunction with the message, as well as for whether they conform to or challenge the conventions of their time.

SPECIAL MATERIAL: MUSIC AND PUBLIC SPEECH

Both music and public speech are texts with other, nonwritten components. Delivery, tone of voice, rhythm, and gestures, for example, cannot be easily reduced to features on a page though scholars have developed a set of transcription symbols used to capture some of these nontextual features (see Figure 6.1). So, while it is common to extract the written words of lyrics or oral talk (formal speeches or informal conversation) and to analyze those written words like other examples of written text, we want to remind you up front that these other, nonwritten features are worth your attention as well when you are working with music or other orally delivered discourse. Similarly the interactions between the words and the other aural features or visual accompaniments to these textual moments can serve to strengthen your analysis because they indicate either consistencies with the message or contradictions/disjunctions to that message. Think, for example, of the facial expressions or tone of voice that clue you in to sarcasm and how a written version of the words said often fails to capture that sarcastic intent.

While the text of both music and speech can be considered using the same strategies as are used in other written texts for the kinds of features discussed earlier, both have a heavier reliance on rhythm, tempo, and rhyme than do other kinds of texts. In formal speeches, whether political campaign speeches or college lectures, speakers usually structure their text to help listeners grasp their meaning more easily. Thus speeches tend to provide an overview of what's to come early on, develop the points with more overt signaling of the different parts provided though words because headings or other stylistic features can only be reproduced aurally through words, and summarize the main points at the end so that listeners remember the key issues. The admonition to "tell them what you're going to tell them, tell them and tell them what you've told them" comes from oral discourse traditions and often seems simply redundant in texts that are presented in a written form and read silently.

Parallel and repetitive phrases (or sounds) are also even more common in oral discourse than in written texts. Like poetry, musical lyrics break sentences into phrases that fit the tempo rather than keeping standard discursive phrasing and word order.[7]

---

[7]Consult a dictionary of literary terms for examples of the many different ways that writers create different affects by manipulating figures of thought (tropes), speech (like chiasmus or metaphors), and sound (such as alliteration and assonance). Your library will most likely also have many similar resources. Try a search with the subject terms "literature- terminology" or "literary form terminology."

FIGURE 6.1 Common transcription symbols used to preserve oral features

[ ]	Square brackets are used to indicate segments of speech that overlap. Left brackets mark the beginning of the overlap and right brackets indicate the end of the simultaneous utterances. These brackets often interrupt sentences or even words to reflect the moments of overlap precisely. Thus, in the following example, Student B starts talking before Student A has finished.

Student A: Did you do all the home [work?]

Student B: [I got ho]me re:ally late.

(0.5)	Numbers in parentheses indicate silence, represented in tenths of a second. Thus, (0.5) indicates 5/10 seconds of silence. Silence is marked both between utterances and within them.
.	A dot is used to indicate a pause that can be heard but not measured accurately.
?, ¿	Punctuation marks are used to reflect delivery rather than grammatical conventions. Commas mark continuing intonation rather than clauses. Inverted question marks indicate a rising intonation stronger than a comma but less than a question.
:	Colons are used to indicate stretching of the sound just before them. The more colons, the longer the stretch. Graphically stretching a word so as to align it with overlapping speech does not indicate that the speaker stretched the word in delivery. Thus,

A: Oh :::[NOW] I get it.

B: [See?]

-	Hyphens indicate self-interruptions or cut-offs
Word	Underlining indicates stress or emphasis, by increased loudness or higher pitch. The more underlining, the greater the stress. Underlining can carry across all or a portion of a word
wOrd	Alternatively, capitalization can indicate louder delivery.
(())	Double parentheses are used to mark off anything the transcriber needs to represent that cannot be reproduced in speech. ((cough)), or ((telephone rings)) or ((whispers))
( )	Blank parentheses indicate segments that the transcriber cannot hear. If the speaker cannot be clearly identified but the context allows a good guess, the speaker identification is put in parentheses.

If you think of the sections of famous speeches that are commonly recognized and remembered—Martin Luther King's "I Have a Dream," Abraham Lincoln's "Gettysburg Address," or John F. Kennedy's "Inaugural Speech," for example—you will surely remember the sections that have strong repetition and striking cadence. Likewise advertising jingles or catch-phrases are at least partly remembered because of their use of repetition, striking tone, memorable phrasing, or pleasing melody.

Vocal quality makes some voices instantly recognizable and thus subject to parody or mimicry. Accent links a speaker to a specific region or country of origin even more strongly than do idiomatic phrases, slang, or regionalisms. Sociolinguists are therefore often interested in such features of speech because they not only influence the communication process

PRACTICE ACTIVITY 6-5

Listening to Oral Speech

Visit any of the Web sites listed in footnote seven and listen to a speech that catches your interest. What features of both content and delivery do you notice even the first time you listen? Replay the speech to see what you notice the second time around that you may have missed. If the speech is a video, try turning off the sound so you can watch facial expressions and gestures in isolation. Make notes on your observations/impressions of this speech.

Consider: Compare the notes of your experience with those of classmates who listened to different speeches. What common patterns exist across different speeches? What questions about these speeches occur to you? How would you investigate those questions?

or alter interpretations of meaning but also are linked to attitudes and perceptions. Similarly common and repeated features of oral exchanges—stock greetings, call/response patterns of some religious groups, rituals for expressing sorrow or offering apologies— are regularly the subject of research as scholars attempt to better understand the complex nature of oral discourse and the influence of talk on social interactions. Because researchers who work with oral discourse often tape record and then transcribe the speech into written text before they begin to analyze the transactions, a number of conventions for transcribing tapes of conversation have been developed to preserve the pauses, interruptions, moments of talking over and other disjunctions that are normal in speech but usually edited out of written discourse. We don't expect that beginning students will undertake a complicated study of oral discourse, but if you use tape recordings for interviews or focus groups and end up transcribing even a small portion of those recordings, you should at least remember to differentiate between pauses and words you can't hear (or choose to omit). Failing to do so will result in having to return to the original tape recording.

Scholars who study performances of music, often in combination with dance, also have to develop ways to represent in writing the complex vocal characteristics of songs in addition to the standard musical scale with its notes, bars, and directive phrases. These scholars also have specialized vocabulary not unlike the range of terms used for describing visual art.[8] Ethnomusicologists such as Professor Michelle Kisliuk[9] are also interested in the social interactions that enable such performances and so work like anthropologists to understand the full context of the musical performances and their meanings in the culture. But you needn't go to distant countries to inquire about the social or cultural functions of music. Mark Jackson's analysis of Woody Guthrie's "This Land Is Your Land," included in the Readings section, demonstrates how the original lyrics served as a social commentary and criticism of class differences during the

---

[8]Glossaries of musical terminology are abundant. See, for example, *The Oxford Dictionary of Musical Terms* by Alison Latham; *Thesaurus of Abstract Musical Properties: A Theoretical and Compositional Resource* by Jeffrey Johnson; and *Musical Terms, Symbols, and Theory: An Illustrated Dictionary* compiled by Michael C. Thomsett.

[9]Although we have not included any assignments that ask that you work with performances, we recommend Kisliuk's discussion and video of BaAka dance/music from Central Africa at http://chnm.gmu.edu/worldhistorysources/analyzing/music/musicq1.html as an example of such work.

PRACTICE ACTIVITY 6-6

Transcribing Oral Speech

Record at least one minute of a television or radio show or commercial that has more than one person speaking. Transcribe this dialogue exchange using the common transcription marks provided in Figure 6.1

Consider: What difficulties do you encounter as you move heard texts onto the printed page? Compare your transcription with those of your classmates. Are the transcriptions similar across different kinds of dialogues? Are some dialogues easier to transcribe than others?

Depression era and how the most critical of these verses dropped out as the song was appropriated by others. University of California Irvine student William Chiriguayo's study titled "'The Rhythmic Cry of the Slave': Black Music and Cultural Identity in America, 1890–1910" combines a close reading of lyrics with historical research to argue for the social and political importance of Negro spirituals in the Jim Crow era.[10]

When scholars work directly with the musical performance rather than with these cultural or social undercurrents of music, they generally consider three major dimensions:

- *Sensory:* Listening to the sound and capturing its quality in writing requires careful attention to different aspects of the sound including consideration of what produces the sound; what qualities of tone, pitch, timbre or harmony that sound has; and how the loudness or intensity of the sound affects the experience.

- *Emotive:* Considering how the features of the music evoke reactions, usually but not always emotional reactions; fast tempos, for example, are upbeat and so cheerful while the slower tempos of funeral marches are more solemn and thus more appropriate for mourning.

- *Structural:* Represented by the movement and composition of rhythms, meter, pitch, order, melody and other formal characteristics of the piece.

SPECIAL MATERIAL: ARCHIVES

In a sense archival research is a natural extension of the archeologist's fieldwork, except carried out with artifacts that have purposely been stored. Although most archival materials are documents, archives can include nontextual artifacts as well. Working with artifacts is discussed in Chapter 3 because not all artifacts are housed in formal archives. In fact it pays to remember that archives vary greatly in their level of formality.

INFORMAL ARCHIVES

A student organization has boxes of papers and junk stuffed at the bottom of an old standing locker. The materials are haphazardly organized. Occasionally, when members want to look up a former decision of the governing council or get ideas for a flyer, they

---

[10]Chiriguayo's study can be found in the Undergraduate Research Journal available on-line at http://www.urop.uci.edu/journal/journal02/02_WilliamChiriguayo/William.pdf.

dig through "The Archive." Archives, you see, take many forms and serve many different purposes. A box of family photographs, your or your parents' tax records, a family Bible swollen with significant documents, photographs or papers marking important occasions, attic boxes of holiday ornaments, a local shop's old records—all these and similar collections are archives, and all record important memories.

What you do with archives, though, depends on your general approach to them. You might approach an informal archive as a user, a general researcher, an archeologist, or a librarian. Often you will approach the archive from a combination of these positions. For a *user*, the archive serves a regular function integrated into daily life. A local shop that has archived financial records may use them if audited by the IRS or when projecting quarterly income; a family with a photograph collection will pull them out from time to time, pass them around, and share memories. A *general researcher* may be investigating the financial well-being of small businesses in the local community, and use the shop's records to further this research, or she may be looking into the history of a particular family and so use the photographs to confirm or discover information about the family. *Archeologists* may be interested in how businesses in a certain area have kept records and what that says about the organization of yearly business cycles, or the ways families build cohesion, and these archives would serve their purposes accordingly. A *librarian* would be interested in organizing and storing materials, and so would be interested in developing an organizational scheme, clearly labeling all documents, and finding a way to index them so people could find what they are after efficiently. Most of us have assumed these different roles in relation to the documents in our lives at one time or another. We know that the roles often overlap: general users who act like librarians will increase their efficiency, for example.

Of course the organization of informal archives varies wildly. Sometimes the records will be meticulous, sometimes in a giant heap. Organizational schemes, even in terms of the order in which a collection of boxes is stacked, often reveal important parts of their purpose, so you should try your best, when working with these kinds of archives, to keep track of their order (or lack thereof) for your own purposes. If you are working with an archive archeologically or as a general researcher, that is, if the archive is as much an object of study as it is a useful and functioning collection, you should maintain and restore the items in it as you found them. And you should handle materials in archives, especially older ones, with care. You never know if future generations will find these materials valuable.

Here are a few things you can do with informal archives:

- List their contents.
- Group them according to different themes.
- Determine their purpose or function: Why have these items been saved or stored?
- Develop a catalog or description of their contents—a finding aid—so future users will be able to find what they are after more efficiently.
- What you do with the archives, however, will depend greatly on your intended use.

LIBRARY AND INSTITUTIONAL ARCHIVES

There are many different kinds of formal and institutional archives: libraries, historical societies or similar organizations, businesses or governmental organizations, public records offices—all keep archives. Some of these institutional archives are open to

FIGURE 6.2 Submitting materials for preservation

The materials you develop or produce as a result of your investigations may be of interest to future historians. In addition businesses and governments, chambers of commerce, tourist offices, zoning boards, as well as local historical associations or museums understand the significance of local history. Tape recordings of oral histories produced during interviews, photographs you take or discover, newspaper clippings or other artifacts that you may be given by private individuals, and, of course, your final essay or article might all be things researchers would love to have available to them for their own projects. If as a result of your work you create an archive, say for a campus organization, then you will have accomplished some important work in preserving cultural memory. Your school, a local organization, an area museum, or a local library might also have an archives division, and you should consider submitting your research materials to that unit if you want to make them available to future generations. Any oral history, or work based on oral history, that you want to submit should have a signed release allowing future researchers access to the tape and/or transcript. Consult the section on Oral Histories in Chapter 4, and the Internet Resources at the end of that chapter for further suggestions about oral histories. Your local archivist may have additional suggestions about preparing your work for submission so it is worth your time to consult with such people early in the process of collecting your materials.

the public, though learning to use them effectively is a different matter. Library archives tend to be among the most restrictive and carefully guarded. Some have individual and idiosyncratic rules; some are very personal extensions of a local archivist, who sometimes has responsibilities other than maintaining the archive; some are themselves large institutions with separate buildings and multiple professional staff members.

Archivists must protect the materials in their collections, and it sometimes seems that using archives is similar to a self-authorizing code; if you are able to overcome the hurdles in your way to finding and getting the materials you want, you prove yourself worthy of their use! No book can take all the difficulty out of using institutional archives, but this section will try to alert you to some of the hurdles you may encounter. Most archivists will be happy to have you using their materials and will do their best to provide you with the help they can so long as you are respectful of their materials and the work they do. Using the archives becomes fairly easy once you get your bearings. Few things will give you a firmer sense of yourself as a scholar, fully vested in your college or university and generating new knowledge, than working with materials that few people before you, if any, have researched.

Library archives will have a set of rules you need to obey. The first thing to know about library archives is that because use really is a privilege, archival librarians restrict access to their collections. There are situations when archivists will deny you access to portions or even to all of a collection; their ability to protect the archival materials under their stewardship is a primary reason archivists have the positions they do. It is critical for all parties involved that you respect archivists' responsibilities, maintain a professional attitude in all your dealings with them, and be ready to communicate as clearly as you can your research interests and/or requirements.

You cannot just wander into the archive and begin pulling materials off the shelf, as you would in the regular library. You will usually need to fill out circulation request forms, asking for certain materials and perhaps providing a rationale for doing so. Archivists, at this point, retrieve the materials from storage and allow you to view them in a reading room. Rarely can you remove archival materials from the reading room. Archivists will often enforce certain rules, for example not allowing backpacks into the reading room, requiring the use of pencils rather than pens, asking that you use a certain color paper for note taking, and restricting photocopying. These rules help archivists protect the materials. So one thing you should start with as you begin working with library or other institutional archives is a healthy respect for other scholars, making sure that you protect these materials so they will continue to be available to everyone.

The cataloging of archival materials is different than the ways books are cataloged in a normal library. This is partly because library archives tend to be organized by *collection*. Certain dignitaries will donate their papers or their personal library to an archive, and the items in those donations all become part of a single collection. Not all collections will be organized by donor—most archives contain a mixture of individual papers, topical collections (e.g., an Early Women Writers collection), and some other organizational scheme appropriate for the materials at hand. The tendency to organize in collections helps to explain some of the difficulties you may face when it comes to searching for and finding materials.

The cataloging of collections varies in level of depth and accuracy, even within one library's records. If you are lucky, the materials within a particular collection will have an overview or description with them, for example a brief biographical sketch of an individual whose papers have been left to a library. Sometimes the materials will be listed within the library's general catalogs, either physical catalogs or computerized ones; often they will not. Archivists may keep separate record sets for different kinds of documents—separating catalog information for manuscripts and books, for instance. Archivists also index their collections in *finding aids*. These are documents that list the boxes and their contents for the various collections in an archive. Finding aids are usually printed and collected in a notebook, or a catalog, and are increasingly available in online form as well.

If you get to know any archival librarians, you will discover that they are always in the process of producing better records and updating searchable databases of their materials. The process is never complete. So you should be prepared to use a few different search techniques, and you will need to take some time learning the systems your archivists have developed. You should also know that when individuals donate materials to library archives, they often maintain private property rights over those materials. Copyright laws and enforcement can be stringent. Consult the archivist if you plan to publish materials or photographs in some form, and be aware that some photocopy or image duplication requests may be turned down because of copyright concerns.

PRACTICE ACTIVITY 6-7

Archive Searching

Visit one of the online archives listed in the Internet Resources at the end of this chapter and experiment with the search engines available there. Alternatively, investigate what kinds of materials are available to you in your local libraries and historical societies. Follow your interests as you scope out what's available and how these materials are indexed.

Consider: What questions occur to you as you browse through these materials? How might you use these materials in an inquiry project?

FIGURE 6.3 **Guidelines for using a library or other institutional archive**

- *Contact the archivists ahead of time.* Let them know who you are and why you want to use the archive, and arrange for an orientation. Sometimes things will work out fine if you just "drop in," but in some situations and under some conditions, you could simply be turned away. If you have an instructor or someone affiliated with the institution that you can use as a resource, it is sometimes useful to make contact through this individual. If your entire class has an archive project, your instructor will likely have made arrangements with the archivist ahead of time. Be sure to find out the times when the archive is open and know that archives are rarely open to users as often or as long as the regular library so plan accordingly.

- *Bring a photo ID.* For entry to most archives, you will need some form of photographic identification. A student ID, in an archive associated with your school, is best.

- *Schedule an orientation session.* You will need to learn the rules and procedures for using this archive, and will also need to learn how to use its cataloging system. Plan to ask questions about and express interest in learning the rules and procedures for this archive at the orientation session. Do not plan to delve too deeply into the collection on your first visit, if at all. You may want to set as a goal for yourself to find and review one item during your initial visit.

- *Plan your trips.* That is trips with an "s." Most people will not find all they need in a single visit, and to tell the truth, you often won't know when your work with a particular archive is complete; there's always more to look into or discover. Many researchers find it useful to plan their trips accordingly. First, know yourself. How long can you realistically sit in the reading room and review the materials you will be looking over? Second, a useful procedure is to find a few things in the catalogs or finding aids that you want to review. Maybe look at one of these things on the first visit. Then, in subsequent visits, you can spend the first half of your time reviewing materials you found the previous visit, and the second half of your time pouring back through the catalogs to find materials to look over the next time. But you should also be flexible. If you discover a box containing "the key" to your project, you will want to use your time to focus attention on it.

- *If you are doing archival research as part of a course, keep your instructor posted.* While completing archival research, you will often discover very interesting

FIGURE 6.3 (Continued)

materials or insights you had not been looking for. You will also likely encounter difficulties you had not anticipated. Communicate with your instructor to be sure those
new avenues you want to explore fit within the context of a course or assignment, or
to figure out ways to overcome difficulties together. Communicating with your instructor is, of course, always a good idea, but such communication is especially helpful
when working with archives.

- *Ask questions.* Working with archives can be disorienting, and no two archives work
  exactly the same. Do not be afraid to ask questions about anything you are unsure of,
  from reading the records in a finding aid, to the correct way to handle items. If you
  think you may have mishandled some materials, notify the archivist right away to
  clear the problem up.

- *Take careful notes.* It is hard, as you will quickly discover, to access the archival
  materials. You never know for sure what aspects of your source materials will be most
  useful to you when you compose an essay about them, and they will usually not be
  immediately available as you are writing. In keeping your notes, be sure to keep careful bibliographic records both for the sake of citing the work and so you can find the
  materials again if you need to. (This really is the whole point of citing work in essays
  anyway—so scholars can help each other find the materials that they use in their
  work.) Many archives will provide you with directions about how to cite materials from
  their collection. Be sure to follow those directions if they are provided.

- *Get to work early on the writing, even in very rough form.* Even when you follow
  the above advice, you will often find that the crucial piece of information is something
  you forgot to take notes on. So you will have to revisit the archive in the middle of your
  composing process. If you are researching in the archives for a paper or presentation
  and leave that paper until the last minute, you will not be able to go back and look up
  the information you need. Remember that archives usually keep much more restricted
  hours than general libraries and that the retrieval process requires additional time.

ETHICAL CONSIDERATIONS

Because researchers who work with texts don't seem to have any impact on live human
beings, it is easy to miss that there are still ethical considerations in the work they do.
Chief among these concerns is the issue of plagiarism and the practice of citing sources
so that others know which words and ideas are the author's and which belong to someone else. Since the data of textual analysis are words on a page and these words can
look just like the words that the analyzer composes, proper use of quotations is essential.
Likewise secondary sources that help the analyzer explain the important features or
context of the primary text are also still words on a page, so ideas or concepts borrowed
from others must be distinguished both from the primary document being analyzed
and from the analyzer's own words and ideas. Obviously, however, working with texts
is not simply a matter of transcribing quotations onto the page and providing citation
information. Instead researchers who work with texts summarize, paraphrase, reorganize,
synthesize, and explicate textual material in a variety of ways. As they do so, they must
keep in mind their responsibility to make such renderings responsibly. Researchers who

work with small sections of text must guard against taking passages, or individual words, out of context not only because they invalidate their own work by appearing to have disregarded the original meaning, but also because the words (or passages) are their primary data and if they extract the data irresponsibly, they can't answer the questions they are interested in pursuing.

A good handbook will provide you with the details of various citations styles, but all have the same intention: provide the information that would allow someone else to locate the source used. Thus all citation styles provide the name of the writer, the title of the piece, the name of the publication, and the date published. Researchers have also developed conventions for handling the difficult process of indicating when a writer has had to change the original in order to make the passage conform to grammatical expectations. When, for example, researchers need to embed someone else's words in a sentence of their own and that embedding requires a small shift in the grammatical structure of the original, the change is indicated in a bracket. Sometimes, because of the way they are presenting the quotation, only the first letter of the quotation is in a bracket, a signal that the researchers have changed the capitalization of that letter (e.g., they are quoting from the middle of a longer sentence). Likewise sometimes a word is added in brackets to make an unclear pronoun or missing subject in the quoted sentence make sense. Researchers also use *sic*, Latin for "so, thus" in parentheses to indicate that a grammatical mistake occurred in the original and is not their fault. Such an indication sometimes draws attention to the mistake, but usually researchers chose to mark a mistake as *(sic)* in order to indicate their faithfulness to the original and their inability to get permission to correct the error.

WORKING ON WRITING FROM TEXTS

Although any researcher may have to work with textual material, those who work primarily with texts must regularly face the difficulty of paraphrasing or summarizing or providing a gloss of general points before they zoom in on the specific features they want to analyze or use as evidence. Such acts of summary happen in the frame as writers provide background about the primary text or highlight the key elements of the theoretical perspective that provides their lens of analysis. Summary can also occur later in the text as writers move from one example to another or turn to secondary sources to support their analysis. As with interview materials, researchers have to decide which parts of these texts they want to paraphrase, which they can incorporate into their own sentences as embedded quotations, and which can only rightly be presented as block quotations. We want to look at these issues of summary and quotation again in the context of working with textual materials, but we think that some of what we said in Chapter 2's overview of working with the words of others and in Chapter 4's discussion of quoting interviews may also be helpful to those working with textual analysis. For textual material, in particular, the key elements become summarizing for your own purposes, accuracy in representing others, and balancing your words with the words of others.

SUMMARIZING FOR YOUR OWN PURPOSES

When James Boyd White puts Greek tragic plays next to Supreme Court opinions to suggest that both play an important role in shaping public meanings and culture, he must necessarily summarize both kinds of texts before moving to the specific features that he wants to compare. To do so White first provides a kind of road map of his plan so as to keep readers with him: "I shall begin with what I assume to be the less familiar form, Greek drama, and then turn to the law." While White might have presented the texts in exactly the same order, his assumption that law would be more familiar is even more reasonable given that he originally wrote the piece for the *Journal of Supreme Court History*. Following a two paragraph overview of the importance of theater to Greek cultural life, White begins his presentation of the first text with a summary of the plot lines in three related performances:

> **I shall begin with** the great trilogy of Aeschylus called the *Oresteia*. **The first play**, the *Agamemnon*, <u>tells</u> the story of that hero's return to Mycenae from the Trojan War, and how he is shamefully killed—in his bath—by his wife Clytemnestra and her lover Aegistheus; **the second play** <u>tells</u> how her son Orestes, commanded by Apollo to avenge this murder of his father, kills his mother; **the third** <u>brings</u> on stage in pursuit of Orestes the Eumenides, the dreadful furies who punish the shedding of kindred blood. Orestes finds refuge in Athens, where he is tried for his act by a court and jury established for the purpose. He is acquitted, for he was acting under divine compulsion in the form of explicit orders from Apollo. **The trilogy thus <u>ends</u> with** the establishment in Athens of courts of justice; courts that will, in the future, break a chain of vengeance such as that which plagued the house of Atreus, and do so by impos-ing sanctions for homicide that themselves do not occasion blood guilt.
>
> **The *Agamemnon* begins with** a watchman in Mycenae waiting, at dawn, for the beacon of light that will announce the victory at Troy.... (p. 598)

We've highlighted in bold type the phrases that help White signal the moves he is making as he progresses from one play to the next. Notice his use of a parallel phrase when he turns from the general summary of the trilogy to the more specific summary of the first play at the beginning of the second paragraph. Notice, too, how the verbs, which we've underlined, help White structure the summary as clearly a summary. But what we find most important about this passage is that the details of the paragraph—the specifics of the three plays—are all intentionally selected to move to the point White wants to make: that these plays are connected to the establishment of courts of justice. We are not suggesting that White is wrong to characterize the plays in this way, or that he is somehow misleading his readers by representing the plays unfairly. Indeed we think that this gloss is certainly accurate, efficient, and crafted to serve the purpose at hand. But other writers with different purposes have summarized the plays highlighting different details. Look, for example, at how Professor Karen Carr summarizes the trilogy for children:[11]

> Aeschylus wrote tragedies about the difficult choices men (not, in his view, women) have to make, and what happens as a result. His most famous plays are the three plays *Agamemnon*, the *Libation Bearers*, and the *Eumenides*. In *Agamemnon*, the king has to decide whether to keep his promise to the other kings, even if it means killing his own daughter. In *Libation Bearers*, that king's son has to decide whether to kill his own mother, because she killed his father. And in *Eumenides*, a jury has to decide whether the same king's son is guilty of murder.

We think that Carr's purposes (and audience) are clearly different from White's, and so it can be little surprise that she highlights different features. Note that she still

---

[11]See http://www.historyforkids.org/learn/greeks/literature/aeschylus.htm.

presents the trilogy one play after another and that her short gloss of each of these plays still serves to illustrate her overarching characterization (or point), though she begins rather than ends the paragraph with her generalization.

In a similar way, Duke University student Stephen Fuller must efficiently summarize the plot of *Something Wicked This Way Comes* before he can move into his Freudian analysis, and he does so in the opening paragraph in the revised version of his essay.[12]

> Ray Bradbury's *Something Wicked This Way Comes* (1962) <u>reads</u> much like a classic horror novel. A carnival train rolls into Greentown, Illinois at midnight, just a week before Halloween. Led by a man named Mr. Dark, the carnival masquerades in the daytime as Cooger and Dark's Pandemonium Shadow Show, attracting visitors with carousels, mirror mazes, and performers. **But** Mr. Dark has a secret: his carnival's magic is real. **And** when night falls, his followers lure a few curious townspeople back to the campgrounds, promising to fulfill their every wish. **But** their wishes bear a heavy cost, and Mr. Dark transforms his victims into exaggerated versions of what they wished to be, **thus** trapping them in the carnival forever. Will Halloway, **however**, detects something sinister in the carnival's attractions and he follows his willful friend Jim Nightshade to the carnival each night, Will's father closely on their heels. Their meddling doesn't come without its own price, **though**, and as they come to face Mr. Dark's legion of grotesque circus attractions, Will and his father must face almost intolerable fear. With Bradbury's omniscient narrator describing their every trepidation, the <u>novel takes on</u> a notably psychological tone and <u>begins to focus</u> not only on good and evil but also on the nature of fear in the individual.

We've again underscored the key phrases where Fuller is signaling his summary of this text, and we've put in bold those words that help Fuller show the contrast between good and evil which is a major point for his analysis to come. Contrast Fuller's summary with this one prepared for Amazon.com by Stanley Wiater:[13]

> A masterpiece of modern Gothic literature, *Something Wicked This Way Comes* is the memorable story of two boys, James Nightshade and William Halloway, and the evil that grips their small Midwestern town with the arrival of a "dark carnival" one autumn midnight. How these two innocents, both age 13, save the souls of the town (as well as their own), makes for compelling reading on timeless themes. What would you do if your secret wishes could be granted by the mysterious ringmaster Mr. Dark? Bradbury excels in revealing the dark side that exists in us all, teaching us ultimately to celebrate the shadows rather than fear them. In many ways, this is a companion piece to his joyful, nostalgia-drenched *Dandelion Wine*, in which Bradbury presented us with one perfect summer as seen through the eyes of a 12-year-old. In *Something Wicked This Way Comes*, he deftly explores the fearsome delights of one perfectly terrifying, unforgettable autumn.

---

[12]Stephen Fuller, "The Freudian Uncanny in Ray Bradbury's *Something Wicked This Way Comes*," *Deliberations: A Journal of First-Year Writing at Duke University*, vol. 6 (Fall 2005): 46–52. available online at http://uwp.aas.duke.edu/writing20/publications/documents/FullerArticle.pdf. An earlier version of Fuller's essay is included at the end of this chapter.
[13]At http://www.amazon.com/Something-Wicked-This-Way-Comes/dp/0380729407.

Wiater's purpose is clearly different from Fuller's, but both provide us with a generalization that identifies the genre and details that help make the central dilemma of the story clear. Our point, again, is that your purpose will help guide which details you select as you write a summary, but that in presenting those details you need to signal your own point so that your readers can see how the text illustrates your point or is relevant to those purposes.

ACCURACY IN REPRESENTING OTHERS

When you summarize, you must take care not to misrepresent the original text. Such misrepresentation is especially frequent when writers turn to secondary texts that serve either as a lens through which they look at other materials, or as the opposing point of view that they are working to refute. Let's look, then, at how some of the writers included in the Readings section handle this difficult move of summarizing a secondary source.

When Michael Frisch tries to explain why students list Betsy Ross first when asked what they remember about American history from colonial times to the Civil War, he turns to cultural studies research and specifically to Catherine L. Albanese's *Sons of the Fathers: The Civil Religion of the American Revolution* (Philadelphia, 1976). Albanese's study helps Frisch to characterize Ross as a mother-figure, not because she makes this point, but because her work defines a symbolic framework for historical figures. Notice in the following passage how Frisch moves from his signal—a move that introduces the relevance of Albanese's work to his own study—to a paragraph summarizing what Frisch takes as the key point of Albanese's research for his purposes, and finally to his own interpretation of the symbolic role of Betsy Ross. Notice, too, that this secondary paragraph, which is his own interpretation, ends with a gesture back to Albanese's work, a gesture that both underscores his point and helps tie this analysis together. We've marked these moves to help you follow them. Here, then, is how Frisch moves from Albanese to his own point:

> Beyond helping us to respect, and thereby understand, a sometimes ludicrous apotheosis that began even in Washington's lifetime, Albanese's discussion provides a context for some final reflections on the essentially religious meaning of Betsy Ross's place in this collective portrait.

Signal to readers of why Frisch is introducing Albanese's study.

PRACTICE ACTIVITY 6-8

Summaries for a Purpose

Write a summary of a book or movie that you know well for the purpose of getting someone else to read that text or see the movie. Write a second summary with the purpose of introducing an analysis of this same text. Write a third summary of no more than a sentence that might serve as an advertisement.

Consider: Compare your three summaries with those written by your classmates. What strategies did you use as you shifted purposes? How do these different purposes change how you characterize the text or select the details to include?

Albanese documents how the revolutionary sons made themselves into Founding Fathers, with Washington the *primus inter pares*, literally the spiritual Father of the Nation. **She also shows how** his spiritual meaning came to obscure his real existence: his wife Martha faded from legendary image and relatively speaking from our memories, because "kindred as was the soul of the father of his country to his wife, it had proved to be far more closely interfused with the structures of meaning and value of his countrymen. Washington . . . had become a grand collective representative, a tribal totem." **And in the process**, fictive and symbolic kin came to replace his real family in popular imagination: **thus** the common celebration of the marquis de Lafayette as the "beloved and 'adopted son.'"

> Summary of Albanese's key point.

Albanese could go no further with the myth, but evidence of the symbolic role of Betsy Ross allows us to complete the picture. **To this end**, it is important to note that the Betsy Ross story is a product of a late nineteenth-century style of religio-mythic craftsmanship. The actual Betsy Ross had, demonstrably, no role whatsoever in the actual creation of any actual flag. **But more important**, her story itself played no part in revolutionary-era tradition or mythmaking even at its most instrumental. **In fact**, the flag story emerged only a century later in Philadelphia, when her descendants sought to create a tourist attraction around the time of the centennial exposition of 1876. The reasons for the emergence of the tale were thus prosaic, not to say mercenary; **but as Albanese reminds us**, however intentional and instrumental, such self-consciousness does not exclude deeper levels of cultural meaning and expression. (p. 397)

> Transition from Albanese to Frisch's own analysis

> Key details of history that Frisch offers as evidence for his interpretation of Ross as a symbol rather than an important historical figure.

> Gesture back to Albanese that also suggests why seeing Ross as a symbol, no matter how that symbolism was created, is important.

This passage is certainly making some of the same moves that we discussed earlier such as selecting details relevant to your own purposes and moving those details of summary toward your own point, even if it takes Frisch a bit longer. Indeed sometimes the move to summarize for your own purposes can take the entire essay, but you ought to be able to track what you are doing in order to see if every sentence is carrying you forward in the analysis. The question, though, is whether Frisch is using Albanese's work responsibly or misrepresenting her in some way. Without reading all of Albanese, it's difficult to say with absolute certainty that Frisch has gotten her work right, and we're certain that in a book-length project like Albanese's, there may be points where scholars disagree either about whether she is right or how to interpret what she is arguing. Still,

Frisch does some important work that helps his readers believe that he is representing Albanese fairly, including:

- Providing complete citation information so his readers can check the source for themselves
- Including some of Albanese's own words rather than trying to represent everything she says himself
- Perhaps most importantly moving between a general gloss and specific details to illustrate that gloss

Let's take a look at this last point more closely by returning to the key paragraph from the passage we quoted before and marking how Frisch includes both generalizations of Albanese's points and specific details to illustrate that generalization.

Albanese documents how the revolutionary sons made themselves into Founding Fathers, with Washington the *primus inter pares*, literally the spiritual Father of the Nation. **She also shows how his spiritual meaning came to obscure his real existence**: his wife Martha faded from legendary image and relatively speaking from our memories, because "kindred as was the soul of the father of his country to his wife, it had proved to be far more closely interfused with the structures of meaning and value of his countrymen. Washington … had become a grand collective representative, a tribal totem." And in the process, fictive and symbolic kin came to replace his real family in popular imagination: thus the common celebration of the marquis de Lafayette as the "beloved and 'adopted son.'"

> Generalization or gloss provided by Frisch

> Specific example of a Founding Father

> Translation of the Latin phrase

> Second feature of the generalized gloss of Albanese's work

> Details which illustrate this second point—symbolic family replaced real life in the cultural memory

Here's how Duke student Stephen Fuller introduced his secondary source, the lens through which he analyzed Ray Bradbury's story:

It is not surprising, then, that a psychoanalytic reading of Bradbury's novel would provide further insight into his message. **Indeed**, Sigmund Freud's 1919 essay "Das Unheimliche" proves highly relevant, considering its focus on fear and the human psyche. **In this famous work, Freud seeks to define "the uncanny," a concept that is "undoubtedly related to what is frightening—to what arouses dread and horror."** At its most basic level, Freud's uncanny is defined by the subconscious recognition of something familiar in the guise of the unfamiliar; some seemingly alien event touches something we have long since repressed and we perceive the uncanny. A Freudian analysis of the uncanny in *Something*

> Introduces the secondary text and the reason for turning to it

> Generalization provided by Fuller

> Restatement of generalization through definition of a key term

> Explanation of key term through additional definition

Wicked This Way Comes ultimately <u>redefines our perception of fear in Bradbury's novel, rooting it not in the evil of the carnival itself, but in the repressed thoughts and tendencies of Will and his father.</u> The major conflict, **then**, becomes the pro-tagonists' attempts to understand and overcome their fear. Only after they do this can they defeat Mr. Dark and rescue the townspeople from his magic. The resolution of this conflict, **as defined by Freud's belief in psychoanalysis, is that fear is ultimately dispelled as our repressed tendencies are allowed to come to the surface.** This notion that the individual can conquer fear through accep-tance aligns powerfully with <u>Mr. Halloway's real-ization that only the individual bears the power to conquer fear by accepting the presence of evil in both the individual and society.</u> **Ultimately**, ana-lyzing *Something Wicked This Way Comes* in the context of Freud's theory of the uncanny **not only** helps the reader to better frame Bradbury's psy-chological treatment of fear, **but also** directly rein-forces his message concerning the nature of fear and the individual's ability to dispel it.

> Details that support the reason for bringing these two texts together

Fuller's use of Freud's theory weaves the two texts together rather than presenting all of first one and then the other, but he nevertheless still makes the moves to provide both generalizations and then specifics as he links these two texts together. This partic-ular paragraph actually serves only as an introduction to a much longer summary of the relevant points in Freud's treatment of the uncanny before Fuller turns his attention back to the fictional work.

Writers make similar moves when they appropriate a secondary source that serves as a counterpoint, or opposition, to their own message. Such uses of source material require similar gestures to gloss the whole, or that part of the whole that is most relevant to your purposes, in a general way. The generalization is then followed with specific details of the source's point, often presented in the original author's own words. Look, for example, at how Janis Edwards and Carol Winkler argue against Michael McGee's narrow formulation of "ideographs," a term they want to appropriate into their analysis of political cartoons. We give you two paragraphs from their text marked as we have earlier summaries/appropriations to make it easier to follow the key moves of gen-eralization and details, but in this case also how these authors are delineating their disagreement with the source.

In 1980 Michael C. McGee formulated the concept of ideographs—culturally-grounded, summarizing, and authoritative terms that enact their meaning by expressing an association of cultural ideals and experiences in an ever-evolving and reifying form within the rhetorical environment. **An ideo-graph's meaning develops through its usages and**

> Introduces secondary sources; note that the key term is followed by a glossing definition/explana-tion that is further developed over the rest of this paragraph

applications, operating as an abstraction and a fragment within the larger rhetorical environment. McGee identifies ideographs as a word or group of words, such as "liberty" or "patriotism," that serve to rhetorically create communities according to ideological constraints and beliefs. By stressing the role of language, **McGee specifically confines the notion of the ideograph to the linguistic realm**.

McGee's assumption that ideographs must be "actual words or terms" lacks a clear rationale (p. 8). **While maintaining** that ideology by necessity is always false and thereby rhetorical, **he insists** that the "clearest access to persuasion (and hence to ideology) is through the discourse used to produce it" (p. 5). **He presumes** that the relevant discourse must be "political language preserved in rhetorical documents," (p. 5) **never addressing** the potential inclusion or exclusion) of nondiscursive forms. **Further, he argues** that ideographs should be restricted to words **because he rejects** propositional logic to explain incidents of "social conflict, commitment, and control" (p. 6). **McGee distinguishes** between the terms and the ideas that become clouded through the use of those terms. **Defining the ideograph** as "language imperatives which hinder and perhaps make impossible pure thought" (p. 9), **he again disregards** the rhetorical potential of visual images. **In the process, he limits** the ideograph to the verbal **rather than** the visual realm. (p. 371)

> Generalized version of the grounds of disagreement—note how this opening sentence echoes the elements highlighted in the previous paragraph that was only summarizing McGee's concept

> Notice how all the specific details that follow the generalization of the disagreement Edwards and Winkler have with McGee are carefully structured with language that makes it clear that they are representing his work and simultaneously demonstrating the key points of contention.

Perhaps you've noticed that we've also been putting key words in boldface type. These are words that help the writers to stitch these paragraphs together, demonstrating in the process the connections they want to make and how different points tie together. We discussed such transition phrases in Chapter 2 as well, so it may be helpful to turn to that section, but if we collect these phrases together, we think you'll see that these writers, though they make the same gestures of generalization and specific details arranged for their own purposes, are nonetheless selecting their words to signal their stance toward the secondary source. Figure 6.4 provides a list of verbs regularly used by writers presenting the words of others. Can you distinguish which ones signal agreement and which ones suggest opposition?

FIGURE 6.4   Words for representing what others have to say

documents, shows, reminds, defines, formulates, develops, identifies, stresses, maintains, insists, presumes, addresses, argues, rejects, distinguishes, disregards, limits, claims, asserts, contends, declares, classifies, recognizes, differentiates, separates, detects, imagines

---

PRACTICE ACTIVITY 6-9

Fair Representation

Find an editorial or letter to the editor that expresses an opinion you disagree with. Write a summary of this position being careful to present it as accurately as you can. Find a second editorial or letter with which you agree and write a second summary. Give both your summaries to a classmate. If you've done a good job of representing the views of others fairly, your classmates should not find any inaccuracies in your summaries but they probably will be able to tell which editorial you oppose.

Consider: Discuss with your classmates the difficulties of representing the views of others when you have strong positive or negative opinions about those views. Can you develop a set of principles for fair representation in paraphrasing?

BALANCING YOUR WORDS WITH THE WORDS OF OTHERS

As we've seen in the examples we've already examined, writers must balance their words with the words of others when incorporating source material, whether they are summarizing a primary or secondary text, using a secondary text as support or arguing against it. Part of that balance comes by signaling how the source text is connected to the point you want to make, but another aspect is deciding which portions of the original can be paraphrased and which should speak for themselves either by embedding key phrases into your own sentences or by providing a block quotation. As we said in Chapter 2 and 4, decisions about quotations are partly a matter of style and partly formed by considering your purpose and audience. Let us remind you, though, of the general principles for quotations that we highlighted in Chapter 2.

- Quoted material must be introduced, usually by providing the source information or some context that links the quotation to the author's own prose.
- Vary the way you introduce quoted material.
- The amount of quoted material should never outweigh the amount of original material written by the author.
- Readers will not read the quotation or understand it in exactly the same way as the writer, so quotations, especially block quotations, should never just be dropped in without comment or analysis by the author.
- If the quotation is the evidence that is being interpreted, the author must demonstrate through analysis exactly how the quoted passage is being interpreted—which details are important, and how those details combine with other portions of the author's analysis to support the conclusions.

In general you should not quote anything that you can paraphrase effectively, but as you've probably noticed in our discussion, writers also quote the original, especially in embedded quotations, to:

- Demonstrate their accuracy in representing the ideas of others
- Provide their readers with the flavor of the original

- Appropriate key terms or concepts
- Preserve the original if it was crafted in a memorable way that can't be duplicated in a paraphrase

One challenge writers have in embedding a quoted word or phrase into their own sentence is making certain that their words work with the words of their source to make a grammatically correct sentence. Substituting single words is usually not a problem, but phrases have to begin and end with words that allow the finished sentence to read seamlessly. Let's say, for example that you want to use this rather famous sentence for your own purposes and have decided to present it as an embedded quotation:

> Ask not what your country can do for you; ask what you can do for your country.

How would you position these words, either complete or in part, within a sentence of your own? Do you begin with your own words and then use the quotation as illustration? Do you start with the quotation and then finish with your own thoughts? Do you break the quotation apart, using it in two different places within your sentence? Do you leave off one of the phrases in order to suggest a new connection? How many different versions can you and your classmates create of grammatically correct sentences that embed the quote differently?

Duke University student Nick Cuneo[14] handles embedding skillfully as he summarizes the debate between Booker T. Washington and W. E. B. Du Bois.

> While Washington advocated for blacks to embrace a Protestant work ethic, a tolerance of segregation, and a submissive attitude in hopes of impressing whites into granting them proper recognition, Du Bois explored the concept of double-consciousness—the "sense of always looking at one's self through the eyes of others," which he claimed black Americans needed to reconcile—and called for blacks to militantly demand their political and civil rights (Du Bois 25).

The overall structure of this sentence, one that has to juxtapose two opposing points of view, follows the form:

> While 1 said a and b, 2 said x and y.

But embedded in this formula is another structure, one that defines a key term by embedding a quotation set off with dashes that interrupt the writer's own sentence. Thus:

> The concept of x—"restated as a direct quote"—verb and object that complete the sentence.

Notice that Cuneo varies this form even further by adding a clause introduced by the subordinator "which" within the dashes, a clause that is not a part of the quoted passage.

It's a complicated sentence structure, then, but one that has parts that are actually rather common. What's particularly noteworthy is how balanced the sentence is, blending both paraphrase and embedded quotation while presenting two opposing points of view and producing a grammatically correct whole.

Gerald Graff and Cathy Birkenstein have an entire book of examples of how writers, especially academic writers, move between their own words and those of their sources

---

[14]Nick Cuneo, "Appeasement, Consciousness, and a New Humanism: Ellison's Criticism of Washington and Du Bois and His Hope for Black Americans," *Deliberations: A Journal of First-Year Writing at Duke University*, vol. 6 (Fall 2005): 24. Available online at http://uwp.aas.duke.edu/writing20/publications/documents/CuneoArticle.pdf.

> ## PRACTICE ACTIVITY 6-10
>
> ### Quoting Alternatives
>
> Work with a paragraph of textual material that you think will be important in your own writing. Present this material first in summary form using only your own words. Then, rewrite your presentation as a block quotation, being careful to introduce and follow the text with your own words. Finally try blending the quoted material into your own sentences using embedded quotations only for the most essential phrases or key terms.
>
> **Consider:** Compare your three versions with those produced by your classmates. Are there any similarities in the strategies you used for each of these forms of quoting? Which versions seem most appropriate for your purposes and why?

presented as templates.[15] We see no need to duplicate their work of laying out common templates here, but we think even those who aren't interested in pursuing a systematic study of such forms can learn to pay attention to how other writers are structuring their sentences. Once you pay attention, a little practice in reproducing the basic structure can help you gain confidence and poise as you blend your words with those of others.

Stephen Fuller produced two versions of his Freudian analysis of Ray Bradbury's story. The second version can be found at Duke University's publication *Deliberations: A Journal of First-Year Writing at Duke University*, Volume 6 (Fall 2006), http://uwp.aas. duke.edu/writing20/publications/documents/FullerArticle.pdf. We've used the revised version for the passages we discussed earlier but we've included below, with Fuller's permission, an earlier and slightly longer version which he produced for his class. It may be useful to compare the two versions and consider what changes Fuller made when he was asked both to shorten his essay and make the "so what?" question clearer to his audience.

STUDENT ESSAY: TEXTUAL ANALYSIS OF LITERARY TEXT

Stephen Fuller is an English major at Duke and was a first-year student when he wrote this essay while taking a writing seminar focused on medieval myths and marvels. Stephen's essay began because it was near Halloween, he had seen Bradbury's book mentioned in one of the class readings, was interested in Freud's use of literature, and remembered seeing a class being taught on the uncanny when he was registering for classes and so was able to interview the professor to discuss his ideas.

The Freudian Uncanny in Ray Bradbury's *Something Wicked This Way Comes*

Stephen Fuller

Yes, it was ugly enough; but if you were man enough you would admit to yourself that there was in you the faintest trace of a response to the terrible frankness of that noise, a dim suspicion of there being a meaning in it which you—you so remote from the night of first ages—could comprehend.—Joseph Conrad, *Heart of Darkness*.

---

[15]Gerald Graff and Cathy Birkenstein, *They Say, I Say: The Moves that Matter in Academic Writing* (New York: W. W. Norton, 2006).

The uncanny, according to Sigmund Freud in his 1919 essay "Das Unheimliche," is "undoubt-edly related to what is frightening—to what arouses dread and horror."[1] Written shortly after the golden age of the ghost story, Freud's now-famous work explores the presence of the uncanny in both contemporary literature and his own case studies. From these numerous examples, he attempted to deduce the origins of uncanny feeling, assuming that all human beings perceive the uncanny through the same psychoanalytic mechanism. Modern psychology, with its emphasis on large sample sizes and scientific objectivity, has largely distanced itself from such abstract psychoanalysis. As a result, Freud's essay has not endured as a scientific work, but is instead celebrated for its philosophical insight into the basis of human fear, bolstered by Freud's already-established theories on primary narcissism, animism, and infantile complexes. Perhaps most importantly, Freud was the first to differentiate between the uncanny in real life and the uncanny in literature, assessing the role of the author and reader in the uncanny effect of the written word. The consideration of such a previously underdeveloped concept, combined with Freud's lucid analysis, makes "Das Unheimliche" a clear theoretical introduction to the psychoanalysis of literature.

More than forty years after the publication of "Das Unheimliche," Ray Bradbury composed *Something Wicked This Way Comes*, the story of two teenage boys facing the pressures of adolescence in allegorical Greentown, Illinois. When a sinister carnival arrives at midnight a week before Halloween, the stage is set for a symbolic conflict between good and evil in which small-town values are tested through the temptations and empty promises of the Cooger and Dark's Pandemonium Shadow Show. Never before had Bradbury strayed so far from his science fiction roots, and many critics reacted negatively to such a drastic change in his work. Exacerbating the issue was Bradbury's increased reliance on a "highly wrought fabric of imagery,"[2] which prompted many to call his writing both bombastic and overly moralizing. Nonetheless, the novel has endured as a classic of modern Gothic fantasy, captivating readers with its cadent prose, flowing imagery, and memorable characters. Indeed, Bradbury himself has referred to the book as "[his] favorite of all the books [he's] ever written."[3]

How does Bradbury develop such a powerful emotional relationship with the reader when the majority of his descriptive power is dedicated to rather abstract discourses on the philosophy of human evil? The most apparent answer is that the novel's allure stems from Bradbury's ability to connect the reader *vicariously* to his story; that is, the reader does not merely recognize fragments of himself in an otherwise foreign story, but instead reacts emotionally to the plot as if he was a part of it. It is within this concept of vicarious association where Freud's theories about the uncanny in literature become applicable, since the primary emotions in *Something Wicked This Way Comes* are of course those of fear, uneasiness, and conscious repression. Bradbury masterfully manipulates these trepidations in the mind of various characters so that uncanny feeling virtually erupts from the page, leading the reader not only to observe it, but to experience it. Supporting this idea of a mutual uncanny is Freud's general theory that the uncanny is not comprised of isolated incidents set off by arbitrary events, but instead has a common psychoanalytical basis present in every human mind. Ultimately, an investigation of the Freudian uncanny in the context of *Something Wicked This Way Comes* provides unique insight into both Bradbury's authorship and the genius of Freud's conceptualization of the uncanny. By evoking apprehensions and fears inherent in the human psyche, he is able to create powerful emotional appeal while simultaneously providing sweeping commentary on the role of evil in everyday society.

Before evaluating the uncanny events of *Something Wicked This Way Comes* in the context of Freud's theory, it would be helpful to present a general summary of his thoughts on the "uncanny," the individual, and society. Perhaps the best place to start is where Freud himself begins his analysis: the etymology of *unheimlich*, the German word for uncanny. *Heimlich* refers to all that is homely and

---

[1] Sigmund Freud, "The Uncanny," *An Infantile Neurosis and Other Works*, vol. XVII, *The Complete Psychological Works of Sigmund Freud*, trans. James Strachey (London: Hogarth Press, 1977), 219.
[2] David Mogen, *Ray Bradbury*, Twayne's United States Authors Series (Boston: Twayne Publishers, 1986), 82.
[3] Ray Bradbury qtd. in *Ray Bradbury* 83.

comfortable, so we are tempted to conclude that *unheimlich*, its opposite, refers to everything that is foreign and inexplicable. This inversion coincides well with the common perception of uncanny events arising from uncertainty. However, *heimlich* also refers to what is hidden, secret, and purposely concealed. This definition is essentially identical to the opposite of the first definition, and *heimlich* thus belongs to two sets of contradictory ideas. Freud's primitive definition of uncanny derives from the inversion of the second *heimlich*, so that *unheimlich* now refers to everything that "ought to have remained secret and hidden but has come to light."[4] Freud's further investigation of the uncanny is largely centered on E. T. A. Hoffman's story *The Sandman*, the focus of which, Freud argues, is the Sandman who tears out children's eyes. Equating the loss of one's eyes with castration, Freud connects his theory of the infantile castration complex[5] to the uncanny effect produced by the fear of ocular "castration," turning the Sandman into the "dreaded father at whose hands castration is expected."[6] Through his explanation of the uncanny in *The Sandman*, Freud implicitly introduces what later will become his first cohesive definition of the uncanny: the uncanny arises "when infantile complexes which have been repressed are once more revived by some impression."[7]

The second definition of the uncanny is based on Freud's conception of phylogenetic (cultural) evolution. Human beings were originally animistic, assigning omnipotence to themselves. With no conception of his own ego, man was convinced that his soul comprised the whole of his conscious existence. With animism came the practice of magic, a rejection of mortality, and the belief in omnipotence of human thought. From this animistic society, a religious society evolved where omnipotence was transferred to gods with whom the individual has some direct relationship. Finally, society has developed (or will develop) into a purely scientific community, in which human omnipotence does not exist and we resign ourselves to the laws of necessity and the inevitability of death. Just as the uncanny arises from the revival of repressed complexes within the individual, it similarly occurs in the context of phylogenetic evolution when primitive beliefs which have been surmounted seem once more to be confirmed. As Freud states, no human being "has passed through without preserving certain residues and traces of [animism] which are still capable of manifesting themselves, and that everything which now strikes us as 'uncanny' fulfills the condition of touching those residues of animistic mental activity within us and bringing them to expression."[8] The division of the uncanny into that of individual origin and that of cultural origin is not a definite one, and many uncanny experiences can derive their power simultaneously from both classes of the uncanny. Yet in both cases, the uncanny is defined by the translation of impressions contained in our societal or individual past to the immediate present; the uncanny again leads back to "what is known of old and long familiar."[9]

More important in the analysis of *Something Wicked This Way Comes* is Freud's division of the uncanny according to whether it was experienced in reality or perceived through literature or art. Because much of literature requires a "suspension of disbelief" on the part of the reader, Freud asserts that "a great deal that is not uncanny in fiction would be so if it happened in real life; and in the second place that there are many more means of creating uncanny effects in fiction than there are in real life."[10] The author, in choosing whether his setting coincides with reality or departs from it, ultimately decides the character of the literary uncanny in the context of his writing. Fairy tales, for example, automatically adapt an animistic system of thought in which magic and wish-fulfillment are not only accepted, but somewhat anticipated. The confirmation of such animistic concepts produces no uncanny effect in these stories precisely because the author's adaptation of such a system negates any possible

---

[4]Freud 225.

[5]That is, that in having an infantile sexual desire for our mothers, we rival our fathers, who threaten castration as a means of ending this conflict. This desire, of course, is repressed as we develop, yet the concept of castration still provokes uncanny fear in every male.

[6]Freud 232.

[7]Freud 249.

[8]Freud 240–241.

[9]Freud 219.

[10]Freud 249.

uncanniness. Of course, the situation is altered when the author pretends to move into the realm of a common reality. In selecting a mundane, realistic setting, the author "deceives us by promising to give us the sober truth, and then after all overstepping it."[11] Freud's supposition that the uncanny effect can be multiplied in fiction depends wholly on this deception, as the reader now reacts to the author's inventions as if they were real experiences. In other words, everything that is uncanny in real life is now similarly uncanny in literature, giving the author the freedom to craft uncanny events without arousing doubt in the gullible reader. By writing in the domain of everyday human existence, the author, says Freud, "has a *peculiarly* directive power over us; by means of the moods he can put us into, he is able to guide the current of our emotions, to dam it up in one direction, and make it flow in another, and he often obtains a great variety of effects from the same material."[12] Bradbury's use of Greentown as his primary setting instead of the carnival itself is a potent example of the method of creating uncanny feeling by allowing common reality to dominate the setting. In his study, Freud also introduces the idea of the importance of the reader's identification with various characters in our perception of the uncanny. Freud's example is derived from a particular story of Herodotus, in which we suspect that a female character might sense uncanniness at one particularly moment but "we have no such sensations, for we put ourselves in the [main character's] place and not hers."[13] Uncanniness in literature is therefore dependent on our relationship with various characters, but by enforcing this relationship through shared emotional experience, it can also strengthen the very bond from which it was derived.

Springing from a discussion of the uncanny in literature, immediate connections can be made between the Freudian uncanny and the characters and themes present in *Something Wicked This Way Comes*. The personalities of Jim and Will correspond to a direct inversion of the Freudian concept of cultural evolution. Jim, born two minutes after Will, is associated with experience, temptation, and death. But while Jim is presented as the more experienced of the two boys, he nonetheless embodies the *less* experienced stages of evolution: the animistic and narcissistic stages.[14] Rebelling against society and tradition, he finds excitement in the carnival's arrival and finds no need to repress any of his desires or uncomfortable feelings. Mr. Halloway recognizes Jim's primitive mind when he reminds Will that Jim "*knows*. He *always* knew. Someone knew before him, a long time ago, someone who had wolves for pets and lions for night conversants. Hell, Jim doesn't know with his mind. But his body knows."[15] Connecting Jim with such a primitive history, we find little uncanny effect in Jim's exploits, primarily because he represses few, if any, thoughts and embodies a primitive belief system with no predecessor to be surmounted.

Will, however, rejects Jim's cavalier attitude and instead prefers the concepts of tradition, civilization, and home. Will is "the last peach, high on a summer tree . . . . They feel good, they look good, they are good. . . . It's just, you know, seeing them pass, that's how they'll be all their life; they'll get hit, hurt, cut, bruised, and always wonder why, why does it happen? how can it happen to *them*?"[16] Often preoccupied with the notion of an "ideal" family, Will constantly upholds the values of a traditional society, repressing any thoughts or experiences that challenge these values. Therefore, much of our impression of the uncanny throughout Bradbury's narrative revolves around the character of Will and his repression of the animism seen in both Jim and the carnival itself. It is not necessary to assign a particular stage of Freudian evolution to Will; it suffices to say that he embodies a society that has already surmounted its animistic tendencies. Brilliantly, Bradbury unites the animistic with the surmounted in the guise of these inseparable best friends, rendering the very notion of Will and Jim's relationship uncanny in itself. More importantly, Bradbury's selectively omniscient point of view

---

[11]Freud 250.
[12]Freud 251.
[13]Freud 252.
[14]From this perspective, the two-minute age gap between Will and Jim seems to take on a symbolic character.
[15]Bradbury 18.
[16]Bradbury 18.

means that the reader senses an almost complete impression of Will's emotions, effecting a smoother translation of Will's uncanny experiences to the uncanny feeling produced in the reader and strengthening the emotional intensity of Bradbury's novel. Just as Freud suggested in his analysis of Herodotus, the relationship between the reader and the character is essential in propagating the literary uncanny.

What ultimately drives the plot of the novel and the uncanny feeling it produces is the arrival of the carnival in Greentown. While the concept of a carnival may seem familiar, Bradbury slowly reveals that its magic is indeed real, and more importantly, incredibly devastating. This concept of physically potent magic and the carnival's position as a possible method of wish-fulfillment produces uncanny effect in that it confirms the animistic belief in what Freud calls "omnipotence of thoughts," that is, that human thoughts can instigate changes in physical reality. Similarly, the infantile element of the carnival's uncanniness is derived from both Will's and the reader's impression of the "over-accentuation of the psychical reality in comparison with material reality—a feature closely allied to the belief in the omnipotence of thoughts."[17] Bradbury further presents the carnival as a confirmation of animism when Tom Fury signals the arrival of the carnival with a lightning rod covered in symbols harkening back to animistic societies, "finely scratched and etched with strange languages, names that could tied the tongue or break the jaw, numerals that added to incomprehensible sums, pictographs of insect-animals all bristle, chaff, and claw."[18] The carnival is at its most uncanny when its various freaks and attractions breach the borders of the familiar town in order to parade through the streets, prompting Jim to announce insightfully: "We never thought! [The carnival] can come *right into town*."[19] The driving force for the carnival is eventually revealed to be the ordinary people who were promised the fulfillment of their desires, but whose wishes ultimately transformed them into circus attractions. The self-perpetuating carnival is in essence a derivation of Freud's idea that the uncanny can arise whenever "a symbol takes over the full functions of the thing it symbolizes."[20] Ms. Foley, for example, is grotesquely transformed into a helpless preadolescent girl after Mr. Dark offers her the opportunity to become young again. Her struggles with age are originally symbolized by the young girl she claims to see in the mirrors of the Mirror Maze. But her situation is most uncanny when Ms. Foley is replaced by her symbolic younger self: that is, the symbol has taken over the full function of the woman whose apprehensions it had previously symbolized.

While the carnival and its powers of temptation can arouse uncanny feeling themselves, there is little doubt that the primary instrument of fear used throughout *Something Wicked This Way Comes* is Mr. Dark's population of carnival people, a terrifying amalgamation of human abnormality. Nowhere in Bradbury's tale does the uncanny have a larger influence on both the characters and the reader than in Jim and Will's various interactions with these quasi-human carnival attractions. The uncanny effect derived from Mr. Dark's sideshow figures is more or less based on our inability to assess the nature of their humanity. Indeed, Ernest Jentsch, one of Freud's primary sources for "Das Unheimliche," similarly ascribes the uncanniness of dolls, wax figures, and other humanoid objects in literature to the "uncertainty whether a particular figure in the story is a human being or an automaton."[21] While Freud rejects Jentsch's association of the uncanny with uncertainty, he nonetheless expounds on Jentsch's theories in considering the uncanniness of epileptic fits and bouts of insanity. These "excite in the spectator the impression of automatic, mechanical processes at work behind the ordinary appearance of mental activity."[22] Within the context of Freud's earlier theories, we may consider that mechanical, inhuman activity in otherwise human form provokes one's sense of primary narcissism, long since repressed through the aging process; primary narcissism, of course, does not coincide well with the idea that the ego is powerless in a body driven by an inhuman, involuntary force, as the narcissistic ego wishes to assign all power to itself.

---

[17]Freud 244.
[18]Bradbury 7.
[19]Bradbury 162.
[20]Freud 244.
[21]Jentsch qtd. in "The Uncanny" 227.
[22]Freud 226.

The various humanoid objects and automata dispersed throughout Bradbury's work serve not only to produce fear within the context of Greentown's populace, but also aid the development of the reader's perception of uncanniness. After all, Freud's conceptualization of the uncanny involves conditions inherent in the psyche of any human being, whether Greentown resident or involved reader. Our first encounter with doll-like objects comes just as the arrival of the carnival train looms on the horizon. Sprinting past Mr. Tetley's cigar shop, Jim and Will recognize Mr. Tetley and the familiar cigar Indian in front of the store. Yet when they speak to him, they are unsettled to see that "now there were two wooden Indians upright in ripe tobacco darkness. Mr. Tetley, amidst his jest, had frozen, mouth open, listening. . . . He heard something far away on the wind but couldn't say what it was. The boys backed off. He did not see them. He did not move. He only listened. They ran."[23] Bradbury has presented a classic example of the uncanny effect of dolls and similar humanoid objects, especially considering the emphasis of such intolerable stillness present in partially human figures and the ambiguous nature of Mr. Tetley's frozen frame. However, Bradbury is able to multiply this effect by first identifying the figure as the familiar Mr. Tetley, then gradually renouncing that identity by revealing Tetley's doll-like immobility. Also, Bradbury's use of short, punctuated sentences notably increases the reader's sense of the uncanny: we can almost hear the patter of fleeing feet or the beating of a frightened heart. The transformation of a familiar human character into an automaton or anthropomorphic being is repeated throughout *Something Wicked This Way Comes*, so that many carnival inhabitants are seen as uncanny not only because they toe the line between the human and the mechanistic, but also because they represent the familiar hidden in the guise of the unfamiliar. Mr. Cooger, for example, is sent backwards on the carousel, his face "melting like pink wax. His hands were becoming doll's hands. His bones sank away beneath his clothes. . . . His face flickered going, and each time around he melted more."[24] Cooger's transmogrification is essentially uncanny because it impresses the malleability of the human form in contrast to the stability of the psyche, thereby confirming animistic beliefs in the soul and its role in defining existence. Bradbury's most potent use of uncanny automata, however, comes with his conception of the Dust Witch. Serving as a blind fortune teller in the carnival's daytime hours, she is transformed at night into an all-seeing, all-feeling being who travels above the town in a hot-air balloon, marking the houses of possible victims with a shiny silver paint. Like the other carnival beings, Bradbury describes her as "peculiarly wax . . . peculiarly alive" and we again perceive the uncanny in the slow, seemingly automatic motion of her hands as she reaches down to "feel the bumps of the world, touch house roofs, probe attic bins. . . . Each soul, a vast warm fingerprint, *felt* different, she could roll it in her hand like clay."[25] Once again, Bradbury encourages the uncanny by blurring the line between human and automaton, by representing action as a mechanistic process, and by confirming the existence of the animistic soul.

Yet our perception of the Dust Witch is most heavily influenced by her blindness, her eyes that "did not see; they were sewn shut with laced black-widow web, dark threads."[26] Beyond the obvious assertion that her physical sight is usurped by an animistic, psychical sight, the basis for the uncanniness of Dust Witch conforms almost perfectly to the Freudian concept of a castration complex, in which "the threat in being castrated in especial excites a peculiarly violent and obscure emotion, and that this emotion is what first gives the idea of losing other organs its intense colouring."[27] Unlike Nathaniel in Hoffman's *The Sandman*, she is not threatened by the tearing out of her eyes: their function has already been eliminated. Instead, the Dust Witch represents the other side of castration: the female with a symbolic inability to see. The association of femininity with visual "castration" is a potent verification of the relationship between the uncanniness of eye injuries and the repressed male fears of being castrated or resembling the female. Ultimately, the Dust Witch is observed as

---

[23]Bradbury 21.
[24]Bradbury 78.
[25]Bradbury 143.
[26]Bradbury 108.
[27]Freud 231.

uncanny because her blindness awakens the repressed infantile castration complex in both the story's male characters and the male reader.[28]

Other instances of uncanny feeling in Bradbury's work are similarly associated with eyes, sight, and the castration complex. Most importantly, one character often identifies another by recognizing the other's eyes, strengthening any uncanny feeling by dramatizing the importance of one's eyes in the conception of the self. When Cooger changes into Ms. Foley's nephew, for instance, his appearance changes drastically, but his eyes remain the same, allowing Jim to recognize him in Ms. Foley's window. Also, the importance of the castration complex is amplified by this resistance of Cooger's eyes to physical change. Besides their obvious connection to the castration complex, eyes can also be thought as uncanny in the character of the Dwarf, whose "idiot camera eyes" affect the observer in a similar fashion to the epileptic fits mentioned by Freud in his discussion of Jentsch. As Jim and Will hide beneath a sewer grille, the Dwarf searches for them, his "face less human, more machine now; in fact, a camera. The shuttering eyes flexed, sightless, opening upon darkness. Tick. Two lenses expanded—contracted with liquid swiftness: a picture-snap of the grille."[29]

Once again, the appearance of mechanical, automatic processes in a seemingly human form makes for particularly uncanny circumstances. The Dwarf's prolonged stare also has a similar effect as Freud's concept of the evil eye. While the glance itself is not uncanny, "what is feared is thus a secret intention of doing harm, and certain signs are taken to mean that intention has the necessary power at its command."[30] In other words, the evil eye involves the replacement of intention with an animistic fulfillment of that intention, causing us again to feel the uncanny as an affirmation of surmounted beliefs.

Closely related to the uncanniness of losing one's eyes is the threat of losing other body parts, which provokes an uncanny reaction because "the threat in being castrated in especial excites a peculiarly violent and obscure emotion, and that this emotion is what first gives the idea of losing other organs its intense colouring." When Will and Jim bring the police to the carnival, hoping to expose its ulterior motives, the Guillotine Man prompts what is perhaps one of Bradbury's most potent uses of the uncanny. With a dummy on the table, the guillotine blade "like a homing hawk scythed down. Whisper-whisk-slither-thunder-rush—wham! The dummy head, chop-cut, fell. And falling, looked like Will's own head, own face, destroyed. He wanted he did not want, to run lift the head, turn to see if it held his own profile. But how could you ever dare do that? Never, never, in a billion years, could one empty that wicker basket."[31] The symbolic projection of Will's own face onto the dummy is a mental consequence of the hugely uncanny feeling aroused in this situation. Not only does Will's reaction to the beheaded dummy reflect the infantile fear of castration, it more importantly has its basis in the overwhelming human fear of death and the dead. Freud asserts that this fear of death and the dead is particularly striking because "almost all of us still think as savages do on this topic," unable to overcome the strength of our original emotional reaction to death and our insufficient understanding of its scientific workings.[32] Indeed, our fear that the dead man is the enemy of the living and wishes to carry survivors off to the underworld plays a large role in our perception of Mr. Electrico, Bradbury's carnival Frankenstein. Impossibly aged after a malfunction of the magic carousel, Cooger is introduced to the skeptical police as Mr. Electrico, the dead man who comes to life with a powerful jolt of electricity. Mr. Dark silently coaxes the "old old dead thing" to "live, live. And the old man came alive. Will yelled himself hoarse. And no one heard. For now, very slowly, as if roused by thunder, as if the electric fire were a new dawn, one dead eyelid

---

[28]The effects of the Dust Witch on the female can be similarly attributed to her blindness. By unconsciously reminding the female reader of her own "castration" and her repressed penis envy, the Dust Witch is perceived as uncanny.

[29]Bradbury 170.

[30]Freud 240.

[31]Bradbury 109.

[32]Freud 242.

peeled itself slowly open."[33] The uncanniness of the situation is heightened by the fact that it was Will who caused the malfunction in the carousel that led to Cooger's three hundred years of aging. Both Will and the reader's fear of the newly revivified creature is therefore compounded by the element of revenge, that is, that the electrified creature will select his killer as the first target. Our fear of Cooger and also of death itself could originate in Freud's belief that "no human being really grasps [his own mortality], and our unconscious has as little use now as it ever had for the idea of its own mortality."[34] Any interaction with the dead causes a revival of this ignorance, which the scientific community has tried to repress with its denial in the existence of spirits and ghosts. The continued existence of such a powerful fear of the dead in modern society, however, greatly undermines any attempts at repression. It is therefore "no matter for surprise that the primitive fear of the dead is still so strong within us and always ready to come to the surface on any provocation."[35] Bradbury himself understood the association between death and the uncanny, employing basic human fears not only to drive the story's main action, but also to imbue his work with powerful emotional appeal.

The primitive fear of death also has implications in one of the most prevalent techniques used in uncanny fiction: doubling. First associated with the uncanny in Otto Rank's 1914 psychoanalytic study *The Double*, the concept was further developed by Freud in "Das Unheimliche." Rank considered the use of shadows and reflections, which affect characters in literature by causing an uncanny cleavage of the ego. In his exploration of the double as uncanny, Freud asserts that in its most primitive form, the double was originally an extension of the primary narcissism dominating the mind of children and primitive societies. The soul doubled the body and in doing so, counteracted human mortality. But once the narcissistic stage has "been surmounted, the 'double' reverses its aspect. From having been an assurance of immortality, it becomes the uncanny harbinger of death."[36] The uncanniness of the double is therefore enhanced whenever doubling involves physical separation and especially when this separation incites physical pursuit or confrontation. Within the context of *Something Wicked This Way Comes*, doubling occurs whenever the carnival's magic transforms a tempted visitor into a grotesque exaggeration of his or her former self. This interpretation of the double is expectedly uncanny, but also benefits from a direct correlation to Freud's general definition of the word. For in the faces of various unfamiliar carnival creatures, Jim and Will are able to recognize fragments of the familiar individuals who submitted to the carnival's powers of temptation. The unfamiliar double derives its uncanniness from its connection to the "old and long familiar," a subtle reinterpretation of Freud's comparison of *heimlich* and *unheimlich*. Tom Fury, for example, is doubled by the Dwarf, whose eyes still hold "the lost bits and fitful pieces of a man named Fury."[37] The uncanny threat of such doubling is undeniable, the double having physically overwhelmed the original form, which vanishes irrevocably.

Figuring prominently in Bradbury's extensive use of doubling is the interaction of Miss Foley and Mr. Halloway with mirrors and the carnival's Mirror Maze. By presenting a palette on which distorted self-images can be projected, mirrors provoke a cleavage of the ego and force an interaction between a character and the doubled mirror image. Mirrors are remarkably uncanny whenever Miss Foley cannot decide whether or not she or her mirrored image is real: "Poor girl. I knew her. 'I *know* you!' I said when I first saw her a minute ago. I waved, she waved. 'Hello!' I ran!—bang! 'Wait!' I said. Oh, she looked so fine, so lovely, so young. But it scared me. 'What're you doing *here*?' I said. 'Why,' I think she said. '*I'm* real. You're *not*!'"[38] Again, doubling is enhanced by the unconscious fear that the doubled image will assume the reality of whatever it doubles. In his consideration of the double in literature, Otto Rank similarly analyzed the uncanniness of mirror reflections, relating such effects to the narcissistic theories of the creation of the world (introduced by Freud), which "just like the later

---

[33]Bradbury 113.
[34]Freud 242.
[35]Freud 242.
[36]Freud 235.
[37]Bradbury 169.
[38]Bradbury 65.

philosophical systems based on the ego, indicate that man is able to perceive the reality surrounding him mainly only as a reflection, or as a part, of his ego."[39] In the context of Freud's theory of the uncanny, mirrors are appropriately uncanny because they create an impression of the narcissistic ego that we continue to repress. The Mirror Maze is an inventive confluence of the uncanniness of mirrors and the uncanniness of repetition. Indeed, the uncanniness of repeated experience is a natural progression from the concept of doubling, which is in effect a single instance of repetition. Freud associates the repetitive uncanny with the feeling produced when a lost hiker continually returns to the same landmark or when one stumbles over the same piece of furniture while navigating a dark room. Our perception of these events as uncanny, says Freud, is directly related to our mind's instinctual impulse to repeat; repetition merely taps into this infantile compulsion and is subsequently uncanny. More importantly, the hopelessness and impotence associated with the repetition of certain experiences suggests that inescapable, mechanistic fate, rather than human will, governs the course of human action. Just as it did in the case of the Dwarf's camera eyes, such presence of mechanical activity induces further uncanny response from the reader.

No discussion of the influence of the uncanny on literature would be complete without considering the relationship between sexuality and uncanny. Sexuality is a crucial issue when considering the use of the uncanny in *Something Wicked This Way Comes*, if only because it plays so heavily into Jim and Will's transition into adolescence. While sexual episodes do not figure prominently in the overall plot, Bradbury includes a noteworthy episode where Jim convinces a stubborn Will to visit what is only described as a "Theater," a window through which the boys see some mysterious sexual interaction. Having already discovered a distaste for such things, his fears come to fruition as he sits watching, "terribly excited, staring in at the Theater, that peculiar stage where people all unknowing . . . stood raw and animal-crazy, naked, like shivery horses, hands out to touch each other. What're they *doing!* thought Will. Why are they laughing? What's wrong with them, what's *wrong*?!"[40] Will's conscious repression of his "terrible excitement" is intimately connected with his visible apprehension, the uncanny Theater not meshing well with his prefigured notions of an ideal society. Will reacts similarly to the flyer proclaiming that the carnival will feature "the most beautiful woman in the world;" and there is little doubt that he senses the uncanny in the presence of such obvious sexual undertones. Yet for all of Freud's associations of familial relationships with sexuality, character relationships in Bradbury's novel feature only small suggestions of Freud's Oedipus complex. There is, of course, Will's vision of his mom as a "creamy pink hothouse rose poised alone in the wilderness," and his hesitations regarding his father, who Will believes threatens his ideas of the maternal and societal ideal.[41] But Bradbury distances Will's uncanny reaction to sexuality from his relationships with his father and mother. Indeed, by the book's end, he is able to sit with his father on the same windowsill, "same size, same weight, colored by the same stars . . . embraced once more with grand fine exhaustion, gasping on huge ingulped laughs which swept their bones together."[42] Bradbury's presentation of such an idealized relationship between father and son leaves so little room for Freud's idea of the dreaded father that any kind of Oedipal analysis seems utterly unfounded. The uncanny in *Something Wicked This Way Comes* is therefore desexualized with relation to Freud's original investigation of the word. This is not surprising, as much of the criticism of "Das Unheimliche" focuses on his overemphasis of sexuality in analyzing the uncanny in literature. Nonetheless, Freud's novel association of the uncanny with repression and the unconscious has overshadowed many of these inconsistencies.

In analyzing *Something Wicked This Way Comes,* we have largely been concerned with the similarities between Freud's theories on the uncanny and the manifestation of such theories in the

---

[39]Otto Rank, *The Double: A Psychoanalytic Study*, trans. Harry Tucker, Jr. (Chapel Hill: U of North Carolina, 1971), 82.
[40]Bradbury 28.
[41]Bradbury 34.
[42]Bradbury 139.

more frightening aspects of Bradbury's novel. But as the earlier consideration of sexuality suggests, we can also learn about both authors by considering the differences between them. Perhaps the most fundamental difference between Freud's psychoanalysis and Bradbury's gothic fiction is in their presentation of morality. Freud's theories on the workings of the human are best categorized as philosophical, yet the scientific, logical undertones in his work leave little room for the consideration of any ideal. On the contrary, Bradbury is undeniably a moralist, considering the relationship of man and evil and suggesting methods through which man can overcome such evil. The uncanny is not the subject of his work, but a methodology through which he is able to provoke an intense emotional reaction from the reader. This reaction ultimately allows him to mask abstract philosophy in the guise of highly-entertaining gothic fiction. The final chapters of *Something Wicked This Way Comes* also reveal that Bradbury may be commenting on the uncanny itself, that is, the role of fear in propagating evil. Mr. Halloway first suggests the connection between the uncanny and morality when he suggests that "being good is a *fearful* occupation; men strain at it and sometimes break in two."[43] Morality in Greentown is defined not by evil itself, but by the human reaction to evil. The ultimate solution to the temptation of evil is, of course, laughter: Mr. Halloway's chuckles save him from the powers of the Dust Witch and a bullet inscribed with a smile ultimately seals her fate. Mr. Halloway's laughter is both a conscious ignorance towards and a direct acceptance of evil, the polar opposite of the repression which gave so much of Bradbury's narrative its uncanny character. As repressed complexes and feelings are forced from the unconscious to the conscious, uncanniness and indeed temptation are dispersed just as the "sun disperses fog."[44] Our acceptance of evil is made bearable by the powers of tradition, of community, and most importantly, of love. Always the philosopher, Mr. Halloway speaks of the time when man finally realized his own mortality, when he realized that "our hour is short, eternity is long. With this knowledge came pity and mercy, so we spared others for the later, more intricate, more mysterious benefits of love."[45] Yet for all of the importance of commiseration and cooperation, Bradbury overwhelmingly emphasizes the role of the individual in dispersing evil: "We got to watch out the rest of our lives. The fight's just begun.' They moved around the carousel slowly. 'What will they look like? How will we know them?' 'Why,' said Dad quietly, 'maybe they're already here.'"[46]

A Freudian reading of Bradbury's *Something Wicked This Way Comes* rationalizes its emotional appeal by linking Bradbury's use of the uncanny with his articulation of mental processes inherent in the mind of any reader. Whether or not Bradbury had intentionally constructed his narrative around Freud's theories of animism, the castration complex, and the like is irrelevant. What matters is his incisive understanding of humanity which allows him not only to manipulate the emotions of the reader, but also to provide compelling commentary on how society and the individual cope with evil. Similarly, the undeniable connection of Bradbury's work to Freud's theory of the uncanny serves as persuasive testimony for the validity of Freud's philosophies and his understanding of the workings of the human mind. Although Bradbury and Freud seem to differ in their presentation of morality, viewing their works in the context of one another enhances the understanding of both authors and their corresponding presentations of humanity.

In his study of uncanny American fiction, Allan Lloyd-Smith explains that writing (and similarly, reading) are actually uncanny themselves. It isn't surprising, then, that Bradbury's writing is so compelling and, as Freud's analysis predicted, that literature and the uncanny would remain so heavily intertwined. For writing "doubles nature, doubles thought, doubles *us*, which reminds us of death; writing animates a dead realm, creates something that seems to be alive." And just like the mirror maze, "writing is a repetition," every word and image reflecting some piece of an overall ideal.[47] As readers

---

[43]Bradbury 135.
[44]Mogen 122.
[45]Bradbury 230.
[46]Bradbury 288.
[47]*Uncanny American Fiction* (New York: St. Martin's Press), 1989.

of fiction, we enter the author's maze expecting nothing more than fiction. But as we stare at the distorted figures in the warped glass, something resonates deep within us. In this unfamiliar reflection, we recognize something "old and familiar." Delighted and disturbed, we continue reading. We have perceived the uncanny.

WORKS CITED

Bradbury, Ray. *Something Wicked This Way Comes*. New York: Avon Books, 1997.

Freud, Sigmund. "The Uncanny." *An Infantile Neurosis and Other Works*. Vol. XVII of *The Standard Edition of the Complete Psychological Works of Sigmund Freud*. Translated by James Strachey. London: The Hogarth Press, 1955.

Jackson, Rosemary. *Fantasy: The Literature of Subversion*. London: Methuen, 1981.

Lloyd-Smith, Allan G. *Uncanny American Fiction*. New York: St. Martin's Press, 1989.

Mogen, David. *Ray Bradbury*. Twayne's United States Authors Series. Boston: Twayne Publishers, 1986.

Rank, Otto. *The Double: A Psychoanalytic Study*. Translated by Harry Tucker, Jr. Chapel Hill: The University of North Carolina Press, 1971.

Samantha Sanderson's oral history of Jenny's experience of the 1999 Columbine school shooting appears at the end of Chapter 4. In the essay that follows, Sanderson returns to her transcript of that interview to examine Jenny's story through the lens of psychology. Though this isn't precisely textual or even rhetorical analysis, we think you'll find the transformation of the original interview worth reading because the attention Sanderson gives to the language of that interview allows her to probe more deeply into what such events mean or how they can be understood.

STUDENT ESSAY: ANALYSIS OF SPOKEN LANGUAGE

Samantha Sanderson is a native of Ohio who transferred to the University of Miami in 2006. A Biochemistry major, Samantha also plays on the university's soccer team. Although Samantha began the composition class where she wrote this essay saying that she was not a very good writer, she discovered that writing was mostly about revising. This essay revises an earlier interview assignment to focus more on analyzing language. You can read the original interview essay at the end of Chapter 4.

The Effects of Columbine

Samantha Sanderson

"Traumatic events are external, but they quickly become incorporated into the mind."—Sandra Bloom, M.D.

The external event that causes extreme anxiety, panic and fear causes the body to react instinctively to protect itself during and after the occurrence is known as a "traumatic event." Defense mechanisms, action, the way one processes information under stress, how we remember things and the development of self-meaning are all psychological mechanisms that the body uses in such situations.

Such an event occurred at a high school in Littleton, Colorado, called Columbine. On April 20, 1999, fellow classmates of students at Columbine, Eric Harris and Dylan Klebold, took the school by storm. Using guns, knives and homemade explosives the two boys ended the lives of twelve students and one teacher before taking their own lives. The survivors from Columbine experienced intense anxiety, panic and fear as this traumatic event unfolded in front of them.

A freshman at the time, Jenny spent five hours in a science closet with a few other students and two teachers. Unknown to Jenny at the time, her neighbor, Danny, had been shot and killed while he was running from the school after helping others to escape. Her experience was personal and from the inside of the school. Using Jenny as an example her story helps to illustrate the internal processes the body uses in such tragic moments, including: defense mechanisms, actions the body takes, how information is processed and how one remembers the incident.

Inside the Mind

Used by Freud in his psychoanalytic theory, a defense mechanism is a tactic that safeguards the mind against feelings and thoughts that are too difficult for the conscious mind to cope with (Van Wagner 1). One of these mechanisms is an inhibitory defense called *Isolation of Affect*; one remains aware of the details of an event but the emotional connection is lost (Richmond 8). Jenny was involved in Columbine but when spoken to about it she did not tear up, get angry or seem bothered by talking about any details, even the death of her neighbor, Danny. She spoke quite frankly of what occurred and said it was horrible, but the emotion was missing from the descriptions that she used to tell her story. Another one of these mechanisms that the body uses is a healthy defense called *Affiliation*. Jenny didn't seem to do this; however, she was the one being affiliated with. "I was holding this girl's hand the whole time we were in the room; she was looking to me to be her rock." The girl's need for a support system is called affiliation; seeking out others for emotional support or physical help (Richmond 6). A third, and final, defensive mechanism that was used post-Columbine was *Repression*; the rejection from consciousness of painful or disagreeable ideas, memories, feelings, or impulse (Dictionary.com). This is illustrated when Jenny says, "I apologize if things seem out of order; I don't think about this day a lot. In fact, sometimes I forget the anniversary of that day." All of these mechanisms were used to create internal safety for the individuals who put them to use.

"When we perceive we are in danger, we are physiologically geared to take action . . . that we respond almost reflexively to save our lives or to protect those we love" (Bloom 5). During these moments of danger, thought processes are put on hold unconsciously and the action one takes is dependent upon instinctive reaction. "I have no idea why I did this, but I rolled onto my left side and tucked my head down. All I wanted was to make sure that if they shot through our window my heart would be protected." Instinctively, Jenny put her heart closest to the floor so it would be the lowest target for a bullet. Her reaction was to try and protect her own life in any way possible. On the other hand, the teachers, who were also authority figures, risked their lives to protect the kids. "One teacher was next to the door, an Exacto knife in hand. I have never seen someone hold a knife with the intent to kill until that moment and I haven't since. The other teacher, the one who had been with Mr. Sanders, was sprawled out over us to protect us." These two teachers used two different methods to protect the children. One was by the door in case the gunmen entered he could attack them and the other just put his body in between where the bullets would come from and the children. Since instinct told these teachers to protect their students, they illustrated their love for their students by risking their lives to keep the children safe. Neither reaction can be classified as better because it is what it is, a reaction. Instinct is something one cannot control.

"When we are overwhelmed with fear, we lose the capacity for speech, we lose the capacity to put words to our experience. Without words the mind shifts to a mode of thinking that is characterized by visual, auditory, olfactory and kinesthetic images, physical sensations, and strong feelings."—Sandra L. Bloom, M.D

Jenny remembered many sounds in her description of what occurred at Columbine that day. For example "the fire alarm sounded," "we heard a lot of popping sounds," and "someone screamed."

Although she heard these things when it came to people talking, she could not remember what people said: "I can't remember specifically but I am pretty sure someone yelled to get back into the classroom" and "the other gunmen started yelling something, I honestly couldn't tell you what he said. . . ." In terms of kinesthetic memory, she remembered holding the girl's hand, rolling onto her left side and being laid on by one of the teachers. Finally, Jenny recalled her strong feelings when a gun was fired and one of the girls screamed. "I remember thinking selfishly that this stupid girl was going to get us killed because we were hiding behind a bookshelf so nobody could see us but now they would know we were there." Memory that only uses the senses is more vivid to those who experience it because one cannot put into words sounds, images or feelings; these things must be experienced to have a full understanding. Perhaps this was why it seemed as though Jenny did not remember things as clearly as one would have thought.

Lastly, when one survives a traumatic event there are many ways a person's line of thinking is changed in the aftermath. One of these is the development of a survivor's mission and/or self-meaning. A survivor's mission is when the survivor of a traumatic occurrence decides that they want to go out and change the world or make everything better. Finding self-meaning is when people realize that they could have died and think that they are here for a reason, they survived for a reason, and from this they develop self-meaning and figure out why they were chosen to stay. Jenny recalls, "Seeing all the people and the efforts they made helped me realize that I wanted to give back just as they had. I have stuck with that and I am graduating with a degree in nursing. I wanted to be a missionary nurse and give back to those in trouble." Jenny has a slight survivor mission to save those in trouble, but she definitely used her situation to her advantage and found self-meaning; she was put here to help people in need. People that go through traumatic experiences do so in different ways and process the experience differently. However, these psychological devices of memory and self-protection are used unconsciously by all people experiencing extreme danger, fear or anxiety. Jenny exhibited a mild case of each mechanism described and clearly her body unconsciously used them all. Some people who are in worse scenarios, or are affected differently, may be diagnosed with post-traumatic stress disorder, where they may have nightmares and flashbacks and feel alone and estranged so much it may interfere with their everyday lives. Fortunately, some will recover well from this disorder; however, others will always remain under the stress and anxiety of this disorder without the ability to be cured. Traumatic events are important and serious. Although the body does most of the work during the event and has its own mechanisms for the aftermath, one must do the work after such an event to fully recover and be at peace with themselves and all that occurred.

WORKS CITED

Bloom, M.D., Sarah L. "Trauma Theory Abbreviated" October 1999. *Community Works*. 15 November 2006. <http://www.sanctuaryweb.com/Documents/Downloads/Trauma%20theory%20abbreviated.pdf>.

"Columbine High School Massacre" Wikimedia Foundation, Inc. 18 November 2006. <http://en.wikipedia.org/wiki/Columbine_High_School_massacre>.

Dictionary.com 2006 Lexico Publishing Group, LLC 15 November 2006. <http://www.dictionary.com>.

Jenny (pseudonym) Personal interview. 10 October 2006.

Richmond, Ph.D., Raymond Lloyd. "The Unconscious" 1997. *A Guide to Psychology and Its Practice*. 15 November 2006. <http://www.guidetopsychology.com/ucs.htm>.

Van Wagner, Kendra. "Defense Mechanism" 2006. *Your Guide to Psychology*, About, Inc., A part of New York Times Company, 15 November 2006. <http://psychology.about.com/od/dindex/g/defensemech.htm>.

Internet Resources

On Textual Analysis:

A glossary of literary theory is maintained by the English Department at the University of Toronto at http://www.library.utoronto.ca/utel/glossary/headerindex.html and the online version of the *Johns Hopkins Guide to Literary Theory and Criticism* at http://www.press.jhu.edu/books/hopkins_guide_to_literary_theory/ are but two of many similar sites.

Robert Harris's *A Handbook of Rhetorical Devices* (http://www.virtualsalt.com/rhetoric.htm) is particularly easy to use and includes examples to illustrate each term. Though less complete, Ted Nellen's Cyber English students maintain the site at http://www.tnellen.com/cybereng/lit_terms/ which includes definitions of many of the most common literary terms with examples.

On Music and Speech

There are several Internet sites where famous speeches have been archived in either written or audio forms. See, for example, http://www.historyplace.com/speeches/previous.htm for examples of many famous historical speeches. http://www.americanrhetoric.com/moviespeeches.htm, a site with movie speeches, and http://www.americanrhetoric.com/top100speechesall.html both include sound recordings illustrating many commonly used rhetorical devices; http://www.history

channel.com/speeches/ has current speeches in the news, as well as historical speeches in categories of arts, entertainment, and culture; science and technology; politics and government; and war & diplomacy; http://gos.sbc.edu/ is a site with speeches by women from around the world.

The Web site sponsored by Sony Music and W. W. Norton Publishers, at http://www.essentialsofmusic.com/glossary/glossary.html, includes audio recordings to illustrate many terms.

On Archives

Many archives, large and small, have been making a variety of materials widely available to the public via the Internet. A good example is the Library of Congress's American Memory Project, which is available at http://memory.loc.gov/ammem/amhome.html.

Harvard University libraries allow archival searching via their OASIS online archival searching at http://oasis.harvard.edu:10080/oasis/deliver/home?_collection=oasis. But most research libraries that include archives have placed a variety of materials as well as much cataloguing information online. You may want to check out Web sites of your school library, local historical society, or local museums to see if they have made archival materials available to you via the Web.

Web Sites Referenced in This Chapter

Carr, Karen *Aeschylus*
http://www.historyforkids.org/learn/greeks/literature/aeschylus.htm

Center for History and New Media, Michelle Kisliuk video and interview
http://chnm.gmu.edu/worldhistorysources/analyzing/music/musicq1.html

Chiriguayo, William "'The Rhythmic Cry of the Slave': Black Music and Cultural Identity in America, 1890–1910"

http://www.urop.uci.edu/journal/journal02/02_WilliamChiriguayo/William.pdf

Cuneo, Nick. "Appeasement, Consciousness, and a New Humanism: Ellison's Criticism of Washington and Du Bois and His Hope for Black Americans." *Deliberations: A Journal of First-Year Writing at Duke University.* Volume 6 (Fall 2005):
http://uwp.aas.duke.edu/writing20/publications/documents/CuneoArticle.pdf

ERIC database
www.eric.ed.gov

http://uwp.aas.duke.edu/writing20/
publications/documents/FullerArticle.pdf

Fuller, Stephen. "The Freudian Uncanny in Ray Bradbury's *Something Wicked This Way Comes*." *Deliberations: A Journal of First-Year Writing at Duke University* Volume 6 (Fall 2005): 46–52.

Wiater, Stanley "Editorial Review: Something Wicked This Way Comes"
http://www.amazon.com/Something-Wicked-This-Way-Comes/dp/0380729407

Links to the Readings

Any of the readings can be analyzed as texts, of course, and because the readings come from different academic disciplines and publications, there are some interesting differences in style and format that will be obvious to readers who conduct a critical analysis of these readings. We invite students at the end of nearly every assignment sequence to read back through their earlier writing to synthesize and analyze their own textual production, but we do not include these assignments in the list that follows. Likewise, though interviews and oral histories are often analyzed as textual moments, we have included such work in the links at the end of Chapter 4 and so do not repeat them here. Listed below, then, are those readings and assignments that make use of textual materials of the kind discussed in this chapter, or that investigate particular kinds of written texts. Archival work is marked with an asterisk; we use the plus sign to indicate work with oral speech or music.

*Bachin, Robin. "Courage, Endurance and Quickness of Decision: Gender and Athletics at the University of Chicago, 1890–1920"

+Jackson, Mark Allan. "Is This Song Your Song Anymore?: Revisioning Woody Guthrie's *This Land Is Your Land*"

+Jones, Jeffrey P. "Forums for Citizenship in Popular Culture"

+Koza, Julia Eklund. "Rap Music: The Cultural Politics of Official Representation"

Len-Ríos, María et al. "Representation of Women in News and Photos: Comparing Content to Perceptions"

*Shackel, Paul A. "Public Memory and the Search for Power in American Historical Archaeology"

White, James Boyd. "Human Dignity and the Claim of Meaning: Athenian Tragic Drama and Supreme Court Opinions"

Assignments Working with Texts

Collective Memory option in Assignment 2 (Spence)
Considering "Public" option in Assignment 4
Cultural Politics and Public Discourse Assignment 5 (Len-Ríos)
Cultural Politics and Public Discourse II: Shaping Values Assignment 3 (White)
Direct Observation option in Assignment 3 and 4
Examining Visuals option in Assignment 5
Expanding a Trends Report option in Assignment 5

Eye on Campus option in Assignment 4 and 6
Gender Investigations Assignment 1 (Len-Ríos)
Histories Official and Unofficial option in Assignment 4
Material Culture Assignment 3 (White)
Representing Community option in Assignment 3; Assignment 5 (White)
Trying Out Interviews option in Assignment 3
Working with Texts

Assignments Working with Archives

Collective Memory Assignment 4 (Shackel)
Considering "Public" Assignment 2 (Shackel);
    option in Assignment 4
Constructing Public Spaces Assignment 3; option
    in Assignment 4; Assignment 5 (Bachin)
Ethnicity in America: Identity option in Assign-
    ment 4
Eye on Campus Assignment 1 (Bachin)
Gender Investigations Assignment 5 (Bachin)

Histories Official and Unofficial Assignment 2
    (Shackel)
Investigating Artifacts Assignment 3
Material Culture Assignment 2 (Bachin)
Reclaiming the Past option in Assignment 3
    (Lewis)
Representing Community Assignment 4
    (Shackel)

Assignments Working with Music and Public Speech

Considering "Public" Assignment 3 (Jones)
Constructing Public Spaces option in Assign-
    ment 2
Cultural Politics and Public Discourse Assign-
    ment 1; Assignment 2 (Koza); Assignment 4
    (Jones)

*Cultural Politics and Public Discourse II: Shap-
    ing Values* Assignment 4 (Jackson)
Humanizing Numbers Assignment 2
Material Culture Assignment 4 (Jackson)
Reading Media Assignment 1 (Jones); Assign-
    ment 2 (Koza)

SAMPLE PROJECTS

The following sample projects are useful for writing courses that ask students to work on a sustained project and learn the methods of inquiry as the need arises. The projects are also useful for programs, courses, or individual teachers who prefer to minimize the attention to readings that aren't either student writing or materials of investigation. Many of these project assignments have variations in the Assignment Sequences that follow, and most of those sequences are linked to readings, so it is certainly possible to find examples of the kind of work we are suggesting in these Sample Projects echoed in the reading selections. As we noted in the Preface, our intent is also to demonstrate several different ways that inquiry projects can be organized to take advantage of research projects that invite national contributions or have local counterparts. We believe that undergraduates can often contribute in meaningful ways to such projects under the guidance of senior researchers and teachers who help blend curricular goals with ongoing research initiatives. Finally many teachers find these projects, or portions of them, work well in conjunction with the Assignment Sequences; and experienced teachers will surely find room to experiment with combinations and connections of their own design and fitting their own local contexts. However, the project assignments are much less structured and so require both students and their teachers to make many of the decisions about audience, purpose, form, and inquiry strategies that are more fully delineated in the Assignment Sequences of the next section. Thus, for many programs, these sample projects will seem most appropriate for more advanced students or for courses taught in conjunction with faculty from relevant disciplines.

PROJECT 1: THE WATER PROJECT

Conceived by Professor Sanjeev Chatterjee, Director of the Center for the Advancement of Modern Media at the University of Miami, *The Water Project* is a collaborative effort centered on highlighting the urgent issues surrounding water in the twenty-first century. While many people in developed countries take clean water and indoor plumbing for granted, an estimated one-sixth of the world's population—some 1.1 billion people—do not have access to this essential resource. Millions die annually from diseases caused by contaminated water, the bulk of them children. An assessment by the World Health Organization in 2000 found that "in the past 10 years, diarrhea has killed more children than all those lost to armed conflict in almost 60 years since the Second World War."

Due to lack of infrastructure in rural areas, millions of other people around the world, mainly women and girls, spend hours each day walking to distant wells, pumps, water holes, lakes, or rivers and then carrying water back to their homes. Nations, meanwhile, vie for control of water sources, particularly in desert regions of the Middle East and Africa. Some political scientists have predicted that water, in the coming century, will be as contended as oil supplies, and wars may well be fought over it.

The United Nations has declared that access to potable water is a universal human right and that governments are obligated to secure and protect this right for their citizens. As part of the effort to raise global awareness of issues surrounding water, Chatterjee and his team produced a twenty-minute wordless film, *One Water*. Featuring footage from India, southern Africa, the Canary Islands, the southern United States, and elsewhere, the film reveals the practical, cultural, and spiritual role this finite resource plays in the lives of people worldwide. A related Web site serves as a clearing house on water issues and sustainability. In 2003 the team began work on a ninty-minute documentary intended for theatrical release. The feature length version debuted on May 9, 2007.

Visit the Web site at http://www.onewater.org
You can see a range of related projects at http://kcim.miami.edu

OPTION 1: *WATER MEMORIES*

As *One Water* demonstrates, water is not merely a physiological need, but has been assigned deep emotional and spiritual meanings. Water figures in innumerable myths and legends, in literature and songs, and in paintings and photographs. Many of us have memories involving water—dancing in a sprinkler on a hot summer afternoon, being awed by a thundering waterfall swollen by spring runoff in the mountains, rocking in a boat on a lake waiting for the fish to bite. What associations do you have with water? Can you identify one or two key memories you have involving water? Were you indoors or outdoors? Drinking it or swimming in it? Write a journal entry in which you develop questions and thoughts regarding these memories, with special regard to your deeper attitudes toward water. If you find that you take water for granted, or have never particularly thought about it, why might that be? After sharing your questions, memories, and attitudes with your classmates, write an essay or memoir that draws on these personal experiences to suggest the significance of water in culture.

OPTION 2: *IDENTIFYING LOCAL WATER ISSUES*

As you can see on the Web site, The Water Project has spawned related projects featuring articles, photos, book and Web site reviews, and interviews related to specific bodies of water such as the Everglades in South Florida. Is there a body of water or a problem with water in your local area that might serve as a focal point for a similar set of investigations and presentations? If so, what are the important issues surrounding that body of water and how can you investigate and then share these investigations with others? If you design materials that could be added to The Water Project Web site, be sure to contact Professor Chatterjee about including them in his project.

OPTION 3: *EXPANDING TEXTUAL MATERIALS AT THE WATER PROJECT SITE*

Examine the articles that have been posted to The Water Project Web site. What's missing from this collection? Add to the collection by investigating and then submitting an article of your own. You might, for example, consider a particular problem (or technological solution), a particular region of the world, songs or visual representations of water, rituals or exploration/development via waterways. You may also want to include links to other Web sites, photographs, or other visual materials as do some of the articles already posted.

OPTION 4: *INVESTIGATING DOCUMENTARIES*

Documentary films bring attention to an issue like water, as you can see in the Web site feature about the presentation made to the United Nations. The Water Project itself is a part of "Modern Media Initiatives for a Sustainable Future." As the creators of the Web site explain, they are "interested in media as a tool to promote change." Investigate the relationship between documentary films and social change. You can do this investigation narrowly, around the issues of water, or more broadly by considering the effect of documentaries on any social change. Here are two ways to proceed:

1. Focus specifically on water and the effect of the documentary *One Water*. What has to happen in order for the problems with water to be solved? Consider such related issues as politics, public policy, international cooperation, or technology.
2. Consider the relationship between documentaries and the issues they raise more generally. You should begin by identifying as many different documentaries as you can and the social issue they were addressing. For the purposes of this assignment, it will be best to concentrate on films that have been out at least one year. Once you have your inventory of possibilities, choose at least three from different time periods or on different subjects, and investigate the reception and/or impact these films had when they were released. Consider, too, how the issues they raised have changed since the release of the documentary.

OPTION 5: *EXPLORING ISSUES OF SUSTAINABILITY*

Consider the problem of "sustainability." Besides water, what else is required if life is to be sustained? With your classmates, brainstorm a list of categories and subtopics connected with sustainability. Choose one of these subtopics and investigate. What is known? What are the problems? What needs to happen? Where are the controversies? Write your investigation in a way that informs others about the specific issue you've investigated but that also considers "sustainability" more generally based on your specific example. If you discover specific features of sustainability that you think Professor Chatterjee should consider adding to his Web site, let him know about your work.

PROJECT 2: LOCAL HISTORY

One of the exciting things about working with local history is you will quickly become one of a handful of experts in a particular area, often *the* expert. So even if you are brand new to a certain locale, investigating and writing about local history can help you learn about the area and is often a genuine contribution to the local community. You need not try to write a local history that covers all areas of the community from the beginning of time. In fact, a closer, more intimate look is often better. You should capitalize on your interests to investigate the history of particular organizations, buildings, and people or to consider a particular moment in time rather than long sweeps of history.

In developing a local history, you may use a variety of the methods covered earlier in this book. You might, for instance, work with archival materials, use interviews to collect oral histories, observe environments carefully, uncover and analyze images. You could also mix investigations into local history with work on public spaces or bodies of water, so a glance at the Assignment Sequences, Readings, and other Sample Projects may be helpful to you.

Whether you concentrate on the school you are currently attending or on the local community, you will probably find that there is more material than you can reasonably deal with in a single term. Thus, collaborating with classmates as you decide on the focus and conduct your investigation will enable you to do more than you could do on your own.

RESEARCHING AND COMPOSING LOCAL HISTORIES

When you begin investigating local history, you will want to have a focus for your investigation—a specific topic or idea you want to discover more about. But you should also be flexible. In the process of investigating your topic, you will discover new and interesting information about topics you had not intended to pursue. If one of these seems more promising than your original idea, check with your instructor to see if changing your focus would be appropriate. As with any project, changes are easier to make early in a process than late. This is one reason why, especially when investigating local history, you need to get an early start.

Composing history, including local history, means telling a story about the past. Historians also tell those stories of the past to make arguments about the significance, cause, or result of particular events; about what the past means to the present; and, sometimes, about how to read the past in new ways. Two issues about writing history that interest current historians may be useful for you to consider as you work on your own local history project. First, current historians are interested in the stories about or by those who have been left out of earlier histories; thus efforts to recover the history of women, minorities, working class, or common people are especially important because they help us understand the fuller picture of the past and reconsider our inherited conceptions. Patricia Nelson Limerick, a current scholar of history, has consistently raised such questions about the untold or ignored past, and she urges those who write history to do so in a way that takes into account the way that myths about the past or a single point of view can distort our understanding of both the past and the present. For Limerick, writing history means telling more than one story, or at least telling a story that acknowledges that different people who lived at a particular time had different vantage points and thus different "truths" to contribute to understanding the events under study.[1]

Second, because historians use narrative, or storytelling, as the primary form for conveying information, they are concerned with how narrative itself might influence meaning. Hayden White, considered the most prominent American scholar working on the connections between historiography and narrative theory, has argued that "story forms not only permit us to judge the moral significance of human projects; they also provide the means by which to judge them, even while we pretend to be merely describing them."[2] In other words, for White, history is always presented as a judgment of the past because historians juxtapose events and offer evidence to support claims, but because the same set of events can be told in different ways by different historians—as tragedy or comedy, for example—*how* historians tell the story teaches readers to consider intentions and whether those intentions were met.

The assignments that follow ask you to construct some sort of narrative. You should identify, as you write, the idea you hope to get across as you compose your narrative. You will have to select from the information that you have uncovered and arrange your selected evidence with both your readers and your point in mind. Thus, even though writing histories means "telling stories," doing so requires you to synthesize multiple sources of information and support the argument or interpretation that *you* find in the material, actions that are the essence of academic writing.

OPTION 1: *BUILDING HISTORY*

Discover and write the history of a local building. The building you investigate may be a local landmark, a particularly uncomfortable classroom building on campus, your school library, or the home you grew up in.

Be sure to explain to its owner or to the person responsible for maintaining it your plans and get permission to physically access the building. You will be doing some snooping around, so you do not want people getting suspicious or calling the police. Begin your investigation by observing the building carefully, noting all of its features that escape your normal recognition. Be sure to tour the building, if it is large. Note its materials, take at least a rough measurement of its dimensions, and sketch it out. Look for alterations, places where the materials do not match or where there is a scar from previous work. Look carefully at the walls, inside and out; the foundation; the windows and windowsills; and the floors, taking notes as you do. Record the current system for heating, ventilating, and air conditioning, and note if there seem to be remnants of an earlier system. Look for indications of age.

Next interview the owner, resident(s), or people associated with the building. If it is a campus building, interview the people responsible for its maintenance and others who have worked in this building for a long time. Use these interviews as opportunities to develop contacts with others whom you will subsequently interview. You'll want to get a sense of the building's functional history, that is, what it was designed to do, how it has been used for that purpose, and how that purpose has changed, but you are also looking for its emotional history, that is, the sorts of human events that have occurred there and the kinds of associations that exist for those who know the building well.

---

[1]See, for example, *The Legacy of Conquest: The Unbroken Past of the American West,* NY: Norton (1987).
[2]"The Narrativization of Real Events," *Critical Inquiry* 7 (1981): 797.

Go to the local or school library, and see if there are published histories of the institution or area that discuss this particular building. Check for newspaper accounts of
important events that you have learned about during your interviews. When appropriate, look in the school archives for photographs or other images of your building. Find
out if there are blueprints and legal descriptions of the property available. If you intend
to complete a thorough history, you should check at the county courthouse or public
records office for deeds, building permits, and other legal records such as plat maps and
tax records. These documents can supplement or verify oral histories, and can provide
you with a wealth of information about the building's construction, use, and ownership
history. (*Note:* You will probably need both the property's legal description and current owner's legal name to find these records. The legal description is not necessarily the
same as its street address, so check deeds or tax records.)

Once you have completed your research, compose a history of your building. You
will have to review your research carefully in order to find the interesting and meaningful story that you want to tell. You will have to consider carefully what meaning you
want your readers to derive from your narrative, and shape the narrative accordingly;
deciding what details to leave out is as important as deciding what details are important
to this story. Include sketches of the layout and any images, such as old or new photographs, which would be useful. Remember to obtain permissions if you use others'
photographs, and to cite your sources for both images and texts.

OPTION 2: *GROUP OR PERSONALITY HISTORY*

Modify the first assignment to focus instead on the history of a local organization or
group, a local personality who has made some kind of contribution to your campus, community, or the world, or a local terrain or space that is somehow interesting or significant.

Local groups might include a campus organization to which you belong, such as
the Filipino Student's Organization or Phi Beta Kappa, or the local chapter of a national
group with which you find affinities or are a member, such as the ACLU or the Feder-
alist Society. This group may have an official historian or archivist you can interview.
Likely, it will not (and your efforts may, if you wish to pursue it, result in the creation
of such an office).

Local personalities are always interesting subjects of exploration. Professors, politicians, business leaders, activists, artists, and benefactors always have stories, often ones that
are interesting and valuable. Professors or other noteworthy people often leave their papers
to a local archive or historical society, and these can be a rich source of investigation. You
can also conduct interviews with people who know or knew this individual, or you may be
able to interview the individual him- or herself even if they have retired. Alternatively you
might want to focus on the history of a specific family, either because of their collective
impact on a community or because their story is somehow typical of the area.

Local terrains or spaces are also surprisingly rich subjects for local histories. You may
live or go to school in an area with a famous natural or historic park—for example, Yel-
lowstone or Valley Forge. Even if there is no specific park, though, many natural phenomena—waterways, mountains, harbors, caves, quarries—have played a significant
role in national and local history. You could focus on the history of a neighborhood, or
a local park, or of a public space. You may also want to explore the archival holdings of
projects already underway, such as those at the Virginia Center for Digital History at
http://www.vcdh.virginia.edu/index.html.

PROJECT 3: PUBLIC SPACE

As urban areas become more and more congested, concern about open, public space for parks and recreation has grown. Many cities have zoning regulations that encourage building owners to design and maintain public spaces such as courtyards, atriums, lobbies, or outdoor landscape and seating areas, often in exchange for waivers of restrictions on height or easements from streets.[3] Likewise many cities have initiatives to put art in public places and thereby improve the quality of the space while increasing public access to art.[4]

Such efforts to improve the quality of public spaces actually have a long history and include both urban areas with the creation of parks, museums, and libraries and the establishment of state and national parks, forests, wetlands, and other wilderness areas.[5] However, the improvement of public spaces is not without controversy, and keeping public spaces open and accessible often runs counter to the mission to preserve these spaces. National Parks and Forests, for example, were established to preserve wilderness areas and have become refuges for wild animals, but visitors to these parks require services such as roads, trails, bathrooms, camping facilities. Construction of such services means less wilderness and even more human traffic.

While organizations like the Project for Public Spaces (http://www.pps.org/) conduct research and offer professional expertise about the design and management of public spaces, students can also have an impact on the use of public spaces and contribute to preservation, cataloging and development efforts. The University of Miami's Florida Public Space Project (http://www.education.miami.edu/succeed/institutes/inspast_iph.htm), for example, has fostered collaborative efforts by high school students and their teachers working to identify and preserve open spaces in South Florida. Likewise students at the University of Virginia's School of Architecture worked for two spring semesters (2001 and 2002) to photograph and map public spaces in Barcelona. You can see their work at http://urban.arch.virginia.edu/lar602-2001/home.html. The University of Toronto also has a Public Spaces project focused more on environmental aspects of public space. Their site is at http://www.utoronto.ca/env/st/pspaces/publicspaces.htm.

In conjunction with government organizations and private organizations and individuals, students and researchers work to protect the environment, acquire additional public spaces, and host events about issues of urban sustainability. Other public space projects focus on historical preservation. At the University of Kentucky, for example, Professor Boyd Landerson Shearer, Jr., has produced two projects centered on the history of the public space represented by segregated parks in the South. His Web site at http://www.uky.edu/Projects/TDA/ includes photos, oral histories, and a documentary video. Another historical project at the University of Kentucky (http://www.uky.edu/Projects/AfricanCem/) features an African American cemetery and includes aerial maps, a detailed walking tour guide, photographs, historical information, and plans for continuing to preserve and research the history of this public place.

---

[3] See Mark Holcolm's *Village Voice* story on a few of NYC's 503 officially designated public spaces at http://www.villagevoice.com/nyclife/0353,amholcomb,49892,17.html.
[4] See, for example, Connecticut's Art in Public Places initiative at http://www.ct.gov/cct/cwp/view.asp?a=2214 &q=293756 and a similar project by Miami Dade County at http://www.co.miami-dade.fl.us/publicart/.
[5] See http://www.cr.nps.gov/history/index.asp for a history of national parks.

The assignments in this project invite you to consider public spaces in your area—their history, the need for them, the resources they require—and to use your research and writing in ways that are appropriate for the space and the goals you and your classmates have for the specific location. While it may be very difficult to have a public space declared for a particular use or to complete its history in a single term, it is very possible to contribute to an ongoing project or to start a new one that others can help develop. Depending on your interests and the needs of your locale, you may well decide to take your project beyond the classroom and the boundaries of the term, continuing the work with the help of organizations, student groups, or public officials.

OPTION 1: *IDENTIFYING PUBLIC SPACE USE*

Working within your local area, identify the public spaces and how they are being used. You may already know of unused spaces, parks, trails, or other areas that provide green space in your community. Use resources like the United States Geographical Survey maps at http://www.usgs.gov/ to help you map the open spaces in your area, and to identify specific open spaces for further investigation. You may also want to locate historical maps, or track changes in topography and development via satellite and other aerial maps. Add to the information that is already available on these open spaces by visiting the site and taking careful observation notes. If you are interested in preserving an open area, you may decide to make an inventory of plant and animal life, as well as chart the use of the area by humans. If you are interested in having the area transformed in some way, a detailed map and chart of features will be important documents to your final presentation/report. Like the work to "map" the historical cemetery featured at http://www.uky.edu/Projects/AfricanCem/, your work may end up being as much discursive as it is visual.

OPTION 2: *TRANSFORMING PUBLIC SPACES*

Choose a particular open and apparently empty or unused space that you believe could be better utilized. This might be a small strip of land, such as the edge of a highway or an abandoned lot, or a much larger parcel of empty space. Working with your classmates, investigate what would be required to transform the space. Who owns the space? How is it zoned? What restrictions apply to how the space can be developed? Whose permission would be required for the transformation to occur? What kind of funding would be necessary? As you consider what would be needed to make the transformation, consider also what the space should be used for and why? Should this space become a park? A playground? An urban garden open to area residents? This project will require you to do many different kinds of writing—letters, perhaps formal reports, applications for grant money to secure funding. The particulars of both audience and form will depend on your particular project. If other groups are already involved in trying to transform the area, be certain to work with them, contributing your ideas and research skills and learning from the experience of those who have been working on the project longer than you have.

OPTION 3: *(RE)NAMING PUBLIC SPACE*

Many local parks, playgrounds, or other open spaces are unnamed and often have little identity within the community. Sometimes, even when they are named, the reason for the choice of name has been lost to the local community. Collect oral histories of those who live near such a space in order to identify either a specific event that has significance in the community or a person with whom local citizens can identify. Once you have thoroughly investigated the history, make an argument for (re)naming the public place, or you might also use the history of the open space to craft a documentary, create brochures or markers or other devices to inform others of this history.

OPTION 4: *PUBLIC SPACE HISTORY*

As an alternative to Option 3, consider areas in your community that have a distinct identity. In Miami, for example, mobile home parks once dotted the landscape because the area was such a popular winter retreat. Now such communities are rare, and the few that survive have interesting but neglected histories. Likewise many college campuses have an area just off campus that attracts students and has an interesting but untold history, often with businesses that have been in existence for decades. Identify and research one of these areas in your community. You'll probably want to make use of existing histories of the region, maps, oral histories, and interviews with long-timers, as well as conduct your own careful observations of the area in question. Your goal in a project such as this one is mostly historical, but along the way you may well discover other preservation or restoration issues, zoning problems, or a need for open green space.

PROJECT 4: ORGANIZATIONAL NEEDS ASSESSMENT

Many organizations both within your college or university and in your local community are starving for information that can help the organization do its job better. Assessing an organization's needs is essentially a matter of inquiry: asking questions and investigating possible answers. Since every organization has a number of strengths as well as areas that could be improved, an *Organizational Needs Assessment* must begin with careful and systematic investigation into the organization itself and proceed to consider possible areas of improvement, concrete recommendations, and presentation of results. Thus the assignments in this project function differently from those in the other sample projects; instead of providing multiple prompts for your investigation, this project is a sequence of assignments that take you from step one to your final formal report.

STEP 1: *IDENTIFYING AN ORGANIZATION*

Brainstorm a list of organizations you might want to know more about or that you have an interest in investigating. You might begin that list with student organizations you belong to or would belong to if you had more time. Consider, as well, nonprofit organizations in the community that you would like to know more about. If you know someone who works at or is involved in an organization, business, or club, add those groups to your list. Be imaginative. Make your list as varied as possible. As you make your list, consider what it is about each of these groups that might be interesting. What kind of work do these groups do that fascinates you? Share you list with your classmates and discuss the possibilities. It's very possible that a group initially identified by someone else will turn out to be your project.

STEP 2: *RESEARCHING THE ORGANIZATION*

Once you have identified an organization you are interested in, investigate the organization. Before trying to interview or observe the group in action, conduct a background investigation by examining public documents. Read through the Internet site for the group, for example, or any written documents they provide to the public. Look for newspaper reports on the organization and its activities. If the local group is a part of a national or statewide organization, be sure to examine documents about this larger group as well and note the formal relationship between the larger group and the local version. This work with texts will allow you to create an archive of relevant documents but will also allow you to create a list of questions and issues for further investigation. Keep careful notes of your work, especially potential interviewees, recognized problems, or controversies.

Once you know the basic, public information about the group, use other inquiry methods to continue your research. You should work both informally—that is, simply collecting more information until you can determine a precise question or focus of research—and formally once you determine that focus. Depending on the group you are assessing, you might:

- Observe the group at work. Attend open meetings of the organization, and the events they sponsor. Visit their offices, showroom, or place of operation.
- Interview key members of the organization, or conduct a focus group session with those the group serves. Collect oral histories from previous members, clients, or others who know of the organization.
- Survey past or present members of the group about their experiences, and/or solicit information from the clients or participants that the group serves.
- Collect appropriate statistics, for example, numbers about membership, budget and expenditures, or activities.

Analyze the data you are collecting throughout the process, looking for key problems that you might consider further and for which you might be able to suggest solutions, as well as for places where you need to do more work. Use your classmates as research colleagues throughout this process. They can help you identify important questions, consider other research methods, and narrow your investigation to a more focused question.

STEP 3: *INCORPORATING SECONDARY SOURCES*

As you conduct your investigation, remember to consult relevant prior research and scholarly articles. Using database search engines such *Academic Search Elite* will allow you to use relevant key terms and limit your search to peer-reviewed (i.e., scholarly) journals.

STEP 4: *NARROWING THE FOCUS*

Once you know your organization well, you should be able to identify a couple of areas that are problematic, that is, issues of concern or areas that need improvement. Narrowing your focus may enable you to form a precise question for further research or to pose a solution to a problem. In either case draw upon your prior work *and* conduct additional research as necessary.

STEP 5: COMPOSING A FIRST DRAFT FOR PEER REVIEW

One of the challenges of this project is to maneuver in rhetorically astute ways, especially since you may well have to communicate bad news. As you do so, you will have to also avoid having your analysis perceived as "intellectual skim milk." After all your audience knows the organization intimately and may well have their own sense of the problems and possible solutions. They may also have a long history with the organization, and they may or may not be open to the perspectives of those they perceive as being less-informed outsiders. Your final report will thus have to establish your authority through a careful blend of humility and confidence. Four key elements to this delicate balance are:

- Using the data gathered in systematic investigation and research rather than relying on general impressions or personal experience and opinion alone
- Integrating secondary sources appropriate to the issues and focus at hand
- Narrowing the focus so that your research is both more precise and less superficial
- Acknowledging the limitations of your work

Sharing an early version of your final report with peers will help you identify whether you are striking the proper tone, explaining effectively, and incorporating appropriate research to substantiate your analysis and recommendations.

STEP 6: FINAL REPORT

Compose your findings in an appropriate form using visuals such as tables, graphs, pie charts, and so forth as appropriate to represent the data you've collected. Because your work may have different audiences, consider carefully both the most appropriate audience(s) and the form your work needs to take to reach that audience most effectively. A final written document will most likely contain:

- *Introduction:* The introduction supplies an overview of the report. Introductions generally include similar basic information, such as a statement of purpose which is simply a sentence or two explaining why you are submitting the report (rationale, justification, objectives); identification of the report's subject matter; explanation of personnel, including the names of others who might be involved in your reporting activity; dates or period of time the report covers; scope of the study; and background information on methods used, definitions of key terms, and limitations of study. As in any introduction, the opening should be crafted to gain the audience's attention and begin to establish the author's credibility/authority.
- *Body/Discussion/Findings:* This part of your work objectively describes your activities and presents the reasons for the recommendations that follow. This is the largest section of the report and requires strong development and organization, especially if you are trying to persuade your audience to accept new ideas. This section should also establish criteria/foundation for the comparison of data.
- *Conclusions/Recommendations:* Your conclusions/recommendations allow you to determine the meaning/significance of your data and to state what decisions you

have made regarding the activities reported. The recommendations section allows you to suggest further actions, to state what you believe should be done next, or to outline what additional research needs to be done. In this section you should go beyond the objective facts as laid out in the discussion section and state the significance of your findings and the action you propose.

STEP 7: ORAL PRESENTATION

Because organizational needs assessments suggest actions or changes that the group should consider, it is common to present the report both in writing and in an oral presentation. Presenting your research orally is not a matter of simply reading what you have written. Nor is it the case that a formal report can be turned into a PowerPoint presentation without also reconsidering how the information should be reorganized, reframed, or rewritten. In fact a PowerPoint presentation may be completely inappropriate for the kind of presentation that best fits your study. Thus, revising the formal report into an oral presentation will require you to rethink audience and purpose and make decisions that fit this new rhetorical situation. It will matter a great deal, for example, whether you are presenting your findings to a single individual in a face-to-face meeting or speaking before a committee or executive board. Likewise, if the oral presentation comes before members of the organization have read your formal report, it will have a different tone and highlight different portions than if the group has read your report and sets up a presentation so you can clarify recommendations and answer questions before they vote to accept (or reject) your proposed solutions. As you prepare for the oral presentation, it may be helpful to:

- Be clear about the purpose, audience, and function of your presentation.
- Select only the most relevant information to highlight, but be prepared to answer questions about details you've omitted.
- Prepare appropriate visual materials—charts, graphs, tables, and so forth—that will help clarify your points and keep your audience focused on your points.
- Practice your presentation several times in front of a mirror or with friends as your audience so you know the material well, can handle the visuals easily, and are comfortable speaking about your work. Remember to make eye contact with everyone so as not to ignore a portion of your audience; you just can't ever know for certain who makes decisions, but you can be fairly certain that no one appreciates being treated as insignificant.
- Prepare note cards or an abbreviated script that will keep you organized without tempting you to read to your audience; do not expect to memorize your presentation or to deliver your material without notes at hand no matter how much experience you've had giving oral presentations.
- Dress appropriately for the presentation. In this situation you are not just a student, but someone with considerable expertise gained from the research you've done. Appropriate dress and demeanor will add to your credibility.

Internet Resources Referenced in Sample Projects and Assignment Sequences

The Water Project: http://www.onewater.org

Knight Center for International Media: http://kcim.miami.edu

Virginia Center for Digital History: http://www.vcdh.virginia.edu/index.html

Project for Public Spaces: http://www.pps.org/

Mark Holcolm's *Village Voice* story on public spaces: http://www.villagevoice.com/nyclife/0353,amholcomb,49892,17.html

University of Miami's Florida Public Space Project: http://www.education.miami.edu/succeed/institutes/inspast_iph.htm

Connecticut's Art in Public Places initiative: http://www.ct.gov/cct/cwp/view.asp?a=2214&q=293756

Miami Dade County's Art in Public Places: http://www.co.miami-dade.fl.us/publicart/

Virginia School of Architecture Barcelona Project: http://urban.arch.virginia.edu/lar602-2001/home.html

University of Toronto Public Spaces Project: http://www.utoronto.ca/env/st/pspaces.publicspaces.htm

History of National Parks: http://www.cr.nps.gov/history/index.asp

Professor Boyd Landerson Shearer, Jr.'s segregated parks in the South: http://www.uky.edu/Projects/TDA/

University of Kentucky African-American Cemeteries Project: http://www.uky.edu/Projects/AfricanCem/

United States Geographical Survey: http://www.usgs.gov/

Census Bureau's *Statistical Abstract of the United States*: http://www.census.gov/compendia/statab/

Federal Statistics: http://www.fedstats.gov/

Government Patent Office: www.uspto.gov

Human Resources Area Files: www.yale.edu/hraf

International Index to Music Periodicals: http://iimpft.chadwyck.com/home

Farm Security Administration-Office of War Information Collection at the Library of Congress: http://memory.loc.gov/ammem/fsowhome.html

ASSIGNMENT SEQUENCES

These sequences are meant to help students and teachers organize their work of inquiry and writing. Each sequence includes assignments that utilize different methods and invite different kinds of revision. In each assignment we encourage students to keep reflective notes, what we call "authorial notes," so that writing processes, strategies, and difficulties become more open to discussion, scrutiny, and reconsideration. Such reflection is an important part of becoming a stronger writer, a writer who knows how to ask others for help and how to reconsider a piece of writing from different perspectives.

Most of the sequences are built around a theme or topic for investigation. A few of the sequences invite work with a primary method as the center of the investigation, but even in these sequences, students can expect to use different methods in combination with the primary method they are encouraged to explore. We have avoided assignments that ask students to pretend to be someone else or to write for a pretend audience; instead we invite students to think about different kinds of audiences that might really be interested in their investigations and to craft documents that are appropriate for those readers and that purpose. In our experience, these assignments produce lots of variety as students develop topics they find interesting but ones that work within the parameters of the suggested method of inquiry. Those common parameters help students to be effective peer reviewers and to learn from each other even as they work with different material and develop very different arguments.

Finally most of the assignments work out of the readings that follow in the next section. Remember that these readings are demonstrating methods of inquiry and investigation, and so they often serve as models for student work, even if imperfect ones. Some of the sequences include assignments that do not build off a reading, though a quick turn to the method chapters will supply examples of readings that use the same method. Our intent in creating some assignments that work without a reading was to open up more space for supplemental reading that teachers might want to include and more time for attending to students' writing as another set of reading materials.

BETWEEN WRITING AND KNOWING

A SEQUENCE WITHOUT READINGS

Although we sometimes think of writing as a transparent medium—our thoughts made visible for others to see—writing is rarely as clear and obvious as we would like. In truth, the way we write shapes the messages we are trying to convey, and the process works in both directions: the way we are able to write shapes the thoughts we are able to have. This sequence asks you to self-consciously "try on" several different ways of writing about issues, each of them representing a different way of knowing. At the same time, this sequence asks that you remain aware of the ways you write so you can recognize the knowledge these forms of communication make possible.

ASSIGNMENT 1: *SPEAKING WITH NUMBERS: A TREND ANALYSIS*

Data from the Census Bureau's normal surveys, including the famous decennial census, are released in the yearly *Statistical Abstract of the United States*. The *Statistical Abstract* will be available in the reference section of most libraries (check with your reference librarian), and is also available on the Internet at http://www.census.gov/compendia/statab/. These reports have several different major sections, including Population, Vital Statistics, Health and Nutrition, Education, Law Enforcement, the Courts and Prison, Geography and the Environment, Elections, Government Finances, National Defense and Veterans Affairs, Social Insurance and Human Services, Labor Statistics, Income and Wealth, Prices, Business, Science and Technology, Agriculture, Natural Resources, Energy, Construction and Housing, Manufactures, Domestic Trade, Transportation, Information and Communications, Banking and Finance, Arts and Entertainment, Accommodation and Food Services, Foreign Commerce and Aid, Puerto Rico and Outlying Areas, and Comparative International Statistics.

Choose one of these sections to explore and begin to dig through the *Statistical Abstract*. One way to approach a section of the *Statistical Abstract* is to browse the list of tables and home in on those tables that present information of particular interest to you. As you look through these data, try to notice where the numbers indicate surprising, shocking, disturbing, encouraging, interesting, or counterintuitive demographic data; relationships; and, especially, trends. Look at the distribution of data at a particular point in time, but also look at how that data have changed over the past five, ten, fifteen, twenty, or more years. See if the tables in the *Statistical Abstract* provide any insight into why such changes have occurred. If your insights or questions lead you to other sections of the report, pursue them. In particular it is often useful to know population totals, provided in "Section 1: Population," when you are thinking about your data. It can be useful to compare the data in the reports for several different years, because they will sometimes provide different comparisons or updated data. You will need to carefully reference these data in your writing, so be sure to take careful notes and make copies, especially if you are using the bound volumes as opposed to the documents available on the Internet.

Once you have a working knowledge of your data, investigate information on this topic provided by at least one other source. One place to look would be at documents provided by other government agencies. For instance, if you were looking at statistics related to infant mortality or AIDS, publications of the Centers for Disease Control and Prevention and the National Center for Health Statistics would be helpful. If you were interested in crime, then the Bureau of Justice Statistics or the data made available through the FBI's famous Uniform Crime Reports might be the place to go. You should start your search at the Fed Stats Web site (http://www.fedstats.gov/), which provides links to statistical data from over one-hundred federal agencies. Reports, both regular and occasional, from many of these agencies will also be available in many libraries.

Produce a written document in which you explain trends related to the subject of your choice to an audience that would find them interesting or useful. Your trend analysis is an argument about what these data, and what changes (or the lack of change) in these data "say" about the country we live in and the people who inhabit it, but the way you present that argument can take different forms. Use the data you have analyzed, presenting the information in tables or charts where appropriate in order to help your readers understand your argument. Make sure that you explain clearly any ways you may have manipulated the data, for instance by finding percentage changes or averages. Whether you notice problems or positive trends or both, you might also provide recommendations about what ought to be done about the trends or characteristics you notice.

When you have completed your writing, write a few authorial notes about your composing process. What was difficult about this work? How was writing about statistics different from other kinds of writing you have done in the past?

ASSIGNMENT 2: *SURVEYING*

College students share a variety of interests and experiences with other people at their schools, across the country, and often throughout the world. Choose an area of concern upon which you believe a survey of college students would help to shed light. Your topic need not be particularly "heavy," and indeed for this project you should steer clear of topics that might bring up painful or disturbing memories in your survey participants. You'll want to review the ethical considerations in Chapter 5 and work with your teacher to select a topic that fits the guidelines of your own institutional research review board. The area of concern can be specific to your campus or can be about college students generally. It can be something college students are interested in, or it can be something people who are interested in college students might want to know. It might be related to the trends analysis you did in Assignment 1, but you needn't feel constrained by that work if it doesn't capture your interest.

Using the steps for conducting surveys outlined in Chapter 5 as a guide, construct a survey to measure the area of concern. Conduct your survey, tabulate and analyze your data, and then report your results in an appropriate written document. Be certain that you not only present your findings but also explain their significance to your readers.

When you have finished your report of survey results, take a few moments to add to your authorial notes. What did you learn about writing from this assignment? What parts of your report would you continue to work on if you had more time?

ASSIGNMENT 3: *WRITING THE UNWRITABLE*

When researchers work to analyze photographs, they embark on a paradoxical project: to explain in writing the things such images do which writing does not do. In order to make this kind of work possible, researchers have to work carefully and closely with a collection of photographs, discovering in the process both how to read them and what they mean. This assignment asks you to experiment with this process by amassing your own collection of photographs. You might use photographs of your own or those that belong to your family, or you might visit an archival collection and select from among that collection. If no other photographs are available to you, select several from magazines or books that are about a similar subject, historical event, or group of people. We think it's best to avoid selecting your photographs from a published book featuring a single artist or topic because such collections often have already done the interesting inquiry work, but you and your instructor may decide that such a publication is appropriate for remixing and reinterpreting, especially in combination with other photographs.

Once you have chosen a collection of at least a dozen or so photographs, present these photos in a written document that demonstrates to others how they can be read. As discussed in the section on visuals in Chapter 3, you might pay special attention to the small details of the image, consider what is just outside the edges of the print, or take into account the various gazes of the subjects in the photo. You'll probably also have to develop other strategies for working with the specifics of your collection. As you work to both read and describe your collection, you'll also need to consider what connections or disjunctions exist between the images in your collection or between your collection and other common photographs. In other words, what makes these images interesting, troubling, surprising, or ordinary? What makes them a collection? Be sure to also consider what you can know and not know from the photographs themselves because some of what you can't know might be worth further investigation and inquiry using other methods.

After you have finished your writing, add to your authorial notes. How was this writing experience like or unlike the earlier work you've done? Which part of this work gave you the most trouble and which parts did you find most pleasurable?

ASSIGNMENT 4: *AN ACADEMIC DIALOGUE*

Sometimes researchers use focus groups as a vehicle for considering attitudes, opinions, and the language differences that become apparent as individuals discuss some issue together. In such an inquiry, the researcher must be careful to start the discussion and keep it focused but without dictating the points the group will consider or the meanings they will argue over. Facilitating a focus group as a research tool requires careful advanced preparation, close listening, thoughtful interventions, and then critical analysis of the recorded conversation in order to determine what all this talk means.

For this assignment, join with people who use a particular thing or medium or space in some kind of "conversation" about how they use it. Your first task will be to set the topic for discussion. Feel free to revisit a topic from a previous paper if you wish, or develop a new topic taken from music, magazines, sports, movies, or television. Remember that while you should select a topic of interest, you should also, as a scholar, study something from which you will be able to develop a critical distance. Your job is neither to defend nor to tear down a particular cultural practice, but to study its dynamics via the way people talk about it. Your second task is to identify a group of individuals to serve as your focus group. It is not necessary for these individuals to already think of themselves as a group; in fact, it is probably better if you don't select a preexisting group like a sorority or sports team because their prior relationships may influence the group dynamics and thus alter the discussion of your topic. You should not use children or teenagers under eighteen for this research unless such work would meet the guidelines of your own institutional research review board and you are able to get parental permission for these children or teens to participate in your study. You should probably also avoid convening a focus group that consists only of your close friends or roommates. Instead think carefully about how the people you invite to participate might represent a particular group, or a range of perspectives, relevant to your topic of inquiry. See Chapter 4 for other suggestions for working with focus group research.

Present the results of your focus group in a written document that considers both the topic you've selected for discussion and the discussion itself in a way that will be of interest to others. You'll want to think carefully about who would be interested in this particular discussion and why, which parts of the discussion those readers would find most compelling, and how to preserve the distinctions and disagreements that arose without simply reproducing an entire transcript. Most important, then, you have to be demonstrating how readers should interpret this conversation and why such talk is worth attending to.

When you have finished your writing, add to your authorial notes. What challenges did you face as you did this assignment? Which parts of your final document seem to be the best and which parts would you revise if you had more time?

ASSIGNMENT 5: *READING OBJECTS*

Researchers who focus on material culture argue for, and try to demonstrate, the deep connections between objects and the beliefs or values of the culture that produces and/or uses those objects. This assignment invites you to try your hand at such work by looking into the life of a particular kind of object. You may choose to work with an historical object if you wish or one from another culture, but you could also work with a commonplace object that you encounter on a regular basis. Your task is to observe that object carefully, consider how its form, function, and cultural significance interact, and investigate as much as you can its genealogy. You may want to see if the object has a patent by going to www.uspto.gov or you might track its origins, especially its links to specific cultures by using the Human Resources Area Files available at www.yale.edu/hraf.

Develop a way of presenting your object in writing so that your readers can "see" it with fresh insight. It may be useful to include photographs or drawings of your object or of the evolution of your object into its current form. Even if you decide to add this additional visual representation, however, you should still spend time fully and accurately describing the object in writing and considering how its design reflects the cultural values of those who use it.

When you are finished with your writing, make additions to your authorial notes. How was writing about an object different from the earlier work you've done in this sequence? Were you able to follow your usual writing processes to complete this work, or did you have to modify your approach in some way? What would you tell others about doing such work that you wish you had known when you began this assignment?

ASSIGNMENT 6: *REWRITING KNOWLEDGE*

The assignments in this sequence have given you the opportunity to grow as a writer and as a researcher. Take these changes into account as you write a document that explores the kinds of insights your work has provided about the relationships between writing and knowing. Begin by looking back over your work, including your authorial notes, to make a list of what writing and research strategies you used in each assignment. Pay careful attention to how you structured each of your written products, how you used illustrations or examples, whether any of your early work got incorporated into later writings. Consider, too, how you developed each of these pieces of writing. What did you do in order to gather material? What difficulties did you have to resolve? Where did you make use of something you already knew how to do, and where did you have to learn to do something new? Your document will need to explain what you would have said about the relationship between knowing and writing before you did this work and what you have to say about that relationship now. To the extent you can, begin to draw connections, rather than distinctions, between the kinds of writing you have completed and the ways of knowing the world that these writing tasks have opened up for you.

The hardest part of this assignment, especially because it comes at the end of the semester and might be used to introduce a portfolio of your writing from the term, is to avoid saying what you imagine your teacher wants you to say. Instead think of your work and your experience the way a researcher would, that is as the data that need to be read, interpreted, and used as examples in a critical argument about the nature of knowing and writing. You might also turn to your classmates for additional data, especially data that complicate the argument you decide to make. Remember to cite your own earlier work and that of your classmates in a form that would allow your readers to easily locate the passage(s) you reference.

COLLECTIVE MEMORY

FRISCH; SPENCE; THELEN; SHACKEL; FRISCH AGAIN; LEWIS

Although it's common to think of memory as belonging to individuals, researchers are also aware of the many ways that memory is shared across age groups, communities, and cultures. Researchers are interested as well in the interactions between what individuals remember and how history is officially recorded or elements of history are forgotten. This sequence invites you to consider several different aspects of collective memory, how it functions, and what forces shape such unifying perspectives.

ASSIGNMENT 1: *EDUCATING MEMORY*

MICHAEL FRISCH, "AMERICAN HISTORY AND THE STRUCTURES OF COLLECTIVE MEMORY: A MODEST EXERCISE IN EMPIRICAL ICONOGRAPHY"

Frisch's informal survey of his students raises questions about the common assumption that schooling shapes our collective memory. On the one hand, his students seem to have much of the same knowledge about American history; on the other hand, Frisch questions whether such knowledge is the result of school lessons alone. Is such shaping true in disciplines other than history? Do students who graduate from American high schools have more or less the same general knowledge of literature, science, art, and music? This assignment invites you to conduct your own informal survey of what people know and determine the level of similarity in various kinds of common knowledge.

You will need to begin by deciding on one or two specific questions that will provide you with the kind of raw data that Frisch was able to collect. You may, if you wish, try the questions Frisch asked so as to update his work, but you needn't limit yourself to historical knowledge. Once you've determined the questions you want to ask, think carefully about the population you want to respond. Are you interested in what the most recent graduating high school class learned and remembers? If so, you can ask your friends and classmates. But, consider expanding your survey to collect data from other generations or from students who were not schooled in the United States. You may want to work with classmates to design the questions and determine how to distribute your surveys and thereby increase the number of responses you will have to analyze. To generate the lists of remembered learning, you'll need to tabulate and analyze the results, and the suggestions in Chapter 5 may be helpful.

Present your analysis of the data in a written form directed to an audience you think appropriate. Follow Frisch's lead in considering what your analysis might mean about memory, education, or the subject matter you chose to investigate. Incorporate graphs or charts that make your findings easier to follow, but don't expect these visuals to substitute for careful written explanation and analysis.

When you have finished your writing, take a few minutes to write some authorial notes about your process. What challenges did you face as you did this work? Try listing the steps of your writing process from the moment you first learned of the assignment to the moment you were ready to turn this work in to your teacher. Where would you alter that process if you were to do similar work again?

ASSIGNMENT 2: *MUSEUMS AS MEMORY*

STEVE SPENCE, "VAN GOGH IN ALABAMA, 1936"

Spence argues that a particular museum exhibit not only captured American's interest enough to make Van Gogh's art work popular, but also influenced the work of other artists such as those who took photographs for the U.S. Farm Security Administration during the Depression. There are two ways to work on extending Spence's work in relation to collective memory.

1. Visit a local museum—art, history, science—or similar institution. Observe the displays carefully, taking notes on the content and design and attending to the various ways that this institution functions to shape conceptions and educate those who visit. You may wish to consider interviewing the personnel associated with the museum or conducting a survey of its patrons.

2. Research the displays shown at other museums during the Depression (or during a different historical period). Pay close attention to the time frame and consider both why those particular exhibits would have been mounted during that period and what people would have been likely to learn from such displays. If possible, interview people who were associated with the museum at that time, or with patrons who saw the exhibits. If such interviews are not possible, see if you can find contemporaneous reviews or other archived records.

Present your research in a written document that explores the connections between museums and their roles as public educators or shapers of memory. You may want to incorporate information from the first assignment, but you will need to rework that information in a way that is appropriate to this new context. Consider using your work to speak back to Spence, expanding his argument to a new site or a different time frame or using your evidence to challenge his conclusions.

When you have completed your work, add to your authorial notes. Did your process change in any way as you worked on this assignment? Where did you make use of what you had learned in the first assignment? What would you do differently if you were to do a similar project in the future?

ASSIGNMENT 3: *REMEMBERING MEMORY*

DAVID THELEN, "REMEMBERING THE DISCOVERY OF THE WATERGATE TAPES"

As Thelen's work clearly demonstrates, people who experience the same events often remember them in very different ways. Memories of these events are also shaped by subsequent events and how those involved recounted their experiences both immediately and over time. This assignment asks you to experiment with Thelen's method of collecting multiple memories of a shared event in order to better consider these aspects of collective memory. There are two ways to proceed with your investigation:

1. Identify two to three individuals who have a shared past experience. The shared event needn't be of widespread historical significance, but might instead be something personal or familial. Interview these individuals separately about their experience and their memory of that event. You'll want to elicit very specific information about who said what, as well as the general details of the event. Because the details are important, narrow your scope to a very specific moment in this past. For example, you might interview your parents about the day of your birth, but not your entire childhood, or you might interview two classmates about a specific event on campus rather than the experiences of an entire year.

2. Select an historical event that happened in the lifetimes of people you know. Interview at least two people about their memories of that specific event, being certain to elicit as many specifics as you can about the memories they retain of the event and how they experienced that event. Again, be certain to narrow your scope. Ask about the Kent State shootings, for example, rather than the entire Vietnam War era.

In either option, be certain to explain to the people you choose to interview how you will be using their memories and their words and get their permission.

Once you have collected at least two memories of the same event, present these stories of the past in a written form that lets you consider the issues Thelen raises about memory and shared history. You needn't agree with Thelen or even mention him in your presentation if it doesn't seem appropriate to the form and audience you've determined is most suitable; in fact you may well find that memories of personal history work in very different ways from the memories of key actors in national history that Thelen is investigating in his consideration of the Watergate tapes.

When you have finished your writing, add to your authorial notes. What writing strategies did you use in this work that you think served you well? Which moments of your final paper are you most pleased with and why?

ASSIGNMENT 4: *MONUMENTS TO MEMORY*

PAUL A. SHACKEL, "PUBLIC MEMORY AND THE SEARCH FOR POWER IN AMERICAN HISTORICAL ARCHAEOLOGY"

Paul Shackel uses newspaper accounts, archival records, and observation of the monument of Robert Gould Shaw to demonstrate how public memory of the past is shaped through the construction of physical monuments and memorials. Choose a local monument or historical landmark, and investigate its creation and history. You may, at first, think that your local community has no such monuments or landmarks, but look closely and you're likely to find plaques on buildings or at the entrance to a park that serve to memorialize its creation, the founder of the company, an important donor, or a local personality. These attributions don't appear without someone, often with community involvement, making decisions about design and placement. You'll need to use historical archives, written histories of the event or person being memorialized, and newspaper accounts of the creation of the monument to reconstruct the interplay of the historical event and the ideological forces that created the monument. As you work to uncover the history of your landmark or monument, be sure to look for evidence of how different memories were being used and shaped in the construction.

Present the history of this monument in a written form that will be of interest to locals who know the monument well and may even know something of its creation, but one that will also interest historians such as Shackel and researchers of collective memory. Should your work lead you to believe that Shackel is incorrect about the role of monuments in shaping public memory or the role of public memory in the construction of monuments, feel free to use your writing to carry on a critical conversation with his work.

After you have finished your writing, take a few minutes to add to your authorial notes. What was different in writing a history of a landmark from representing the memories of others? How would you approach this kind of project in the future?

ASSIGNMENT 5: *IMAGES AND MEMORY*

MICHAEL FRISCH, "AMERICAN HISTORY AND THE STRUCTURES OF COLLECTIVE MEMORY: A MODEST EXERCISE IN EMPIRICAL ICONOGRAPHY"

In the second part of Frisch's article, he speculates that part of what students remember about history may be coming from common images rather than from their actual study of history. Images help us to remember some parts of the past and forget others by encapsulating the event or the people without the contradictions of competing versions. This assignment invites you to work with images as a way of complicating one of your earlier investigations and in order to consider collective memory in yet another way. There are two ways to take up this challenge.

1. Return to the survey you conducted in Assignment 1 and locate an image, perhaps from an advertisement, that evokes one or more of the associations you found to be common. Analyze this photograph carefully and incorporate it into a revision of your original writing from Assignment 1. You might want to share the image with respondents, or a population of respondents similar to those you used originally. Be alert to the possibility that the image (and the reactions to it) will not support your original analysis. What can account for such differences if they exist? As you incorporate the image into a revised version of your earlier writing, think carefully about where it should enter your work and how you will refer to it in your prose.

2. Return to the interviews you conducted in Assignment 2. Collect several images that illustrate the remembered event. Analyze those images carefully. Consider showing them to each of your interviewees and asking them to respond. Pay attention to differences you can determine in the narrative memories and the visual record, as well as to any additions to the accounts that result from seeing the image. Revise your original written document from Assignment 2 to incorporate one or more of the visual images. Consider carefully where these images should enter your work and what their presence does to your understanding of historical memories.

When you have completed your revision, take a few minutes to add to your authorial notes. What did you learn about writing by doing this revision? Did your writing process change in any way as you added these visual images, or were the steps you took similar to your usual approach to writing assignments?

ASSIGNMENT 6: *RECOGNIZING FORGOTTEN MEMORY IN PHYSICAL STRUCTURES*

PEIRCE LEWIS, "COMMON LANDSCAPES AS HISTORIC DOCUMENTS"

Lewis's article demonstrates how the physical structures of a community can be read as signs of an otherwise forgotten (or ignored) shared past. Such reading is complicated, and Lewis warns us both at the beginning and again at the end that simple observation of the physical landscape can produce a caricature rather than real understanding, that good fieldwork takes considerable preparation, and that landscape observation can raise more questions than it answers. With these cautions in mind, select a particular community or portion of a community that you are interested in, and follow Lewis's lead in reading its landscape, particularly the elements of buildings that indicate a prior life.

Like Lewis and his students, you will want to consult maps of the location you have selected and gain a perspective of the whole from some higher vantage point—a hill or tall building where you can see the entire lay of the land. If you cannot find maps or a vantage point from which to see the wider landscape, look for aerial photos or satellite shots of the area which are easily available on the Internet. You will also need to spend time on the ground, observing and taking notes of what you observe at the street level, in different parts of the area you've selected, and with attention to different aspects of buildings or other structures in the location. You will also need to spend time in the library, tracing the elements of architectural style to particular periods of community development and history. Feel free to take photographs or make sketches to remind you of your observations and incorporate these visuals into the final writing. You might also choose to work with one or more of your classmates, conducting your observations together and helping each other to ask questions and speculate on the features you can observe. In some communities it is possible to take walking or riding tours with a local historian. You may want to take advantage of such a service, but do not allow the tour to substitute for your own careful observations, note taking, and question posing.

Once you have observed the location carefully and as fully as possible in the time you have available to you, write a detailed account of your observations as a way of demonstrating its links to the past, or the way this area has erased (or forgotten) its past. Your writing should be a demonstration of what Lewis calls "reading the landscape," but it should also be a continuation of your consideration of collective memory and the problems of forgetting.

When you have completed your writing, add to your authorial notes. What new strategies did you employ in this assignment? Could you use any of those strategies if you were to revise your earlier work?

ASSIGNMENT 7: *REFLECTING ON COLLECTIVE MEMORY*

Read through the work you've done in this sequence, including your authorial notes. What do you understand now about collective memory that you didn't know or wouldn't have thought of in quite the same way before? Using specific examples from your own work or from that of your classmates, present what you've learned about the topic of collective memory in an appropriate written form. Be certain to cite your work and that of your classmates in a way that will allow your readers to locate the original material easily. This reflective writing might serve to introduce the various assignments you've already done, but it should also stand alone, making an argument of its own that synthesizes this work and uses it for a new purpose. Consider sharing your authorial notes with members of your class in order to compare experiences. Is there any evidence that the experience of these assignments created a collective memory about writing among your classmates?

CONSIDERING "PUBLIC"

Shackel; Jones; NEA

"Public," as a term that represents a larger collective (as in "the public good" or "public opinion") and that creates a distinction from "private" or "personal," appears at first glance to be simple enough. But if we start asking questions about this term as it is commonly used, both the term and what it means become much more complicated. What does it mean, for example, to have "public spaces" in a culture that promotes individual ownership? What role does the distinction between a public sphere and a private one serve? How are our ideas about "the public" formed? Who is "the public" in public opinion and how did their opinion get formed? This sequence asks that you consider such questions carefully and systematically—like a researcher—and then to consider the implications of your work in order to make arguments, advance theories, or offer a more meaningful definition of this term and its many uses. The assignments in this sequence ask you to use the methods of different disciplines, however, so your work will allow, even force, you to view your topic—in this case the specific term "public"—from multiple perspectives.

ASSIGNMENT 1: *CONSIDERING PUBLIC SPACE*

Conduct an investigation of a local area that serves as a "public space." You could choose a place on your college campus or somewhere in the surrounding community, such as a park, pedestrian mall, or civic center. No matter what place you choose, it's important that it be open to human interactions. Thus, a turnpike or interstate highway is public but not particularly useful for this assignment because individuals do not get out of their cars and interact (except in times of crisis). The rest stops alongside the highway, however, are public spaces where interaction is possible, even though it might not be desired. Your work will involve careful observations, and Chapter 3 will help you develop different strategies for those observations. For your investigation to be complete, you must not simply record your experiences as a member of this local community or as a bystander. Instead use close and systematic observations, perhaps working with others in your class to observe at different times or from different positions.

Once you have collected your observations about this public space, present your research in writing as an example of interpreting a public space. You will need to push beyond simply reporting what you observe to make an argument about how this place functions as a public space, for example. You will also need to consider who would be interested in your work and choose an appropriate format for that audience and material. You might consider such questions as: What kinds of human interactions occur in this space? Do the physical features of the space contribute to those interactions or impede them? You may want to consider the public space you observed alongside the spaces observed by your classmates in order to think more critically about the nature and meaning of public spaces. How does your space, as one of a network or system of public spaces, contribute, or fail to contribute, to a public life that is distinct from our private lives?

When you've finished your writing, take a few minutes to make some authorial notes about your writing process. What did this assignment teach you about writing? How did it let you use what you already knew about writing?

ASSIGNMENT 2: *CONSIDERING PUBLIC MEMORY*

PAUL A. SHACKEL, "PUBLIC MEMORY AND THE SEARCH FOR POWER IN AMERICAN HISTORICAL ARCHAEOLOGY"

Paul Shackel uses newspaper accounts, archival records, and observation of the monument of Robert Gould Shaw to demonstrate how public memory of the past is shaped through the construction of physical monuments and memorials. Choose a local monument or historical landmark, and investigate its creation and history. You may, at first, think that your local community has no such monuments or landmarks, but look closely and you're likely to find plaques on buildings or at the entrance to a park that serve to memorialize its creation, the founder of the company, an important donor, or a local personality. These attributions don't appear without someone, often with community involvement, making decisions about design and placement. You'll need to use historical archives, written histories of the event or person being memorialized, and newspaper accounts of the creation of the monument to reconstruct the interplay of the historical event and the ideological forces that created the monument. Be sure to look for evidence of the power of the elite group, whoever they might be, as well as evidence that that power was resisted or countered by others as this example of public memory was constructed.

Present your findings as a written history of this monument in a form that will be of interest to locals who know the monument well and may even know something of its creation, but also for historians such as Shackel who are less interested in the particular monument than they are in how monuments function to construct a public memory and an historical past. Should your work lead you to believe that Shackel is incorrect about the role of monuments in shaping public memory or the role of public memory in the construction of monuments, feel free to use your writing to carry on a critical conversation with his work.

When you're done with your written account, take a few minutes to add to your authorial notes. What challenges did you face in this assignment? How would you resolve those difficulties if you had more time?

ASSIGNMENT 3: *CONSTRUCTIONS OF "PUBLIC"*

JEFFREY P. JONES, "FORUMS FOR CITIZENSHIP IN POPULAR CULTURE"

For Jones, our public life, especially our citizenship, is shaped through our interactions with popular culture, especially the media. However, because different subgroups of the media imagine "the public" very differently, the conception of "public" is also different. By choosing two distinct popular forums—*Politically Incorrect with Bill Maher* and *This Week with Sam Donaldson*—Jones points to the distinctions between serious news and comedic entertainment. Jones also suggests that there are numerous such sites of difference to investigate. This assignment asks that you take up Jones's work and investigate one of these other sites, seeing if his observations and conclusions hold true with other topics and in other kinds of popular/public forums, and then considering how your work might revise Jones's argument about the conception of the public embedded in popular media. There are two ways to proceed with your investigation:

1. Begin by selecting a topic of public discussion that is occurring in more than one kind of public forum. Like Jones, record the conversations in at least two different forums—talk shows, editorial pages, stand-up comedies, Internet sites, and so on—and analyze the differences in both the nature of the discussion and the way these sites are constructing "the public" who is interested in the topic.

2. Choose any two closely related media sites on the same day (or span of days), and record the topic of conversation and the construction of the interested "public" that is visible there. You might choose to follow two monologues on late night television, for example, or the cover story on two weekly newsmagazines. If you choose this option, you will have not only the differences in how the topic is discussed and how the public is constructed but also differences in what was considered important enough to talk about on a particular day. Be careful to avoid reruns since that will make it impossible to compare accurately.

Whichever of the two ways you select, present your analysis as a written response to Jones using specific details and examples from your study. Feel free to disagree with Jones; perhaps his study was atypical or current media interactions are very different from those of the Clinton scandal. It will probably be helpful to consider how your work helps you to define "the public" and how this definition differs from the "public" you referred to in the earlier assignments.

Once you've finished your writing, add to your authorial notes. Which moments of your final paper are you most pleased with and which would you rework if you could? What did this assignment teach you about writing?

ASSIGNMENT 4: *CONSIDERING "PUBLIC" CONSTRUCTIONS*

Another way to think about popular culture and its ability to shape individual or collective conceptions is to consider the various *practices* that are allowed or promoted as appropriate for public venues rather than only the *talk* within public venues. This assignment asks you to investigate a particular public practice and consider what consequences that practice has for particular groups or for our collective (or public) mind-set.

You will need to determine a particular public practice, event, or spectacle which is generally regarded positively but which you suspect has a negative side or negative consequences. You might consider, for example, various kinds of entertainment (sporting events, concerts or theatrical events, pageants, contests) or rituals (rites of passage, ceremonies, observances), but you'll want to narrow your investigation to a particular type of event rather than to a general category. Observe that practice firsthand, but also consider collecting information by surveying or interviewing participants and by reading about the event or practice you are investigating. Though you will already have an idea of the negative side of this practice, you will want to collect information that confirms or contradicts your suspicions, and you will need to remain open to the possibility that there is something else going on that was not immediately visible to you.

Write your description and analysis of this practice or event as a way to consider how it impacts on individuals, groups of individuals, and on the larger public psyche. Your task is not to argue for or against this practice, but rather to consider what the practice says about our culture and about how we think about the people or groups who are involved with it. You may decide that you *do* want to argue against this practice or that the practice is appropriate, but that should take a secondary position in your writing to the analysis and deliberation you offer of its significance to the public. As you develop this written document, you'll need to consider the direct and invoked audiences carefully and may find the discussion of these issues in Chapter 2 helpful.

When you are finished with your writing, make additions to your authorial notes. Did this assignment alter your usual writing process in any way? What do you think your work could teach other students about writing?

ASSIGNMENT 5: *CONSTRUCTING "PUBLIC" THROUGH RESEARCH*

NATIONAL ENDOWMENT FOR THE ARTS, "TRENDS IN LITERATURE PARTICIPATION, 1982–2002"

The NEA is clearly troubled by its findings that the "public" is reading less literature than it had in previous years. It seems particularly worried that young people are reading less literature for pleasure. This assignment asks you to do two things: (1) conduct a simple survey of your own to see if the NEA's assessment of trends is accurate for the group you survey. You will need to decide how to phrase questions, tally results, and make comparisons that challenge and extend the work done by the NEA (in other words, don't try to ask exactly the same questions in exactly the same way the NEA researchers did since their definitions of "reading," "literature," or "leisure" may be part of what you want to investigate); and (2) consider how the NEA research and your own work is constructing a "reading public."

When you have finished designing, conducting, and analyzing your survey, present your work as a written response to the NEA in a form that fits your imagined audience. You might also use this written document as a further example (or contradiction) of your earlier work on either public citizens or the influence of popular culture on individuals. In either case, you should feel free to use appropriate examples and arguments from your earlier writings, as well as to rework your earlier ideas in light of your new findings.

Once you've finished your writing, make additions to your authorial notes. How was this work different from what you've done in the past? How did you adjust your usual writing process or your writing style to accommodate these differences?

ASSIGNMENT 6: *DEFINING "PUBLIC"*

This final assignment asks that you take careful stock of the work you have done through-out the term. Using examples from your previous writings, write a document in which you define "public," especially in relation to those things which are not public—private space, private lives, individualism, and so on. Use this writing to introduce a portfolio of your work for this term showing both how your own thinking has evolved over the term and how your work represents you as a writer and as a researcher of the term "public" and its many uses. Incorporate your authorial notes if they seem appropriate evidence of the arguments you are making about your work, and consider borrowing examples from the work of your classmates with proper citation to the original writer. The most difficult aspect of this assignment is avoiding writing only what you think your teacher wants to hear. Instead think of your work as a researcher would, that is, as evidence that needs to be read and interpreted carefully without avoiding those parts that are problematic.

CONSTRUCTING PUBLIC SPACES

LEWIS; BACHIN

This sequence asks you to try out the various ways that researchers work with and within physical spaces as you consider the meanings that those spaces have to individuals, groups, and a larger public. Because public spaces are built and revised at particular moments of history, by particular groups and for particular purposes, their meanings are usually lay-ered and subject to interpretation.

ASSIGNMENT 1: *MAPPING THE TERRAIN*

PEIRCE LEWIS, "COMMON LANDSCAPES AS HISTORIC DOCUMENTS"

Lewis's article is a condensed version of an eight-hour field trip to a small town in cen-tral Pennsylvania, and he warns us both at the beginning and again at the end that sim-ple observation of the physical landscape can produce a caricature rather than real understanding, that good fieldwork takes considerable preparation, and that landscape observation can raise more questions than it answers. With these cautions in mind, select a particular community or portion of a community that you are interested in and that might serve as the centerpiece of your work for this sequence. Then follow Lewis's lead in reading the landscape.

Like Lewis and his students, you will want to consult maps of the location you have selected and to gain a perspective of the whole from some higher vantage point—a hill or tall building where you can see the entire lay of the land. If you cannot find maps or a vantage point from which to see the wider landscape, look for aerial photos or satellite shots of the area. You will also need to spend time on the ground, observing and taking notes of what you observe at the street level, in different parts of the area you've selected and with attention to different aspects of buildings or other structures in the location. Feel free to take photographs or make sketches to remind you of your observations and incorporate these visuals into the final writing. You may want to visit your location more than once, at different times of the day or on different days of the week. You might also choose to work with one or more of your classmates, conducting your observations together and helping each other to ask questions and speculate on the features you can observe. In some communities it is possible to take walking or riding tours with a local historian. You may want to take advantage of such a service, but do not allow the tour to substitute for your own careful observations, note taking, and question posing.

Once you have observed the location carefully and as fully as possible in the time you have available to you, write a detailed account of your observations that includes the questions you have about this area and its features. Your writing should be a demonstration of what Lewis calls "reading the landscape," but it should also be a kind of beginning map of what you would like to know about the place you have chosen.

When you have finished your work, take a few minutes to write some authorial notes. What process did you use for writing this account? Was this writing different in any way from writing you have done in the past?

ASSIGNMENT 2: *THE FUNCTION OF SPACE*

In this assignment you will return to the community or to a part of the community you selected in your first assignment and consider the function that one of the public areas serves in that location. You can use any public, open area where people are likely to interact as the site for your investigation. Thus, a park, civic center, public transportation system, open-air market, or even the student center on your campus might be a space of public interaction in the locale you've selected.

Your task is to again observe, focusing on human interactions, but you may also add to your observations by interviewing individuals, conducting a survey, or noting the discourse that happens in this space. You may again find it helpful to take photographs that you can return to later or incorporate into your writing. Work to discover something of the *function* of this particular public space, especially in relation to the community or location you are investigating. If you are working with your classmates on the location, consider doing this assignment on multiple public spaces within your research area and then comparing your data to look for patterns or distinctions.

Once you have collected your observations and other data, present your research in writing as an example of interpreting a public space. It might be helpful to consider such questions as, What function does this public space fill, and how does it work? Are the physical features of this space contributing to the ways humans use that space or the interactions that occur there? You may want to consider the public space you observed alongside the spaces observed by your classmates in order to think more critically about the nature and meaning of public spaces. How does your space, as one of a network or system of public spaces, contribute, or fail to contribute, to a public life that is distinct from our private lives?

When you are finished with your writing, add to your authorial notes. Did your writing process change in any way as you completed this assignment? What did you learn about writing or about yourself as a writer as you worked on this assignment?

ASSIGNMENT 3: *SPACES CONSTRUCTING COMMUNITY*

In this assignment you will have the opportunity to return to the public space you worked with in Assignment 2 or to choose another public space within the community you are researching. In either case your task is to add history to your observations and to deepen your consideration of the function of public spaces.

You might use interviews, newspaper clippings, or archival materials to describe the history of this particular public space and its impact on both individuals and the community. No matter how insignificant the space you select might seem to be, it still has a history and that history will enable you to raise new questions and make new or revised claims about both the particular space and the larger location you are investigating. Thus you should choose additional methods of investigation that are appropriate to the space you have selected.

As you write your history, feel free to borrow from the earlier pieces you have written as you think necessary or appropriate. The final document should, however, be more than a simple addition to those earlier pieces, for you should now be providing your readers with history rather than descriptive observation. If appropriate to the location you select, you might consider recasting your investigation into a different form suitable for a nonacademic audience. You might, for example, write your history as a tourist guide or chamber of commerce feature article.

Once you've finished your writing, make additions to your authorial notes. What challenges did you face in this assignment? How would you use what you learned from this work if you were to do a similar assignment in the future?

ASSIGNMENT 4: *EMPTY SPACES*

In this assignment you should investigate some of the usually ignored spaces of the location you are investigating. There are lots of spaces that we routinely pass through without really stopping to see what's there. Likewise every community has areas that are less pristine, perhaps even "eyesores," but it takes some work to figure out why these spots are the way they are. Without taking any unreasonable risks, spend some time in such a location within the community you are investigating. Consider interviewing those who live, work, or pass through this location. You might also investigate the history of this space to determine if it has always been the way it is now or if some particular event or policy contributed to its decline or abandonment.

Write an account of this space in a way that will help others appreciate it and see it as something more than "empty" or common space. Include pictures in your account if that seems appropriate or useful to the point you want your readers to understand from your account. If it seems appropriate, consider casting your research in a form that speaks to a nonacademic audience.

When you are finished with your account, make additions to your authorial notes. Which parts of your writing are you most pleased with and why? Which parts would you alter if you could and why?

ASSIGNMENT 5: *BUILDING AND REVISING COMMUNITY*

ROBIN BACHIN, "COURAGE, ENDURANCE AND QUICKNESS OF DECISION: GENDER AND ATHLETICS AT THE UNIVERSITY OF CHICAGO, 1890–1920"

Bachin works with archival materials of various kinds to write a history of a particular building that serves as an example of a set of ideas—in this case, ideas about gender and athletics—that were operating at the time the structure was built. Your task in this assignment is to write another history of a particular aspect of the community you are investigating, but this time a history that focuses on the beliefs and values of the community as represented in the decisions the community has made about how to use its physical spaces.

Though you may not be fortunate enough to have a particularly rich archive or a single building that can serve as an example of a shift in values or ideas as Bachin did, it is still possible to consider community values through the use of physical spaces and structures. If you do have such resources, by all means feel free to follow Bachin's lead and write the history of the place and the values it reflects. If such a resource is not immediately apparent in the location you are investigating, pay close attention to artwork, architectural styles, and the various functions of the structures that are present. Consider the evolution of these structures or changes in land use within your research area, changes that may be discernable by comparing maps or photographs from different time periods or consulting the zoning records. In any case you'll need to begin with your close observations and add additional information gleaned from archives, interviews, architectural analysis, or comparisons of historical records.

Present your work as a written history of the community's values, borrowing as seems appropriate from the work you've done in earlier assignments. Incorporate illustrations of the archival documents or current structures if that seems appropriate.

Once you've finished writing, take time to add to your authorial notes. What was different about this kind of writing in comparison to what you've done earlier? What do you think your work could teach others about writing?

ASSIGNMENT 6: *COMPOSITE*

You've now considered your research location from many different angles—up close, through landscapes and buildings, and via public and ignored spaces. For this assignment write a composite of your location drawing from all the work you've done. You might decide on a particular format for your composite—a tourist guide, for example, or a brochure, or a feature article for a local publication—or you might write the composite as an introduction to the collection of writing you've done in this sequence. In either case you will have to make choices about what to include, what to rearrange, and what to make of what you've discovered. What can you say now about public spaces and their construction that you could not say at the beginning of this work? What can you say about this particular community that you couldn't have said before?

In a separate piece of writing, consider what you've learned about writing and what you still need to learn. If you are using these pieces as an introduction to a final portfolio of your term's work, try to avoid saying only what you think your teacher wants to hear. Instead look at your work as a researcher would, that is, as evidence that needs to be interpreted but that may not tell a unified story or make only one coherent argument.

CULTURAL POLITICS AND PUBLIC DISCOURSE

KOZA; LOWE; JONES; LEN-RÍOS ET AL.

What is public discourse or speech? How do we define these terms: *public* and *speech*? Is it possible to understand the goals (and perhaps the hidden agendas) of those who engage in public discourse? This sequence asks you to stretch the way you think of and write about public speech and invites you to use various methods of analysis.

ASSIGNMENT 1: *COMMON AREAS*

For this assignment, choose a place where similar social interactions tend to occur—perhaps a coffee shop, a common area in the dormitory, the hallways of classroom buildings—and use careful observation to investigate how this space of social interaction functions. You should pay close attention to groups and how they interact in this space, but don't overlook individuals and whether they are allowed into group interactions or keep to themselves. Take notes on both the conversations that occur there and on the location itself, and consider returning to the area at different times of the day or different days of the week to see if the patterns you notice are consistent. You will need to respect the privacy of others, of course, so you should either get those you observe to agree to have their words included in your final paper, or describe any conversations you "overhear" without details that would allow individuals to be identified.

Begin by sitting in the location you've chosen for at least thirty minutes at a time when the place is busy enough for you to be able to observe multiple interactions and overhear the talk that is going on. You'll need to take notes, make a sketch of the physical layout, and keep track of the topics of conversation and the patterns of interaction. You may notice that small groups cluster together or that everyone who enters interacts with the same person. Try not to narrow your focus too quickly because you should examine the role of both individuals and groups as they interact in this location.

Write an account of the social interactions that occur in the common area you have chosen. As you work to represent what you've observed, determine what patterns if any exist and what meaning can be attached to the interactions you've observed in this location. You'll also need to think carefully about the ethical issues involved and be sensitive to the privacy of the individuals you observed even though their actions and talk happened in public.

When you are finished with your account, take a few minutes to write some authorial notes. What process did you use to write this piece? What challenges did you face in completing this work?

ASSIGNMENT 2: *MUSIC AND THE MEDIA*

JULIA EKLUND KOZA, "RAP MUSIC: THE CULTURAL POLITICS OF OFFICIAL REPRESENTATION"

In her article, Koza brings together the roles of the artist, audience and the media and demonstrates how rap music has become a "cultural artifact" because of the way it is treated in the media. This assignment asks you to extend and test Koza's work by working with other kinds of music or other representations of music in the media. You can proceed with your investigation in one of two ways.

1. Following Koza's example, choose a musical genre or movement which you find interesting, perhaps a current style or something from a past decade. You'll need to track how this musical genre is presented in the media. Is it considered mainstream or is it "other"? Have there been any changes in the music or in the way the music has come to be perceived over time?

2. Koza's analysis deals with articles that appeared in magazines through 1992. Extend her work by examining other media or current magazines (even the same titles she worked with) to see if they deal with rap in the same way as Koza claims. Collect articles on rap and rappers from publications Koza did not include but from the same years as her study, or examine current issues of *Time* or *Newsweek* to determine if any changes have occurred in the ways these magazines represent rap/rappers since Koza completed her study.

Write a document that responds to Koza and updates her work with your additional findings. Your goal is to explore music as a "cultural artifact," especially the impact it has had on its culture and on subsequent (or future) generations. It might be helpful to consider such questions as: How does your work complicate Koza's argument? What differences and similarities appear across time?

When you have finished your writing, add to your authorial notes. What writing strategies did you use in this assignment that you did not use in the earlier assignment? What changes occurred in your writing process?

ASSIGNMENT 3: *MANIPULATED IMAGES*

MELANIE LOWE, "COLLIDING FEMINISMS: BRITNEY SPEARS, 'TWEENS,' AND THE POLITICS OF RECEPTION"

Lowe's article allows us to better understand the dynamic conversation that exists between an artist and her audience, even if they are never in the same room. As Lowe's research indicates, Britney Spears manipulates her image(s) to try to satisfy the needs of her varied public, but in doing so seems to alienate her target audience, which is not naïve about the conflicting messages Spears delivers. Test Lowe's work by extending it to another famous person—a politician, athlete, pop culture star—who has had more than one image over his/her career.

Begin by collecting examples of the shifts in image, informing yourself as well as you can about the details of the personality you've selected and preparing questions for discussion using the guidelines in Chapter 4. Then assemble a focus group to discuss this person. You needn't have a group who are all "fans" of the person you've chosen, but everyone in your group should know about the person and be able to recognize that the image has shifted over time. Following Lowe's example, solicit conversation about the person, specifically the image this person has portrayed at various times. You might consider such questions as: What differences were important to members of your group and why? How did they read these shifts at the time they were occurring, and how do they read them now? You should spend thirty minutes to one hour with your focus group in order to generate enough data for your analysis.

Write your findings as a response to Lowe and as a way to consider further how ordinary people understand the shifting images of those who are famous. You'll want to think carefully about the various audiences for this piece and how to present the conversation accurately but for your own purposes.

Once you've completed your writing, make additions to your authorial notes. What challenges did you face in this assignment? What would you do differently if you were to do a similar project in the future?

ASSIGNMENT 4: *BLURRING BOUNDARIES*

JEFFREY P. JONES, "FORUMS FOR CITIZENSHIP IN POPULAR CULTURE"

Near the end of his article, Jones challenges his readers to extend the work he has already undertaken. There are at least two ways to do so:

1. Begin by selecting a topic of public discussion that is occurring in more than one kind of public forum. Record the conversations in at least two different forums—talk shows, editorial pages, political cartoons, stand-up comedy routines, Internet sites, and so on—and analyze the differences in how the topic is presented, paying special attention to the blurring of boundaries between "news" and "entertainment."

2. Choose any two closely related media sites on the same day (or span of days) and record the topic of conversation. You might choose to follow two monologues on late night television, for example, or the cover story on two weekly newsmagazines. In this case you will have not only the differences in how the topic is discussed but also differences in what was considered important enough to talk about on a particular day. Be careful to avoid reruns since that will make it impossible to compare.

Present your analysis as a written response to Jones using specific details and examples from your study. Feel free to disagree with Jones; perhaps his study was atypical, or current media interactions are very different from those of the Clinton scandal. Remember that responding to a prior piece of research doesn't always require that you summarize or even mention the original author; such issues depend on the genre and audience you choose for your work. It might be useful to consider how your work helps you think about the topic itself and the media's responses to that topic.

When you've completed your writing, add to your authorial notes. What do you think your work could teach other students about writing? What do you think you still need to learn about writing?

ASSIGNMENT 5: *MEDIATED DIFFERENCE*

María Len-Ríos et al., "Representation of Women in News and Photos: Comparing Content to Perceptions"

As Len-Ríos and her colleagues demonstrate, news media reflects more than the news; cultural norms and differences of power are perpetuated in the ways news gets portrayed. As these scholars suggest, gender is not the only power difference that may be visible upon close scrutiny. This assignment asks you to extend Len-Ríos's study in one of two ways:

1. Repeat the analysis of how (and where) women are represented in the news using a local publication—either a city newspaper or your campus paper.
2. Extend the analysis by considering race/ethnicity, class, or age. You might choose to do your analysis with a local paper, or consider a national (or international) publication.

Present your results in writing, using specific examples to illustrate the patterns that you find most significant. Though you may choose not to present your work in the formal social-science format used by Len-Ríos, you should be certain to explain your methods and the limitations of your work as you make your argument.

When you are finished with your writing, take a few minutes to add to your authorial notes. How is this work different from what you have done earlier? How has your writing process changed since the beginning of the term?

ASSIGNMENT 6: *PUBLIC DISCOURSE REVISITED*

At this point in the semester, you have worked with different approaches—observation, focus-group interviews, and textual analysis—to understand public speech and the different forms it can take—speech, image, song, news. Drawing from your work in the preceding assignments, write a final document in which you analyze the impact public speech has on individuals and on the culture. Consider in particular the way that we, your readers, can learn to be better "listeners" when exposed to these various forms of public speech. Feel free to incorporate moments from your earlier work as appropriate, but rework those excerpts for this new context. You may wish to bring in examples from the work of your classmates to support or complicate your own work, but be certain to give credit to the original writer if you do so.

When you have finished this writing, add to your authorial notes. How was writing a synthesis different from the earlier assignments? Which passages of your work are you most pleased with, which would you rework if you had more time and why?

ASSIGNMENT 7: *REFLECTION*

Write a reflective piece centered on what you've learned about writing from these assignments. You'll want to review the authorial notes you've been keeping throughout the sequence but also to reread the formal pieces of writing you've produced. The most difficult part of this reflection, especially since it comes at the end of the term and may be used to introduce a portfolio of your work, is to avoid saying only what you think your teacher expects you to say. Instead consider your work as a researcher would, that is, as evidence that needs to be interpreted but probably cannot be made to tell only one story or to mean only one thing. When you cite from your earlier work, be certain to do so in a way that will make it easy for your readers to find the original passages.

CULTURAL POLITICS AND PUBLIC DISCOURSE II: SHAPING VALUES

FRISCH; THELEN; WHITE; JACKSON; EDWARDS & WINKLER

Another way to consider cultural politics and public discourse is to focus more specifically on discourse that aims to shape values and opinions. Political debates and advertisements are two examples where efforts to influence opinions and shape values (or behavior) are easily visible even if the techniques employed are not always straightforward. There are other forms of persuasion and influence that are not so overt. For example, school courses, visual images, and music are not generally considered primarily efforts to persuade or shape values. Likewise, sometimes in the midst of a politicized debate, values or beliefs are at stake in addition to whatever public policy issue is under discussion. This sequence invites you to examine such examples of discourse for their underlying features and to consider the many and varied ways in which our cultural values are shaped or called into play.

ASSIGNMENT 1: *EDUCATIONAL DISCOURSE*

MICHAEL FRISCH, "AMERICAN HISTORY AND THE STRUCTURES OF COLLECTIVE MEMORY: A MODEST EXERCISE IN EMPIRICAL ICONOGRAPHY"

Frisch's informal survey of his students raises questions about the common assumption that schooling shapes our collective memory. On the one hand, his students seem to have much of the same knowledge about American history; on the other hand, Frisch questions whether such knowledge is the result of school lessons alone. Is such shaping true in disciplines other than history? Do students who graduate from American high schools have more or less the same general knowledge of literature, science, art, and music? This assignment invites you to conduct your own informal survey of what people know and determine the level of similarity in various kinds of common knowledge.

You will need to begin by deciding on one or two specific questions that will provide you with the kind of raw data that Frisch was able to collect. You may, if you wish, try the questions Frisch asked so as to update his work, but you needn't limit yourself to historical knowledge. Once you've determined the questions you want to ask, think carefully about the population you want to respond. Are you interested in what the most recent graduating high school class learned and remembers? If so, you can ask your friends and classmates. But consider expanding your survey to collect data from other generations or from students who were not schooled in the United States. You may want to work with classmates to design the questions and determine how to distribute your surveys to increase the number of responses. To generate the lists of remembered learning, you'll need to tabulate and analyze the results. The suggestions in Chapter 5 may be helpful.

Present your analysis of the data in a written form directed to an audience you think appropriate. Follow Frisch's lead in considering what your analysis might mean about memory, education, or the subject matter you chose to investigate. If your work leads you to think Frisch is wrong in some way, use your writing and the research you've done to speak back to him.

After you've finished make additions to your authorial notes. What do you think your work could teach others about writing? What do you think you still need to learn to do to make your writing more effective?

ASSIGNMENT 2: *HISTORICAL DISCOURSE*

DAVID THELEN, "REMEMBERING THE DISCOVERY OF THE WATERGATE TAPES"

Although few of us are key actors in historical events, we all live through historical moments that end up shaping our perspectives and values. Your task in this assignment is to identify such an important historical moment and interview at least two different people who lived through that event. You might find brainstorming with your classmates useful. Narrow the events to be as specific and self-contained as possible. Thus, rather than trying to interview someone about all of World War II, for example, you should narrow your scope to one key event within the war: D-Day, or the bombing of Hiroshima, or Kristallnacht.

As you select the people you will interview, think carefully about how they will provide you with different perspectives. While people of different ages might easily have different perspectives, your topic might be better explored by locating people of the same age who were living in different locations during the event you want them to remember. Use the suggestions in Chapter 4 to help you prepare for and conduct your interview, being certain to solicit information about how the historical event changed or continued to influence your interviewee after the initial event.

Once you've collected these accounts, analyze them carefully, and present them in writing. Follow Thelen's lead to consider what is significant about these memories or the aftermath of the event rather than simply relating the event itself. It might be helpful to consider such questions as: Who or what has shaped the memories of the people you interviewed? What do the differences in their memories or subsequence experiences suggest about the way that history works to shape our cultural values?

When you have finished your work, add to your authorial notes. In what ways was your writing process different in this assignment than in those you've done before? Which passage in your writing are you most satisfied with and which part would you rework if you had more time?

ASSIGNMENT 3: *JUDICIAL AND LITERARY DISCOURSE*

JAMES BOYD WHITE, "HUMAN DIGNITY AND THE CLAIM OF MEANING: ATHENIAN TRAGIC DRAMA AND SUPREME COURT OPINIONS"

White uses a close reading of Greek tragedies and the Supreme Court opinion in *Cohen v. California* to argue that both serve as exemplars of the kind of public discourse that lets us be our best selves. Test and extend White's work in one of two ways:

1. Attend a theatrical performance, and secure a copy of the written play to analyze as a site of public discourse. Do contemporary plays (or at least this play) function in the same ways as White outlines for Greek tragedies? What aspects of the play make it an appropriate form of public discourse, and how does it work to shape the audience's understanding of the issues it addresses? If you cannot attend a live play, you can try the same approach with a film or video, but you'll need to have access to the script version or be able to replay key scenes in order to capture and represent the exact language.

2. Select another Supreme Court opinion to analyze. Does it make the moves White describes? How does it answer the questions White poses at the end of his essay?

In either of these options, you will be reading the text closely and critically, with attention to its language and how it constitutes the world and invites its audience to imagine the issues with which it is concerned.

Present your reading of the text in a written document showing others how to read this text as an example of White's characterizations of ideal discourse. Do not expect your readers to already be familiar with White's work, however, so consider carefully whether and how to incorporate White's writing into your own document. If you think White is wrong, you might also use your work to speak back to him.

When you've finished your writing, take a few minutes to make some authorial notes about your process. Which portions of this work did you find easy and where did you run into challenges or difficulties? What might you do differently if you have a similar writing project to complete in the future?

ASSIGNMENT 4: *MUSICAL DISCOURSE*

MARK ALLAN JACKSON, "IS THIS SONG YOUR SONG ANY MORE?: REVISIONING WOODY GUTHRIE'S 'THIS LAND IS YOUR LAND'"

This assignment asks you to work closely with a particular piece of vocal music to present its history and to consider how it functions to shape cultural values or perspectives. There are two ways you can focus your research.

1. Think back to the songs you learned as a child, especially the ones you sang in school or other organized venues such as church or scout meetings. Investigate one of those songs to uncover its history, its reception, any alternative versions, and the way it has been used for different purposes. Do not expect this kind of information to be in one location. You may have to compare different versions printed in various songbooks, search for biographical information about the composer or performers, or look for scholarly articles in databases such as the International Index to Music Periodicals at http://iimpft.chadwyck.com/home.

2. Consider the genre of protest songs that function to galvanize public opinion or inform listeners about a particular issue. The Vietnam War spawned a number of such protest songs, but that is certainly not the only possibility. Choose one of these songs to investigate, being certain to research how the song has been appropriated for other purposes.

3. Perhaps you know of a particular song that reflects an effort, like Woody Guthrie's "This Land," to comment on social conditions of its time. Research the

song and its artist, being certain to consider any alternative versions or appropriations that have arisen.

Once you have collected as much information as you can in the time you have to work, present a written history of your song, being certain to read and interpret the lyrics. Use Jackson's work as a guide, but do not be discouraged if the song you've selected doesn't have as rich or controversial a history as Guthrie's "This Land." No matter what song you've chosen, your primary task is to consider how it worked to educate those who heard and sang it.

When you've finished with your writing, add to your authorial notes. What challenges did you face in doing this assignment? How would you use what you've learned about writing to approach similar tasks in the future?

ASSIGNMENT 5: *VISUAL DISCOURSE*

JANIS L. EDWARDS AND CAROL K. WINKLER, "REPRESENTATIVE FORM AND THE VISUAL IDEOGRAPH: THE IWO JIMA IMAGE IN EDITORIAL CARTOONS"

As Edwards and Winkler demonstrate, editorial cartoons are something more than images and not quite the same as written editorials or political commentary. Their research concentrates on a particular image that appears across cartoons about a number of different topics, but it is also possible to focus careful attention on the cartoons about a single topic, or featuring a single recognizable figure. Your task in this assignment is to experiment with analyzing editorial cartoons for yourself.

You may, if you wish, return to the historical event you used in Assignment 2 or focus on the political controversy you used in Assignment 1, but you needn't be limited to either of these choices. If you have no topic, figure, or image that you are interested in following through cartoon imagery, consider analyzing the cartoons of a single newspaper, cartoonist, or those that appeared in various publications on a particular date. You should collect as many cartoons as you can but certainly no fewer than five before you begin to analyze them. The suggestions in Chapter 3, particularly the checklist in Figure 3.8 should be helpful.

Present your analysis of the political cartoons you've collected in writing as carefully and completely as you can. You aren't just turning the visual images into a discursive version, however, since your writing should make an argument about the significance of these cartoons as vehicles that shape and reflect cultural beliefs and values and that aim to influence, persuade, or critique.

Once you've finished your writing, make additions to your authorial notes. Did your process change in any way as you did this assignment? How is the writing you did in this assignment different from what you've produced earlier? Could you use any of the strategies you used in one assignment to make your other writing stronger?

ASSIGNMENT 6: *REFLECTION*

Drawing on the work you and your classmates have done in this sequence, write a document that makes an argument about cultural politics and public discourse. Use specific examples from your earlier work, or rework pieces of your earlier writing for this new purpose. Consider, for example, what you can say now about the relationship between these various forms of public discourse and cultural values that you would not have known to say before. What other questions or problems have arisen from your work, and how might you continue with the investigation of those questions if you had more time? What would you need to learn to do in order to answer those questions? Your work should not simply repeat what you expect your teacher wants to hear. Instead treat your own writing and that of your classmates as a researcher would, that is, as evidence that needs to be synthesized and analyzed and that may be problematic in some way.

DIRECT OBSERVATION

A SEQUENCE WITHOUT READINGS

This assignment sequence invites you to work with observation in a variety of ways and then to revise your work by adding other kinds of data to your observations, working with classmates to duplicate studies, altering the audience or purpose for your writing, or shifting your gaze to refocus your work. Throughout the process you are encouraged to keep authorial notes so that at the end of the sequence you can reconsider the kinds of inquiries you've been able to do with observation as your major methodology.

ASSIGNMENT 1: *OBSERVING AS AN ANTHROPOLOGIST*

Try observing like an anthropologist or ethnographer by selecting an event or public place where human beings gather. Use one or more of the strategies suggested in Chapter 3 to record your observations. Remember that ethical practice requires that you consider the vulnerability of your subjects. Observing behavior in a public place with no illegal activities going on is fine; observing drug use at a private party probably is not. Do not observe children under eighteen unless you have clearance to do so from your school's institutional review board, which is responsible for approving human subjects' research. Be sensitive to cultural differences if you choose to observe rituals that hold religious or cultural significance to the group you are observing. Ask permission, be as discreet and nonintrusive as possible, and show respect for the people you are observing and their practices.

Once you've collected your observation "data," write the account of your observation to share with your classmates. As you work with your observation account, you'll want to ask questions about the significance of this work. When you are finished, take a few minutes to make some authorial notes. You might consider, for example, such questions as: What did you learn from observing this event or place? What questions did your observations generate for you? What significance would you claim for the event or the location based on your observations?

ASSIGNMENT 2: *OBSERVING AS A NATURALIST*

Try your hand at being a naturalist observer by selecting a place where you can observe insects, birds, or other wildlife in action. For this practice it is best not to use a pet. Observing a single creature will be easier than trying to focus on an entire group, though if interactions between your selected creature and others occur, you'll want to note those. Do not interact with the subject of your observation. A zoo, aviary, or park may be a good location for this observation. If you can find nothing else to observe, consider investing in a goldfish (usually very inexpensive and easy to keep) or try using the zoocam sites mentioned in the Internet Resources at the end of Chapter 3. Take notes on what your selected creature does over at least a thirty-minute period. If possible, repeat your observations periodically over several days.

Write up your observations as a naturalistic account in as complete a form as you can (i.e., this is not just a set of notes). Include a visual (sketch or photograph). As you work with this writing consider such questions as: What did you learn from observing this creature? What questions did your observations generate for you? If you wanted to continue to observe this same subject, are there particular questions you would hope to answer? If so, how would you structure your observation to get answers to those questions? When you are finished, add to your authorial notes. How is observing a place different from observing a live creature?

ASSIGNMENT 3: *SUGGESTED REVISION:*
ADDING TO OBSERVATION

Go back to the observation account you wrote in either Assignment 1 or 2. Revise one of these earlier accounts of observing by supplementing with another source of information. You might get information from an informant, check other research studies to see if your results are typical, or add statistical information. As you add this additional information, consider how you should reveal your own presence in your writing.

Once you've made the revisions, take a few minutes to make some authorial notes that you can share with your classmates or your instructor. In your author notes, consider: What does the addition do for your original account? What new questions does your return to the observation data generate for you?

ASSIGNMENT 4: *SUGGESTED REVISION:*
SHIFTING YOUR GAZE

Revise one of your earlier accounts of observing by returning to one of the features that was on the sidelines originally and making that side feature the center of a new investigation. You will still use your observations, of course, but you will also need to add other research methods such as interviews to thoroughly investigate this new direction. You should feel free to incorporate portions of your previous writing as appropriate, but most likely the new direction will require a fresh start in both your thinking and writing.

Once you've finished your revision, write a few more authorial notes that can be shared with your classmates or your instructor. In these notes, consider: Why was this focus peripheral in your initial account, and why did you choose it as the focus of your shifting gaze? What happened to the original account as you made this shift?

ASSIGNMENT 5: *SUGGESTED REVISION:*
DUPLICATION TO TEST CONCLUSIONS

Using one of your classmates' accounts as a starting point, repeat that observation as closely as you can arrange. You will be trying to prove either that your classmate's conclusions about the significance of this event or place are accurate or that your classmate is wrong in some way. In other words you will go into the observation with a theory and an objective in mind. Once you've repeated the actual observation and collected your own set of observation notes, write your account making references to your classmate's account. Be certain to cite your classmate's account appropriately as you make your own conclusions about significance.

After you've written your account, write authorial notes in which you consider: How does having a theory change your observation practices? What did you leave out because of this focus that might have been more interesting but would have taken you in a different direction? How does your classmate respond to your account?

ASSIGNMENT 6: *SUGGESTED REVISION: DUPLICATION AND COLLABORATION*

Revise the account you provided in Assignment 5, but do so in collaboration with the classmate whose work prompted yours. The object is to blend together the two observations into one account that both of you think is accurate and fair to your own individual observations. You will have to consider how to balance your different conclusions as well.

Once you have finished your collaborative observation account, write separate authorial notes in which you consider: How is working with a coauthor different from working alone? What choices did you make about focus, details, and conclusions that would not have been possible without collaborating?

ASSIGNMENT 7: *SUGGESTED REVISION: MOVING OUTSIDE THE CLASSROOM*

Revise any of the work you've done so far to make the account more than just a class assignment. Such a revision should make your observation account understandable to an audience outside your class, but you will have to decide who that audience is and why they would want to read what you have to say. Depending on what you decide to revise, and what audience you think would be interested in your work, the form of presentation will change. You might, for example, write your account as a trail guide to a park you've observed, as a feature essay for a local newspaper or magazine, as an argument about the function of a particular place, or as a letter to potential donors soliciting funds for the zoo.

When you have finished your piece for an audience outside the classroom context, spend some time writing authorial notes to consider: How is writing for "publication" different from the work you've done for classes? Why did you choose the piece you did? How did you decide on the audience and format of your piece? What other options for "publication" do you see in the work you or your classmates have done with observation?

ASSIGNMENT 8: *REFLECTIVE PRACTICE: DRAWING CONCLUSIONS FROM EXPERIENCE*

Reread the various pieces you've written using inquiry through observation. Be certain to consider the authorial notes you've written as well. Then write a reflective piece about your work that could serve to introduce these pieces if they were collected together. You might consider such issues as: What have you learned about observing that would not be obvious to someone who had never written an observation account? How did the revisions you undertook complicate your view of this research method? What ethical issues arose for you as you worked with inquiry through observation? Provide specific examples by citing or quoting examples from your own or your classmates' work.

You might also speculate about further work that might be done by considering such questions as: If you were going to continue any of the projects you've done so far, what would you choose? How would you pursue this next step in your inquiry, and what do you think you would have to learn how to do in order to take this next step? Why? What would you do differently if you were starting over with these projects? Why? What are the limitations of observation as a method of inquiry, and what are its advantages? Resist the tendency to say what you think your teacher wants to hear. Instead continue to write as a researcher as you turn your critical eye back on your own work.

ETHNICITY IN AMERICA: IDENTITY

DILWORTH; CHAVEZ; YUNG

We all know that America is made up of many different ethnic groups, that its image is of a melting pot of diverse cultures, and that this simplistic image is often undercut by a harsher reality of clashes in culture and stereotypes about ethnic identity. This sequence gives you the opportunity to consider aspects of ethnicity in American culture from the vantage point of different academic disciplines. Although different ethnic groups are considered in the readings, you may wish to concentrate your investigation on a single ethnic group or on those who are of mixed ethnicity. In any case your work should lead you to be able to say something complex and original about ethnicity and its relation to American culture by the end of the term that you cannot say as you begin.

ASSIGNMENT 1: *RELICS OF IDENTITY*

LEAH DILWORTH, "'HANDMADE BY AN AMERICAN INDIAN': SOUVENIRS AND THE CULTURAL ECONOMY OF SOUTHWESTERN TOURISM"

Dilworth's investigation of an artifact representing American Indians of the southwest raises questions about the nature of identity and how some ethnic identities are transformed to become souvenirs of particular regions. Souvenirs don't always represent ethnic groups; in fact lots of souvenirs are replicas of buildings (e.g., the Empire State Building) or of geographic features (Niagara Falls or the Grand Canyon might be examples). For this assignment you need to consider the relationship between the souvenirs that represent your region and the issues of identity and representation raised by Dilworth. You can proceed in one of two ways:

1. Begin by visiting a store that sells souvenirs to tourists. If you cannot visit such a store in your community or near a local tourist site, consider the section of your campus bookstore that sells memorabilia of your college and its sports teams. Take notes on the various kinds of souvenirs available, paying attention especially to the reoccurring images marketed as being representative of the region or some aspect of the locale. Select one of the souvenirs that seems typical, and produce a written document in which you describe and investigate the meaning of this souvenir in relation to the region. You might consider such questions as: Does your souvenir function in the same way as the ones Dilworth describes? How is the region or one of its ethnic groups being marketed through this souvenir?

2. Consider the ethnic groups in your area and how they are represented to tourists of your region. Collect examples of this representation in souvenirs, postcards, travel promotions, and other artifacts of marketing. Once you have collected several examples, produce a written document to present and investigate the relationship between the marketing of ethnicity and the region being represented. You might consider such questions as: What's honored in these representations, and what's ignored? Who benefits from this kind of marketing, and what consequences does it involve? You should consider your work an extension and challenge to Dilworth so you needn't agree with her, but you should aim for the same level of examination of these artifacts and their meaning.

When you've finished with your writing, take a few minutes to make some authorial notes about your writing process. Try listing the steps you followed as you did this work. Where do you think you might have altered your process so as to be more efficient or thorough? Which parts of your writing process seem to you to be most effective and why?

ASSIGNMENT 2: *PICTURING ETHNICITY*

LEO CHAVEZ, "DEVELOPING A VISUAL DISCOURSE ON IMMIGRATION"

Chavez's project is to trace attitudes about immigration through a close examination of the images of immigrants on American magazine covers. This assignment asks you to experiment with Chavez's method of reading visual images in newsmagazines and to test his work by focusing on a particular ethnic group rather than on immigration more generally.

You will need to begin by collecting several images to work with. You might know of events in which the immigrant group you are interested in was "in the news"; if so, you can scan through the news magazines of that period to collect your images. Alternatively you might search the Reader's Guide or another index of popular magazines for articles about the ethnic group and find images associated with those articles. For the purposes of this assignment, you may also choose to include political cartoons or caricatures, or advertisements where the ethnicity is clear. In any case you should try to have images from different publications and from different years if possible.

Once you have a collection of images, look for patterns and surprises using the guidelines in Chapter 3 to help you analyze. Present your analysis in a written document that includes a close and careful reading of at least two specific examples, as well as a description of the overall patterns you uncover. You will want to make sense of how this particular group is represented in the media, and you will want to consider what that representation suggests about American culture. You may include copies of the images in your writing, but those images should not take the place of your careful description and interpretation.

When you've finished your work, add to your authorial notes. What did you do differently as you worked on this assignment, and what were you able to keep of your usual process? How is the writing you produced for this assignment different from the writing you produced for Assignment 1? What accounts for those differences?

ASSIGNMENT 3: *TELLING STORIES*

JUDY YUNG, "'A BOWLFUL OF TEARS' REVISITED: THE FULL STORY OF LEE PUEY YOU'S IMMIGRATION EXPERIENCE AT ANGEL ISLAND"

As Yung's work demonstrates, life stories are complicated, layered, and not always told in the same way over time or to different people. Your task in this assignment is to retell someone's story of immigration to America or at least to a new community within America. Feel free to select a story from someone who represents the ethnic group you have worked with in Assignments 1 or 2 if that is possible and interesting to you.

You may be able to interview an appropriate immigrant directly, as Yung did, but you might also choose to tell the story of someone not available to you by using archival records or secondhand accounts. In fact, even if you are able to conduct an interview, you should also locate other versions of the immigrant's story in diaries, letters, histories, or family stories told second- or even third-hand. You should aim to collect at least two versions of the story to blend together to form your written account.

Present your work in writing in a form that fits the material you've collected and the argument you think this story might make. You might, for example, consider the relationship of this particular story to the larger story of immigration, or you might show how a particular moment in history is represented by this individual's story. You may wish to consider how issues of class or gender are also embedded in this story of immigration.

When you're finished with your writing, make additions to your authorial notes. Which parts of this assignment did you find challenging, and which parts were easy? How did the challenges you faced alter your writing process or your style? If you were to do a similar project in the future, what would you do differently and why?

ASSIGNMENT 4: *HISTORY AND ETHNICITY*

The oral history of one person is different from the history that might be told of the collective group that person represents because the larger history has to make generalizations or look for recurring patterns that might not be reflected in the individual's story. This assignment asks you to move from the particular examples toward a larger history of any of the ethnic groups you've represented in earlier assignments.

Select one of those earlier pieces and add interviews, statistical information, or other additional research to what you've already learned in order to move from the particular examples to a more generalized history, or to put the particular into the context of the general. If you have managed to work with the same group for each assignment, this is your opportunity to combine the individual documents into a single account. As you write this compounded history, though, consider the meaning that those not in the ethnic group might find in this particular story. What does the experience of this ethnic group say about American culture and its values?

When you've completed your historical account, add to your authorial notes. What questions arose for you as you did this assignment that you were not able to pursue? What method of inquiry would you use to follow up on those questions if you had more time?

ASSIGNMENT 5: *REFLECTING ON ETHNICITY*

For your final assignment in this sequence, read through the work you have done so far. You might want to consider the work done by your classmates as well. Write a piece that draws on these examples of ethnicity in America and introduces the collection of work you have done this term, being certain to cite this work in a way that would allow your readers to locate the original writing. You'll want to consider what can be said about ethnicity, about America as a country of different ethnicities, and about the different methods of working to investigate ethnicity that you've tried out in these assignments. In a separate piece of writing, consider what you've learned about writing and yourself as a writer. Use your authorial notes and your own earlier work to illustrate your analysis. The hardest part of this assignment is to avoid saying only what you think your teacher expects you to say. Instead work with your own writing as a researcher would, that is, seeing this work as evidence that needs to be interpreted but that may be problematic in some way.

ETHNICITY IN AMERICA II: DEFINING AMERICA

A SEQUENCE WITHOUT READINGS

How is America defined by its ethnic groups? How can scholars understand the ethnic experience and its contributions to American culture? This sequence asks you to work with individual and collective identities to consider ethnicity as a shaping force in American life.

ASSIGNMENT 1: *ORAL HISTORIES*

Using your region or institution as a starting point, interview someone who might be said to represent an interesting facet of statistical information about the ethnicity of your area. This individual might be a member of an ethnic group or someone who is knowledgeable about the ethnic groups of your area. Your goal is to supplement and provide a personalization of the numerical profile of your community. Write your account as both an oral history and a response to the numbers—whatever those numbers might be.

When you've finished your writing, take a few minutes to write some authorial notes about your writing process. Try listing the steps you took to complete this assignment. As you look back on that list, where would you approach the task differently if you were to do a similar project in the future?

ASSIGNMENT 2: *ETHNIC INTERACTIONS*

Where do different groups in your locale interact? Using close observation, interviews, and archival materials, write an account of such a scene of ethnic interaction. You needn't be concerned with major ethnic groups if the interactions that interest you are of a more local kind. Perhaps there is a place on your campus where different groups of students find common ground or set aside differences in order to enjoy the moment. In your account be certain to consider both what contributes to this particular location being a scene of interaction and what such interactions produce.

Once you've finished your writing, add to your authorial notes. What strategies did you use to complete this assignment that you didn't need to use in the first assignment? What could your work teach other students about writing?

ASSIGNMENT 3: *UP CLOSE AND PERSONAL*

Locate, observe, interview, and write about an individual who operates in the crossroads of difference in your locale. This person might serve to unite a portion of the community through the services he provides, or she might reflect the history of the community or its changing demographics. The individual you choose may or may not represent an ethnic minority. Your task here is to consider up close and personal some feature of the local community represented through a single individual. Present your work in writing using an appropriate form for the material you've collected.

When you've finished your writing, add to your authorial notes. What questions arose for you in this assignment that you were not able to pursue? If you had more time, how would you continue this inquiry?

ASSIGNMENT 4: *PHOTOGRAPHS OF "OTHERS"*

In this assignment you will need to work with a collection of images culled from popular culture. You might be interested in looking at how a number of different ethnic groups are portrayed in a magazine or newspaper, or you may want to consider collecting only images of a particular ethnic group from a number of different publications. You may want to work with classmates to cover as many different publications and as broad a time frame as possible, and then to divide up the photographs you collect in a way that make sense to your interests and the material you find. In either case you should collect as many different examples as you can and plan to use at least three of them in your final written presentation of your work.

Present your analysis of these photographs as carefully and completely as you can, but be certain to move beyond a simple description to analyze how these photographs construct "others" or "ethnicity" in America. The section on working with visual materials in Chapter 3 will be helpful as you consider how to analyze the meaning embedded in the images you've collected. You may also find that your images do not tell a single, unified story but rather can be interpreted in different ways depending on how they are arranged and which ones you omit as atypical. Consider carefully how to deal with these multiple interpretations and how to present the most compelling interpretation even as you acknowledge the contradictions to that viewpoint.

When you're finished with your written analysis, add to your authorial notes. How is your writing or your writing process changing in response to the methods you are using or the tasks the assignments require of you? Which strategies might you be able to use if you were to revise your work?

ASSIGNMENT 5: *REFLECTION ON ETHNICITY IN AMERICA*

In this sequence you've had the chance to look at different representations of ethnicity and to explore different methods of representing and interpreting ethnicity in American culture. What have you learned that you did not already know? How has your understanding of ethnicity or of American culture been influenced by the work you've done? Write a paper that can serve as both an introduction to the work you've done so far and as an example of careful deliberation of the issues of ethnicity in American culture and life. You'll need, then, to turn a critical eye on both the content of your writing and on your work as evidence of your learning and ability. Be certain to cite this earlier work in a way that allows your readers to locate the earlier passages. The most difficult part of this assignment is to avoid saying what you think your teacher expects you to say. Instead keep working as a researcher would, that is, treating your own writing as evidence that must be interpreted but that probably is problematic in some way.

EXAMINING VISUALS

A SEQUENCE WITHOUT READINGS

This assignment sequence asks you to work with different kinds of visual materials and then to revise your work in various ways. Throughout the process you are encouraged to consider the primary distinction that separates visual material into *art* and *not-art*. By keeping authorial notes of your processes and insights, you should be able by the end of the sequence to comment in an informed way on the challenges and potential of inquiry projects built around visual materials.

ASSIGNMENT 1: *WORKING WITH FORMAL ART*

Visit a museum or art gallery. Browse in the museum or gallery until you find a painting or other piece of two-dimensional art that appeals to you. It is important for later assignments that you select two-dimensional art rather than a piece of sculpture or an artifact, but you may choose to work with a piece done in any medium you wish—oils, acrylics, water colors, photography, and so forth. Without consulting the information tag, consider why you are drawn to this particular piece of art. What of your own background, experiences, or education influenced you to be attracted to this particular piece? Was it the subject that appealed to your system of values? Perhaps the appeal was a rational one, based on your exposure to history or artistic education. Maybe the appeal was emotional, reminiscent of a significant memory, or aesthetic, engaging the senses in texture, hue, composition. Spend at least ten minutes making notes or free writing about the nature of your interest in this piece. When you have done so, you can consult the information tag or museum directory and record the title, artist, and other information about the piece. Finally make additional notes about the work using the strategies outlined in the subsection about working with visual materials in Chapter 3. A copy of the painting may be helpful to you later, so check the museum gift store for a postcard reproduction or ask if you can take your own photo of the piece. Remember, however, that photographs cannot capture the textures or other details of paintings so be certain that you have detailed notes to return to as you write.

Using your notes, write a description of the piece with enough detail that others can visualize it or recall having seen it themselves. Consider why the piece is worth attending to and what more you would like to know about it. In other words pose the kinds of questions that a full inquiry into the piece might answer.

When you have finished your writing, make some authorial notes about your experience working with formal art. What was difficult or particularly easy about this assignment? How did the assignment to write about the piece influence the way you saw this work of art?

ASSIGNMENT 2: *WORKING WITH OTHER VISUAL IMAGES*

For this assignment you will need to select images that are not examples of the formal art found in galleries or museums, that is, a kind of visual material you did not work with in Assignment 1 but that is still two-dimensional. You might select, for example, graffiti, newspaper or magazine images, illustrations in children's books or textbooks, advertisements, or packaging. The category of images you choose should be public rather than private (thus, no photos from your own family albums, but school yearbooks would be fine). Once you have decided on a general kind of image, browse through several samples representing the category to find at least one example that catches your interest and that seems worth further investigation. Take careful notes of the image so that you can describe it fully, but consider as well the context of the image. You might consider such questions as: Where does it appear and how does it seem to function? If there is any text associated with the image, what is the relationship between the two? If the image appears in conjunction with other images, how do you interpret those surrounding images? What is the economic, social, or political connection/use of the image? Who benefits from this image and who does it represent? These questions do not necessarily apply to all images, and your image may suggest a different set of questions altogether, so treat these questions merely as suggestions.

Present the image you have selected in a written document with enough detail that others can imagine it or recall having seen it. Present its context as well, and help your readers to become curious about the image or the way it has been used. You may decide to add a copy of the image into your writing, but don't let its presence substitute for the writing you'll need to do.

When you are finished with your writing, make some authorial notes about your experiences. How did considering the context of the visual material change what you noticed? How was working with visual material that was not classified as "art" different from the work you did with formal art? How do you understand this distinction now that you have written about both art and visuals that are not usually seen as art?

ASSIGNMENT 3: *WORKING WITH PERSONAL PHOTOGRAPHS*

Select at least four photographs from your personal (or family) collection. You may take new pictures for this project or select ones from personal albums. Be sure to get permission to use these images if they include subjects other than yourself, or you may prefer to use a collection of photos from archival holdings in the public domain. See the suggestions in the section on visuals in Chapter 3 if you have difficulty finding appropriate images. If such photographs are not available to you, go to a magazine that you can dismantle, and choose at least four pictures that are not a part of advertisements but that are related in some way.

Using the collection of photographs you have selected, create a written document that both describes these photos and uses them as illustration. Your writing might be primarily narrative, but it needn't be confined to that. You might, instead, write to consider why these images are significant, what they say about the people who took them, or how they reflect an historical moment or era. Be sure to include copies of the images at appropriate points within your writing.

When you have completed your writing, spend several minutes making notes about your experience. What differences, if any, were apparent to you as you worked with photographs rather than other visual material? How did your personal memories shape your selection or interest in the photographs, and how did you manage that memory in order to produce your document?

ASSIGNMENT 4: *ANALYZING MOVING IMAGES*

Select one clip from a video or film in which the images seem to you particularly powerful. You will need to be able to view the moving images without their accompanying sound, whether that sound is a spoken narrative, dialogue from the characters, or a musical score. The clip you select should be relatively short, certainly no more than a minute or two, but it can come from any form of moving image you like, including home movies, television shows or advertisements, music videos, online streaming videos, documentaries, or feature films. Take careful notes on the images themselves, the sequence in which they occur, and the way they segue together. Look for the *motif*, the recurring image that dominates the segment or scene. Notice the angle of filming, whether the camera pans or stays stationary, and how your vision is directed both within each shot and across the clip as a whole.

Using your notes, produce a written document that describes the clip fully enough that your readers can visualize it and recognize it if they saw it. Your task is not just to describe the content of the clip, or even its technique, but rather to consider what makes it powerful and effective enough to be worth closer attention and inquiry.

When you are finished with your writing, make some authorial notes about your experience working with moving images. How was this assignment similar and different from the others you have done? What happens to individual images when they are blended into a moving sequence?

ASSIGNMENT 5: *SUGGESTED REVISION: ADDING SECONDARY SOURCES*

Choose one of the images you've worked with in the earlier assignments. Your task is to add appropriate additional information so that your description becomes a fuller analysis or argument about the images you've selected. You might, for example, investigate the symbolism connected to the piece, its history, or its place in the body of work associated with the artist, or you might want to consider what has been left out of the personal photos you worked with, or how the small details of the images can be read independently of the larger image.

The challenge of this assignment is to avoid simply writing a report of the image, amassing a series of facts or comments that others have already written. Instead you will need to follow a path of your own interest or curiosity and make that path interesting and relevant to your classmates. In the end, however, you are using the description with which you began to produce a new piece of writing that makes an argument about the visual material you have chosen. Thus, while you should certainly feel free to keep portions of your earlier writing that still seem relevant, you should also rework that material as you incorporate information and shape the argument.

When you have finished your writing, make some additional authorial notes about your experiences. What difficulties did you encounter as you searched for appropriate secondary materials to add to your earlier work? What interesting directions did you abandon and why? What leads would you follow if you had more time to work on this project?

ASSIGNMENT 6: *SUGGESTED REVISION: COMPARING IMAGES*

This assignment asks that you add another image to the one you have been considering in Assignment 5 and use that additional image to make the argument or interpretation you are advancing stronger. You might, for example, choose another image from the same artist, contrast the original image to one from the same category, juxtapose two images from the same time period or from the same stylistic tradition, consider how another piece of artwork employs similar symbols for similar or different purposes, or reflect on how different photographers capture different aspects of the same scenes or events. You may, if you think it relevant to your original selection, consider a copy or reproduction or satire of the original image.

As you revise your earlier writing, then, you will need to do more than tack on a description of the new image. Rather, you will need to select the addition intentionally for what it can add to the argument or the analysis you have been developing, and you will need to spend enough time with the additional image that your readers can see it fully and understand why it is important to your argument. In fact, depending on the material and the argument you are making, you may well decide that a very different form of presentation is necessary.

As before, when you are finished with the writing, make some additions to your authorial notes about the experience of working with this additional image. What issues arose as you incorporated this new image into your writing and thinking? If you chose to work with a reproduction or satire of the original, what elements of the original were lost in the translation into the new work?

ASSIGNMENT 7: *SUGGESTED REVISION: COLLABORATION*

Working with your classmates, determine what patterns exist among the images you have chosen to work with and the arguments you have been making. Perhaps you have several examples of images in popular culture, multiple illustrations of the way pictures are used to preserve family memories, or several cases of symbolism in formal artistic representations. Borrowing from the work of your classmates, revise the piece of writing you have been working on to include these other images and the arguments/interpretations your classmates have been making. You may find in the process that you have to abandon your original argument and rethink the meaning or significance of all of the images you think are connected, or it may be possible to account for the differences you find by reconsidering the context that makes these images appear to be of the same kind when they are really quite different. Be certain to cite any material that you appropriate from your classmates as you produce this new written document.

As you've done before, spend some time making authorial notes when you have finished your writing. What insights did this assignment give you about your original argument or the ways you had been looking at images? What possibilities did you consider but abandon as you reshaped your writing, and why did you make those choices?

ASSIGNMENT 8: *SUGGESTED REVISION: MOVING OUTSIDE THE CLASSROOM*

Consider how the work you have been doing might be useful outside the classroom. Would the museum or gallery that displays the pieces you've written about be interested in your work? Would the city council find your inquiry into neighborhood graffiti useful in their discussions about prohibiting such expressions? Would members of your family appreciate your document featuring family photos? Revise one of your earlier pieces of writing to address this new audience and different purpose. Remember that not all writing takes the form of essays, so feel free to create a brochure, gallery guide, or newsletter—whatever seems most appropriate for the material you've been investigating and the audience(s) you think might find your work interesting.

When you have finished your new document, write a few authorial notes about the differences in the finished product, the audience you've imagined for this piece, and the processes you used to move your work outside the classroom setting. How did your understanding of the images shift as you moved your work into this new context or adjusted to this new audience?

ASSIGNMENT 9: *REFLECTIVE PRACTICE: DRAWING CONCLUSIONS ABOUT VISUAL MATERIALS*

Turn back to the work you have done throughout this sequence, and read through your various drafts and authorial notes. Then, write a reflective piece about your work that could serve to introduce these pieces if they were collected together. You might consider such issues as: What have you learned about working with visual materials that would not be obvious to someone who had never written about such material? How did the revisions you undertook complicate your view of the images you chose to work with? How did the choices you made reflect your own interests, and how were they shaped by contingencies such as the available time or the resources you could locate? What would you say are the challenges and the possibilities of working with different kinds of visual images? Provide specific examples by citing or quoting examples from your own or your classmates' work.

EXPANDING A TRENDS REPORT

A SEQUENCE WITHOUT READINGS

This assignment sequence begins by having you do a trends report on a topic of interest from the *Statistical Abstracts* and then asks you to revise that work by conducting other kinds of inquiries. Throughout the process you are encouraged to keep authorial notes of your processes and insights, and to use these notes as well as your own and your classmates' writings at the end of the sequence to reconsider what can be learned by working with numbers and what difficulties arise when researchers do so.

ASSIGNMENT 1: *TRENDS REPORT*

The U.S. Census Bureau releases a *Statistical Abstract of the United States* every year. The *Statistical Abstract* will be available in the reference section of most libraries, and is available on the Internet at http://www.census.gov/compendia/statab/. If you would prefer to work with statistics from another country, see the suggestions in the Internet Resources at the end of Chapter 5. You may, if you wish, choose to work with a statistical abstract from an earlier time period, but to do so you'll need to consult your own library's holdings. Many libraries have earlier editions of government reports as well, and some of these data have been converted to electronic texts or microfiche. These reports have several different major sections, including Population, Vital Statistics, Health and Nutrition, Education, Law Enforcement, the Courts and Prison, Geography and the Environment, Elections, Government Finances, National Defense and Veterans Affairs, Social Insurance and Human Services, Labor Statistics, Income and Wealth, Prices, Business, Science and Technology, Agriculture, Natural Resources, Energy, Construction and Housing, Manufactures, Domestic Trade, Transportation, Information and Communications, Banking and Finance, Arts and Entertainment, Accommodation and Food Services, Foreign Commerce and Aid, Puerto Rico and Outlying Areas, and Comparative International Statistics.

Choose one of the sections to explore and begin to dig through the *Statistical Abstract*. One way to approach your report section is to browse the list of tables and select those tables that present information that is of particular interest to you. As you look though these data, try to notice where the numbers indicate surprising, shocking, disturbing, encouraging, interesting, or counterintuitive demographic data, relationships, or, especially, trends. Look at the distribution of data at a particular point in time, but also look at how the data have changed over the past five, ten, fifteen, twenty, or more years. See if the tables in the *Statistical Abstract* provide any insight into why. If your insights or questions lead you to other sections of the report, pursue them. In particular it is often useful to know population totals, provided in "Section 1: Population," when you are thinking about your data. In looking over the data, follow some of the examples provided in Chapter 5. Be sure to take careful notes and make copies, especially if you are using the bound volumes as opposed to the documents available on the Internet. It can be useful to compare the data in the reports for several different years, because they will sometimes provide different comparisons or updated statistics.

Once you have a working knowledge of your data, investigate information on this topic provided by at least one other source. One place to look would be through documents prepared by other government agencies. For instance, if you were looking at statistics related to infant mortality or AIDS, publications of the Centers for Disease Control and Prevention and the National Center for Health Statistics would be helpful. If you are interested in crime, then the Bureau of Justice Statistics or the FBI's famous Uniform Crime Reports might be the place to go. As the Internet Resources at the end of Chapter 5 suggests, a good place to start your search is at the Fed Stats Web site (http://www.fedstats.gov/), which provides links to statistical data from over one-hundred federal agencies.

Present your work in a written document in which you explain trends related to the subject of your choice. Your trend analysis is primarily an argument about what these data mean, and/or about what the changes (or the lack of changes) in the data "say" about the country we live in, the people who inhabit it, or the issues we face. Use the data you have analyzed, presenting the information in tables or charts where appropriate in order to help your readers understand your argument. Make sure that you explain clearly any ways you may have manipulated the data, for instance by finding percentage changes or averages. It's perfectly acceptable to make an argument about how these trends ought to be understood, even if you cannot offer solutions to any problems that these trends suggest. The NEA report "Trends in Literature Participation, 1982–2002" available in the Readings section may be a useful guide for your work.

When you have completed your writing, take a few minutes to make some authorial notes about your experiences. What challenges did you encounter as you conducted your trend analysis? How was the writing you did for this assignment different from previous writing you've done?

ASSIGNMENT 2: *SURVEY OF COLLEGE STUDENTS*

As a college student, you share a variety of interests and experiences with other people at your school, across the country, and indeed throughout the world. Choose an area of concern upon which you believe a survey of college students would help to shed light. This area of concern can be specific to your campus or can be about college students generally. The area of concern can be something college students are interested in, or it can be something people who are interested in college students might want to know. Consider the topic or issue you want to work with carefully so that you do not select an issue that might lead to ethical problems for the participants or require you to wait for formal approval from an institutional research board. Following the steps outlined in Chapter 5 Part II, construct survey questions to measure some aspect of the area of concern you have chosen. Then administer your survey, tabulate the results, and analyze the data. The article by Frisch and the document by Rosina at the end of Chapter 5 provide examples that might guide your work.

Present the results of your study in writing, being certain to clearly explain the methodology you have used and provide a detailed description of your research process. Any data you refer to should be clear, and you should include graphics when and where appropriate and useful. Make certain, however, that your report does more than simply present data or tell the story of your process. Instead your writing should build an argument about the significance of that data and/or draw attention to the importance of your findings. Depending on the nature of your study, you may or may not want to present a set of recommendations as well. Be sure to include a section, perhaps near the end, where you explain possible shortcomings (or limitations) of your approach to your question or topic and suggest what further research needs to be done to resolve confusions, overcome these shortcomings, or follow-up on your results.

When you have finished the account of your study, add to your authorial notes to record your experiences with conducting the survey. What did you learn from designing and conducting your survey? What would you do differently if you were beginning the project again? What did you learn about writing as you did this assignment?

ASSIGNMENT 3: *REVISION: COMBINING RESEARCH METHODS*

In the first assignment of this sequence, you used available census data to demonstrate possible trends. In the second, you constructed your own survey of college students based on a topic of your choice. For this option, revisit the work you completed in the second assignment, and supplement it with census or other government data of the kind you investigated in the first assignment. You might have to be creative in determining exactly where and how such data will be useful to you. Use this demographic data to test, extend, supplement, or revise the conclusion you were able to draw in the second paper.

When you have finished your revision, take a few minutes to make authorial notes that you can share with a classmate or instructor. What did adding the demographic data do for or to your argument? How has the emphasis of your work shifted? What new questions has adding this perspective raised about your work? How would you want to pursue these new questions?

ASSIGNMENT 4: *REVISION: CASE STUDY INTERVIEWS*

Revisit the work from one of your previous pieces of writing and supplement it with two or more in-depth interviews. Your goal is to provide more specific details that flesh out the generalizations of the population you've already written about. Chapter 4 will help you to prepare for and develop these interviews. The readings in this collection by Judy Yung, Rina Benmayor, or David Thelen might serve as useful examples of working with interview materials. But even a quick look at these examples will illustrate that interviews can be presented in very different forms, so think carefully about how you want these personal accounts to appear on the page. As you work on this piece of writing, then, you may well decide to experiment with a different form of presentation, or to shift your intended audience.

When you have finished writing, make additional authorial notes about your experiences. How was completing these case study interviews different from completing surveys? What kind of information were you able to gather from the surveys that you couldn't get from the interviews? What advantages did the interviews provide? Now that you have talked with individuals, what questions do you wish you had pursued in the original survey?

ASSIGNMENT 5: *REVISION: YOUR TURN*

In your authorial notes for the previous two assignments, you identified new questions and different methods for pursuing those methods. In a sense you have already devised your own research program. Pursue this research program. Investigate the new kinds of questions you have, using appropriate methods for doing so. You may want to redesign your survey or create a new one. You may want to pursue more interviews, conduct an observation, or complete additional library research. Use the methods chapters in this text to help you where appropriate. Present your work in writing using a form that fits the material and your intended audience and purposes.

After you have completed this revision, add to your authorial notes. How has your project grown since you first began thinking about this topic? Do you find the work getting easier or more difficult, and why? What discoveries have you made as a writer that have surprised you?

ASSIGNMENT 6: *REVISION: COLLABORATING WITH CLASSMATES*

In this assignment you will work with classmates in one of two ways.

1. There may be interesting overlaps in the surveys you and one or more of your classmates have done. These overlaps may provide reinforcement for your interpretations or they may complicate your earlier work through contrast. Using the work of at least two classmates (you can be one of the two), write a document that makes use of both. You will want to check with the original author(s) throughout the process to be certain that you are not misrepresenting their work, and you will need cite the work of your classmates just as you would cite published authors. Your task is not to erase the differences in these different surveys, but to consider what can be said about college students in the light of both that cannot be said if only one of the two is presented.

2. An alternative to blending two surveys together is to work with a partner to reassess the data they have collected. In this case you and a partner will trade raw data and see what else can be said about the work that the original author

did not already say. Do not relinquish the survey questionnaires themselves, but rather provide your partner with the tables of data that you created to tabulate the survey forms. As you write your assessment, feel free to incorporate the original author's work, with proper citation, as appropriate to either support your own analysis or critique the original data assessment.

Present your work in writing using a form that is appropriate for your material and purpose. In some cases it will be appropriate for you and your partner to be cowriters in addition to being coresearchers.

When you have finished your collaborative work, write additional authorial notes about your experience. What did you learn from collaborating with a classmate in this way? What strategies did you have to use as a writer that you did not use when you weren't collaborating? What new questions about your own work occurred to you as you worked with your classmate's study?

ASSIGNMENT 7: *REVISION: MOVING OUTSIDE THE CLASSROOM*

Choose any of the work you have completed so far and revise it for an audience outside the classroom. You need not use the most recent version of your research as the basis for this revision. One possibility is to repackage your research into a proposal to the dean of student life at your university to make some change you feel would benefit students, or you could produce a feature article for a student newspaper. In developing this "real world" context, think carefully about who would care about your research and why. As you revise, think about all the ways the format, content, and style of your presentation will have to change to meet this audience's expectations. It may be helpful to review the discussion of audiences addressed and audiences invoked in Chapter 2 as you make the decisions about presenting your work in writing.

When you have finished your piece for an audience outside the classroom context, spend some time writing authorial notes to consider: How is writing for "publication" different from the work you've done for classes? Why did you choose the piece you did? How did you decide on the audience and format of your piece? What other options for "publication" do you see in the work you or your classmates have done?

ASSIGNMENT 8: *REFLECTIVE PRACTICE: WORKING WITH NUMBERS, WORKING WITH PEOPLE*

Reread the various pieces you've written, making sure to consider the authorial notes as well. Then, write a reflective piece about your work that could serve to introduce these pieces if they were collected together. You might consider such issues as: What have you learned about working with these various methods that would not be obvious to someone who had never written about such material? What has been gained through the statistical representations of people, and what through more direct personal accounts? What are the disadvantages of each approach? How did the revisions you undertook complicate your view of your research? What advances in your writing do you think show the most potential as foundations for further progress? What kinds of problems, complications, mistakes or failures have you encountered, and what have you learned from them? Provide specific examples by citing or quoting examples from your own or your classmates' work.

You might also speculate about further work that might be done by considering such questions as: If you were going to continue any of the projects you've done so far, what would you choose? Why? How would you pursue this next step in your inquiry, and what do you think you would have to learn how to do in order to take this next step?

EYE ON CAMPUS

BACHIN; BENMAYOR; FRISCH

A college campus, like any other community, is an interesting physical and social place. It has a history, serves a variety of functions, and brings together a collection of people; it is a place ripe for investigation. This sequence invites you to examine your own college community, to consider its members, especially your fellow students, and write documents that attest to the significance of your campus.

ASSIGNMENT 1: *WRITING HISTORY*

ROBIN BACHIN, "COURAGE, ENDURANCE AND QUICKNESS OF DECISION: GENDER AND ATHLETICS AT THE UNIVERSITY OF CHICAGO, 1890–1920"

Because looking at the past gives us distance, we are often able to notice what would otherwise be difficult to see, especially attitudes or common assumptions of the time. Bachin works with a particular building and the archival history behind it in order to expose attitudes about women's athletics in a previous generation, attitudes that must have seemed "normal" or "typical" at the time the women's gymnasium was constructed. Your task in this assignment is to find some aspect of the history of your institution and tell its story.

You might want to select a building, as Bachin did, but you might also investigate and write about a particular organization, the creation of a particular department or program, or a particular controversy on your campus at some earlier time. Use university archives, campus newspapers or yearbooks, or histories of your institution to gather the data to be analyzed and presented for your readers.

Present the history in such a way that your readers learn something of the attitudes of this previous time and how those attitudes might still echo in your current campus community through its buildings, traditions, or commonplace structures. Incorporate specific examples from your search, but don't simply summarize or describe each of these sources in turn. Instead look for the patterns and disjunctions that help you make sense of the material you've gathered.

When you have finished writing this history, take a few minutes to write some authorial notes about your experience. What was unusual, difficult, or interesting about this kind of writing? Did your usual writing process change in any way?

ASSIGNMENT 2: *WRITING PEOPLE*

RINA BENMAYOR, "NARRATING CULTURAL CITIZENSHIP: ORAL HISTORIES OF FIRST-GENERATION COLLEGE STUDENTS OF MEXICAN ORIGIN"

Using demographic data about your institution, select a group that is in some way significant. You might choose, as Benmayor did, a particular ethnic group or first-generation students on your campus, or it may be more appropriate on your campus to select students of a particular religious affiliation, those from a particular region, or members of a particular major.

Once you've decided on the group whose experiences you would like to investigate, develop a list of theoretical questions about the group similar to those Benmayor posed. Notice Benmayor's reference to "some studies" which indicates that she knew about research concerning her group that had happened in other locations. Also note that she does not limit herself to assumptions, but rather entertains seemingly conflicting explanations of experience and data. Translate your critical questions into more straightforward and colloquial interview ones, as described in Chapter 4. Next choose an individual who is in some way representative of the group you are investigating and whose story you think would provide you with a greater understanding of the group. Set up and conduct the interview following the guidelines described in Chapter 4.

Present your work in writing but not as a simple transcript of the interview. Instead use a combination of exact quotation and paraphrase to communicate the most revealing parts of your subject's story, that is, the information that best responds to your initial research questions. Use the oral history you have collected to begin to draw conclusions about this group on your campus and perhaps indicate what additional research would complement your findings and/or explain the potential practical uses for your interview data and analysis.

When you are finished with your writing, add to your authorial notes. What strategies did you use to write this paper that you did not have to use in Assignment 1? What could your work teach others about writing?

ASSIGNMENT 3: *ASSESSING STUDENT KNOWLEDGE*

MICHAEL FRISCH, "AMERICAN HISTORY AND THE STRUCTURES OF COLLECTIVE MEMORY: A MODEST EXERCISE IN EMPIRICAL ICONOGRAPHY"

Frisch's informal survey of his students raises questions about the common assumption that schooling shapes our collective memory. On the one hand, his students seem to have much of the same knowledge about American history; on the other hand, Frisch questions whether such knowledge is the result of school lessons alone. Is such shaping true in disciplines other than history? Do students who graduate from American high schools have more or less the same general knowledge of literature, science, art, and music? This assignment invites you to conduct your own informal survey of what people know and determine the level of similarity in various kinds of common knowledge.

You will need to begin by deciding on one or two specific questions that will provide you with the kind of raw data that Frisch was able to collect. You may, if you wish, try the questions Frisch asked so as to update his work, but you needn't limit yourself to historical knowledge. You might, for example, consider what students know about some aspect of popular culture, your campus or community, or some current event. Once you've determined the questions you want to ask, think carefully about the population you want to respond. Are you interested in what the most recent graduating high school class learned and remembers? If so, you can ask your friends and classmates. But if you suspect that students of different ages or from different regions will be significant to your study, you will have to figure out how to collect those distinctions as you do your survey.

Once you've gathered the information from your survey, present your analysis of the data in writing. Follow Frisch's lead in considering what your analysis might mean about students or about the nature of the information you were asking about.

When you're finished with your work, add to your authorial notes. How is writing with numerical information different from the earlier writing you've done? What part of your work do you like the best and why? Which part would you like to improve and how might you do so?

ASSIGNMENT 4: *VIEWING STUDENTS*

How are students represented in popular media? There are at least two ways you might go about answering this question.

1. Collect images of your campus from a number of different sources—the official Web site and brochures, newspaper coverage of campus events, current and past examples of yearbooks—and analyze those images carefully and completely. You might find the work of Chavez helpful to you in addition to the section on working with visual images in Chapter 3.

2. Collect representations of students and student groups more generally rather than limiting yourself to either visual images or to your campus. Consider focusing on a particular magazine or set of magazines over an extended period of time and tracking changes in how students are represented as Koza does in her consideration of the representations of rap music.

Once you have your collection of either images or textual representations of students, analyze this material carefully, and present your work in a piece of writing that considers the place of "students" in our culture. You might consider such questions as: What features of student life are present in these media portrayals, and what is missing? What function do "students" as a group seem to serve? Be certain to consider the various ways the material might be interpreted rather than settling for a quick or simplistic view that might ignore contradictions or examples that seem atypical.

Once you've completed your writing, make additions to your authorial notes. What strategies did you use as a writer that might make earlier pieces of writing better? What did you learn about writing that you might be able to use in future assignments?

ASSIGNMENT 5: *STUDENT VIEWS AGAIN*

What behavior or practice of students on your campus seems to you to be typical of your generation but not so typical of those who came before you? Perhaps there is a form of technology that is impacting the behavior of your classmates. Alternatively, consider the features of your campus that influence student behavior there in unique ways. Perhaps the location of your campus has a direct impact on social interactions. Your task in this assignment is to consider some aspect of student behavior or social interaction that you think is either unique to your campus or typical of your generation. Conduct a study or a series of interviews that helps explain why this behavior or interaction exists.

Another possibility is to return to the survey you conducted in Assignment 3, and expand it by giving it to another group. You might, for example, want to compare students to nonstudents and so give the same survey to faculty members, or you might be interested in comparing students who live on campus with those who commute and so need to revise your survey in order to capture this comparison.

In either case you will need to present your work in full detail and explain its significance to others. Remember that your audience will likely include both students and those who are interested in student life. Be careful to acknowledge any limitations in your research that might alter your interpretations and suggest areas for future investigation.

When you're finished with your writing, add to your authorial notes. Why did you make the choices you made in this assignment? If you were going to continue to develop this project, how would you do so? What additional questions would you pose, or what other methods do you think you should employ?

ASSIGNMENT 6: *REVISITING EYES ON CAMPUS*

Researchers rarely use a single methodology in isolation, but instead regularly combine direct observations with archival work, oral histories with survey data, or surveys with textual analysis. This assignment asks you to return to one of the assignments you've already completed and add to your work some other form of investigation that enriches your inquiry. Whichever initial assignment you choose to return to, your work in this assignment should move the initial project in directions that are of interest to you and that help move your writing out of the classroom to a larger audience of readers who are interested in your institution or college life and students more generally.

When you've finished your revision, take a few minutes to reflect on your experiences by adding to your authorial notes. What challenges did you face in doing this revision? Why did you make the choices you made? What other possibilities do you see for moving your work outside the classroom?

ASSIGNMENT 7: *REFLECTION*

Return to the work you've done in this sequence, especially to your authorial notes. What have you learned? Use your writing and authorial notes as evidence that helps you build a written argument for how your writing can be interpreted as a sign of your learning and of your ability. Be careful not to read your work too simplistically by eliminating the contradictions or alternative interpretations. In other words don't just talk about the places where your work is exemplary, but instead consider it as you have other research data that need to be interpreted and analyzed and that may include atypical elements.

GENDER INVESTIGATIONS

LEN-RÍOS ET AL.; EDWARDS AND WINKLER; LOWE; BACHIN; YUNG

Many scholars are interested in how gender influences culture, values, perceptions, or experience. In this sequence you are invited to extend the work of scholars who have investigated gender in different ways or to focus prior scholarly models more specifically on gender issues. In each case you will be trying to understand how cultural attitudes about women are reflected, perpetuated, or revised.

ASSIGNMENT 1: *MEDIA REPRESENTATIONS*

MARÍA LEN-RÍOS ET AL. "REPRESENTATIONS OF WOMEN IN NEWS AND PHOTOS: COMPARING CONTENT TO PERCEPTIONS"

As the authors of this study explain, newspapers reflect social norms. Close attention to how newspapers portray women can therefore help us understand cultural values. Extend Len-Ríos's work by conducting your own content analysis of a local newspaper or other publication. You may want to work in collaboration with your classmates in order to consider different publications (a city paper in comparison to your campus paper, for example), or to extend the scope of your content analysis (looking at more than one section of the paper perhaps). You may choose to focus on images or textual features or both, but your goal, like that of Len-Ríos and her colleagues, is to consider how the publication you've chosen represents women.

Present your findings using specific examples and interpreting details to make a claim about their significance. You needn't, however, follow the same formal social-science research format as Len-Ríos for presenting your work, though you certainly could.

When you are finished writing your content analysis, take a few minutes to add to your authorial notes. What difficulties did you encounter as you did this work? What would you do differently if you were beginning a similar project in the future?

ASSIGNMENT 2: *UNDERSTANDING PERCEPTIONS OF MEDIA*

MARÍA LEN-RÍOS ET AL., "REPRESENTATIONS OF WOMEN IN NEWS AND PHOTOS: COMPARING CONTENT TO PERCEPTIONS"

In the second part of Len-Ríos's study, the researchers compare their content analysis to how readers and staff perceive the newspaper's representation of women. Extend your work from Assignment 1 by conducting a similar survey of readers and/or workers. Since Len-Ríos doesn't explain precisely what questions she asked to gauge perceptions, you will have to develop an appropriate survey using the material in Chapter 5 as a guide.

Present your findings by revising your earlier written document to incorporate this new dimension, but consider carefully how to work in this new material rather than just tacking it on to what you already have. You will want to pay particular attention to how this new information might impact or even transform your interpretations and arguments about significance.

When you have finished your revision, add to your authorial notes. What did you learn from this work that surprised you? How did your writing process change as you worked on a revision rather than a new project? Could any of the strategies you used in this assignment be useful in assignments that aren't revisions?

ASSIGNMENT 3: *INDIVIDUAL MEDIA REPRESENTATIONS*

JANIS L. EDWARDS AND CAROL K. WINKLER, "REPRESENTATIVE FORM AND THE VISUAL IDEOGRAPH: THE IWO JIMA IMAGE IN EDITORIAL CARTOONS"

Edwards and Winkler are interested in how political cartoons make use of a recognizable image like the flag raising at Iwo Jima. Because political cartoons reflect cultural norms *and* offer criticism, they are a more complicated form of media representation than we considered in Assignment 1. Follow Edwards and Winkler's lead to collect a set of political cartoons focused on either a single public woman (e.g., Hillary Clinton, Condolizza Rice, or Barbara Bush) or on a particular woman's issue (the ERA, women in the military, or working mothers). Analyze those images carefully using the suggestions in Chapter 3, particularly Figure 3.8 as a guide.

Present your work in a written document that uses specific examples to show readers how to understand the pattern(s) of the whole. In other words use your examples to make an argument about the importance of this form of cultural representation and commentary.

When you have finished your writing, take a few minutes to add to your authorial notes. What challenges did you encounter in this assignment? How would you resolve these difficulties if you had more time? What part of your work do you like the best and why?

ASSIGNMENT 4: *UNDERSTANDING PERCEPTIONS AGAIN*

MELANIE LOWE, "COLLIDING FEMINISMS: BRITNEY SPEARS, 'TWEENS,' AND THE POLITICS OF RECEPTION"

Lowe's investigation uses a focus group of "tweens" to consider how these young girls understand and reconcile Britney Spears's contradictory public images. At the heart of her study, then, is a question about the impact of media representations on the formation of young women. For this assignment, use your work from Assignment 3 to raise similar questions about how a group of readers perceive either the person or the issue you focused on.

Like Lowe, you will need to define a demographic (e.g., recent white male college graduates), convene a focus group of appropriate participants, and pose questions that allow this group to discuss their impressions and how those impressions have been formed. Like Lowe, you'll need to prepare carefully so you can offer particular examples for your group to consider. Lead the conversation so as to elicit the *kind of talk* that will answer questions you are interested in considering.

Present your work in a written document that argues for the significance of your focus group's perceptions. Include both the specific visual examples and appropriate comments from your discussion to support your interpretation or argument rather than producing a full transcript of the group's conversation.

When you finish your writing, add to your authorial notes. What do you think others could learn about writing from your work? What do you think you still need to learn about writing, and how will you do so?

ASSIGNMENT 5: *GENDERED SPACES OR OBJECTS*

ROBIN BACHIN, "COURAGE, ENDURANCE AND QUICKNESS OF DECISION: GENDER AND ATHLETICS AT THE UNIVERSITY OF CHICAGO, 1890–1920"

Bachin uses both historical archives and close observation to demonstrate how a building designed for women incorporated a cultural shift in gender roles by mediating between old and new expectations. Do more recent buildings show any of these same signs of mediation, especially the mediation of new expectations and old values? Are the physical spaces meant to be used by only one gender—restrooms or hair salons, for example—designed or decorated differently than those spaces meant to be used by either or both genders?

As you consider these questions, choose specific buildings or parts of buildings in your area that you can observe carefully and fully. If possible, find the original architectural drawings and any archival records of the building's construction or renovation to supplement your study. Another possibility is to consider a concrete artifact that isn't a building, perhaps some object that had been considered suitable for only one gender but is now used by both men and women. How did the object change either in design or aesthetics as it made this transition? Your task in this assignment is to consider the connections between physical spaces or physical objects and cultural values as you extend Bachin's work with new and different examples.

Present your work in writing with careful attention to the specific details as you explain how your chosen example reflects shifts in cultural norms. You may include illustrations if you wish, but these should not take the place of careful description and analysis.

When you've finished your writing, add to your authorial notes. What parts of your work are you most satisfied with and why? Which parts would you do differently if you wrote a similar account in the future?

ASSIGNMENT 6: *PERSONAL PERCEPTIONS*

JUDY YUNG, "'A BOWLFUL OF TEARS' REVISITED: THE FULL STORY OF LEE PUEY YOU'S IMMIGRATION EXPERIENCE AT ANGEL ISLAND"

As Lee Puey You's story illustrates, personal stories are an important way that scholars come to understand the hidden histories of places and events. The details of an individual life are inflected by the cultural attitudes of their time, and Lee Puey You's life is certainly no exception. In particular, cultural attitudes about women resonate throughout her decisions and her experiences trying to immigrate to this country. Your task in this assignment is to find an individual who can shed light on some aspect of the work you've done in prior assignments and conduct a similar interview.

You might, for example, be able to interview a woman who works for the publication you examined in Assignment 1 and 2, or you may be able to find an individual who helped design the building or object you analyzed in Assignment 5. Use the guidelines in Chapter 4 to help you prepare for the interview.

Present the interview as an oral history that stands alone, or use it in conjunction with the material you already have. In either case your task is to produce an interesting and effective piece of writing that makes use of the interview data you've collected.

When you have finished writing this new piece, add to your authorial notes. How is a personal interview different from the other kinds of methods you've used? What aspects of this work were the most interesting? Challenging? Fun? How could you make use of personal accounts if you were to revise your other writings from this sequence?

ASSIGNMENT 7: *REFLECTION*

Look back over the assignments you've done in this sequence, and reread your authorial notes. Using this material as the "data" to be analyzed, write a paper that considers what you've learned about gendered research and about writing. The challenge of this assignment is to avoid saying what you think your instructor expects, and instead to consider critically and carefully both the possibilities and limits of the research and writing you've done. Incorporate specific examples either from your own work or that of your classmates, giving appropriate citations to the original writing. This writing might certainly serve to introduce a portfolio of your term's work, but it should also be capable of standing alone; it should develop an argument or interpretation from the specific examples you are considering and say something more about gender than you would have been able to say at the beginning of the term.

HISTORIES: OFFICIAL AND UNOFFICIAL

SHACKEL; THELEN

What or who makes history? Why are some versions of past events given the status of "official" truths and other, often more common or locally known, versions treated as "unofficial"? How is it that some locations come to be landmarks or receptacles of community memory, and what does such a distinction do for these locations? Likewise what stories lurk behind official landmarks or are hidden away in the memories of ordinary people? This sequence invites you to explore various sites of history—both official and unofficial histories—and to consider in the process how history comes to be shaped, remembered, and shared.

ASSIGNMENT 1: *UNOFFICIAL LANDMARKS*

For this assignment your goal is to write a history of a local landmark or public space. You might certainly choose an "unofficial" landmark that somehow represents a community or a portion of a community rather than a place that is featured in tourist guides or other more official documents of your area. Conduct careful observations and interview key actors to develop an understanding of both the story of the place itself and the people associated with it. Using the material you've gathered, produce a written document explaining the history of this location for readers who may be locals who know the place well themselves but also for those who are interested in history more generally.

When you've finished writing, take a few minutes to write some authorial notes. What was your process for completing this assignment? Was that process different in any way from your usual writing process? What questions arose as you worked on this project that you might be interested in pursuing if you had more time?

ASSIGNMENT 2: *OFFICIAL LANDMARKS*

PAUL A. SHACKEL, "PUBLIC MEMORY AND THE SEARCH FOR POWER IN AMERICAN HISTORICAL ARCHAEOLOGY"

Paul A. Shackel offers a perspective on the development and maintenance of public memory, arguing that Americans' memory of "the past is often reinforced by landscapes, monuments, commemorative ceremonies, and archeology." Central to Shackel's argument is the idea that official public monuments and ceremonies can "serve individual or collective needs and can validate the holder's version of the past," which often ultimately "serve[s] the dominant culture by supporting existing social inequalities." From this perspective, our understanding of history is informed by these monuments and the ideological principles they support. As his discussion of the controversies surrounding several public spaces indicates, social and political authority play a crucial role in determining the images, narratives, and historical documentation that become a part of the official public space.

This assignment asks that you test and extend Shackel's work by uncovering the history of a piece of local public art, a monument, a building or a similar public object that serves as an official landmark in your community. The object should be something physically close enough that you can visit and observe with a fresh set of eyes as you become more and more acquainted with its history. Investigate the history of this object and any controversies surrounding it. Find who commissioned it, who designed and completed it, and how it was made. Search local newspapers to find reviews or accounts of dedication ceremonies. To the extent possible, interview people connected to your chosen landmark, including, perhaps, some of its critics and supporters, those responsible for maintaining it, those responsible for designing and/or building it, or the people responsible for the public space where it lives. If possible, dig in local archives to see if there is other information related to this object. One question to ask interviewees would be whether they know where documents related to this object are—or if they have any they could provide you. And you may want to conduct an informal survey, either of the general public or of local experts, to understand their take on this object. Be alert to indications that there are different versions of history being melded together or displaced in the construction or maintenance of this landmark and that public memory is being shaped by its presence.

Present your findings as a social history of the public object you have chosen but also as a way of considering Shackel's claims. Aim not simply to provide a chronology or to dump a set of facts in your readers' laps. Instead, in writing this piece, you will want to find a clear focus, an interesting "hook," a particular point of view on this history. Select from among the information you have gathered to present this interesting background story to your readers *and* to consider what such hidden history might mean to the community or to historical understanding in general. You might consider such questions as: Whose interests are being served, or whose beliefs are being reinforced by this landmark? What kind of public memory is being created? What alternative pasts or interpretations have been forgotten or left out?

When you're finished with your writing, add to your authorial notes. What new strategies did you use as you worked on this project? What choices did you make as you wrote and why? Did you leave out, or leave unexplored, details that might be worth returning to at some point?

ASSIGNMENT 3: *HISTORICAL PERSPECTIVES*

DAVID THELEN, "REMEMBERING THE DISCOVERY OF THE WATERGATE TAPES"

Although few of us are key actors in historical events, we all live through historical moments that end up shaping our perspectives and values, and our memories of those events constitute a kind of unofficial history that may or may not match the official histories available in textbooks, government documents, or scholarly records. One of the reasons historians are so interested in oral histories is because individual memories and experiences of historical events can provide both detail and contrary perspectives. Your task in this assignment is to identify an important historical moment and interview someone who lived through that event. You might find brainstorming with your classmates useful because you will need to narrow your moment in history to be as specific and self-contained as possible. Thus, rather than trying to interview someone about all of World War II, for example, you should narrow your scope to one key event within the war: D-Day, or the bombing of Hiroshima, or Kristallnacht.

As you prepare for your interview, you'll need to know the official versions of this event and use that information to solicit response from your interviewee. Use the suggestions in Chapter 4 to help you prepare for and conduct your interview, being certain to solicit information about how the historical event changed or continued to influence your interviewee after the initial event. Once you've collected these accounts, analyze them carefully and present them in writing. Follow Thelen's lead to consider what is significant about these memories or the aftermath of the event rather than simply relating the event itself. Who or what has shaped the memories of the person you interviewed and what do the memories or subsequent experiences suggest about the way that history works to shape our cultural values?

Once you've completed your writing, make additions to your authorial notes. What surprised you as you worked on this assignment? What moments of your work are you most satisfied with and why? What would you do differently if you could?

ASSIGNMENT 4: *RETHINKING HISTORY*

Sometimes writers use history to provide a frame or context for an argument that has nothing to do with history. Consider, for example, how Shackel's examination of monuments is really less about the history represented by these structures than about the politics that shape their construction, or consider how Thelen's work uses the details of the Watergate affair to demonstrate the complex ways individuals make sense of their experiences and remember them years later. Such uses of history require deep knowledge on the part of the writer who must select, summarize, and reframe historical information for a different purpose.

This assignment invites you to return to one of the histories you've written in the earlier assignments and to reframe that history in order to make an argument of some other kind. What that other argument is going to be depends, of course, on the work you have done, but it may also require you to do more—to interview others, conduct a survey, collect another oral history, or to spend more time in the library. Feel free to borrow from the work you've done before, but you will probably not be able to incorporate your earlier work wholesale; rather you will need to rewrite, summarize, omit some information, and add new in order to serve your new purpose.

When you've finished your writing, add to your authorial notes. How was revising different from the original writing? What do you think your work could teach others about writing?

ASSIGNMENT 5: *SYNTHESIS AND REFLECTION*

Reread the work you have done in this sequence, and write a document that can serve as an introduction to this work if it were collected together but that might also stand on its own as a piece that considers carefully the distinctions represented by "official and unofficial history." Use examples from your own work or that of your classmates as you write, being certain to cite the work you use in a way that your readers could locate the original pieces. You should be able to consider the ways public spaces reflect, reinforce, shape, or distort public history and community identity. You should also be able to say something about the way individuals experience or remember history, and how writers construct history or reshape it to fit their own purposes. Your writing, then, is both an opportunity to reflect on and synthesize the work you have done so far, and an occasion to say something more about the nature of history and historical writing than you could have said at the beginning of this sequence of work.

HUMANIZING NUMBERS

A SEQUENCE WITHOUT READINGS

A great deal of the information presented to and assessed daily by scholars, businesspeople, and the average consumer takes the form of percentages, data tables, charts, graphs, and other numerical presentations. Television commercials affirm that "nine out of ten" dentists prefer this or that toothpaste; scientists proclaim that x percentage of the population is at risk for a virus; and the U.S. government releases mounds of statistical data about the American people every year. This sequence uses such statistics as a springboard from which to embark upon an exploration of what lies beyond them— using public speech, interviews, and visual materials—to, in effect, complement the numbers with a "human" dimension and assess the efficacy of these diverse modes of inquiry.

ASSIGNMENT 1: *TRENDS REPORT*

The U.S. Census Bureau releases a *Statistical Abstract of the United States* every year. The *Statistical Abstract* will be available in the reference section of most libraries, and is available on the Internet at http://www.census.gov/compendia/statab/. If you would prefer to work with statistics from another country, see the suggestions in the Internet Resources at the end of Chapter 5. You may, if you wish, choose to work with a statistical abstract from an earlier time period but to do so you'll need to consult your own library's holdings. Many libraries have earlier editions of government reports as well, and some of these data have been converted to electronic texts or microfiche. These reports have several different major sections, including Population, Vital Statistics, Health and Nutrition, Education, Law Enforcement, the Courts and Prison, Geography and the Environment, Elections, Government Finances, National Defense and Veterans Affairs, Social Insurance and Human Services, Labor Statistics, Income and Wealth, Prices, Business, Science and Technology, Agriculture, Natural Resources, Energy, Construction and Housing, Manufactures, Domestic Trade, Transportation, Information and Communications, Banking and Finance, Arts and Entertainment, Accommodation and Food Services, Foreign Commerce and Aid, Puerto Rico and Outlying Areas, and Comparative International Statistics.

Choose one of the sections to explore and begin to dig through the *Statistical Abstract*. One way to approach your report section is to browse the list of tables and select those tables that present information that is of particular interest to you. As you look though these data, try to notice where the numbers indicate surprising, shocking, disturbing, encouraging, interesting, or counterintuitive demographic data, relationships, or, especially, trends. Look at the distribution of data at a particular point in time, but also look at how the data have changed over the past five, ten, fifteen, twenty, or more years. See if the tables in the *Statistical Abstract* provide any insight into why. If your insights or questions lead you to other sections of the report, pursue them. In particular it is often useful to know population totals, provided in "Section 1: Population," when you are thinking about your data. In looking over the data, follow some of the examples provided in Chapter 5. Be sure to take careful notes and make copies, especially if you are using the bound volumes as opposed to the documents available on the Internet. It can be useful to compare the data in the reports for several different years, because they will sometimes provide different comparisons or updated statistics.

Once you have a working knowledge of your data, investigate information on this topic provided by at least one other source. One place to look would be through documents prepared by other government agencies. For instance, if you were looking at statistics related to infant mortality or AIDS, publications of the Centers for Disease Control and Prevention and the National Center for Health Statistics would be helpful. If you are interested in crime, then the Bureau of Justice Statistics or the FBI's famous Uniform Crime Reports might be the place to go. As the Internet Resources at the end of Chapter 5 suggests, a good place to start your search is at the Fed Stats Web site (http://www.fedstats.gov/), which provides links to statistical data from over one-hundred federal agencies.

Present your work in a written document in which you explain trends related to the subject of your choice. Your trend analysis is primarily an argument about what these data mean, and/or about what the changes (or the lack of changes) in the data "say" about the country we live in, the people who inhabit it, or the issues we face. Use the data you have analyzed, presenting the information in tables or charts where appropriate in order to help your readers understand. Make sure that you explain clearly any ways you may have manipulated the data, for instance by finding percentage changes or averages. It's perfectly acceptable to make an argument about how these trends ought to be understood, even if you cannot offer solutions to any problems that these trends suggest. The NEA report "Trends in Literature Participation, 1982–2002" available in the Readings section may be a useful guide for your work.

Note that since this sequence asks that you build upon this trends report assignment throughout the semester, it is important to take the time to carefully select a topic that truly interests you and seems worth exploring in depth.

When you have finished your writing, make a few authorial notes about your writing process and your experience of working with numbers. What challenges did you face, and how did you resolve them? What parts of your work are you most pleased with, and what would you work on further if you had the time?

ASSIGNMENT 2: *WHO'S SAYING WHAT?*

Although there are varying conceptions of what is characterized as "public speech," at the core of all discourse is a rhetorical situation comprised of audience, speaker, and message. This rhetorical relationship is constructed through *ethos*, an appeal based on the speaker's authority; *logos*, an appeal to the audience's reason; or *pathos*, the appeal to the audience's emotion. Clearly, then, public speech involves human interactions even when it uses statistical data of the type you examined in Assignment 1.

To complete this assignment, you will first need to identify one or two examples of public speech that correspond to your trend analysis, for instance, a speech in which a political figure discussed the topic represented by your numerical analysis, or a press release issued by an organization or individual in which the topic was featured. You might also find a transcript of an interview or newspaper article in which an individual "speaks" publicly about your trend.

Write a paper in which you examine your selection(s) of public speech, taking into account how *ethos*, *logos*, and *pathos* might account for what was said and *how* it was said, as well as for what was not spoken. Evaluate how this example of public speech functions as a vehicle for conveying information and what the piece(s) of public speech you found contribute to your understanding of the trend you selected. You may choose to incorporate some of your work from the previous assignment, but your goal is to write a piece that can stand alone, that is, one that can be understood by someone who has not read your previous paper.

When you have finished your writing, add to your authorial notes. You might consider how adding public speech influenced your prior analysis of the data and the argument you made in your previous piece, or how public speech compares to the use of statistics and numbers as a means of conveying knowledge.

ASSIGNMENT 3: *CASE STUDY: INTERVIEW*

Unlike statistics that categorize people into groups, case studies focus on individuals in order to consider how those generalities actually apply to individual lives. Likewise while most public speech is uttered by those with authority or fame, case studies present the voices of ordinary people. This assignment asks that you find an individual who somehow relates to the trend analysis you explored in your first two papers and to interview that individual as a specific "case" of your trend.

Using the guidelines described in Chapter 4, interview the person you have identified, and use that data to expand upon your understanding of the topic/trend you have been investigating. Begin your writing by providing the necessary context—explaining whose narrative you will be providing, why you selected this person, and so on, and then present those parts of the interview that seem most pertinent to your trend analysis. It may be helpful to use a combination of transcript, question and answer format (with exact quotations), and paraphrase. As in your previous writings, consider how these new data affect the conclusions and observations you made in your previous analyses, and so revise your argument accordingly.

When you are finished with this work, make authorial notes about your experience. What difficulties did you encounter in writing from interview data, and how did you resolve those problems? What did you learn from the interview that you had not expected based on the earlier work you had completed?

ASSIGNMENT 4: *ADDING VISUALS*

Scholars use visual materials in two ways: analyzing existing images and creating visuals themselves. For this assignment, choose one of these approaches to enhance your ongoing trend analysis. If you decide to analyze existing images—including photographs, paintings, cartoons, or films—begin with a description and analysis of the image(s) selected. Not all trends lend themselves to incorporating images in this way; the NEA report on trends in literary reading probably could not turn to an analysis of visual images, but a trend report concerned with immigration might produce something like Chavez's analysis of magazine depictions of immigration. If your trend lends itself to including an analysis of visual images, you might consider such questions as: How do the images relate to the trend? How does the visual representation affect your previous conception of the topic? If possible, include the visual materials in your new writing, adding captions as appropriate.

If you choose to create visual materials (photographs, charts and graphs, etc.), you will have to decide what aspects of your work can benefit from visual representations and what visuals are best to represent that work. You will still need to reconsider how including visual materials alters your previous conceptions of the topic, whether the information needs to be reorganized, and what captions are necessary to make the visual material understandable. The discussion of these issues in Chapter 5 may help you get started.

When you are finished adding visuals to your document, take a few minutes to write an additional authorial note that describes your process and analyzes the result. How does the visual representation effect your previous conception of the topic? How do the captions you wrote mediate between the visual and the larger discursive document? What other visual materials would you include if you had more time?

ASSIGNMENT 5: *MOVING OUTSIDE THE CLASSROOM*

This assignment asks that you consider how to move your work outside the classroom to address a larger audience. You may select any of your earlier work to revise, or you may want to devise a composite form that draws on more than one of the specific assignments you've already completed. Remember that the forms for nonacademic work are variable and that research in such settings can be presented in a number of ways. You might, for example, want to write a proposal for specific action, present your findings as a feature for a local newspaper or magazine, or construct a more formal report for a government agency or business.

When you have completed your work, take a few minutes to add to your authorial notes. What differences in your writing process were necessary in order to transform your research for a nonacademic audience? What do you think you did well in this transformation, and what problems did you encounter? What other possibilities did you consider, and how did you choose from among the options you considered?

ASSIGNMENT 6: *REFLECTION AND REVISION*

Your task in this assignment is to provide a commentary on the work you've done in this sequence. Begin by reading through all of your written products and the authorial notes you constructed at the end of each assignment. What have you learned about the topic you chose and about how to represent the human side of numbers? As far as you can tell, was your work on your topic similar to the work your classmates did on their topics? Present your analysis, synthesis, and reflection as a new document that comments on these aspects of writing about and studying numbers, but one that can serve to introduce a reader to the collection of work you have produced, as well as to the topic you have been investigating. If you incorporate passages from your own writing or from the work of your classmates, be certain to cite them in a way that would allow your readers to locate the original passages.

INVESTIGATING ARTIFACTS

A SEQUENCE WITHOUT READINGS

This assignment sequence asks you to experiment with artifacts as subjects of inquiry and then to revise your work in various ways. Throughout the process you are encouraged to keep authorial notes of your processes and insights so that by the end of the sequence you can comment in an informed way on the challenges and potential of inquiry projects involving artifacts.

ASSIGNMENT 1: *DESCRIBING AN ARTIFACT*

Investigating an artifact must begin with the selection of an object that you find intriguing enough to sustain your interest. You might select an historical object, one that represents a particular culture, or one that seems commonplace but significant for what it conveys about cultural or historical values. Buildings, monuments, pieces of art—especially public sculpture—can also be considered "artifacts" and often have interesting histories or are surrounded by controversies. Assignment 2 asks you to work with those, so for this assignment, we ask that you stick with something smaller and man-made. Likewise, though photographs or other two-dimensional images can be treated as artifacts, we think it is best for the purposes of this assignment that you work with other material. The articles by Dilworth and Prown might serve to guide you in analyzing the object you select, and the section in Chapter 3 on working with artifacts provides specific strategies you may find helpful.

Begin by writing a complete description of the artifact based on your own direct observations. Take measurements, note the composition and construction, attend to the details that might reflect age, style, or artisan. Present your description in writing as completely as you can, but include your speculations about why these details might be important or what they seem to signify. In other words begin to generate questions that you expect your investigation of the artifact to answer. You may include photographs or drawings if you wish, but these should not take the place of your thorough written description.

When you are finished with the description, write an authorial note about the process you used to decide on an object to investigate and any problems you encountered in writing the description.

ASSIGNMENT 2: *DESCRIBING A BUILDING OR OTHER STRUCTURE AS AN ARTIFACT*

In this assignment turn your attention to a local building or piece of public art. As in writing about a smaller artifact, your description will rely on careful and detailed observations. You will probably not, however, be able to take exact measurements. If you are working with a building, consider both the inside and outside, the larger impression and small details of the architecture. If you are working with a piece of public art, you'll want to include details of setting as well as the object itself. In either case ask permission of the owner or manager of the space before you begin so that your note taking, photography, and "snooping around" don't create suspicion that causes you trouble. Present your description in writing with attention to the kinds of questions that you would like to be able to answer by the time you are done with your inquiry. Use drawing or photographs as supplements to the written word.

After your description is complete, write an authorial note in which you consider how working with a larger artifact was different from or similar to working with a small object. What strategies of observation were the same in both cases, and what did you have to do differently? Which of these descriptions do you find yourself most interested in investigating and why?

ASSIGNMENT 3: *SUGGESTED REVISION: EXPANDING WITH HISTORY*

Your object (or building) has a history, and your job in this assignment is to find sources of information that can fill in that past. Using either the smaller artifact you described in Assignment 1 or the building or work of art you wrote about in Assignment 2, expand your description by adding history. You might conduct an interview, go to the archives, or research similar objects in books. Local archives may have letters about the building or piece of artwork, announcements of groundbreaking or dedication ceremonies, architectural drawings or directions to the artist when the work was commissioned, or records of public hearings, rezoning efforts, or fund-raising campaigns.

If you decide to work with your smaller artifact, you may have to rely on less direct information. Instead of trying to find a book about the specific object you are investigating, you may need to consider how the object would be classified in order to find relevant details. Let's say, for example, that you are investigating a sword that has been in your family for several generations. Rather than hunting for books just on swords, you might look for texts with illustrations of military weapons and then for sections on cavalry weapons, or you may notice that the handle is silver and so be able to locate information about how silver work was done in the years you know the sword was created. Often owners can tell you some details that will help you establish a date of construction or how it was acquired.

In either case rewrite your description to incorporate the new information. Consider how the history you have uncovered has answered any of your earlier questions or generated new ones. What can be said now about the significance of the artifact you've chosen?

When you are finished with your revision, write a new set of authorial notes to report on your difficulties and what you have learned in doing this revision. What would you do if you had more time to continue your investigation? What other bits of information did you learn along the way that caught your interest but did not fit with your current investigation?

ASSIGNMENT 4: *SUGGESTED REVISION: COMPARING OTHER OBJECTS*

Chances are strong that several of your classmates are working with similar objects or with materials from the same time period. Choose one of the objects from a classmate that seems related to your own work, and working with the written descriptions and histories that your classmate has written, revise your account to include this other object. You will have to decide whether the objects are contrasts of one another, close relatives with lots in common, or only distant cousins—present or created at the same time but having little else in common. You will also have to make decisions about which object should take the primary position in your new writing and which will serve in the backup role, or if both can occupy the page equally. Your decisions will be influenced, of course, by what you've decided is the importance (or meaning) of the objects you are working with and whether you agree with your classmate's assessment of the meaning of his/her object in relation to your own.

When you are finished with your written account of these two objects, add to your authorial notes. Did incorporating a second artifact change your perception of the original object you were investigating? What helped you make the decisions you had to make about presenting these two objects together?

ASSIGNMENT 5: *SUGGESTED REVISION: MOVING OUTSIDE THE CLASSROOM*

Rework either the full history and description piece you wrote for Assignment 3 or the comparison account you completed in Assignment 4, but for a new audience. You might, for example, revise your historical account of a locale building or piece of artwork for your campus paper, reconstruct the description of an historical artifact for a museum guide, or alter your comparison piece to become an editorial for a local paper. How you move your writing outside of your class is intimately connected to both the artifact you are investigating and the meaning you have found in it. You will have to decide who cares about this object and why and then choose a form of writing that fits the material, purpose, and imagined audience. The piece you end up with may not be as long as your earlier work, and you may have to find new ways to present the history (e.g., using graphics) but this revision will nevertheless draw upon all the work you have done so far.

When you are finished, you should again add to your authorial notes. What difficulties did you encounter, and how did you resolve them? What did you learn by repositioning the description, history, and comparison for a different audience?

ASSIGNMENT 6: *SUGGESTED REVISION:*
COLLABORATION

Working with either the comparison account you wrote in Assignment 4 or the document you created for Assignment 5, join with a classmate to create a joint document you both think adequately represents your objects and your analyses of those objects. If you decide to work with the comparison account, you needn't work with the classmate whose object you originally compared with your own artifact, though you may choose to do so. If you are working with the documents you created for Assignment 5, you will have to agree on a shared audience, or construct a single document that will work for both of your intended audiences. In any case you should be making decisions jointly, sharing the tasks of editing and rewriting, and contributing equally (though perhaps in different ways) to the finished product.

After you have finished the collaborative document, write individual authorial notes about your experience. What did you learn from your classmate in the process of working together? What did you teach your classmate that you think s/he didn't already know? What was different about your writing process when you were writing with a partner from when you write alone?

ASSIGNMENT 7: *REFLECTIVE PRACTICE: DRAWING*
CONCLUSIONS FROM EXPERIENCE

Reread the various pieces you've written about artifacts. Be certain to consider the authorial notes you've written as well. Then write a reflective paper about your work that could serve to introduce these pieces if they were collected together. You might consider such issues as: What have you learned about working with artifacts that would not be obvious to someone who had never written about such material? How did the revisions you undertook complicate your view of your research? Provide specific examples by citing or quoting examples from your own or your classmates' work.

You might also speculate about further work that might be done by considering such question as: If you were going to continue any of the projects you've done so far, what would you choose? How would you pursue this next step in your inquiry, and what do you think you would have to learn how to do in order to take this next step? Why? What would you do differently if you were starting over with these projects? Why? What are the difficulties of working with artifacts and what is their potential?

MATERIAL CULTURE

Prown; Bachin; White; Jackson; Lutz and Collins

Many of us are familiar with the idea of analyzing a culture's texts, images, and music to reveal things about the people behind these artifacts, what they dream, and what they value. However, other kinds of objects may reveal similar kinds of cultural knowledge. This sequence asks you to observe elements of the material world and to begin reading this material world in its cultural variety and richness. The assignments will ask you to think about objects and the ways people use objects to shape our interactions with each other.

ASSIGNMENT 1: *READING OBJECTS*

Jules David Prown, "The Truth of Material Culture: History or Fiction?"

Prown argues for, and tries to demonstrate, the deep connections between objects and the beliefs or values of the culture that produces and/or uses those objects. Using Prown's essay as a model, look into the life of a particular kind of object and develop a way of presenting that object in writing so that your readers can "see" it with fresh insight. You may choose to work with an historical object if you wish or one from another culture, but you could also work with a commonplace object that you encounter on a regular basis. Your task is to observe that object carefully and describe it fully as you consider how its form, function, and cultural significance interact. You may want to see if the object has a patent by going to www.uspto.gov or you might track its origins, especially its links to specific cultures by using the Human Resources Area Files at www.yale.edu/hraf.

Develop a way of presenting your object in writing so that your readers can "see" it with fresh insight. It may be useful to include photographs or drawings of your object or of the evolution of your object into its current form. Even if you decide to add this additional visual representation, however, you should still spend time fully and accurately describing the object in writing and considering how its design reflects the cultural values of those who use it.

When you have finished your writing, take a few minutes to make some authorial notes. Try listing the steps you followed to complete this assignment. Did you need to alter any of your usual writing processes or strategies?

ASSIGNMENT 2: *READING STRUCTURES*

Robin Bachin, "Courage, Endurance and Quickness of Decision: Gender and Athletics at the University of Chicago, 1890–1920"

Bachin uses both historical archives and close observation to demonstrate how a building designed for women (but doing an activity associated at the time with men) incorporated this cultural shift by mediating between old expectations and new ones. Do more recent buildings show any of these same signs of mediation, especially the mediation of new expectations and old values? Are the physical spaces meant to be used by only one gender—restrooms or hair salons, for example—designed or decorated differently than those spaces meant to be used by either or both genders? Does the building have spaces that mediate generational gaps or religious differences? Perhaps the art work included in the structure reflects a compromise between aesthetics and community identity, or between cultural values such as freedom of speech versus the prohibition against government support for religion. As you consider these questions, choose specific buildings or parts of buildings in your area that you can observe carefully and fully. If possible, find the original architectural drawings, and any archival records of the construction or renovation to supplement your study.

Present your findings in a written document that explains the connections between physical spaces and cultural values as you extend Bachin's work with new and different examples. You may add illustrations if you wish, but these should not take the place of the written description and analysis.

When you've finished your writing, add to your authorial notes. What parts of your work are you most satisfied with and why? Which parts would you do differently if you wrote a similar history in the future?

ASSIGNMENT 3: *READING COMMON TEXTS*

JAMES BOYD WHITE, "HUMAN DIGNITY AND THE CLAIM OF MEANING: ATHENIAN TRAGIC DRAMA AND SUPREME COURT OPINIONS"

As James Boyd White demonstrates, textual materials like court opinions are sites where cultural values can become visible if we know how to look for and interpret the signs of their existence. This assignment invites you to test and extend White's work by locating and closely reading another kind of textual material that seems to you to participate in constructing our culture.

You may want to consider other specific forms of governmental texts such as legislative acts, or other forms of protest speech like bumper stickers or T-shirts, or you might stretch White's work into new arenas by considering other commonplace textual material such as cookbooks, etiquette manuals, wedding guides, parenting books, signposts, or packaging. You may, if you wish, concentrate your work on a particular historical period, or compare historical forms of the genre you select to current versions. Whatever genre of textual material you decide to examine, collect several examples to analyze and work with at least three different examples in your final written presentation.

Present your analysis in writing being certain to provide, as White does, both the context for this commonplace textual material and specific examples of how the text reflects and constitutes cultural values. Use your work to speak back to White, challenging his conclusions or extending his analysis in a new direction.

Once you've completed the piece, make additions to your authorial notes. What's the difference in writing about textual material and writing about an object? What strategies did you use in this assignment that you might be able to incorporate into your earlier work?

ASSIGNMENT 4: *READING MUSIC*

MARK ALLAN JACKSON, "IS THIS SONG YOUR SONG ANY MORE?: REVISIONING WOODY GUTHRIE'S 'THIS LAND IS YOUR LAND'"

This assignment asks you to work closely with a particular piece of vocal music to present its history and to consider how it functions to shape cultural values or perspectives. There are three ways you can focus your research.

1. Think back to the songs you learned as a child, especially the ones you sang in school or other organized venues such as church or scout meetings. Investigate one of those songs to uncover its history, its reception, any alternative versions, and the way it has been used for different purposes. Do not expect this kind of information to be in one location. You may have to compare different versions printed in various songbooks, search for biographical information about the composer or performers, or look for scholarly articles in databases such as the International Index to Music Periodicals at http://iimpft.chadwyck .com/home.

2. Consider the genre of protest songs that function to galvanize public opinion or inform listeners about a particular issue. The Vietnam War spawned a number of such protest songs, but that is certainly not the only possibility. Choose one of these songs to investigate, being certain to research how the song has been appropriated for other purposes.

3. Perhaps you know of a particular song that reflects an effort, like Woody Guthrie's "This Land," to comment on social conditions of its time. Research the song and its artist, being certain to consider any alternative versions or appropriations that have arisen.

Once you have collected as much information as you can in the time you have to work, present a written history of your song being certain to read and interpret the lyrics and its material life. Use Jackson's work as a guide, but do not be discouraged if the song you've selected doesn't have as rich or controversial a history as Guthrie's "This Land." No matter what song you've chosen, your primary task is to consider how it worked to educate those who heard and sang it.

When you're finished with your writing, add to your authorial notes. Has anything surprised you as you've worked on this sequence? Where do you see changes in your writing?

ASSIGNMENT 5: *READING PHOTOGRAPHS*

CATHERINE A. LUTZ AND JANE L. COLLINS, "THE PHOTOGRAPH AS AN INTERSECTION OF GAZES"

Lutz and Collins demonstrate how photographs can be read and interpreted as "stories about looking" and they are particularly interested in how American readers of *National Geographic* magazine looked at photographs of foreign peoples and in the process were led to consider the identities of these "others" as well as their own. Extend and test

Lutz and Collins's work by collecting your own set of photographs and analyzing them through a close reading of one or more of their features.

You should start by deciding on a category of photographs to investigate. You could, for example, consider public photos like those included in magazines, used to illustrate news stories, or featured in travel brochures, or you might want to focus on family photographs, school pictures, or drivers' license shots. In any case, you should collect as many different examples of the type you choose as you can and plan to use at least three different examples in your final written report. You may want to work with classmates to cover as many different categories of photographs, publications, and time frames as possible, and then compare your readings of the material culture represented by photographs.

Present your analysis of these photographs in writing as carefully and completely as you can. Follow Lutz and Collins's lead to consider some particular aspect of these photographs which suggests a pattern that reveals underlying cultural values or perspectives. Present this feature carefully, using your specific examples to explain how the feature works as a part of the material culture of photographs.

Once you're finished with the writing, make additions to your authorial notes. What do you think your work could teach others about writing? Which moments of your writing would you like to do better if you could, and what would such an improvement require?

ASSIGNMENT 6: *REVISING MATERIAL CULTURE*

Reread the work you have done so far, and consider what you have learned. How is reading material culture like and not like other kinds of reading you do? Write a paper that can serve to introduce the different pieces of writing you have produced, a paper that takes stock of what you have learned and how you have learned it, but that also considers the role of material culture in understanding humans and/or culture. If you incorporate specific passages from your earlier work, be certain to cite them in a way that would allow a reader to locate the original.

READING MEDIA

JONES; KOZA; CHAVEZ; LEN-RÍOS ET AL.; EDWARDS AND WINKLER; LOWE

What impact do the media have on our perceptions of ourselves and others? How can we be better readers of media, and thus better consumers of media information?

ASSIGNMENT 1: *WATCHING CRITICALLY*

JEFFREY P. JONES, "FORUMS FOR CITIZENSHIP IN POPULAR CULTURE"

For Jones, our public citizenship is shaped through our interactions with popular culture, especially the media. However, popular media are not all the same. Different subgroups of the media imagine "the public" very differently. By choosing two such distinct popular forums—*Politically Incorrect with Bill Maher* and *This Week with Sam Donaldson*— Jones points to the distinctions between serious news and comedic entertainment. Jones also suggests that there are numerous sites of difference to investigate. This assignment asks that you take up Jones's work and investigate one of these other sites to see if his observations and conclusions hold true with other topics and in other kinds of popular/ public forums. There are two ways to proceed with your investigation:

1. Begin by selecting a topic of public discussion that is occurring in more than one kind of public forum. Record the conversations in at least two different forums— talk shows, editorial pages, stand-up comedies, Internet sites, and so on—and analyze the differences in both the nature of the discussion and the way the site is constructing the "public" who is interested in the topic.

2. Choose any two closely related media sites on the same day (or span of days) and record the topic of conversation. You might choose to follow two monologues on late night television, for example, or the cover story on two weekly newsmagazines. In this case you will have not only the differences in how the topic is discussed and how the public is constructed but also differences in what was considered important enough to talk about on a particular day. Be careful to avoid reruns since that will make it impossible to compare.

Present your analysis as a written response to Jones using specific details and examples from your study. Feel free to disagree with Jones; perhaps his study was atypical or current media interactions are very different from those of the Clinton scandal. How does your work help you think about the topic itself and the media's responses to or coverage of that topic?

When you've finished your writing, take a few minutes to write some authorial notes about your process. Try making a list of the steps you followed to complete this assignment. Was this process different in any way from your usual writing process? How would you do things differently if you were starting again knowing what you know now?

ASSIGNMENT 2: *READING CRITICALLY*

JULIA EKLUND KOZA, "RAP MUSIC: THE CULTURAL POLITICS OF OFFICIAL REPRESENTATION"

Koza's work shows how something new—in this case, rap music—gets evaluated even as it is presented to a public audience. By shifting the critique of the music away from the sections of the media usually associated with music, rap became a political and social threat rather than simply a new form of expression. Your task in this assignment is to see if the same kinds of shifts happen in media representations of other controversies or new forms of cultural expression.

Begin by selecting a controversy or criticism that, like rap music, can be easily traced in the media. You might consider issues of cultural expression commonly associated with younger generations such as tattoos, body piercing, hair styles, or particular articles of clothing. Or, you may want to consider other, earlier forms of music such as jazz, hip hop, or rock and roll and examine media from the relevant time period. You may want to select something that at the time it emerged represented something "new" and "unusual" (such as motorized cars in the early twentieth century or cell phones in the

1980s and 1990s). Using Koza as a guide, collect examples of the media representation of the phenomenon you've chosen, paying careful attention to where the articles appeared, what they said, and how they characterized the issues. You should follow the representation of your chosen focus over several years and in different kinds of media.

Using the material you've collected, create a written document that presents the representation as both a social history of the phenomenon you've chosen and as an interpretation of the role of media in representing and shaping the reception of this phenomenon. Your writing should be of interest to both readers who are interested in the topic you've selected (like rap music) and to those who are students of media even if they are not particularly interested in the topic.

Once you've finished the piece, make some additions to your authorial notes. What portions of your work are you most satisfied with and why? What portions would you rework if you could?

ASSIGNMENT 3: *READING IMAGES CRITICALLY*

LEO CHAVEZ, "DEVELOPING A VISUAL DISCOURSE ON IMMIGRATION"

Chavez's work suggests that the media plays an important role in shaping the attitudes or perceptions of the general public, but Chavez concentrates on how the visuals in print media play this role. Return to the topic you used in Assignment 1, or select a new topic that has figured predominantly or regularly in the media and amass a collection of visual images similar to those Chavez finds in magazine covers. You may be able to use magazine covers as Chavez did, but your visuals needn't be limited to covers since any visual material can be read for how it is representing the topic.

Once you have collected several images, present your analysis in writing. Like Chavez, you will want to read not only the overt messages being conveyed in your visual collection but also the subtleties conveyed by placement and other rhetorical choices. Feel free to use material from your earlier writing if that seems helpful in presenting your analysis. Your task is to present the visual material and how that material has shaped the representation of the topic you have selected, but also to consider how the visuals "advertise" the issue or the underlying ideology of the publication or its imagined audience.

Once you've completed the document, make additions to your authorial notes. What challenges did you face working with visual materials and how did you resolve those difficulties? What changes would you make if you were beginning the assignment again knowing what you now know?

ASSIGNMENT 4: *READING PERCEPTIONS OF MEDIA IMAGES*

MARÍA LEN-RÍOS ET AL., "REPRESENTATION OF WOMEN IN NEW AND PHOTOS: COMPARING CONTENT TO PERCEPTIONS"

Len-Ríos and her colleagues do a content analysis that is similar to the work done by Chavez, but they then survey both readers of the newspaper and the staff members of the publications they have examined to see if perceptions match the actual patterns of portrayal they have discovered. Extend your work in Assignment 3 by developing a survey of perceptions. Since it may be difficult to survey staff members of the publications you have been examining, target your survey to readers. You will want to use the material in Chapter 5 to help you design, conduct, and analyze your survey.

Present your findings in writing, incorporating material from your earlier documents as seems appropriate. You may, if you wish, alter the genre you use for the presentation, but you need not produce the formal social-science form that Len-Ríos and her colleagues use.

When you have finished your work, add to your authorial notes. What portions of doing a survey did you find most interesting? Most difficult? How did the earlier material change as you reworked it into this new context? Are any of those changes worth keeping even if you eliminated the survey?

ASSIGNMENT 5: *READING MEDIA'S APPROPRIATIONS OF IMAGES*

JANIS L. EDWARDS AND CAROL K. WINKLER, "REPRESENTATIVE FORM AND THE VISUAL IDEOGRAPH: THE IWO JIMA IMAGE IN EDITORIAL CARTOONS"

As Edwards and Winkler demonstrate, editorial cartoons are something more than images and not quite the same as written editorials or political commentary. Their research concentrates on a particular image that appears across cartoons about a number of different topics, but it is also possible to focus careful attention on the cartoons about a single topic, or featuring a single recognizable figure. Your task in this assignment is to experiment with analyzing editorial cartoons for yourself.

You may, if you wish, return to one of the topics you've used in earlier assignments, but you needn't be limited to these if some other issue or image seems to you more compelling, interesting, or curious. If you have no topic, figure, or image that you are interested in following through cartoon imagery, consider analyzing the cartoons of a single newspaper, cartoonist, or those from a particular date. You should collect as many cartoons as you can but certainly no fewer than five before you begin to analyze them. The suggestions in Chapter 3, particularly the checklist in Figure 3.8, should be helpful.

Present your analysis of the editorial cartoons you've collected in writing as carefully and completely as you can. You aren't just turning the visual images into a discursive version, however, since your writing should make an argument about the significance of these cartoons as vehicles that shape and reflect cultural beliefs and values and that aim to influence, persuade, or critique.

When you're finished with your writing, add to your authorial notes. What could your work teach others about writing? What do you think you need to learn to do to improve your writing?

ASSIGNMENT 6: *THE WAY OTHERS HAVE "READ" THE TOPIC*

MELANIE LOWE, "COLLIDING FEMINISMS: BRITNEY SPEARS, 'TWEENS,' AND THE POLITICS OF RECEPTION"

In her piece about Britney Spears, Melanie Lowe uses focus groups as part of an argument about the significance (or lack thereof) of media representations of personal identity. Assemble a focus group, and assess their knowledge of one of the topics you've worked with in earlier assignments. The material in Chapter 4 will help you prepare for the focus group discussion and consider who you should invite to participate. In general you will be concerned with such questions as: What does your group have to say on the topic? What do they know? What do they not know? What are the sources of their information? What are their general opinions on the topic? You should spend thirty minutes to one hour with your focus group in order to generate enough data for your analysis.

Write a paper that ties together the findings from your focus group with your previous research and writing on this topic. In light of all of your previous research, how do you think media representations have contributed (or not contributed) to the opinions you discovered in the members of your focus groups. Can you make a direct or indirect connection between media representations and what individuals know/believe/feel on your topic? Feel free to use any relevant parts of your earlier writings, but make sure those recycled sections are framed and revised to contribute effectively to this new piece of writing. Remember that you don't have to use all of the comments from the discussion since you aren't producing a transcript of that event but rather using this material as data to be interpreted.

Once you've completed the paper, make additions to your authorial notes. If you were able to incorporate passages from your earlier writing, how did you decide what to use and how to rework it? If you didn't reuse any of your earlier writing, what kept you from doing so?

ASSIGNMENT 7: *RECONSIDERING MEDIA IMPACT*

Read through the documents you have written this term, and consider what you can say now about media that you could not have said at the beginning of the term. Write a paper that can serve to introduce your collection of work to those who might be interested in media or the topics you've chosen to investigate. The hardest part of this assignment is to avoid saying only what you think your teacher expects you to say. Instead treat your work as evidence, and read it as a researcher would. When/if you incorporate passages of your earlier work, be certain to cite it appropriately.

RECLAIMING THE PAST

YUNG; EDWARDS AND WINKLER; LEWIS; PROWN; FRISCH

This sequence asks you to experiment with various ways of investigating history, including collecting oral histories, working with historical images, digging in archival records, and closely examining historical artifacts. While it may be possible to do each assignment with a different topic or focus, you will probably learn more and have a better sense of working with historical methods if you choose a single event or time period to investigate throughout these assignments.

ASSIGNMENT 1: *TELLING AND RETELLING*

JUDY YUNG, "A BOWLFUL OF TEARS' REVISITED: THE FULL STORY OF LEE PUEY YOU'S IMMIGRATION EXPERIENCE AT ANGEL ISLAND"

Oral histories can be both powerful and misleading, detailed additions to a general history or truncated accounts that raise more questions than they answer. Your task in this assignment is to try your hand at collecting an oral history. Because this sequence is asking you to work with the past, you should interview someone from a different generation. There are at least two ways to begin:

1. Decide first on the topic or moment in history that you want to investigate, and find a person to interview who has something to contribute from their first hand experience. You might choose a particularly memorable event or period of time as a starting point, but be open to the possibility that what your informant has to tell is actually a story of daily, normal life during that period of time. Using the discussion of Oral Histories in Chapter 4 as a guide, prepare questions in advance and be certain to get written permission from your informant to both tape record the interview and to use it in your writing.

2. You may know an informant who you think will be interesting no matter what topic they choose to tell you about. An older member of your family, a member of your campus community who has been around long enough to see some important changes, or a person who is new to your area might be likely sources of interesting stories. Again, prepare in advance, be certain to get permission to use the material you collect, and stay open to interesting yet unexpected directions.

Present your oral history in writing, providing as much of the contextual detail as necessary to help your readers understand both the informant and the story they are telling.

When you're finished, take a few minutes to write some authorial notes. What challenges or surprises did you encounter in this assignment, and how did you handle them? What would you do differently if you could?

ASSIGNMENT 2: *WORKING WITH IMAGES OF THE PAST*

JANIS L. EDWARDS AND CAROL K. WINKLER, "REPRESENTATIVE FORM AND THE VISUAL IDEOGRAPH: THE IWO JIMA IMAGE IN EDITORIAL CARTOONS"

Using the historical period you used for Assignment 1, collect editorial cartoons that comment on and critique the events of this period or that you think reflect the issues of concern during this time frame.

You may want to narrow your focus to a particular region of the country and the newspapers of that region, or you may want to follow a single controversy or public figure in order to keep your work manageable. If no particular event seems to lend itself to this assignment, consider collecting the cartoons that appeared in different publications during the same week. Plan to collect at least five examples of cartoons that you can read closely. Look for patterns across the collection, as well as the nuances of the individual cartoons. The guidelines in Figure 3.8 should be helpful.

Present your work in writing. The document you produce should not simply turn the visuals into a discursive account since your object is to consider the significance of these images and how they reflect the period and its concerns. You are, then, making an argument about how to understand this past via these cartoons.

When you have finished your work, add to your authorial notes to record difficulties, changes in your writing processes, and/or interesting facets of your work that you had to leave out of your final document. What strategies did you use in this assignment that you did not use in collecting or presenting the oral history?

ASSIGNMENT 3: *RECLAIMING THE PAST IN PHYSICAL STRUCTURES*

PEIRCE LEWIS, "COMMON LANDSCAPES AS HISTORIC DOCUMENTS"

Lewis's article demonstrates how the physical structures of a community can be read as signs of an otherwise forgotten (or ignored) past. Such reading is complicated, and Lewis warns us both at the beginning and again at the end of his piece that simple observation of the physical landscape can produce a caricature rather than real understanding, that good fieldwork takes considerable preparation, and that landscape observation can raise more questions than it answers. With these cautions in mind, select a particular community or portion of a community that was constructed during the time period you are investigating, or one that shows signs of that time period even if only in reproduction.

If you are working with original architecture, you will want to consult maps of the location you have selected and gain a perspective of the whole from some higher vantage point—a hill or tall building—where you can see the entire lay of the land. If you cannot find maps or a vantage point from which to see the wider landscape, look for aerial photos or satellite shots of the area. You will also need to spend time on the ground, observing and taking notes of what you observe at the street level, in different parts of the area you've selected and with attention to different aspects of buildings or other structures in the location. You will need to spend time in the library as well, tracing the elements of architectural style to particular periods of community development and history. Feel free to take photographs or make sketches to remind you of your observations and incorporate these visuals into the final writing. You might choose to work with one or more of your classmates, conducting your observations together and helping each other to ask questions and speculate on the features you can observe. In some communities it is possible to take walking or riding tours with a local historian. You may want to take advantage of such a service, but do not allow the tour to substitute for your own careful observations, note taking, and question posing.

If you are working with architectural elements that are reproductions rather than original constructions, you will probably need to spend even more time in the library (or in the archives of city offices) to determine why these particular elements from the past have been incorporated into newer buildings. Don't neglect, however, the work of direct observation. Again, use photographs and sketches to remind you of your observations and to provide illustrations for your written account.

Once you have observed the location carefully and as fully as possible in the time you have available to you, write a detailed account of your observations as a way of demonstrating its links to the past, or the way this area has erased (or forgotten) its past. Your writing should be a demonstration of what Lewis calls "reading the landscape," but it should also be a continuation of your consideration of how we can (or do) reclaim the past.

Be certain to add to your authorial notes when you are done with your account. You might consider such issues as: How is your writing process changing as you move to different kinds of historical investigation? What parts of your work are you particularly pleased with, and which parts would you do differently if you had more time? What questions have arisen as you do your investigations that you simply haven't been able to answer?

ASSIGNMENT 4: *WORKING WITH ARTIFACTS*

JULES DAVID PROWN, "THE TRUTH OF MATERIAL CULTURE: HISTORY OF FICTION?"

Your task in this assignment is to add to your historical project by working carefully and closely with an object from the same period of time or that is relevant in some way to the work you have been doing. You may have to visit a museum to locate an appropriate artifact, and you will probably have to think creatively in order to find an interesting and appropriate object to examine. If you must, step outside the moment in history that you have been working with so far and choose an object from a different time that you find intriguing in some way.

Following Prown's lead, describe the object fully and in detail, and consider both its function and its underlying ideology in a written document. What makes this object an "artifact" of a particular historical period? That is, what marks it as *historical*? Present your work, with or without accompanying illustrations, so that anyone interested in history or in the culture represented by your artifact can learn something by attending to it under your guidance.

When you have finished your descriptive analysis, add to your authorial notes anything new you've learned about working with historical materials or writing history from this assignment. What do you think your work could teach others about writing or about history?

ASSIGNMENT 5: *ASSESSING HISTORICAL MEMORY*

MICHAEL FRISCH, "AMERICAN HISTORY AND THE STRUCTURES OF COLLECTIVE MEMORY: A MODEST EXERCISE IN EMPIRICAL ICONOGRAPHY"

Frisch's informal survey of his students demonstrated what might be called the "common knowledge" of a particularly broad period of American history—the beginning through the Civil War. Your task in this assignment is to find out what people know and/or remember about the time period you have been investigating by conducting a similar survey.

Think carefully about how to frame the survey question(s) to solicit an appropriate list of "common knowledge." You may want to consult history books, especially textbooks, to see what issues, people, or events are regularly included and compare this coverage to what your survey respondents remember. The material in Chapter 5 should help you think about the issues involved in designing, conducting, and analyzing your survey.

Once you've generated the lists of remembered learning, present your analysis of the data in a written document. Follow Frisch's lead in considering what such remembered history tells us about schooling and/or our collective understanding of the period you have been investigating. While some of your earlier writing may be incorporated, the focus of this piece of writing should be on the survey data you've collected.

When you are finished with your writing, add to your authorial notes. How is working with survey data different from the other forms of historical work you've done? What strategies did you use in this assignment that might be useful in revising your earlier work?

ASSIGNMENT 6: *REFLECTION ON HISTORY*

Turn to the authorial notes you have been keeping throughout the sequence, and write a paper that can introduce your other work and that comments on the experience of reclaiming the past through historical writing. What have you learned, and how is that learning visible in the writing you have produced? The hardest part of this assignment is to avoid saying what you think is expected. Instead, treat your work as evidence that needs to be interpreted just like any other historical evidence.

REPRESENTING COMMUNITY

BACHIN; SHACKEL; WHITE

This sequence asks you to investigate a single community, examining its physical aspects, its common practices, and the values implied in those practices.

ASSIGNMENT 1: *COMMUNITY SPACES*

ROBIN BACHIN, "COURAGE, ENDURANCE AND QUICKNESS OF DECISION: GENDER AND ATHLETICS AT THE UNIVERSITY OF CHICAGO, 1890–1920"

Robin Bachin's history of the women's gymnasium at the University of Chicago demonstrates how a physical space can embody cultural values, even when those values are in transition. Though Bachin uses archival records, she is also presenting her own close observations of the physical features of one building. This assignment asks you to conduct your own investigation of a local area that serves as a "public space" and develop an argument about how that space functions within the community relying on close observation as your primary method of investigation.

You could choose a place on your college campus or somewhere in the surrounding community like a park, pedestrian mall, or civic center. No matter what place you choose, it's important that it be open to human interactions. Thus a turnpike or interstate highway is "public" but not workable for this assignment because individuals do not get out of their cars and interact (except in times of crisis). The rest stops alongside the highway, however, are public spaces where interaction *is* possible, even though it might not be desired. Refer to the suggestions in Chapter 3 for observation strategies and consider working with classmates in order to extend your observations across different days or times of day. For your investigation to be complete, you must not simply record your experiences as a member of this local community or as a by-stander. Instead use close and systematic observations and consider what meaning you can derive from this space, even if you cannot see how it represents the kind of cultural values in transition that Bachin is concerned with.

Once you have collected your observations about this public space, write a document in which you present your research as an example of interpreting a public space. You will need to push beyond simply reporting what you observe to make an argument about how this place functions as a public space. What kinds of human interactions occur in this space? Do the physical features of the space contribute to those interactions or impede them? You may want to consider the public space you observed alongside the spaces observed by your classmates in order to think more critically about the nature and meaning of public spaces. How does your space, as one of a network or system of public spaces, contribute, or fail to contribute, to a public life that is distinct from our private lives?

When you've finished the writing, take a few minutes to make some authorial notes. What process did you follow to complete this writing assignment? How was that process different from, or similar to, your usual process?

ASSIGNMENT 2: *COMMUNITY MEMBERS*

Locate, observe, interview, and write about an individual who operates in the crossroads of difference in your locale. This person might serve to unite the community through the services he provides, or she might reflect the history of the community or its changing demographics. Your task here is to consider some personality of the local community and the interactions of its members as reflected in the life of this individual.

Present the story of this individual who operates at the crossroads of your community in writing and in a way that would be interesting to those who are members of the community, as well as to those who might not know it personally. If you include photographs, be certain not to let these visuals substitute for written description and analysis.

When you're finished, make additions to your authorial notes. How is writing about an individual different from, or similar to, writing about a location?

ASSIGNMENT 3: *SHARED VALUES AND COMMUNITY PRACTICES*

This assignment asks that you turn from the concrete community represented by individuals or physical spaces to the more *invisible* community formed by shared values and believes. Those beliefs and values are shaped, at least in part, by the kinds of practices that are allowed or promoted as appropriate. This assignment asks you to consider what invisible communities exist within the physical community you have been investigating, that is, what practices serve to shape an invisible community of values and beliefs within the physical locale of your earlier work?

You might begin by making a list of the common practices of your community. For campus communities, such items as going to class, attending sporting events, hanging out in the cafeteria might all be on your list. But push beyond these common items to consider the full range of behaviors members of your physical community engage in as well as whether those practices divide members of the physical community into smaller communities of shared values and beliefs. Once you have a fairly complete list, choose one public practice, event, or spectacle that is generally regarded positively but that you suspect has a negative side or negative consequences. Observe that practice first hand, but also consider collecting information by surveying or interviewing participants and by reading about the event or practice you are investigating. You will already have an idea of the negative side of this practice and you will want to collect information that confirms or contradicts your suspicions, but you will also need to remain open to the possibility that there is something else going on that was not immediately visible to you.

Write your description and analysis of this practice or event as a way to consider how it impacts on individuals or groups and how it constructs a community based on shared beliefs or values. Your task is not to argue for or against this practice, but rather to consider what the practice says about "community" and about how we think about the people or groups who belong to this community. You may decide that you *do* want to argue against this practice or that the practice is appropriate, but that should take a secondary position in your writing to the analysis and deliberation you offer of its role in shaping community. As you develop this written document, you'll need to consider the direct and invoked audiences carefully and may find the discussion of these issues in Chapter 2 helpful.

Once you've finished your writing, make additions to your authorial notes. What strategies did you use in this assignment that might be useful to you if you were to revise your earlier work?

ASSIGNMENT 4: *CONFLICT AND COLLECTIVITY*

PAUL SHACKEL, "PUBLIC MEMORY AND THE SEARCH FOR POWER IN AMERICAN HISTORICAL ARCHAEOLOGY"

As Shackel's work makes clear, there is often a history behind everyday objects, public art, or objects that represent us, and that history is often contested because members of a physical community may not be members of the same invisible community who share common values and beliefs. Members of these different ideological communities have to come together and coexist in physical proximity, and so their differences are often glossed over or rendered invisible unless one knows how to look carefully and see the compromises. The different ideological communities may be so at odds that they separate physically as well. Using the community you have been working with and whatever archival records or history you can uncover, present the fuller story of some aspect of the physical community where different groups or interests have had to negotiate their differences or compromise in a common task.

Work with Shackel as a guide and become an historical archaeologist. This is not precisely the same as writing about what is ordinarily missed, but it is closely related. You might begin by consulting existing histories of your community, but you might also turn to concrete objects such as buildings or landmarks because such objects are often sites of community compromise. To write a history of a concrete object, landmark, or monument, you need to have historical documents, differing accounts, and evidence to show your readers that the traces of this history are actually still present, if they only knew how to see them. Such documents may be available in archival holdings, or you may have to cull them from newspaper accounts or interviews with those who remember.

When you have done as much investigation as you can in the time you have available, write a document that tells the story as a history *and* as an argument about the significance of that history to the larger community you are investigating. The genre you choose for your writing will depend, of course, on what methods you've used and what you've been able to find.

When you're done with your writing, add to your authorial notes. Is there some aspect of your work that you are particularly satisfied with? Why? What portions would you rework if you could?

ASSIGNMENT 5: *COMMUNITY INSTITUTIONS*

JAMES BOYD WHITE, "HUMAN DIGNITY AND THE CLAIM OF MEANING: ATHENIAN TRAGIC DRAMA AND SUPREME COURT OPINIONS"

White uses a close reading of Greek tragedies and the Supreme Court opinion in *Cohen v. California* to argue that both are sites where community values are constructed through discourse. In a sense White's work is concerned with the kind of "invisible" community shaped by values and beliefs that you considered in Assignment 3. Test and extend White's work in one of three ways:

1. Attend a theatrical performance and/or secure a copy of the written play to analyze as a site of public discourse. Do contemporary plays (or at least this play) function in the same ways as White outlines for Greek tragedies? What aspects of the play make it an appropriate form of public discourse, how does it work to shape the audience's understanding of the issues it addresses and how does it construct the community? If you cannot attend a live play, you can try the same approach with a film or video.

2. Select another Supreme Court opinion to analyze. Does it make the moves White describes? How does it answer the questions White poses at the end of his essay? How does the case you are working with construct or represent community?

3. Identify another textual artifact of the community you considered in Assignment 3. Working closely with one or more examples, present these texts as reflective of the values and beliefs you considered before. How does the text either enact or contradict those beliefs? How does the text construct and represent its community?

In either of these options, you will be reading the text closely and critically, with attention to its language and how it constitutes the world and invites its audience to imagine the issues with which it is concerned.

Present your reading of the text in writing. You should focus on demonstrating how the text you've chosen functions as an example of public discourse that constructs and represents the community and its values, showing others how to read this text as an example of White's characterizations of ideal discourse. Do not expect your readers to already be familiar with White's work, however. And if you think White is wrong, use your work to speak back to him.

When you're finished, add to your authorial notes. What kind of language did you use to complete this assignment? What do you think your work could teach others about writing? What would you like to learn about writing from someone else in your class?

ASSIGNMENT 6: *RECONSIDERING COMMUNITY*

Drawing on the work you have done so far as well as the work of your classmates, write a paper in which you make an argument about your community, about how your community functions, and what stories it tells about itself. In other words consider community as both a physical space with identifiable characters and as an invisible collection of shared memories, beliefs, and values which sometimes have to be negotiated in order for the physical space to be shared. Your writing might incorporate pieces of your earlier work, or serve to introduce those pieces. If you make use of work your classmates have done as evidence, be certain to cite that work appropriately.

TRYING OUT INTERVIEWS

A SEQUENCE WITHOUT READINGS

This assignment sequence asks you to conduct interviews and then to revise your work in various ways. Throughout the process you are encouraged to keep authorial notes of your processes and insights so that by the end of the sequence you can comment in an informed way about the challenges and potential of interviewing as a method of inquiry.

ASSIGNMENT 1: *INTERVIEW AS EXPLORATION*

Following the practical and ethical guidelines discussed in Chapter 4, conduct an interview to explore one or more theoretical questions. Use conversational questions to interview one of the subjects you've identified as appropriate for your investigation.

Write a paper in which you present an argument about the significance of your interview data. First, introduce your topic and your research questions. Explain what drew your attention to the topic as a way to secure your audience's interest. Next, explain your methodology in detail. For instance, whom did you interview, and why did you select this individual? How did you develop your questions? When presenting your findings, use both exact quotations and paraphrase, and be sure to analyze each of the quotations you incorporate.

When you have finished presenting your interview and arguing for its significance, take time to write a few authorial notes about your experience. You might consider: What did you learn about your research questions through this interview? What other steps might you take to further explore the subject—perhaps using other inquiry methods presented in this text?

ASSIGNMENT 2: *INTERVIEW TO FILL IN GAPS*

The introduction to Chapter 4 mentions that interviews can be useful in finding information that is not included in published accounts or in considering perspectives typically left out of official versions. Find a recent newspaper or popular magazine article on a current event or topic of interest to you, read it carefully, and develop a list of questions it leaves unanswered and a list of individuals whose viewpoints have been excluded. Try to find answers to your queries and/or fill in the missing standpoint using an appropriate interview.

Although you already have a sense of the topic your interview will investigate, take the time to develop a set of theoretical/research questions, as well as the corresponding conversational ones. In other words, you can't simply ask your subject their answer to the one missing question, or ask them to tell you their account of the event or topic reported in the original article. Conduct your interview and transcribe your session. Write a paper in which you present and examine your interview findings, that is, present the missing material.

When you have finished your paper, add to your authorial notes. Consider: How do your interview findings help you explain why the question you identified had been left unanswered by the media or authors you read? Why had the missing viewpoint been excluded? Who or what determines the kind of information that is included and whose voice is heard? What other steps might you take to further explore the subject?

ASSIGNMENT 3: *SUGGESTED REVISION:*
FOLLOW-UP INQUIRY

Go back to the interview paper you wrote in Assignment 1 and follow-up on your response to the question, "What other steps might you take to further explore the subject?" In other words, take some of the steps you felt would help you gain a fuller understanding of your research question. Feel free to use any of the inquiry methods described in this text. Use this new information to enhance and reconsider your first paper. It is acceptable to reuse those portions of your first paper that are still relevant, but be certain to rework those sections you choose to incorporate so your finished work is unified in tone and style.

After you've finished making your revision, add some authorial notes about your experience. You might consider: How did this additional research impact your original analysis of the transcript? What's still left to be explored, and what other methods would you need to use in order to answer the questions you still have (or the new ones that have arisen)?

ASSIGNMENT 4: *SUGGESTED REVISION: TAILORING TO AN AUDIENCE*

When writing Assignment 2, you may have found that one of the reasons specific content or perspectives were excluded was because the piece was trying to reach a general audience. As explained in the segment "What Does Audience Have to Do with It?" in Chapter 2, authors must examine their audience and tailor their writing accordingly. For this assignment, rewrite one of your earlier papers for a different audience. You might, for example, represent your work for a specific discipline, redirect your work to a younger audience, or revise the piece to speak more directly to one gender rather than both. How you shift audience will, in part, depend on your topic. Spend some time researching your intended audience by looking at other publications that are designed for these readers. Remember that shifting audience may require additional research, as well as changes both big and small in the presentation of your material and ideas.

When you have finished writing for this new audience, take a few minutes to make some authorial notes. What did you learn about the subject by reframing your writing toward this new group of readers? What challenges did you face as you made this transformation?

ASSIGNMENT 5: *SUGGESTED REVISION: COLLABORATION*

Although you and your classmates may have been working from different theoretical questions and surely have interviewed different people, there are very likely some connections in your work. Working in teams, identify papers in your class that speak to one another, or that address related issues. Then, again in teams of at least two people, develop a plan for merging the perspectives of this work together. You may need to add additional research or use interview material that you eliminated earlier as you reframe your work. Your task, though, is to write a paper in collaboration with others, being certain that none of the original authors feel that their work has been misused.

Alternatively, trade transcripts of one of your first two interviews with a classmate. Using the transcript of an interview you did not conduct, write a paper that makes use of this material. You might, for example, see a different point of significance in the piece, or you might combine the transcript with information from other sources that are different from those your classmate used. As you write from your colleague's material, be certain to check any unclear details, to acknowledge his/her work in providing you with the transcript, and to cite the original author if you decide to incorporate any of that writing in your own paper.

When your work is complete, add to your authorial notes. Be certain to record any difficulties you encountered using a transcript of an interview you did not conduct or working in collaboration with others. Consider also how your view of your own earlier work changed as you worked with someone else's material.

ASSIGNMENT 6: *SUGGESTED REVISION: MOVING OUTSIDE THE CLASSROOM*

Revise any of the work you've done so far to make the account more than just a class assignment. Such a revision should make your interviews understandable to an audience outside your class, but you will have to decide who that audience is and why they would want to read what you have to say. Depending on what you decide to revise, and what audience you think would be interested in your work, the form of presentation will change. You might, for example, rewrite your account as a feature essay for a local newspaper or magazine, as a letter to the editor about missing points of view, or as a guide for younger writers on writing collaboratively.

When you have finished your piece for an audience outside the classroom context, spend some time writing authorial notes to consider: How is writing for "publication" different from the work you've done for classes? Why did you choose the piece you did? How did you decide on the audience and format of your piece? What other options for "publication" do you see in the work you or your classmates have done with interviews?

ASSIGNMENT 7: *REFLECTIVE PRACTICE: RECONSIDERING INTERVIEWING*

Reread the various pieces you've written using interviews. Be certain to consider the authorial notes you've written as well. Then write a reflective piece about your work that could serve to introduce these documents if they were collected together. You might consider in your paper such issues as: What have you learned about interviewing that would not be obvious to someone who had never conducted an interview? How did the revisions you undertook complicate your view of this research method? What ethical issues arose for you as you worked with interviews? Provide specific examples by citing or quoting examples from your own or your classmates' work.

You might also speculate about further work that might be done by considering such questions as: If you were going to continue any of the projects you've done so far, what would you choose and why? How would you pursue this next step in your inquiry, and what do you think you would have to learn how to do in order to take this next step? What would you do differently if you were starting over with these projects? What are the limitations of interviewing as a method of inquiry, and what are its advantages? Remember to consider your own development as a writer, including what new strategies you learned for working on your writing; how your writing changed over the term; and where you still have work to do to make your writing more effective.

VISUAL RHETORIC: PHOTOGRAPHS

LUTZ AND COLLINS; SPENCE; EDWARDS AND WINKLER; CHAVEZ

This sequence invites you to consider the construction and use of photographs as a form of knowledge. How do researchers examine photographic images, and what do they expect to learn from them? How have photographers been influenced by other forms of art? What do historical photographs tells us that might be ignored or overlooked in other historical records and accounts? Finally, how do photographic images represent the physical world and the people who inhabit it?

ASSIGNMENT 1: *PHOTOGRAPHS OF "OTHERS"*

CATHERINE A. LUTZ AND JANE L. COLLINS, "THE PHOTOGRAPH AS AN INTERSECTION OF GAZES"

Lutz and Collins demonstrate how photographs can be read and interpreted as "stories about looking," and they are particularly interested in how American readers of *National Geographic* magazine looked at photographs of foreign peoples and in the process were led to consider the identities of these "others" as well as their own. Extend and test Lutz and Collins's work by collecting your own magazine photographs of those who would be considered "other."

You may decide to use the *National Geographic* as Lutz and Collins did but to concentrate on photographs of American ethnic groups rather than foreign populations, or you could consider photographs of children in magazines meant for adults. In any case, you should collect as many different examples as you can and plan to use at least three of them in your final written report of your work. You may want to work with classmates to cover as many different publications and as broad a time frame as possible, and then divide up the photographs you collect in ways that make sense to your interests and the material you find. The material in Chapter 3 should help you think about how to analyze your visual collection, looking for patterns across the group, as well as the particulars about the individual photographs.

Present your analysis of these photographs in writing as carefully and completely as you can. Follow Lutz and Collins's lead to consider "gaze" and how it works in your photographic collection, but do not be afraid to speak back to them, showing them how your examples fit or challenge their conclusions.

When you're finished with your writing, take a few minutes to make some authorial notes. What process did you use to complete this assignment? Was that process different from your usual way of writing?

ASSIGNMENT 2: *PHOTOGRAPHS AND ART*

STEVE SPENCE, "VAN GOGH IN ALABAMA, 1936"

As Steve Spence's analysis of Van Gogh's paintings and Walker Evans's photographs make clear, photographic images often borrow from techniques of more traditional art work. Your task in this assignment is to experiment with these connections, using Spence's work as a guide. There are at least three ways to do this work:

1. Select several photographs from those produced by the other photographers who contributed to the Farm Security Administration–Office of War Information Collection available at the Library of Congress Web site at http://memory.loc.gov/ ammem/fsowhome.html. Work closely with the images you have selected to read

the images themselves as examples of artistic expression and to consider how they may reflect stylistic features typical of the artist who took them. To do this last step, you will have to spend some time in the library finding out what you can about the individual artist.

2. Gather together other photographs from a similar time period or by the same photographer. Consult the suggestions in Chapter 3 for possible sources of such photographs. Examine your collection for patterns of similarity in design, composition, or technique. Research enough of the history of the context of these photographs that you can offer an explanation of what may have influenced these similarities.

3. Visit an exhibit of photographs in an art museum or gallery. Take careful notes of the details of these images, looking especially for any common patterns across the collection. Research as much as possible the context for the creation of these images, including any information you can find about the photographer or the creation of the exhibit. You may have to rely on the museum guide or identifying labels for this information, but consider interviewing the curator or artist for additional background information.

Present your reading of your photographic collection in writing using at least two different images as evidence of an argument you want to advance about how to read them. Draw on the historical research you've done, and if appropriate, include references to works of art. As you work to read and present these images, you'll also want to consider the differences and similarities between photography and other forms of art.

When you're finished, add to your authorial notes. What difficulties or surprises did you encounter as you worked on this assignment? What would you do differently if you were beginning again knowing what you now know?

ASSIGNMENT 3: *APPROPRIATIONS OF PHOTOGRAPHIC IMAGES*

JANIS L. EDWARDS AND CAROL K. WINKLER, "REPRESENTATIVE FORM AND THE VISUAL IDEOGRAPH: THE IWO JIMA IMAGE IN EDITORIAL CARTOONS"

The famous photograph of Iwo Jima is not the only image that has been appropriated for other uses. In fact historical photographs are often appropriated as decorations for restaurants, turned into posters and postcards, altered or imitated in advertisements, or, as Edwards and Winkler demonstrate, refigured in editorial cartoons. Work with your classmates to identify as many examples of photographic reuse and appropriation as you can. Then, working closely with two or more of these appropriations, consider whether the particular photographic image works, as Edwards and Winkler claim the Iwo Jima image does, as an ideograph. It may well be the case that this other image functions differently, and does not meet the criteria for a visual ideograph as outlined by Edwards and Winkler. But consider why the image would be appropriated or reused. What does its reuse tell us about the past that produced it and the present that continues to circulate this image?

Present your analysis as completely as you can in writing so that your audience will understand both how to read these appropriations and what the act of appropriation means. Use your work to speak back to Edwards and Winkler, extending their work or pointing out how they may be wrong, but in a way that readers who do not know Edwards and Winkler's work can understand.

Add to your authorial notes when you're finished. What parts of your work are you most satisfied with and why? What would you rework if you could?

ASSIGNMENT 4: *VISUAL DISCOURSE AND POPULAR MEDIA*

LEO R. CHAVEZ, "DEVELOPING A VISUAL DISCOURSE ON IMMIGRATION"

Chavez is interested in the use of visual images, often photographic images, that serve to represent a topic of interest in the popular media. His careful analysis required a systematic tracing of these images on the covers of popular magazines, categorizing the results into patterns, and then considering what those patterns say about our culture and the media that informs and represents us.

Your task in this assignment is to follow the photographic images that accompany some other topic of repeated media interest. You needn't limit yourself to magazine covers, but you should collect examples from as long a time span as possible and from at least three different publications. You may find it helpful to work with classmates to identify a topic to analyze and then to systematically collect photographic images from the publications you find most applicable to your topic. The material in Chapter 3 should help you think about patterns across the collection, as well as the features of individual photographs.

Present your findings, using at least three different images in your final document, with close attention to the specific features of the images and to how these images reflect the coverage of the topic you are following. You task is not merely to describe these images, but to analyze them and their function. As you make your argument, you may find that you are agreeing with Chavez, extending his work into another area, or that you are speaking back to Chavez, contradicting his conclusions by considering a different topic. If it seems useful to refer to Chavez in your own analysis, remember that your readers will not necessarily know his work or understand it in the same way that you do.

When you're finished, add to your authorial notes. What could your work teach others about writing? What would you like to learn about writing from others?

ASSIGNMENT 5: *COLLABORATION*

Although you and your classmates have been working on different projects, using different images, and writing individual papers, there are probably some interesting connections in the work you are doing. Work with your classmates to identify the possibilities for combining the work you've been doing to stretch your analysis, provide additional or contrasting examples, or otherwise complicate your investigations.

Then, working in teams of at least two writers/investigators, write a paper that draws upon the earlier work produced by you and your classmates. You will need to be certain to reference this earlier work appropriately and to work closely with the original authors to be certain that your analysis does not misrepresent their investigations. You need not agree with their interpretations or accept their original arguments without question; instead your challenge is to produce a new text that is both accurate and novel.

When you are finished with this collaborative paper, add to your authorial notes. How is writing in collaboration with others different from writing on your own? What did you learn from your classmate(s) that you might be able to use in future assignments? What did your classmate(s) learn from you?

ASSIGNMENT 6: *MOVING BEYOND THE CLASSROOM*

Look back at the work you've done so far, and select one of these earlier pieces to revise for an audience that is outside your classroom. Who might be interested in the investigations into photographs that you've done? What form of presentation would let you speak to these potential readers? You might, for example, compose a photographic essay that combines text and images. You might write a feature article for a local magazine or newspaper. You might reframe your work to be a museum or gallery guide for an exhibit, or you might present your work with magazines as a lesson in critical reading aimed at younger students.

When you are finished with this revision for a non–classroom audience, add to your authorial notes. What difficulties did you encounter in moving your investigations outside the academic arena? Which parts of your work are you especially pleased with, and which parts seem to you to still need more work? Are there any strategies you used in producing this revision that might be useful if you were to revise the original documents for an academic audience?

ASSIGNMENT 7: *REFLECTING ON PHOTOGRAPHS*

Reread the work you have done in this sequence. Using examples from your own work as well as that of your classmates, write a paper that synthesizes what you have learned about the visual rhetoric of photographs. What can you say now that you wouldn't have known to say about photographs before? What have you learned about writing and incorporating visuals into your writing, and where is there still more work to be done if you had more time? Use your paper as a way of introducing the collection of writing you have done in this sequence, but also as a piece of writing that makes an argument about some aspect of photographic images or the visual rhetoric they employ.

WORKING WITH TEXTS

A SEQUENCE WITHOUT READINGS

This sequence asks you to experiment with different kinds of texts and to write about them using different methods of textual analysis. We expect that Chapter 6 will be helpful and that the kinds of texts we invite you to work with in this sequence will not require you to read hundreds of additional pages. At the end of your investigations, you should be able to say something about the challenges and possibilities of working with textual inquiry.

ASSIGNMENT 1: *WORKING WITH EDITORIALS*

Begin by conducting a simplified content analysis of editorials or letters to the editor in a particular publication. You might want to work with classmates to examine a local newspaper over time, or you might choose a professional journal that includes letters or a response section and/or has an editorial as a regular feature. Use your content analysis to help you select a particular editorial to work with more closely. Using the guidelines in Chapter 6 to assist you, present your close reading of this text with particular attention to its rhetorical moves, language, and structure. If you can use the content analysis to identify patterns or recurring themes, feel free to do so. Your analysis should demonstrate how to read the editorial as a typical or unusual example, or otherwise make an argument about why such a piece of prose is worth our attention.

When you are finished with your writing, take a few minutes to make some authorial notes about your experience doing this assignment. What was your process for completing this writing? Would you change any of this process if you were to repeat similar work in the future?

ASSIGNMENT 2: *EDITORIALS AS EVIDENCE*

Return to one of the editorials you worked with in Assignment 1 and consider it as a piece of evidence. If you think of it, for example, as an historian would, what does this editorial say about this particular moment in history? Or think of it as a sociologist, cultural anthropologist, or linguist would. You may need to return to your content analysis and select additional pieces that support your sense of this piece as evidence of a particular kind. And you may need to do work in the library to develop this context for the particular editorial you have selected. Revise your analysis from Assignment 1 to re-present this text as evidence in a new piece of writing.

Once you have finished your revised analysis, add to your authorial notes. How was working on this revision different from the original composing process?

ASSIGNMENT 3: *CHILDREN'S BOOKS*

Select a book intended for small children. This may be a book that you remember well from your own childhood or one you borrow from a library. Picture books will probably work best for this assignment, because longer works will give you more text than you can reasonably analyze. Obviously wordless picture books are not suitable. Reread the book carefully, paying attention to its structural features as a piece of literature. You may want to attend to the interaction between the images and the written language, but there may be other features that seem to you more interesting or curious. Present your analysis in writing as an example of close reading, demonstrating to your own readers how to attend to such a text and how it functions as a piece of literature.

When you're finished, add to your authorial notes. What strategies of writing have you learned from this assignment that you could apply to other kinds of writing you have been asked to do in different courses or in life?

ASSIGNMENT 4: *CHILDREN'S BOOKS RECONSIDERED*

Return to the book you worked with in Assignment 3, and consider it not as literature but as a cultural object. For example, consider such questions as: How does this book construct childhood? How do its images represent adults? What does its publication history tell us about its culture? What values does the story celebrate or challenge? How does the book fit within the lifework of its author? You may want to draw upon the books used by your classmates to strengthen or complicate the meaning you think this book suggests when viewed as a cultural object. Present your analysis in writing, reworking your earlier close reading as appropriate to this new inquiry.

Once you've completed the paper, make additions to your authorial notes. How is the process of writing about books as literature different from writing about them as cultural objects?

ASSIGNMENT 5: *WORKING WITH FORMAL SPEECHES*

Select a famous speech that you find interesting enough and compelling enough to examine closely. The speech should be available to you in writing so you can read it repeatedly, but if it is also available in an audio format, such a recording may be useful to your analysis as well. Present your close reading of the rhetoric of this speech in a written document that shows others how to do such work. What features of this speech make it memorable enough to warrant the label "famous"?

When you're done, add to your authorial notes. What challenges or surprises have you encountered in these assignments and how did you handle them? What would you do differently if you could?

ASSIGNMENT 6: *TRACING APPROPRIATIONS*

For this assignment you'll need to work with a single memorable phrase, one that is well known and easily recognized. These phrases may actually be longer than a single sentence, like "Go Ahead. Make my day," or "To be or not to be. That is the question." It may be a portion of what was originally a longer sentence such as "I have a dream," or "Life is like a box of chocolates." If the speech you worked with in Assignment 5 contains such a phrase, feel free to work with it. Otherwise you might select a phrase from a movie, play, or advertisement that you know is regularly repeated in other contexts. Your task in this assignment is to trace the appropriations or reuses of this phrase to the best of your ability. You might begin with a Google search, but don't forget to search databases for newspapers, academic publications, and general magazines. You should also try searching for variations of the phrase or its subsections. Once you've collected as many of these variations and reuses as you can, present your work in writing as you consider what such reuse says about the meaning of the phrase or the significance of its origin to our culture.

When you're finished with your writing, add to your authorial notes. What parts of your work are you most satisfied with and why? What parts would you rework if you could?

ASSIGNMENT 7: *RECONSIDERING WORK WITH TEXTS*

Reread the work you've done in this sequence. Drawing on specific examples from your own work or that of your classmates, write a paper that reconsiders the possibilities and limitations of working with texts. The difficult part of this assignment, especially since it comes at the end of the term and may be used to introduce a portfolio of your writing, is to avoid saying what you think your teacher expects. Instead think about your work as a collection of specific textual cases that need to be interpreted and then considered as evidence just as you've been doing with other kinds of texts all term.

READINGS

Courage, Endurance and Quickness of Decision: Gender and Athletics at the University of Chicago, 1890–1920

Robin F. Bachin

Robin Bachin's research and teaching explores American urban, environmental, immigration, sport, and cultural history. The Charlton W. Tebeau Associate Professor of History, Dr. Bachin also serves as Director of the American Studies Program at the University of Miami, where she has been awarded prizes for her scholarship and for her teaching. This article originally appeared in *Rethinking History: The Journal of Theory and Practice*, an academic journal that provides a forum for historians of all disciplines who challenge traditional ways of conceptualizing and researching history. Because the piece was originally published in Great Britain, it follows stylistic conventions and spellings that are different from those used in American publications.

INTRODUCTION

A March 1900 editorial in the *University of Chicago Record* addressed a current debate among students and faculty about the role of athletics at the University. The article responded to the proposition 'That the Present Increasing Interest in Athletics at the University is Undesirable'. Those in favour of the proposition argued that athletics led students to neglect college work, to be introduced to unhealthy influences, and to subject the University to public scandal. Those opposed countered that athletics and physical exercise were desirable because they led to 'courage, endurance, and quickness of decision', and that athletic training was 'beneficial morally as well as physically' (AAS 18: 2).

Most students favoured the latter position, as did the president of the University, William Rainey Harper. Increasingly by the turn of the century, male intercollegiate athletics were becoming a central feature of collegiate life and played an important role in structuring male sociability on campuses across the country (Lester 1995; Miller forthcoming; Park, 1989: 123–68; Rader 1983:

75–86; Smith 1988: chapters 9 and 10). This change took place both at all-male colleges and at coeducational institutions like the University of Chicago. It was unclear, though, what role women would play in these athletic programmes and in coeducational collegiate culture more broadly. Female leaders at the University of Chicago, including Dean of Women Marion Talbott and women's athletic director Gertrude Dudley, fought hard to ensure women's participation in sports, and to secure funds for facilities like a gymnasium for women. Yet battles over women's access to athletics at the University illustrate broader tensions within the new coeducational university over its commitment to providing equal and inclusive programmes of study and extracurricular activities for men and for women (Balsamo 1995; Faragher and Howe 1988; Gordon 1990; Horowitz 1987; Newcomer 1959; Rosenberg 1982; Russett 1989; Solomon 1985).

This article addresses the gendered assumptions about men and women's roles within the University. Specifically, I highlight how notions of men and women's physical capacities, their patterns of sociability and the physical spaces they occupied on campus manifested the mark of gender differences. Debates over the role of athletics at the University illustrate the continued belief in the unique needs and roles of men and women, even within a coeducational institution. These pervasive assumptions of difference forced female students and educators to walk a fine line between providing for the 'special needs' of women, and fighting for equal status within all University programmes, including athletics, in the Progressive Era. Moreover, the spatial dimension of these debates about gender illustrated how the presence of the female body in a space often perceived as 'male' (the university campus) led to the creation of plans intended to circumscribe women's place so as not to 'overfeminize' and thereby undervalue university education (Ainley 1998; Colomina 1992; Duncan 1996; Massey 1994). Examining collegiate culture through the lens of athletics exposes many of the assumptions about gender difference that structured the modern university. Highlighting the material culture of the university offers a useful tool in rethinking the process by which these assumptions become inscribed in the built environment, helping both to reflect and reify complex and often contradictory cultural attitudes.

DEBATING GENDER AND ATHLETICS IN PROGRESSIVE-ERA AMERICA

Athletics was a central feature of the overall mission of the University of Chicago from the start. President Harper believed that through athletics he could foster a spirit of collegiate culture many critics claimed was missing from the new research university. Rooting for the college team, according to Harper and other promoters of intercollegiate athletics, would unite students in a common cause and create the bonds so integral to college life historically. Promoters touted loyalty to the team as a central feature of college athletics and one of its greatest contributions to academic life. Students could take these qualities with them into the world outside the ivory tower and into the modern corporate workplace.

5   Harper demonstrated his strong support for university athletics when he hired Amos Alonzo Stagg, former Yale Divinity School student who played football under legendary coach Walter Camp, the 'father of American football'. Harper named Stagg football coach and Director of

Physical Culture even before the University opened, and football practice began the day classes officially started, 1 October 1892. In his 1896 Convocation address, Harper emphasized his belief that athletics should be a central feature of the modern university, and explained how the athletic programme would fit within the broader mission of the institution:

> The athletic work of the students is a vital part of the student life. Under the proper restrictions it is a real and essential part of the college education. The athletic field like the gymnasium is one of the University's labouratories, and by no means the least important one.

(Harper 1896: 212)

Harper went on to link college spirit and team loyalty directly to manhood and morality. He stated, 'In the director of the work of college athletics, Mr. Stagg, we have an example of earnest and conscientious manhood which exerts a powerful influence among the men themselves toward right conduct and right living' (Harper 1896: 212).

Both Stagg and Harper invoked the rhetoric of 'muscular Christianity' in order to articulate the central role competitive sports played in promoting the best attributes in college students. Muscular Christianity emerged in the mid-nineteenth century as a male concept that linked exercise, health and hygiene with moral purity and national strength. It combined millennial ideas about human perfectibility with health reform programs designed to purify 'the race'. Social reformer Thomas Wentworth Higginson, among others, found that the physical degeneracy he witnessed in mid-nineteenth-century American society mirrored the moral degeneracy he wished to overcome. As Borish points out, 'Physical degeneration represented a spiritual and medical problem. In health reform ideology, renovating the spiritual and physical condition of Americans became essential for bettering individuals and the nation alike' (1987: 140).

By the turn of the century, this rhetoric of muscular Christianity shifted slightly, with athletics serving the interests of morality and nationalism, but also of the modern corporate workplace. University of Chicago faculty, for example, illustrated how the values and discipline learned on the athletic field would have important applications within society at large. For Alonzo Stagg the drive to win further promoted principles of conduct that would transcend the football field. He explained:

10   It will be a pleasure to create a strong college spirit which means so much to a boy's life. And last and best of all, it will give me such a fine chance to do the Christian work among the boys who are sure to have the most influence. Win the athletes of any college for Christ, and you will have the strongest working element attainable in college life.

(Stagg to family, 20 January 1891, in Storr 1966: 179. See also Stearns 1914: 148–52; Stewart 1914: 153–60)

University of Chicago sociologist Albion Small agreed, stating that 'athletic sports in our colleges are among the most important moralizing influences at our disposal' (Small 1900: 42). Chicago English Professor Robert Herrick also highlighted the role of athletics in creating loyalty, both to the university, and to the nation. He argued that team sports helped (male) students 'feel the exhilaration and loyalty to the scope of the institution as men working shoulder to shoulder in a new country, planning for a brilliant future' (Herrick 1895: 416). By making sports a prominent feature of university culture, college presidents and athletic directors helped reshape the focus of higher education, joining academic achievement with physical prowess in the creation of the nation's new class of educated white-collar workers.

University of Chicago faculty were not the only Americans championing the virtues of athletics at the turn of the century. Many American civic, political and business leaders argued that athletics and teamwork could serve as an antidote to the growing discomfort of many American intellectuals with the rise of modern bureaucratic culture and urban life. During a time when established religious ideals were challenged by the new scientific theories of Darwin, Freud and Nietzsche, many Americans searched for salvation through 'authentic' experiences. This feeling of 'weightlessness', as cultural historian Lears calls it, led many like Theodore Roosevelt to see in 'the cult of strenuosity' and 'muscular Christianity' a means to unite a seemingly divided self and find intense experience through physical activity (1981: 32, 108–9; Mrozek 1983, 1989: 18–46). A *New York Times* editorial captured this faith in the potential of physical exercise

to overcome what many regarded as the effeminacy of modern urban commercial culture:

A weakly, sickly, flabby race may be a pleasing spectacle to theorists who live chiefly in the clouds, but for the destiny yet lying before us we cannot have too much of the attributes which are popularly included in the word 'manliness'.

(*New York Times* 28 August 1869)

This passage clearly emphasizes the gendered underpinnings of the cult of strenuosity. It highlights the connection many leading Americans, including Roosevelt, drew between rough, competitive sport and the reassertion of manhood in a nation on the brink of imperial greatness.

Yet these prescriptions for physical exercise 15 included women as well. Some scientists stressed the need for exercise, especially among college-educated women, so they could effectively carry out the expected demands of motherhood. University of Chicago sociologist William I. Thomas, in *Sex and Society: Studies in the Social Psychology of Sex*, argued that women's participation in athletics was essential as an antidote to neurasthenia and other aliments suffered by elite and middle-class white women as a result of their 'passive' social role (Thomas 1907. See also Atkinson 1987: 38–57; Fellman and Fellman 1981; Lee 1983; Lenskyj 1986: chapters 1–2; Lunbeck 1994; Morantz-Sanchez 1985; Messner and Sabo 1990; Russett 1989; Smith-Rosenberg 1985; Verbrugge 1988).

Dr Dudley Allen Sargent, director of the Hemenway Gymnasium at Harvard University and founder of the Sargent School for Physical Education, pointed to the enormous benefits of sports for women, including 'concentration, accuracy, alertness . . . perseverance, reason, judgment . . . grace, poise, suppleness, courage, strength, and endurance' (Sargent 1912: 72. See also Hall 1885: 496; Ballintine 1898: 29).

These advocates of women's exercise echoed the ideas of earlier women's health reformers, including Catharine Beecher and Francis Willard, by linking women's physical health with their ability to carry out their duties as wives and mothers. The 'cult of true womanhood', which maintained that women's proper sphere was in the home providing nurture and maintaining piety among all members of the household, required women to be both morally and physically robust. This idea was the women's equivalent of muscular Christianity, and its proponents highlighted how a woman's physical well-being was tied directly to her roles as wife and mother. According to Beecher and her sister Harriet Beecher Stowe, exercise offered women a chance to enhance their daily lives while at the same time taking more control over their domestic duties:

> Young girls can seldom be made to realize the value of health, and the need of exercise to secure it, so as to feel much interest in walking abroad, when they have no other object. But, if they are brought up to minister to the comfort and enjoyment of themselves and of others, by performing domestic duties, they will constantly be interested and cheered in their exercise by the feeling of usefulness and the consciousness of having performed their duty.

(Beecher and Stowe: 1870, 117)

Temperance advocate Frances Willard even pointed to the liberating elements of exercise that would allow women to learn more about their bodies and therefore be better able to prepare themselves for motherhood (Willard 1991). While Beecher's and Willard's advocacy of exercise was framed within the narrow limits of the cult of true womanhood, they nonetheless challenged the idea that physical weakness was an essential element of the female constitution (Beecher 1856, 1874; Borish 1987; Rossiter 1982; Sklar 1973).

20   By the turn of the century, several female physicians and scientists broadened this interpretation of the role of exercise for women, illustrating how control over one's body could be liberating in other realms of life as well. Female scientists like Helen Bradford Thompson (who studied with James Angell at Chicago) linked their pioneering studies in physiology and social psychology to the New Woman. Challenging ingrained beliefs about the inherent inferiority of women, these scientists demonstrated how slight sex differences were in terms of both physical and mental abilities (Gordon 1990; Rosenberg 1982: 54–83; Rossiter 1982: 51–72; Solomon 1985: 103). Physical exercise (as well as intellectual stimulation), according to these studies, was beneficial for both men and women. While fitness and health were the foundations of prescriptions for women's exercise, some female reformers and scientists such as Thompson and Eliza Mosher saw women's liberation as a potential result of increased understanding

and control of their bodies (Cahn 1994: chapters 1–2; Eisen 1991: 103–20; Gleason 1999; Guttmann 1991; Horowitz 1984, 1987; Stanley 1996; Twin 1979, 1985: 193–217; Vertinksy 1990).

In a *Ladies Home Journal* series, entitled 'What Has College Done for Girls?', writer Edith Rickert highlighted the benefits and drawbacks of higher education for women, and included a discussion of athletics among college women. Rickert based her series on interviews with hundreds of women who had attended college between 1849 and 1909. Respondents to Rickert's survey stressed the importance of physical education in allowing college women to preserve 'the balance of a sound mind in a healthful body'. Many respondents also believed that women's specific needs should be more directly addressed in college. 'That is', according to Rickert, 'the special handicaps of women should be more carefully weighed in the scheme of physical training, particularly athletics, and this training should be directed more definitely toward the strength that is needed for motherhood rather than the muscularity that shows up well in contests' (Rickert 1912b: 23). She explained how some alumnae complained that 'the spirit of athletics has crept into gymnasium work, and that muscularity is encouraged . . . at the expense of the physiological work needed by women' (Rickert 1912a: 12).

Many women, along with men, believed that physical exercise for women ought to be used to improve their health, fitness and, by extension, beauty, but that athletic competition was an altogether separate matter, one which could introduce masculine characteristics such as competitiveness, aggression and even violence into women's activities. While numerous physicians, both male and female, stressed the importance of exercise for women's physical and mental well-being, they were less sympathetic to the idea of women engaging in competitive sports. Indeed, Vertinsky argues that women physicians subscribed to the idea that women's exercise should be moderate and non-competitive, 'and that it should develop fitness for motherhood rather than strength for independence' (Vertinsky 1990: 149–58).

In his *Ladies Home Journal* article, 'Are Athletics Making Girls Masculine? A Practical Answer to a Question Every Girl Asks', Dudley Sargent recognized the fear that many Americans expressed about how competitive sports could undermine women's femininity and pose a threat to the race. 'Many persons honestly believe', he stated, 'that athletics are making girls bold, masculine and overassertive; that they are destroying the beautiful lines and curves of her figure' (Sargent 1912: 72). Indeed, Sargent argued, women who excelled in competitive sports may have inherited male physiological features. This was necessarily so, he pointed out, because only by taking on 'masculine attributes' could success in certain forms of sporting competition be achieved. While Sargent believed that some degree of competition was beneficial, he criticized the prospect of women engaging in rough, contact sports that would threaten their health, and he argued for rules changes that would take into account the different physical and emotional capacities of men and women (Sargent 1912: 72).

COLLEGIATE CULTURE, GENDER AND ATHLETICS AT THE UNIVERSITY OF CHICAGO

This tension between athletics as a means of healthful exercise and as a form of sports competition structured early debates about women's athletics at the University of Chicago. When the Department of Physical Culture and Athletics was organized on 1 October 1892, members highlighted the importance of tending to the physical fitness of all students. Part of the General Regulations of the University stated, 'All students will be examined as to their physical condition on entering the University, and at intervals during the course'. The University physician would make the examination, and provide each student with a detailed written report 'indicating constitutional weaknesses, and forms of exercise desirable and undesirable for the individual in question'. The regulation stipulated that Alonzo Stagg, as the director of the Department of Physical Education, 'give his personal attention, not only to the organization and training of athletics teams . . . but especially to the physical training of each student, in so far as it is practicable' (Division of Physical Culture and Athletics, AAS 18: 10).

The Women's Division of the Department of Physical Education, under the leadership of Gertrude Dudley, embraced the role of exercise in improving physical fitness, and dealt cautiously with the issue of competitive sports for women. The purpose of the Women's Division was 'to assist each student either to maintain or raise her health standard; to provide her with wholesome types of recreation

which she will enjoy; and to enable her to acquire a sufficient degree of skill in some individual sport to provide her after graduation with a leisure time recreation—perhaps more than one' ('Statement Concerning the Women's Division of the Department of Physical Education,' n.d. AAS: 18–10). Professor Dudley met with each student to discuss recommended physical education programmes, and made suggestions for personal health habits, sleep, food and exercise regimen. Dudley worked in conjunction with Dean of Women Marion Talbot, furnishing her with a list of all female students who 'in her opinion, were not in average physical condition'. Women engaged in rowing, tennis, golf, swimming, ring hockey and calisthenics to stress the 'corrective' aspects of individual exercise over team competition (BPCA 1: 1 Minutes, 6 October 1894).

The Women's Department stressed not only health and fitness for women as its goals, but also the creation of a new sphere of female sociability at college. Women physical educators provided instruction in a variety of activities that the female students selected themselves, and which allowed for 'differing degrees of physical fitness'. According to the Women's Division of the Department of Physical Education, 'In all of the teaching, emphasis is placed on the Joy of activity. If a student seems unable to get that result, change of activity is not only suggested but urged' ('Statement Concerning the Women's Division of the Department of Physical Education', AAS 18: 10). Regarding the possibility of competition, Dean Marion Talbot advised the Board of Physical Culture in 1894 that 'contests in women's training' should be 'very carefully watched and guarded' (BPCA 1: 1 Minutes, June 1894).

By 1904, though, team sports had become a central feature of the physical culture programme for women, and included basketball, baseball, captain ball and field hockey. This change resulted largely from the emerging belief that *controlled* competition (not intercollegiate competition) possessed social benefits for women athletes. Dudley stressed that team-sports, when the element of competition was moderated, provided college women with a sense of belonging. By becoming a member of a team, she argued, women could feel an integral part of a group: 'The early realization of a definite place in the life of a large University is important, especially in a non-residential campus like Chicago with so large a proportion of women living at home' (BPCA 1: 1 Minutes, June 1894. See also Dudley and Kellor 1909). Team sports offered this element of co-operation and comradeship.

The rules for intramural basketball highlighted this emphasis on democracy, sociability, and belief in the need to protect women's health. Women's basketball was played in colleges and universities throughout the nation by the turn of the century, structured by a variety of rules modifications first introduced by Sendra Berenson, Director of Women's Physical Culture at Smith College in 1901.[1] When asked by Alonzo Stagg which rules for basketball the Chicago women employed, intramural coach Marie C. Ortmayer responded that they used the American Amateur Athletic Union rules with two modifications: 'No one shall tackle the ball after a fair catch by the opposite side . . . and only forwards throw for the basket. This is our rule for two reasons; 1. Educational 2. Physical — where all throw too great a strain for women' (Stagg to Ortmayer 8 January 1909 AAS 12: 22). In 1903 the National Conference of Deans of Women made clear these connections between promoting female sociability and teamwork, and limiting athletic competition. The Conference adopted resolutions that highlighted these goals. 'Resolved, that the social life shall be regulated and that the tests of good health and high scholarship should be applied' to be sure female students are not engaged in 'social dissipation'. 'Resolved, that intercollegiate athletic contests for women are not approved' ('Resolutions III and IV, Adopted by the Conference of Deans of Women', BTUC 3: 6, 3–4 November 1903).

Part of the admonition against female intercollegiate competition resulted from the increased evidence of scandal and corruption plaguing male athletic competition, especially in intercollegiate football. Female physical educators argued that women's athletics represented the true spirit of the amateur ideal, as opposed to male competition increasingly intertwined in a web of commercialism and professionalism. Scandal regarding the amateur status of football players — at the University of Chicago and at other leading institutions — illustrated the extent to which big-time athletics had the potential to undermine the educational values and ideals of the university experience (Bond 1912: 70–1; Gems 1997: 101; Lester 1995: 72–91; Miller forthcoming; Oriard 1993; Smith 1988). According to many female educators, women's model of athletic engagement, emphasizing co-operation and participation, served as an

antidote to the more brutal and commercial tendencies within male competition, emphasizing winning. These discussions also prompted many educators to question how the values associated with sports were being promoted or corrupted on college campuses.

Yet despite the efforts of educators like Gertrude Dudley, the spirit of competition continued to flourish on college campuses, even after years of scandal in football. Moreover, as football became one of the leading sources of campus pride — at the University of Chicago and throughout the nation — and as victory served to promote greater alumni loyalty and fundraising, women's athletics were further marginalized from collegiate culture. Instead, collegiate athletics increasingly placed women on the sidelines, showing support for and loyalty to their male counterparts on the field. Demia Butler, a member of the first class at the University of Chicago, recalled a visit to the Beatrice, the apartment house rented for female students, by Stagg and Joseph Raycroft, a quarterback for the team who would become Assistant Professor of Physical Culture (and who also married Demia's sister Elizabeth). Stagg and Raycroft sang songs, entertained the women and invited them to attend a football game the next day in Washington Park. A week later, the Beatrice hosted a reception where Stagg spoke about the demands of football. Butler recalls, 'After he told us of the great physical, mental, and moral strength the game demanded, and what a fine discipline it is in all the times, we were prepared to enjoy it with greater zest than ever' (DDB 8, 10, 17 October 1892).[2]

The idea that women best served the athletic programme as sideline fans, instead of as active participants, was apparent in discussions over women's participation in the Athletic Department's portion of the annual Spring Program in 1913. Stagg asked Dudley and the female students to participate in the Athletic Department events by putting on a series of Maypole Dances. He reminded her that 'the women's work for several years has been receiving approximately $2,000 from the athletic fund. . . . The athletic fund, as you know, is created entirely by the receipts from the men's athletic contests. The women have shared in its beneficence without really giving a single income-producing event' (Stagg to Dudley, 9 May 1913, AAS 11: 8). What he did not tell Dudley, but shared with Athletic Department physician Dudley Reed, was that he believed the Maypole Dance could raise a great deal of money for the athletic fund. He explained to Reed that 'last year four thousand people paid twenty-five cents at Illinois to see the dances put on by the women in their May Day Festival. You can readily see from the success of the affair at Illinois what the prospects are for Chicago' (Stagg to Reed, 9 May 1913, AAS 12: 9).

The discussion about the Spring Festival reflects the increasingly common notion that women's athletics were of secondary importance to male inter-collegiate competition, and that female athletes best served the sports programme by being ornamental spectacles. In Dudley's response to Stagg she expressed her appreciation for the generosity that Stagg had shown the Women's Department in the past. Her objection to co-ordinating the Maypole Dances focused on the fact that she wanted the female athletes to participate in Woman's Day activities at the festival. Dudley, along with Marion Talbot, wanted to showcase the achievements of women in all aspects of University life. In addition, Dudley argued that if women were to participate in the athletic programme, she wanted it to be as athletes, not as dancers (Dudley to Stagg, 27 May 1913, AAS 11: 8). While dance was a regular part of the women's physical culture programme, Dudley did not wish to see it used as a means of representing women's athletics at the University of Chicago. She recognized that the Maypole Dance had the potential to create a titillating spectacle of women's bodies rather than a celebration of female athletic achievement. Stagg recalled, though, that at the first festival, held three years earlier, several male faculty members objected to the hockey game put on by the women. Apparently, they 'objected to having the women exhibit publicly', and the Board of Athletics supported the faculty position. Stagg added that for the current year's events there most likely would be no objection to some feature of the women's work, and in the past the dances have been a success (Stagg to Reed, 9 May 1913, AAS 12: 9).[3] The female body, then, became an object of public display, showcasing femininity and beauty rather than athleticism, skill and strength. In short, the female body became a commodity in the service of the increasingly commercialized male athletic programme that relied on spectators and gate receipts for a large portion of its funding.

Ironically, it was Marion Talbot, Dean of Women, who led one of the initial efforts to create university cheers in support of the football team. She held a competition among the female students for 'the best gridiron lyric'.[4] The Beatrice served as a site of pre-game rallies and post-game parties, with football players mixing with female students under the supervision of herself and Stagg (DDB, 17 October 1892). The women's support of male athletics did not, however, undermine their genuine efforts to promote women's athletics. They recognized, as did University of Chicago President Harper and other university leaders, that football was becoming not only a major source of fund-raising, but also a defining element of collegiate culture. The increasingly elaborate rituals that surrounded football games not only structured student social life but also served as mediums for generating and expressing loyalty to the University and fostering the collegial spirit Harper sought to create.

GENDER AND THE PHYSICAL SPACES OF ATHLETICS AT THE UNIVERSITY OF CHICAGO

The question of loyalty to the University, and women's role in promoting it, became a central issue in efforts to improve the facilities available to women for athletics. Dudley, and female alumnae, regularly lamented the lack of adequate facilities for women. Stagg and Dudley engaged in constant battles over financial appropriations for female athletics from the University's athletic funds. A series of letters over several years shows that there was no clearly designated amount of funding set aside for women's athletics. In a 1910 letter to Stagg, for example, Dudley explained that in the past year, the women have used only $98.13 from the athletics fund, and that amount was on requisition. She asked, 'Do you not think we might arrange to have at least one quarter of the athletic funds for the use of the women?' (Dudley to Stagg, 17 April 1910, AAS 11: 8).[5]

A campaign launched by the Alumnae Club to raise funds for a women's gymnasium highlighted women's loyalty to the University, and their desire to have the University repay this loyalty with a women's building. A pitch in the *University of Chicago Magazine* in 1912 exclaimed, 'Oh, Chicago! It is time to wake up, time to take advantage of this love and loyalty while it is yours. Give us a woman's building worthy of this great institution, worthy of the women who crowd your halls, a place where every girl might have a fair chance' ('A Permanent Building' 1912: 207). The article pointed to the poor facilities and dearth of equipment for women's athletics. It mentioned

how University women needed to use a corner of the library for a gymnasium in the early days, as well as lecture rooms in Ellis Hall and Cobb Hall. Alumnae also recounted the lack of field space for women's outdoor athletics. Indeed, letters from Dudley to Stagg recount the lack of field space for women's outdoor sports, including hockey. In a 1905 letter, Dudley wrote, 'Once again I have to trouble you about space'. In another letter, she questioned why the athletic fund provided for the upkeep of Marshall Field, the main athletic field that hosted intercollegiate football games, but not for any other spaces used by women, and asks that someone from Buildings and Grounds be assigned to the women's field. By June of 1910, the Superintendent of Buildings and Grounds agreed to turn over vacant ground (south of Greenwood Hall, between 60th and 61st streets) for women's use, but could not guarantee upkeep.[6] Physical facilities at the University became contested spaces when male and female sports became the focus of their use.

These battles over space continued after the new state-of-the-art men's facility, Bartlett Gymnasium, opened with great fanfare in 1904 (figure 1). Even before the gym was built, the Committee on Buildings and Grounds voted that 'the women should not occupy a portion of the new gymnasium, even temporarily' (BPCA 1: 1 Minutes, 2 February

1901). Administrators evidently felt that the physical culture activities of men and women needed to be strictly regulated and kept distinct, both in terms of programmes and in terms of the use of space. Indeed, it was clear from the start that Bartlett was designed to be a monument to manly sports. During his convocation address in 1900, Harper announced plans for the new building. 'A father will erect this building, which shall be dedicated to the work of the physical upbuilding of young men, in memory of his son taken suddenly from life in the midst of a splendid and vigorous young manhood'. Board of Trustee member A. C. Bartlett eventually donated $150,000 for the gymnasium dedicated to 'The Advancement of Physical Education and the Glory of Manly Arts' (Harper 1900: 348).[7]

The design of the building reinforced this glorification of masculine virility and a space solely for male athletics. The entranceway contained a stained glass window above the main door that depicted triumphal tournament scenes from Sir Walter Scott's *Ivanhoe* (figure 2). The entry also featured an Arthurian mural picturing medieval stick and sword fights, suggesting the links between male athletic competition and medieval honour (figure 3). In addition, a stone relief on the north side of the building showed two rams butting heads, and recalled one of the speeches given on

FIGURE 2   Stained glass window in Bartlett Gymnasium depicting scene from Sir Walter Scott's *Ivanhoe*. Edward C. Sperry, 1904. Courtesy of Special Collections, Joseph Regenstein Library, University of Chicago.

FIGURE 3   Mural in Bartlett Gymnasium depicting medieval tournament. Courtesy of Special Collections, Joseph Regenstein Library, University of Chicago.

opening day in 1904 in which men were described as 'the noblest of animals', and celebrated for their 'tough muscles and steady nerves, vital force and elastic vigor' (Seidel and Taylor 1998: 43).

All of this celebration of manliness, and its embodiment in the gymnasium's design, clearly marked it as off limits to women. The lack of adequate facilities for women, however, led Stagg and Harper to agree to open the natatorium to women for swimming on Monday afternoons (Stagg to Harper, 12 May 1904, AAS 9: 8; 'The Women's Department, 1904–05 Physical Culture Report', pp. 12–13, AAS 18: 12). But the rest of women's athletics laboured under the same constrained conditions until they could secure enough funds for a building of their own. The Women's Athletic Association offered subscriptions and staged a variety of plays to purchase equipment, and worked at forging relationships with donors that might lead to the construction of a gymnasium for women. Along these lines, the Gymnasium Committee of the Alumnae Club asked Chicagoans, 'Isn't there among us some large-hearted, public spirited Chicago man or woman who, recognizing our needs, will feel honored to have his or her name carved above the entrance to a women's building?' ('A Permanent Building' 1912: 207).

They found a supporter in LaVerne Noyes, a prominent Chicago businessman who wished to endow a building in honour of his deceased wife. Noyes told Stagg, and later University President Harry Judson, that he would give $300,000 to be used, in part, for a women's gymnasium. Julius Rosenwald of Sears, who would become one of the largest contributors to the University, also made a gift toward the building (Stagg to Dudley, 17 July 1913, AAS 11: 8). Upon hearing of the gifts, members of the Women's Athletic Association exclaimed, 'The millennium for University women seems at last to be at hand. We are to have a gymnasium and a club house!' (Letter enclosed in Stagg to Dudley, 17 July 1913, AAS 11: 8).

Indeed, unlike Bartlett Gymnasium's focus on virility and competition, the new women's gym would be structured around patterns of appropriate female physical activity and sociability. Marion Talbot and Gertrude Dudley, along with several female faculty and students, contributed ideas for the design of the building to the architects Shepley, Rutan and Coolidge (RCBG 24: 12; see also Block 1983: 123). Ida Noyes Hall was built to resemble a Tudor manor house, with elegant interior details that symbolized women's domestic arts (figure 4). The Hall contained a large Common Room, as well as a library, social rooms for serving refreshments, offices for women's

FIGURE 4 Ida Noyes Hall. Shepley, Rutan, and Coolidge, 1916. Courtesy of Special Collections, Joseph Regenstein Library, University of Chicago.

clubs and a sun parlour. It also included a personal service department, with provisions for shining shoes and giving manicures. The Hall featured a swimming pool, a game room, two bowling alleys and a large room for 'corrective gymnasium work' (Goodspeed 1916: 441–2). The latter room was finished off with a large mural depicting the *Masque of Youth*, led by the Spirit of Gothic Architecture, illustrating, according to University Professor Edith Flint Foster, that 'beauty ought to be educative' (figure 5; see Block 1983: 123).

The dedication remarks delivered to celebrate the opening of Ida Noyes Hall further underscored the gendered differences between it and Bartlett Gymnasium. At the cornerstone ceremony on 18 April 1915, Marion Talbot spoke about the joy and importance of seeing this building come to fruition and emphasized the important role it would play in the lives of University women: 'Here self-discovery and self-control will lead to social co-operation and mutual understanding . . . Tolerance, sympathy, kindness, the generous word and the helpful act . . . will be the contribution of the women who go forth from Ida Noyes Hall to take part in the upbuilding of the new civilization which is to come' (Marion Talbot, 18 April 1915, quoted in Goodspeed 1916: 441; see also The Committee on the Dedication of Ida Noyes Hall, MTP 5: 3). The gymnasium would serve to enhance feminine characteristics, not detract from them, and further reinforce women's role as the guardians of co-operation instead of competition.

CONCLUSION

Promoters of women's athletics walked a fine line between seeking equal access for women and safeguarding the femininity of female athletes. At the same time, they attempted to ensure that women's bodies did not become commodified and placed in the service of male commercial athletics. Dudley's efforts to secure funds and facilities for women illustrated her commitment to the goals of equal participation and athletic opportunities supposedly at the heart of the mission of the new coeducational institution. Yet it soon became clear, both in athletics and in other curricular programmes, that the University's commitment to coeducation did not necessarily mean it supported integration of men and women, or even similar courses of study for them. Indeed, the construction of separate facilities for men's and women's athletics gave physical expression to the stark differences in the ideals and goals for men and women, not only in their involvement with sports, but in their lives more generally. That women like Gertrude Dudley and Marion Talbot fought at once for greater access to previously male domains, and for recognizing women's 'special needs' within the university, illustrated the multiple ways in which women needed to position themselves to gain a place in the modern research university. These women leaders negotiated the constraints placed upon them and developed their own vision of female athletics at the University of Chicago. Their efforts went not only toward securing facilities and funds for women's programmes, but also in reshaping perceptions about

FIGURE 5   Mural in Ida Noyes Hall, *The Masque of Youth*, depicting the Spirit of Gothic Architecture. Jessie Arms Botke, 1918. Courtesy of Special Collections, Joseph Regenstein Library, University of Chicago.

the proper relationships between gender and athletics, women and higher education.

The athletic programme at Chicago, in short, embodied many of the trends shaping higher education in the Progressive era. It highlighted the scientific element of exercise in the promotion of health, fitness and 'good living'. At the same time, it reflected the increasingly important role of commercialism in shaping the spectacle of college sport, especially football. By structuring rituals and ceremonies around collegiate football, universities linked sport with fund-raising and public visibility, thereby tying promotion of the university directly to sports. In doing so, they contributed to the commodification of athletics that would lead sport to become more and more at odds with the professed educational and moral mission of higher education. This process also contributed to the continued inequities between men's and women's sporting programmes within the university. Both the scientific and the commercial aspects of athletics served to reify gender differences on college campuses by

circumscribing appropriate forms of physical and social activity for women, especially on coeducational campuses. Yet athletics also opened up new possibilities for women, to use scientific notions of fitness and health to take greater control over their own bodies, and to shape new models of collegiate sociability based more on (female) ideals of co-operation than on (male) competition. These ideals transcended the playing field and found their way into curricular programmes within the University, and at times into women's public roles within the city.

ACKNOWLEDGEMENTS

The author would like to thank Linda Borish, Gerald Gems, Steven Riess and Barbara Tischler for comments on earlier versions of this article. Part of the research for this article was funded by a Mellon Foundation Postdoctoral Fellowship at the Newberry Library and a Max Orovitz Summer Research Award from the University of Miami.

Notes

1. Historian Susan Cahn discusses the process by which women's rules were codified. Smith College Athletic Director Sendra Berenson sought to draw up a single set of rules of play for women's basketball, since in the 1880s and 1890s there were numerous variations, with rules set by each school's athletic directors. In 1899 Berenson organized the National Women's Basketball Committee under the auspices of the American Physical Education Association. Through the Spalding Sporting Goods company, the Committee issued the first women's rules book in 1901. The rules called for six players per side, and three regions of the court. Players were designated as forwards, centres or guards and were confined to their section of the court. No physical contact was allowed and players could dribble only once. Female physical educators tried to thwart attempts by local business people to sponsor competition among women's teams, seeing that as a threat to the amateur ideal and femininity of sport (see Cahn 1994: 86–7; see also Berenson 1901). For a discussion of the role of women's basketball in collegiate culture at Oberlin, see Horger (1996: 256–83) and Hult and Trekell (1991).

2. The women could attend the football game only if they went 'in a body, accompanied by the Dean', and watched from the sidelines. See Marion Talbot, 'Women's Houses at the University of Chicago: Their Origin and Meaning', 1933, typescript in MTP 4: 13.

3. Dudley expresses her desire to help in any way possible, and show the loyalty of the female students to the athletic programme, but only if their participation does not detract from their preparations for Woman's Day events (Dudley to Stagg, 27 May 1913, AAS 11: 8).

4. Talbot quoted in the *Chicago Interocean*, 8 October 1902 (see also Talbot 1936; Lester 1995: 36–7). Historian Robin Lester suggests that this cheer competition illustrated how 'women were working out their peculiar role as major athletic advocates on the American campus' (p. 36). He also recounts a story about Agnes Wayman, the captain of the women's basketball team and assistant instructor in the women's gymnasium at the University of Chicago Settlement. She evidently spoke at a rally for the defeated Chicago football team in which her words helped console the players after their loss. Lester points out that there were few options for women with the ban on

intercollegiate athletics, and suggests that cheerleading and rallying around the football team were the only ways for women to take part in this aspect of collegiate culture. Yet he does not address the constant struggles among Talbot and Dudley to challenge and redefine the roles of women in athletics, and in collegiate culture more broadly. For further discussion of women's roles as cheerleaders, see Hanson (1995: Chapter 1).

5. In 1905, Stagg had urged Harper to create a separate fund for women's athletics by using a one-time contribution of $500 from the General Athletic Fund, along with an additional $500 that the Women's Athletic Association would raise. That money would be invested, and the income from it used to support women's athletics (see Stagg to Gertrude Dudley, 18 February 1905, AAS 11: 8). Apparently this plan was never implemented, as Dudley continually had to ask Stagg for funds to help pay for the female coaches, whose salaries came from fund-raisers sponsored by the Women's Athletic Fund, the General Athletic Fund and the

General Appropriations funds of the University (see Stagg to Trevor Arnett, Vice President and Business Manager of the University of Chicago, 23 February 1907, AAS 8: 4).

6. See 'Report of the Department of Physical Culture, Women's Department, 1892,' AAS 18: 10; Dudley to Stagg, 29 May 1905, AAS Papers. Box 11, folder 8; see also M. H. MacLean, Superintendent of Buildings and Grounds, to Stagg, 10 June 1910, AAS 11: 8. Borish points out that other institutions in Chicago faced similar concerns about providing athletic facilities for women, but used different strategies than those chosen by the University of Chicago (1999: 240–70).

7. The dedication is above the door of the gymnasium facing the front entrance. The building included a swimming pool, professors' exercise room, general gymnasium and running track, and lockers and showers. The total cost of the building was $238,000, the remainder coming from a Rockefeller subscription of 1895 (Goodspeed 1916: 249).

References

University of Chicago Manuscript Collections

AAS Amos Alonzo Stagg Papers, Special Collections, Joseph Regenstein Library.

BPCA The Board of Physical Culture and Athletics, Minutes, vol. 1, 1893–1908, Special Collections, Joseph Regenstein Library.

BTUC Correspondence of the Board of Trustees of the University of Chicago, vol. 1, 1890–1913, Special Collections, Joseph Regenstein Library.

DDB Diary of Demia Butler, Special Collections, Joseph Regenstein Library.

MTP Marion Talbot Papers, Special Collections, Joseph Regenstein Library.

RCBG Records of the Committee on Buildings and Grounds, Special Collections, Joseph Regenstein Library.

Ainley, R. (ed.) (1998) *New Frontiers of Space, Bodies, and Gender*, New York: Routledge.

Adelman, M. L. (1990) *A Sporting Time: New York City and the Rise of Modern Athletics, 1820–1870*, Urbana, IL: University of Illinois Press.

Atkinson, P. (1987) 'The feminist physique: physical education and the medicalization of women's education',

in J. A. Mangan and R. J. Park (eds) *From 'Fair Sex' to Feminism*, London: Frank Cass, 38–57.

Atlantic Monthly (1914) 'Athletics and morals', no author cited February: 145–8.

Ballintine, H. I. (1898) 'Out-of-door sports for college women', *American Physical Education Review* March: 29.

Balsamo, A. (1995) 'Forms of technological embodiment: reading the body in contemporary culture', in M. Featherstone and R. Burrows (eds) *Cyberspace/Cyberbodies/Cyberpunk: Cultures of Technological Embodiment*, London: Sage, 215–37.

Beecher, C. (1874) *Educational Reminiscences and Suggestion*, New York: J. B. Ford and Company.

———(1856) *Physiology and Calisthenics for Schools and Families*, New York: Harper & Bros.

———and Beecher Stowe, H. (1870) *The American Woman's Home*, New York: J. B. Ford & Company.

Berenson, S. (ed.) (1901) *Line Basket Ball, or Basket Ball for Women*, New York: American Sports Publishing Company.

Block, J. F. (1983) *The Uses of Gothic: Planning and Building the Campus of the University* of Chicago, 1892–1932, Chicago: University of Chicago Press.

Bond, W. S. (1912) 'Summer baseball', *University of Chicago Magazine* IV: 70–71.

Borish, L. J. (1987) 'The robust woman and the muscular christian: Catharine Beecher, Thomas Higginson, and their vision of American society, health, and physical activities', *The International Journal of the History of Sport* 4: 139–54.

——(1999) ' Athletic activities of various kinds': physical health and sport programs for Jewish American women', *Journal of Sport History* 26: 240–70.

Cahn, S. K. (1994) *Coming on Strong: Gender and Sexuality in Twentieth-Century Women's Sport*, New York: The Free Press.

Cole, C. (1993) 'Resisting the Canon: feminist cultural studies, sport and technologies of the body', *Journal of Sport and Social Issues* 17: 77–97.

Colomina, B. (ed.) (1992) *Sexuality and Space*, Princeton: Princeton Architectural Press.

Dudley, G. and Kellor, F. A. (1909) *Athletic Games in the Education of Women*, New York: Henry Holt and Company.

Duncan, N. (ed.) (1996) *BodySpace: Destabilizing Geographies of Gender and Sexuality*, New York: Routledge.

Eisen, G. (1991) 'Sport, recreation and gender: Jewish immigrant women in turn-of-the-century America (1880–1920)', *Journal of Sport History* 18: 103–20.

Faragher, J. M. and Howe, F. (eds) (1988) *Women and Higher Education in American History*, New York: W. W. Norton and Company.

Fellman, A. C. and Fellman, M. (1981) *Making Sense of Self: Medical Advice Literature in Late Nineteenth-Century America*, Philadelphia: University of Pennsylvania Press.

Gems, G. R. (1997) *Windy City Wars: Labor, Leisure, and Sport in the Making of Chicago*, Lanham, MD: Scarecrow Press.

Gleason, W. A. (1999) *The Leisure Ethic: Work and Play in American Literature, 1840–1940*, Stanford: Stanford University Press.

Goodspeed, T. Wakefield (1916) *A History of the University of Chicago*, Chicago: University of Chicago Press.

Gordon, L. (1990) *Gender and Higher Education in the Progressive Era*, New Haven: Yale University Press.

Guttmann, A. (1991) *Women's Sports: A History*, New York: Columbia University Press.

Hall, L. M. (1885) 'Physical training of girls', *Popular Science Monthly* XXVI: 496.

Hanson, M. E. (1995) *Go! Fight! Win! Cheerleading in American Culture*, Bowling Green, OH: Bowling Green University Popular Press.

Haraway, D. (1985) 'A manifesto for cyborgs: science, technology, and socialist-feminism in the 1980s', *Socialist Review* 80: 65–107.

Harper, W. R. (1916) 'Convocation Address, Sept. 18, 1900', in T. Wakefield Goodspeed, *A History of the University of Chicago*, Chicago: University of Chicago Press, p. 348.

——(1976) 'Convocation Address, July 1, 1896', in W. M. Murphy and D. J. R. Bruckner (eds) *The Idea of the University of Chicago: Selections from the Papers of the First Eight Chief Executives of the University of Chicago from 1891 to 1975*, Chicago: University of Chicago Press.

Herrick, R. (1895) 'The University of Chicago', *Scribner's Magazine* XVIII: 397–417.

Horger, M. (1996) 'Basketball and athletic control at Oberlin College, 1896–1915', *Journal of Sport History* 23: 256–83.

Horowitz, H. L. (1984) *Alma Mater: Design and Experience in the Women's Colleges from their Nineteenth-Century Beginnings to the 1930s*, New York: Alfred A. Knopf.

——(1987) *Campus Life: Undergraduate Culture from the End of the Eighteenth Century to the Present*, Chicago: University of Chicago Press.

Hult, J. S. and Trekell, M. (1991) *A Century of Women's Basketball: From Frailty to Final Four*, Reston, Va.: National Association for Girls and Women in Sport.

Lears, T. J. Jackson (1981) *No Place of Grace: Antimodernism and the Transformation of American Culture, 1880–1920*, New York: Pantheon Books.

Lee, M. (1983) *A History of Physical Education and Sports in the USA*, New York: John Wiley and Sons.

Lenskyj, H. (1986) *Out of Bounds: Women, Sport, and Sexuality*, Toronto: Women's Press.

Leslie, B. W. (1992) *Gentlemen and Scholars: College and Community in the 'Age of the University', 1865–1917*, University Park, PN: Penn State University Press.

Lester, R. (1995) *Stagg's University: The Rise, Decline, and Fall of Big-Time Football at Chicago*, Urbana, IL: University of Illinois Press.

Lunbeck, E. (1994) *The Psychiatric Persuasion: Knowledge, Gender, and Power in Modern America*, Princeton, NJ: Princeton University Press.

Massey, D. (1994) *Space, Place, and Gender*, Minneapolis: University of Minnesota Press.

Messner, M. and Sabo, D. (eds) (1990) *Sport, Men and the Gender Order: Critical Feminist Perspectives*, Champaign, IL: Human Kinetics.

Miller, P. B. (forthcoming) *The Playing Fields of American Culture: Athletics and Higher Education, 1850–1945*, New York: Oxford University Press.

Morantz-Sanchez, R. M. (1985) *Sympathy and Science: Women Physicians in American Medicine*, New York: Oxford University Press.

Mrozek, D. J. (1983) *Sport and American Mentality, 1880–1910*, Knoxville: University of Tennessee Press.

——(1989) 'Sport in American life: from national health to personal fulfillment, 1890–1940', in K. Grover (ed.) *Fitness in American Culture: Images of Health, Sport, and the Body, 1830–1940*, Amherst: University of Massachusetts Press, 18–46.

Newcomer, M. (1959) *A Century of Higher Education for American Women*, New York: Harper & Brothers.

New York Times (28 August 1869)

Oriard, M. (1993) *Reading Football: How the Popular Press Created an American Spectacle*, Chapel Hill: University of North Carolina Press.

Palmieri, P. A. (1995) *In Adamless Eden: The Community of Women Faculty at Wellesley*, New Haven: Yale University Press.

Park, R. J. (1989) 'Healthy, moral, and strong: educational views of exercise and athletics in nineteenth-century America', in K. Grover (ed.) *Fitness in American Culture: Images of Health, Sport, and the Body, 1830–1940*, Amherst: University of Massachusetts Press, pp. 123–68.

Pronger, B. (1998) 'Post-sport: transgressing boundaries in physical culture', in G. Rail (ed.) *Sport and Postmodern Times*, Albany: SUNY Press, pp. 277–98.

Rader, B. G. (1983) *American Sports: From the Age of Folk Games to the Age of Spectators*, Englewood Cliffs, NJ: Prentice-Hall.

Rickert, E. (1912a) 'What has the college done for girls: has the college injured the health of girls?' *Ladies Home Journal* 29 January: 11–12.

——(1912b) 'What has the college done for girls: how can the woman's college be bettered' *Ladies Home Journal* 29 April: 23–4.

Rosenberg, R. (1982) *Beyond Separate Spheres: Intellectual Roots of Modern Feminism*, New Haven: Yale University Press.

Rossiter, M. W. (1982) *Women Scientists in America: Struggles and Strategies to 1940*, Baltimore: Johns Hopkins University Press.

Russett, C. Eagle (1989) *Sexual Science: The Victorian Construction of Womanhood*, Cambridge, MA: Harvard University Press.

Sargent, D. A. (1912) 'Are athletics making girls masculine? A practical answer to a question every girl asks', *Ladies Home Journal* 29 March: 72.

Seidel, L. and Taylor, K. (1998) *Looking to Learn: Visual Pedagogy at the University of Chicago*, Chicago: David and Alfred Smart Museum of Art.

Sklar, K. K. (1973) *Catharine Beecher: A Study in American Domesticity*, New Haven: Yale University Press.

Small, A. (1900) *University of Chicago Record* V: 42.

Smith, R. A. (1988) *Sports and Freedom: The Rise of Big-Time Athletics,* New York: Oxford University Press.

Smith-Rosenberg, C. (1985) *Disorderly Conduct: Visions of Gender in Victorian America*, New York: Alfred A. Knopf.

Solomon, B. M. (1985) *In the Company of Educated Women: A History of Women and Higher Education in America,* New Haven: Yale University Press.

Sperber, M. (1993) *Shake Down the Thunder: The Creation of Notre Dame Football*, New York: Henry Holt.

Stanley, G. K. (1996) *The Rise and Fall of the Sportswoman: Women's Health, Fitness, and Athletics, 1860–1940*, New York: Peter Lang.

Stearns, A. E. (1914) 'Athletics and the school', *Atlantic Monthly* February: 148–52.

Stewart, C. A. (1914) 'Athletics and the college', *Atlantic Monthly* February: 153–60.

Storr, R. J. (1966) *Harper's University: The Beginnings*, Chicago: University of Chicago Press.

Talbot, M. (1910) *The Education of Women*, Chicago: University of Chicago Press.

——(1936) *More Than Lore: Reminiscences of Marion Talbot,* Chicago: University of Chicago Press.

Thomas, W. I. (1907) *Sex and Society: Studies in the Social Psychology of Sex*, Chicago: University of Chicago Press.

Twin, S. L. (1979) *Out of the Bleachers: Writing on Women and Sport*, Old Westbury, NY: Feminist Press.

——(1985) 'Women and sport', in D. Spivey (ed.) *Sport in America: New Historical Perspectives*, Westport, CN: Greenwood Press, pp. 193–217.

University of Chicago Magazine (1912a) 'A permanent building for the women of the university', 4 May: 204–7 no author.

——(1912b) 'What shall we do about intercollegiate athletics?', *University of Chicago Magazine* IV: 135–42 no author.

Verbrugge, M. H. (1988) *Able-Bodied Womanhhood: Personal Health and Social Change in Nineteenth-Century Boston*, New York: Oxford University Press.

Vertinsky, P. A. (1990) *The Eternally Wounded Woman: Women, Doctors, and Exercise in the Late Nineteenth Century*, Manchester: Manchester University Press.

Willard, F. E. (1991) *How I Learned to Ride the Bicycle*, Sunnyvale, CA: Fair Oaks Publishing {reprint *of A Wheel Within a Wheel*, 1895}.

Narrating Cultural Citizenship: Oral Histories of First-Generation College Students of Mexican Origin

Rina Benmayor

Rina Benmayor is a Professor in the Institute of Human Communication at California State University, Monterey Bay. In addition to teaching courses in Latina/o and Hispanic literature and culture, Dr. Benmayor is the cofounder and codirector of the CSUMB Oral History and Community Memory Institute and Archive, a public repository with over two hundred hours of interviews on the history of the Monterey Bay area. This essay originally appeared in a special issue of the independent journal *Social Justice* that focused on state and national efforts to control learning and how educators were devising innovative practices that resisted "standards" and instead promoted educational rights.

When I was in high school, I worked in the summers. Not because my parents made me . . . it was me, I wanted to do it. I wanted to have money for myself and to help them out. It was in the summer that I got a letter from ETS [Educational Talent Search], asking me to come to a program called FOCUS. It is a mini bridge program preparing us for college. . . .[1] I did it for a week and then I went back to work in the broccoli fields in Greenfield. All of a sudden, I got a call on the walkie-talkie. I was putting the boxes of broccoli together in the trailer. It was my supervisor's brother. He said "Pedro, I got some news for you." He hands me the walkie-talkie. [My supervisor on the other end] told me he got a call that I got accepted [to the university]. I was pretty happy! I told my mom. She started screaming! She was packing broccoli. She stopped and said she was very proud of me. It was good. All she could do was smile. She was so happy. Her dream for me to go to college was going to be complete (Student interview, González, 2000).

The "Broccoli Story," as I have dubbed it, is one of my favorites among more than 80 hours of oral histories with first-generation college students on our campus. In a graphic and poignant way, Pedro González captures the pride and hope that going to college represents for so many Mexican-origin[2] students and their parents. I always think of this story as I drive through the patchwork fields in the region. How many of the women and men I see stooping over this green gold are dreaming these dreams for their children?

Pedro's story also reminds me of why I joined the founding faculty of California State University, Monterey Bay (CSUMB). This new university was envisioned specifically to serve the historically underrepresented in higher education—low-income, working-class students from ethnic, racial, and im/migrant backgrounds. Given its geographic location at the edge of the Salinas Valley in California, I knew that many of my new students would be the daughters and sons of migrant *mexicana/o* farm workers, who work the fields to put food on our tables every day. Young women and men of Mexican heritage comprise 25% of our student body, and most of them are the first in their families to attend college, sometimes the first to graduate from high school.[3] The opportunity to combine professional and political purposes in one coherent effort remains very seductive.

Along with its emotional force, the "broccoli story" draws me in with its subtexts, interpretive possibilities, and theoretical potential. The story is about a personal and collective dream of achieving a college education. It makes a point of affirming a strong sense of responsibility to family, which for students often takes the form of continued contributions to the family economy, as well as role modeling, paving the way to higher education for younger siblings. These commitments shape Mexican-origin students' goals and aspirations in very significant ways. Pedro was not in the fields when telling this story. He was at the university library, constructing his account. He could tell the story because at that time he was living it.

How do I, as an oral historian, faculty member, and informal ethnographer on my own campus, interpret this story? Does it merely assert the culturally gendered role of the independent male provider? Or is the story really about how first-generation students of Mexican origin construct and fulfill that educational dream? How do they negotiate the transformative experience of higher education? Are they "losing their culture" to upward mobility, as some studies would claim? Do they experience college as a process of deracination? Or are they negotiating multiple cultural worlds in integrative ways, venturing into the unknown world of higher education to bring new resources to their cultural communities? What do they say about the university's support of their commitments and needs?

My oral history students and I have been asking these questions for several semesters, interviewing first-generation students of Mexican origin on our campus. Students have published their collectively authored research findings in two extensive Web pages (Oral History, 1998; 2000). Nourished by my students' interpretations, much secondary literature, and by the interviews, I now reflect on these questions, proposing that the narratives of first-generation Mexican-origin students on our campus express emerging claims for cultural citizenship (Flores and Benmayor, 1997; Benmayor, 1997; Benmayor et al., 1997).[4] Applied to

our campus context, claiming cultural citizenship means affirming the right *as Mexican-origin students* to receive quality education, to be on college campuses in significant numbers, and to be appropriately supported in their academic and career development. In other words, it is the right to first-class student status. More important, students of Mexican origin want to be valued for the cultural "assets" they bring to the 21st-century university, such as bilingualism, cross-cultural knowledge, and transnational experience. Instead, they find that traditional frameworks of assessment often stigmatize bilingual and bicultural students as academically deficient. Students of Mexican origin want to help shape the curriculum, the values, and the multicultural life of the university. They want the university to acknowledge and share their commitments to family and community, as well as support their personal goals and dreams.

The stories of first-generation students on our campus challenge hegemonic arrangements of meritocracy. At the same time, they affirm a subjectivity shaped by what Henry Giroux (1997: 125) calls "different cultural logics"—logics that are counter-hegemonic and affirm different epistemologies, cultural standpoints, and historical experiences.[5] The stories of first-generation Mexican-origin students at CSUMB articulate a cultural logic in which the value of education is measured not by individual class mobility or increased economic power, but by the collective advancement and well-being of their subordinated communities. Cultural citizenship becomes a particularly useful framework for analysis, then, as it articulates specific cultural logics and practices with collective claims for cultural rights, empowerment, and full belonging.

WHY CULTURAL CITIZENSHIP?

Cultural citizenship refers to "the ways people organize their values, their beliefs about their rights, and their practices based on their sense of cultural belonging rather than on their formal status as citizens of a nation" (Silvestrini, 1997: 44).[6] Framed in opposition to hegemonic legal citizenship, cultural citizenship describes "the claims of social, human, and cultural rights made by communities which do not hold state power and which are denied basic rights by those who do" (Inter-University Program,

1988: 2). Claims for cultural citizenship often go beyond those rights already enjoyed by "first-class" citizens. Disenfranchised, racialized, subordinated, and excluded peoples become what Stuart Hall and David Held (1990) call "new citizens," creating new rights, often not formally recognized by the law. Based on ethnicity, race, class, gender, sexuality, and other defining social identities and binding solidarities, claims for cultural citizenship question, disrupt, and re-map national projects, creating new rights and new ways of practicing citizenship itself.

In his introductory essay to *Latino Cultural Citizenship* (Flores and Benmayor, 1997: 37), Renato Rosaldo cautions that "too often social thought anchors its research in the vantage point of the dominant social group and thus reproduces the dominant ideology by studying subordinated groups as a 'problem' rather than as people with agency—with goals, perceptions, and purposes of their own." Cultural citizenship places at the center the ways in which subordinated groups perceive, affirm, and claim their rights and their cultural responsibilities. Drawing on their distinctive cultural assets, subordinated communities struggle to affirm equal inclusion and new rights to reshape civil society in more egalitarian, democratic, and creative ways. Going beyond pluralism, then, cultural citizenship destabilizes the essentialized idea of a unified "American" cultural logic and instead presents a cultural dynamic in perpetual tension.

10   A borderlands paradigm, cultural citizenship converses with liberation philosophies in education (Freire, 1972, 1973; hooks, 1994; Giroux, 1997, 1992; McLaren, 1997). Education has always been fundamental to the formation and reproduction of citizenship in the modern nation-state (Bourdieu, 1977; Banks, 1997; Aronowitz, 2000). Similarly, education and language have long been primary sites of cultural contestation and new citizenship for Latinas/os in the United States.[7] Chicana/o scholars have produced considerable research and writing on the experience of Latina/o students in higher education (Olivas, 1986; Rendón, 1992; Valdés, 1996; Cuádraz, 1996; Solórzano and Villalpando, 1999, among others). Though this body of scholarship does not explicitly use the framework of cultural citizenship, it speaks to the critical importance of cultural standpoint and what Moll and Vélez-Ibáñez call funds of knowledge (1990).[8] Moving beyond old immigrant-based paradigms of assimilation and social integration, this scholarship calls for a consideration of ethno-cultural values and practices, racialized histories and experiences, and complex gender roles as critical factors in understanding how minoritized students experience college. Solórzano and Villalpando propose, for example, that for students of color, marginality is not just a site of domination. Citing bell hooks (1990: 153), they frame marginality as a site of resistance and empowerment (1999: 304). Cultural citizenship captures this nexus, as it describes the cultural dynamics and logics through which subordinated communities construct claims, affirm their sense of rights and entitlements, and act to transform margins into centers. How, then, does cultural citizenship manifest itself among Mexican-origin students on the CSUMB campus?

WHY FIRST GENERATION?

Given our distinctive campus community, an oral history research class on first-generation college students made sense in many ways.[9] The topic offered a unique opportunity for my students to engage in action research and contribute to the development of this new university's outreach, recruitment, and retention programs. Students' testimonies provide deeper insight into how they negotiate the experience of college. At the same time, they serve administrators and planners as a report card on the campus' success in serving the student population that is at the core of its vision and that, according to the latest census figures (Martinez and Garcia, 2001), is mushrooming. From another perspective, teaching a class on the topic of first-generation college students opens up interesting curricular and pedagogical opportunities.

The Project

The course I designed was titled, "Oral History and Community Memory: First in My Family to Go to College." I taught it twice, in spring 1998 and spring 2000. In total, students in the course interviewed 63 first-generation students. Of the interviewees, 41 were of Mexican origin, six were African American, one was Asian American, and 15 were white, representing diverse European ethnic origins.[10] Of the Mexican-origin students interviewed, 30 were female and 11 were male.[11] Many participated in our "Summer Bridge" program between high school and college; others were community college transfer students. Most interviews ran an hour in length and were audio recorded either on campus or in student housing. Interviewees signed consent forms, authorizing the use of their name or a pseudonym.[12] All the interviews are archived in the CSUMB Oral History and Community Memory Archive (1999), in analog and digital formats.

Drawing from secondary sources and their own personal histories, students in the class developed interview guides, focusing on what they felt were the most important aspects of the first-generation experience. The guide included topics like the memory of high school, expectations of college, the transition to college, financial aid, other kinds of support, cultural identity, and future goals. These topics guided the research and analysis, shaping the final study that each class produced. In addition, the class of 2000 was able to divide their inquiry into three cohorts: frosh, sophomores, and juniors, capturing important differentials within the academic and social experience of college. These studies are published on the Web and reflect what students interpreted to be of greatest significance (Oral History Student Websites, 1998; 2000). Students also publicly presented their research findings and recommendations on campus. Their studies stand as a unique contribution to the critical literature on first-generation college students, as they are the only "published" studies on the subject collaboratively authored by students.

When I Told Him I Was Thinking of Going to College, He Laughed: Memory, Cultural Community, and Rights

Memory is where cultural citizenship and oral history meet. Remembrance involves reclaiming legacies of struggle (Giroux, 1997: 153–154). Thus, speaking a memory of exclusion is part of the process of voicing rights. Prompted by questions like, "*Did high school prepare you for college? Did anyone encourage you to go to college? Did anyone discourage you?*" our narrators began to construct a collective memory of their educational pasts, paying tribute to those who supported and encouraged them and indicting institutional neglect. We heard uplifting stories about exceptional teachers or counselors:

15   There were a couple of professors that really encouraged me; they saw in me a person that was capable of achieving in what she [laughing] wanted. They would recommend me for different programs. They would tell me, "Here is this scholarship; you should apply for it." A lot of information I got from teachers. They were a big change in my life. They recommended me. They were like really good role models (Student interview, Patty Delgado, 1998).

The reason why I'm here is because I had a good counselor I guess in high school. One time I was walking down the halls and he approached me and said, what I'm going to do after high school? I had just, at that point I was thinking of going to a community college, Hartnell; and you know, he took me into his office and looked at all my stuff and told me to apply here—that I had a good chance of getting in. So he gave me all the forms and I just applied and I'm here (Student interview, Wilfredo Vargas, 2000).

However, the "exceptional teacher/counselor" stories were overpowered by strong memories of discriminatory treatment, particularly from counselors:

...My counselor in high school, she just gave me the classes she wanted. She never said, "Oh, this is a college course, oh, this not going to help you." Basically, I got it myself.... I guess she had something against me. Because every time I went to see her, she was really angry and in a bitchy mood, and I think she treated me bad [sic] (Student interview, Gregorio X, 1998).

My counselor actually never told me I could go to college and when I told him I was gonna, I was thinking about going to college, he laughed. So you know he pretty much laughed, like not just smile, he laughed (emphasized), you know (Student interview, César Mora, 2000).

Stories like these sparked emotional class- 20 room discussions, as most students in the class remembered similar experiences in high school. Students spoke angrily about being ignored or led to believe they were not smart, and thus not worthy, or that they did not belong in college or have a right to a university education.

Being marked as exceptional or being ignored are the two extremes of the same system of stratification. Yet, despite the fact that our first-generation students were made to feel invisible, students did not invoke victimization. Their narratives often counterbalanced exclusion with a strong affirmation of cultural resources as sources of support. Their accounts speak of parental encouragement, even when the experience of college was not part of the family history. Patty Delgado's response is representative of the majority of our interviewees:

> They were really proud of me. They encouraged me. When I needed to go take a test for college or anything, they were always there for me. My mother, I asked her, "Mom, can you take me to take this test?" She had to work that day and she went and asked for the day off. She even told me if they wouldn't allow it, she would quit the job. Just so that I would take a test! (Student interview, Delgado, 1998).

Interestingly, María X makes an important distinction between encouragement and concrete mentoring, both of which she received outside of school:

> Usually what encouraged me to go to college was my parents . . . but, in high school, like teachers or counselors never told me you know, they never encouraged me. So, I always got the encouragement to go to college outside, not inside, school (Student interview, María X, 1998).

25 Interviewees reported that their strongest sources of mentoring and support came from the affirmative action recruitment programs that entered the school, but were not a formal part of the institution:

> I think that the *Yo Puedo* program, that was like a really inspiring experience for me because, um, that was the time when I first heard the word college. . . . I didn't know like if I wanted to go to any CSU or a U.C., but that was the first time that the word college was placed in my mind (Student interview, María Lupe Figueroa, 2000).

I wanted to go to Hartnell [Community College], but then one of my Migrant Education counselors pulled me out of class one day, and she told me I had good grades, a good grade point average, and that I could attend college, other than a community college. . . . So she helped me out by getting applications, going on fieldtrips, visiting universities, and talking to people, to counselors . . . students at the universities. Basically, getting to know more of the life of a university. . . . Because, like I said, I wasn't planning, and if it wasn't for Miss Arroyave . . . (Student interview, Gregorio X, 1998).

In high school, I was involved in *Educational Talent Search*. Well, I was involved in it since seventh grade. In seventh and eighth grade, they helped us with homework and tutored us. Then from ninth grade to twelfth grade, they just, well especially in our senior year, they helped us fill out the applications to come to the university. The federal aid applications, the EOP application. Then the ACT and the SAT. Everything that you have to take. Then ninth grade through tenth grade we did academic plans. We had to write down what classes we were taking, as if they were preparing us to go to a university (Student interview, Sandra Chavarín, 2000).

I think that ETS served a really good motivational, you know, part for me. I would get called out of class and we would, you know, have one of the [ETS] counselors come and say, "these are the classes that you have and these are the ones that you need to take." When the application period came, I was really busy and they really helped me, I mean, they were so helpful that they sent applications for me. And it was just like, it was great. They helped me write my essay and it was really good, and plus they always offered programs and fieldtrips, and stuff like that. So they were a nice chunk of the portion of the people that helped me come to school (Student interview, Merlyn Calderón, 1998).

Of course, we were interviewing students who, 30 for the most part, were recruited to our campus through Educational Talent Search or Migrant Education, so their responses were not surprising. However, from a cultural perspective, the "biased" sample still makes a valid point. Born in the era of civil rights, these programs are highly successful in recruiting and serving low-income, first-generation, immigrant students, or those ethnically underrepresented in higher education. Once in college, first-generation students can work as outreach recruiters and counselors in local middle and high schools.[13] This circular network supports students financially, emotionally, and culturally. In motivating middle and high school youth to consider college, student recruiters motivate themselves to stay in college and succeed. They look to the Mexican-origin staff of these programs as surrogate parents and role models. Consequently, Mexican-origin high school and college students readily identify these programs as a sustaining part of their "cultural community." Patricia Morales interprets their function as community advocacy:

> I think ETS plays a big role because that's some of the people that helped me back home. They helped me, they informed me about financial aid, how to apply, and the different programs available and all that. They do because at the same time that they are informing the kids, they are making the parents aware. Like that, for their next child, they will be able to encourage more and give more support to them (Student interview, Morales, 1998).

Migrant Education provided Yolanda X with a model for how she might fulfill her desire to contribute to her community:

> I had one role model that I still admire up to this date. He was a Migrant Counselor, Mr. Cárdenas. He encouraged me a lot. He is helping a lot of migrant students get to high school and that is what I would like to do. And he told me that after I finish college, it would be nice to take his place.
>
> **How did it make you feel after he said that?**
>
> It made me feel that he had a lot of faith in me. That he knew me very well, as well as I knew him. He knew that one day I would come back to the high school or anywhere around the community and help other kids

as well and that is my focus because he encouraged me. That is why I want to go back.

(Student interview, Yolanda X, 2000).

Parental encouragement, caring teachers, and 35 the outreach programs loomed large in our interviewees' memories. Many said that without these programs, they would not be in the university today. Interviewees clearly identified their cultural sources of support and acknowledged the feelings of entitlement, self-confidence, and empowerment they had gained. Consequently, they began to picture themselves and the generations to come as *belonging* in the university. Articulating this sense of entitlement and belonging is the first step in forming a real and an *imagined* community of first-generation Mexican-origin students in higher education. It is also the first step toward affirming the right to belong on their own terms.

THE VISION, IT'S NOT GETTING DONE: CULTURAL CITIZENSHIP ON CAMPUS

At its heart, cultural citizenship is a construction of belonging and community entitlement from the perspective of subordinated groups. Drawing upon one's own cultural resources to build that sense of entitlement expands and transforms the public space. Once in the university, how did our first-generation interviewees negotiate this new environment and construct a framework for belonging?

In analyzing the data, students in the class of 2000 distinguished the concerns of frosh, sophomores, and juniors. They found that in the first year, students were preoccupied with adjusting to new academic expectations and being away from home. Sophomores voiced stronger concern over experiences in the classroom and the availability of academic and financial support, tutoring and mentoring, financial aid, and job opportunities. Juniors were more openly critical of the university and spoke more about expanding their networks, future careers, and world vision (Oral History Student Web Pages, 2000).

When asked what sources of support they found on campus, the frosh said that the Summer Bridge program, Educational Talent Search, Migrant Education, and clubs like M.E.Ch.A

(Movimiento Estudiantil Chicano de Aztlán) or
Mujeres de Maíz provided students with a second
familia on campus, a site of cultural comfort (on
concepts of *familia* and cultural community, see
Benmayor et al., 1997: 182–189).[14] Miriam Rivera
was asked:

**Do you feel like you have a lot in common
with the students here on
the CSUMB campus?**

Actually, the ones I can relate to are the
ones from ETS. We just bonded.
40   Everybody just had something in
common. And with other students here at
CSUMB, I guess I don't talk to them enough
to find out if I really relate to them, but with
the ETS people I do.

**Do you think that has to do with your cul-
ture, being Hispanic?**

Yeah, I think it does. I think it does, and the
family, how you grow up, because there's a
lot of similarities.

So you're bilingual?

Uh huh, yeah.

**And most of the people in ETS are bilingual
too?**

Uh huh.

Does that offer you some support?

Yeah, I think it does. You feel comfortable.
You feel like you're at home, yeah

(Student interview, Rivera, 1998).

45   Students' testimonies confirm what Troy
Duster (1991) reported a decade ago in his campus study of diversity at U.C. Berkeley. Ethnic clusters are one of the ways first-generation students
construct a space of cultural belonging and peer
support on campus.

Outside the safe space of a second *familia*,
however, do Mexican-origin first-generation students feel integral to the university? An important
part of our research included inquiry into issues of
identity, diversity, and representation. When asked
if they felt their ethnic group was well represented
on campus, interviewees generally said yes, with
the exception of those from urban cities.[15] Students
from local rural cities like Salinas and Watsonville

said that the university was their first experience in
a diverse, multicultural environment:

> . . . like in my high school, there's no
> diversity at all. So when I came here, I was
> really like "Oh!" . . . And I liked it, you know.
> It's different, everybody's different. . . . In
> my high school, like 99.9% are Mexican
> Americans. . . . So I like that here it's diverse
> (Student interview, Miriam Rivera, 1998).

Some who came from metropolitan contexts like
Los Angeles sometimes found ethnic groupings on
campus uncomfortable. Angélica X said:

> I just had friends from everywhere. And then
> I came here. And it was just so weird to see
> how . . . there's a group of Mexicans and
> then there's a group . . . but I didn't see any
> integration between them. And I didn't know
> if it was because, okay, they are just friends
> or they have other friends of other races. But
> just going to the cafeteria, I saw that, and I'd
> go to the store and I'd see it. . . . It made me
> feel really weird (Student interview,
> Angélica X, 1998).

Paradoxically, Angélica dealt with her feeling of   50
alienation through a very culturally marked practice. Since she did not find the diverse community
she expected on campus, she turned to the Mexican
community in nearby Salinas. One can read her
discomfort with the campus environment as a critique of imbalanced representation among students of color and a discomfort with physical
isolation. Constructed on an old military base (Fort
Ord), CSUMB is radically different from a city
school, where the boundaries between school and
the daily life of the community are more porous.
Ironically, the Service Learning program, which
links courses with related community service, provided her with a connection to the very ethnic community she rejected on campus:

> I just think it is really important to know
> the people around you, like the new people
> and your new community. . . . That's why I
> think Service Learning is great because it
> gets you out there (Student interview,
> Angélica X, 1998).

The classroom is one of the primary sites
where students negotiate cultural identity and

diversity. Across our sample from frosh to juniors, students like Carlos Armenta report receiving a high degree of personal attention from faculty, which has been very intentional on our campus:

> You know I think what really makes it different here is a lot of the professors are real down to earth. Real. I think that's probably why I look up to a few of them. . . .

When you say down to earth, do you mean like they can relate to you or—

Yeah. . . or it's the class environment. It's not like. . . if you don't get it, too bad. . . . They'll sit and take the time to make sure that you know it. . . . They talk with you just like normal people. . . . I think that's what really makes it nice, because the community is small; I mean, you can have that one-on-one interaction with the teachers. . . . It's not, you know, like at other colleges where it's one professor to 300 students (Student interview, Armenta, 2000).

55   However, first-generation Mexican-origin students are also highly sensitive to treatment that imposes difference upon them. María X vividly remembers her experience of being "othered" in the classroom:

> . . . I never thought I was gonna see that. In one of my classes we were all scheduled to do an essay . . . so . . . the teacher, after he read them, I guess he was kind of disappointed. . . . But what I didn't like was that he went in that day and he started talking Spanish. And . . . there's like five or six Hispanics—they're Mexicans—and the rest are a different race. . . . So, he started speaking Spanish and saying that he could understand that it was difficult for us to write a good paper because English wasn't our first language. . . . The other people didn't understand Spanish. Well, what did he try to say, you know? That we're not that good like the other people? Like our papers weren't that good? . . . I understand that maybe because our language wasn't English, our first language, but he didn't have the right of speaking Spanish. He could have told us, you know, in private, not in front of all of them [the class] and like embarrass us. . . . A lot of

my friends, we felt offended because of that. . . . I guess the reason he tried talking in Spanish was just for us to understand, not the rest of them [the class], you know. . . .

So, are you affected by that experience?

It was a disappointment. . . . It made me feel bad, because it made me feel that I am here as one of *those persons* . . .

> (Student interview, María X, 1998).

Students also spoke out about racism outside the classroom, testifying to a fragile sense of belonging that Mexican-origin students feel, despite their numbers. Pedro recalled:

> Well on Monday, there was a rally on racism, which I thought was really great. Everyone was there. It was the first time that I felt united with the whole campus. . . . I mean, a lot of the students got together the rally because of the hate email toward them [in this case African Americans], but there has [*sic*] been others directed at the Latino community, too. My friend sent an email wanting to start a Latino Business Club. Well, somebody took this as an opportunity to bash Latinos with racist comments and suggestions like having a white male business club with the directors being David Duke and Adolph Hitler (Student interview, González, 1998).   60

Incidents like this caused students to question the campus' ability to live up to its own multicultural vision. Students expressed an acute awareness of class boundaries and differential treatment, even when it did not involve them directly:

> Frankly, I think the Vision Statement . . . has not been met. . . . When it tries to be met, it gets challenged with a lot of racism and it all falls through the cracks. . . .

> . . . We have the Migrant Program . . . [but if] we look back at the records, we see . . . the director . . . doesn't have any support. He has moved from building to building and now he is at a dorm, basically. That is where he has his office. . . . That is my main concern with the Vision Statement, not being realized with my race, my group.

There's a lot of us who don't have the money to go to a university. . . . This university says it's offering that chance to people, but it doesn't go out there and grab other people that are low income. If you look at [other] students here, . . . their parents are full of money and . . . they're doing stuff just to have fun. And *they* are not wasting any money, their *parents* are. And *we* have people here paying their own tuition. . . . I think my main concern with the Vision Statement, it's not getting done (Student interview, González, 2000).

Critiques of racist or degrading treatment are emerging claims for cultural citizenship on campus. Students hold the institution accountable, asking it to "walk the talk." Mexican-origin students feel personally violated by disrespect either to themselves or to one of their community. The cultural values of *respeto*, *dignidad*, and *confianza* are deeply engrained in their upbringing and acquire added potency in situations where they feel marginalized or excluded (Rosaldo, 1997; Benmayor et al., 1997; Valdés, 1997; Vélez-Ibáñez, 1983; Lauria-Perricelli, 1964). They are conscious of the ever-present danger of renewed invisibility. Their call for the Vision can be read as an affirmation of cultural citizenship, of the right of Mexican-origin students to be respected and supported as core members of the university community. Whether in class, in their jobs, in their *familias*, through campus activism, or through speaking out in these interviews, students expressed their right to be on campus, their right to be supported, and to be treated equally, with cultural respect. First-generation Mexican-origin interviewees were acutely aware of what "gets done" and what does not, and in the end, gave the campus a mixed report card.

SO I WANT TO MAKE THE CONNECTION: CULTURAL CITIZENSHIP AS CULTURAL RESPONSIBILITY

65 Within the education literature, empirical studies on first-generation students generally focus on issues of access, cognitive development, performance, persistence, outcomes, and class mobility (Lamont and Lareau, 1988; McDonough, 1991; Terenzini et al., 1996; Walpole, 1998; Boatsman,

2000).[16] Although most contemporary studies take into account Bourdieu's (1977) concepts of "cultural capital" and "habitus,"[17] as mediating factors in class mobility, relatively little has been written on cultural dynamics, epistemologies, and practices among first-generation students of specific racial/ethnic groups (Lara, 1992; Sidel, 1994; Rochlin, 1997; Shibazaki, 1999).

In an often-cited essay that aims to explore the more "intimate" cultural dynamics of the first-generation experience, Howard London (1992: 5) contends that "the cultural challenges faced by first-generation students are not limited to the classroom, but include the difficulties of redefining relationships and self-identity." Using old separation theory, London argues that "'moving up' requires a 'leaving off' and a 'taking on,' the shedding of one social identity and the acquisition of another" (1992: 8). He concludes that:

> It is only when we see that negotiating cultural obstacles involves not just gain but loss—most of all the loss of a familiar past, including a past self—that we can begin to understand the attendant periods of confusion, conflict, isolation, and even anguish reported by first-generation students (1992: 10).

Although this analysis accounts for some of the cultural tension that first-generation students experience, its framework is fundamentally assimilationist, assuming a linear trajectory of upward mobility—that students will experience a "molting process" and painfully shed their old cultural skins as they gradually achieve social and economic mobility.[18] The language is telling: that college marks a *separation*, a *loss of a familiar past*, a *loss of a past self*, a *break* with the past, a *traumatic* period of *confusion, conflict, isolation, anguish* [emphasis added]. Such language is closely associated with "deficit" thinking, stressing first-generation students' problems and obstacles in successfully negotiating college (Terenzini et al., 1996).

Drawing from new thought in ethnic studies, cultural studies, and critical race theory, Chicana/o scholars offer radically different frameworks of interpretation with regard to Mexican-origin and other students of color (Solórzano and Villalpando, 1999; Cuádraz, 1996; Rendón, 1992; Valdés, 1997; Moll, Vélez-Ibáñez, and Greenberg, 1990). Daniel Solórzano and Octavio Villalpando suggest that "redefining relationships and self-identity" may not accurately describe or explain the experience of first-generation students of color:

70   ...The assumption that they [first-generation students] succeed largely because of their ability to conform to the dominant cultural norms of a college environment ignores much of their current and historical experiences in higher education. . . . Some students of color have developed what we call critical resistant navigational skills to succeed in higher education. Many of these skills do not stem from students' conformist or adaptive strategies, but emerge from their resistance to domination and oppression in a system that devalues their ethno and sociocultural experiences (1999: 306).

Instead of measuring the achievement and success of first-generation students through a social mobility paradigm, Chicana/o scholarship recognizes the ways in which working-class students of color use their cultural resources — their funds of knowledge — to actively resist that paradigm.

Our interviews support the need for new frameworks to understand the experiences of first-generation students of Mexican origin. In constructing themselves as cultural citizens in the university, our interviewees were claiming rights and assuming cultural responsibilities. Although students spoke about difficulties negotiating college and home life, they did not express a sense of anguish or fragmentation. Instead, they attested to a desire to integrate their multiple cultural worlds, aspirations, and responsibilities. Rather than separate from family, many of our interviewees embraced their various positionalities, seeking to become effective students, family advocates, and community builders. For example, in her interview, María Lupe Figueroa acknowledges ways in which college has changed, but not alienated her:

I think my ideas have changed in the way that I see things that I didn't see before. . . . Like my little sister used to tell me when I go home, "Lupe, I don't know what is happening to you. You're like Lupe, but you're not Lupe. . . ." So, I think they are seeing that side of me that I am changing. But I am trying to change in a positive way, that I can inform them and educate them just by sharing my experiences [learning] in the classroom. . . .

Like, don't be racist. Don't criticize people because of the way they look. . . . First, hear their story and hear what they have to say, and then [draw] your own conclusion or make your decision. So, in terms of the community, they look at me and I feel like some kind of pressure because all the time they are like, "Oh, she's going to college. Look at the family. They are not rich, but she is in college. . . ." So, I am like, "Okay, now I have to make it. . . ." Because of me, but also . . . because of my family, because of my community, because I do want to help my community. I do want to go back and help and serve, and be like a resource for them. So, I want to make the connection between like community and my family, with education, with college life (Student interview, Figueroa, 2000).

From Lupe's standpoint, education is about making a difference in one's home community. Almost every Mexican-origin student we interviewed expressed this sense of mission. Agency and memory dialogue with each other to produce this integrated subjectivity. As children of *mexicano* farm workers and working-class families, students spoke from the experience of second-class or noncitizenship. Reminiscences of growing up in a farmworker family are determining for many students. Wilfredo Vargas explains:

You mentioned that you had the support   75
from your parents, that they didn't want you
to suffer what they suffered. What did you
mean by that?

Well, both my parents, when they got here they worked in the fields. My father, he worked at [sic] cauliflower and my mother worked in the strawberries. And I don't know if you know about working in the strawberries. It's not the best job, and they both come in late, you know, dirty and stuff, and I hardly ever see them until seven. And, yeah, they would tell me, "You don't want to go that way and your education is the answer" (Student interview, Vargas, 2000).

For Juanita López, the painful awareness of her parents' sacrifice motivates her:

I think that I'm in college because it was like a goal and a challenge that I wanted to put myself through. . . . Because both of my parents worked in the agricultural fields and I would see them get up early in the morning, five in the morning, maybe four in the morning, come [home] late, seven, eight, nine. My dad, at times I would be asleep by the time he got home. So, I knew that I wanted something different for myself (Student interview, López, 2000).

Memory shapes the students' advocacy and they are aware that by going to college they are building new funds of knowledge, new family practices, new histories, and new memory. Responding to London's claims about separation from family and culture, we asked students whether they or their parents felt that by coming to college they were "losing their culture." Some said:

80   I think we gain our culture! I think we learn more about where we come from. I now know a lot of things I didn't know in the past (Student Interview, Gregorio X: 1998).

I remember . . . a lot of people would say [about college], "You'll lose yourself. You're going to forget you're Mexican." I would say, "Why? That's dumb!" Here [at this campus] . . . we're not the majority and we didn't lose it. My family knows I haven't lost it. We are always in organizations, marching [in protest], or doing this or that. If that were the case, I wouldn't be teaching at a bilingual school (Student interview, Anonymous, 1998).

Honoring family and culture is one of the strongest assets Mexican-heritage students bring with them to college. Yet, the mainstream literature often positions the family environment as a liability. A commonly voiced claim is that parents are unable to guide their children through the exigencies and stresses of an educational system in this country. In this deficit mode of analysis, emphasis is placed on what students lack, while ignoring the cultural assets they bring to the educational environment.

Guadalupe Valdés' ethnographic study of immigrant Mexican families (1997: 169–189) provides important insight into how they prepare children to survive and succeed in school. Life chances, Valdés argues, are connected to cultural environment and social conditions that immigrant families experience in countries of origin. Families who migrate from rural Mexico come from "a world where relationships and human ties are far more important than options or choices" (p. 171). Consequently, reciprocal relationships, security, trust, continuity, and being part of a larger entity with a shared history are values that take precedence over the ethos of individualism encountered in the U.S. Though parents may not have the education or the time to become more intimately involved in their children's formal schooling, they school their children in another way. Children receive cultural nurturing and connection to family history and values, which they readily identified in their narratives as a source of pride and a strategy for empowerment.

It is not surprising, then, that so many of our narrators expressed deeply rooted collective concepts of "payback," "role modeling," and "return to community." Acutely aware of being "the first" inspires them to want to return to community, to guide younger generations, and prevent them from becoming casualties of a tracking system that relegates poor students of color to vocational training or community college at best.[19] In this regard, Sandra Chavarín speaks to the importance of role modeling:

How do you feel now about the community that you came from?

. . . The people that live there are farm   85
workers that have kids going to school. . . . Farm workers go from sunrise to sunset, so they are never with their kids. Except for a little while before bed. So most of the kids are off track. They just go to school, but they don't know what they are doing. . . . They don't know what's going on. So they are just lost, or afraid. So I think they need more role models to go in there and tell them, "My parents were farm workers. I also went to school in Mexico, but now I'm going to a university." That they can do the same thing when they get older. Just helping them settle down and start helping them realize what they want to do.

How do your brothers and sisters feel about being in college?

I haven't ever asked them that question. . . . But I think that my little sisters give me support. Especially the little one that's nine years old. She tells me that she wants to be like me. That she wants to be a teacher and wants to go to college. And it's so funny of her because I cut my hair and she goes, "I want to cut my hair like you." She just tells me she wants to be like me. I think she's the one that gives me the most support, because then I think that if I do finish college and become a teacher or other professional job, then she's going to be looking at me . . .

(Student interview, Chavarín, 2000).

Benjamín Jiménez tutored elementary school kids in East Salinas, which has helped him think about becoming a teacher. In going out to the community, he says:

You're being a role model to individuals if you work with students like I do. . . . I just tell them, "I graduated from Gonzales. I'm local." You know . . . I understand what is going on with them . . . and their parents like know that the only thing is education. And they would push the student. . . . "You have to go to college. You have to study, you have to study." The students . . . realize, "Oh, I can't be like my parents, I have to be . . . better than my parents." That's how I was, you know. I can't be like a farm [worker] . . . like just drive tractors, just spray fertilizers on the ground. . . . [I have to be] something . . . more helpful for myself and for the community (Student interview, Jimenez, 2000).

90   In our interviews, students commonly used phrases like "becoming a role model," "going back," "giving back," and "paying back." María X articulates the concept of payback:

My experiences with Educational Talent Search have been great. . . . They helped me a lot coming here, to say, "I want to go to college." I feel like they reward[ed] me, so now I'm paying back that reward by helping other students in high school get prepared for college (Student interview, María X: 1998).

Asked what his goals were after college, Pedro González responded:

Get a career in my major, Art. . . . I'm not sure what kind of job it will be, but as soon

as I get that job, I will try to make life easier for my parents. In other words, helping them with their payments. Try to encourage my brothers to keep on going . . . to university. . . . My main goal is just helping out my family. That's a big part of my life. They were there when you needed them. They're just there for me and I just want to pay them back (Student interview, González, 1998).

These expressions are part of the vernacular language of cultural citizenship. As ethnographers, cultural studies scholars, and oral historians point out, vernacular language is a symbolic signifier. Grossberg (1994: 20) suggests that one "must listen for the 'stutterings,' the unexpected dialects and misspeakings, the unpredicted articulations, within the hegemonic culture. . . , which may enable the mobilization of peoples' memories, fantasies, desires. . . . " Through culturally coded terms, students affirm an awareness of their historically subordinated class location and a sense of their social responsibility as path breakers, for their families and younger siblings as well as for the extended community.

Within the framework of cultural citizenship, providing role models, mentoring the next generations, and giving back to family are expressions of political agency. The first-generation Mexican-origin students we interviewed are all engaged in some act of "return." They do so from the cultural logic of reciprocity, but also from the conviction that every child of Mexican origin in the U.S. has the right to a college education. This right is framed not merely as a hypothetical or a possibility, but as a demand—on the family, the community, on themselves to be active cultural agents and pave the way, and on the educational system to provide access and insure their success.

Many of our interviewees cited their long- 95 term career goals as returning to their communities to be teachers, counselors, principals, social workers, or small business owners. These professions are rooted in older agrarian concepts of community mutual aid. Rather than a separation from collective commitments, college represents an opportunity for Mexican-origin students to gain new cultural capital to "capitalize" on their cultural funds of knowledge and apply them professionally. Largely, the career goals they seek represent social benefit to their communities. In this regard, for Mexican-origin first-generation students on our campus, individual upward mobility does not appear to be the ultimate goal. Instead, they hope to reinforce reciprocal relations and build collective welfare.

THE CLASSROOM AS A SITE OF CULTURAL CITIZENSHIP

Cultural citizenship shaped these reflections and transformed my pedagogy. The decision to give the class a unifying topic and organize it around a collaborative project was predicated on my hope that students would feel personally invested and intellectually passionate about researching the experiences of first-generation students and the role of our university in serving them. I assumed that all students, first generation or not, would feel a personal stake in an investigation that placed their lived experiences at the center. Given their insider status as college students and as members of a shared university community, their lived experiences could be valued as intellectual capital. Although I hoped the class would resonate for every student, given our campus demographics I was seeking to offer first-generation students, and particularly Mexican-origin students, a central platform of expertise. I wanted the course to provide a space for them to validate the deeper cultural logics, experiences, and funds of knowledge they bring to the table, guiding our analyses in unique ways. I tried to situate this project within what bell hooks (1994: 13) calls "engaged pedagogy" and what Grossberg describes as "a pedagogy of risk and experimentation" and a "politics of praxis," where student protagonism is at the fore:

> Praxical pedagogy . . . attempts to offer people the skills that would enable them to understand and intervene in their own history, to challenge the institutional relations of power. . . . Students should gain some understanding of the world in which they exist . . . , construct and reconstruct their world in new ways . . . , [and] draw unexpected maps and possibilities (1994: 16).

In 1998 and 2000, over half the students in the class were the first in their families to go to college. Both times, students jumped into the topic without reserve. They listened to each other's life stories with enormous respect, and in their discussion demonstrated a great sensitivity to their multiple standpoints. Everyone learned from each other, but particularly from the first-generation Mexican-origin students in the class. All students engaged the secondary readings passionately and critically. They knew when the readings rang true and when they didn't, when they were lacking in analysis, and when they were insightful. Class conversations were emotional, didactic, and culturally affirming. Mexican-origin students were not in the minority and they were not rendered invisible. Their experiences were at the center of the investigation. This arrangement allowed my students and me to position ourselves in a more complex, dialogic relationship as collaborators, co-scholars, and interlocutors engaged in applied learning and action research. The classroom became an affirming space of cultural citizenship within the university.

Emulating our narrators, the final part of our class mission was to return our research to them and the university community. The practice of community oral history is never complete without engaging in some form of knowledge reciprocation. It is a litmus test of ethical accountability and intellectual honesty. The class of 1998 published their study as a special issue of the student newspaper. In 1998 and 2000, the classes designed public forums and scripted them so that everyone had a part. Interviewees, other students, administrators, and faculty attended these events (Oral History Student Web Pages, 1998; 2000; video clips and photographs are included in the sites). In spring 2000, the students concluded their presentation with a set of "Recommendations and Action Plan" (Oral History Student Web Pages, 2000). Recommendations focused on recruitment and retention of "Vision" students, and included improving outreach materials, establishing a mentorship program for parents, hiring EOP counselors, and designing premajor advising with the academic departments. Also called for were increasing job opportunities on campus, strengthening Summer Bridge and the Academic Skills Assistance Program, establishing a visionary language-support program for second-language learners, and conducting large-scale recruitment of students and faculty who embody the University Vision. Their final words were: "Embrace the Vision; Live up to the Vision; Hurry up!" (Oral History Student Web Pages, 2000). Students demonstrated how oral history can be action research.

CONCLUSION

100 With this study, I am proposing a cultural framework for interpreting the educational stories of first-generation Mexican-origin students who are rooted in histories of migration, rural farm labor, and working-class economies. As the demographics of California unfold, it becomes more urgent and imperative for educational institutions and faculty to understand who their students are, what aspirations and commitments they hold, and what assets they bring to the classroom and the larger society. It is important to know that first-generation Mexican-origin students need peers, mentors, and role models for *familia* on campus, and that they need appropriate structural supports that enable them to thrive. It is equally important to know that as students from subordinated communities, their social commitments shape their personal aspirations in deep and abiding ways. They do not break off from their families and in many ways resist the "American dream" of individual upward mobility, and instead are deeply concerned with improving the life chances of their families and communities. They simultaneously look back and forward. Given the high stakes, students have a right to expect that higher education will be responsive to their presence, their needs, and their goals.

This analysis also points to limitations in mainstream studies of first-generation college students. The beauty of examining the experience of first-generation Mexican-origin students through the lens of cultural citizenship is that this framework allows for, indeed requires, a close reading of students' cultural discourses and practices. The ethnography of cultural citizenship involves articulating memory, language, narratives, and discourses in specific settings and historical contexts with cultural and political agency. Concepts of "cultural logic," "funds of knowledge," "cultural capital," and "habitus" are very useful for describing how first-generation students negotiate their college experience, apply existing and newly acquired assets, and integrate their trajectories with those of their families and communities. Cultural citizenship acknowledges that cultural practices have profoundly political stakes and that agency is deeply informed by cultural meanings.

As first-generation Mexican-origin college students negotiate a better future for themselves, their families, and their communities, they are constructing and affirming their cultural citizenship. Woven throughout their stories is a fundamental claim to the right to shape the educational experience in ways that are culturally meaningful and socially productive for their communities. They claim a right to higher education in cultural terms, recognizing the importance of distinctive cultural values, funds of knowledge, logics, and histories to their futures as a community and as citizens. The affirmation of culturally relevant education and commitments to community public service may seem anachronistic in our region, in light of the young millionaire success stories in nearby Silicon Valley. Our narrators reveal, however, a fundamental process of turning histories of cultural and economic subordination into empowering integrative spaces in which students negotiate and interconnect multiple allegiances, without having to cut any ties or limit their aspirations. As they model through cultural citizenship the possibility of an integrated, subject position, first-generation college students of Mexican origin challenge institutions and ideologies to follow suit.

Notes

1. Educational Talent Search is a national program that recruits low-income, working-class students in middle and high schools to be the first in their families to go to college. Students are mentored for college preparation throughout their secondary education. FOCUS was the first summer bridge program at California State University, Monterey Bay. Fourteen first-generation students spent two weeks on the campus during the summer in an intensive program that acquainted them with college life and academic expectations. Currently, the Summer Bridge program has expanded to 40 students and is an intensive six-week residential program of workshops and classes that gives students the advantage of entering their first year with 10 academic credits completed.

2. I prefer "Mexican origin" to "Mexican heritage" since heritage may suggest a more

remote cultural connection to Mexico than is the case among most of our interviewees. In this study, "Mexican-origin" describes: (1) students who are children or grandchildren of *mexicana/o* families from rural Mexico (predominantly from the states of Guanajuato, Jalisco, and Michoacán), who have been employed in the U.S. as agricultural farm workers (migrant or not), or who have moved into low-paying service-sector jobs; (2) students who are third generation in the United States, perhaps English dominant, whose parents may occupy lower managerial positions within the labor market. Most of our interviewees come from rural towns and cities in California, with some from urban or suburban environments. Mexican-origin students on our campus self-identify as *mexicana/o* (those born and perhaps raised in Mexico and who migrated with their parents to the U.S.), Mexican American or Hispanic (those whose parents have been here for several generations and who have looser cultural ties to Mexico, as well as those whose ancestry is native to Alta California), and Chicana/o (students who embrace a political consciousness and identity regardless of migration or native ancestry).

3. Most come from the Tri-County region, especially from the rural Salinas Valley. Their parents may work in the fields, either as pickers or irrigators, or in low-paid service-sector jobs, especially if they came to the valley in the last 20 years. Some families are native to the region or have lived there for generations. Although they may be small entrepreneurs (restaurant or grocery store owners), or work in civil service, they are still working class and live within modest means.

4. This article is the beginning of what I hope will become a larger study, perhaps a series of articles or book chapters, stemming from this research. I am currently examining how gender intersects with class and ethnicity in our students' narratives and the implications of gender in my larger analysis.

5. In his discussion of schooling and ideology, Giroux (1997: 125) distinguishes between cultural difference and integrative pluralism. Within the ideology of integrative pluralism,

he argues, cultural difference is seen as a source of conflict and tensions to be overcome in the interest of creating unity and cooperation. This approach, he proposes, "erases the respect for the autonomy of different cultural logics and any understanding of how such logics operate within asymmetrical relations of power and domination."

6. The term "cultural citizenship" began to appear in anthropology and the cultural studies literature in the late 1980s. As most terms, it has varied interpretations. The definition I use was developed collaboratively by a group of Latina/o scholars conducting ethnographic research in Chicana/o, Mexican American, Puerto Rican, and mixed Latina/o communities (see Inter-University Program, 1988; Flores and Benmayor, 1997). We describe and theorize ways in which Latinas/os across the country have responded to historical marginalization and institutionalized racism.

7. The following is a good example of how claims for cultural citizenship in education have created new rights. After much lobbying, in October 2001, the California legislature and the governor passed into law a bill enabling the large numbers of undocumented youth who qualify for admission to colleges and universities to be admitted and eligible for state financial aid.

8. For Moll, Vélez-Ibáñez, and Greenberg (1990: 33–40), funds of knowledge are "constituted through the historical experiences and productive activities of families and shared or distributed through the creation of social networks for exchange." They argue that social and intellectual resources that comprise the funds or knowledge in a community can have an impact on education, when these are recognized, tapped, and schools and classrooms are organized to take advantage of such community knowledge.

9. I am indebted to our former colleague, Michelle Slade of the Service Learning Institute, for making me aware of the current demographics in our surrounding communities regarding first-generation college students. She planted the seed for our class and strongly supported our community collaborations.

10. Students selected interviewees either from the Summer Bridge program lists or from personal friends who were first generation. We attempted to build ethnic diversity into each cohort of interviewees; however, aside from the significant representation of Mexican-origin students on campus, our sample does not proportionally represent the campus' ethnic diversity.

11. These numbers are not proportional representations of male/female Mexican-origin students on our campus, but of the larger female populations in the incoming Summer Bridge Program cohorts. Approximately 60% of the CSUMB student body are female, a statistic that has remained fairly constant since 1998; approximately 62% of Mexican-origin students are female. My thanks to Juan Avalos, Director of Institutional Research, for this data.

12. Pseudonyms are indicated by a fictitious given name and the surname "X." Students were also given the option of non-consent for use of their interviews in any educational research.

13. At least half of the Mexican-origin students we interviewed had paid jobs as recruiters or peer counselors for Educational Talent Search or Migrant Education.

14. To date, the CSUMB campus does not support a Greek system of sororities and fraternities, organizations that also sometimes provide students with "a home away from home."

15. The rural/urban split was evident among African American students as well. African American students from the cities were struck by what for them looked like a lack of diversity, particularly the under-representation of African American students on campus.

16. I wish to express my thanks to Anne-Marie Núñez and Rebecca Burciaga, graduate students in the School of Education at UCLA, for assisting me in identifying several doctoral dissertations and unpublished papers on first-generation college students.

17. Bourdieu defines "cultural capital" as "symbolic wealth socially designated as worthy of being sought and possessed" (1977: 488) and "habitus" as a "system of dispositions which acts as a mediation between structure and practice" (1977: 487). Both concepts are widely used in the literature to help explain the dynamics of reproduction of social inequality in education.

18. The contemporary literature on first-generation students strongly challenges the attainability of the "American dream." Class stratification and low economic status are widely understood to be significant variables in the persistence and success of first-generation college students. Class stratification, the deployment of "cultural capital," and the cultural mediations of "habitus" are seen as intersecting constraints that limit upward mobility and call into question the usefulness of the concept altogether (Walpole, 1998; Boatsman, 2000).

19. Students in the class of 2000 reported: "We discovered from our research that some of our interviewees were automatically put into the tracking system because of language barriers, past behavioral problems, or race. . . . All of our interviewees made some reference to how the tracking system made it more difficult to receive the attention and support necessary to be successful in high school or continue to a four-year institute [*sic*]" (Oral History Student Web Page, 2000: http://classes.csumb.edu/HCOM/HCOM350-02/world/hsl.html).

References

Anzaldúa, Gloria 1986 *Borderlands, La Frontera: The New Mestiza*. San Francisco: Aunte Lute.

Aronowitz, Stanley 2000 *The Knowledge Factory: Dismantling the Corporate University and Creating True Higher Learning*. Boston: Beacon.

Banks, James A. 1997 *Educating Citizens in a Multicultural Society*. New York: Teachers College Press.

Benmayor, Rina 1997 "Education, Cultural Rights, and Citizenship." Cathy J. Cohen, Kathleen B. Jones, Joan C. Tronto eds., *Women Transforming Politics*. New York: New York University Press: 187–204.

Benmayor, Rina, Rosa M. Torruellas, and Ana L. Juarbe 1997 "Claiming Cultural Citizenship in East Harlem: *Si esto puede ayudar a la comunidad mia. . . .*" William

V. Flores and Rina Benmayor (eds.), *Latino Cultural Citizenship*. Boston: Beacon: 152–209.

Boatsman, K. C. 2000 "How College Mediates Upward Mobility: Social and Cultural Reproduction in Action." Paper presented at the Annual Meeting of the American Educational Research Association, New Orleans, April.

Bourdieu, Pierre 1977 "Cultural Reproduction and Social Reproduction." Jerome Karabel and A.H. Halsey (eds.), *Power and Ideology in Education*. New York: Oxford University Press: 487–510.

California State University, Monterey Bay 1994 *Vision Statement*. At www.csumb.edu/vision.

Cuádraz, Gloria Holguín 1996 "Experiences of Multiple Marginality: A Case Study of Chicana 'Scholarship Women.' " Caroline Turner, M. Garcia, A. Nora, L.I. Rendón (eds.), *Racial and Ethnic Diversity in Higher Education*. New York: Simon and Schuster Custom Publishing: 210–222.

Duster, Troy 1991 *The Diversity Project: Final Report*. Berkeley, CA: University of California.

Flores, William V. and Rina Benmayor 1997 *Latino Cultural Citizenship: Claiming Identity, Space, and Rights*. Boston: Beacon Press.

Freire, Paulo 1973 *Pedagogy of the Oppressed*. New York: Herder and Herder.

———1972 *Education for Critical Consciousness*. New York: Seabury.

Giroux, Henry A. 1997 *Pedagogy and the Politics of Hope: Theory, Culture, and Schooling: A Critical Reader*. Boulder, CO: Westview Press.

———1992 *Border Crossings: Cultural Workers and the Politics of Education*. New York; London: Routledge.

Giroux, Henry A. and Peter McLaren 1991 *Between Borders: Pedagogy and the Politics of Cultural Studies*. New York; London: Routledge.

Grossberg, Lawrence 1994 "Introduction: Bringin' It All Back Home—Pedagogy and Cultural Studies." Henry A. Giroux and Peter McLaren (eds.), *Between Borders: Pedagogy and the Politics of Cultural Studies*. New York, London: Routledge: 1–25.

Hall, Stuart and David Held 1990 "Citizens and Citizenship." Stuart Hall and Martin Jacques (eds.), *New Times: The Changing Face of Politics in the 1990s*. London, New York: Verso: 173–188.

hooks, bell 1994 *Teaching to Transgress: Education as the Practice of Freedom*. New York: Routledge.

———1990 *Yearning: Race, Gender, and Cultural Politics*. Boston: South End Press.

Inter-University Program for Latino Research, Culture Studies Working Group 1988 "Draft Concept Paper on Cultural Citizenship." Unpublished.

Lamont, Michele and Annette Lareau 1988 "Cultural Capital: Allusions, Gaps, and Glissandos in Recent Theoretical Developments." *Sociological Theory* 6: 153–168.

Lara, J. 1992 "Reflections: Bridging Cultures." Stephen L. Zwerling and Howard B. London (eds.), *First Generation Students: Confronting the Cultural Issues*. New Directions for Community Colleges 80. San Francisco: Josie Bass: 65–70.

Lauria-Perricelli, Antonio 1964 "*Respeto, Relajo*, and Interpersonal Relations in Puerto Rico." *Anthropological Quarterly* 37: 53–67.

London, Howard B. 1992 "Transformations: Cultural Challenges Faced by First-Generation Students." L. Steven Zwerling and Howard B. London (eds.), *First Generation Students: Confronting the Cultural Issues*. New Directions for Community Colleges 80. San Francisco: Josie Bass: 5–12.

Martinez, Anne and Edwin Garcia 2001 "With Most Dramatic Mix, California Is America's Melting Pot." Census 2000, a *Mercury News* Special Report. *San Jose Mercury News* (Friday, March 30): 1A, 20A.

McDonough, Patricia M. 1991 *Who Goes Where to College: Social Class and High School Organizational Context Effects on College-Choice Decision Making*. Unpublished doctoral dissertation, Stanford University.

McLaren, Peter 1997 *Revolutionary Multiculturalism: Pedagogies of Dissent for the New Millennium*. Boulder, CO: Westview Press.

Moll, Luis C., Carlos Vélez-Ibáñez, and James Greenberg 1990 *Community Knowledge and Classroom Practice Combining Resources for Literacy Instruction: A Technical Report from the Innovative Approaches Research Project*. Washington, D.C.: U.S. Dept. of Education, Office of Educational Research and Improvement, Educational Resources Information Center: 33–40.

Olivas, Michael A. 1986 *Latino College Students*. New York: Teachers College Press.

Oral History and Community Memory Student Web Pages 2000 http://classes.csumb.edu/HCOM/ HCOM350-02/world/index.html.

———1998 http://classes.csumb.edu/HCOM/ HCOM314S-01/world/index.html.

Oral History and Community Memory Institute and Archive Website 1999 http://hcom.csumb.edu/ oralhistory/index.html.

Rendón, Laura 1992 "From the Barrio to the Academy: Revelations of a Mexican American 'Scholarship Girl.' " L. Steven Zwerling and Howard B. London (eds.), *First Generation Students: Confronting the Cultural Issues*. New Directions for Community Colleges 80. San Francisco: Josie Bass: 55–64.

Rochlin, Jay M. 1997 *Race and Class on Campus: Conversations with Ricardo's Daughter*. Tucson: University of Arizona Press.

Rosaldo, Renato 1997 "Cultural Citizenship, Inequality, and Multiculturalism." William V. Flores and Rina Benmayor (eds.), *Latino Cultural Citizenship*. Boston: Beacon Press: 27–38.

Scott Roberts, J. and George C. Rosenwald 1994 "Ever Upward and No Turning Back: Social Mobility and Identity Formation in First-Generation College Students." Dan P. McAdam, R. Josselson, and A. Lieblich (eds.), *Turns in the Road: Narrative Studies of Lives in Transition*. Washington, D.C.: American Psychological Association: 121–150.

Shibazaki, Kozue 1999 *Ethnic Identity, Acculturation, Perceived Discrimination, and College Adjustment in Mexican Americans*. Dissertation, Texas Tech University.

Sidel, Ruth 1994 *Battling Bias: The Struggle for Identity and Community on College Campuses*. New York: Viking Press.

Silvestrini, Blanca 1997 "The World We Enter When Claiming Rights: Latinos and Their Quest for Culture." William V. Flores and Rina Benmayor (eds.), *Latino Cultural Citizenship*. Boston: Beacon Press: 39–53.

Solórzano, Daniel G. and Octavio Villalpando 1999 "Critical Race Theory, Marginality, and the Experience of Students of Color in Higher Education." Carlos A. Torres and Ted Mitchell (eds.), *Emerging Issues in the Sociology of Education: Comparative Perspectives*. New York: SUNY Press: 299–319.

Terenzini, Patrick T., L. Springer, P.M. Yaeger, E.T. Pascarella, and A. Nora 1996 "College Students: Characteristics, Experiences, and Cognitive Development." *Research in Higher Education* 17,1: 1–22.

Valdés, Guadalupe 1997 *Con Respeto: Bridging the Distances Between Culturally Diverse Families and Schools*. New York, London: Teachers College Press.

Vélez-Ibáñez, Carlos 1983 *The Cultural Systems of Rotating Credit Associations Among Urban Mexicans and Chicanos*. New Brunswick, N.J.: Rutgers University Press.

Walpole, Mary Beth 1998 *Class Matters: How Social Class Shapes College Experiences and Outcomes*. Doctoral Dissertation, University of California, Los Angeles.

Student Interviews. 2000 CSUMB Oral History and Community Memory Archive

Albarrán, Mireya, HCOM74, HCOM350S, 130.

Armenta, Carlos, HCOM 51, HCOM350S, 150.

Chavarín, Sandra, HCOM58, HCOM350S, 157.

Figueroa, María Lupe, HCOM48, HCOM350S, 148.

González, Pedro, HCOM77, HCOM350S, 104.

Jiménez, Benjamín, HCOM66, HCOM350S, 126.

López, Juanita, HCOM50, HCOM350S, 116.

Mora, César, HCOM56, HCOM350S, 156.

Rivera, Miriam, HCOM62, HCOM350S, 118.

Vargas, Wilfredo, HCOM54, HCOM350S, 153.

Yolanda X, HCOM64, HCOM350S, 161.

———1998

Anonymous student.

Angélica X, HCOM05, HCOM314S, 105.

Calderón, Merlyn, HCOM 01, HCOM314S, 101.

Delgado, Patty, HCOM15, HCOM314S, 115.

González, Pedro, HCOM04, HCOM314S, 104.

Gregorio X, HCOM03, HCOM314S, 103.

María X, HCOM20, HCOM314S, 120.

Morales, Patricia, HCOM22, HCOM314S, 122.

Rivera, Miriam, HCOM18, HCOM314S, 118.

Developing a Visual Discourse on Immigration

Leo R. Chavez

Leo Chavez is a Professor of Anthropology at the University of California, Irvine, where he also serves as the Director of the Chicano/Latino Studies Program and The Center for Research on Latinos in a Global Society. Dr. Chavez's research explores a range of issues connected to transnational migration. This essay was originally published as a chapter in his 2001 book *Covering Immigration: Popular Images and the Politics of the Nation* which details how American media and pop culture present immigrants. Using anthropology, sociology, and cultural studies, Dr. Chavez's analysis suggests that media images reflect the national mood and influence national discourse about immigration.

To produce images is to produce identity.

Octavio Getino, La tercera mirada

Culture is the material site of struggle in which active links are made between signifying practices and social structure. . . . Because culture is the contemporary repository of memory, of history, it is through culture, rather than government, that alternative forms of subjectivity, collectivity, and public life are imagined.

Lisa Lowe, Immigrant Acts

Images on popular magazine covers provide an excellent window into issues of importance in a society. As artifacts of popular culture, magazine covers are ubiquitous yet seldom thought about, especially in a systematic way.[1] We casually glance at them in their neatly ordered rows as we shop for groceries or browse through them in bookstores and newsstands or choose among them as we wait in a doctor's or dentist's office. We often pause for a moment when a magazine cover catches our attention, then plunge quickly into the interior articles. And yet, despite our lack of attention, the images on magazine covers are not empty of meaning.

This analysis begins with a search for preliminary patterns in the material under study. The state of the economy appears to have influenced a pattern of timing and frequency of immigration-related magazine covers. As graph 2.1 indicates, periods of economic recession somewhat foreshadow a concern with immigration (Cornelius 1980). There have been five economic recessions of various lengths since 1965.[2] The first recession occurred between December 1969 and November 1970, as the Vietnam War–related inflation, taxes, and credit-rates all went up. Between November 1973 and March 1975 another recession was ushered in by rising inflation as wage and price controls were lifted and OPEC quadrupled the price of crude oil. Oil prices and inflation soared again between January 1980 and July 1980. Then, between July 1981 and November 1982, the nation was gripped by a major recession as inflation rates rose steeply, and the money supply was tightened in response. Between July 1990 and March 1991, another recession hit the country, from which some states, particularly California, would take many years to fully recover. Except for the 1969–70 period, each of these periods of economic recession was followed by an increase in the number of magazine covers devoted to the topic of immigration, a concern that then receded until the next recession. Indeed,

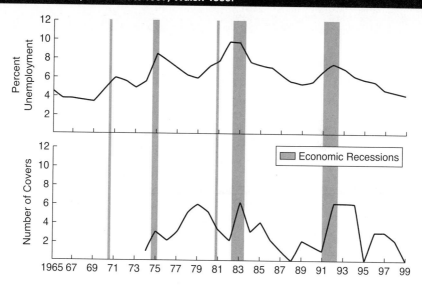

Graph 2.1 Number of magazine covers per year and annual unemployment rates, 1965–99.
Sources: **Espenshade and Hempstead 1996; U.S. Bureau of the Census,** *Statistical Abstracts of the United States***; Rosenblatt 1997; Walsh 1999.**

the focus on immigration as a cover story begins in 1974, during a period of recession.

Graph 2.1 also presents the annual fluctuations in the rate of national unemployment over the same period.[3] Following the 1974 recession and the peak high unemployment rate of 1975, the unemployment rate fell each year until 1979. In spite of this downward trend, however, unemployment generally stayed above the pre-1975 highs. The post-1974 rise in the number of magazine covers on immigration occurs during this downturn in the unemployment rate. The number of magazine covers fell in 1980, 1981, and 1982, as the rate of unemployment began to rise again. The peak high unemployment years of 1982 and 1983, and the still relatively high levels of unemployment for 1984 through 1986, are matched with an increase in coverage of immigration-related issues. As the unemployment rate fell in 1988 to 1989, so too did magazine coverage. Rising unemployment and the recession of 1991 were followed by high numbers of magazine covers on immigration-related issues. As the unemployment rate dropped to new lows in 1995 and beyond, the number of covers on immigration also dropped.

Public opinion on immigration and the frequency of magazine covers on the topic are also intertwined (graph 2.2).[4] In 1980, attitudes favoring less immigration reached an all-time high. This occurred during a recession, but also following three years of increasing media attention to immigration as cover stories. Public opinion favoring reduced immigration declined after passage of the 1986 immigration law (IRCA), just as the number of magazine covers declined. The percentage of the nation's public favoring reduced immigration rose to almost 70 percent during the early 1990s, corresponding to both an economic recession and the rise in the number of covers devoted to immigration. Both public opinion and the number of magazine covers fall in the postrecession, post 1995 part of the decade. The state of the economy, public opinion, and media coverage appear to be engaged in a tightly choreographed dance, each leading and following at various times.

IMAGES AS AFFIRMATIVE OR ALARMIST ABOUT IMMIGRATION

In order to explore other patterns, I classified the magazine covers based upon their use of images that were affirmative, alarmist, or neutral toward immigration. Affirmative covers use images and text in a way that celebrates immigrants, typically tying them to the nation's identity (e.g., America as a nation of immigrants) or present images that

5

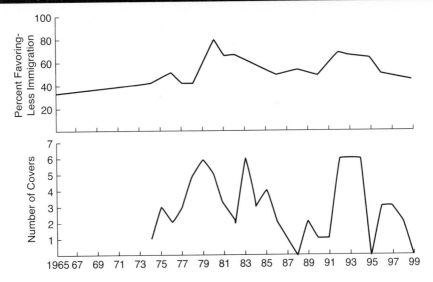

Graph 2.2 Number of magazine covers per year and percentage of Americans favoring less immigration. *Sources:* Espenshade and Hempstead 1996; Simon and Lynch 1999; *U.S. News and World Report* 13 October 1980, 7 July 1986, 23 June 1993; *Business Week* 13 July 1992; *Newsweek* 9 August 1993; *Time* Fall 1993; CBS/*New York Times* Poll September 1995; Gallup Poll 1995, 1999.

appeal for compassion, especially for refugees. Covers raising an alarm about immigration typically use images and text to suggest problems, fears, or dangers raised by immigration, such as population growth, demographic changes, a lack of assimilation, a breakup of the nation, or the death of the nation. Alarmist covers may also feature words such as "invasion," "crisis," and "time bomb" that characterize immigration as a threat to the nation or that appeal to fears and anxieties about immigration. Neutral covers do not make an obvious statement of affirmation or alarm or were seemingly balanced in their message. Whenever it was not obvious if a cover was affirmative or alarmist, it was assigned to the neutral category, the logic being that it is better to be conservative when in doubt. This classification is admittedly subjective. However, the classification was also undertaken independently.[5] The issue of how other readers interpreted the message of the covers is further discussed in Chapter 9, which examines reactions from 298 students at the University of California, Irvine, to the covers.

This exercise suggests a "first impression" or "quick message" about immigration issues suggested by what Barthes calls the denotive level of the message on the covers. An initial read,

however, may change with more in-depth analysis that expands on the interpretation to the connotive level of meanings about the larger society and culture (see Chapter 3 for a discussion of denotive and connotive levels of analysis). Magazine covers are often made up of layers of images and text that express complex messages, juxtaposing affirmative and alarmist messages, or underlying an alarmist message below an ostensibly affirmative message. The result is a complex message alluding to narratives (Barthes's "mythologies" or even ideologies) of the nation, its people, its values, and its identity.

In addition, it must be emphasized that this initial classification is not meant to suggest that "affirmative" means that the magazine's editorial position was pro-immigration or that the use of alarmist images means that the magazine was anti-immigration. Alarmist imagery and text, for example, can be used to send a message about the perils of continued immigration or as a critique on the economic system that "exploits" immigrant workers, suggesting sympathy for immigrants. Presenting such issues may be guaranteed to raise the interest of readers— and thus possibly increasing the number of the magazine's consumers—regardless of, or even because of, their personal stand on immigration policies. It must be stressed that these preliminary classifications are for heuristic purposes only; they need to be judged against deeper interpretations. Before moving to a fuller reading of the images, however, I need to address the general patterns suggested by this initial reading of the magazine covers.

Seven magazine covers (9 percent) conveyed neutral or balanced messages about immigration. Nineteen magazine covers (25 percent) used affirmative images and text to present issues related to immigration, and fifty covers (66 percent) used alarmist imagery, metaphors, adjectives, or other symbols. Alarmist covers, in this sense, were two-and-a-half times as common as affirmative covers. Even if neutral covers were included with affirmative covers, alarmist covers would still be about double their number. Most of the magazines published covers that at times were affirmative and at other times were alarmist. In terms of the "big three," *Newsweek* and *Time* magazines were about balanced in their presentations; alarmist covers did not exceed the number of affirmative and neutral covers combined. *U.S. News and World Report*, with 71 percent of its covers classified as alarmist, relied more on alarmist imagery and text than the other two magazines. The use of alarmist and affirmative imagery did not generally follow a pattern based on conservative or liberal ideology of the magazine. *Atlantic Monthly*, the *New Republic*, the *Nation*, and the *Progressive* more often used alarmist than affirmative or neutral images and text on their covers dealing with immigration. The *Progressive* and the *Nation* used alarmist imagery as a way of raising critiques of existing anti-immigrant attitudes and policies, as will be discussed later.

An important pattern that emerges from the survey has to do with the timing of the covers that portray immigration with affirmative or alarmist images and text. An examination of the ten magazines for the thirty-five-year period after 1965 reveals a pattern of increasingly alarmist portrayals of immigration. Ten of the nineteen magazine covers (53 percent) conveying an affirmative image were published during the 1970s, compared to six (32 percent) published in the 1980s and three (16 percent) between 1990 and the end of 1999.

10   This downward trend from the 1970s for affirmative covers stands in marked contrast to the decidedly increasing trend in magazine covers to use alarmist images and text. Only nine (18 percent) of the forty-eight magazines with alarmist covers were published in the 1970s, compared to

nineteen (38 percent) in the 1980s and twenty-two (44 percent) between 1990 and 1999. In addition, alarmist covers are not evenly distributed across time. They appear in cycles. For example, all but one of the nineteen alarmist covers that appeared in the 1980s were published between 1980 and 1985. In 1986, President Reagan signed into law the Immigration Reform and Control Act, which was to reduce undocumented immigration. It was not until 1989 that another alarmist cover was published by one of these ten magazines. After 1989, there followed a number of alarmist covers leading up to the passage of the 1996 immigration and welfare reform laws (discussed in Chapter 7), and then a precipitous drop off in frequency occurred between 1995 and 1999.

THE NATION'S BIRTHDAY AND THE MAGAZINE COVERS

The linear unfolding of historical time is not the only way events can be ordered. Cultures also have ritual cycles that repeat season after season (Bloch 1989). National holidays are examples of rituals that are imbued with cultural rules concerning the appropriate ways to honor them and the meanings they are intended to convey about society. National magazines appear to consciously or unconsciously follow those rules. Thirteen of the nineteen affirmative covers (68 percent) appeared in the month of July. Only one neutral (14 percent) and four alarmist (8.5 percent) magazine covers appeared in a July issue of one of the magazines surveyed. Or put another way, 68 percent of the covers appearing in July were affirmative of immigration.

July 4th, of course, is the day the United States celebrates its birthday. The nation of immigrants narrative as a founding narrative is fundamental to the identity of the nation. It takes on quasi-religious stature during the month of July, as it becomes associated with patriotism, the birth of the nation, and the subsequent peopling of the continent. July, therefore, becomes a time to speak affirmatively of immigrants and to show compassion for the plight of immigrants, especially refugees. It is a "feel good" moment.

For example, *Newsweek*'s 4 July 1977 cover featured a portrait of a white family wearing clothing that suggests the late 1800s to early 1900s. The family appears to include a grandmother carrying the youngest child of the central family in the picture. Their ethnic background appears to be southern or eastern European. The portrait is three-quarters framed with stars evocative of those on the American flag. The text reads: "Everybody's Search for Roots." This image captures an immigrant history narrative that is affirmative in its romanticization of past immigration as family oriented, working class, and European. To be efficacious, the cover relies on the pervasive cultural stereotype of the European immigrant family, a stereotype that is now seen in the positive light of the distant past. This affirmative reading of past immigration does not reflect the often alarmist view of the immigrants at the time of their arrival. Nonetheless, the image works in the contemporary period because it now carries an important message about America's identity. It is a comfortable reminder that the nation is a united family with an immigrant history and identity. The cover also comes on the heels of the extremely popular television show "Roots," about an African American family's history from slavery to emancipation. Consequently, this cover can also be read as a not-so-subtle reminder that the nation's immigrant history has been collectively imagined as having white or European roots, largely ignoring the mostly forced immigration of Africans.

The use of the photographic portrait of a family is an important part of the cover's success in conveying the nation and its past in terms that are easily understandable and reassuring. With the invention of photography, the family portrait has become the key image used by families to tell the world about themselves, as whole, integrated, and enduring, even when the everyday reality may not be as rosy as the photograph. It was in relation to family portraits that Pierre Bourdieu commented, "Photography itself is most frequently nothing but the *re*production of the image that a group produces of its own integration" (Bourdieu 1965, 48; quoted and translated in Krauss 1990, 19). *Newsweek*'s cover takes this symbol of family unity to the level of the nation.

July is also a time to appeal to America's com- 15 passion for the downtrodden and less fortunate, especially those "huddled masses yearning to breathe free." Five of the affirmative covers appearing in July had refugees on their covers. For example, on 2 July 1979, *Newsweek*'s cover dealt with the "Agony of the Boat People." The image is of Vietnamese men, women, and children who appear to be waiting, huddled together, with tired expressions on their faces. Some children and men

FIGURE 1 *Newsweek*, 4 July 1977. "Roots."

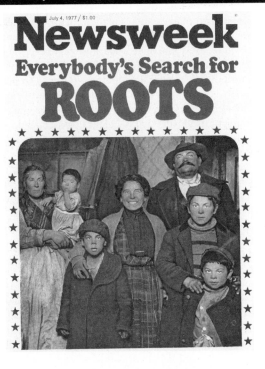

wear no shirts. There is no background, just faces and bodies of people that appear poor and weary. *Time* magazine's cover of that same year (9 July 1979) also pictured a multitude of refugees in the upper right-hand corner. The caption read "Refugees: Tragedy of the homeless." *U.S. News and World Report* (9 July 1979) weighed in with its July feature on refugees. Its cover text expressed "America: Still the Promised Land" as a boatload of Asians stared longingly at the Statue of Liberty.

The self-congratulatory nature of July magazine issues dealing with immigration is readily apparent in headlines such as "Still the Land of Opportunity?" which appeared on *U.S. News and World Report*'s cover on 4 July 1983. Although framed as a question, the image of the American flag flowing in the wind with sunlight radiating from behind it left little doubt that the answer was a resounding "Yes!" In similar fashion, *U.S. News and World Report*'s 7 July 1986 cover proudly claimed "Only in America" above a beautiful multicolored painting of the Statue of Liberty's head. The cover suggests that the nation still beckons immigrants and offers them opportunities for success, which is then detailed in the magazine's feature article. On this birthday, America's generosity toward immigrants is celebrated. Immigrants can easily become enveloped in the spirit of patriotism and as a symbol of America at her best: a nation that takes in all people and allows them to make a place for themselves and their families.

Newsweek magazine's 7 July 1980 cover captured these sentiments. The cover text announcing "The New Immigrants" is printed on a birthday ribbon that also includes white stars on a red, white, and blue background. The ribbon frames the picture of an Asian woman carrying her baby on her back. The woman, a Hmong living in Providence, Rhode Island (we learn inside the magazine), smiles pleasantly at the camera. An American eagle perches atop the picture and text. The woman's happy expression, the ribbon, and the colors all converge in an overall image of birthday exuberance and optimism; the "nation of immigrants" is alive and well as the new, multicultural immigrants are happily becoming Americans.

Multiculturalism was also affirmatively represented on *Time* magazine's 8 July 1985 cover of a special issue on the topic. The cover text read, "The Changing Face of America." A mosaic of

FIGURE 2 *U.S. News and World Report,* **9 July 1979. "America: Still the Promised Land."**

FIGURE 3 *Newsweek,* 7 July 1980. "The New Immigrants."

FIGURE 4 *Time,* 8 July 1985. "The Changing Face of America."

faces of different racial and ethnic backgrounds fills the entire cover. The faces look quietly but expectantly to the right, as if perhaps looking toward the future, wondering what it will bring. They do not appear demanding or aggressive; they simply wait, hopefully, but seriously. Their position also suggests that they could be standing just outside a door, waiting to be invited in, metaphorically raising the question: Will they be accepted into the nation's "imagined community"? All but one of the twenty-six heads has black or dark hair. One woman is blond. The changing face of America is decidedly nonwhite, in the European sense of the word. While this may be a subtle message about the changing demographics resulting in increasing minority populations, especially Asians and Latinos, it is not overtly alarmist in its depiction of these "new faces." America as the nation of immigrants, as the country that will somehow continue to function as a melting pot, still exudes from this birthday issue. This is the future, the image suggests, for which these immigrants longingly wait.

The dark side of multiculturalism can also be suggested implicitly, even when the surface image is affirmative. For example, *American Heritage* magazine's cover of February/March 1992 has a photograph of men, women, and children dressed in dark, serious clothing gazing up at a figure of the Statue of Liberty with a statue of President Abraham Lincoln standing next to her. At the foot of the statues is a sign that reads "The Wanderer Finds Liberty in America." Behind and above the people is an American flag. The clothing, the room, and the photograph itself all suggest that these are European immigrants who came to America in the late 1800s or early 1900s. In other words, this is a romantic vision of past (white European) immigrants gazing at two of America's grandest icons. The immigrants, the image suggests, look affirmatively toward becoming American. The text reads: "What Should We Teach Our Children about History? Arthur Schlesinger, Jr., on the multiculturalism furor." The "history" in the text refers us immediately to the old "historical" photographic image. Here is history, and the message the image and text convey is that past immigrants longed to become American rather than maintain their cultural differences, that is, rather than pursue multiculturalism. Although affirmative in its ostensible portrayal of immigrants, the cover suggests that history and the contemporary "furor" over multiculturalism are not in agreement; in fact,

they collide. Multiculturalism is counter to the romanticized historical narrative of assimilation and the melting pot. And indeed, this is exactly Schlesinger's message in the accompanying article.

The issue of multiculturalism can be raised in a seemingly neutral way and yet convey implicit undertones that suggest that certain immigrant groups lack a will to assimilate. The simple and beautiful photograph on the cover of *American Heritage* magazine's December 1978 issue captures a Chinese man in ethnic dress walking down an urban street, in front of a store with vegetables in woven baskets. The text reads: "San Francisco, 1900." Ostensibly, the cover is neither affirmative nor alarmist, simply a historical photograph that accompanies an article on the photographer and the photographs. However, the image can also be read as capturing not just a historical moment but as raising questions about assimilation and cultural retention by Chinese immigrants. The clothes and the street scene make the geographic context ambiguous. Is it China or America? Only the text defines the geographic location of the pictured event. Once the location is established, the image suggests that China has been plopped down, intact and immutable, in San Francisco.

The image captures the "Otherness" of Chinese immigrants at the turn of the century. It also says something about 1978, which was the time Asian immigration was on the rise. In a way, this cover is the opposite of the previous cover, which used a historical image of European immigrants to convey a romanticized assimilation/melting pot narrative. In this image, the foreignness of the Chinese man in America suggests that his goal is not to blend into the melting pot and that society will have a difficult task assimilating him. His portrayal is that of the classic Chinese "sojourner," as described by Paul Siu (1987) in his account of the Chinese in Chicago during the early decades of the twentieth century. Sojourners were immigrants whose orientation remained faithful to life and memories of their native homes and who therefore eschewed acculturation into American life.

GENDER AND RACE

There is also a nonrandom pattern of gender representations on the magazine covers. Males account for 225 (79 percent) of the 284 immigrants whose gender was decipherable on the covers with

photographic images.[6] Males also accounted for fourteen (70 percent) of the twenty nonimmigrants on the magazine covers. Nonimmigrants were mostly INS or other governmental agents. Illustrations and cartoons were counted separately and only when gender was clearly observable. Males accounted for fifty-five (73 percent) of the seventy-five illustrations of immigrants, and fifteen (100 percent) of the fifteen nonimmigrants. While there may be a margin of error due to the difficulty of counting people in some images, the majority representation of males on the covers is clear.

The breakdown of the people represented on the covers by race and ethnicity is also interesting. Whites accounted for twenty-six (10 percent) of the 266 immigrants for whom race was clear (once again illustrations were counted separately). Most of these were in photographs taken of European immigrants early in the twentieth century. Whites accounted for twelve (71 percent) of the seventeen nonimmigrants, mostly government officers, on the covers. None of the fifty-five illustrations was of white immigrants, but eight (69 percent) of the thirteen illustrations of nonimmigrants were white. There were sixty African Caribbean immigrants

(23 percent) found on the covers, but most of these (fifty-four) were on one cover, which featured a long line of black immigrants waiting in an open-air detention area to be processed by INS agents. Two of the nonimmigrants were African Americans. African Caribbeans accounted for twenty-five (46 percent) of the fifty-five illustrations of immigrants, but all of these were on one cover, that of the Statue of Liberty drowning in a sea of immigrants with black figures in boats floating around her. There was only one African Caribbean among the illustrated nonimmigrants.

Asians accounted for 106 (40 percent) of the immigrants on the magazine covers. The large number of Asians is related to the frequent image of a mass of people when depicting refugees. This visual technique is discussed in Chapter 4, but suffice it to say that the large frequency of Asians on the covers is directly related to their association with refugee flows. Two (12 percent) of the seventeen nonimmigrants were Asians, and only five (9 percent) of the illustrations of immigrants and none of the illustrations of nonimmigrants were Asians. There were sixty-nine (26 percent) Latin American, mostly Mexican, immigrants on the covers. Only one (7 percent) of the nonimmigrants appeared to be Latin American. Twenty-five (45 percent) of the fifty-five illustrations of immigrants and three of the twelve nonimmigrants were Latin American.

25   In sum, magazine covers dealing with immigration since 1965 have followed two basic patterns. First, magazines have increasingly used alarmist images, issues, and implications of immigration on their covers to communicate a message to consumers. This pattern supports Harvey's (1989) argument that as social and economic conditions change, so, too, does the way society represents the world and itself to itself. While this pattern is one that could be said to be sensitive to historical changes that society is experiencing, the same could not be said of the second pattern, which is one that is sensitive to deeply embedded cultural assumptions about the nation and our identity as a people. The emergence of July as the month with many affirmative representations of immigration, immigrants, and refugees suggests the unconscious power of culture to influence behavior. I imagine

that there is no explicit rule that says "Thou shalt not speak ill of immigrants in July" on a placard in the editorial offices of the nation's popular magazines, and yet this is a pervasive pattern in the thirty-five-year period I have examined.

While the month of July is the repository for most affirmative portrayals of immigration on the nation's popular magazine covers, alarmist treatments of immigration can be found during the remaining eleven months. Many of the same themes—multiculturalism, demographic change in America's racial and ethnic makeup, the nation as melting pot—raised in the affirmative presentations of immigration reappear, but with a decidedly alarmist take. Additional issues, images, and metaphors also become increasingly prominent on the covers. In particular, the survival of the "nation," the U.S.-Mexico border, "illegal" immigrants, and national sovereignty emerge as key issues. Before proceeding to a closer reading of the magazines and their covers, it is important to first elaborate the theoretical framework that informs my reading, which is the topic of the following chapter.

Notes

1. Anthropologists have been particularly absent from studies of American popular culture (Traube 1996).
2. *Newsweek* (10 November 1997, 42) summarized these periods of economic recession.
3. Sources for Graph 2.1: Espenshade and Hempstead 1996; U.S. Bureau of the Census, *Statistical Abstracts of the United States*, various issues; Rosenblatt 1997; Walsh 1999.
4. Sources for Graph 2.2: Espenshade and Hempstead 1996; Simon and Lynch 1999; *U.S. News and World Report* 13 October 1980, 7 July 1986, 23 June 1993; *Business Week* 13 July 1992; *Newsweek* 9 August 1993; *Time* fall 1993; CBS/*New York Times* Poll September 1995; *Chicago Tribune* 3 April 2000.

5. I coded the covers first and then asked Juliet McMullin, an advanced graduate student at UC Irvine whose area of research is not directly related to immigration, to make an independent coding of the magazine covers. We agreed on all but three of the cover's classifications, an agreement of 96 percent. As social science graduate student and professor, we have, perhaps, learned to read in similar ways. Undergraduate students, as discussed in the final chapters, were more varied in their readings.
6. People on the cover were counted only if their characteristics were decipherable; partial heads or unclear features were not counted. The frequencies are, therefore, conservative.

Works Cited

Bourdieu, Pierre 1965. *Un art moyen: Essai sur les usages sociaux de la photographie.* Paris: Editions de Minuit.

Cornelius, Wayne A. 1980. America in the era of limits. Working Paper No. 3. La Jolla: Center for U.S.-Mexican Studies, University of California, San Diego.

Espenshade, Thomas J., and Katherine Hempstead 1996. Contemporary American attitudes toward U.S. immigration. *International Migration Review* 30: 535–71.

Getino, Octavio 1977. *La tercera mirada: Panorama del audiovisual latinoamericano.* Buenos Aires: Paidós.

Krauss, Rosalind 1990. A note on photography and simulacrum. In *the critical image: Essays on contemporary photography*, edited by Carol Squiers, 15–27. Seattle: Bay Press.

Lowe, Lisa 1996. *Immigrant acts: on Asian American cultural politics.* Durham: Duke University Press.

Rosenblatt, Robert A. 1977. U.S. jobless rate is 4.7%, a 24-year low. *Los Angeles Times* 8 November, sec. A, p. 1.

Simon, Rita J., and James P. Lynch 1999. A comparative assessment of public opinion toward immigrants and immigration policies. *International Migration Review* 33: 455–68.

Siu, Paul C. P. 1987. *The Chinese Laundryman: A study in social isolation.* New York: New York University Press.

Traube, Elizabeth G. 1996. "The popular" in American culture. *Annual Review of Anthropology* 25: 127–51.

U.S. Bureau of the Census 1991. *Race and Hispanic origin, 1990 census profile.* Washington, D.C.: U.S. Department of Commerce.

Walsh, Mary Williams 1999. Soft growth in jobs makes markets jump. *Los Angeles Times* 4 September, sec. A, p.1.

"Handmade by an American Indian": Souvenirs and the Cultural Economy of Southwestern Tourism

Leah Dilworth

Leah Dilworth is a Professor of English at Long Island University. She received her PhD in American Studies from Yale University and wrote her first book on the representations of Native Americans and the notions of "primitive" that underlie these discursive and visual images. Her interest in how primitive cultures were represented via artifacts led to her current work on "collections" and especially how collections teach non-natives about Indian culture via material objects. This essay appeared in *The Culture of Tourism, the Tourism of Culture: Selling the Past to the Present in the American Southwest*, a 2003 book that arose from a symposium on tourism in the Southwest hosted by the Clements Center for Southwest Studies at Southern Methodist University.

No-one is interested in other people's souvenirs.

—Susan Pearce, Museums, Objects, and Collections

At the risk of proving Susan Pearce right, I'm going to begin by writing about two souvenirs that belong to me.

The first is a souvenir of my childhood. It is a kachina purchased for me by my parents at a trading post in Tuba City, Arizona, while we were on a family vacation to the Grand Canyon when I was about ten years old. I had a collection of dolls at home that friends and relatives had given to me. The dolls were mainly from "foreign" lands, where these adults had traveled. At some point in the mounting excitement as we prepared for the vacation, my parents told me that they would like to buy me a kachina "doll" to add to my collection. I had no idea what a kachina was or who the Hopis were, but it sounded neat, and it thrilled me that my parents seemed to place so much importance on it. I remember Tuba City as a great disappointment, basically a dusty cross-roads. The trading post, though, was interesting, full of all sorts of exotic items. Behind a counter were shelves filled with kachinas, which I thought were strange looking and not very appealing. After talking to the white saleslady, my parents selected two for me to

choose from. Measuring about a foot tall each, they had human bodies but odd, robotlike heads. I had no idea how to choose; these were alien objects, completely beyond my ken. One was new looking and was holding a bow and arrow and cost $20; the other held a rattle and what looked like a deer antler and seemed a bit faded. It cost $18. As I stood between my parents, unable to decide, the saleslady offered some information: the faded one had been used by a Hopi family. This seemed meaningful to my parents, and I could feel the balance tip in favor of the "used" kachina. Relieved, I said I would take that one. Back home, the kachina quickly became my prized possession. It was too tall to fit on the shelf with the other dolls, so I put it on a shelf by itself. There it seemed to reign over all my other childish possessions. I decided that the kachina would be the one thing out of all my belongings I would save if our house were burning down.[1]

The other souvenir I want to discuss was given to me by a coworker at my part-time proofreading job while I was in graduate school. He knew I was interested in southwestern Indian things, and

when he came across this object at a garage sale in Philadelphia, he bought it for a dollar. The object is, I suppose, another souvenir doll, representing a miniature Navajo weaver seated before a loom. The weaver is wearing a purple velvet blouse and a beaded necklace. She sits on a piece of real sheepskin, and beside her is a swaddled baby doll. There is a half-completed weaving on the loom. On the bottom of the base of this object is a bright orange sticker that reads "HAND MADE BY AN AMERICAN INDIAN."

As souvenirs of the Southwest, these objects reveal, first, some of the major themes of tourism in the region and, second, how souvenirs function, how they carry or make meaning. I want to examine the meanings these two objects suggest and then look at the wider significance of the production and consumption of Indian-crafted objects in the "cultural economy of tourism." "Handmade by an American Indian" is the standard trope for authenticity in this economy, and I'd like to spend some time unpacking it, looking first at the significance of the "handmade" and then at how

Indian and tourist identities are constructed within the markets for Indian arts and crafts.

Susan Stewart defines souvenirs as "traces of authentic experience."[2] This definition includes not only objects made for purchase by tourists but also any objects that serve as reminders or evidence of an authentic experience. My kachina is such a "trace" of our family's trip to a place redolent of authenticity: in the touristic Southwest the desert landscape represents a kind of raw yet sublime nature; the natives are "primitives" untouched by modernity. That trip took us out of our ordinary life and permitted us a brush with an authentic, exotic place. The kachina's connection with that vacation, the last we took as a family, was probably its most powerful association for me for years, and it can prompt several narratives about my past, as it did above. So part of its significance is that it "tells" about me and my past. It is a nostalgic object that suggests the loss of childhood, and in the "intimate distance" between the present and the past, the adult and the child, lies its power to make meaning.[3] The kachina prompts me to formulate a narrative

FIGURE 2 Souvenir Navajo weaver. Author's "collection."

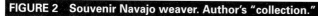

FIGURE 2 Souvenir Navajo weaver. Author's "collection."

to bridge that distance, and in this way it allows me to be a tourist of my own life.[4] The kachina helped me begin to construct the narrative of my life, a narrative of authentic experiences I could revisit through telling it.

The kachina also signifies Hopi culture; as part of my childhood doll collection, it "represented" one of many exotic cultures, in the same way that the doll wearing a sari in my collection represented India. The kachina domesticated my experience of "otherness";[5] when it became part of the interior of my childhood room, it reflected the interior of my childish mind. In buying the kachina for me, I think my parents were trying to "furnish" both my room and my mind, suggesting that I incorporate something "Indian" into my white, bourgeois self. This primitive presence in my childhood room also spoke to my capacity to outgrow my own primitive state. In a kind of magical logic, incorporating this "other" would contribute to my own growing power.

But I think I was also aware that the kachina signified another narrative, about the Hopi family who had used it and my relation to them. I vaguely

perceived that there was something inequitable going on in the transaction I had been a part of. What had prompted the Hopi family to sell the kachina? What circumstances might lead my family to sell my dolls? I was very dimly aware that this situation was somehow connected to a shameful history of white exploitation of Indian people; the transaction seemed illicit. Furthermore, the kachina seemed to have a life and a history: from its origins in the Hopi family, it had briefly, sadly, fallen into the state of being a commodity, and we had rescued it. Although as tourists we constantly saw evidence that we were in the land of the Indians, we never met any; this transaction was as close as I would come to an encounter with any "natives."

Since I acquired it, the kachina has stayed with me, still a loaded presence, like a troubling foster child. It now "lives" in my Brooklyn apartment, where I have arranged a number of souvenirs and family "heirlooms" to suggest an "Indian corner" in a nineteenth-century gentleman's library. It seems that the only way I can remain comfortable with this object is to frame it within a context that creates an ironic distance even as it creates a narrative about "me."

It is in some ways easier for me to discuss the Navajo weaver doll. Unlike the kachina, it does not narrate an authentic southwestern experience of mine. The only personal narrative I can attach to it is how it was given to me. It was at one time, probably, a trace of someone's trip to the Southwest, but now it has become disassociated from that narrative. Nevertheless, it is still a souvenir; it was made to be a souvenir and came already loaded with a narrative that recapitulates the attractions of the Southwest. First it represents Indian artisan labor, a major attraction since the turn of the century. Along with the "olla maiden," Indian artisans (mainly potters, weavers, and silversmiths) have been central icons in the creation of the Southwest as a cultural region. Indian arts and crafts have signified authenticity to generations of non-Indian Americans and are a vital part of the region's economy.[6] The souvenir doll "tells" about the production of Navajo weavings. It replicates in miniature the typical iconography of Navajo weavers: a scene of domestic industry, with the product near completion. (Other steps in the production of weavings, such as shearing the wool, carding, spinning, or dyeing, were almost never depicted in the tourist literature. Certainly the spectacle of a weaver *buying* yarn to weave was never shown.) The miniaturization of the weaver aestheticizes and eternalizes the labor depicted and suggests that this is antiquated, primitive labor, frozen and cut off from modernity and lived experience.[7]

10 In addition, the object has a wonderful "meta" aspect: the sticker on the bottom guarantees that the object, which *represents* Indian hand labor, was "hand made by an American Indian." I love that it's a sticker, too, a mechanically reproduced label added to a handmade object to assure the buyer of its authenticity. Although the object shows evidence of handwork, the sticker effectively separates out that quality and then reapplies it to the object by means of some adhesive. This process speaks about how the characteristics of "authenticity" have always been defined and maintained by non-Indians. Who put the sticker there? By what authority? The sticker prompts questions about how the object was produced. Who wove the blanket? Was it the same person who made the doll? Was he or she Navajo? Was the souvenir produced on an assembly line, with one person making

the weaving, one the doll, and another assembling them? What about the distinction between the "handmade" and the "mass-produced"? What kind of craft or labor is making souvenirs? What does this say about the value of Native American labor? Why does the assurance of handcraft add value? The final irony is that the doll has no hands. I like to think it's a joke, a refusal by the person who made the doll to capitulate totally in being reduced to a pair of hands.

"HANDMADE . . ."

Of all Indian-made objects and products, the souvenir is the lowliest. Anthropologist Nancy Parezo distinguishes the different external markets for Indian arts and crafts in descending order of value: ethnographic/archeological specimens; fine art; crafts ("home decorations and gifts"); and finally souvenirs.[8] Although any object can serve as a souvenir, Parezo refers here to objects produced for tourist markets. The characteristics of these objects contradict what is valuable in the other markets: the singular, the handmade, the "detailed." Parezo says souvenirs "require simplification and mass production, since the extra expense of the addition of time-consuming, intricate details brings no economic, return. . . . Indeed monies obtained from souvenirs are considered by makers as wages."[9] Wage labor does not signify authenticity; wage labor is "alienated" labor. In contrast, Indian artisanal labor signifies a kind of authenticity based on the idea that the primitive artisan thinks with his or her hands, that the mark of the hand is "honorific" in a world of mass-produced goods.[10] Indian craftwork seems to be an unmediated form of production, in which the artisan is bound by tradition and nature rather than capitalist markets. In fact, for the last hundred years and more Native American craftspeople in the Southwest have been participating in the marketplace, responding to the demands of tourists and collectors. The influences of these markets have been well documented, but the idea that something is handmade by an American Indian prompts a kind of willful blindness, a fantasy of the auratic magic of such objects.[11] The production of objects intended for sale to tourists admits that Indian people are engaged with the marketplace. It suggests that Indians can actually "see" tourists, that they are not inward looking or blind to modernity.

In her essay "How 'They' See 'Us': Native American Images of Tourists," folklorist Deirdre Evans-Pritchard notes that Native Americans have observed closely the significance of their exchanges with whites. She finds that jokes Native Americans tell about tourists and anthropologists often hinge on the whites' desire to commodify Indian cultures: "Reifying culture is fundamental to cultural tourism and fits well with the general sense in Indian folklore that the whiteman is a slave to consumerism."[12] The Hopi filmmaker Victor Masayesva, Jr., has often addressed this tendency to reify, to turn the abstract into the material or concrete, in the markets for Indian arts and crafts. His short film *Pott Starr* (1990) begins with an image of an "olla maiden" going to fill her olla with water at a stream.[13] As she walks, she is replaced by an animated olla with arms and legs. The joke is that Indian women are objectified but also that Indian-crafted objects are subjectified, animated by the culture they supposedly "embody." This tendency to animate Indian-crafted objects is evident in the touristic expectation that Indian objects "tell stories." Evans-Pritchard notes that many artisans use symbols to create an aesthetic effect, but they will sometimes tell a tourist a story associated with a work, because this is what the tourist expects.[14] This expectation may derive from the ethnographic approach to objects as metonymic, or *representative* of cultures (like the dolls in my childhood collection), but it also suggests a fantasy of playing Indian: the tourist can reanimate the object by retelling the Indian's story. Later in *Pott Starr* the animated olla is seen walking in downtown Santa Fe. The camera then follows a white woman in cowboy boots, Navajo-style skirt, and concha belt. She approaches the Native American vendors under the portal of the Palace of the Governors. We see her hand, with red polished nails and turquoise rings, reaching down from the top of the screen in slow motion. Then we see her from the vendor's point of view, bending and reaching—not looking at the camera, but at the objects, which are out of sight. Finally we see that the woman is reaching for an olla, which disappears in a flash. In addition to parodying the grasping, consuming white tourist or collector who refuses to see Indian subjectivity, the scene suggests that what she desires is, ultimately, unavailable.

The question of what tourists desire is compelling. In her poem "The Living Exhibit Under the Museum's Portal," Nora Naranjo-Morse suggests that what tourists want is confirmation of what they already know. "Visitors looking for mementos to take home, / that will remind them of the curiously / silent Indians, wrapped tightly in colorful / shawls, just like in the postcards."[15] Tourists buy souvenirs from Indians arranged in a "living exhibit," who look just like Indians seen on picture postcards, which can serve as souvenirs themselves. Such representations of Indians circulate in what Guy Debord has called a "spectacle," "a social relation among people, mediated by images."[16] In the spectacle of Indian artisanal labor, touristic desire is created and fulfilled in a self-perpetuating, repetitive cycle, and as the "represented," Indians are "curiously silent."

In the touristic economy, the tourist is mobile and spectating, and everything the tourist sees is subject to appropriation. Photography allows this almost literally, but the purchase of goods is redolent of an exchange with the natives—even if what is purchased is not of native manufacture. In the cultural as well as monetary economy of tourism, shopping is an important activity. It drives the economic engine of the industry, but it also recapitulates a powerful cultural narrative of exploration, contact, and exchange with alien beings. In the Southwest, the Columbian exchange and its historical consequences are lurking within this narrative. What is the wish to reenact this exchange, culturally speaking? An imperialist power play? A longing for authenticity? For contact with the other? With the self? A nostalgic wish for wholeness?[17] Probably each of these longings comes into play at some point.

More and more I agree with sociologist Dean MacCannell's assertion that touring is a trope for a modern state of being, that "'the tourist' is one of the best models available for modern-man-in-general."[18] The desiring, roving, spectating, consuming tourist is the embodiment of the late capitalist individual. Touring is a performance of "life,"[19] inscribed within consumer capitalism. The meaning of this performance only becomes clear upon returning home, at which point the tourist begins to construct a narrative of the experience. Stewart notes that souvenirs "allow one to be a tourist of one's own life." One tours the museum, or collection, of one's experiences: an interior furnished with souvenirs, a life collected, inspected, cataloged, interpreted, and finally narrated. In the process of

15

narration, the self is performed; it is a performance of re-collected experience. This may be why other people's souvenirs hold no appeal. Detached from their narratives, they fail to signify authenticity. Signification is emptied out, and they are material reminders of the tenuous and ephemeral ways we construct our sense of self.

". . . BY AN AMERICAN INDIAN"

Which brings me to the Indian Arts and Crafts Act of 1990. The act was passed by the House and Senate on October 27, 1990, and George Bush signed it on November 29. Cosponsored by Senator Ben Nighthorse Campbell (Republican-Colorado) and then Representative Jon Kyl (Republican-Arizona), the act expands the powers of the Indian Arts and Crafts Board (IACB), an agency of the U.S. Department of the Interior, and directs the IACB to promote the economic welfare of Indians through development and expansion of markets for arts and crafts. In addition, it mandates the IACB to create and administer a system of trademarks and to set standards of "'genuineness and quality.'" But the crux of the law makes it illegal "to offer or display for sale or sell a good, with or without a Government trademark, in a manner that falsely suggests it is Indian produced, an Indian product, or the product of a particular Indian or Indian tribe or Indian arts and crafts organization, resident within the United States."[20] The act imposes big fines if the law is broken: a first-time individual offense can result in a $250,000 fine and five years' imprisonment; for an entity such as a corporation the first-offense fine is $1 million. Subsequent fines start from $1 million for an individual and $5 million for a nonindividual offender.[21]

In support of this bill, Senator Nighthorse Campbell explained that Indian art is "the only ethnic art form in the United States that is badly plagiarized.... Arts and crafts are one of the most important industries on reservations. This is also a consumer protection bill: when people buy Indian art they have a right to know that an Indian made it."[22] Indeed, a lot of money is at stake: American Indian–style arts and crafts earn an estimated $1 billion a year, and 10 percent of that is siphoned off by fake products.[23] If "handmade by an American Indian" is the standard trope for authenticity, the trope for inauthenticity is "made in Taiwan"—or Hong Kong or Indonesia or Mexico.

The intent may be benign, but the Indian Arts and Crafts Act is very troubling in the way it codifies Indian identity. The act defines "Indian" as "any individual who is a member of an Indian tribe; or for the purpose of this section is certified as an Indian artisan by an Indian tribe." "Indian tribe" is defined as a federally or state-recognized Indian tribe, band, nation, Alaska native village, or another organized group or community.[25] One of the problems with this definition is that many Native Americans are not registered with any tribe. Most critics of the act cite instances in which someone is Indian by blood but not officially certified. For example, the artist Kay WalkingStick has pointed out that some tribes recognize matrilineal descent (like the Hopi), some patrilineal (like the Salish). If a person had a Hopi father and a Salish mother and was born off the Salish reservation, that person could register with neither tribe. Furthermore, even though the act leaves the certification of artisans and questions of membership up to the discretion of each tribe, the history of regulating tribal membership is complicated and riven by racism, corruption, and resistance. For example, to be a member of the Cherokee tribe, one has to have the enrollment number of an ancestor who registered as a Cherokee with the federal government at the turn of the century. For many reasons, not all Cherokees at the turn of the century did this.[26]

One of the most cogent responses to the act came from the artist Jimmie Durham, who identifies himself as Cherokee but lacks an enrollment number. Two of his exhibitions scheduled for 1991 were canceled because the institutions were worried about being prosecuted under the new law. Durham recognized that the terms of authentic Indian identity, as well as the definitions of authenticity in the Indian art market, have long been in the hands of the colonizers, and the Indian Arts and Crafts Act serves to enforce those terms and that tradition. In response to the act, Durham wrote an open letter in which he declared that "authenticity is a racist concept which functions to keep us enclosed in 'our world' (in our place) for the comfort of a dominant society."[27]

Cultural products made by Indians are authenticated not just in terms of whether a particular individual made them (as are objects in the non-Indian art markets); the ethnic identity of the maker must also be authenticated. This is the particular aim of the Indian Arts and Crafts Act, and the regulations, which went into effect in 1996, make it clear that this identity is tied to race. The regulations state that if an artisan is not a certified member of a tribe, he or she can be certified by a tribe as a "non-member Indian artisan." In order to be so certified, the artist must be of the "Indian lineage" of a tribe.[28] Also, someone who is not a certified member or a "non-member Indian artisan" may describe him or herself as of "Indian descent, Native American descent,"[29] or tribal descent. Furthermore, in its response to the public commentary on the regulations, the Indian Arts and Crafts Board specified that someone's "adoption by an 'Indian spiritual leader' or tribal member does not necessarily make that person a member of a recognized tribe."[30] The key terms here are *ancestry* and *descent*. Blood is the authenticating factor in Indian identity.

Why is this problematic? I think mainly for the reasons Jimmie Durham suggested, that racial identities are restrictive and easily controlled by others. Indian artists, like most people, are forever negotiating between what Werner Sollors has called achieved and ascribed identities,[31] but in the art markets the identity "Indian artist" is defined by ethnicity and tradition, both of which are conceived of as inheritable, or ascribed. Nora Naranjo-Morse also comments on this dilemma in the poem "Mud Woman's First Encounter with the World of Money and Business." She writes about selling her figures to a gallery owner, who asks, "Who is your family? / Are any of them well known in the Indian art world?"[32] Here Naranjo-Morse confronts the market's demand for blood. As she has pointed out in an interview, this line of questioning boils down to: "Are you sellable?"[33] She questions the relevance of her descent to the work under negotiation and recognizes that the object is being evaluated not in terms of her labor and talent, but in terms of the exact quality of her "Indianness." The other question Naranjo-Morse implies is, Would any gallery owner ever put such questions to an Anglo artist?

This conception of an inheritable Indian artistic tradition rests on the notion of race as inescapable and telling. The markets for Indian art demand blood as the mark of authenticity and operate on the assumption that "blood will out." No matter how "individualistic" or "nontraditional" the object, it will tell on its maker. In the words of Clara Lee Tanner in the 1988 book *Beyond Tradition:* "Even the most contemporary work usually includes some hint of heritage."[34]

In the ethnic art market, Indian blood signifies the inescapable, the natural—and the market's demand for it naturalizes tradition as a kind of timeless inheritable magic. For most of this century Indian artists and artisans have not been recognized as historical agents; instead the market insists that they do what they do naturally and that artists, dealers, and collectors are participating not in a real market, but in a kind of benign magical exchange, in which a mystical essence that has rubbed off on the object from the caress of an Indian hand can be accumulated by the buyer. In these exchanges, the object of desire represents continuity and perhaps a connection with an imagined "other" and past. This continuity is represented by a racialized notion of tradition rather than by any notion of tradition as a function of human history, as a process that is complicated by conflict and disruptions.

Which brings me back to the problem of reification. In addition to the racialized notion of authenticity, Jimmie Durham has argued that the European conception of identity is tied to ownership. "European culture's emphasis on the sovereign subject and its private property is alien to a Native American concept of the self as an integral part of a social body whose history and knowledge are inscribed across a particular body of land."[35] The image of the "sovereign subject and its private property" brings to mind the tourist and his or her souvenirs, subject to the possessive gaze and interpretation of the self. And in the markets for Indian arts and crafts identity becomes a commodity. Thus the Indian Arts and Crafts Act calls for a system of trademarking to ensure authenticity. As a reporter in *The Albuquerque Tribune* noted, after a meeting held by the Indian Arts and Crafts Association in 1997 to discuss the law, "Copyright, trademarks and the issue of intellectual property emerged as keys to controlling ownership of symbols, designs and cultural heritage."[36] The possibility of a Navajo trademark is already under discussion in the Navajo Tourism Department.[37] Behind these discussions about "cultural heritage" and authenticity lie notions of culture and identity in which "culture" is a kind of inheritable property, but it is property that can't be disposed of or even controlled (except by the government) because it is tied to race.[38]

Because tradition and culture are racialized in the markets for Indian arts and crafts, objects that circulate in those markets become less metonymic and more synecdochic, like trophies.

As I have tried to show, not only are Indian people objectified, but also Indian-crafted objects are "subjectified," or animated by ethnicity. The Luiseño artist James Luna has addressed issues of objectification and subjectivity in many of his works. In a 1986 installation called *Artifact Piece* he exhibited himself, sedated on barbiturates, in a museum case. In addition to a display of "artifacts" from his life, the scars on his body were annotated.[39] This, he seems to be saying, is where the objectification and appropriation of Indian culture leads you. What kind of "cultural property" is this? The exhibit also speaks about Native Americans as part of the tourist spectacle. He serves himself up for the touristic gaze but in a way that makes the voyeurism of this gaze clear and uncomfortable for the viewer. Is he a trophy of the hunt? A souvenir? But even as he offers himself as an artifact or trophy, he also recapitulates a kind of touristic narrative inside the case. The scars and artifacts are souvenirs of his life; they construct a narrative of his life. But his "present absence" complicates matters. He is a living human "subject," but he is drugged, unable to narrate the souvenirs himself.

He seems to be enacting a fear that lurks in the souvenir, in horror stories such as "The Monkey's Paw," in which Susan Stewart notes, "The danger of the souvenir lies in its unfamiliarity, in our difficulty in subjecting it to interpretation. There is always the possibility that reverie's signification will go out of control here, that the object itself will take charge, awakening some dormant capacity for destruction."[40] Luna presents the uncomfortable possibility that the object might reanimate itself and assert its subjectivity as a historical agent, wreaking revenge for the violence done to it.

In his 1993 short film, *History of the Luiseño People,* Luna probes the question of Indian identity further.[41] Nothing much happens in the film; it simply shows Luna at home on the La Jolla reservation making phone calls to friends and relatives on Christmas Day. As he talks on the phone, he smokes cigarettes and consumes the better part of a six-pack of beer. We hear only his side of the phone conversations. A TV in the room is showing the movie *White Christmas.* The film refuses all the stereotypes of Indians. Luna is emphatically not being picturesque. The film offers an unsatisfactory

FIGURE 3   James Luna, *The Artifact Piece* (detail), 1986, San Diego Museum of Man.

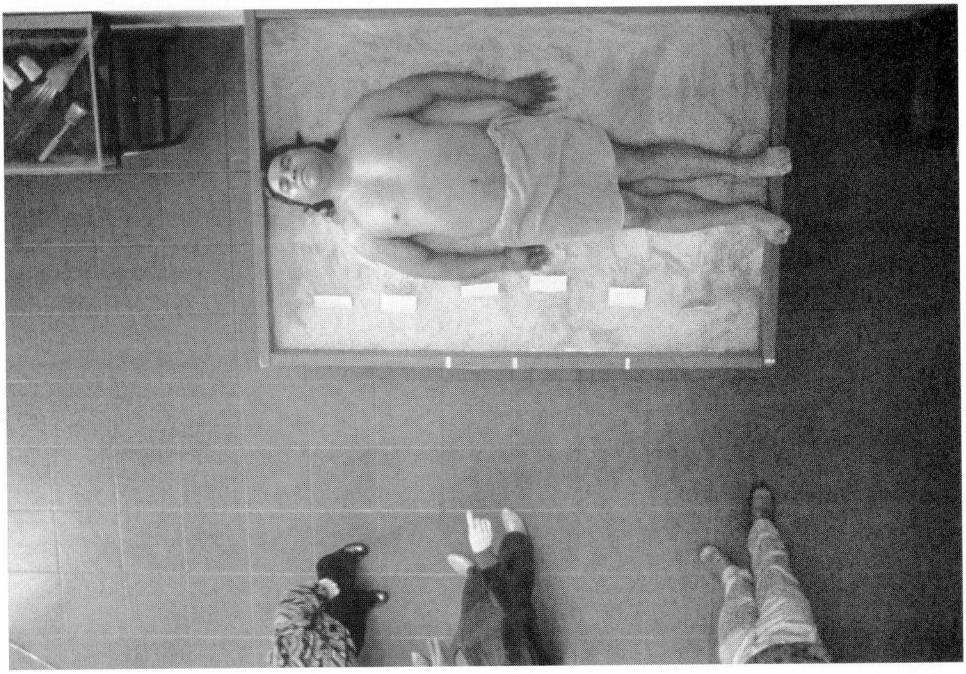

FIGURE 4 Nora Naranjo-Morse, *A Pueblo Woman's Clothesline*, 1994, Heard Museum, Phoenix, Arizona.

encounter with an "Indian." As a tourist, the viewer is seeing into the "back regions" of the attraction, but the spectacle fails, and the viewer becomes a voyeur.[42] This encounter won't leave the tourist with a souvenir or even a narrative. Instead Luna shows us someone who looks like a poor American. While the film addresses the real problems of poverty and alcoholism among Native Americans, Luna is also concerned with questions of identity and representation. He does not present himself as "representative"; it's impossible to generalize about the identity the film presents; what we see is much too specific. He is one man in a particular historical situation.

I'd like to conclude with an image of one more object that is "handmade by an American Indian." Nora Naranjo-Morse's *A Pueblo Woman's Clothesline* (1994) also speaks to a notion of identity that is situated in the world as it is. The *Clothesline* is rooted in the ground, but the flags it flies are constantly changing. It suggests the texture of a Pueblo woman's life as it is actually lived and the kind of domestic and political labor that has not "traditionally" appeared in the marketplace. The object escapes commodification. Like James Luna's *Artifact Piece* or the arrangement of souvenirs in my living room, the *Clothesline* offers narratives of endless variation that speak about ownership and commodification and the body. But Naranjo-Morse's piece makes the point that identity is situated within history and that it is negotiated and performed every single day.

Notes

The epigraph at the beginning of this chapter is from Susan Pearce, *Museums, Objects, and Collections: A Cultural Study* (Leicester: Leicester University Press, 1992), 72.

1. I have written about the significance of this kachina at greater length in an article, "Re-Collections of a Texan Girlhood," *Journal of the American Studies Association of Texas* 28 (October 1997): 1–3. Thanks to *JASAT* editor John Tisdale for permission to republish passages from the article.

2. Susan Stewart, *On Longing: Narratives of the Miniature, the Gigantic, the Souvenir, the Collection* (Durham, N.C.: Duke University Press, 1993), 135.

3. Ibid., 140.

4. Ibid., 146.

5. Ibid., 134.

6. Leah Dilworth, "The Spectacle of Indian Artisanal Labor," in *Imagining Indians in the Southwest: Persistent Visions of a Primitive Past* (Washington, D.C.: Smithsonian Institution Press, 1996): 125–72.

7. Stewart, *On Longing*, 144.

8. Nancy Parezo, "A Multitude of Markets," *Journal of the Southwest* 32 (winter 1990): 563–75.

9. Ibid., 572.

10. Thorstein Veblen, *The Theory of the Leisure Class* (New York: Penguin, 1986): 161.

11. For influences of markets on Indian crafts, see J. J. Brody, "The Creative Consumer: Survival, Revival and Invention in Southwest Indian Arts," in *Ethnic and Tourist Arts: Cultural Expressions from the Fourth World*, ed. Nelson H. H. Graburn (Berkeley: University of California Press, 1976), 70–83; and Molly H. Mullin, "Consuming the American Southwest: Culture, Art, and Difference" (Ph.D. diss., Duke University, 1993).

12. Deirdre Evans-Pritchard, "How 'They' See 'Us': Native American Images of Tourists," *Annals of Tourism Research* 16 (1989): 92.

13. Victor Masayesva, Jr., *Pott Starr*, videocassette, 6 min., IS Productions, Hotevilla, Ariz., 1990.

14. Evans-Pritchard, "How 'They' See 'Us,'" 95.

15. Nora Naranjo-Morse, *Mud Woman: Poems from the Clay* (Tucson: University of Arizona Press, 1992): 29–30.

16. Guy Debord, *Society of the Spectacle* (Detroit: Red and Black, 1983), 4.

17. Susan Stewart considers these longings in relation to the body and notes that according to Baudrillard, the exotic object is linked to the "anteriority" of childhood and its toys (*On Longing*, 146).

18. Dean MacCannell, *The Tourist: A New Theory of the Leisure Class* (New York: Schocken Books, 1989), 1.

19. Stewart, *On Longing*, 146.

20. *Indian Arts and Crafts Act of 1990, U.S. Code*, vol. 25, sec. 305a (1999).

21. Gail K. Sheffield, *The Arbitrary Indian: The Indian Arts and Crafts Act of 1990* (Norman: University of Oklahoma Press, 1997), 12.

22. Michelle Quinn, "Ethnic Litmus Test a Problem for American Indian Artists; Arts," *Los Angeles Times*, 18 June 1992, Home Edition, F1.

23. These estimates were quoted in ibid., 1; and T. D. Mobley-Martinez, "Indians to Act on Fake Art," *Albuquerque Tribune*, 25 January 1997, A1.

24. Sheffield, *The Arbitrary Indian*, 13.

25. Kay WalkingStick, "Indian Arts and Crafts Act: Counterpoint," in *Native American Expressive Culture* (Washington, D.C.: Akwekon Press and National Museum of the American Indian, 1994), 116.

26. Ibid., 115–16.

27. Richard Shiff, "The Necessity of Jimmie Durham's Jokes," *Art Journal* 51 (fall 1992): 75–76.

28. *Code of Federal Regulations*, Title 25, part 309.4 (a) (1).

29. Ibid., 309.3 (c).

30. Indian Arts and Crafts Board, "Protection for Products of Indian Art and Craftsmanship," *Federal Register* [on-line] 61, no. 204 (October 1996): 54553, wais.access.gpo.gov, quoted in Ron McCoy, "Federal Indian Arts and Crafts Regulations Take Effect," *American Indian Art Magazine* 22 (spring 1997): 88.

31. Werner Sollors, *Beyond Ethnicity: Consent and Descent in American Culture* (New York: Oxford University Press, 1986), 5–6.

32. Naranjo-Morse, *Mud Woman*, 35.

33. Stephen Trimble, "Brown Earth and Laughter: The Clay People of Nora Naranjo-Morse," *American Indian Art* 12 (autumn 1987): 64.

34. Clara Lee Tanner, introduction to *Beyond Tradition: Contemporary Indian Art and Its Evolution*, by Jerry D. Jacka (Flagstaff, Ariz.: Northland Publishing, 1988), 36.

35. Shiff, "Jimmie Durham's Jokes," 76.

36. Mobley-Martinez, "Indians to Act on Fake Art," A1.

37. Duane A. Beyal, "Tourism Office Hosts Unique Forum to Examine Arts and Crafts Issues," *Navajo Times*, 14 May 1998, A2. However, as of May 2000, the Indian Arts and Crafts Board has not finalized the regulations on trademarking under the act.

38. As of May 2000, the Indian Arts and Crafts Board, the entity charged with enforcing the Indian Arts and Crafts Act of 1990, had not prosecuted any cases under the act due to budgetary restrictions. Matt Kelley, "Tribes: Gov't Not Enforcing Laws," 17 May 2000, Associated Press Online, <http://dailynewsyahoo.com/h/ap/20000517/pl/indian_knock-offs_i.html>, 18 May 2000.

39. Carla Roberts, "Object, Subject, Practitioner: Native Americans and Cultural Institutions," *Native American Expressive Culture* (Washington, D.C.: Akwekon Press, 1994), 24. See also Lucy Lippard, *Mixed Blessings: New Art in Multicultural America* (New York: Pantheon Books, 1990), 198.

40. Stewart, *On Longing*, 148.

41. James Luna, *History of the Luiseño People*, videocassette, 27 min., dir. Isaac Artenstein, 1993. When I saw this movie for the first time, at the Margaret Mead Film Festival at the American Museum of Natural History in 1994, it was listed in the program as *I've Always Wanted to Be an American Indian*, which is also the title of a photo essay by Luna. The photographs in the essay depict places on the La Jolla reservation along with demographic statistic about the people who live on the reservation. I still like this title for the film best. See James Luna, "I've Always Wanted to Be an American Indian," *Art Journal* 51 (fall 1992): 18–27.

Many thanks to Emelia Seubert, assistant curator, Film and Video Center, National Museum of the American Indian, Smithsonian Institution, for screening this and other films for me.

42. MacCannell, *The Tourist*, 94–96.

Representative Form and the Visual Ideograph: The Iwo Jima Image in Editorial Cartoons

Janis L. Edwards and Carol K. Winkler

Janis L. Edwards is an Associate Professor of Communication Studies at the University of Alabama. Her research focuses on the connections between contemporary rhetorical theory and political discourse and the rhetorical dimensions of media, visual rhetoric, and gender. Carol K. Winkler is the Associate Dean of Humanities at Georgia State University. Her scholarship focuses on presidential rhetoric involving foreign policy. This essay originally appeared in the *Quarterly Journal of Speech,* a peer-reviewed publication of the National Communication Association. The journal focuses on essays that consider the theory and criticism of human communication and is particularly interested in understanding the rhetorical and cultural aspects of different forms of communication.

Much has been written about the iconic power of Joe Rosenthal's 1945 photograph of the flag-raising at Iwo Jima. This scholarship, however, insufficiently accounts for the rhetorical function of this image as it is appropriated in an unusual number of recent editorial cartoons. Building upon rhetorical theory addressing repetitive form and visual metaphor, we propose a concept of representative form. Exemplifying representative form, the parodied Iwo Jima image operates as an instance of depictive rhetoric that functions ideographically.
Key words: political cartoons, ideograph, Iwo Jima, icon, visual metaphor

On February 23, 1945, Joe Rosenthal, a photographer working for the Associated Press, climbed a rough volcanic hill on a Pacific island of Iwo Jima. He hoped the view from the summit would allow for some good shots of the military activity in the area, and he got one. Along with three other photographers and a film cameraman, Rosenthal snapped a picture of a large American flag being hoisted into place, a picture that would become one of the most famous and controversial American photographs ever made. The story of this photograph has invited scholarly attention among those interested in the visual artifacts of American culture. Our interest in the image, however, is not in its historical context, but in its appropriation by editorial cartoonists in the present day. The image of those five Marines and one Navy Corpsman raising the flag has appeared in recent editorial cartoons[1] so frequently that it was derided as a visual cliche by David Astor (1993) in the magazine of the American Association of Editorial Cartoonists.

While the term "cliche" may be pejorative, the repetitive use of the Iwo Jima image is what initially inspires investigation into its rhetorical aspects, for rhetorical analyses often involve a search for recurrent patterns. The cultural salience of the image also compels attention. Images used strategically in the public sphere reflect not only beliefs, attitudes, and values of their creators, but those of the society at large. Cartoonists must use cultural references that readers can easily understand or, as Roger Fischer predicts, "risk almost certain failure, for obscurity and snob humor are fatal to the medium" (1996, p. 122).[2] Yet, our sample of cartoons shows that in more than fifty instances, cartoonists have reached back half a century to appropriate Rosenthal's patriotic cultural icon in service of an art directed at iconoclasm rather than sanctification.[3]

The assumptions common to research in iconology raise more questions than they resolve regarding the rhetorical experience provoked by the parodied Iwo Jima image. The term "icon" proves problematic in this case because, despite its variant meanings and aspects,[4] the presumptive definition usually focuses on factors of representation by concrete resemblance. In describing visual studies as "iconology," Lester Olson (1987) defines icon as "a visual representation so as to designate a type of image that is palpable in manifest form and denotative in function" (p. 38). W. J. T. Mitchell (1986) and Ernst Gombrich (1996) similarly emphasize the quality of resemblance in iconographic study. Writings on the editorial cartoon, specifically those by Gombrich (1963) and Sol Worth (1981), call attention to the importance of denotation in establishing recognizability and subsequent interpretation of a caricature's meaning.

If representation proceeds from resemblance, the cartoon parodies of Iwo Jima should denote and represent the historical moment of February 23, 1945, as it occurred on Mt. Suribachi.[5] This denotative reading of the Iwo Jima image, however, is incongruent with the nature of political cartoons. Cartoonists concern themselves with contemporary subjects; the Iwo Jima flag-raising is a fixed moment in past history. The historical reference to Iwo Jima in editorial cartoons does not provide a theme, in the manner of a motif, but serves as a reference point for other themes. The image functions as visual topos, a visual reference point that forms the basis of arguments about a variety of themes and subjects.

The rhetorical experience of the parodied Iwo Jima image is not defined so much, then, by the denotative function of the iconic image, but by the abstracted qualities of the image as symbol. Paul Messaris (1994) notes the presence of ambivalence in parodied images, which he calls an ineffability that pushes an image beyond its concrete, motivated constraints, allowing for elasticity in application and interpretation. The visual image thus becomes more of an abstraction, an available site for the attachment of multiple connotations serviceable in multiple contexts. We contend that the Iwo Jima image, as appropriated and parodied in recent editorial cartoons, is a special type of symbolic form that represents an essence of cultural beliefs and ideals at a high level of abstraction. As such, we will argue, the parodied image constitutes an instance of depictive rhetoric that functions ideographically.

Our argument proceeds in three stages. First, we review literature on visual form and repetitive form that provides suggestive, but limited, explanations for the power and rhetorical function of this recurring visual image. Then, we consider the metaphoric properties of the image and argue that metaphor is not sufficient to explain the image's use in the parodied context. Instead, we articulate a concept of *representative form* to more fully account for the rhetorical experience and function of the parodied Iwo Jima image in cartoons. Third, we isolate the ways in which the parodied image functions as visual ideograph in editorial cartoons, thus challenging the assumption that only verbal expressions can fulfill such a rhetorical function. In the process, we expand Michael C. McGee's (1980) definition of the ideograph, posit potential differences between verbal and visual ideographs, and explore how the context of cultural parodies functions to express ideographic forms.

THE IWO JIMA IMAGE AS VISUAL FORM

The power of the Iwo Jima image in editorial cartoons necessarily draws from the visual and symbolic power of Joe Rosenthal's photograph, which depicts the raising of an 8' by 4'8" American flag by five Marines and a Navy Corpsman to mark the successful capture of Mt. Suribachi, an early moment in a protracted battle for the strategically located Pacific Island of Iwo Jima. This large flag replaced a smaller flag that had been planted earlier that day as Americans first reached the summit.[6] The second, more visible flag signaled the patriotic significance of the battle at this strategic place, an effort that would take weeks to complete and kill more than 20,000 Japanese and nearly 7,000 American soldiers, including three of the six men depicted in Rosenthal's picture and the Marine camera operator who made a motion picture record of the event.[7]

Previous scholars have identified meaningful compositional features of the photograph in an effort to account for its power and impact as a memorable image. Parker Albee & Keller Freeman (1995), Lance Bertelsen (1989), and Vicki Goldberg (1991) note the emphatic diagonal element of the flagpole and the vaulted perspective with the sky as backdrop as significant compositional elements. Kevin Leary & Carl Nolte (1995) suggest the strong, "sculptural" lighting makes some detail stand out in sharp relief, even as the men's faces are obscured in shadow. Following from Roland Barthes (1977) we might say the pose of the photograph connotes a sacred effort, as the bodies strain in unified action and the hands reach heavenward in lifting the flag, which is caught in a moment of unfurling. These interpretations of the image's visual form are consistent with theoretical propositions concerning a universal vocabulary of graphic or compositional features, summarized by Evelyn Hatcher (1974) and Paul Martin Lester (1995). They note that the elemental dynamic quality of the diagonal lines and the triangular form of the image are particularly vital, suggesting movement, energy, determination, virility, and strength. Directionality and placement are also significant, according to the grammar identified by Gunther Kress and Theo van Leeuwen (1996). The flag, symbolizing the American ideals of liberty, equality, and democracy, is moving toward the upper space in the frame—the space of the ideal, a place, as Goldberg (1991) suggests, that is "waiting to be filled" (p. 142).

Other compositional features signify more symbolic notions of communal effort, egalitarianism, and patriotism. Paul Fussell (1982) and George Roeder (1993) posit that the group effort and the obscured faces[8] speak to common cause and communal involvement. James Guimond (1991) asserts that photographs published in mass outlets at that time, as Rosenthal's was, function to embody common values and goals that would unite the public. The spontaneous photograph was embraced as an embodiment of a culturally preferred interpretation of war's heroism and valor.[9] Additional symbolic connotations derive from one feature of the image, the American flag. Bertelsen (1989) argues that military flag fetishism plays a role in the canonical reception of Rosenthal's photograph by inducing patriotic associations.

10   No doubt, the compositional and symbolic associations of Rosenthal's photograph contribute to its resonance with the American public. The flexibility of interpretation as cartoonists omit, distort, and add to the original composition without losing its recognizability attests to the image's visual power. But any number of images display dramatic compositional elements or possess historical and symbolic significance, yet have not emerged as recurrent visual topoi to the extent we have seen with the Iwo Jima image in recent cartoons.

The Iwo Jima Image as Recurring Form

Unsatisfied that the account of Rosenthal's photograph as a distinctive image fully accounts for the rhetorical import of the image as visual topos in political cartoons, we examined literature on repetitive form to search for an explanation for the image's modern day resonance. Karlyn Campbell and Kathleen Jamieson's (1978) insights into form and genre appeared relevant, given that generic criticism "permit[s] the critic to generalize beyond the individual event which is constrained by time and place to affinities and traditions across time" (p. 27), and Fischer (1990, 1995) has previously recognized the generic features of political cartoons. But, as before, a generic interpretation of the Iwo Jima's recurrence in editorial cartoons was insufficient to explain the rhetorical application of the image. Unlike genre, which depends on recurrent situational elements that prompt recurrent substantive and stylistic elements, our sample displays the Iwo Jima image within a wide variety of contexts. While military settings predominate, more than a third of our sample uses the image in non-military references.

Beyond the lack of situational constraint, the lack of a constellation of recurrent stylistic and substantive elements renders any interpretation of the parodied image as genre suspect. Campbell and Jamieson insist that a constellation of elements should be present for an artifact to meet the audience's expectations associated with a specified genre. Our sample reveals that the formal elements of the Iwo Jima image are frequently omitted, distorted, or substituted during the parody operation. The cartoonists substitute elephants, rats, veterans in wheelchairs, etc., for the Marines; gas tanks, George Bush, eating utensils, a baseball bat, a Christmas tree, and alternative flags for the American flag; and pedestals, a trash can, and Bosnian quicksand for the rubbled peak of Mt. Suribachi. In one cartoon, the only remaining formal feature of Rosenthal's image is the summit's terrain which, like many of our examples, lacks the fusion of dynamic elements necessary for a successful application of genre, but appears to still have utility for the cartoonist in providing a resonant image for the audience.

While the concept of genre has limited applicability to the Iwo Jima image in editorial cartoons, the repeated presentation of the image, as well as its concrete nature, signal its categorization as depictive rhetoric. Michael Osborn (1986) defines depictive rhetoric as "strategic pictures, verbal or nonverbal visualizations, that linger in the collective memory of audiences as representative of their subjects when rhetoric has been successful" (p. 79). In the functions of depictive rhetoric (to present, intensify, facilitate identification, implement, and reaffirm identity), we discover a close correlation with the function of the Iwo Jima image as it appears in cartoons. Osborn (1986) declares that, through repeated presentations, depictive rhetoric generates "pictures for sharing that can be transmitted quickly and precisely by the mass media" (p. 89). The Iwo Jima image as rhetorical depiction would appear to be an instance where cartoonists use graphic lessons from the past to identify solutions for present decisions.

Osborn (1986) further defines the particular symbols of depiction as culturetypes which, grounded in cultural specificity, "authorize arguments and social practices" (p. 89) through their status as shared, communal symbols. The Iwo Jima photographic image as national icon is recalled in the depictive function of reaffirmation of identity, where symbols serve as "moral markers [that] fill our minds again with their radiance and power, and coronates them as basic premises that ought to govern moral reasoning" (Osborn, 1986, p. 95).

15 Among forms of figuration known as culturetypes, Osborn (1994) lists icons, which he defines as concrete embodiments of an abstraction, implying that this is a suitable label for nonverbal rhetorical depictions. According to Osborn (1986), icons also acquire a "secular sacredness" among the public (p. 82). Certainly, the original photographic image of Iwo Jima inspired a reverential attitude, demonstrated by its widespread popularity and achievement of the Pulitzer Prize in the months following initial publication. But the parodied use of the image in cartoons is distinctly irreverent. Furthermore, the decontextualization and elasticity that characterizes the parodied image suggests that its meaning is not grounded in what it concretely represents or denotes, but in its more general and abstract function.

THE IWO JIMA IMAGE AS REPRESENTATION

When conceived as an abstraction, the parodied Iwo Jima image moves into the representational realm. It functions symbolically to represent events and subjects that expand beyond the historical constraints of the original battle at Iwo Jima. Specifically, the role of metaphor and representative form appear relevant to this broader conceptualization of image's resonance.

Metaphor

When a familiar figure is placed in a new, incongruent, context, it is not uncommon to assume that metaphor is the functional rhetorical operation. Messaris (1997) makes this assumption about the Iwo Jima image as parodied in a motion picture advertisement, and similar conclusions could be drawn regarding Iwo Jima parodies in editorial cartoons. Recent research on political cartoons, although subject-centered,[10] strongly suggests the potentials of metaphor as an explanatory framework for the functions of symbolic imagery in cartoons.[11] Through the use of subversive mimicry, which often involves a metaphorical transformation, cartoonists offer debunking parodies of their subjects.

Carl Hausman (1989) notes that "one of the marks of a metaphor is that its particular conjoining of terms is integral to its significance. This indispensability of the expression as it is initially articulated must be sustained if the expression is to be regarded as a metaphor" (p. 14). However, in many of these cartoons, the Iwo Jima image is not indispensable to meaning, but is replaceable. Frequently, the Iwo Jima image is used as a sign for the military, rather than a metaphor that creates a new conception through a transforming mutual adjustment between tenor and vehicle. This use of sign, rather than metaphoric adjustment, is evident in a group of cartoons about gays in the military. Dennis Renault of the *Sacramento Bee,* for example, draws the group of Iwo Jima Marines as a sign for a generic military organization being reviewed by the military establishment for homosexual infiltration (see Figure 1). However, any relationship between yesterday's heroes and today's military policies and population is not metaphorically constructed as a matching and transformation process where qualities of one are mapped onto the other, and there is no specific and evident referral to the military of yesterday. The configuration of the soldiers into the familiar pose of the Iwo Jima image functions more as a sign, assisting the viewer in quickly identifying the military context.

Where Renault's soldiers in the Iwo Jima pose stand for the rank-and-file under review by the military establishment, Bill Schorr, in a 1993

FIGURE 1   Dennis Renault, *Sacramento Bee*

'Wait! Before we take the picture – Is anybody gay?'

cartoon, converts the flag-raising soldiers into representatives of the military establishment through their collective effort to keep the closet door closed on the gay issue (see Figure 2). Any reference to the original Iwo Jima image is an implicit and vague contrast between the heroic accomplishments of yesterday's military and today's concern with the sexual orientation of its members. This contrast reflects a common rhetorical strategy used by editorial cartoonists, identified by Denise Bostdorff (1987), where cartoonists provide perspective by incongruity. But incongruity as a factor is neither consistent nor explicit. A metaphor, to be clear, should function explicitly. The cartoon plays off the familiarity of the military context of the Iwo Jima configuration more than it alludes to the metaphorical meaning of that image in relationship to the cartoon's subject — gays in today's military.

20   In some other cartoons that refer to the military, the comparison with the heroes at Iwo Jima is a strictly ironic one, indicative of the perceived weaknesses of today's military "antiheroes." For example, some of the more recently published cartoons in our study make reference to criminal sexual misconduct — the rape of an Okinawan girl by

American soldiers or sexual harassment against female military members. In these cases, no indication exists that the group of soldiers patterned visually after the Iwo Jima Marines stands for anything other than themselves, but there is an implied contrast with the more positive values exhibited by "yesterday's" military. Similarly, two cartoons in our sample depict today's military members as self-absorbed, media-oriented, and cynically shallow in contrast to the selfless, dedicated heroes represented in Rosenthal's 1945 photograph.

Some cartoons are structured more clearly as metaphors. If the heroism of Iwo Jima is only a dream, it is a daydream of Bill Clinton's, as envisioned by Wayne Stayskal (1995). In this cartoon, Clinton metaphorically transforms himself into the heroic World War II Marines who are raising a proud flag over Haiti. Several other cartoonists recall the heroism of the Iwo Jima soldiers as they convey laudatory comments about the U.S. military's role in providing famine relief to Somalia. While some parodied references to the Iwo Jima image are metaphoric, the relationship induced between the image and its referenced subjects is not consistent across our sample.

SCHORR/from the Kansas City Star

Representative Form

The limitations of compositional symbolism, visual metaphor, and genre theory in providing a comprehensive explanation for the Iwo Jima image's rhetorical significance in contemporary editorial cartoons and the suggestion that, as a cliched image, its representative qualities have transcended the denotative prompts us to consider the question of representation more directly. We propose that the Iwo Jima image is a special type of visual presentation that, through a combination of determined visual features and symbolic attributions, constitutes a representative form. A representative form transcends the specifics of its immediate visual references and, through a cumulative process of visual and symbolic meaning, rhetorically identifies and delineates the ideals of the body politic.

In proposing the idea of a representative form, we refer to two related constructs which inform the concept: Burke's "representative anecdote" (1969a) and S. Paige Baty's (1995) "representative character." Although an anecdote is a formal feature, the representative anecdote is not merely a reductive element featured in the text. Rather, as Barry Brummett (1984) notes, the representative anecdote may be a filter identified by the critic in the course of reconstructing discourse. In a sense, cartoonists function as cultural critics; some have chosen the Iwo Jima image, not because it is literally embedded in the discourse of the Gulf War, gays in the military, presidential campaigns, etc., but because it provides a perspective on the situation. Burke considers the representative anecdote to demonstrate the aspects of representation and reduction by fulfilling the requirements of an explanatory language of human motives. It serves as a discussion point or frame offering a prototype that Burke (1969a) argues, "sums up action" (p. 61) in accounting for the varieties of human nature or envisioning future conditions. Representative stories outline strategies for human responses to situations, or "equipments for living" (Burke, 1957, p. 262). Because they aim at collective understanding they are "sufficiently generalized to extend far beyond the particular combination of events named by them in any one instance" (Burke, 1957, p. 260). Burke (1969a) notes, "a given calculus must be supple and complex enough to be representative of the subject matter it is designed to calculate. It must have scope. Yet it must also possess simplicity, in that it is broadly a reduction of the subject matter" (p. 60).

The Iwo Jima image functions similarly in editorial cartoons. Visually, its compositional power can be likened to a kind of simplicity, which allows for recognizability of the abstract symbolic allusions we bring to the photograph from our understanding or knowledge of World War II. Yet the image also possesses sufficient complexity to be applicable to a wide variety of military and nonmilitary subjects and is supple enough to withstand and accommodate frequent visual distortions and alterations. The anecdotal nature of the Iwo Jima flag-raising is not predominantly represented in the cartoons. Even for those five in our sample that implicitly or directly recall the history of Iwo Jima, the formal image is paramount, for rather than depict a specific moment of heroic achievement, they coalesce a set of abstracted attitudes about communal effort, patriotism, and militarism that transcend the facts of the event. The Iwo Jima image functions representatively in cartoons, then, not as anecdote, but as visual form.

25   The transcendence of the particular to a representation of the general is also outlined in Baty's concept of the representative character, extended from work by Robert Bellah, Richard Madsen, William Sullivan, Ann Swidler, and Steven Tipton (1985). In their construct, a person (character) is abstracted and elevated to the status of a cultural figure, and becomes a surface for the articulation of the political character, embodying cultural ideals. As Bellah et al. (1985) have described the concept,

> A representative character is more than a collection of individual traits or personalities. It is rather a public image that helps define, for a given group of people, just what kinds of personality traits it is good and legitimate to develop. A representative character provides an ideal, a point of reference and focus, that gives living expression to a vision of life (p. 39).

Like the Iwo Jima image, a representative character originates in actuality and specificity, but is abstracted into a symbol or concentrated image, and provides an explanatory model for human motive.

Baty further charts the process for how such a cultural figure comes to represent and articulate the political character. Rather than characterize these figures as static representations, Baty posits that they are "reconstructions that reveal the nature of conversations about the present even as they draw on materials from the past.... [They point] to inclusions and exclusions made in the greater construction of a national identity" (p. 49). For Baty, the representative character is a featured element of mass-mediated modes of remembering that reconstitute the space of politics each time they are invoked. Such representations help articulate the fast-paced space of politics, and "allow for building and expressing forms of community" (Baty, p. 41). At the same time, each invocation of a representative character adds to the definition of the character.

In a similar way, we would argue that each use of the Iwo Jima image, as parodied in editorial cartoons, contributes to the meaning of the image and to the way in which the image defines and constructs a political and ideological reality. Although the U.S. government singled out the surviving men depicted in Rosenthal's photograph as embodiments of heroic ideals, the specific individuals do not give the image its rhetorical force. For one thing, the personal stories of the flagmen are characterized by death and self-destruction as well as heroism. Moreover, their individual identities are obscured in the photograph in the cartoons. Again, the symbolic import of the total visual form is representative, not indicative of the individual characters who are present in the visual form. In this sense, the form becomes abstracted, creating a new perception or concept that is grounded in the original meaning, while transcending it.[12] As Chris Jenks (1995) describes the process, "To abstract implies a removal, a drawing out from an original location, and an enforced movement of elements from one level to another. Abstraction, then, involves the transposition of worlds. . . . The new world, the created level, the (re)presentation, provides the potential arena for the manipulation and control of images. Images become infinitely malleable once freed from their original context, whilst still retaining significations within that original context" (p. 9).

The abstraction that allows for the Iwo Jima image's flexibility and applicability to various contexts creates new worlds of signification in what the Iwo Jima image represents. It also recalls the original context in some indirect referential, and continuously reifying way, suggesting that the Iwo

Jima image functions rhetorically as an ideograph, rather than an icon.

THE IWO JIMA IMAGE AS VISUAL IDEOGRAPH

30 In 1980 Michael C. McGee formulated the concept of ideographs—culturally-grounded, summarizing, and authoritative terms that enact their meaning by expressing an association of cultural ideals and experiences in an ever-evolving and reifying form within the rhetorical environment. An ideograph's meaning develops through its usages and applications, operating as an abstraction and a fragment within the larger rhetorical environment. McGee identifies ideographs as a word or group of words, such as "liberty" or "patriotism," that serve to rhetorically create communities according to ideological constraints and beliefs.[13] By stressing the role of language, McGee specifically confines the notion of the ideograph to the linguistic realm.

McGee's assumption that ideographs must be "actual words or terms" lacks a clear rationale (p. 8). While maintaining that ideology by necessity is always false and thereby rhetorical, he insists that the "clearest access to persuasion (and hence to ideology) is through the discourse used to produce it" (p. 5). He presumes that the relevant discourse must be "political language preserved in rhetorical documents," (p. 5) never addressing the potential inclusion (or exclusion) of nondiscursive forms.[14] Further, he argues that ideographs should be restricted to words because he rejects propositional logic to explain incidents of "social conflict, commitment, and control" (p. 6). McGee distinguishes between the use of terms and the ideas that become clouded through the use of those terms. Defining the ideograph as "language imperatives which hinder and perhaps make impossible pure thought'" (p. 9), he again disregards the rhetorical potential of visual images. In the process, he limits the ideograph to the verbal rather than the visual realm.

McGee outlines four characteristics that constitute his formal definition of an ideograph. Based on an application of these characteristics, we argue that the Iwo Jima image, originally disseminated by governmental sources, is a "non-ideographic use" (p. 15) of the image. A review of recent popular history as represented through editorial cartoon depictions, however, reveals modern day usages of the Iwo Jima image do fall within the definitional

and functional boundaries of the ideograph, the "language term" requirement notwithstanding. The image has become a discourse fragment that multiple publics appropriate for diverse purposes.

Ordinary Term in Political Discourse

McGee contends that the ideograph must be "an ordinary language term found in political discourse" (p. 15). He argues that ideographs in their ordinary sense garner much of their power precisely because they are not reserved for the political elite. They are "transcendent, as much an influence on the belief and behavior of the ruler as on the ruled" (p. 5). The artifacts which expose ideographs are not limited to academic treatises and documents recording the words of the nation's leadership. McGee suggests that critics examining a particular ideograph look to "popular history" (p. 11), such as novels, films, plays, songs, and grammar school history to trace the chronological expansions and contractions of such terms.

On one level, the Iwo Jima image does appear to qualify as "an ordinary image" (McGee, p. 15). Rosenthal's photo was widely published within days of Suribachi's capture. Government officials subsequently used both the photographic image and the surviving men depicted in it to nurture Americans' personal involvement in the war effort. Although the Iwo Jima image's power arguably evokes a narrative about heroism, the rank and file Marines' obscured faces and diverse backgrounds form a representation of the common citizen/warrior, enhancing the "ordinary" quality of the image.

Unlike the present day usage of the Iwo Jima, 35 however, the first mass dissemination of Rosenthal's photograph was reserved for the nation's leadership. The original photograph was a product of a liberalized censorship policy ordered by Admiral Kelly Turner in response to a Washington directive that the Navy pursue a more aggressive policy of press coverage related to Pacific Ocean military activities. After negotiating with the Associated Press to use the photograph as the official image of the flag-raising without cost, the Marines subsequently used the visual symbol for war bond drives and Marine recruiting. The photograph appeared on 3,500,000 posters and 15,000 panels, as recorded by Joe Rosenthal and W. C. Heinz (1955). On July 11, 1945, the federal government issued an official postage stamp bearing the image of the Iwo Jima flag-raising. The flag itself was treated as a national relic during the

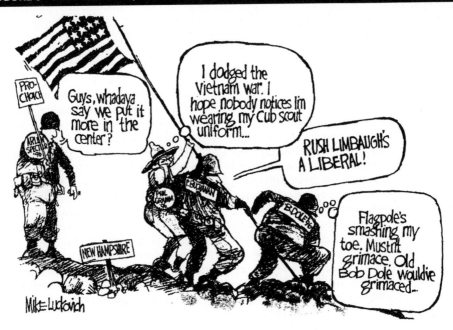

FIGURE 3 Mike Luckovich, *Atlanta Constitution*

Seventh War Loan Drive (Albee & Freeman, 1995). While the early uses of the photograph, and subsequent monument, undoubtedly qualify as ordinary visual images with high public recognizability, neither garnered the power commensurate with regular use in political discourse by both elite and non-elite sources.

The use of the Iwo Jima image as visual material within the context of editorial cartoons, however, disseminates the ordinary visual image into both elite and non-elite public discourse. With access to national audiences, editorial cartoonists arguably have "as much influence on the belief and behavior of the ruler as on the ruled" (McGee, p. 5). William Gamson and David Stuart (1992) propose that the wide syndication of cartoons provides their creators with a national forum for addressing the public, and a segment of scholarship argues that such a forum has public influence.[15]

All of the cartoons using the Iwo Jima image parody aspects of political decision-making to some degree. Nearly one-third (17 of 53) of the cartoons we surveyed directly address political campaigns or public opinion on political issues. In one, Mike Luckovich (1995) transforms the soldiers of Iwo Jima into the New Hampshire primary challengers for the 1996 Republican Presidential nomination to parody the lack of unity evident in the GOP leadership (see Figure 3). Each candidate has an independent concern: Arlen Spector advocating a more centrist position, Pat Buchanan proclaiming even right-wing talk show hosts as liberal, Phil Gramm worried about his war record, and Bob Dole concerned about distancing himself from his past. In other cartoons by Doug Marlette (1994) and Bill Schorr (1995), the focus shifts to questioning the day-to-day decisions of the nation's chief executive. In these parodies, the cartoonists remove some soldiers from the image to signify military budget cutbacks. As these illustrations suggest, the Iwo Jima image has been appropriated from the exclusive control of the ruling elite to those who would parody the nation's leadership.

Abstraction Representing Collective Commitment

McGee's second characteristic of an ideograph is that it must be a "high-order abstraction representing collective commitment to a particular but equivocal and ill-defined normative goal" (p. 15). The abstraction is necessary to distinguish between those publics that fall within the social control motivated by the term and those that fall outside those parameters. The equivocal normative goal is necessary to ensure that the ideograph could never be empirically verifiable; the ambiguity allows the ideograph to be more inclusive of groups that might otherwise feel excluded.

As already argued, the compositional and symbolic representations of Rosenthal's original photograph constitute a visual abstraction reminiscent of the national unity required for success in war efforts. The use of a large amount of empty space in the background, the anonymity of the soldiers' faces, and the reliance on the flag as an icon for patriotism, all contribute to the Iwo Jima image as a form representing collective commitment to shared ideals.

40   The appeal to collective commitment embodied in Rosenthal's photograph also serves as an abstraction to "a particular but equivocal and ill-defined normative goal" (McGee, p. 15). Initially, the government used the photograph to serve as a public relations vehicle for celebrating the capture of the Japanese stronghold, and as the official symbol of the Seventh War Loan Drive. However, the symbolic interpretations of the image, as noted earlier, tapped into broader, inchoate notions of heroism, honor, and patriotism which proved transcendent, and permitted its force to expand beyond its utility for a given war effort, resulting in a broader public subscription to cultural ideals.

Within the context of editorial cartoons, the use of the Iwo Jima image retains the representative quality of collective commitment, while focusing that commitment towards equivocal and ill-defined normative goals. The use of the Iwo Jima image across our sample of editorial cartoons demonstrates the elasticity and abstractness of this image in its application. When applied to military contexts in editorial cartoons, the Iwo Jima image functions to comment on collective commitment required for a wide range of modern usages of the nation's armed forces. Where referring to humanitarian relief efforts such as Somalia, the United States flag is transformed into a bag of grain, a sack of food, or a spoon. When coupled with protracted ethnic struggles such as Bosnia, the rocky terrain of Mt. Suribachi is replaced with a swampy quicksand. In proposed military interventions that lack the full support of foreign citizenries, such as Haiti, the soldiers prop up Aristide rather than the Stars and Stripes.

The cartoons analyzed in our sample suggest that the image of Iwo Jima has come to represent collective commitment to normative goals that transcend the military environment. In a 1989 cartoon published in the *Los Angeles Times,* Paul Conrad replaces the terrain of Mt. Suribachi with the pinnacle of the U.S. Supreme Court Building, the soldiers with five of the nation's Supreme Court justices, and the intact United States flag with a half-burned United States flag. The caption on the cartoon reads: "Monument to the First Amendment" (see Figure 4). Here, Conrad uses the visual image of Iwo Jima to expose the irony of those who support a flag-burning amendment for patriotic reasons.

While the Iwo Jima image accommodates application to a wide array of political contexts, the precise normative goal being represented defies an easy explanation. Democracy, freedom, liberty, patriotism, military preparedness, and equality of opportunity are all components of the representation, but no single language term sums up the interpretations of the image. The Iwo Jima image, like its verbal counterparts, "liberty" and "patriotism," functions as "a high-order abstraction representing collective commitment to particular but equivocal and ill-defined goal" (McGee, p. 15).

Warrants Power/Guides Behavior

McGee maintains that an ideograph also "warrants the use of power, excuses behavior and belief which might otherwise be perceived as eccentric or antisocial, and guides behavior and belief into channels easily recognized by a community as acceptable and laudable" (p. 15). He dispels the widely-held notion that ideology is discussed as propositional logic in the public arena.

Even when Rosenthal's famous photograph 45 first appeared in public forums, the use of the image was an attempt to warrant behavior that could be deemed as antisocial. Without an alternative frame in which to interpret the event, the public might have considered the large number of casualties that the military leadership was willing to sacrifice in the capture of Iwo Jima (6,281 dead; 19,217 wounded) to be unacceptable. Placed within the frame of collective, heroic effort embodied in Rosenthal's photograph, however, the battle of Iwo Jima—expressed metonymically through the Mt. Suribachi flag-raising—comes to represent the success that is achievable through collective sacrifice. Viewed from this perspective, the cost of military engagement becomes an indicator, if not evidence, for the acceptability of U.S. risk-taking during wartime.

In the context of contemporary editorial cartoons, the Iwo Jima image is used to parody

MONUMENT TO THE FIRST AMENDMENT

governmental actions for the purpose of highlighting whether they are acceptable or antisocial in nature. Instead of guiding "behavior and belief into channels easily recognized by a community as acceptable and laudable," the parodied image functions to expose the "eccentric or antisocial" (McGee, p. 15). It further highlights unwarranted attempts by the government to call for collective sacrifice. Richard Morin (1990) provides an illustration in one of his cartoons printed during the Persian Gulf War (see Figure 5). Rather than climb the hilly terrain of Mt. Suribachi, the soldiers struggle along the oil fields of Saudi Arabia, an ally of the United States. Raising an oversized gas pump in place of the Stars and Stripes, the cartoon belittles the motivation for U.S. involvement in the Gulf War to be one of economic self-interest.

Repeatedly, editorial cartoonists manipulate the flag in the Iwo Jima image to parody the less than noble motivations that govern American society. Our sample reveals that cartoonists transform the flag into a dollar sign to symbolize the greed of those in the drug trade, into a campaign banner to underscore the political agenda of Gulf War supporters, into a gas tank or gas gauge to reveal the oil interests motivating U.S. military defense of Saudi Arabia, into a poll indicator to signify the political agenda behind the invasion of Haiti, and into the figure of Aristide to expose the political motivations behind U.S. military intervention in Haiti. Rather than function as a subject of parody itself, in these cartoons the Iwo Jima image serves as a point of comparison for determining what is an "acceptable and laudable" use of governmental power (McGee, p. 15).

Culture-Bound

The final characteristic McGee identifies for the ideograph is that it must be culture-bound. He insists that society's interactions with ideographs work to define and exclude groupings of the public. He claims that members who do not "respond appropriately to claims on their behavior warranted through the agency of ideographs" will experience societal penalties (pp. 15–16).

From the initial release of Rosenthal's photograph for public consumption, the Iwo Jima image came to represent the ideals of American

culture. Karal Ann Marling and John Wetenhall (1991) describe how the soldiers themselves contribute to cultural definition embodied in the image: "That the group indeed included a son of immigrants, an Indian, boys from the Midwest, the plains, the East, only confirmed the representative character of the image" (p. 9). In addition to reinforcing the American heritage of a melting pot of diverse cultures, the image of Iwo Jima relies on the American flag, the cultural icon of patriotism.

The use of irony in editorial cartoons makes 50 the medium particularly suited to society's infliction of penalties on individuals who might ignore or misuse the ideograph. The question of society's tolerance of cultural diversity serves as an example. Bill Schorr (1993) uses the Iwo Jima image to expose the military's own intolerance for gender diversity. Instead of raising the flag, the grouped Marines harass a female recruit by peering under her skirt (see Figure 6). Schorr juxtaposes the

military's current intolerance for diversity with the celebrated ideal of cultural heterogeneity embodied in the Iwo Jima image.

Perhaps the most obvious linkage of the Iwo Jima image to American culture involves a cartoon by Steve Benson for the *Arizona Republic* (1995a). Above the visual image of the cartoon, a caption reads, "As the nation reflects, memories return of the opening day, the struggle in the sand, the deafening roar—and Americans ponder the things that, to them, matter most" (see Figure 7). In this case, though, it isn't the sand and roar of the heroic battlefield, but the playing field that "matters most" as our soldiers join together to raise a dominant symbol of American culture—the baseball bat.[16]

CONCLUSIONS

As a representative form, the parodied Iwo Jima image transcends its historical referents, gains meaning from its subsequent symbolic associations, and helps create and reaffirm the identity of the body politic through its ideographic functions. Like representative anecdotes and representative characters, such forms provide instructive perspectives on varied, multiple situations by summing up the culturally-defined essences of human motivations.

This conceptualization of representative form extends conventional interpretations of how visual images function within societal contexts. Rather than serve in an iconic relationship to a verbal referent, representative forms perform as visual ideographs. While our review of related literature uncovers no specific discussion of ideographs relative to visual forms, we do find implicit assumptions about the nature of the relationship. Like McGee, Osborn (1986, 1994) emphasizes the implicit verbal features of the ideograph by setting it apart from its companion construction—the icon. Osborn implicitly assigns a verbal quality to ideographs when he contrasts them with the concrete qualities of icons; ideographs and icons are positioned as rival terms, a view consistent with the commonplace definition of icon as picture representation.[17] Even though both the icon and the ideograph are culturetypes in Osborn's view, the terms are not interchangeable. To consider the icon as an embodiment of the ideograph is to establish a hierarchical relationship whereby the icon primarily illustrates that which is already linguistically manifested in the ideograph. The ideograph is more authoritative because it expresses a concept that an icon can only reconstruct through illustration.[18] Following this line of thought, the icon's relationship to the ideograph is circumvented; it can only redescribe and imitate the meaning of the ideograph, which *stands for* something. The ideograph, as a verbal expression, is privileged because language is often considered paradigmatic for meaning. Maria Mayenova (1981) typifies this view in saying, "I regard iconic signs in general as being of a derivative, lame character, requiring verbal intervention" (p. 134). In this view, the icon may refer to the ideograph, but ideographs do not refer to icons, and must be preceded by language to obtain meaning.[19]

Osborn may have foreseen a stronger symbolic potential for icons in asserting "the *combination* of ideograph and icon may be especially potent in popular discourse, because it offers the virtues of both abstract and concrete rhetorical expression" (1994, p. 93). In the cartooned Iwo Jima image, we find these virtues coexistent and transcendent. We do not deny the denotative aspects of these visual parodies. We do propose, however, that the function of denotative representation associated with icons is a secondary feature of the totalized rhetorical function of these images. More significantly, the images are symbols realized as representative forms that transcend univocal denotative reference. Similarly, metaphor may operate as a presentational mechanism in these cartoons, but it is transcended as the source of rhetorical invention by the more abstract symbolic aspect of representative form.

Confirmation that certain visual images can function as ideographs, rather than be confined to the more restricted representational territory of icons, emerges in light of previous scholarship on repetitive form. Unlike recurrent forms operative in rhetorical genres, representative forms such as the parodied image of the Iwo Jima flag-raising transcend particular groupings of symbolic or rhetorical contexts. The situations prompting the use of the parodied Iwo Jima image are not wholly recurrent; instead they vary from military to political to entertainment contexts. Even the military-related themes span domestic and international arenas with subjects ranging from motives for war to questions of military policy and from actions by individual soldiers to the conduct of the media. Like McGee's example of equality, the parodied Iwo Jima image is "paramorphic, for even when the [image] changes its signification in particular circumstances, it retains a formal, categorical meaning, a constant reference to its history as an ideograph" (p. 10).

Our examination of the Iwo Jima image would readily concede that, in many cases, visual images bear an iconic relationship to the ideas they represent. If either the elite or the non-elite are influenced by the image exclusively, or the purposes of the image are clearly defined and unequivocal, or the image lacks the elasticity to accommodate meanings beyond its contextual specifics, the image fails to meet the requirements of the ideograph. Only in its appropriation does the influence of the image transcend the domain of the political elite to affect both the nation's leadership and its citizenry.

Appropriation and recontextualization appear to be central features of the transformation of visual images into representative forms. By choosing the situational context for the use of the image, the editorial cartoonist identifies the times and places that warrant ideological judgement. Like McGee's verbal ideographs, representative forms garner their meaning through the description they provide to situations.[20] Editorial cartoons present politicized contexts that, through satire, irony, and parody, motivate differing senses of community. The cartoonist can elevate actions through complementary comparison to the visual ideographs, i.e. equating humanitarian relief in Somalia to the valor of World War II by transforming the flag into a spoon feeding the hungry. Or, the parody can denigrate actions that fail to meet the moral standards established by the ideology, i.e. underscoring the economic rather than the moral justification for entering the Persian Gulf conflict by transforming the flag into a gas pump or gas gauge. By replacing the heroic Marines at Iwo Jima with distinctly unheroic businessmen or political operatives, or with wheelchair-bound soldiers suffering from war's less glorious effects, cartoonists provide an ironic counter-perspective that questions the boundaries of ideological concern.

Not only does the parodied context of a representative form identify the specific circumstances which inspire the ideology's application, it also draws attention to key elements of the ideology at issue. Cartoonists direct the audience's attention by the addition, omission, substitution, and/or distortion of visual elements. Changes made to the flag within the image, for example, can applaud or denounce the motivations used by the nation's leadership to call for collective effort. Manipulation of the Iwo Jima servicemen can focus attention on who constitutes (or does not constitute) the cultural membership of the ideology. Alterations in the terrain of the Iwo Jima image can prompt the audience to consider the degree of sacrifice called for in the ideological application.

The ability of cartoonists to alter visual images arguably distinguishes the verbal from the visual ideograph. Unlike the verbal version, visual ideographs can appear to members of the culture in a variety of forms through the addition, omission, and distortion of their component elements. For the audience to respond to an image manifested in an array of forms, they must have a prior memory or recognition of the original. By comparing the cartoonist's rendition of the image to the memory of the original form, the audience can participate in the reinforcement of the ideograph's categorical meaning, and the creation of the expansions and contractions that result from its parodied contexts. Since words have a limited capacity for manipulation before their recognizability is lost, the opportunity for potential audience participation in the linguistic realm is comparatively small.

60   The comparative potentials of visual and verbal ideographs also relate to the ability of the visual realm to embody iconic images. A single language term usually lacks an iconic relationship between the letters of its makeup and a situational referent. Visual ideographs like the Iwo Jima image can embody icons such as the American flag to bolster tenets of the ideology at work. The inclusion of these icons can both constrain and expand the meaning of representative forms. Representative forms in parodied contexts, then, would appear to have persuasive potentials unavailable to their linguistic counterparts.

At this point we are unprepared to identify definitively other visual images that function ideographically as representative forms. Messaris (1994) has identified a small number of widely parodied, resonant images (such as Grant Wood's *American Gothic* and Flagg's "I Want You" poster of Uncle Sam) that might serve as a basis for future study of images that serve as representative forms. To Messaris's list we might add Mt. Rushmore and specific photographic records of the Vietnam War.

Although we agree with Mitchell (1994) that "visual experience ... might not be fully explicable on the model of textuality" (p. 16) and that visual images and language resist conflation, this study illuminates the value of considering visual images in light of existing rhetorical constructs and emphasizes the importance of continued attention to visual forms of rhetorical experiences. Rather than marginalizing visual studies within the communication discipline, as Sonja Foss (1992) warns is inevitable when visual images are compared with the properties of discursive symbols, we believe the case for the visual ideograph affirms the value of multi-strategic inquiry into rhetorical acts and artifacts.

Notes

The authors wish to note that while co-authorship sometimes implies a differentiation between primary and secondary contributions to a research project, this essay is the result of a collaboration of mutual contribution. An earlier version of this essay was presented at the 1994 SCA Convention in New Orleans. The authors wish to thank Judy Butler and Cameron Murray for their research assistance on this project, as well as Janette Kenner-Muir and Celeste Condit for their helpful comments.

1. In this study, we define an editorial cartoon as a graphic presentation typically designed in a one-panel, non-continuing format to make an independent statement or observation on political events or social policy (as opposed to illustrating a written editorial). Such cartoons are a type of graphic art which regularly appear on newspaper editorial and op-ed pages, and which are typically created by a person employed on a newspaper staff, but may be distributed through syndication. We located fifty-eight editorial cartoons published between 1988 and 1996 which used the Iwo Jima image in reference to a current event or concern. Our sample consisted of cartoons collected from newspapers, from periodical and book collections of cartoons, and, in two cases, directly from a syndicate source, but all meet the above definitional criteria. In this essay, we use the terms "political cartoon" and "editorial cartoon" interchangeably.

2. In making the same point about the necessity of recognizable reference points, Medhurst

and DeSousa (1981) identify literary/cultural allusions, political commonplaces, recognizable character traits, and situational factors as the "inventional storehouse" of cartoonists.

3. Despite the fame of Rosenthal's photograph, its contemporary recognition value is unclear, as those who would personally remember the events of World War II are replaced by those familiar only with collective memory. Messaris (1994), for example, in an informal survey of 29 college students, found that not quite half could accurately place the image in historical context. Similar results occurred in our own survey of 78 students responding to a cartoon version of the image, although we speculate recognition might be greater among an audience more representative of the general population in age distribution.

4. See, for example, a discussion of verbal icons in Leff and Sachs (1990), "Words the most like things: Iconicity and the rhetorical text;" and J.A. Campbell (1990), "Between the fragment and the icon: Prospect for a rhetorical house of the middle way" in *Western Journal of Communication* 54. In calling Rosenthal's photograph an "icon" we refer to the definition of icon as a highly symbolic, canonical, emblematic figure or object of uncritical devotion.

5. For example, Olson's (1987, 1990, 1991) investigation of iconic images such as political cartoons focused on early visual representations of the American colonies in artifacts of the historical moment.

6. The effort to claim the summit took four days, but by the time Rosenthal took his picture, the fighting was in hiatus. That Rosenthal photographed the *second* flag-raising is the crucial factor in controversies about the authenticity of the photograph. The facts of the two flag-raisings, and their photographic record, are recounted in detail in Albee and Freeman (1995), *Shadow of Suribachi: Raising the Flags on Iwo Jima*, and Thomey (1996), *Immortal Images: A Personal History of Two Photographs and the Flag Raising at Iwo Jima*. Additionally, we drew historical information from accounts in Bertelsen (1989), Dart (1995), Marling & Wetenhall (1991), Rosenthal (1995), Rosenthal & Heinz (1995), and Ross (1986).

7. At least eleven photographs taken by six photographers, in addition to film shot by Bill Genaust, captured the two flag-raisings and the subsequent scene at Suribachi from a variety of perspectives. Rosenthal himself took two additional pictures at the summit that day.

8. The exact identity of the men remained uncertain for some time after Rosenthal's picture was published.

9. See, for example, Gregory and Lewis (1988) and Bertelsen (1989).

10. These subject categories include presidential campaigns and candidates as in (Edwards, 1997, 1995; DeSousa & Medhurst, 1982; Hill, 1984; Kenner-Muir, 1986; Sewell, 1993); other political figures (Bostdorff, 1987; DeSousa, 1984; Templin, 1995); religion (Sewell, 1987; Edwards, 1988); and wartime enemies (Edwards, 1993).

11. See, for example, (Bostdorff, 1987; DeSousa, 1984; Edwards, 1993, 1995, 1997; Hill, 1984; Kenner-Muir, 1986; DeSousa & Medhurst, 1982; Medhurst & DeSousa, 1981; Sewell, 1993; and Worth, 1981).

12. Fischer's (1995) analysis of the use of the Lincoln Monument in editorial cartoons also reflects the idea of a representative form, yet the centrality of Lincoln as an American figure retains aspects of the representative character, which would seem to impede the abstraction of the Lincoln Monument. In other respects, cartoonists' visual exploitation of the monument, as argued by Fischer, is conducted to ends similar to their use of the Iwo Jima image—it is held up as ideal against which lesser men are measured.

13. In this sense, they are similar to Weaver's (1953) and Burke's (1969b) articulation of "ultimate terms" which embody propositions through their place in a constellation of terms that progress sequentially.

14. Burke (1969b) provides a rationale for the potential of the visual ideograph in suggesting that nonverbal meanings take on the nature of words.

15. See also Bohrmann, Koester, and Bennett (1978), Langeveld (1981), and Root (1996).

16. The linkage between militarism and masculine sport may itself be revelatory of currents in American culture that substantiate the Iwo Jima image as a meaningful ideograph.

For discussions of the intersections of masculine culture and paramilitarism, especially during the time frame when our sampled cartoons were published, see L. E. Boose (1993) and J. W. Gibson (1994).

17. Argan (1980), J. A. Campbell (1990), Mitchell (1986), Olson (1983); and Steakley (1983) employ the term "icon" in this sense.

18. Gombrich (1963) echoes Osborn's interpretation of the relationship between language and image when he specifically says of cartoons that they are "merely [the tangible expression] of what language has prepared" (p. 128).

19. The view that pictures can only have meaning through their illustrations of words is common, particularly in the realm of photography theory, but it has been challenged by Barthes (1977), who maintained that an image may function as the principle message which is rationalized by words.

20. J. A. Campbell (1990) maintains that we come to understand the rhetorical function of ideographs through their performances, as they "enact what they mean" (p. 367).

References

Albee, P. B., Jr. & Freeman, K. C. (1995). *Shadow of Suribachi: Raising the flags on Iwo Jima.* Westport, CT: Praeger.

Argan, G. C. (1980). Ideology and iconology (R. West, Trans.) In W. J. T. Mitchell (Ed.), *The language of images* (pp. 15–23). Chicago: University of Chicago Press.

Astor, D. (1993, Summer/Fall). Jack and Joel hack the hackneyed. *The Association of American Editorial Cartoonists Notebook*, 12–13.

Barthes, R. (1977). The photographic message. *Image, music, text* (S. Heath, Trans.). New York: Hill and Wang.

Baty, S. P. (1995). *American Monroe: The making of a body politic.* Berkeley, CA: University of California Press.

Bellah, R. N., Madsen, R., Sullivan, W. M., Swidler, A., & Tipton, S. M. (1985). *Habits of the heart: Individualism and commitment in American life.* Berkeley, CA: University of California Press.

Benson, S. (1995, February). [Cartoon]. *Arizona Republic.*

Bertelsen, L. (1989). Icons on Iwo. *Journal of Popular Culture, 2,* 79–95.

Bohrmann, E. G., Koester, J., & Bennett, J. (1978). Political cartoons and salient rhetorical fantasies: An empirical analysis of the '76 presidential campaign. *Communication Monographs, 45,* 317–329.

Boose, L. E. (1993). Techno-muscularity and the boy eternal. In M. Cooke & A. Woollacott (Eds.), *Gendering war talk* (pp. 67–106). Princeton, NJ: Princeton University Press.

Bostdorff, D. M. (1987). Making light of James Watt: A Burkean approach to the form and attitude of political cartoons. *Quarterly Journal of Speech, 73,* 43–59.

Brummett, B. (1984). Burke's representative anecdote as a method in media criticism. *Critical Studies in Mass Communication, 1,* 161–176.

Burke, K. (1969a). *A grammar of motives.* Berkeley, CA: University of California Press.

Burke, K. (1969b). *A rhetoric of motives.* Berkeley, CA.: University of California Press.

Burke, K. (1957). *The philosophy of literary form: Studies in symbolic action.* (Revised Edition) New York: Vintage Books.

Campbell, J. A. (1990). Between the fragment and the icon: Prospect for a rhetorical house of the middle way. *Western Journal of Communication, 54,* 346–376.

Campbell, K. K. & Jamieson, K. H. (1978). *Form and genre: Shaping rhetorical action.* Falls Church, VA: Speech Communication Association.

Conrad, P. (1989, June). [Cartoon]. *Los Angeles Times,* p. B7.

Dart, B. (1995, February 20). 'Grateful' nation thanks survivors of Iwo Jima. *Atlanta Journal-Constitution,* p. 16.

DeSousa, M. A. (1984). Symbolic action and pretended insight: The Ayatollah Khomeini in U.S. editorial cartoons. In M. J. Medhurst & T. W. Benson (Eds.), *Rhetorical dimensions in media: A critical casebook* (pp. 204–230). Dubuque, IA: Kendall/Hunt.

DeSousa, M. A. & Medhurst, M. J. (1982). Political cartoons and American culture: Significant symbols of campaign 1980. *Studies in Visual Communication, 8,* 84–97.

Edwards, J. L. (1988). Keepers of the flame: Rhetorical themes in recent editorial cartoons on religion. Paper presented at the Eastern Communication Association, Baltimore, MD.

Edwards, J. L. (1993). Metaphors of enmity in Gulf War political cartoons. *Ohio Speech Journal, 30,* 62–75.

Edwards, J. L. (May, 1995). Wee George and the seven dwarfs: Caricature and metaphor in campaign '88 cartoons. *INKS Cartoon and Comic Art Studies,* 26–34.

Edwards, J. L. (1997). *Political cartoons in the 1988 presidential campaign: Image, metaphor, and narrative.* New York: Garland Press [forthcoming].

Fischer, R. A. (1990). The Lucifer legacy: Boss Tweed and Richard Nixon as generic sleaze symbols in cartoon art. *Journal of American Culture, 13,* 1–19.

Fischer, R. A. (1995, February). The 'monumental' Lincoln as an American cartoon convention. *INKS Cartoon and Comic Art Studies,* 12–25.

Fischer, R. A. (1996). *Them damned pictures: Explorations in American political cartoon art.* North Haven, CT.: Archon Books.

Forceville, C. (1996). *Pictorial metaphor in advertising.* London: Routledge.

Foss, S. (1992). Visual imagery as communication. *Text and Performance Quarterly, 12,* 85–96.

Fussell, P. (1982). *The boy scout handbook and other observations.* New York: Oxford University Press.

Gamson, W. A. & Stuart, D. (1992, March). Media discourse as a symbolic contest: The bomb in political cartoons. *Sociological Forum,* 55–86.

Gibson, J. W. (1994). *Warrior dreams: Violence and manhood in post-Vietnam America.* New York: Hill & Wang.

Goldberg, V. (1991). *The power of photography.* New York: Abbeville Press.

Gombrich, E. H. (1963). *Meditations on a hobbyhorse.* Chicago: University of Chicago Press.

Gombrich, E. H. (1996). Aims and limits of iconology. In R. Woodfield (Ed.) *The essential Gombrich* (pp. 457–484). London: Phaidon Press Limited.

Gregory, S. W., Jr. & Lewis, J. M. (1988, Fall). Symbols of collective memory: The social process of memorializing May 4, 1970, at Kent State University. *Symbolic Interaction,* 213–233.

Guimond, J. (1991). *American photography and the American dream.* Chapel Hill, NC: University of North Carolina Press.

Hatcher, E. P. (1974). *Visual metaphors: A methodological study in visual communication.* Albuquerque, NM: University of New Mexico Press.

Hausman, C. R. (1989). *Metaphor and art: Interactionism and reference in the verbal and nonverbal arts.* New York: Cambridge University Press.

Hill, A. (1984). The Carter campaign in retrospect: Decoding the cartoons. In M. J. Medhurst & T. W. Benson (Eds.), *Rhetorical dimensions in media: A critical casebook* (pp. 182–203). Dubuque, IA: Kendall/Hunt.

Jenks, C. (Ed.) (1995). *Visual Culture.* London: Routledge.

Kaplan, S. J. (1990). Visual metaphor in the representation of communication technology. *Critical Studies in Mass Communication, 7,* 37–47.

Kaplan, S. J. (1992). A conceptual analysis of form and content in visual metaphors. *Communication, 13,* 197–209.

Kenner-Muir, J. (1986). *Political cartoons and synecdoche: A rhetorical analysis of the 1984 Presidential campaign.* Unpublished doctoral dissertation, University of Massachusetts, Amherst.

Kress, G. and van Leeuwen, T. (1996). *Reading images: The grammar of visual design.* London: Routledge.

Langeveld, W. (1981). Political cartoons as a medium of political communication. *International Journal of Political Education, 4,* 343–371.

Leary, K. and Nolte, C. (1995, February 19). The shot of a lifetime. *San Francisco Chronicle,* Sunday section, p. 3.

Leff, M. and Sachs, A. (1990). Words the most like things: Iconicity and the rhetorical text. *Western Journal of Speech Communication, 54,* 252–273.

Lester, P. M. (1995). *Visual communication: Images with messages.* Belmont, CA: Wadsworth Publishing Company.

Luckovitch, M. (1995). [Cartoon]. *The Atlanta Constitution.*

Marlette, D. (1994, Winter). [Cartoon]. *Notebook of the AAEC,* 25.

Marling, K. A. & Wetenhall, J. (1991). *Iwo Jima: Monuments, memories, and the American hero.* Cambridge, MA: Harvard University Press.

Mayenova, M. R. (1981). Verbal texts and iconic-visual texts. In W. Steiner (Ed.), *Image and code* (pp. 133–137). University of Michigan.

McGee, M. C. (1980). The 'ideograph': A link between rhetoric and ideology. *Quarterly Journal of Speech, 66,* 1–16.

Medhurst, M. J. and DeSousa, M. A. (1981). Political cartoons as rhetorical form: A taxonomy of graphic discourse. *Communication Monographs, 48,* 197–236.

Messaris, P. (1994). *Visual "literacy": Image, mind, and reality.* Boulder, CO: Westview Press.

Messaris, P. (1997). *Visual persuasion: The role of images in advertising.* Thousand Oaks: SAGE Publications.

Mitchell, W. J. T. (1986). *Iconology: Image, text, ideology*. Chicago: University of Chicago Press.

Mitchell, W. J. T. (1994). *Picture theory: Essays on verbal and visual representation*. Chicago: University of Chicago Press.

Morin, R. (1990, August 20). [Cartoon]. *Political Pix*.

Olson, L. C. (1983). Portraits in praise of a people: A rhetorical analysis of Norman Rockwell's icons in Franklin D. Roosevelt's 'Four Freedoms' campaign. *Quarterly Journal of Speech, 69*, 15–24

Olson, L. C. (1987). Benjamin Franklin's Pictorial Representations of the British Colonies in America: A study in rhetorical iconology. *Quarterly Journal of Speech, 73*, 18–42.

Olson, L. C. (1990). Benjamin Franklin's commemorative medal, *Libertas Americana*: A study in rhetorical iconology. *Quarterly Journal of Speech, 76*, 23–45.

Olson, L. C. (1991). *Emblems of American community in the revolutionary era: A study in rhetorical iconology*. Washington, D.C.: Smithsonian Institute Press.

Osborn, M. (1986). Rhetorical depiction. In H.W. Simons & A. A. Aghazian (Eds.), *Form, genre, and the study of political discourse* (pp. 79–107). Columbia, SC: University of South Carolina Press.

Osborn, M. (1994). The invention of rhetorical criticism in my work. In W. L. Nothstine, C. Blair, & G. C. Copeland (Eds.), *Critical questions: Invention, creativity, and the criticism of discourse and media* (pp. 82–94). New York: St. Martin's Press.

Renault, D. (1993, January 27). [Cartoon]. *Sacramento Bee*, p. B6.

Roeder, G., Jr. (1993). *The censored war: American visual experience during World War Two*. New Haven, CT: Yale University Press.

Root, J. R. (1996). *Is a picture worth a thousand words? A Q methodological study of political cartoons*. Unpublished doctoral dissertation, University of Houston, Texas.

Rosenthal, J. (1995, May 31). [Telephone interview with author].

Rosenthal, J. & Heinz, W. C. (1955). The picture that will live forever. *Collier's Magazine*. 18 Feb, pp. 62–67.

Ross, B. D. (1986). *Iwo Jima: Legacy of Valor*. New York: Vintage Books, 1986.

Schorr, B. (1993, February 7). [Cartoon]. *The Sacramento Bee*, p. Forum 5.

Schorr, B. (1994). [Cartoon]. In C. Brooks (Ed.), *Best editorial cartoons of the year, 1994 edition*. (p. 8). Gretna, LA: Pelican Publishing Company.

Schorr, B. (1995, July 23). [Cartoon]. *San Francisco Examiner & Chronicle*, p. 8.

Sewell, E. H. (1987). Exorcism of fools: Images of the televangelist in editorial cartoons. In M. Fishwick & R. B. Brown (Eds.), *The God pumpers: Religion in the electronic age* (pp. 46–59). Bowling Green, OH: Bowling Green State University Popular Press.

Sewell, E. H. (1993). Editorial cartoon images of Bill Clinton in the 1992 Presidential campaign. Paper presented at the meeting of the Speech Communication Association, Miami, FL.

Stayskal. (1995, March). [Cartoon] *Tampa Tribune*.

Steakley, J. D. (1983). Iconography of a scandal: Political cartoons and the Eulenburg affair. *Studies in Visual Communication, 9*, 20–51.

Templin, C. (1995). The political cartoon and the President's wife: Bashing Hillary. Paper presented at the meeting of the International Society for Humor Studies, Birmingham, England.

Thomey, T. (1996). *Immortal images: A personal history of two photographers and the flag-raising on Iwo Jima*. Annapolis, MD: Naval Institute Press.

Weaver, R. (1953). *The ethics of rhetoric*. Chicago: Henry Regency.

Worth, S. (1981). *Studying visual communication*. L. Gross (Ed.). Philadelphia: University of Pennsylvania Press.

American History and the Structures of Collective Memory: A Modest Exercise in Empirical Iconography

Michael Frisch

Michael H. Frisch is a Professor and Senior Researcher in the History Department at SUNY Buffalo. His research interests include oral and public history, urban/social history especially deindustrialization, and the implications of new digital technologies on historical understanding and teaching. He is currently at work on digital software for indexing and annotating audio and video documentation of oral histories. Dr. Frisch works with interdisciplinary students in the Center for the Americas at Buffalo and serves on the advisory boards of several local and national organizations. This essay originally appeared in *The Journal of American History,* a publication of the Organization of American Historians. An earlier version of this essay was presented at the Symposium on Memory and History at Baylor University in February 1988. It was subsequently published with slight modifications as part of a collection of essays authored by Professor Frisch entitled *A Shared Authority* (SUNY Press, 1990).

For over a decade now, I have been accumulating some fascinating data on the images of American history that my students have carried around in their heads before entering my classroom. The term *data* may be misleadingly scientific, and I am not even sure my hunting and gathering process deserves to be called research, since it began playfully, as little more than a tonic designed to fortify student recruits setting out on their uncertain trek across the arid reaches of the standard survey course. Increasingly, however, I have come to sense that there may be some broader meaning, or at least interest, in the picture gradually emerging from this experimentation.

That sense has been recently sharpened by loud alarums—the very lively debate about American education's role in the ominously accelerating historical amnesia reportedly afflicting high school and college students. As it happens, my modest experiments in what can be called "empirical iconography," conducted well before that debate emerged, address its concerns quite directly, providing a certain reassurance in the face of the jeremiads while raising some disturbing questions of a rather different sort.

Let me begin with some brief frame-setting observations about the problem at hand. I will then turn to a straightforward unfolding of my quasi-scientific data combined with some unlicensed flights of exegetical excess. I will conclude by returning to the contemporary debate about American education and historical memory, in order to see how different it may appear after our excursion into the realm of the collective historical subconscious, or at least that portion of it embodied in the responses of over one thousand students at the State University of New York at Buffalo (SUNY-Buffalo) over the past decade.

As a general matter, discussions of historical memory have not been very clear about the relation of individual-level processes—what and how we remember, whether about our own or more broadly historical experience—and the processes of collective memory, those broader patterns through which culture may shape the parameters, structure, and even the content of our sense of history. My impression is that the two levels of discussion have remained relatively separate, the former engaging more those concerned with psychology, education, language, and to an extent oral history, the latter of interest to cultural historians.

5   The current debate about history, culture, and education in American life has brought these differing aspects of memory together, since it focuses on what individuals know about history, how they come to know (or not know) it, and what this says about our collective culture, in terms of both cause and broader effect. I will presume a certain familiarity with the recently discovered crisis of cultural illiteracy, which seems to have struck a genuine chord of some kind. Two basic texts by the prophets Allan Bloom and E. D. Hirsch, Jr., have been improbable best sellers for many months, and there has been widespread discussion of documents such as *A Nation at Risk,* the report of the National Commission on Excellence in Education, and *American Memory: A Report on the Humanities in the Nation's Public Schools,* by Lynne V. Cheney, the chairman of the National Endowment for the Humanities. All have worked their way into newsweekly cover stories and extensive television news reports. The most recent sensation, Diane Ravitch and Chester E. Finn, Jr.'s *What Do Our Seventeen-Year-Olds Know?* has seemed to offer the hard epidemiological evidence on which the declaration of a cultural health emergency has been based.[1]

    This literature is far from uniform, but for present purposes it is possible to identify at least three linked propositions sounded consistently in all these works, and others in the same vein. The first, already noted, is that our students and young adults are woefully ignorant of the most basic orienting facts of history, particularly our own American history, much less its larger meanings, with the result that the strings of a shared cultural memory have been cut. The second proposition is that this severing of memory is a direct consequence of a failure of education, of the diminished place of history education in the curriculum at every level, and of a deterioration in the pedagogy by which we teach whatever history has managed to survive. The final proposition, a derivative of the first two, is that unless there is a drastic change in the quantity and quality of the teaching of history, the only issue will be whether we collapse from internal disintegration before we are overwhelmed by economic and political threats from without. Indeed, the most apocalyptic critics mirror the homophobic Right in its view of Acquired Immune Deficiency Syndrome (AIDS), seeing the amnesia epidemic as at once a threat to our survival and a kind of divine judgment on a culture gone wrong.

All three propositions involve history and memory, and all turn out, on close examination, to be something short of self-evident, at least in the sense in which they are usually advanced. The last mentioned, of course, is so dependent on a particular ideological world view as to be beyond the critical discussion appropriate in this forum. The first two, however, can be stated in objective, even quantitative, form, and are amenable to both internal and external test.

The evidence I present today is offered in this empirical spirit. As for the first, root proposition, my data challenge the amnesiac conclusion itself, quite directly. While my tables can lay little claim to scientific validity, in at least one respect they address the central question more squarely than most of the well-funded research on which the current debate rests. Ravitch and Finn's title notwithstanding, the major survey work has pursued a kind of inversion of Howard Baker's famous Watergate query: What don't the students know and since when haven't they known it? But to

---

[1]The best sellers, of course, are E. D. Hirsch, Jr., *Cultural Literacy: What Every American Needs to Know* (New York, 1987); and Allan Bloom, *The Closing of the American Mind: How Higher Education Has Failed Democracy and Impoverished the Souls of Today's Students* (New York, 1987). The 1987 study by the chairman of the National Endowment for the Humanities is Lynne V. Cheney, *American Memory: A Report on the Humanities in the Nation's Public Schools* (Washington, 1987), which follows the 1983 report of the National Commission on Excellence in Education, *A Nation at Risk: The Imperative for Educational Reform* (Washington, 1983). Both are available from the U.S. Government Printing Office. The new study is Diane Ravitch and Chester E. Finn, Jr., *What Do Our Seventeen-Year-Olds Know? A Report on the First National Assessment of History and Literature* (New York, 1987). For a representative example of the mass-mediated digestion of this debate, see the cover story, "What Americans Should Know," *U.S. News and World Report,* Sept. 28, 1987, pp. 86–94.

answer such questions, even assuming the validity of the dubious survey instrument, is not necessarily to discover the other side of the coin, to see and understand what they *do* know.[2] However inadvertently, my somewhat whimsical investigation may have stumbled on some very different results because it began as an attempt to map that very terrain, to explore an interior historical landscape exactly as presented by students.

In fact, the expedition has revealed an environment so strikingly uniform as to cast a significant shadow over the remaining proposition — that pedagogy and curriculum are critical variables in the structuring of American memory. My evidence suggests that our students' historical memory may not, in fact, be shaped so much by their education or lack of it as by collective cultural mechanisms and structures we need to understand better. In that sense, the research bears quite directly on a central focus of recent cultural studies, the concept of "civil religion." Those studies argue the existence in American culture of a set of shared beliefs, myths, "meaning systems," and historical images forming a functionally religious structure, and inquire into the content, origins, and functions of the complex, both as a general cultural concept and in terms of its particular American meaning.[3]

Because so much prior discussion has relied on literary, rather than empirical, evidence of the very existence, much less shared acceptance, of such core cultural beliefs, my data may help advance the inquiry. Cultural analysis, in turn, has much to contribute to our understanding of the broader relation of history to memory. Unless we can bring those two far-from-identical concepts together in a clearly demarcated arena, we will have difficulty penetrating an increasingly strident public discourse in which they are being pressed into the service of some not-so-hidden agendas. But if the debate is approached with careful curiosity and the conceptual tools commonly found in our scholarly workshops, it may be possible to get closer to the core of legitimate concern in it. Even more, I believe this may be one of the rare instances where the benefits flow both ways — where the heat of a particular polemic can generate light sufficient to illuminate some of the issues.

Let me describe my classroom laboratory. Over a decade ago, I was first assigned to take my turn conducting the first semester of our standard year-long American history survey course, from the beginning through the Civil War. As one who had been teaching the relatively exotic specialty of urban and social history, I realized that this would be an initiation in which I would have to teach materials that most of my students had previously encountered, in what I presumed to be high school versions that were parochial at best and grossly distorted at the expected worst. With all the arrogance of a beginner, I expected my major task to be the clearing of a forest of facts, names, dates, and conventional concepts in order to build, out of the logs of American experience, a city of insight and understanding.

As a way to survey the wilderness before me, I began the very first class with a spot quiz: I asked the students to take out blank paper and to write down, without undue reflection, the first ten names that popped into their heads in response to the prompt "American history from its beginning through the end of the Civil War." Assuming that the lists would be predictably presidential, starting with George Washington, after the students had finished I suggested that the experiment be repeated, but this time excluding presidents, generals, statesmen, or other figures in official public life. I hoped that the two lists in combination would be a reasonable approximation of the image of American history brought into the class. The quiz was anonymous, I assured them, simply a way to obtain, via free association, a kind of collective portrait of our starting point. My intention was to fashion, out of the collated answers, an opening lecture contrasting this high school image to the university-level alternative we would develop during the semester.

The results were in some ways quite surprising, which encouraged me to repeat the quizzes each time I taught the course. I have now run eight

10

[2]See two useful reviews of Ravitch and Finn, *What Do Our Seventeen-Year-Olds Know?* that develop this point: Deborah Meier and Florence Miller, "The Book of Lists," *Nation*, Jan. 9, 1988, pp. 25–27; and Etta Moser, "What They Do Know," *ibid.*, 27–28.

[3]The best single discussion, as well as the best case study application, is Catherine L. Albanese, *Sons of the Fathers: The Civil Religion of the American Revolution* (Philadelphia, 1976). See also Hirsch, *Cultural Literacy,* 98–103, for a discussion especially relevant to the context of this essay.

such surveys, between 1975 and 1988, involving over 1,000 students in groups ranging from 40 to 270. That is a sufficiently substantial base, I think, to justify taking a close look at the results.

Tables 1 and 2 present two representative surveys' tally for the first question, one from 1984 and the other from my current class in the fall 1988 semester. The parenthetic figures are the number of students mentioning each name. (About 95 took the quiz in 1984 and 220 in 1988.) I should note that the free association mechanism worked dramatically. Many students listed only five or six names and then froze, their minds a blank, although they realized on seeing the lists later that they "knew" virtually every name anybody had mentioned. It is, of course, the difference between those names recognized and those immediately leaping to mind that students of culture, with backing from the psychologists, may find most interesting. The phenomenon also helps compensate for a methodological deficiency: In a more serious analysis, it would be important to analyze the order of mention as well as the frequency, but as that was beyond my statistical resources, I sought an approximation by limiting the time available and by encouraging students to stop when their minds began to go blank, rather than to fill up all ten places through more deliberate concentration.

The first tables are unsurprising, an array of mostly political and military figures crystallizing around the major defining events of United States history, the Revolution and the Civil War. There is little here to suggest anything other than the dutiful, civics-focused high school history courses whose residue I had expected to find. But as we shall see, the other results cast the lists in a somewhat different light.

Table 3 presents an eight-time comparison of answers to this question. The lists are of unequal length because of frequent ties, and because each survey rank orders all those names receiving at least three to six mentions, depending on the size of the class—wherever it falls ordinally, the last name marks a dropping-off point; all those below it received only relatively isolated mentions.

TABLE 1   Responses to Question One: 1984
(Question One: Write down the first ten names that you think of in response to the prompt, "American History from its beginning through the end of the Civil War.")

Rank	Name	Frequency	Rank	Name	Frequency
1	G. Washington	83	21	T. Paine	5
2	A. Lincoln	76	22	J. Davis	4
3	T. Jefferson	70	23	N. Hale	4
4	B. Franklin	52	24	J. Monroe	4
5	R. E. Lee	37	25	B. Arnold	3
6	U. S. Grant	31	26	J. Cabot	3
7	J. Adams	30	27	C. Cornwallis	3
8	C. Columbus	22	28	G. A. Custer	3
9	P. Revere	22	29	George III	3
10	J. Hancock	16	30	Lafayette	3
11	J. Smith	10	31	F. Magellan	3
12	A. Jackson	9	32	S. Adams	2
13	J. Q. Adams	7	33	D. Boone	2
14	J. W. Booth	7	34	A. Burr	2
15	A. Hamilton	7	35	H. Clay	2
16	B. Ross	7	36	T. Edison	2
17	P. Henry	6	37	F. S. Key	2
18	J. Madison	6	38	D. Madison	2
19	A. Jackson	5	39	Pocahontas	2
20	Lewis & Clark	5	40	H. Tubman	2

The first tables are unsurprising, an array of 15

TABLE 2 Responses to Question One: 1988
(Question One: Write down the first ten names that you think of in response to the prompt, "American History from its beginning through the end of the Civil War.")

Rank	Name	Frequency	Rank	Name	Frequency
1	G. Washington	197	22	H. Tubman	8
2	A. Lincoln	192	23	George III	7
3	T. Jefferson	140	24	F. S. Key	7
4	B. Franklin	102	25	T. Edison	6
5	J. Adams	78	26	P. Henry	6
6	U. S. Grant	70	27	J. P. Jones	6
7	R. E. Lee	64	28	J. Q. Adams	5
8	A. Jackson	58	29	Lafayette	5
9	C. Columbus	49	30	W. T. Sherman	5
10	J. Hancock	37	31	A. Burr	4
11	J. Madison	25	32	F. Douglass	4
12	P. Revere	25	33	T. J. Jackson	4
13	A. Hamilton	22	34	A. Johnson	4
14	T. Paine	19	35	W. Penn	4
15	B. Ross	17	36	H. B. Stowe	4
16	G. A. Custer	11	37	D. Boone	3
17	J. Smith	11	38	C. Cornwallis	3
18	B. Arnold	9	39	S. Douglas	3
19	J. W. Booth	9	40	N. Hale	3
20	J. Monroe	9	41	Lewis & Clark	3
21	S. Adams	8	42	D. Madison	3
			43	M. Standish	3

The results confirm the initial impression of any one year, but the uniformity is quite striking. Considering first the "top ten" of each list, we find six names appearing every year (Washington, Thomas Jefferson, Abraham Lincoln, Ulysses S. Grant, John Adams, and Benjamin Franklin). As charted in Table 4, four other names rank in the top ten in five of the eight years: Robert E. Lee, Paul Revere, John Hancock, and Andrew Jackson.

All told, only 14 different names appear in the 80 slots (10 each year for eight years) at the top of the lists. To be in social-scientific fashion, I have calculated measures of the diversity and consensus on these lists. (See Table 5.) The maximum number of possible top ten names (80) minus the minimum possible (10) yields a maximum "spread" of 70. Subtracting from the actual total number of names in the 80 slots (14) that same minimum (10) yields an *actual* spread of 4. To provide a standardized base for comparison, dividing actual spread by the potential maximum yields an index

on a scale where 0.00 represents total lack of diversity (the same ten names each year) and 1.00 represents total diversity (no names appearing on more than one year's list). This I will declare, only slightly tongue-in-cheek, to be the Diversity Index: for question one's top ten, it is a minuscule 0.057.

The Consensus Index is less complex—those names appearing *every* year in the top ten as a percentage of all names appearing *any* year in the top ten: 42.9 percent. Perhaps more indicative is the Five-Plus Consensus Index: 71.4 percent of the names that ever appeared in the top ten did so in five or more of the eight years surveyed.

Moving from the top ten to consider the full lists, we find slots for 132 names, but only 24 different ones appearing, resulting in a Diversity Index of 0.036—*lower* than that for the top ten. This is an important indication that the degree of diversity does not increase as one proceeds down the list. Of the 24 names, 10 (41.7 percent) appear every year and 15 (62.5 percent) in five of the eight

TABLE 3 Question One: Eight Samples
(Question One: Write down the first ten names that you think of in response to the prompt, "American History from its beginning through the end of the Civil War.")

1975	1976	1978	1982	1983	1984	1985	1988
1. G. Washington	1. G. Washington	1. G. Washington	1. G. Washington	1. G. Washington	1. G. Washington	1. G. Washington	1. G. Washington
2. T. Jefferson	2. T. Jefferson	2. T. Jefferson	2. A. Lincoln	2. A. Lincoln	2. A. Lincoln	2. A. Lincoln	2. A. Lincoln
3. A. Lincoln	3. A. Lincoln	3. A. Lincoln	3. T. Jefferson	3. T. Jefferson	3. T. Jefferson	3. T. Jefferson	3. T. Jefferson
4. U. S. Grant	4. B. Franklin	4. B. Franklin	4. B. Franklin	4. B. Franklin	4. B. Franklin	4. J. Adams	4. B. Franklin
5. R. E. Lee	5. J. Adams	5. U. S. Grant	5. J. Adams	5. U. S. Grant	5. R. E. Lee	5. B. Franklin	5. J. Adams
6. J. Adams	6. U. S. Grant	6. R. E. Lee	6. U. S. Grant	6. R. E. Lee	6. U. S. Grant	6. U. S. Grant	6. U. S. Grant
7. B. Franklin	7. P. Revere	7. J. Adams	7. A. Jackson	7. J. Adams	7. J. Adams	7. P. Revere	7. R. E. Lee
8. J. Madison	8. J. Hancock	8. A. Jackson	8. J. Hancock	8. J. Hancock	8. C. Columbus	8. R. E. Lee	8. A. Jackson
9. A. Hamilton	9. A. Jackson	9. C. Columbus	9. R. E. Lee	9. P. Revere	9. P. Revere	9. A. Jackson	9. C. Columbus
10. J. Smith	10. A. Hamilton	10. P. Revere	10. P. Revere	10. A. Jackson	10. J. Hancock	10. J. Hancock	10. J. Hancock
11. C. Columbus	11. R. E. Lee	11. J. Hancock	11. J. Madison	11. C. Columbus	11. J. Smith	11. C. Columbus	11. J. Madison
12. B. Ross	12. B. Ross	12. J. Smith	12. C. Columbus	12. J. Madison	12. A. Jackson	12. A. Hamilton	12. P. Revere
13. P. Revere	13. P. Henry	13. George III	13. G. A. Custer	13. A. Hamilton	13. J. Q. Adams	13. J. Madison	13. A. Hamilton
	14. J. Madison	14. J. Madison	14. T. Paine	14. J. Monroe	14. J. W. Booth	14. J. Smith	14. B. Ross
	15. C. Columbus	15. B. Arnold	15. A. Hamilton	15. P. Jones	15. A. Hamilton	15. J. Q. Adams	15. G. A. Custer
				16. G. A. Custer	16. B. Ross	16. George III	16. J. Smith
				17. P. Henry	17. P. Henry	17. J. Monroe	17. B. Arnold
					18. J. Madison	18. B. Ross	18. J. W. Booth
						19. J. W. Booth	19. J. Monroe

TABLE 4   Question One: Eight Sample Summary
(Question One: Write down the first ten names that you think of in response to the prompt, "American History from its beginning through the end of the Civil War.")

| | | | | *Rank in Year:* | | | | | Years on |
Name	1975	1976	1978	1982	1983	1984	1985	1988	List
1. G. Washington	1	1	1	1	1	1	1	1	8
2. A. Lincoln	3	3	3	2	2	2	2	2	8
3. T. Jefferson	2	2	2	3	3	3	3	3	8
4. B. Franklin	7	4	4	4	4	4	5	4	8
5. U. S. Grant	4	6	5	6	5	6	6	6	8
6. J. Adams	6	5	7	5	7	7	4	5	8
7. R. E. Lee	5	11	6	9	6	5	8	7	8
8. P. Revere	13	7	10	10	9	9	7	12	8
9. C. Columbus	11	15	9	12	11	8	11	9	8
10. J. Madison	8	14	14	11	12	18	13	11	8
11. A. Jackson		9	8	7	10	12	9	8	7
12. J. Hancock		8	11	8	8	10	10	10	7
13. A. Hamilton	9	10		15	13	15	12	13	7
14. J. Smith	10		12			11	14	17	5
15. B. Ross	12	12				16	18	15	5
16. G. A. Custer				13	16			16	3
17. P. Henry		13			17	17			3
18. J. Monroe					14		17	20	3
19. J. W. Booth						14	19	19	3
20. T. Paine				14				14	2
21. J. Q. Adams						13	15		2
22. George III			13				16		2
23. B. Arnold			15					18	2
24. J. P. Jones						15			1

TABLE 5   Eight Sample Analysis

Question One	Top Ten	Total List
A Total Names	14	24
B Maximum Possible Names	80	132
C Minimum Possible Names	10	20
D Maximum Possible Spread (B-C)	70	112
E Actual Spread (A-C)	4	4
F Diversity Index (E/D)	0.057	0.036
G Names on List All Eight Yeats	6	10
H Eight-Year Consensus Index (G/A)	42.9%	41.7%
I Names on List Five Years or More	10	15
J Five-Plus Consensus Index (I/A)	71.4%	62.5%
K Consensus Decay Index [(J.1-J.2)/J.1]		0.125

years. Both the Diversity Index and the Consensus Index, then, suggest that the overall similarity of the lists is hardly accounted for by the very famous names at the top but spreads relatively evenly through the full range of names my students list year after year.

Perhaps the most culturally revealing characteristic of the lists is their almost exclusively political and military cast, focused on epochal events. In class discussion, we have frequently noted the kinds of people missing from the survey: religious figures, for instance, or artists, philosophers, or scientists. It is hard to imagine a similar poll in England or Italy or China or Chile being quite so relentlessly political, public, and heroic. That narrow focus certainly seemed to say something about American culture, but it is not inconsistent with my original expectation that what I was measuring was the result of high school history curricula focused on our civic traditions and formal institutions. The dramatic uniformity from year to year, however, suggested something else—perhaps an unexpected level of indoctrination, or a deeper set of cultural structures at work on the collective imagination of students year after year.

The results of the second set of surveys offer some powerful evidence for the latter hypothesis, and some provocative suggestions as to the content and meaning of those cultural structures. The most recent surveys are presented in Tables 6 and 7, a compendium of near-legendary characters whom most Americans encounter in grade school, if anywhere on the educational spectrum; more generally, the figures on the list are the stuff of popular culture rather than school curricula.

I must admit that the first time I encountered such results, I was quite surprised. Indeed, the students were surprised and a little embarrassed themselves: again, they all claimed to "know" something about the more sophisticated names mentioned even once. Yet it seemed clear that when confronting the blank page, many of them had reached back beyond their recent experience and listed figures imaginatively encountered a good bit earlier, or outside of school altogether.

TABLE 6 **Responses to Question Two: 1984**
(Question Two: Write down the first ten names that you think of, excluding presidents, generals, statesmen, etc., in response to the prompt, "American History from its beginning through the end of the Civil War.")

Rank	Name	Frequency	Rank	Name	Frequency
1	B. Ross	37	19	A. G. Bell	3
2	P. Revere	25	20	G. W. Carver	3
3	H. Tubman	15	21	F. Douglass	3
4	Lewis & Clark	14	22	J. Hancock	3
5	J. W. Booth	11	23	W. Penn	3
6	D. Madison	10	24	M. Standish	3
7	J. Smith	10	25	M. Washington	3
8	F. S. Key	8	26	S. B. Anthony	2
9	Pocahontas	8	27	C. Attucks	2
10	H. B. Stowe	7	28	A. Burr	2
11	D. Boone	6	29	D. Crockett	2
12	T. Edison	6	30	N. Hale	2
13	B. Franklin	6	31	C. McCormick	2
14	R. Fulton	6	32	F. Nightingale	2
15	B. Arnold	5	33	T. Paine	2
16	C. Barton	5	34	M. Pitcher	2
17	J. Brown	5	35	Sacajawea	2
18	J. P. Jones	4	36	W. Scott	2

TABLE 7   Responses to Question Two: 1988
(Question Two: Write down the first ten names that you think of, excluding presidents, generals, statesmen, etc., in response to the prompt, "American History from its beginning through the end of the Civil War.")

Rank	Name	Frequency	Rank	Name	Frequency
1	B. Franklin	124	21	M. Washington	9
2	B. Ross	74	22	Pocahontas	8
3	Columbus	63	23	E. Whitney	8
4	P. Revere	63	24	P. Henry	7
5	J. Hancock	33	25	G. W. Carver	6
6	H. Tubman	33	26	M. Standish	6
7	Lewis & Clark	25	27	D. Madison	5
8	T. Edison	17	28	F. Nightingale	5
9	J. W. Booth	16	29	N. Turner	5
10	F. S. Key	15	30	A. G. Bell	4
11	T. Paine	13	31	J. Brown	4
12	S. B. Anthony	12	32	A. Burr	4
13	N. Hale	12	33	D. Crockett	4
14	A. Hamilton	12	34	George III	4
15	J. Smith	12	35	J. P. Jones	4
16	F. Douglass	10	36	S. Clemens	3
17	H. B. Stowe	10	37	J. Jay	3
18	B. Arnold	9	38	Dred Scott	3
19	D. Boone	9	39	M. Twain	3
20	W. Penn	9	40	Uncle Tom	3

This impression is confirmed, to put it mildly, by comparing the answers to this second survey in the eight different years. (See Table 8.) The lists are so consistent in character, and even in individual composition, as to suggest that they stem from something beyond the high school classroom. They suggest, as a closer examination can illustrate, that the free association method was opening to view evidence of a very particular cultural imprinting independent of whatever degree of sophistication the students had encountered in high school. To explore the nature and content of that particularity, we need to examine this ad hoc pantheon more closely.

25   At first glance, it is the uniformity that is the most striking. In fact, given the absence of the focusing presence of Lincoln, Washington, and Jefferson, the similarity of the lists is really astonishing. To repeat the previous analysis, we find here that only 20 different names appear in the top ten for the eight years, out of the 80 possible, for a Diversity Index of 0.14—not as low as for question one, but still strikingly diminutive.

Two of the top ten are the same in all eight years: Betsy Ross, the apocryphal creator of the first American flag, and Paul Revere, the horseback-borne messenger of revolution. Another six rank in this grouping in at least five of the seven years: Christopher Columbus; John Smith, the leader of the first successful colonial settlement in Virginia; Eli Whitney, inventor of both interchangeable parts and the cotton gin and hence a symbol of the rise of both northern industry and southern slave society; Meriwether Lewis and William Clark, explorers of the American West who are counted as one—they have become almost a fused individual in the memories of students, always listed together as "Lewis & Clark" or, more than once, Lewis N. Clark; the frontiersman Daniel Boone; and Harriet Tubman, the heroic escaped slave who returned to lead others to freedom, whose presence is the one sign that a century-old pantheon has begun to respond to the recent recognition of blacks as agents of change, not merely objects of misfortune, in American history.

TABLE 8 Question Two: Eight Samples
(Question Two: Write down the first ten names that you think of, excluding presidents, generals, statesmen, etc., in response to the prompt, "American History from its beginning through the end of the Civil War.")

1975	1976	1978	1982	1983	1984	1985	1988
1. B. Ross	1. B. Ross	1. B. Ross	1. B. Ross	1. B. Ross	1. B. Ross	1. B. Ross	1. B. Franklin
2. P. Revere	2. P. Revere	2. E. Whitney	2. P. Revere	2. P. Revere	2. P. Revere	2. P. Revere	2. B. Ross
3. C. Columbus	3. C. Columbus	3. D. Boone	3. J. Smith	3. Lewis & Clark	3. H. Tubman	3. H. Tubman	3. C. Columbus
4. J. Smith	4. E. Whitney	4. P. Revere	4. T. Edison	4. J. Smith	4. Lewis & Clark	4. C. Columbus	4. P. Revere
5. Pocahontas	5. T. Paine	5. Pocahontas	5. E. Whitney	5. T. Edison	5. J. W. Booth	5. F. S. Key	5. J. Hancock
6. B. Arnold	6. H. Tubman	6. C. Columbus	6. D. Crockett	6. J. W. Booth	6. D. Madison	6. J. Smith	6. H. Tubman
7. Lewis & Clark	7. J. Smith	7. Lewis & Clark	7. C. Columbus	7. H. Tubman	7. J. Smith	7. Pocahontas	7. Lewis & Clark
8. D. Boone	8. Lewis & Clark	8. J. Smith	8. H. Tubman	8. E. Whitney	8. F. S. Key	8. Lewis & Clark	8. T. Edison
9. E. Whitney	9. B. Arnold	9. R. Fulton	9. D. Boone	9. D. Boone	9. Pocahontas	9. E. Whitney	9. J. W. Booth
10. D. Crockett	10. D. Boone	10. T. Edison	10. F. S. Key	10. T. Paine	10. H. B. Stowe	10. B. Franklin	10. F. S. Key
11. F. S. Key	11. Pocahontas	11. A. Hutchinson	11. N. Turner	11. Pocahontas	11. D. Boone	11. J. W. Booth	11. T. Paine
12. T. Paine	12. F. S. Key	12. D. Crockett	12. F. Nightingale	12. M. Washington	12. T. Edison	12. T. Paine	12. S. B. Anthony
13. J. P. Jones	13. J. Brown	13. F. Douglass	13. T. Paine	13. C. Columbus	13. B. Franklin	13. M. Washington	13. N. Hale
14. N. Hawthorne	14. J. P. Jones	14. C. McCormick	14. J. W. Booth	14. B. Arnold	14. R. Fulton	14. C. Attucks	14. J. Smith
15. H. B. Stowe	15. Lafayette	15. N. Hawthorne	15. P. De Leon	15. A. Burr	15. B. Arnold	15. J. Brown	15. F. Douglass
16. R. Williams	16. J. W. Booth	16. H. Tubman	16. Sitting Bull	16. F. Douglass	16. C. Barton	16. G. W. Carver	16. H. B. Stowe
17. M. Standish	17. D. Crockett	17. H. B. Stowe	17. M. Washington	17. Sitting Bull	17. J. Brown	17. S. B. Anthony	17. B. Arnold
18. G. W. Carver	18. R. Fulton	18. V. Balboa	18. E. Allen	18. J. Hancock	18. J. P. Jones	18. D. Boone	18. D. Boone
	19. G. W. Carver	19. G. W. Carver	19. G. W. Carver	19. F. S. Key	19. A. G. Bell	19. N. Hale	19. W. Penn
				20. G. W. Carver	20. G. W. Carver	20. P. Henry	20. M. Washington
					21. F. Douglass	21. M. Pitcher	21. Pocahontas
					22. J. Hancock	22. M. Standish	22. E. Whitney
					23. W. Penn	23. H. B. Stowe	23. P. Henry
					24. M. Standish		24. G. W. Carver
					25. M. Washington		25. M. Standish

Considering the entire list, in a total of 168 possibilities, only 46 different names are listed, and of them 17 appear in at least five of the eight years and 5 appear every year. Our Diversity Index for question two's full list is thus 0.15, inconsequentially higher than the 0.14 for the list's top ten. The diversity and consensus indexes for question two are of course considerably lower than for the canonical list of question one, but that is unsurprising since the second question prompts responses unconstrained by the familiar political pantheon. In fact, it is remarkable that the indexes are as low as they are, given the infinite range of possible responses. It is especially significant that the diversity and consensus in the top ten list for question two do not alter very much when the full range of responses is considered. Indeed, by at least one measure (which in a last fit of social science I will call the Consensus Decay Index, or CDI), there is more consistency between the top ten and the full list on question two (a CDI of 0.076) than on question one (a CDI of 0.125, nearly 65 percent higher). That is to say, on question two there is a slower increase than on question one in the variation encountered as we move away from the most popular images at the top. This means there is actually more consistency in the images students have offered over the years in response to the second question.

It is hard to know how much we can generalize from the uniformity of these lists, or how much interpretive weight they can bear. Perhaps all this is merely an artifact of my western New York sample, or the curriculum of New York State's primary and secondary schools; I would be the first to concede that a similar survey in Waco, Texas, for example, would produce a somewhat different list. But I believe regional variation would be far less than might be expected, and that the consistency of the lists—arguably closer to the heart of their significance than the precise content—might well be as striking. I think the free association producing the lists is tapping a very particular kind of cultural memory, one whose hold is general rather than a product of particular associations. For instance, the most famous local citizen in national life—Millard Fillmore, a lamentable president but a great Buffalonian, whose name inescapably graces city streets, districts, and public institutions—has not made the list even once. Beyond that, Buffalo is a heavily ethnic city, and many of our students come from a highly self-conscious Polish-American community; Casimir Pulaski is paraded every year and his name is certainly well known to such students. Yet he has rarely been mentioned on any list *at all*, nor do the tallies suggest much imprint of any other ethnic identification.

There is some more positive and empirical support for my claim of generality in one carefully controlled replication of the survey in another locale. After learning of my experiment and discussing it in correspondence, the cultural geographer Wilbur Zelinsky tried it on a large group of his own students at the Pennsylvania State University—an institution not terribly far from Buffalo, but not in an identical culture area either, and one whose students are shaped by a different precollege curriculum. Even with the accumulating weight of my own evidence, we were both astounded by the results in Pennsylvania: on questions one and two alike, thirteen of the top fifteen names were identical to those on my Buffalo surveys, appearing in nearly identical rank order, headed once again by the unsinkable Betsy Ross. The tiny differences in the lists almost disappeared in the fuller list of twenty or so: William Penn turns out to be the only figure who holds a very different place in the Pennsylvania rankings. Zelinsky's lists even reproduce some of the peculiarities of mine, such as the curiously misplaced presence of George Washington Carver and Thomas Edison, who belong in a different time period, and the Americanization of Florence Nightingale, who belongs on another continent.

In addition, Zelinsky added one methodological flourish whose products bear usefully on the broader issues I raised earlier: he asked his students to note whether they had ever taken a college American history course before (roughly 30 percent had, and 70 percent had not). Given the cultural importance that many attach to exposure to history courses in the curriculum, it is interesting to ask what changes when Zelinsky's responses are tallied under these headings.

The answer is absolutely nothing; the lists compiled by both groups of students are virtually identical in composition and even rank order. Some individual names obtain slightly higher support from students exposed to college history courses (Samuel Adams and Jefferson Davis on question one, Davy Crockett and John Wilkes Booth on question two), while others gain proportionally more of their votes from students without that background (George Washington Carver and William Penn). But the breakdown of support for most of the names shows only the most modest divergence from the breakdown of the class as a whole. There is a final poetic justice in the fact that the one figure on question two at absolute dead center, listed in absolutely identical proportions by history and non-history students alike, is none other than Betsy Ross. Whatever students may or may not have learned in college history courses (and, as I shall argue, high school history courses) seems to have little to do with the images drawn forth by this exercise[4]

Having mollified the gods of empiricism, let us turn to the task of explaining in broader cultural terms the patterns we have uncovered. Each list profiles a strikingly consistent pantheon of generally received and recalled cultural heroes, legends, and near-mythic figures. Quite apparently, we are examining here evidence of cultural transmission, perhaps as mediated through the primary schools and popular culture. Accordingly, my introductory lecture has had less to do with the high school curricula I had expected to engage in battle than with what I came to pose, for the students, as a kind of anthropological question: "If all you knew about American culture was what you could deduce from this list, what would you know?"

Thus viewed as a cultural artifact, the profile offered in each list is anything but random. Rather, it stands as a dramatic elaboration of what Catherine L. Albanese has termed the "presumption of newness" at the core of the American myth.[5] Indeed, what we see here is a broadening of that theme into an ongoing fixation on creation myths of origin and innovation.

In this, myth must be understood as the driving force behind history: John Smith and Pocahontas were real, of course, but manifestly it is the mythic scene in which the "love" of the Indian "princess" saves the explorer from a "savage" death that accounts for the high-ranking presence of both figures in the imagination of my students. Such a mythic framework reaches out to the explorers, from Columbus to the Siamese-twin Lewis & Clark, who define the nation by "beginning" its history, their "discovery" of space really a beginning of America's historical time, again and again. It includes both the revolutionary progenitors and the practical inventors like Whitney who are remembered as initiators of America's distinctive epoch of technological time.

It is interesting, in this regard, to note the rank of the inventor Edison, in fourteenth place on the question two summary tally, near the top, and the place of the black botanist Carver, who brings up the rear almost every time and who is the only figure *never* to appear in the top ten who *always* ranks on the overall list. (On Zelinsky's poll, he is the single figure most disproportionately listed by students who had not taken history courses.) As figures from the late nineteenth and early twentieth centuries, both Edison and Carver represent an overriding of the instructions to focus on an earlier time period. It hardly seems coincidental, given contemporary anxiety about ungraspable technological change and uncontrollable corporate organization on a worldwide scale, that the *only* regularly repeated chronological "mistakes" are these comfortable symbols of practical genius and human-scale progress.

And for a white society shuttling between racial guilt and fear, the symbol of Carver has always offered an additional all-too-convenient balm. The myth of the patient experimenter, the "credit to his race" who discovered manifold new uses for the lowly peanut, has long obscured the reality of a man whose acquiescence in the racism of the early twentieth-century United States stands in dramatic contrast to the resistance offered by contemporaneous black leaders like W. E. B. Du Bois and even Booker T. Washington. One wonders if that posture may have contributed more than his modest scientific accomplishments to Carver's not-quite-natural selection for immortality in the evolution of American memory.

There is also something beyond coincidence in the recurrence of John Wilkes Booth and Benedict Arnold, who represent for an innocent nation the serpent-traitors whose evil also sets history in

[4]I much appreciate Professor Zelinsky's interest in the problem and his sending me the data from his March 1, 1984, survey of a Geography 1 class of 115 students. This material is discussed and presented with his kind permission. Wilbur Zelinsky to Michael Frisch, March 5, 1984 (in Michael Frisch's possession).
[5]Albanese, *Sons of the Fathers*, 9, 28.

TABLE 9 Question Two: Eight Sample Summary
(Question Two: Write down the first ten names that you think of, excluding presidents, generals, statesmen, etc., in response to the prompt, "American History from its beginning through the end of the Civil War.")

Name	Rank in Year: 1975	1976	1978	1982	1983	1984	1985	1988	Years on List
1. B. Ross	1	1	1	1	1	1	1	2	8
2. P. Revere	2	2	4	2	2	2	2	4	8
3. J. Smith	4	7	8	3	4	7	6	14	8
4. D. Boone	8	10	3	9	9	11	18	18	8
5. G. W. Carver	18	19	19	19	20	20	16	24	8
6. C. Columbus	3	3	6	7	13		4	3	7
7. Lewis & Clark	7	8	7		3	4	8	7	7
8. H. Tubman		6	16	8	7	3	3	6	7
9. E. Whitney	9	4	2	5	8		9	22	7
10. Pocahontas	5	11	5		11	9	7	21	7
11. F. S. Key	11	12		10	19	8	5	10	7
12. J. W. Booth		16		14	6	5	11	9	6
13. T. Paine	12	5		13	10		12	11	6
14. T. Edison			10	4	5	12		8	5
15. B. Arnold	6	9			14	15		17	5
16. H. B. Stowe	15		17			10	23	16	5
17. M. Washington				17	12	25	13	20	5
18. R. Fulton		18	9			14			4
19. D. Crockett	10	17	12	6					4
20. F. Douglass			13		16	21		15	4
21. M. Standish	17					24	22	25	4
22. B. Franklin						13	10	1	3
23. J. Hancock					18	22		5	3
24. J. P. Jones	13	14				18			3
25. J. Brown		13				17	15		3
26. S. B. Anthony							17	12	2
27. N. Hawthorne	14		15						2
28. N. Hale							19	13	2
29. Sitting Bull				16	17				2
30. W. Penn						23		19	2
31. P. Henry							20	23	2
32. J. Madison						6			1
33. A. Hutchinson			11						1
34. N. Turner				11					1
35. F. Nightingale				12					1
36. C. McCormick			14						1
37. C. Attucks							14		1
38. P. De Leon				15					1
39. A. Burr					15				1
40. Lafayette		15							1
41. R. Williams	16								1
42. C. Barton						16			1
43. E. Allen				18					1
44. V. Balboa			18						1
45. A. G. Bell						19			1
46. M. Pitcher							21		1

TABLE 10 Eight Sample Analysis		
Question Two	*Top Ten*	*Total List*
A Total Names	20	46
B Maximum Possible Names	80	168
C Minimum Possible Names	10	25
D Maximum Possible Spread (B-C)	70	143
E Actual Spread (A-C)	10	21
F Diversity Index (E/D)	0.14	0.15
G Names on List All Eight Years	2	5
H Eight-Year Consensus Index (G/A)	10.0%	10.9%
I Names on List Five Years or More	8	17
J Five-Plus Consensus Index (I/A)	40.0%	37.0%
K Consensus Decay Index [(J.1-J.2)/J.1]		0.076

motion—necessary preludes to the transcendent triumph of good. As these observations suggest, the list is not only composed of quasi-mythic figures: as a collective portrait, it has a kind of mythic structure and completeness itself, a character confirmed by its re-creation year after year in nearly identical terms.

But the most compelling indication of this character is the nearly unshakable hold of Betsy Ross on the first place position—she tops the list in seven of the eight classes, and her decline to second place this past semester is actually the exception that proves the rule. My graduate assistant notes that I seem to have omitted the "statesmen" prompt from the list of those to be excluded on question two's list, thus accounting for Franklin's triumph and John Hancock's uncharacteristically high rank on question two. (Always fixtures on question one, both were usually omitted from the second list by students given the intended exclusionary prompt in other years.) In any event, Betsy Ross's position at the top is truly phenomenal, a record that cries out for explanation as it has occasioned a good deal of discussion in my classes each year. Even given everything said so far, it is still not immediately apparent why this *particular* mythic figure has been discovered so much more frequently than others by the searching beam of free association memory.

Part of the explanation may lie in a kind of psychological/feminist interpretation generated by one class discussion. Perhaps the command to produce names of those not in positions of public power led the genderized imaginations of students

through the following sequence: Nonpublic means domestic and private; domestic and private means women; women means Betsy Ross. I think there may be something to this, though it still begs a number of questions. The framework of civil religion and comparative mythology provides some additional insights, however, and all combined may serve to make the Betsy Ross hegemony less mystical and more instructive.

The flag, of course, is the primary symbol of what is distinctive about the United States. It represents the core of our nationality—that political identity declared and constituted in the epochal revolutionary experience whose artifactual, yet genuine, religious content Albanese has documented so powerfully. As Marshall Smelser has written, the flag "has assumed a moral value transcending the mundane purposes of national identification. As a tribal totem, it satisfies the real and almost universal hunger for a public symbol of spiritual kinship above and invulnerable to the contentions and changes of politics—and for which no other totem is available to the United States."[6] If that is true, there is a nice logic to Betsy Ross's preeminent place in a structure of creation myth figures and heroic progenitors; she represents the most inclusive symbol of national identity, an identity perhaps more fragile and in need of shoring up than other national identities because of its uniquely political character.

The Ross hegemony also helps to bring the presidential list of question one within the interpretation developed here, for its figures are also

[6]*Ibid.*, 261–62n51.

more powerful as symbols of political cohesion and identity than as historical figures per se. Indeed, Washington himself "absorbed and unified the elements from the classical and Christian past, becoming for Americans, a divine man."[7] Beyond helping us to respect, and thereby understand, a sometimes ludicrous apotheosis that began even in Washington's lifetime. Albanese's discussion provides a context for some final reflections on the essentially religious meaning of Betsy Ross's place in this collective portrait.

Albanese documents how the revolutionary sons made themselves into Founding Fathers, with Washington the *primus inter pares,* literally the spiritual Father of the Nation. She also shows how his spiritual meaning came to obscure his real existence: his wife Martha faded from legendary image and relatively speaking from our memories, because "kindred as was the soul of the father of his country to his wife, it had proved to be far more closely interfused with the structures of meaning and value of his countrymen. Washington . . . had become a grand collective representative, a tribal totem." And in the process, fictive and symbolic kin came to replace his real family in popular imagination: thus the common celebration of the marquis de Lafayette as the "beloved and 'adopted son.' "[8]

Albanese could go no further with the myth, but evidence of the symbolic role of Betsy Ross allows us to complete the picture. To this end, it is important to note that the Betsy Ross story is a product of a late nineteenth-century style of religio-mythic craftsmanship. The actual Betsy Ross had, demonstrably, no role whatsoever in the actual creation of any actual first flag. But more important, her story itself played no part in revolutionary-era tradition or mythmaking even at its most instrumental. In fact, the flag story emerged only a century later in Philadelphia, when her descendants sought to create a tourist attraction around the time of the centennial exposition of 1876. The reasons for the emergence of the tale were thus prosaic, not to say mercenary; but as Albanese reminds us, however intentional and instrumental, such self-consciousness does not exclude deeper levels of cultural meaning and expression.[9]

It is hard to avoid the speculation that the latter-day invention of the mythic Betsy Ross—and her immediate public enshrinement—came as a kind of needed supplement to the revolutionary myth, a final step in the humano-centric articulation of essentially religious beliefs and experiences. If George is the Father of the Country—of the nation, of all the American sons and daughters—then surely Betsy Ross exists symbolically as the Mother, who gives birth to our collective symbol.

One can go further. If Washington is, indeed, a surrogate for God the Father, the meaning of Betsy Ross is unmistakable: she stands for the Blessed Virgin Mary in the iconography of our civil religion. A plain woman is visited by a distant god and commanded to be the vehicle, through their collaboration, of a divine creation. And indeed, in the classroom pageants enacted by generations of American school-children over the past century, that is exactly what we see: Washington calls on the humble seamstress Betsy Ross in her tiny home and asks her if she will make the nation's flag, to his design. And Betsy promptly brings forth—from her lap!—the flag, the nation itself, and the promise of freedom and natural rights for all mankind.

There is a final note of confirmation for this hypothesis in the rather after-the-fact addition of Betsy Ross to our national mythology. For the cult of the Virgin Mother was itself a rather late development in Christian theology, a medieval elaboration of an undeveloped dimension of the Gospels, a statement, perhaps, that for a fully satisfying religious symbolism, Sons and Fathers were not quite enough. If I seem to overinterpret what are, after all, trite relics from grade school primers, then I ask you to remember Albanese's caution that the contrivance or superficiality of myth-making does not necessarily deny, and may even tend to confirm, its deeper cultural functions.

That observation provides a pivot on which to return to our initial questions—the relevance of this exploration in historical trivia for the august debates on history and education that loom so large in contemporary discussion.

On one level, my results can be read as a confirmation of the diagnosis that something is seriously

---

[7] *Ibid.,* 158–59.
[8] *Ibid.,* 172, 170.
[9] See the full and interesting account in Joseph Jackson, *Encyclopedia of Philadelphia* (Harrisburg, 1931). 1054–55.

The certificate* records a contribution to the "Endowment Fund for the preservation of the Historic House in which the First Flag of the United States of America was made." Wreath-encircled representations of Betsy Ross's house and grave flank a painting (enlarged below). Behind it the sun rises; on its beams rides an American eagle, clutching arrows and the E Pluribus Unum streamer.

* The original certificate Dr. Frisch used in his essay could not be located for reprinting here, so a copy of another certificate has been used courtesy of the Betsy Ross Historical House, Philadelphia.

wrong. If college students cannot come up with lists showing more depth and grasp than these; if college courses—as Zelinsky's data suggest, or even high school courses, as the overall survey demonstrates—have so little impact, then surely we are in some kind of trouble. The almost childish character of the revealed pantheon seems quite consistent with the diagnosis that we are producing generations for whom a meaningful national history in even some of its richness and complexity is not an accessible resource. And as such, the survey can only reinforce the resonance many history teachers must feel when they encounter the documented ignorance that so exercises former Secretary of Education William J. Bennett, Diane Ravitch, Lynne Cheney, et al. Everyone who teaches history must have his or her own horror story that seems to confirm the ominous collapse of rope bridges across the generation gap.[10]

---

[10]My personal favorite is Professor Manning Marable's report of the black student in a black studies class who came up to ask, "Now, who is this Malcolm the Tenth, and what was he king of, anyway?" (Professor Marable confirmed this anecdote in a conversation in Buffalo in February 1987.) This is instructive in indicating that the problem of cultural loss, whatever else it may mean, is a shared one, not simply a matter, as usually presented, of the dominant culture's heritage being insufficiently respected by those held to be in need of its ministrations.

This reproduction of *Birth of Our Nation's Flag* appears on the elaborate certificate of membership (above) that the American Flag House and Betsy Ross Memorial Association issued to Charlotte Kromm in 1919. The certificate has sobering relevance to the politics of past and present cultural literacy campaigns: Kromm, a German American, may have taken out membership less to advance historic preservation than to affirm the loyalty of German Americans, much impugned during World War I. *Certificate courtesy of Donald A. Ritchie.*

Birth of Our Nation's Flag.

As I have argued, however, the surveys are more interesting when taken as evidence of what students do know, rather than what they don't. If the results say little one way or the other about how much history the students surveyed may actually know, they are evidence that cultural imagery seems to be reproduced in our young people with startling consistency and regularity. And this conclusion casts something of a shadow over the current jeremiads, whose core concerns, I would argue, are at bottom more fundamentally cultural and political than educational. This point is worth at least brief examination by way of conclusion.

The sermons being preached in this crusade are difficult to deal with as texts, because they slide so fluidly along a spectrum of analysis ranging from the high-minded and humanistic to the crudely political and instrumental. At the former end, we find the calls for exposure to the complexity

of historical studies, for the cultivation of the critical mind, and for provision of the basic orientation to the real world and its history that citizens need to understand the present and make intelligent choices in the future. It is hard to see how anyone could fail to be shocked by the documented effects on students of an almost willful indifference to the value of historical consciousness and training, and the effects on teachers, especially in the secondary schools, of decades of overemphasis on pseudoprofessional training programs and methods at the expense of subject and substance.

It is a different matter when those unexceptionable themes are given a more particular emphasis: that students need not just more of history, but rather more of "our" national history. To a degree, the argument still holds: citizenship in a democracy requires the critical skills that such

training should provide, and a certain core familiarity with the history and geography of one's country is arguably essential to knowing what the society is all about. But in most formulations, the educational critique is sufficiently expansive to suggest a different animus behind it: the problem is that our students are spending too much time on "them"—the rest of the world, global and comparative studies, and so forth—rather than on the "us" at home. And to the extent they do study "us," it is the wrong us—too much emphasis on social history, people outside ruling elites, minorities, and women, rather than on the political and military core of national tradition.

That emphasis is held to be problematic, both symptom and cause of a fragmentation of national unity, cohesion, and will in the face of grave political, economic, and military threats from without, and even from within. Virtually every one of the core documents slips into this mood sooner rather than later, after the appropriate genuflections at the altar of humanism and the critical spirit. The issue is put starkly in terms of American competitiveness, the Cold War, and the danger of ethnic and linguistic pluralism run rampant.

Since I haven't the time to demonstrate this point by citing chapter and verse from the new scriptures, let me instead offer a single picture. This lead page from a 1985 *New York Times Magazine* article by Ravitch touches every base. The headline announces the problem in its most generalized form—the "Decline and Fall of Teaching History." The subhead slides into the Americanization of the cultural literacy problem, masking the shift of focus with syntax that raises concern about plain old literacy at the *Times:* "An ignorance or indifference about studying our past has become cause for concern." And finally, there is the picture, suspended between the two: a teacher leads a small group discussion in a global studies course that is, elsewhere in the article, an object of ridicule. Manifestly, the picture is intended to illustrate both "decline and fall" and "ignorance and indifference." Yet the class seems lively and intense; the lesson

plan on the blackboard behind the teacher carries the outline for what could be a satisfying history lecture in any college course. What, then, is the picture doing here? Could it have anything to do with the fact that the teacher is black, the students black and perhaps Hispanic, and the planned lesson a discussion of Russia on the eve of the 1917 Revolution?[11]

I submit that the page captures perfectly the tension between the explicit text, couched in broadly acceptable abstract terms about history, and the deeply political subtext of the current educational crusade. Beneath the huffing and puffing about historical studies lies a fear not dissimilar to that propelling the "Americanization" efforts that so dominated education and politics in the United States in the early years of the twentieth century, fueled by a terror of immigrant cultures and concern for the future of the Anglo-Saxon race and heritage. It is fascinating how often, in the current litany, those educational efforts are taken to represent a kind of golden age to which we should return.

If all this has a quaint ring so soon after the Statue of Liberty centennial, the explicit cold war fixation strikes a much more ominous tone: Secretary Bennett has grounded his own critique of the schools, for example, on the proposition that they have embraced the doctrine of, in Jeane Kirkpatrick's term, "moral equivalence," willfully offering education "designed to prevent future generations of American intellectuals from telling the difference between the U.S. and the U.S.S.R."[12]

In such formulations, educational reform has been given a highly ideological definition: the point of education is not individual but national; the object of improvement in training in history is the production of obedient, patriotic citizens who share a set of presumptions about the United States, its people, economy, and relation to the other nations of the world. The argument has traveled a long way from its humanistic origins, arriving at a point where education and indoctrination—cultural and political—seem almost indistinguishable.

[11]Diane Ravitch, "Decline and Fall of Teaching History," *New York Times Magazine,* Nov. 17, 1985, pp. 50, 52, 54, 56, 101, 117.

[12]Walter Goodman, "Conservatives' Theme: The West is Different," *New York Times,* May 5, 1985, sec. 1, p. 21, a report on an anticommunism conference, the first event sponsored by the State Department's new and controversial Office for Public Diplomacy.

Indeed, in one of the more remarkable documents in the current literature, they *are* indistinguishable. Sidney Hook's 1984 lecture "Education in Defense of a Free Society" is a kind of *Ur-text* of the cultural literacy movement, outlining a set of themes that reappear again and again, less baldly, in the writings and speeches of Bennett, Ravitch, Cheney, and others. To Hook the issue is "whether we possess the basic social cohesion and solidarity today to survive the challenge to our society . . . posed by the global expansion of Communism"; the role of the schools—primary and secondary especially—is to generate sufficient loyalty through what he freely acknowledges is an embrace of propaganda and indoctrination (critical thought comes later, he says). In the final analysis, "no institutional changes of themselves will develop that bond of community we need to sustain our nation in times of crisis without a prolonged schooling in the history of our free society, its martyrology, and its national tradition."[13]

Hook's explicit reference to martyrology, tradition, and the need for cultural indoctrination in the primary and secondary schools brings us back to Betsy Ross and the tables of data I have been discussing here. According to Hook, Bennett, Cheney, Ravitch, and others in what William Greider has called the "Bloom and Doom" school, we are in trouble on every front: the crisis of historical amnesia, the decline of formal studies in history, and the deterioration of critical thinking are taken to be linked to a presumed corrosion of national spirit and will, evidenced in a declining respect for and awareness of the binding symbols of national tradition at the most basic levels. Such critics see no contradiction in calling for both patriotic indoctrination under the umbrella of a culturally binding nationalism and intellectually challenging studies in history. The assumption is that a shared cultural memory and historical consciousness ought to be close to the same thing, or at least linked in some developmental or cumulative sense.[14]

The evidence I have presented suggests that this philosophically dubious proposition is also without foundation empirically. Whatever the deeper knowledge and grasp of history among my students, there is no indication in the data that the chords of cultural memory, in terms of the hold of national historical symbols, have weakened in the slightest. In fact, the consistency and extraordinary uniformity in the images offered up by these students indicates that the president, Secretary Bennett, and their followers have little cause for concern: the structure of myth and heroes, martyrs and mothers, is firmly in place.

This does not mean there is no crisis in the teaching of history, no deficiency in the historical consciousness with which our young people perceive the swiftly changing world around them. It does suggest, however, that frantic injections of cultural symbolism are not needed and almost certainly will not be the solution to the epidemic; if anything, the lesson is that indoctrination and education need to be more effectively decoupled, not conflated. For students who already hold lists of heroes deep in their imaginations need a sense that history is populated by three-dimensional human beings, the famous as well as the forgotten, who live in and act on a real world that is always changing.

In the tension between such a vision and the grade-school pantheon students dutifully remember for my surveys each year, there is a suggestion of what most history teachers in the trenches already know: that alienated students cannot be bullied into attention or retention; that authoritarian cultural intimidation is likely to be met by a further and more rapid retreat; and that there may well be, in that alienation itself, statements about the claims of the present on the past worth our respect, attention, and response. I have concluded in my own teaching that the evidently massive, uniform subsurface reefs of cultural memory are, in this sense, part of the problem, not resources for a solution.

---

[13]Sidney Hook, "Education in Defense of a Free Society," *Commentary,* 78 (July 1984), 17–22, esp. 21, 22. Hook delivered the speech on receiving the Jefferson award for "intellectual achievement in the humanities," bestowed as its highest honor by the National Endowment for the Humanities.

[14]The reference is to a witty review of Bloom, *Closing of the American Mind:* William Greider, "Bloom and Doom," *Rolling Stone,* Oct. 8, 1987, pp. 39–40. For other relevant critiques, see Martha Nussbaum, "Undemocratic Vistas," *New York Review of Books,* Nov. 5, 1987, pp. 20–26; and Robert Pattison, "On the Finn Syndrome and the Shakespeare Paradox," *Nation,* May 30, 1987, pp. 710–20.

As such, however, those structures merit immense respect from pedagogic navigators. They tell us a great deal about our culture, its resources, and its often problematic hold on the imagination of students—and on citizens as well, to judge from the power in the 1988 presidential campaign of some of the very icons discussed in this essay. My ongoing experiment in the survey course has convinced me that we need to realize what we are up against, in the classroom and in political life more broadly. We must understand the depth of the cultural symbolism our students and fellow citizens carry inside them long before entering our classrooms, if ever they do. Appreciating the powerful grip of collective cultural memory becomes a necessary first step if we are to help our students to understand the real people and processes of history, to locate its reality in their lives, and to discover the power and uses of historical imagination in the present.

Is This Song Your Song Anymore?: Revisioning Woody Guthrie's "This Land Is Your Land"

Mark Allan Jackson

Mark Allan Jackson is an Assistant Professor of English at DePauw University in Greencastle, Indiana. This essay was originally written when Dr. Jackson was a graduate student at Louisiana State University and is part of a project that became the 2007 book *Prophet Singer: The Voice and Vision of Woody Guthrie*. In addition to several other scholarly essays, Dr. Jackson has compiled two CD collections for the West Virginia University Press' Sound Archive Series: *John Handcox: Songs, Poems, and Stories of the Southern Tenant Farmers Union* and *Coal Digging Blues: Songs of West Virginia Miners*. Originally this essay was published in *American Music,* a quarterly publication featuring articles on American composers, performers, musical events, and the music industry.

After drifting around New York for almost two months at the beginning of 1940, sleeping on a succession of friends' couches, and busking for tips in Bowery saloons, songwriter and political activist Woody Guthrie settled into the shabby surroundings of Hanover House, a hotel located near the jumble and noise of Times Square. There, on February 23, he wrote "God Blessed America," whose six verses ended in the refrain "God blessed America for me." Afterward, he did not show much interest in the song and did not perform it often.[1] Then sometime before the end of April 1944, when Moses Asch first recorded him singing it, Guthrie decided to change the title to "This Land Is Your Land" and the refrain to "This land was made for you and me."

Over the years, this song has surpassed simple popularity and found its way into our national consciousness, evidenced by a great many Americans' familiarity with the melody. Many people can sing all or part of the chorus—and a few even know Woody Guthrie wrote the song. This recognition cannot be attributed directly to its commercial achievement, however. For example, if we look to *Billboard* magazine as a typical measurement of a song's commercial status, we find none of the many versions of "This Land" has reached the top ten, forty, or even hundred in terms of sales. Yet even without this type of commercial success, it has become as Clifton Fadiman describes Guthrie and his work as a whole: "a national possession, like Yellow-stone or Yosemite, and a part of the best stuff this country has to show the world."[2] In time, "This Land" has risen to the same status of such American songs as "The Star-Spangled Banner," "America the Beautiful," "My Country' Tis of Thee" ("America"), and "God Bless America." Much like these other songs, through varied and sometimes subtle means, "This Land" has entered the bloodstream of our nation's cultural body.

No matter how Americans first encounter the song, however, the version they hear always contains vivid and idyllic references to "the redwood forest" and a "golden valley," to "diamond deserts" and "wheat fields waving." If we compare the verses most of us are familiar with to those in the original version of the song, differences appear, however. In the very first written version, the fourth and sixth verses address aspects of our society Guthrie finds disturbing:

> Was a big high wall that tried to stop me
> A sign was painted said: Private Property,
> But on the back side it didn't say nothing—
> God blessed America for me.
>
> One bright sunny morning in the shadow of
> the steeple

By the relief office I saw my people —
As they stood hungry, I stood there wondering if
God blessed America for me.[3]

The sentiments expressed here, detailing restriction and want, differ greatly from the celebratory vision of America shining through the popular three-verse/chorus version.[4] The omission of these verses also removes the song's initial dissenting and questioning voice and leaves behind a praising remnant, one that sings more like a national anthem than its intended purpose — a musical response to and protest against Irving Berlin's "God Bless America."

5   Considering the prominent status "This Land" holds in our culture, it is important to those exploring the American experience to understand how one dominant version of the song came to be known by the American populace and how its meaning has been changed by different contexts throughout its life. While looking into the song's past and popularity, we also need to examine the original lyrics and those from other versions and contrast them with the words of the popularized creation. This analysis will also produce new insight into Guthrie. Over the years, his image has become clouded by hyperbole from both ends of the political spectrum. Since "This Land" remains the main means through which the American people have encountered his voice and vision, it offers the single best vantage point to attempt to understand the man who wrote it and the country he tried to sing about.

In that Guthrie initially intended "This Land" as a critical musical response to "God Bless America," a brief discussion of Berlin's song — its origins and acceptance by Americans — will provide an idea of just what inspired the creation of Guthrie's most popular work. To find the beginning of "God Bless America," we must travel back to 1917, when young Irving Berlin — who was in the army at the time — wrote and directed the musical *Yip! Yip! Yaphank* as a military fund-raiser. As part of this production, he wrote "God Bless America," which his biographer Laurence Bergreen calls an "unashamedly patriotic anthem."[5] The unmitigated patriotism of the song was so obvious that even Berlin believed it inappropriate for this particular production. The *New York Times Magazine* quotes him as saying, "everyone was emotionally stirred and realized what we were up against. It seemed

like carrying coals to Newcastle to have a bunch of soldiers come out and sing it."[6] As a result of these apprehensions, he cut it from the show and filed it away with his other unused manuscripts — where it stayed for over twenty years.

In late 1938, with another war in Europe looming ever closer, popular singer Kate Smith asked Berlin for a song that would stir patriotic fervor to use on her Armistice Day radio broadcast. After a few abortive efforts to produce a new tune, he remembered the song cut from *Yip! Yip! Yaphank* and decided to rework it to fit the current situation. First, he took the line "Guide her to the right with a light from above" from the original song and changed it to "Through the night with a light from above" because when the song was originally written, Berlin says, "'to the right' had meant 'to the right path,'" but in 1938 it meant "the political Right."[7] The second change shifted it away from being a war song. "Make her victorious on land and foam, God bless America, my home, sweet home" became "From the mountains to the prairies to the oceans white with foam, God Bless America, my home, sweet home."[8] Even with these changes, the opening vision of "storm clouds gather[ing] far across the sea" still remains, invoking a fearful image. Then comes the push for "allegiance" from a voice that uses "us" to establish the speaker as being with the listener. After asking for all to "be grateful for a land so fair," the speaker finally calls for a unifying prayer:

> God bless America, land that I love.
> Stand beside her and guide her through the
>   night with a light from above.
> From the mountains, to the prairies, to the
>   oceans white with foam.
> God bless America, my home sweet home.[9]

Although this final version remains nationalistic, Berlin's revisions do make the song less jingoistic than its earlier incarnation.

After making these changes, Berlin offered "God Bless America" to Smith. Supposedly, she read the manuscript and blurted out, "Irving, do you realize you've written the second 'Star-Spangled Banner'?"[10] Smith first sang the piece on November 11, 1938, during her highly rated radio program on CBS. Almost immediately, the song established itself at the top of the Hit Parade and could be heard on radios throughout America. The sheet music also did well, staying in the top fifteen in sales for almost six months in the first half of 1939.[11] But these typical signs of popularity do not show how deeply the American people accepted the song in the late 1930s. Within a few months, Smith's comment on first hearing the song seemed prophetic when it actually did take on some of the trappings of our national anthem. On Memorial Day in 1939, the assembled sports fans at Ebbits Field in Brooklyn stood and even took off their hats for "God Bless America," just as they had earlier for the "Star-Spangled Banner."[12]

10   Not everyone held Berlin's song in such high esteem, however. As he traveled north from Texas to New York City in early 1940, Woody Guthrie heard Berlin's song "in Pampa [Texas], in Konawa [Oklahoma], on car radios, in diners, and it seemed that every time he stopped in a roadhouse for a shot of warm-up whiskey some maudlin joker would plunk a nickel in a jukebox and play it just for spite," according to his principal biographer, Joe Klein.[13] For Guthrie, Kate Smith was singing a song about America, a song celebrating this country, that did not completely jibe with what he had witnessed or had lived. He knew firsthand that not everyone had reason to be "grateful for a land so fair" nor had everyone experienced an America that could reasonably be called their "home sweet home."

Looking at Guthrie's personal history, several important reasons for his dissatisfaction with the song's sentiments appear. First, he had already been a "Dust Bowl refugee" (a term he hated), even if he had never been driven off a farm by dust, drought, or mechanization—just as he had never worked in western fields alongside his fellow Okies. But he had ridden the rails and highways with those who had left behind their homes in the South and Southwest for an uncertain future out West. He had also seen and talked to the landless migrant laborers toiling in the fields when he toured California's farming communities above Los Angeles during the late 1930s. During these wanderings, he heard the migrants' stories of hardship and saw their weatherbeaten, old-before-their-time faces, much the same faces we can see in thousands of Farm Security Administration photographs taken during the Depression. Although not a photographer, he too captured their suffering and beauty, but with words:

> I did keep my eyes on you, and kept my ears open when you came close to me. I saw the lines chopped across your face by the troubles

in time and space. I saw the wind shape your face so the sun could light it up with thoughts and shadows. I remember your face as it was when I saw you.[14]

More explicitly in another prose piece, he wrote, "I saw the hundreds of thousands of stranded, broke, hungry, idle, miserable people that lined the highways all out through the leaves and the underbrush."[15] His own eyes easily told him that these people had been little blessed by America. But the suffering he saw and lived did not end in the nation's farming communities.

During the course of his travels, Guthrie also found that America's cities had their own brand of ills, which would be another reason for his problem with Berlin's song. Just as he had in the fields of California, he saw the angry reaction to the Okies pouring into urban and new suburban landscapes of Los Angeles. Later, when he first moved to New York, he traveled down to the Bowery. According to Klein, "instead of unemployed Okies just passing through" such as those he had encountered on Los Angeles' Skid Row, he found "hardcore alcoholics groveling for pennies."[16] Flop houses, cheap bars, and relief agencies—these were the sights of the city, just as dust clouds, repossessed farms, and migrant laborers were those of the country. Human misery was a constant in both, though. This panorama of misery did not add up to an America blessed for everyone.

Guthrie's once-inchoate political awareness also began flowering around the time he wrote the song that would eventually become "This Land." He started connecting the poverty in the nation's fields, skid rows, and elsewhere to the exclusions and unfairness of the distribution of wealth in America. For example, using the tune to "So Long, It's Been Good to Know You" and a sentiment similar to "I Ain't Got No Home in This World Anymore," he found a voice for these newfound notions in "I Don't Feel at Home on the Bowery No More," also written in early 1940. He wrote, "Once on this Bowery I used to be gay." Next, he juxtaposed images of the decrepit Bowery with those of opulent Fifth Avenue and ended the song with the lines "since I seen the difference 'tween the rich and the poor / I don't feel at home in the Bowery no more." In an endnote he dedicated the song "to the bum situation up and down every Skid Row and Bowery Street in this country."[17] To Guthrie, the great gulf between the wealthy and the poor stood out more boldly in New York than it ever had elsewhere.

15   This difference in class status also manifests itself in the personal situations of Berlin and Guthrie. A full quarter century before "God Bless America" made its successful public debut, Berlin rose from immigrant poverty to great wealth. Then, during the 1930s, he was part of a New York social circle left largely untouched by the Great Depression. In contrast, Guthrie suffered through his sister's death, his father's financial failure, the late 1920s boom/bust cycle of Oklahoma's oilfields, the institutionalization and death of his mother, dire poverty, dust storms, and a number of other personal hardships. His early tragedies, his low-budget travels across the whole of America in the mid- and late 1930s, the sights that met him in the fields of California, and his time on Skid Row in Los Angeles and on the Bowery in New York, gave him a greatly different perspective on the state of America than that of Berlin.

Somewhat surprisingly considering these class differences, both Berlin and Guthrie held similar beliefs concerning the source and power of songs; they both believed songs represented the common discourse of Americans. In fact, their comments on this issue strongly jibe. Guthrie wrote, "A song ain't nothing but a conversation fixed up to where you can talk it over and over without getting tired of it," while Berlin said, "A good popular song is just sort of the feeling and conversation of people set to music."[18] Much as did Berlin, Guthrie believed songs have the power to influence people and to tell their own truths back to them. However, Guthrie also thought songs can point to suffering and explain how to lessen it. In late 1940, he expressed this view with poetic suppleness in a letter sent to Alan Lomax: "A folk song is whats wrong and how to fix it or it could be whose hungry and where their mouth is or whose out of work and where the job is or whose broke and where the money is or whose carrying a gun and where the peace is."[19] Both songwriters believed their work gave the people of America a voice that could speak, moan, or holler out their minds and feelings. Listening from different vantage points, Guthrie and Berlin channeled wildly disparate voices.

By the time he first traveled to New York, Guthrie had already put the sights and experiences of the Dust Bowl into songs such as "So Long, It's

Been Good to Know You," "Dust Storm Disaster," and "Dust Pneumonia Blues." He had also explored and exposed the harsh reality of the California-as-promised-land myth in "Do Re Mi" and "Dust Bowl Refugees." He performed these songs, along with less politicized material, on the radio at KFVD in Los Angeles. In response, thousands of people wrote him, many of them expressing support for his reflections on the Great Depression and sympathy for those down and out. These people told him he had said their words and amplified them. When he heard Berlin's paean to the unmitigated, the unmarred magnificence of America, Guthrie understandably realized that the song neglected to address many people's pain, that it failed to document any of the injustices and suffering that stretched along with the land "from the mountains, to the prairies, to the oceans white with foam." But he did not have to remain silent in his dissent; he had the talent to counter Berlin's song with one of his own.

Soon after arriving in New York, Guthrie began to transmute his feelings about "God Bless America" into song. Like many folksingers before him, Guthrie often hung his lyrics on the tunes of others. As a result, much speculation as to the source for the melody for "This Land" has arisen, with candidates ranging from the old Baptist hymn "Oh My Lovin' Brother," the Carter Family's "Little Darling, Pal of Mine," the gospel song "When the World's on Fire," or even "You Are My Sunshine."[20] However, none of these suggestions completely satisfies—any or none could have been Guthrie's musical inspiration. Yet the debate over the melody's origins shifts the emphasis away from the song's lyrics. For it must be realized that Guthrie believed the worth of any song to be in the words, not the music: "If the tale the ballad tells is worth the telling, the tune makes very scant difference."[21] He only demanded that the tune used could be easily sung and played by everyone, and "This Land" fits his own criteria. The tune he used (or even created) can be sung by almost anyone since it stays within one octave—unlike Berlin's song, which ranges over an octave and a half. In addition, not only does the song remain in G major throughout, but both the chorus and verses use the same chords and in the same sequence. Any beginning player can easily handle "This Land."

Moving away from the tune and with Guthrie's emphasis on language in mind, let us look to the words of the six-verse song originally titled "God Blessed America" to see the vision of America he created to counter Berlin's song:

> This land is your land, this land is my land,
> From California to the New York island,
> From the redwood forest to the Gulf Stream waters;
> God blessed America for me.
>
> As I was walking that ribbon of highway
> And saw above me that endless skyway,
> And saw below me the golden valley, I said:
> God blessed America for me.
>
> I roamed and rambled, and I followed my footsteps
> To the sparkling sands of her diamond deserts,
> And all around me a voice was sounding:
> God blessed America for me.
>
> Was a great high wall there that tried to stop me
> A sign was painted said: Private Property,
> But on the back side it didn't say nothing—
> God blessed America for me.
>
> When the sun come shining, then I was strolling
> In wheat fields waving, and dust clouds rolling;
> The voice was chanting as the fog was lifting:
> God blessed America for me.
>
> One bright sunny morning in the shadow of the steeple
> By the relief office I saw my people—
> As they stood hungry, I stood there wondering if
> God blessed America for me.[22]©

20 Running the gamut from a laudatory to a discordant vision, these lyrics offer a far more complete depiction of America—detailing both its beauties and its ills—than does "God Bless America."

In the opening verse (which later became the chorus), Guthrie lays out the space of his canvas: "From California to the New York island / From the redwood forest to the Gulf Stream waters," which strongly suggest Berlin's lines, "From the mountains, to the prairies, / to the oceans white with foam." Guthrie then begins a catalog of beauty that includes an "endless skyway," a "golden valley," "sparkling sands," "diamond deserts," and "wheat fields waving." But in this beautiful landscape full of lush images, we find "dust clouds rolling," most likely the same ones he sings about in some of his Dust Bowl ballads. Other scenes definitely point to less pleasant realities. Verses four and six criticize the selfishness of private property and show the very real need for public relief. In bold contrast to Berlin's song, here the bad of America appears along with the good. Songwriter and activist Ernie Marrs well explains the range of the song's images: "All together, I don't know of another song so full of love for these United States, recognition of the injustices in them, and determination to do something about the latter."[23]

Unlike the hymns from which its underlying musical structure might have come, this song does not look to God for explanation of these differing images and definitely does not turn to Christianity for hope in resolving them. It offers a nation containing both beautiful vistas and hungry people standing in shadow; however, the conflicts between these very different images are not resolved. The final refrain continues in this uncertainty since it shifts from a statement to a question through the addition of the simple introductory phrase "I stood there wondering if." With this moment of doubt occurring at the very end of the song, it allows the audience the space to create its own answer, which is very different from the commanding tone of the prayer and beseeching ending of "God Bless America."

In effect, Guthrie implicitly acknowledged in his song that the ills he saw in this country were but a part of the American experience as a whole; yet he also admitted that some of his excitement came from this understanding. In a letter to Marjorie Mazia, he wrote, "The world I've seen is alive and interesting, not because its perfect and pretty and eternal, but because it needs my fixin', so does the land" and then added that this realization allowed his own shortcomings and mistakes to be removed:

> When I let my mind dwell on such truths, I seem to float up like a balloon, way up high somewhere. And the world and the work and the trouble and the people, seem to be goin' as a bunch in such a good direction, that my own little personal lead weights and drawbacks, miscues, mistakes, and flounderin' around

seem to fade away; rubbed out like a finger rubbin' out a wild pastel color.[24]

For Guthrie, understanding the bad and the good of the people and the country allows for personal transcendence and redemption. Thus, the America he wrote of does not exclude the ugly in order to emphasize only the beautiful; he linked the two and worked to increase the latter while decreasing the former. Therefore, the later omission of the protest verses of "This Land" due to their criticism of America is not in keeping with his all-encompassing vision.

25   However, Guthrie's drive for honest expression, which did include criticism of the country he loved, was at odds with a powerful segment of the American political scene. At the time of the song's writing, these forces actually were growing in power and influence. For example, in May 1938, Congress created the Dies Committee, which eventually mutated into the House Un-American Activities Committee. Another example of curtailment of freedom of expression occurred in June 1940 when Congress passed and President Roosevelt signed the Alien Registration Act, also known as the Smith Act. Through a number of general restrictions on civil liberties and freedom of speech, this act worked to quell socialist and communist protest against the war in Europe and America's growing part in it. Before the act passed, the *New York Times* described it as pulling together "most of the anti-alien and anti-radical legislation offered in Congress in the last twenty years."[25] Restrictions against any type of domestic protest grew even more insidious during a desperate scramble to condemn all radicals during the Communist witch hunts of the late 1940s through the early 1960s. The challenging nature of the protest verses in the original version of "This Land" not only put Guthrie at odds with Berlin and those who gave America unadulterated support but also put him in some danger of prosecution if those in power so desired, as evidenced by the later trials and tribulations of other left-leaning composers and songwriters such as Hans Eisler and Pete Seeger.

It is doubtful, however, that this possibility would have entered Guthrie's thoughts in early 1940, especially considering how little interest he showed in "This Land." Much like Berlin with "God Bless America," Guthrie did not immediately realize the popular potential of his new song and did

not record it until the spring of 1944. During a marathon session in March and April, Guthrie and a smattering of other artists including Cisco Houston, Sonny Terry, Bess Lomax, and Leadbelly recorded a number of songs for Asch Records (later to become Folkways); one was the first recorded version of "This Land." By this time, Guthrie had replaced the original title and refrain of "God Blessed America" with "This Land Is My Land" and "This land was made for you and me" respectively. In addition, he decided to use what had been the first verse as the chorus, which he also used to open and close the song. Of the protest verses, this particular version of the song contains only the one criticizing private property; and it remained unreleased until 1997, when it first appeared on *This Land Is Your Land: The Asch Recordings,* vol. 1.[26]

Nevertheless, the song did not become fixed in Guthrie's mind even after this session, for he created another version of "This Land" that same year. From December 1944 until February 1945, Guthrie had a weekly fifteen-minute show on radio station WNEW in New York. On this program, he used "This Land" as the theme song and also included it in the mimeographed songbook *Ten Twenty-Five Cent Songs by Woody Guthrie,* which he hawked on the show. Just as in the version recorded for Asch, Guthrie used the first verse of the original as the chorus and included variants of the second, third, and fifth verses. While subtracting the two original protest verses, he did add a new one:

> Nobody living can ever stop me,
> As I go walking my freedom highway.
> Nobody living can make me turn back.
> This land was made for you and me.[27]

The rebelliousness of this verse does place it more in the protest vein than the other three standard verses and the rousing, everybody-knows-it chorus. Still, this verse found little or no circulation for decades. Guthrie's friend Gordon Friesen, a leftist writer and fellow Oklahoman, noted in 1963 that he "has yet to hear or see anywhere outside of Woody's little mimeographed book his final verse."[28] This verse does not express the direct criticism toward some of America's harder realities found in the two omitted verses, however. As far as the author's intentions for this version, we do not have to speculate. In the songbook's introduction, he writes, "the main idea about this song is, you think about these Eight words all the rest of your life and they'll come a bubbling up into Eighty Jillion all Union. Try it and see. THIS LAND IS MADE FOR YOU AND ME."[29]

Neither of these two early versions had much impact though. Instead, another eventually became the standard. According to Jeff Place of the Ralph Rinzler Archives, this particular version came out of some 1947 sessions Guthrie laid down after he returned to New York City from a trip to Portland. Only the three verses and the chorus that eventually comprise the popular version appear here. This take appeared on the 1951 album *This Land Is Your Land,* the first commercial pressing of the song. Even Pete Seeger, who worked closely with Guthrie throughout the 1940s and early 1950s, says he originally heard the song on this record.[30] Subsequently, this version found its way onto at least thirteen other albums and CDs.[31]

30   Despite this landmark recording, though, Guthrie continued to change the song. During a brief session for Decca Records on January 7, 1952, he recorded yet another version of "This Land." Here, the chorus remains largely the same as before; and out of the three verses used here, two are variants of those already mentioned. However, the third does offer new lyrics:

> I can see your mailbox, I can see your
>   doorstep
> I can feel my wind rock your tip top tree top
> All around your house there my sun beam
>   whispers
> This land was made for you and me.[32]

By the time he made this recording, Guthrie showed distinct signs of the hereditary disease Huntington's chorea—resulting in a halting and somewhat disjointed performance. Consequently, Decca never issued this version although it did eventually find its way onto the box set *Songs for Political Action* in 1996.[33]

The reasons for all these additions and subtractions are not readily apparent from any of his writings, but comments made by Moses Asch to interviewer Israel Young may give us some idea of Guthrie's methodology. Asch said Guthrie "would often use the words but change the tune. He'd make two or three versions of the thing 'til the right tune came to him. He always used a folk tune to the words he created." Asch sometimes had a

hand in making these changes, even to Guthrie's best-known composition: "I made suggestions. 'This Land Is My Land' [*sic*] and some of the songs from *Songs to Grow On* (FC7675) were worked on right at the studio. He had a concept, and then through discussion it evolved into something."[34] In mentioning "This Land" in conjunction with the *Songs to Grow On* selections, Asch probably refers to the 1947 sessions in particular since Guthrie recorded both these children's songs and the now-standard version of "This Land" around the same time. But with the deaths of Guthrie and Asch, we will never know just exactly the extent of, or motivation for, any suggested changes.

In time, the 1947 recording became authoritative text although Guthrie may not have wanted it to achieve this dominance. In fact, several plausible reasons exist for the exclusion of the protest verses in the other recordings that have nothing to do with self-censorship. First, by the time of this first recording for Asch, the relief problem in America had largely disappeared due to the advent of World War II and the jobs it created. Therefore, Guthrie may have dropped the verse referring to relief because it no longer had as much relevance to the current situation in America as when he first wrote it. Second, Guthrie often forgot or changed words, depending on his mood and memory. Klein states, "Occasionally Woody might screw up the words or music irretrievably (sometimes he'd actually have trouble remembering which tune went with which set of words) and they'd [Guthrie and Asch] have to start over again."[35] Third, his overall approach does not suggest that any one performance of a song, whether recorded or not, had precedence over any other—just as the folk tradition from which he came never fully respected or acknowledged the authority of any one version of a song and expected all songs to change from performer to performer and even from performance to performance. Therefore, Guthrie might have thought that any version he recorded would stand among several possibilities for the song.

Around the same time as the 1951 Asch release, the now-standard version of "This Land"—still lyrical and beautiful—began entering America's cultural bloodstream from a number of other sources. Not surprisingly, the protest verses were mostly forgotten, as was feared by their author. This fear manifests itself in one of the most arresting moments in Klein's *Woody Guthrie: A Life.*

Here, Woody's son Arlo speaks of one particular afternoon when his father came home to the family apartment in Howard Beach from the Greystone Park Hospital, where he stayed most of the time due to the ravages of his illness. There, in the apartment's small backyard, his hands trembling uncontrollably from a disease that would eventually kill him, Guthrie taught his young son the two protest verses of the original version of "This Land Is Your Land" and the "Nobody living can ever stop me" verse for fear that if Arlo did not learn them, "no one will remember." Soon after, Arlo began to sing the verse about private property, although this practice did not have much of an impact on the general perception of the song until the late 1960s.[36]

35   Pete Seeger also points to Arlo's story as evidence of Guthrie's dissatisfaction with the song's presentation. Seeger adds to this story, however, that Guthrie knew schoolchildren were learning only select verses of the song while his other lyrics were ignored, for he quotes Guthrie as saying to Arlo, "they're singing my song in the schools, but they're not singing all the verses. You write 'em down now."[37] Indeed, one version of Guthrie's song did slowly find its way into America's classrooms. In the late 1940s and early 1950s, several liberal private schools in the New York City area, such as the Little Red School House and the Brooklyn Community School, began to use some of Guthrie's songs as part of their general music curriculum. Harold Leventhal, who was Guthrie's manager, notes that the teachers and the students in these schools "took these songs with them when they left, particularly 'This Land.'"[38] As a result of being disseminated in these schools and by these teachers, the song became well known in liberal circles in general. However, the song's influence did not end in small private schools; it eventually became known in America's public schools, too.

In 1951, Guthrie, then noticeably experiencing the effects of Huntington's chorea, recorded tapes of hundreds of his songs for Howie Richmond, his music publisher. One of these tapes contained a version of "This Land" similar to the one Guthrie recorded for Decca, and Richmond supposedly recognized the potential of the song. In fact, confident of its appeal, he made a version of it available with out cost to some scholastic publishers producing songbooks in an attempt to make it a national standard. Klein describes Richmond's

plans as "a classy, low-key strategy, with the advantage of being both high-minded and astute."[39] Due to Richmond's actions, the song gained enough status in the classroom to become known as an alternative anthem. By 1966 Leventhal felt confident enough to say it was "almost a second anthem to thousands of students."[40] More recently, one critic echoed and amplified Leventhal's opinion when he wrote, "Plenty of progressive-school pupils already think Woody Guthrie's populist jingle is the national anthem," although he added, "the tune is a little too Barney the Dinosaurish."[41] Alan Lomax had a higher opinion of the song, for he used it to open the first annual Music in Our Schools Day in 1975. By this time, the song had become a standard that most children knew and could sing. For a couple of incredible minutes, millions of schoolchildren all across the country joined together on "This Land" through the miracle of live television transmission. Nevertheless, the version used in this momentous broadcast, the same version used throughout the majority of American school-rooms, left the protest verses unsung and unknown.

Along with the thrum of support due to the appearance of the song in schools came the added weight of commercial publications. Textbooks were not the only source for a hardcopy of the lyrics of the shortened version. Throughout the 1950s and 1960s, printed versions of "This Land" appeared in several forms. In 1954 the song first showed up in the pages of *Sing Out!*, the well-known folk music magazine. Those who missed this issue had another opportunity five years later when it appeared in *Reprints from Sing Out!*, vol. 1, *1959* and then three decades later in the *Collected Reprints from Sing Out!* vols. 1–6, *1959–1964.*[42] All three times, the editors noted that the text followed the lyrics sung on the 1951 Folkways album, further proof that this one recorded version by Guthrie was held as the standard. Even when the published lyrics were not transcriptions from this one recording, the words captured generally adhere to it.

In 1956 Guthrie's own music publishers, Ludlow Music/TRO Richmond, finally decided to copyright the lyrics to "This Land" and put them out in sheet music. Two years later, "This Land" also appeared in the songbook *California to the New York Island,* which included all of the script and songs from the first of many tributes to Guthrie. Following the organization of the March

17, 1956, show at Pythian Hall in New York, the songbook ended with the pretty but politically passive version of "This Land."[43] In 1963 Ludlow Music eventually brought out its own songbook, *Woody Guthrie Folk Songs: A Collection of Songs by America's Foremost Balladeer,* which Pete Seeger edited. Here "This Land" occupies the prominent opening selection. Also that same year, in the May 1 issue of *Variety,* Leventhal printed it as part of a greeting from Guthrie to the once-controversial and blacklisted Weavers on the occasion of their fifteenth anniversary.[44] No matter how many magazines, songbooks, or other publications included the lyrics of "This Land" until the late 1960s, the shortened version almost always appeared.

This situation also repeats in the work created by those musicians covering Guthrie's song. The first documented instance of a group reproducing this song occurred around 1949, when director Robert DeCormier and his Jewish Young People's Folksingers Chorus began performing it.[45] Since then, a wide array of artists—whose views range across the political spectrum—have sung "This Land" in styles as varied as bluegrass and bop, country and choral.[46] Although some of these performers have revised "This Land," they largely sang and still sing only the popular lyrics in performances. However, the past omission of the protest verses by artists with close ties to Guthrie—such as Pete Seeger and Ramblin' Jack Elliot—surprise more than the work produced by commercially driven singers. These performers do not fear singing controversial material. Actually, they would seem to be eager to include any politically charged verses penned by the man many consider the father of contemporary folk protest.

40   Overall, though, these omissions do not surprise in that the protest verses were available from only three little-known sources until the 1960s: Guthrie's original handwritten lyric sheet, the unissued 1944 Asch recording, and the mimeographed songbook *Ten Twenty-Five Cent Songs by Woody Guthrie.* None of these sources contained all three of the protest verses, however. Almost completely unknown and scattered, these lyrics got little notice. In contrast, the shortened version of the song began its slow drumbeat with the Folkways version, its subsequent rereleases, its place in school texts, and its exposure through other publications and other artists' recordings.

As the song's recognition and reputation grew, so did opportunity for criticism, even from left-leaning musicians and writers. The earliest published reaction to "This Land" appears in *The Bosses' Songbook: Songs to Stifle the Flames of Discontent,* a 1959 collection of folk and leftist song parodies. Compiled by folkstyle singer Dave Van Ronk and Richard Ellington, these songs poke fun at old-left personnel, such as Pete Seeger, and their positions—particularly those stemming out of some folksingers' past affiliations with the American Communist Party and assorted unions. Some of these parodies used such well-known songs as "Wreck of the Old '97" and "Columbus Stockade" as musical structures and even copied a few lines from the originals. Although the preface to this songbook includes the disclaimer that these songs "were done for fun and meant to be sung for fun," some of the works included not only use various folksongs' melodies but also directly parody the ideas expressed in these songs. For example, "When Johnny Comes Marching Home" becomes "When Johnny Comes Hobbling Home" and offers a less than positive view of the brave warrior returning from war. In examples more important to this discussion, the book also contains direct parodies of three Guthrie songs. The version of "Jesus Christ" offered here depicts a savior who becomes an avid Marxist and a Judas who becomes a labor spy, while in the "Modern Union Maid," the title character fears radicals enough to stick to both her conservative union and Harry Truman.[47]

The third parody, "This Land Is Their Land," offers a take on America that strangely echoes the viewpoint expressed by Guthrie in the often-omitted verses of his song. The first verse of the parody opens with the observation, "This land is their land. It is not our land." It then lists the material goods and comforts the wealthy in America have, concluding that "This land is not for you and me." In the next verse, the focus shifts from a discussion of the rich to the plight of the poor and begins "As I was walking that endless breadline / My landlord gave me a one-week deadline."[48] The image of want here is similar to that expressed in the sixth verse of the original version of Guthrie's song: "In the shadow of the steeple / By the relief office I saw my people / As they stood hungry." Of course, the author(s) of the parody probably would not have known these lyrics in that they were not readily available to the public at this time.

The parody does not end here, however. The final verse begins with the lines "So take your slogans and kindly stow it, / If this is our land you'd never know it," which reads as a direct rejoinder to the attitude found in the popular version of "This Land." Here, the song offers an alternative to passive acceptance: "Let's join together and overthrow it."[49] In effect, the parody's last stanza goes beyond simply pointing out some of society's ills and questioning whether "This land was made for you and me," as Guthrie's original version did, and becomes incendiary, advocating revolution. Even without the parody's similarities to the original version of "This Land" or its revolutionary ending, the rest of the lyrics would still contradict the bright vision of America found in the popularized version of Guthrie's song.

Despite this criticism of "This Land," the popular version basically remained unchallenged. In fact, when Guthrie finally died on October 3, 1967, his earlier fears had definitely been realized, for none of the original verses had ever been released in wide-access recorded or published versions. As it turned out, Guthrie missed by just a few years the resurgence of his protest verses. Beginning in the latter part of the 1960s, they started to appear in a few publications, performances, and recordings through the efforts of some members of the folkstyle community who discovered the exclusion. For example, in a January 1968 article he wrote for the leftist musical journal *Broadside,* Ernie Marrs claims, "So far as I know, the first time anyone sang all six verses of ["This Land"] on the air was when I sang them on KPFA-FM, in Berkeley, California, in the spring of 1960." He adds in the same piece that he confronted Pete Seeger with the omitted verses: "When I came across that page in Woody's old KFVD notebook in 1959, I made a copy of it and showed it to Pete Seeger." Finally, Marrs accuses Seeger of not supporting the use of the verses, even going as far as quoting him as saying, "They're good verses. But the short version's been around so long now, and is so well known, that nobody would believe he wrote these."[50]

However, Seeger had already published all of Guthrie's protesting verses from "This Land" in *American Favorite Ballads: Tunes and Songs as Sung by Pete Seeger* in 1961, although these lyrics did not gain much notoriety by their inclusion in this little-known songbook. In the later months of 1968, perhaps egged on by Marrs's comments, *Sing*

Out! (for which Seeger was a member of the editorial advisory board and a columnist) published the two omitted original verses along with two 1954 photographs of Guthrie looking shaggy and disheveled.[51] Gone is the little hobo bard; in his place appears the proto-hippie, a biologically but not ideologically damaged forefather of the protest singers of the sixties. These pictures and lyrics strike out from the page, demanding attention. And some people did pay attention. In the final years of the 1960s, Pete Seeger, Arlo Guthrie, and other folkstyle singers began making the protest verses an essential part of the song again.

The first time one of the lost verses showed up in a major performance occurred at the end of the 1970 Hollywood Bowl memorial concert for Guthrie. As can be heard in a recording of the concert, singer Odetta opens up "This Land" with a slow but powerful slide through one of the popular verses. Later in the song, actor Will Geer (better known as Grampa Walton from the 1970s television series) jumps in, while Odetta and the other performers back off, and recites a brief but often-quoted passage from a speech Guthrie wrote up for his opening show on WNEW in December 1944, the same show on which he used "This Land" as a theme song. During a moment of synchronicity, Geer emphasizes the line, "I am out to sing songs that will prove to you that this is your world," while the chorus chants the refrain, "This land was made for you and me." Finally, everyone pulls back and Arlo takes the third and final verse of the evening alone. He sings,

> As I went walking, I saw a sign there.
> And on the sign it said, "No Trespassing."
> But on the other side, it didn't say nothing.
> That side was made for you and me.[52]

This important moment, along with several other songs and readings from both the 1968 Carnegie Hall and 1970 Hollywood Bowl memorial concerts, appears on the 1972 album *A Tribute to Woody Guthrie,* which contains the first instance of any of the song's protest verses being included on a commercially released recording.[53] Similar to the 1956 tribute concert, these two memorial shows also found themselves represented in a songbook. In 1972, Ludlow Music and Woody Guthrie Publications brought out *A Tribute to Woody Guthrie,* which followed the lead of the second concert by including the verse Arlo sang along with the other two protest verses.[54]

During this same period, Pete Seeger and other folkstyle performers began adding their own verses to the song in an attempt to represent and comment on the changing problems of America. In a July 1971 article for the *Village Voice,* Seeger notes that he had created numerous verses for the song, such as the following one:

> Maybe you been working just as hard as
>   you're able
> And you just got crumbs from the rich
>   man's table
> Maybe you been wondering, is it truth or
>   fable
> This land was made for you and me.

In the same article, Seeger also pointed to other professionals' and amateurs' creative efforts to reshape and to keep current "This Land." For example, he offered an added verse by Jerry J. Smith:

> We've logged the forests, we've mined the
>   mountains
> We've dammed the rivers, but we've built
>   fountains!
> We got tin and plastic, and crowded free-
>   ways,
> This land was made for you and me.

50 This verse does not stand alone in pointing out environmental degradation. Other new verses created by Seeger that appear here do much the same, along with other writers' verses that pointed out additional ills faced by America. Seeger also included two verses in Spanish by Alberto O. Martinez, showing the song's potential for crossing cultural boundaries and reaching an ever-changing, multicultural national audience.[55]

Others also discovered newly created verses and published them. Irwin and Fred Silber cobbled together several for inclusion in their extensive 1973 folksong anthology, *Folksinger's Wordbook.* Of the six verses tendered there, three had already been quoted by Seeger earlier and two others had come from the parody included in *The Bosses' Songbook.* However, a verse called the "GI Vietnam version" had never appeared in print before:

> This land is your land
> But it isn't my land,
> From the Mekong Delta
> To the Pleiku Highland,
> When we get shot at

> The ARVN flee,
> This land was meant for the V.C.![56]

Overall, the folkstyle community seemed to welcome these additions, just as long as they were in keeping with the sentiments of the song's creator. In fact, Seeger believes "the best thing that could happen to the song would be for it to end up with hundreds of different versions being sung by millions of people who do understand the basic message."[57] Decades before, Guthrie himself acknowledged the need for artists to shift and add to songs so as to keep them current. He wrote, "this bringing them up to date is what keeps a folk song a folk song, it says whatever needs to be said, or as much as the law allows, at the time when it needs to be said."[58] Certainly, the additions mentioned above show how easily his song could be altered and reshaped so as to connect it to contemporary issues and move it further away from the American nationalist jingle it had, in part, become.

Looking back to Seeger's article again, we find not one but two new verses by Country Joe McDonald, who released a Guthrie tribute album called *Thinking of Woody Guthrie* on Vanguard Records in 1969. Here are the verses Seeger included:

> As I was walking that ribbon of highway
> I heard the buzzing of a hundred chain saws
> And the Redwoods falling, and the loggers
>   calling
> This land was made for you and me

> As I went walking the oil-filled coastline
> Along the beaches fishes were choking
> The smog kept rolling, the populations
>   growing
> This land was made for you and me.[59]

One year before the publication of Seeger's article, McDonald and his group the Fish had become the center of nationwide attention due to their Woodstock performance of the Vietnam protest song "I Feel Like I'm Fixin' to Die Rag" and their signature salute, known as "The 'Fish' Cheer," which involved spelling out the word "fuck" to the great glee of the assembled crowd. As a result, McDonald's voice became synonymous with protest in the late 1960s. Therefore, his use of Guthrie's song to include his thoughts on environmental dangers in America brought together two well-known voices of protest. In fact, all the performers who added comments on the ills of 1960s and '70s America to "This Land" helped to keep it current and alive, resulting in the reenergizing of Guthrie's work. These discoveries and additions are not surprising if we look at what was happening at this time in some sectors of popular music.

55   Beginning in the early 1960s, more and more music that offered criticism or even displayed open hostility toward the status quo in America became available—not only to young people through college radio and little-known recordings but also, although somewhat later, to all ages through mainstream radio stations and well-established recording companies. A major source of this protest came from the pen and voice of Bob Dylan, who was himself greatly influenced by Guthrie's work. However, Dylan's protests and interest in Guthrie did not stand alone. Along with Dylan, many other performers—such as Phil Ochs, Tom Paxton, Joan Baez, and Peter, Paul, and Mary—pointed out the injustices they saw around them, using song as their medium, just as Guthrie had done. These artists also often included his songs in their performances and on their recordings.

After the late 1960s and early 1970s, songs containing lyrics explicitly protesting establishment values and regulations became, and continue to be, more commonplace than in Guthrie's era. Yet even in this environment, the once-lost lyrics of "This Land" could have a far-reaching impact, if only to challenge the authority of the popular version. From this time on, the once completely unknown verses became more and more accessible in publications, performances, and recordings—providing a counterinfluence to the popular version that continued its steady and unabated drumbeat.

One source of this drive came from Guthrie's music publisher, Ludlow Music/TRO Richmond, which did much to help in bringing all the lyrics to public notice. The early 1970s saw a change in the sheet music of "This Land" that Ludlow Music put out. It began to include all the verses of the song, albeit only on the middle-voice pieces, while those for high and low voice continued to include only the popular verses.[60] Since 1963, this firm has put out five Woody Guthrie songbooks, of which four contain all the known verses. The inclusion of the three protest verses in *101 Woody Guthrie Songs, Including All the Songs from "Bound for Glory,"* does not surprise since this songbook appeared in conjunction with the release of the United Artists film version of Guthrie's autobiographical novel, *Bound for Glory.* The film's soundtrack includes two of the protest verses, which is in keeping with the project's emphasis on Guthrie's leftist politics.[61]

Another film project on Guthrie also used the protest verses. The Arlo Guthrie–hosted 1984 documentary, *Woody Guthrie: Hard Travelin',* ends with a sing-along jam on "This Land" that overlays images of Guthrie and those interviewed during the course of the film. But what stands out the most here are the lyrics sung. Along with the well-known chorus and the verse that begins "As I roamed and rambled," all three protest verses are included. Arlo and Joan Baez trade off on the verse about private property, while Pete Seeger alone handles the verse mentioning the need for relief. Then Arlo finishes up with the verse beginning with the line, "Nobody living can ever stop me."[62] With the emphasis on these lesser-known verses, the documentary's end focuses on Guthrie's more radical lyrics and brings attention to the song's dissenting voice.

After this rediscovery and dissemination of the once-lost protest verses, many recordings and publications of the song still excluded them. One of the most surprising of these instances occurred on the 1988 Grammy-winning album *A Vision Shared: A Tribute to Woody Guthrie and Leadbelly* put out by CBS Records. As performed here by Pete Seeger, Sweet Honey in the Rock, Doc Watson, and the Little Red School House Chorus, "This Land" remains fairly faithful to the version released in 1951, the only change being the repeating of the chorus between all the verses and twice at the end.[63] As a result, the continued reinforcement of the popular version leaves it firmly entrenched in the public mind. However, its meaning began to be shifted and molded through its contextualization by various cultural forces.

Soon after the protest lyrics resurfaced, Pete   60 Seeger explained the reasoning behind his belief that they should be put before the public. He writes,

> I and others have started singing [these expunged verses]. We feel that there is a danger of this song being misinterpreted without these old/new verses being added. The song could even be co-opted by the very selfish interests Woody was fighting all his life.[64]

Actually, at the time of Seeger's writing, the cultural symbolism of the popular version of the song had already been co-opted. For example, during the late 1960s, both the Ford Motor Company and American Airlines used the verses lauding America in their advertising campaigns, selling their wares while the song played on in seeming acceptance and agreement. Some attempts, however, have been thwarted, such as when the U.S. Army requested the song's use as part of their recruiting campaign. Considering their political tendencies, the Guthrie family balked at this proposal, and the plan was never carried out.[65]

Just as commercial and conservative forces have shaped the message of the popular version of the song, so have progressive forces because it has the potential to offer up a protesting voice, just as the song's original lyrics do. Unlike the original version, though, the popular version offers this voice in ambiguous language, thus requiring a particular context to release a radical message. In effect, this radicalized context would energize the expurgated version of this song, or any song. In *Minstrels of the Dawn,* Jerome Rodnitzky writes, "Within the subversive, righteous atmosphere that permeated their [the folk-protest singers] performances, it mattered not what they sang. There, a simple patriotic song like 'God Bless America' could take on the colorings of a radical hymn." A telling and specific example of how context can control the perception of a song as protest comes from leftist historian Howard Zinn. He notes that during a May 1971 gathering in Washington, D.C., to protest the Vietnam War, the police arrested six people who were peacefully walking down the street and singing "America the Beautiful."[66]

Simply presenting the popular version of "This Land" in certain environs could reestablish an effect similar to its original purpose and make it a powerful leftist statement of unity and pride or of environmental protectionism. When Guy Carawan performed it at NAACP meetings in the 1950s, the song could be heard and sung with the hope that one day America would indeed be "made for you and me."[67] Here, the refrain all at once becomes a question and a demand. More important, sung before this group and in this context, "This Land" offers an idea of revolutionary import in the 1950s: America belongs equally to black and white. Although somewhat less striking than in the last example, even the use of the song

in advertisements can offer a progressive agenda. In the 1980s, country singer Loretta Lynn recorded a version that appeared on national radio and television advertisements for the National Wildlife Federation.[68] Placed in this context, the images of "the redwood forest," "golden valley," "diamond deserts," and "wheat fields waving" encourage pride in the American landscape and urge us to work to protect it and the wildlife that inhabits it from destruction. In effect, the popular version of the song becomes an environmental rallying cry.

In a further and more telling example of how trappings surrounding the presentation of the song can shape it in different ways, we can look at "This Land" in the context of the national conventions of America's two dominant political parties. In what might be considered the highpoint of its use in liberal mainstream politics, the singing of "This Land" immediately followed George McGovern's famous 3 a.m. "Come Home, America" acceptance speech at the 1972 Democratic National Convention in Miami. According to one observer, the song filled the hall and helped make it" "come alive with an emotion of oneness" to such a degree that her "feelings of discontent were blotted out by the music and singing."[69] Later, the song even became McGovern's theme song in his presidential bid. But who could disagree that the song must have taken on a completely different meaning when the 1960 Republican National Convention featured it, especially considering Richard Nixon became the party's chosen candidate. Certainly, Guthrie's political sympathies and Nixon's red-baiting tendencies are incompatible, yet it is doubtful that many at this convention would have known about the politics of the song's author. Additionally, it is easy to imagine that the overwhelmingly white, Protestant, middle and upper-class crowd would not hear the "you" of the song as referring to anyone other than Americans very much like themselves.

Nevertheless, even in a political environment that would have completely pleased Guthrie, the song can be interpreted in undesired ways. It could even be seen as a colonialist statement, as an incident involving Pete Seeger in June 1968 testifies. During much of that month, Seeger was in Washington, D.C., staying at Resurrection City, a camp organized by Dr. Martin Luther King as part of his Poor People's Campaign. One night, Seeger participated in a sing-along that had a strange turn concerning "This Land." He writes that when he and singer/organizer Jimmy Collier began singing it, "Henry Crowdog of the Sioux Indian delegation came up and punched his finger in Jimmy's chest, 'Hey, you're both wrong. It belongs to me.'" Then Collier stopped and questioned whether the song should go on. At this point, "a big grin came over Henry Crowdog's face. 'No, it's okay. Go ahead and sing it. *As long as we are all down here together to get something done*'" (emphasis in original).[70]

This incident affected Seeger noticeably. Bernice Reagon, Seeger's friend and a founding member of the Freedom Singers, remembers his reaction and even expresses a theory about it:

> That song was the basis of the American dream—coming in and building a country, freedom, blah, blah. I felt that in '67 and '68, all that **got** smashed to smithereens. . . . I remember Pete talking constantly about that exchange with . . . Collier around Chief Crow Dog, and how he then had a hard time doing "This Land Is Your Land." It felt like he didn't know *what* to sing . . . he was not sure what his function was.[71]

Not only could the "very selfish interests Woody was fighting all his life" that Seeger mentions make a mockery of the song, but history itself could make the song tell a lie—or at least point out a promise not kept and an entire people displaced. Somehow though, Seeger did find some function for himself and the song, although he had to add an extra verse written by Cappy Israel to do so:

> This land is your land, but it once was my land
> Before we sold you Manhattan Island
> You pushed my nation to the reservation,
> This land was stole by you from me.[72]

Immediately after singing this verse, Seeger would tell the story about the problems the song sparked in Resurrection City. Here, Seeger recontextualizes the song by adding the above verse that strains against some of the other unity verses and by explaining how some of the song's sentiments can easily be seen as exclusionary. Considering the song's heavy use in the past decades as nationalistic jingle, a concentrated effort is still needed to push the song in a direction more in keeping with its creator's intentions, especially since Guthrie never had a chance to perform the song after its rise or to say who could sing it.

Even if Guthrie were alive today, it would be impossible for him to control the meaning of "This Land." Once an artist releases a song into the bloodstream of America, it can flow anywhere and be used in many different ways. As music critic Greil Marcus notes, "Good art is always dangerous, always open-ended. Once you put it out in the world you lose control of it; people will fit it into their lives in all sorts of different ways."[73] These myriad interpretations may not match the original sentiment the artist intended for the work. Not only songs but even contemporary artists' own images can and have been appropriated. For example, during the 1984 presidential campaign, the Reagan re-election juggernaut briefly used Bruce Springsteen and his song "Born in the USA" for its own nationalistic purposes, completely ignoring the singer's politics and misrepresenting the song's lyrics—particularly the ironic chorus. Eventually, Springsteen felt driven to make a very public effort to regain control of his image and his song.[74] Unlike Springsteen, though, Guthrie did not have the opportunity to combat the shifting politics of "This Land." He remained hospitalized from the mid-1950s on, with no hope of recovery. Thus, he had little or no control over the song's presentation or contexualization.

The reason for the continued minimization of the protest verses, however, may not be due to the lack of access to these lyrics but rather to the American public's inability to deal adequately with the abuses that Guthrie documented in them. English songwriter Billy Bragg believes, "One of the problems America has about Woody is he don't beat around the bush—he looks America in the eye and says what he says. And these are questions America cannot bring itself to focus on today, let alone in the Thirties; the questions he asked have still not been answered."[75] The final question of the original version of "This Land" remains as relevant today as when Guthrie first put it to paper back in 1940.

Since Guthrie's comments, criticisms, and questions continue to be applicable to contemporary America, then those encapsulated in the little-known protest verses of his most popular song should be brought more forcefully to the public's attention, which some of the examples mentioned above show is an achievable goal. Just as all songs, all texts, remain malleable, so does the seemingly intractable popular form of "This Land." It can be added to; it can be changed. In fact, the mere act of acknowledging all of Guthrie's verses changes "This Land" forever. Realizing how the song has come to us, how it has been shifted in time, gives "This Land" new meaning. It becomes a song with a history rather than a set of lyrics to mumble through at some public occasion. In addition, realizing that the song has changed and shifted from its beginning may provide those who care about Guthrie's art and his complete vision the impetus to change the song once again. In effect, simply because one

of the song's many voices has shouted down the others does not mean that this situation is permanent—the voices of the other verses can be heard more clearly. Their volume merely needs adjusting through their inclusion in more performances and publications so that they may gain a more complete hearing—creating a situation where one version no longer has dominant status over any other and allowing the American public the opportunity to choose for itself which lyrics it wants to sing.

Notes

Many people and institutions should be acknowledged for their help in making this essay possible. My deepest gratitude goes to Dr. John Lowe and Dr. Frank DeCaro of Louisiana State University for their detailed criticism and unyeilding support. In addition, I would like to thank Jeff Place at the Ralph Rinzler Archives in the Center for Folklife and Cultural Heritage for giving me guidance through its Woody Guthrie Collection, just as I want to give a nod of appreciation to Nora Guthrie and the staff at the Woody Guthrie Archives for their kind assistance. The staff at the Library of Congress' American Folklife Center have also helped guide me in my research into "This Land Is Your Land," and Judy Bell of TRO Richmond has not only given me help in my research but has also graciously commented on this essay. Finally, I would like to thank this journal's anonymous reviewers for their many suggestions.

1. Original in Songs 1, Box 3, Folder 27, Woody Guthrie Archives, 250 West 57th Street, New York, N.Y. (hereafter WGA). Pete Seeger states he first heard the song from a recording rather than from Guthrie first-hand. Pete Seeger, "A Tribute to Woody Guthrie," in Woody Guthrie and Kathy Jakobsen, *This Land Is Your Land* (New York: Little, Brown, 1998), 30. Additionally, when working with him in labor reform circles in California, Seema Weatherwax assumed Guthrie had not written "This Land" when they visited the migrant camps around Los Angeles in early 1940, because he never performed it for the laborers or their families. Seema Weatherwax, interview by Jane Yett, "In Touch with the Human Spirit: On the Road with Woody Guthrie," *Californians* 10, no. 4 (1993): 33.

2. Clifton Fadiman, "Minstrel Boy," *New Yorker* 19, no. 5 (March 1943): 68.

3. Songs 1, Box 3, Folder 27, WGA.

4. Generally, the popular version consists of the following chorus and three verses:

(Chorus)
This land is your land, this land is my land,
From California to the New York island;
From the redwood forest to the Gulf Stream waters,
This land was made for you and me.

As I was walking that ribbon of highway,
I saw above me that endless skyway,
I saw below me that golden valley.
This land was made for you and me.

I've roamed and rambled, and I followed my footsteps
To the sparkling sands of her diamond deserts;
And all around me a voice was sounding:
"This land was made for you and me."

When the sun came shining and I was strolling
As the wheat fields waving and the dust clouds rolling.
As the fog was lifting, a voice was chanting,
"This land was made for you and me."©

5. Laurence Bergreen, *As Thousands Cheer: The Life of Irving Berlin* (New York: Viking Press, 1990), 155.

6. "What Makes a Song: A Talk with Irving Berlin," *New York Times Magazine*, July 28, 1940, 7.

7. Charles Braun, "Let's Waive 'The Star-Spangled Banner,'" *Fact* 2, no. 1 (Jan.–Feb. 1965): 8.

8. Bergreen, *As Thousands Cheer*, 370.

9. Irving Berlin, *Songs of Irving Berlin* (Milwaukee: Hal Leonard Corporation, 1998), 16.

10. David Ewen, *The Story of Irving Berlin* (New York: Henry Holt and Co., 1950), 124; and Michael Freedland, *A Salute to Irving Berlin* (London: W. H. Allen, 1986), 178.

11. The sheet music sales figures from this period appear in the following issues of *Variety* magazine in 1939: Feb. 15, no. 12; Feb. 22, no. 13; March 1, no. 9; March 8, no. 10; March 15, no. 9; March 22, no. 5; March 29, no. 6; April 5, no. 11; April 19, no. 6; April 26, no. 7; May 3, no. 10; May 10, no. 10; May 17, no. 13; May 24, no. 8; May 31, no. 12; June 7, no. 13; June 28, no. 13; July 12, no. 13.

12. "Footnotes on Headliners," *New York Times*, July 14, 1940, 4.

13. Joe Klein, *Woody Guthrie: A Life* (New York: Delta, 1999), 140–41.

14. Woody Guthrie, *Sing Out!* 17, no. 6 (Dec–Jan. 1967–68): 4.

15. Woody Guthrie, *American Folksong* (New York: Oak Publications, 1961), 4.

16. Klein, *Woody Guthrie*, 142.

17. Woody Guthrie, "I Don't Feel at Home on the Bowery No More," Box 2, Folder 3, Woody Guthrie Collection, in the Ralph Rinzler Archives, Center for Folklife and Cultural Heritage, Smithsonian Institution, Washington, D.C. (hereafter WGC).

18. Woody Guthrie, *Born to Win* (New York: Macmillan, 1965), 146; and "Irving Berlin Tells Adela Rogers St. Johns: 'I'd Like to Write a Great Peace Song,'" *New York Journal American*, Sept. 4, 1938, E:3.

19. Woody Guthrie, letter to Alan Lomax, Sept. 19, 1940, Box 1, Correspondence Folder, Woody Guthrie Manuscript Collection, American Folklife Center, Library of Congress, Washington, D.C. In this quotation and in all others used in this article, Guthrie's idiosyncratic prose style and spellings have been retained.

20. Klein, *Woody Guthrie*, 144; Guy Logsdon, "Notes on the Songs," *This Land Is Your Land: The Asch Recordings*, vol. 1 (Smithsonian Folkways Records, 1997): 10; and Guy Logsdon, "Woody's Roots," *The Music Journal* (Dec. 1976): 21.

21. Woody Guthrie, "Mario Russo," in Box 4, Folder 2, WGC.

22. Songs 1, Box 3, Folder 27, WGA.

23. Ernie Marrs, "The Rest of the Song," *Broadside*, no. 8 (January 1968): 8.

24. Woody Guthrie, letter to Marjorie Mazia, December 17, 1942, 4–6, in Songs 2, Notebook 11, WGA.

25. "Army, Navy Back Bill to Hit Aliens," *New York Times*, April 13, 1939, 92.

26. *This Land Is Your Land: The Asch Recordings*, vol. 1, track 14.

27. Box 2, Folder 1, WGC.

28. Gordon Friesen, "Woody Guthrie: Hard Travellin'," *Mainstream* 16, no. 8 (1963): 5.

29. Box 2, Folder 1, WGC.

30. Jeff Place, interview with author, March 31, 1999. Side 1, track 1, to *This Land Is Your Land* (Folkways Records, 1951); Seeger, "Tribute to Woody Guthrie," 30.

31. Side 2, track 1, *Bound for Glory: The Songs and Story of Woody Guthrie* (Folkways Records, 1956); side 1, track 1, *Songs to Grow On: American Work Songs*, vol. 3 (Folkways Records, 1961); side 7, track 10, *The Folk Box* (Elektra Records, 1964); side 1, track 1, *The Greatest Songs of Woody Guthrie* (Vanguard, 1972); side 2, track 1, *Bonneville Dam and Other Columbia River Songs* (Verve/Folkways, 1966); side 2, track 1, *This Land Is Your Land* (Folkways Records, 1967); side 5, track 10, *World of Popular Music: Folk and Country* (Follett Publishing Company, 1975); side 2, track 5, *Original Recordings Made by Woody Guthrie* (Warner Brothers, 1977); side 2, track 7, *Folkways: The Original Vision* (Smithsonian Folkways, 1988); track 1, *Troubadours of the Folk Era*, vol. 1 (Rhino Records, 1992); track 2, *Folk Hits Around the Campfire* (K-Tel, 1995); track 15, *American Roots Collection* (Smithsonian Folkways, 1996); track 1, *This Land Is Your Land: The Asch Recordings*, vol. 1 (Smithsonian Folkways Records, 1997).

32. Woody Guthrie, "This Land Is Your Land" (Decca, January 1952). A recording of this track is held by the Ralph Rinzler Archives.

33. Disc 10, track 31, *Songs for Political Action,* complied by Ronald Cohen and Dave Samuelson (Bear Family Records BCD 15720, 1996).

34. Moses Asch, interview by Israel Young, "Moses Asch: Twentieth Century Man, Part II" *Sing Out!* 26, no. 2 (1977): 26.

35. Klein, *Woody Guthrie,* 286.

36. Ibid., xii, 458.

37. Pete Seeger, *Where Have All the Flowers Gone* (Bethlehem, Pa.: Sing Out Publications, 1993), 142.

38. Harold Leventhal, interview with author, October 16, 1998.

39. Judy Bell, interview with author, Nov. 28, 2001, and Klein, *Woody Guthrie,* 375. Examples of the publishers are Birchard, Silver Burdett, and Ginn, as noted by Judy Bell in an interview with author, Nov. 3, 2000.

40. John Cashman, "Folk Hero," *New York Post,* April 19, 1966, p. 27, col. 1.

41. Hendrick Hertzberg, "Star-Spangled Banter," *New Yorker* 73, no. 20 (July 21, 1997): 5.

42. *Sing Out!* 4, no. 7 (1954): 3; *Reprints from Sing Out!* vol. 1, ed. by Irwin Silber (1959), 1; and *The Collected Reprints from Sing Out! (1959–64),* vols. 1–6, ed. Irwin Silber, Paul Nelson, Ethel Raim, Pete Seeger, and Jerry Silverman (Bethlehem, Pa.: Sing Out! Publications, 1990), 4.

43. Woody Guthrie, *California to the New York Island: Being a Pocketful of Brags, Blues, Bad-Men, Ballads, Love Songs, Okie Laments and Children's Catcalls by Woody Guthrie,* ed. Millard Lampell (New York: The Guthrie Children's Trust Fund, 1958), 45.

44. Woody Guthrie, *Woody Guthrie Folk Songs: A Collection of Songs by America's Foremost Balladeer,* ed. Pete Seeger (New York: Ludlow Music, 1963), 7. *Variety,* May 1, 1963, 75.

45. Seeger, *Where Have All the Flowers Gone,* 143.

46. The better known of these artists include Paul Anka, Harry Belafonte, the Brothers Four, Glen Campbell, David Carradine, the Mike Curb Congregation, Jim Croce, Bing Crosby, Jack Elliot, Lester Flatt and Earl Scruggs, Connie Francis, Arlo Guthrie, the Harvesters, Ella Jenkins, the Kingston Trio, the Limeliters, Loretta Lynn, Jay and the Americans, Country Joe McDonald, the Mormon Tabernacle Choir, the New Christy Minstrels, Odetta, Peter, Paul, and Mary, Tex Ritter, Earl Robinson, Pete Seeger, the Staple Singers, Bruce Springsteen, the Tarriers, the Wayfarers, the Weavers, and Glen Yarborough.

47. *The Bosses' Songbook: Songs to Stifle the Flames of Discontent,* 2nd ed., collected and edited by Dave Van Ronk and Richard Ellington (New York: R Ellington, 1959), 3, 14, 18.

48. Ibid., 22.

49. Ibid.

50. Marrs, "The Rest of the Song," 8 and 9.

51. *American Favorite Ballads: Tunes and Songs as Sung by Pete Seeger* (New York: Oak Publications, 1961), 30; "Woody Guthrie/Another Image," *Sing Out!* 18, no. 4 (Oct.–Nov. 1968): 34.

52. *A Tribute to Woody Guthrie* (Warner Brothers Records, 1972), track 27.

53. Ibid.

54. *A Tribute to Woody Guthrie* (New York: Ludlow Music, 1972), 65.

55. Pete Seeger, "Portrait of a Song as a Bird in Flight," *Village Voice* (July 1, 1971): 5.

56. Irwin Silbert and Fred Silber, eds., *Folksinger's Wordbook* (New York: Oak Publications, 1973), 315.

57. Seeger, "Portrait of a Song as a Bird in Flight," 5.

58. Woody Guthrie, letter to Columbia Recording Company, ca. June 1942, Box 1, Correspondence Folder, WGC.

59. Seeger, "Portrait of a Song as a Bird in Flight," 5. However, it was only in a version of this article in his 1993 book *Where Have All the Flowers Gone* (p. 145) that Seeger actually attributed the first of these verses to McDonald.

60. Judy Bell, interview with author, February 1, 1999.

61. Woody Guthrie, *101 Woody Guthrie Songs, Including All the Songs from "Bound for Glory"* (Ludlow Music, Inc. 1977), 86–88. *Bound for Glory,* directed by Hal Ashby (United Artists, 1976). Rereleased by MGM/UA Home Video (1991).

62. *Woody Guthrie: Hard Travelin'* directed by Jim Brown (Ginger Group and Harold Leventhal Management, 1984). Rereleased on MGM/UA Home Video (1986).

63. Track 14, *A Vision Shared: A Tribute to Woody Guthrie and Leadbelly* (CBS Records, 1988).

64. Seeger, *Where Have All the Flowers Gone,* 143.

65. Tom Burton, interview with author, March 2, 1999.

66. Jerome L. Rodnitzky, *Minstrels of the Dawn: The Folk-Protest Singer as a Cultural Hero* (Chicago: Nelson Hall, 1976), 146; Howard Zinn, *Postwar America: 1945–1971* (Indianapolis: Bobbs-Merrill, 1973), 179.

67. Peter D. Goldsmith, *Making People's Music: Moe Asch and Folkways Records* (Washington, D.C.: Smithsonian Press, 1998), 360.

68. Wayne Hampton, *Guerrilla Minstrels: John Lennon, Joe Hill, Woody Guthrie, Bob Dylan* (Knoxville: University of Tennessee Press, 1986), 243.

69. Kristi Witker, *How to Lose Everything in Politics Except Massachusetts* (New York: Manson and Lipscomb, 1974), 135.

70. Seeger, *Where Have All the Flowers Gone,* 144.

71. David Dunaway, *How Can I Keep from Singing: Pete Seeger* (New York: McGraw-Hill, 1981), 276.

72. Seeger, "Portrait of a Song as a Bird in Flight," 5. However, it was only in his 1993 book *Where Have All the Flowers Gone* (p. 145) that Seeger actually attributed this verse to Cappy Israel.

73. Greil Marcus, *Mystery Train: Images of America in Rock 'n' Roll Music* (New York: E. P. Dutton, 1976), 125.

74. For particulars concerning this issues see Dave Marsh, *Glory Days: Bruce Springsteen in the 1980s* (New York: Pantheon Books, 1987), 255, 260–64, 266, and Jon Wiener, *Professors, Politics and Pop* (London: Verso, 1991), 309.

75. Quoted by Mark Rowland, "Notebooks of Plenty," *Musician,* no. 236 (July 1998): 23.

Forums for Citizenship in Popular Culture

Jeffrey P. Jones

Jeffrey P. Jones is an Assistant Professor in the Department of Communication and Theatre Arts at Old Dominion University in Norfolk, Virginia. Dr. Jones's research focuses on media, politics, and civic culture. He teaches courses in television and society, mass media and popular culture, and media activism. Dr. Jones also writes a media-watch column for a Norfolk-area alternative publication, *Portfolio Weekly*. This essay was originally published in 2001 in *Politics, Discourse, and American Society: New Agendas,* a book featuring original research by young scholars working in the area of political communication. In 2004, Dr. Jones published *Entertaining Politics,* a book that tracked the blurred lines between serious television and satirical talk shows to demonstrate the role of media in public life and how Americans understand television and politics.

Four men walk into a bar: Jesse Ventura, Ross Perot, Donald Trump, and Warren Beatty, each dressed as a political candidate. The five regulars at the bar offer their opinions: The *New York Times* reporter summarily dismisses them; Larry King wildly celebrates them; Jay Leno jokingly exploits them; Joe Public is somewhat intrigued by them; and the research scholar at the end of the bar ignores them.

What sounds like a bad joke is actually a somewhat accurate representation of how recent commentators have reacted to the increasingly blurred boundaries between popular culture and politics. Although we have witnessed a profound change in how formal politics appears in popular culture—including its appearance at times *as* popular culture—the academic community has generally turned a blind eye to how such changes are shaping political culture in the United States.

To speak of separate realms for the "serious" business of politics on the one hand and "entertainment" culture on the other is simply no longer possible, at least in the public's eye. Witness the following: politicians acting like celebrities (appearances on David Letterman and Arsenio Hall); politicians' personal lives scrutinized as if they were celebrities (Bill Clinton's impeachment and Bob Livingston's dethronement); news media acting like tabloids (circulating Clinton's supposed illegitimate child rumor); tabloids acting like news

media (the Gennifer Flowers story in *The Star*); entertainment programs featuring politics (Comedy Central's *Indecision 2000* and *Politically Incorrect with Bill Maher*); political news as soap opera (the Clinton impeachment and the Clarence Thomas hearings); former politicians becoming talk show hosts (Mario Cuomo and Jesse Jackson); talk show hosts becoming politicians (Jesse Ventura and Pat Buchanan); new forms of political talk programming that include the voices of laity in place of or alongside "experts" (CNN's *TalkBack Live*); and young adults receiving more of their political news from Jay Leno than from Dan Rather. Although one might argue that many of these occurrences are not unprecedented, never has there been such a confluence of these improbable events.

Of special concern is the overall lack of attention these phenomena have received by scholars. While the expansion and institutionalization of cultural studies in the last twenty years has resulted in important examinations of "the political" in society, those studies rarely examine the impact of culture on "official," institutional politics. Similarly, traditional political communication research has far too rarely employed the theoretical insights gained from cultural studies, retaining its primary focus on traditional institutional political players and processes (elite-elite interactions or elite-lay interactions) with little recognition of how these agents are (or are not) incorporated into the everyday lives of citizens. These two academic camps have kept their respective campfires bright, although with seemingly little interest in appropriating the illuminating light coming from nearby campers.

5   An important new agenda for political communication research is this: scholars must study how popular culture is trying to shape political culture and vice versa. That includes the recognition of how popular culture affects political meaning in a consumer-driven society. As the mass media increasingly encode "the political" as entertainment offerings, these encodings become popular sites for the formation of common knowledge about politics. As such, we should no longer dismiss the late-night comedian/talk show host's characterizations of our politicians. Nor should we dismiss the seriousness of public reaction to celebrity entrants into formal politics as political candidates. No longer can we dismiss the politician's sense that popular cultural venues are good ways of reaching his or her constituency. And no longer should we dismiss new forms of radio and television talk shows as duping, distracting, and diverting citizens from the "real" business of politics. As culture industries continue to search for new means of profit making through diversified programming—including new encodings of politics as entertainment—we must recognize that the viewing audience may not find these offerings any less legitimate (or farcical) than the newscasters and pundits who traditionally shape and reflect political meaning through the media. Alan Wolfe, in a book review article in the early 1990's, made the argument with special effect.

Americans are increasingly oblivious to politics, but they are exceptionally sensitive to culture. . . . Politics in the classic sense of who gets what, when and how is carried out by a tiny elite watched over by a somewhat larger, but still infinitesimally small, audience of news followers. The attitude of the great majority of Americans to such traditional political subjects is an unstable combination of boredom, resentment, and sporadic attention. . . . Culture, on the other hand, grabs everyone's attention all the time. . . . Because they practice politics in cultural terms, Americans cannot be understood with the tool kits developed by political scientists. (Wolfe 1991, quoted in Grossberg 1992)

As Wolfe suggests, we must examine how citizens practice politics in cultural terms. One example offered here could easily be dismissed as "farcical entertainment"—the talk show *Politically Incorrect with Bill Maher*. Although produced as competition to other entertainment shows, political discussion programs (such as *P.I.*) that feature the voice of the laity offer *alternative* political interpretations of political events not found in traditional forums. As such, those "meanings" may be more *meaningful* to the average citizen/television viewer than those developed by political elites whose legitimacy has been severely challenged in the last two decades. Because most political communication research on media focuses on elite-elite interactions (that is, the dance between politicians and the press) or elite-lay interactions (that is, public opinion polling, voter reactions to campaign advertising, etc.), we have a special opportunity to step outside the bounds of the traditional to take seriously the interactions *among laity* within the mass media.

I situate this new agenda in recent writings that have begun to explore the notion of "cultural citizenship." Next, I examine two types of television talk show texts, both centered on the Clinton-Lewinsky scandal, to exemplify how popular cultural texts can produce very different meanings from those produced by the elite-based media. Next, an entertainment-based program featuring lay political discussion, *Politically Incorrect with Bill Maher,* will be compared to the discourse found on *This Week with Sam Donaldson and Cokie Roberts,* with a special focus on the sense-making strategies employed by each show's discussants/participants. Finally, the chapter offers suggestions for ways in which this new agenda might be pursued to produce new insights into the maintenance of citizenship in popular culture.

NOTIONS OF "CULTURAL CITIZENSHIP"

Some scholars are beginning to grapple with the importance of popular culture as a primary site for the maintenance of public interest in, and development of common knowledge of, politics. While focused more on citizenship than on popular culture, Michael Schudson's recent writings examine how citizens contend with the political information they encounter daily, regardless of whether that information could be categorized as "serious" (for example, news) or "entertainment." Schudson contends that modern citizens "monitor" politics and political information in a crowded media landscape, as opposed to an earlier model of "informed" citizenship in which the ideal citizen was expected to gather and process political information in a rational-critical manner. Because the monitorial citizen is bombarded with loads of information, he or she "engages in environmental surveillance more than information-gathering. . . . Monitorial citizens scan (rather than read) the information environment in a way so that they may be alerted on a very wide variety of issues for a very wide variety of ends and may be mobilized around those issues in a large variety of ways" (Schudson 1998a, 311, 310).

10   Schudson's new model of citizenship is bolstered by research that explores the use of media in everyday life. This research suggests that consumers attend to media (and the information content they employ) in haphazard, partial, distracted, and combinatory ways (Bausinger 1984; Lull 1988; Silverstone and Hirsch 1992). If Schudson is correct, citizens may read about issues or events in the newspaper, watch *Nightline* to see what policymakers are saying, and then tune in to *Politically Incorrect* to see what "common sense" other public personalities offer on the matter. Or they may only pay scant attention to all three if nothing "significant" is occurring. The entertainment packaging of political discourse, then, does not necessarily diminish public interest and awareness, but provides another venue through which sense is made of public affairs.

In the field of television studies, several authors have begun to explore the interrelationships between television entertainment and political citizenship, although none has advanced anything approximating a full theory of "cultural citizenship." John Hartley, for instance, refers to media content as *democratainment*, "the means by which popular participation in public issues is conducted in the mediasphere" (Hartley 1999, 209). The audiences for this fusion, according to Hartley, are "citizens of media," a concept to "connect political participation with media-readership" (206–207). Hartley's exploration of these concepts is part of a larger project to understand changes occurring in the transformation of a public-service

model of broadcasting in an age dominated by private media ownership, resulting in what he calls "do-it-yourself" citizenship, or semiotic self-determination. That is, Hartley is interested in how citizens use television as a "transcultural teacher" to educate themselves about what it means to be a citizen of Britain, Australia, etc. In his usual style as provocateur, though, Hartley's concepts are quite short on specifics, data, or further theorization.

Toby Miller (1998) extends the analysis of cultural citizenship through his writings on film. Miller is interested in the moments in which "the popular and the civic brush up against one another," and his work examines the "intersection of textual, social, and economic forms of knowledge with the popular under the sign of government" (Miller 1998, 4, 12). His attention is directed to what he calls "technologies of truth," in essence, the "popular logics for establishing fact." Miller recognizes that it is through citizen interaction with these technologies (media) that meaningful development and maintenance of citizenship occurs. As he notes, "when these technologies congeal to forge loyalty to the sovereign state through custom or art, they do so through the cultural citizen, who steps, sits, and shits outside the formalities of the Constitution, a citizen in need of daily maintenance through lore as much as its homonym." More than simply an alternate version of hegemony theory, Miller applies Foucault's theories of governmentality to examine the "consumer—citizen couplet" and the ways in which "the population knows itself and its duties" (17–18).

In sum, there is a growing recognition among scholars of the increased importance of popular culture for the day-to-day relationship between citizens and their government. As I have noted here, however, this relationship needs considerably more examination. After providing an illustration of the type of research this new agenda might produce, I offer some thoughts on the types of questions further research in this area might address.

Before moving forward, however, it is necessary to define what is meant by the terms "political culture" and "popular culture." I define *political culture* as the beliefs and behaviors citizens hold toward what is permissible and expected from their system of governance (Berger 1989). I use the term *popular culture* to refer to the mass-produced, usually commodified, offerings of culture industries for consumption by viewers, audiences, subscribers, and consumers, often through the mass media. Although it is possible to argue with both of these definitions, they are offered simply to locate more precisely the characteristics and arenas of operation being dealt with here.

MAKING SENSE OF POLITICS THE CASE OF TWO TALK SHOWS

15 As a means of illustrating what is at stake for audiences who attend to differing presentations of politics on television, I have chosen two different forms of political talk shows—one incorporating discussions by Washington insiders and journalists, the other centered around discussions by celebrities and other nonexperts on politics. Specifically, I examine four weeks of programming on *Politically Incorrect with Bill Maher (P.I.)* from January 26 through February 3, 1998, and August 10 through 21, 1998. The first two weeks encompass the period when revelations of President Clinton's affair with White House intern Monica Lewinsky (and his subsequent denial of any wrongdoing) went public. The second two weeks surrounded the president's admission of the affair to the American people and his testimony before a grand jury. Both of these dates were high-water marks in the scandal, especially with regard to public interest in the matter. The first was the "gossip" period when revelations and rumors were swirling about what the president did or might have done. The second covers the period in which the president finally admitted and apologized for his transgressions.

The pundit show examined is *This Week with Sam Donaldson and Cokie Roberts* aired during the same time frame.[1] *This Week* is hosted by two senior broadcast journalists, and the roundtable discussion includes a former top White House official and advisor to President Clinton (George Stephanopoulos), an editor of a conservative weekly journal of political opinion (Bill Kristol), and a conservative syndicated columnist (George Will). All three guests are active in Republican and Democratic policy circles, though none is an officeholder.

Politically Incorrect with Bill Maher is also a roundtable discussion show specifically dedicated to the discussion of politics and contemporary social issues. Hosted by the comedian Maher, guests typically include comedians, actors/actresses,

authors/journalists, activists, musicians, athletes, pundits, lawyers, entrepreneurs, the occasional politician, and "citizen panelist." Most of the participants are "public persons," but they are often not celebrities in the formal sense of the word. Foremost, though, is their general lack of "expertise" about politics. They tend to bring to the discussion the same understanding and sense of politics (however weak or strong that might be) as that held by the program's viewers. Indeed, the expertise of the show's guests is not what gains them admission to the program. Instead, the show tries to assemble a diverse mix of people from various sections of public culture, hoping that their differences in viewpoints will create an interesting discussion, a televised cocktail party with an odd mixture of guests, if you will.

THIS WEEK WITH SAM DONALDSON AND COKIE ROBERTS

One of the distinguishing features of the discourse on *This Week* is the high level of agreement among the participants. For an issue like the Clinton scandal that was so discordant in American society, there was relatively little disagreement over what the scandal "meant" at any given time, on the show. The participants' fundamental concern was for the political system, or the "constitutional order" as they referred to it. The issue that drove that concern was the threat to the system resulting from Clinton's lying. The explanation offered for this threat was the weak moral character of Bill Clinton, or "this man" as George Will often referred to the president.[2] And, finally, the discussants based their conclusion on the fundamental faith, despite continued evidence to the contrary, that the American people would do the "right" thing (that is, stop supporting Clinton) once they realized the "truth."

From the time the scandal broke as a story until the president's confession some seven months later, the primary issue these pundits discussed was "did Clinton lie?" If he did, they contended, his presidency was through.

January 25

SAM DONALDSON: If he's not telling the truth, I think his presidency is numbered in days. This isn't going to drag out. We're not going to be here three months from now talking about this. Mr. Clinton, if he's not telling the truth and the evidence shows that, will resign, perhaps this week.

August 16

GEORGE STEPHANOPOULOS: It all depends on what he does tomorrow. I think if he tells the truth and comes forward to the American people, he can at least go on with his presidency.

GEORGE WILL: The presidency is over.

There was relatively little interest in *what* the president lied about or *why* he lied, questions that were of utmost importance on *Politically Incorrect*. Instead, lying itself was deemed unacceptable. The act of lying was considered so serious that its occurrence alone meant the president would have to leave office; hence, the unanimous predictions for his early departure. Lying, their arguments suggested, was harmful in two ways. First, it damages the president's ability to lead as a politician, to advance a political agenda, and the necessary moral leadership of the office.

August 23

COKIE ROBERTS: There is the question of can he govern if he stays in office? Can he go up and twist an arm and get a bill?

GEORGE STEPHANOPOULOS: He can govern, but he can't advance his agenda.

Second was the threat Clinton's supposed lying presents to the political system:

January 25

GEORGE WILL: This man's condition is known. His moral authority is gone. He will resign when he acquires the moral sense to understand. . . .

August 23

BILL KRISTOL: To let him stay now, I think, is fundamentally corrupting.

GEORGE WILL: The metastasizing corruption spread by this man is apparent now, and the corruption of the very idea of what it means to be a representative.

BILL KRISTOL: The president is at the center of the constitutional order. Credibility in him matters.

February 1

GEORGE WILL: This is a great uncontrolled experiment now under way about having vulgarians in the most conspicuous offices in the republic. And it can't be good.

20   The explanation given for why Clinton lied was simple—he had no moral character; he was a "vulgarian," a "lout." As George Will argued, "he can't tell the truth. . . . I mean, that's the reasonable assumption on the evidence informed by the context in which it occurs, which is six years of evidence of his deceit."

The pundits continued to exhibit a fundamental faith that the American public would ultimately agree with them about what was right and wrong. With "lying" as the centerpiece premise, the pundits maintained the hope that eventually the public would realize the wrongs that had been committed and rise up to punish the president. Ultimately, their conception of "the people" was quite paternalistic, although not condescending. For instance, George Will seemed to suggest that the people would recognize the right thing to do (what the political class already knew) once the Starr report was made public: The public, he argued, "will not be able to change their mind. . . . Once that report [by Kenneth Starr] is written and published, Congress will be dragged along in the wake of the public" (August 23). They saw a good and virtuous public, although one that was a bit naïve and unsophisticated. As Bill Kristol stated, "I think it is that the American people are nice people. They're too nice, in fact, too trusting" (February 1). This was a public fashioned in their own image, with little connection to what ordinary Americans were actually saying about the scandal.

August 23

GEORGE WILL: But beneath the argument there's a visceral process. And it has to do with the peculiar intimacy of the modern presidency. Because of television, the president is in our living rooms night after night after night. And once the dress comes in and once some of the details come in from the Ken Starr report, people—there's going to come a critical mass, the yuck factor—where people say, "I don't want him in my living room anymore."

In summary, the pundits on *This Week* reduced the scandal to one fundamental question—did the president lie? If he did—which they all assumed was true because of Clinton's supposed pattern of deceit—then it would be necessary for him to depart the office, either willingly or unwillingly. The foundation of legitimacy in American democracy, they suggested, was based on the president's telling the truth; should the president violate that cornerstone principle, then the system would remove him. It was also assumed that the public shared the same understanding of how the system works, and that they would ultimately respond in a fitting manner.

What led to such formulations is that these pundits used "political sense" for assessing political matters. By political sense I mean a learned understanding of how politics works, what actions and behaviors are admissible, correct, justifiable, and workable; an acquired sense of what matters and what does not. Political sense is like any other intellectualized system—legal sense, scientific sense, artistic sense—a philosophy or an intellectual worldview. "Philosophy," Gramsci argues, is "official conceptions of the world" that are "elaborated, systematic, and politically organized and centralized" (Gramsci 1988, 360). Practitioners of politics are trained (through schooling and professional experiences) to think in certain ways about how the system works.[3] Political sense is different from common sense in that it is a conscious creation of an abstracted mode of thinking. As John Dewey notes,

> Science is the example, par excellence, of the liberative effect of abstraction. . . . The liberative outcome of the abstraction that is supremely manifested in scientific activity is the transformation of the affairs of common sense concern which has come about through the vast return wave of the methods and conclusions of scientific concern into the uses and enjoyments (and sufferings) of everyday affairs; together with an accompanying transformation of judgment and of the emotional affections, preferences, and aversions of everyday human beings. (Dewey and Bentley 1949, 282)

25   The political sense used by the pundits of the "political class" (to use George Will's term) is the product of just such a transformation, an alteration of the "emotional affections, preferences, and aversions of everyday human beings" into an abstraction with its own set of rules and understandings about what is valid, right, just, and legitimate. According to political sense, politics in a representative democracy is centered around the contract between the polity and the trust they bestow on their elected officials to conduct the affairs of state in an honest and open fashion, operating in the

people's best interest. Political legitimacy in such a system is based on public trust. A politician caught in a lie has naturally betrayed that trust. The pundits argued that the president was at the center of the constitutional order; for him to violate that order threatens the whole system and everyone in it. The pundits recognized that the political system was fragile but they had faith that the constitutional system would purge individuals who betrayed that trust.

Those who employ political sense maintain a systematic logic—a structured understanding of the workings of a complex political system that guarantees the functioning of democracy. Within that system, though, the public is only one of several factors. Executive leadership, legislative agendas, and political parties are also crucial to the system's functioning. But the public was also key. The political sense employed by these pundits led to a paternalistic view of the public—a public that is good and decent, but one that would need to overcome its naiveté to understand the seriousness of Clinton's violations. The pundits' faith was therefore not in the people per se but in the system itself. The public's role in the scandal was simply to acquiesce to what the system needed to do—to purge itself of sin. This type of systematic logic was so strong that the pundits were almost incapable of recognizing those who felt differently; that is, an overwhelming majority of the public was not interested in having the system purge itself. Indeed, "the public" was a pure abstraction for the pundits, whereas the political "players" (whom they all knew) and the functioning of the arenas in which they operate (with which they were already thoroughly familiar) were much more real.

What the pundits could not entertain was the idea that citizens might employ a different logic of politics altogether. The fact that many citizens considered Clinton's lying about sex to be a private matter and not a public concern should lead us to examine more fully the "common sense structures" of the people themselves. If the pundits had tuned into *Politically Incorrect,* they would have seen a quite different public than the one the pundits themselves had constructed. The citizens on *P.I.* knew quite well that the president was lying. For them, however, the issue was not "did he lie?" but "what did he lie about?" Because they featured the second question, the public did not respond in ways the pundits had imagined.

POLITICALLY INCORRECT
WITH BILL MAHER

If there was a high level of agreement among the pundits on *This Week,* the discussions on *Politically Incorrect* were much more fractious, with no unified conclusions to the debates offered. Despite the great variety of guests, the arguments made by the panelists tended to coalesce around several issues, with quite similar arguments appearing time and again. The primary focus for most panelists was not on the political system but on how Clinton as president should be judged. That is, most discussions focused on assessing Clinton as a legitimate or illegitimate president in light of his "wrongdoing"—were his activities a threat to leadership itself or were his activities innocuous? The fundamental issue in the scandal was Clinton's sexual affair and his lying about it. Most panelists assumed he lied, but the focus of his lying was not when or where he lied, or even that he lied, but what he lied *about.*

Because the lying was about sex, the arguments split over how to assess Clinton—as a human being (which made the actions normal, comprehensible, fathomable, and ultimately benign) or as a moral leader (which made the actions unacceptable, unfathomable, and therefore a threat). At a broader level, those assessments were based on whether the lying was seen as a public or private matter, and ultimately hinged on concerns over the politicization of private life.

January 29

JOLEY FISHER *(actress):* We don't have to know about it. I don't want to hear about other people's orgasms unless I'm involved [laughter, applause, cheers].

August 17

MICHAEL MOORE *(director):* He didn't have to tell the truth in January. You don't have to answer a question nobody has a right to ask. [applause] It's nobody's business.

30   Another defense of Clinton was based on conceptions of human nature. Although Clinton may be guilty of lying, some panelists suggested, he couldn't help it because the need for sex—and lots of it—was part of the male nature. Clinton did this,

they argued, because he is a man, and it is a simple fact that men, in their efforts to fulfill these human needs, have extramarital sex and lie about it. Furthermore, that behavior is understandable, if not justified, because men need sex more than women. Behavior and agency are explained in essentialist terms:

August 18

STAR PARKER *(author):* We are a land of law. And if man starts to do whatever he wants to, then so is everybody else. And when you do it from the highest office so are the lowest.

DONZALEIGH ABERNATHY *(actress):* They have been doing it already. They have been doing it since the beginning of time. . . . It's the nature of men. They need to cast their seed everywhere they can.

Panelists who did not embrace essentialist arguments sometimes resorted to claims that *all* humans are fallible and therefore deserving of mercy:

August 17

MICHAEL MOORE *(director):* We are human beings. Have you ever made a mistake? Have you ever made a mistake?

JACKIE COLLINS *(author):* Yeah, but I'm not president, Michael.

MICHAEL MOORE: Well, but you're a public figure. You're a public figure. You're in the press.

JACKIE COLLINS: I am not the president. The president we expect something more of.

Other panelists advanced the argument that Clinton was just a regular guy, an average American like everyone else. Instead of exalting Clinton as a distant leader, these panelists embraced the notion that their leader was just like them. It was not his higher moral stature that garnered their respect (or the lack thereof in both instances), but rather his position as both a political leader *and* a regular guy that inspired them. Many citizens, that is, fashioned the president in their own image.

January 29

COOLIO *(rapper):* What it really is, is that he's human, and that's why people like Clinton because he's showing that 'I'm human. O.K., I had an affair, whether I admit it or not, or whether I did it or not, I'm human.'

DENNIS PRAGER *(talk radio host):* Exactly! A guy called my show and said, "Dennis, Clinton is the sort of guy I can see drinking beers with and chasing women with."

But arguments also ensued over Clinton's position as leader and role model, and the relationship of lying to leadership.

January 29

BILL MAHER: Over and over again, the polls say [the people] think he had an affair, and they don't care. So what they're saying is, let him live, we don't need him as a role model. We'll look to ourselves for our own moral guidance. [applause]

BRAD KEENA *(political analyst):* But it's important that we don't normalize this kind of behavior and that's what we're allowing to happen. . . . I think it is time to have a president, to elect a president who is a role model, someone who has good moral values.

Some panelists extended the conception of Clinton-as-leader a step further, invoking the metaphor of the country as a family. In this metaphor, Clinton was the "father" of the country, the people were his "children," and the White House (the site of the indiscretions) the family's "home."

January 26

EARTHA KITT *(singer/actress):* The president is head of the family. He sets an example for the rest of us. If he can't live by moral standards, then what does he expect of us?

August 13

JEFFREY TAMBOR *(actor):* Any household can look within their own selves and their families and say, "There have been transgressions in my family." There are transgressions here. And the smart thing to do is separate the presidency from the man.

35   The arguments on *Politically Incorrect* form a central dialectic—the tension that exists between the desire to separate Clinton-the-man from Clinton-the-leader. When viewed as a *leader*, a split occurred between those who argued that:

A.   *Leaders and the people have different rules.* These discussants invoked history (all presidents have done this), explained power (men in power have affairs the world over), and made his job performance more important than his off-the-job activities (he can do whatever he wants if he's doing a good job).

B.   *Leaders are not exempt from the rules guiding the people.* Presidents get no special treatment when it comes to moral behavior.

When viewed as a *human*, a split occurred between those who argued that:

C.   *Clinton should represent the people by being better than them as a moral person.* He should be a model for how the people should behave.

D.   *Clinton is no different from the people be represents.* He has the same flaws, he does the same foolish things that all humans do.

It seems that panelists wanted it both ways—Clinton was like the average person and unlike the average person, with special rules and with the same rules. Despite their contradictory positioning, both liberal and conservative guests tended to adopt these dual stances. The more liberal voices tended to use both arguments A and D (different rules as a leader, but Clinton the man is no different than the rest of us), while conservatives tended to use both arguments B and C (leaders have the same rules as the people, yet as a man he has different rules; he should be better than us). From the perspective of political culture in the 1990s, these positions seem grounded in populist premises (for instance, the suspicion of political elites disconnected from the people; a desire to have politicians behave like the people) and the culture wars (elites who don't lead, who have no morals). These positions also represent the contradictory and disjointed dimensions of commonsense thinking that Gramsci (1988), Geertz (1975), and other theorists of common sense have described so well.

MAKING SENSE OF COMPETING SENSE

The panelists on *P.I.* utilized common sense to understand politics—elements derived from everyday experiences, other belief systems, and intellectualized philosophical concepts. Citizens on

P.I. often employed arguments which included claims to universality, claims based on personal or group experience which defined the situation in universalistic terms: "*Everyone* does this," "*All* politicians lie," "*Never* trust a liar," "*All* families have problems," "*All* men are this way." These claims to universality render the common sense reliable, constantly reassuring citizens that "this is the way of the world." Clinton is not exceptional, such persons argued; the case is not exceptional either. Its universality was the key to understanding it.

The most prominent themes in citizens' arguments over the scandal were conflicts over whether the Clinton affair was a public or a private matter. For those who argued the latter, the liberal notions of freedom and individuality were embedded in their arguments. Similarly, for those who argued the former, republican notions of responsibility and community came to bear. Rarely were these concepts enunciated as theoretical postulates, but rather as beliefs about how the world works. As Billig et al. note, "within the ideology of liberalism is a dialectic, which contains negative counter-themes and which gives rise to debates. These debates are not confined to the level of intellectual analysis; both themes and counter-themes have arisen from, and passed into, everyday consciousness. And, of course, this everyday consciousness provides the material for further intellectual debate" (Billig et al. 1988, 27). American liberalism battles republicanism here, yet these ideological formulations appeared simply as common sense: "This is none of your business"; "This is between him and his wife"; "If his wife is O.K. with it, what concern is it of yours?" "He did this in our house, the people's house"; "What type of example does this set for the people/the children?" "Lying is lying, so how can we trust a liar?"

40   Panelists did not argue on the basis of political sense—the chief law enforcement officer lying, the implications for systems of justice, the precedent this sets for future presidents, etc. Instead, they used accessible terms that not only made sense but that made the scandal interesting to discuss. In other words, the terms and conditions of the Clinton scandal (for example, sex, lying, adultery, cigars, dresses, semen, fellatio) favored the application of common sense (certainly in ways that the Savings & Loan scandal did not). People could *relate* to this kind of politics, for it had resonance with their own lives. As one guest on *P.I.*

intimated, "You know, I've been following this [scandal] 'cause I haven't seen *All My Children* in a long time."

This latter remark is telling in that it exemplifies how politics is becoming fused with entertainment and consumer culture. As a result, the sense making found in those realms will increasingly be used when it comes to formal politics. Politics in American society, that is, has come to center around the activities of politicians as celebrities. David Marshall argues that "the celebrity offers a discursive focus for the discussion of realms that are considered outside the bounds of public debate in the most public fashion. The celebrity system is a way in which the sphere of the irrational, emotional, personal, and affective is contained and negotiated in contemporary culture" (Marshall 1998, 72–73). He goes on to argue that "celebrities. . . . are intense sites for determining the meaning and significance of the private sphere and its implications for the public sphere. . . . The private sphere is constructed to be revelatory, the ultimate site of truth and meaning for any representation in the public sphere. . . . Celebrities . . . are sites for the dispersal of power and meaning into the personal and therefore universal" (247).

By making politics personal and universal, the invitation is made to treat all politics on these same terms. *Formal* political sense about how politics functions therefore comes to be seen as nonsense, and publics revert to the sorts of thinking used in other realms of their everyday existence. Defenders of Clinton appealed to the commonsense "truth" of the private realm, including essentialist claims about a man's needs or human biology, or personal identification with Clinton because of his human frailties. For some guests, Clinton-as-celebrity was easier to judge than Clinton-as-leader and politician. Clinton's actions as a celebrity seemed all too familiar when compared with other celebrities. For instance, the foibles of Bill Clinton, and actor Hugh Grant's sexual misconduct, come to be seen in similar ways when such criteria are used for judgment.

But as Joshua Gamson points out, the celebrity sign is composed of oppositional characteristics that allow for different readings, depending on the situation. "Contemporary celebrity," he notes, "is composed of a string of antinomies: public roles opposing private selves, artificial opposing natural, image opposing reality, ideal opposing typical, special opposing ordinary, hierarchy opposing equality" (Gamson 1994, 195). As the analysis above suggests, these are *exactly* the means through which *P.I.* panelists attempted to read Clinton as a political celebrity—Clinton as special or ordinary, equal to the people or better than the people, an ideal leader or a typical American, etc. Pundit discourse based on political sense, a perspective that didn't position Clinton as a celebrity but as a politician required to play the game of politics by certain rules, was much more unified in how to make sense of the scandal.

The means through which talk show guests think through the political matters of the day will greatly affect the realities they create, as will the discursive frames of the two types of television. The political sense of *This Week* tended to stifle debate, efficiently organizing the scandal around a particular set of meanings apart from which other explanations made no sense. This particular ordering framed Clinton as a systemic threat, and the integrity and continuity of the system necessitated his exit from the system. Alternative means of making sense of the scandal, however rare, were not entertained. On *P.I.*, however, the Clinton scandal became an opportunity for citizens to explore a range of interpretations about the changing relationships between leaders and the public. Commonsense thinking led panelists to explore what Clinton as (fallen) archetypal hero meant for America—is this scandal just about him, an amoral and selfish baby boomer, or is the public implicated in some way? It also led citizens to investigate the nature of leadership and political privilege and the normative expectations that should exist given contemporary social realities. Those investigations, in essence, raised fundamental questions affecting citizens' relationships with their government, matters rarely considered on the pundit program.

45   What this study suggests, then, is that entertainment-based programming can offer alternative forums for citizens to make sense, in their own language, of politics at any given moment. These forums become a site through which common knowledge can be developed, even during the pursuit of entertainment pleasure. They become a site where citizens need not segregate their "private" lives and pleasures from their simultaneous role as "public" beings. They become a site where the values, meanings, and sense used in their private lives can have direct bearing on politics itself.

ADVANCING THE NEW AGENDA

To further the agenda sketched out here, numerous sites within popular culture should be examined. While this chapter has focused on television talk shows as an important genre for cultural citizenship, the analysis should be extended to other sites—stand-up comedians and the monologues of late-night talk show hosts, comedy channels, Internet discussion and parody sites, and magazines such as *George,* which intentionally obfuscate the boundaries between politics and popular culture. Examining the content of these genres can provide important insight into the types of civic knowledge citizens encounter about their government on a daily basis.

But the study of politics in popular culture should not be an end in itself. Indeed, what the study of culture can contribute to our understandings of politics begins by returning to the arena of electoral politics itself. That is to say, these examinations should ultimately lead us to rethink traditional issues in the study of formal politics (questions traditionally entertained by political scientists). Those issues lie primarily in the areas of *political behavior* and *political culture.* In terms of political behavior, we must begin to question how traditional modes of interaction with politics may have changed. For instance, do these new sites of citizenship affect political attitude formation? Do they affect voting behaviors? Do they influence citizens' attitudes, opinions, and behaviors more than news shows and pundit talk shows? Do citizens feel more engaged or involved with politics when attending to political information packaged in a more common vernacular? Do these new sites affect how, when, and where citizens talk about politics among themselves? In short, how do these cultural presentations of politics affect the *practices* of representative democracy?

Questions of political cognition are also important here: do citizens develop different types of "knowingness" in this narrow-casted media environment, and how does this environment affect "common knowledge" about politics? How do factors with great currency in popular culture (for example, celebrity) affect citizen evaluation of politicians (what one critic calls "celebriticians") (Gabler 2000)? In short, if politics is increasingly attended to in the realm of culture, we must ask how political participation and behavior are affected as a result.

The second set of questions this new agenda raises concerns American political culture. Not only should we recognize how politics is played out in popular culture but also the converse: how the language of popular culture can become the language of politics. We have already witnessed events such as Bill Clinton's saxophone on the *Arsenio Hall Show,* his fielding questions on MTV about the types of underwear he wore, the eerie relationship between art and life in films like *Wag the Dog,* the usage of rock music in political campaign events, and the embrace of radio performer Rush Limbaugh by the 104th Congress. These phenomena exemplify ways in which political players use the symbolic material of popular culture in the conduct of political activity. Whether these events are trivial or significant needs to be determined.

50   One of the most important questions with regard to voters, however, is the ways in which the dominant language of pop culture—the ethos of consumption—may be shaping our political culture. As political party affiliation and loyalty decline and as the number of independent voters increases, as politics becomes not something one does with other people but what one watches on television, how much does the selection of politicians for political office resemble models of consumer choice? With the surprising popularity of populist candidates such as Ross Perot and Jesse Ventura,

we should begin to question how the culture of consumption might be leaching into the political mainstream. Are voters now becoming "bored" with politics just as they become bored with long-running sitcoms? Why should a voter's relationship to the politics she watches on television be any different from her relationship to other programming found there? And then there is the practiced question: Does a populist leadership style play better in attracting bored but hopeful voters? We should ask whether these pop culture forums help shape expectations of a more "relational" style of political leadership for voters (for example, Reagan as loveable grandfather, Clinton as drinking buddy, George W. Bush as fraternity brother)?[4] The point to be made here is that the boundary between cultural practices and traditional politics may have eroded entirely by now. Scholars would be wise to examine if this is so.

What is ultimately at stake is a better understanding of how American democracy is manifested, attended to, and maintained through cultural practices in the daily mediascape. We must alter our conceptions of political citizenship as being determined solely through traditional means, and look more carefully at the fluid interchange of politics and culture in everyday life. The forums for citizenship contested in popular culture are a good place to begin that investigation.

Notes

1. Actual broadcast dates are January 25, February 1, August 16, and August 23, 1998. The analysis was conducted from transcripts of these broadcasts.
2. Will's usage of "this man" is similar to Clinton's usage of "that woman," referring to Monica Lewinsky, in his denial of the affair. Both are semantic moves to distance themselves from the object of referral. In Will's case, he seeks to distance Clinton from any *legitimate* place in the political system.
3. Of the pundits on *This Week,* for instance, both of Roberts's parents served in Congress.

Kristol's father is the conservative intellectual Irving Kristol. Will's wife was a manager in Bob Dole's 1996 presidential campaign. Stephanopoulos was a senior advisor to President Clinton, and Donaldson has been a senior White House reporter for over two decades.
4. Ronald Lee argues that political leaders in this new era of politics are "feeling conduits" for voters; they must embody the voters' interests in a visceral way (Lee 1994).

References

Bausinger, H. 1984. Media, Technology and Daily Life. *Media, Culture, and Society* 6: 343–351.

Billig, M., S. Condor, D. Edwards, M. Gane, D. Middleton, and A. Radley. 1988. *Ideological Dilemmas: A Social Psychology of Everyday Thinking.* London: Sage.

Dewey, J. and A. F. Bentley. 1949. *Knowing and the Known.* Boston: Beacon.

Gabler, N. 2000. The Celebriticians. *George* (December/January): 108–111, 124.

Gamson, J. 1994. *Claims to Fame: Celebrity in Contemporary America.* Berkeley: University of California Press.

Geertz, C. 1975. Common Sense as a Cultural System. *Antioch Review* 33 (spring): 5–26.

Gramsci, A. 1988. *An Antonio Gramsci Reader,* edited by David Forgacs. New York: Schocken Books.

Grossberg, L. 1992. *We Gotta Get out of This Place.* New York: Routledge

Hartley, J. 1999. *Uses of Television.* London: Routledge.

Lee, R. 1994. Images of Civic Virtue in the New Political Rhetoric. In *Presidential Campaigns and American Self Images,* edited by A. H. Miller and B. E. Gronbeck. Boulder, Colo.: Westview press.

Lull, J., ed. 1988. *World Families Watch Television.* Newbury Park, Calif.: Sage.

Marshall, P. D. 1998. *Celebrity and Power: Fame in Contemporary Culture.* Minneapolis: University of Minnesota Press.

Miller, T. 1998. *Technologies of Truth: Cultural Citizenship and the Popular Media.* Minneapolis: University of Minnesota Press.

Schudson, M. 1998a. *The Good Citizen: A History of American Civic Life.* New York: Free Press.

———. 1998b. In All Fairness: Definitions of Fair Journalism Have Changed over the Last Two Centuries. In *What's Fair? Media Studies Journal* (spring/summer).

Silverstone, R., and E. Hirsch, eds. 1992. *Consuming Technologies: Media and Information in Domestic Spaces.* New York: Routledge.

Rap Music: The Cultural Politics of Official Representation

Julia Eklund Koza

Julia Eklund Koza is a Professor of Music Education at the University of Wisconsin, Madison. She is interested in equity and social justice, especially how these issues are reflected in education, music, and music education. Her research also considers corporate influences on music education. She has served as chair of her department since 1998, yet maintains an active publishing record and serves on the editorial board of several journals. This essay was originally published in *Sound Identities: Popular Music and the Cultural Politics of Education*, a book that focused on the critical role popular culture plays in shaping the social identity of school-aged youth.

INTRODUCTION

Rap music has been in existence for at least twenty years and has been called "the most significant popular innovation" of the past two decades (Leland, 1992d, p. 59), but American music educators have rarely welcomed this diverse and potentially powerful genre into official school knowledge. Instead, for many, rap epitomizes what they have dedicated their careers to opposing. According to a growing body of educators, however, a compelling case can be made for giving serious and respectful attention to many dimensions of popular culture, including rap.[1] Educators who acknowledge that rap is a significant aesthetic experience for countless American students and recognize the merits of understanding and valuing the cultural experiences students bring with them call for a broadened definition of legitimate school knowledge, one that recognizes rap as a significant cultural artifact. As forays into the complexities of cultural politics reveal connections between official knowledge and power, the problems resulting from unquestioned acceptance of traditional definitions of legitimate school knowledge have become clearer. Ignoring or denouncing popular culture—the culture of the people—sends elitist messages about whose understandings of the world do or do not count, both in schools and in the dominant culture. Thus, educators should care about rap, because disregarding this important art form may help to perpetuate dominant power relations. Furthermore, popular culture sometimes serves as a venue for cultural critique, specifically of institutions and the power regimes that support them. Schooling is one such institution, and it is imperative that educators, ensconced as we are, seriously ponder the voices critical of this institution and the regimes of power that shape it.

The uninformed educator who seeks to better understand rap music quickly discovers that the genre has received scant attention in scholarly circles, particularly in music. This silence is a commentary on whose knowledge is deemed most legitimate in academe. More importantly, however, it enlarges the role of the general media as educators of educators on rap. Because the general media may be playing a central role in shaping educators' understandings and attitudes, the manner in which the media represent rap and hip hop culture is of considerable importance.

In the process of becoming more rap literate, I became intrigued by media coverage of the genre and decided to embark on an exploration of this coverage. To that end, I did a close reading of all rap-related articles that appeared in three American weekly news magazines during the ten-year period from January 1983 through December 1992; the three magazines I examined were *Newsweek*, *Time* magazine, and *U.S. News and World Report*.

In the following analysis, I will uncover some of the ways that discourses of domination, including inside/outside binaries that construct the outside as the undesirable other, speak through these texts, reinforcing and reinscribing unequal power relations along lines of race, social class, and gender. I will argue that in their representations of rap, rappers, and rap fans, these news magazines participated in a construction and commodification of otherness, integrally related to the perpetuation of hegemony. Construction of otherness was accomplished not only through specific textual content but also by means of what television media specialist John Fiske calls "generic characteristics" or "conventions" of news reporting (1987, pp. 282–283).

REPRESENTATION AND POWER

This analysis is based on the assumption that representations are social constructs and on the premise that mass media representations are commodities designed to be marketed to and consumed by vast audiences. The significance of representation, specifically mass media representation, lies in its relationship to power, a relationship that bell hooks explores in her books *Yearning: Race, Gender, and Cultural Politics* and *Black Looks: Race and Representation*. hooks discusses the critical role media representations play in shaping people's perceptions of themselves and others,[2] and she ties specific representations of race to the perpetuation of unequal power relations:

5   There is a direct and abiding connection between the maintenance of white supremacist patriarchy in this society and the institutionalization via mass media of specific images, representations of race, of blackness that support and maintain the oppression, exploitation, and overall domination of all black people (hooks, 1992, 2).

She calls for "radical interventions," for "fierce critical interrogation" of representations, and for "revolutionary attitudes about race and representation" (1992, p. 7, p. 5). hooks' observations about the relationship between power and representation, and her call for new attitudes, are relevant not only in discussions of race, but also in those of social class and gender.

BINARY CONSTRUCTIONS AND OPPRESSION

Examining how oppressive representations are constructed can be a part of the fierce critical interrogation that hooks recommends. Some constructions use what John Fiske calls deep-structure binary oppositions, and what feminist Diana Fuss describes as inside/outside oppositions that depict the outside as the alien, excluded, lacking, or contaminated other (Fiske, 1987, pp. 131–134; Fuss, 1991, pp. 1–3). Fiske explains that deep-structure abstract binaries, such as good/evil, are "metaphorically transformed into concrete representations," such as middle class/lower class, order/lawlessness, light/dark, and masculine/feminine. Fiske points to the theorizing of Roland Barthes, who argued that such binaries are part of a myth-making that serves dominant classes in capitalist societies (Fiske, 1987, p. 132, p. 134). Fuss relates inside/outside rhetoric to regimes of power by stating that

> The figure inside/outside, which encapsulates the structure of language, repression, and subjectivity, also designates the structure of exclusion, oppression, and repudiation. This latter model may well be more insistent to those subjects routinely relegated to the right of the virgule—to the outside of systems of power, authority, and cultural legitimacy (1991, p. 2).

Fuss maintains that the inside/outside figure can never be completely eliminated, but it can be "worked on and worked over—itself turned inside out to expose its critical operations and interior machinery" (1991, p. 1).

STRATEGIES OF CONTAINMENT AND THE NEWS

10   In addition to relating narrative structures such as binary oppositions to the maintenance of unequal power relations, Fiske explains how "generic characteristics" or conventions of news reporting tend to reinforce dominant ideologies, specifically through controlling or limiting meaning. Fiske considers news to be a commodity and news reporting a highly ideological practice, and he maintains that a myth of objectivity tends to obscure the ideological intent of such reporting (1987, pp. 281–283, p. 285, p. 288). He enumerates

several general characteristics or conventions of news reporting that he contends are strategies of control and containment; the list includes selection, categorization, metaphor, negativity, and inoculation. Selection and categorization involve decisions about what does or does not constitute news. Fiske points out that to discuss news in terms of "events" gives news an aura of naturalness; however, selection, which is the means by which events become news, is a cultural process (Fiske, 1987, pp. 282–293). Through selection and categorization, events are placed into the categories of news or not news; categorization also refers to sorting news into subcategories and to placing events on a "conceptual grid" (1987, pp. 286–287). Fiske says that such subcategories are "normalizing agents," and as I will show later, choice of category may influence how an event is read and interpreted. Metaphor, according to him, is a sense-making mechanism; choice of metaphor affects how news is understood (1987, pp. 291–293). Negativity is the tendency for the news to focus on the negative or the "bad"; he comments on the ideological messages underlying the convention of focusing on bad news:

> What is absent from the text of the news, but present as a powerforce in its reading, are the unspoken assumptions that life is ordinarily smooth-running, rule- and law-abiding, and harmonious. These norms are of course prescriptive rather than descriptive, that is, they embody the sense of what our social life ought to be rather than what it is, and in doing this they embody the ideology of the dominant classes (Fiske 1987, p. 284).

Finally, inoculation is a metaphor for allowing radical voices to be heard in controlled doses. This practice surrounds the news with an aura of objectivity, but Fiske says it tends to strengthen rather than challenge "the social body" (1987, p. 291).

SELECTING THE GENERAL MEDIA SOURCES

Before turning to a discussion of how narrative structures and news conventions operated in the texts I examined, let us briefly consider the magazines themselves. *Newsweek*, *Time*, and *U.S. News* are the three most widely circulated news magazines in the United States and Canada. According to 1991 statistics, *Time*'s paid circulation was

4,073,530; the circulation for *Newsweek* was 3,224,770 and for *U.S. News* was 2,237,009 (*Information Please Almanac*, 1993, p. 310). All three magazines are published weekly, all of them may be classified as information rather than entertainment magazines, and two of them, *Time* and *Newsweek*, regularly feature a music/arts column. As Fiske has noted in regard to television, information and entertainment are "leaky" classifications. He points out, however, that in spite of this leakiness there are "very real differences" in the approaches and understandings that audiences and producers bring to these genres (Fiske, 1987, 282). Information magazines were chosen for this study because of the understandings that audiences likely would bring to such texts.

Rap and rap-related subject headings in *Readers' Guide Abstracts*, which indexed articles for the ten-year period from January 1983 through December 1992, were used to find pertinent articles. Thirty-nine articles were located and read. During subsequent readings, as part of my analytical strategy, excerpts were placed in one or more thematic categories. I acknowledge that my against-the-grain readings are situated in this selection scheme and, thus, partial and incomplete. Furthermore, I recognize that as a white, middle-class female, I hold multiple positions, and I realize that these positions helped shape what I did or did not see.

SELECTION AND SILENCE

One way to begin to understand how rap was represented is to examine patterns of coverage in the three magazines (Table 1).

Clearly, *Newsweek* provided the most consistent and extensive coverage while *U.S. News*, which did not have an arts/music section, spoke only rarely about the subject. Although the magazines are independent from each other, Table 1 shows that they displayed remarkably similar patterns of decision making regarding when rap was or was not considered newsworthy. During the seven years prior to 1990, the magazines were nearly silent on the subject, and no articles were published during the years 1984, 1985, or 1988. Two sudden increases in coverage occurred during the same years in all three magazines, and those were the only years when *U.S. News* published any rap articles. Perhaps the most dramatic revelation from this portion of my analysis is that one-third of the

TABLE 1	Frequency of Rap Article Publication, by Year			
Magazine Year	*Time*	*Newsweek*	*U.S. News*	*Total*
1983	1	1	0	2
1984	0	0	0	0
1985	0	0	0	0
1986	1	1	0	2
1987	0	1	0	1
1988	0	0	0	0
1989	0	1	0	1
1990	3	7	2	12
1991	2	3	0	5
1992	7	6	3	16
Total	14	20	5	39
Arts Section	Yes	Yes	No	

thirty-nine articles published during the ten-year period appeared in the four months in 1992 immediately following the Rodney King verdict and the Los Angeles response to that verdict.[3] After those four months, coverage disappeared completely from *U.S. News* and dropped dramatically in the other two magazines. I will discuss the foci of some of these articles a bit later; but for now, let us consider the silences, particularly the silences in the two magazines featuring an arts/music column.

Patterns of coverage can reveal what Fiske calls the strategies of selection and categorization—in this instance, the categorization of rap music as news or not news. As I indicated earlier, Fiske maintains that these strategies are based in ideology. For many years, even those magazines featuring a music/arts column did not think rap was newsworthy; perhaps they did not think rap was art, at least not art of sufficient merit to deserve their attention. Silences and sparse coverage indicate that the magazines were in doubt about whether rap was "socially *legitimate*" cultural capital, to use Michael Apple's phrase (1979, p. 6). The lengthy span when these widely read magazines relegated rap to the right of the virgule in the news/not news or art/not art binary is a reflection of whose knowledge was deemed worth knowing, and thus, indirectly, a commentary on power relations. In this instance, the role of race and social class as influential factors in the selection and categorization processes should not be overlooked.

SUBCATEGORIZATION: RAP AS A CULTURAL ARTIFACT

Another pattern emerged when I examined which news subcategory was selected when information about rap was published. Rap was more frequently discussed in the music/arts section than in any other single news category in the two magazines that featured such a section. However, in both of these magazines, articles about rap appeared *outside* the music/arts section *in the majority of cases* (e.g., in "Lifestyle," "Nation," "Living," "Sports," etc.)[4] In *U.S. News*, the magazine not featuring a music/arts section, rap articles appeared most often under the "Society" heading.

As Fiske has noted, choice of news category influences the ways that information is understood:

> The categorization of news and its consequent fragmentation is a strategy that attempts to control and limit the meanings of social life, and to construct the interests of the western bourgeoisie into 'natural' common sense. Compartmentalization is central to news's strategy of containment (Fiske, 1987, p. 287).

Placing discussions of rap in categories other than the music/arts sections contributed to a construction of rap as a sociological phenomenon, as political discourse, or as reportage rather than as an art form, and, thus, it changed the terms in which rap was discussed. Regardless of whether articles appeared in or out of the arts/music section, however, there was very little discussion of the music itself, aside from its lyrics. Little attention was paid to its history, its formal characteristics, or even to the practice of sampling, which is a rich and complex musical component of rap. These absences further contributed to rap's construction as a sociological phenomenon, subject to intense social analysis. Thus, even if the magazines recognized that rap is an art form (as opposed to "not art"), they did not discuss it as such, and certainly not in terms apparently reserved for "high art." The few journalists to compare rap and "high art" placed rap on a much lower plane. For example, in a scathing critique of N.W.A.'s explicit lyrics, Jerry Adler wrote, "The outrageous implication is that to *not* sing about this stuff would be to do violence to an artistic vision as pure and compelling as Bach's" (Adler, 1990, p. 58). George F. Will distanced rap from "high art" music by suggesting it was ludicrous to compare negative responses to 2 Live Crew to the riots that followed early performances of Stravinsky's *Rite of Spring* (Will, 1990, p. 64).

Of course, rap is a socially constructed cultural artifact, as is all music; however, a double standard appears to exist, which can be made visible by comparing the terms in which Euro-American high art music is usually discussed to those used for rap. Recent attempts to regard high art music as a sociological phenomenon have often met with sharp criticism and considerable resistance, at least from within academe.[5]

One dissimilarity between the left and right sides of the high art/popular art binary is that a myth of transcendence tends to accompany the high art position, and the myth appears to insulate high art from discussion constructing it as a cultural artifact. Thus, the myth accords high art music a measure of freedom from the intense scrutiny and sociological analysis to which rap, constructed as popular art, not art, or bad art, was frequently subjected. This myth of transcendence suggests (falsely, of course) that "high" or "great" art does not participate in the racism, misogyny, homophobia, or glorification of violence with which rap was frequently associated and for which it was harshly criticized. A handful of the magazines' discussions of attempted censorship of rap lyrics shattered this myth by pointing out that a net designed to catch rap would also snag much "high art" music. Ira Glasser, executive director of the American Civil

Liberties Union, was quoted as saying that there are no words in 2 Live Crew "that have not appeared in books or in serious literature" ("Should dirty lyrics," 1990, p. 24). Ironically, although Glasser supported 2 Live Crew's rap, he also categorized it as not serious and, thus, relegated it to the right side of the virgule.

Of course, the myth of transcendence does not completely insulate "high art." For example, controversy over the Mapplethorpe exhibit made the news during the same period as discussions of 2 Live Crew's lyrics. However, the strength of the myth of transcendence may have aided the Mapplethorpe case; significantly, the gallery showing Mapplethorpe's pieces was acquitted of all obscenity charges while the record store owner who sold 2 Live Crew albums was convicted, a point not lost on Peter Plagens, who wrote about the court decisions in a *Newsweek* article entitled "Mixed Signals on Obscenity" (1990, p. 74).

Pierre Bourdieu (1984) theorized about the role that distinctions between high and popular art play in the perpetuation of unequal power relations along social class lines. These distinctions, and their relationship to power, need to be taken into account when considering representations of rap; in addition, however, the role that these distinctions play in perpetuating unequal power relations along racial lines also should be examined.

RAPPERS, RAP FANS, AND OTHERNESS

Rappers

Now that we have considered some of the ways that strategies of selection and categorization placed rap on the right side of the virgule in inside/outside binaries, let us turn to actual textual content, specifically to that which constructed rappers and rap fans. Rap was generally represented as a genre by and for black, urban, adolescent, males who were poor or from the working class. Evidence of inside/outside binaries was in abundance in comments about rappers' race and social class, the binaries variously taking the form of high/low, good/bad, here/there, and up/down. Rap was usually associated with the right side of the virgule, and with lack or want. For example, Jay Cocks relied upon high/low binaries when he reported that rap "began as a fierce and proudly insular music of the American black underclass (1992, p. 70). David Gates, in his description of rap as "a communiqué from the 'underclass'—or less euphemistically, poor blacks," equated poverty (specifically being "under") with being black. Gates also painted a picture of want and lack when he described athletes and rappers as "the only credible role models for inner-city kids"; since most athletes and rappers are male, his comment has sexist overtones as well (Gates, 1990a, p. 60). In several sources, rap was described as coming from the ghetto, a term not only suggesting a place apart, but also a place of otherness, at least from a white, Anglo-Saxon, Protestant perspective. This place of otherness was represented as dangerous; for example, N.W.A.'s music was described as a "rap mural of ghetto life, spray painted with blood" (Cocks, 1991, p. 78). One source said rap originated in the "cauldron of New York City's underclass," a phrase evoking images of simmering, poisonous brews (Thigpen, 1991, p. 71). Articles that called rap the music from the streets were connecting it to a specific social-class location; however, as a location of otherness, streets were represented as undesirable places associated with crime, poverty, offal, and moral degradation. For example, one reference explained that a "new musical culture, filled with self-assertion and anger, has come boiling up from the streets. Some people think it should have stayed there" (Adler, 1990, p. 56). The statement not only placed streets on the low side of an up/down binary but also suggested that rap had changed social location and had moved to an unnamed "higher" ground. Finally, the headline "America's Slide into the Sewer," which George F. Will chose for his anti-rap essay, suggested that America, however defined, had participated in a downward movement to a place reserved for offal (Will, 1990, p. 64). We can assume that Will was describing a moral slide; however, sewers are found in or under the streets, and streets represent a social location.

A second component in the construction of rappers was an emphasis on the meteoric rises to fame and fortune that resulted from rap's popularity and success. Rap was represented as an enormously profitable venture, but mixed messages were sent about whether such profit was good. Rap's critics argued that rappers were making fortunes on obscenity and getting rich on offensiveness. Much attention was paid to the successes of controversial groups such as N.W.A. (Adler, 1990, p. 56; Gates, 1990b, p. 52; Leland, 1992b, p. 48). In

addition, critics and proponents alike sometimes listed ways that rappers and those affiliated with the sales and promotion of rap were spending their money. For example, rap impresario Russell Simmons was described as "livin' large. His empire brings him an income of $5 million a year" (Simpson, 1992, p. 69). The article enumerated some of his possessions, including a bullet-proof Rolls-Royce and a triplex penthouse. Simmons, the magazine reported, buys Cristal champagne, and abstract art. Sports cars, a private jet, exotic trips, a home in Hollywood, and expensive jewelry were among the other possessions associated with rappers (Cocks, 1990, p. 73; Donnelly, 1992, p. 68; Bard, 1987, p. 71; Gates, 1990a, p. 607). Philanthropic efforts were reported occasionally, but more often than not, the magazines focused on rappers' predilections for luxury items. In addition to symbolizing success and wealth, however, the belongings mentioned can also represent extravagance, excess, and unprincipled spending, at least to a middle-class eye.

Another element complicating the representation of successful rappers was the implication that rap is a quasi-legal means of making money, a just-barely-legal way to acquire capital. The tone was set by references to some rappers' past criminal activities. For example, 2 Live Crew's Luther Campbell was described as an "ex-gang leader turned entrepreneur," and Ice-T was reported to have been very successful as a hustler, spending $500 on sneakers before he changed careers (Gates, 1990b, p. 52; Donnelly, 1992, p. 68). Such reports set the stage for portrayals of rap as "the safe and legal road to riches" (Gates, 1990a, p. 61). One article quoted Ice-T lyrics indicating that friends in crime were now making more money in music (Donnelly, 1992, p. 68). Another reported that one quarter of rap's "homeboys end up in serious trouble with the law" (Gates, 1990a, p. 60).

Some links between successful rappers and crime were more subtle. For example, when N.W.A.'s attitude was described as "jaunty and sullen by turns; showy but somehow furtive, in glasses as opaque as a limousine window and sneakers as white as a banker's shirt," subtle connections were made between N.W.A., crime, and otherness (Adler, 1990, p. 56). The words "sullen" and "furtive" set an ominous tone. Next, reference was made to signs of fortune that have also come to represent criminal activity. Limousines with opaque windows are symbols of wealth, but they also are associated with pimps and drug dealers. Opaque glasses, long worn by highway patrol officers, also suggest drug use and inaccessibility. White banker's shirts are a symbol of legal acquisition of capital, but N.W.A. members were not wearing banker's shirts; instead, they donned sneakers.

30   Reports indicating that some successful rappers, including impresario Russell Simmons, Tracy Marrow (Ice-T), and members of Public Enemy had not come from poverty, but instead had roots in the middle class (Simpson, 1992, p. 69; Donnelly, 1992, p. 68; Leland, 1992b, p. 49), contributed to a representation of rappers as impostors and charlatans, shrewd but unscrupulous business people, who furthered their own interests at the expense of a long list of victims, among them women and poor black people. Of course, rather than recognizing that all musical performances are just performances, such arguments assumed that some are and others are not. One critic charged that Ice-T's heavy metal single *Cop Killer* was not "an authentic anguished cry of rage from the ghetto," but rather a "cynical commercial concoction designed to titillate its audience with imagery of violence"; *Cop Killer*, the critic claimed, is "an excellent joke [by Ice-T and Time Warner, the parent corporation] on the white establishment" (Kinsley, 1992, p. 88). Another article described impresario Simmons as sensing the commercial potential when others thought rap was a gimmick (Simpson, 1992, p. 69). In a discussion of an N.W.A. album released in 1991, N.W.A's mystique was said to pay "no attention to where criminality begins and marketing lets off" (Leland, 1991, p. 63). Finally, when Sister Souljah spoke at a convention of Jesse Jackson's Rainbow Coalition in 1992, and presidential candidate William Clinton criticized Souljah, one commentator unflatteringly represented all three figures (Jackson, Souljah, and Clinton) as self-serving, bottom-line business people whose primary interest was furthering their own careers; the essay was entitled "Sister Souljah: Capitalist Tool" (White, 1992, p. 88). The proposition that rappers are entrepreneurs, not artists, overlooked the possibility that they could be both; furthermore, it did not address the reality that most, if not all, artists are by necessity entrepreneurs as well.

      Ironically, stories of rappers' entrepreneurialism and success, bootstrap stories that would make Horatio Alger proud, sometimes were viewed with

mistrust and suspicion. Controversial rappers, at least one of whom was a card-carrying member of the Republican party,[6] were amassing wealth by serving up conservative political fare that embraced "old-fashioned social norms (even in its take on gender roles and homosexuality . . .)" (Leland, 1992b, p. 52). Ironically, these conservative voices were being vilified and rebuked by other conservatives. Thus, rappers' acquisition of wealth and their concomitant shift in social-class status did not necessarily change the representation of these rappers as outsiders. This representation can be explained, in part, in terms of power relations. If successful black rappers are viewed as a threat to hegemony and a challenge to some white middle-class values, specifically to beliefs about who is entitled to capital, how it should be acquired, and how it should be used, then mixed or negative portrayals of these rappers may be seen as attempts to reinforce dominant ideology and to keep black people "in their place."

Rap Fans

As mentioned earlier, rap was represented as originating in a specific place of otherness; lines of distinction were drawn in terms of race, social class, and gender. However, as the decade advanced, the magazines indicated that some types of rap were traversing some of these lines; the race and social class of the typical fan were shifting, but the age and sex generally were not. Some articles said these shifts or expansions began in the mid-1980s, but the movement may have started several years earlier.[7] When an article published in 1990 told parents that rap can be heard booming from "your kid's bedroom," the kid in question could have been either black or white (Gates, 1990a, p. 60). As early as 1990, articles began recognizing that music by rap's most controversial groups, for example, Public Enemy and N.W.A., was being consumed primarily by white, middle-class, suburban, adolescent males (Gates, 1990a, p. 61; Cocks, 1991, p. 78). By contrast, according to John Schecter, editor of the hip-hop journal *The Source*, N.W.A. was not liked by most black people (Cocks, 1991, p. 75).

      Audience shift or expansion was discussed most extensively in articles appearing during the final three years I analyzed, 1990–1992; this shift may help explain the dramatic increase in 1990 of the magazines' coverage of rap. The scope of the expansion was alluded to in a statement made in 1992 by rapper

Tupac Shakur, who opined that rap was no longer a black movement but rather a youth movement (Leland, 1992a, p. 53). Throughout the final three years, however, the perception lingered that rap was, first and foremost, by and for black people.

The term often used to describe the movement of rap's popularity from one racial and social-class group to another was "crossover," and the place to which rap crossed was often called "the mainstream." Inside/outside binaries were evident throughout these discussions. The mainstream, the inside of the binary, was white, middle class, and male. Journalists spoke of rap crossing over from black America "into the mainstream of popular culture" (Gates, 1990c, p. 68). Impresario Russell Simmons was described as moving rap "from the streets of the inner city into the white mainstream of American pop culture" (Simpson, 1992, p. 69). Journalist John Leland mentioned rap's "trip to the white mainstream" (1992b, p. 51), and Jay Cocks talked about "why ghetto rage and the brutal abuse of women appeal to mainstream listeners." Cocks later gave a profile of the typical fan that provided clues about who constituted the mainstream; fans were white, middle class, teenage, and male (Cocks, 1991, p. 78).

35   Inside/outside binaries took several forms in discussions of rappers and rap fans, one of which was a we/they binary to which the moral judgments good/bad were often explicitly or implicitly attached: At times, "they" were rappers, and at other times, fans. For example, an article appearing in 1990, the year when crossover began receiving substantial attention, was entitled "Polluting Our Popular Culture." The article described popular culture as "the air we breathe," and 2 Live Crew was termed "a pesky new pollutant"; the journalist, John Leo, called for the elimination of the "2 Live Pollutants" from "our air." In this we/they structure, popular culture was owned by an unspecified "us," and "they," 2 Live Crew, were a foreign contaminant. "They" were rappers and rap music from whom rap fans, constructed as "our daughters," needed to be protected. Leo, in a question that displayed a protect-the-women-and-children logic, queried, "Why should our daughters have to grow up in a culture in which musical advice on the domination and abuse of women is accepted as entertainment?" (Leo, 1990, p. 15). Leo's question appears to be a color-blind plea to all parents; however, in an article focusing on 2

Live Crew's controversial lyrics, group leader Luther Campbell observed that he had been making similar albums for years and had received no complaints from the "decency police" until white kids started listening (Gates, 1990b, p. 52). Apparently, protecting daughters was not much of an issue with these watchdog groups until "our daughters" were white. Leo's question is an excellent one; however, as feminist musicians know, serving up the domination and abuse of women as entertainment is not unique to rap or to popular music; much Euro-American high art music does the same. Leo's decision to single out rap indicated that the genre was on the outside of the inside/outside binary, a position offering less protection from scrutiny.

Yet another example of the we/they binary was seen in a scathing criticism of rap fans, whom journalist Jerry Adler described as "working-class" and "underclass" youths "who forgot to go to business school in the 1980s." Adler placed himself in the otherwise unspecified category of "we" and argued that "we" cannot talk to "them," the rap fans. Adler characterized fans as stupid and uninformed; he maintained that if they "had ever listened to anything except the homeboys talking trash," if they had studied and read, "*[t]hen* we might have a sensible discussion with them; but they haven't, so we can't" (Adler, 1990, p. 59).

An especially ugly manifestation of the inside/outside binary was seen in discussions distancing rap from civilization. For example, in a diatribe focusing largely on rap, George F. Will implied that rappers are lower animals (Will, 1990, p. 64). Shortly thereafter, Jerry Adler equated civilization with control and rap with chaos when he wrote, "Civilized society abhors [rap] attitude and perpetuates itself by keeping it under control" (1990, p. 57). A letter to the editor responded to the issue in which Adler's article appeared by chastising *Newsweek* for publishing any information about rap. Calling it a "bestial and obscene" subculture, the reader fumed, "I realize that these creatures [rappers] have the right to express themselves. . . . However, you seem to have forgotten your responsibility to your readers to keep within the bounds of decency."[8] To suggest, as these passages did, that members of a predominantly black group such as rappers are uncivilized, low animals is to invoke a racism as old as colonialism itself.

The Other of Others

Some rap and rappers were routinely criticized for making hateful or demeaning comments about whole groups of people. The groups most frequently mentioned were women, gays, Korean immigrants, Jews, whites, and the police; however, from time to time rap also was denounced for furthering hatred toward blacks through the commodification of racist images of black people. With the exception of the police, the groups mentioned were defined in terms of race, social class, gender, sexual orientation, or ethnicity. Social class was described as a separating factor when black people were divided in opinion on the subject of rap. Discussions of black opposition to rap shattered the myth of a unified black voice; however, they also contributed to the perception that rap had and deserved little support from important segments of the black community; anti-rap sentiment was thus portrayed as transcending race. Paradoxically, people who may have viewed themselves as disenfranchised others—women, gays, Asian immigrants, and Jews—were summoned to join powerful dominant groups—whites and the police—in an improbable coalition against rap. In short, not only were rappers and rap fans often represented as the others in inside/outside binaries, they also were constructed as the other of others. A quotation by bell hooks applies: "Black youth culture comes to stand for the outer limits of 'outness' " (1992, p. 34).

RAP AND NEGATIVITY

It would be inaccurate and misleading to say that every article openly opposed all rap. Indeed, making generalizations about the overall tone of the articles was extraordinarily difficult. It usually was impossible to simplistically categorize an article as patently pro or con, positive or negative. I can say that *U.S. News* had a prevailing attitude toward rap because anti-rap sentiments were expressed in every article; furthermore, four of the five articles were patently opposed to the rap discussed. However, when speaking about the other two magazines, especially about *Newsweek*, which presented the most extensive coverage of rap, there is an ever-present danger of being reductive. In all three magazines an image of balanced reporting, of including multiple viewpoints, was created;

one way of accomplishing this was by using side-by-side pro and con arguments. The image of balance confounded attempts to analyze and generalize, and it implied that the magazines were not in the business of telling readers what to think. However, Fiske probably would describe these pro/con presentations as examples of inoculation, of allowing radical voices to speak in controlled environments.

Even though the articles were difficult to characterize and often presented the image of balance, most of them nevertheless participated in reinforcing dominant ideologies through the strategy of containment that Fiske calls negativity. Evidence of this negativity surfaced when thematic content of the articles was analyzed. The vast majority of articles made reference to at least one of the following themes: violence, obscenity, hatred, crime, gangs, and anger. Such references appeared in all *U.S. News* articles and in more than 85% of those published by *Time* and by *Newsweek*. Thus, even when articles were sympathetic to rap, they usually reinforced a link between rap and specific negative themes. A corollary representation was that controversy is rap's constant partner. Concentrating on the negative, focusing on a circumscribed list of rap topics, and constructing rap as controversial, were means by which these magazines placed readers in a position where they likely received a skewed vision of rap, a vision that nearly obliterated its diversity. The vastness of rap and its extraordinary variety—illustrated, for example, by the existence of groups such as DC Talk, composed of students from conservative evangelist Jerry Falwell's Liberty University—was lost in a reductive wash (Rabey, 1991, p. 50). In its relentless search for the negative and the controversial, the reporting made generalizations about the whole after looking at only a very small part. It centered on a few controversial groups rather than on the complete genre, and characteristics of the former tended to be ascribed to the latter. Coverage almost invariably obscured the reality that the rappers and rap discussed were neither necessarily representative nor the most popular with the majority of rap fans. The rare qualifying statement, such as, "The vast majority of rap is healthy," or "Rap is so vast, you can't really categorize it anymore," was barely audible amid the clatter of negativity (Leo, 1992, p. 19, p. 50).

NEGATIVE IMAGERY AND THE REPRESENTATION OF RAP

Even when articles did not specifically refer to negative themes, they nevertheless sometimes constructed rap as bad in roundabout ways, for example, through use of imagery. As Fiske states, choice of image, specifically of metaphor, influences the understandings people bring to texts. There was imagery of poison and pollution. For example, one headline read "Rap Music's Toxic Fringe" (Leo, 1992, p. 19). In a similar vein, an article suggested that the recording industry was telling consumers to "buy a gas mask or stop breathing"; it described rap as sending "venomous messages" disguised as "harmless fun" (Leo, 1990, p. 19). There also were images of violence, anger, and fear. Ice-T's poetry, it was said, "takes a switchblade and deftly slices life's jugular" (Donnelly, 1992, p. 66). A simile laced with racism described rap attitude as being "as scary as sudden footsteps in the dark" (Adler, 1990, p. 57). Even descriptions of the music itself sometimes relied on violent imagery. For example, a journalist wrote of "the thumping, clattering scratching *assault* [my emphasis] of rap" (Adler, 1990, p. 56). Another said that the group B.W.P served up "a vengeful brand of radical black feminism" in a "snarling hard-core style" (Thigpen, 1991, p. 72).

War metaphors were used occasionally. One passage called rap music "a series of bulletins from the front in a battle for survival," and another referred to members of Public Enemy as "racial warriors" (Leland, 1992b, p. 6, p. 49). In what was perhaps the most vivid example, an image of war was evoked when conservative actor Charlton Heston likened Ice-T to Adolf Hitler, a comparison made at a Time Warner shareholders' meeting held in 1992 (Leland, 1992c, p. 51). By equating a rapper with a war figure who personifies evil of mythic proportions, Heston and the journalist who reported the event constructed Ice-T as the enemy in a battle of good against evil.

RAP, REPRESENTATION, AND RACE

The significance of the magazines' negativity and negative representations becomes clearer when one considers that theorists have linked both negativity and negative representation to power relations. John Fiske asserted that negativity is a strategy of containment that tends to reinforce dominant ideologies.

Specifically, Fiske noted, ideological practice is evident in news reporting's predisposition to construct "the bad" as an aberration in dominant culture but as normal for others. Fiske commented on the relationship between "otherness," negativity, and power:

> There is, of course, a connection between elitism and negativity: the positive or 'normal' actions of elite people will often be reported whereas those without social power are considered newsworthy only when their actions are disruptive or deviant. In representing the dominant as performing positive actions and the subordinate as performing deviant or negative ones the news is engaging in the same ideological practices as fictional television (Fiske, 1987, pp. 285–286).

Because there is a relationship between representation and power, negative representation that consistently links a black cultural product and black performers to violence, obscenity, hatred, crime, gangs, and anger, and that thus represents hip hop culture as the undesirable other, must be viewed as a factor contributing to the maintenance of white supremacy. Tricia Rose, who has explored some of the complex cultural politics of rap, speaks of a "sociologically based crime discourse" that surrounds "the political economy of rap" (Rose, 1991, p. 277). Rose asserts that opposition to rap is grounded in fear:

> Young African Americans are positioned in fundamentally antagonistic relationships to the institutions that most prominently frame and constrain their lives. The public school system, the police, and the popular media perceive and construct them as a dangerous internal element in urban America—an element that if allowed to roam about freely will threaten the social order, an element that must be policed. The social construction of rap and rap-related violence is fundamentally linked to the social discourse on Black containment and fears of a Black planet (Rose, 1991, p. 279).

According to Rose, this white fear, born in the days of slavery, is of loss of white control, specifically through black uprising or revolt; the fear informs constructions of black people, especially of young black males, who are seen as threats "to the social order of oppression," threats that must be restrained or controlled (1991, pp. 283–284, p. 289).

FEARS OF A BLACK PLANET AND THE DISCOURSE OF CONTAINMENT

With Rose's analysis of the cultural politics of rap music in mind, let us examine two cases from the magazines in which the negative representations of rap, rappers, and rap fans seemed clearly linked to fears of a black planet and the social discourse of containment. I will begin with a close reading of George F. Will's essay, "America's Slide into the Sewer," in which Will stepped beyond the observation that some rap lyrics speak of violence to suggest that 2 Live Crew lyrics induce violence. In this article, Will associated rap with an actual act of violence, the brutal rape in 1989 of a Central Park jogger. It is from rap groups like 2 Live Crew, Will suggested, that young men such as the accused rapists learn that sexual violence against women is enjoyable: "Where can you get the idea that sexual violence against women is fun? From a music store, through Walkman earphones, from boom boxes blaring forth the rap lyrics of 2 Live Crew." To prove his point, Will interspersed horrifyingly graphic excerpts of courtroom testimony from the rape case with shockingly explicit rap lyrics from 2 Live Crew. He connected the rapists to rap fans by citing common characteristics of both groups: "Fact: Some members of a particular age and social cohort—the one making 2 Live Crew rich—stomped and raped the jogger to the razor edge of death, for the fun of it." To bolster his argument he quoted the *Washington Post*'s Juan Williams, whom he identified as "black and disgusted"; Williams excoriated 2 Live Crew, claiming the group is "'selling corruption—self-hate—to vulnerable young minds in a weak black America'" (Will, 1990, p. 64). Williams supported his allegation that American black families are falling apart by citing statistics indicating that half of all black children are raised in single-parent households headed by women.

Will charged that liberals are the tools of unscrupulous corporations, which have sold "civil pollution for profit." America's priorities are wrong, Will argued, because protecting black women receives less attention than saving endangered fish: "America today is capable of terrific intolerance about smoking, or toxic waste that threatens trout. But only a deeply confused society is more concerned about protecting lungs than minds, trout than black women. We legislate against smoking in restaurants; singing 'Me So Horny' is a constitutional right" (Willis, 1990, p. 64). Will's parting comments indicated that he believes protection of black women will be accomplished by exercising more control over groups such as 2 Live Crew.

The Central Park rape was horrible and 2 Live Crew's lyrics are graphic and misogynistic; however, these realities do not change the fact that Will's argument was not only flawed, sexist, and elitist but also showed evidence of a racist fear of a black planet. To begin to excavate the racism, sexism, and elitism implicit in Will's essay, the reader must keep in mind a critical piece of information about the Central Park rape: the jogger was white and the attackers were black. Will made no reference to the race of either party, but this information was generally known and widely reported. Thus, Will chose as his example of crime and violence an event that was laden with prejudicial meaning and was a classic scenario for evoking white racist fears. The Central Park rape reinforced the racist perception that young black adolescents are dangerous, out of control, and sexually violent; the event appeared to confirm the belief that uncontrolled, young black adolescents are a threat to vulnerable (female) white America.

Next, Will linked this meaning-laden rape to a black cultural product, even though he did not present one scintilla of evidence suggesting the accused rapists had ever listened to 2 Live Crew or to any form of rap music. Even if Will had found such evidence, he would have faced the formidable task of establishing causation. He grounded his case on the argument that the accused rapists were of the same "age and social cohort group" making 2 Live Crew rich but never articulated salient features of that cohort group. Will and Williams apparently assumed that race was one of those salient features, an assumption encountered in Williams' statement that 2 Live Crew was selling corruption to the black community. However, as noted previously, information reported elsewhere in 1990 indicated that the typical fan of controversial rap groups was a young, white, middle-class boy from the suburbs. Thus, Will's characterization of "social cohort group" probably was flawed. Significantly, his characterization tended to perpetuate negative stereotypes of black adolescents while it permitted members of the social cohort group most likely to listen to explicit rap—white, middle-class boys from the suburbs—to emerge unscathed.

When Will asked the question "Where can you get the idea that sexual violence against women is fun?" he failed to list a whole array of sources unrelated to black music, and in so doing, constructed rap music as the culprit. He did not acknowledge that young males in American society can learn misogyny from countless sources in the dominant culture, the most influential of which are probably outside the boundaries of entertainment. There is implicit racism in Will's decision to single out a black cultural product but never to mention heavy metal, country, opera, and the classical fare typically sung in high school choirs, which often are at least as misogynistic (if perhaps not as graphic) as 2 Live Crew.

Will appears to have attempted to construct his argument as one that transcends race. For example, he included a sentence criticizing Andrew Dice Clay, whom he carefully described as a white comedian. However, that sentence was the only one to indict a white cultural product, and it was dwarfed by the extensive coverage given to 2 Live Crew. Will also appears to have tried to protect himself from the accusation of being racist by quoting a black spokesperson. However, Juan Williams' unflattering assessment of the state of black families and his sexist but commonly believed assumption that single-parent families headed by women are not strong, worked to reinforce white racist constructions of black families as bad families. bell hooks has commented on similar constructions:

> …African-Americans need to consider whose interests are served when the predominant representation of black culture both on television news and in talk shows suggests that the black family is disintegrating and that a hostile gender war is taking place between black women and men (hooks, 1990, 73).

55   Finally, in a particularly patriarchal gesture, Will constructed himself as a protector of black women; one significant aspect of this construction was that it came in response to the rape of a white woman. By placing himself in that role, Will depicted black women as the weak or vulnerable

"others" who need to be protected by the strong, more powerful white man. Protected from what? According to Will, from violence caused by black music, his assertion simply assuming that music-induced violence exists. His unspoken, racist message is that trouble in the lives of black people is caused by black people, in this case, by black musicians. Arguments such as Will's deflect attention away from real issues and substantive discussion of the kinds of change that would be necessary to alter the lived realities of many black women's lives. Whose interests are served by such deflection? Greater control of black discursive terrain would tend to reinforce dominant power relations; substantive change that might bring real improvement would threaten hegemony.

Some of the racial politics of Will's essay become visible when one examines the list of who looks bad in this article, that is, who was portrayed as the evil, lacking, or undesirable other. First, there were the rapists, whom the newspapers had widely reported were black. Next, there was rap music, which was generally regarded as a black cultural product, followed by 2 Live Crew, a black rap group. Fourth, there were 2 Live Crew fans, who were assumed to be black (probably incorrectly). In all of these representations, negativity was achieved by linking black people or cultural products to brutality, sexual violence, and amorality. Fifth, there were black families, specifically those headed by women, and finally, there were unscrupulous liberals and corporations, groups whose racial constitutions were not reported. Will's superficial attempts to present himself as color-blind did not mask the racism, elitism, and sexism in his constructions of black people as dangerous, undesirable, others.

Fears of a black planet and a discourse of containment were evident not only in Will's choice of the Central Park rape as the crime to discuss and in his negative constructions of black people and black cultural products, but most significantly, in his cries for more regulation of black discursive terrain. Ironically, a spurious link between rap and actual violence was the foundation for this cry. Will claimed that more control would benefit black women, but the question of whose interests are served and who stands to benefit from black containment typically elicits answers other than black women.

Finally, Will accused liberals and corporations of participating in a pornography of violence for profit. However, news also is a marketable commodity, and an inspection of Will's article for signs of what was being sold there reveals that such accusations may also justifiably be leveled at him. For example, his decision to write about brutal violence, and to include graphic excerpts of the trial transcripts and lyrics, suggests that he himself was participating in this very commodification.

Rap coverage in the four months immediately following the Rodney King verdict and response was a second example in which representations of rap, rappers, and rap fans as the "bad other" seemed clearly linked to fears of a black planet and the social discourse of containment. As I mentioned earlier, the three independent magazines made very similar decisions about when rap and rappers were newsworthy, and all concluded that hip hop culture was big news in the four months immediately following the Rodney King verdict and the Los Angeles response. A rapper, Sister Souljah, even made the cover of *Newsweek* in June 1992. I am not suggesting the publishers were malicious, nor do I subscribe to conspiracies theories. However, in the case of the articles appearing during that four-month period, the timing of this extensive coverage, even if it was coincidental, was of the essence. Through timing alone, rap once again was linked to controversy and violence, and was thus represented as the undesirable other.

60 The question of why the magazines decided to give rap such extensive coverage during those four months, and why the coverage would nearly disappear after August or September, is an interesting one. Most of the articles appearing during this period focused on (1) a comment about killing whites that rapper Sister Souljah reportedly made at a convention of Jesse Jackson's Rainbow Coalition, or (2) Ice-T and a boycott of Time Warner proposed by police in response to the rapper's heavy-metal single *Cop Killer*. The reproaches leveled at these performers were not new: critics accused the musicians of condoning or inciting hatred and violence. In addition, several rap articles mentioned the Rodney King verdict and response. Typically such references explored the relationship between rap, the verdict, and the response (Leland, 1992a, pp. 52–53; 1992b, p. 48, p. 52; Leo, 1992, p. 19; Zuckerman, 1992, p. 80). Some articles spoke of rap presaging the events; others

suggested it contributed to, orchestrated, or incited the insurgence. Just as George Will had done earlier, some journalists were suggesting the unlikely, namely that "bad" art was responsible for real-life events.

If we naturalize the news by saying it is merely about events and if we assume that the Souljah and Ice-T events just coincidentally happened in the wake of the verdict and response, then we lose sight of the role that the cultural process of selection plays in the reporting of news. However, if we assume that the Los Angeles response tapped the deep-seated white fears of which Tricia Rose spoke, then extensive coverage of controversies surrounding black musicians and a black cultural product is less puzzling, especially when the controversy included allegations of promoting or inciting hatred toward whites and the police. A statement in *Time* by Doug Elder, a Houston police officer spearheading the boycott of Time Warner, not only reverberated with white fears but also constructed rappers (and perhaps rap fans) as the dangerous enemies, the evil outsiders in a mythic opposition of good against evil: "'You mix this [*Cop Killer*] with the summer, the violence and a little drugs, and they are going to unleash a reign of terror on communities all across this country'" (Donnelly, 1992, 66).

On August 4, 1992, Ice-T announced that he was withdrawing *Cop Killer*, a decision he reportedly made after employees of Warner Brothers Records, the subsidiary of Time Warner that had distributed *Cop Killer*, had received bomb or death threats. If the controversy over this single is constructed as a standoff between the police and Ice-T, and if this standoff is viewed as a racist concretization of deep-structure myths, then the headlines "Ice-T Melts" and "The Ice-Man Concedeth" sent the message that "good" had prevailed over "evil" (Leland, 1992c, p. 50; "Ice-T Melts," 1992, p. 23). The melting imagery obviously was a play on Ice-T's name; however, images of melting also send messages about power. The Wicked Witch in *The Wizard of Oz* lost her magical powers when she melted. When people melt, they are reduced, weakened, made invisible, or rendered impotent. Ice-T had not merely made a decision to withdraw a single; instead, according to the headlines, he had conceded and melted.

The *Newsweek* article reporting Ice-T's decision spoke of mounting fears that skittish corporations would exercise more internal control over future releases. The Time Warner corporate board, the article reported, "is demanding tighter control of what gets made." Journalist John Leland expressed the concern that self-censorship would stifle "controversial ideas before they can ever enter public debate" (1992c, p. 51). Thus, limitations on discursive terrain, on published space, appeared to be a long-lasting outcome of one of the 1992 controversies. Such self-censorship is significant because, as Tricia Rose maintains, control over the art form is a form of containment; self-censorship is another manifestation of what Rose called the "institutional policing to which all rappers are subject" (Rose, 1991, p. 276).

For the most part, 1992 coverage of rap ended with Ice-T's announcement. Rap once again was relegated to the "not-news" category, and the news gaze glanced elsewhere. Significantly, the tone of the two rap articles that appeared in the final months of 1992 was distinctly different from that of most others. One article constructed rap as an extraordinarily successful exportable commodity, and the other spoke largely of a new style, dancehall, that was said to be rapidly supplanting rap (Cocks, 1992, pp. 70–71; Leland, 1992d, p. 59). Both articles intimated that rap was on its way out.

When assessing whose interests were or were not served by the extensive coverage given to rap in the four months immediately following the King verdict and response, it is important to remember that news itself is a marketable commodity. Not only did these magazines link rap to violence and controversy, but the companies owning them profited from such representations, and thus, participated in their own version of what bell hooks calls "the commodification of Otherness" (1992, p. 21). There was potential for Time Warner to reap double benefits, first, from sales of *Cop Killer*, and, second, from sales of Time magazine's coverage of the controversy.

There was no indication that the magazines viewed themselves as being in any way responsible for the reduction in discursive terrain that was a promised result of the Ice-T controversy. Journalists rarely reflected on the role they, or the media in general, played in the perpetuation of specific representations of rap, rappers, or rap fans; furthermore, there was little or no discussion of the potential damage media representations might cause.

Only one article, an interview with high school students, mentioned media representations of rap and hip hop culture. In this article, several high schoolers indicated that newspapers and other media, obsessed with controversy and negativity, have played a significant role in shaping rap's bad image (Leo, 1992a, pp. 50–51).

THEORIES ON THE APPEAL OF CONTROVERSIAL RAP TO WHITE MALES

Before closing, let us consider a final related question: Why is explicit, controversial rap especially popular among white, middle-class, suburban males? One theory is that stereotypical constructions of blackness, prevalent in rap, help define whiteness. According to this theory, consuming the "other," in this case listening to rap music, is a transgressive act, performed in defiance of dominant white norms. David Samuels writes,

> Rap's appeal to whites rested in its evocation of an age-old image of blackness: a foreign, sexually charged, and criminal underworld against which the norms of white society are defined, and by extension, through which they may be defied (1991, p. 25).

Thus, for whites, listening to rap may be an expression of adolescent rebellion and a symbol of opposition. A foray into otherness, according to bell hooks, may be viewed by adolescents as a way out of alienation:

> Masses of young people dissatisfied by U.S. imperialism, unemployment, lack of economic opportunity, afflicted by the postmodern malaise of alienation, no sense of grounding, no redemptive identity, can be manipulated by cultural strategies that offer Otherness as appeasement, particularly through commodification (hooks, 1992, p. 25).

Opinions have differed, however, about whether acts of transgression principally reinforce or challenge dominant power relations. Peter Stallybrass and Allon White, for example, argue that transgression tends to unravel dominant discourses: "Transgression becomes a kind of reverse or counter-sublimation, undoing the discursive hierarchies and stratifications of bodies and cultures which bourgeois society has produced as the mechanism of its symbolic dominance" (1986, pp. 200–201). Another perspective is provided by hooks, who maintains that consuming otherness for pleasure is a means by which discourses of dominance are reinforced:

> When race and ethnicity become commodified as resources for pleasure, the culture of specific groups, as well as the bodies of individuals, can be seen as constituting an alternative playground where members of dominating races, genders, sexual practices affirm their power-over in intimate relations with the Other (hooks, 1992, p. 23).

To rebut the assumption that consuming rap is unproblematically counterhegemonic, Samuels points out that although black music historically has been a "refuge from white middle-class boredom," in earlier times forays by whites into black music required face-to-face contact; with the advent of records and videos, whites can now consume without contact. One significant dimension of this no-touch mode of consumption is control; controversial rap can offer exciting, but safe, appearances of danger — semblances of street experience — to consumers who never leave the comfort of their suburban living rooms (1991, p. 29). Media, to use Bakhtinian terminology, have enabled carnival to be transformed into spectacle, and this transformation alters power relations. Records and videos, thus, provide a vantage point similar to that offered by the nineteenth-century balcony, which, Stallybrass and White have observed, was a location from which the bourgeoisie "could both participate in the banquet of the streets and yet remain separated" from it and above it (1986, p. 126).

Some scholars have indicated that fascination with the other is an inevitable consequence of binaries that construct otherness as evil, bad, or disgusting. For example, Stallybrass and White indicate that "disgust always bears the imprint of desire. These low domains, apparently expelled as 'Other', return as the object of nostalgia, longing, and fascination." Furthermore, these margins and sites of otherness may be viewed as growth plates, historically serving as sources of creativity from which the bourgeoisie have drawn sustenance (1986, 191, p. 21). The appeal of rap may thus be its imaginative, creative potential.

Finally, it may be argued that the text, which is what renders some rap controversial, is of little importance to many rap fans, who are drawn to the genre because of its strong, mesmerizing beat and its potential for dancing. Those who forward this explanation argue that white appeal is unrelated to rap's explicit texts and stereotypical representations of race. Perhaps no single factor accounts for rap's appeal to specific groups. However, the topic is an interesting one and merits much further consideration.

CONCLUSION

Through an analysis of *Time, Newsweek*, and *U.S. News and World Report*, I have explored how concretizations of deep-structure binaries and general characteristics of news reporting have constructed rap, rappers, and rap fans as the deviant, lacking, undesirable, or evil other. I have examined links between specific representations of hip hop culture and the perpetuation of dominant power relations along lines of race, social class, and gender. Specifically, I have explored how these representations were related to fears of a black planet and to discourses of containment. Finally, I have suggested that the magazines themselves engaged in a commodification of otherness, as well as a commodification of violence, and that these news sources did not openly acknowledge their own role as participants in the construction of representations that tend to perpetuate hegemony. In revealing some of the weaknesses of these magazines' coverage of rap, I have also pointed to drawbacks of relying heavily on such media for information about the genre. Like it or not, however, the general media are educating all of us, and television, newspapers, and magazines may be the sole sources of information about rap for a large portion of the population.

Learning about rap from second-hand sources such as the general news media, given the prevalence of the myth that news reporting is objective, presents a special array of problems for educators. These problems may be particularly serious if media information substitutes for actual experience with the genre. As I mentioned at the outset, some circles are urging educators to become more rap-literate and to include rap in official school knowledge. Ironically, however, current goals and conventions of news reporting appear to result in media representations that may bolster narrow beliefs about what constitutes legitimate school knowledge and fuel suspicion of popular culture.

Because these magazines' representations are in many respects problematic, educators need to subject them to the "fierce critical interrogations" of which bell hooks speaks, especially as they make decisions about whether and how to include rap in the school curriculum. These fierce critical interrogations are of paramount importance, not only as an essential ingredient when consuming entertainment, but also, as we have seen here, when we consume the news.

Notes

1. For interesting work on the relationship between popular culture and education, see Giroux & McLaren 1989.
2. See, for example, hooks (1990, p. 73, p. 220).
3. In *Time*, six of seven articles were published after the LA response, and five of seven appeared in the four-month window. This within-window count did not include an article appearing in the May 4, 1992 issue. Although the date of the issue technically qualified the article, I assume the issue went to press before the verdict. In *Newsweek*, five of six were published after the LA response. All three 1992 *U.S. News* articles appeared in the window.
4. In 25 of the 39 articles, discussions appeared in a classification other than arts/music. Eleven of twenty *Newsweek* articles were not in music/arts, and nine of fourteen *Time* articles appeared elsewhere.
5. One obvious example of this resistance is negative response to feminist musicologist Susan McGlary's ground-breaking analyses and deconstructions of opera and symphonic music. For a scathing assessment of McGlary, see Van Den Toorn (1991).
6. N.W.A.'s Eazy-E reportedly "contributed $1,000 to join the Republican Senatorial Inner Circle"; see Leland (1991).
7. For discussions indicating the shift occurred in the middle of the 1980s, see Barol (1992) and Gates (1990c). Jay Cocks (1983) talked about rappers sometimes performing for mostly white audiences in 1981, and Donnelly (1992) said Ice-T held performances for "mostly white crowds" as early as 1982.
8. See correspondence from Eichelmann (1990). Ironically, the same issue included several letters from irate rap fans who charged that Leo had treated rap unfairly.

References

Adler, J. (1990, March 19). The rap attitude. *Newsweek*, p. 58.

Apple. M. (1979). *Ideology and curriculum*. London: Routledge.

Barol, B. (1992, June 29). The kings of rap, together. *Newsweek*, p. 71.

Bourdieu, P. (1984). *Distinction: A social critique of the judgement of taste*. Cambridge, MA: Harvard University Press.

Cocks, J. (1983, March 21). Chilling out on rap flash. *Time*, p. 73.

Cocks, J. (1990, August 13). U can't touch him. *Time*, p. 73.

Cocks, J. (1991, July 1). A nasty jolt for the top pops. *Time*, p. 78.

Cocks, J. (1992, October 19). Rap around the globe. *Time*, p. 70.

Donnelly, S. (1992, June 22). The fire around the ice. *Time*, p. 68.

Eichelmann, H. (1990, April 9). Letters. *Newsweek*, p. 13.

Fiske, J. (1987). *Television culture*. New York: Routledge.

Fuss, D. (1991). Inside/out, In Fuss, D. (Ed.). *Inside/out: Lesbian theories, gay theories* (pp.). New York: Routledge.

Gates, D. (1990a, March 19). Decoding rap music. *Newsweek*, p. 60.

Gates, D. (1990b, July 2). The importance of being nasty. *Newsweek*, p. 52.

Gates, D. (1990c, December 3). Play that packaged music. *Newsweek*, p. 68.

Giroux, H. & McLaren. P. (Eds.). (1989). *Critical pedagogy, the state, and cultural struggle*. Albany, NY: State University of New York Press.

hooks, bell. (1990). *Yearning: Race, gender, and cultural politics*. Boston, MA: South End Press.

hooks, bell. (1992). *Black looks: Race and representation*. Boston, MA: South End Press.

Information Please Almanac: Atlas and Yearbook. (1993). Boston: Houghton Mifflin.

Kinsley, M. (1992, July 20). Ice-T: Is the issue social responsibility. *Time*, p. 88.

Leland, J. (1991, July 1). Number one with a bullet. *Newsweek*, p. 63.

Leland, J. (1992a, May 11). The word on the street is heard in the beat. *Newsweek*, p. 53.

Leland, J. (1992b, June 29). Rap and race. *Newsweek*, p. 48.

Leland, J. (1992c, August 10). The iceman concedeth, *Newsweek*, p. 51.

Leland, J. (1992d, September 7). When rap meets reggae. *Newsweek*, p. 259.

Leo, J. (1990, July 2). Polluting our popular culture. *U.S. News and World Report*, p. 15.

Leo, J. (1992a, June 29). The lowdown on hip hop: Kids talk about the music. *Newsweek*, p. 50.

Leo, J. (1992b, June 29). Rap music's toxic fringe. *U.S. News and World Report*, p. 19.

Plagens, P. (1990, October 15). Mixed signals on obscenity: Mapplethorpe passes but 2 Live Crew doesn't. *Newsweek*, p. 74.

Rabey, S. (1991, June 24). Rhymin' and rappin' 4D King. *Christianity Today*, p. 13.

Rose, T. (1991). Fear of a black planet: Rap music and black cultural politics in the 1990s. *Journal of Negro Education*, 60, 32–77.

Samuels, D. (1991, November 11). The rap on rap. *The New Republic*, p. 25.

"Should dirty lyrics be against the law?" (1990, June 25). *U.S. News and World Report*, 24.

Stallybrass, P. & White, A. (1986). *The politcs and poetics of transgression*. Ithaca, NY: Cornell University Press.

Thigpen, D. (1991, May 27). Not for men only. *Time*, p. 71.

Van Den Toorn, P. (1991). Politics, feminism, and contemporary music theory. *The Journal of Musicology*, 9, 3, 275–299.

White, J. (1992, June 29). Sister Souljah: Capitalist tool. *Time*, p. 88.

Will, G. (1990, July 30). America's slide into the sewer. *Newsweek*, p. 64.

Zuckerman, M. (1992, June 29). The Sister Souljah affair. *U.S. News and World Report*, p. 80.

Representation of Women in News and Photos: Comparing Content to Perceptions

María E. Len-Ríos, Shelly Rodgers, Esther Thorson, and Doyle Yoon

María Len-Ríos, Shelly Rodgers, and Esther Thorson are all faculty members of the Strategic Communication Program at the University of Missouri's School of Journalism. Dr. Len-Ríos's research focuses on public perceptions and decision making, and she is particularly interested in Web site communication, health issues and underrepresented populations. Dr. Rodgers's work focuses on Internet advertising and promoting healthy behaviors. Professor Thorson serves as Associate Dean for Graduate Studies and Research, and Director of Research for the Reynolds Journalism Institute. Her research is concerned with health communication, advertising, the effects of news, and media economics. Doyle Yoon is an Assistant Professor at The Gaylord College of Journalism and Mass Communication at the University of Oklahoma. His research interests include cross-cultural Web-based communication, advertising and media effects, and brand advertising. This article was originally published in the *Journal of Communication*, a publication of the International Communication Association.

This study uses a feminist framework of masculine cultural hegemony to examine the representation of women in two newspapers—a medium-sized newspaper (Study 1) and a larger newspaper (Study 2). Surveys gauged news staff and news reader perceptions of female representation in news content to determine if perceptions matched content-analysis findings. Content-analysis results revealed a greater proportion of males than females in both content and photos for both studies. Female staffers were more likely than their male counterparts to perceive this disparity, and news readers perceived an even greater disparity than the news staff. News staffs were less likely to perceive disparities in the editorial, travel, and entertainment sections. We discuss the findings in relation to cultural hegemony and the representation of women in the news.

More than half of the U.S. population and labor force is female, yet women are often underrepresented in studies of news content (Greenwald, 1990; Potter, 1985; Rodgers & Thorson, 2000, 2003). One explanation for the underrepresentation of women is that reporters preserve hegemonic cultural norms. When journalists cover stories deemed newsworthy by political and societal elites, most of whom are males, journalists reproduce societal norms privileging men. This explanation supports feminist arguments that cultural hegemony is pervasive and accepted as commonplace (Danner & Walsh, 1999)—even in the newsroom.

Malhotra and Rogers (2000) defined cultural hegemony as "the phenomenon of a dominant and oppressive cultural order being adopted by a

This research was supported by a Ford Foundation grant to the Missouri School of Journalism. The authors thank Frances E. Gorman for her assistance in manuscript preparation. Correspondence should be addressed to María E. Len-Ríos, Missouri School of Journalism, University of Missouri-Columbia, 179A Gannett Hall, Columbia, MO 65211-1200; lenriosm@missouri.edu.

majority of people because of the ubiquitous nature of the mass media and advanced capitalism" (p. 410). If newspapers serve as the record of the day, yet underrepresent women, then they unwittingly contribute to public consent of masculine cultural hegemony. Women are thus symbolically excluded from an important cultural symbol of power. As Van Zoonen (1998) noted, "Because the news is made by men, it is thought to reflect the interests and values of men too" (p. 34). Therefore, news may often reflect and reinforce symbols of a patriarchal society.

This study examines the representation of women in newspaper content and compares it to the perceptions of news staff and readers to further explore the concept of masculine cultural hegemony. We compare content to perceptions rather than actual demographics because occupational statistics (e.g., the number of females in elite societal positions) tend to represent the outcomes of a patriarchal system. Rather, by examining both male and female perceptions, we get a better sense of attitudes toward the system and determine how well content matches perceptions. This is not to say actual demographics do not matter; they do. However, for our analysis, perceptions reflect fewer institutional biases than occupational statistics.

Fenton (2000) called for scholars to "examine production, content and reception as connected and integrated within transnational, national and personal socioeconomic realities and in a way that is manageable within the practical constraints of empirical research" (p. 724). We do so by using data triangulation from news staff perceptions (producers), news stories and photos (content), and newspaper readers' perceptions (reception) of the representation of women in the news of two newspapers, a medium-sized one (Study 1) and a larger one (Study 2).

THEORETICAL FRAMEWORK

5   The origin of the term "hegemony" can be traced back to the early 20th-century Italian Marxist Antonio Gramsci. Gramsci felt that the power of hegemony resided in the conformity to prescriptions developed by social institutions: "It follows that hegemony is the predominance obtained by *consent* rather than force of one class or group over other classes" (Femia, 1981, p. 24, emphasis in the original).

Hegemony is sustained through socialization (e.g., learned stereotypes) and also by societal structures (e.g., work hours, child care duties), which both work to preserve the class or group in power. Social psychology research on gender stereotypes supports the view that power relations are integral components of gender stereotypes. Carter, Branston, and Allan (1998) defined gender stereotypes as "standardized mental pictures which provide sexist judgments about women such that their subordinate status within patriarchal society is symbolically reinforced" (p. 6). In other words, stereotypes about women are used to keep women in subordinate roles.

A vast literature illustrates that women are perceived as more communal (e.g., caring, sensitive, giving) and that men are viewed as more instrumental (e.g., assertive, aggressive, dominant). As Van Zoonen (1998) observed, women in newsrooms often write stories that pertain to human interest, entertainment, or culture rather than to crime or politics.

Conway and Vartanian (2000) found that power is used to define gender and social status. Their study reinforces the idea that perceptions of gender and status, inextricably linked, perpetuate cultural hegemony. People associate masculinity with high status (i.e., power) and femininity with low status. Through cultural hegemony and learned stereotypes, men and women often choose stereotyped roles and assign them to others. Van Zoonen (1998) showed that female journalists believe topics of interest to women—"'human interest' news, consumer news, culture, education and upbringing, and social policy" (p. 35)—are often given short shrift. Hence female journalists, from Van Zoonen's view, select traditional female-stereotyped topics.

Cultural feminists view gender as a contrast of the intellectual-rational and the physical-emotional. They argue that the intellectual realm, historically, has supported the Caucasian male in a position of power, while society has defined women by their bodies (e.g., women serve to bear children). Thus, according to cultural feminists, men were masters of the mind and women's status was tied to the womb (Cirksena & Cuklanz, 1992). Naturally, news belongs to the realm of intellect—a realm created for man, not woman.

The news is indelibly linked to gender and 1(power. The newspaper claims to reflect societal reality and that of the world (Williams, 2002). Appearing in the newspaper is deemed special and noteworthy. Presence in the news relays and reinforces one's status. Those of higher social status appear more often in the news. Research also suggests that reporters cover social movements differently and reinforce a group's lower status. Some scholars argue that the underrepresentation of women in news coverage has been a male hegemonic response to the U.S. women's movement (Danner & Walsh, 1999; Malhotra & Rogers, 2000). By overlooking women, or marginalizing them as emotional radicals, news organizations assign them lower status and bar them from debate.

Feminist media scholars do not agree on how to achieve equal representation for women in news content. In fact, feminist philosophies differ on how to approach equality. U.S. feminists have preferred the radical or liberal feminist viewpoint (Walby, 1997). As Van Zoonen (1991) explained, liberal feminists argue that parity in public representation will ultimately lead to the acceptance of women in public life. Liberal feminists believe women can achieve equality through the current system (Rakow & Kranich, 1991), whereas radical feminists argue for societal changes (Walby, 1997).

We ground our argument in the middle of these feminist philosophies. We believe that equal representation is a precursor to greater equality, but that representation is a product of attitudes and beliefs ingrained by decades of cultural hegemony.

LITERATURE REVIEW

Many studies have found that women are underrepresented in news stories (Rodgers & Thorson, 2003; Rodgers, Thorson, & Antecol, 2001), front pages (Gibbons, 2000; Potter, 1985), the *New York Times Magazine* ("Marginalizing," 1996; Zoch & Turk, 1998), business sections (Davis, 1982; Greenwald, 1990), and news photographs (Blackwood, 1983; Miller, 1975; Rodgers & Thorson, 2000). In fact, Potter's study of newspapers from 1913, 1933, 1963, and 1983 found that the proportion of women portrayed decreased over time.

According to theories of cultural hegemony, the class or group that is in power works to preserve its power. If news represents the important events of the day and societal truth, then we would expect it to reflect a more masculine society and one that relies more on men to relay the "truth." Therefore, if masculine cultural hegemony is in effect, we expect to mirror previous findings that show women underrepresented in news stories and photos for both newspapers.

Based on the concept of cultural hegemony 15 and previous findings, the following hypothesis is proposed for both newspapers (Study 1 and Study 2):

> H1: There will be proportionally more males than females in news stories and news photographs.

The underrepresentation of women is connected to news production. Journalism classrooms are becoming predominantly female (Golombisky, 2002), yet the proportion of female journalists to male remains stable. Van Zoonen (1998) argued that "the gender of journalists is relatively unimportant for the way news looks" (p. 35), yet McLaughlin (1993) argued, "The media apparatus will not change until its workers learn to 'see' differently and to offer new 'ways of seeing'" (p. 615). Even though the number of women in the newsroom may increase, underrepresentation may still prevail.

Some studies have indicated that female journalists provide modest differences in story framing and source selection (Kahn & Goldberg, 1991; Zoch & Turk, 1998), whereas other studies have shown that female journalists do not differ greatly from their male colleagues (Lavie & Lehman, 2003; Merritt & Gross, 1978; Turk, 1987).

Kahn and Goldberg (1991, p. 195), in a content analysis, found that female reporters more often discuss stereotyped female traits (e.g., "passive," "gentle," "compassionate") when covering female senatorial candidates than they did to describe male candidates. This shows that female reporters characterized women more stereotypically than male reporters and supports psychological research that suggests we are socialized to choose stereotypical roles. Zoch and Turk (1998) studied 10 years of news in three Southern newspapers and showed that both male and female reporters tend to rely on official sources; however, female reporters cite female sources more frequently.

Conversely, in a study that compared male and female women's page editors at large metropolitan papers, Merritt and Gross (1978) found that both males and females selected traditional female-stereotyped content to include in the women's pages. Turk (1987) uncovered similar results through a quasi-experimental study on sexist bias in newswriting. She found no significant differences based on the reporter's or source's gender. Lavie and Lehman (2003) studied editors' story selection for seven Israeli newspapers and found few differences by gender in headline selection and importance given to news topics.

20   Van Zoonen (1994) suggested that "gender itself is not a sufficient factor to explain the professional performance and values of female journalists" (p. 55). Lavie and Lehman (2003) offered that a lack of gender differences may mean that women entering journalism self-select themselves for the profession and so have similarities with their male colleagues. The authors suggested that newspaper reading develops news values or that journalists aim to please readers by writing what they think readers want to read.

Rodgers and Thorson (2003) studied the representation of women in news stories in a small, a medium-sized, and a large newspaper. They found that female reporters used females as sources more often than male reporters did. They also discovered differences associated with the newspaper's size: Females working at larger newspapers were socialized to report stories similarly to their male colleagues more so than at smaller newspapers.

Because socialization is part of the larger process of cultural hegemony, we might expect that gender stereotypes and attitudes toward gender roles would lead reporters to represent men more in "masculine" news sections and women more in "feminine" sections. Studies have found that men substantially outnumber women in sports news (Davis, 1982, Rodgers & Thorson, 2000). Therefore, we posed the following research question:

> RQ1: Will females appear proportionately less often than men in stereotypically male sections of the newspaper (e.g., business and sports) and more often in stereotypically female sections of the newspaper (e.g., entertainment)? How will women be represented in "gender neutral" sections of the paper (e.g., front page, local)? Are the findings replicated for the larger newspaper (Study 2)?

To inform us of how news staffs perceive the representation of women in their newspapers, we asked the following research question:

> RQ2: How do male and female news staffs perceive the frequency with which females appear in news photos? What are their perceptions of the newspaper's coverage of females across news sections (Study 1)? Are the findings replicated for the larger newspaper (Study 2)?

Again, to examine if cultural hegemony affects news reader perceptions of each gender differently and to determine how news readers perceive the representation of women in newspapers, we asked the next research question:

> RQ3: Will male and female newspaper readers' perceptions of the representation of females in news photos, stories, and the business section differ (Study 1)? Are the findings replicated for the larger newspaper (Study 2)?

Our next research question compared process, 25 content, and reception. To study how representation is perceived, we focused on the most obvious symbol of representation in the newspaper: the news photo. When people read the newspaper, most often people view the photos even if they do not read the news stories (Blackwood, 1983). Photos have a greater impact on memory, as they break the monotony of the printed page. To address the perceptions of the representation of women in photos, we asked the following question:

> RQ4: How will the perceptions of both news staff and readers compare to the actual representation of females in news photos, as determined by content analysis (Study 1)? To what extent is this comparison replicated in the larger newspaper (Study 2)?

Our final research question addressed whether the perceptions of news staff have changed over time. Differences in staff attitudes by age may represent shifts in attitudes. If cultural hegemony has weakened over the years, younger news staff should think diversity is important in newsworthiness.

> RQ5: Is the age cohort of the news staff associated with perceptions of greater importance placed on diversity in news content?

The following section explains the methods used for our content analysis and surveys.

METHOD

This study used a triangulated approach, which involves using several different research methods and data to inspect the same basic principle (Babbie, 2001). Researchers use several methods to probe one issue in methodological triangulation and multiple data sets to get at a broader truth in data triangulation (Oppermann, 2000). This does not always entail asking the same question, but rather looking at the same phenomena from several vantage points. By using three data sources and two methods, we increased our external validity (Jick, 1979).

We used content analysis and telephone surveys as our primary methods. A medium-sized, midwestern U.S. newspaper (circ. about 200,000) was content analyzed in Study 1 and a census of the staff was conducted. Readers of the newspaper were selected for the telephone survey using a random-digit-dialing method. The same method was employed in Study 2, which replicated Study 1 using a larger, midwestern U.S. newspaper (circ. about 475,000). We use the labels Study 1 and Study 2 to distinguish between studies. All analyses use a .05 level of significance. Percentages are rounded.

Content Analysis

30 **Sample** A random sample of three constructed weeks (21 issues) was selected from February 1998 to March 1999 for Study 1. A similar sample was constructed during the same time period for Study 2. A constructed sample ensures that each day of the week is equally represented to control for differences due to special issues or days (e.g., Sunday) with more news. Two constructed weeks of a 1-year period is considered a sufficient sample to yield reliable estimates of local stories (Riffe, Aust, & Lacy, 1993, p. 139). However, because we coded all stories and photos, not just local stories, we examined a more conservative sample of 3 weeks for 1 year. Thus, we coded all news stories and photos for 21 issues each for Study 1 and Study 2.

Unit of Analysis and Intercoder Reliability

The individual was the unit of analysis for coding gender and role, and the entire section was the unit of analysis for coding newspaper sections. Three graduate students coded the variables. Coders achieved complete agreement on each variable, Scott's *pi*s of 1.0.

Coding Categories *Gender.* Gender was defined as the formal classification by which nouns are grouped and inflected or changed in form so as to reflect certain syntactic relationships. Nouns and third-person singular pronouns were distinguished according to sex. The coders determined gender by examining first names and/or looking for physical features to indicate gender in photos. When gender could not be determined (e.g., "Pat" or "Chris"), coders selected a "cannot tell" category.

Section. A newspaper section was defined as a distinct part or division of the newspaper separated from other distinct part(s) or division(s). There were seven sections identified: front, local, business, sports, editorial, entertainment (including the calendar of events section), and travel.

Telephone Surveys

Samples of News Staffs *Study 1.* A census of the newsroom, taken during July and August 1999, yielded 100 telephone surveys with newsroom staff at the medium-sized newspaper. The response rate was 62%. The average age of respondents was 40 (SD = 9.53). The sample was 52% male and 48% female. Of the news staff sample, 49% were reporters, 34% were editors, and 18% held other occupations (photographers, graphic designers, etc.).

Study 2. A total of 274 telephone surveys were conducted with newsroom staff at the large newspaper between August and October 1999. The census yielded a response rate of 77%. The average age of respondents was 43 (*SD* = 8.77). The sample was 60% male and 41% female. For news staff, 42% were reporters, 39% were editors, and 19% held other positions (photographers, graphic designers, etc.).

Compared with national newsroom statistics, our samples of daily staff were slightly more female. According to the 2000 Newsroom Census of the American Society of Newspaper Editors (ASNE), women constitute 40% of newsroom staff and about 37% of staff at dailies (2000, 2001). Surveys for both Study 1 and Study 2 were conducted by a professional research center at a university in the midwestern U.S.

Newspaper Reader Sample The survey center 35 also conducted 657 telephone interviews with newspaper readers between March and April

2000 using a random-digit-dialing method. Surveys of the news readers of both papers in Study 1 and Study 2 were conducted simultaneously. To categorize respondents as readers by newspaper, respondents were asked how many days a week they usually read newspaper X. Respondents who read the paper more than once a week were counted as readers. If they read more than one newspaper equally, they were randomly assigned to answer questions for one newspaper. The response rate was about 48%.

Demographics for the newspaper readers of Study 1 were as follows: Average age was 47 years old (SD = 15.29). The sample was 45% female, 55% male. According to the Audit Bureau of Circulation's 2002 reader profile (the closest date available for reader data), Study 1's readers are 52% female and 48% male. Our respondents were more male. Also, 56% of news readers were younger than 45 years old, so our sample was a little older.

Study 2 readers were an average of 45 years old (SD = 15.38). The sample was 51% female and 49% male. According to the Audit Bureau of Circulation's 2000–2001 reader profile, Study 2's readers are 51% female and 49% male. This matches our sample. In addition, the Audit Bureau reported that 58% of Study 2's readers are under the age of 45 and 42% of readers are older than 45, which is comparable to our sample's mean age.

VARIABLES OF INTEREST

Newspaper Staff Survey

The news staff survey addressed questions on the general representation and presence of females in the content of news stories, news photos, and newspaper sections.

Representation of Women Across Newspaper Sections On a scale of (1) *poor* to (5) *excellent,* the news staff was asked to respond to the following question: "How well do you think the following sections of the newspaper show the role of women in modern life?" The question was repeated for each of the following sections: front, local, business, sports, editorial, entertainment, and travel.

Frequency of Photo Coverage of Women Using a four-point Likert scale (strongly agree, somewhat agree, somewhat disagree, strongly disagree), respondents were asked their agreement with two statements: "Photos in [newspaper] show a good cross-section of men and women" and "A majority of photos are of men rather than women."

Importance of Diversity Considerations To answer RQ5, we used the same four-point Likert scale to record news staff responses to the following statement: "[Newspaper] should cover newsworthy events without diversity considerations." This question measured cultural attitudes.

Newspaper Reader Survey

Interviewers asked news readers to respond to the following items using the same four-point Likert scale that was used for the news staff.

Representation of Women in News Stories Perceived representation of females in news stories was measured in two ways: generally for the entire newspaper and specifically for one section of the newspaper. The statement, "A story in [newspaper] is just as likely to be about men as women," measured general perceptions of representativeness, whereas the statement, "There are just as many women as men featured in [newspaper's] business section" measured perceptions of representation for that specific section.

Representation of Women in News Photos Perceived representation of females in news photos was measured with the statement: "There aren't nearly as many photos of women in the [newspaper] as there are photos of men."

FINDINGS

Hypotheses

Hypothesis 1 predicted males would appear proportionally more than females in news stories and photos. This was confirmed in Study 1. Coders classified a total of 4,851 individuals in news stories. Of these, 79% (N = 3,825) were males, and 18% (N = 897) were females. Gender could not be identified for 3% (N = 129) of the individuals. A total of 2,193 were coded in news photographs, and of these, 67% (N = 1,459) were males and 30% (N = 663) were females. Three percent (N = 71) could not be identified.

A similar pattern emerged in Study 2; a total of 6,175 individuals were coded in news stories. Of these, 4,659 were males (75%), and 1,304 were females (21%). The gender of 212 individuals (3%) could not be identified. A total of 2,640 were coded in news photographs, and of these, 1,783 were males (68%) and 717 were females (27%). Gender could not be identified for 140 individuals (5%).

Research Questions

RQ1 addressed whether females appear proportionately less often than men in stereotypically male sections of the newspaper and more often in stereotypically female sections. We ran two separate chi-square analyses to study photos and text. To account for the large disparity in frequencies of men and women in news content, we examined text using proportions of total male or female appearances. From H1, we knew that women appear far less than men, but when they do appear, we wanted to know if they are more often stereotypically represented.

Looking at text first in Study 1, females (8%) appeared proportionally more than males (2%) in the entertainment section, a stereotypically female section. Females (8%) appeared proportionately less than males (9%) in the business and sports sections (F-9%, M-31%), stereotypically male sections. Table 1 shows the differences were statistically significant, $x^2(5, N = 4,719) = 319.18$, $p < .0001, r = -.11$. The same findings were revealed in Study 2. There were proportionally fewer

females (8%) than males (11%) in the business and sports (F-10% and M-26%) sections and proportionally more females (10%) than males (4%) in the entertainment section. As with Study 1, the differences were statistically significant $x^2(5, N = 5,963) = 299.47, p < .05, r = -.03$. In "gender neutral" sections of the paper, females appeared proportionally more often in local sections for both Study 1 and Study 2, although there were mixed findings for the front section (see Table 1). Examination of frequencies shows that women appear substantially less often in all sections except the entertainment section.

In news photos, a similar pattern of findings emerged. There were proportionally fewer females (9%) than males (31%) in the sports but not the business (F-6%, M-6%) section and proportionally more females (16%) than males (9%) in the entertainment section (see Table 2). Again, these differences were statistically significant, $x^2(5, N = 2,117) = 156.20, p < .0001, r = .003$. Thus, RQ1 was supported in Study 1 in all instances that were examined except one (business photos). In "gender neutral" sections of the paper, women were proportionally represented almost as often as men in photos in the front sections and proportionally more often in the local

TABLE 1 Percentage of Males and Females in News Content for Different Newspaper Sections

Section	Study 1				Study 2			
	M%	*(N)*	*F%*	*(N)*	*M%*	*(N)*	*F%*	*(N)*
Front	34%	(1297)	37%	(327)	37%	(1739)	34%	(442)
Local	17%	(664)	34%	(305)	19%	(881)	33%	(425)
Business	9%	(359)	8%	(68)	11%	(502)	8%	(107)
Sports	31%	(1186)	9%	(79)	26%	(1204)	10%	(127)
Entertainment	2%	(68)	8%	(67)	4%	(179)	10%	(124)
Other	7%	(249)	4%	(50)	3%	(154)	5%	(79)
TOTAL	100%	(3823)	100%	(896)	100%	(4659)	100%	(1304)

For Study 1: $x^2 = 319.18, df = 5, p < .0001, r = -.11$.

For Study 2: $x^2 = 299.47, df = 5, p < .05, r = -.03$.

TABLE 2 Percentage of Males and Females in News Photos for Different Newspaper Sections

	Study 1				Study 2			
Section	*M%*	*(N)*	*F%*	*(N)*	*M%*	*(N)*	*F%*	*(N)*
Front	26%	(373)	25%	(164)	27%	(480)	28%	(202)
Local	3%	(183)	24%	(156)	14%	(253)	19%	(139)
Business	6%	(90)	6%	(41)	4%	(75)	3%	(21)
Sports	31%	(450)	9%	(57)	32%	(569)	9%	(64)
Entertainment	9%	(131)	16%	(105)	14%	(249)	28%	(200)
Other	15%	(227)	21%	(140)	9%	(156)	13%	(90)
TOTAL	100%	(1454)	100%	(663)	100%	(1782)	100%	(716)

For Study 1: $x^2 = 156.20$, $df = 5$, $p < .0001$, $r = .003$.

For Study 2: $x^2 = 180.81$, $df = 5$, $p < .01$, $r = .06$.

sections. However, frequencies show men were represented substantially more often across all categories except for the entertainment section.

Similar findings were revealed in Study 2. There were proportionally fewer females (3%) than males (4%) in photos in the business and sports (F-9%, M-32%) sections and proportionally more females (28%) than males (14%) in photos in the entertainment section $x^2(5, N= 2,498) = 180.81$, $p < .01$, $r = .06$ (see Table 2).

RQ2 examined whether male and female news staffs' perceptions differ in the frequency and representation of females in photos and across newspaper sections. Our findings revealed that more female (72%) than male (60%) staff agreed that a majority of news photos were of men. Males were more likely to strongly disagree (M-24%, F-4%). A chi-square analysis revealed a significant difference, $x^2(3, n = 92) = 8.66$, $p= .034$, $r= .29$. Female staffers were more likely than males to rate the coverage of females poorer for every news section examined. Table 3 shows the differences were statistically significant for all sections except editorial, M: $M = 3.49$, $SD= 0.99$; F: $M = 3.16$, $SD = 1.02$), $t(94) = 1.63$, $p = .11$ (two-tailed), $r = .17$,

power $= .37$, and travel, M: $M = 3.65$, $SD = 1.0$; F: $M = 3.33$, $SD = 0.77$), $t(74) = 1.51$, $p = .14$ (two-tailed), $r = .17$, power $= .32$.

Study 2, which replicated Study 1, revealed similar findings. Overall, female staff (74%) agreed more than male staff (54%) that a majority of photos were of men, $x^2(3, n= 267) = 15.956$, $p= .001$, $r=.23$. Female staffers were more likely than male staff to rate the coverage of females as poorer for every section except travel, M: $M = 3.76$, $SD=0.91$; F: $M = 3.82$, $SD = 0.92$), $t(243) = -.49$, $p = .62$ (two-tailed), $r = .03$, although the differences were only significant for the front, business, and sports sections (see Table 4). No differences were found of perceptions of women in the local, M: $M = 3.51$, $SD= 0.75$; F: $M = 3.35$, $SD = 0.91$), $t(237) = 1.52$, $p= .13$ (two-tailed), $r = .09$, power $= .34$; editorial, M: $M = 3.58$, $SD = 0.91$; F: $M= 3.41$, $SD = 0.95$), $t(256) = 1.47$, $p = .14$ (two-tailed), $r = .09$, power $= .31$; or entertainment sestions, M: $M = 3.88$, $SD = 0.90$; F: $M = 3.73$, $SD = 0.81$), $t(267) = 1.32$, $p = .19$ (two-tailed), $r = .08$, power $= .26$.

RQ3 had three parts. First, RQ3 asked whether news reader gender was associated with perceptions of how frequently females appeared

TABLE 3   Mean Differences of Staff Perceptions by Gender and News Section for Study 1

News section	Male	Female	df	t	r	power
Front	3.42 (0.80) n = 52	3.02 (0.90) n= 47	97	2.36*	.23	.65
Local	3.56 (0.75) n = 52	3.21 (0.91) n= 47	97	2.07*	.21	.53
Business	3.63 (1.13) n = 51	3.13 (1.22) n= 46	95	2.08*	.21	.54
Sports	3.08 (1.25) n = 52	2.40 (1.04) n= 42	92	2.80**	.28	.79
Editorial	3.49 (0.99) n = 51	3.16 (1.02) n= 45	94	1.63	.17	.37
Travel	3.65 (1.00) n = 43	3.33 (0.77) n= 33	74	1.51	.17	.32
Entertainment	3.78 (0.88) n = 52	3.26 (1.00) n= 47	96	2.80**	.28	.79

Note. Mean scores are based on a five-point scale where 5 = excellent and 1 = poor. Standard deviations are in parentheses.

$* < .05$, two-tailed. $** < .01$, two-tailed.

TABLE 4   Mean Differences of Staff Perceptions by Gender and News Section for Study 2

News section	Male	Female	df	t	r	power
Front	3.52 (0.75) n= 162	3.14 (0.92) n= 111	271	3.69**	.22	.96
Local	3.51 (0.75) n= 162	3.35 (0.91) n= 111	237	1.52	.09	.34
Business	3.29 (1.13) n= 159	2.88 (1.22) n= 105	262	3.52**	.21	.94
Sports	2.90 (1.05) n= 162	2.04 (0.98) n= 105	265	6.67**	.38	1.0
Editorial	3.58 (0.91) n= 153	3.41 (0.95) n= 105	256	1.47	.09	.31
Travel	3.76 (0.91) n= 141	3.82 (0.92) n= 104	243	-0.49	.03	.08
Entertainment	3.88 (0.90) n= 160	3.73 (0.81) n= 109	267	1.32	.08	.26

Note. Mean scores are based on a five-point scale where 5 = excellent and 1= poor. Standard deviations are in parentheses.

$* < .05$, two-tailed. $** < .01$, two-tailed.

in news photos. Study 1 survey findings showed that more female (48%) than male (38%) readers agreed that women were less often in photos, $x^2(3, n = 272) = 9.1, p = .05, r = -.15$. A similar finding emerged in Study 2. More female (60%) than male (48%) readers agreed there were not nearly as many photos of women as men, $x^2(3, n = 582) = 17.55, p = .001, r = -.15$.

The second part of RQ3 examined whether male and female readers' perceptions would differ with regard to the number of females relative to males in stories. The survey in Study 1 showed that more male (80%) than female (75%) readers agreed that news stories were as likely to be about males as females, although the differences were not statistically significant, $x^2(3, n = 311) = 2.10, p = .55, r = .06$. A similar pattern emerged in Study 2. More male (73%) than female (64%) readers agreed that a story in the newspaper was just as likely to be about men as women, $x^2(3, n = 632) = 26.73, p < .001, r = .08$.

55 The third part of RQ3 asked whether male and female readers perceived differences in the representation of women in the business section. There were no significant differences between genders in either study, Study 1: $x^2(3, n = 282) = .90, p = .83, r = .03$; Study 2: $x^2(3, n = 591) = 3.61, p = .31, r = .05$. However, 46% of newspaper readers in Study 1 and more than 58% in Study 2 agreed that the business sections represented women less than men.

RQ4 compared the perceptions of news staffs and news readers of female representations with the actual content. This was accomplished by examining the percentage of individuals who either strongly agreed or disagreed with survey items. Two anchors were used to simplify the analysis, allowing for comparison of perceived representations from the survey to actual representations from content analysis.

The content analysis revealed a greater number of males than females in both text and photos for both newspapers, that is, Study 1 revealed a 4-to-1 male to female ratio in news text and a 2-to-1 male to female ratio in news photos. In other words, the "actual" representation of gender was skewed toward males. This finding was replicated in Study 2. With this baseline in mind, we examined whether news staff and news readers sense a similar disproportionate weighting toward males. To accomplish this, we studied survey items about representation of women in news photos—the most read and salient news features.

The news staffs in Study 1 were more likely to strongly agree (23%) than strongly disagree (4%) that their newspaper showed a good cross section of men and women in news photos. The news readers in Study 1 strongly agreed less (13%) and strongly disagreed (12%) more than news staff that there were as many females as males in news photos. News staff thought they represented women well in news photos whereas news readers agreed less.

A similar pattern emerged in Study 2. News staff strongly agreed (28%) more than disagreed (4%) that their newspaper showed a good cross section of males and females. However, the news readers in Study 2 strongly agreed less (13%) and strongly disagreed (12%) more that there were as many photos of women as men. So again, more news staff perceived they were doing a good job representing women in news photos, whereas news readers were more likely to disagree. Put another way, news readers' perceptions seem more consistent with actual representation than news staffs' perceptions because females were clearly found to be underrepresented.

Our fifth and final research question 60 addressed news staff perceptions of the importance of diversity in news coverage by age cohort. As noted previously, cultural hegemony is thought to represent cultural attitudes shaped partly by socialization. As culture changes, we may expect to see a shift by age. In Study 1, news staffs responded to whether they should cover newsworthy events without regard to diversity. We ran simple cross tabulations with age cohort (18–45 and > 45) and agreement. The chi-square was significant $x^2(3, N = 93) = 10.91, p = .012, r = .17$. For the news staff in Study 1, older staff members agreed (76%) more than younger staff (45%) that newsworthy events should be covered without consideration of diversity. The same analysis was conducted for Study 2 and replicated Study 1 to a smaller extent $x^2(3, N = 257) = 11.54, p < .01, r = .15$. Fifty-seven percent of those 18 to 45 agreed and 65% of those older than 45 agreed. It appears that older news staff believe diversity should be less of an issue when deciding if a story is newsworthy than do younger news staff.

DISCUSSION

Based on the content analyses of both Study 1 and Study 2, we can conclude that the newspapers studied here reflect the masculine cultural hegemony that prevails in U.S. culture. About three quarters of the individuals in news stories were men. Additionally, about two thirds of photos featured men. By providing men more of the news hole, journalists confer power to men. Although we have focused on gender, similar findings have been found concerning class, age, and ethnicity/race (Rodgers & Thorson, 2003). Can women achieve equality without equal representation in the U.S. cultural symbols of societal power? Even if women touted an alternative press, "separate but equal" may still not change the power differential.

Our findings for Study 1, echoed in Study 2, show that newspapers also sustain gender stereotypes by showing women in more "feminine" news sections and men in more "masculine" sections. We also found exceptions. Women appeared proportionately the same in business photos in Study 1, and the frequency of women and men in the entertainment sections was nearly equal, although women appeared proportionately more. Furthermore, staffs thought coverage of females was poorer in most sections except editorial, travel, and entertainment. Staffs knew they represented women in entertainment—a female-stereotyped section.

In regard to sports, both content and perceptions were in the same direction, suggesting that socialization and institutional structures (more male access to organized sports) may contribute to differences and stereotyped news coverage.

More than half of all news staff reported that news photos were more often of men rather than women. In Study 1, more than two thirds of staff reported a majority of photos were of men, with female staffers agreeing significantly more than men. Female staffers in Study 2 agreed nearly one fifth more than male staffers that a majority of photos were of men. This suggests that female staffers notice underrepresentation more than men.

When compared, news readers in both studies agreed less than news staff that women appeared equally in news photographs. Readers' perceptions more closely matched news content than those of news staff. Society has changed over time as women in the workforce have increased; however, the number of women in the newsroom has remained steady. Statistics in 1999 from the Bureau of Labor showed 73% of women and 84% of men worked in the metropolitan areas where the newspapers in this study are located. Our findings may reflect cultural differences based on differences in workforce experiences between staffers and readers.

We found age was an important moderator of news staffs' perceptions of the importance of diversity considerations. This finding suggests that as younger generations move through the newsroom hierarchy, cultural socialization (e.g., up-bringing, journalism education) may change newsroom attitudes if individuals shape a new form of newsroom socialization.

By examining news content, news staff, and news reader perceptions, we have provided a broader picture of how news represents women. Triangulation has offered us a look at the issues from different perspectives. We have studied similar questions in two newspapers to see if the findings affirm our theoretical perspective. In line with our theory, we found underrepresentation and gender stereotyping, and that news readers are more likely to perceive these problems.

Our study has its limitations. The two midwestern U.S. newspapers we studied may not be representative of others. Our survey measures were single-item measures. Future studies should use multiple-item constructs. In addition, our data were staggered. We first examined news content, then newsroom perceptions, and finally news reader perceptions. It could be that there were changes in content and perceptions between study times that affected the results. It is also possible that the newspapers changed substantially over the past 5 years. However, with stable newsroom demographics, with research spanning several decades indicating similar results, and with little culture shift in the United States, we believe masculine cultural hegemony would still be supported today. If news readers and staff are continually socialized to see certain types of news as gendered, then there is little expectation for change. Consistent with feminist theory, future research should use qualitative techniques to track cross-cultural training and news-room socialization to determine how they actually influence newsroom decisions.

The American Press Institute and the Pew Center for Civic Journalism (2002) may shed additional light on this issue. They have found that news staffs of both genders held similar attitudes, but identified "career-conflicted" and "career-confident" women. The authors suggest that career-conflicted news staffers worry about sexism and lack of opportunity and are less satisfied, whereas career-confident women expect to remain in journalism and have strong mentors. The results show some female staffers to be concerned about gender stereotyping and opportunities, whereas others had mentors to help them, perhaps allowing them to work better within the system.

Bridge (1994, p. 18) suggested that media "reflect cultural behavior and attitudes" and "influence such trends." For newspapers to stop perpetuating masculine hegemony, news staffs and readers must recognize their part in perpetuating the dominant power structure.

References

American Press Institute and the Pew Center for Civic Journalism. (2002, September 26). *The great divide: Female leadership in U.S. newsrooms.* Retrieved November 18, 2003, from http:// www.pewcenter.org/doingcj/research/r_apipewstudy.pdf

American Society of Newspaper Editors (ASNE). (2000, April 12). *Newsroom employment drops again; diversity gains.* Retrieved April 24, 2004, from http://www.asne.org/index.cfm?ID=1458

American Society of Newspaper Editors (ASNE). (2001, April 3). *2001 ASNE census finds newsrooms less diverse: Increased hiring of minorities blunted by departure rate.* Retrieved April 24, 2004, from http://www.asne.org/kiosk/diversity/2001Survey/2001CensusReport.htm

Babbie, E. (2001). *The practice of social research* (9th ed.). Belmont, CA: Wadsworth/Thomson Learning.

Blackwood, R. E. (1983). The content of news photos: Roles portrayed by men and women. *Journalism Quarterly, 60,* 710–714.

Bridge, J. (1994, January). The media mirror: Reading between the (news) lines. *The Quill, 22,* 18–19.

Carter, C., Branston, G., & Allan, S. (1998). Setting new(s) agendas: An introduction. In C. Carter, G. Branston, & S. Allen (Eds.), *News, gender and power* (pp. 1–9). London: Routledge.

Cirksena, K., & Cuklanz, L. (1992). Male is to female as _____ is to _____: A guided tour of five feminist frameworks for communication studies. In L. Rakow (Ed.), *Women making meaning: New feminist directions in communication* (pp. 18–44). New York: Routledge.

Conway, M., & Vartanian, L. R. (2000). A status account of gender stereotypes: Beyond communality and agency. *Sex Roles, 43,* 181–199.

Danner, L., & Walsh, S. (1999). "Radical" feminists and "bickering" women: Backlash in U.S. media coverage of the United Nations Fourth World Conference on Women. *Critical Studies in Mass Communication, 16,* 63–84.

Davis, J. (1982). Sexist bias in eight newspapers. *Journalism Quarterly, 59,* 456–460.

Femia, J. V. (1981). *Gramsci's political thought: Hegemony, consciousness, and the revolutionary process.* Oxford, UK: Clarendon Press.

Fenton, N. (2000). The problematics of postmodernism for feminist media studies. *Media, Culture and Society, 22,* 723–741.

Gibbons, S. J. (2000, Fall). News analysis: Women still don't rate in *The New York Times* coverage, *Media Report to Women, 28,* 5.

Golombisky, K. (2002). Gender equity and mass communication's female student majority. *Journalism & Mass Communication Educators, 57,* 53–66.

Greenwald, M. S. (1990). Gender representation in newspaper business sections. *Newspaper Research Journal, 11,* 68–73.

Jick, T. D. (1979). Mixing qualitative and quantitative methods: Triangulation in action. *Administrative Science Quarterly, 24,* 602–611.

Kahn, K. F., & Goldberg, E. N. (1991). Women candidates in the news: An examination of gender differences in U.S. senate campaign coverage. *Public Opinion Quarterly, 55,* 180–199.

Lavie, A., & Lehman-Wilzig, S. (2003). Whose news? Does gender determine the editorial product? *European Journal of Communication, 18,* 5–29.

Malhotra, S., & Rogers, E. M. (2000). Satellite television and the new Indian woman. *Gazette, 62,* 407–429.

Marginalizing women: Front-page news coverage of females declines in 1996. (1996). *St. Louis Journalism Review, 26, 5,* 11.

McLaughlin, L. (1993). Feminism, the public sphere, media and democracy. *Media, Culture and Society, 15,* 599–620.

Merritt, S., & Gross, H. (1978). Women's page/lifestyle editors: Does sex make a difference? *Journalism Quarterly, 55,* 508–514.

Miller, S. H. (1975). The content of news photos: Women's and men's roles. *Journalism Quarterly, 42,* 70–75.

Oppermann, M. (2000). Triangulation—A methodological discussion. *International Journal of Tourism Research, 2,* 141–146.

Potter, W. J. (1985). Gender representation in elite newspapers. *Journalism Quarterly, 62,* 636–640.

Rakow, L. F., & Kranich, K. (1991). Woman as sign in television news. *Journal of Communication, 41,* 8–23.

Riffe, D., Aust, C. F., & Lacy, S. R. (1993). The effectiveness of random, consecutive day and constructed week sampling in newspaper content analysis. *Journalism Quarterly, 70,* 133–139.

Rodgers, S., & Thorson, E. (2000). "Fixing" stereotypes in news photos: A synergistic approach with the *Los Angeles Times. Visual Communication Quarterly, 55(7),* 8–11.

Rodgers, S., & Thorson, E. (2003). A socialization perspective on male and female reporting. *Journal of Communication, 53(4),* 658–675.

Rodgers, S., Thorson, E., & Antecol, M. (2001). "Reality" in the *St. Louis Post-Dispatch. Newspaper Research Journal, 21(3),* 51–68.

Turk, J. V. (1987). Sex-role stereotyping in writing the news. *Journalism Quarterly, 64,* 613–617.

Van Zoonen, L. (1991). A tyranny of intimacy? Women, femininity, and television news. In P. Dahlgren & C. Sparks (Eds.), *Communication and citizenship: Journalism and the public sphere in the new media age* (pp. 217–235). London: Routledge.

Van Zoonen, L. (1994). *Feminist media studies.* London: Sage.

Van Zoonen, L. (1998). One of the girls? The changing gender of journalism. In C. Carter, G. Branston, & S. Allen (Eds.), *News, gender and power* (pp. 33–46) London: Routledge.

Walby, S. (1997). *Theorizing patriarchy.* Oxford, UK: Blackwell.

Williams, J. H. (2002). The purposes of journalism. In W. D. Sloan & L. M. Parcell (Eds.), *American journalism: History, principles, practices* (pp. 3–13). Jefferson, NC: McFarland.

Zoch, L. M., & Turk, J. V. (1998). Women making news: Gender as a variable in source selection and use. *Journalism & Mass Communication Quarterly, 75,* 762–775.

Common Landscapes as Historic Documents

Peirce Lewis

Peirce Lewis is Professor Emeritus of Geography at Pennsylvania State University. Dr. Lewis has graduate degrees in geography and history and studied American rural and urban landscapes for four decades before his retirement. He is particularly interested in how ordinary people shape their landscape, the American love of transportation, and transportation technologies. Professor Lewis served on many editorial boards, and was awarded prizes for his scholarship and his teaching. This essay was originally published in *History from Things: Essays in Material Culture* which arose from a conference at the Smithsonian in 1989 that focused on how scholars from different disciplines used objects to understand the past.

Tangible objects form a challenging and stubborn kind of historic record. They challenge us because they are there—and because we know, as an article of faith, that those objects have meaning, if we are only clever enough to decipher it. They are stubborn because they simply refuse to go away, by their very presence demanding to be interpreted. To human geographers no form of material artifact is more stubborn, more tantalizing, or potentially more illuminating than the vast disorderly collection of human artifacts that constitute the cultural landscape.

The idea is simple to define but daunting in the enormity of its scope. By *cultural landscape* geographers mean the total assemblage of visible things that human beings have done to alter the face of the earth—their shapings of the earth with mines and quarries and dams and jetties; the ubiquitous purposeful manipulation of the earth's vegetative cover in farms, forests, lawns, parks, and gardens; the things humans build on the earth, cities and towns, houses and barns, factories and office buildings; the spaces we create for worship and for play. Cultural landscape includes the roads and machines we build to transport objects and ideas, the fences and walls we erect to subdivide land into manageable units and separate portions of the earth from one another, the monuments we build to celebrate ourselves, our institutions, our heroes, and our ancestors. Cultural landscape, in short, is everything that humans do to the natural earth for whatever purpose but most commonly for material profit; aesthetic pleasure, spiritual fulfillment, personal comfort, or communal safety.[1]

Human landscapes differ in appearance from place to place for the self-evident reason that all cultures have certain collective ambitions about the way the world should operate and because they possess peculiar means of achieving those goals of profit, pleasure, and safety. Simply because cultures are peculiar, their landscapes are peculiar too. And, of course, because cultures change through time, their landscapes also change. Those landscapes become in effect a kind of document, a kind of cultural autobiography that humans have carved and continue to carve into the surface of the earth.

It follows, necessarily, that if landscape is a document, we ought to be able to read it in a manner analogous to the way we read written documents. We are driven to try to read the language of landscape partly because it is the primary evidence created by people who often left behind no written records of their day-to-day activities and partly because there is so much of it that the validity of its messages can be tested by that most powerful of tests—internal consistency. It does not follow, however, that cultural landscape is an easy document to read, nor does it follow that it is complete. It was, after all, not meant to be read, nor are people accustomed to reading it. Large parts of the document are missing (especially the older parts), and our contemporaries are constantly messing with what remains—altering it, erasing it, redesigning it. Cultural landscape has many of the qualities of a gigantic palimpsest, a huge ragged informal document written by a host of people with various levels of literacy, repeatedly erased and amended by people with different motives and different tools at their disposal. Rarely, however, did the creators of landscape think of themselves as writing a document, nor did they suspect that anyone would try to read it. This quality of artlessness is, to a large degree, what makes cultural landscape such a rich document but also such a valuable one.

5   But how can one learn to read cultural landscape? What can one expect to learn from the exercise? And how can one test the validity of ideas based on evidence from that landscape?

LEARNING BY DOING: READING THE LANDSCAPE OF A SMALL TOWN

I have been wrestling with these problems for more than twenty years. Every year at Pennsylvania State University I teach an introductory course on the American cultural landscape to a hundred or so undergraduate students, none of them tutored in these matters.[2] The students come from all over campus—from architecture and landscape architecture, mathematics and history, electrical engineering and dairy husbandry; they are, in effect, a random grab from the population of a very large public university. It has not occurred to many of those students that landscape is something other than a disorderly assemblage of miscellaneous objects. To most of them landscape is merely something to cast their eyes across—sometimes in approval, sometimes in disgust—but most often to take for granted, except when particular items in the landscape impinge on ordinary day-to-day life—the location of dormitories and classrooms and dining halls, the pattern of streets and paths that lead most efficiently to a favorite bookstore or disco or pizza joint or romantic liaison. Except under unusual circumstances most students view ordinary landscape simply as a time-consuming obstacle that lies between where they are and where they want to be, to be crossed as quickly as possible but otherwise ignored. It almost never occurs to those students—as it almost never occurs to most Americans—to look at that landscape questioningly, to inquire how it came to be, to ask

what it has to tell us about the folk who made it: ourselves and our cultural ancestors.

My job with those students is simple to state but not so easy to execute: to persuade them that landscape can be read and that the enterprise is worth undertaking. Most students are skeptical of both propositions. They do not believe that landscape can be read, partly because it has never occurred to them but, more important, because they have never seen anybody do it. It has never occurred to them that the human landscape can be viewed as a form of cultural autobiography—a source of ideas and information about themselves and their society that is often hard to obtain in other ways.

Over a good many years of teaching the course I have discovered only one effective means of persuading them, and that is to take them physically into that landscape and show them during the course of a one-day field trip what a finite bit of that world has to teach them. Before we sally forth, I ask them to arm themselves with a bit of vocabulary, having mainly to do with the history of American architecture and building technology, and then follow me around for a day while we jointly ask questions about what we see, trying to get some reasonable answers and trying, insofar as we can, to test those answers to see if they are valid.

The place we go to try out these ideas is a small town about a dozen miles from my university campus, a place called Bellefonte, Pennsylvania. Its population is not quite ten thousand, so it is small enough that the mind can get around it and the eye can grasp it as a whole. But it is complex enough to be challenging and old enough (it was founded about two hundred years ago) to contain a good deal of historical diversity. Like many small towns, it does a fair variety of things. It is the county seat of Centre County, and it has been an economic and social hub for a good-sized and fairly prosperous farming district. From time to time it has had its share of manufacturing, chiefly a lively iron industry that flourished for much of the nineteenth century. In sum, it is fairly typical of many semianonymous small American towns.[3]

This essay is a vicarious trip to Bellefonte and   10 is aimed to demonstrate a few things that a common American landscape can reveal. There is some risk in trying to do this. To condense into a short printed essay what takes about eight hours of constant looking and talking and thinking to show the students obviously runs some risk of caricature. And a few black-and-white illustrations cannot really do justice to the multicolored three-dimensional variety and complexity of the real landscape. (Indeed, photographs taken from a single perspective and framed by linear borders cannot help but pull things out of context, something that one constantly seeks to avoid in an enterprise where context is crucial to the understanding of the subject.) But, at the risk of caricaturing the town or, even worse, caricaturing the act of landscape reading, what follows is a small sample of the things one can see on a one-day excursion into the ordinary cultural landscape of an American small town.

PUTTING THINGS IN CONTEXT: THREE LEVELS OF MAGNIFICATION

If there is a single rule about the interpretation of landscape (or any other artifact for that matter), it is, I submit, to view it in its context of place and time — of geography and history, if you please. Context, of course, is what pathologists look for when they examine cells under a microscope at a low level of magnification but with a large field of vision. Before looking at the details of a cell, pathologists want to see where the cell is, what kind of tissue is around it. Only when they understand that are they ready to increase the level of magnification and look in detail at the cell's internal anatomy.

We approach Bellefonte in the same way by getting two composite bird's-eye views of the town from nearby hilltops — one at a considerable distance, another closer in. Only then do we descend into the streets of the town for a final close-up look.

Fortunately for this exercise, Bellefonte is a fairly hilly place, and a good view of the town can be had from several hilltops nearby. That is not always the case, of course, and that is why students of landscape typically start an exercise of this kind by seeking out a vantage point — a high building or firetower perhaps — to obtain a composite view of the place to be studied. Maps and aerial photographs, of course, serve much the same purpose (Figure 1). At various scales they are wonderfully useful devices to help us simplify and generalize our ideas about large complicated places and, above all, to see them in their larger geographic context.

Two Views from a Distance

From the top of a hill in the prosperous farmland outside Bellefonte one can get a sweeping view of the town and its surroundings (Figure 2). Even at this low level of magnification one can make some educated guesses about the place. The town commands the entrance of a gap in a mountain ridge where a little stream has cut a notch through that ridge. It requires little imagination to guess that the town's prosperity, such as it is, has derived from command of transportation routes through that gap. Prima facie the town seems to be a market center and, one is inclined to guess, a social center too, like so many other American towns that grew up at the junction of roads. What else it may be this distant view does not reveal, but it invites questions that can be answered only by stepping up the level of magnification and getting a closer view of the town.

From a second hilltop, Half Moon Hill, a knoll that overlooks the railroad station and commercial district, one can make out the general outlines of the town's main industrial, commercial, and residential districts. In the foreground, along Spring Creek and the railroad tracks, is a string of large nineteenth-century industrial buildings, many apparently in an advanced state of decay. (We wonder about what kind of industry flourished there and why it is no more, and we remind ourselves to take a closer look at the banks of the creek when we descend into the town.) On the edge of that industrial district, also near the creek, is the railroad station. The town's main street, High Street, leads uphill from the railroad to the courthouse, a commanding white building with a self-consciously classical porch. Much of the commercial district is strung out along High Street between the railroad station and courthouse. Even at this distance one suspects that those two buildings served as functional anchors — politics at one end of the street, commerce at the other. Indeed, from the hilltop one can make out two bulky hotels: one (the Bush House) across the street from the railroad station, the other (the Brockerhoff) across the street from the courthouse. One is inclined to guess that the railroad hotel might have served commercial travelers — drummers and the like. Equally, it seems plausible that the courthouse hotel was the seat of a good deal of unofficial political activity.

On the hills beyond the commercial district rises the town's main residential area. Even from this distant hilltop there is evidence of residential segregation. To the left (the north side of town) the residential area is a bosky kind of place, and one can spot the characteristic profile of Norway spruces, a tree much beloved by high-style romantic landscape designers of the late nineteenth-century in

FIGURE 1   Maps are singularly useful devices not merely to show where things are located but also to place them in their geographic contexts. This figure is excerpted from the U.S. Geological Survey's 1908 "Bellefonte, Pennsylvania, Quadrangle" (1:62, 500) and shows the town's location with respect to Bald Eagle Mountain, which bisects the map WSW-ENE. Notice the funneling of roads, railroads, and waterways through the water-gap carved by Spring Creek between Milesburg and Bellefonte. All photographs in this chapter by Peirce Lewis.

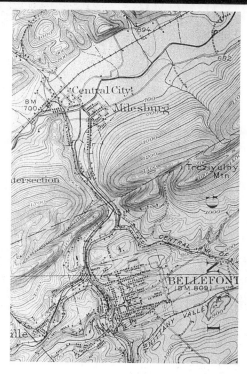

America. This man-made forest is punctured by several church steeples and mansard roofs, green with verdigris—signs of Victorian money and Victorian good taste. To the right (the south side of town), however, the residential area of Bellefonte is substantially different, even though it lies about the same distance from the center of town and one presumes that it was built about the same time. Landscaping is scantier, and the fashionable late Victorian architecture is totally absent. From the hilltop it is hard to make out much detail, but most of the houses on the south side of town are blocky, unadorned, rectangular two-story houses—the I-houses and watered-down Georgians that had been fashionable in colonial and early national Pennsylvania but had gone out of style among the affluent elite by the time of the Civil War (Figure 3).[4] In short, the north side of Bellefonte was keeping up nicely with late nineteenth-century national styles,

as one would expect in the establishment part of town (Figure 4). But Victorian fashion evidently did not reach the south side, and one is led to guess at a substantial schism between the establishment north side and the working-class south side. To be sure, both are parts of the same town, but one suspects that they occupied two very different worlds—different incomes, different ethnic backgrounds, different religions, and different social structures.

Later on, when we descend into the town, those guesses will be corroborated. The fashionable churches of north-side Bellefonte are all establishment Protestant denominations, while the churches of south-side Bellefonte are Roman Catholic and fundamentalist Protestant. We will also learn, later on, when we read the gravestones in the Catholic cemetery in the middle of south-side Bellefonte, that most of those Catholics are late nineteenth-century

FIGURE 2 Panoramic view of Bellefonte from a hilltop about a mile south of town. Rising beyond the town is Bald Eagle Mountain, broken by the water gap carved by Spring Creek (left middleground). The command of routes through the gap gave Bellefonte its economic and social reason for being; like most American cities and towns, it prospered because it commanded a route junction.

arrivals: mainly Irish, Germans, and most recently Italian. Most of those Italians, we can learn from conversations on the street, came from the *Mezzogiorno* (Calabria, mainly) and Sicily. That was desperately poor country in the late nineteenth century, of course, and one guesses that those southern Italians who came to Bellefonte were poor folk, hardly people who were plugged into the town's middle-class Protestant society. By contrast, we can get some flavor of the non-Catholic side of town (again later on) by reading the names on Bellefonte's imposing Civil War monument in front of the courthouse. The monument carries hundreds and hundreds of names (supposedly every man who served even temporarily in the Union Army is listed), but there are no Italian names on the rolls and few Irish names. One must conclude that early nineteenth-century Bellefonte was inhabited largely by Anglo-Saxon Protestants, and it is natural to suppose that during the nineteenth century at least and perhaps later the town's affluent elite derived from that group.

Maximum Magnification: The View from High Street

We can learn more about the history of Bellefonte by descending from our lofty perch into the streets of the town. By so doing we raise the level of magnification one last notch to discover what can be learned along the three-block stretch of High Street between the railroad station and the courthouse—in effect, the old center of the town.

The railroad station itself, a modest but respectable Stick Style building with Queen Anne touches, plainly dates to somewhere around the beginning of the twentieth century. Across the street is the Bush House Hotel, a substantial four-story Italianate building that bears a blue plastic sign proclaiming it was built in 1868. Historic signs made of plastic are not always the most reliable sources of information, but this one seems plausible. The architectural style is right for the Civil War decade. Furthermore, for a hotel obviously associated with the railroad station the date is consistent with what we know about American railroad history.

FIGURE 3   Simple two-story Georgian houses were the fashionable norm in early nineteenth-century Pennsylvania, but they continued to be built and inhabited by unfashionable people almost until 1900, when the elite were emulating the latest Gothic, Italianate, and Queen Anne styles that issued regularly from Philadelphia, New York, Boston, and London. This is blue-collar south-side Bellefonte.

FIGURE 4   A sample of fashionable Victorian architecture from affluent north-side Bellefonte, built about the same time as the unfashionable Georgian houses in figure 3.

The Pennsylvania Railroad's Main Line was finished between Philadelphia and Pittsburgh in the mid-1850s, and it makes sense that branch lines were built to outlying places like Bellefonte within a few years. The size and modest grandeur of the Bush House, in short, is a measure of the railroad's impact on the town's economy, and its dignified facade allows us to conclude that the railroad brought not just money but ideas of Victorian style as well. The railroad, in short, was not merely an economic shot in the arm but also Bellefonte's window on a larger world of ideas and style.

20   The present railroad station, however, clearly was built twenty or thirty years later than the hotel, and one has to suppose that it was an updating of an earlier station. From the look of the new station Bellefonte as late as the 1890s was trying to keep up with national and international styles of the times and doing so with some success.

A century ago this zone between the hotel and the railroad station was surely a hive of economic and social activity. Today is another story. The railroad station is closed and has been taken over by the Chamber of Commerce, which is using it for offices. The hotel is closed too, except for its bar and dining room, and its current owners have painted the exterior and added the plastic signs, as well as some Williamsburg embellishments obviously meant to signify its historicity. Unlike the original designers of these buildings, who knew very well what they were doing, the current custodians have a fuzzier idea of style and history. Since 1868, one suspects, at least some of the connections with the world of ideas have come unplugged.

Today, the immediate environs of the hotel and railroad station are fairly bleak. The ground floor of the hotel contains a row of shop windows, but only about half of the shops are occupied and those by low-rent occupants: a county relief agency and a cut-rate optometrist. Across the street, in sharp contrast with the Italianate elegance of the hotel, are an ill-tended and optimistically large parking lot and a city park. The park has been planted with grass and a few trees and furnished with a newly built gazebo and a civic fountain. Both park and parking lot are fairly recent, judging from the patina of the asphalt, the size of grease spots on the pavement of the parking stalls, and the modest stature of the Colorado blue spruces

on the edge of the park. Even on a nice day, however, the park is not heavily used, and the parking lot is never full, despite the attractive rate of three-hour parking for 25 cents.

Alongside the hotel, however, there is other evidence of those earlier, more prosperous days. In the grass of the city park one can pick out a pattern of old railroad ties that makes it clear that these were railroad yards. Alongside the yards and immediately behind the hotel is a small canal that parallels Spring Creek and is fed by waters impounded behind a dam just upstream. One suspects that this might have been a navigation canal in prerailroad days, but that suspicion is quickly discarded. Standing in the middle of the canal, built Malay-style on pylons in the water, are several buildings that stand as mute testimony to two things: the value of adjacent real estate, which must have been the incentive for this amphibious building, and the unnavigability of the canal. One is left with the necessary conclusion that this was a millrace, generating power for industrial buildings alongside Spring Creek. That, of course, was a typical arrangement during the early days of the Industrial Revolution, and it worked in much the same way as the mills on the Merrimac River at Lowell and Lawrence and Manchester. Today, only one of Bellefonte's mills survives, a large brick vaguely Gothic affair now occupied (as mills tend to be these days) by an up-scale restaurant and a neighborhood bar that offers a variety of imported and designer beers. A set of concrete piers crosses the millrace at an extremely acute angle, requiring one to conclude that a railroad bridge originally connected the mills between the creek and the millrace with the main railroad yards. Here, as in so many other parts of America, history is a ghostly presence, but with the help of artifacts and imagination we can reconstruct the scene in our minds—the constant comings and goings, trains backing and filling amid sulphurous clouds of bituminous smoke, laborers coming and going to work at the now-ruined mills, baggagemen and commercial travelers hauling luggage between the railroad station and the newly built hotel. That century-old image differs wrenchingly from today's scene of desolation and abandonment, but it helps explain the elegance of the hotel and railroad station and a fair number of other buildings in Bellefonte's downtown that were built about the same time.

For Bellefonte was indeed an elegant place, at least in the last third of the nineteenth century. Along High Street between the railroad station and the courthouse are several other commercial buildings executed with care and competence and designed in the latest styles of the times. The Bush Arcade, for example, slightly uptown from the hotel, is a three-story commercial block done in the picturesque-eclectic style of the day and bearing a date stone of 1888 (Figure 5). The arcade is finished with bas-relief tile, finely laid brick, and the same kind of Gothic towers, Romanesque windows, and brownstone piers that were being used in the mansions of Fifth Avenue in New York at about the same time. Like many of Bellefonte's downtown buildings, it exudes pride, optimism, money, and a tone of substantial urbanity. The Bellefonte of 1888, one has to suppose, was a place that was elegantly up to date, knew it, and took pride in the fact.

25   That prosperous town of the 1880s, however, was a quite different sort of place than it had been earlier in the nineteenth century. One does not need to look far for evidence of that earlier town. In various places along High Street are four-square Georgian buildings, made of rough-cut local limestone, that obviously predate the episode of Victorian prosperity generated by the railroad. In the middle of town a few of those buildings are more or less intact, although several have been equipped with showcase windows with the help of steel I-beams to keep their upper floors from collapsing. Others of the same vintage were obviously updated in the period of the great prosperity, mostly between 1870 and 1900. That updating took a variety of forms: Many of High Street's most exuberant Italianate buildings, for example, turn out really to be Georgian when viewed from the side (Figure 6). In other instances those older Georgian buildings simply had their roofs raised and were furnished with Queen Anne dormers, fish scales, and a proper Queen Anne roof pitch. But the shape and proportions of those Georgian buildings are unmistakable, even though they are hard to date with any exactitude. We can be sure, however, that they

FIGURE 5   The Bush Arcade (1888) is one of several imposing eclectic buildings along High Street between the railroad and the courthouse, each built according to the best stylistic canons of the day. The shop windows have recently been "historicized" with snap-in Williamsburg mullions but to little avail. Two of the shops stand empty; the new "historic" tenants include a card and trophy shop, the Bellefonte Area Youth Center, and a karate parlor.

FIGURE 6 A fashionable Italianate house of the 1870s turns out to be pre—Civil War Georgian when viewed from the side. Georgian architecture had been the urban fashion in Pennsylvania for 150 years but was suddenly eclipsed by the parade of national architectural styles that came crowding in all over America from the mid-nineteenth century onward.

come from pre–Civil War days, since they are of the same style that Pennsylvanians had been building with conservative persistence ever since William Penn set foot on the shore of the Delaware River in 1682 and had continued to build well into the nineteenth century, long after Georgian architectural styles had ceased to be fashionable in Boston and Philadelphia and New York. Here in Bellefonte the best we can say is that they are pre—Civil War, but that is saying a good deal. When we map those Georgian buildings, we can describe a small, conservative, and not very fashionable town, about three by three square blocks (see Figure 1). It is the town that obviously predated the arrival of the railroad, a small agricultural market town of no great wealth and no great pretensions. The arrival of the railroad, then, was not just another incident in the town's ongoing history. It arrived like a barrage of revolutionary cannon fire.

One way to see the effects of that revolution is to stand on the steps of the courthouse and look around. Across the street is the town's largest hotel and most imposing building, the Brockerhoff

House, closed in 1958 but recently revamped as a county residence for elderly folk (Figure 7). In architectural style the lower three floors of the Brockerhoff are simple Italianate, just like the Bush House down the street, and it was presumably built about the same time. The upper floor and roof, however, have been redesigned in the manner of the 1890s, and the style can best be called eclectic (to put it mildly): a combination of neo-Gothic and neo-Romanesque with additional Gothic touches that seem to derive from Felipe II by way of the Schwartzwald. If a designer of cuckoo clocks had tried his hand at designing hotels, this is presumably what he would have done in 1890—and in Bellefonte did.

The Brockerhoff is a metaphor for the period of Bellefonte's greatest prosperity, for it was finished with modest grandeur after the Civil War and then flamboyantly renewed about the turn of the century. The Brockerhoff, as well as the buildings across the street, is a second redefinition of the small agricultural market town of the early nineteenth century whose Georgian fringes are clearly visible from the Civil War monument in front of the courthouse.

FIGURE 7   **The Brockerhoff House, c. 1867. The lower three floors are conventional Italianate, not unlike the Bush House, built about the same time three blocks down High Street. The upper story and roof were remodeled according to picturesque eclectic canons of the 1890s.**

There is ample evidence that from the Civil War to the turn of the century Bellefonte was growing bigger but also perhaps more cosmopolitan. Indeed, if Bellefonte's landscape tells us anything, it is that small towns were not necessarily unsophisticated towns. A sign erected in front of the courthouse by the Pennsylvania Historical and Museum Commission notes that Bellefonte was the residence of five Pennsylvania governors during the nineteenth century; one of them, whose statue stands proudly in front of the Civil War monument, was James Curtin, a man who helped keep Pennsylvania loyal to the Union during the grim days between the shelling of Fort Sumter and the Battle of Gettysburg. Curtin was no parochial figure; he was a respected figure in national politics and was appointed U.S. minister to Russia after the war, shortly after the purchase of Alaska. It was no accident that this gifted powerful man called Bellefonte his home. The Bellefonte of 1867 was no backwater.

But it was no paradise either. The county historical society, of course, makes much of Bellefonte's architectural treasures and for good

reason. Many are substantial and sophisticated. Along High Street, however, there are elements of the landscape that lead one to suspect that wealth and sophistication were not unmixed blessings. Three institutions, all located within a block of the courthouse, are familiar features in the American small-town landscape: the BPOE, the YMCA, and the WCTU. It is easy to dismiss them all as quaint or insignificant; none seems to possess much social relevance in these closing days of the twentieth century. But it is worth recalling what each of those three institutions did and the social pathologies that each reflected. In nineteenth-century America each performed different functions from those they do today, and taken together their presence on High Street tells a somber story about this picturesque little town.

Consider the BPOE, for example. The Benevo- 30 lent and Protective Order of Elks was founded for the same reason that the Independent Order of Odd Fellows, the Red Men, and the Woodmen of the World were founded—to care for the widows and orphans of members who had been killed in accidents or died of typhoid and to provide dignified Christian burials that a fatherless family without life insurance could not readily afford.[5] Those fraternal lodges were, in effect, the precursors of life insurance companies and social security agencies. They were invented to help rural folk, who were flocking from farms into the new cities of industrializing America, cope with the unfamiliar physical and social hazards of new cities and new factories—in effect, cope with a whole new society that was being born before their eyes. It was a society that offered unforeseen opportunities but unforeseen perils as well, a cruel, dangerous society in which heretofore rural people needed protection and needed it badly. The BPOE was just one form of such protection.

Across the street the YMCA performed a similar function. Undergraduate students at my university grew up in a twentieth-century world where the YMCA is commonly viewed as a place of recreation for adolescents and where children are taken by their parents on Saturday mornings to learn how to swim. But in the nineteenth century the YMCA was a crucially important institution. It provided safe haven for innocent young men,

fresh from the farm, who had come to find new jobs but found as well a quite pathological urban environment. This environment offered opportunities that the overcrowded farmland did not, which is, of course, why the young men came. (Young women came too, and they formed the YWCA.) But the burgeoning cities and towns of nineteenth-century America were easy places for those fresh-faced farm boys and girls to lose their money, their virtue, their health, and even their lives. The YMCA and the YWCA sought to avert such disasters by providing the young single newcomer a clean safe place to sleep, cheap nourishing meals, and some protection against the evils of the street. It is worth remembering that syphilis and gonorrhea were not joking matters before the invention of sulfa drugs and penicillin. The YMCA's safe Christian environment was not a luxury for young people in nineteenth-century American towns: It was an indispensable form of protection against an environment that those innocent rural youngsters had never seen before.

FIGURE 8 Shutters for street-level windows. The house, which fronts on High Street only a block from the courthouse and the majesty of the law, dates to the early nineteenth century, a time when urban shutters needed to be shuttable. Urban lawlessness did not originate in the twentieth century.

Across the street the WCTU building gives evidence of yet another pathology. The history of prohibition in the United States is a complicated business. One would hardly know that, however, by listening to contemporary pop historians, who have persuaded many Americans (including most of my students) that Prohibition was a silly experiment, imposed on the nation by ignorant extremists. According to that same story, the Women's Christian Temperance Union was largely a collection of hatchet-wielding fanatics.

The WCTU headquarters on High Street in Bellefonte casts considerable doubt on the premises of that pop history. The building, which bears a 1903 date stone, is a large, formal brick and brownstone pile, which bespeaks money, taste, and serious purpose. In Bellefonte, as in many other parts of America, the WCTU was a serious institution, for the simple reason that alcoholism was a serious matter in nineteenth-century America. It is easy enough in the late twentieth century to snicker at those Grant Wood women with their thin lips and grim dedication to the suppression of fun. But institutions such as the WCTU in Bellefonte do not arise without good reason. Indeed, one must conclude that the abuse of alcohol in places like Bellefonte perhaps was not quite as amusing as W. C. Fields later tried to make it seem.

Considered in isolation, none of these three institutions allows profound conclusions about the nature of nineteenth-century Bellefonte. But seen as a group and in the context of a burgeoning urban place, the BPOE, the YMCA, and the WCTU reflect a time and an environment that resembles not at all the roseate image of Norman Rockwell's small-town America. Nor is that the only evidence. All along High Street the shutters of early and mid-nineteenth-century houses are workable things, and they mean business (Figure 8). They are picturesque enough today, and on the town's well-policed streets they are seldom closed. But they do close, and they do work, and one can surmise that in a nineteenth-century town that required the BPOE and the YMCA and the WCTU all in the space of one block to deal with just a few of its social pathologies those shutters were put there for a reason.

LESSONS FROM THE LANDSCAPE

35 High Street in Bellefonte is not unique among the main streets of small-town America, and Bellefonte is not unique either. But that is precisely the point.

Its ordinary human landscape has things to tell us, not only about one small town in the mountains of central Pennsylvania but also about the larger world of nineteenth-century America. There is evidence all up and down the street that the urbanization of nineteenth-century America was more than just a change in scale of economic enterprise, more than just a shift in population. The Bellefontes of the nineteenth century were often rich, exhilarating places, but they were also wrenching, dangerous places for a nation that, to borrow Richard Hofstadter's words, was born in the country and moved to the city.[6] It was more than just a move from one place to another; Americans, after all, have always been on the move. This was a move from one world to another. And the Bellefontes of America formed crucial stepping stones on America's century-long conversion from a rural world to an urban one.

But that move is over now, and the landscape of Bellefonte's main street makes it obvious that the currents of history have swirled by the town and left it on the shore, beached, like so much other historical detritus in America's throw-away society. Many of its downtown store windows are empty; its downtown parking lots stand waiting for cars that seldom come; buildings such as its old opera house command rents so low that a cut-rate furniture store has taken up residence there and a wholesale beer distributor has its warehouse at the rear. Both these enterprises are (to use the jargon of social science) space-consumptive, which is simply another way of saying that in a prosperous place rents would long since have forced them to the outskirts, where land is cheap. If the WCTU and BPOE are indicators of nineteenth-century social pathology, the location of a wholesale beer distributor and a large cut-rate furniture store on what ought to be prime commercial land is an equally clear sign of twentieth-century economic pathology.

An essay such as this can only hint at the wealth of information that the landscape of a place such as Bellefonte contains. But it suggests, perhaps, some of the benefits and some of the problems of trying to read history from the evidence of ordinary human landscapes.

The benefits, I think, are clear enough. Information derived from direct observation of landscape is, in the old-fashioned sense of the term, primary data; in fact, it is hard to imagine any data that are more primary. Just as important, the data are abundant—indeed, sometimes superfluously abundant beyond any scholar's reasonable needs. But that abundance allows us to assemble huge bodies of data that by their very volume are convincing. Finally, and of surpassing value, the data are in their geographical context. By and large, things are where things were with respect to one another, albeit with some notable exceptions. As geographers have been insisting for a long time, location matters.

And what are the limitations, the defects, in this material geographical record? In my own work and that of fellow landscape readers the most serious defects are likely to reside in ourselves—the occasional failure to remember that landscape, like any artifact, is an incomplete record, that we cannot hope to write a complete history of any place on the basis of artifacts outdoors, any more than archaeologists can hope to write a complete history of Troy, no matter how deeply they may dig, no matter how thoroughly they may sift the diggings. A huge volume of material is simply gone. There is, as well, a common temptation to be glib: to assert relationships between artifact and idea that the evidence itself simply does not support. Rarely in the real world of material objects does "this" mean "that."

40   Then, too, no scholar can expect to ask questions of the landscape or to get reasonable answers without prior knowledge and without preparation. J. Hoover Mackin, late professor of geomorphology at the University of Washington and perhaps the most brilliant fieldworker I have ever had the privilege of knowing, used to tell his students, "What you get out of fieldwork is in exact pro-

portion to the knowledge you take into the field." Landscape will not provide answers to questions that are not asked, and it cannot be expected to provide good answers unless questions are carefully and intelligently framed. The wise student of landscape reads deeply, thinks long, and plans carefully before sallying forth into the complicated world of geographic reality.

Finally, as with any other method of historical inquiry, reading evidence from landscape demands a constant willingness to be skeptical. Like most artifacts, common landscapes pose more questions than they are likely to answer. But such questions, in turn, can be among the most powerful tools a scholar can possess. Sometimes they force us to look again, to seek other evidence that can corroborate or contradict our hypotheses; sometimes they send us back to the archives to see what others have said about the things we can only suspect on the street; inevitably they send us out to seek first-hand information through careful interviews with knowledgeable old-timers and look again at things we had previously only glanced at.

But in the last analysis, I think, the attempt to derive meaning from common human landscapes possesses one overwhelming virtue. It keeps us constantly alert to the world around us, demanding that we pay attention not just to some of the things around us but to all of them—the whole visible world in all of its rich, glorious, messy, confusing, ugly, and beautiful complexity.

And that, to my way of thinking, may be its greatest virtue.

Notes

1. There is a considerable literature bearing on this subject. Two avenues into the subject are a collection of essays edited by D. W. Meinig, *The Interpretation of Ordinary Landscape* (New York: Oxford University Press, 1979), and my bibliographic essay, "Learning Through Looking: Geographic and Other Writings about the American Cultural Landscape," *American Quarterly* 35, no. 3 (1983):242–261, reprinted in Thomas J. Schlereth, ed., *Material Culture: A Research Guide* (Lawrence: University Press of Kansas, 1985), 35–56.

2. My course is not unique. Although I know of no university department formally called landscape studies, a small informal band of

scholars teaches a variety of similar courses elsewhere in various university departments; examples are those taught by Paul Groth in the landscape architecture department at the University of California at Berkeley, John Stilgoe in the American studies department at Harvard University, John Jakle in the geography department at the University of Illinois, and John Fraser Hart in the geography department at the University of Minnesota. There are many others, but most owe their contemporary form to the pioneer work of John Brinckerhoff Jackson, founder of the magazine *Landscape* and its editor from 1951 to 1968 and himself the teacher of celebrated courses at Berkeley and Harvard. The single best appreciation of Jackson and his work is Donald Meinig's "Reading the Landscape: An Appreciation of W. G. Hoskins and J. B. Jackson," in D. W. Meinig, ed., *The Interpretation of Ordinary Landscape* (New York: Oxford University Press, 1979), 195–244. Meinig's essay contains a fairly complete bibliography of Jackson's seminal work up to 1978.

3. For a historical-geographical profile of Bellefonte, see Peirce Lewis, "Small Town in Pennsylvania," *Annals of the Association of American Geographers* 62, no. 2 1972): 323–351, reprinted in J. F. Hart, ed., *Regions of the United States* (New York: Harper and Row, 1974), 323–351.

4. Fred Kniffen, "Folk Housing, Key to Diffusion," *Annals of the Association of American Geographers* 55 (1965):173–193. See also Peirce Lewis, "Common Houses, Cultural Spoor," *Landscape* 19, no. 2 (1975):1–22.

5. For an excellent account of how these organizations worked, see Richard H. Schein, "A Geographical and Historical Account of the American Benevolent Fraternal Order" (master's thesis, The Pennsylvania State University, 1983).

6. Richard Hofstadter, *The Age of Reform*, especially Chapter 1, "The Agrarian Myth and Commercial Realities" (New York: Knopf, Vintage Books, 1955), p. 23.

Colliding Feminisms: Britney Spears, "Tweens," and the Politics of Reception

Melanie Lowe

Melanie Lowe is an Assistant Professor of Musicology at the Blair School of Music at Vanderbilt University in Nashville, Tennessee. Dr. Lowe is also an affiliate member of the faculties of American Studies and Women's and Gender Studies. Her research focuses on eighteenth-century music, popular culture, and music media. Her 2007 book, *Pleasure and Meaning in Classical Symphony*, considers how audiences of different classes and from different times and cultures understand and enjoy music. This essay originally appeared in *Popular Music and Society*, an academic journal publishing research using various methodologies or approaches to understand music of any genre or time and its influence.

Video games, cartoon violence, and "shoot-em-up" action movies provoke school shootings. Ever-shrinking supermodels and actors encourage eating disorders. Heavy metal music lures boys to Satanism and suicide. Hollywood teaches girls passivity and submission. Or so we learn on the nightly news.

Scores of studies that seem to support an influence of media content on audience beliefs and behavior drive our ever-current "blame-the-media" political climate. These high-profile studies, many of them policy oriented, typically conclude that the social well-being of a particular group is endangered by the frequent depiction of violence, sex, sexism, racism, consumerism, and even light "PG" violence or sexual innuendo. Concerning body image and the health of women and girls, effects researchers tend to concentrate most intensely on the role that advertising, fashion magazines, and celebrities—actors and super-models in particular—play in shaping female body perception. Feminist writing, particularly in the 1970s and early 1980s, often argues that images of women in subordinate, passive, or even nontechnologically savvy roles encourage societal adherence to patriarchal notions of femininity. The popular press itself, typically the perpetrator in media crimes, now frequently toes the line. The cover of the February 14, 2000 *People Weekly*, for example, reads: "Pop princess Britney Spears: Too sexy too soon? Little girls love her, but her image makes some moms nervous." The message is loud and clear: Mom, be nervous; be very, very nervous.

Much recent academic literature in communications studies, however, challenges the direct influence of media content suggested by mainstream effects research. Connections between what an audience takes in and how it thinks and behaves are complex, ambiguous, and highly dependent on individual identity, family and peer groups, and social relationships. Postfeminist criticism likewise questions a cause-and-effect approach, particularly the images-of-women theorizing that dominated second-wave feminism. No longer do we assume an unproblematic relationship between image and audience, one in which the text clearly transmits meaning and the viewer easily decodes it. Taking cues from literary criticism, academic writers about film, comic books, literature, soap operas, professional wrestling—in short, nearly any and all artifacts of popular culture—increasingly understand meaning not as something intrinsic to a text but rather realized and performed by an audience. Meaning is constantly negotiated and highly dependent on context of consumption and identity of consumer.

In this qualitative study of early adolescent girls and their complex relationship to singer Britney Spears, I engage this audience not as passive recipients of questionable material but as active agents in the creation of their own culture. The girls are active readers of media texts, and, in the ethnography that follows, I consider issues of meaning, constructions of identity, and their social practice of being teen pop's target audience.

ATTACKING BRITNEY

5   During the summer of 1999 I conducted focus-group sessions with groups of five to six early-adolescent middle-class girls. The general topic for discussion in all of the focus group sessions was "their" music, the current teen pop. And, in 1999, teen pop could be summed up in four names: 'N Sync, Backstreet Boys, 98°, and Britney Spears. The most striking early event in *every* conversation was a very strong reaction to teenage pop sensation Britney Spears, *Rolling Stone*'s crowned "Teen Queen" (Daly 60). As soon as one girl mentioned her name, the others would jump into the conversation, and, with excited, raised voices, rip Ms. Spears to shreds:

> [Emily, who had left the room briefly, enters.]
>
> **ANNE:** We're talking about Britney Spears.
> **EMILY:** She's slutty!
> . . .
> **RACHEL** [TO MELANIE]: Did you see the pictures in *Rolling Stone*? She looks really trashy.
> **ANNE:** Slore!
> **BRENDA:** Slore!
> **ANNE AND BRENDA:** Slore slore slore slore slore slore whore!
> **MELANIE:** Is that a new word?
> **ANNE:** Slut and whore together! [laughing]

"Slut," "Whore," and "Slore" (an elision of slut and whore) were the first words out of their mouths. There was no such reaction to Christina Aguilera, another teenage pop star, or to Brandy, Monica, or Maya. The hunks in 98° and heartthrob Justin Timberlake of 'N Sync were neither here nor there. For these girls, Britney Spears is a tough and touchy subject.

At first we might argue that by calling Spears a "whore" the girls are enabling their own subordination. As Cowie and Lees first recognized, labels like "whore," "slut," and "slag" are not only applied to women and girls unfairly, but, with the opposite constructs "virgin," "pris," and "drag," form a discursive dichotomy that is used to describe nearly all female behavior, sexual and oth-

erwise. While the girls Cowie and Lees interviewed recognized such labels as degrading and unjust, they nevertheless used the words themselves in much the same way as the boys did, thereby perpetuating the discursive process that controlled them. It is certainly possible to read the abject language hurled at Britney Spears by her female fans in this light and be disheartened by how little has changed in the twenty years since Cowie and Lees's study of working-class girls in London. But, in conversation about Britney Spears, what struck me most was not the girls' casual use of cruel and demeaning language, but the intensity of their emotion: they were *angry*. Although they may feel some discomfort with the no-win situation set up by the good girl/bad girl, slag/drag, or virgin/whore dichotomy that has plagued women for ages, what distresses them most is finding this good girl/bad girl combination within Spears herself.

They desperately want to believe Spears's good-girl image and projected naïveté, but (most of the time) they seem to know better. Because of the clashing photographic images, contradictory messages in her music, and inconsistencies in the course of her career, the girls don't know which is the real Spears—the pure and wholesome Britney they meet in *Teen People* or the Lolita they discover in *Rolling Stone*, the chaste Britney of "Sometimes" or the lusty Britney of ". . . Baby One More Time." Unlike Madonna, we don't read Spears as using such ambiguity and self-conscious play with traditional constructs of femininity to challenge or undo dominant gender codes. And, unlike Madonna's fans of the 1980s, Spears's fans of today seem not to feel empowered by any overt expressions of her sexuality. In the end, the girls deem Britney Spears a "whore" not because they find her attire inappropriate or her behavior raw, but largely because she affects "innocent" at the same time. As we shall see, the frustration and anger they feel on account of these conflicting Britneys reflect a deeper dilemma for today's early adolescent girls—the main consumers of teen pop: their feminist consciousness colliding with a postfeminist culture.

METHODOLOGY

Most focus groups met in private rooms at YMCA Teen Center summer programs or summer camps. I conducted this fieldwork during the summer at camps rather than during the academic year at schools because I was hoping for as relaxed and casual an atmosphere as possible. I chose to work with focus groups rather than conduct one-on-one interviews for several reasons. First and foremost, I wanted to experience something of teen-pop culture in action—early adolescent girls talking to each other rather than to me directly about the music and pop stars that interest them. As Barbara Bradby demonstrates in her study of preteen girls and Madonna, "the place to investigate the work women do in relation to texts of femininity," particularly resistance to patriarchy and dominant discourses of femininity, "is in the local, social organization of talk" (Bradby 70). I was also hoping that the girls would get into the role-playing and dancing they reportedly did at home, and indeed they did, putting on quite a show at times! (It is hard to imagine such activity happening in an interview situation.) A final reason for choosing focus groups over interviews was practical: these girls were at summer camp and did not want to be taken out of an activity to speak with some stranger. They were, however, quite excited to be able to just hang out together, leave the boys behind (for the moment), listen to music, and talk about anything they wanted. All in all, I found them engaging, imaginative, informative, and refreshingly uninhibited.

10   Setting up these sessions required the usual formalities and meetings with center directors, but once I was on site with the girls I tried to be as casual as possible. As a young, middle-class white woman, who is reasonably well plugged into their culture (I worked for several years as the pre- and early-teen unit leader at a suburban day camp), I consciously strove not to be seen as "teacher" but someone more like an older sister or friend. Although I am around fifteen years older than the girls in the focus groups, I tried to dampen the sense of generational difference by dressing as they did (mostly cut-off shorts and T-shirts), wearing little or no makeup (even though, of course, most of the girls wear eyeliner, mascara, and lipstick or gloss), and remaining on the same physical level as they were on at all times. Usually we all sat on the floor together or lounged on gym mats. I avoided standing before the group and addressing them like a teacher or counselor might. By the end of the sessions, particularly in the two groups profiled below, I felt we had achieved a certain intimacy. The rapport we developed seemed, to me, something like

friendship for the moment. I believe we had each other's confidence. But still, my own position and power in relation to the girls inevitably influenced every aspect of the sessions despite my attempts to minimize this power differential. In my reading of the relationships between these girls and teen-pop culture, I remain conscious of and attempt to relay how my presence, power, and positioning affected the discourse.

Because my previous experiences with preteen girls and camcorders resulted in some of the girls playing to the camera and others feeling overly self-conscious about their appearance, I audio-taped rather than videotaped the focus-group sessions. At first, many of the girls were fixated on the fact that they were being audiotaped. After I showed them my tape recorder and turned it on for the session, one girl would grab the recorder and speak (well, more like shout) into it and then pass it to her friends. At the beginning of a few of the sessions (in fact, in both of the sessions that make up the primary fieldwork for this ethnography), some of the girls played like they were interviewing each other, and then, once they got into this role-playing game, they would pass the recorder around and introduce themselves. This particular game proved quite valuable to me. I did not have to put them on the spot up front and ask them too many questions about themselves. They provided their own introductions. This also gave me a clear example of each girl speaking (mostly) alone. Many times during the transcription process, particularly when it was difficult to tell who was speaking, I referred back to these introductions to be sure I was hearing whom I thought I was hearing.

The transcriptions that follow are written out as a drama script. No single word or phrase was omitted, and I have represented the significant pauses in their speech—pauses that occurred when they seemed to be searching for words, didn't want to finish a phrase, were looking to a friend for support, etc.—with an em-dash (—). Most dialogue excerpts are unbroken, but, to avoid overly long excerpts and the risk of overwhelming the reader with detail unrelated to the main argument presented here, a few of the excerpts have been abbreviated. Omitted were only those bits of the conversation in which the girls got off the topic being considered, were distracted by something outside the group or room, or started up a private conversation on a different subject with another girl in the focus group. If a digression was significant itself or seemed an attempt to avoid or sidestep an issue, I left it in. An ellipsis (...) represents any omitted material. Quite often, more than one girl spoke at a time. The most significant cleaning up I did during the transcription process was to write out each girl's "lines" intact rather than to try to preserve the layered effect of the dialogue. In other words, I am privileging content over time in my representation of the conversations.

The sessions all started similarly. I introduced myself briefly, told them a little about what I was up to, and asked them if they were interested in talking about music. Then, after the tape recorder routine, I got the girls talking about music with a few questions about what radio stations they listen to, who their favorite artists are, what they like about these artists or their music, etc. Once the talking started, I hoped the girls would take the conversation wherever they wanted to, and generally they did. I tried not to lead so much as listen. However, at certain points, when the girls touched on an issue I found particularly significant, I asked them direct questions or brought out some materials for them to consider—CDs, videos, pictures, magazines, and the like. At these moments, the girls spoke to me somewhat more formally and more seriously. During the review, transcription, and analysis of the audiotapes, I listened carefully for how my direct address may have altered the group dynamic, affected their interactions with each other, or colored their responses. In general, I didn't hear their speech become more stilted, awkward, inhibited, or embarrassed at these moments. They didn't hesitate or clam up either. I'm quite confident that, for the most part, they weren't simply telling me what they thought I wanted to hear or what they thought would be considered legitimate. But still, my presence, particularly during instances of direct questioning, may have encouraged the girls to give particularly mature, thoughtful, and sophisticated answers (see Buckingham). My participation in the focus group sessions necessarily forms part of any analysis.

Profiles of Two Focus Groups

All dialogue excerpts are taken from transcripts of the audiotapes of meetings with two focus groups. I met both groups of girls at YMCA Teen Centers in the Nashville, Tennessee area. Although the majority of the girls have lived in Nashville for most of their lives, I found their conversation, con-

victions, and aspirations not at all unlike those of girls I met who grew up in other parts of the United States. I chose to center this discussion on the issues raised by these two focus groups largely because I was able to spend more time with them than any other group. When it comes to teen-pop culture in the United States, boundaries are not drawn geographically so much as by gender and age. As evidenced by the contribution African-American girls brought to our conversations, both black and white girls are consumers of teen pop and participate in its culture. Because there were no Latina, Asian-American, or Native American girls in any of the focus-group sessions, and because I chose not to seek them out actively, I cannot speak for their engagement with teen pop. But, since I found those taking part in teen-pop culture to be mostly middle- to upper-class girls, I would also speculate that demographics would break down more by socioeconomic class than race.

Figure 1 shows the profiles of the two focus 15 groups. Although the girls assured me they wouldn't mind if I used their real names, I have nonetheless changed their names to conceal their identities.

FROM ADMIRATION TO ENVY

The music, videos, photographs, career, images, etc. of Britney Spears, as well as videos and articles about her in music and teen magazines, eventually became the main topic of discussion in the sessions with these two focus groups. At the time, Spears was at the top of the pop charts and practically owned the coveted Number One spot on MTV's *Total Request Live*; so, it isn't all that surprising that she is the female popstar today's "tweens" (an advertising-industry term for those people between childhood and adolescence) have followed most closely. The girls have memorized every word of every song, and they can do every dance step in her videos. They know the most obscure "facts" about her life and rise to teen stardom. Jessica always carried a Discman and several CDs in her bag, and, despite the fact that she was among the most vocal in the full-on takedown of Spears, . . . *Baby One More Time*, Spears's debut album, was always with her wherever she went.

Because of her carefully constructed thirteen-year-old girl-next-door image, most girls see Britney Spears as a peer, an equal, but one who's become an international popstar. And, despite the fact that

FIGURE 1   Profiles of the focus groups

Focus group 1

Rachel, Jessica, Wendy, and Anne go to public schools.

Rachel, 14 yrs, 10th grade

Jessica, 13 yrs, 8th grade

Brenda, 13 yrs, 8th grade

Wendy, 13 yrs, 8th grade

Anne, 13 yrs, 8th grade

Emily, 13 yrs, 8th grade

Emily and Brenda go to private schools.

Rachel, Jessica, Brenda, Anne, and Emily are white.

Wendy is African-American.

Jessica and Brenda have boyfriends.

Rachel and Brenda have cell phones and pagers.

All girls have lived in Nashville suburbs for most of their lives.

Focus group 2

Allison, Catherine, Julie, and Monique go to public schools.
 Kara goes to a private school.

Allison, 12 yrs, 6th grade

Catherine, 12 yrs, 7th grade

Julie, 13 yrs, 8th grade

Monique, 13 yrs, 8th grade

Kara, 12 yrs, 7th grade

Allison, Julie, and Kara are white.

Catherine and Monique are African-American.

Allison, Monique, and Kara have lived in Nashville
 suburbs for most of their lives.

Julie is a self-described "army brat" and has lived all over the
 United States, as well as in Latin America.

Catherine is from Pasadena, California.

twenty minutes earlier they had nothing complimentary to say about the singer, they imagine—even fantasize—about spending time with her.

ANNE: Britney Spears is, like, down to earth.

JESSICA & RACHEL: Yeah—

ANNE: And she's not trying so hard to be popular.

WENDY: She was at the Cool Springs Mall.

MELANIE: Did you guys go see her when she was there?

ANNE, JESSICA, WENDY, & RACHEL: No—

ANNE: But it would be cool if she moved here—we could hang out!

(Focus group 1)

CATHERINE: If you see them by themselves, like, I saw this thing on Britney Spears, I saw, like, you know, how they have a making-the-video thing, I saw one on Britney Spears and at the end of the video she's not as fake as she seems. She's playing with her friends—she's playing with her friends, or playing cards or something and she's laughing with them. She's not wearing any makeup; she looks like she just got out of bed and didn't even do her hair. She was wearing pants and some Adidas shirt and it's not like—she's not always part of the media.

KARA: And she loves her family but she can't really be with her family because she's on tour.

CATHERINE: She's like us but she can't be because she's famous.

(Focus group 2)

The girls also see Britney Spears as someone who's always wanted to be a star and worked hard to accomplish that goal:

EMILY: She took lessons, you know, she practices. She was on the Mickey Mouse Club and took singing lessons since she was like three.

RACHEL: And dancing lessons.

EMILY: So, I mean, she knew she wanted to be a singer. And she went to a singing school in New York I think so she practiced hard.

(Focus group 1)

They have tremendous respect for her accomplishments. Despite their earlier vicious attack, they seem to both like and admire the singer.

20   The girls are also envious of Spears's appearance, celebrity, and success, and they practically admit this themselves. Jessica, who seems confident and reasonably happy with her appearance, likes how Spears looks and confesses that she wouldn't mind looking like Britney Spears. But behind her approval lies some resentment and, like the other girls, she quickly finds something to criticize.

JESSICA: I mean, I would want to look like her—I mean, I know I could never look like that—her hair and—I mean, she's pretty without makeup and all but she like overdid it. I used to wear really really dark eyeliner.

MELANIE: You don't anymore?

JESSICA: No, it looks really trashy—I mean, I think I look better now.

RACHEL: Yeah, you do.

(Focus group 1)

Catherine, who aspires to be a singer herself, reveals some envy of Spears, but quickly criticized the singer's choice of clothing:

CATHERINE [TO MELANIE]: Know what? Ever since I was five, I think, I wanted to be a singer and like all these people that are— like—are like Britney Spears and all the guys who try to show off their bodies—that kinda steered me away from wanting to be a singer or whatever. I mean I would love to be like Britney Spears but if I was a singer I wouldn't do that. It shouldn't matter how much publicity they can get from that, I wouldn't dress like a whore.

(Focus group 2)

Rachel, too, who is slightly overweight, voices first envy and then, in what is likely a reference to Spears's alleged breast-augmentation surgery, disapproval and even disgust:

RACHEL: I mean, I would want to look like her, but not like that! She looks like she wants to be another Pamela Anderson—you see

pictures of Pamela Anderson and she's so— she's all falling out and like that.

(Focus group 1)

But simple admiration turned to jealously doesn't seem to account for the sustained intensity and anger of the girls' initial attacks. Something larger and more disturbing than the latest antics of a favorite pop stars seems to be fueling their fire. As we shall see, in some ways, these girls feel betrayed by Britney Spears. And while on the surface this might seem a simple and obvious response—not unlike the betrayal felt when one girl abandons her group of friends for a more "popular" group, one higher in their school's social order—the forces that set up these girls' feelings of betrayal are considerably distant from the source. It's not the *personal* betrayal of a friend these girls are experiencing, but an *ideological* one, rooted in conflicts within their own culture. If we listen carefully to how early adolescent girls view the world around them, particularly the world as presented in mass media, and respect their observations, opinions, and politics, they themselves lead us to at least one significant source of their anxiety and confusion.

GIRL-POWER FEMINISM

At one point during a meeting with focus group 2, The Offspring's song "Why Don't You Get a Job?" came on the radio and, when the girls finally stopped singing along, they explained why they thought the song had a good message. Kara put it succinctly:

KARA: It's saying "do it yourself, don't just rely on some guy."

(Focus group 2)

Although the girls in the focus groups want noth- 25 ing to do with the Spice Girls (anymore, that is), they believe that the Spice Girls had a "good message" and that "girl power" is alive and well. For them, "girl power" is code for a certain type of feminism—girl solidarity, self-sufficiency, and equality. They believe that they should defend each other and stick together, they want careers so they don't have to "rely on some guy," and they expect girls and boys, women and men, to be treated equally in all situations. Perhaps surprisingly, the girls seem to have acquired much of their feminist conviction from mass media.

In terms of media representations and constructions of possibility, it's a pretty good time to be a middle-class, twelve-year-old girl in suburbia, United States. With thoughts of high school right around the corner and college a near certainty for many, adolescent girls can look to an unprecedented number of women and find strength, brains, and confidence—from Madeline Albright on the world stage to the U.S. Women's Soccer Team with their World Cup victory, and from television's "Lisa Simpson" and "Daria" to "Agent Scully" and medical student "Lucy Knight." When asked about the course they saw their lives taking after high school, most of them answered by mentioning career aspirations. And several of the careers they envision themselves pursuing bear a striking resemblance to those of female characters on their favorite television shows—from doctor (*ER*) to lawyer (*Ally McBeal*) to forensic scientist (*The X-Files*). They see these careers as true possibilities. After all, they have, in their words, "good role models"—from Mom, who is a lawyer, to MTV's Daria, who will surely become one.

Although the girls don't call it such, they also notice gender inequity all around them. And it gets them fired up, as revealed in their lengthy accounts of how girls and boys are treated differently in their schools. Nearly every conversation eventually turned to school at some point, and before long I was witnessing lively and animated girl-gripe sessions that covered everything from the sexism they experience in physical education classes to the skimpy outfits they believe some cheerleaders are forced to wear.

> **EMILY:** The guy teachers, like in PE, they treat you so much differently.
>
> **RACHEL:** They have, like, guy stuff and girl stuff.
>
> **MELANIE:** So you want to do the guy stuff too?
>
> **BRENDA:** I don't necessarily want to *do* the guy stuff, but I think they should treat us equally and not different.
>
> **EMILY & RACHEL:** Yeah—
>
> **EMILY:** The guys think they're stronger and that's because the PE teachers let them do all the stronger stuff—so they get stronger and we just, like—'cause we never get to do any of the hard stuff, so we just, like—
>
> **RACHEL:** I mean, I don't want to do the hard stuff, but I just think—

> **EMILY:** They just give us the easy stuff. . . .
>
> **RACHEL:** We'd rather do all the same thing.
>
> **EMILY:** So that's the reason we're not as strong as the guys are—we grew up thinking that we weren't as strong—so when we get to, like, middle school we're doing, like, the weaker stuff—so obviously we're not going to be stronger and the guys come at us with stuff like that.
>
> **RACHEL:** Yeah
>
> (Focus group 1)

> **KARA:** The cheerleaders in my school, they get the skirts too big so that they will go down lower.
>
> **CATHERINE & JULIE:** Yeah
>
> **CATHERINE:** My grandmother, she sews a lot and she has to sew them so that they come down further. They're too short and they don't like them—and then also when I was a cheerleader—they said that they bought the same size, every one was the same size, for everyone, and they were all small or whatever, so for some people they were 8 inches too high or whatever and they did that on purpose—they bought a size too small for everyone because these skinny girls and—
>
> **MELANIE:** So, who was "they"?
>
> **CATHERINE:** The coach, Coach Morantz, he is, oh God, such a jerk—like, on the softball team we said "why can't we go in the batting cage?" and he said "you are girls, go get me some lemonade and cookies and come back and we'll talk"—and he was such a jerk—he's so sexist, it's not even funny and he's the one who orders all this stuff so we had to have someone come to our school and take out the skirts because they were so tight.
>
> (Focus group 2)

In these conversations the girls' complaints of gender inequity ring loud and clear.

The girls also voice concern about the objectification of women. For example, they don't approve of the risqué outfits Britney Spears wears with increasing frequency, and they worry about the influence her attire might be having on younger girls, particularly their younger sisters. They condemned her performance at the Kids' Choice Awards, for instance, broadcast May 1, 1999 on Nickelodeon, as particularly inappropriate for kids. (Spears performed without a bra—or so it might appear—in a skin-tight and translucent, *very* highly cropped t-shirt, revealing not only the new shape and size resulting from her recent "growth spurt" but much detail as well.)

> **KARA:** She did this like little kids tour thingy
>
> **JULIE:** The Kids' Choice Awards.
>
> **KARA:** And she wore this really skin tight shirt and—
>
> **JULIE:** She doesn't wear a bra!
>
> **KARA:** You could see everything.
>
> (Focus group 2)

30 But what disturbed the girls even more than Spears's revealing outfit was the reason they suspect she wore it.

> **MELANIE:** If you could see everything, why did she wear it?
>
> **KARA:** To show off her boob job! OK, guys see boobs, jugs, or whatever you want to call it in a little booty they see is tight, they just go—like their jaw falls and their eyes go "wooooo."
>
> **ALLISON** [LAUGHING, JUMPING UP AND DOWN]**:** Boing boing boing!
>
> (Focus group 2)

> **BRENDA:** Because she had that—surgery—breast enhancement. She should let them grow—you know—naturally.
>
> **RACHEL:** She's 17, so you know—she should just wait and see.
>
> **ANNE:** Most of her fans are guys, that's probably why she did it, to make her look sexier—and for the guys—to make them look at her more.
>
> **BRENDA:** All the guys, they like—[giggling and hesitation]
>
> **RACHEL** [LAUGHING]**:** The bigger the better!
>
> (Focus group 1)

The girls explained that by "bouncing" around, showing off her "fake boobs" and body, Britney Spears is sending a terrible message to the young girls in the audience. In this short dialogue excerpt, Catherine cuts right to the heart of the matter:

> **JULIE:** Her chest was sticking out, what a huge surprise—it's like—
>
> **CATHERINE:** It's only your boobs and butt that matter.
>
> (Focus group 2)

And finally, Rachel, Wendy, and Jessica articulate clearly the impact they think other women's choices can have on their lives. Here, they're discussing the clothing choices of Brenda's older sister, of whose behavior the girls obviously disapprove. (Brenda's sister is eighteen years old and has three children by two fathers.)

> **BRENDA:** She dresses like my sister.
>
> **MELANIE:** How old is your sister?
>
> **BRENDA:** She's 18—she has three kids
>
> **RACHEL:** Oh my God!
>
> **BRENDA:** And I think that's—that's crazy—she's getting married and I'm really happy about that, but—she should stop dressing like that.
>
> **JESSICA** [LAUGHING]**:** What do you think she'll wear for her wedding?
>
> **BRENDA:** It makes her look loose.
>
> **JESSICA:** It makes her look like a slut!
>
> **RACHEL:** And it makes us—like—all women are sluts.
>
> **WENDY:** The people who don't dress like that, it makes us look bad.
>
> **JESSICA:** Like a slut!
>
> (Focus group 1)

These girls are quite articulate when it comes to condemning patriarchal values. They complain about sexism, recognize the objectification of women's bodies, and worry about the impact media images and messages might be having on younger girls. They also fret about how other girls' attire and behavior might affect how they are perceived and treated. Although, as mentioned above, I took certain measures to dampen the sense of power differential during the focus-group sessions, my presence and role as an adult researcher may have invited such "adult" comments (see Buckingham). Still, as I hear them, the girls—Catherine, Kara, and Rachel in particular—sound like young feminists.

CELEBRATING BRITNEY: "SOMETIMES"

That the girls possess such feminist convictions makes it all the more surprising when they swing back into their defend-and-celebrate-Britney mode. I found particularly interesting—and quite perplexing—the reasons they articulated for which songs they believe have good messages and which songs have bad ones. (This judgment has nothing to do with whether they like the songs; they enjoy them all.) When we first started talking about particular songs, most of the girls said that "Sometimes," the second and then-current hit from Spears's debut album, was their favorite one. The lyrics to "Sometimes," sung by Spears as a direct address to a (presumably) male "you," seem to communicate quite clearly a girl's dismay that her boyfriend is moving too fast and her hope that he'll slow down and wait for her. She explains that she wants to be with him and wants to trust him, but also wants him to know why she comes off as "shy" and "moves away" every time he comes too close. Although the sentiment of the chorus—that all she desires is to be with him constantly, to hold him, and to treat him right—might not sit entirely comfortably with many women, the song's "message" strikes me as reasonably palatable, particularly for teen pop. Once the girls informed me that it was their favorite, I expected to hear them applaud the girl in the song's assertiveness for telling the guy to take things at her speed, not his.

35   But that's not at all what the girls in focus group 1 hear in this song.

> **MELANIE** [TO **EMILY**]: So, what is your favorite song?
>
> **EMILY:** "Sometimes."
>
> **WENDY:** Yeah, "Sometimes."
>
> **MELANIE:** Why that one?
>
> **EMILY:** I just like the concept—because she's like different at different times. She has a lot of different personalities.
>
> **WENDY:** Yeah, she's different in that one.
>
> (Focus group 1)

I was surprised and confused by this response during the session, but the conversation was moving on, so I let it go and the girls kept chatting. Later, while reviewing the audiotapes, I came to understand what the girls meant. On the one hand, from watching them sing along nicely with the verses but *belt* out the chorus, it's clear that, for them, the song *is* the chorus. So forget the story. By "concept" of the song, Emily seems to mean that, literally, sometimes "Britney" runs, sometimes "Britney" hides, and sometimes "Britney" is scared. In other words, as she sees it, Britney Spears's character in this song is different at different times,

and she likes seeing her many sides. But Wendy's follow-up comment is particularly interesting, and suggests that there is another layer of interpretation, another possible meaning in play. For Wendy, like many of the other girls, Spears does not act or play a character external to herself when she sings. She is always Britney Spears and it's Spears herself singing these words. So Wendy seems to mean that in "Sometimes" Spears shows a different side of *her* personality than she does *in her other songs.*

The music, perhaps even more than the words, invites Wendy's reading of the song. Musically, "Sometimes" was quite unlike Spears's other two current hits, ". . . Baby One More Time" and "(You Drive Me) Crazy." While all three are slickly produced pop tunes, the latter two have a pop-R&B flavor, driving dance beats, and edgy synthesized instruments. Spears's voice is at times distant and hollow (likely run through a mid-pass filter). The former is pure bubblegum pop. It lacks rhythmic drive even though its tempo is not that much slower than the other two (think high-school prom "slow dance"), and the backing track is fuller, with smoother and rounder synthesized instruments. Here, Spears's voice sounds somewhat more natural. The positive message the girls find in "Sometimes" lies not so much in the song itself, but rather in its contrast—both lyrical and musical—with Spears's other songs. In the end, the girls celebrate the many sides of Britney, and the idea, communicated musically, that she has different "personalities."

CONDEMNING BRITNEY: ". . . BABY ONE MORE TIME"

While the girls applaud the notion that Spears's personality would have many different facets, they don't necessarily approve of each one individually. Even though they hardly pay attention to a song's "story" and become quite excited when *any* Britney Spears tune comes on the radio or television, they are none the less troubled by the singer's "I'll-do-anything-to-get-my-boyfriend-back" tunes, particularly the title track ". . . Baby One More Time." In the lyrics, we learn of a relationship gone bad and the girl's revelation that the reason she breathes is this boy. She confesses that there's nothing she wouldn't do for him and that she wants him to show her how he wants "it." Her loneliness is killing her, she explains, and because when she's not with him she loses her mind, she demands a sign—in short, the song's hook: "Hit me baby one more time."

Here, as in "Sometimes," Spears is singing to a male "you," only this time the message received is quite different. The girls don't like Britney throwing herself at some guy and are particularly concerned about the possible meanings of one line in specific: "Hit me baby one more time." We talked extensively in the focus group sessions about that line, and it's obvious that some of the girls had talked about it before—either at home or with friends.

> **RACHEL:** Hit me baby one more time—my mom says that—
>
> **BRENDA:** In the video she's like drooling over this guy—
>
> **RACHEL:** I think it's about an ex-boyfriend that she wants back.
>
> **JESSICA:** I think it's like—I don't really want to say this but—[laughing]—
>
> **BRENDA:** In the video, at the end, she's like drooling all over this basketball player.
>
> **RACHEL:** Not in the video he isn't, but in real life he's her cousin.
>
> **WENDY:** I think Britney Spears should, like—like—I think she's really desperate and she needs, like—somebody to, like—to care for her and, like—and, like, take her around and everything.
>
> **JESSICA:** [still laughing] she wants more sex! Come on, baby, give me some more!
>
> (Focus group 1)

> **ALLISON:** Hit me so I can tell that you love me still, I don't know.
>
> **JULIE:** In the video, on the bleachers, it's her cousin she's looking at, it's her cousin!
>
> **MELANIE:** So what's the whole song about?
>
> **ALLISON, JULIE & MONIQUE:** Sex! [laughing]
>
> **MELANIE:** Does it have a story?
>
> **ALLISON, JULIE & MONIQUE:** no! [laughing]
>
> **ALLISON:** Hit me again! Lay me lay me lay me!
>
> (Focus group 2)

40 In the end, although they say the song has no story, the girls obviously have some sense of its narrative. "...Baby One More Time" is, to them, about lust. As they see it, Britney wants it, and wants it bad. She's desperate and they're disappointed. But, despite their disapproval of its message, they smile and laugh

when they hear it, dancing and singing along. At these moments, the social process of being teen pop's audience involves *not* reading or consuming a text individually but experiencing it together. The girls could be singing nonsense and still perform this communal activity.

CONFLICTING BRITNEYS AND COLLIDING FEMINISMS

The greater conflict starts to come into focus, however, when we recognize that for the girls to celebrate Spears's different "personalities," she needs to embody *both* lust and purity, virtue and vice. And, further, they recognize the potential power of Spears's bad-girl persona. When we consider the wider context for the girls' active readings of these texts their confusion seems imminent.

In the middle of conversation about clothing, Kara shocked me, proclaiming:

> **KARA:** If a guy thinks you're sexy, you can get him to do anything.
>
> (Focus group 2)

I found startling not her directness or acuity, but her seeming approval of the implications of this statement. While the girls feel offended and angry when women's bodies are objectified in media, many of them are surprisingly empowered by the idea that women themselves might *choose* to use their own bodies for personal or—in the case of Britney Spears—professional gain.

Several girls mentioned that all of their guy friends "hate" Spears's music, but bought her album anyway. Why? For the pictures inside, particularly the one in which . . .

> **ALLISON:** She's humping the chair!
>
> **JULIE:** I have a male friend who obsesses over her and one day a girl passed it [the . . . *Baby One More Time* album jacket] out on the bus and he unfolded it like that and he was kissing it.
>
> **KARA:** I have this friend and he puts it over his bed and he took another one . . . he's got like four copies and he cut out each picture and, like, pasted it on his pillow. I am *not* joking.
>
> (Focus group 2)

The girls are quite ambivalent about this clear 45 objectification of Spears. They explain that the singer wants to sell albums and, with that photograph, she doubled her sales because all the guys would buy it too. They applaud this other type of "girl power" as well—in this case, Spears's ability to suggest or assume an alternate identity, manipulate men, and get what she wants: the top-selling pop album of 1999.

In the end, though, what gets the girls frustrated, upset, and finally angry—what compels them to trash the singer they respect, admire, and adore—is that she presents them with an irreconcilable difference. They celebrate Spears's ambition and success, a response that jibes with their "girl-power" feminism. And their postfeminist awareness allows them to accept Spears's adoption of a more sexual persona for the moment, especially when it gives her power. But at the same time they feel they must condemn Spears for her "whore" image, as their more traditional feminist convictions dictate. They see a conflict that can't be resolved. How can you celebrate and condemn the same thing?

The girls' intelligent readings and discussions of Larry Busacca's and Albert Sanchez's . . . *Baby One More Time* album-jacket photographs and David Lachapelle's photographs in the April 15, 1999 *Rolling Stone* shed telling light on the social and cultural forces that give rise to their Britney Spears conflict. At its heart is the collision of their feminist convictions with a postmodern sense of self—one that consciously constructs distinct identities for different contexts and meanings.

When the girls became fixated on Britney Spears in the focus group sessions, I brought out some materials I thought they might look at and discuss. Rachel immediately snatched the *Rolling Stone* from my hand and tore through the magazine looking for the "slutty" photographs, eager to share them with the rest of the group. A few of the girls had already seen the article and photographs, but they enthusiastically went through them again, one by one, pointing out and describing with quite colorful language and very loud voices nearly every feature of the photographs: from Spears's clothing, hair, makeup, and body to the props, settings, and other people in the backgrounds. The girls also passed around the unfolded compact-disc liner from Spears's debut album (in focus group 1, they passed around *two* copies—mine and Jessica's), shouting, pointing, and even at one point slapping the photographs on it.

In Larry Busacca's main photograph inside the Britney Spears . . . *Baby One More Time* album,

Britney, wearing tight blue jeans and a white tank top, cocks her head back and to the right, straddles an open-back chair and sports a warm and "innocent" smile; her hair falls softly around her face, covering much of her neck and shoulders while hiding her tank-top straps. David Lachapelle's photograph for the cover of the April 15, 1999 *Rolling Stone* features Britney, made up with dark blush and heavy eye shadow and eye liner, lying on satin sheets in a push-up bra and hot pants; she is talking on the phone and looking provocatively into the viewer's eyes; a Teletubby stuffed animal is tucked under her right arm. Among Lachapelle's several photographs accompanying the article inside is one taken in Spears' own childhood bedroom: a heavily made-up Britney, wearing a push-up bra, hot pants, and high heels, eyes the viewer seductively; scattered around her feet and on the desk/dresser behind her are dolls, stuffed animals, and other such trappings of suburban girlhood. In another photo, Britney looks lustfully over her right shoulder while pushing a little girl's pink bicycle away from the viewer; her attire consists of a tight, elastic, strapless pink top and *very* short, white hot pants; the word "BABY" is sewn twice in sequins on the seat of the pants—once on each cheek.

The intensity of the girls' reactions to the photographs was fascinating, almost shocking. And the words they use to describe what they saw are colorful and explicit. 50

MONIQUE: My legs are open for you.

KARA: I'm sexy, come and get me, my boobs are hanging out, let's go!

MELANIE: What did you say?

CATHERINE: I would love to stick my tongue down your throat!

MELANIE: You think that's what that one says.

CATHERINE: Yes!

MELANIE: OK

. . . .

KARA: I can be sporty too, for all you sporty guys.

CATHERINE: She looks like she's turning her head over so that you can see a little more than you're supposed to—like, if that was a bigger picture—I think you'd be able to see a little more than you want to.

MELANIE: OK, yeah, these are obviously kind of small.

KARA: Um, my shirt's down real low, can you see? Um, I'm sporty for all the sporty guys. I have a lot of different personalities, come and check them out.

(Focus group 2, discussing photographs inside the Britney Spears . . . *Baby One More Time* album)

RACHEL: They're awful.

JESSICA: Oh my God! That is so uncalled for!

BRENDA: That's tacky.

JESSICA: Oh my God!

RACHEL: Well, her pants are posed and—

BRENDA: Pressed all like so that picture right here, like, that's all that hits you.

MELANIE: Yeah, OK.

ANNE: Like she's wanting to be desired for by guys.

JESSICA: That's just awful.

RACHEL: The thing is, she's got all baby dolls acting like she's in a little girl's room and then she—she looks like she's older and stuff.

JESSICA: Oh my God!

WENDY: Ewww!

RACHEL: Her eyeliner is so heavy.

ANNE: I know, look at her eyeliner—

JESSICA: That's tacky! That's not cute, that's tacky!

ANNE: She looks like—she's like trying to be like, OK, like she's wanting to be desired for by guys.

(Focus group 1, discussing the *Rolling Stone* "bedroom" photograph)

MONIQUE: Oh my God!

ALLISON: Whore!

JULIE: Oh my God!

ALLISON: She looks like a prostitute standing on the corner.

KARA: Twenty-dollar whore! Blow job!

CATHERINE: I think she looks like a slut.

KARA: She looks like a baby, can't you tell, it's written on her butt!—Come and get me!

MONIQUE: Yeah, and look, there's an ass cheek! You see the cheek?

KARA: Come and get me! Come on, baby, come on!

ALLISON: Oh baby!

MONIQUE: There's a butt cheek.

KARA: Come on and get me baby!

(Focus group 2 discussing the *Rolling Stone* "bicycle" photograph)

I was nearly overwhelmed by the girls' reactions to these photographs. For several minutes they shouted angrily and hurled all sorts of invective at the Britney Spears they saw in these pictures, especially those published in *Rolling Stone*. But after this initial knee-jerk condemnation of Spears's "slutty" appearance they engaged in quite a thoughtful analysis of the photographs. In fact, by the time they were finished looking at them, the girls in both focus groups had significantly revised their thinking. While at first the girls felt that, as Rachel put it when speaking of Brenda's sister (quoted above), "it makes us—like—all women are sluts," in the end, they in fact claim the opposite: they have no problem with Spears (or anyone else) dressing in lingerie or the tightest and shortest of shorts, *as long as she wasn't made to dress like that by her manager or anyone else.* (Whether Spears was or wasn't is for my analysis of their analysis irrelevant.)

JULIE: No, she [Spears] doesn't even look comfortable in that. Janet Jackson wears tight clothes, but not like that, she doesn't look comfortable in those.

MELANIE: So, it sounds like comfort is an issue for you.

JULIE: If they're comfortable and feel pretty and sexy and they wear it with pride and dignity then who cares. You can tell that if she was not doing that for a shot then she wouldn't be wearing those clothes. Janet Jackson you can see almost anywhere, I don't care what it is, she looks so comfortable, like she's got it.

KARA: Yeah, if you've got it—that's fine!

(Focus group 2)

RACHEL: Her producers put her up to that.

BRENDA: On the TV and, you know—she said she didn't want to do these pictures.

MELANIE: So do you think she shouldn't have done it?

BRENDA: She can decide if she wants to do it or not.

ANNE: If I was her I would not have done that but if I wanted to do that, I would have.

(Focus group 1)

The girls don't want someone forcing Spears to dress in revealing clothing, but they don't want someone telling her not to either. They believe women should dress however they feel comfortable, and if Britney Spears feels "pretty and sexy" in those clothes—if a woman can wear them with "pride and dignity"—that's fine. The bottom line is that women should dress how they want to.

Curiously, though, they are less forgiving when Spears tries to look younger than she really is, when she puts on her "Catholic school girl" persona, as the girls call it. But ultimately, in what turns out to be quite a sophisticated reading of these texts, they are not bothered by Spears's assumption of either the "whore" or the "Catholic school girl" persona individually. As Emily said, you can have "different personalities." Rather, the girls are bothered by a *clash* of the two personae: a conflict of signifieds within the same frame.

> **CATHERINE:** Oh my God, that little bike. Oh my God.
>
> **JULIE:** She has a little tricycle.
>
> **MONIQUE:** And when she puts her leg up on it—ohhhh!
>
> **JULIE:** Girl! Aghhh! Stop it!
>
> **CATHERINE:** OK, hold it. She's 17. She's 16, 17? And she has baby on her butt, I mean, come on, and then she has a tricycle, she's about to get on it—
>
> **JULIE:** The image she's got is trying to be—
>
> **ALLISON:** Let me be sexy with the tricycle—get on the tricycle and go, baby, go! [pumping her hips, laughing]
>
> **JULIE:** is, like, trying to be all mature and, like, sexy and the bicycle is—and the bicycle is just implying that she's a little person who doesn't know what the heck she's doing and that she's not mature enough—
>
> **KARA:** I think that these little—
>
> **JULIE:** The picture— she's trying to make her look more mature, like more sexy, but—
>
> **ALLISON:** Yeah, that's a sexy prostitute picture—and look, her butt cheek's hanging out!
>
> **CATHERINE:** But you know what—I think that pictures like these or whatever, these pictures

that you have, these pictures look, make her look worse.

(Focus group 2, discussing the *Rolling Stone* "bicycle" photograph, conversation continued)

> **CATHERINE:** She has china dolls on top—ohh—ewww—
>
> **ALLISON:** I'm gonna be like a china doll with breasts.
>
> **CATHERINE:** But you know what, this, OK, this—
>
> **KARA:** China doll—I think this one is called "I'm a big china doll with breasts, come and get me!"
>
> **CATHERINE:** Because she has a tricycle, that image is baby, and then she has all these toys and stuff—
>
> **MONIQUE:** Teletubby—
>
> **CATHERINE:** And that's baby also—so I think that these are like [inaudible—others talking over her] but do you pose with short shorts and, um, showing your stomach and your boobs pushed up to your neck, I mean, do you want that on your record?
>
> **JULIE:** Have you heard that commercial about those girls who wear short shorts or something like that?
>
> **KARA:** I can't push them up that far—
>
> **JULIE:** They won't go! [pushing up her own breasts]
>
> **KARA:** But what this [*Rolling Stone* cover photo] says to me is I'm a little cutie, come and get me, I'm, yeah, I've got my little stuffed animals going—but, I don't know, that's says too much, that's—that's—
>
> **CATHERINE:** I think all these pictures make her image look worse.

(Focus group 2, discussing all of the *Rolling Stone* photographs)

In the end, what offends the girls most is not the push-up bra, hot pants, or stilettos, but their combination with the baby dolls, a "tricycle," and the Teletubby. Likewise, it's not the innocent smile and head-tilt, but her wearing of this expression while "humping a chair." The girls seem frustrated not by a limitation or subordination rooted in the good girl/bad girl, slag/drag, or virgin/whore dichotomy, but rather by the projection of two such opposites *concurrently*. These "tweens" will accept only so much of a decentered self: it's fine to wear masks, but please, wear only one at a time.

BEYOND BRITNEY

If the girls I got to know in 1999 are at all "typical," today's early adolescent, middle-class, suburban girls—many of whom have cell phones, beepers, and boyfriends—are smart and sophisticated young feminists. Indeed, they are quite articulate when it comes to condemning patriarchal values and resist conforming to traditional ideals of femininity. They actively read the many media texts they take in each day, often scrutinizing those they find troublesome or confusing. Their individual readings of various media texts frequently frustrate them, particularly when their feminist consciousness engages the increasingly decentered self of pop culture and postfeminism.

And yet they seem able to separate their disapproval from their enjoyment of those texts that confuse and anger them. At times, particularly when they are hanging out with friends, they hear but don't *listen*, see but don't *read*. In other words, their social practice of being teen pop's target audience allows them to maintain strong feminist convictions and still enjoy songs, videos, and any other texts that don't jibe with their politics.

Will their feminist convictions fade? Will they stop voicing resistance? Will they succumb to the passivity and submission mainstream effects research argues they are taught by mass media? Will they experience "the loss of voice, the narrowing of desires and expectations, the capitulation to conventional notions of femininity" so compellingly recounted in the many disturbing studies of adolescent girls (Brown 7)? Well, most of the girls gave me their home phone numbers. Those who didn't gave me their cell phone numbers. And I have a standing invitation to meet with them again sometime in the future. So who knows how their lives, opinions, and values might change? But for now, at least, for the "tweens" I got to know in 1999, relationships between image, music, mass media, sexuality, and socialization exist in a state of constant flux at the point of reception rather than a state of absolute signification at the source. Today's girl is the woman not yet determined.

Works Cited

Bradby, Barbara. "Freedom, Feeling and Dancing: Madonna's Songs Traverse Girls' Talk." *Gendering the Reader.* Ed. Sara Mills. New York: Harvester Wheatsheaf, 1994. 67–96.

Brown, Lyn Mikel. *Raising Their Voices: The Politics of Girls' Anger.* Cambridge, MA: Harvard UP, 1998.

Buckingham, David. "What Words Are Worth: Interpreting Children's Talk about Television." *Cultural Studies* 5 (1991): 228–45.

Cowie, Celia, and Sue Lees. "Slags or Drags." *Feminist Review* 9 (1981): 17–31.

Daly, Steven. "Britney Spears: Inside the Heart and Mind (and Bedroom) of America's New Teen Queen." *Rolling Stone* 15 Apr. 1999: 60ff.

The Photograph as an Intersection of Gazes

Catherine A. Lutz and Jane L. Collins

Catherin A. Lutz is a Professor of Anthropology with a joint appointment in the Watson Institute for International Studies at Brown University. Dr. Lutz's many different research projects share a concern for the question of how better to understand power and inequality in different cultural settings. Jane L. Collins is the Evjue-Bascom Professor of Women's Studies and Rural Sociology at the University of Wisconsin, Madison. She also serves as Director of the Women's Studies Program. Professor Collins's research focuses on the intersection of cultural studies and the political economy of development. This essay is from the book *Looking for America: The Visual Production of Nation and People*, but was also a part of the book-length project *Reading National Geographic* authored by Lutz and Collins. *Looking for America*, a 2004 publication, focused on tracing how visual materials can be read to better understand American national identity and different experiences of America from the 1860s to the end of the 21st century.

If photographs are messages, the message is both transparent and mysterious.

(Sontag 1977: 111)

All photographs tell stories about looking. In considering the *National Geographic*'s photographs, we have been struck by the variety of looks and looking relations that swirl in and around them. These looks—whether from the photographer, the reader, or the person photographed—are ambiguous, charged with feeling and power, central to the stories (sometimes several and conflicting) that the photo can be said to tell. By examining the "lines of sight" evident in the *Geographic* photograph of the non-Westerner, we become aware that it is not simply a captured view of the *other*, but rather a dynamic site at which many gazes or viewpoints intersect. This intersection creates a complex, multidimensional object; it allows viewers of the photo to negotiate a number of different identities both for themselves and for those pictured; and it is one route by which the photograph threatens to break frame and reveal its social context. We aim here to explore the significance of "gaze" for intercultural relations in the photograph and to present a typology of seven kinds of gaze that can be found in the photograph and its social context: the photographer's gaze (the actual look through the viewfinder); the institutional magazine gaze, evident in cropping, picture choice, and captioning; the reader's gaze; the non-Western subject's gaze; the explicit looking done by Westerners who may be framed with locals in the picture; the gaze returned or refracted by the mirrors or cameras that are shown in local hands; and our own academic gaze.

THE GAZE AND ITS SIGNIFICANCE

The photograph and the non-Western person share two fundamental attributes in the culturally tutored experience of most Americans; they are objects at which we *look*. The photograph has this quality because it is usually intended as a thing of either beauty or documentary interest and surveillance. Non-Westerners draw a look, rather than inattention or interaction, to the extent that their difference or foreignness defines them as noteworthy yet distant. A look is necessary to cross the span created by the perception of difference, a perception which initially, of course, also involves looking. When people from outside the Western world are photographed, the importance of the look is accentuated.[1]

A number of intellectual traditions have dealt with "the gaze," looking or spectating as they occur in photography and art. Often these types of analysis have focused on the formal features of the photograph alone, excluding history and culture. While we are critical of several of the perspectives on gaze that we review below, to view photographs as having a certain structure can be consistent with an emphasis on an active and historical reader. In other words, we will argue that the lines of gaze perceptible in the photograph suggest the multiple forces at work in creating photographic meaning, one of the most important of which is readers' culturally informed interpretive work. One objective of our research has been to test the universal claims of certain of these theories about gaze by looking at actual cases of photographs being taken, edited, and read by individuals in real historical time and cultural space. Nonetheless, the interethnic looking that gets done in *National Geographic* photos can be conceptualized by drawing on a number of the insights of these analyses.

Feminist film theory, beginning with Mulvey (1985), has focused on the ways in which looking in patriarchal society is, in her words, "split between active/male and passive/female. The controlling male gaze projects its phantasy on to the female figure which is styled accordingly (1985: 808). The position of spectator, in this view, belongs to the male and allows for the construction of femininity. John Berger (1972) has treated the gaze as masculine. He points out that contemporary gender ideologies envisage men as active doers and define women as passive presence, men by what they do to others, women by their attitudes toward themselves. This has led to women's focusing on how they appear before others and so to fragmenting themselves into "the surveyor and the surveyed.... One might simplify this by saying *men act* and *women appear*. Men look at women. Women watch themselves being looked at ... [and] the surveyor of woman in herself is male" (1972: 46–7; see also Burgin 1986).

Mulvey and Berger alert us to the ways in which the position of spectator has the potential to enhance or articulate the power of the observer over the observed. Representations produced by the artist, the photographer, and the scientist in their role as spectators have permanent, tangible qualities and are culturally defined as quasi-sacred. Both Mulvey and Berger point out that it is the social context of patriarchy, rather than a universal essential quality of the image, that gives the gaze a masculine character.

Recent critiques of these views take issue with the simple equation of the gaze with the masculine, with the psychoanalytic emphasis of this work and its concomitant tendency to universalize its claims and to ignore social and historical context, as well as its neglect of race and class as key factors determining looking relations (de Lauretis 1987; Gaines 1988; Green 1984; Jameson 1983; Tagg 1988; Williams 1987). These critiques make a number of proposals useful in examining *National Geographic* photographs. They suggest, first, that the magazine viewer operates within a racial system in which there are taboos on certain kinds of looking, for example, black men looking at white women. Gaines (1988) forcefully suggests that we need to rethink ideas about looking "along more materialist lines, considering, for instance, how some groups have historically had the license to 'look' openly while other groups have 'looked' illicitly" (1988: 24–5). She also argues that those who have used psychoanalytic theory claim to treat looking positions (viewer/viewed) as distinct from actual social groups (male/female) even while they are identified with gender, and in so doing, "keep the levels of the social ensemble [social experience, representational systems, and so on] hopelessly separate."

Work on women as spectators suggests that viewers may have several possible responses to images, moving toward and away from identification with the imaged person and sometimes "disrupt[ing] the authority and closure of dominant representations" (Williams 1987: 11; compare Burgin 1982). This research suggests that looking need not be equated with controlling; Jameson argues that there may be legitimate pleasures in looking at others that are not predicated on the desire to control, denigrate, or distance oneself from the other. More broadly, we can say that the social whole in which photographers, editors, and a diversity of readers look at the non-Western world allows no simple rendering of the spectator of the magazine, including the spectator's gender.

Much feminist analysis of the power of gaze has drawn on the psychoanalytic theorizing of Lacan (1981). While it carries the dangers of a universalizing focus, Lacan's view of the gaze can be helpful as a model for the *potential* effects of looking. Lacan speaks of gaze as something distinct from the eye of the beholder and from simple vision: it is that "something [which] slips . . . and is always to some degree eluded in it [vision]" (1981: 73); it is "the lack." The gaze comes from the other who constitutes the self in that looking, but the gaze the self encounters is "not a seen gaze, but a gaze imagined by me in the field of the Other" (1981: 84). Ultimately, however, the look that the self receives is "profoundly unsatisfying" because the other does not look at the self in the way that the self imagines it ought to be looked at. The photograph of the non-Westerner can be seen as at least partially the outcome of a set of psychoculturally informed choices made by photographers, editors, and caption writers who pay attention at some level to their own and the other's gaze. Their choices may be made in such a way as to reduce the likelihood of the kind of disappointment Lacan mentions. What can be done in the photograph is to manipulate, perhaps unconsciously, the gaze of the other (by way of such processes as photo selection) so that it allows us to see ourselves reflected in their eyes in ways that are comfortable, familiar, and pleasurable. Photographs might be seen as functioning in the way Lacan says a painting can, which is by pacifying the viewer. What is pacified is the gaze, or rather the anxiety that accompanies the gap between our ideal identity and the real. This taming of the gaze occurs when we realize that the picture does not change as our gaze changes. In Lacan's view, we are desperate for and because of the gaze, and the power of the pictorial representation is that it can ease that anxiety. Photos of the ethnic other can help relieve the anxiety provoked by the ideal of the other's gaze and estimation of us.[2]

Homi Bhabha (1983), on the other hand, argues that the gaze is not only crucial to colonial regimes, but that a tremendous ambivalence and unsettling effect must accompany colonial looking relations because the mirror which these images of the other hold up to the colonial self is "problematic, for the subject finds or recognizes itself through an image which is simultaneously alienating and hence potentially confrontational" (29). "There is always the threatened return of the look" (1983: 33). In Bhabha's terms, the look at the racial other places the viewer in the uncomfortable position of both recognizing himself or herself in the other and denying that recognition. Denial leaves "always the trace of loss, absence. To put it succinctly, the recognition and disavowal of 'difference' is always disturbed by the question of its re-presentation or construction" (1983: 33). From this perspective, which borrows from Lacan and Freud, colonial social relations are enacted largely through a "regime of visibility," in which the look is crucial both for identifying the other and for raising questions of how racist discourse can enclose the mirrored self as well as the other within itself. The photograph and all its intersections of gaze, then, is a site at which this identification and the conflict of maintaining a stereotyped view of difference occurs.[3]

Foucault's analysis of the rise of surveillance in modern society is also relevant to understanding the photographic gaze, and recent analyses (Green 1984; Tagg 1988) have sharply delineated ways in which photography of the other operates at the nexus of knowledge and power that Foucault identified. Foucault pointed to psychiatry, medicine, and legal institutions as primary sites in which control over populations was achieved. His novel contribution was to see these institutions as exercising power not only by coercive control of the body but by creating knowledge of the body and thereby forcing it "to emit signs" or to conform physically and representationally to the knowledge produced by these powerful institutions. The crucial role of photography in the exercise of power lies in its ability to allow for close study of the other and to promote, in Foucault's words, the "normalizing gaze, a surveillance that makes it possible to qualify, to classify and to punish. It establishes over individuals a visibility through which one differentiates them and judges them" (1977: 25).

In the second half of the nineteenth century, photography began to be used to identify prisoners, mental patients, and racial or ethnic types. According to Tagg, its efficacy lies not so much in facilitating social control of those photographed but in representing these others to an audience of "non-deviants" who thereby acquire a language for understanding themselves and the limits they must observe to avoid being classed with those on the outside. Foucault's analysis might suggest that the gaze of the *Geographic* is part of the "capillary system" of international power relations allowing for the surveillance, if not the control, of non-Western people. The magazine's gaze at the third world operates to represent it to an American audience in ways that can but do not always shore up a Western cultural identity or sense of self as modern and civilized. The gaze is not, however, as singular or monolithic as Foucault might suggest. In itself, we might say, a look can mean anything, but lines and types of gaze, in social context, tend to open up certain possibilities for interpreting a photograph and to foreclose others. They often center on issues of intimacy, pleasure, scrutiny, confrontation, and power.[4]

A MULTITUDE OF GAZES

Many gazes can be found in every photograph in the *National Geographic*. This is true whether the picture shows an empty landscape; a single person looking straight at the camera; a large group of people, each looking in a different direction but none at the camera; or a person in the distance whose eyes are tiny or out of focus. In other words, the gaze is not simply the look given by or to a photographed subject. It includes seven kinds of gaze.[5]

The Photographer's Gaze

This gaze, represented by the camera's eye, leaves its clear mark on the structure and content of the photograph. Independently or constrained by others, the photographer takes a position on a rooftop overlooking Khartoum or inside a Ulithian menstrual hut or in front of a funeral parade in Vietnam. Photo subject matter, composition, vantage point (angle or point of view), sharpness and depth of focus, color balance, framing, and other elements of style are the results of the viewing choices made by the photographer or by the invitations or exclusions of those being photographed (Geary 1988).

Susan Sontag argues that photographers are usually profoundly alienated from the people they photograph, and may "feel compelled to put the camera between themselves and whatever is remarkable that they encounter" (1977: 10). *Geographic* photographers, despite an expressed fundamental sympathy with the third world people they meet, confront them across distances of class, race, and sometimes gender. Whether from a fear of these differences or the more primordial (per Lacan) insecurity of the gaze itself, the photographer can often make the choice to insert technique between self and his or her subjects, as can the social scientist (Devereux 1967).

Under most circumstances, the photographer's gaze and the viewer's gaze overlap. The photographer may treat the camera eye as simply a conduit for the reader's look, the "searchlight" (Metz 1985) of his or her vision. Though these two looks can be disentangled, the technology and conventions of photography force the reader to follow that eye and see the world from its position.[6] The implications of this fact can be illustrated with a photo that shows a Venezuelan miner selling the diamonds he has just prospected to a middleman (August 1976 [Figure 1]). To take his picture, the photographer has stood inside the broker's place of business, shooting out over his back and shoulder to capture the face and hands of the miner as he exchanges his diamonds for cash. The viewer is strongly encouraged to share the photographer's interest in the miner, rather than the broker (whose absent gaze may be more available for substitution with the viewer's than is the miner's), and in fact to identify with the broker from whose relative position the shot has been taken and received. The broker, like the North American reader, stands outside the frontier mining world. Alternative readings of this photograph are, of course, possible; the visibility of the miner's gaze may make identification with him and his precarious position more likely. Ultimately what is important is the question of how a diverse set of readers respond to such points of view in a photograph.

The Magazine's Gaze

This is the whole institutional process by which some portion of the photographer's gaze is chosen for use and emphasis. It includes (1) the editor's decision to commission articles on particular locations or issues; (2) the editor's choice of pictures; and (3) the editor's and layout designer's decisions about cropping the picture, arranging it with other photos on the page to bring out the desired meaning, reproducing it in a certain size format to emphasize or downplay its importance, or even altering the picture. The reader, of course, cannot determine whether decisions relating to the last two choices are made by editor or photographer. The magazine's gaze is more evident and accessible in (4) the caption writer's verbal fixing of a vantage on the picture's meaning. This gaze is also multiple and sometimes controversial, given

FIGURE 1   The gaze of the camera is not always exactly the same as the gaze of the viewer, but in most *Geographic* photographs the former structures the latter in powerful ways. In this August 1976 photograph of a Venezuelan diamond transaction, the viewer is strongly encouraged to share the photographer's interest in the miner rather than in the broker. Photograph by Robert Madden. © by National Geographic Society. Reprinted courtesy of National Geographic Society.

the diverse perspectives and politics of those who work for the *Geographic*.

The Magazine Readers' Gazes

As Barthes has pointed out, the "photograph is not only perceived, received, it is *read*, connected more or less consciously by the public that consumes it to a traditional stock of signs" (1977: 19). Independently of what the photographer or the caption writer may intend as the message of the photo, the reader can imagine something else. This fact, which distinguishes the reader's gaze from that of the magazine, led us to investigate the former directly by asking a number of people to look at and interpret our set of photos. Certain elements of composition or content may make it more likely that the reader will resist the photographic gaze and its ideological messages or potentials. These include whatever indicates that a camera (rather

than the reader's eye alone) has been at work—jarring, unnatural colors, off-center angles, and obvious photo retouching.

What *National Geographic* subscribers see is not simply what they get (the physical object, the photograph) but what they imagine the world is about before the magazine arrives, what imagining the picture provokes, and what they remember afterwards of the story they make the picture tell or allow it to tell. The reader's gaze, then, has a history and a future, and it is structured by the mental work of inference and imagination, provoked by the picture's inherent ambiguity (Is that woman smiling or smirking? What are those people in the background doing?) and its tunnel vision (What is going on outside the picture frame? What is it, outside the picture, that she is looking at?). Beyond that, the photo permits fantasy ("Those two are in love, in love like I am with Stuart, but they're bored there on the bench, bored like I have been even in love" or "That child. How beautiful. She should be mine to hold and feed.").

The reader's gaze is structured by a large number of cultural elements or models, many more than those used to reason about racial or cultural difference. Cultural models that we have learned help us interpret gestures such as the thrown-back shoulders of an Argentinean cowboy as indicative of confidence, strength, and bravery. Models of gender lead to a reading of a picture of a mother with a child as a natural scenario, and of the pictured relationship as one of loving, relaxed nurturance; alternatively, the scene might have been read as underlaid with tensions and emotional distance, an interpretation that might be more common in societies with high infant mortality. There is, however, not one reader's gaze; each individual looks with his or her own personal, cultural, and political background or set of interests. It has been possible for people to speak of "the [singular] reader" only so long as "the text" is treated as an entity with a single determinate meaning that is simply consumed (Radway 1984) and only so long as the agency, enculturated nature, and diversity of experience of readers are denied.

20   The gaze of the *National Geographic* reader is also structured by photography's technological form, including a central paradox. On the one hand, photographs allow participation in the non-Western scene through vicarious viewing. On the other, they may also alienate the reader by way of the fact that they create or require a passive viewer and that they frame out much of what an actual viewer of the scene would see, smell, and hear, thereby atomizing and impoverishing experience (Sontag 1977). From another perspective, the photograph has been said (Metz 1985) to necessarily distance the viewer by changing the person photographed into an object—we know our gaze falls on a two-dimensional object—and promoting fantasy. Still, the presumed consent of the other to be photographed can give the viewer the illusion of having some relationship with him or her.

Finally, this gaze is also structured by the context of reading. How and where does the reader go through the magazine—quickly or carefully, alone or with a child? [. . .] In a less literal sense, the context of reading includes cultural notions about the magazine itself, as high middlebrow, scientific, and

pleasurable. Readers' views of what the photograph says about the other must have something to do with the elevated class position they can assume their reading of *National Geographic* indicates. If I the reader am educated and highbrow in contrast to the reader of *People* magazine or the daily newspaper, my gaze may take on the seriousness and appreciative stance a high-class cultural product requires.

The Non-Western Subject's Gaze

There is perhaps no more significant gaze in the photograph than that of its subject. It is how and where the other looks that most determines the differences in the message a photograph can give about intercultural relations. The gaze of the other found in *National Geographic* can be classified into at least four types; she or he can confront the camera, look at something or someone within the picture frame, look off into the distance, or not look at anything at all.

The gaze confronting camera and reader comprises nearly a quarter of the photos that have at least some non-Western locals in them.[7] What does the look into the camera's eye suggest to readers about the photographic subject? A number of possibilities suggest themselves.

The look into the camera must at least suggest acknowledgment of photographer and reader. Film theorists have disagreed about what this look does, some arguing that it short circuits the voyeurism identified as an important component of most photography: there can be no peeping if the other meets our gaze. The gaze can be confrontational: "I see you looking at me, so you cannot steal that look." Others, however, have argued that this look, while acknowledging the viewer, simply implies more open voyeurism: the return gaze does not contest the right of the viewer to look and may in fact be read as the subject's assent to being watched (Metz 1985: 800–1).

This disagreement hinges on ignoring how the 25 look is returned and on discounting the effects of context inside the frame and in the reader's historically and culturally variable interpretive work. Facial expression is obviously crucial. The local person looks back with a number of different faces, including friendly smiling, hostile glaring, a vacant or indifferent glance, curiosity, or an ambiguous look. Some of these looks, from some kinds of ethnic others, are unsettling, disorienting, and perhaps often avoided. In *National Geographic*'s photos, the return look is, however, usually not a confrontational or challenging one. The smile plays an important role in muting the potentially disruptive, confrontational role of this return gaze. If the other looks back at the camera and smiles, the combination can be read by viewers as the subject's assent to being surveyed. In 38 percent of the pictures of locals where facial expressions are visible (N = 436), someone is smiling (although not all who smile are looking into the camera), while a higher 55 percent of all pictures in which someone looks back at the camera include one or more smiling figures.

The camera gaze can also establish at least the illusion of intimacy and communication. To the extent that *National Geographic* presents itself as bringing together the corners of the world, the portrait and camera gaze are important routes to those ends. The other is not distanced, but characterized as approachable; the reader can imagine the other is about to speak to him or her. The photographers commonly view the frontal shot as a device for cutting across language barriers and allowing for intercultural communication. The portrait is, in the words of one early *Geographic* photographer, "a collaboration between subject and photographer" (National Geographic Society 1981: 22). In published form, of course, the photographed person is still "subjected to an unreturnable gaze" (Tagg 1988: 64), in no position to speak.

The magazine's goal of creating intimacy between subject and reader contradicts to some extent its official goal of presenting an unmanipulated, truthful slice of life from another country. Virtually all the photographers and picture editors we spoke with saw the return gaze as problematic and believed that such pictures ought to be used sparingly because they are clearly not candid, and potentially influenced by the photographer. They might also be "almost faking intimacy," one editor said. Another mentioned that the use of direct gaze is also a question of style, suggesting more commercial and less gritty values. The photographer can achieve both the goals of intimacy and invisibility by taking portraits which are not directly frontal, but in which the gaze angles off to the side of the camera.

To face the camera is to permit close examination of the photographed subject, including scrutiny of the face and eyes, which are in common-sense parlance the seat of the soul—feelings, personality, or character. Frontality is a central technique of a documentary rhetoric in photography (Tagg 1988: 189); it sets the stage for either critique or celebration, but in either case evaluation, of the other as a person or type. Editors at the magazine talked about their search for the "compelling face" in selecting photos for the magazine.

Racial, age, and gender differences appear in how often and how exactly the gaze is returned and lend substance to each of these perspectives on the camera gaze. To a statistically significant degree, women look into the camera more than men, children and older people look into the camera more often than other adults, those who appear poor more than those who appear wealthy, those whose skin is very dark more than those who are bronze, those who are bronze more than those whose skin is white, those in native dress more than those in Western garb, those without any tools more than those who are using machinery.[8] Those who are culturally defined as weak—women, children, people of color, the poor, the tribal rather than the modern, those without technology—are more likely to face the camera, the more powerful to be represented looking elsewhere. There is also an intriguing (but not statistically significant) trend toward higher rates of looking at the camera in pictures taken in countries that were perceived as friendly towards the United States.[9]

To look out at the viewer, then, would appear to represent not a confrontation between the West and the rest, but the accessibility of the other. This interpretation is supported by the fact that historically the frontal portrait has been associated with the rougher classes, as the Daumier print points out. Tagg (1988), in a social history of photography, argues that this earlier class-based styling was passed on from portraiture to the emerging use of photography for the documentation and surveillance of the criminal and the insane. Camera gaze is often associated with full frontal posture in the *Geographic*; as such, it is also part of frontality's work as a "code of social inferiority" (Tagg 1988: 37). The civilized classes, at least since the nineteenth century, have traditionally been depicted in Western art turning away from the camera and so making themselves less available.[10] The higher-status person may thus be characterized as too absorbed in weighty matters to attend to the photographer's agenda. Facing the camera, in Tagg's terms, "signified the bluntness and 'naturalness' of a culturally unsophisticated class [and had a history which predated photography]" (1988: 36).

These class-coded styles of approach and gaze before the camera have continued to have force and utility in renderings of the ethnic other. The twist here is that the more civilized quality imparted to the lighter-skinned male in Western dress and to adult exotics who turn away from the camera is only a relative quality. Full civilization still belongs, ideologically, to the Euroamerican.

Whether these categories of people have actually looked at the camera more readily and openly is another matter. If the gaze toward the camera reflected only a lack of familiarity with it, and curiosity, then one would expect rural people to look at the camera more than urban people. This is not the case. One might also expect some change over time, as cameras became more common everywhere, but there is no difference in rate of gaze when the period from 1950 to 1970 is compared with the later period. The heavy editorial hand at the *Geographic* argues that what is at work is a set of unarticulated perceptions about the kinds of non-Westerners who make comfortable and interesting subjects for the magazine. *National Geographic* editors select from a vast array of possible pictures on the basis of some notion about what the social/power relations are between the reader and the particular ethnic subject being photographed. These aesthetic choices are outside explicit politics but encode politics nonetheless. A "good picture" is a picture that makes sense in terms of prevailing ideas about the other, including ideas about accessibility and difference.

In a second form of gaze by the photographed subject, the non-Westerner looks at someone or something evident within the frame. The ideas readers get about who the other is are often read off from this gaze, which is taken as an index of interest, attention, or goals. The Venezuelan prospector who looks at the diamonds as they are being weighed by the buyer is interested in selling, in making money, rather than in the Western viewer or other compatriots. The caption supplies details: "The hard-won money usually flies fast in gambling and merry-making at primitive diamond camps, where riches-to-rags tales abound." [A] picture of the Marcos family . . . shows both Ferdinand and Imelda happily staring at their children, assuring the audience of their family-oriented character.

A potential point of interest in our set of photographs is the presence of a Western traveler. In 10 percent of such pictures, at least one local looks into the camera. Yet in 22 percent of the pictures in which only locals appear, someone looks into the camera. To a statistically significant degree, then, the Westerner in the frame draws a look away from those Westerners beyond the camera, suggesting both that these two kinds of Westerners might stand in for each other, as well as indexing the interest they are believed to have for locals.

Third, the other's gaze can run off into the distance beyond the frame. This behavior can suggest radically different things about the character of the subject. It might portray either a dreamy, vacant, absent-minded person or a forward-looking, future-oriented, and determined one. Compare the photo of three Argentinean gauchos as they dress for a rodeo (October 1980) with the shot of a group of six Australian aborigines as they stand and sit in a road to block a government survey team (November 1980). Two of the gauchos, looking out the window at a point in the far distance, come across as thoughtful, pensive, and sharply focused on the heroic tasks in front of them. The aboriginal group includes seven gazes, each heading off in a different direction and only one clearly focused on something within the frame, thus giving the group a disconnected and unfocused look. It becomes harder to imagine this group of seven engaged in coordinated or successful action; that coordination would require mutual planning and, as a corollary, at least some mutual gazing during planning discussions. Other elements of the photograph which add to this impression include their more casual posture, three of them leaning on the truck behind them, in contrast with the gaucho picture in which each stands erect. In addition, the gaze of the aborigines is by no means clear, with gaze having to be read off from the direction of the head. The fuzzy gaze is a significant textual device for reading off character, alienation, or availability. Character connotations aside, the out-of-frame look may also have implications for the viewer's identification with the subject, in some sense connecting with the reader outside the frame (Metz 1985: 795).

Finally, in many pictures no gaze at all is visible, either because the people in them are tiny figures lost in a landscape or in a sea of others, or because the scene is dark or the person's face covered by a mask or veil. We might read this kind of

35

picture (14 percent of the whole sample) as being about the landscape or activity rather than the people or as communicating a sense of nameless others or group members rather than individuals. While these pictures do not increase in number over the period, there has been a sudden spate of recent covers in which the face or eyes of a non-Western person photographed are partly hidden (November 1979, February 1983, October 1985, August 1987, October 1987, November 1987, July 1988, February 1991, December 1991). Stylistically, *National Geographic* photographers may now have license to experiment with elements of the classical portrait with its full-face view, but the absence of any such shots before 1979 can also be read as a sign of a changing attitude about the possibilities of cross-cultural communication. The covered face can tell a story of a boundary erected, contact broken.

A Direct Western Gaze

In its articles on the non-Western world, the *National Geographic* has frequently included photographs that show a Western traveler in the local setting covered in the piece. During the postwar period, these Western travelers have included adventurers, mountain climbers, and explorers; anthropologists, geographers, botanists, and archaeologists; United States military personnel; tourists; and government officials or functionaries from the United States and Europe, from Prince Philip and Dwight Eisenhower to members of the Peace Corps. These photographs show the Westerners viewing the local landscape from atop a hill, studying an artifact, showing a local tribal person some wonder of Western technology (a photograph, a mirror, or the camera itself), or interacting with a native in conversation, work, or play. The Westerner may stand alone or with associates, but more often is framed in company with one or more locals.

These pictures can have complex effects on viewers, for they represent more explicitly than most the intercultural relations it is thought or hoped obtain between the West and its global neighbors. They may allow identification with the Westerner in the photo and, through that, more interaction with, or imaginary participation in, the photo. Before exploring these possibilities, however, we will speculate on some of the functions these photographs serve in the magazine.

Most obviously, the pictures of Westerners can serve a validating function by proving that the author was *there*, that the account is a firsthand one, brought from the field rather than from library or photographic archives. In this respect the photography sequences in *National Geographic* resemble traditional ethnographic accounts, which are written predominantly in the third person but often include at least one story in the first person that portrays the anthropologist in the field (Marcus and Cushman 1982). For this purpose, it does not matter whether the Westerner stands alone with locals.

To serve the function of dramatizing intercultural relations, however, it is helpful to have a local person in the frame. When the Westerner and the other are positioned face-to-face, we can read their relationship and their natures from such features as Goffman (1979) has identified in his study of advertising photography's representation of women and men—their relative height, the leading and guying behaviors found more often in pictured males, the greater emotional expressiveness of the women, and the like.[11] What the Westerners and non-Westerners are doing, the relative vantage points from which they are photographed, and their facial expressions give other cues to their moral and social characters.

Whether or not the gaze of the two parties is mutual provides a comment on who has the right and/or the need to look at whom. When the reader looks out at the world through this proxy Westerner, does the other look back? Rich implications can emerge from a photo showing two female travelers looking at an Ituri forest man in central Africa (February 1960 [Figure 2]). Standing in the upper left-hand corner, the two women smile down at the native figure in the lower right foreground. He looks toward the ground in front of them, an ambiguous expression on his face. The lines of their gaze have crossed but do not meet; because of this lack of reciprocity, the women's smiles appear bemused and patronizing. In its lack of reciprocity, this gaze is distinctly colonial. The Westerners do not seek a relationship but are content, even pleased, to view the other as an ethnic object. The composition of the picture, structured by an oblique line running from the women down to the man, shows the Westerners standing over the African; the slope itself can suggest, as Maquet (1986) has pointed out for other visual forms, the idea of *descent* or decline from the one (the Western women) to the other.

A related function of this type of photo lies in the way it prompts the viewer to become self-aware,

FIGURE 2   Photographs in which Western travelers are present encode complete messages about intercultural relations. The nonreciprocal gazes in this February 1960 picture encode distinctly colonial social relations. Photograph by Lowell Thomas, Jr. Reprinted courtesy of National Geographic Society.

not just in relation to others but as a viewer, as one who looks or surveys. Mulvey (1985) argues that the gaze in cinema takes three forms—in the camera, in the audience, and in the characters as they look at each other or out at the audience. She says that the first two forms have to be invisible or obscured if the film is to follow realist conventions and bestow on itself the qualities of "reality, obviousness and truth" (1985: 816). The viewer who becomes aware of his or her own eye or that of the camera will develop a "distancing awareness" rather than an immediate unconscious involvement. Applying this insight to the *Geographic* photograph, Mulvey might say that bringing the Western eye into the frame promotes distancing rather than immersion. Alvarado (1979/80) has also argued that such intrusion can reveal contradictions in the social relations of the West and the rest that are otherwise less visible, undermining the authority of the photographer by showing the photo being produced, showing it to be an artifact rather than an unmediated fact.[12]

Photographs in which Westerners appear differ from others because we can be more aware of

ourselves as actors in the world. Whether or not Westerners appear in the picture, we *are* there, but in pictures that include a Westerner, we may see ourselves being viewed by the other, and we become conscious of ourselves and relationships. The act of seeing the self being seen is antithetical to the voyeurism which many art critics have identified as intrinsic to most photography and film (Alloula 1986; Burgin 1982; Metz 1985).

This factor might best account for Westerners retreating from the photographs after 1969. Staffers in the photography department said that pictures including authors of articles came to be regarded as outdated and were discontinued. Photographer and writer were no longer to be the stars of the story, we were told, although text continued to be written in the first person. As more and more readers had traveled to exotic locales, the *Geographic* staff realized that the picture of the intrepid traveler no longer looked so intrepid. While the rise in international tourism may have had this effect, other social changes of the late 1960s contributed as well. In 1968 popular American protest against participation in the Vietnam

War reached a critical point. Huge antiwar demonstrations, the police riot at the Democratic convention, and especially the Viet Cong's success in the Tet offensive convinced many that the American role in Vietnam and, by extension, the third world, would have to be radically reconceptualized. The withdrawal or retreat of American forces came to be seen as inevitable, even though there were many more years of conflict over how, when, and why. American power had come into question for the first time since the end of World War II. Moreover, the assassinations of Malcolm X and Martin Luther King, and the fire of revolt in urban ghettoes, gave many white people a sense of changing and more threatening relations with people of color within the boundaries of the United States.

45   Most of the non-*Geographic* photos now considered iconic representations of the Vietnam War do not include American soldiers or civilians. The girl who, napalmed, runs down a road towards the camera; the Saigon police chief executing a Viet Cong soldier; the Buddhist monk in process of self-immolation—each of these photographs, frequently reproduced, erases American involvement.

The withdrawal of Americans and other Westerners from the photographs of *National Geographic* may involve a historically similar process. The decolonization process accelerated in 1968 and led Americans (including, one must assume, the editors of *National Geographic*) to see the third world as a more dangerous place, a place where they were no longer welcome to walk and survey as they pleased. The decreasing visibility of Westerners signaled a retreat from a third world seen as a less valuable site for Western achievement, more difficult of access and control. The decolonization process was and is received as a threat to an American view of itself. In Lacan's terms, the other's look could threaten an American sense of self-coherence, and so in this historic moment the Westerner, whose presence in the picture makes it possible for us to see ourselves being seen by that other, withdraws to look from a safer distance, behind the camera.

The Refracted Gaze of the Other: To See Themselves as Others See Them

In a small but nonetheless striking number of *National Geographic* photographs, a native is shown with a camera, a mirror, or mirror equivalent in his or her hands. Take the photograph of two Aivilik men in northern Canada sitting on a rock in animal skin parkas, one smiling and the other pointing a camera out at the landscape (November 1956). Or the picture that shows two Indian women dancing as they watch their image in a large wall mirror. Or the picture of Governor Brown of California on Tonga showing a group of children the Polaroid snapshots he has just taken of them (March 1968).

Mirror and camera are tools of self-reflection and surveillance. Each creates a double of the self, a second figure who can be examined more closely than the original—a double that can also be alienated from the self, taken away, as a photograph can be, to another place. Psychoanalytic theory notes that the infant's look into the mirror is a significant step in ego formation because it permits the child to see itself for the first time as an other. The central role of these two tools in American society—after all, its millions of bathrooms have mirrors as fixtures nearly as important as their toilets—stems at least in part from their self-reflective capacities. For many Americans, self-knowledge is a central life goal; the injunction to "know thyself" is taken seriously.

The mirror most directly suggests the possibility of self-awareness, and Western folktales and literature provide many examples of characters (often animals like Bambi or wild children like Kipling's Mowgli) who come upon the mirrored surface of a lake or stream and for the first time see themselves in a kind of epiphany of newly acquired self-knowledge. Placing the mirror in non-Western hands makes an interesting picture for Western viewers because this theme can interact with the common perception that the non-Western native remains somewhat childlike and cognitively immature. Lack of self-awareness implies a lack of history (Wolf 1982); he or she is not without consciousness but is relatively without self-consciousness. The myth is that history and change are primarily characteristic of the West and that self-awareness was brought to the rest of the world by "discovery" and colonization.[13]

In the article "Into the Heart of Africa" (August 1956) a magazine staff member on expedition is shown sitting in his Land-Rover, holding open a *National Geographic* magazine to show a native woman a photograph of a woman of her tribe [Figure 3]. Here the magazine serves the role of reflecting glass, as the caption tells us: "Platter-lipped woman peers at her look-alike in the mirror of *National Geographic*." The *Geographic* artist smiles as he watches the woman's face closely for signs of self-recognition; the fascination evident in

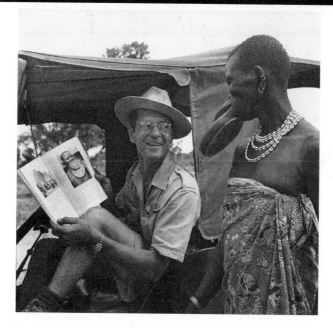

his gaze is in the response of the woman, perhaps the question of how she "likes" her image, her own self. An early version of this type of photo a quarter of a century earlier shows an explorer in pith helmet who, with a triumphant smile, holds up a mirror to a taller native man [Figure 4]. He dips his head down to peer into it, and we, the viewers, see not his expression but a redundant caption: "His first mirror: Porter's boy seeing himself as others see him." By contrast with the later photo, the explorer's gaze is not at the African but out toward the camera, indicating more interest in the camera's reception of this amusing scene than in searching the man's face for clues to his thinking. It also demonstrates the importance of manipulating relative height between races to communicate dominance. In the same genre, a Westerner in safari clothes holds a mirror up to a baboon (May 1955). Here as well, the *Geographic* plays with boundaries between nature and culture. The baboon, like third-world peoples, occupies that boundary in the popular culture of white Westerners (see Haraway 1989); its response to the mirror can only seem humorously inadequate when engaged in the ultimately human and most adult of activities, self-reflection.

The mirror sometimes serves as a device to tell a story about the process of forming national identity. National self-reflection is presumed to accompany development, with the latter term suggesting a process that is both technological and psychosocial. The caption to a 1980 picture of a Tunisian woman looking into a mirror plays with this confusion between individual and nation, between the developing self-awareness of mature adults and historically emergent national identity: "A moment for reflection: Mahbouba Sassi glances in the mirror to tie her head-band. A wife and mother in the village of Takrouna, she wears garb still typical of rural women in the region. Step by step, Tunisia has, by any standards, quietly but steadily brought herself into the front rank of developing nations."

Cameras break into the frame of many *National Geographic* photographs. In some, a Westerner is holding the camera, showing a local group the photograph he has just taken of them. Here the camera, like the mirror, shows the native himself. Frequently the picture is handed to children

crowding happily around the Western cameraman. Historically it was first the mirror and then the camera that were thought to prove the superiority of the Westerner who invented and controls them (Adas 1989). In many pictures of natives holding a mirror or camera, the magazine plays with what McGrane (1989) identifies with the nineteenth century European mind, the notion "of a low threshold of the miraculous [in the non-Western native], of a seemingly childish lack of restraint" (1989: 50).

In other pictures, the native holds the camera. In one sense, this violates the prerogative of the Western surveyor to control the camera, long seen as a form of power. In an analysis of photographs of Middle Eastern women, Graham-Brown (1988) provides evidence that colonial photographers were motivated to keep local subjects "at the lens-end of the camera" and quotes one who, in 1890, complained, "It was a mistake for the first photographer in the Pathan [Afghanistan] country to allow the natives to look at the ground glass screen of the camera. He forgot that a little learning is a dangerous thing" (1988: 61). The camera could be given to native subjects only at the risk of giving away that power.

Pictures in *National Geographic* that place the camera in other hands, however, merely suggest that the native's use of the camera is amusing or quaint. A broad smile graces the face of the Aivilik man above who uses the camera lens to view the landscape with a companion. At least one caption suggests that, although the subject goes behind the camera—in 1952 a young African boy looking through the viewfinder—what he looks out at is the imagined self at whom the Western photographer has been looking moments before: "Young Lemba sees others as the photographer sees him."

Such pictures were more common in the 1950s. We can detect a change, as decolonization proceeded, in the simple terms with which the problem is depicted in an amazing photograph from August 1982 [Figure 5]. It sits on the right-hand side of the page in an article entitled "Paraguay, Paradox of South America." The frame is nearly filled with three foreground figures—a white female tourist standing between an Amerindian woman and man, both in native dress, both bare-chested. The three stand close together in a line, the tourist smiling with her arm on the shoulder of the sober-faced native woman. The

tourist and the man, also unsmiling, face off slightly toward the left where a second camera (besides the one snapping the photo for the magazine) takes their picture. The caption asks us to look at the natives as photographic subjects: "Portraits for pay: A tourist poses with members of the Macá Indian tribe on Colonia Juan Belaieff Island in the Paraguay River near Asunción. The Indians charge 80 cents a person each time they pose in a photograph."

This rare photograph invites us into a contradictory, ambiguous, but, in any case, highly charged scene. It is not a pleasant picture, in contrast with more typical *Geographic* style, because it depicts the act of looking at unwilling subjects, suggesting the voyeurism of the photograph of the exotic, a voyeurism *doubled* by the presence of a second photographer. Further, the picture's ambiguity lies in its suggestion that we are seeing a candid shot of a posed shot, and that we are looking at the other look at us though in fact the Indian gaze is diverted twenty degrees from ours. This unusual structure of gaze draws attention to the commodified nature of the relationship between looker and looked-at. The Indians appear

unhappy, even coerced; the tourist satisfied, presumably with her catch. Here too an apparent contradiction—the diverted gaze and its candid appearance suggest that the *National Geographic* photographer took this picture without paying, unlike the tourists; the caption suggests otherwise.

The photograph's potentially disturbing message for *National Geographic* readers is muted when one considers that the camera has not succeeded so much in representing the returned gaze of indigenous peoples as it has in taking the distance between Western viewer and non-Western subject one step farther and in drawing attention to the photographer (and the artifice) between them. A symptom of alienation from the act of looking even while attention is drawn to it, this photo may exemplify a principle that Sontag says operates in all photography: "The photographer is supertourist, an extension of the anthropologist, visiting natives and bringing back news of their exotic doings and strange gear. The photographer is always trying to colonize new experiences or find new ways to look at familiar subjects—to fight against boredom. For boredom is just the reverse side of fascination: both depend on being outside rather than inside a situation, and one leads to the other" (1977: 42). Avoiding boredom is crucial to retaining readers' interest and therefore membership.

One could also look at the photograph from a 1990 issue on Botswana showing a French television crew—in full camera-and-sound gear and from a distance of a few feet—filming two Dzu Bushmen in hunting gear and authentic dress. The Frenchmen enthusiastically instruct the hunters in stalking posture, and the caption critiques them, noting that they have dressed up the natives (who otherwise wear Western clothing) for the benefit of European consumers. While this photograph is valuable in letting the reader see how images are constructed rather than found, its postmodern peek behind the scenes may also do what Gitlin notes contemporary journalism has done: engaged in a demystifying look at how image makers control the face political candidates put forward, they encourage viewers to be "cognoscenti of their own bamboozlement" (1990).

Ultimately the magazine itself is a mirror for the historical, cultural, and political-economic contexts of its production and use. That context is reflected in the magazine's images, but not in a simple, reflective way, as either the objectivist myth of the nature of cameras and mirrors or as the Althusserian notion of a "specular," or mirrorlike ideology (in which the subject simply recognizes him- or herself) would have it. It is perhaps more in the form of a rippled lake whose many intersecting lines present a constantly changing and emergent image.

The Academic Spectator

60 In one sense, this gaze is simply a subtype of the reader's gaze. It emerges out of the same American middle-class experiential matrix with its family of other cultural representations, its formal and informal schooling in techniques for interpreting both photograph and cultural difference, and its social relations. We read the *National Geographic* with a sense of astonishment, absorption, and wonder, both as children and, in a way that is different only some of the time, as adults. All of the looks embedded in the pictures are ultimately being filtered for you the reader through this, our own gaze. At times during this project, we have looked at the reader of an American magazine who is looking at a photographer's looking at a Western explorer who is looking at a Polynesian child who is looking

at the explorer's photographed snapshot of herself moments earlier. While this framing of the seventh look might suggest that it is simply a more convoluted and distanced voyeurism, it can be distinguished from other kinds of readers' gazes, including the voyeuristic and the hierarchic, by both its distinctive intent and the sociological position (white, middle class, female, academic) from which it comes. Its intent is not aesthetic appreciation or formal description, but critique of the images in spite of, because of, and in terms of their pleasures. We aim to make the pictures tell a different story than they were originally meant to tell, one about their makers and readers rather than their subjects.[14] The critique arises out of a desire "to anthropologize the West," as Rabinow (1986) suggests we might, and to denaturalize the images of difference in the magazine in part because those images and the institution which has produced them have historically articulated too easily with the shifting interests and positions of the state. The strong impact of the magazine on popular attitudes suggests that anthropological teaching or writing purveys images that, even if intended as oppositional (certainly not always the case), may simply be subsumed or bypassed by the *National Geographic* view of the world.

A suspicion of the power of images is inevitable, as they exist in a field more populated with advertising photography than anything else. The image is experienced daily as a sales technique or as a trace of the commodity. That experience is, at least for us and perhaps for other readers, transferred to some degree to the experience of seeing *National Geographic* images.

Our reading of theory has tutored our gaze in distinctive ways, told us how to understand the techniques by which the photographs work, how to find our way to something other than an aesthetic or literal reading, suggesting that we view them as cultural artifacts. It also suggested that we avoid immersion in the many pleasures of the richly colored and exotically peopled photographs, as in Alloula's reading of Algerian colonial period postcards. He notes his analytic need to resist the "aestheticizing temptation" (1986: 116) to see beauty in those cards, a position predicated in part on a highly deterministic view of their hegemonic effect. Alternative, more positive views of the political implications of visual pleasure exist, a view which Jameson (1983) and others argue is achieved in part by unlinking a disdain for popular culture products from the issue of pleasure. Validating both seemingly contradictory views, however, would seem to be the fact that the seductiveness of the pictures both captures and instructs us. We are captured by the temptation to view the photographs as more real than the world or at least as a comfortable substitute for it, to imagine at some level a world of basically happy, classless, even noble others in conflict neither with themselves nor with "us." These and other illusions of the images we have found in part through our own vulnerability to them. The pleasures are also instructive, however. They come from being given views, without having to make our own efforts to get them, of a world different, however slightly, from the American middle-class norm. The considerable beauty with which those lives are portrayed can potentially challenge that norm.

CONCLUSION

The many looking relations represented in all photographs are at the foundation of the kinds of meaning that can be found or made in them. The multiplicity of looks is at the root of a photo's ambiguity, each gaze potentially suggesting a different way of viewing the scene. Moreover, a visual illiteracy leaves most of us with few resources for understanding or integrating the diverse messages these looks can produce. Multiple gaze is the source of many of the photograph's contradictions, highlighting the gaps (as when some gazes are literally interrupted) and multiple perspectives of each person involved in the complex scene. It is the root of much of the photograph's dynamism as a cultural object, and the place where the analyst can perhaps most productively begin to trace its connections to the wider social world of which it is a part. Through attention to the dynamic nature of these intersecting gazes, the photograph becomes less vulnerable to the charge that it masks or stuffs and mounts the world, freezes the life out of a scene, or violently slices into time. While the gaze of the subject of the photograph may be difficult to find in the heavy crisscrossing traffic of the more privileged gazes of producers and consumers, contemporary stories of contestable power are told there nonetheless.

Notes

1. The same of course can be said for other categories of people who share a marked quality with the non-Westerner, including physical deviants (Diane Arbus's pictures, for example), the criminal (Tagg 1988), and, most commonly, women (Goffman 1979).

2. The differences between painting and photography are also important. The gaze cannot be altered at will or completely to taste, and so the looks that are exchanged in *National Geographic* photographs can be seen as more disappointing and less pacifying than are, for example, Gauguin's pictures of Polynesian women.

3. This analysis resembles the less psychoanalytically freighted work of Sider on the stereotype in Indian – white relations. Sider frames the problem as one of "the basic contradiction of this form of domination—*that it cannot both create and incorporate the other as an other*—thus opening a space for continuing resistance and distancing" (1987: 22).

4. Ellsworth's research (e.g., 1975) on gaze in natural and experimental contacts between people (conducted in the United States) has been central in making the argument for a thoroughly contextual view of looking relations in the discipline of psychology.

5. An early typology of the gaze from a colonial and racist perspective is found in Sir Richard Burton's accounts of his African expeditions, during which he felt himself to be the victim of "an ecstasy of curiosity." Wrote Burton: "At last my experience in staring enabled me to categorize the infliction as follows. Firstly is the stare furtive, when the starer would peep and peer under the tent, and its reverse, the open stare. Thirdly is the stare curious or intelligent, which generally was accompanied with irreverent laughter regarding our appearance. Fourthly is the stare stupid, which denoted the hebete incurious savage. The stare discreet is that of Sultans and greatmen; the stare indiscreet at unusual seasons is affected by women and children. Sixthly is the stare flattering—it was exceedingly rare, and equally so was the stare contemptuous.

Eighthly is the stare greedy; it was denoted by the eyes restlessly bounding from one object to another, never tired, never satisfied. Ninthly is the stare peremptory and pertinacious, peculiar to crabbed age. The dozen concludes with the stare drunken, the stare fierce or pugnacious, and finally the stare cannibal, which apparently considered us as articles of diet" (Burton in Moorehead 1960: 33). One can imagine a similarly hostile categorization of white Westerners staring at exotics over the past centuries.

6. Some contemporary photographers are experimenting with these conventions (in point of view or framing) in an effort to undermine this equation. Victor Burgin, for example, intentionally attempts to break this down by making photographs that are "'occasions for interpretation' rather than … 'objects of consumption' " and that thereby require a gaze which more actively produces itself rather than simply accepting the photographer's gaze as its own. While one can question whether any *National Geographic* photograph is ever purely an object of consumption, the distinction alerts us to the possibility that the photographer can encourage or discourage, through technique, the relative independence of the viewer's gaze.

7. This figure is based on 438 photographs coded in this way, 24% of which had a subject looking at the camera.

8. These analyses were based on those photos where gaze was visible, and excluded pictures with a Westerner in the photo. The results were, for gender (N = 360) x^2 = 3.835, df = 1, p < .05; for age (N = 501) x^2 = 13.745, df = 4, p < .01; for wealth (N = 507) x^2 = 12.950, df = 2, p < .01; for skin color (N = 417) x^2 = 8.704, df = 3, p < .05; for dress style (N = 452) x^2 = 12.702, df = 1, p_2 <.001; and for technology (N = 287) x^2 = 4.172, df = 1, p < .05. Discussing these findings in the photography department, we were given the pragmatic explanation that children generally are more fearless in approaching photographers, while men often seem more wary of the camera than women, especially when it is wielded by a male photographer.

9. In the sample of pictures from Asia in which gaze is ascertainable (N = 179), "friendly" countries (including the PRC after 1975, Taiwan, Hong Kong, South Korea, Japan, and the Philippines) had higher rates of smiling than "unfriendly" or neutral countries (x^2 = 2.101, df = 1, p = .147). Excluding Japan, which may have had a more ambiguous status in American eyes, the relationship between gaze and "friendliness" reaches significance (x^2 = 4.14, df = 1, p < .05).

10. Tagg (1988) notes that the pose was initially the pragmatic outcome of the technique of the Physionotrace, a popular mechanism used to trace a person's profile from shadow onto a copper plate. When photography took the place of the Physionotrace, no longer requiring profiles, the conventions of associating class with non-frontality continued to have force.

11. Goffman (1979) draws on ethological insights into height and dominance relations when he explains why women are almost always represented as shorter than men in print advertisements. He notes that "so thoroughly is it assumed that differences in size will correlate with differences in social weight that relative size can be routinely used as a means of ensuring that the picture's story will be understandable at a glance" (1979: 28).

12. The documentary filmmaker Dennis O'Rourke, whose films *Cannibal Tours* and *Half Life: A Parable for the Nuclear Age* explore third-world settings, develops a related argument for the role of reflexivity for the image maker (Lutkehaus 1989). He consistently includes himself in the scene but distinguishes between simple filmmaker self-revelation and rendering the social relations between him and his subjects, including capturing the subject's gaze in such a way as to show his or her complicity with the filmmaker. O'Rourke appears to view the reader's gaze more deterministically (for instance, as "naturally" seeing the complicity in a subject's gaze) than do the theorists considered above.

13. Compare the pictures of natives looking into a mirror with that of an American woman looking into the shiny surface of the airplane she is riveting in the August 1944 issue. It is captioned, "No time to prink [primp] in the

mirror-like tail assembly of a Liberator." The **issue** raised by this caption is not self-knowl**edge (W**estern women have this) but female **vanity,** or rather its transcendence by a woman who, manlike, works in heavy industry during the male labor shortage of World War II. Many of these mirror pictures evoke a tradition in Western art in which Venus or some other female figure gazes into a mirror in a moment of self-absorption. Like those paintings, this photo may operate "within the convention that justifies male voyeuristic desire by aligning it with female narcissistic self-involvement" (Snow 1989: 38).

14. Our interviews with readers show that they do not always ignore the frame but also sometimes see the photograph as an object produced by someone in a concrete social context.

References

Adas, Michael. 1989. *Machines as the Measure of Men.* Ithaca: Cornell University Press.

Alloula, Malek. 1986. *The Colonial Harem.* Minneapolis: University of Minnesota Press.

Alvarado, Manuel. 1979/80. Photographs and narrativity. *Screen Education* (Autumn/Winter), 5–17.

Barthes, Roland. 1977. The Photographic Message. In *Image-Music-Text,* trans. S. Heath. Glasgow: Fontana.

Berger, John. 1972. *Ways of Seeing.* London: British Broadcasting Corporation and Penguin Books.

Bhabha, Homi K. 1983. The Other Question—Homi K. Bhabha Reconsiders the Stereotype and Colonial Discourse. *Screen,* 24:6, 18–36.

Burgin, Victor (ed.). 1982. *Thinking Photography.* London: Macmillan.

Burgin, Victor. 1986. *The End of Art Theory: Criticism and Post-Modernity.* London: Macmillan.

De Lauretis, Teresa. 1987. *Technologies of Gender: Essays on Theory, Film, and Fiction.* Bloomington: Indiana University Press.

Devereux, George. 1967. *From Anxiety to Method in the Behavioral Sciences.* The Hague: Mouton.

Ellsworth, Phoebe. 1975. Direct Gaze as Social Stimulus: The Example of Aggression. In P. Pliner, L. Krames, and T. Alloway (eds.), *Nonverbal Communication of Aggression,* 53–75. New York: Plenum.

Gaines, Jane. 1988. White Privilege and Looking Relations: Race and Gender in Feminist Film Theory. *Screen,* 29:4, 12–27.

Geary, Christaud M. 1988. *Images from Barnum: German Colonial Photography at the Court of King Njoya, Cameroon, West Africa, 1902–1915.* Washington, DC: Smithsonian Institution Press.

Gitlin, Todd. 1990. Blips, Bites and Savvy Talk. *Dissent,* 37, 18–26.

Goffman, Erving. 1979. *Gender Advertisements.* New York: Harper & Row.

Graham-Brown, Sarah. 1988. *Images of Women: The Portrayal of Women in Photography of the Middle East, 1860–1950.* London: Quartet Books.

Green, David. 1984. Classified Subjects. *Ten/8,* 8:14, 30–7.

Haraway, Donna. 1989. *Primate Visions: Gender, Race, and Nature in the World of Modern Science.* New York: Routledge.

Jameson, Fredric. 1983. Pleasure: A Political Issue. In Fredric Jameson (ed.), *Formations of Pleasure,* 1–14. London: Routledge.

Lacan, Jacques. 1981. *The Four Fundamental Concepts of Psycho-Analysis.* New York: Norton.

Lutkehaus, Nancy. 1989. "Excuse me, everything is not airight": On Ethnography, Film, and Representation. An Interview with Filmmaker Dennis O'Rourke. *Cultural Anthropology* 4, 422–37.

Maquet, Jacques. 1986. *The Aesthetic Experience.* New Haven: Yale University Press.

Marcus, George, and Dick Cushman. 1982. Ethnographies as Texts. *Annual Review of Anthropology,* 11, 25–69.

McGrane, Bernard. 1989. *Beyond Anthropology: Society and the Other.* New York: Columbia University Press.

Metz, Christian. 1985. From *The Imaginary Signifier.* In G. Mast and M. Cohen (eds.), *Film Theory and Criticism: Introductory Readings,* 782–802. New York: Oxford University Press.

Moorehead, Alan. 1960. *The White Nile.* New York: Harper & Brothers.

Mulvey, Laura. 1985. Visual Pleasure and Narrative Cinema. In G. Mast and M. Cohen (eds.), *Film Theory and Criticism: Introductory Readings,* 803–16. New York: Oxford University Press.

National Geographic Society. 1981. *Images of the World: Photography at the National Geographic.* Washington, DC: National Geographic Society.

Rabinow, Paul. 1986. Representations Are Social Facts: Modernity in Anthropology. In J. Clifford and G. Marcus (eds.), *Writing Culture,* 234–61. Berkeley and Los Angeles: University of California Press.

Radway, Janice. 1984. *Reading the Romance.* Chapel Hill: University of North Carolina Press.

Sider, Gerald. 1987. When Parrots Learn to Talk, and Why They Can't: Domination, Deception, and Self-Deception in Indian-White Relations. *Comparative Studies in Society and History*, 29, 3–23.

Snow, Edward. 1989. Theorizing the Male Gaze: Some Problems. *Representations*, 25 (Winter), 30–41.

Sontag, Susan. 1977. *On Photography*. New York: Dell.

Tagg, John. 1988. *The Burden of Representation: Essays on Photographies and Histories*. Amherst: University of Massachusetts Press.

Williams, Anne. 1987. Untitled. *Ten/8*, 11, 6–11.

Wolf, Eric. 1982. *Europe and the People without History*. Berkeley and Los Angeles: University of California Press.

Trends in Literature Participation, 1982–2002

National Endowment for the Arts

The National Endowment for the Arts is an independent federal agency created by Congress in 1965 to support excellence in the arts, bring art to the people, and enhance art education. The NEA provides grants to support the arts, conducts research, and partners with other agencies and individuals to support initiatives related to the arts. This article is a part of the report *Reading at Risk: A Survey of Literary Reading in America*, which represents the findings of the literature section of the Survey of Public Participation in the Arts conducted by the Census Bureau in 2002 at the NEA's request. The survey asked seventeen thousand adult Americans about their reading of literature for pleasure.

Over the past 20 years, the U.S. has experienced significant demographic change. The population has grown considerably since 1982 and is becoming increasingly racially and ethnically diverse. Recent waves of immigration have come from a wide range of countries. The Census Bureau noted in a recent report that "the minority population grew 11 times more rapidly as the white non-Hispanic population between 1980 and 2000."[1] The changing demographics of the United States ensure continued change in literary and artistic circles and in public participation in literature and the arts.

Myriad other social and economic transformations have also taken place since 1982. For example, technological change has increased in intensity over the past 20 years. In 1982, personal computers were a relatively new phenomenon, and the Internet was a small network. Now, computers and the Internet are readily available in many homes and in most workplaces. Videogames have also proliferated since the early 1980s, a time when Atari sets were fairly new. These changes, along with the growth in network, cable, and satellite television and the advent of video rentals, have had a significant impact on people's time use over the past 20 years. As early as the 1980s, fears were expressed that the U.S. was becoming a "nation of watchers" rather than a "nation of readers."[2] In the late 1990s, the Center for the Book in the Library of Congress chose "Building a Nation of Readers" as its National Reading Promotion Campaign theme. By the time of the 2002 SPPA, public participation in literature faced very real challenges born out by the Survey's findings.

This chapter examines changes in literary reading in the 1982, 1992, and 2002 Surveys of Public Participation in the Arts, and relates these changes to literary, social, and cultural trends in American society. Results from statistical tests (chi-square) are also presented in this chapter in order to examine whether the changes in literary reading between 1982, 1992, and 2002 are statistically significant.[3]

CHANGES IN LITERATURE PARTICIPATION

Literary reading in America has not grown since 1982. In fact, it is the strong growth in the population that has allowed the overall number of people

---

[1] *Demographic Trends in the 20th Century*, Census 2000 Special Report issued November 2002.
[2] See, for example, President Reagan's Radio Address on Education, September 8, 1984, available at http://www.reagan.utexas.edu/resource/speeches/1984/90884a.htm.
[3] The chi-square statistic can be used to test whether the literary reading rates of Americans in various groups (e.g., men, women, Hispanic Americans, white Americans, etc.) are independent of the year the sampling was done. Within each group, a statistically significant chi-square statistic would indicate that the literary reading rates were significantly different between the years tested.

reading literature to remain stable at about 96 million between 1982 and 2002.[4] Along with these figures, Table 17 shows that there has been a substantial decrease in the percentage of people reading literature, from 57 percent in 1982 to 47 percent in 2002, a decline of 10 percentage points.

CHANGES IN POETRY READING AND LISTENING

5 During the 1990s, the growth in popularity of live readings, poetry slams, and other forms led some to speculate about a revitalization of poetry in America.[5] If such revitalization is occurring, it is not apparent in the figures from the 1982, 1992, and 2002 Surveys of Public Participation in the Arts. A comparison of the poetry readers and listeners in these years (see Table 18) shows that, despite significant population growth, the number of people reading poetry or listening to a poetry reading decreased from about 34 million in 1982 to just under 30 million in

2002. This amounts to a loss of more than 4 million people, or 13 percent of the 1982 audience for poetry.[6] The percentage of people reading poetry or listening to poetry decreased substantially, from about 20 percent of adults in 1982 and 1992 to 14 percent in 2002.

CHANGES IN PERSONAL CREATIVE WRITING

Contrary to the overall decline in literary reading, the number of people doing creative writing—of any genre, not exclusively literary works—increased substantially between 1982 and 2002. In 1982, about 11 million people did some form of creative writing. By 2002, this number had risen to almost 15 million people (18 or older), an increase of about 30 percent.[7]

The percentage of people doing creative writing increased by a much smaller amount, from just fewer than 7 percent of adults in 1982 to just greater than 7 percent in 2002. Table 19 shows the trends in creative writing activity.

TABLE 17 Literary Reading, U.S. Adults, 1982, 1992, and 2002

	1982	*1992*	*2002*	*Change 1982 to 2002*
Number reading literature (in millions)	95.6	100.3	96.2	0.6
American population 18 or older (in millions)	168.0	185.8	205.9	37.9
% reading literature	56.9%	54.0%	46.7%	−10.2

[4]In 1982, only one question was asked regarding literary reading: "During the last 12 months, did you read novels, short stories, poetry or plays?" In 1992 and 2002, three separate questions were asked: "During the last 12 months, did you read any plays?"; "During the last 12 months, did you read any poetry?"; and "During the last 12 months, did you read any novels or short stories?" Respondents who said "yes" to any of these three questions in 1992 or 2002 are included in Table 17. In all three years, a statistically representative sample of Americans was surveyed. In 1982 and 2002, there were about 17,000 survey respondents, compared to about 13,000 in 1992. It should be noted that the estimate of 96 million literary readers differs from the 93.3 million estimate that appears on page 2, Table 1, of *Research Report #45, 2002 Survey of Public Participation in the Arts*, because it is based on the revised estimate of the 1982 adult population, 168 million, and not the 164 million originally provided by the Census Bureau.
[5]See, for example, "10 Years After, Poetry Still Matters" in *The Chronicle of Higher Education*, September 27, 2002.
[6]In 1982, only one question was asked regarding poetry reading and listening: "During the last 12 months, did you read, or listen to a reading of, poetry?" In 2002, two separate questions were asked: "During the last 12 months, did you read any poetry?" and "During the last 12 months, did you listen to a reading of poetry, either live or recorded?" Respondents who said "yes" to either of these questions in 2002 are included in Table 18.
[7]The creative writing question asked did not vary much between 1982 and 2002. In 1982, the wording was: "During the last 12 months, did you work on any creative writings such as stories, poems, plays and the like? Exclude any writing done as part of a course requirement." In 1992 and 2002, the wording was: "With the exception of work or school, did you do any creative writing such as stories, poems or plays during the last 12 months?"

TABLE 18   Reading or Listening to Poetry, U.S. Adults, 1982, 1992, and 2002

	1982	*1992*	*2002*	*Change 1982 to 2002*
Number reading or listening to poetry (in millions)	33.8	38	29.5	−4.3
% reading or listening to poetry	19.8%	20.5%	14.3%	−5.5

CHANGES IN CREATIVE WRITING CLASSES OR LESSONS

Table 20 shows that the number of people who indicated that they had ever taken a creative writing class or lesson decreased from 30 million in 1982 to 27 million in 2002.[8] The percentage of people taking creative writing classes or lessons at some point in their lives also decreased, from 18 percent of adults in 1982 to 13 percent in 2002.

FACTORS IN THE CHANGES IN LITERATURE PARTICIPATION

Due to higher overall levels of education in America over the past 20 years and the correlation between literature participation and education, one might think that there would have been an increase in the popularity of literature since 1982. However, an analysis of the demographic characteristics of literary readers in 1982, 1992, and 2002 shows a widespread decline in the literary reading rates of people from a range of demographic backgrounds.

In fact, literary reading rates decreased for men, women, all ethnic and racial groups, all education groups, and all age groups.

The results of the statistical test (chi-square) 10 confirm the significance of the widespread decline in literary reading. The statistical test shows that, between 1982 and 2002, there were statistically significant decreases in literary reading for the following demographic groups:

- men and women;
- Hispanic Americans, white Americans, African Americans and other ethnic groups;
- people in all categories of educational attainment; and
- the three age groups under 45 (18–24, 25–34, and 35–44).

There are some differences in the rates of decline among different demographic groups. For example, the decrease in literary reading was more pronounced among men than among women. Figure 5 illustrates a decrease in the male literary reading rate from 49 percent to 37 percent, a drop of

TABLE 19   Creative Writing, U.S. Adults, 1982, 1992, and 2002

	1982	*1992*	*2002*	*Change 1982 to 2002**
Number doing creative writing (in millions)	11.5	13.7	14.4	2.9
% doing creative writing	7.0%	7.4%	7.1%	0.1

* The amounts in the change column are calculated from non-rounded figures. Because of rounding, the amounts in this column may not equal the difference between the figures in the other columns.

---

[8]The question regarding creative writing lessons or classes did not change between 1982 and 2002. In all three years, the wording was: "Have you ever taken lessons or classes in creative writing?"

TABLE 20 Creative Writing Classes or Lessons, U.S. Adults, 1982, 1992, and 2002

	1982	1992	2002	Change 1982 to 2002
Number ever taking creative writing classes or lessons (in millions)	29.5	29	27.3	−2.2
% ever taking creative writing classes or lessons	18.0%	15.6%	13.3%	−4.7

12 percentage points.[9] In contrast, the female literary reading rate decreased from 63 percent to 55 percent, a drop of 8 percentage points. Figure 5 also illustrates the overall decline in literary reading, from 56 percent in 1982 to 47 percent in 2002.

GENDER

The gap in the literary reading rates between women and men increased between 1982 and 2002. In 1982, the literary reading rate among women (63 percent) was 14 percentage points higher than the rate among men (49 percent). The difference increased to 17 percentage points in 2002, with 55 percent of women and 38 percent of men reading literature. Changes in the *number* of people reading literature depend on two main factors: changes in the literary reading rate and changes in population. Because of the overall 21 percent increase in the population

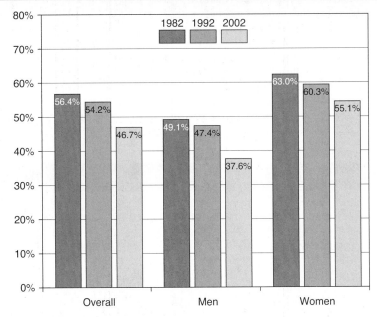

FIGURE 5 Literary Reading Rates by Gender, 1982, 1992, and 2002 Americans 18 Years of Age or Older

Source: 2002 Survey of Public Participation in the Arts

---

[9]This drop in percentage points should not be confused with the "percentage decrease." The drop in percentage points is simply the difference between the literary reading rates in 1982 and 2002. The percentage change relates the difference in rates to the initial reading rate. The percentage change in the proportion of men reading literature was 24 percent between 1982 and 2002, while the percentage change was 13 percent for women.

TABLE 21	Literary Reading by Gender, 1982, 1992, and 2002 (Millions of U.S. Adults)				
	1982	*1992*	*2002*	*Change*	*% Change*
Men	39.5	42.2	36.9	−2.6	−6.6%
Women	56.8	58.5	59.1	2.3	4.0%

(18 years of age and older), the trends in the number of people reading literature were not as strongly downward as the changes in the literary reading rates.

Different demographic groups saw varying rates of population growth and differing changes in literary reading rates between 1982 and 2002.

Consequently, changes in the number of people reading literature varied between demographic groups. Table 21 shows that the number of male literary readers decreased slightly, from 39 million in 1982 to 37 million in 2002. The number of American women reading literature increased slightly, from 57 million to 59 million between 1982 and 2002.

RACE AND ETHNICITY

Among all four ethnic and racial groups examined, 15 the literary reading rate decreased most strongly among Hispanic Americans. At 36 percent, the literary reading rate of Hispanic Americans was the lowest of all ethnic and racial groups in 1982. This rate decreased by 10 percentage points to 26 percent in 2002. Figure 6 shows that there were significant, but lower, rates of decline in literary reading among white Americans (−8.4 points), African Americans (−5.2), and people of Other ethnic and racial origins (−6.5).

The gap between the literary reading rates of white and Hispanic Americans increased slightly between 1982 and 2002. In 1982, 60 percent of

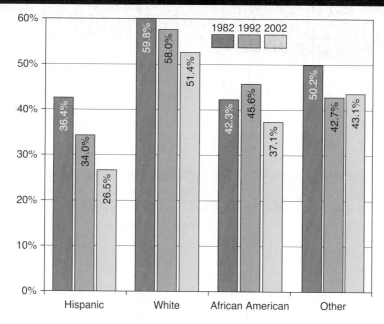

FIGURE 6   Literary Reading Rates by Ethnicity and Race, 1982, 1992, and 2002 Americans 18 years of age or older

1982 1992 2002

Hispanic: 36.4%, 34.0%, 26.5%
White: 59.8%, 58.0%, 51.4%
African American: 42.3%, 45.6%, 37.1%
Other: 50.2%, 42.7%, 43.1%

Source: 2002 Survey of Public Participation in the Arts

white Americans and 36 percent of Hispanic Americans read literature, for a difference of about 23 percentage points. In 2002, the difference was 25 percentage points.

The gap between the literary reading rates of white and African Americans decreased slightly, from 17 percentage points in 1982 to 14 percentage points in 2002. The gap between the literary reading rates of white Americans and people from other ethnic groups also decreased slightly between 1982 and 2002. In 1982, the gap was nearly 10 percentage points; in 2002, the gap was 6.5 percentage points. At the same time as the literary reading rate decreased very strongly among Hispanic Americans, there was also a sharp increase in the Hispanic American population. Given this population increase, the number of Hispanic Americans reading literature increased by nearly 3 million between 1982 and 2002. This increase, which amounts to nearly 75 percent of the number of Hispanic American literary readers in 1982, is the largest increase in the number of readers from any ethnic or racial group.

There was also significant growth in the African American population and in the population from other ethnic groups. Because of these important demographic shifts, the number of readers from African American and other backgrounds increased between 1982 and 2002. In contrast, the number of white Americans reading literature fell by more than 6 million between 1982 and 2002. In summary, because of the changing demographics of the U.S., there was an increase in the number of literary readers from all ethnic and racial groups *except* white Americans.

These changes in the number of literary readers are highlighted in Table 22. White Americans represented 80 percent of literary readers in 2002,

down from 87 percent in 1982. African Americans constituted 9 percent of **literary** readers in 2002, a slight increase from 8 **percent** in 1982. Hispanic Americans comprised 6 **percent** of literary readers in 2002, up from 4 percent in 1982. Finally, Americans from other ethnic and racial groups represented 4 percent of literary readers in 2002, an increase from 2 percent in 1982.

EDUCATION

Figure 7 illustrates that the literary reading rate 20 decreased significantly for people with all levels of educational attainment. In fact, the literary reading rate decreased by 15 percentage points or more for those in all except the lowest education group (grade school only).

The gap between the literary reading rates of college graduates and high school graduates remained large but stable between 1982 and 2002. In 1982, the difference between the reading rates of college graduates (82 percent) and high school graduates (54 percent) was about 28 percentage points. By 2002, after a significant drop in the literary reading rates of both groups, the gap was 29 percentage points.

Despite the sharp decreases in literary reading at all education levels, rising levels of education in American society led to an increase in the number of literary readers who had some college education or a college degree. Table 23 shows that the number of readers with a college degree or graduate education increased by about 12 million. The number of literary readers with some college education increased by about 4 million. There were decreases in the number of literary readers at the three other education levels. In particular, the number of literary readers with a high school education decreased by 9 million.

TABLE 22 Literary Reading by Ethnicity and Race, 1982, 1992, and 2002 (Millions of U.S. Adults)					
	1982	*1992*	*2002*	*Change*	*% Change*
Hispanic	3.4	5.2	6	2.6	74.7%
White	83.3	83.5	77	−6.2	−7.5
African American	7.6	9.5	8.8	1.2	15.4
Other	2	2.4	4.1	2.2	111.5

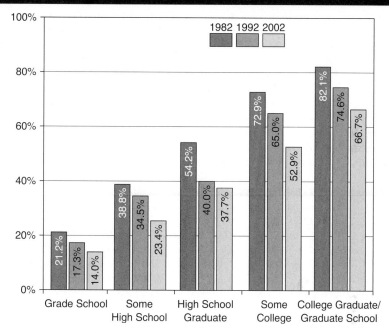

FIGURE 7 Literary Reading Rates by Education, 1982, 1992, and 2002 Americans 18 Years of Age or Older

Source: 2002 Survey of Public Participation in the Arts

AGE GROUPS

Although literary reading rates decreased between 1982 and 2002, the only statistically significant decrease was for those 18 to 44 years of age. While all three age groups under age 45 dropped in percentage, for those adults 18 to 24 years of age, the literary reading rate decreased from nearly 60 percent in 1982 to 43 percent in 2002—a drop of 17 percentage points.

Young adults are reading much less than they used to. Making literary reading appeal to teenagers also appears to be a significant problem. Long-term reading assessments, summarized by the National Institute for Literacy, show that:

- a smaller percentage of 13- and 17-year-olds read for fun daily in 1999 than in 1984;
- a smaller percentage of 17-year-olds saw adults reading in their homes in 1999 than in 1984; and

TABLE 23 Literary Reading by Education, 1982, 1992, and 2002 (Millions of U.S. Adults)

	1982	1992	2002	Change	% Change
Grade school	4.2	2.4	1.6	−2.5	−60.9%
Some high school	9.9	7.6	4.7	−5.2	−52.6
High school graduate	33.1	32.6	24	−9.1	−27.5
Some college	26.1	27.2	30	4	15.2
College graduate / Graduate school	23.5	31.1	35.6	12.2	52.0

- a greater percentage of 17-year-olds were watching three or more hours of television each day in 1999 than in 1978.[10]

25 For those in the 25 to 34 age group, literary reading decreased by more than 14 percentage points, from 62 percent in 1982 to 47 percent in 2002. The literary reading rate among those 35 to 44 years of age decreased by 13 percentage points, from 60 percent in 1982 to 47 percent in 2002.

A close examination of Figure 8 also reveals a shift in the popularity of literary reading between 1982 and 2002, especially among the younger age groups. In 1982, the 25 to 34 age group had the highest literary reading rate (62 percent), followed by the 18 to 24 and the 35 to 44 age groups (each 60 percent). In 2002, the literary reading rate of people under 45 did not rank as highly among the seven age groups. In 2002, the 18 to 24 age group had a literary reading rate (43 percent) that placed it sixth among the seven age groups. The 48 percent literary reading rate of those between 25 and 34 ranked third among all age groups, while the 47 percent rate for people between 35 and 44 ranked

fourth. People between 45 and 54 had the highest literary reading rate in 2002 (52 percent). For people between 55 and 64, the literary reading rate of 49 percent placed this group second among the seven age groups. The literary reading rates of those between 65 and 74 (45 percent) and people 75 and older (37 percent) ranked these groups fifth and seventh respectively.

In 1982, reading literature peaked between ages 18 and 34, gradually falling off as readers aged. In 2002, fewer younger people are reading literature; the peak age group is 45–54, with sloping off rates at both ends of the spectrum.

Population growth and aging led to increases in the number of people reading literature in all age groups 35 or older. The increase in the number of literary readers was largest for those between the ages of 45 and 54 (this age group encompasses the largest share of the baby boomer cohort). There were more than 7 million more literary readers in this age category in 2002 than in 1982. This is about double the increase in the number of literary readers between the ages of 35 and 44. For those 55 and older, the increase in the number of

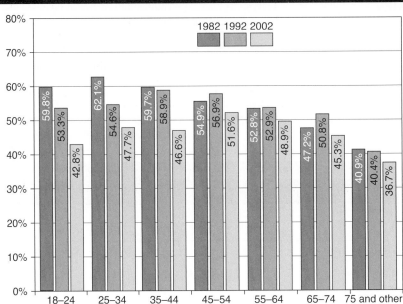

FIGURE 8   Literary Reading Rates by Age, 1982, 1992, and 2002 Americans 18 Years of Age or Older

Source: 2002 Survey of Public Participation in the Arts

---

[10]See the National Institute for Literacy's online, *Reading Facts* available at www.nifl.gov.

TABLE 24 Literary Reading by Age, 1982, 1992, and 2002 (Millions of U.S. Adults)					
	1982	*1992*	*2002*	*Change*	*% Change*
18 to 24	17.8	12.9	11.4	−6.3	−35.7%
25 to 34	24.9	23.1	17.6	−7.3	−29.2
35 to 44	17	23.4	20.5	3.5	20.7
45 to 54	12.7	15.8	20.1	7.4	58.4
55 to 64	12	11.3	12.6	0.6	5.0
65 to 74	7.8	9.3	8	0.2	2.5
75 and older	4.1	5	5.7	1.6	39.3

literary readers was fairly small. There were significant decreases in the number of literary readers in the 18 to 24 and 25 to 34 age groups. Not only have the percentages fallen for young adults, but the actual numbers of young readers have fallen, despite overall population grown. See Table 24 for full details.

An important question about literary reading concerns trends in age cohorts over time. This section compares the literary reading rates by age in 1982 with the age groups to which those people would belong in 2002. As an example, the literary reading rate of 25 to 34 year olds in 1982 was 62 percent. In 2002, this group of people would have been between 45 and 54. The literary reading rate of this group in 2002 was under 52 percent, a decrease of more than 10 percentage points. Table 25 shows that there has been a substantial decrease in literary reading between 1982 and 2002 for every age cohort. In fact, all of the age cohorts have seen decreases of about 10 percentage points or more since 1982.

OTHER LEISURE ACTIVITIES

A comparison of the 1982, 1992, and 2002 Surveys 30 of Public Participation in the Arts shows that time spent watching TV has remained stable for those 18 and older. In 1982 and 1992, the average amount of TV watched per day was 3.0 hours. This decreased slightly to 2.9 hours per day in 2002. These figures suggest that TV watching may not be an important factor in the overall decrease in literary reading.

Movies are a popular leisure activity in the United States, but the percentage of people going to at least one movie in a year decreased slightly over the past 20 years, from 63 percent in 1982 to 60 percent in 2002. Although this seems to show that literary reading is not being replaced by

TABLE 25 Literary Reading by Age Cohort, 1982 and 2002 (Millions of U.S. Adults)			
	1982	*2002*	*Change*
18–24 in 1982/35–44 in 2002	59.8%	46.6%	−13.2
25–34 in 1982/45–54 in 2002	62.1	51.6	−10.5
35–44 in 1982/55–64 in 2002	59.7	48.9	−10.8
45–54 in 1982/65–74 in 2002	54.9	45.3	−9.6
55–64 in 1982/75 and older in 2002	52.8	36.7	−16.1

moviegoing, it should be noted that it is possible that those who went to the movies in 2002 may have gone to more movies per year (than movie-goers in 1982), leaving them with less time to read literature.

Watching movies at home is also very popular, with many people setting up full "home theaters" to watch movies acquired through satellite or cable connections or the rental of videotape and digital video disks. In 1982, videocassette recorders were just starting to achieve widespread home popularity. Between 1985 and 2000, annual consumer spending on television, radios, and sound equipment increased by 68 percent, from $371 per household in 1985 to $622 in 2000. In comparison, annual spending on reading increased by only 4 percent, from $141 per household in 1985 to $146 in 2000.[11]

SUMMARY OF TRENDS
IN LITERATURE PARTICIPATION

The statistics presented in this chapter clearly demonstrate that there has been a widespread decline in literary reading over the past 20 years. There were significant decreases in the literary reading rates of Americans from a wide range of demographic groups, including:

- men and women;
- people from all ethnic and racial groups;

- people with all levels of educational attainment; and
- those under age 45.

Poetry suffered between 1982 and 2002 with fewer people reading poetry or listening to live poetry readings or recordings. Creative writing is one of the few literary activities in which a higher percentage of people participated in 2002 than in 1982.

Although nearly half of Americans read literature in 2002, literary participation is clearly less popular than it used to be, possibly due to competition for entertainment time and money from a range of other options, including videogames, movies, and the Internet. Consumer spending data show a significant increase in spending on television, radios, and sound equipment between 1985 and 2000. Because of the overall increase in the population between 1982 and 2002, the trends in the number of people reading literature were not as strongly downward as the changes in the literary reading rates.

For all who are interested in reading habits in America—from the book industry, literacy organizations, and arts funders to governments and businesses that depend on a well-educated, literate workforce—the trends presented in this chapter point to the importance of attracting and exciting readers from a broad range of demographic groups.

---

[11]U.S. Census Bureau, *Statistical Abstract of the United States: 2002*, Table 1212, p. 748.

The Truth of Material Culture: History or Fiction?

Jules David Prown

Jules Prown is the Paul Mellon Professor Emeritus of American Art and Material Culture at Yale University. A faculty member of the History of Art Department at Yale for many years, Professor Prown also served as the curator of several museums and galleries, was on the editorial board for several journals, and was active in professional organizations. In addition he served on numerous advisory boards, including the Whitney Museum of American Art in New York City, the National Humanities Institute, and the National Museum of American Art at the Smithsonian. This essay was originally published in *History from Things: Essays in Material Culture,* which arose from a conference at the Smithsonian in 1989 that focused on how scholars from different disciplines used objects to understand the past.

Material culture is just what it says it is—namely, the manifestations of culture through material productions. And the study of material culture is the study of material to understand culture, to discover the beliefs—the values, ideas, attitudes, and assumptions—of a particular community or society at a given time. The underlying premise is that human-made objects reflect, consciously or unconsciously, directly or indirectly, the beliefs of the individuals who commissioned, fabricated, purchased, or used them and, by extension, the beliefs of the larger society to which these individuals belonged. Material culture is thus an object-based branch of cultural anthropology or cultural history.

What material do we study in material culture? Obviously we study things made by human beings—a hammer, a card table, a plow, a teapot, a microscope, a house, a painting, a city. But we also study natural objects that have been modified by human beings—stones arranged into a wall, a garden, a prepared meal, a tattooed body. We may even study unmodified natural objects, as Cyril Stanley Smith has done, to understand better the relationship between the structure of human-made things and the structure of natural things in the physical universe in which we live.

Objects made or modified by humans are clumped together under the term *artifact*. That word connects two words—*art* and *fact*—reflecting its double Latin root. The word *art* derives from *ars, artis* (skill in joining), and *fact* derives through *factum* (deed or act) from *facere* (to make or to do), emphasizing the utilitarian meaning already implicit in the word *art*; thus, skill or knowledge is applied to the making of a thing. This verbal conjunction introduces an issue that often derails material culture discussions, namely the relationship between artifacts and art. The term *art* refers to objects whose primary initial purpose has been to represent, to memorialize, to induce veneration, elevation or contemplation, to provide access to or influence supernatural forces, to delight the eye, or otherwise to affect human thought or behavior through visual means. Many cultures do not have a special category of objects identified as art. In our culture, art is what we say is art, including ethnographic and technological objects that were not created as art but that have been aestheticized by being placed in museums or other special collections.

There are two ways to view the relationship between art and artifact—inclusive and exclusive. The inclusive approach asserts that just as the word *art* is incorporated in the word *artifact*, so too are all works of art, as fabricated objects, by definition artifacts. Some even hold that the terms are interchangeable. Several years ago the art historian Irving Lavin of the Institute for Advanced Study set forth a series of what he termed "assumptions" about art, leading to a definition of art history.[1] "The first assumption," he wrote, "is that anything man made is a work of art, even the lowliest and most purely functional object." For Lavin, and for an increasing number of art historians, art is equatable with artifacts, the material of material culture.

5 Several scholars have observed that any artifact—and the inclusive view would mean any work of art as well—is a historical event. This brings me to the first part of this paper's subtitle—history. An artifact is something that happened in the past, but, unlike other historical events, it continues to exist in our own time. Artifacts constitute the only class of historical events that occurred in the past but survive into the present. They can be reexperienced; they are authentic, primary historical material available for firsthand study. Artifacts are historical evidence.

Artifacts, like other historical events, do not just happen; they are the results of causes. There are reasons why an object comes into existence in a particular configuration, is decorated with particular motifs, is made of particular materials, and has a particular color and texture. Peter Gay, in the introduction to his book *Art and Act*, identified three types of historical causation that apply to artifacts just as to other historical events. These he calls craft, culture, and privacy. The first, craft, refers to tradition. Things are done or made in the way they were done or made previously. This is obviously true about artifacts whose artists and craftspeople are trained in art schools or apprenticeships, learn from design books, and learn from other objects. The second type of causation, culture, refers to the mind of contemporary culture—prevailing attitudes, customs, or beliefs that condition the ways in which things are said, done, or made. It refers to the world in which both maker and consumer lived and which affected their values. People are a product of their time and place. The third causal factor, privacy, refers to the individual psychological makeup of the person who made the object; it might be entirely conformist and therefore reflective of contemporary

society, or it might be quirky or eccentric, producing an original, novel, or idiosyncratic result.

The objective of a cultural investigation is mind—belief—the belief of individuals and the belief of groups of individuals, of societies. There are surface beliefs, beliefs of which people are aware and which they express in what they say, do, and make, and there are beliefs that are hidden, submerged. If we may return to etymology for a moment, beliefs that are on the surface are *sur-face* or *super-ficial* (on the face). The cultural analyst wants to get at hidden beliefs, at what lies behind surface appearance, behind the mask of the face. What lurks behind the face is our quarry—mind. A culture's most fundamental beliefs are often so widely understood, so generally shared and accepted, that they never need to be stated. They are therefore invisible to outsiders. Indeed, they may be beliefs of which the culture itself is not aware, and some of them may be so hard to face that they are repressed.

Mind, whether individual or cultural, does not reveal itself fully in overt expression; it hides things from others, and it hides things from itself. It can express itself in complex or elliptical ways. Just as some of the secrets of the physical world cannot be observed directly but only through representations—DNA, quarks, black holes—so secrets of the mental world—the world of belief—are manifest only in representations. Dreams are one example of the representations of hidden mind, of the expression of meaning in masked form. The capacity of human beings to process the unnoticed material of daily life into fictions that surface in dreams suggests to me that human beings constantly create fictions unconsciously, using the language of fiction—simile, motonomy, synecdoche, metaphor. I wish to suggest that like dreams artifacts are, in addition to their intended function, unconscious representations of hidden mind, of belief. If so, then artifacts may reveal deeper cultural truth if interpreted as fictions rather than as history. I realize that an analogy between dreams and artifacts as expressions of subconscious mind is not self-evident; indeed, it seems unlikely. Let me develop the case further.

Because underlying cultural assumptions and beliefs are taken for granted or repressed, they are not visible in what a society says, or does, or makes—its self-conscious expressions. They are, however, detectable in the way things are said, or done, or made—that is, in their style. The analysis of style, I believe, is one key to cultural understanding.[2] What do I mean by style? The configuration of a single object is its form. When groups of objects share formal characteristics, those resemblances or resonances constitute style. In the practice of art history, the study of those characteristics is called formal or stylistic analysis. When it is used in practice to discriminate between objects, it is often called connoisseurship. That term is unfortunately maligned because it seems to smack of preciousness and elitism. But in fact connoisseurship is a powerful scholarly tool, permitting rapid distinctions between what is true and what is false. I know of no other field of historical inquiry in which it is possible to achieve such rapid and precise analytical results as connoisseurship, which enables an analyst to say immediately and with assurance that this chair is Philadelphia, 1760–70, made by X, or this chest is Essex County, Massachusetts, probably Ipswich, about 1670, from the workshop of Y, or this table is a forgery, a cultural lie.

10   Whereas iconography, the analysis of subject matter, serves an art historian well in discerning and tracking linkages of objects across time and space, the analysis of style facilitates the identification of difference, of elements that are specific to a place, a time, a maker. Why is this so? Because form is the great summarizer, the concretion of belief in abstract form. A chair is Philadelphia of the 1760s because it embodies elements of what was believed in Philadelphia in the 1760s, and that formal pattern is what enables an analyst to determine the truth of the chair. It follows logically that formal patterns should also allow an analyst to reverse the process: to consider the beliefs, the patterns of mind, materialized in the chair. Instead of analyzing the concrete formal expressions of belief to determine the authenticity of the chair, the concrete formal expressions of an authentic chair are analyzed to get at belief. When style is shared by clusters of objects in a time and place, it is akin to a cultural daydream expressing unspoken beliefs. Human minds are inhabited by a matrix of feelings, sensations, intuitions, and understandings that are nonverbal or preverbal, and in any given culture many of these are shared, held in common. Perhaps if we had access to a culture's dream world, we could discover and analyze some of these hidden beliefs. In the absence of that, I suggest that some of these beliefs are encapsulated in the form of things, and there they can be discerned and analyzed.

Style is most informative about underlying beliefs when their expression is least self-conscious, and a society is less self-conscious in what it makes, especially such utilitarian objects as houses, furniture, and pots, than in what it says or does, which is necessarily conscious and intentional. Purposive expressions—for example, a diplomatic communique or an advertisement—may be intended to deceive as well as to inform. It is just here that the inclusive approach accepting a close linkage or even identification between art and artifact causes problems. The function of art is to communicate—whether to instruct, record, moralize, influence, or please. In this abstract mode of operation it resembles literature more than it does other physical artifacts. It is self-conscious, intentional expression. An icon of Saint Francis of Assisi or a representation of the Madonna and Child may be intended to arouse religious sentiments, to persuade, or even to convert; a portrait may be intended to flatter. Art may be true or deceptive; in either case it is intentional. Works of art are conscious expressions of belief, fictions composed of a vocabulary of line and color, light and texture, enriched by tropes and metaphors. As cultural evidence, works of art have many of the same liabilities as verbal fictions with their attendant problems of intentionality. The distinction between art and artifact is that artifacts do not lie. That is an exaggerated way to put it, but it makes the point. Card tables and teapots, hammers and telephones—all have specific functional programs that are constants, and the variables of style through which the program is realized are unmediated, unconscious expressions of cultural value and beliefs.

However, it is in what we call art—whether painting, sculpture, literature, theater, dance, music, or other modes of aesthetic expression—that societies have expressly articulated their beliefs. Because material culturalists are interested in objects as expressions of belief and because art is specifically material that is expressive of belief, it would be absurd to exclude art from material culture. Although we may attach special importance to uncovering deep structures of belief that may underlie the conscious, articulated top layer of belief, we cannot simply exclude the most obvious expressions of belief—art, literature, and so forth—from cultural analysis because they are self-conscious. So if an

inclusive approach that identifies art and artifact closely is unsatisfactory, so too is an exclusive approach that would pry art completely away from artifacts as unsuitable for material culture analysis.

For those of us who think that as material culturists we are "doing history" with objects, it is a sobering corrective to realize that in one sense history consistently uses small truths to build large untruths. History can never completely retrieve the past with all its rich complexity, not only of events but of emotions and sensations and spirit. We retrieve only the facts of what transpired; we do not retrieve the feel, the affective totality, of what it was like to be alive in the past. History is necessarily false; it has to be. On the other hand, literature can weave small fictions into profound and true insights regarding the human condition. It can re-create the experience of deeply felt moments and move us profoundly. It can trace inexorable patterns of cause and effect in fiction and concentrate the largest universal truths into myth.[3]

I suggest, then, that deep structural meanings of artifacts can be sprung loose by going beyond cataloguing them as historical facts to analyzing

them as fictions, specifically artistic fictions. While hierarchically art is a subcategory of artifact, analytically it is useful to treat artifacts as if they were works of art. Viewing all objects as fictions reduces the distinction between art and artifacts.

As an example, I will analyze a single artifact 15 (Figure 1). This object is 6 3/8 inches high, 4 3/4 inches wide at the widest part of the body, and 7 7/8 inches wide from spout tip to handle. It is wider than it is high and could be inscribed within a rectangle. The primary material is pewter, although the handle and lower ring of the finial are of wood. There is a small hole in the top of the lid, and inside the vessel there is a circular arrangement of small holes where the spout joins the body.

The vessel is divided by a horizontal line three-fifths of the way up where the lid rests on the body. The lid and the body also are subdivided by horizontal moldings, the lower one exactly midway between the base and the top of the handle and at a height exactly equal to the total height of the lid. Viewed from the side the object presents a series of S-curves, including the handle, the spout, and the outlines of the body, the lid, and the finial.

The spout and the handle rise above the rim. The vessel stands on a raised base 3/8 inch high.

Seen from the top (Figure 2), the object presents a series of concentric circles surrounding the finial. The spout, finial, hole, hinge, and handle are aligned to form an axis through the vessel at its largest dimension.

The object consists of five separate parts—lid, body, handle, spout, and finial. The lower section of the body is a flattened ball, the upper part a reel. The lid is bell-shaped and surmounted by a finial that echoes in simplified form the shape of the vessel—a flattened ball surmounted by a reel, with a hemisphere above.

Setting aside previous knowledge, it could nonetheless be deduced that this hollow-bodied object is a vessel or container, that the larger opening at the top revealed when the lid is opened is used to put some substance into the vessel, and that the spout is used to redirect that substance into a smaller container. The small holes in the body at the base of the spout suggest that the contained substance is strained in the act of pouring to retain in the vessel particles larger than the holes. The fact that the spout rises above the rim suggests that the substance contained is liquid, since if the spout were below the rim, liquid would overflow when the vessel were full. The use of wood in the handle and in the finial, which is grasped to open the lid, suggests that the liquid may be hot, since wood is not as good a conductor of heat as metal. The fact that an attached rim raises the bottom of the pot off the surface on which it stands also suggests that the contents may be hot.

Manipulating the object suggests the use of 20 the handle and the finial. Opening the lid indicates that the finial makes contact with the handle, and the absence of wear suggests that the handle, and perhaps the finial disk as well, is a replacement. The bell shape of the lid suggests sound, and actual sound results from opening and closing the lid.

When respondents have been asked to express their feelings about this object following extended analysis, they have used such words as "solid," "substantial," "cheerful," "comfortable," "grandmotherly," and "reliable." The object evokes recollections, and the identification of the links between the object and the memories of experience for which it stands as a sign is the key to unlocking the cultural belief embedded in it. If you ask what in the object triggered such words as "solid," "substantial," and "reliable," respondents

FIGURE 2   Detail of pewter teapot by Danforth. Yale University Art Gallery, Mabel Brady Garvan Collection

will note that the object is wider than it is high and that the flattened ball of the lower part gives it a squarish and bottom-weighted appearance, suggesting stability. The responses are based on experience of the phenomenal world. The words "cheerful," "comfortable," and "grandmotherly" reflect more subjective life experiences that also can be located with some precision by asking questions based on the previously deduced evidence. Under what circumstances do we drink warm liquids? When we are cold, warm liquid warms us inside; when we are hot, it causes perspiration that evaporates, cooling the body surface. We drink hot liquids when we are ill—soup or tea—again because they make us feel better, perhaps by promoting perspiration and helping break a fever. When we are ill and incapacitated, warm liquids are often brought to us, and the care of another person is comforting. Hot liquids are also drunk on social occasions. Drinking coffee and tea is marked by a sense of well-being that derives from the stimulation of the drink itself, by the physical act of giving or pouring and receiving, and frequently by conversation. Drinking hot liquids and talking seem to go together.

James Fernandez has written of the importance of metaphor to anthropologists in decoding culture, a process he referred to punningly as "antrope-ology."[4] Although he was discussing verbal metaphors, several of his discriminations are applicable as well to the understanding of how artifacts function as metaphorical expressions of culture. He distinguishes between two kinds of metaphor—structural metaphors, which conform to the shape of experience and thus resemble actual objects in the physical world, and textual metaphors, which are similar to the feelings of experience. Structural metaphors are based on physical experience of the phenomenal world; textual metaphors are based on the emotive experience of living in that world.

The object, which we can now refer to as a teapot since our analysis of it is complete, invokes multiple textual metaphors—cheerful, comfortable, reliable, grandmotherly, and so forth—metaphors based on the feelings of experience. It also embodies structural metaphors based on the shape of experience. The lid and finial, for example, can be read as a bell metaphor. And the bell shape suggests calling—whether by a dinner bell or ringing from a sick

bed—calling for and receiving help or comfort or sustenance. Another structural metaphor, equally obvious, is less easily retrieved, however, perhaps because repressed. If you ask the respondent (or the analyst asks him- or herself) to identify the Ur-experience, the earliest human experience of ingesting warm liquids, the immediate response is as a baby feeding from a mother's breast. Structural analogies between the shape of the lower section of the body of the vessel and the female breast now become evident. And when the object is viewed from above, with the finial at the center like a nipple, the object is even more breastlike (Figure 2). The teapot is revealed, unexpectedly, as a structural metaphor for the female breast.

Fernandez defines a metaphor as a sign, a combination of image and idea located between a signal and a symbol, between perception and conception. A signal invokes a simple perception that orients some kind of action or interaction. A picture of a teapot could function literally as a signal hanging outside a tea room beckoning the tourist to enter; at a tea party the teapot itself serves as a signal for pouring and serving. At the other end of the scale, a symbol triggers a conception whose meaning is fully realized. A common denominator linking the various circumstances cited earlier in which warm liquids are ingested is that all involve an act of giving and receiving, which is, in its largest social sense, the act of charity.[5] A teapot, fully conceptualized in meaning, could become a symbol of the act of giving, of charity. One can envision a page in an emblem book with an image of a teapot, a symbol of charity, and an accompanying moralizing text.

Located between signal, a simple perception, and symbol, a fully realized conception, the teapot by itself stands as a sign, a metaphor both structural and textual. It embodies deeply felt but unconceptualized meanings relating to giving and receiving, to such things as maternal love and care, oral gratification, satisfaction of hunger and thirst, comforting internal warmth when cold or ill, and conviviality. And it is thus as a sign or metaphor that the teapot works as evidence of cultural belief.

If artifacts express culture metaphorically, what kinds of insight can they afford us? What, for example, does the teapot tell us about belief? The object has given us a clue that the drinking of tea, and perhaps the entire ceremony of tea drinking, may be related metaphorically to the fundamental human act of giving and receiving and has the potential of being a symbol of generosity or charity, of *caritas*. The humanness as well as the humaneness of the act is suggested in this teapot by the fact that the liquid is encased in an organic, breastlike form. But, as we well know, a teapot can be precisely the opposite in form (Figure 3); it can deny the humanly anatomical or personal aspect of giving, or charity, and by using purely inorganic, intellectual, geometric forms deny personal involvement and emphasize the cerebral character of the act. In so doing it conveys something about the different character of a different culture.[6]

The fundamental structural linkage of warm liquids, breast feeding, and charity—the human metaphor—suggested to us by our study of a single teapot is now understood to be a formal potential for all vessels used to pour out hot liquids. The extent to which it is generated, tolerated, or rejected by a culture is an index of one aspect of that culture's belief. Objects are evidence, and material culture enables us to interpret the culture that produced them in subjective, affective ways unachievable through written records alone. They did not write much about breasts in the late eighteenth century,

and even less about the linkage between breasts and charity, but the metaphorical language of teapots conveys a livelier and perhaps truer picture. What we have perceived in the teapot are indicators of beliefs about giving and receiving, generosity, charity, and definitions of the self in relation to others. Can one go on to describe with greater precision the terrain of cultural belief expressed by artifacts? The most persistent metaphors in objects of which I have become aware relate to such fundamental human experiences as mortality and death; love, sexuality, and gender roles; privacy (seeing and being seen) and communication; power or control and acceptance; fear and danger; and, as here, giving and receiving.

Metaphors, Fernandez says, locate beliefs in what he calls the "quality space" of a culture.[7] Among several formulations he noted as to how metaphors locate belief is one that accords closely with the polarities of belief I have encountered in my analysis of American artifacts, that articulated by W. T. Jones as seven "axes of bias."[8] These "axes" are lines of predisposition, along the calibration of which beliefs are situated. They are static-dynamic, order-disorder, discreteness-continuity, process-spontaneity, sharp-soft, outer-inner, and other world-this world. (The first

FIGURE 3   Teapot, silver. Loring Bailey (American, 1740–1814). Hood Museum of Art, Dartmouth College, Hanover, N.H. Gift of Frank L. Harrington, Class of 1924

term in each opposition cited applies more to the neoclassical Bailey teapot, the second to the Danforth teapot, but in varying degrees). I wonder whether it would not be possible to graph these points, an admittedly subjective exercise, to arrive at abstractions of artifacts that would constitute a type of cultural fingerprint.

It should be understood that the analysis of artifacts as fictions to discover otherwise unexpressed cultural beliefs does not so much answer questions as raise them. Artifacts make us aware affectively of attitudes and values; they provide only limited amounts of data. In the language of semiotics, they are artistic signs articulating a climate of belief; they are often poor informational signs. But the questions they pose are authentic ones, arising from the primary evidence of the artifact rather than being imposed by the investigator.

30   If artifacts materialize belief, then it follows that when a society undergoes a traumatic change, that change should manifest itself artifactually. Perhaps the most clearly defined moment of social change in our country occurred at the time of transition from colony to nation; that is the change signalled in the configuration of these two teapots.[9] We can corroborate the connection by looking at two stylistically similar expressions in a different type of object. A pre–Revolution New York Chippendale or rococo card table (Figure 4) is irregular, organic, curvilinear, jutting into and penetrated by ambient space, heavy, and decorated with carved leafage, shells, claw and ball feet, and rope gadrooning. It has wells for counters, recesses at the corners for candlesticks, a drawer to hold cards and counters, and a baize cover to protect the surface, make it easier to pick up cards, and keep them from sliding. A post–Revolution Federal or classical revival card table (Figure 5) is regular, geometrical, self-contained, light in weight and structure, and decorated on its smooth veneered surfaces with inlaid images of flowers and eagles. It has three fixed and one fly leg; two sides have legs in the center, and two sides are open. Questions arise. Did women in dresses tend to sit at the open sides and men in trousers take the sides with the center legs, which they could straddle? If so, if two men and two women played, the player across the table was always of the opposite sex. In the games played, was the opposing player a partner or an adversary, or was each player out for him- or herself? A player at a Chippendale table (Figure 4) is drawn into closer physical proximity to the other players,

FIGURE 4   Card table (American, New York, 1760–70). Yale University Art Gallery, Mabel Brady Garvan Collection

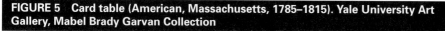

FIGURE 5   Card table (American, Massachusetts, 1785–1815). Yale University Art Gallery, Mabel Brady Garvan Collection

in part because the sides, although bowed in the center, are recessed from the corners. The sensation of closeness is especially pervasive if one is forced to circle one's legs around the solid protruding cabriole leg in the center of three of the four sides, becoming literally wrapped up with the table. The other players are near, their faces loom large, their voices are close, their aromas are pervasive, as is the warmth and smell of the candles at either elbow. There is a sense of intimacy, of coziness, reinforced by the warmth of the nearby candles, the soft baize covering, and a sheltered trove of private wealth in a well—a kind of security, like food in a bowl or money in one's pocket.

We are aware of the reality of physical substances—the sturdiness and weight of the table, the solidity of elements carved of mahogany that replicate organic elements in the natural world, such as rope carvings, leafage, shells, and claws clutching balls. We are comforted by the real, natural environment of substantial, tangible things. The functionalism of the table is reassuring. Places are carved out for candlesticks, counters, even players. The sinuous curves of solid organic forms that surround the player suggest not only the natural world but also the complexity of

human relations within that world. Deviousness might be a natural and not unfriendly part of the game—it is a fact of life, like sinuous curves in nature. The table suggests a culture in which value is placed on and pleasure derived from substantial things—the realities of the world and of life as well as warm, complex, intimate human relations.

The Federal card table (Figure 5) seems to substitute the mental for the physical, fragility for substantiality, intellectual geometry for organic complexity, aloofness for intimacy. Forms are slender and orderly; surfaces are sheer and planar; clarity and regularity replace complexity and sinuousness. The decorative elements on Federal card tables tend not to be real things but pictures of things—inlay—abstract images rather than the things themselves. Projecting sides often serve to keep each player at a slight distance from the table. The players are thus farther away from each other. Objects on the table surface are less secure, less rooted, set on a flat, all-purpose surface rather than nestled into designed concavities. The entire enterprise is cooler, more distant, more abstract, and in a sense more tentative, less friendly. It is almost as if at the Chippendale table one tries to win real property from intimates, to put their goods in your pocket, while at the Federal table one attempts to win intellectual supremacy over adversaries and perhaps money in a more abstract form.

An investigation now could go in many directions; a particularly promising one would be a study to see whether the actual games played during the pre–Revolution and post–Revolution periods changed and how these changes, if any, related to relations between men and women, ideas about independence and authority, private and corporate entrepreneurship, generosity and greed, hostility and friendship, and a host of other attitudes, values, and beliefs imbedded in the artifacts and acted out in the games people played.

Obviously not all belief can be retrieved. An artifact is embedded in its culture and embodies some of that culture's beliefs. We are deeply embedded in another culture, and our understandings are colored by its beliefs. One great advantage of the study of material culture is the extent to which it provides a way to overcome the problem of cultural perspective by establishing the broadest possible base of commonality. A society we would study had its set of beliefs, its culture, while we who would seek to understand that culture are the products not only of a different cultural environment but of a complex of cultural environments. Each of us is pervaded by the beliefs of our own particular groups—nationality, place of residence, class, religion, politics, occupation, gender, age, race, ethnicity, and so forth. We all have biases of which we are not aware, convictions that we accept as unquestioningly as the air we breathe. The issue that haunts all cultural studies is whether it is possible for us to step outside our own cultural givens, our own time and place, and interpret the evidence of another culture objectively—that is, in terms of the individuals and society who produced it rather than in our own terms. If not—if we are irredeemably biased by our own unconscious beliefs, if we are hopelessly culture-bound to our own time and place—then all efforts to interpret other cultures should be avoided since our interpretations will inevitably be distorted.

35   The problem is a problem of mind. We are trying to understand another culture whose patterns of belief, whose mind, is different from our own. Our own beliefs, our mindset, biases our view. It

would be ideal, and this is not as silly as it sounds, if we could approach that other culture mindlessly, at least while we gather our data. This is the great promise of material culture: By undertaking cultural interpretation through artifacts, we engage the other culture in the first instance not with our minds, the seat of our cultural biases, but with our senses. Figuratively speaking, we put ourselves inside the bodies of the individuals who made or used these objects; we see with their eyes and touch with their hands. To identify with people from the past or from other places empathetically through the senses is clearly a different way of engaging them than abstractly through the reading of written words. Instead of our minds making intellectual contact with their minds, our senses make affective contact with their sensory experience.

Certainly it is true that sense perceptions filtered through the brain may also be culturally conditioned. But although commonality of sense perception cannot be proven either empirically or philosophically, certain conclusions can be drawn on the basis of the shared neuro-physiological apparatus of all human beings, which is not culturally specific and has evolved only slowly over time, and also from the inescapable commonalities of life as lived. All humans undergo a passage from birth, through nurturing and aging, to death. En route they experience the realities of the physical world: gravity, a sense of up and down, an awareness of night and day, of straight, curved, and crooked, of enclosure and exclusion. Through the channels of the senses they taste sweet, sour, and bitter; smell the acrid and the fragrant; hear sounds loud and quiet; perceive through touch the difference between rough and smooth, hot and cold, wet and dry; and see colors and shapes. They know hunger and thirst, illness and health, pain, sexual passion, bodily functions, loss and discovery, laughter and real tears. The human body constantly provides a sense of scale. It all adds up to a tremendous body of experience that is common and transcultural. This experience is transformed into belief that finds material expression in artifacts, the analysis of which—material culture—provides privileged paths of access for us to an understanding of other peoples and other cultures, of other times and other places.

Notes

Part of this essay is derived from a paper given at a conference on North American material culture research, sponsored by the Institute of Social and Economic Research, Memorial University of Newfoundland, and Winterthur Museum, St. John's, Newfoundland, June 1986, and published in *Living in a Material World: Canadian and American Approaches to Material Culture*, edited by Gerald L. Pocius (St. John's: Institute of Social and Economic Research, Memorial University of Newfoundland, 1991).

1. "The Art of Art History," *Art News*, October 1983.
2. For more on this, see my "Style as Evidence," *Winterthur Portfolio* 15, no. 3 (Autumn 1980): 197–210.
3. Henry Glassie resolved this paradox by viewing history as myth, as art, in his article "Meaningful Things and Appropriate Myths: The Artifact's Place in American Studies," *Prospects* 3 (1977):1–49, reprinted in Robert Blair St. George, *Material Life in America, 1600–1860* (Northeastern University Press: Boston, 1988).
4. James Fernandez, "The Mission of Metaphor in Expressive Culture," *Current Anthropology* 15, no. 2 (June 1974):119–45.
5. The Roman legend of Cimon and Pero, known as the legend of Roman charity, tells of the daughter who visits her elderly father starving in prison. She nourishes him by feeding him from her own breast.
6. Although the Danforth teapot is in the Queen Anne style, it may well be as late in date as the Bailey teapot. One would expect that contemporaneous teapots would be similar in form, and the formal opposition of these two pots would seem to undercut the claim that difference in form conveys difference in cultural character. Apparent anomolies that arise in material culture study pose questions—What is the explanation for the formal difference of contemporary objects?—and it is precisely such questions that stimulate further investigation, new thinking, and enlarged understandings. Pursuit of the question was beyond the scope of the present paper because of time constraints, but what is involved here is a difference in technologies required by the difference in materials (the Danforth pot is pewter; the Bailey pot is silver) relating to significant differences in stylistic persistence between rural Connecticut (Danforth) and the urban Boston region (Bailey). Retention of a colonial style half a century later might well suggest a hypothesis about post–Revolution Connecticut, a particular part of Connecticut, or a particular clientele that would need to be tested more widely.
7. I am not comfortable with the spatial or topographical model for imaging cultural belief, but neither is Fernandez.
8. W. T. Jones, *The Romantic Syndrome* (Martinus Nijhoff: The Hague, 1961).
9. This section develops ideas introduced in "Style as Evidence," 200ff.

Public Memory and the Search for Power in American Historical Archaeology

Paul A. Shackel

Paul A. Shackel is the Director of the Center for Heritage Resource Studies and Professor of Anthropology at the University of Maryland, College Park. Prior to joining the University faculty, Professor Shackel worked for the National Park Service for seven and one-half years. His research focuses on material culture and how people use objects to establish identity and forge social relations. Professor Shackel uses history and anthropology to consider American monuments. He is especially interested in what these artifacts mean to national identity; how they reflect gender, race, class, and power relationships; and how such relationships change over time. This essay was originally published in *American Anthropologist*, a publication of the American Anthropology Association.

How Americans remember the past is often reinforced by landscapes, monuments, commemorative ceremonies, and archaeology. These features and activities often help to create an official public memory that becomes part of a group's heritage. I suggest that public memory can be established by (1) forgetting about or excluding an alternative past, (2) creating and reinforcing patriotism, and/or (3) developing a sense of nostalgia to legitimize a particular heritage. These categories are not mutually exclusive, and the lines that separate these categories may not always be well defined. I show how post–Civil War American landscapes, monuments, and commemorative activities helped to reinforce racist attitudes in the United States that became part of the official memory. African Americans have struggled to revise the official memory of the Civil War, although the power to change this memory has been situational and not always successful. *[commemoration, memory, material culture, historical archaeology, landscapes]*

Americans often turn to the past to explain current social conditions, to comf1ort themselves, to build self-esteem, and to create cultural pride. What aspects of the past are remembered and how they are remembered and interpreted are important issues that allow us to see how public memory develops. Memories can serve individual or collective needs and can validate the holders' version of the past. In the public arena they can be embedded in power to serve the dominant culture by supporting existing social inequalities. It is common for subordinate groups explicitly or implicitly to challenge the dominant meanings of public memories and create new ones that suit their needs. Often, the success of these challenges is situational, depending upon context and social and political power.

In 1925 Maurice Halbwachs formally introduced the concept of memory in the creation of history. He remarked that a collective memory develops when individuals seek the testimony of others in order to "validate their interpretations of their own experiences, to provide independent confirmation (or refutation) of the content of their memories and thus confidence in their accuracy" (in Thelen 1989:1122). Other individuals are needed as a second reference in order to establish a frame of reference and to create recollection. People experience and remember or forget collectively, and they figure out how to interpret these experiences. They develop a collective memory by molding, shaping, and agreeing upon what to remember, although this process may not be always consciously planned. A collective memory becomes public when a group has the resources and power to promote a particular past. These histories mask or naturalize inequalities through material culture, such as memorials, museums, and the built landscape. Inequalities can be also promoted or challenged through commemoration ceremonies.

In archaeology some important works that critically evaluate the production of history include those written by Trigger (1989), Leone et al. (1987), and Shanks and Tilley (1987). These works evaluate the management and use of prehistoric and historic resources. They view the production of historical consciousness as an outcome of the struggle between groups. I found the production of a collective memory intriguing when examining the development of the industrial town of Harpers Ferry, West Virginia (see Shackel 1994b, 1999, 2000, in press). For instance, until very recently, all of the town's histories written in the twentieth century stop documenting the town just after the Civil War era. It is easy to come away with the impression that the town reached its economic zenith in the 1850s and 1860s and that the town had virtually disappeared after the Civil War (Shackel 1996). Almost all of these histories proclaim that Harpers Ferry should be remembered only because of its role in the surrender of 12,500 Union troops to Stonewall Jackson and the events that surround John Brown (excerpt Gilbert 1984, 1999). A historical archaeology of the town shows that it did survive and that it became a major regional industrial center until the 1920s. It thrives today as a tourist town (Shackel 1993, 2000). Many of the people who remained in Harpers Ferry after the Great Depression had a working-class background that extended into the Victorian era as all of the industrial entrepreneurs were gone by the late 1930s. I think it is not an accident that Harpers Ferrians, mostly merchants and working-class families, ignored much of the town's Victorian industrial history. The postbellum industrial entrepreneurs who controlled the town's economy and labor opportunities were northerners and did little for Harpers Ferry's working-class families, except to take their rent money and extract their labor at very low wages. While the town had industrial success, people chose to forget their exploitation as well as their relatives' (Shackel 1994a).

This phenomenon, masking a class or a group history when developing a collective memory, is well documented in other communities. For instance, in Lawrence, Massachusetts, Sider (1996:48–83) describes a workers' history of resistance and strikes that has been repressed by community memory. In this mill community, the Strike of 1912, euphemistically called the "Bread and Roses Day," was branded by the Catholic Church as instigated by the most "unsavory immigrants" (quoted in Sider 1996:52). Strike leaders were intimidated throughout their lives by supervisors and industrialists. Community leaders focused on the strike, rather than the working conditions that provided the rationale for the strike. More important, the testimony of the factory working conditions by a 14-year-old girl in front of Congress was also suppressed from historical consciousness (Cameron 1993, 1996).

As these examples demonstrate, public memory is more a reflection of present political and social relations than a true reconstruction of the past. As present conditions change socially, politically, and ideologically, the collective memory of the past will also change. The control of a group's memory is often a question of power. Individuals and groups often struggle over the meaning of memory as the official memory is imposed by the power elite (Teski and Climo 1995:2). For instance, Handler and Gable's 1997 *The New History in an Old Museum* serves as an excellent example of deconstructing the production of history in an outdoor museum like Colonial Williamsburg. They reveal that the museum's interpretation of the colonial era is a way to reinforce social inequalities in contemporary society. This sentiment, that the histories told at Colonial Williamsburg are a product of public memory, has been expressed by others (Leone 1981; Wallace 1981). Anthropologist Michel-Rolph Trouillot (1995:15) also produces a compelling argument about taking a critical approach to historical accounts. Taking accounts that range from Columbus Day to the Haitian revolution for independence, he notes that the past can only be understood in the context of the present. He recognizes that during the production of history power operates in a way that silences subaltern groups.

Historians, too, have seen memories as being subjective to group interests. Influential works by David Lowenthal (1985), Michael Frisch (1990), David Glassberg (1990), Michael Kammen (1991), John Bodner (1992), and Edward Linenthal (1993) have guided public historians into addressing issues that show the connectedness between memory and

5

power. These works show that we cannot assume that all groups, and all members of the same group, understand the past in the same way. The same historical and material representation may have divergent meanings to different audiences (Glassberg 1996:9–10; Lowenthal 1985). A struggle to create or subvert a past often develops between competing interest groups (see, for instance, Neustadt and May 1986; Peterson 1994). Different versions of the past are communicated through various institutions, including schools, amusements, art and literature, government ceremonies, families and friends, and landscape features that are designated as historical. Public memory does not solely rely on professional historical scholarship, but it is usually influenced by various individuals and institutions that support the collective memory.

In particular, I am interested in the various ways memory takes shape on the American landscape and how it is influenced by race, and power. After the American Civil War sectional bitterness existed, and to some extent it continues today. By the end of Reconstruction the political importance of the war refocused (Foster 1987:68–69; McConnell 1992:108). Blue–Grey reunions from the 1880s became a form of selective memory rather than forgiveness (McConnell 1992:190). The African American memory of the war continually lost ground to a new and growing dominant ideology, led by people like Oliver Wendell Holmes Jr. and later Theodore Roosevelt. An integrated collective memory became unacceptable to the majority of white Americans. They interpreted the war as a test of a generation's valor and loyalty toward a cause. The Lost Cause mythology argued that the Confederacy was never defeated but, rather, was overwhelmed by numbers and betrayed by some key generals (Blight 2001).

While the Victorian era had been a healing period between the North and the South, greater schisms developed in this country that divided people along lines of class and ethnicity. The era is recognized by many as the "decade of patriotic offensives among native-born, white members of the American middle class" (McConnell 1992:207). Exclusionary groups dominated the era. Americans created clubs and organizations at a rate never seen before or after in U.S. history. Associations developed for group protection and the wealthy increasingly excluded other groups (Hobsbawm 1983:292–293). Social Darwinism and scientific racism became the popular paradigms in intellectual circles, and African American

participation in society and their role in the Civil War minimized. Commemoration ceremonies of the war often celebrated the great white hero memorialized with statues of generals on horseback or a generic-looking single soldier that stood in a town center (O'Leary 1999).

Recognizing various types of power is valuable when examining issues related to the creation of public memory, race, and the American landscape. Eric Wolf (1990) describes four modes of power: "the first is power as the capability of a person; the second is power as the ability of a person to impose upon another interpersonally; the third is tactical power which controls social settings; and the fourth is structural power, which allocates social labor" (in Little 1994:23). The first mode is what Miller and Tilley (1984) describe as "power to" and the remaining they call "power over." Contextualizing the use of power in relationship to public memory allows us to recognize the complexity of the use of power and its connections to public memory.

Many of the studies in public memory can be viewed within the context of tactical power, which controls social settings. The control over the uses and meanings of material culture, and the exercise of "power over," can be accomplished in several ways. Memory can be about (1) forgetting about or excluding an alternative past, (2) creating and reinforcing patriotism, and/or (3) developing a sense of nostalgia to legitimize a particular heritage. These categories serve as an organizational point to see the relationship between power and the construction of public memory. They allow us to see that objects and landscapes that historical archaeologists and public historians often view have different meanings to different people and groups at different times. These categories are not mutually exclusive. The public memory associated with highly visible objects is always being constructed, changed, and challenged, and at all times power and the challenge to power are situational. Below, I provide background and a case study for each category, all from a Civil War context and related to how landscapes reflect and reinforce the ideals of race and power through heritage and patriotism.

AN EXCLUSIONARY PAST

Elements of the past remembered in common, as well as elements of the past forgotten in common, are essential for group cohesion (Glassberg 1996:13). While collective memory can be about forgetting a past, it often comes at the expense of a subordinate group. Those who are excluded may try to subvert the meaning of the past through alternative histories, or they may also strive for more representation in the form of a more pluralistic past. When Americans reflect on the traditional meanings associated with a collective national memory, it has focused on elites and traditional heroes. The perception of many is that American history is linear and straightforward. This uncomplicated story occurs only when we leave others out of the picture. This "sacred story with strong nationalist overtones... derived much of its coherence from the groups it ignored or dismissed" (Leff 1995:833; also see Nash et al. 1998:100). Those who disagree with a multicultural history have claimed that

> It is difficult ... to see how the subjects of the new [social] history can be accommodated in any single framework, let alone a national and political one.... How can all these groups, each cherishing its uniqueness and its claim to sovereign attention, be mainstreamed into a single, coherent, integrated history? [quoted in Nash et al. 1998:100–101]

I have seen this attitude among some historical archaeologists and historians who believe that the only reason for preserving Civil War battlefields is for commemorating the dead and for studying battlefield logistics. They refuse to see the relevance of incorporating social history to view the Civil War in its larger context. Multicultural perspectives, like addressing the issues of slavery at a national battlefield, are reprehensible to some Civil War scholars (see Smith 1999). There is the perception that the Civil War is all about loyalty to a cause, a sentiment that developed in the late nineteenth century that excluded African Americans from the Civil War story. It is a feeling that remains strong among many conservative scholars.

We often find that while accounts of ordinary people and subaltern groups do not necessarily find their way into official accounts, they can persist and create an alternative minority view. This view has a function to legitimize and stabilize a claim to a history (Fields 1994:153). While many federally funded museums extol the glories of economic and social progress as a result of industry, many working-class members view the preservation

of old buildings and ruins as an attempt to save a degrading phase of human history. Robert Vogel of the Smithsonian Institution notes, "The dirt, noise, bad smell, hard labor and other forms of exploitation associated with these kinds of places make preservation [of industrial sites] ludicrous. 'Preserve a steel mill?' people say, 'It killed my father. Who wants to preserve that?'" (quoted in Lowenthal 1985:403). Therefore, while individual dissenting views on the true benefits of industrialization exist, the federal government remains strong in supporting ideas of industrial progress at national parks such as Lowell and Saugus in Massachusetts and Hopewell and Steam Town in Pennsylvania. In many of these cases archaeology has played a major role in supporting the official history.

Following, I provide a case study of how a community created an official history of an event in the Civil War at the expense of another group. In particular, a white officer was commemorated in the form of a statue that minimized the role of the African American troops that he commanded. Only through protest and the rise of the Civil Rights movement did the forgotten history of the troops become part of the official memory.

CASE STUDY: THE REMAKING OF THE ROBERT GOULD SHAW MEMORIAL

The Robert Gould Shaw Memorial sits on the Boston Common to commemorate the colonel who led the first African American Northern volunteer regiment into battle during the American Civil War. The memorial to Shaw with a representation of the 54th Massachusetts Infantry has stood for over a century with its meaning controlled by the white community. It demonstrates and reinforces the memory of their community's historic patriotic and abolitionist commitment.

On May 28, 1863, Shaw and the 54th Massachusetts Volunteer Infantry marched to Boston's Battery Wharf, where they sailed for the Sea Islands off Charleston, South Carolina. The world watched the soldiers since it was the first Northern-raised African American regiment. After a two-night march through rain and shifting sands, with insufficient rations, an exhausted Shaw accepted the order to lead an immediate attack on Fort Wagner. At dusk, on July 18, the Massachusetts 54th led the assault. Six hundred troops charged across a narrow spit of sand against a strong earthwork. Shaw was one of the first to fall, but his troops pressed on. More than half reached the inside of the fort, and they were able to hold Wagner's parapet for an hour before being driven off by the Confederates. Other white regiments attacked that night, but they also failed. The assault on Fort Wagner that day left 1,515 Union casualties compared with 181 on the Confederate side.

News of the assault on Fort Wagner by the 54th Massachusetts became widely known in the North, and Shaw and the deeds of his fallen men were transformed into martyrdom. The *New York Tribune* wrote that the battle "made Fort Wagner such a name to the colored race as Bunker Hill had been for ninety years to the white Yankees" (from McPherson 1988:686). The *Atlantic Monthly* wrote, "Through the cannon smoke of that black night the manhood of the colored race shines before many eyes that would not see" (from McPherson 1969). The 54th had proven that African Americans could fight honorably. Shaw's death was a family loss and a moral contribution by Boston to preserve the Union and fight for emancipation.

Shaw became one of the Civil War's most celebrated legends. More than 40 poems have been written about Shaw and they helped to solidify his martyrdom. Plans for a Shaw monument began in 1865 with a formal meeting held in Boston. Many delays occurred as key proponents of the memorial died, but in 1884, a commission appointed a young, well-known artist, Augustus Saint-Gaudens, for the Shaw memorial project.

Saint-Gaudens labored sporadically on the monument for 13 years, and he finally unveiled it on "Decoration Day," May 31, 1897. At the ceremony 65 veterans of the 54th Massachusetts marched up Beacon Hill past the Robert Gould Shaw Memorial. It was the first soldier's monument to honor a group rather than a single individual, although an explicit hierarchy exists in the representation. The memorial places the colonel in the center among his troops. Shaw is on horseback with his fatigue cap on. The African American soldiers serve as a backdrop. They are ready for battle with rifles over their shoulders, and the procession is led by a drummer boy. Above them is an allegorical figure with laurel branches in one hand and poppies in the other. The work was immediately hailed as a great success by many art critics.

In 1916 Freeman Murry lauded the sculpture as a "memorial to man, race, and a cause." Murry remarked that Saint-Gaudens's work will "tower above the color line" (1916:166). Murry's interpretation—that the Shaw monument would help dismantle the racial boundaries that were so prevalent in the early twentieth century—puzzles some scholars. For instance, modern art scholars, like Albert Boime (1990), point out Saint-Gaudens's racist tendencies. He created the Shaw monument in the context of strong racial and ethnic tensions in the late-nineteenth-century United States. The development of Jim Crow legislation in the late nineteenth century made it increasingly difficult for African Americans to achieve equality—in the North and the South.

While creating the monument, Saint-Gaudens filled his studio in New York with African American subjects from the surrounding neighborhood. Reinforcing a contemporary stereotype, Saint-Gaudens wrote that "they are very likable, with their soft voices and imaginative, though simple, minds" (1913:334–335; see Boime 1990:208). Saint-Gaudens's son, Homer, describes an incident of his father's substandard treatment of African Americans. Homer noted, "I believe he could detect a change of two degrees from his favorite amount of heat, when woe betides the darkey who tended stove" (Saint-Gaudens 1913:133).

While contemporary critics claimed his sculpture as an act of "newborn American patriotism" (Taft [1924]1969:304) and said that it would "tower above the color line" (Murry 1916:166), there were other contemporary voices that contested the meaning of the Shaw monument. Based on what we know about Saint-Gaudens's feelings about African Americans through his writings, it is difficult to see him as very sympathetic toward African Americans, and it becomes even more difficult to see his work as an expression of the abolitionist sentiment. The Shaw memorial is just that, a memorial to Robert Gould Shaw, and the African American troops serve as a background to the subject. It is a monument that remembers one of Boston's Brahman elite and the role that the elite played in the abolitionist movement.

A contemporary critic, Charles Caffin, wrote in 1913 that Saint-Gaudens "portrays the humble soldiers with varying characteristics of pathetic devotion. The emotion [is] aroused by intent and steadfast onward movement of the troops, whose dog like trustfulness is contrasted with the serene elevation of their white leader" (1913:11). There is no doubt that the white officer is the central figure in the monument. Shaw is elevated on horseback and "sharing the upper zone with the allegorical Angel of Death who bears Victory and Sleep" (Boime 1990:209). Shaw is portrayed as noble and sits erect in his saddle. Boime concludes that Saint-Gaudens was successful "in establishing a visual 'color-line' that guarded white supremacy" (1990:211). The hegemony of the powerful is explicit and noticeable.

In the late twentieth century the tone and meaning associated with the monument have become even more muddled. A rededication of the monument in 1981 placed in stone on the back of the monument the names of the 281 African American soldiers who died in the assault of Fort Wagner. This act provides some recognition to the foot soldiers. Later that decade, the critically acclaimed movie *Glory* brought further recognition to the role of African Americans in the Civil War.

25   In May 1997, Boston held a public ceremony that celebrated the 100th anniversary of the unveiling of the Shaw memorial. Several prominent African Americans spoke at this 100th anniversary rededication. President Benjamin Payton of Tuskegee University, Professor Henry Louis Gates Jr. of the Du Bois Institute at Harvard University, and General Colin Powell all remarked on the splendid beauty of the monument and saw the portrayal of the troops in a positive and uplifting light (Blatt et al. 2000).

Art historian Kirk Savage remarked that the memorial is an excellent blend between soldier and general. Savage argued that they are not "listless," as described by Boime (1990) but, rather, determined. The troops do not lose their humanity. He notes that the soldiers look well drilled and each looks very different. They are individuals who wear their uniforms in various fashions. The horse glides and towers, and the soldiers are weighed down by their equipment as they lean forward: "Saint-Gaudens was able to elevate the white hero without demoting the black troops" (Savage 1997:203). African Americans never had this representation of individuality before. While Saint-Gaudens was racist in his memoirs, Savage remarks, he made the infantrymen individuals, and the memorial is not a racist monument. Savage

proposes that what Saint-Gaudens was thinking about had no bearing on his sculpture. He notes that Saint-Gaudens "treated racial differences openly and with dignity, asserting a 'brotherhood' of man. And yet it registered, compellingly and beautifully, the transcendence of the white hero in that of brotherhood" (1997:204). Savage does not believe that there can be different readings of the same piece of material culture and he claims that Caffin's (1913) and Boime's (1990) argument "cannot be sustained without a serious misreading of the sculpture itself" (Savage 1997:256 n. 97).

While Savage believes that there can only be one reading of the monument, I believe that the importance and significance of the Shaw memorial is that it can be read in various ways and different people will ascribe diverse meanings to it, depending upon the memory they have associated with the event. Saint-Gaudens created this statue in a racist era, and he used the white colonel to dominate the foreground of the memorial. He also gives African Americans significant representation in the memorial, a rare phenomenon for the era. The events of the civil rights movement of the mid – and late twentieth century, along with the Civil Rights Act, have given African Americans a greater representation in our public memory, and the Shaw memorial centennial celebration, backed by many prominent political and social figures, also helped to solidify and sanctify a new public meaning and memory of the memorial. For instance, the newspaper *USA Today* reported on the ceremonies, and it did not even mention Robert Gould Shaw when describing the memorial but, rather, only mentioned the 54th Massachusetts Infantry. No longer do public-funded institutions, like the National Park Service, speak only about the Robert Gould Shaw Memorial, but they now include the name of the 54th Massachusetts Infantry when referencing the monument. It is part of the dominant culture's changing view of the Civil War and its willingness to include African American history in the public memory of this country's heritage.

COMMEMORATION AND THE MAKING OF A PATRIOTIC PAST

Another way to control the past is to create a public memory that commemorates a patriotic past. The official expression is concerned with promoting and preserving the ideals of cultural leaders and authorities, developing social unity, and maintaining the status quo. Those in control of the official memory interpret the past and present reality in a way that helps to reduce competing interests (Bodner 1992:13). Government agencies have traditionally advanced the notion of "community of the nation while suppressing authentic local group memories and collective identities" (Glassberg 1996:12). The goal of the official public memory is to produce obedient, patriotic citizens. "The argument," remarks Michael Frisch, "has traveled a long way from its humanistic origins, arriving at a point where education and indoctrination—cultural and political—seem almost indistinguishable" (1989:1153).

The Enola Gay exhibit at the Smithsonian Institution is an excellent example of how the government suppressed an alternative view on the grounds that it was not patriotic. The original plans for the exhibit ran counter to the collective memory of powerful lobbying groups. The original draft text interpreted the horrors of the atomic bomb. Veterans' groups and lobbying groups convinced the U.S. Congress and the president of the United States to place political pressure on the Smithsonian Institution to change the exhibit. The revised exhibit conformed to the traditional patriotic view that claimed that it was necessary to drop the bomb to save American lives. The exhibit portrayed the flight crew as patriots and heroes (see *Journal of American History* 1995).

30   While collective memories are sometimes challenged, the ideals of the official memory must be supported through ceremonies and commemorations if their ideas and histories are to be long lived. One of the most popular commemorative events in U.S. history is the commemoration and reinterpretation of the American Civil War battlefields and landscapes. The struggle over which patriotic past the nation should celebrate was being settled by the end of Reconstruction, and it solidified through the early and mid–twentieth century. David Blight writes,

> Historical memory . . . was not merely an entity altered by the passage of time; it was the prize in a struggle between rival versions of the past, a question of will, of power, of persuasion. The historical memory of any transforming or controversial event emerges from cultural and political competition, from

the choice to confront the past and to debate and manipulate its meaning. [1989:1159]

From the late nineteenth century through most of the twentieth century, recognizing African American participation in the Civil War became increasingly limited as the southern revisionist movement gained momentum. Southern whites gained tremendous political and social power after Reconstruction, and they developed a southern patriotic past that could overcome historical humiliation. They created a glorious past of honor and dedication to a cause, while excluding African Americans from the story except to mention their faithfulness to the regime of the Old South (Aaron 1973:332–333).

Patriotism promotes and preserves the ideals of cultural leaders and authorities to develop social unity and maintain social inequalities in society. Officials in charge of creating patriotic histories present a past that reduced competing interests (Bodner 1992:13). They create the notion of community and heritage while suppressing the local memories of competing interest groups. The establishment of a patriotic past is evident with the development of the Civil War centennial movement.

CASE STUDY: THE CIVIL WAR CENTENNIAL AND THE BATTLE AT MANASSAS

In the 1950s and 1960s Americans looked for a unifying theme that could bring some peace and tranquility to the growing antagonism between races and regions. The era was marked by violence and grief as racial issues tugged at the fragile seams that held this nation together. For instance, in September 1962 more than a thousand angry whites rampaged across the University of Mississippi campus to protest the admission of the campus's first black student. President Kennedy sent several hundred federal marshals to protect the student. The mob killed two men, more than two dozen marshals were wounded, and 120 people were wounded amid considerable property damage (Cohodas 1997). These were not isolated incidents, but they were indicative of race relations at the time.

During this era of racial tensions, Civil War Round Tables in 1957, successfully petitioned

Congress to create a Civil War Centennial Commission. The commission used the anniversary of this historic event to promote nationalism and patriotism. It fashioned memories of past conflict and tried to transform them into symbolic struggles for unity. Abroe explains that the recollection of a heroic past could easily provide a diversion from the racial and political unrest sweeping through the country: "With citizens' attention fixed upon subversive threats—real or imagined—to democratic institutions, the vision of a United States tested and fortified in the crucible of civil conflict offered reassurance that the nation could meet any crisis and emerge victorious" (1998:22). President Eisenhower wrote the Civil War Centennial Commission and urged it to

> Look on this great struggle not merely as a set of military operations, but as a period in our history in which the times called for extraordinary degrees of patriotism and heroism on the part of the men and women of both North and South. In this context we may derive inspiration from their deeds to renew our dedication to the task which yet confronts us—the furtherance, together with other free nations of the world, of the freedom and dignity of man and the building of a just and lasting peace. [1960a]

35   Karl Betts, who became the first executive director of the national commission, was joined by Ulysses S. Grant III. Both men had military backgrounds. At the Civil War Centennial meetings it is clear that the ideas of the Lost Cause were embedded in the national public memory of the Civil War. Grant explained that the Civil War could not be forgotten and that the Confederates were also Americans "who were heroically fighting for what they thought was right" (Minutes of the Civil War Centennial Commission 1960). Heroism allowed for the common foot soldier to be recognized, but it also provided an example of how ordinary citizens followed the orders of their leaders. They fought for a larger political structure without question (Bodner 1992:209).

The opening ceremonies of the centennial celebration were held in New York City, where a group gathered at the Grant Memorial. There, Major General Grant gave a speech that stressed that the Civil War was important since it showed the ability of the country to reunite (*New York Times* 1961:1). That same day, opening ceremonies

were held in Lexington, at Robert E. Lee's grave site. Congressman William Tuck of Virginia noted that after the war Lee urged Southerners to strengthen the Union (*New York Times* 1961:1).

Allan Nevis, a professional historian, and James I. Robertson, former editor of *Civil War History*, became the new commission leaders in 1961. Nevis declared the mission of the commission:

> Above all, our central theme will be unity, not division. When we finally reach the commemoration of Appomattox, we shall treat it not as a victory of a defeat, but as a beginning of a century of increasing concord, mutual understanding, and fraternal affection among all the sections and social groups. [Minutes of the Civil War Centennial Commission 1961]

The Civil War centennial celebrated dedication and loyalty to a cause while the issue of slavery played little or no role at all during commemoration events. The commission could not totally ignore the racial divisiveness within the country, and on September 22, 1962, it sponsored an event at the Lincoln Memorial to commemorate the centennial of the Emancipation Proclamation. The ceremonies marked more than the symbolic end to slavery, and white national unity became the overriding theme once again. The Kennedy administration was reluctant to take a major political stance at the event while racial tensions boiled in this country. At the time Kennedy contemplated reelection, and he did not want to offend white southerners. The audience did listen to a recording of President Kennedy. He emphasized patriotic themes and commended African Americans for working on civil rights issues within the framework of the Constitution. He praised African Americans for their struggle to make life better for their people: "He thought it remarkable that despite humiliation and depravation, blacks had retained their loyalty to the nation and 'democratic institution'" (*New York Times* 1962:1, 50; Bodner 1992:211).

Centennial celebrations occurred at many national parks, including Manassas National Battlefield Park on July 21, 22, and 23, 1961. Reenactment gatherings often attracted up to 100,000 spectators, and at Manassas, nearly 200,000 people observed the three-day event. In August 1960, President Eisenhower wrote the First Manassas Corporation that the event "will serve to remind all

Americans that the bonds which now unite us are as precious as the blood of young men" (1960b). A 1961 pamphlet, called "Grand Reenactment," advertising the event described the importance of the battle in American history. It stated that the "reenactment will commemorate in action, sight, and sound the courage and devotion demonstrated here in 1861 and the need for similar dedication in the years to come."

40   The Centennial Commemoration program adopted the "Lost Cause" sentiment, claiming: "Today's commemorative spectacle has the objective of reminding you of our common heritage — and indeed of reminding the world — that our people have always been willing to fight and to die if need be for their beliefs — and their principles." Whether fighting for the Union or the Confederacy, "they were all deeply in love with their country. And the country they loved was America."

While the reenactment received praise from the press, others criticized the event as "a celebration rather than an event commemorating a tragic event in our history. The 'Coney Island' atmosphere that concession stands created behind the spectator section was objectionable" (see Volz 1961:12). Another citizen noted "that even though great pains were taken to present a historically accurate event, as it was, comparatively few people came away really understanding what took place" (see Volz 1961:12).

Manassas National Battlefield Park has always been about the history of the battles (the First Battle of Manassas and the Second Battle of Manassas), and National Park Service historians at the park have not been willing to expand the interpretation of the park to incorporate social history into the story of the park. The centennial celebrations were about Confederate victories and the reconciliation between whites. These celebrations ignored some of the broader issues surrounding the war, like slavery, emancipation, and the use of African American troops in the Civil War. These topics are still not fully addressed in the park today, and park cultural resource managers and historians have continued to take steps to reinforce and glorify a Confederate past by erasing any forms of African American history from the battlefield landscape (see Martin et al. 1997).

NOSTALGIA AND THE LEGITIMATION OF AMERICAN HERITAGE

Another way to create memory is to develop a sense of heritage. Citizens of the early American republic resisted the development of an American collective memory and frowned upon the commemoration of a sacred past. Adherence to republican values in the early nineteenth century produced tensions between democracy and tradition. John Quincy Adams noted, "Democracy has no monuments. It strikes no medals. It bears the head of no man on a coin" (in Everett [1836] 1972:38). In the antebellum era, Americans saw the United States as a country with a future rather than a glorious past worth commemoration. They believed in the value of succeeding without patronage or family influence. Emerson wrote that Americans were "emancipated from history, happily bereft of ancestry, untouched and undefiled by the usual inheritances of family and race" (quoted in Lowenthal 1996:55).

Because of the resistance to create an American heritage, large-scale commemoration activities began slowly after the middle of the nineteenth century. The Mount Vernon's Ladies Association (formed in 1856) and the Ladies' Hermitage Association (1889) are important early preservation groups involved in the American historic, preservation movement. Women were the primary custodians of American heritage, and they took pride in demonstrating their care and, therefore, patriotism for America's past. Those who did not have ancestral roots could join other groups, like the Patriotic League of the Revolution (formed in 1894). Their goal was to "create and promote interest in all matters pertaining to American history, to collect and preserve relics of the period of the American Revolution, and to foster patriotism" (from Kammen 1991:267).

Until the 1890s the U.S. government did little 45 to assist historic preservation or to create a national collective memory. From 1880 through 1886, eight bills were introduced to Congress to preserve historic lands, but none was enacted. In the 1890s Congress finally authorized the establishment of five Civil War battlefields as national military parks to be administered by the Defense Department — Chickamauga, Antietam, Shiloh, Gettysburg, and Vicksburg. Several Revolutionary

War sites were also added. By 1906, protection became available for prehistoric ruins with the establishment of the Antiquities Act. These events are an important indication of America's growing need to create a useable heritage.

This national movement helped to develop and foster a collective memory and national heritage. Heritage creates a useable past and it generates a precedent that serves our present needs. More recently the political uses of heritage have been made very explicit within Western culture. We live in a society whose thirst for nostalgia seems unquenchable. Kammen (1991:214–219) calls the creation of Americans' consciousness for historic preservation since the 1950s the "heritage phenomenon." Heritage connotes integrity, authenticity, venerability, and stability. While "history explores and explains pasts it grows ever more opaque over time; heritage clarifies pasts so as to infuse them with present purposes" (Lowenthal 1996:xv).

Heritage is one way to create community and cultural continuity. A nation uses heritage to create a collective memory in order to look for more innocent and carefree days by selectively remembering. We remember what we perceive as good and forget the rest. False notions of the past may be upheld in order to create and sustain national mythology. For instance, David Lowenthal brings to our attention the myth behind the founding of Londonderry (Derry). Contrary to local belief, the city was not founded by St. Columba, and the famed siege of 1689 was only a blockade: "But Derry folk dote on these founding fables all the more because they are fabulous" (Lowenthal 1996: 129).

Closely linked with the idea of heritage is nostalgia. Nostalgia for things that are reminders of earlier days has replaced the early American republic's ideals for progress and development. Nostalgia is about nurturance and stewardship. Beleaguered by loss and change, Americans remember a bygone day of economic power. They have angst about the loss of community. In a throwaway society, people are looking for something more lasting (Lowenthal 1996:6). Massive migrations of the last 200 years have also sharpened our needs and feelings of nostalgia. Tens of millions of people have sought refuge outside of their native lands, fleeing hunger, violence, and hatred. Rural people have increasingly migrated to urban areas. People have been cut off from their own past, and they are increasingly seeking their roots (Lowenthal 1996:9).

The celebration of America's heritage can often be read from the American landscape, and it can be reinforced through material culture, such as museums and monuments. Following is an example of how a southern patriotic group used commemoration and a monument to reinforce nostalgia in order to legitimize southern bigotry. African American groups have challenged the placement of the monument in a visible and public place, and they have struggled to change the meaning of the event that the memorial commemorates.

CASE STUDY: THE HEYWARD SHEPHERD MEMORIAL

After the Civil War, Southerners created more 50 monuments to their defeat than any other civilization in history. It is their dedication to the Lost Cause, justifying their actions during the Civil War, that created the proliferation of these markers (McPherson 1982:488). The idea of the "Lost Cause" survived through the twentieth and now into the twenty-first century. It is kept alive by southern patriotic groups like the United Daughters of the Confederacy (UDC) and the Sons of Confederate Veterans (SCV). These southern heritage groups were, and still are, engaged in cultural warfare to establish a "Confederate tradition." This tradition focuses on the white South's view of history, appreciation for the rule by the elite, a fear of the enfranchisement of African Americans, and a reverence for the Confederate cause (Foster 1987:5). From the late nineteenth century, this paradigm has preached racial separation and the virtues of an aristocratic South. The Lost Cause mythology argued that the Confederacy was never defeated but, rather, they were overwhelmed by numbers and betrayed by some key generals. The Lost Cause has been compared to the Ghost Dance of the Plains Indians whereby southerners created "a dream of a return to an undefeated confederacy" (Foster 1987:47,60). This mythology won in the battle to control the public memory of the Civil War (Blight 1989:1162–1163; Connelly and Bellows 1982; Holmes 1962:4–5, 76).

A monument to Heyward Shepherd, an African American killed by John Brown's raiding party on Harpers Ferry, is an important example of how one group consciously excluded another group's memory of the past. Brown, a famous abolitionist known for fighting against slavery in Kansas, had come to Harpers Ferry in October 1859. His goal was to capture the U.S. arsenal where guns were stored for the U.S. Army. Brown believed that once enslaved African Americans heard that he captured the arsenal they would abandon their plantations and come to his aid. Brown would supply escaped slaves with weapons and they would march south, freeing slaves along the way. No slaves joined Brown's revolt; Brown and his men were captured, and many of his men were found guilty of treason and hanged.

It is ironic that Heyward Shepherd became the first casualty of Brown's raid. Although the stories are not clear, it appears that he was shot in the back as he tried to flee from Brown's raiding party. The memory of Heyward Shepherd, controlled by the white press, became an important tool to justify the Lost Cause sentiment. The *Virginia Free Press* reported, "He was shot down like a dog. A humble negro as he was, his life was worth more than all of the desperadoes of the party, and his memory will be revered, when theirs will only be thought of with execution" (1859:2). The newspaper continually reinforced the martyrdom of a faithful African American who worked diligently in a white-dominated society (*Virginia Free Press* 1867, 1879, 1884).

The UDC decided in 1905 that a "Faithful Slave Monument" would be one way that southerners could create and control a public memory of the conditions of slavery. A "Faithful Slave Monument" was a vehicle to counter the memory created by northerners about the South and the institution of slavery. The UDC believed that it was important to erect a monument "to the faithful old slaves who remained loyal and true to their owners in the dark days of the sixties and on through the infamous reconstruction period" (*Confederate Veteran* 1905:123). The monument would tell future generations "that the white men of the South were the negro's best friend then and that the men of the South are the negro's best friend to-day" (*Confederate Veteran* 1905: 123–124).

During the beginning of the Great Depression there was a new sense of xenophobia that swept through the country, and African Americans found themselves further segregated and oppressed by Jim Crow legislation. In 1931, the town council in Harpers Ferry unanimously agreed to allow the "Faithful Slave Monument" to be erected in town. Ceremonies occurred in October 1931, and Henry T. McDonald, president of Storer College, an African American college, participated in the unveiling of the memorial. The president general of the UDC, Elizabeth Bashinsky, spoke about her devotion to the Confederate flag and remarked how the "black mammy" loved her white "chilluns." She also believed that the slaves in the United States did not violently rise against their masters, like they did in Haiti, because they were well clothed, fed, and housed; treated kindly; and taught Christianity. Bashinsky noted that Heyward Shepherd "gave his life in defense of his employer's property, and in memory of many others of his race who were loyal and true during a period that tried men's souls. . . . Heyward Shepherd's conduct was honorable just, and true, and merits the praise we bring him" (*Confederate Veteran* 1931:411). After Bashinsky's speech the memorial was unveiled. Part of the memorial inscription reads:

> As a Memorial to Heyward Shepherd,
> Exemplifying The Character And
> Faithfulness of Thousands Of
> Negroes Who, Under Many
> Temptations Throughout
> Subsequent Years of War, So
> Conducted Themselves That
> No Stain Was Left Upon a Record
> Which Is The Peculiar Heritage
> of The American People, And An
> Everlasting Tribute to The Best
> in Both Races. [UDC 1931:58–59]

The inscription angered many African Americans, and McDonald's participation in the ceremonies was immediately attacked by several members of the African American community (Andrews 1931). Max Barber remarked that McDonald should have been "shocked and disgusted" at the statements made at the ceremony and that he erred in participating in an event coordinated by "a bunch of unregenerated rebels" (*Pittsburgh Courier* 1931). W. E. B. Du Bois wrote in *Crisis* (1932) that the dedication was a "proslavery celebration" and called McDonald's participation in the event "disgraceful."

In the 1950s the National Park Service (NPS) acquired the Heyward Shepherd Memorial along with the building it stood against in Lower Town Harpers Ferry. Funding became available for building renovations in the mid-1970s, and in 1976 the buildings adjacent to the Heyward Shepherd Memorial underwent construction. The NPS removed the memorial to its maintenance yard so it would not get damaged. In 1981 the Heyward Shepherd Memorial was moved back to its original location, although the NPS covered it with plywood when it received reports of possible plans to deface the monument (Meyer 1995:C2). The NPS found itself between two opposing organizations. The National Association for the Advancement of Colored People (NAACP) viewed the monument as offensive, and the UDC and the SCV wanted the monument uncovered and displayed to the public.

Mrs. Dewey Wood of the UDC believed that the message on the monument is clear in its meaning. She remarked, "Why should the NAACP be opposed to this? It is a monument to one of their people. . . . There were 40,000 slaves in Maryland, and none of them came to [John Brown's] support. They were loyal to their people. . . . I really don't know what they find offensive about it" (in White 1989:4). Efforts to have all groups—UDC, SCV, NAACP, and the NPS—reach a compromise to uncover the monument failed.

On January 13, 1994, Elliot Cummings, Commander, Maryland Division, SCV, wrote to Senator Jesse Helms, Republican, South Carolina, complaining that the monument, a form of southern heritage, was covered "for reason of political correctness." He argued against an interpretive sign next to the monument to explain its historical context: "This is the exact same line used by the perverters of history at the Smithsonian to justify a distorted story line about the Enola Gay. . . . This kind of thinking jeopardizes the heritage of all of us" (Cummings 1995).

The NPS received a congressional inquiry from Helms (Helms 1995) and political pressure forced it to remove the plywood covering. Beside the monument stands interpretive signage to create a context for the monument. The reaction to the inscription on the monument belies the oppressing memories this monument represents. Cummings demanded that the national park give the monument back to those who paid for it (the UDC and the SCV) or remove the interpretive

wayside sign. "My position is that the monument should not be interpreted," said Cummings. "They should be allowed to exist as they are and people should be allowed to make whatever interpretation they want. . . . Do I get to put an interpretive plaque on the Lincoln Memorial saying this man was responsible for the deaths of 250,000 Southerners and usurped the Constitution?" (quoted in Bailey 1995:22).

While these southern heritage groups have fought to have the monument redisplayed in the national park, and are fighting to remove any contextual material associated with the object, blacks are arguing to remove the memorial from public display in order to erase some of the landscape reminders of the Jim Crow era. The president of the West Virginia chapter of the NAACP, James Tolbert remarked, "I don't think it's history. I think it is a misrepresentation of the life and role of Heyward Shepherd. We don't think that the Daughters of the Confederacy and the Sons of the Confederacy had that much love for Negroes" (quoted in Deutsch 1995:1A). During its August meeting, the NAACP chapter passed a resolution that condemned the monument (Bailes 1995:A1). Tolbert later added, "I believe it should be taken by crane to the Potomac River and dropped at the river's deepest point" (quoted in Deutsch 1995:9A; *Jet Magazine* 1995:22–23).

The erection of the Heyward Shepherd Memorial is a way that the SCV and the UDC used nostalgia to legitimize southern bigotry. While African Americans were not pleased with the erection of the Heyward Shepherd Memorial in 1931, they continue to battle with the UDC and the SCV over the meaning of the monument and the memory of slavery. The presence of the memorial in lower town Harpers Ferry is a reminder of the racism that existed in America during the Jim Crow era, and its placement in the national park, on view to the public, threatens African Americans' wishes to remove these signs of bigotry on the American landscape. African Americans feel that the monument legitimizes a racist heritage and successfully excludes a memory of the cruelties of slavery. They fear that its meaning may become part of the official public memory. It is obvious that the lack of political clout has hampered the success of the West Virginia NAACP.

CONCLUSION

There is a growing literature related to how archaeology is used to create a particular memory and instill nationalism in almost all parts of the globe including Asia (Edwards 1991:1–23; Glover 1999; Ikawa-Smith 1999:626–629; Pai 1999:619–625; Pak 1999:613–618), the Pacific region (Spriggs 1999:109–121), the Middle East (El-Haj 1998:166–188), Mesoamerica (Mazariegos 1998:376–386), Scandinavia (Scott 1996:321–342), and Greece (Brown 1994:784–796; Hamilakis 1996:117–129, 1999:303–320). Archaeology has a long tradition of supporting national programs and creating a past that justifies national territories and/or particular pasts (Anderson 1991:163–185; Kohl 1998:225; Scham 1998:301–308; Trigger 1989). Using historical archaeology to help prop official histories is not new to Americans as many projects had their beginnings during times of instability or times of social and economic crises. For instance, a major historical archaeology project began in the United States in the late nineteenth century when labor increasingly challenged the practices of capitalism. In 1897, the Association for the Preservation of Virginia Antiquities, which owns portions of James Island, uncovered the brick foundations of the 1639 church at Jamestown, the first permanent English settlement in the New World. During the Great Depression, in 1934 the NPS initiated excavations at Jamestown with the main goal of architectural reconstruction. This work, undertaken by J. C. Harrington from 1936 through the 1940s, continued under the direction of John Cotter in the 1950s (Cotter 1958; Cotter and Hudson 1957).

Excavations at St. Mary's City, Maryland's first capital, were also begun in the 1930s, pioneered by H. Chandler Forman, who worked there intermittently from 1936 to 1965 after he left Jamestown (Shackel and Little 1994). While the first capitals of Virginia and Maryland received early attention by archaeologists, Virginia's second capital did as well. Sponsored by the Rockefeller Foundation, excavations at Williamsburg from the 1930s also catered to architectural restorations (Derry and Brown 1987; Nöel Hume 1983:29).

Jamestown and Williamsburg, in particular, provide examples of government and private interest, respectively, in creating a memory of a historic past. For instance, at Jamestown the NPS presents the town not only as the first permanent English settlement in the New World but also as the birthplace of modern democracy. The first representative legislative assembly in America convened at Jamestown from 1619 until it was moved in 1699 to Williamsburg (Hudson 1985:48). At Williamsburg, the Rockefeller Foundation celebrates the ideals of the planter elite as timeless and inevitable American values (Wallace 1981:68–78; Patterson 1986). While each site celebrates Anglo-American history, non-European (and other European) peoples whose histories were inextricably linked with the British (and other Europeans) have been largely ignored or glossed over. Neither American Indians nor African Americans figured in the initial vision of the Jamestown and Williamsburg restorations. However, in the 1980s the Colonial Williamsburg Foundation made substantial strides in incorporating the lives of those "others" (e.g., black slaves, servants, and women in general) in restoration, archaeology, research designs, and public presentations (Handler and Gable 1997). An increasing awareness exists among the public, probably through greater exposure to critical histories, that the ideals of the planter elite were not "natural" in the sense of being inevitable, or timeless, but were embedded in their own contemporary social and political realities.

There would be much less to say about historical archaeology in the Chesapeake were it not for the likes of the Rockefeller Foundation (Colonial Williamsburg), the Association for the Preservation of Virginia Antiquities (Jamestown), the Thomas Jefferson Memorial Foundation (Monticello), and the Mount Vernon Ladies Association (Mount Vernon). However, it is also very clear that all of these archaeologies help to reinforce the ideals of the official history and help to create stability and justify inequalities in society today.

The analysis of the construction of history and public memory has taken on a renewed interest, especially when dealing with memory of the recent past and justification for the present (see, for instance, Blake 1999:423–435; Daynes 1997; Peri 1999:106–124). Many scholars are paying considerable attention to the memory of a generation that is coming to a close, the histories associated with World War II (Epstein 1999; La Capra 1998), and the creation of modern Europe in the post–World War II era (Markovits and Reich 1997). Remembering the Vietnam era has also occupied the scholarship of memory in recent years (see, for instance, Hass 1998).

How we remember and reinterpret a past also serves to create ethnic identities for communities, such as African Americans (Bethel 1997; Fraser 1998), native peoples in Mexico (Florescano 1994), and people of rural Australia (Goodall 1999:160–190). Selective memory of the past has also been used by groups to create and justify racism and ethnic cleansing (Coslovich 1994; Larson 1999:335–362).

Memory can be about (1) forgetting about or excluding an alternative past, (2) creating and reinforcing patriotism, and/or (3) developing a sense of nostalgia to legitimize a particular heritage. These strategies become important for the construction and legitimation of social groups, particularly nation-states (Alonso 1988:40; Anderson 1991; Hobsbawm and Ranger 1983). It becomes important in creating national histories and in inspiring nationalism (see, for instance, Howe 1999:222–239; Nora 1999). Nation-states tend to be rooted in tradition, and this memory of the past appears to be "so 'natural' as to require no definition other than self assertion" (Hobsbawm and Ranger 1983:14). Official histories of a nation require consensus building and the construction of a history from multiple, often conflicting memories (Anderson 1991:163–185; Kohl 1998:225; Scham 1998:301–308; Trigger 1989).

Public memory can be viewed as tactical power that controls social settings. Competing groups ceaselessly battle to create and control the collective national memory of revered sacred sites and objects. Different group agendas often clash causing the established collective memories to be continuously in flux. Some subordinate groups can subvert the dominant memory, other groups compromise and become part of a multivocal history, while others fail to have their story remembered by the wider society. The tensions between and within groups who struggle for the control over the collective public memory is often situational and ongoing since the political stakes are high. Those who control the past have the ability to command the present and the future.

70 "Culture may be seen as memory in action as we live and enact our version of the real living world. Habitual ways of doing things are almost automatic, for we act as we have acted before, and ultimately as we have been taught to act" (Teski and Climo 1995:2). We learn through actual instruction and imitating patterns that we have observed as they surround us at all stages of life. Social actors actively know the way society operates and individuals act within a preexisting structure, or

habitus (Bourdieu 1977; Giddens 1979). Habitus is the interaction between the unconscious and physical world that is learned and reinforced through interaction. Symbols play an important role in structuring relations of hierarchy and classification systems. Using past experience and the ability to read the meanings of objects allows one to accept or reject the use and meaning of the object and the creation of a particular past.

Material culture, in the form of statues, monuments, museums, artifacts, or landscapes, has some ascribed meaning—past and present—associated with it, and these meanings vary between individuals and interest groups. This material culture can be transformed into sacred objects when serving the goals and needs of any group. The three case studies presented above show how conflicting memories developed around the Heyward Shepherd Memorial, the Civil War Centennial and Manassas National Battlefield Park, and the Robert Gould Shaw Memorial. All of the case studies are about the situational use of power and the ability to use resources to control public memory. In none of these cases has a consensus been reached; rather, groups struggle to have their meaning become part of public history. In the case of the Heyward Shepherd Memorial groups like the UDC and the SCV, the NAACP, and the NPS are fighting over the control for the meaning of a particular past. In this case, NPS representatives placed the monument on display with an interpretive sign that provides some contextual information. A consensus was not reached between the different groups regarding a solution for redisplaying of the monument. The federal government imposed a solution and secured control over the interpretation of the monument. During the late 1950s and early 1960s, an era of great civil strife, the Civil War centennial commemorations became a vehicle to create the notion of obedience and loyalty to a cause. This message was reinforced through public displays and ceremonies. What became clear during these celebratory events was that African American issues played a subservient role to the larger issues of white reconciliation. At Manassas National Battlefield, as well as in many other national parks, African Americans have never had much of a voice at the national park. At the Robert Gould Shaw Memorial the African American community has been very successful in challenging the power of the meaning of the monument. The recent dedication has reaffirmed the power of the African American community and the meaning of the monument has become a memorial about the black soldiers rather than the white colonel. It is a monument that has become an integral part of African American heritage related to the American Civil War.

In all of these case studies the power of the African Americans to assert themselves and become part of the official meaning varies significantly. While the civil rights movement and the Civil Rights Act allow blacks to gain some control over their official memory, it is important to look at the situational context of power. Blacks have had little power to claim representation at Manassas, a park that historically celebrated two Confederate victories. At Harpers Ferry, the NAACP struggles to gain control over the meaning of a UDC monument, although their efforts have not succeeded since they have had little political clout and they are fighting against an organization that has the backing of U.S. congressional leaders, like Senator Jesse Helms. In Boston, the presence of powerful black leaders like President Benjamin Payton of Tuskegee University, Professor Henry Louis

Gates Jr. of the Du Bois Institute at Harvard University, and General Colin Powell gave legitimacy to the control of the meaning of the Shaw Memorial.

While there is always a strong movement to remove subordinate memories from our national collective memory, minority groups continually struggle to have their histories remembered. The clash over the control of public history occurs in some of the most visible places on the landscape, like national monuments and national parks. They are the arenas for negotiating meanings of the past (see for instance Linenthal 1993; Linenthal and Englehardt 1996; Lowenthal 1996). The past is always in flux, with competing interests always trying to take control over the collective meaning. The meaning of the American landscape is continually being contested, constructed, and reconstructed.

Note

Acknowledgments. Matthew Reeves, Barbara Little, Charles Orser, and three anonymous reviewers provided suggestions on an earlier draft of this article. I appreciate their time and thoughtful comments.

References Cited

Aaron, Daniel. (1973) The Unwritten War: American Writers and the Civil War. New York: Knopf.

Abroe, Mary Munsell. (1998) Observing the Civil War Centennial: Rhetoric, Reality, and the Bounds of Selective Memory: Understanding the Past. CRM21(11):22–25.

Alonso, Ana. (1988)The Effects of Truth: Re-Presentations of the Past and the Imagining of Community. Journal of Historical Sociology 1(1):33–57.

Anderson, Benedict. (1991) Imagined Communities: Reflections on the Origins and Spread of Nationalism. London: Verso Press.

Andrews, Matthew Page. (1931) Letter to Henry T. McDonald. McDonald Collection Box 4, Folder 3. October 12. On file, Harpers Ferry National Historical Park, Harpers Ferry, WV.

Bailes, Marc. (1995) NAACP Seeks Response from Park Service, Calls Monument Offensive. The Journal, October 1:A1–A2.

Bailey, Rebecca. (1995) Harpers Ferry Sign Angers Some. Civil War News, August: 22–23.

Bethel, Elizabeth R. (1997) The Roots of African-American Identity: Memory and History in Free Antebellum Communities. New York: St. Martin's Press.

Blake, C. N. (1999) The Usable Past, the Comfortable Past, and the Civic Past: Memory in Contemporary America. Cultural Anthropology 14(3):423–435.

Blatt, Martin, Thomas Brown, and Donald Yacovone. (2000) Hope and Glory: Essays on the Legacy of the Fifty-Fourth Massachusetts Regiment. Amherst: University of Massachusetts and Massachusetts Historical Society.

Blight, David W. (1989) "For Something beyond the Battlefield": Frederick Douglass and the Struggle for the Memory of the Civil War. Journal of American History 75(4):1156–1178.

———(2001) Race and Reunion: The Civil War in American Memory. Cambridge, MA:Belknap Press of Harvard University Press.

Bodner, John. (1992) Remaking America: Public Memory, Commemoration, and Patriotism in the Twentieth Century. Princeton: Princeton University Press.

Boime, Albert. (1990) The Art of Exclusion: Representing Blacks in the Nineteenth Century. Washington, DC: Smithsonian Institution Press.

Bourdieu, Pierre. (1977) Outline of a Theory of Practice. Cambridge: Cambridge University Press.

Brown, K. S. (1994) Seeing Stars: Character and Identity in the Landscapes of Modern Macedonia. Antiquity 68:784–796.

Caffin, Charles H. (1913) American Masters of Sculpture: Being Brief Appreciations of Some American Sculptors and of Some Phase of Sculpture in America. New York: Doubleday, Page.

Cameron, A. (1993) Radicals of the Worst Sort: Laboring Women in Lawrence, Massachusetts, 1860–1912. Urbana: University of Illinois Press.

———(1996) Comments on "Cleansing History." Radical History Review 65:91–97.

Cohodas, Nadine. (1997) The Day the Band Played Dixie: Race and Liberal Conscience at Ole Miss. New York: Free Press.

Confederate Veteran. (1905) Monument to Faithful Slaves. Confederate Veteran 13 (March):123–124.

———(1931) Heyward Shepherd. Confederate Veteran 37 (November):411–414.

Connelly, Thomas L., and Barbara L. Bellows. (1982) God and General Longstreet: The Lost Cause and the Southern Mind. Baton Rouge: Louisiana State University Press.

Coslovich, Marco. (1994) I Percorsi della Sopravvivenza: Storia e Memoria della Deportazione della "Adriatisches Kustenland." Milan, Italy: Mursia.

Cotter, John L. (1958) Archaeological Excavations at Jamestown, Virginia. U.S. National Park Service Archaeological Research Series, 4. Washington, DC: National Park Service.

Cotter, John L., and Paul Hudson. (1957) New Discoveries at Jamestown. Washington, DC: Government Printing Office.

Cummings, Elliot G. (1995) Letter to Jesse Helms. Heyward Shepherd Folder. January 30. On file, Park Historian, Harpers Ferry National Historical Park, Harpers Ferry, WV.

Daynes, Gary. (1997) Making Villains, Making Heroes: Joseph R. McCarthy, Martin Luther King, Jr. and the Politics of American Memory. New York: Garland Publishing.

Derry, Linda, and Marley R. Brown III. (1987) Excavation at Colonial Williamsburg Thirty Years Ago: An Archaeological Analysis of Cross-Trenching behind the Peyton-Randolph Site. American Archaeology 6(1):10–19.

Deutsch, Jack. (1995) War of Words Erupts over Monument. Daily Mail, November 28:1A, 9A.

Du Bois, W. E. B. (1932) No title. Crisis 41(January): 467.

Edwards, Walter. (1991) Buried Discourse: The Toro Archeological Site and Japanese National Identity in the Early Postwar Period. The Journal of Japanese Studies 17:1–23.

Eisenhower, Dwight D. (1960a) Letter to the Civil War Centennial Commission, 6 July 1959. In First Manassas (a Prospectus), a Commemorative Reenactment of a Great Moment in History, a Ceremony Officially Opening the Civil War Centennial Years 1961–1965. On file, Manassas National Battlefield Park, Manassas, VA.

———(1960b) Letter to Major General James C. Fry, First Manassas Corporation. On file, Manassas National Battlefield Park, Manassas, VA.

El-Haj, Nadia Abu. (1998) Translating Truths: Nationalism, the Practice of Archaeology, and the Remaking of Past and Present in Contemporary Jerusalem. American Ethnologist 25(2):166–188.

Epstein, C. (1999) The Production of "Official Memory" in East Germany: Old Communists and the Dilemmas of Memoir-Writing. Central European History 32(2):181–201.

Everett, Edward. ([1836]1972) Orations and Speeches on Various Occasions. New York: Arno Press.

Fields, Karen. (1994) What One Cannot Remember Mistakenly. In History and Memory in African-American Culture. Genevieve Fabre and Robert O'Meally, eds. pp. 10–163. New York: Oxford University Press.

Florescano, E. (1994) Memory, Myth, and Time in Mexico: From the Aztecs to Independence. Albert G. Bork, trans. Austin: University of Texas Press.

Foster, Gaines M. (1987) Ghosts of the Confederacy: Defeat, the Lost Cause, and the Emergence of the New South, 1865 to 1913. New York: Oxford University Press.

Fraser, Gertrude J. (1998) African American Midwifery in the South: Dialogues of Birth, Race, and Memory. Cambridge, MA: Harvard University Press.

Frisch, Michael. (1989) American History and the Structure of Collective Memory: A Modest Exercise in Empirical Iconography. Journal of American History 75(4): 1131–1155.

———(1990) A Shared Authority: Essays on the Craft and Meaning of Oral and Public History. Albany: State University of New York Press.

Giddens, Anthony. (1979) Central Problems in Social Theory: Action, Structure and Contradiction in Social Analysis. London: Macmillan Press.

Gilbert, David. (1984) Where Industry Failed: Water-Powered Mills at Harpers Ferry. Charleston, WV: Pictorial Histories Publishing.

———(1999) Mills, Factories, Machines and Floods at Harpers Ferry, West Virginia, 1762–1991. Harpers Ferry, WV: Harpers Ferry Historical Association.

Glassberg, David. (1990) American Historical Pageantry: The Uses of Tradition in the Early Twentieth Century. Chapel Hill: University of North Carolina Press.

———(1996) Public History and the Study of Memory. The Public Historian 18(2):7–23.

Glover, Ian C. (1999) Letting the Past Serve the Present—Some Contemporary Uses of Archaeology in Viet Nam. Antiquity 73(281):587–593.

Goodall, H. (1999) Telling Country: Memory, Modernity and Narratives in Rural Australia. History Workshop Journal N47 (spring):160–190.

Hamilakis, Yannis. (1996) Antiquities as Symbolic Capital in Modern Greek Society. Antiquity 70:117–129.

———(1999) Stories from Exile: Fragments from the Cultural Biography of the Parthenon (or "Elgin") Marbles. World Archaeology 31(2):303–320.

Handler, Richard, and Eric Gable. (1997) The New History in an Old Museum: Creating the Past at Colonial Williamsburg. Durham, NC: Duke University Press.

Hass, Kristin A. (1998) Carried to the Wall: American Memory and the Vietnam-Veterans-Memorial. Berkeley: University of California Press.

Helms, Jesse. (1995) Letter to Marilyn Merrill. Heyward Shepherd Folder. April 3. On file, Park Historian, Harpers Ferry National Historical Park, Harpers Ferry, WV.

Hobsbawm, Eric. (1983) Introduction: Inventing Tradition. In The Invention of Tradition. Eric Hobsbawm and Terrence Ranger, eds. pp. 1–14. Cambridge: Cambridge University Press.

Hobsbawm, Eric, and Terence Ranger, eds. (1983) The Invention of Tradition. New York: Cambridge University Press.

Holmes, Oliver Wendell. (1962) Occasional Speeches. Mark DeWolfe Howe, comp. Cambridge, MA: Belknap Press of Harvard University Press.

Howe, S. (1999) Speaking of '98: History, Politics and Memory in the Bicentenary of the 1798 United Irish Uprising. History Workshop Journal 47:222–239.

Hudson, Paul. (1985) Jamestown: Birthplace of Historical Archaeology in the United States. Journal of the Archaeological Society of Virginia 40(1):46–57.

Ikawa-Smith, Fumiko. (1999) Construction of National Identity and Origins in East Asia: A Comparative Perspective. Antiquity 73(281):626–629.

Jet Magazine. (1995) Monument to the First Black Killed at Harpers Ferry Raid Draws Criticism. Jet Magazine, September 18:22–23.

Journal of American History. (1995) History and the Public: What Can We Handle? A Round Table about History after the Enola Gay Controversy. Journal of American History 82:1029–1140.

Kammen, Michael. (1991) Mystic Chords of Memory: The Transformation of Tradition in American Culture. New York: Knopf.

Kohl, Philip L. (1998) Nationalism and Archaeology: On the Constructions of Nations and the Reconstructions of the Remote Past. Annual Review of Anthropology 27:223–246.

La Capra, Dominick. (1998) History and Memory after Auschwitz. Ithaca, NY: Cornell University Press.

Larson, P. M. (1999) Reconsidering Trauma, Identity, and the African Diaspora: Enslavement and History Memory in 19th-Century Highland Madagascar. William and Mary Quarterly 56(2):335–362.

Leff, Mark H. (1995) Revisioning United States Political History. American Historical Review 100:833.

Leone, Mark P. (1981) Archaeology's Relationship to the Present and the Past. In Modern Material Culture: The Archaeology of Us. Richard A. Gould and Michael B. Schiffer, eds. pp. 5–14. New York: Academic Press.

Leone, Mark P., Parker B. Potter Jr., and Paul A. Shackel. (1987) Toward a Critical Archaeology. Current Anthropology 28(3):283–302.

Linenthal, Edward T. (1993) Sacred Ground: Americans and Their Battlefields. Urbana: University of Illinois Press.

Linenthal, Edward, and Tom Engelhardt. (1996) History Wars: The Enola Gay and Other Battles for the American Past. New York: Henry Holt.

Little, Barbara J. (1994) People with History: An Update on Historical Archaeology in the United States. Journal of Archaeological Method and Theory 1(1):5–40.

Lowenthal, David. (1985) The Past Is a Foreign Country. Cambridge: Cambridge University Press.

———(1996) Possessed by the Past: The Heritage Crusade and the Spoils of History. New York: Free Press.

———(1997) History and Memory. The Public Historian 19(2):31–39.

Markovits, Andrei S., and Simon Reich (1997) The German Predicament: Memory and Power in the New Europe. Ithaca, NY: Cornell University Press.

Martin, Erika, Mia Parsons, and Paul A. Shackel. (1997) Commemorating a Rural African-American Family at a National Battlefield Park. International Journal of Historical Archaeology 1(2):157–177.

Mazariegos, Oswaldo Chinchilla. (1998) Archaeology and Nationalism in Guatemala at the Time of Independence. Antiquity 72(276):376–386.

McConnell, Stuart. (1992) Glorious Contentment: The Grand Army of the Republic, 1865–1900. Chapel Hill: University of North Carolina Press.

McPherson, James M. (1969) Foreword. *In* A Brave Black Regiment: History of the Fifty-Fourth Regiment of Massachusetts Volunteer Infantry 1863–1865. New York: Arno Press and the New York Times.

———(1982) Ordeal by Fire: The Civil War and Reconstruction. New York: Knopf.

———(1988) Battle Cry of Freedom: The Civil War Era. New York: Oxford University Press.

Meyer, Eugene L. (1995) As Civil War Monument Returns, So Does Controversy. Washington Post, July 10: C1, C2.

Miller, Daniel, and Christopher Tilley. (1984) Ideology, Power, and Prehistory: An Introduction. *In* Ideology and Power in Prehistory. Daniel Miller and Christopher Tilley, eds. pp. 1–15. Cambridge: Cambridge University Press.

Minutes of the Civil War Centennial Commission. (1960) Records of the Civil War Centennial Commission. R.G. 79, Box 22, January 5, 1960. Washington, DC: National Archives.

———(1961) Records of the Civil War Centennial Commission. R.G. 79, Box 21, December 4, 1961. Washington, DC: National Archives.

Murry, Freeman H. M. (1916) Emancipation and the Freed in American Sculpture: A Study in Interpretation. Washington, DC: Freeman Murry.

Nash, Gary B., Charlotte Crabtree, and Ross E. Dunn. (1998) History on Trial: Culture Wars and the Teaching of the Past. New York: Knopf.

Neustadt, Richard, and Ernst May. (1986) Thinking in Time: The Uses of History for Decision-Makers. New York: Free Press.

New York Times. (1961) No title. New York Times, January 9:1.

———(1962) No title. New York Times, September 22:1, 50.

Nöel Hume, Ivor. (1983) Martin's Hundred. New York: Alfred A. Knopf.

Nora, Pierre. (1999) Realms of Memory: Rethinking the French Past. Arthur Goldhammer, trans. New York: Columbia University Press.

O'Leary, Cecilia Elizabeth. (1999) To Die For: The Paradox of American Patriotism. Princeton: Princeton University Press.

Pai, Hyung, II. (1999) Nationalism and Preserving Korea's Buried Past: The Office of Cultural Properties and Archeological Heritage Management in South Korea. Antiquity 73(281):619–625.

Pak, Yangjin. (1999) Contested Ethnicities and Ancient Homelands in Northeast Chinese Archaeology. Antiquity 73(281):613–618.

Patterson, Thomas C. (1986) The Last Sixty Years: Toward a Social History of Americanist Archaeology in the United States. American Anthropologist 88(1):7–26.

Peri, Y. (1999) The Media and Collective Memory of Yitzhak Rabin's Remembrance. Journal of Communication 49(3):106–124.

Peterson, Merrill. (1994) Lincoln in American Memory. New York: Oxford University Press.

Pittsburgh Courier. (1931) Heyward Shepherd Memorial. Pittsburgh Courier, October 24.

Saint-Gaudens, Homer. (1913) The Reminiscences of Augustus Saint-Gaudens. 2 vols. New York: Century Co.

Savage, Kirk. (1997) Standing Soldier, Kneeling Slaves: Race, War, and Monument in Nineteenth-Century America. Princeton: Princeton University Press.

Scham, Sandra A. (1998) Mediating Nationalism and Archaeology: A Matter of Trust? American Anthropologist 100(2):301–308.

Scott, Barbara G. (1996) Archaeology and National Identity: The Norwegian Example. Scandinavian Studies 68:321–342.

Shackel, Paul A. (1994a) Archaeology in Harpers Ferry National Historical Park. West Virginia Archaeologist 1–2:1–11.

———(1994b) Memorializing Landscapes and the Civil War in Harpers Ferry. *In* Look to the Earth: An Archaeology of the Civil War. Clarence Geier and Susan Winter, eds. pp. 256–270. Knoxville: University of Tennessee Press.

———(1996) Culture Change and the New Technology: An Archaeology of the Early American Industrial Era. New York: Plenum Publishing.

———(1999) Public Memory and the Rebuilding of the Nineteenth-Century Industrial Landscape at

Harpers Ferry. Quarterly Bulletin: Archeological Society of Virginia 54(3):138–144.

———(2000) Archaeology and Created Memory: Public History in a National Park. New York: Kluwer Academic/Plenum Publishing.

———(In press) Rediscovering Harpers Ferry's Post-Bellum Histories. *In* Proceedings of the Symposium on Culture—History of the Mountainous Eastern United States. Eugene B. Barfield, ed. Harrisonburg, VA: Archaeological Society of Virginia and the U.S. Department of Agriculture—Forest Service.

Shackel, Paul A., ed. (1993) Interdisciplinary Investigations of Domestic Life in Government Block B: Perspectives on Harpers Ferry's Armory and Commercial District. Occasional Report, 6. Washington, DC: Department of the Interior, National Capital Region Archaeology Program, National Park Service.

Shackel, Paul A., and Barbara J. Little. (1994) Archaeological Perspectives: An Overview of Chesapeake Historical Archaeology. *In* Historical Archaeology of the Chesapeake. Paul A. Shackel and Barbara J. Little, eds. pp. 1–15. Washington, DC: Smithsonian Institution Press.

Shanks, Michael, and Christopher Tilley. (1987) Re-Constructing Archaeology. Cambridge: Cambridge University Press.

Sider, G. M. (1996) Cleansing History: Lawrence, Massachusetts, the Strike for Four Loaves of Bread and No Roses, and the Anthropology of Working-Class Consciousness. Radical History Review 65:48–83.

Smith, Steven. (1999) Preserving American Battlefields: What's the Point? Paper presented at "Commemoration, Conflict and the American Landscape: An Archaeology of Battlefield and Military Landscapes," University of Maryland, College Park, November 12.

Spriggs, Matthew. (1999) Pacific Archaeologies: Contested Ground in the Construction of Pacific History. The Journal of Pacific History 34(1):109–121.

Taft, Lorado. ([1924]1969) The History of American Sculpture. New York: Arno Press.

Teski, Marea C., and Jacob J. Climo. (1995) Introduction. *In* The Labyrinth of Memory: Ethnographic Journeys. Marea C. Teski and Jacob J. Climo, eds. pp. 1–10. Westport, CT: Bergin and Garvey.

Thelen, David. (1989) Memory and American History. Journal of American History 75(4):1117–1129.

Trigger, Bruce. (1989) A History of Archaeological Thought. Cambridge: Cambridge University Press.

Trouillot, Michel-Rolph. (1995) Silencing the Past: Power and Production of History. Boston: Beacon Press.

United Daughters of the Confederacy—National Chapter (1931) Report of the Faithful Slave Memorial Committee. *In* Minutes of the Thirty-Eighth Annual Convention of the United Daughters of the Confederacy. pp. 58–61. Jacksonville, FL, November 17–21.

Virginia Free Press. (1859) No title. Virginia Free Press, October 27: 2.

———(1867) No title. Virginia Free Press, May 23: 2.

———(1879) No title. Virginia Free Press, November 29: 2.

———(1884) No title. Virginia Free Press, November 13: 2.

Volz, J. Leonard. (1961) Draft Memorandum, from J. Leonard Volz, Regional Chief of Visitor Protection, to Regional Director. Critique—Reenactment of the Battle of First Manassas. August. On file, Manassas National Battlefield Park, Manassas, VA.

Wachtel, Nathan. (1986) Memory and History, Introduction. History and Anthropology 2(October):2–11.

Wallace, Anthony. (1981) Visiting the Past: History Museums in the United States. Radical History Review 25:63–96.

White, Rodney A. (1989) The Monument in the Box. The Journal's Weekend Magazine, The Martinsburg Journal 12(23):4, 11.

Wolf, Eric. (1990) Distinguished Lecture: Facing Power—Old Insights, New Questions. American Anthropologist 92:586–596.

Van Gogh in Alabama, 1936

Steve Spence

Steve Spence is an Associate Professor of English and media studies at Clayton State University in Morrow, Georgia, just outside Atlanta. Dr. Spence teaches courses in new media studies, media production, and cultural studies and serves as the Program Director for the BA in Communication Media Studies. He is currently working on several video and new media productions, as well as a book-length examination of how Martin Luther King's images and words have been preserved. This essay first appeared in the interdisciplinary journal *Representations*. Published by the University of California Press, *Representations* has been known since its inception in 1983 as a place for trend-setting work in history, literature, art history, social theory, and anthropology.

It is the camera that today reveals our disasters and our claims to divinity, doing what painting and poetry used to do and, we can only hope, will do again.

—Lincoln Kirstein, 1938[1]

In October 1935, the American photographer Walker Evans took a permanent position with the agency that would become the U.S. Farm Security Administration (FSA). A month later, New York's Museum of Modern Art (MoMA) opened the nation's first major exhibition of work by the Dutch painter Vincent van Gogh. Both are signal moments in American art history. While the MoMA opening initiated a string of events that eventually would make van Gogh an American icon, Evans's work over the next eighteen months is generally regarded as his definitive contribution to American photography.[2] The FSA assignments themselves undoubtedly provided the key provocation for this extraordinary creative streak; however, Evans's approach to these assignments owes a great and largely unacknowledged debt to the MoMA exhibition. Although I know of no direct record that Evans either saw the van Gogh show or explicitly acknowledged its influence on his government photography, the circumstantial evidence for such influence is clear in the facts of Evans's life, in the photographs themselves, and in the texts that shaped their creation and reception.

It does no disservice to the quality of Evans's photography to note that his career benefited from the influence of well-placed friends among MoMA's executive staff. In the early 1930s, Evans lived in New York and traveled in a social circle that included many of the young museum's curators, directors, and advisory council members, including Alfred Barr, Thomas Mabry, Dorothy Miller, and Lincoln Kirstein.[3] The museum began hiring Evans to photograph its exhibitions in 1930, and in 1933 MoMA's architectural galleries displayed thirty-nine of his photographs of Victorian houses — the result of a collaborative project conceived by Kirstein.[4] During his eighteen months with the FSA, Evans maintained close contacts with MoMA, and this relationship bore fruit in the 1938 single-artist exhibition *American Photographs*, a first both for the museum and for Evans. In 1935–36, then, Evans's tours throughout the South coincided with an increasing nationwide recognition of a triumph both for the artist van Gogh and for Evans's friends at MoMA.

In itself, of course, this historical parallel offers no evidence that the painter's work influenced the photographer's. Indeed, at first glance few visual artists share less in common. Van Gogh was a painter of storm and stress; the reviews considered here are unanimous in emphasizing his drama,

551

color, and energy. The most consistent notes in Evans's imagery, on the other hand, are reticence and stasis. With few exceptions, Evans worked in sharp-focus, black-and-white photography, usually with a large-format architectural camera that leant itself to static subject matter. Most of his photographs avoid dramatic angles and strong tonal contrasts, concentrating instead on straight lines and muted, middle-range tones. Reviewers often emphasized this technique's distance from the painterly tradition (labeling it "antigraphic," for example), and Evans himself encouraged this line of evaluation. However, Evans also consistently sought venues for and encouraged readings of his photography as specifically *modern* art. It is here that van Gogh's nineteenth-century drawings and paintings and Evans's twentieth-century photography begin to converge.

Although critics have previously noted only an isolated similarity linking these two artists, both Evans's photographic practice and contemporary evaluations of it depended on a particular and pervasive interpretation of van Gogh that conjoined documentary realism and modernist idealism. This understanding developed, I will demonstrate, both within and as a response to the "van Gogh phenomenon" of the middle 1930s—a widespread mass-cultural celebration of van Gogh sparked by the MoMA exhibition.

5   This influence did not end with Evans, however, and that brings me to a second, larger point. The van Gogh phenomenon—fundamentally a set of texts and interpretive practices that spanned the divide between modernism and mass culture—provides a template vital to the understanding of the 1930s documentary movement in general. Van Gogh's influence on Evans represents only a single moment in a broader trend: the dependence of thirties documentary photography on the fine arts. Throughout the decade, documentary photography traveled alongside reproductions of artistic masterpieces in the same mass-media and artistic circles, and their proximity shaped valuations of both the photography and the art. In these years, for example, van Gogh became a documentary artist whose great strength lay in his sympathetic and accurate vision of agricultural life and labor. In a similar manner, the painter's empathetic persona infused the photographic record promoted by the New Deal, reinforcing the photography's aesthetic and moral authority and, therefore, its rhetorical effect. Thirties documentary claimed the mantle of

science, but it did so within a discourse that mobilized the aesthetic, expressive, and visionary resonance of modernist art. It was from this contradictory mixture—a combination enabled by the mingling of mass culture and high art in the decade's photographic media—that documentary drew its persuasive power.

To elucidate this argument, I first take up the van Gogh phenomenon, examining the process that transformed an obscure nineteenth-century Dutch painter into the most celebrated artist of the European tradition. I then investigate the visual parallels linking paintings and drawings from the van Gogh exhibition to some of Evan's most renowned documentary photographs. Finally, I analyze the textual accompaniments to Evans's work, with a particular emphasis on an extraordinary and influential interpretation of Evans's imagery—James Agee's contribution to *Let Us Now Praise Famous Men*, a collaborative documentary book on the lives of three families of Alabama tenant farmers. A close examination of *Praise*'s text demonstrates that Agee read Evans's documentary practice as nothing less than a revolutionary means of visual representation, one appropriate to a new stage of modernity. And like Evans himself, in forging this new vision Agee drew on the aesthetic and political resonance of van Gogh's example.

THE VAN GOGH PHENOMENON

Opening on 5 November 1935, MoMA's single-artist exhibition *Vincent van Gogh* presented 127 drawings, watercolors, and oil paintings by the artist on three floors of the museum's townhouse at West 53rd Street. Originally scheduled for six months and seven venues, the exhibition finally closed its second installation at MoMA fourteen months later. Its extended tour included ten cities, and by September 1936 more than fifty others had offered to serve as host. More than 900,000 people attended the show (including 227,000 in San Francisco alone), an audience that surpassed the total for any previous single-artist exhibition in U.S. history.[5] In the process, van Gogh's blockbuster success secured the six-year-old museum's status as one of America's most influential cultural institutions. As one historian noted, "It is unlikely—indeed, inconceivable—that any other art exhibition has ever had such an immediate impact on the public taste as the van Gogh show."[6]

Van Gogh's appeal astonished both supporters and opponents, who struggled with one of the questions that concerns this essay: Why van Gogh? What fueled the enormous appeal of this particular painter at this moment in American history? Or, as a newspaper columnist in Cleveland put it, "Just what combination of circumstances is it that causes people to flock in swarming multitudes to see the works of a single crazy Dutch painter as if he were a combination of Ringling Bros. Circus, Jack Benny and a two-headed horse?"[7]

The motive forces behind such widespread appeal were surely heterogeneous, and what follows will not attempt to answer this question definitively. A clear contributing factor, however, was the merchandising frenzy that surrounded the exhibition, fed in part by the new museum's "expert press-agentry."[8] The show's popular success, for example, generated two reprintings of *Lust for Life*, Irving Stone's 1934 fictionalized biography; a *Reader's Digest* condensation of that novel; reproductions in the Sunday rotogravure sections of major newspapers across the country; multiple new editions reproducing van Gogh's paintings; a popular edition of the artist's letters to his brother Theo; and a vogue for the painter's palette and iconography in the period's fashions, shop-window displays, and advertising.

Shoppers walking down Fifth Avenue in the fall of 1935, for example, would discover that MoMA was not alone in appreciating van Gogh's broad appeal. Within weeks of the exhibition's opening, *ART news* commended the results of the commercial vogue that accompanied it:

> Seldom has an exhibition aroused such enthusiasm as that at the MoMA and never within our memory has there been such constant visual reinforcement from unexpected sources. ... Now prints of the greater part of the artist's oeuvre appear so inescapably in window after window that even the casual stroller is likely to gather without effort impressions that equal in extent those usually obtained by earnest students from special brochures and books.[9]

Led by Saks Fifth Avenue, New York's retailers capitalized on van Gogh's sudden popularity, integrating his palette and style into their window displays and their merchandise.[10] Some readers condemned *ART news* for praising such commercial exploitation, but others supported it on populist grounds:

> I feel that art is not only for the "privileged few" who visit art galleries, but also for the world at large and I believe that our country would benefit greatly by having more shop windows making use of the decorative values of Van Gogh. ... If the colors and styles of today are to be chosen from the palette of Vincent Van Gogh, I think that here is a just cause for much rejoicing.[11]

Of course, such an argument runs counter to the *l'art pour l'art* formalism that became MoMA orthodoxy after World War II. These merchandising initiatives promoted a thing that Americans learned to call kitsch, and in traditional histories of American modernism this is the opposite of "art." Because MoMA often appears in such histories as the standard-bearer of an elitist and hermetic formalism, the suggestion that the museum supported this trend might seem surprising.[12] Nevertheless, in the 1930s *l'art pour l'art* represented only one among a diverse array of competing aesthetic faiths, and good evidence suggests that MoMA encouraged the commercial frenzy that grew up around its exhibition.[13] In the context of the Great Depression's economic and cultural crises—a moment when the boundaries separating institution art from mass culture blurred considerably—both the museum and its canonical modernists could be seen as vital contributors to commercial culture. That the museum would support this blending of commerce and art should not surprise us, since its original charter claimed that encouraging the application of the modern arts "to manufacture and practical life" would be a central aspect of the new museum's mission.[14] Through its van Gogh exhibition, the museum achieved this goal with unprecedented success.

Although MoMA's publicity campaign for the exhibition met strong criticism from within the museum community, Alfred H. Barr, the museum's founding director, proved to be at least ambivalent about encouraging the painter's mass appeal.[15] In a contemporary press release, for example, Barr argued that van Gogh's popularity among "the great aesthetically naive public" was "just what the artist himself would most passionately have desired."[16] As this quotation suggests, both van Gogh's "passionate desires" and the wellsprings of his contemporary appeal proved to be contentious topics in the wake of MoMA's success. The exhibition, "hailed by the radical press no less than by the fashionable periodicals," became the site of an explicitly political debate that attempted to make sense of the contradictory legacies inscribed within the painter's biography and oeuvre.[17] Rather than through any authoritative resolution, however, it was these contradictions themselves that made the painter a Depression-era icon.

In short, Vincent van Gogh found a huge and passionate American audience in the middle thirties because the fundamental discontinuities of his art and life resonated with the contradictions of a society reeling from economic meltdown. Basic categories of knowledge and evidence were in crisis, and within this contested terrain the image of the modern artist as impassioned and truthful seer took on resonant importance. The artistic subject "van Gogh" came to stand for a social vision that could reconcile irreconcilables, bridging the divide that separated nature from culture, art from science, fine art from vernacular, and the metaphysical from the physical realms. And because these reconciliations remained imaginary, Depression-era discussions of van Gogh's achievements took on a characteristically ambivalent form.

FROM THE BORINAGE TO ARLES

Vincent van Gogh's life and oeuvre are both marked by a number of false starts and discontinuities. Born in 1853 and raised in southern Holland, van Gogh embarked on numerous careers and failed, during his lifetime, in all of them. Van Gogh worked first as a picture salesman at a family gallery, then as a bookseller, a teacher, an evangelical minister to poor miners in Belgium, and, finally, in the last ten years of his life, as an artist. His paintings themselves demonstrate unusual shifts of style and subject matter. In the 1930s this variety was read (as it often is today) as a split between early and late periods, divided at 1886, when van Gogh moved to Paris and encountered impressionism firsthand. Van Gogh's drawings and paintings before this period demonstrate the strong influence of the early Dutch masters and later realists including Honoré Daumier and Jean-François Millet. Their emphasis is on draftsmanship, tonal variation, and genre scenes, while their palette draws from a muted range of blacks, grays, browns, and greens. In Paris, the most fundamental elements of van Gogh's art transformed. Contrasts of color replaced those of tone, an emphasis on painting replaced drawing, and the early concentration on the lives of proletarian and agricultural laborers shifted to a more varied range of landscape, still life from nature, and portraiture. Present-day assessments of van Gogh's oeuvre generally privilege these later canvases, most created in the French provincial towns of Arles and St. Rémy during the final five years of the painter's life.

Compared to present-day evaluations, however, the most widely circulated interpretations of the 1930s gave great weight to van Gogh's early work in Belgium and the Netherlands. Irving Stone's 1934 *Lust for Life*, for example, devoted more than eighty pages to van Gogh's evangelical and artistic ministries to the Belgian miners in the Borinage, while abbreviating or ignoring many of his later, more artistically productive periods.[18] In 1936, Stone published articles in conjunction with the MoMA openings in New York and San Francisco, and his approach is apparent in many other reviews as well. As a result, drawings and paintings that are today treated as preliminary and unschooled were often given an attention equal to that of the later, postimpressionist canvases. One final, broad tendency in the period's interpretations merits notice here. Despite the numerous shifts and discontinuities in van Gogh's life—and despite a simultaneous understanding of van Gogh's oeuvre as bifurcated by the encounter with impressionism—1930s readings of van Gogh were also marked by attempts to articulate the artist's life and art as a unitary narrative of struggle toward redemption.

An important part of the answer to "Why van Gogh?" lies in these two contradictory tendencies. The painter's depression-era popularity depended on this structural dichotomy between the early and late periods, read as a narrative of contest and reconciliation. Their combination in the work of a single artist enabled viewers to stage van Gogh's oeuvre as a scene of revolutionary struggle. In such readings, the artist's tortured, visionary personality acted as the middle term of a hoped-for dialectical synthesis—between a suffering realism associated with an earthy, agricultural past and a transcendent idealism connected to a redeemed, modernized future.

American interpretations of van Gogh's art did not, of course, spring up fully formed in response to the MoMA exhibition. As Carol Zemel has demonstrated in her groundbreaking *The Formation of* 20 *a Legend: Van Gogh Criticism, 1890–1920*, a substantial critical tradition was already established in Europe before van Gogh's full-scale introduction to the American public in 1935–36.[19] Critical reactions to the MoMA show followed the major themes of this tradition, stressing

- a symbolist aesthetics that emphasized painterly form—color, line, and brushstroke—and a subjectivist and mystical idealism;
- a biographical approach that read van Gogh's life as a parable of romantic alienation and unrecognized genius, in which the paintings became expressive records of the artist's struggle, heroism, and redemption; or
- a socialist reading that emphasized van Gogh's debt to the earlier realist movements in Holland and France, finding in the painter's art and life the embodiment of anticapitalist, communitarian ideals.

Occasionally these interpretations appeared in relatively unmixed form. A review in the radical journal *Art Front*, for example, took a purely socialist standpoint, dismissing the "color-occultism" of van Gogh's postimpressionist period in favor of his early work among the poor: "In our own day, van Gogh might not have found his original efforts to speak to the working people in whose society he lived so inconsistent with the movement of art."[20] In contrast, Herbert McBride of the *New York Sun* valued only the later canvases, which he read as the products of mystical ecstasies, moments when the painter "left all earthy, animal attributes behind him, and became pure spirit, giving out emanations entirely unexplainable to us lesser mortals." Absent this otherworldly inspiration, McBride argued, van Gogh was "an exceedingly commonplace painter."[21]

In general, however, reactions to the MoMA show were more discordant. Most reviews praised both the early and the later work, and most did so by mixing elements of two or more of the approaches that I have labeled symbolist, biographical, and socialist. This complexity is itself significant, and I will delineate its layers and effects through close readings of three important reviews of the exhibition: first, from the *New York Times*, then as now the source of American journalism's most authoritative art criticism; second, from the communist weekly *New Masses*, an important venue in light of van Gogh's continuing status as a "people's artist"; and third, from a lengthy article published in the *American Magazine of Art* that attempted to draw together van Gogh's early and late periods as the combined legacy of "the real Vincent, the social visionary, the brilliantly lucid thinker, the revolutionary artist."[22] Because these three reviews register tensions characteristic of many others, they repay careful scrutiny.

The overt structure of the argument presented by the *New York Times*'s reviewer Edward Alden Jewell, for example, is dialectical.[23] Jewell articulates van Gogh's early career as the first stage in a confrontation of polar opposites: the artist, aspiring to pure spirit, confronts nature, both in his recalcitrant materials and in the prosaic material world of his peasant subjects. Jewell then posits moments of triumphant synthesis, as van Gogh catches "fugitive glimpses of a beauty *that can transfigure everything*" (emphasis added). These fleeting moments bring heaven to earth, gratifying van Gogh with visions of "a real ideal life." The swirling line and hallucinogenic color of the later canvases—for Jewell the "fullest splendor" of van Gogh's art—therefore become images of synthesis and fulfillment. However, a close reading of the review demonstrates that Jewell's proposed dialectic unravels by its end, entangled within the text's contradictory valuations of van Gogh's working-class subject matter.

In sum, the ground of Jewell's evaluation changes dramatically as it moves from the Dutch period to the later work in France. The early *Potato Eaters* (Figure 1), for example, is celebrated for its evocation of smoke and potato steam; Jewell consistently praises such images for their fidelity to the meanings of the pictured scenes. Later work is praised for its innovative brushstroke and unique "signature." In both sections, van Gogh's sinuous line and self-taught figuration become meaningful, but in works like *The Potato Eaters* they signify the painter's solidarity with the men and women portrayed, while in later canvases they become signs of a uniquely expressive personality. The review thus shifts ground from mimesis to expression, but Jewell blurs these essentially contradictory valuations of art through references to van Gogh's "sincerity." The word appears throughout the review, and the morality Jewell discovers in van Gogh's earnest struggle allows him to claim that the works are simultaneously faithful representation and impassioned, transcendent expression. Finally, the reviewer suggests that museum

FIGURE 1 **Vincent van Gogh, *The Potato Eaters*, 1885. Oil on canvas, 82.5 × 114.5 cm. Van Gogh Museum (Vincent van Gogh Foundation), Amsterdam. This painting is indexed as F82 in the standard catalogue raisonné: J.-B. de la Faille, *The Works of Vincent van Gogh: His Paintings and Drawings,* rev. ed. (New York, 1970). Captions for other works by van Gogh list the catalogue number in parentheses.**

patrons who identify with the ethical core of van Gogh's artistic project—tortured, aspiring, passionate, and sincere—take on the moral authority ascribed to the artist himself, an authority that Jewell earlier equated with the poverty and humility of agricultural labor.

25   Thus, although the realist aura attributed to van Gogh's early work seems to disappear by the end of the review, it in fact sustains Jewell's aesthetics. True feeling for the artworks can only be achieved by a penetration *through* the canvas and into the "tortured, aspiring heart" of the human subject posited on its other side. This movement is framed as a transcendence of material resistance, and Jewell first envisions the artist as its agent, confronting his peasant models and painterly media. The marks of van Gogh's struggle are left on the canvas, and these are endowed with a Christian, utopian resonance. Finally, the sympathetic audience embraces this tortured artistry, completing their journey into van Gogh's tortured heart.

    Jewell's final emphasis on the artistic personality was not uncommon in the 1930s, and it is not surprising to find such a reading in a mainstream

venue like the *New York Times*. What distinguished the van Gogh show from other exhibitions, however, was the breadth of its appeal. What might surprise, for example, is the point-by-point resemblance to Jewell's van Gogh demonstrated by the artistic persona constructed by the communist weekly *New Masses*.

    Like Jewell's, Stephen Alexander's van Gogh is the hero of a moral crusade, struggling toward visions of something very like "the real ideal life." And like Jewell, Alexander presents this vision as the combined product of van Gogh's early and late periods. Alexander claims van Gogh for "the great tradition of revolutionary art," arguing that his entire oeuvre reflects a single, coherent goal:

> Both his early work and his later, impressionist paintings are complementary aspects of a single fundamental attitude. Van Gogh was in search of truth. Violently, uncompromisingly in search of truth. He loved humanity and nature warmly and with passionate intensity. . . . He set down on canvas and in drawings his straight forward

observations and knowledge of life about **him in** essentially the same manner ... **whether** it was a weaver at work, a peasant **woman's** head, or a vase of flowers.[24]

The key to van Gogh's truth is once again empathy, and the signs of this empathy are once again the marks of the painter's "crude, sincere, and direct methods." Like Jewell, Alexander equates the paintings' seeming crudity with their creator's sincerity. The weaver referred to by Alexander, for example, is probably the *Weaver: Interior with Three Windows*, painted fifteen months before *The Potato Eaters* and hung near the later canvas in the MoMA installation. Like *The Potato Eaters*, the *Weaver* uses blocky, simplified forms and a flattened, unconventional perspective to portray a working-class figure within a darkened interior. The result is a grim and foreboding image of the artisan's working life, and Alexander pours scorn on those who rejected or ignored it during van Gogh's life:

30   What need had a smug, effete mercantile bourgeoisie for these deeply sympathetic, tragic statements of the lives of the working class on the walls of their luxury homes? They would have none of this awkward, uncouth lout ... who did not know how to draw, nor the meaning of art. (30)

Here again, van Gogh's awkward draftsmanship is taken as a sign of inspired difference, a sympathetic identification that supports and sustains his canvases' realism. In the following sentence, however, Alexander assimilates the dramatically different *Sunflower* canvases under the same sign: "Van Gogh's dynamic, radiant statements about nature were no better received than his earlier statements about humanity" (30).

For Alexander, then, all of van Gogh's varied, modernist challenges to the artistic tradition—simplified figuration, flattened perspective, and dazzling, discordant color—become signifiers of the artist's revolutionary perception and moral authority. Despite their differences, the *New Masses* and the *New York Times* made similar linkages between conflict, passion, truth, and painterly form. While Alexander privileges the painter's early realism and Jewell the later postimpressionism, both critics depend on a synthesis that crosses the polar oppositions of a realist/idealist divide. Van Gogh's work becomes a record of the painter's lifelong battle to transcend a vale of suffering, marking his struggle toward (for Alexander) "a decent and a better world" and (for Jewell) a "real ideal life."

The correspondence submerged within these competing stories of opposition, confrontation, and Christlike passion—both tales spun around a Dutch artist who had died almost a half century before—became more explicit in a long article published a few months later in the *American Magazine of Art*. Like Jewell and Alexander, Gertrude Benson presented van Gogh as a brilliantly perceptive seer, a revolutionary artist whose artistic vision manifests a synthesis of idealist and materialist oppositions. It was this combination, Benson argued, that fueled the MoMA exhibition's phenomenal success.

Between 1929 and 1936, Benson writes, American audiences lost interest in "refinements of form and color for their own sake, in abstract invention and construction, in easel-egocentricities":

35   The economic débâcle brought with it the rediscovery of the subject, and, in a sense, the rediscovery of van Gogh. A man who could write in 1882—"To stroll on wharves, and in alleys, and in streets, and in the houses, waiting rooms, even saloons—that is not a pleasant pastime unless for an artist. As such one would rather be in the dirtiest place where there is something to draw than at a tea party with charming ladies. Unless one wants to draw ladies, then a tea party is all right even for an artist"—such a man is curiously in tune with our own age.[25]

As this passage signals, the Great Depression forms a constant background for Benson's evaluation of van Gogh; in both form and content, the passage reflects the documentary aesthetic that shaped public discourse about the economic crisis. Benson builds her appeal to van Gogh's realism around a quotation from the artist's letters, reinforcing the documentary factuality of this evocation of "the dirtiest places." However, like Jewell, Benson simultaneously registers a lack of ease; the qualifications "in a sense" and "curiously" manifest a significant tension.

It is indeed curious to claim the painter of the *Starry Night* and the *Night Cafe* as a realist; yet these equations of crudity, sincerity, and realism echo in multiple thirties reactions: "What remains, and pulls him through, is something stirring about the struggle, something that flows from an impassioned search after truth. ... it is the prosaic realist who ultimately prevails, crude, hampered, but indomitably honest."[26] Or again, from the journal *Parnassus*: "What if van Gogh has no chic, in the sense of slickness? He had what is infinitely better— sincerity, zeal, and vision."[27] Or, as Alexander of the *New Masses* put it in short, "His simplicity was tantamount to a fanatic honesty" (29). The realism of van Gogh was, for the 1930s, an *impassioned* realism, grounded in the poverty and misery of the artist's life, and signified by the marks of intensity in his art. As the quotations here suggest, this "stirring struggle," "zeal," and "fanatic honesty" supported van Gogh's claims to truth.

As a result, van Gogh's persona takes its place among the reliable, passionate eyewitnesses peopling the subgenre William Stott identifies, in *Documentary Expression and Thirties America*, as "vicarious" documentary reportage.[28] In such texts, the impassioned reactions of a first-person narrator were meant to guide the audience's feelings about the events portrayed. Noting the period's fascination with Walt Whitman's "I am the man, I suffer'd, I was there," Stott writes, "To be trustworthy, a speaker needed to be the man or a firsthand witness; if he had suffered also, it would help" (36).

For widespread American audiences during the thirties, van Gogh's suffering clearly supported the authenticity of his pictures. "Tortured Soul," for example, a *Reader's Digest* condensation of Irving Stone's biography, portrayed van Gogh's life in the Borinage as one long, anguished process of identification: "Now he was living like the miners, eating the same food, sleeping in the identical bed. . . . At last he was one of them, and had won the right to bring them the Word of God."[29] Stone's concurrent emphasis on van Gogh's Christian evangelism, however, suggests the second, idealist side of the painter's appeal. Like Benson, Stone equates the impulses that led van Gogh to Christian ministry with those that took him to Arles as a postimpressionist painter. Both journeys became the quests of a utopian visionary. Unlike Stone's abrupt conflation, however, Benson's reading of the later canvases consistently places van Gogh within a contested social terrain. Sustained by the sturdy provincialism of his line and the lyrical mysticism in his palette, van Gogh emerges as both man-of-the-people and utopian socialist. His oeuvre figures, simultaneously, a forthright, earthy realism and a prophetic idealism. It is on this unstable combination that van Gogh's extraordinary appeal was founded, and it is on this same combination that documentary expression depended.

WALKER EVANS: ART AND THE MACHINE

At President Roosevelt's prompting, in 1935 the U.S. Congress created a new federal agency, the Resettlement Administration (RA), to address the agricultural crises brought on by the Great Depression and a series of widespread natural disasters. Although the world of New York museums and art galleries might seem remote from such a project, in its first year the RA allocated part of its $277 million budget to a task that seemed remarkable, even at the time.[30] While devoting most of its energies to removing small farmers from overcultivated land, the agency also hired a corps of photographers to make a comprehensive record of America's agricultural regions and their inhabitants. The result of this initiative is an archive of more than seventy-seven thousand photographs, today housed in the Library of Congress.

Many other federal agencies employed photographers, of course, both before and after the New Deal. What made this project extraordinary was the fact that the RA claimed to be creating both historical documents *and* works of art:

> There are three ways of evaluating photographs: as a mere record; for their immediacy and news value; as works of art. . . . In the photographic work of the Resettlement Administration it was decided to submit all material to the three foregoing criteria.[31]

In June 1936, the RA claimed success. Its photography's unprecedented popularity "in the press, the literature, and in the art circles of the United States" fully justified this novel approach.[32] This was the same span of months during which the nation became fascinated with Vincent van Gogh, whose images of rural and provincial folk began to seem "curiously in tune" with the contemporary moment.

More so than other documentary photographers, Walker Evans can illuminate this congruence of painting and photography. My reading of Evans is not, however, a part of the critical tradition that seeks to distinguish his practice either from the aims of his federal employers or from the work of other documentary photographers. As the RA's *First Annual Report* suggests, the agency encouraged all of its photographers to pursue artistic aims, and the extraordinary work produced by FSA photographers including Dorothea Lange, Arthur Rothstein, and Ben Shahn testifies to the success of this approach. However—and largely due to his special relationship with MoMA—Evans's photography circulated more frequently within explicitly high-art contexts; as a result, a close reading of the texts that surrounded Evans's work helps make visible the appeals to artistic iconography and poetics that underlay most of the period's documentary photography. And for Evans in particular, the van Gogh phenomenon sparked by MoMA's blockbuster success provided the key artistic context.

45   The most fundamental similarity linking van Gogh and Evans lies in their shared emphasis on agricultural life and labor, and two metonymic representations of that labor are the source of a frequently remarked parallel. Evans's photograph of *Floyd Burroughs' Work Boots*, made in 1936, echoes the theme of several paintings made by van Gogh between 1886 and 1888, including the *Still Life: A Pair of Shoes* that was a part of the MoMA exhibition. Both images present a pair of well-worn shoes within a flat, horizontal plane,

and both share obvious similarities in treatment and angle of vision. A number of critics have commented on this parallel, but none have noted that Evans's explicit homage points toward a more comprehensive influence.[33]

Although Evans did not make such overt reference to a particular artwork in any other photograph, his portrayal of rural and provincial life invites constant reference to van Gogh's. In *Farm Kitchen, Alabama* (Figure 2), for example, Evans presents a collection of objects sitting foursquare on bare wooden flooring. The fine grain of the print reveals the objects' rich and varied textures while maintaining a characteristically narrow, middle-tone range. The space is lit to emphasize the objects' three-dimensional solidity, yet the minimal shadows limit reference to a context outside the frame. As a result, the stove, chair, containers, and utensils recall similar objects in *Vincent's Bedroom at Arles* (Figure 3), a painting that Evans had admired at MoMA's inaugural exhibition in 1929.[34] In both images, the diagonal lines of floor and walls lend an energy to the enclosing space, while the objects' strong outlines and muted tones endow them with a solidity and static serenity. The effect is that of

FIGURE 2   Walker Evans, *Farm Kitchen, Alabama*, 1936. Gelatin silver print, 23.5 × 18.5 cm. Farm Security Administration Collection, Library of Congress, Washington, D.C. (LC-USF342-8143A).

a portrait; in both images, the homely objects of provincial life take on the aura of subjectivity that Walter Benjamin has posited as the hallmark of fine-art objects.

These parallel visions of rural and provincial spaces extended to their inhabitants. During the same period that Evans recorded the interior shots discussed here, for example, he made another photograph, called *Alabama Tenant Farmer Wife*, that recalls a pen-and-ink drawing included in the MoMA exhibition (Figure 4). In this 1883 drawing, van Gogh uses hatching to shade both the background and the woman's clothing and face, and a lightly pigmented wash softens the contrast between ink and paper. The result is a softened, striated texture that merges the figure with its background. In his 1936 portrait of tenant farmer Allie Mae Burroughs, Evans made a number of choices that resulted in a cognate image (Figure 5). First, in the print made for the 1941 edition of *Let Us Now Praise Famous Men*, Evans closely cropped the negative around the woman's head and

shoulders, resulting in a closeup framing, like van Gogh's, dominated by the figure's head and upper torso. Second (and unlike most of his other portraits), Evans here kept the unpainted wooden background in sharp focus. Combined with the close cropping, this makes the horizontal grain of the weathered pine boards an integral part of the image. At least one contemporary observer noted the echoes in figure and ground: "the sharp horizontals of eyebrows, eyes and mouth...are repeated in the three parallel shadows of the clapboard wall behind, and...the camera's light emphasis on the early wrinkles and the puckered forehead . . . are delicately repeated in the grain of the wood."[35]

The same critic, Lionel Trilling, also stressed that Evans's photograph presented a flatly lit, full-frontal *portrait*: "It was 'sat for' and 'posed' ...the sitter gains in dignity when allowed to defend herself against the camera" (100). In her direct gaze and expression, Trilling argues, Burroughs "refuses to be an object at all—everything in the picture

FIGURE 4   Vincent van Gogh, *Head of a Woman with Dark Cap* 1883. Pen and ink on ordinary paper, washed, 21 × 13.5 cm. (F1073). Courtesy of the Kröller-Müller Museum, Otterlo.

FIGURE 5   Walker Evans, *Allie Mae Burroughs, Wife of a Cotton Sharecropper, Hale County, Alabama / Annie Mae Gudger*, 1936. Gelatin silver print, 24.4 × 19.2 cm. Courtesy of the J. Paul Getty Museum, Los Angeles.

proclaims her to be all subject" (101). This reading emphasizes qualities that distinguish Evans's photograph from van Gogh's earlier drawing. Rather than as a specific individual, van Gogh's figure is cast as an emblematic, generalized "peasant woman" through his use of side lighting, indirect gaze, and meditative expression.

This was not the limit of either Evans's or van Gogh's variations on the tradition of portraiture, however. The subjectivity of Allie Mae Burroughs was not always as apparent as Trilling seemed to assume. For example, in the 1938 *American Photographs* exhibition, Evans chose to caption the photograph "Alabama Tenant Farmer Wife." This vocational label—a standard practice for all FSA photographers—marked Burroughs's visage as a generic type rather than an individual portrait. And, like Burroughs's the other men and women pictured in *American Photographs* become representatives of social types: "American Legionnaire," "Cuban Ship Loader," "Flood Refugee," and "Main Street Faces."

50   A similar generalized portraiture was also standard practice for the later van Gogh; most of the forty-nine portraits he painted in Arles are presented as icons or emblems of social roles (for example, shepherd, soldier, lover, and postal worker). Like the ones in *American Photographs*, van Gogh's various figures "seem like those of stock characters in a social primer or an *encyclopédie*, and, taken together, they constitute a social panorama of Provençal citizens."[36]

Moreover, these parallel approaches yielded similarly complex results. Both artists borrow from the tradition of portraiture, for example, to give the men pictured in *Portrait of an Actor* (Figure 6) and *Landowner* (Figure 7) an individualist aura. At the same time, the generic labels mark the men as emblematic of their type or class, and both portraits mix conflicting signs of authority and disrespect. The haughty stare and cravat of the *Portrait of an Actor*, for example, are undermined by van Gogh's treatment of both the suit and face. The suit is dashed off in bold, simplified lines that suggest cartoonlike forms of caricature, while the fleshy features of the actor's face are subtly distorted and incomplete. A viewer could easily conclude that the hauteur is the result of theatrics, or wine, or both. In

FIGURE 6   Vincent van Gogh, *Portrait of an Actor*, 1888. Oil on canvas, 65 × 54.5 cm. (F533). Courtesy of the Kröller-Müller Museum.

FIGURE 7   Walker Evans, *Landowner*, 1936. Gelatin silver print, 23.5 × 18.5 cm. Farm Security Administration Collection, Library of Congress, Washington, D.C. (LC-USF342-8127A).

a similar manner, the *Landowner's* square stance and direct, faintly hostile stare combine with the suit and necktie to suggest economic and social authority. At the same time, these marks are rendered vaguely ridiculous: the man's slumped posture; rumpled, poorly fitting suit; and equivocal gaze all undercut the figure's claim to authority.

Finally, though—and despite the many other direct parallels that appear throughout Evans's FSA photography—the most comprehensive influence Evans took from van Gogh is not manifest in any particular painting or photograph. Instead, it lies in the two artists' systematic blending of vernacular, mass-cultural, and modernist artistic styles. Van Gogh's *La berceuse*, for example, combines the bold outlines and flattened, simplified forms of vernacular art with a flamboyantly modernist palette (Figure 8). As the reviews cited earlier demonstrate, 1930s audiences often read such uses of vernacular form as signifiers of van Gogh's identification with his rural and provincial models. At the same time, however, *La berceuse's* palette added discordant references. In a letter to his brother, van Gogh compared the canvas to "a chromolithograph from a cheap shop," thereby claiming the populist appeal of brightly colored,

inexpensive, mass-manufactured art. The MoMA exhibition paired the canvas with this quotation, and the museum argued that these aspects of the painter's art signified both van Gogh's modernism *and* his populism: "For it is only recently that his gay, decorative, exaggerated color, his tortured drawing, his flat, unconventional perspective and the direct and passionate emotionalism have attracted rather than repelled the general public."[37]

Like van Gogh, Evans constructed an avant-garde aesthetic that appropriated the forms of vernacular and mass-cultural figuration. In both artists' work, these traditions are transformed through incorporation into resolutely modernist projects. The bold lines and flat planes rendered by Evans's *Butcher Sign, Mississippi* (Figure 9), for example, share a family resemblance with the chair and figure in *La berceuse;* both images recontextualize the iconography of self-taught, vernacular painting and crafts. The *Butcher Sign* may stand for a host of such images in Evans's oeuvre—the FSA archive documents his methodical search for such folk iconography.[38] And like van Gogh, Evans integrated vernacular iconography into a style that resonated with modernity. A MoMA press release for *American Photographs*, for example, argued that

FIGURE 8 Vincent van Gogh, *La berceuse* (*Madame Roulin*), 1888–1889. Oil on canvas, 92 × 73 cm. (F504). Courtesy of the Kröller-Müller Museum.

FIGURE 9 Walker Evans, *Butcher Sign, Mississippi*, 1936. Gelatin silver print, 17.6 × 19.8 cm. Courtesy of the J. Paul Getty Museum.

The word modern in its truest sense aptly characterizes Mr. Evans' work as it is "straight" photography, so factual that it may almost be called functional. Its insistence is upon the utmost clarity and detail of the image. Combined with this technical skill is Walker Evans' genius for composition.[39]

55   Evans's genius for composition established its modernism in at least two ways. It was, first of all, "anti-graphic." A reviewer applied this label to Evans's 1935 exhibition at Julian Levy's gallery in New York, and it was taken up by Lincoln Kirstein's article in *American Photographs*.[40] The phrase suggested that the camera's mechanical nature allowed its operators to break free from the stifling weight of the painterly tradition. As machine, the camera could reveal ways of seeing different from—and more in tune with modernity than—images created by the human hand. Evans's photographs jolted viewers out of their visual complacency through the "shock-value" of unexpected angles of vision and juxtapositions of objects. But despite the shock, the photographs presented their subject matter as "still real and without distortion."[41]

This aura of realism resulted from Evans's deliberate choice of rectilinear angles, repetitive imagery, and geometric form. The photographer's preferred tool was an architectural camera that allowed him to correct for optical distortion. The results are evident in photographs like *Negro Church, South Carolina, 1936*, whose ruler-straight lines are more regular than those that would be seen even by a human observer standing in front of the church. Evans composed dozens of such images; their repetition, regularity, and linearity signified the inhumanly clear vision of a functionalist, utilitarian, "machine-age" modernism.

Second, Evans's practice claimed the mantle of modernism through a surrealist juxtaposition of disparate objects. Like the combinations of vernacular craftsmanship and mechanical precision evident in his architectural photographs, these juxtapositions often combined signifiers of the timeless and the new. His *Interior Detail, West Virginia Coal Miner's House* (Figure 10), for example, brought together the curvilinear arcs of a handmade rocking chair with the machine-cut angles

FIGURE 10   Walker Evans, *Interior Detail, West Virginia Coal Miner's House / Coal Miner's House, Scotts Run, West Virginia*, 1935. Gelatin silver print, 23.6 × 16 cm. Courtesy of the J. Paul Getty Museum.

and photorealism of advertising signage. Evans was particularly drawn to such combinations of mass culture and folk craftsmanship, but the trope is widespread throughout the period's documentary photography. As James Guimond has observed, such images expressed "the strange mixtures of times, activities, and cultural influences that mingled and jostled with one another in the FSA photographers' America."[42] However, these discordant combinations of visual styles—vernacular, mass-cultural, and high-art modernism—did more than simply express the contradictions of the age; the readings of Evans and van Gogh considered here suggest that they also enforced the rhetorical impact of both van Gogh's art and FSA photography. In short, both the paintings and the photographs appealed simultaneously to nostalgia for a mythic past and to an embattled faith in a better future.

For thirties audiences, however, one fundamental difference distinguished van Gogh's art from documentary photography. van Gogh signified the past in two ways: his artistic innovations were those of a previous generation, and his folk models were the peasants and townspeople of a distant place and time. The objects of Evans's camera, on the other hand, were very much alive, understood to be living and working in the cotton-growing regions of the South. By mobilizing visual tropes borrowed from Vincent van Gogh, in other words, Evans created complex and contradictory modern emblems: real pictures of disintegration and desperate need, which simultaneously figured a politically resonant, utopian hopefulness.

The best record of this complexity lies in the text that has become the privileged gloss on Evans's depression-era practice: the 481 pages of *Let Us Now Praise Famous Men*, written by James Agee as a complement to Evans's documentary portrait of three rural families in Alabama.[43] In early 1936, Agee recruited Evans for this documentary project on sharecropping in the American South. The FSA agreed to free Evans for the assignment, and that summer he and Agee traveled to Alabama, located three "representative" families, lived with and near these families for several weeks, and then returned to New York. Although not published until 1941, Agee's final version of the experience offers the best source for consideration of the textual and conceptual environment in which Evans worked. Agee's contribution to *Praise* is important in its own right, but a full treatment is beyond the scope of my argument here. As a frame for Evans's image-making, however, Agee's text demonstrates that the van Gogh phenomenon deeply marked the contextual environment surrounding Evans's praxis.

Like Agee and Evans in 1936, van Gogh sought out and created images that emphasized the back-breaking effort, humility, and everyday hardships of agricultural workers. Van Gogh's letters invested this project with a moral fervor, and this closely parallels the tone and emphasis of Agee's contribution to *Praise*. For example, the following quotation appeared as the epigraph to *Dear Theo*, the best-selling collection of van Gogh's letters published in 1937:

> The figure of a labourer—some furrows in a ploughed field—a bit of sand, sea and sky—are serious subjects, so difficult, but at the same time so beautiful, that it is indeed worth while to devote one's life to the task of expressing the poetry hidden in them.

It is difficult to imagine a better epigraph for *Let Us Now Praise Famous Men*, published four years later. Notably, the context of van Gogh's assertion emphasizes its embattled, insistent tone.[44] Both this tone and van Gogh's characterization of his subject matter—difficult, beautiful, and, above all, serious—echo throughout Agee's prose, and these are only the first of dozens of close textual parallels. Throughout *Praise*, Agee combines this passion with a painter's concentration on form and color, and this obsessive attention to sensory detail gives the text its most distinctive trope. A passage from another of van Gogh's letters, also published in the 1937 *Dear Theo*, offers a representative analogue:

> The people here instinctively wear the most beautiful blue that I have ever seen. It is coarse linen which they weave themselves, warp black, woof blue, the result of which is a black-and-blue-striped pattern. When this fades, and becomes somewhat discoloured by wind and weather, it is an infinitely quiet, delicate tone which just brings out the flesh colours. (336)

Compare this to Agee's lyrical description of the structure and tone of the tenant farmers' denim overalls:

> [Through hard use, the] whole shape, texture, color, finally substance, all are changed. The

shape, particularly along the urgent frontage of the things, so that the whole structure of the knee and musculature of the thigh is sculptured there; . . . The texture and the color change in union, by sweat, sun, laundering . . . into a region and scale of blues, subtle, delicious, and deft beyond what I have seen elsewhere approached except in rare skies, the smoky light some days are filmed with, and some of the blues of Cézanne. (267)

This excerpt comes from Agee's four-page description of overalls, part of a thirty-page chapter called "Clothing." The explicit reference to Cézanne should not obscure the great debt Agee's prose owes to that of another postimpressionist. The most characteristic tropes in *Praise*'s text—an artist's attention to sensory detail, infused with a deeply Christian, passionately expressed preference for the realities of the working poor—Agee found in van Gogh's letters.[45]

From the van Gogh *phenomenon* that exploded simultaneously with its composition, Agee's text took a final, compelling, and cautionary tale. *Praise*'s rhetorical framework is structured by its reaction to the commercial frenzy for van Gogh's images and words. Although Agee's prose is clearly literary in its roots and aspirations, the text repeatedly expresses anxiety about *Praise*'s likely reception:

> Above all else: in God's name don't think of it as Art.
>
> Every fury on earth has been absorbed in time, as art, or as religion, or as authority in one form or another. . . . Official acceptance is the one unmistakable symptom that salvation is beaten again . . . and is the kiss of Judas. (15)

70 The blending of Christian and artistic themes here once again recalls van Gogh, but the text's disavowal of art does not. The trope marks a distinguishing element in *Praise*'s rhetoric, one articulated in reaction to the mass-cultural assimilation of van Gogh and other representatives of "high art":

> People hear Beethoven in concert halls, or over a bridge game, or to relax. . . . van Gogh is the man who cut off his ear and whose yellows became recently popular in window decoration. . . . Kafka is a fad; Blake is in the Modern Library. (14)

This reaction against the mass-cultural absorption of high art haunts Agee's contribution to *Praise*. It is worth stressing again that in the years Agee's text took shape, this conjunction was most apparent in the mainstream fascination with van Gogh. *Praise*'s disgust with the "castration" of great artists—"one by one, you have absorbed and have captured and dishonored, and you have distilled of your deliverers the most ruinous of all your poisons"—recalls the *New Masses* reviewer's contempt for the bourgeois audiences of the van Gogh exhibition: "What perversion of history and the meaning of a great artist. What bitter irony."[46] The *New Masses* reacted by claiming van Gogh for revolutionary art, arguing that artists aligned with the Communist Party continued van Gogh's search for truth "in a more organized, clear, and conscious manner."[47] Agee reacted by creating *Praise*'s text—a work of dense, heterogeneous, and difficult prose, clearly indebted to modernist formal experimentation, yet one that insistently disavowed the label "art."

American literary critics have been slow to recognize that Agee's rejection of the category "art" is itself a characteristic trope of many kinds of modernism. Because the various movements of the historical avant-garde occupy a more secure niche in the art-historical canon, it is not surprising that an art historian first made this point in relation to Agee's text. Identifying the rhetoric of a socially conscious, utilitarian modernism within *Praise*, Margaret Olin argues that the book can best be read as a site of interchange between "two modernist discursive modes," documentary and "hermetic art."[48] Although Olin does not pursue the point, this combination closely resembles the radical formalism that characterized avant-garde movements like Soviet constructivism: an outwardly focused, socially engaged artistic praxis that aligned formalist experimentation with social revolution. Nor was this resemblance as distant as it might at first appear. In a short list of artistic influences cited in 1938, *Time* magazine aligned Evans with the constructivist film-maker Dziga Vertov.[49]

Like the constructivists, in 1937 Agee defined modern art as the linkage of formal experimentation and radical politics: "Any new light on anything, if the light has integrity, is a revolution."[50] Continuing the optical metaphor, Agee argued that a strictly Marxian lens was limited, and, moreover, "a willingness to use and still more to try to invent or perfect still other lenses may well become all but obligatory and can in any case scarcely avoid being useful."[51] In *Praise*, published four years later, the metaphors of light and lenses became explicitly photographic:

75   One reason I care so deeply about the camera is just this. So far as it goes . . . and handled cleanly and literally in its own terms, as an ice-cold, some ways limited, some ways more capable, eye, it is, like the phonograph record and like scientific instruments and unlike any other leverage of art, incapable of recording anything but absolute, dry truth. (234)

In *Praise*, the camera becomes the central instrument of Agee's attempt to forge nothing less than a radically new way of seeing and knowing. However, both this passage's passionate advocacy *and* its repetitive qualifications are characteristic of Agee's references to the camera. The anxieties expressed about the reception of great artists like van Gogh are equally apparent in Agee's discussion of photography. Through its misuse, Agee complains, this "central instrument of our time" has spread a "nearly universal . . . corruption of sight" (11).

These perceived limits of science and art, photography and the printed word, are the motivation for the text's obsessive return to the language and example of van Gogh. Responding to the author's own experiences in Alabama and to Evans's photographic portrayals of it, Agee's text effectively transfers the structure of van Gogh's early and late periods—empathetic, suffering realism counterpoised with an ecstatic, transcendent idealism—into the dialectical oppositions that mark *Praise*. Agee reaches toward a particular synthesis of science and fine art, combining the objective realism of the camera with the visionary Christian humanism he associates with van Gogh.

Such contradictory imbrications of art and science, past and future, vernacular, mass, and modernist traditions mark Agee's text as very much of its time; similar patterns are manifest within the broader fascination with the nation's countryside and agricultural workers. In short, documentary photography aroused great passion during the depression because it provided a stage for a bitter political and cultural struggle over the requisites of modernity. What is striking about thirties readings of Evans's photography is their explicit partisanship, particularly when compared to recent interpretations of the photographer as somehow blithely indifferent to the political warfare waged through his imagery. Writing in *American Photographs*, for example, Lincoln Kirstein claimed that Evans's attitude was that of "a member revolting from his own class" (197). The photographer Ansel Adams made a similar point in a different way: "[*American Photographs*] gave me a hernia. I am so *goddam* mad over what people think America is from the left tier."[52] While Adams's photography celebrated the nation's natural beauty, Evans recorded its social schizophrenia.

Notably, despite Evans's "anti-graphic" preference for the iconography of poverty and decay, his Depression-era defenders made frequent references to high art, usually in support of the photographer's moral authority. For example, a review of the *American Photographs* exhibition in Los Angeles discovered in Evans a clarity and compassion reminiscent of Rembrandt: "There are people who will insist that we should not look at poverty or starvation or frustration because these are too ugly. It was said of Rembrandt too."[53] Evans's blending of "historical documents" and "works of art," in other words, served as a weapon in hard-fought battles over the proper role of government in addressing the poverty, starvation, and frustration caused by the Great Depression.

Because the American South played a pivotal   80 role in Franklin Roosevelt's New Deal coalition— and because the South was Walker Evans's chosen terrain—the photographer's particular combinations of modernist, mass-cultural, and vernacular forms took on a compelling political edge. In 1938, after eight years of debilitating economic crisis and six years as president, Roosevelt declared the American South to be "the Nation's No. 1 economic problem."[54] Southern poverty fed conditions that held the entire nation in the grips of depression, Roosevelt argued, and the president charged one of the New Deal's public relations arms, the National Emergency Council, to prepare a brief, persuasive tract that would make his case for change. At the time, per capita income in the wealthiest southern state ranked below that of the poorest state outside the region. Millions of southerners lived on the edge of starvation, and southern tenant farmers were the poorest of the poor, often enduring lives of abject misery. Seeking an image that would resonate with a public that must be moved to action, the council drew a remarkable parallel. Many of the South's tenant farmers, the *Report on Economic Conditions of the South* noted, are "living in poverty comparable to that of the poorest peasants in Europe."[55]

There can be no doubt which images of European peasantry came to mind first in 1938. These were images whose accuracy was ensured by their creator's moral authority, grounded in Vincent van Gogh's Christlike image of suffering and self-sacrifice. They were also images with powerful political resonance. Locating European peasantry on American soil challenged the centuries-old Jeffersonian ideal of citizen-farmers, a keystone of arguments made by the New Deal's many southern opponents. In appeals that resonated with broad streams of *American* ideology, southerners led by the Vanderbilt Agrarians posited agricultural society as a fertile, arcadian space that sustained both material abundance and a democratic, classless society. The equation of southern tenant farmers and European peasants argued, in contrast, that southern agriculture perpetuated a rigid caste system that chained farmers to lives of poverty and exploitation.[56]

However, while van Gogh helped underscore the *Report*'s portrait of southern society as brutalizing and pathological, the allusion accomplished a further task as well. For audiences in the 1930s, van Gogh's imagery combined earthy populism with brilliant modernism—his empathetic visions of agricultural folk stood beside dazzling painterly innovations, vital with the energies of a redeemed modernity. In the photography promoted by the New Deal—claiming, simultaneously, to be both artworks and historical documents—similar juxtapositions proved to be extraordinarily persuasive.

Notes

1. Lincoln Kirstein, "Photographs of America: Walker Evans," in Walker Evans, *American Photographs* (New York, 1988), 192.
2. Evans's interpreters generally accord enormous weight to these eighteen months with the FSA. See, for example, Pare Lorentz, "Putting American on Record," *Saturday Review of Literature*, 17 Dec. 1938; and John Szarkowski, introduction to *Walker Evans* (New York, 1971).
3. Belinda Rathbone, *Walker Evans: A Biography* (Boston, 1995), 63.
4. Ibid., 63, 85.
5. Press release 92136–20. Museum of Modern Art Archives. Department of Circulating Exhibitions. Vincent van Gogh exhibition II.1/1(9), 1. "The van Gogh Exhibit," *Life*, 15 Feb. 1937, 32–35.
6. Russell Lynes, *Good Old Modern* (New York, 1973), 135.
7. William F. McDermott, "McDermott on van Gogh," *Cleveland Plain Dealer*, 12 April 1936. This and many of the other reviews cited in this essay are collected in an unpaginated scrapbook compiled by MoMA's president, available in the museum's archives: A. Conger Goodyear, "van Gogh Exhibition," *Goodyear 37*. Microfilm reproductions of MoMA's Goodyear and Public Information scrapbooks are also available from the Archives of American Art, New York.
8. "All-Time High: Modern Museum," *American Magazine of Art*, Feb. 1936, 120.
9. "Art Progenies," *ARTnews*, 10 Nov. 1935, in Goodyear, "van Gogh Exhibition," no page.
10. In January 1936, Saks Fifth Avenue dedicated ten storefront windows to reproductions of van Gogh's paintings paired with clothing and accessories inspired by the painter's oeuvre. Photographs of these displays are included in MoMA's Public Information scrapbooks (microfilm reel MF 6, frames 696–700). For newspaper clippings that illustrate the same trend in advertising and department stores throughout the nation, see, for example, MF 6, frames 692–94, 701, 759, 938, 979.
11. Lawrence Stevens, "Letters," *ARTnews*, 8 Feb. 1936, in Goodyear, "van Gogh Exhibition," no page.
12. On MoMA's curatorial history, see Christopher Phillips, "The Judgment Seat of Photography," in *The Contest of Meaning*, ed. Richard Bolton (Cambridge, Mass., 1989), 14–47; Serge Guilbaut, *How New York Stole the Idea of Modern Art*, trans. Arthur Goldhammer (Chicago, 1983); and Mary Anne Staniszewski, *The Power of Display* (Cambridge, Mass., 1998).
13. Personal correspondence housed in the museum's Department of Registration archives also supports this conclusion. See van Gogh exhibition (no. 44), "Dept. and Catalogue Material File, Corresp. o–z."

14. A. Conger Goodyear, *The Museum of Modern Art: The First Ten Years* (New York, 1943), 15–16.

15. Alice Marquis, *Alfred H. Barr, Jr.* (Chicago, 1989), 134.

16. Press release 122735–43. Museum of Modern Art Archives. Department of Circulating Exhibitions. Vincent van Gogh exhibition II.1/1(9), 2.

17. Gertrude R. Benson, "Exploding the van Gogh Myth," *American Magazine of Art* 29, no. 1 (1936): 7.

18. Sjraar van Heugten, "Vincent van Gogh as a Hero of Fiction," in *The Mythology of Vincent van Gogh*, eds. Kodera Tsukasa and Yvette Rosenberg (Tokyo, 1993), 165.

19. Carol M. Zemel, *The Formation of a Legend: van Gogh Criticism, 1890–1920* (Ann Arbor, Mich., 1980).

20. Harold Rosenberg, "Peasants and Pure Art," *Art Front*, Jan. 1936, 6.

21. Herbert McBride, "The Art of Vincent van Gogh," *New York Sun*, 9 Nov. 1935, in Goodyear, "van Gogh Exhibition," no page.

22. Benson, "Exploding the van Gogh Myth," 6.

23. Edward Alden Jewell, "Realm of Art: The Warfare That Was Van Gogh," *New York Times*, 10 Nov. 1935, sec. 9, 9. Subsequent citations all refer to page 9. Jewell's approach follows the dialectical interpretation presented by Julius Meier-Graefe, *Vincent van Gogh*, trans., John Holroyd-Reece (New York, 1933).

24. Stephen Alexander, "In Search of Truth," *New Masses*, 26 Nov. 1935, 29.

25. Benson, "Exploding the van Gogh Myth," 7.

26. Royal Cortissoz, "The Emotional Art of Vincent van Gogh," *New York Herald Tribune*, 10 Nov. 1935, in Goodyear, "van Gogh Exhibition," no page.

27. James W. Lane, "Current Exhibitions," *Parnassus* 7, no. 7 (Dec. 1935), in Goodyear, "Van Gogh Exhibition," no page.

28. William Stott, *Documentary Expression and Thirties America* (Chicago, 1986), 33–45.

29. Irving Stone, "Tortured Soul," *Reader's Digest*, March 1936, 119.

30. U.S. Resettlement Administration, *First Annual Report* (Washington, D. C., 1936), 173.

31. Ibid.

32. Ibid.

33. Some of the most interesting commentaries are found in Stott, *Documentary Expression*, 273–75; T. V. Reed, *Fifteen Jugglers, Five Believers* (Berkeley, 1992); Fredric Jameson, *Postmodernism, or, the Cultural Logic of Late Capitalism* (Durham, N. C., 1991); and Suzanne Bloom and Ed Hill, "Borrowed Shoes," *Artforum*, April 1988, 111–17.

34. James R. Mellow, *Walker Evans* (New York, 1999), 104.

35. Lionel Trilling, "Greatness with One Fault in It," *Kenyon Review* (Winter 1942): 100.

36. Carol Zemel, *van Gogh's Progress* (Berkeley, 1997), 88.

37. Press release 122735–43, 2.

38. A useful compilation of such images appears in Walker Evans, *Walker Evans: Signs* (Los Angeles, 1998).

39. Untitled press release. Museum of Modern Art Archives. Department of Circulating Exhibitions. Walker Evans II.1/34 (12), 2.

40. Howard Devree, "In the Galleries: A Reviewer's Week," *New York Times*, 28 April 1935, sec. 10, 7. Kirstein, "Photographs of America," 192.

41. Devree, "In the Galleries," 7.

42. James Guimond, *American Photography and the American Dream* (Chapel Hill, N. C., 1991), 134.

43. James Agee and Walker Evans, *Let Us Now Praise Famous Men*, 2d ed. (Boston, 1969). All subsequent citations are from this edition and will appear as page numbers given in parentheses within the text.

44. Irving Stone, *Dear Theo: The Autobiography of Vincent van Gogh* (Boston, 1937), 173.

45. Agee notes that he read van Gogh's letters in a 26 Dec. 1935 letter, shortly before he took on the assignment that became *Praise*. See James Agee, *Letters of James Agee to Father Flye* (New York, 1962), 75.

46. Agee and Evans, *Praise*, 14. Alexander, "In Search of Truth," 29.

47. Alexander, "In Search of Truth," 30.

48. Margaret Olin, " 'It Is Not Going to Be Easy to Look into Their Eyes': Privilege of Perception in *Let Us Now Praise Famous Men*," *Art History* 14, no. 1 (1991): 92.

49. "Recorded Time," *Time*, 3 Oct. 1938, 43.

50. James Agee, "Art for What's Sake," *New Masses*, 15 Dec. 1936, 48.

51. Ibid.

52. Ansel Adams quoted in Lynes, *Good Old Modern*, 158.

53. Arthur Millier, "Photo Shows Greet Camera Centenary," *Los Angeles Times*, 15 Jan. 1939, in "American Photographs by Walker Evans 1/1," Museum of Modern Art Archives, Department of Circulating Exhibitions, Walker Evans II.1/34 (12), no page.

54. David L. Carlton and Peter A. Coclanis, eds., *Confronting Southern Poverty in the Great Depression: The Report on Economic Conditions of the South with Related Documents* (Boston, 1996), 1.

55. Ibid., 46, 21, 22.

56. Although one-third of tenant farmers were African American in 1938, publicity for the New Deal often ignored the systematic racial oppression that intertwined with economic oppression in the South. Agee's attempts to confront his own culpability in rendering black southerners invisible are discussed in Michael Staub, "As Close as You Can Get: Torment, Speech, and Listening in *Let Us Now Praise Famous Men*," *Mississippi Quarterly* 61, no. 2 (1988): 147–60. The most comprehensive study of African Americans in FSA photography is Nicholas Natanson, *The Black Image in the New Deal* (Knoxville, 1992).

Remembering the Discovery
of the Watergate Tapes

David Thelen

David Thelen is a Distinguished Professor Emeritus of History at the University of Indiana. Professor Thelen served on the editorial board of several journals and received many awards and recognitions during his long career. The author of numerous books and articles, Professor Thelen served as editor of the *Journal of American History*, the premier scholarly publication in the field of American History, from 1985–1999. These essays were originally published in 1989 in that journal, a publication of the Organization of the American Historians in existence for over eighty years, and were part of a special edition focused on memory and American history.

INTRODUCTION

On Friday, the thirteenth of July 1973, in the ornate Senate Caucus Room, the Senate Watergate Committee was completing two months of televised hearings into illegal campaign activities during the 1972 election. The faces of the seven senators and the leading counsels had become familiar to Americans, who were growing increasingly troubled by the revelations and charges that appeared on the news each night. Only two weeks earlier former White House counsel John Dean had testified in exquisite detail about elaborate steps taken by the administration of Richard M. Nixon to hide its connections to illegal activities. Nixon denied Dean's charges. Who, everyone wondered, was telling the truth? How would the truth be determined?

Across the street on that same afternoon five little-recognized people headed for an appointment in the basement of the Dirksen Senate Office Building in room G-334. None of them expected that the meeting was going to be much different from other preliminary interviews between Watergate Committee staffers and current and former White House employees. To the Democratic staffers, Scott Armstrong and Gene Boyce, the Republican staffer, Donald Sanders, and the stenographer, Marianne Brazer, the interview was just the latest in a crowded week of fishing for information that might reveal whether Richard

Nixon or John Dean was telling the truth. To the witness, Alexander P. Butterfield, a former administrative aide at the White House, the interview was a distraction between his work that morning at the Federal Aviation Administration, where he was the chief, and a ceremonial function the next day at a new air traffic control center in New Hampshire, and, four days after that, an object of greater anticipation, his official visit to the Soviet Union. As they started the conversations around the green felt-covered table no one imagined that some four hours later the staffers would emerge with the way to determine who was telling the truth, that they were to discover something that would lead to the president's resignation.

What follows are the recollections of the three people who created the discovery that afternoon.

Scott Armstrong came to that interview as an investigator with a bent for advocacy and journalism. While a student at Harvard Law School, he had worked for a consulting firm that investigated firms holding government contracts. Before coming to the Watergate Committee, he had been a car dealer and, most recently, deputy coordinator of the New England Correctional Council, a group that attempted to introduce new approaches to penology. Since high school he had been a good friend of the *Washington Post*'s Watergate investigator, Bob Woodward, who had helped him get the appointment as investigator for the Senate committee. His work for the Watergate Committee and particularly his questioning of Butterfield added to his reputation as an investigator. He went on to assist Woodward and Carl Bernstein with *The Final Days* and then to become an investigative reporter for the *Washington Post* from 1976 to 1984, with time off to coauthor an exposé of the Supreme Court, *The Brethren*, with Woodward. In 1985 he created the National Security Archive, which he currently directs, to assemble and disseminate "national security" information that it acquires from the United States government.

Donald Sanders had honed his investigative skills as a detective and legislative investigator. After graduating from the University of Missouri School of Law, doing legal work in the Marine Corps for two years, and practicing law (including as city attorney) in Columbia, Missouri, Sanders joined the Federal Bureau of Investigation (FBI) in 1959. For ten years he was an investigator and supervisor for the FBI. In 1969 he became chief counsel for the House Internal Security Committee (newly reformed from the notorious House Committee on Un-American Activities), which he served until he joined the Senate Watergate Committee. Although Nixon's friends never forgave him for asking the question that revealed the existence of the tapes, Sanders believes that his work in probing Watergate actually improved his career opportunities. He went on to investigate the security of nuclear plants for the Nuclear Regulatory Commission, to lobby senators for the Pentagon, and to direct investigations for the Subcommittee on Investigations of the Senate Intelligence Committee (1977–1979) and the Senate Ethics Committee (1979–1982). In 1983 he returned to Columbia, Missouri, to practice law.

Alexander Butterfield came to the White House in 1969 following a distinguished career in the air force. Although he loved flying planes (and was a much-decorated pilot), he had also served as an aide to leading military officials. He rose through the ranks of aides to become a White House military aide for the secretary of defense in the Johnson administration. His old classmate at the University of California, Los Angeles, H. R. Haldeman, chose him as his chief administrative aide in the Nixon administration. Haldeman's offer promised an important administrative challenge,

as well as an opportunity for even better jobs after he left the White House. In March 1973 he was glad to move from the White House back to his original interest, aviation, becoming chief of the Federal Aviation Administration. What happened to him as a result of his revelations is part of the story he tells in the following conversation.

The participants concluded during the interview that Butterfield's revelation marked a "historical" moment and sensed that they would be asked to reconstruct it. Each went about the reconstruction a bit differently. Sanders kept detailed notes during the course of the interview. Almost immediately afterward, chief minority counsel Fred Thompson asked for his notes, and Sanders never saw them again. Three days after the interview he constructed a new account of the meeting itself, of his question, and of Butterfield's response. He has used that 1973 reconstruction as a basis for part of the account published here.

Armstrong acquired the notes taken during the interview by stenographer Marianne Brazer. Since Brazer did not take shorthand, her notes were not so much a verbatim transcript as a record of the questions and answers she thought significant recorded as accurately as she could write them down during the give-and-take. Armstrong used Brazer's notes as the basis for an account he wrote in December of 1974 for Bob Woodward and Carl Bernstein to include in *The Final Days*.[1] According to Armstrong, Woodward and Bernstein used much of this account in their book. Armstrong has drawn heavily on the 1974 memorandum, elaborating on the context, partisan setting, and his own role and perceptions in this account for the *Journal*.

Butterfield routinely made notes of his own activities. He examined Brazer's notes three weeks after the interview. As he began to think of writing a more formal account or giving an elaborate interview to a journalist, he arranged a discussion on May 31, 1974, in which he, Sanders, and Armstrong compared their memories of what had happened on July 13, 1973. In 1975 Butterfield did write an account that he envisioned as part of the introductory chapter of a book he hoped—and still hopes—to complete at some future point. He brought no notes to our meetings and said in 1988 that he did not use his notes and 1975 account as prompts for any of his recollections.

---

[1] Compare pages 1234–44 of Armstrong's account in this issue with Bob Woodward and Carl Bernstein. *The Final Days* (New York, 1976). 54–57.

10   Historians concerned with what actually happened in room G-334 on that afternoon fifteen years ago may well be struck by the discrepancies and even occasional inaccuracies in the accounts that follow. Perhaps the most dramatic discrepancy in the accounts is that each of the major participants remembers differently "the" question that led a reluctant Butterfield to acknowledge the tapes' existence. There are also what appear to be errors of fact. In our conversations Butterfield recalled that it was H. R. Haldeman who had asked him to install the White House taping system, when it had actually been Lawrence Higby. Butterfield also recalled that he had received his summons to testify in public while he was at a barbershop in the Ritz-Carlton Hotel, when the hotel was actually called the Sheraton-Carlton. Although historians generally believe that such minor memory lapses are the natural result of the passage of time since the event being recalled, Scott Armstrong gave dramatic evidence that the workings of memory are far more complex. Within less than an hour after the interview ended he told chief majority counsel Sam Dash that he, not Don Sanders, had asked the question that led Butterfield to disclose the taping system. At stake was whether Butterfield would be a Democratic witness, with Democrats receiving the right to ask him to reveal the tapes in public session, or a Republican witness. "I literally was sure I'd asked that question," Armstrong recalls. For the next eighteen months he was positive that Sanders had "fabricated" his claim to asking "the" question and that Dash had surrendered to a desire to maintain a nonpartisan aura when he accepted Sanders's account and allowed the minority (Republican) staff lawyer Thompson to ask Butterfield "the" question in public. Armstrong only concluded that his recollection was inaccurate eighteen months later when he examined Brazer's notes of the interview. Even to this day Armstrong believes that Butterfield was thinking about Armstrong's earlier question when he answered Sanders.

What is interesting for a conception of history that places memory close to its center is not that there are errors and discrepancies in accounts published fifteen years after an event, but how each of the participants has created a different narrative from the same original event in the years since 1973. Rather than our customary concern with what actually happened in room G-334, we can focus on which parts of the story each participant "forgot," "remembered," and reshaped, when and why. Since 1973 Armstrong has associated with people who value investigative skills and who also applauded the disclosure of the tapes and Nixon's resignation. As he has evolved the story, he likes to emphasize his overall strategy for interviewing witnesses and his use of a White House memo as the factors that led Butterfield to answer the question. He likes to see himself as the active creator of the disclosure. Most of Sanders's associates have likewise applauded his role. Butterfield, on the other hand, has associated with people who think that he toppled a great president and has paid a high price in his career for his disclosure. Not surprisingly, he has constructed a memory in which in 1973 he passively, even reluctantly, "remembered" and then disclosed the tapes in response to questions posed by others.

Even as each participant reshaped a story over time to meet different needs of the moment, each believed that the latest story was a vivid, unchanged, and accurate record of precisely what had occurred in room G-334. Armstrong's anger at Sanders and Dash for depriving him of the credit he positively remembered that he was entitled to was one example. As Butterfield reflected on one of my questions and prepared a written elaboration and modification of his original recollection six weeks later, he prefaced his new version with: "I have to tell you that my recollections have been and are very clear. They really are." The need to see memories as vivid and unchanging interacts with participants' constant testing and reshaping of memories in response to new needs and perceptions to make memory a creative process.

CHRONOLOGY

June 17, 1972—Five men arrested after breaking into the Democratic National Committee headquarters in the Watergate complex.[2]

June 22, 1972—Nixon denies White House involvement.

September–October 1972—*Washington Post* in many stories links Watergate defendants to

---

[2]Chronology taken from Woodward and Bernstein, *Final Days*, 457–61; J. Anthony Lukas, *Nightmare: The Underside of the Nixon Years* (New York, 1976); and Congressional Quarterly, *Watergate: Chronology of a Crisis* (Washington, 1975).

White House and to the Committee for the Re-election of the President (CREEP).

January 8–30, 1973 – Trial of seven men indicted for Watergate burglary. Five plead guilty. E. Howard Hunt and G. Gordon Liddy are convicted by jury.

February 7, 1973 – Senate establishes select committee to investigate Watergate.

March 1973 – Butterfield leaves White House to become administrator of Federal Aviation Administration.

March 23, 1973 – Judge John Sirica reports that Watergate defendant James McCord charged he and other burglars were put under "political pressure" to plead guilty by higher-ups who approved the break-in and that perjury was committed in their trial.

April 30, 1973 – Nixon announces resignations of H. R. Haldeman, John D. Ehrlichman, Attorney General Richard Kleindienst, and firing of White House Counsel John Dean.

May 17, 1973 – Senate Watergate Committee begins nationally televised hearings.

May 18, 1973 – Archibald Cox is named special prosecutor.

June 25–29, 1973 – Dean testifies before Watergate Committee and accuses the president of participation in cover-up.

July 13–16, 1973 – Butterfield reveals existence of White House tapes and testifies before Watergate Committee.

July 23, 1973 – Cox subpoenas recordings of nine presidential conversations and meetings. Senate Watergate Committee subpoenas five tapes.

July 26, 1973 – Nixon refuses to turn over subpoenaed tapes.

August 29, 1973 – Judge Sirica rules Nixon must turn over tapes.

October 10–12, 1973 – Vice President Spiro Agnew resigns, and Nixon nominates Gerald R. Ford as vice president.

October 12, 1973 – U. S. Court of Appeals upholds Sirica's decision that Nixon must surrender tapes.

October 20, 1973 – "Saturday Night Massacre" in which Cox is fired as special prosecutor and Attorney General Elliot Richardson and Deputy Attorney General William Ruckelshaus resign in protest.

October 23, 1973 – White House announces that subpoenaed tapes will be turned over but soon reveals that some tapes were missing and others had been partially erased.

March 1, 1974 – Grand jury indicts Haldeman, Ehrlichman, and five others in the cover-up. It names Nixon as "unindicted co-conspirator."

April 11, 1974 – House Judiciary Committee subpoenas forty-two tapes as part of deliberations over possible impeachment of Nixon.

April 18, 1974 – Special Prosecutor Leon Jaworski subpoenas an additional sixty-four tapes.

April 30, 1974 – Nixon releases edited transcripts of tapes sought by Judiciary Committee but announces he will not release those sought by Jaworski.

July 24, 1974 – U. S. Supreme Court rules that Nixon must turn over sixty-four tapes to Jaworski.

July 27–30, 1974 – Judiciary Committee passes three articles of impeachment.

August 9, 1974 – Nixon resigns.

WATERGATE REMINISCENCES

Donald G. Sanders*

Sixteen years have passed since the burglary of the Democratic National Committee headquarters in the Watergate Office Complex in Washington, D.C. The arrests of the burglars occurred in the very early hours of a Saturday morning, June 17, 1972. The Sunday edition of the *Columbia* (Missouri) *Tribune* had no report of the event. In the Monday *Tribune* there was a brief report at the bottom of page 1. Over the next week there was only one small follow-up story – on page 12. This initial treatment of the event by the press was not unusual. There was no immediate sense that this was the predicate for something very serious.

To view Watergate in perspective it is essential to remember that it occurred when presidential power was great – the weakening from Vietnam was still incipient. John F. Kennedy and Lyndon B. Johnson had been very powerful, dynamic executives. Richard M. Nixon's first term in office vastly consolidated power in the White House. I had

---

*Donald G. Sanders now practices law in Columbia, Missouri, with the firm of Shurtleff and Froeschner. He also serves as one of three commissioners on the governing body of Boone County, Missouri. This remembrance, in modified form, was originally prepared for delivery as an oral address.

already worked on the congressional staff for four years, and I specifically recall learning, in contrast to what I had been taught in high school civics, that the legislative branch was not nearly an equal to the executive branch. In such basic matters as congressional efforts to obtain executive branch witnesses for routine hearings or to gain access to even unclassified files, the executive branch response was cavalier. While Congress was already approving hundreds of millions of dollars for executive branch computers, for example, Congress itself was still in the Model A Ford category.

15   What I am leading to is the proposition that one did not then lightly contemplate serious battle with the White House nor lightly contemplate accusations of serious misconduct within the White House. And if one did, in contrast to the situation today, there was little expectation that access could be gained to White House documents, or that White House staff would not invoke executive privilege if called to testify. There was a very different aura about the infallibility and inaccessibility of the White House. The balloon had yet to be punctured.

I say this to underline how I felt, and to give you a sense of the pervasive disbelief that filled the room, soon after the Watergate Committee was organized, when Sen. Lowell Weicker (the Connecticut Republican on the committee) stated in a closed-door meeting that he felt culpability for the break-in could extend all the way to Bob Haldeman. Mind you, he wasn't even accusing the president—but to think that he was virtually accusing the president's right-hand man. Most of us were incredulous.

After reading of the arrest of the burglars in the Democratic National Committee office, I had a persistent feeling that it was more than a rogue operation. I thought surely it would prove to be a conscious design of the Committee for the Reelection of the President to gather political intelligence. I had absolutely no thought that it might extend into the White House. It did not seem remarkable to me that one campaign committee should try to collect data on another, but I was shocked that it involved breaking and entering. As the months passed, it seemed strange that the news accounts revealed no firm tie to the leaders of the reelection committee.

It was of paramount importance to the White House to keep the lid on until the November election. The White House strategy was to present the appearance that there was no one of higher rank

than Gordon Liddy involved. In reality Liddy had cleared his illegal activities, and his $200,000 budget, with the executive director of the reelection committee, Jeb Magruder, and the attorney general of the United States, John Mitchell—still in office, but serving as the de facto head of the reelection committee. Moreover, before the break-in, Liddy's overall plan for covert intelligence had been reported to Haldeman by John Dean.

And so, when the grand jury indictment of the burglars was made known in September 1972, with just fifty-two days to go to the election, the Department of Justice made the phenomenal pronouncement that there was no evidence of higher-up culpability.

When I learned in January 1973 that the Senate   20 was forming an investigative committee, I made application for a staff position. I had been in Washington nine years, five at the headquarters of the Federal Bureau of Investigation (FBI) and four working as chief counsel for Congressman Dick Ichord (a Missouri Democrat). Of course, I would have liked to become chief counsel for Sam Ervin or Howard Baker. That was not to be. But despite my previous service with a House Democrat, my employment record attracted Baker and his new Chief Counsel, Fred Thompson. My job was to be deputy minority counsel.

I was impressed by Howard Baker's earnest instructions at one of my earliest meetings with him that we were to turn over every possible stone and, in his precise words, "let the chips fall where they may." My admiration and respect for Baker continued to grow. In public his behavior is gentlemanly and statesmanlike; he is exactly the same in private. While he deeply hoped the Republican National Committee, a distinct entity from the reelection committee, was not involved in the illegal conduct (it was eventually proved that it was not), he nevertheless urged us on to get all the facts. Baker served a vital role as negotiator and mediator between the committee and the White House and in disputes in the Senate between the Republican and Democratic parties.

Staff work began around the first of March 1973. We started with only slightly more than had been in the press. While hiring went on, Fred Thompson and I spent nights reading news reports—piecing together a mosaic of what was already known and who the key players were. We compiled a list of leads to be investigated. Some work had been started by a Senate subcommittee headed by Edward M. Kennedy and the House Banking and Currency Committee under Wright Patman. They withdrew when we began. Our objective was to try to trace a line of authority upward from Liddy.

In 1987, as the Iran-Contra affair was revealed, there was news coverage about Lt. Col. Oliver North's secretary, Fawn Hall. It shouldn't come as any surprise where we chose to start. Sure, with Gordon Liddy's secretary. When the big fellows refuse to talk with you, there's usually a coterie of others around them without whom they couldn't function. I must say, however, that attitudes about the inviolability of a personal secretary's knowledge have changed some since then. There were never any legal constraints on what a secretary could disclose, except for classified information or possibly something specified by contract, but there may have once been an unwritten code of honor about secrets she knew. Liddy's secretary had a melodious name: Sally Harmony. I conducted the interview with Sally Harmony, but I felt secret twinges of conscience in asking her to reveal her boss's business. It seemed somewhat akin to invading the attorney-client relationship.

Several sessions were required with Harmony. She lied at first to protect Liddy. She was not quite as eager as Fawn Hall. Eventually, she revealed that Liddy gave her wiretapped recordings of telephone conversations to transcribe, and that he sent political intelligence information to Jeb Magruder. She told us that Liddy was under the supervision of Magruder and John Mitchell, although on paper Liddy was shown as legal counsel to the finance director. Liddy went to the trouble of ordering a special printing of stationery with brightly colored borders, emblazoned with his code word "Gemstone," which Harmony used to prepare reports of wiretapped conversations. The purpose of the stationery was to alert those to whom it was sent to be discreet in handling it. Harmony took the bill for this stationery directly to Magruder. He approved it but told Harmony to destroy the invoice. Bit by bit, the Watergate conspiracy was being pieced together.

As an aside, in speaking of Sally Harmony, I'm reminded of a rather unkind joke that circulated among staff and press concerning the way in which one committee senator questioned witnesses in the public hearings. As was customary, this senator had his staff assistant prepare questions for the senator to use in the hearings. Unfortunately, the senator had a habit of paying more attention to his questions than to the witness's answers. The story goes thus: "Now, Mrs. Harmony, tell me, did Gordon Liddy meet with John Mitchell on April 2, 1972?" Answer: "No, sir." Next question: "Well, then, tell me, Mrs. Harmony, what did they discuss?"

One other early witness is of interest. She was the secretary to Liddy before Harmony—in January and February 1972, in the crucial period when Liddy was presenting to the attorney general, in the very office of the attorney general, his elaborate plans for political kidnaping, mugging, bugging, burglary, and prostitution. The secretary told me she recalled Liddy carrying into his office a thick pack of poster boards of large dimension, perhaps three feet by four feet. These were the graphic aids he used in his presentation to the attorney general.

The big break in the case however was the letter of Jim McCord to Judge John Sirica. McCord, you will recall, had been the hands-on supervisor of the burglary crew. As a Central Intelligence Agency (CIA) veteran, he did not like the indications that the CIA was being blamed for the burglary. Neither did he relish an impending stiff sentence from Judge Sirica, nor the information he had been hearing that some other defendants were receiving financial assistance.

McCord had no firsthand knowledge of the involvement of Liddy's superiors, but he had hearsay helpful to investigators. He accused Magruder of perjury before the grand jury, and he alleged that Magruder, Mitchell, and Dean had participated in the planning for covert intelligence. McCord's letter generated an epidemic of nervousness in Washington, and several individuals started talking.

The most notable witness was John Dean, who had frequent contact with the president. He testified for several days. In one of his scenarios, he said that in a conversation with the president in one of the president's offices, the president drew him to a corner of the room and in a quiet voice told Dean that he, Nixon, had been foolish in discussing clemency for one of the burglars with Chuck Colson. Dean seemed to suspect that there was some White House recording capability, but the discovery of it did not occur until two weeks later—on Friday the thirteenth, July 13, 1973.

30   Senator Ervin's staff scheduled an interview with Alexander Butterfield at 2:00 P.M. on July 13. It was to be held in a small, secure, windowless room in the basement of the Dirksen Senate Office Building. The room was big enough for only a desk, a table, and several chairs. Butterfield was then head of the Federal Aviation Administration, but he had been an assistant to Haldeman, and as such he had occupied a very small office immediately adjoining the Oval Office. It was his job to control, absolutely, the president's schedule, that is, to make it work. If someone was due to see the President at 1:12 P.M., Butterfield was responsible for ushering the person in at 1:12 P.M. He was the pivot point for papers and persons going into and out of the Oval Office.

Butterfield had been scheduled for interview for two reasons: (1) he was one of a number of persons who had frequent contact with the president and key staff such as Haldeman, and (2) he could specifically provide insights to the White House methods for preserving on paper what transpired in the Oval Office.

I participated in the interview of Butterfield as Senator Baker's representative. Ervin's staff sent one attorney, an investigator, and a secretary. The investigator was Scott Armstrong, who later coauthored with Bob Woodward the best seller exposé of the United States Supreme Court entitled *The Brethren*. Bob Woodward was a very close friend of Armstrong. He was the *Washington Post* reporter who wrote *All the President's Men* with Carl Bernstein.

Scott Armstrong and the other attorney questioned Butterfield for about three hours concerning Nixon's office routine. Armstrong had a document from the White House containing some summaries of Dean's conversations with Nixon. It would be logical to question how they were constructed. Of course, they could have been put together immediately after a meeting by personal recollections and by reference to notes. But there was another dimension to the quality of those summaries, it seemed to me. I couldn't put my finger on it, but they had a measure of precision that went beyond those possibilities.

I had a fixed agreement with Ervin's staff; I would not interrupt or interfere with their conduct of an interview, and they were not to interfere with mine. Once they were finished, I would have whatever time I wanted for questioning. So, for three hours I simply listened and took notes, knowing that eventually it would be my turn.

As the minutes passed, I felt a growing cer-   35 tainty that the summaries had to have been made from a verbatim recording. I wondered whether Butterfield would be truthful if asked about a hidden recording system. I thought surely if such a system existed, the president would never have said anything incriminating on record. I wondered, if it existed, how it could therefore be of any value—remarks on it would be self-serving. Or, to consider it from a positive viewpoint, remarks on it would prove the president's innocence—in other words, contradict what John Dean was alleging. But if there were exculpatory recordings, why hadn't the president revealed the system and used it to his advantage? I was mystified that Ervin's staff hadn't asked Butterfield about tape recordings. I seriously considered the consequences of Butterfield revealing, in answer to *my* question, that there were recordings. If they were incriminating, did I want on my shoulders the fate of the presidency? It all seemed quite enormous. But Baker had said to let the chips fall where they might. It occurred to me that Butterfield would soon walk out of the room and this opportunity might not repeat itself. No matter how limited the circle of persons who would know of a recording system, I was sure Butterfield had to be included.

There was one other factor in my reasoning. I had served five years in FBI headquarters, on the fourth floor of the Department of Justice building, just below J. Edgar Hoover's fifth-floor suite. For years I heard comments about a built-in recorder in Hoover's office for use on occasions when he needed to preserve what was said. It was inconceivable to me that the office of the president (via the Secret Service) hadn't availed itself of a technological process that the FBI had.

And so my time came. It was no "cool-hand Luke" at work. My heart was pounding and my breath was shortened as I began questioning. I had resolved to go through with it only minutes before. I decided, for some unknown reason, not to bluntly ask if there was a tape recording system. After a few preliminaries, I asked Butterfield if he knew of any reason why the president would take John Dean to a corner of a room and speak to him in a quiet voice, as Dean had testified. His reply was stunning; he said, "I was hoping you fellows wouldn't ask me that. I've wondered what I would say. I'm concerned about the effect my answer will have on national security and international affairs. But I suppose I have to assume that this is a formal, official interview in the same vein as if I were being questioned by the committee under oath." I said, "That's right." He continued, "Well, yes, there's a recording system in the White House." We were all thunderstruck. Butterfield said the president wanted this kept absolutely secret, but he felt he had no other choice.

The system had been installed, he said, on Nixon's instructions, probably for historical use. There were microphones in the Oval Office, the Cabinet Room, the president's office in the Executive Office Building, the Lincoln Sitting Room on the second floor of the White House, in Aspen Lodge at Camp David, and in the telephones in all those rooms except the Cabinet Room.

When Butterfield finished it was 6:30. Knowing Armstrong's reputation for leaks, I asked Ervin's staff for renewed promises of secrecy. I then tracked down Fred Thompson at the pub across the street. Naturally, he was having a beer with a newsman. If I had appeared excited, the reporter would have been alerted, so I ordered a beer and engaged in small talk for a while. Eventually, I asked Fred to step outside. On the street corner I told him the story, and he ran to telephone Senator Baker. I went home, late again for dinner. Senator Baker called me at home on Sunday for a firsthand account because Butterfield wanted to meet with him.

40   On Monday, after first resisting a committee subpoena, Butterfield testified before the committee in public, and you saw him on television. I couldn't believe we had kept the story from the *Washington Post*. We hadn't. I heard later through the grapevine that the *Post* had the story, but not enough corroboration to print it.

The battle for access to the tapes, and their erasures and disappearances, is another story, as is the impeachment proceeding. But the process was now irreversible.

FRIDAY THE THIRTEENTH

Scott Armstrong*

In May of 1973, a few members of the Democratic staff of the Senate Committee on Presidential Campaign Activities—Sam Dash, Jim Hamilton, Marc Lackritz, Terry Lenzner, and I—began interviewing John Dean in extensive (some as long as ten hours) secret sessions usually taking place in the recreation room of his Alexandria, Virginia, home. Dean had left the White House abruptly the month before, when it became apparent that he was likely to be made the scapegoat for the Watergate affair. His attorneys had sought and received a tentative agreement that in return for receiving from the committee immunity from the use of his congressional testimony against him in court, Dean would provide a complete account and documentation of his activities. To assure that Dean was willing to cooperate and that his story was credible and not self-serving, the staff interviewed him at length during mornings, afternoons, and evenings. Dean's account was extraordinary in both detail and scope and was often backed up by memoranda, particularly where Dean's account went into intelligence abuses not directly connected with the Watergate break-in. As Dean told his story in secret, the majority staff went out and interviewed other witnesses to corroborate it.

In late May, with the hearings already two weeks underway, Marc Lackritz and I insisted on taking Sam Dash to lunch at the Monocle restaurant next to the Dirksen Senate Office Building where we worked. We were deeply disturbed that the interviewing of possible corroborating witnesses was not systematic. Those interviewed were not being asked the full complement of relevant questions. Worse still, many important witnesses, such as secretaries, clerks, and functionaries, were being overlooked. We suggested to Dash that a template of standard questions be drawn up for every interview. I drew a chart (what we came later to call a "satellite chart") of the key witnesses who had come into contact with Dean and about whom Dean was to testify publicly. I then drew several sample charts of every individual we knew worked

*Scott Armstrong is executive director of the National Security Archive in Washington, D.C. He was principal assistant to Bob Woodward and Carl Bernstein in the research and writing of *The Final Days*, and some portions of the following article appear in that book. Those portions appear in *The Final Days*, copyright © 1976, by Bob Woodward and Carl Bernstein, reprinted by permission of Simon and Schuster.

for, or was regularly in touch with, each satellite witness. We suggested that a systematic effort be made to identify everyone who could add something to confirm or refute Dean's testimony. Dash enthusiastically agreed.

Back in our office we started our investigative template with questions about each individual's daily routine and responsibilities, hoping to commit interviewees to telling us what they would know about in the normal course of business before we posed the tougher questions. We developed chart after chart of prospective witnesses. As Dean's public testimony approached, scheduled for the end of July, the public hearings called on the key witnesses about whom Dean would testify. In preparation for each such witness, the staff met privately in a downstairs interview room with his staff, secretaries, and so forth, hoping to find clues to back or defeat Dean's story.

45   In general, the minority (Republican) staff was not told what Dean had told us beyond the summaries prepared for the full committee in order to get him granted immunity. This was primarily because of several incidents early on in which Sen. Howard Baker's staff had been caught leaking things back to the White House (one staff member was fired for it). Moreover, Dean had told the majority staff that when he was still in the White House he had worked out a deal with Baker himself to help the White House sabotage the hearings. The longer we held back what Dean had told us, the more anger the minority staff felt. But as we interviewed the satellite witnesses, the committee ruled that the majority staff must take along a member of the minority staff. Thus the minority staff was developing its own knowledge of Dean's forthcoming testimony.

As Dean's testimony approached, his credibility increased with the majority staff. Detail after detail that he had provided in secret sessions was confirmed. In one case, Dean's recollection of what the participants in a cover-up meeting at LaCosta County Club wore—two noncomplementary plaids for which Dean recalled not only the colors but also the names of the Scottish clans—caused a reluctant witness to remember the meeting and verify Dean's account. In short, Dean's testimony was being corroborated in every respect except one. There were no records or individuals except H. R. Haldeman and John D. Ehrlichman that could verify Dean's account of his meetings with President Richard M. Nixon.

We believed we had a brief reprieve when Dean's testimony was delayed at the request of the White House until after the San Clemente summit with Leonid Brezhnev. The delay provided yet another week to interview those close to Dean. Indeed, we got more corroboration, but not for Dean's meetings with the president. Dean testified for an entire week and was grilled closely by both sides. At the time, it was not clear to the majority staff how the minority members of the committee were quite as well prepared as they were. Certain details closely held by the majority until the last minute were appearing at the heart of well-thought-out (uncharacteristically so) questions by minority members Baker and Edward Gurney as well as by minority chief counsel Fred Thompson, not known for thinking on his feet.

Dean's story appeared to hold up, but it was rapidly becoming a case of his testimony against the president's publicly stated account to the contrary. During the following week, several witnesses, testifying in great detail about Dean's meetings with the president, suggested that Dean's account was largely correct except for his tendency to blame Nixon for the cover-up. That was Dean's idea, executed by Dean and kept from the president by Dean.

The temperature was in the nineties in Washington on Friday, July 13, 1973, as former attorney general John Mitchell testified publicly in the Senate Caucus Room in the Old Senate Office Building. As Dean's former boss, Mitchell was doing a splendid job of explaining away some of what Dean had said, admitting other parts, and flatly insisting he was lying about the rest. Downstairs and across the street in room G-334 of the new Senate office building (the Dirksen building), I was getting regular updates about the public hearings as I prepared to interview an obscure, retired air force colonel named Alexander Butterfield. Butterfield had worked closely with both Haldeman and Ehrlichman, the key witnesses who would be coming up two weeks later. Time was running out to find some corroboration for Dean's accounts of his meetings with the president. If anyone other than Haldeman and Ehrlichman knew the truth about those meetings, it was likely to be Butterfield. Moreover, Butterfield might know about something else we had discovered just after Dean testified. Unknown to the majority staff, Fred Buzhardt, Nixon's special counsel to handle the hearings, had secretly dictated to Minority Chief Counsel Fred Thompson over the phone a listing of Nixon's meetings with Dean and a summary of Nixon's account of those meetings. Although plainly a summary, it contained extensive verbatim and near verbatim quotes. Although they were in most cases in agreement with Dean's testimony, they usually added a remark or two that suggested an interpretation more favorable to the president. The summary had been circulated only to key minority staff. But one of the minority staff had accidently left it out on a desk at night, where it was picked up by a majority staff clerk and provided to the majority staff, including myself, who were now trying to determine how best to use it strategically before the minority staff learned that we had it.

50   The fact that this summary had been prepared prior to Dean's public testimony suggested several interesting things. First, the passages chosen— almost exactly paralleling Dean's testimony—gave it a high likelihood that someone (I assumed Thompson and/or Baker) had leaked the summary of Dean's testimony about his meetings with the president back to the White House. Second, the president had personally corroborated most of what Dean had said or had evidence in the form of notes or dictated recollections that corroborated it, better evidence than the committee now had. Third, that evidence, if it vindicated the president in the same manner as the summary, would be a striking refutation of Dean if it could be authenticated as contemporaneous. And if it appeared to have been altered or to have been created after the fact, that could be a further step in the obstruction of the committee's inquiry and thus damning of the president.

Although he had recently left the White House staff to become the head of the Federal Aviation Administration (FAA), Butterfield, throughout the period about which Dean had been testifying, had been a deputy assistant to the president in charge of the paper work and records that moved into and out of the Oval Office. If anyone had seen notes of conversations or seen accounts of the conversations created later, it would probably have been Butterfield. It was my hunch that Butterfield could at the very least tell whether or not the Buzhardt account had been created from the president's recollection alone or whether there was evidence lying behind it. If there was evidence behind it, the committee would have a good claim to demand and perhaps even get the evidence

before Haldeman and Ehrlichman testified. If it was from the president's own account, there were some important questions to be asked of Haldeman and Ehrlichman about how they refreshed their own recollections. In any case, the committee was building a case to request the president himself testify as a witness—a virtually unprecedented confrontation.

The room had only one small air-conditioning vent, and it was oppressively hot. The chairs and table were stained with grease from fast-food meals. Wastebaskets spilled over with cigarette butts and packages and sandwich wrappings. The carpet was filthy. (Janitors were barred from entering for fear that someone might plant an eavesdropping device.)

The session was to be conducted by myself, as lead majority committee investigator, and Donald Sanders, a former Federal Bureau of Investigation (FBI) agent who was the deputy counsel to the Republican minority and their lead investigator. Sanders was an example of the best the FBI can produce. A polished questioner, he was also an excellent listener. Whereas many investigators allowed their totally partisan views to enter their questions, Sanders was professional, playing it straight down the middle. He was also the only minority investigator willing to sit patiently through my long list of template questions. Other minority investigators, unable to stop such interviews, tried to obstruct them by leaving before I had completed the questions. That had hurt the minority several times when routine questions four hours into the interview hit pay dirt, which the minority did not learn about for days or weeks. (It was in this manner that the minority failed to learn for more than three months about the majority's discovery of the connection between the hundred thousand–dollar gift from Howard Hughes to Nixon's confidant Bebe Rebozo and the Watergate break-in and subsequent cover-up.) The interview recorder was Marianne Brazer, the most conscientious and competent of a highly talented stenographic pool. In addition, I was backed up by Gene Boyce, a majority counsel.

One of the few witnesses to appear without counsel, Butterfield impressed me with his military manner and his excellent memory. With his hands folded in front of him, he considered each question carefully. He looked directly at me; he spoke in calm and even tones. He had resigned his commission as an air force colonel to work for Haldeman in the White House. He described Haldeman and Haldeman's odd relationship with Nixon in candid, almost clinical terms. His respect for each had been deeply tempered by a contempt for their manner and style. We reviewed his daily routine. I asked Butterfield to describe every mechanism for documenting the president's day. He seemed to enjoy this rare opportunity to talk about the responsibilities with which he had been charged.

55　　But his candor and memory were not much help in determining whether it was John Dean or Richard Nixon who was lying. Butterfield's job and his access to the president were matters of routine. "Did you see or hear anything which indicated to you that the president was involved in the alleged effort to keep the facts from the public?" I asked Butterfield. "No, but the way the White House operated it could have happened, certainly." Butterfield paused to reflect. "The series of meetings in questions [with Dean] didn't begin until February 1973. I was phasing out of my job and getting ready to leave for the FAA. I can't document anything or prove anything. I don't remember Watergate being anything," Butterfield said.

I was deeply disappointed that we were not going to get a more knowledgeable account of the Dean/Nixon relationship. I asked how good the president's memory was. Good, Butterfield replied, but he rarely had to rely on it. A talking points memo was always provided for the president, whether it was for a meeting of state, a telephone call, a postscript to a letter. Usually he was offered three alternatives—the middle one was always the one he was supposed to pick—but nothing was left to chance.

Butterfield told a joke about how rigid the system of preparing talking points memos for the president was. Butterfield recalled an instance in which the president and most of the senior staff were in Florida. Butterfield sent down a reminder that over the weekend Vice President Agnew would be celebrating his birthday. Butterfield suggested in a brief note to Haldeman that the president call Agnew and wish him a happy birthday. Back from Key Biscayne came the request from Haldeman for a talking points memo. Butterfield complied:

1.　Happy Birthday to you.
2.　Happy Birthday to you.

3.　Happy Birthday Dear:
　　Alternative 1: Spiro　Agree _____
　　　　　　　　　　　　Disagree _____
　　Alternative 2: Ted　Agree _____
　　　　　　　　　　　　Disagree _____
　　Alternative 3: Mr. Vice President
　　　　Agree _____ Disagree _____
4.　Happy Birthday to you.

Trying to make the most of the situation, I returned to Butterfield's expertise on the president's office routine and decided to spring the Buzhardt material. There were actually two documents: one memorandum listed the times, dates, locations, and participants for all the Dean-Nixon conversations; another described the substance of Dean's calls and meetings with the president. I started with the first. "We received a listing from the White House of the conversations between the president and Dean, which we understand are from the president's diaries," I began. Where could these materials come from?

"We have three types of back-up materials from which these listings could be constructed," Butterfield said. "The switchboard operators kept track of all phone calls to and from the president. Secret Service personnel, ushers, and secretaries record who comes and goes from the president's office. Staff members prepare memos for the president before each formal meeting with outsiders, outline the purpose and points to be covered, and then prepare another memo after each meeting, summarizing the tone of the meetings and any commitments made." All this was put together into a daily log for the president—where, when, and with whom he had met.

"Would there be a file on the substance of 60 each meeting with staff members?" I asked, repeating the question he had previously answered. "If the staff member was in alone or only with other White House staff members, there would probably be no memo written. If there was a highly significant meeting, the president might say, 'Write this up.'" How did these results of meetings generally get recorded? Butterfield said if a guest, whether a head of state or an official from Capitol Hill, were visiting, the junior staff person attending the meeting would take notes and submit a memo for the record. Because most head of state meetings were not attended by any staff member besides Henry Kissinger, Nixon's national security adviser,

Kissinger owed over three hundred such memos to the chron-file.

If there were no outside guests, the most junior staff person in the room would do a memo to the file, but only insofar as action was called for. Thus Haldeman would be the only source of notes in his meetings with the president. If Ehrlichman were there too, then he, not Haldeman, would decide what notes to keep and what to submit for the file. If Dean joined the three, then Dean would be the notetaker. Generally, each person meeting with the president kept the notes of his meetings in his own files.

I then turned to the second type of memo that Buzhardt had dictated to the Republican minority counsel — the president's version of his conversations with Dean. Pulling out a typed transcript of the summary, I asked Butterfield — without telling him where we had gotten it — where such an account might have originated. Could it have been from someone's notes of the meetings?

Butterfield glanced over the document. He paused several times to remark how detailed the account was. He lingered over it, picking it up off the table and setting it down neatly in front of him. Each time, he looked up at me and then Sanders, as if expecting us to say something more about the document. I thought Sanders seemed surprised that I had the Buzhardt summary, but he said nothing. It was not until that moment that it occurred to me that I did not know if Sanders himself had ever seen the document. It was possible the minority had not shared it with their own investigators.

"Somebody probably got the information from the chron-file and put it down," Butterfield said finally. As he continued to read, he was asked whether the summary described the kinds of meetings the president would ask someone to write up. No, he responded, again picking up the memo. I asked him if this type of information could come from any of the systems he had described to us before. In each case, he said no, it was too detailed.

65   Resuming his reading, Butterfield arrived at the account of the March 21, 1973, meeting and stopped. He noted aloud that the summary stated that Dean had told the president that E. Howard Hunt was trying to blackmail Ehrlichman. Butterfield was surprised. He pointed out to me that the next sentence included an actual quote: "The President said how could it possibly be paid, 'What makes you think he would be satisfied with that?' "

"Where did you get this?" Butterfield asked, glancing quickly back and forth between Sanders and me. "Mr. Buzhardt provided it to the committee. Could it have come from someone's notes of a meeting?" I asked. "No, it seems too detailed," Butterfield replied. "Was the president's recollection of meetings good?" "Yes, when I came I was impressed," Butterfield replied. "He is a great and fast learner. He does recall things very well. He tends to overexplain things."

"Was he as precise as the summary?" I asked. "Well, no, but he would sometimes dictate his thoughts after a meeting." Butterfield offered his earlier explanation. "How often did he do so?" I asked. "Very rarely," Butterfield said. "Were his memos this detailed?" I asked. "I don't think so," Butterfield said.

"Where else could this have come from?" I pressed. Butterfield stared down at the document. Slowly, he lifted it an inch off the table. "I don't know. Well, let me think about this awhile." He pushed the document toward the center of the green felt–covered table. He seemed troubled. I assumed he was reluctant to tell us about some file system that he had just remembered. I began drafting up sample subpoena language for these newly revealed systems. Gene Boyce asked a few follow-up questions.

Don Sanders began by turning the questioning into other areas. I was surprised he didn't follow up on possible ways to explain where the Buzhardt memo had come from.

"Did the president ever note an article in a news summary and write it in the margin?" asked Sanders. "Yes," Butterfield said. "Did he ever write 'Get this guy'?" "Yes. Not necessarily in those words. He is profane, but in a nice sort of way," Butterfield responded. "Do you recall when he said 'Get this guy'? Do you remember the phrase he used?" Sanders asked. "He said several times, 'I remember his — he's no good' — oftentimes referring to news people," Butterfield said. "Sometimes he'd write something like 'Ziegler should get wise to this guy.' "

Then Sanders began asking questions derived directly from Dean's testimony. I assumed that he was going to give his best shot at trying to document the president's innocence. I began to note the direction of Sanders's questions. He led to his question cautiously by recalling for Butterfield Dean's testimony. "Dean indicated that there might be some facility for taping," Sanders said. "He said that on April 15 in the president's EOB office he had the impression he was being taped, and that at the end of the meeting the president went to a corner of the room and lowered his voice as if he was trying to stay off the tape himself while he discussed his earlier conversation with Colson about executive clemency. Is it possible Dean knew what he was talking about?" Sanders asked.

I assumed Sanders was after additional examples that the Joint Chiefs of Staff were spying on the president, a fact that had been revealed earlier in our hearings, or trying to support Howard Baker's favorite thesis that the Central Intelligence Agency (CIA) arranged Watergate to entrap Nixon.

Butterfield thought for a moment, trying to frame a response to a complicated question. Then, glancing back and forth between Sanders and me, as if he were somehow trapped, he leaned over to the center of the table and picked up the Buzhardt account of the Dean-Nixon meetings.

"No, Dean didn't know about it," Butterfield said at last. Turning directly to me as if he were now answering the long-pending question, Butterfield continued. "But that is where this must have come from," Butterfield said, glancing frantically from one to another of us in the room to see if we had previously known what he was talking about. "There is a tape in each of the president's offices." Butterfield continued. "It is kept by the Secret Service, and only four other men know about it. Dean had no way of knowing about it. He was just guessing." "You do know about it, don't you; someone else must have told you about it?" Butterfield asked.

70   "Yes," I said, lying. "But we are not sure who knows what, so please tell us what you know and who else knows about it."

"Then, for forty-five minutes, Butterfield described the taping system in detail. Gradually he realized that he was not being trapped by us but that we had not heard about the system before. Butterfield became increasingly concerned that his trip the following week to the Soviet Union where he would sign the first civil air pact between the United States and the Soviet Union would be canceled. He did not want to be the one to publicly reveal the taping system. I assured him we would try to get someone else to testify to it. In the meantime, I asked him to say nothing to anyone until we called him. When the interview ended, I raced upstairs with Phil Hare to brief the Democratic majority's chief counsel, Sam Dash.

Dash was ready to leave for the evening; he was pulling his office door shut as we arrived.

Followed by Gene Boyce, I pushed him back into his office over his objection. "I have to get home right away," Dash said. "Sarah [Sam's wife] insisted that tonight I must be home for dinner at a reasonable hour." I learned later that it was Sam and Sarah's anniversary.

"Sam," I blurted out, "Nixon taped all his conversations, apparently including those with Dean." Dash stood dumbfounded for a moment just as we had less than an hour before. "Let me call Sarah." Within a few minutes, I briefed Dash, and he called Senator Ervin to relay the news. Ervin asked Dash to brief his chief political aide, Rufus Edmisten.

Dash told us to move cautiously to verify the system's existence before the White House heard about Butterfield's revelation. I believed that the Watergate inquiry would be over one way or another in a matter of days or weeks.

Meanwhile, I had learned from a minority staffer 80 that Sanders had located his boss, Fred Thompson, at a bar in the Carroll Arms Hotel, talking to two reporters. Later we learned that after Sanders relayed word of the discovery to Thompson, Thompson called and tipped off Buzhardt. Over the weekend Butterfield contacted Baker, who told him to contact the White House. Over the weekend, I briefed Terry Lenzner, Marc Lackritz, Jim Moore, and Lee Sheehy, key majority (Democratic) staff members, about the existence of the tape system. The five of us spent the weekend developing background information about the others who according to Butterfield, knew about the taping system.

A preliminary decision was made to attempt to verify what use had been made of the system and the status of the tapes since Butterfield had left the White House. We felt we needed to secure this information without tipping off the White House that the committee knew about the existence of the tapes and thus providing an opportunity for complete or partial destruction of this unique evidence. Our theory was that if we could document the existence of tapes of the crucial meetings with Dean and others, the president would be forced to choose, on one hand, between refusing to turn them over and immediately resigning or, on the other hand, turning them over to the committee and either being cleared or condemned in the committee's hearings. The key, we decided, was to get the Secret Service agent who had installed and maintained the system before the committee to testify in secret that the taping system existed, that the tapes were still in the custody of the Secret Service. If certain tapes had been checked out for use or were missing or were altered or destroyed, it was better to find out before the White House was aware of the significance of the inquiry. If others had heard the tapes, they could be questioned about their substance. If any of the tapes were altered or destroyed, the staff reasoned, the president would be accountable for tampering with evidence of constitutional magnitude.

Other staff were concerned that the Butterfield information had come too conveniently. Was it possible Sanders was orchestrating the discovery for Nixon's benefit? they wondered. I argued that the order and context of the interview led me to believe that Sanders had asked the question spontaneously and that Butterfield was truly caught unawares.

I called the head of the Secret Service unit that had installed the system, Al Wong. Wong agreed to appear for a secret staff interview on Monday. I called Haldeman's aide, Larry Higby, and asked him to come in on Monday afternoon. Steve Bull, Nixon's closest aide, was unavailable. After we had taken informal statements from each with a stenographer present, we would move quickly on Tuesday—before Butterfield was scheduled to leave for the Soviet Union—to get the best-informed and most authoritative witnesses to testify before an executive session of the committee. That way we would have the president boxed into a clear choice between denying or providing to the committee the best evidence available on his guilt or innocence.

The next Monday, Baker, without revealing his weekend role in urging Butterfield to tell the White House what had happened, urged the committee to call Butterfield as a witness immediately. With the exception of Dash and Edmisten, the other key majority staff were busy Monday morning tracking down other Secret Service agents, Higby, and Bull to testify. By the time they heard about Baker's proposal, it was too late to effectively oppose; I was instructed to call Butterfield to testify publicly that afternoon. I objected to Dash that by calling Butterfield publicly first we would lose our opportunity to find out from other witnesses what tapes did and did not exist and whether and by whom they had been used in preparing the president's defense, including the

Buzhardt memo. I believed that if we did not get answers to these questions first, we would be bogged down in months of executive privilege claims. It was too late, Dash indicated. The committee had decided to proceed with the facade of bipartisan support.

Just before noon on Monday, I smuggled Butterfield into the small conference room in the basement of the Dirksen office building where we had interviewed him the previous Friday. He was still trying to talk us out of using him as the principal witness. Before he even completed his reasons, Senator Ervin and Sam Dash had arrived with Senator Baker and Fred Thompson. After recovering with Butterfield the basic elements of his testimony about the taping system, Ervin, Baker, and Thompson left. Dash took me aside and told me for the first time that Baker had claimed to Ervin that the Butterfield revelation had come spontaneously in answer to Sanders's question alone.

I repeated to Dash the context in which the interview had taken place. Butterfield had seemed to me to be a reluctant witness who had responded negatively to Sanders's question and positively to the pending question about the Buzhardt memo. While Butterfield was the best witness to the existence of the tapes, he was an even better witness on the subject of the Buzhardt memo and the attempt to use it secretly through the committee's minority. If Butterfield was to be called to testify, it should be in the context that he had revealed the tapes, i.e., that the tapes could be the only possible source of the detail contained in the Buzhardt memo. Butterfield should be questioned by Dash, the majority chief counsel, as a majority witness, I insisted. It was again too late, Dash explained. In the interests of comity, Butterfield would be treated as a minority witness.

I escorted Butterfield from room G-334. We had slipped unnoticed into the room, but a battery of television reporters greeted us as we emerged. I hurried Butterfield down the hall to the Senate Caucus Room. Leslie Stahl had the presence of mind to notice the name tag on his briefcase as we fled down the hallway. Why was the director of the FAA going to be testifying? she shouted after us.

I sat behind Ervin and Baker as Thompson questioned Butterfield, fuming that as a result of Baker's interference it would now take considerably longer to learn what was on the tapes.

Butterfield concluded his televised testimony by noting, "This matter which we have discussed here today, I think, is precisely the substance on which the president plans to present his defense." Butterfield was, of course, right; that had been the plan all along. However, the president ended up spending more energy over the next thirteen months defending the tapes than using them in his defense.

CONVERSATIONS BETWEEN ALEXANDER P. BUTTERFIELD AND DAVID THELEN ABOUT THE DISCOVERY OF THE WATERGATE TAPES

Introduction

The following document originated from a three-hour taped conversation between Alexander P. Butterfield and me at the O'Hare Hilton in Chicago, on June 22, 1988. After thinking over what he had said in Chicago, Butterfield called me on July 15 to elaborate his answer. We then taped a one-hour telephone call on August 8, during which he was at a motel in Cedar Rapids, Iowa, and I was at the *Journal* office in Bloomington. I then edited and spliced the two transcripts into a single document, which I forwarded to him for his comments and elaborations. On October 12 he returned a heavily edited revision. I then suggested revisions to his revision in which I left untouched most of his proposed changes but asked him to restore some of his omissions and inserted a few exchanges from our earlier conversations that I had not incorporated into the original transcript. Those changes he accepted with only minor alterations.

90   In my conversations with Butterfield I became acutely aware that what we were creating was not so much an accurate record of what Butterfield had said, done, and felt in 1973, but a collaboration based on our different needs in 1988. I wanted our product to illustrate for this special issue how he used his memory creatively, and he wanted to tell his story in his way. Over the course of the summer each of us came to understand and want to help the other meet his needs, but we were both conscious throughout of our different purposes.

The memories that informed our respective contributions to the collaboration were shaped by our different experiences and associations between 1973 and 1988. I had a vivid memory of the excitement

I had felt as I had watched Butterfield testify on television that the White House had been taped. That revelation, not Butterfield as a person, was what I recalled. On the few occasions when I had thought back to the revelation—as when I read a published transcript to prepare a lecture or when I speculated about Nixon with friends (most of whom had not admired Nixon)—I had found only confirmation for my 1973 impression that Butterfield had only answered a question.

Butterfield's world, on the other hand, contained many Nixon supporters. He has had to formulate explanations to people who condemn him for contributing to Nixon's forced resignation, and, more importantly, to himself for the high personal and professional toll this revelation has taken. His memories in 1988 struck me as answers he has constructed over fifteen years to questions posed (and prices exacted) by those who think he never should have disclosed the tapes, not (as my memories have been) to the concerns of those who have cheered that revelation.

When I first approached Butterfield for what I expected would be a single interview, I expected that the transcript would be the triumphant, perhaps even inspiring, story of a truth teller. The story that is printed here certainly contains elements of that view, but it also is a rather sad story of a man whose life was badly, if temporarily, wounded by the events of 1973. The difference between my expectation and his story reflects the different ways the people we have associated with since 1973 have viewed his revelation. It also reveals how even now he tests, confirms, modifies, and reshapes his memory against new experiences, associations, and perceptions. He reported in 1988 that he would very much like to go on a camping trip with John Ehrlichman and John Dean in which they would test and compare memories of their White House years.

I got the clear impression that Butterfield had told, retold, and rehearsed many parts of this story many times since 1973. On several different occasions he used the same language to describe the same events. He has testified before millions of watchers and on the public record to some of these events. As he told his story in 1988, he seemed to be quoting some of these earlier accounts. Some of these rehearsed and public statements have not changed. There were a few times, however, when

I would like to thank Matthew Derr for his assistance in the research and preparation for this project.

I asked things that led him to question his memory, to reflect in new ways about what he might have thought or felt. The best example is our lengthy exchange about whether he felt regret, as he expressed it in 1973, or relief, as he now thinks possible, at his revelation of the tapes. After we opened this question in our June meeting, he thought a great deal about it, calling me three weeks later to express his new recollection, and then drafting a statement that he read to me in August. By October he acknowledged that our particular collaboration had led him first to reconstruct things a bit differently and then to decide to make public his new conclusion.

95   The transcript itself was a collaboration. I spliced 130 double-spaced pages from two conversations into a single 20-page narrative in question-and-answer form. I had been particularly struck in our Chicago conversation by how much Butterfield's memories of that incident and of the White House generally seemed colored by the military culture from which he came. And I was struck by the prices he had paid for his revelation. Those impressions shaped the portrait that I edited from our conversations. He, in turn, was concerned that he not sound whiny or bitter (for many of his associates from that period had gone to prison) and that he sound responsive and articulate in his answers to my questions. Most of the changes he introduced were changes in style, not in substance or tone. They were so extensive, however, that fewer than half of his words in this printed transcript were the literal words he uttered during our conversations. He removed most of the references to the negative consequences of his revelation, but I persuaded him to reinsert them for the final draft. In each of our conversations about his 1973 Senate testimony about the taping system he brought up his 1974 testimony before the House impeachment hearing. I could not see the relevance, but when he prominently repeated the 1974 association in reacting to a transcript that omitted it, I decided that it was such a integral part of his memory of the Watergate revelation that our joint story should feature that particular recollection in his final summing-up of the points he wanted our story to tell.

In deciding to let the final product reflect an ongoing process of creation rather than a literal record of what we said on any particular occasion I have sided with those oral historians who emphasize the collaborative, cumulative, and creative aspects to the construction of memory. Even though I thought the record would be more revealing if it included a few of the things Butterfield said to me privately (and negotiated with him—sometimes successfully—to restore those points), I thought he deserved the right to put his story in the language in which he wanted it presented to *Journal* readers. At the same time I tried to illustrate the lines along which his memory evolved over time. I particularly wanted to report his conclusion that his recollections were vivid over the last fifteen years even as he interpreted his feelings in a new way.

Conversations

DAVID THELEN: What were some of your impressions of working in the White House in the years before Watergate?

ALEXANDER BUTTERFIELD: Well, I had worked even earlier in the Johnson White House, roughly twenty hours a week as a lieutenant colonel and military assistant for White House matters in the office of the secretary of defense. When the White House came to the Defense Department for anything at all—a press release, military airlift, a mercy mission, anything—the request would in all likelihood come to my desk; and I would attend to it, get it done. This was in the 1965–66 time frame. Then later, in January 1969, I became an appointee of President Nixon and served in a civilian capacity as Bob Haldeman's immediate deputy. Haldeman was what they call today the chief of staff or chief of the White House staff. But as a matter of interest, there was no such term then, and I'm surprised its use has become so common. To the best of my knowledge and recollection, the White House, by tradition, was not to have any military flavor. The point was always made not to publicize the fact that there were military people, apart from aides, working in the White House. Yet, it's true, there always are a good many military people assigned there sort of unbeknownst to the public. But to have come up with the title "chief of staff" for the president's principal or senior assistant was in my opinion highly inappropriate. It makes it sound as though you've got a Prussian army headquartered there, running America military style.

But back to my duties in the Nixon White House. In many ways I was a jack-of-all-trades, but responsible essentially for the smooth running of the president's official day, and for all White House administration. That, I think, pretty well sums up the essence of what I did on a day-to-day basis. Oh, I was also the secretary to the cabinet.

DT: Did anything strike you as noticeable about the atmosphere there as a place to work?

AB: As the son of a military officer and having been one myself for a full career, some twenty-one years in the air force, I was surprised by how many things were done for the president that had to do, not with the issues of the day, but with image, with manipulating the public's perception of the president. I was surprised by the emphasis placed on "image," and by the extent to which aides and image makers plotted and planned. For example, we had a number of people who did nothing but cut clippings from newspapers from cities and towns all over America just to get little human interest stories that they might inject the president into; human interest stories that would be sure to make big news in Dubuque, or Duluth, or Peoria. For instance, they'd have the president spend all one morning calling "little people" around the country who had made news in their own locals . . . like a call to a third grade school teacher in Nashville to tell her how wonderful he thought it was that she took her class to the museum or to the zoo, or whatever. And of course the fact that the president of the United States called a local (Peoria) schoolteacher would play very big indeed in Peoria's newspapers and on Peoria's radio and TV stations. It was strictly an image-making activity to enhance the president's image, to promote the president's humanism, to touch the people with his warmth and thoughtfulness, and it worked. I remember on one occasion they planned a large presidential rally. And someone, to give the president maximum visibility, said, "Let's put him on top of a car." I was present at this session and I thought to myself, "I can't believe these idiots." They're actually going to put the president on top of a car, so the entire crowd can see him. And you probably know that the president didn't stand very well on terra firma as it was. He was just not a graceful or athletic man; and now, to want to put him up on a car roof and ask him to wave . . . well! So in the pictures in the newspapers of this particular incident, there he is, doing this strange balancing act on a Volkswagen roof and looking downright weird in the process. He was sort of teetering backward and waving a funny wave. At any rate, those kinds of things took up all kinds of time

and were considered to be of great importance. And *that* I was not used to.

DT: Let's move on to the decision in 1971 to install a taping system.

AB: OK. There wasn't much to it. Bob Haldeman came into my office one day and said that the president wanted a taping system installed that would record everything that was said in the Oval Office, in the Cabinet Room, on the telephones he used most frequently (that would mean the telephones in the Oval Office, in the Lincoln Sitting Room, and [in] the president's office over in the EOB). And let me make a point here: He didn't have to tell me that it was for historical purposes. I just knew from working there and from being so close to the president that he was extremely conscious of history, of the historical aspect of things. As a matter of fact, we already had in place a system whereby a staff member, a particular staff member, would sit in on each meeting the president had, and then, immediately after the meeting ended, go back to his office and dictate a memo describing the meeting's substance and mood. That's how nuts, crazy, they were—or I should say, he was, the president—about history. These memos were called "memos for the President's file." So when I was asked to install a taping system, I said [to myself], "Ahh, another attempt to record history in the making. I wonder if the president realizes it'll duplicate the efforts ongoing to collect and maintain our memos for the president's file."

DT: You said they installed it for historical purposes.

AB: Yes. Without question.

DT: To keep a record?

AB: Yes, I was sure of that. The second thing Haldeman said to me, apart from giving me the basic assignment, was: "Be sure that WHCA doesn't do the work." WHCA was—and is—the White House Communications Agency, which was run then by a three-star army general named Starbird, General Starbird. But my point here is that Haldeman, who had this great and noticeable disdain for the military, who looked down on the military (as do a great many civilians in the higher echelons of the federal government), wanted to be sure that the military didn't install the taping system the president wanted. Many Kennedy holdovers on the Johnson staff just plain did not like the military. They thought that anyone in the military was an absolute dummkopf. Nixon was that way, too, incidentally. He felt uncomfortable around repetition of military people. He, too, felt deep down they were dumb bastards. Anyway, Haldeman said, "Have anyone but WHCA do the project." That meant that I was to call on the Technical Security Division of the Secret Service. The fellow who ran that division, Al Wong, said: "Well, Mr. Butterfield, we sure don't like to get into this, but of course we'll get it done right away." I said, "What do you mean when you say you don't like getting into this?" He then alluded to the fact that Johnson had had some kind of a taping system, and that other presidents had, too. He seemed only to intimate that over the years the experience was that such systems were more trouble than they were worth. He hinted, too, that technically it was wrong, maybe even a little illegal, to be taping officials of our government and other governments without their knowledge. I think that's a rather important point there. I don't think a lot of these young staff men who were asked to do things really sat down to think: Wait a minute. They're asking me to do thus and so. Now strictly speaking, in a legal sense, that's not cricket. But you don't think that. You think the man, the great man, wants me to do it. I can't do it fast enough. I should make it very clear here that Wong was not digging in his heels. He was only telling me what his views were—that these recording systems often became a pain in the neck, more of a waste of time than anything really useful.[1]

DT: Now here were these memos to the president's file, and here were these tapes. Did anyone ever listen to them or read them?

AB: No one ever listened to the tapes once the taping system was installed; that is, not while I was at the White House . . . up until March 15 of '73.

DT: They just accumulated in a pile? They were just not part of the working White House?

AB: No, that's right.

DT: I mean Nixon wouldn't say, Gee, I would like to go back and hear what the president of Mexico said or something like that?

AB: No, no, no.

DT: Did Nixon ever acknowledge to you your role with the tapes?

AB: No, but in fact it's funny because he is such a strange, strange fellow. I remember hearing Haldeman say in a 1975 interview that he thought Nixon was the strangest man he'd ever met. I was glad to hear Bob express himself that way. It helped me realize that I wasn't crazy, for I'd felt for some time, even then, that Nixon was the strangest man I'd ever met, too.

DT: What do you mean by that?

AB: Huh? What do I mean by that? I could give you a hundred examples, but we'd go too far from the subject if I started. Well, here's one example. You just asked me if Nixon ever mentioned the tapes once they were in. At the end of the day when the taping system installation was completed, Haldeman asked me to brief the president sometime before he left the Oval Office for the day. So I went in and said: "Mr. President, the taping system that Bob said you wanted is in place now, and I've thoroughly checked it out. It works fine, and I would like now to check you out, to at least brief you on the locations of the microphones, etc." He looked up, gave me a sort of blank stare, and said, "Oh, hmmm, ahh, hmmm, ahh, oh well, ahh." In other words, he didn't want to talk about it. That was the way he often communicated, and you had to know him awfully well to get his drift. Now in this case, his expressed disinterest wasn't because he viewed the taping system as a sinister thing. He just didn't want or need to get back into it. He had given the order. He was glad it was in, and that was that. But at the same time he knew he needed to know something about how it worked. It was the kind of petty little thing he didn't want to have to turn and talk to me about. So just to put the words in his mouth, so he wouldn't have to say the words himself or deliberate on this thing, I said: "We will do it about seven o'clock this evening, when you get ready to leave for the day." So, starting about 6:00 P.M., I kept an

---

[1]DT: In *Nightmare: The Underside of the Nixon Years*, J. Anthony Lukas writes that it was Higby who told you that the president wanted a tape recording system set up in the Oval Office and Cabinet Room and to make sure you don't go to the military and all that. Is that your recollection, too, that it was Higby who asked?

AB: Yes, it was Higby rather than Haldeman, personally. I may have said "Haldeman" a few times, but Higby, Haldeman's immediate or closest staff aide, was like Haldeman's spokesman. He issued instructions to most of the White House staffers almost daily, but you knew that if Higby asked something of you, it was being asked in the name of Haldeman.

DT: So when Higby talked you thought you were basically talking to Haldeman?

AB: Yes.

eye on him feeling pretty sure that he'd try to sneak away. When I thought he was ready to leave, I just barged in with the day's final batch of papers and walked him through it. And all the while, he never said a word. Now, is that strange?

DT: Well, there must have come a point—especially as John Dean started to appear—when you thought: I know a way that we can confirm or refute Dean's claims. The record is there on the tapes.

AB: Yes, yes, OK, yes. Several people who know this story and who look back on the events of July '73 have said, "Gee, didn't you think that?" I did, but only fleetingly. I don't recall ever pondering over the matter. Please keep in mind that everyone was working like a son of a bitch. People don't just sit around and discuss newspaper stories—not anyone I know. We all worked from early morning to 9:00 and 10:00 and 11:00 P.M. day in and day out. I was a loyal Nixon man and a strong supporter. That's another reason I wouldn't be inclined to doubt or wonder about the president's veracity. In March of '73 I became administrator of the Federal Aviation Administration and was especially busy getting settled in there when in June, I think, John Dean began his long testimony.

I'll tell you all I thought of as I listened to Dean. "Everything John is saying makes perfect sense. I know the 'White House System' as well as anyone, and everything he's saying fits." But again, strange as it may seem, I did not follow the thought any further. I didn't let myself take the time to look deeper into the matter. Subconsciously, I may have had some suspicions about Richard Nixon, even then, quite early on, but only subconsciously. Otherwise, I was totally loyal.

DT: Would there have come a time when you would have thought that these tapes—or maybe the memos for the president's file you were talking about earlier—would refute or confirm somebody's story?

AB: I knew about [Nixon's] suspicion of everyone. I had learned by working there in the inner sanctum for so long that this was part of Nixon—part of his strangeness. He had deep resentments of people—resentments that seemed to have deepened over the years. If some senator or congressman weren't toeing the mark or were ultraliberal in his views or vocally anti-Nixon or had crossed Nixon in the past (he remembered those things like an elephant), he would say, "I don't want that son of a bitch to get any favors. Do you hear me? NOT a goddamned one."

I knew, for instance, that they felt Ted Kennedy might have a girl friend or two. The president wanted to, and did eventually, order the Secret Service to report on Teddy's activities. Naturally that's not the Secret Service's job; they (the agents) don't like to be put in those kinds of positions. But that's only an example of what went on—little sort of sneaky things like that were a far cry from my former "clean Gene" military world. But I must say, I took it in stride. I didn't, you know, think it was anything terribly shocking. I wasn't *that* naïve.

DT: But you knew one thing that very few people knew. You knew there was a tape being made of all these conversations to prove that either Nixon was right or Dean was right.

AB: Yes, and I thought about that. I thought that if those tapes were exposed—if that deep dark secret ever came to light—it would blow the whole issue, the whole national dilemma out of the water. When I was asked to come up to Capitol Hill [on Friday, July 13, 1973] and talk to some staff investigators of the Senate Watergate Committee, I knew very well that disclosure of the tapes information would be like a bombshell nationally and internationally. And because the taping system at the White House was known by only nine people, I made a conscious decision before going into that session not to reveal the taping system's existence unless, I want to repeat that, unless I were asked a very direct question pertaining to such a system. And of course I have to tell you I felt that that was highly unlikely. I never dreamed they would ask a question having anything to do with the subject of taping or recording conversations. But if I were asked a direct question about the taping system, I would, of course, answer appropriately. I knew in my mind that I would do that.

DT: Did you have any questions you thought they were much more likely to ask you about?

AB: No, I didn't prepare at all. I went up there on Friday afternoon directly from work. I didn't have to prepare. I knew what I knew, and I didn't know what I didn't know. They said they were going to ask me about how the White House works, how the staff functions. I guess I knew that about as well as anyone.

DT: Some people in that White House probably would have denied it or tried to evade it if asked. Why did you decide you would acknowledge it if you were asked?

AB: I never thought that I *couldn't* tell. You know what I mean? It seems so dumb now. People have pointed out to me that I could have taken the Fifth Amendment or something. I don't know about that kind of thing. I really don't. I mean I am not that kind of guy. This was a major investigation, and, if you want to get technical about it, Richard Nixon had said time and time again in public forums: "I want all of my people to come forward and be straightforward and open and honest. I want all the facts to come out." Well, I sort of knew that that was baloney, yet he was saying it, loudly and clearly.

The decision wasn't all that conscious. I simply knew I wouldn't lie. I would never lie. This may sound a little corny now, but this was an official investigation. I would never have *thought* of lying, whether under oath or not. But incidentally, I see now that I have been in the business world for a good many years that a hell of a lot of people do lie. Sometimes it seems that everyone lies, or would if money were involved. I didn't learn this until I was fifty-five years old. My whole upbringing was different. My father wouldn't have lied if his life had depended on it. I can't tell you how straight my parents were. In fact, I clearly recall my dad paying back the government a portion of his travel allowance when he spent less than was alotted, or authorized, for a particular trip. He was a career naval aviator, a Naval Academy graduate.

The Interview

[*This is the account Butterfield wrote six weeks after our interview in Chicago.*]

AB: The session with the investigators began around 2:00 P.M. on Friday, July 13, 1973. And almost immediately I was shown a paper which appeared to me to be a transcript from the tapes. Well, I couldn't have been more surprised, though I don't think I expressed or demonstrated my surprise to my principal interrogator [Scott Armstrong]. It was a typed, seemingly verbatim, conversation the president was having with someone (I don't recall the other initials; it seems to me it was John Dean now that I think about it) and the question put to me was, "Where would something like this have come from?" I suppose you could argue about how direct that was as a question, but no one had mentioned tapes, no one had mentioned recording devices, or even indicated that such was on his mind so I responded as though I too were puzzled. I allowed as how the president

had quite a fantastic retentive ability, but that that particular paper I was holding in my hand seemed almost too detailed for one to have dictated its contents from memory. Then I mentioned that the president had kept a small mobile recording device in his desk drawer and occasionally dictated, on those small "tape belts," brief personal letters to friends, relatives, and others — letters which Rose Woods, his secretary, typed up for his signature. But I added that the transcript I was being shown was obviously not one of those "brief personal letters." So I sat there and scratched my head as though I were puzzled. And I was in a way. I couldn't believe that this was a transcript from the hidden recording system; yet what else could it be? Then, almost immediately, and to my great relief, the subject was dropped. It was as though the transcript had not been very important. The interview moved on to other matters, to things I knew very well. I am referring to the administration of the White House, how the office of the president and the president's staff really worked, what the president's relationship was to members of his staff, what the relationships were one staff member to another, that type of thing. Well, some four hours later, it had to be close to 6:00 P.M., Don Sanders, the staff member representing the minority counsel, spoke. He'd been relatively quiet up to that point. He said, "Mr. Butterfield, getting back to that paper you were shown at the outset of this session, you mentioned the fact that the president had a small mobile dictating machine in his desk drawer. Was there ever any other kind of voice recording system in the president's office?" Those are close to his exact words, and I think you'll have to admit, as I did at the time to myself, that that indeed constituted a direct question. And there was just no way that I could be evasive or give a vague answer. It was either yes or no. I recall precisely my response. I said, "I hoped you all wouldn't ask that question. Yes, there was another recording system in the Oval Office." "Where was it?" he said. "Well, it was a rather extensive system," I said. "In the Oval Office it was in two locations. There were microphones imbedded in the top of the president's desk and on fixtures over the mantel above the fireplace at the far end of the room, that is, at the opposite end of the room from the president's desk. There were also microphones in the Cabinet Room, and in the president's Executive Office Building (EOB) office, and on several of the president's most frequently used telephones."

Some people have asked since why I responded as I did, but that's an easy question for me to answer now. I thought it was easy to answer then, too. Because it was the truth; because he, Sanders, was a member of an official investigative body; because any other course of action would have been deceptive; because Richard Nixon (whether he meant it or not) had long since counseled his White House aides publicly to be cooperative and forthright with investigators; and, as if to emphasize his sincerity on that score, he had only some two months earlier released all of his aides from the executive privilege rule. Finally, I answered truthfully because I am a truthful person. I used to play that down to some considerable extent, but I see no reason to invent other reasons for having been open and honest and direct once the sixty-four-dollar question was put to me.

And the reason I prefaced my response to Don Sanders's question with the statement, "I hoped you wouldn't ask that question," was because of the adverse impact I knew the news would have around the world . . . within diplomatic and other circles. For instance, British prime minister Harold Wilson, Golda Meir, and a host of other world leaders would know that their conversations with our president, in his office, had been surreptitiously recorded. The nation would clearly suffer embarrassment, as would the president. That concerned me—the nation's image and the president's image. It concerned me greatly. But I didn't feel I had the luxury of choice in this matter.

DT: Did you feel relieved when they didn't get into the tapes after Armstrong finished? Or did you feel disappointed when they didn't get into the tapes?

AB: Now you've brought up an interesting question. You've touched on an issue I've never before mentioned. I was just thinking coming in here today that I would have to admit to some suspicion going back to my White House days. I didn't think a lot in mid-1973 about John Dean being right and the president being wrong; but I thought to myself—often, as a matter of fact—that the tapes ought to be brought to light so that we could clear up this long and debilitating national mess. I certainly didn't see it as a means to put the screws to a president I enjoyed serving and very much respected. I just kept thinking, "Why doesn't the president refer to the tapes? Why don't we get on with the simple process of clearing this matter up?"

So, as I say, you asked an interesting question there. I had already said to myself that I was going to answer the big question if it were put to me directly. And I had already diverted the one not-so-direct question, and now the same subject, the same question, was coming at me again. But this time, this fellow, Don Sanders, was asking about as directly as one could ask. Was there or was there not any kind of a taping system ever? Immediately after Sanders asked his question about a taping system, I said, "I am sorry you asked that question." Well, it's just possible that sub-consciously I wasn't sorry. It's just possible that my impatience for the facts of the matter to be known, and for the debating to end, had its influence. I don't know; it's a psychological thing. Perhaps deep down I was delighted he asked that question. But then the initiative was his, not mine. And I'm as sure as I know I'm sitting here that if he hadn't asked, I would never have volunteered.

AB: [*Butterfield elaborated on this answer six weeks later.*] I remember occasional, but only occasional, feelings of impatience at the time John Dean was testifying publicly in the summer of 1973. I found myself at times wanting something to happen, wanting the impasse, the debate, the stalemate, to end. What I'm saying, I think, is that I sense now in 1988 that I may have had a subconscious desire then, in 1973, to see an end to the debacle. There was a debilitating factor or aspect to the affair and knowing much or all of it could be brought to a close by the simple revelation of the hidden taping system, I was impatient. Do I think the subconscious impatience guided me? I'm not sure; I don't think so. I think I was guided by those things I mentioned early in our conversation. I was, however, strangely relieved. In speaking of this whole matter of impatience and the feeling of relief once the tapes information was out, I dare say that *most* people experienced a sense of relief. It was as though we had broken through a logjam and were now going to get on with it. I don't know if even the relief was a conscious thing in my case. It was just that I had this sense, subconsciously, that it sure would be great if everything would come out in the open. All one would have to do is expose the secret recording system. Then lo and behold, I'm in the docket and being asked the lead-in question. Does that mean that I somehow guided the event? I don't think so.

DT: After you revealed the tapes you must have thought something different than before Sanders asked the question. Did you think: Holy cow, the whole complexion of this issue is going to change, the Watergate Committee's actions are going to change, the press and so on, when it gets out?

AB: I knew very well that the complexion of the whole investigation was going to change, that the emphasis would shift immediately from who said what to whom to getting transcripts of the tapes, or the tapes themselves. I knew also how momentous the news would be. But perhaps naïvely, I thought the news, for a while at least, might be contained; and with that in mind, the first thing I did was gather Armstrong, Sanders, and the others right after the interview and express my hope that they would handle what they had heard from me wisely . . . because of the embarrassment such news would surely bring to the president and the country. I actually said to them (it really was naïve, wasn't it?) that it would never do for this to get out to world leaders and others. I recall feeling upset—maybe depressed is the word—that I had been forced by circumstances, to preempt the president. I didn't know what in the hell was going to happen. But then I felt that I needed to talk to someone on the committee so I went to see Howard Baker a day and a half later, on Sunday [July 15].

DT: Why did you choose Howard Baker?

AB: Because he was the Republican leader of the committee, and I felt I knew him sufficiently well to tell everything that was on my mind. Moreover, I wanted to go to someone senior on the Republican side.

DT: Did you assume that he would know right away what you had said and would be discussing it with the White House?

AB: I didn't know that. I was a little naïve about that, too. When I went to see him that Sunday afternoon, I told him the whole story as though he knew nothing. But of course he knew it all and had known it within hours of the event on the previous Friday.

DT: He acted like he hadn't heard it?

AB: Yes, and now that I think about it, had he let me know right away, he could have saved me a lot of time. After I went through the entire story, I said to Howard, "I wish this thing weren't out. It's so big. How are you committee members going to contain it?" "Well," he said, "it's going to have to come out eventually." Then I said, "I sure as hell don't want to testify before the [full Ervin] Committee [about the tapes]. Perhaps you could get Haldeman to do that. I'm so peripheral to this Watergate business. Haldeman knows about the system and he's already a central figure." "Oh," he said, "I don't think you'll have to testify before the committee."

DT: Baker said that?[2]

AB: Yes, he did. In fact, he said he'd lend a hand to quell the idea if it gained momentum. I felt pleased, as though I had a partner, someone in my corner. Then on Monday, July 16, I'm getting my hair cut prior to my scheduled departure for the Soviet Union the next day. I was at the barbershop at the Ritz-Carlton Hotel, watching the committee hearings on the barbershop TV. The phone rang, and it was for me. Committee staffer Jim Hamilton said: "Mr. Butterfield, we'd like you to come up to the committee. We are going to put you on this afternoon." Well, I was surprised to say the least. I'd felt comfortable after having talked to Howard Baker. Why hadn't I heard from Howard? What the hell was this all about? I felt myself getting angry. So, I said to Hamilton, "No way am I coming up there. I've talked to Howard Baker about this, and he said I probably would not have to testify publicly. So don't look for me. I won't be there. Besides you're interrupting my haircut." I then hung up. Then, within a half minute I saw this guy on the tube walk onto the dais where the committee members were sitting, walk back behind the row of senators, stop at Senator Ervin's chair, and lean over and whisper in Ervin's ear. I actually saw him whisper into the old man's ear, and Ervin—you know how he had those eyebrows?—I could see those eyebrows go whoop, whoop, whoop, up and down; and it was a strange feeling, for I knew precisely what he was hearing—this guy Butterfield said no way is he coming up here. Well, no

---

[2]Howard Baker argued before the committee that Butterfield should be called immediately as a witness, and he insisted—successfully—that Butterfield be a Republican witness because Donald Sanders, a Republican staffer, had elicited the crucial information. See Scott Armstrong, "Friday the Thirteenth," *Journal of American History*, 75 (March 1989), 1234–44.

doubt the senator wasn't used to having people talk to him like that, even indirectly, so sure enough, a minute or two later the barbershop phone rang again. It was Hamilton. He said very calmly, "Mr. Butterfield, I have talked to Senator Ervin about what you said." I said: "I know, I saw you on television." Hamilton replied, "Senator Ervin told me to tell you that if you aren't up here in his office by 12:30 today, he'll have federal marshals pick you up on the street." Well, having seen this fellow on TV was funny, and it made me lighten up a bit. I apologized for my tough talk earlier and told him I'd be there . . . which I was. We moved to a small room. There was Senator Ervin, Senator Baker, Sam Dash, and Mr. Thompson, plus, as I recall one or two of the underlings. Howard was sort of apologetic. I sat on the table and spoke first. I said, "I am a very peripheral person here, but this is so big. I meant it when I said I didn't want to testify publicly. I think that if the taping system has to be made public, one of you all should simply announce it; or you should ask someone like Haldeman, who is already one of your witnesses, to give you the details."

DT: Why were you worried about it coming from you rather than Haldeman?

AB: I don't know. I don't know. Maybe because in my view it would give the appearance of me sort of running in the back door. I just felt that it wasn't up to me. At any rate, they said no, we have talked it over and we understand your point, Mr. Butterfield, but no way is it going to be contained. It is going to come out, and the best way for it to come out is for you to reveal it just as you did last Friday. You are the one who told us; therefore you are the one who should tell the nation. So I said: OK, all right, let's go. I went in the washroom, washed my face, combed my hair, looked at myself in the mirror, and remember pausing for a second or two. Then I said to myself, son of a bitch, here goes. I didn't know precisely what I was going to say. But I knew I was going to answer questions, and I knew I wasn't going to have any trouble answering them. Yet I wanted to say more. I wanted to get a message to the president somehow. I wanted him—especially him—to know and appreciate how all of this had come about.

DT: How did this revelation, do you think now, in retrospect fifteen years later, change your life?

AB: It made it tough, I suppose, for a while. As it happened, I hadn't come to the White House to go on to a cushy job and make big money. That was not my motivation. Having come from a military family, and having been in the military, myself, for some twenty-one years, money was clearly not my orientation. It was hard for me to leave the military in a way because I had had my cap set to go to the top. And, admittedly, I had been on a fairly fast track. But, yes, I did think the White House experience would in some ways be an enhancement to my new civilian career. And, yes, as a result of Watergate, it was not. So, while I've had a few tough years, I can't complain too loudly. Just look at all the colleagues of mine who went to prison. They have to have had a hell of a lot tougher time than I did. My case, where Watergate was concerned, was so different. I was neither a good guy nor a bad guy. I was an enigma. Business executives didn't rush in to pick up those who were involved with Watergate and dust them off and give them nice cushy jobs out in the private sector. So, generally speaking, those first ten years for me were not happy. In fact, it was a fairly miserable period. I think the inner sanctum, the Nixon lovers, are down on me to this day, as I am sure he is, because I screwed things up. But I doubt they understand the context in which all of this occurred.

DT: Do you ever talk about these events with people from the Nixon White House?

AB: I see Ehrlichman every now and then. I have dinner with him occasionally in Santa Fe.

DT: Do you ever talk about this stuff with him?

AB: Yes, I have a little bit with him, and with John Dean, too.

DT: Well, what do you say as you think back?

AB: We haven't gotten into too much. But I'd like to. I'd like to get them both alone. I would love to go off on a camping trip with Ehrlichman and Dean and hash everything out, but of course those two wouldn't go on the same camping trip. My guess is that they dislike each other still.

DT: Thinking of your cold-shoulder treatment by the Nixon White House . . .

AB: And I'd have to tell you by the Ford White House as well.

DT: Do you think the reputation, this decision, affected your chances of getting jobs?

AB: Without question. As I said, CEOs of companies don't want anything to do with you if they think you may be the subject of new and surprising revelations. One has to recapture his self-esteem. I don't think I actually lost my self-esteem, but I had to keep thinking: I am a good guy, and I have had bosses in the past under different conditions who thought I did a superb job for them. But while thinking this and telling myself how great I was, I was noticing on the job market that CEOs I knew personally were shying away from me.

But I'm not going to sit here now in 1988 and be a bleeding heart. Things are just fine now. In fact, now I look back and feel very good indeed about the course of actions I chose—and about myself—and I rather enjoy looking the jerks, the people I know put selfish personal interests before probity, squarely in the eye. I feel that I have so much more than they do.

DT: Do you ever wonder why Nixon didn't burn the tapes after you revealed their existence?

AB: He didn't burn the tapes, when the chance was there, for one very simple reason. He didn't dream that he'd ever have to. He felt certain that there would be no need. He didn't know the snowball coming downhill was as big as it was, or that it was getting bigger by the day ... nor did he know how fast it was moving. The president's perception of the mounting trouble was not accurate because the White House never listens. There's so much power there, at the White House; there really is. You can pick up the phone and call almost anywhere and people will get in line to talk to you. You can do so much. You can have such tremendous influence, and on such a scale. It's almost awesome. So I don't think Mr. Nixon ever dreamed that the Watergate issue would come unraveled or get to the point where it might be wise not to have tapes around.

Significance

AB: I guess I told you that in this Trivial Pursuit game I'm "the man who revealed the existence of the tapes." That will be with me always. And of course I don't like that description or identification because it connotes or implies a foreknowledge of wrongdoing. It leads people to believe that I may well have been out to dump the president, that I went to the investigators, not that they came to me. Well maybe in 1974, but definitely not in 1973. But getting back to the Trivial Pursuit game, to me it's a shame the identifying statement can't read, "He was one of the few people who answered questions honestly."

DT: Well, if you could write the Trivial Pursuit question for you, what would you say? "The man who just told the truth"?

AB: Yes, something like that. This is not worth belaboring, but suffice it to say that I'd like truth or honesty or integrity to be the emphasis. After all, that's the way it really was. Why should it now be twisted? I didn't go forward saying to myself, "Here's a chance to be famous because, like George Washington, I chopped down the cherry tree." It seems funny, strange actually, that what I did is exactly what all of us are supposed to do—what we teach our children to do—and yet that side of it, the simple motivation to be forthright, never came out. What came out was that things seem sinister, dirty, suspicious.

DT: Now, knowing all that happened, would you have tried to avoid the summons?

AB: No. I'm glad I didn't try to avoid the summons.

DT: You're glad?

AB: Yes. I felt good about it then because I knew in my heart it was right. It was perfectly OK to tell what I knew to be the case. And human nature being what it is, I'm not sorry that I might have some little place in history here, even though I realize that it's not the kind of place in history that might be admired by Nixon's progeny. It's not as though I went to my death for my country or burned at the stake like Joan of Arc or shot down thirty-nine enemy airplanes or something like that. My role was quite simple.

Butterfield added this comment when he returned the edited transcript in October 1988:

Let me summarize here the essence of the three principal points that I want to make:

1. In 1973 I did not go to the Watergate Committee; it came to me. I did not want to testify publicly and, in fact, refused until subpoenaed. I did not ask the questions; I only answered them.

2. While I do not feel that my memory of the events of 1973–74 has faded *or* that my perspectives have changed. I do realize *now* that during the fairly long period of John Dean's testimony before the Ervin Committee, I was, at times, impatient for the truth ... which I knew the tapes would reveal. There was obviously a debate going

on nationwide. Was the president involved, as Dean was telling us . . . or was the president free of complicity? I knew, of course, that the tapes would provide the answer, and in some strange, deep-down, almost subconscious way was relieved by having the direct question asked of me by Mr. Sanders . . . even though I heard myself say first in response, "I'm sorry you gentlemen asked that question." In fact, I was sorry—very sorry—for the several reasons I've already mentioned, yet simultaneously there was this sense of relief that at last the taping system would be known, and with it the honest answers to a myriad of questions concerning the commission of illegal acts.

3. While I was very much a Nixon man and fan and an ardent and loyal appointee up to and through my July 1973 testimony, I was quite less than that a year later when I went before Peter Rodino's House Judiciary Committee as its first of eight witnesses. I then had a purpose and a cause. I knew, or at least felt I knew, that if the committee voted one or more articles of impeachment, Richard Nixon, understanding that the House would follow, would be wise enough to close shop and step down. I was sure that what I had to say would greatly influence the committee membership and that no combination of wily tactics by Mr. St. Clair, the renowned Boston attorney representing the president, could throw me off course or render ineffective my factual contradictions of Nixon's oft-repeated lines about his negligence in monitoring and supervising his zealous aides, and about his preoccupations with the affairs of state.

Human Dignity and the Claim of Meaning: Athenian Tragic Drama and Supreme Court Opinions

James Boyd White

James Boyd White is a Professor of English and an Adjunct Professor of Classical Studies as well as the L. Hart Wright Collegiate Professor of Law at the University of Michigan. Professor White practiced law in Boston before beginning his teaching career at the University of Colorado Law School and then the University of Chicago Law School before moving to Michigan. The author of several books, Professor White published this essay in 2002 in the *Journal of Supreme Court History*, a publication of the Supreme Court Historical Society. Professor White's writings consistently connect the legal and literary worlds through rhetorical analysis and cultural criticism.

I am going to bring together what may seem at first to be two extremely different institutions for the creation of public meaning, namely classical Athenian tragedy and the Supreme Court opinion.[1] My object is not so much to draw lines of similarity and distinction between them, as a cultural analyst might do, as to try to capture something of what I believe is centrally at work in both institutions, in fact essential to what each at its best achieves. I can frame it as a question: How is it that the best instances of each genre (for I will be talking only about the best) work to resist the ever-present impulse to trivialize human life and experience—certainly well known in our own era—and instead confer upon the individual, and his or her sufferings and struggles in the world, a kind of dignity? I think that something like this is in fact the core of the most important achievements of both institutions, and that in both cases it is simultaneously imaginative (or literary) and political in nature.

I mean not to make an especially original or controversial point, but to call upon a familiar and widespread intuition. I assume that we all sometimes have the feeling that what we are reading—or watching or hearing—trivializes human experience, reducing it to something unimportant or insignificant and stimulating a kind of cynicism

or despair. But of course we also sometimes have the opposite feeling, that the expression or action to which we are exposed—the Bach cantata, the painting by Vermeer, the poem by Keats or Dickinson—somehow dignifies or exalts the human, marking out possibilities for significance in life, in our lives, that can serve as a ground of hope in a universe full of confusion and suffering. We can't easily explain how it happens, but in the first case we come away somehow ashamed of being a human being, in the second, proud and glad to belong to such a species.

Speaking of my own experience, and I hope yours too, at least some theatrical productions, and some Supreme Court opinions too, give me the second (and better) kind of response, and in this talk I want to explore how and why that happens. I shall not summarize my conclusions now except to say that a large part of my attention will be on the way in which both the dramas and the opinions I shall examine imagine human beings as speaking creatures—on what, that is, they make speech mean. This will lead me to suggest at the end what I mean as a major point, that it is in our capacity for claiming meaning for experience that our deepest dignity lies, and that it is in the denial of that capacity, and what it says about us, that the essence of trivialization can be found.

I shall begin with what I assume to be the less familiar form, Greek drama, and then turn to the law.

5 First, some background. In Athens the performance of tragedy was a highly public and intensively competitive event which occurred in its full grandeur only once a year, at the great festival of Dionysus. Only three dramatists were permitted to compete; they were chosen several months ahead of time, and given that period in which to perfect the performance of the four-play sequences they had submitted. What we might call "rehearsal" was no small or casual matter; it cost roughly as much to train a chorus for a single set of plays as it did to keep a warship at sea for a year, and rich men were called upon by the state to bear this burden. The plays were performed at the Theater of Dionysus next to the Acropolis; they were then judged by officials or by the crowd, with prizes of great honor awarded for the best play, best actor, best chorus, and so forth.[2]

The tragic theater was a cultural form, an occasion for the making of public and shared meaning, that had certain ways of working. These were naturally realized differently by different playwrights and in different plays, but running through this body of work there are three important strands that I would like to bring to your attention. As we shall later see, these three strands, perhaps surprisingly, have analogues in some of the best opinions of the Supreme Court.

BRINGING THE REMOTE INTO THE CIRCLE OF ATTENTION

I shall begin with the great trilogy of Aeschylus called the *Oresteia*. The first play, the *Agamemnon*, tells the story of that hero's return to Mycenae from the Trojan War, and how he is shamefully killed—in his bath—by his wife Clytemnestra and her lover Aegistheus; the second play tells how her son Orestes, commanded by Apollo to avenge this murder of his father, kills his mother; the third brings on stage in pursuit of Orestes the Eumenides, the dreadful furies who punish the shedding of kindred blood. Orestes finds refuge in Athens, where he is tried for his act by a court and jury established for the purpose. He is acquitted, for he was acting under divine compulsion in the form of explicit orders from Apollo. The trilogy thus ends with the establishment in Athens of courts of justice; courts that will, in the future, break a chain of vengeance such as that which plagued the house of Atreus, and do so by imposing sanctions for homicide that themselves do not occasion blood guilt.

The *Agamemnon* begins with a watchman in Mycenae waiting, at dawn, for the beacon of light that will announce the victory at Troy—for Clytemnestra has arranged for fires to be lit on mountain top after mountain top, to bring this news across the sea in a single night. Next, the chorus, in a song about the events that have led up to the present, tells how Agamemnon, on his way to Troy ten years earlier, his fleet held in harbor by adverse winds, sacrificed his daughter Iphigenia to persuade the gods to let him go—a terrible crime that Clytemnestra will later invoke as a justification for her own terrible crime. Soon after, a messenger arrives to describe the sack of Troy, in his vivid account bringing directly before the other characters within the play—and before the audience in Athens, too—these remote and perilous happenings.

I wish to draw attention here to a rather simple fact, namely, that the drama brings into the space we call the theater, and before the minds of the people of Athens, imagined events that are distant in both time and place. Thus the audience is here asked to imagine Mycenae at the time of the fall of Troy, Troy itself, the chain of mountain tops running from Troy to Mycenae, the sacrifice of Iphigenia ten years earlier, and so on.[3]

In an age of television, movies, newspapers, 10 and the Internet, it may be difficult to see this for the surprising and powerful cultural phenomenon it was, for we are besieged with communications that invite us to imagine the remote and distant. But these plays took place in a different kind of world, one in which this was a real invention. In bringing on stage, and into the conscious imaginings of the people, events that were remote in time and space, the drama invited the audience to connect themselves to the distant. This was, I think, one of the central functions of the Athenian theater, and it had a perhaps surprising political and ethical significance.[4]

Think, for example, of another play by Aeschylus, *The Persians*. This tells the story of the great naval battle at Salamis, at which the Athenians destroyed the Persian invaders. Writing ten years after the battle, Aeschylus locates the action of his play surprisingly in Persia itself, where we see the royal women of Persia awaiting news of the expedition. The audience sees these events, not from the point of view of Athens, as a wonderful triumph, but from the point of view of the Persian women, for whom it is a disaster and with whose suffering one must sympathize. Of course, the audience is really Athenian, so they actually see it both ways at once—they are forced to do so—and that double vision is a central part of the meaning of the play.

At the climax of *The Persians*, a messenger reports the story of the battle itself, to which he was an eyewitness—telling how the Persians were tricked into rowing around the island of Salamis all night, then penned into a narrow bay from which they could not escape. These events in fact took place just a few miles away from Athens—the audience can see the mountains of Salamis from their seats—which means that in this play, occuring in Athens but set in Persia, Athens itself is brought on stage, simultaneously into the imagined world of Persia and the real world of Athens itself. The play thus makes Athens look at itself as it appears to others.

In setting the play up this way, Aeschylus is I think talking to his citizens about their own world, simultaneously stimulating pride in their great victory and disciplining that pride by the recognition of the terrible loss it brought to others. He is also telling the Athenians that they should guard against the heady overconfidence that might otherwise naturally arise in them from the victory. In a real sense this play is thus a teaching play, teaching the public something crucial about its moral situation, as the *Oresteia* taught it something about its central institutions—in both cases, by bringing to awareness what is distant in time and space, and morally distant too.

It is not just that the theater carries distant events before the consciousness of the people. It brings into the light of day facts—or forces or ideas or impulses—that are normally repressed or hidden: the reality of the experience of the Persian women, for example, or of the murdered Iphigenia, or the psychic and moral forces represented by the Furies in the *Eumenides*—monstrous deities who normally live out of sight, underground, so hideous in the performance, says one account, that women miscarried at the sight of them. Perhaps the most famous example of this habit of bringing on to the stage what in a deep sense is felt to belong off it is the *Oedipus Tyrannos* of Sophocles, where, as Freud helped us see, some of the most profound and disturbing of human psychological forces are brought directly into the consciousness of the audience, as it contemplates Oedipus' violation of the central taboos against incest and parricide.

A particularly striking instance of this impulse lies in the theater's treatment of women. In the world of Athens, women had a legal and social position mainly as the possessions of men, whether fathers or husbands; even in procreation they were imagined to contribute nothing to the child except a kind of oven in which the male seed could grow; and they themselves had no property and no civil rights. Yet by all three dramatists they are represented on stage as psychological and moral actors who are in every sense (except power) the equal of men. It may be indeed that such figures as Antigone and her sister Ismene, Phaedra, Medea, and Alcestis are the most deeply and fully realized women in Western literature until Shakespeare, perhaps even Jane Austen. It is hard to know how fully to explain this phenomenon, but I think it is another expression of the general impulse to put on stage what is real but unseen—a part of life that is normally excluded from the vision of the male citizens who made up most of the audience.[5]

In all of these ways the drama works as a way of expanding and intensifying our sense of what it means to be human, making it possible to pay attention to what we had not fully seen before. This kind of drama is not merely a kind of entertainment, but a major public and political event, one of the purposes of which, at the hands of the three great geniuses whose work we have, is educative and transformative.

I want now to turn from Athenian tragic drama to the form we call the judicial opinion, especially the opinion of the Supreme Court of the United States. There are, of course, obvious differences between these forms of speech and life, but I think there are also significant parallels. What we call the Supreme Court is in an important sense not this building, nor the nine men and women who sit on the Court, nor even all those who have done so in the past, but an entity that exists primarily in cultural and imaginative and political space. It is a public arena, bounded by its own structures and rules, one function of which is to bring certain stories and the problems they present into public attention, not for the sake of entertainment but in some sense for education or enlightenment. Likewise, it has its own sense of time, in which the remote is brought into the present. The time and space it creates and within which it works are in a sense of its own making; it is the Court itself that gives significance and reality to these dimensions of its existence; and it does so in the form which its great Chief Justice Marshall did much to invent, the opinion of the Court.[6]

Like the ancient theater of Athens, the Court is thus an institution for the making of shared and public meaning. What is more, it shares the more particular feature I have just described, for it too regularly brings into the circle of public attention events and people and places that are normally overlooked or excluded or just not seen. This is in fact one of its central functions.

As a way of exploring how this works in a particular instance, I now turn to *Cohen v. California*, a famous First Amendment case to which I shall refer throughout this article.[7] Its facts reflect the era of the Vietnam War, including protests against it. The defendant, Paul Robert Cohen, wore a jacket bearing the words "Fuck the Draft" while walking down a corridor of the Los Angeles municipal courthouse. He was then arrested and convicted of violating a California penal statute that made it an offense to "maliciously and willfully disturb the peace or quiet of any neighborhood or person ... by ... offensive conduct." The defendant engaged in no other conduct alleged to disturb the peace. The state court imposed a penalty of thirty days in jail. The Supreme Court, in an opinion by Justice Harlan, reversed the conviction.

20 The judicial process here brings into a zone of public awareness material that is normally unseen, most obviously and dramatically, and perhaps a bit embarrassingly, in the use of the word "fuck"—a word which although known, I assume, to almost all English speakers, is normally used only on certain kinds of occasions, with certain kinds of audience, and is definitely excluded from most formal discourse, certainly the discourse of the Supreme Court of the United States. Justice Harlan marks the distance between this term and the language of the Supreme Court—and the decorous conversation he seeks to establish with his readers—by the way he recites the facts of the case, not in his own words but those of the California court: "On April 26, 1968, the defendant was observed in the Los Angeles County Courthouse in the corridor outside of division 20 of the municipal court wearing a jacket bearing the words 'Fuck the Draft' which were plainly visible."[8] He thus quotes the language but distances himself from it.

This is not the only way in which the repressed or unknown is brought by the opinion in *Cohen* to a place where it can be seen and thought about and responded to in a new and deeper way. Mr. Cohen's story was from almost all other perspectives a trivial one, a minor skirmish in the national war about the war. He was not, so far as I know, otherwise an important person in the world, but just a young man opposed to the draft. This was a case of no political or public significance until the Court made it so, saying that despite the apparent triviality of the event the issues presented here—presented, that is, by the lawyers, and seen and articulated by the Court in this very opinion—"are of no small constitutional significance."[9]

This process—giving significance to the apparently insignificant—is a major part of what the Court regularly does. Think, for example, of a case like *Powell v. Texas*,[10] where an alcoholic pauper was thrown into jail overnight to sober up, to all the actors as minor and routine an event as occurs in police work; the Supreme Court made this the object of learned, and contrasting, reflections on the conditions upon which the state may punish conduct as criminal, especially conduct arising from disease, in a set of opinions that might have remade criminal law in this country.[11] In this case—as in every criminal procedure case, in nearly every First Amendment case, and throughout the law, really—the unimportant is made important. This has its own political meaning, for it says that there is no case too small, no person too insignificant to be worthy of potential attention. Here and elsewhere the Court makes big law by attending to small events. No one is excluded on principle.

When a dramatist invokes what is physically or morally distant, we naturally ask what he will make of it: What meaning will he claim for the story of Iphigenia or the looting of Troy or the events at the Persian court? The answer will always lie in particularities of writing and performance. In the same way, when Mr. Cohen's story is brought into the theater of the courtroom, we ask what it will be made to mean by the lawyers and by the Court, and this, too, is of necessity a highly particular matter, tied intimately to the facts of the case. For, as every lawyer knows, we do not and cannot know ahead of time the cluster of arguments on both sides by which the law will work in a particular case, which the Court must in turn resolve, and which it will use and transform in its own opinion.

This particularity requires a kind of attention, makes possible a kind of invention, different from the kind of talk usual in political or theoretical debate. What is happening in the *Cohen* case, from one perspective, is just another event in the long struggle over the meaning of the Vietnam War. But the law cannot think in such terms; it must fashion itself to meet the particularities of the case as these emerge in thought and argument. And when the bright light of attention is focused on what we have not seen, or not seen clearly, it almost always reveals a complexity and richness of significance that we had missed, thus putting in question, among other things, our own prior habits of mind and imagination. In the *Cohen* case, the large issue—that of the draft and the war itself—is, of course, on everybody's mind. What the law does here is take a tiny fragment of that larger story, this simple act of protest, and examine it not in the terms of the national political debate—prowar or antiwar—but as a constitutional problem, to be analyzed, argued, and decided in the terms established by this branch of the law. This means, as we shall soon see, that an essential part of the opinion will be a delineation of these terms, an account of the universe of meaning established by the First Amendment and the cases decided under it.

25 Like the drama, then, the opinion not only brings before us what is remote in time and space but in doing so creates a world of imagination, simultaneously drawn from the world we otherwise know and an alternative to it. The idea in both cases is not to offer the audience an escape into fantasy, but to create an imagined reality that can run against the "real world," both to test it and to be tested by it. In both forms, particularity is essential to the art; and in both forms, the created order is at once final and tentative: final because it reaches a conclusion, comes to an end; tentative because the rest of life continues, creating an ever-changing context that will challenge or confirm the imagined order in new and different ways.

MOVEMENT TO DISCOVERY BY DRAMATIC OPPOSITION

Perhaps a more familiar feature of Greek tragedy is that it lives and works dramatically, by the interaction between different characters speaking out of their respective situations in different voices. This too was a real invention, for the first forms of drama were purely choral performances; at first one actor was added to the chorus, then another, then finally, by Sophocles, the third.[12]

The opposition of character to character is so much the soul of what we think of as drama, then and now, that it is hard to appreciate the force and originality of the invention. Think, for example, of the opposition between Creon and Antigone over the relative authority of the city's decrees and those of the timeless and unwritten laws that the young woman invokes; or of the confrontation between Orestes and the Furies at his trial for the murder of Clytemnestra; or, in the play that bears her name, of the intense struggle between Medea and Jason. Or, to shift nearer our own world, think of Shakespeare's *Hamlet*, which can be seen as a set of antagonistic conversations between Hamlet and others—Gertrude and Claudius and Polonius and Laertes and Horatio—each defining somewhat differently the meaning of the past they share and of contemplated future action too. The question the play presents is, what kind of sense can be made of a world defined by such contrasting possibilities of speech and meaning?

It is equally obvious that, with us at least, the law works in a similar way: by the opposition of character against character, plaintiff against defendant, each representing a different vision of the world—and of the law—and seeking to establish its own as the dominant one. The central legal institution we call the hearing works by a disciplined opposition that is intended to lead, and sometimes does, to deeper understanding, indeed, to the revelation of central questions theretofore obscured by our ignorance, or by our habits of thought and imagination.[13] It is not simply that play and trial work by opposition, but that the opposition leads the participants and the audience to new discoveries, about what has happened and what it means, about what ought to happen, about who these people are and ought to be.

As the play often takes as its subject a familiar story from mythology or history, which is told in such a way as to reveal new possibilities of meaning, so the hearing often begins with a set of preconceived ideas—in the parties, judge, and lawyers alike—about the facts and their significance, about the law and its bearing upon them; these are tested and complicated in argument and sometimes completely transformed. When the play and the hearing work well, they are both processes that carry us by the force of opposition from a position defined by our preexisting expectations into quite different and often surprising terrain. This happens in *Cohen* itself: this is a case to the facts of which lots of people, including judges and lawyers, would have highly predictable responses, pro or con, and one of the functions of the opinion is to complicate these responses, perhaps beyond recognition, by the discipline of the body of thought and law developed under the First Amendment.

30   I shall not belabor this point of comparison, which seems plain enough as it stands, but wish to make a particular point about the way the law works in this respect. It is true that in *Cohen*, as usual in American law, the lawyers for the two sides create a drama of opposition that the Court will in turn address. But notice that Cohen himself is not a participant in this conversation. His original speech—the slogan on his jacket—is reported by others, but he himself has no opportunity to say what it should be said to mean in the language of the law. That is the task in the first instance of the lawyers, then of the courts. Unlike Orestes or Oedipus, Cohen is a real flesh-and-blood person, with his own ways of talking, his own vision of the meaning and perhaps the necessity of what he did, and none of this is present in the legal argument, especially on appeal.

The law thus provides a second language, into which the languages and experiences of ordinary life must be translated. The people of the law will locate and define what happened in the real world in these terms, placing what Cohen himself actually said and did in a larger context, which will in turn do much to shape the kind of meaning that can now be claimed for Cohen's words. The law is in this way a cultural process, working on the raw material of life—the injury to the body or the psyche, the failed business, the broken marriage, the vulgar words in the courthouse—to convert it into something else, something of its own: the occasion for the assertion of a certain sort of meaning. It is a kind of translation.

One of the striking features of the opinion in *Cohen*, and one of its great merits, is that it acknowledges this fact about itself: the difference between ordinary language and legal language is not erased or elided, as it usually is, but made inescapably prominent. In addition to the usual dramatic opposition between the lawyers, there is

thus another overt tension, between two registers of discourse and between the people who speak in these different ways: between Mr. Cohen, wearing his jacket with its blunt-spoken legend into the municipal courthouse, and Justice Harlan, speaking as he does in elaborate and sophisticated legal terms about that event. On one side, we have the crude and simple phrase, a gesture of contempt and defiance that seems to express the view that nothing else need be said, to claim that this is a wholly adequate response to the issue of policy it addresses, indeed the only proper response. On the other side, we have a mind of great fastidiousness and care, defining, by the way it works through the issues, a set of crucial cultural and social values: the values of learning, of balance and comprehensiveness of mind, of human intelligence, of depth of understanding. Nothing could seemingly be further from the mind exemplified in this elegant, complex, civilized composition than the kind of crude speech it protects.[14] And by creating in his own voice a tone that respects ordinary canons of decency in expression, then incorporating this vulgarism within it, Justice Harlan performs, at the level of the text, just what he says the First Amendment requires of society in places like the courthouse: the toleration of what we normally exclude or suppress.

In this way, while protecting the speech Justice Harlan distances himself from it, defining himself and the Court as different from, indeed, opposed to, the values—the sense of self and other, the idea of public thinking and speaking—expressed by it. It is this distance that enables him credibly to say at one point that the tolerance of "cacophony" required by the First Amendment may be a sign of strength, not weakness, in the society that is capable of it. This is a message that he does not merely articulate but performs or enacts throughout the whole opinion, for he simultaneously protects Cohen's speech and exemplifies ways of thinking and talking that are at the other end of the spectrum. Do not imagine from this opinion that you might be well advised to use language like that on Mr. Cohen's jacket in addressing the Supreme Court, or that to display such a jacket in a courtroom might be immune from sanction.

It is important to notice in this First Amendment case that the kind of speech that the opinion exemplifies and values in its own performance is not really "free speech," but the opposite of that, highly regulated and constrained: by the principle of judicial authority, which requires serious attention to earlier cases and to the tensions between them; by a conception of excellence in legal thought, which shapes the kind of attention Justice Harlan gives to those cases; and by canons of civilized and rational discourse, including grammar and syntax, which govern the forms of expression. It is, in fact, this very quality of Harlan's opinion that makes its protection of Cohen's slogan so significant and important: it is protecting something very different from itself, and in doing so it defines the kind of toleration the First Amendment has at its center. Yet when it does so it recognizes, almost of necessity, that this other utterance has a force and value which may be missing from the opinion itself; indeed, it almost necessarily suggests that there may be times when the right response to a political situation is not more reason not more civilization, but the kind of verbal gesture one cannot quite imagine Justice Harlan, as he defines himself here, ever making.

35   For there are points in this opinion at which one might be less inclined to call Harlan's manner of speech "elegant" or "sophisticated" than "stuffy" or "stilted"—as for example, when he says that we should remember that human speech "conveys not only ideas capable of relatively precise, detached explication, but otherwise inexpressible emotions as well," and goes on to add that the Constitution should not be assumed to have little or no regard for this "emotive" function which "may often be the more important element of the overall message sought to be communicated."[15] When I hear this, I at least have the feeling that I am in the presence of highly overformal speech, the workings of a mind that is at the moment constricted by its own commitments to a certain kind of thought. But this very fact has its dramatic and literary function, for it enacts for us what it might mean to insist as California wants to do, that Cohen should be compelled to translate his utterance into more formal and generally acceptable speech—this would make him sound like me, Harlan is in effect saying, and it would bleed what he says of all its life and vigor.

We can see now that the other impulse I mentioned, the bringing on stage of that which is unrecognized or alien or perhaps taboo, is at work through the entire opinion. Harlan brings on this phrase, this moment, not only to protect it, but to establish a dramatic tension with it, a tension that validates it as well as tolerates it. One is reminded of Shakespeare's capacity to see the world from every point of view, in this sense to humanize every monster. Even Caliban, the subhuman creature who tries to rape Miranda and destroy Prospero, is given his moments of sympathy, and more than sympathy—of unique and beautiful expression.

CLAIMING MEANING FOR EXPERIENCE

In addition to its way of imagining the distant and remote and its way of working by dramatic opposition, Greek tragedy has a third feature, harder to define than the others but no less important, not only for Athens but in its consequences for the literary and dramatic imagination ever since. What I have in mind is a certain sort of speech in which a speaker looks back over his experience as a whole—and thus our experience too—seeking to find a meaning in it, to claim a meaning for it, and such a meaning as will enable him or her to shape his or her future speech and conduct in a coherent and valuable way.

Not all dramatic speech has this quality. Much of it consists of simple response to events, in the form of lamentation or the expression of joy or worry; some of it consists of denunciation, or manipulation, or planning, or the giving of orders— think of Creon speaking to Antigone—or the pursuit of clarification, as in *Oedipus*. All of these gestures can of course, be ways of giving meaning to experience, but they have not quite the quality I seek to define which includes a kind of summing up, a self-consciousness, an effort to imagine the whole world and oneself and others within it, to see one's story as a whole and among other stories. It is the full performance of a gesture that is begun over and over in human experience, both in our own lives and on the stage, but rarely taken to completion.

Let me give two brief instances. In *Oedipus at Colonus*, the blind and aged man finds at last a home in the sanctuary of Colonus on the edge of Attica. The townspeople in the chorus are afraid of him and wish to drive him off; Creon, his brother in-law, comes from Thebes to seize and bring him back to that city, to ensure that he will be buried there and thus confer on Thebes the benefits which an oracle has promised to the place that receives his body. Oedipus himself is filled with a sense of cost and loss, of his own status as an object of fear and taboo, but he also displays a remarkable serenity, an integrity of mind; and towards the end, in an argument with Creon, he surprisingly asserts his essential innocence. He looks back over his entire life and claims new meaning for it. He was, he says, the object of a divine decree from birth that he should do these unspeakable things—how then, can it have been his fault? He did not know who it was he killed, or who it was he was marrying; and when he did kill he acted in self-defense. He has—and he knows it—violated the deepest of taboos and is by this fact eternally marked; but he also sees that in another and deeper sense he is innocent as well. The action of the play confirms this sense of his own deep innocence in two ways: first, in Theseus' expulsion of Creon and acceptance of Oedipus into the territory of Athens; then, in Oedipus' own apotheosis, his conversion by divine power on his death into a kind of quasi-deity himself.

40   Or consider the *Ajax* of Sophocles. The story here takes place during the Trojan War, just after the death of Achilles. The armor of Achilles is given by the leaders, Agamemnon and Menelaus, not to Ajax, who is sure he de serves this mark of honor, but to Odysseus, in what Ajax regards as an act of fraud. Filled with fury and a sense of injury, Ajax sets forth at night to kill Odysseus and the two leaders, the only response this man of war and honor can possibly imagine. Athena sees him do this, and deludes him into thinking that a herd of sheep and goats are the enemies he seeks; he slaughters them, delighted at his revenge; but then he gradually returns to sanity, surrounded by the corpses of these animals, a laughingstock to the whole world, utterly humiliated. The course for him is plain, and he faces it clearly and with characteristic courage: "It's a contemptible thing to want to live forever.... Let a man nobly live or nobly die."[16] The meaning of his situation is that he should die and be done with it.

Tecmessa, the woman with whom he lives and by whom he has had his only son, pleads with him not to end his life, for the moment he dies she and their son will become slaves of others, which will be horrible for themselves and a humiliation both to Ajax' parents, who are still alive, and to his own memory. Ajax at first rejects her claim, but he is in fact affected by what she says, and when he returns to the stage after a choral ode lamenting his decision, he speaks in a wholly different way, not from inside his misery of the moment but from outside, at an enormous distance, philosophical or religious in kind.

> Strangely the long and countless drift of
>   time
> Brings all things forth from darkness into
>   light,
> Then covers them once more. Nothing so
>   marvelous
> That man can say it surely will not be—
> Strong oath and iron intent come crashing
>   down.
> *My* mood, which just before was strong and
>   rigid,
> No dipped sword more so, now has lost its
>   edge—
> My speech is womanish for this woman's
>   sake;
> And pity touches me for my wife and child . . .

So, he says, he will go to the shore of the sea and purify himself, hiding his sword in the sand.

> From now on this will be my rule:
>   Give way
> To Heaven and bow before the sons of
>   Atreus.
> They are our rulers, they must be obeyed.
> I must give way, as all dread strengths give
>   way.
> In turn and deference. Winter's hard-packed
>   snow
> Cedes to the fruitful summer; stubborn
>   night
> At last removes, for day's white steeds to
>   shine.
> The dread blast of the gale slackens and gives
> Peace to the sounding sea; and Sleep, strong
>   jailer.
> In time yields up his captive. Shall not I
> Learn place and wisdom?

This is an extraordinary speech. It represents an enormous shift of mind and feeling, from a self-centered despair to an acceptance of his lot, which is in turn based at least in part on a recognition of the claims and experience of others. Ajax can now see Tecmessa, not merely as a possession, but as a person with whose experience he can sympathize. His virtue has so far been to be without pity; now he can pity. What is more, he now sees his present defeat not as a single, unique, and humiliating event, but as part of the larger order and process of the world, in which all dread and powerful things give way in the end: winter, and night, and storms, and sleep, and wakefulness. We live amidst cycling emergences and withdrawals, dominances and submissions, of which this event is only one. His humiliation is thus stripped of social and moral significance and made a fact, a fact of nature, like death itself.

This speech is, therefore, an answer to a central question the play presents, which is how one can possibly live in a world in which life is so utterly subject to chance, even malicious destruction. The answer is ultimately a matter of voice and character, of imagination and speech. Ajax lives in a world of uncertainty and destruction; but he can see that and say it, and in doing this can see himself, not as a unique heroic ego, but as part of a set of processes larger than he; and all this enables him to accept his life, and its conditions.[17]

45   There is enacted in this speech an impulse that is perhaps first made part of the Western inheritance here in the tragic drama of Greece: the impulse to stop, to sum up life as a whole and to try to make sense of it, to claim a meaning for it; to try to imagine the world and oneself within it in such a way as to make meaningful action possible — whether that action is the kind of suicide upon which Ajax first resolves, and later, perhaps still under the destructive spell of Athena, commits, or whether it is the kind of life in connection with others that he, in this speech, for a moment, imagines.

What is more, this kind of speech is, I think, essential to the deepest contribution of tragic drama, which is, as Hegel said, to give dignity to human life by recognizing and enacting the possibility that the human mind — the self or soul — can maintain its integrity even, or especially, at the moment of its dissolution.[18] It is such an act of character and imagination that enables Oedipus to overcome and transform what he has done; that enables Prometheus, chained to the rock, to maintain a moral and psychological superiority to the Zeus who tortures him; and that enables Ajax, for a moment at least, to accept and live with the humiliation thrust upon him by fate and the gods. It is in the human capacity for speech of a certain kind that human dignity most deeply resides: speech that invokes what is distant and remote and brings it before the mind, where it can provide material and a point of view from which the culture, and

the self, can be criticized; speech that moves, as the play and trial both do, by opposition and contrast into new perception and understanding; and speech, like that of Ajax or Oedipus, that seeks to sum up experience and claim a meaning for it.

To return once more to *Cohen*, I want now to suggest that in writing his opinion for the Court, as, in a sense, in any judicial opinion of any real quality, Justice Harlan is expressing very much the same impulse, in a different context, that we saw at work in Ajax and Oedipus: the desire to sum things up, to tell again the story of the past, to imagine the world and its people, all in ways that will make possible coherent speech, intelligible and appropriate action. For part of the duty of the Court is to say how this case should be talked about in the language the Court has made — in this instance, the language made in cases decided under the First Amendment. To do this, it must attend to the entire authoritative past created by the Court and do so with the duty of resolving so far as it can the tensions it discovers within it, with the aim of asserting, for the moment, that justice has been done. It must use this language to make a claim both to coherent speech and to appropriate action.

How does Justice Harlan, speaking for the Court in the *Cohen* case, attempt to do these things? Here is a brief outline of what might be called the argumentative structure of his opinion.

He begins a bit like a modernist painter sculpting out negative space by telling what, in his words, this case "does *not* present" (emphasis in original). First, he says this is a case in which the state seeks to punish, not conduct that is associated with speech, but speech itself.[19] Likewise, it does not involve a statute directed at the special need for decorous speech and conduct in the courthouse or its precincts, but one of general applicability. This means that no special deference is due any judgment of the legislature as to the proper control of speech in the halls of a courthouse, for no such judgment has been made.[20] And, despite the sexual vulgarity of the central term employed, this is not an obscenity case, for the expression is in no way erotic.[21] Furthermore, the phrase in question does not qualify as the sort of expression the Court has termed "fighting words," unprotected by the First Amendment, for it was not a direct personal insult. Nor is a prohibition of this phrase justified by the fact that it was forced upon "unwilling or unsuspecting viewers," as a "captive audience"; to justify suppression on such grounds, the government must show that "substantial privacy interests are being invaded in an essentially intolerable manner," which is not the case here.[22]

50 Harlan thus runs through nearly the entire body of potentially relevant First Amendment law, only to put it aside on the grounds that it does not bear on the case before him. That is, he simultaneously admits the surface relevance of the arguments he states and denies their real force in this case. He is here addressing and resolving the sort of argumentative opposition between lawyers I referred to earlier, and it is important to say—although it would take too long for me to show that it is so—that none of the points he dismisses is without some merit, none of his own positions beyond argument. He recognizes what can be said the other way, but is, at the same time, exercising a power—the power of a language-shaper—to determine its scope and basis and reach.

All this is, for him, a kind of brush-clearing that opens up what he regards as the real issue in the case, which is whether California may "excise, as 'offensive conduct,' one particular scurrilous epithet from the public discourse." It cannot do so, he first says, on the theory advanced by the court below, namely that it is "inherently likely to cause a violent reaction," for that is simply not the case.[23] However, there is a second theory supporting the conviction, which in his view commands more respect and attention: namely, that the states may suppress this "unseemly expletive" in an effort to "maintain what they regard as a suitable level of discourse within the body politic."[24]

He begins his examination of this question at a highly general level, reimagining as it were the first premises of the legal universe. First, he says, we must make this judgment with an understanding of the purpose of the constitutional right of free expression: "It is designed and intended to remove governmental restraints from the arena of public discussion, putting the decision as to what views shall be voiced largely in the hands of each of us, in the hope that such freedom will ultimately produce a more capable citizenry and more perfect polity, and in the belief that no other approach would comport with the premise of individual dignity and choice upon which our system rests."[25] This is a lovely and economical statement, drawn

from a more extended one, the famous dissent of Justice Brandeis in *Whitney v. California*,[26] to which Harlan makes reference. The result of this freedom, Harlan goes on to say, "may often appear to be verbal tumult, discord, and even offensive utterance."[27] But these are side effects of what a broader debate enables us to achieve, and "that the air may at times seem to be filled with verbal cacophony is, in this sense, not a sign of weakness, but of strength."[28]

Then, in turning to the particulars of this case, Harlan makes two central points. First he says that the result contended for by the prosecution would confer "inherently boundless" powers on the state. For if this word can be excised from public speech, where is the power to stop? What he means is that there is simply no principled way to distinguish between this particular term and others. This view rests on an important understanding of the nature of language, namely, that words cannot be sorted like peas or bolts, according to size or weight. They have a life that is more mysterious and multidimensional, more context-dependent, than such a view would allow.

Second—and central to the ultimate meaning of the case—Harlan says that to force a translation of Cohen's utterance into more socially presentable speech would strip it of much of its significance. For human speech, he says in a passage I quoted earlier, "conveys not only ideas capable of relatively precise, detached explication, but otherwise inexpressible emotions as well"; and we cannot believe that the Constitution has "little or no regard" for this "emotive function, which practically speaking, may often be the more important element of the overall message sought to be communicated."[29] And even if this is not true, he thinks that it would be too facile to assume that one "can forbid particular words without also running a substantial risk of suppressing ideas in the process."[30]

Note the tension here. First Harlan says that 55 speech does more than express "ideas," and that what he calls its emotional content is crucial to its value; then he returns to the topic of "ideas," saying that we cannot be confident that the suppression of vulgarity would not involve the suppression of "ideas," as though ideas are the important things after all. He thus reaffirms the distinction between ideas and feelings he has just criticized; but the earlier criticism—insisting on the value of emotive expression—continues to work, thus transforming his point from its rather crude statement about "ideas" to a crucial recognition that our language about language is itself inherently limited and constricting. What unites his two perceptions, despite the tensions between them, is his sense that we cannot be confident that we can know how the meaning of language works, certainly not so confident that we can inflict surgery on an utterance without running the risk of destroying its life.

This is the most important part of the meaning of the Court's opinion: a sensitivity to the fact that meaning and form are inseparable. It is a familiar truth of literary criticism that the meaning of a poem or a play or a novel, or any other work of art, lies not in any restatement of it into other terms—in any message or idea—but in its performance, in the life and experience it creates for its audience or viewer. In adopting and performing this position in the law, Harlan takes an enormously significant step away from the view that the First Amendment should be held to protect only speech that contributes to the marketplace of "ideas," and especially of political ideas. Of course Cohen's own speech is deeply political; but the way the Court imagines and resolves his case makes the amendment reach much further, to the protection of art and perhaps—as one might wish to do in the case of Greek drama—to a dissolution of the simple distinction between political and nonpolitical, as the opinion dissolves the distinction between ideas and feelings.

There is thus this additional connection between the opinion in *Cohen v. California* and the Greek dramas with which we began, that *Cohen* provides a language and an authority for the protection of these plays and others like them. It is not only itself a drama; it is a way of thinking about drama.

In comparing the form of classic Greek tragedy and that of the Supreme Court opinion, my hope has been to begin to establish a somewhat clearer sense of the ways in which they work as institutions for the making of collective meaning. One idea is that increased understanding of these matters might lead to deeper criticism, and perhaps even to better performance of the judicial opinion. The three points of comparison made here, for example, can be seen to generate questions that can be brought to the reading and criticism of any judicial opinion.

1. To what extent does this opinion bring into the circle of public awareness persons or events or other material that are normally repressed, ignored, or overlooked? Does it do this with the kind of particularity that will bring to the surface something new and problematic, and thus become the occasion for growth and change, both in our perceptions of the world and in the law?

2. Does it work in an explicit way by dramatic opposition and development (as opposed, for example, to the deductive application of theory)? In particular, how far does the Court recognize that its own language of description, argument, and conclusion has, as it were, a shadow version opposed to it, represented by the losing side? For the Court does its job, not just by reasoning to a result, but by recognizing the force and reality of other views, other ways of imagining and speaking. And does the Court find a way to create significant dramatic tensions within its own opinion, as Harlan does with respect to what I have called the two registers of discourse reflected here?

3. Does the Court find a way to sum up the law and claim a meaning for it, and, if so, with what kind and degree of coherence? In a First Amendment case, for example, we can ask whether the Court has a workable view of the aims and principles of that text, which in turn requires a view of the nature of human speech, and of language itself; whether it has a way of imagining the Constitution as a whole, and the roles of the various actors within it—legislatures, juries, other courts, itself; whether it offers, in short, a way of imagining this case and the law and the larger society that will enable it to reach a result which it can claim to be just, not only in some technical way, but truly just. And in all three dimensions of meaning we shall be interested not only in the Court's explicit statements or arguments, but, as I have tried to suggest with respect to Harlan's opinion in *Cohen v. California*, in the meaning of the performance enacted in the opinion itself.

I think that the desire for meaning of the kind that is reflected in the speeches of Oedipus and Ajax is the deepest impulse from which literature comes, and that it lies at the heart of our hopes when we approach a judicial opinion, especially a Supreme Court opinion. But the impulse is even more general than that, for we ourselves participate in it in our own lives and imaginations. Every human being shares the desire to find a way of describing and claiming meaning for his or her experience—at the most general level, a way of imagining the world, and herself (or himself) and others within it, that will make possible coherent speech and valuable action, even in the face of the deep uncertainties and injustices life necessarily presents.[31] The process is never complete, for the future lines of the story we are telling are necessarily unknown to us; but we know that when they come they will certainly, like the murder of Agamemnon or the madness of Ajax, give new meaning to what is past. As we do this, we work against two deep fears: that the story we shall then be able to tell will have a meaning that is intolerable to us—or no meaning at all.

60   To discover shape and coherence and significance in a work of art—or law—presents us with an acute form of this problem, for it simultaneously stimulates the desire for meaning of the kind I mean and reminds us that our experience, our story—like that of Agamemnon—is necessarily incomplete. In this way it is the function of art, and law too, to challenge life at its imaginative center.

To test out the depth and pervasiveness of the human desire to discover a way to claim meaning for one's experience, imagine for the moment that we could not claim meaning for our experience; that all our speech was reducible—as, indeed, certain strains of thought in our own world would reduce it—to something called information. Under these conditions, instead of what we call meaningful speech, we would send signals that communicated particular desires or aversions, expressed a willingness or a refusal to engage in a course of conduct, and so on. We could make offers, pay bills, get the car fixed, go to the hair-dresser, buy a suit, order a dinner, arrange for sexual gratification, watch or play baseball, but we could not say what any of these things means to us. We could not justify our decisions, or explain our preferences, we could only act on them; we could not engage in the kind of conversation by which we discover who we

are, what we desire, or should desire, what kind of life we live and want to live. Life could go on as a series of exchanges, and expression as a set of signals that make the exchanges possible. But such an existence would in the most important sense not be human, for it would omit the most deeply human form of speech, which is the effort to define our experience and claim a meaning for it. Description, explanation, justification: these are for us essential activities of mind and language.

As we have seen, the form we call the opinion of the Supreme Court—like the drama—is a cultural institution that works to teach the public: in part by bringing into the zone of collective attention that which is distant or remote, unseen and particular; in part by the way it works through dramatic opposition, with character poised against character, voice against voice; in part by the way it seeks to give meaning to the events thus examined, locating them in a larger context and a larger story, running back in time and including, potentially, all the elements of its institutional memory. It does this in a language fashioned for the purpose, in which the Court—like Ajax or Oedipus— claims, or struggles to claim, that it can describe, explain, and justify its decision in an appropriate way, one that will make possible coherent speech and meaningful action in the future. And like the drama it has the potential, at least—in my view, realized in cases like *Cohen* and many others, though not all—to enhance our sense of the dignity of human life and experience, in resistance to those forces, in this and every age, that would trivialize these things.

In the judicial opinion and the drama alike, we are thus exposed to imaginations that, at their best, confront the deep uncertainties of the world, of language and the mind, but nonetheless create orders, in language, that run against those uncertainties. But in each—the speech of Ajax, the play that bears his name, the opinion in *Cohen*—the order is tentative, temporary, soon to be replaced by others, or redefined as the context that gives it meaning changes. In this way, both forms call upon us, as readers, to engage in our own versions of this fundamental activity of imagination and language: Become a maker of order yourself, they tell us, become one who claims meaning for our shared experience, or the possibility will be lost.

Notes

1. This paper was originally delivered as a lecture to the Supreme Court Historical Society, 13 December 2000.
2. For a brief account, *see* the articles on *choregia* and Greek tragedy in **The Oxford Classical Dictionary**, 3rd ed., S. Hornblower and A. Spawforth, 1538–1542 (1996).
3. The way this works practically is that the audience is first asked to imagine that the space before it, the theater, is of a different time and place, in this case Mycenae; then, by speech and song, events in places and times remote from that one are also brought before the mind of the audience.
4. Of course, there were other forms that did something like this especially the *Odyssey*, one of the foundational texts of this culture, which invited the audience to imagine both the world of Odysseus and then, through his speeches about his travels, a world beyond that. But the drama does this in a much more immediate way, inviting the audience in believe that what they are seeing and hearing in real time, on this spring morning, are the events of long ago or far away. The *Odyssey* told of remote events; the drama acts them out.
5. For an account of the ways in which such characters can nonetheless be seen to serve the needs of a male-dominated culture, *see* Helene Foley, **Female Acts in Greek Tragedy** (2001). On the place of women in the theater, *see* **Literature in the Greek and Roman Worlds,** O. Taplin, ed., 127–132 (2000).
6. That it is through the judicial opinion that the Court does these things is too obvious, I think, for argument. Imagine, for a moment, that it had been forbidden to write opinions, that its judgments had to stand on their own, undefined and uninterpreted. This would destroy the possibility of law as we know it. Of course, a case matters in part because of its outcome, especially to the parties; but to the rest of us this outcome matters largely because of what it is made to mean, in the first instance by the Court that decides it, then by later Courts and commentators. The case does not have a meaning automatically, that is, but is given meaning through the opinion that describes, explains, and justifies the outcome. As a teacher once said to a writing class, "The facts do not speak for themselves. You have to speak for them." So too it is with the results reached by the Supreme Court. It is the opinion that gives significance. For elaboration of this point, *see* "What's an Opinion For?" in my **From Expectation to Experience: Essays on Law and Legal Education**. Chapter 4 (2000).
7. 403 U.S. 15 (1971). One of the peculiarities of a First Amendment opinion is that it is speech about speech, which means that the Court is always exemplifying its own version of the activity it is protecting (or not protecting). This in turn holds out the possibility of a tension, productive or unproductive, between the speech of the citizen in question and that of the Court. For the Court may talk *about* speech one way, yet imply—or seem to imply—a very different sense of it, of its possibilities and dangers, in its own performance. That will in fact be true here.
8. *Id.* at 16.
9. *Id.* at 15. Notice, too, as I said earlier, that the imagined world in which this story is placed reaches far in space and time alike. In space, it reaches out to Los Angeles and the county jail, to bring what happens there into the circle of public attention that the Supreme Court defines. And it reaches back in time, too, as we shall soon see, when the Court tries to explain its decision, as it must, in the terms and understandings established by earlier decisions. Everything the Court has ever done is of potential relevance; that inheritance must be examined, thought about, and reorganized into a system of thought that will give appropriate and tolerable meaning to the events before it.
10. 392 U.S. 514 (1968).
11. I say "might have" because, in the event, the Court backed away from the possibilities opened up in *Powell*. Nonetheless, that case had real force in focusing thought on the

problem of criminal responsibility and doing so in a highly constructive way.

12. *See* Aristotle, **Poetics**, IV 10–17.

13. *See* Robert P. Burns, **A Theory of the Trial** (1999); Milner Ball. "The Play's the Thing: An Unscientific Reflection on Courts Under the Rubric of Theater." 28 *Stanford Law Review* 81 (1975).

14. I have spoken as though Cohen's gesture were simply a crude vulgarity, and the question were whether or not to tolerate it. This is, in a sense, of course true, but there are also respects in which his utterance was in its own way highly mannered. In a footnote, Justice Harlan explains that Cohen went into a courtroom where a trial was proceeding and, before he did so, took off his jacket and folded it up so that the slogan was not visible. Whatever his feelings may have been, from an objective point of view this was an act of respect for the courtroom and the judicial process. A policeman present suggested that the court hold him in contempt, but the judge sensibly refused, 403 U.S. 15, 19 n. 3 (1971).

15. *Id.* at 26

16. All quotations from **Ajax** are from the translation by John Moore, in **Sophocles, v. II,** David Grene, ed. (1957).

17. This is, at least, what it looks like when the speech is given, but shortly afterwards Ajax retires to the sea coast not to bury his sword, but to fall upon it, as a suicide. Is the speech quoted above, then, all deception, meant perhaps to placate for the moment Tecmessa and the chorus of sailors from Salamis, his countrymen? So some take it, but that would be odd in a person as utterly direct and forthright as Ajax is throughout. Yet how is one, then, to explain the suicide? One possibility, and in my view a strong one, is that the suicide is the continuing work of Athena. (Soon a messenger will report the words of Calchas, the seer, that if Ajax can be kept safe within his tent for this one day, Athena will harass him no more [lines 758–759].) On this view, the speech is sincerely meant when given; its intention is undone by the force of Athena's curse. But this would reduce Ajax's suicide by making it in a sense involuntary. And who could imagine him actually submit-

ting to Menelaus and Agamemnon? A third reading is suggested by Bernard Knox, namely that the first part of the speech, quoted above, is actually a soliloquy in which Ajax truly articulates his vision of the world; but this is not a vision that he accepts, quite the reverse of that. The language about reverencing the Atreidae, for example, shows how impossible acquiescence would be. The speech in this way confirms his resolve to leave this impossible life. *See* Bernard Knox. **Word and Action: Essays on the Ancient Theater** 134–141 (1979). For other views, *see* C. M. Bown **Sophoclean Tragedy** 39–46 (1944) and R. P. Winnington-Ingram, **Sophoclean: An Interpretation.** 46–55 (1980).

These are all plausible interpretations, none of them without difficulty, presenting choices for the director and actor. For my present purposes it is not necessary to try to resolve the tensions among them, for they all involve the speaker summarizing a way of imagining the whole world and himself within it, whether this is done directly, or with an intention to deceive, or as a way of discovering how impossible for him the truth he is discovering actually is. But I will say, for what it is worth, that the idea that this speech is straight deception, though shared by many, seems to me simply wrong.

18. For an elaboration, *See* Michelle Gellrich, **Tragedy and Theory: The Problem of Conflict since Aristotle** (1988).

19. This is not a self-evidently obvious proposition, for one might easily think the Constitution could draw a line between speech say on a street corner, or in a newspaper, and speech that takes the forms of slogans emblazoned on a jacket and displayed in a courthouse. But that is actually part of Harlan's point, for in those cases the state would be punishing the *manner* of speech, not its content or substance, which, if defined as a communication that opposes participation in the Vietnam War or the military draft, is immune from suppression. The question, then, is whether this is an appropriate time, place, or manner regulation.

20. What is more, there is no notice in this statute that the courthouse is a special place, governed by special rules. "No fair rending

of the phrase, 'offensive conduct,' can be said sufficiently to inform the ordinary person that distinctions between certain locations are thereby created." 403 U.S. at 19.

21. He puts this point as a question of fact: "It cannot be plausibly maintained that this vulgar allusion to the Selective Service System would conjure up such psychic stimulation in anyone likely to be confronted with Cohen's crudely defaced jacket." *Id,* at 20.

22. The phrase on Cohen's jacket is not comparable to "the raucous emissions of sound trucks" outside one's residence, for "those in the Los Angeles courthouse could avoid further bombardment of their sensibilities by simply averting their eyes." *Id.* at 21. Harlan concludes that this is no basis for suppression, especially where there is no evidence that "persons powerless to avoid appellant's conduct did in fact object to it" (*id.* at 22) and where the legislature has not focused attention on the issues presented by the captive auditor, but "indiscriminately sweeps within its prohibitions all 'offensive conduct' that 'disturbs any neighborhood or person' (*id*). Here Harlan does find a way to give force to objections that might have been made to the statute on its face, but he does so not in an abstract way but in the context defined by the

particulars of this case. The statute may thus be valid in other cases, but not as applied to this conduct in this case—at least not without a showing of a legislative judgment made on the issues presented here.

23. *Id.* at 22–23. He makes this point—in the first instance, at least—as a question of fact, and finds the government's case wanting. "We have been shown no evidence that substantial numbers of citizens are standing ready to strike out physically at whoever may assault their sensibilities" by such "execrations." There may be some people "with such lawless and violent proclivities," but that does not constitute a sufficient basis for the regulation of speech. To hold that it did would amount to the "self-defeating proposition" that to avoid censorship by a "hypothetical coterie of the violent and lawless" the state may impose that censorship itself, 403 U.S. at 23.

24. *Id.*

25. *Id.* at 24.

26. 274 U.S. 357, 372 (1927)

27. *Id.* at 24–25.

28. *Id.* at 25.

29. *Id.* at 26.

30. *Id.*

31. For a fuller explication of this theme, *see* my recent book, **The Edge of Meaning** (2001).

"A Bowlful of Tears" Revisited: The Full Story of Lee Puey You's Immigration Experience at Angel Island

Judy Yung

Judy Yung is a Professor in the American Studies Department at the University of California, Santa Cruz. Professor Yung specializes in Asian American studies, ethnic studies, oral history, and women's studies. Her 1999 book, *Unbound Voices: A Documentary History of Chinese Women in San Francisco*, combines oral histories with letters, essays, poems, autobiographies, speeches, testimonials, and photographs. Professor Yung has won several national awards for her research. This essay was originally published in *Frontiers*, a feminist journal committed to publishing a wide array of scholarly work, personal essays, and cross-disciplinary perspectives on women's history, cultural theory, art, and criticism.

In 1975, a few years after the discovery of Chinese poems on the walls of the immigration barracks at Angel Island, I embarked on an oral history project with historian Him Mark Lai and poet Genny Lim to document the story of Chinese detention at Angel Island during the exclusion period. After conducting forty-five interviews with ex-detainees and staff and translating one hundred thirty-five of the Chinese poems, we published *Island: Poetry and History of Chinese Immigrants on Angel Island, 1910–1940*. Although none of the poems was written by women, we conducted eight interviews with women, offering us a rare opportunity to hear their versions of the story as well.[1]

One of the women we interviewed was Lee Puey You, who had immigrated to the United States in 1939. She was denied entry by immigration authorities and detained at Angel Island for twenty months before she was deported. She gave us a detailed and moving account of her long stay at Angel Island. It was her refrain, "I must have cried a bowlful of tears," that I used in the title of my first article on the experiences of Chinese immigrant women at Angel Island in *Frontiers*. Little did I know then how much more complicated and sad her full story was and how our lack of experience as oral historians had made us overlook the gendered effects of exclusion on women's

lives. In hindsight, we should have asked more open-ended as well as follow-up questions; covered more of her entire life history; considered race, class, gender and memory dynamics in our line of questioning and analysis; and compared her testimony to the transcripts in her immigration file at the National Archives.[2]

The following rewrite and analysis of the interview that we conducted with Lee Puey You in 1975 as part of the *Island* book project is intended to provide a fuller picture of a Chinese woman's experience at Angel Island, told in her own words, as well as a better understanding of how we can best reclaim our past through oral history. The 1975 interview is compared with a second interview with Lee that was conducted ten years later for a film production, *Carved in Silence*, to show what was overlooked in the first interview and the different results that come from working in the medium of film. Excerpts from a third interview conducted by an immigration officer in 1955, when Lee was threatened with deportation for fraudulent entry, are included at the end to reveal the full tragic story of her immigration and life in America that she withheld from us. I did not come across this last interview until after Lee's death in 1996.[3] While I can respect Lee Puey You's sense of privacy and desire to protect her family and us from the painful circumstances of her immigration, I include the full story here with the permission of her daughters as a testimony to the strength of character that Lee displayed in confronting institutional racism and sexual exploitation. Against such odds, she must have cried more than a bowlful of tears in her lifetime.

"A BOWLFUL OF TEARS": FIRST INTERVIEW FOR THE BOOK *ISLAND*

In 1975, we were lucky to find Lee Puey You through a mutual friend of her daughter Daisy Gin. We had heard she was detained on Angel Island for close to two years, probably the longest stay of any Chinese detainee in the history of the Angel Island Immigration Station. And she was willing to be interviewed. So one Saturday afternoon, Him Mark Lai and I, fully equipped with tape recorders and a list of questions, paid Lee Puey You a visit in her North Beach flat in San Francisco. I remember she welcomed our questions and thoughtfully answered them one by one until we ran out of questions after an hour or so.

5   In many ways hers was both a common and a unique story about detention life at Angel Island. Lee Puey You was born in Chung Tow village in Chungshan (Zhongshan) District, Guangdong Province, in 1916. She was twenty-three years old when she immigrated to the United States in 1939, posing as the daughter of a U.S. citizen. Once admitted, she was to marry a Chinese immigrant in the United States and prepare the way for the rest of her family to come. Unlike most Chinese women immigrating at this time, she was well educated and thus had an easier time memorizing the coaching book for the interrogation. She expected to be detained at Angel Island for a few weeks until she successfully passed the physical examination and interrogation. However, because of discrepancies in her interview and that of her alleged father, she was denied entry.[4]

Slated for deportation, Lee Puey You was told by her "relatives" that they would hire an attorney to appeal her case to higher authorities in Washington, D.C., and that she needed to be patient. The appeal went from the U.S. District Court to the U.S. Circuit Court of Appeals, and finally to the U.S. Supreme Court, without success. By this time the war against Japan had escalated in China, and the United States was about to enter

World War II on the same side as China. The hope was that Lee would be allowed to land because it would be too dangerous to send her back to China. Instead, after twenty months of confinement at Angel Island, she was deported to Hong Kong. Here, her story took another unique turn. In 1947 she returned to the United States posing as a war bride to marry the same man. The immigration station at Angel Island had since closed and been moved to San Francisco, and the Chinese Exclusion Act had been repealed. This time, she was allowed to enter immediately. But the twenty months of prison-like detainment at Angel Island had been forever etched into her mind and heart.[5]

When we interviewed Lee Puey You thirty years after her ordeal at Angel Island, she told us repeatedly how she was made to feel like a criminal and how often she cried in anguish and out of frustration. We found that because she had been there for such an unusually long time and because she was an educated woman, Lee observed and understood the detention experience at Angel Island more thoroughly than her peers. She remembered in detail the backgrounds of the women and their emotional state of mind, the poetry on the barrack walls, the interrogation process, and the ways women coped with imprisonment. Mindful of the psychological scars of Angel Island that she still bore, Him Mark Lai and I treaded carefully, perhaps too cautiously, in asking our prepared list of questions. As a result, we saw only a partial picture of the circumstances of her immigration to the United States. Nevertheless, the following is what she told us about what happened to her at Angel Island. The original interview in Chinese has been translated into English and edited to eliminate redundancies and to allow for an organized flow, but the tone and substance of the interview remain hers. Whenever helpful, I have included interview questions and editorial comments in brackets.

I didn't want to come to America but I was forced by circumstances to come. My mother had arranged a marriage for me. I had a passport to come [as a daughter of a U.S. citizen] when I was 16, but I didn't come until I was 23, after the Japanese attacked China.[6] They bombed Shekki and everywhere and there was nowhere to hide so I had to come to America. But my fate was not good. I had never seen my fiancé before, but I knew he was a lot older than me. He said he would give me the choice of marrying him or not after I arrived. My mother wanted me to come so that I could bring the family over later. Because of that, I was afraid to oppose the arranged marriage. I had to be a filial daughter. The situation forced me to sacrifice everything to come to America.

In 1939 I arrived at Angel Island. They told us to put down our luggage [in the storage shed] *and then they directed us to the wooden building. We were allowed to bring only a small suitcase of clothes. There must have been over one hundred people. The men had their dormitories and the women had theirs. They assigned us to beds* [two-tiered bunk beds] *and there were* gwai poh [foreign devil women] *to take care of us. We slept there and had three meals a day. Everyday we got up at about 7:00. They yelled, chow, chow. You know those* gwai poh. *They would wake us up and take us to the dining room for breakfast. Usually a plate of vegetables and a plate of meat catering to the Chinese palate. Nothing good. Sometimes scrambled eggs, sometimes vegetables mixed with meat. Their food was pretty bad, not very tasty. But then most people didn't eat their food. Many had relatives in the city who sent Chinese dishes, barbecued duck and pork, packages of food every day. After we ate, they took us back and locked the doors. That's all. Just like in jail. Followed us out and followed us back, then locked the doors. They treated us like criminals. They were always afraid that we would go over to the men's side and talk to them* [and thereby corroborate testimonies] *or that we might escape or commit suicide. Where would we escape to? I never saw anyone try suicide, but people did cry for death because they were suffering so.*

There was nowhere to go. Just a little hallway that was fenced in for us to sun, exercise, or play ball. No longer than my hallway here [about fifteen feet]. *The men's exercise area was larger. There was a long table put there for us to use for writing or sewing. From the windows we could see the boats arrive daily at about 9:30 or 10:00 in the morning. At the end of the day we would watch the inspectors and newly released immigrants leave the island on the same boat. That's all.* [How did you pass the time?] *Sometimes I read or knitted, made some clothes, or slept. When you got up, it was time to eat again. Day in and day out, eat and sleep. Many people cried. Everyone there cried at least once.* [The men gambled and had music, how about the women?] *No,*

no mah jongg, *no recreation. Once a week they allowed us to walk out to the storage room where our luggage was kept* [to retrieve things]. *That allowed us to stretch and breathe in some fresh air. We walked around a bit and then returned.* [Were you allowed to write letters to your relatives?] *Yes, but they examined your letters before mailing them. The same for letters coming in. They opened them to see if there was any coaching information. Any packages or food that were sent to us had to be examined too. Then the* gwai poh *would call our name and deliver the package to you.*

[Any other regulations?] *Well, when you got sick you were supposed to tell the* gwai poh. *They would send you to the hospital until you got well. They always gave you laxatives, which tasted awful. After a few days, you came back. We couldn't have any visitors, but there was a Miss Moore* [Maurer], *a Protestant woman who came once or twice a week. She was pretty old. Sometimes she brought me yarn or fabric. She was very nice to me. I still remember her. At Christmas time she gave us gifts. The staff there were pretty nice to me too because I had been there for such a long time. They allowed me in and out of their office.* [Did they ever threaten or punish anyone?] *Sometimes when they called you to get up to go eat and you didn't feel well enough, they would force you to. They won't let you stay in bed. Or they would make you go to the hospital. But they never hit anyone. They might scold you but they never punished anyone. Sometimes the girls would scold back and they would get into an argument. But some were very nice to us.*[7]

[Did you remember seeing any poems on the walls?] *Yes, there were some written* [not carved] *on the walls. It was like songs people would sing.* [Did you write any yourself?] *Not on the wall, but I did write poetry to console myself. I would write and cry at the same time. You know, sitting at Angel Island I must have cried a bowlful of tears. It was so pitiful.*

[Were there other immigrants who were not Chinese there?] *There were a few Japanese and Korean women. They lived in a different room next to ours. We had no contact with them. The Japanese were looked up to. They came and went in a day or two. That's probably because we Chinese didn't have the proper papers.*[8]

[Was it comfortable living there?] Of course not! We had a bed to sleep in and the bathrooms were adequate, but it was so noisy with so many people—fifty or sixty women at one time and a few young children besides. Sometimes the people next to you talked or people would cry in the middle of the night so you couldn't sleep. It was very noisy. Sometimes people didn't get along and argued, but because we were in the same fix, we were generally good friends. We shared food and helped each other out even though I couldn't understand the Sze Yup dialect. Often, those who had been there awhile cried when they saw others leave. So you started to cry. It was very sad.[9]

[The men had their Self-Governing Organization that lodged complaints for them, did the women?] No, we didn't. The women did not dare complain [about the food or the treatment]. If you didn't like the food, the only thing you could do is not eat their food and get your own [from relatives in San Francisco]. Or you could buy things at the small store [in the dining room]. You could buy almost anything there—canned fish, fermented bean cakes, fruit, ice cream, cookies. As a new arrival, you're like a stupid pig, not knowing anything. Whatever they told you to do, you did. There was no recourse for protest.

[What was the interrogation like?] People said that coming to America was like going to heaven, but it was so difficult. You had to memorize all the coaching information—background on your grandparents, your home and neighbors, the distance between places, you know, how many ancestral halls, temples, everything. It was just like in school. You had this vast amount of information to learn. How many brothers and sisters does your father have? What are the names of your uncles? What were their occupations? When did they return to China? Have you ever seen them? When did your grandparents die? Where were they born? Lots of questions and answers going back three generations.

Two or three weeks after my arrival, I was called in for the interrogation. I knew I would be interrogated, but I was still nervous when the time came. There was a typist, an inspector, and an interpreter; three in all. It took three days. We started at 9:30 or 10:00 in the morning. At 11:30 or 12:00 there was a lunch break. Then we went back at 1:00 until 4:00.

They asked me about my grandparents, which direction the house faced, which house I lived in, how far from one place to another. It took a long time because they had to interrogate the witnesses too. After they asked me questions, they would ask my father, then my uncles, and then the two witnesses. That's why it took two or three days. [Were the interrogators hard on you?] Sometimes the interpreters were cranky. When I said I wasn't sure or I didn't know, they would tell me to say yes or no. They just treated us like criminals.

After the interrogation, if you failed, they didn't tell you. But when you were allowed to see your father or witnesses, you knew they were going to deport you. You see, if I had passed I won't have had to see the witnesses. I would have been immediately called to land, to gather my things and leave. That's how it usually was. Relatives later told me that they would appeal my case to the higher courts in Washington, D.C. They told me to be patient. My appeal failed the first time and then a second time. They were hoping that when the war finally hit the United States, I would be released. But instead, I was stuck on Angel Island for twenty months. I was there the longest. Most people stayed three weeks or so. Those on appeal left after a few months. But my case was more crooked [complicated] because my paper father had reported twins and it wasn't true. So I wasn't landed.[10]

[Did anything unusual happen while you were there?] Right before I was deported, there was a fire in the middle of the night. We saw flames and inhaled smoke. Everything was burnt in the women's barracks. It was pretty bad so we had to run over to the hospital to live for awhile. Then they moved us to that immigration building on Washington Street [in San Francisco]. A few weeks later, I was deported to Hong Kong.[11]

[Upon reflection, how do you feel about what happened at Angel Island now?] Before, that was the system. There was nothing you could do about it. That was the American law then, how can you go against it? But this is how I look at it now. If things checked out at the American consul's in Hong Kong, they should let us come. If not, they shouldn't let us come. That would have spared us suffering twenty days aboard ship, seasickness and all, and then *imprisonment at Angel Island. In my case, I had to endure twenty months of prison-like confinement. And then to be deported back to Hong Kong, how sad!*[12]

CARVED IN SILENCE: SECOND INTERVIEW FOR A FILM PRODUCTION

In 1984, when filmmaker Felicia Lowe decided to make *Carved in Silence*, a film about the Chinese immigration experience at Angel Island, I suggested Lee Puey You as a possible subject. Felicia wanted to follow the stories of three immigrants in the format of a docudrama but was having trouble finding ex–detainees who were willing to tell their story on camera and who would come across well on film. Lee agreed to be filmed, and I signed on as a historical consultant to help with the research and interviews. Working with Felicia, I learned that film requires a different approach to interviewing. Although the historical background was important, it was the emotional connection that really mattered.[13]

My job was to sit right below the camera and ask open-ended questions that would evoke memories of Angel Island and encourage Lee Puey You to speak expressively but succinctly into the camera. Short answers in a monotonous tone or long answers that skirted the questions would be deadly in this situation. I learned to be both solicitous and persistent in my line of questioning, to rephrase my questions and ask good follow-up questions in order to steer her in the right direction. Felicia was already familiar with Lee Pucy You's story from reading the transcript of our earlier interview with her and from interviewing Lee herself a number of times. She knew which stories she wanted Lee to tell on camera. My part was to draw these stories out of Lee as spontaneously as possible, even though we reshot some of the answers a number of times. Although Lee Puey You's voice would be dubbed over in English, Felicia intended to do an exact translation and stay as close as possible to the tone and wording of her responses, which, to her credit, she did accomplish in the final edit of the film.

10   The following excerpts from a series of interviews with Lee Puey You in preparation for the filming of *Carved in Silence* show what we learned by pursuing a different line of questioning. In particular, we hear about her life before and after Angel Island, the dire family conditions that forced her to agree to marry a stranger in America, and the poetry she saw in the bathroom of the women's barracks. Since the building that housed the women at Angel Island burned in the 1940 fire, we had given up hope of ever finding any Chinese poetry by women. Yet, here was Lee Puey You, reciting one of the poems she had written while at Angel Island, proving that not all Chinese immigrant women were illiterate at the time. Moreover, Felicia prodded her to tell us how she felt having to appear naked before a white male physician, something we had failed to ask in our 1975 interview. She also got Lee to analyze how her upbringing and education in China helped her to endure the twenty long months of confinement at Angel Island.

Then came that unforgettable moment on film when Lee Puey You broke down and began to cry while recalling her return voyage to China. It was totally unexpected, and we caught it on film. While it is to Lee's credit as an interviewee that she was willing and able to tell her own story on film as effectively as she did, it still takes a good interviewer and filmmaker to make this possible—to establish the rapport, ask the right questions, and edit the interview so that the significant points are made within a broader historical context. Compared to our cautious approach in interviewing Lee for the book *Island*, Felicia was persistent about exploring Lee's unique background and capturing her emotional response to detention life and deportation on film. The following excerpts from the interview with Lee Puey You have been translated from Chinese into English and edited for an organized flow, but the integrity of her voice has been retained. As before, I have left certain questions in brackets to show what prompted her to answer as she did.

[What were your reasons for coming?] *My mother wanted me to come to America so that later on, I could bring my brothers and sisters over to America. At the time, the Japanese were bombing my village. That was another reason why I fled my country.* [How was your family doing then?] *When I was very young, my father was a wealthy farmer. A flood destroyed all his land and he lost all his money. It was then that our family changed. My brother had to go to work to support me and my mother. I saw how hard he worked, just one job. It was* barely enough. Finally I decided to listen to my mother. I would come to America first and then later help my brother and the rest of the family to come over. That was what my mother had always wanted. Here, there was a future. In China we were just too poor and there was nothing we could do.

[What were your preparations before you came to America?] *My mother had a girlfriend in our village who wanted to introduce me to her cousin for marriage. She wanted me to come to America to marry him so she bought me a false paper.*

[Tell me about your trip to the United States.] *From my village, I went to Hong Kong. I stayed with relatives in Hong Kong for six months until I got the papers from America to come. Then I got on a big ship and was on it for nineteen days. I thought it would be very easy for me to land in America. Instead, I had to go to Angel Island.*

[Could you describe the physical examination?] *When the doctor came, I had to take off all my clothes. It was so embarrassing and shameful. I didn't really want to let him examine me, but I had no choice. Back in China, I never had to take off everything, but it was different here in America. I found it very strange.*

[Tell me about the interrogation.] *The interrogators frightened me. There were two or three Westerners along with one Chinese at the interrogation. Just looking at them made me scared and nervous. I didn't know what to do or how to act around them. They asked me questions that I could not answer, even how many feet our house was from the house next door. I was bewildered and didn't know how to answer them.*

[Were the rest of the women scared like you?] *Everyone was feeling low. We all suffered emotionally. No one had any energy. We slept all day. So much mental anguish. You know, we cried more than anything else. It was hard and time went by so slowly. When I was in China, I didn't know it would be so hard in America. Everybody said that coming to America was like going to heaven, but at* Angel Island *they treated the Chinese as if we were criminals, like we were all thieves and robbers. Because I was there so long, all the new arrivals would ask me questions about Angel Island. They all wanted to learn from my experience. We sympathized and tried to help each other out.*

[What else gave you the strength to endure such sadness and hardships?] *Sometimes I tried to analyze myself, to understand my inner feelings and emotions. Sometimes I wrote poems to express my feelings. That helped to release some of the tension.* [Were there many poems written on the walls of the women's barracks?] *The bathroom was filled with poems expressing sadness and bitterness. They were about how hard the stay at Angel Island was, how sad and depressed the women were, not knowing when they would be allowed to leave the island. During one of my more painful moments, I wrote this poem:*

遠 涉 重 洋 到 美 洲

離 別 家 鄉 與 親 朋

誰 知 困 在 木 樓 中

不 知 何 日 得 出 頭

*From across the Pacific Ocean to America
I left my village and all my loved ones.
Who would have thought I would be imprisoned in this wooden barrack?
I do not know when I will ever be set free.*

In my darkest moment of sadness, I could only turn to God for help. I just prayed everyday. That was the only way I could bear those hardships. I had no choice but to be strong. I had to take care of myself so that I might survive. I had to fulfill my duty as a filial daughter. That was all![14]

[Tell us how your father influenced your life.] *When I was little, my father always told me what to do and how things worked. At fourteen years old, I knew how to lease and how to rent out land. I was considered quite smart. During the poor times, I learned how to dig up plants and roots for cooking. I also knew how to catch fish. I was very capable and helped my mother quite a bit.*

[Tell us about your schooling.] *I went to school and studied history. We even had a special teacher to teach us the Chinese classics. I have a very good brain so I was able to absorb all the material. This was probably what gave me the extra strength to endure life on Angel Island. It gave me a better understanding of people and of the world. My father always said it was a pity that I was born a girl and not a boy. I had a good business head and was able to help him. I became a housewife after I got married. But I encouraged my husband to buy stocks, a business, and real estate. I had no interest in just staying home and cleaning house. Even today, my goals in life are more like a man's.*

[Why were you on the island so long?] *My case had to go through two appeals in Washington, D.C. My mother's girlfriend was determined that I stay in America. She did not care how much money or how long it would take. As long as there was a string of light, she wanted me to hang on. I was the only one to stay on Angel Island for such a long time. Twenty months. Anyone else would have just gone back home to China.*[15]

[How did you feel when you found out about your deportation?] *My heart felt very heavy. I had no face [was ashamed] to see my family back home. My spirit was broken. During my trip back to China on the boat, my heart hurt so much that I finally had to put some rice, some hot rice, against my chest to ease the pain inside (sobs). The anguish that I had suffered is more than anyone can bear. I can't begin to describe it. Then all of a sudden, I had a dream. My appeal was successful! It was like a message from God. Then my heart was at peace. So that's my story from start to finish. It took me fourteen years to come back to America, fourteen long, long years.*[16]

[How was your life when you returned to America the second time?] *It was a lot easier than life in China. As long as you are willing to work hard, you can make a better living in America. I consider myself lucky that I did not have to work too hard in America. We had a grocery store, and since there were enough people working in the store, I was not needed. Later on, after my father-in-law passed away and my brother-in-law left, that left only my husband and me to run the store. I would work every day from 7 a.m. to 9 p.m., fourteen hours a day, seven days a week. But I only did that for five or six years. Now my life is quite settled. I saved enough money to buy a building so that I can live in one apartment and rent the rest of the units out. I should be able to take care of myself for the rest of my life.*

[Tell me how you finally sponsored your family over to America.] *My mother had wanted me to come to America, hoping that later on I would somehow bring the rest of the family over. Twenty years later, my mother, my brother, his wife and their four children, my sister and her husband and children rode a ship and came to America. It cost me thousands of dollars, but my mother's hopes have finally been fulfilled! Now all of them are doing well. They all have good jobs and their own homes. And all the children have finished college and are making good money. Everyone is happy and my responsibility to them is finally over.*

"IN THE MATTER OF YIM TAI MUEY": THIRD INTERVIEW WITH INS

Sixteen years after the second interview for the film *Carved in Silence*, I came to a different understanding of Lee Puey You's immigration experience and life in America. It had not been as "easy" as she had said. By then, Lee had passed away, and I turned to her daughters, Daisy and Debbie Gin, for help in clarifying some discrepancies in her interviews. Based on the immigration files that Daisy and Debbie found at the National Archives, we learned that in 1955 someone blew the whistle and reported her illegal entry to the Immigration and Naturalization Service (INS). A warrant for her arrest was issued on the grounds that the immigration visa she had used to enter the country in 1947 had been procured by fraud. She was ordered to appear before the INS to show cause as to why she should not be deported. The stakes were just as high as they had been for her at Angel Island in 1939, but this time she had the benefit of an attorney to represent her interest, as well as the support of her second husband, Fred Gin, whom she had married in 1953. She was also apparently prepared to tell the whole story. According to the transcript, part way through the interrogation and at the prompting of her attorney, she said through the interpreter, "I wish to volunteer the whole facts in the case." Then she proceeded to tell the following story:[17]

I was born in Cr 5-5-3. My name was Lee Puey You at birth. When I was about 13 years old my father died and he did not leave us anything and my family was very poor. It was during the war and my family was having a hard time to make a living. One day a cousin of Woo Tong talked to my mother and told her that he has a cousin in the United States whose wife died recently and that he would like to remarry again and asked my mother whether she was willing to consent to having her daughter marry his cousin in the United States. Later Woo Tong's cousin tell my mother to have a photograph of me to send it to Woo Tong to see whether he liked me or not. Some time later Woo Tong's cousin came and told me that I was to go to the United States under the name of Ngin Ah Oy as a daughter of a son of a native—I was known as Yim Tai Muey at that time—and that after I came to the United States I was to marry Woo Tong as his wife, and I came to the United States in 1939. When I arrived here in San Francisco, I was detained at Angel Island for almost two years. During all of that time I had a very hard time and I was very sad, and every time that someone was released from there I felt sick all over again. I did not know what was happening to my case. I even attempted

suicide. Then later I was deported back to Hong Kong. On my way back to Hong Kong I wanted to commit suicide again, but I was thinking about my mother, of the hard times we had together. When I arrived back in Hong Kong, I sold rice on the street in Hong Kong. I was having a very hard time because it was during the war at that time. My mother told me that we have used some of Woo Tong's money and no matter how hard a time I am having I must not get married. She already promised my marriage to Woo Tong. She said that I should wait until after the war, when she could correspond with Woo Tong again and that he will make arrangements for me to go to the United States again. After the war, in about 1947, Woo Tong came to Hong Kong and he came to our house and talked to my mother. Later then, we invited some friends for dinner; then my mother told me it was considered as my marriage ceremony with Woo Tong. Then Woo Tong told me of his plan to bring me to the United States. He said I was to get a marriage certificate with Sai Chan and said I was to come to the United States as Sai Chan's wife and said he would accompany me to the United States. After Sai Chan and I obtained our marriage certificate from the American Consular Office in Hong Kong, he told me that I must go to a husband and wife relationship with him before he could bring me to the United States. I objected to that, but he forced me into that, so I lived with him as man and wife in Hong Kong. Sai Chan and I came to the United States together in 1947. After we arrived in the United States, he took me to Woo Tong's place at 1141 Stockton Street and he left me there. When I get there I learned Woo Tong's wife was still living and that I was not actually to be Woo Tong's wife, but his concubine. I objected to it, but there was nothing I could do because I was now here in the United States. I did not know of anyone to go to for aid, so I stayed with him. During all those times I was living there, I was treated very badly by his wife. She treated me as a slave girl. I had to do all kinds of work in the house, take care of her, and I also had to take care of one of Woo Tong's buildings. On January 8, 1949, I gave birth to a daughter fathered by Woo Tong. While I was in the

Stanford Hospital during my maternity period, Woo Tong made all the arrangements for me. He filled out the birth certificate for my daughter, and he filled out the father's name as Sai Chan. Woo Tong died August 18, 1950, in San Francisco. After he died, his wife forced me to continue to work for her. When Woo Tong died, he did not leave money or anything for my daughter and myself. I met Fred Gin in about 1953 and learned his wife had passed away several years before. I found he was a person of good character. I went with him about six months before we got married. I went to Reno and obtained a divorce decree from Sai Chan to clear the record on January 16, 1953. Fred Gin had two sons by his first wife in the United States and after we were married, I bore him a daughter on February 4, 1955.[18]

Then followed a series of humiliating questions regarding her moral character, specifically her sexual relationships with Sai Chan and Woo Tong:

Q: During the few days you lived with Woo Tong after that dinner [in Hong Kong], did you have sexual intercourse with him?

Q: [After you were admitted to the United States and started living with Woo Tong] did you immediately have sexual intercourse with Woo Tong?

Q: When did you last have sexual intercourse with Woo Tong?

Q: After you obtained a marriage certificate with Sai Chan, did you voluntarily submit to relationships with him?

Lee Puey You admitted to no wrongdoing and insisted that she was just following her mother's orders, that she had agreed to marry Woo Tong believing he was a widower, and that Sai Chan had forced her to have sex with him after their wedding. In the cross-examination by her attorney, Lee emphasized her newfound happiness at being married to Fred Gin:

Q: What would happen if you were separated from Fred and the rest of your family?

A: I would have a hard time, because I have no one else to go to if I should be separated from my family.

Q: Would Fred go with you in the event you should be deported?

A: I will not allow him to go with me even if willing, because I don't want him to sacrifice his life for me.

Q: Would you take your blood daughters Eva and Daisy if you were separated from Fred?

A: No. I will leave them in the United States. Even if they have to beg or starve in the United States, I would leave them because the living conditions here in the United States are better.[19]

When asked by the INS officer if she had anything further to add before the hearing came to a close, she said:

I just wish to say that you give me a chance so that I can remain in the United States to be with my family. I found happiness after I married Fred Gin. Prior to that time the wrongdoing was not due to my fault. I was just obeying my mother, which she make all the arrangements with Woo Tong that I apply for a marriage certificate as the wife of Sai Chan to come to the United States.

The INS officer was evidently not convinced or moved by her testimony and ordered her deported on grounds that her immigration visa had been procured by fraud and that "she [had] lived in an adulterous relationship with Woo Tong" while still married to Sai Chan. Lee Puey You did not give up. She hired another attorney to appeal the decision on her behalf. First, the attorney argued that she was "not innately a bad person of criminal tendencies . . . but a mere pawn—indeed a slave—of men who deserve severe condemnation." Next, he pointed out that because her marriage to Sai Chan, a citizen veteran, was consummated and deemed valid, she had immigrated legitimately as a war bride. Evidently persuaded by the attorney's arguments, the Board of Immigration Appeals sustained Lee Puey You's appeal and terminated the deportation proceedings on March 25, 1956. She became a naturalized U.S. citizen in 1959, which paved the way for her to send for her family from China.

Lee Puey You's full story sheds light not only on the complexities and ordeal of immigration for Chinese women at Angel Island, but also on how we can best reclaim that past through oral history. Conceptions of race, class, and gender all played a part in determining who immigrated and their treatment upon arrival. Because of poverty and war conditions at home, and out of filial duty, Lee sacrificed her own happiness in agreeing to marry a man who was thirty years her senior in order to immigrate to the United States. In the process, class and gender inequities placed her in a vulnerable position, to be sexually exploited by men such as Woo Tong and Sai Chan. Then, because of race, class, and gender biases in the exclusionary laws, Lee could come to the United States only by posing as a dependent member of the exempt classes. As such, she was subjected to a double test. In claiming her right to land as the daughter of a U.S. citizen, she had to reconfirm her alleged father's exempt status as well as prove that their relationship actually existed. Later, when she was accused of fraudulent entry as a war bride and threatened with deportation, she had to prove the legitimacy of her marriage to a citizen veteran as well as her moral character by answering humiliating questions about her sexual life. In these ways, race, class, and gender dynamics made the immigration process more difficult for Chinese women like Lee Puey You than for any other group of immigrants during the exclusion period.

In interviewing Lee Puey You, it was important that Him Mark Lai and I were Chinese-speaking, culturally sensitive, and well informed about Chinese American history. For these reasons, we were able to establish rapport with her and encourage her to talk freely about her twenty-month ordeal at Angel Island. But being novice oral historians and overly polite at the time, we missed out on the opportunity to learn the full impact of exclusion on her life and how she was able to overcome racial and gender oppression. Working with Felicia Lowe on the film *Carved in Silence* made me realize how important it is to be persistent and analytical in our line of questioning. What influential forces shaped her life and helped her to cope with detention at Angel Island?

Even after knowing this, we did not get the full tragic story. It had not occurred to any of us to question the validity of her story, to read between the lines, to compare the interview with her testimony in the records of the National Archives, or even to ask her daughters what they knew. What made her hide the truth from us? Would she have told us the whole story if we had probed further or showed her the immigration record? Although aware of the pain that full recall might have caused

her, I believe that she would have told us more if we had only persisted. In not doing our job well as critical oral historians, we missed the opportunity to better understand her life as well as to vindicate the wrongs committed against her.

Nevertheless, one thing is for certain: Lee Puey You was not a passive victim but an active agent in the making of her own history. She chose to talk to us and then selectively to tell us what she did. That showed good judgment and self-control. After three appeals and deportation to Hong Kong, she ultimately succeeded in her goal of landing in America and sending for her family. That took patience and tenacity. Even though both Sai Chan and Woo Tong betrayed her, she kept her word and went through with the marriages. That showed strength of character. And when threatened with deportation again, she persisted in fighting to the extent of telling and reliving the sordid details of her horrendous past. That required courage and forbearance on her part.[20]

In finally being able to hear her full story, I believe we come to a better understanding of and appreciation for the struggles and triumphs of our foremothers. Lee Puey You's story is an important part of the larger American story, indeed a challenge to the master narrative of the immigration saga, and a reminder that reclaiming our past as women requires a special approach to doing oral history.[21]

The following is an unedited translation of a Chinese letter that Lee Puey You wrote to her alleged father while at Angel Island. It was found in the women's barracks soon after the Board of Special Inquiry denied her admission into the United States on May 6, 1939. When confronted with this piece of evidence in a gut-wrenching interview before the Board, Lee repeatedly denied that she had written it and refused to provide a sampling of her handwriting for verification. But two hours later, she relented, asked to see the head inspector, and admitted to writing it. According to the Board's report, "this incident furnishes convincing proof that the applicant will lie deliberately and repeatedly in her testimony in this matter whenever she considers it to be to her advantage to do so." Evidently, the Board disregarded the positive aspects of Lee Puey You's character as revealed in the letter and chose instead to focus only on the letter as further evidence that she should be denied admission:

Yesterday I received a box of canned food and a letter, which I have noted. Some days ago I had received some foodstuff twice and a Chinese-American calendar which is very useful and which I have hung on the wall.

The foodstuff you sent me is very good, but I would ask you not to spend so much to buy food to send me, because I cannot eat so much. Send me some calico, if you have it.

The hotel expenses must be very great, and then you have to appeal the case to Washington. That means money and anxiety on your part. I do not mind to prolong my stay here in order to get landed. I do not know whether you have understood the testimony in this case or not. If you do not know it all, you can write the word "mei" on the edge or in the bottom of a box of food you might send me, and when I see it I will understand. Write that word plainly, so that I will send it to you by some one who will be landed later. I want to tell you the answers I gave to the questions,

so that you may know them and advise me concerning my answers. If you have understood it, I do not wish to talk about it now. When some one goes to the city, I will send it to you by him (or her).

Every time you sent me something, the officer tore away the name on the side and kept it until the next day. When you send me things, you can write "sent by Ngim Lin," but that's not important. I am glad to know you have sent mother a letter and some money. Your last letter said that the case had been appealed to Washington, and that costs you money and gives you anxiety. Please get me a beginner's book to learn how to write English, so that I may make use of my time here.

To my father Ngim Lin, C/O maternal uncle Woo Tong. (Note: The Chinese paper from which the above translation is made is a draft of a letter, rather poorly written, but the translation is substantially and almost literally correct. Interp. H. K. Tang, 5-19-39).

Notes

This article was originally published in slightly different form in *Asian/Pacific Islander American Women: A Historical Anthology*. ed. Shirley Hune and Gail Nomura (New York: New York University Press, 2003). It is written in memory and in honor of Lee Puey You. My thanks to Daisy and Debbie Gin for sharing their mother's story and immigration file with me; to Michael Frush for his assistance at the National Archives and Records Administration—Pacific Region (San Francisco); and to Ruthanne Lum McCunn for her careful reading of an earlier draft of this essay.

1. The exclusion period began with the passage of the Chinese Exclusion Act of 1882, which barred the further immigration of Chinese laborers to the United States, and ended with the repeal of the act in 1943. Between 1910 and 1940, during the time that the Angel Island Immigration Station was in operation, Chinese immigrants were singled out for long detention and subjected to physical examinations and grueling interrogations in order to prove their legal right to enter the country. Him Mark Lai, Genny

Lim, and Judy Yung, *Island: Poetry and History of Chinese Immigrants on Angel Island, 1910–1940* (San Francisco: HOC DOI Project, Chinese Culture Foundation of San Francisco, 1980; Seattle: University of Washington Press, 1991).

2. Judy Yung, "'A Bowlful of Tears': Chinese Women Immigrants on Angel Island," *Frontiers: A Journal of Women Studies* 2:2 (1977): 52–55. The National Archives and Records Administration—Pacific Region (San Francisco) holds thousands of immigration case files relating to the enforcement of the Chinese Exclusion Act at Angel Island that can be made available to family members and researchers. For details, see Waverly Lowell, "Chinese Immigration and Chinese in the United States: Records in the Regional Archives of the National Archives and Records Administration," National Archives and Records Administration, Reference Information Paper 99 (1996).

3. At my suggestion, Daisy and Debbie Gin looked up their mother's immigration records at the National Archives and

Records Administration—Pacific Region in San Bruno, California, and were able to uncover three separate files: documents pertaining to her interrogation at Angel Island in 1939 (Ngim Ah Oy, Folder 39071/12-9, Chinese Departure Case Files, San Francisco District Office, Immigration and Naturalization Service, record group 85); the legal briefs of three separate appeals to higher courts not to deport her ("In the Matter of Ngim Ah Oy on Habeas Corpus," folder 23099R; Admiralty Files, San Francisco District Office, Immigration and Naturalization Service, record group 85); and documents pertaining to her deportation hearing in 1955 ("In the Matter of Yim Tai Muey," folder A6824153, Alien Registration Files, San Francisco District Office, Immigration and Naturalization Service, record group 85). The staff at the National Archives could not locate the immigration file of her entry as a war bride in 1947.

4. Chinese wanting to immigrate to the United States during the exclusion period found ways to circumvent the Chinese Exclusion Act by posing as members of the exempt classes—merchants, teachers, students, officials, tourists, and those who claimed derivative U.S. citizenship. Relatives or professionals in the field prepared coaching books for prospective immigrants, giving questions and answers about one's background that immigration officials might ask. For a detailed description of a coaching book, see Judy Yung, *Unbound Voices: A Documentary History of Chinese Women in San Francisco* (Berkeley: University of California Press, 1999), 32–56.

5. The War Brides Act of 1945 was amended in 1947 to allow Chinese American veterans to bring their wives to the United States.

6. In 1937, after Japan's vicious attack on China, war was formally declared between the two countries, Shekki (Shiqi) is the county seat of Chungshan (Zhongshan) District in Guangdong Province. Her fiancé was thirty years her senior.

7. Deaconess Katharine Maurer (1881–1962) was appointed by the Methodist Episcopal Church in 1912 to administer to the needs of immigrants at Angel Island. She was known as the Angel of Angel Island.

8. Because of the diplomatic influence of the Japanese government, and because the Japanese generally had passports and papers to verify their identities, they faced few delays at Angel Island.

9. Most of the women were from the Sze Yup districts of Guangdong Province (Sunwui, Toishan, Hoiping, and Yanping), while Lee Puey You was from Chungshan District, where the Lung Do dialect was spoken.

10. The final report in Lee Puey You's immigration file cited numerous discrepancies in her own testimonies about her birth date and in her "paper father's" testimony about his family background and the exact birth dates and different names given to his twin children (Lee Puey You was supposedly the older twin child).

11. Lee Puey You is probably referring to the immigration building at 630 Sansome Street near Washington Street, where she was detained in 1947 on her second attempt to enter the United States. After the fire in 1940, Chinese detainees were temporarily housed at 801 Silver Avenue in San Francisco.

12. Indeed, beginning in the 1950s, decisions on one's eligibility for admission into the United States were made at the port of departure.

13. Felicia Lowe, *Carved in Silence* (San Francisco: Felicia Lowe Productions, distributed by Cross Currents Media, 1987).

14. According to Daisy Gin, her mother never converted to Christianity but was always open to all belief systems.

15. According to Lee Puey You's immigration file, her lawyer actually filed three appeals on her behalf—first to the U.S. District Court, then to the U.S. Circuit Court of Appeals, and finally to the U.S. Supreme Court.

16. It took Lee Puey You fourteen years to come to America, counting from 1932, when she was betrothed and first issued a visa, to 1947, when she was finally admitted into the United States as a war bride.

17. Yim Tai Muey is the name that Lee Puey You used to enter the United States as a war bride in 1947. Lee Puey You gave her testimony in Chinese. Through an interpreter, the

transcript was rendered in English. I have intentionally quoted the transcript as is and not corrected any of the grammatical errors in it.

18. "Cr" refers to the Chinese Republic, which was established in 1912. Lee Puey You was born in the fifth year, fifth month, and third day of the Chinese Republic, or June 3, 1916, according to the Western calendar. Sai Chan (the pseudonym I chose to use in compliance with INS regulations) is a U.S. citizen and World War II veteran.

19. At the time of the INS interview, Lee Puey You's youngest daughter, Debbie Gin, had not yet been born.

20. Similarly, according to her daughter Daisy Gin, Lee Puey You led a courageous and a very "in character" struggle with cancer before she died in 1996: "She underwent a mastectomy in 1985 and would insist on taking the bus to her chemotherapy sessions on her own, only to take a taxi afterwards to play *mah jongg* in some Chinatown alley! She then underwent a very major operation for pancreatic cancer in 1990, where most of her digestive system was removed. She was given a prognosis of only six months to a year, even with repeated chemotherapy. She surprised and was marveled by her surgeon and physicians when she passed the five-year mark. She waved off medical advice about diet and diabetes-control measures and said that she knew how to take care of her own body" (e-mail communication to author on September 10, 2000).

21. See Sherna Gluck, "What's So Special about Women? Women's Oral History," *Frontiers: A Journal of Women Studies* 2:2 (1977): 3–17; and Judy Yung, "Giving Voice to Chinese American Women," *Frontiers: A Journal of Women Studies* 19:3 (1998): 130–56.

CREDITS

PHOTO CREDITS

TEXT CREDITS

Page 14, Figure 1.3: Adapted from Berke, Jacqueline. Twenty Questions for the Writer: A Rhetoric with Readings, 2nd edition. New York: Harcourt Brace Jovanovich, Inc., 1976. **Page 60, Figure 3-8:** Courtesy of Jonathan Burak. **Pages 75–78:** Reprinted by permission of Hattie Wellington. **Pages 78–82:** Reprinted by permission of Christopher Perin. **Page 92, Figure 4.1:** Adapted from Kvale 133. **Pages 106–108:** Reprinted by permission of Bryan McLucas. **Pages 114–117:** Reprinted by permission of Samantha Sanderson. **Pages 152–156:** Reprinted by permission of Kenny Rosina. **Pages 192–202:** Reprinted by permission of Stephen Fuller. **Pages 202–204:** Reprinted by permission of Samantha Sanderson. **Pages 309–323:** Rethinking History 5:1 (2001), pp. 93–116. © 2001 Taylor & Francis Ltd. **Pages 324–341:** Social Justice; December 2002; 29, 4: Social Science Module, p. 96. **Pages 342–352:** Covering Immigration: Popular Images and the Politics of the Nation. University of California Press. Copyright © 2001 The Regents of the University of California. **Page 343:** Sources: Espenshade and Hempstead, 1996; U.S. Bureau of the Census, Statistical Abstract of the United States; Rosenblatt 1997; Walsh, 1999. **Page 344:** Espenshade and Hempstead, 1996; Simon and Lynch, 1999; U.S. News and World Report 13 October 1980; 7 July 1986; 23 June 1993; Business Week 13 July 1992; Newsweek 9 August 1993; Time Fall 1993; CBS/New York Times Poll September 1995; Gallup Poll 1995, 1999. **Pages 353–363:** The Culture of Tourism, The Tourism of Culture: Selling the Past to the Present in the American Southwest. Hal K. Rothman, ed., University of New Mexico Press (2003). **Pages 364–382:** Quarterly Journal of Speech 83 (1997): 289-310. © 1997 Taylor & Francis Ltd. **Pages 383–403:** The Journal of American History, Vol. 75, No. 4 (March 1989), 1130-1155. **Pages 404–421:** American Music, Vol. 20, No. 3 (Autumn 2003), 249-276. **Pages 422–433:** Politics, Discourse, and American Society: New Agendas. Rowman & Littlefield Publishers (2001). **Pages 434–450:** Sound Identities: Popular Music and the Cultural Politics of Education. Peter Lang Publishing (1999). **Pages 451–463:** Journal of Communication, 55(1), pp. 152–168. March 2005. Copyright © 2005 International Communication Association. Reprinted by permission. **Pages 464–477:** History from Things: Essays in Material Culture. Smithsonian Institution Press (1993). **Pages 478–491:** Popular Music and Society, Vol. 26, No. 2 (2003). © 2003 Taylor & Francis, Ltd. **Pages 492–510:** Catherine A. Lutz and Jane L. Collins, "The Photograph as an Intersection of Gazes," in Lutz and Collins, Reading National Geographic. University of Chicago Press, 1993, pp. 187–216. © 1993 by the University of Chicago Press. Reprinted with permission. **Pages 511–520:** Reading at Risk: A Survey of Literary Reading in America (2004), pp. 21–28. National Endowment for the Arts. **Pages 521–531:** History from Things: Essays in Material Culture. Smithsonian Institution Press (1993). **Pages 532–550:** American Anthropologist 103 (3): 655-670. Copyright © 2001 American Anthropological Association. **Pages 551–571:** Representations, No. 75 (Summer 2001), pp. 33–60. Copyright © 2001 The Regents of the University of California. **Pages 572–596:** The Journal of American History, Vol. 75, No. 4 (Mar., 1989), 1130-1155. **Pages 597–611:** Journal of Supreme Court History, Vol. 27:1, pp. 45–64. (2002). **Pages 612–624:** Frontiers, Vol. 25, No. 1 (2004). Reprinted by permission of the author.

INDEX

W

Wellington, Hattiek, 72, 74–78
White, Hayden, 212
White, James Boyd, 168
    assignments using, 244,
       284, 297
    summary in, 36–38, 182–85,
       597–611
Wiater, Stanley, 184
Wood, Grant, 63
Writing. *See* Summary; Peer
    Review; and Student
    Essays. *See also* Literacy

about reading, 10
and habits of mind, 2
and rhetorical choices, 10,
    20–46
and the internet, 18
choosing language, 73–74
from numbers, 145–51
from observations,
    suggestions, 73
from texts, 182–92
including graphics, 149–51
interviews, 102–6
questions in, 11–12

role in inquiry, 1, 3–6, 6, 11,
    16, 51
role of reading in, 6–8, 9–10
value of, 3

Y

Yung, Judy, 89
    assignments using, 252, 263,
       271, 291, *612–624*